Visit our *Finance in a Canadian Setting* ... for a wealth of on-line resources to help maxim... experience. Study tools and the latest dev... finance world are made available throug...

APPENDICES

The following appendices are located on the website and form an important link with the text:
- Appendix I: The Tax Environment
- Appendix II: BCE Inc. Annual Report 1999
- Appendix III: Compounding and Discounting Tables

POWERPOINT SLIDES

PowerPoint presentations highlighting key concepts for each chapter of the text are included on this site. Review them in preparation for lectures or use them while studying for tests and exams.

WEB CASES

These cases allow you to identify and use important on-line information as you work your way through each scenario.

RESEARCH QUESTIONS

These are designed to strengthen your analytical skills and encourage you to use a variety of resources as you investigate diverse financial situations.

ON-LINE QUIZ

Take this self-test as you prepare for an upcoming quiz or exam. You will receive your grade and immediate feedback, which includes page references to the text, should you want further details on the topics covered in each question.

WEB LINKS

Links to companies and organizations mentioned in the text, as well as finance-related sites, are listed for quick reference.

CAREERS IN FINANCE

A list of potential careers in the finance and related sectors will point you in the right direction as you plan for your future.

GLOSSARY

Definitions of finance terms found in the text are featured on this site.

Other on-line resources to help you as you progress through the book, include:
Excel Spreadsheets • Summary of Notations and Formulae • Chapter Summaries • FAQs

AND MUCH MORE!

WILEY

SIXTH EDITION

Finance in a Canadian Setting

FINANCE *in a* CANADIAN SETTING

SIXTH EDITION

Peter Lusztig
University of British Columbia

W. Sean Cleary
Saint Mary's University

Bernhard H. Schwab
University of British Columbia

JOHN WILEY & SONS CANADA, LTD

Toronto · New York · Chichester · Weinheim · Brisbane · Singapore

National Library of Canada Cataloguing in Publication Data
Lusztig, Peter A., 1930–
    Finance in a Canadian setting

6th ed.
Previously published under title: Managerial finance in a Canadian setting.
Includes index.
ISBN 0-471-64185-5

1. Business enterprises—Finance. I. Cleary, W. Sean (William Sean), 1962–
II. Schwab, Bernhard, 1942– . III. Title. IV. Title: Managerial finance in a Canadian setting

HG4090.L8 2001   658.15   C2001-930270-3

Production Credits
Acquisitions Editor: John Horne
Publishing Services Director: Karen Bryan
Developmental Editor: Michelle M. Harrington
Editorial/Production Assistant: Michelle L. Love
New Media Editor: Elsa A. Passera
Senior Business Marketing Manager: Janine Daoust
Cover Design and Text: Interrobang Graphic Design Inc.
Senior Graphic Designer: Ian J. Koo, John Wiley & Sons Canada Ltd
Printing and Binding: Tri-Graphic Printing Limited

Printed and bound in Canada
10 9 8 7 6 5 4

John Wiley & Sons Canada, Ltd.
22 Worcester Road
Etobicoke, Ontario M9W 1L1
Visit our Web site at: www.wiley.com/canada

WILEY

ABOUT THE AUTHORS

Peter Lusztig is a graduate of the University of British Columbia (B.Comm.), the University of Western Ontario (MBA), and Stanford (PhD) and is the recipient of an honorary CGA. He joined the Faculty of Commerce in 1957, and served as Dean between 1977. Between 1955 and 1957 he was the administrative assistant to the VP, Finance at B.C. Electric. He has taught at the Pacific Coast Banking School (University of Washington) and for a number of years at the Banff School of Advanced Management — co-sponsored by UBC, and at the Nestle Company sponsored management school (known as IMEDE) in Lausanne, Switzerland, and for the Certified General Accountants Association of British Columbia.

Dr. Lusztig served as one of three Commissioners on the 1966-68 B.C. Royal Commission on Automobile Insurance, was the sole Commissioner of the B.C. Commission of Inquiry on the Tree Fruit Industry, chaired the recent Federal/Provincial Governments' Asia Pacific Initiative Advisory Committee and during the Fall of 1991, he was a Senior Advisor to the B.C. Ministry of Economic Development, Small Business and Trade. He was a Public Governor of the Vancouver Stock Exchange and a member of its Executive Committee. In the past, he served as a director of the Laurier Institution and was on the board of Canfor Corporation. He has served on the board of Tree Island Industries, a founding director of ICBC, and a trustee of the Vancouver General Hospital and the VGH Foundations.

Dr. Lusztig retired form the University of British Columbia in 1995. Since that time, he has been the Federal Government's appointment to the B.C. Treaty Commission. He is Dean Emeritus of the Faculty of Commerce at the University of British Columbia, and is on the boards of Royal Sun Alliance, Western Insurance, and Quebec Insurance—ROINS Financial Holdings.

W. Sean Cleary is Associate Professor of Finance at Saint Mary's University in Halifax, Nova Scotia. Dr. Cleary graduated with his MBA from Saint Mary's University in 1989, and with his PhD in finance from the University of Toronto in 1998. He has completed level II of the Chartered Financial Analyst (CFA) program. He has also completed the Canadian Securities Course (CSC) as well as the Investment Funds Institute of Canada (IFIC) Mutual Fund Course.

Dr. Cleary has taught numerous university finance courses, including Investments, Introductory Finance, Corporate Finance and Mergers and Acquisitions at Saint Mary's University, the University of Toronto, Ryerson Polytechnic University, and the University of Lethbridge over the past 10 years. He has also taught seminars preparing students to write the Canadian Securities Course for the past six years.

Dr. Cleary is the Canadian author of *Investments: Analysis and Management*, Canadian Edition by W. Sean Cleary and Charles P. Jones. He is also the author of *The Canadian Securities Exam Fast Track Study Guide*, published by John Wiley & Sons Canada, Ltd. He has published articles in *The Journal of Finance*, the *Canadian Journal of Administrative Sciences*, and the *Canadian Investment Review*, in addition to receiving research funding from the Social Sciences and Humanities Research Council of Canada (SSHRC). He has also prepared chapters for professional courses and delivered seminars for the Canadian Securities Institute.

Bernhard Schwab is Professor of Business Administration at the Faculty of Commerce and Business Administration, University of British Columbia, teaching both in Corporate Finance and Business Strategy. He received his Dipl.-Ing. in electrical engineering at the Technische Hochschule in Munich (1963). Subsequently, he pursued graduate studies in economics and business administration at the University of Munich and the University of California in Los Angeles, where he obtained his MBA (1965) and PhD (1967).

Dr. Schwab has been at the University of British Columbia since 1968, with visiting appointments at universities in Europe and Australia. He has taught in a variety of professional and executive programs in North America, Europe, Asia, and Australia and has received the Teaching Excellence Award of the Faculty of Commerce. Dr. Schwab has published numerous articles in both academic and professional literature including journals such as the *Harvard Business Review*, *Sloan Management Review*, *Journal of Finance*, *Journal of Financial and Quantitative Analysis*, *Columbia Journal of World Business*, *Policy Options* and others. He is a member of the Financial Executives Institute.

PREFACE

INTRODUCTION

Since the first edition was published, the vision for this book has been to be the only finance text to address the specific needs of a Canadian audience. The goal has been simple: To provide students and instructors with a text that was Canadian, that bridged the gap between financial theory and practice, and that was clearly written and current.

Financial theory has developed rapidly in recent years affecting curriculum content, classroom presentation, and current financial practice. The increased reliance on economic theory and quantitative analysis has made it even more critical to bridge the gap between academics and practitioners. Thus, the focus of this book has been on relating the theory of finance and its assumptions and conclusions to the world of the practitioner.

Widely used across Canada throughout five editions, instructors and students alike have commented that the book's strengths include:

- strong Canadian content
- a clear writing style, structure, and layout
- thorough coverage of theory and practice
- excellent examples and cases
- comprehensive end-of-chapter problem sections
- an integrated discussion of international finance

In this, the Sixth Edition, the goals have been to build upon these strengths, to make the book more accessible and user-friendly for students and instructors, and to enhance the presentation and organization of material. Additionally, we have addressed technology—both in its impact on the field of finance, and by providing tools to assist in teaching and learning.

The book is written for the first course in investments at universities and colleges, and is a useful supplement for students planning to enroll in the CSC. Standard prerequisites include basic accounting, economics, and introductory finance. A course in statistics is very useful but not absolutely essential. We have sought to minimize formulae and to simplify difficult material, consistent with a presentation of the subject that takes into account current ideas and practices. Relevant, state-of-the-art material has been simplified and structured specifically for the benefit of the student.

SIXTH EDITION ENHANCED FEATURES

Based on the comments of reviewers and users of the Fifth Edition, the presentation has been strengthened to more accurately reflect the needs of instructors and students. The goal is to provide the most complete and up-to-date coverage of introductory finance in Canada.

Streamlined Discussion

Wherever appropriate, discussions were streamlined and the writing style enhanced to make the material more reader-friendly.

Re-organization of Topics

Several changes were made to the organization of topics to enhance the flow of material and to assist in teaching and understanding. These include:

- Coverage of valuation, risk and return, and portfolio theory are now divided into three distinct chapters. This will allow students to better understand these critical foundation topics of financial theory.

- Part 5 "Long-Term Sources of Funds" has been reorganized into two distinct chapters on debt/preferred equity and common equity.

- Chapters on financial statement analysis, funds flow analysis, and forecasting are now discussed early in the presentation to provide students with the necessary background to deal with subsequent topics in the book.

Complete Update

Financial theory and examples have been completely updated. Examples from real-world organizations have been expanded throughout and real financial data is used wherever appropriate to help bridge the gap between theory and practice. Many "hot topics" are incorporated to pique students' interest.

International Coverage

Coverage of international material remains uniquely integrated throughout the book. This material is now highlighted to stress its importance by incorporating the "Global Finance" icon wherever discussion of international finance occurs.

Derivatives

Highly regarded in the Fifth Edition, this book continues to have the most complete coverage of derivatives available, including a complete chapter on treasury risk management.

NEW FEATURES

Many new features have been added to the Sixth Edition to enhance the learning experience, to strengthen the textual discussions, and to further bridge the gap between theory and practice. Almost all are unique to *Finance in a Canadian Setting*.

Chapter Opening Vignettes
Each chapter now begins with a brief snapshot of an actual Canadian company and how they are applying the chapter material in real-world settings.

Chapter Overviews
Each chapter also begins with a graphical overview of the chapter material demonstrating how the various sections relate to each other.

Perspectives Boxes
New Perspectives Boxes demonstrate both the corporate and investor perspectives of financial theory and discuss how key concepts are viewed by both internal and external users of financial information. This unique tool will benefit students no matter where their career path may take them as managers and users of financial information.

Finance in the News Boxes
Finance in the News boxes present students with articles covering financial issues found in today's news media.

BCE Running Case
A Running Case developed from the financial data of BCE Inc. is included at the end of each Part. Additionally, the BCE Annual Report, from which the data is gathered, is available to view and print at www.wiley.com/canada/lusztig. The Running Case provides the opportunity to analyse a company using tools and techniques from a variety of chapters.

Career Choices Appendix
The Appendix to Chapter 1 includes a brief overview of many of the career possibilities available to finance students. Feedback from reviewers has been very favourable to this addition, since it addresses many of the questions posed by finance students who enroll in their first finance course.

PROBLEM MATERIAL

The end-of-chapter problem material has been completely updated and enhanced, and continues to be the most comprehensive problem set available. This has been enhanced by the addition of Greg MacKinnon of Saint Mary's University as Problems Author.

Questions and Problems
All questions and problems have been completely re-worked and expanded. They are now reorganized to provide instructors with better flexibility in assigning material.

Spreadsheet Problems
A number of key problems are available in Excel format and help integrate the use of spreadsheets in learning and understanding finance.

Problems with Solutions
The Sixth Edition continues to provide practice problems with solutions to assist students in their problem solving skills. Many are now available on the Lusztig website at www.wiley.com/canada/lusztig.

Running Case
As described above, a Running Case developed from the financial data of BCE, Inc. is found at the end of each Part.

Internet Cases
A variety of Internet Cases are available on the Lusztig Website at www.wiley.com/canada/lusztig. These cases will be updated on a continual basis and will expand student's use of the internet in studying and understanding finance.

ADDITIONAL RESOURCES

A wide variety of new additional resources is now available with the Sixth Edition to assist instructors in their course delivery and students in understanding the material.

Instructor's Resource CD
An Instructor's Resource CD is available to instructors teaching from the Sixth Edition and includes a completely new set of instructor's supplements. The CD includes:

- Instructor's manual
- Solutions manual
- PowerPoint ™ slides
- Computerized Test Bank prepared by Michael Inglis of Ryerson Polytechnic University
- Data for spreadsheet problems

All items are completely new. Instructors should contact their local Wiley representative for more information.

Website
A comprehensive and fully integrated website is available and includes a variety of additional resources for both students and instructors. This website will be updated every semester to ensure that information, data, and links are current and up-to-date. Detailed information on the variety of features found on the website is included on the inside front-cover of this book. The website can be found at www.wiley.com/canada/lusztig.

Student Resource Manual
Students seeking further aids to study can purchase the Finance in a Canadian Setting Student Resource Manual. This manual contains a variety of additional demonstration problems, practice problems with solutions, study outlines, chapter summaries, and

resources for additional study. You can ask your bookstore to order a copy for you (ISBN: 0-471-64633-4) or you can purchase it directly from the Wiley website at www.wiley.com.

Corporate Finance 101 Software

This powerful software tool, created by Zoologic Inc. and available exclusively through Wiley, is a valuable aid to any finance student. Corporate Finance 101 ™ teaches the fundamental concepts of corporate finance in an interactive environment, including how to allocate resources, how to find the optimal capital structure, and how to develop a dividend policy. Randomly-generated exercises allow students to check their progress as they go. Corporate Finance 101 ™ (ISBN: 0-471-33308-5) is available for purchase on the Wiley website at www.wiley.com.

USING FINANCIAL INFORMATION

In contemporary business programs in Canada, many instructors comment on the need to focus more on the use and analysis of financial information to provide students with stronger decision-making and analytical skills when they enter the workforce. Many programs have been reshaped in this manner. One of the underlying themes of this new edition is to better prepare students with the tools, skills, and understanding they will need as managers and/or users of financial information. Such enhancements as the reorganization of topics, the addition of the *Perspectives* boxes, and the inclusion of a Running Case are all included to better prepare students as future managers.

ACKNOWLEDGEMENTS
SIXTH EDITION

Finance in a Canadian Setting Sixth Edition is the result of an extensive team of individuals who have all contributed toward making this edition into the most exciting ever. I am indebted to the comments and feedback from users and reviewers who provided feedback on the previous edition and on the manuscript for the Sixth Edition. Those reviewers are:

Arshad Ahmad, *Concordia University*

Ben Amoako-Adu, *Wilfrid Laurier University*

Larry Bauer, *Memorial University of Newfoundland*

Nalinaksha Bhattacharyya, *University of Manitoba*

Trevor W. Chamberlain, *McMaster University*

Alex Faseruk, *Memorial University of Newfoundland*

Brian Furzecott, *Georgian College*

Eldon Gardner, *University of Lethbridge*

Charles Mossman, *University of Manitoba*

Michael A. Perretta, *Sheridan College*

Ian Rakita, *Concordia University*

This edition has benefited from the input of a number of contributors without whose effort this book would not be possible. I would like to thank:

Greg MacKinnon, Running Case and Problems Author

Michael Inglis, Computerized Test Bank Author

Elizabeth d'Anjou, Vignette Author

Donald E. Stoyle, Solutions Checker

Morgan Fudge, Website Content

I would like to thank my wife Helen, my children Jason, Brennan, Brigid, and Siobhan, and my parents Bill and Beryl for their support. Thanks to Gordon Dixon at the University of Lethbridge for his tax expertise, and to my colleagues Greg MacKinnon, Greg Hebb, and Francis Boabang for their input and feedback. I would also like to thank my assistants, Kim Phillips and Morgan Fudge, for their capable efforts. Finally, I would like to acknowledge the support and direction provided by the Wiley production team, with special acknowledgements to John Horne, Michelle Harrington, Janine Daoust, and Elsa Passera. They are true professionals who have helped to keep me on track throughout the entire process.

W. Sean Cleary
February 2001

BRIEF CONTENTS

The following Appendices and the Glossary are located on the website at:
www.wiley.com/canada/lusztig and form an important link with the text.

Appendix I   The Tax Environment
Appendix II   BCE Inc. Annual Report 1999
Appendix III   Compounding and Discounting Tables

Glossary

CONTENTS

The following Appendices and the Glossary are located on the website at:
<u>www.wiley.com/canada/lusztig</u> and form an important link with the text.

Appendix I The Tax Environment

Appendix II BCE Inc. Annual Report 1999

Appendix III Compounding and Discounting Tables

Glossary

Overview of Financial Management

In Part 1, we discuss the objectives of financial mangement, and the financial environment. Chapter 1 provides an overview of finance and the major functional areas of finance. It also discusses the goals of financial management and the importance of agency costs. Chapter 2 describes the structure of Canadian and global financial systems and the functions provided by financial intermediaries.

What Beer's All About— Shareholder Value

In 1998, Molson Company made headlines in the business press across the country with its startling new strategic plan: to brew beer.

Since Molson has been brewing beer in Canada since 1786, this may not seem like an especially newsworthy event. But for most of the past thirty years, the company had been pursuing a strategy of diversification, acquiring significant stakes in Diversey (a chemical company), Beaver Lumber, and Home Depot. As the millennium drew to a close, the company's management decided on a complete "reinvention of the organization," starting with the premise "back to beer."

Molson announced four central corporate goals for this new strategy. First among them was aligning the interests of employees with shareholders. (The other three were operating strategically, reducing the cost base while improving productivity, and growing globally.)

As the clout of large investors grows, putting shareholder value at the top of the corporate agenda has become more and more common. And often, maximizing shareholder returns involves "corporate clarity," focusing on one business. These former conglomerates become "tangerines," to be taken apart in sections. The message from investors, wrote James Darroch in *Report on Business* magazine, is that "they are the asset allocators and they do not need corporate CEOs doing their jobs of finding a good portfolio mix."

Molson lost no time implementing its turnaround. On April 30 1998 the company sold its 25% interest in The Home Depot Canada; by June 30 it had signed an agreement to dispose of its last non-beer retail holding, Beaver Lumber. Departing CEO James Arnett announced, "We, at Molson, can now focus exclusively on increasing shareholder value through our brewing and related activities."

And so they did. With the proceeds from these sales and further financing, Molson repurchased the partial stakes in some of its operations and brands that it had sold off in preceding years. It became once again a brewery, pure and simple. The company even moved the offices of its top executives back to its Montreal building on Notre Dame St., site of its 18th-century brewery.

By the first quarter of fiscal year 2000, the new strategy was showing impressive results. Earnings from continuing operations were up 49%; revenue for the quarter increased 4% to $697.5 million; and brewing operating profit was up 15.5%. "This is a great way to start off the new fiscal year," said Daniel J. O'Neill, President and Chief Executive Officer of Molson. "We are positioning Molson for future sustainable growth for the benefit of our shareholders," he added.

chapter 1

Financial Management and the Financial Objectives of the Firm

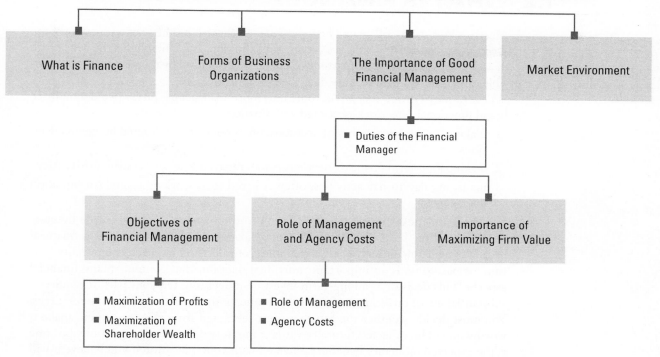

Learning Objectives

After studying this chapter, you should be able to:

1. *Define financial management, and give two reasons why it is important.*
2. *Name three reasons why simple profit maximization is not a satisfactory economic objective for financial managers.*
3. *Discuss the two main categories of criticisms of simple share price maximization as a corporate objective.*
4. *Examine agency relationships, and outline the potential associated costs.*

1.1 INTRODUCTION

This chapter provides an overview of the discipline of finance including a discussion of the major functions of financial management. It also discusses the financial objectives of the firm and the framework within which financial managers operate. It is important to have an understanding of the goals that motivate financial decision-making as well as the constraints faced by financial managers since the quality of financial decisions can be judged only if one has a clear objective in mind.

1.2 WHAT IS FINANCE?

Merriam Webster's Collegiate Dictionary defines finance as "the science or study of the management of funds."[1] This is a very broad definition, and it highlights the wide range of activities associated with the study of finance as evidenced by the vast number of possible careers in this field that are described in Appendix 1-A.

In order to divide this broad topic into more manageable pieces, we define three broad functional categories associated with finance:

1. making long-term investment decisions, often referred to as capital budgeting decisions
2. making long-term financing decisions, often referred to as capital structure decisions
3. managing day-to-day activities, often referred to as working capital (or liquidity) management

While this text devotes much attention to the financial decisions made by businesses, the three basic elements of financial management apply equally to financial decisions made by individuals. For example, your decision to enrol in university full-time or part-time is an important individual decision that contains many financial aspects. This decision is a long-term investment decision. On your part, it requires a substantial initial investment of money and time, both of which are valuable resources. You must decide whether the future rewards expected from this investment make it worthwhile. The expected future rewards come in two forms. The most obvious one is the expected monetary benefits associated with your education if you believe it will enable you to earn a higher income. However, there are also very important intangible benefits that you can expect to realize, and these intangibles may be more important for many individuals. For example, you may believe that the education itself will bring you self-satisfaction and/or will enable you to obtain a job that you will enjoy. You must weigh the costs of obtaining these expected future benefits against your other alternatives, which may include working full-time at an existing job or looking for full-time employment without a degree. We will discuss the ways to analyse this decision from a financial point of view.

One of the main considerations in your decision to attend university—your investment decision—will be how you will finance this endeavour—your financing decision. In

---

[1] Source: Merriam Webster website at http://www.m-w.com/dictionary/htm. Accessed May 16, 2000.

other words, if you cannot find a way of financing your education, you will be unable to pursue this opportunity. This is a long-term financing decision because you will be concerned with paying for the courses both now and in the future as well as sustaining yourself and any dependents you have. You may decide to liquidate some investments you now own, work while attending school, obtain student loans or scholarships, or some combination of these alternatives. From a financial perspective, you should weigh the costs of these financing alternatives against your expected future benefits and also consider the earnings you forego by attending school. Remember, time is money!

Finally, once you have decided to invest in your education and have established a mechanism for financing this pursuit, you must manage your day-to-day finances. (Of course, this is true whether or not you attend university.) For example, if you finance a substantial portion of your education through student loans, and the advances are received through periodic instalments, you must employ a strategy to allocate your funds properly during the intervals between instalments. Otherwise, you may be forced to seek alternative financing, forego some of life's pleasures (or necessities), or even become a reluctant adherent to the all-too-familiar Kraft Dinner diet.

The example above discusses the financial aspects associated with one particular decision. Individuals will face many such choices throughout their lives, some of greater magnitude and some that are less important. Large companies make such financial decisions on a regular basis. Irrespective of their importance, frequency, or who is making the choices, the basic framework for these financial resolutions is essentially the same—only the situations and details change. Before considering the importance of financial management in greater depth, we introduce the three basic forms of business organizations.

FORMS OF BUSINESS ORGANIZATIONS   1.3

The **sole proprietorship** is a business that is owned and operated by one individual. It is not recognized as a separate legal entity (from the owner) for tax and legal purposes. All the profits go to the owner, so the income generated from the proprietorship is taxed as personal income at the owner's individual tax rate. In addition, the owner faces **unlimited liability** with respect to the business. This means that the proprietor is liable for any and all obligations incurred by the business, and the amount of the owner's personal liability is not restricted to the amount of money the individual invests in the business. Proprietorships are easy to establish, but they are limited in size by their ability to generate investment capital for growth. As a result, while the number of proprietorships exceeds that of the other types of business organizations by a wide margin, the dollar volume of sales produced by these type of businesses and the value of their assets is trivial compared to those of corporations.

Partnerships involve two or more owners, at least one of whom is responsible for the operation of the business. The details of the organization of the partnership are described in a partnership agreement, which outlines details regarding each partner's responsibilities and share of the profits. There are two types of partnerships: **general partnerships** and **limited partnerships**. In a general partnership, all of the partners face unlimited liability with regard to the partnership obligations, and most (or all) of them are involved in the day-to-day operation of the business. In addition, the partners face "joint and several liability," meaning that all the partners are jointly liable for the sum of the obligations of the partnership, but each partner is also "severally" liable for this entire amount on his or her own.

Limited partnerships must have at least one general partner who is involved in the day-to-day operations and faces unlimited liability. The limited partners cannot participate in the business operations, and their liability is limited to the amount they invest in the partnership. In other words, the most they can lose is what they invest in the business.

Partnerships are very similar to proprietorships in that they are not recognized as separate legal entities, the income from the partnership is taxed as personal income, and general partners face unlimited liability. In addition, the amount of capital that can be raised by partnerships is also limited.

While **corporations** represent a small percentage of the total number of businesses in Canada, they dominate in terms of assets and dollar volumes of sales. Corporations are not as easy to establish or maintain as proprietorships or partnerships. They are formed by filing documents with the appropriate government agency. Once incorporation has been approved, the corporation will come into existence after the government agency issues a charter for the company in the form of letters patent, a memorandum of association, or articles of incorporation. Companies may incorporate federally under the *Canada Business Corporations Act* or provincially under appropriate provincial statutes. A company that incorporates provincially can carry on business in that province but may require additional licensing to carry on business outside that province. The decision of where to incorporate will be based on where the company does business and upon the regulation it will face under relevant provincial or federal laws.

Unlike proprietorships and partnerships, corporations are recognized as separate legal entities that can enter into legal contracts and own property. Profits are taxed based on corporate tax rates, and the owners face **limited liability** (i.e., their liability is limited to the amount they invest in the corporation). A distinguishing feature of corporations is the separation of ownership from management. Corporations are owned by individuals who hold shares in the company. While company managers usually own some shares in the company, there are also usually a large number of shareholders who do not have any direct involvement in the management of the corporation. These shareholders exert their influence over the corporation (at least in principle) by electing the board of directors. The directors, in turn, determine the firm's strategic direction, pick its management team, and monitor their actions. Transferring one's ownership stake in a corporation is relatively straightforward. Owners (shareholders) only need to sell their shares to another investor. This contrasts with proprietorships, which must sell the entire business. With partnerships, if one or more of the partners wants to get out, a new business must be established and a new partnership agreement drawn up.

In summary, corporations have many potential advantages that have led to their growth and dominance of business activity including the following:

1. Corporate tax laws may be more attractive in some circumstances thus allowing tax deferral or avoidance.

2. The separation of ownership from control allows corporations to obtain the best available management team (at least in principle).

3. Limited liability makes ownership more attractive to shareholders.

4. Transfer of ownership is relatively easy.

Limited liability and the ease of ownership transfer make it relatively easy for corporations to attract investment capital since potential investors know that their exposure to loss is limited and that they can cash out any time if they need the cash or are unhappy with the direction in which the company is headed. In fact, the ability to access capital markets is probably the most important feature of corporations because it enables them to grow.

While this text focuses on financial management as it pertains to corporations because of their dominance of business activity, most of the same underlying principles are applicable to proprietorships, partnerships, and individuals.

IMPORTANCE OF
GOOD FINANCIAL MANAGEMENT

1.4

Successful firms have long recognized the need for effective financial management and for having significant financial expertise among their senior executives. Over the years, the importance of finance in corporate management has grown, and today's presidents and chief executive officers invariably have significant financial expertise. The importance of financial management is reflected in the annual reports of most companies, which have specific finance-related objectives (such as maximizing shareholder wealth) included in their corporate mission statements.[2]

There are several reasons for the importance and scope of finance. First, the scale of operations of business firms has expanded greatly in recent years. The growing significance of large corporations and the increasing size of investments highlight the importance of long-range financial planning. Second, the widespread diversification of products and the global nature of today's business environment have increased the complexity of managing a business. Instead of companies with one division and a few products, we now have multiproduct, multidivisional, and multinational corporations. The effective control of such diverse operations has required a substantial strengthening of the finance function particularly in an environment that has been characterized by increasing economic uncertainties and the globalization of business activities. Even those companies that concentrate their efforts primarily in domestic markets must be aware of the threat of competition from foreign competitors and products. As a result of the above developments, financial executives increasingly participate in formulating and implementing broad corporate strategy. Financial decisions directly affect the risk and profitability of a firm. Risk and profitability, in turn, critically determine the company's relative success in a competitive marketplace.

---

[2] We will discuss corporate objectives and the maximization of shareholder wealth in greater detail in Section 1.6.

Organizationally, the finance function is handled in a variety of ways, and the financial executive's specific role will vary according to the nature of the business, the size of the firm, the financial executive's ability, and the abilities of the other officers and directors. However, because financial decisions affect the destiny of the entire business, financial management is treated somewhat differently from other functional areas and is generally viewed as part of the central management of the enterprise. As a consequence, even in the most decentralized firms with independent management of operations perhaps in various parts of the world, financial management tends to remain fairly centralized.

Although the finance function is well developed in most larger enterprises, the frequent lack of financial expertise has become a serious deficiency in many smaller businesses. Here, the position of a financial executive may not even exist, and the president is left to assume all financial duties. Unfortunately, in many small firms, a president's competence in financial matters may be limited; he may be one of the original promoters of the company who either developed a new product idea or has a marketable technical competence. For example, computer companies are often formed by computer scientists or programmers, mining and oil companies by geologists, and manufacturing firms by inventors and engineers. The high failure rates experienced by small businesses in Canada can be attributed at least in part to a lack of financial expertise among management.

Duties of the Financial Manager

Today's financial officer is oriented toward the future performance of the enterprise. In contrast to the traditional accountant who is more concerned with keeping an up-to-date record on past operations, the financial executive is more likely to participate in forecasting and forward planning. In an environment that is characterized by complexity, rapid change, and a high degree of uncertainty, this responsibility for future planning and performance places increasing pressures on financial managers. Therefore, they must

- be thoroughly familiar with financial and accounting theory and practice
- be continually involved in the development of information systems by which data are made available in a timely fashion and in a form that facilitates decision-making
- understand the strengths and limitations of computers
- have an adequate knowledge of the newer analytical techniques in order to participate effectively in decision-making
- generally be familiar with the non-financial aspects of business
- be well versed in economics in order to assess current developments in financial markets, movements of interest and foreign exchange rates, and changes in price levels and in the general level of economic activity

In the economic environment of the new millennium, further skills that have been deemed increasingly important are the ability to contain costs and to foster productivity improvements in the face of increasingly intense price competition and a deepened understanding of the international business environment. Required international expertise is no longer restricted to an arms-length financial control of foreign operations but ranges from an in-depth understanding of business conditions and opportunities in a wide range of countries to the overall management of risk in an international context. Finally, financial managers must have sound business judgement in order to make good decisions in areas in which information is likely to be incomplete, theoretical developments have often remained controversial, and past experience may have limited applicability.

The financial executive typically is involved in all areas of finance outlined in Section 1.2. The financial manager's main responsibilities are the procurement of funds to support the ongoing operations and planned investments of the firm (treasury functions) and control over the disbursements of funds to ensure efficiency and adequate returns (controllership function). In this sense, the finance function links and coordinates the liability side (financing and interfacing with financial markets) and the asset side (investments to satisfy consumer needs) of the balance sheet. These relationships are depicted in Figure 1.1.

FINANCIAL MANAGEMENT

- Markets/institutions
- Individual sources
- Cost of capital
- Financing strategy, captial structure
- Dividend policy

Procurement of funds
Treasury

Financial management

Disbursement of funds

- Internal investments (capital budgeting)
- Mergers/acquisitions

Controllership

Controls of operations

- Financial analysis
- Financial planning
- Performance measurement evaluation, management
- Working capital and liquidity management
- Risk management

FIGURE 1.1

Financial Management

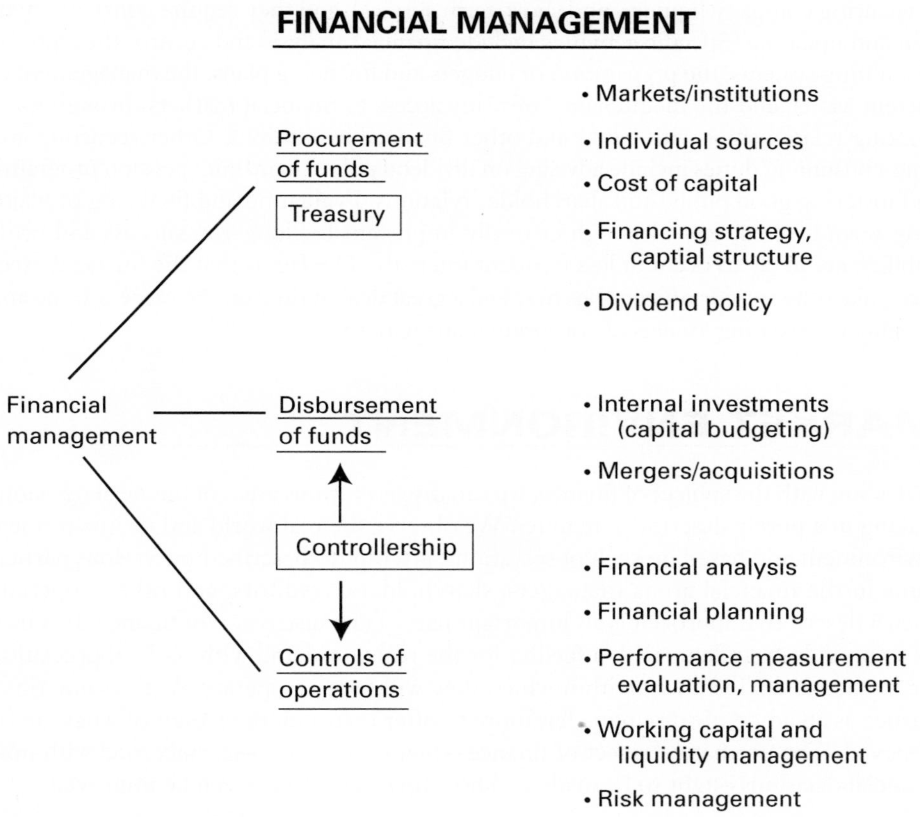

P E R S P E C T I V E S

Corporate Manager

It is important for managers to monitor current and expected future market conditions when making decisions regarding financing, investments, dividends, mergers, and managing day-to-day risks.

Investor

Individual investors should be aware of their own financial constraints as well as expected future market conditions before making any financial decisions such as allocating funds for investment purposes or borrowing for consumption purposes.

Financial planning, working capital management, and risk management are critical in ensuring company liquidity and short-term survival, and they require constant attention and updating. Specific activities include financial analysis and control through the accounting systems, the preparation of budgets and financing plans, the management of current assets, and the maintenance of ready access to financial markets through good working relationships with banks and other financial institutions. Other recurring and time-consuming duties include advising on dividend policy, managing pension programs, and fostering good public and shareholder relations. Evaluation and financing of major long-term investments, although critically important for long-run success and profitability, are likely to occur at less frequent intervals. The fact is that the financial executive, like other senior officers, has to spend a great deal of time on the more routine and possibly less exciting aspects of corporate management.

1.5 MARKET ENVIRONMENT

In dealing with the subject of finance, we can discuss various areas of financial decision-making in a purely descriptive manner. We observe the real world and its institutional environment and based on such observations, attempt to describe how various participants in the financial arena (managers, shareholders, creditors, and others) operate. Such a descriptive approach is an important part of any discussion of finance. It is useful in providing students with a feeling for the real world and with some appreciation for the actual environment within which they will have to operate. At the same time, finance as an academic discipline has more to offer than a mere recount of what can be observed. The normative aspect of finance—financial theory—is concerned with how financial decisions ought to be made and how financial practice can be improved.

A prerequisite for the development of financial theory is the formulation of financial objectives. Clearly, we can only term a decision as good, bad, better, or worse if we have some standard against which we can measure performance. The purpose of developing financial objectives is to provide such a standard. In this section, we review the philosophy and framework of free markets and discuss the implications of the market environment for the formulation of financial objectives.

Much of the economic system of industrialized nations is based on the philosophy of free markets. This free-market framework is illustrated schematically in a simplified form in Figure 1.2. Businesses obtain funds by selling securities such as stocks or bonds in financial markets in which investors allocate their savings to the purchase of securities so as to maximize their wealth. Companies then allocate the funds received to capital investments such as plant and equipment in order to maximize their own wealth by satisfying consumer demand for goods and services. This system is appealing because it allows for free investor and consumer choice, with businesses simply reacting to the collective choices made by market participants.

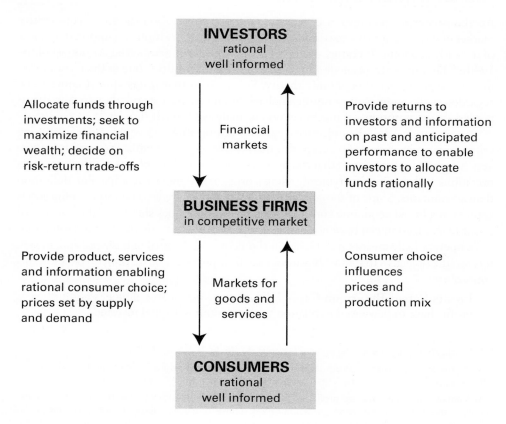

FIGURE 1.2

Simplified Framework for a Free-Market Economy

The free-market system also has important underpinnings in economic theory that date back to Adam Smith.[3] Thus, one can show that under the assumptions of perfect markets (implying, for example, perfect competition, rational and well-informed investors and consumers, and prices that capture all external costs or benefits), this system leads to an efficient allocation of resources in the economy. Businesses that best serve consumer interests capture an increased share of the market and reap higher returns. Investors are attracted to such firms and thus make additional funds available to them, thereby ensuring that financial resources are allocated to ventures and organizations that most efficiently serve the economic preferences of society.

1.6 OBJECTIVES OF FINANCIAL MANAGEMENT

Maximization of Profits

An almost stereotyped response regarding the objectives of business in a competitive market environment is the maximization of profits. This position is reinforced by some of the early economic literature on the subject. To quote one respected economist of the 1940s: "That the entrepreneur aims at maximizing his profits is one of the most fundamental assumptions of economic theory. So much so that it has almost come to be regarded as the equivalent of rational behaviour and we have a vested interest in maintaining this assumption—it makes economic analysis so much simpler."[4]

In recent decades, the objective of profit maximization has come under increasing criticism even by those who accept the framework of private enterprise and free markets. We note in this context that the notion of profits itself is subject to different interpretations with economists typically using a broader and more encompassing definition than accountants. Some of the concerns arise when the narrow accounting definition is applied in a broad economic context.[5] Specifically, the critics show that the concept of profit maximization can have not only conceptual flaws but can also be too ambiguous to be operationally meaningful. Hence, it should not be the goal of business, and, in fact, it is not the objective that most businesses say they pursue. The three main issues in this context are:

1. **Profits Versus Return on Capital**: From an owner or shareholder's point of view, profits have to be viewed in relation to the amount of capital invested.

---

[3] A. Smith, *An Inquiry into the Nature and Causes of the Wealth of Nations*, (1776).

[4] T. Scitovsky, "A Note on Profit Maximization and Its Implications," *Review of Economic Studies* (1943–44), p. 57.

[5] Accountants typically measure profits as the residual gain that accrues to equity investors after deducting interest on debt but before provision of any returns on equity capital. Economists view profits as the residual gain left after a fair-market-determined return (including possible premiums for risk) has been provided on all capital (including equity) invested. If we use this broader economic definition, many of the inconsistencies that we discuss below disappear since economic profits can be linked to an increase in shareholder wealth much more readily than accounting profits.

2. **Timing of Cash Flows**: The occurrence of profits is not a one-time event. Rather, most businesses anticipate a stream of profits over time. Thus, any operational objective ought to incorporate the "time value of money" that allows for profits to be compared and traded off across different time periods.

3. **Risk**: Any stream of anticipated profits is subject to risk. If a financial objective is to be operationally meaningful, it will have to allow for the explicit evaluation of risk.[6]

We discuss each of these points in turn.

1. Profits Versus Return on Capital

Clearly, conceptual inconsistencies may arise if accounting profits are not related to the amount of capital invested or to the number of shares outstanding since the wealth position of owners or shareholders can suffer even when total profits increase. For example, a company can always increase its aggregate profits by raising additional capital through the sale of more common shares and by investing the proceeds in projects that yield positive rates of return. If, however, such returns are below the average returns that the firm earns on its existing investments, a reduction in earnings per share will result. Such a dilution in earnings per share may suggest an inappropriate interpretation of profit maximization because the original shareholders are now worse off.

TOTAL PROFITS VERSUS EARNINGS PER SHARE

EXAMPLE

An enterprise has 1,000 common shares outstanding and after-tax profits of $1,000 per year yielding earnings per share of $1. Assume that a further 1,000 shares are sold that net the company $7,000 and that the proceeds are then invested to generate an additional after-tax profit of $500 per year. Thus, although total profits have increased significantly to $1,500 per year, the position of the original shareholders has been diluted because earnings per share have dipped from the original $1 to $0.75.

We conclude that profits have to be viewed in relation to capital invested if they are to guide financial decision-making. This issue is related to that of dividend policy. So long as profits that are retained in the business can be invested to earn a positive return, earnings per share can be increased by retaining all profits and never paying dividends. Obviously, however, it would not be in the best interest of shareholders if a firm retained earnings only to invest surplus funds in a low-yielding savings account at a bank. Although earnings per share would increase modestly, shareholders would rather see the company distributing its excess cash through dividend payments. Shareholders could then reinvest the funds themselves in more productive ventures. The return on capital invested by a firm—whether it is raised externally through the sale of new securities or internally through retained earnings—should always be commensurate with reasonable

---

[6] A fourth issue that could be raised in this context is whether owners in their evaluation of an enterprise are mainly concerned with profits as defined by accountants or economists, cash flows, or dividends. Although important, this issue is more technical than the issues presented above, and we postpone its discussion to the appropriate places in Chapters 6, 10, and 17.

shareholder expectations in a given market environment. If it is not, disappointed investors will sell their shares and channel their funds elsewhere. As a consequence, the company's stock price will fall, and shareholders will see their wealth position erode.

2. Timing of Cash Flows

Two key dimensions of almost any financial decisions are time and risk. These variables are at the core of financial decision-making and will be recognized in every major section of this text. Typically, financial decisions entail a stream of uncertain future cash flows. For example, if a firm undertakes an investment such as building a new plant or acquiring another company, it does so on the expectation that the project will generate a stream of future cash flows that over time, will both repay the investment and provide a fair return. Similarly, if an investor buys a security such as a common share, she does so in anticipation of future cash flows in the form of dividends and/or capital gains. We will discuss the time value of money in detail in Chapter 5. At this stage, we simply note that because money can be invested to earn a return, identical dollar amounts received at two different points in time do not have the same economic value. A dollar received today can be reinvested immediately and earn interest. Consequently, it is worth more than a dollar received sometime in the future. The statement of profit maximization ignores this fundamental time dimension and fails to provide any operational guidance on how we should trade off profits across different time periods. To illustrate, one investment may promise moderate but fairly immediate returns, whereas a second project may entail a lengthy start-up period but offer the potential for significant long-term gains. The two projects may be mutually exclusive, which means that if you choose one, you cannot choose the other and vice versa. If a financial objective is to be operationally meaningful, it will have to provide guidance on how to decide between such alternatives.

3. Risk

Uncertainty or risk is the other key factor that affects financial decisions. As we know, the future is inherently uncertain, and any investor who relies on a stream of estimated future cash flows is subject to risk. Even the most carefully prepared projections may fail to materialize, and actual cash flows may exceed or fall short of original estimates. However, not all investments are subject to the same degree of risk. For example, the returns associated with government bonds are much more predictable than those expected from an investment in an Internet company's stock. Similarly, at the level of a firm, an investment to automate part of a well-known production process may result in more predictable returns than an investment that entails launching a new and untried product. Most market participants—investors and managers alike—are not indifferent to risk, but they view it as something negative to be avoided or reduced whenever possible. As a consequence, investors in financial markets generally demand a higher expected return, or a risk premium, in order to invest in risky securities. Again, the concept of profit maximization ignores these well-documented preferences of decision-makers with regard to risk.

Maximization of Shareholder Wealth

We would like to find a financial objective that overcomes the ambiguities and conceptual shortcomings of profit maximization. The key question in this context is whose value judgements one should rely on in developing time preferences and risk attitudes that are needed for the evaluation of streams of uncertain future cash flows. In the context of the free-market framework, the only justifiable source for such judgements is the market itself, and the time value and the risk attitudes that ought to guide managerial decision-making are those observed in the marketplace.[7] The time value of money is reflected in interest rates, and market trade-offs between risk and expected returns will be considered in detail in subsequent chapters. We will see that these market preferences are measurable by, for example, relating statistically expected or average returns for various types of securities to risk or variations in those returns over time.

In order to specify financial objectives, we next need to translate such market preferences regarding time and risk into variables that are operationally meaningful at the level of the firm. The standard mechanism through which market preferences are reflected in economics is price—share price in our case because common shares are certificates that confer ultimate ownership rights in the company. If we substitute the maximization of the firm's share prices for profit maximization, we overcome most of the ambiguities discussed above. This is because the objective of share price maximization incorporates both the time and risk dimensions that are so critical in financial decisions.

For example, assume that a business does not abide by market preferences in selecting its investment projects and is overly liberal in accepting risky projects that do not promise commensurate returns. Once investors perceive such a shift in investment policy, they will start selling their shareholdings in the firm and reinvesting in companies where the trade-off between risk and expected returns is more consistent with their preferences. As a consequence, share prices will drop until the anticipated returns are once again in line with market preferences. Similarly, if a firm is overly stringent in its acceptance criteria for new investments, it will reject some opportunities that the market will support. These projects will be taken up by competitors, and the company will have sacrificed growth potential. This will be reflected in a less than optimal share price.

Assuming rational and well-informed investors, the objective of financial management in a free-market framework should be the **maximization of shareholder wealth** as reflected in share prices.[8] Even if some shareholders should become dissatisfied with

---

[7] This assumes that markets are reasonably efficient in assessing this information and reflecting it in security prices. The issues surrounding the notion of market efficiency and the information contained in share prices will be discussed at some length in Chapter 9.

[8] The maximization of shareholder wealth through share prices can be formulated and expressed in various ways. Thus, one can think about maximizing the price per individual share, the total market value of the firm's outstanding common equity, or the company's total market value of all outstanding securities (including debt and preferred shares). It can be shown that in theory, all these formulations of maximizing shareholder wealth are essentially equivalent and will lead to the same actions and results. See H. Levy and M. Sarnat, "A Pedagogic Note on Alternative Formulations of the Goal of the Firm," *The Journal of Business* (1977), pp. 526–28. For a firm with a given set of investments and operations, this implies that the number of shares outstanding is given and remains constant. For example, a company could alter its share price through stock repurchases or stock splits without affecting the wealth position of the individual shareholder or the total market value of its outstanding equity. We exclude from consideration such manipulations of stock price that are essentially affected by altering the number of shares outstanding rather than by increasing the economic value of the firm.

the policies being pursued perhaps because their preferences differ from those that prevail in the market, their interests will be served since they can now sell their shares for a good price and pursue other activities that they find more suitable. Hence, we can essentially separate the decisions that management makes in running the firm, which ought to be guided by aggregate market preferences as outlined above, from preferences that individual shareholders may have. This **concept of separation** is important for financial management because it implies that the financial executive need not be concerned with individual shareholder reactions to policies but only with the aggregate judgement of the marketplace.

EXAMPLE

THE SEPARATION OF MANAGEMENT DECISIONS FROM INDIVIDUAL SHAREHOLDER PREFERENCES

Assume that a company has paid a regular dividend over the past few years, but this year, because of new technological developments, management has exciting new investment and growth opportunities. Because these imply substantial funding requirements, management decides to suspend its dividend payments temporarily in order to retain as much as possible for reinvestment. Most shareholders regard this as good news and expect to receive increased dividends in the future. As a consequence, the share price increases from the previous level of $50 to $60 per share. An individual shareholder, who has come to rely on the regular dividend payments to supplement her income, is quite distraught by the announcement. However, since aggregate market reaction is positive, this investor still stands to gain. She can sell her shares, realize the capital gain, and reinvest the increased amount in a similar firm that provides regular dividend payments. The company's decision, being guided by market reaction as reflected in share price, has made everyone better off even if it is at odds with individual shareholder preferences.

The above example illustrates that financial (and other) markets act as information processors combining the views of many shareholders together into one measure—namely share price. By monitoring share price movements, management can measure investors' reactions to corporate decisions and other happenings that affect the firm.

For other organizational forms of business for which no share certificates exist such as partnerships or sole proprietorships, the goal of maximizing the owner's wealth as expressed, for example, by the market value of the business if it were to be sold is much more difficult to justify. For example, a sole proprietorship should be operated to maximize the overall well-being (or utility) of its owner. This may involve turning down chances to increase the value of the company if the cost in terms of lost leisure or risk is unacceptable. Furthermore, the concept of maximizing firm value may also no longer be entirely appropriate once we deal with organizations such as co-operatives or Crown corporations. Other concerns that are not market-related may play important roles in their management.

As the above example illustrates, the usefullness of value maximization as a guiding principle grows out of the way financial markets process information. If the views of many owners need not be combined into a signal to management, the concept loses validity.

Although much stronger conceptually than profit maximization, even the objective of share price maximization does have critics. The criticisms fall into two broad categories:

1. **Operational Difficulties in Maximizing Share Prices**: Even if one basically accepts the free-enterprise framework, the arguments outlined above hinge on the assumption of rational and well-informed investors with behaviour patterns that are reasonably predictable by management. If we move from this idealized view into real-world markets with all their complexities and imperfections, share price maximization may once again embody conceptual ambiguities that could stand in the way of allowing it to become an operational goal for business decisions.

2. **Limitations of the Free-Market Framework**: More general questions exist regarding the validity of the free-market framework and its underlying assumptions in today's society. These include, for example, concerns about market imperfections and failures, the power and role of management, and issues around economic and market efficiency.

We review both of these issues below.

1. Operational Difficulties in Maximizing Share Prices

The consequences of having shareholders that may not always be well informed and rational are best illustrated through examples. Most firms can increase reported profits in the short run by curtailing discretionary expenditures such as research and development, advertising, and perhaps even maintenance. Clearly, if such curtailments are drastic, they will jeopardize the company's competitive position in the longer run. However, if shareholders misinterpret the sudden increase in profitability, share prices could react positively and actually go up only to collapse once information regarding the firm's real situation filters through to the investment community. Similarly, as the recent Bre-X fiasco attests, it is well known that false or incomplete information regarding exploration results can cause short-term speculative booms in the prices of mining stocks. Also, investors attitudes—like public opinion in other areas—may simply be volatile and subject to irrationalities and mass psychology without good economic reason. A good example of this is the explosion in the prices of high-technology stocks (such as Internet companies) during 1999 and the first three months of 2000. During this period, a number of companies increased their value by more than 100 percent (and even as much as 500 percent or more) based on the expectation that some of them would dominate future business activity and to a large extent on speculation. This trend was reversed in April 2000 when the speculative bubble burst, and many stocks lost more than 50 percent of their value in a matter of days.

Clearly, actions that might maximize share prices in the short run but that are not based on substantive economic realities will not serve the best long-term interests of either the firm and its owners or society. On the contrary, they can bring about a misallocation of resources by misled investors and thereby promote inefficiencies. To exclude such undesirable effects, it is normally argued that companies should strive to maximize share prices *over the long run*. This implies that short-run fluctuations caused by, for example, investor ignorance or irrationality should not dominate considerations in choosing between alternative financial policies.[9]

Making allowances for the possibilities of both a lack of information and short-term shareholder irrationality still does not remove all obstacles. In order to use share prices as a guide for evaluating decisions, we would need to know what influences share prices and how financial markets react to various financial policies. Given that most financial and economic theories are based on the objective of share price maximization, it is understandable that the issue of valuation—or what determines the value of securities—has received considerable attention, and a great number of statistical studies have been conducted that attempt to relate share prices to other financial variables. At the same time, impressive advances have been made on the theoretical front to derive how financial assets ought to be priced if one assumes that markets are efficient and perfect. The results of these efforts will be reviewed in detail in the appropriate sections of this book. In spite of all the advances, however, the issue of valuation remains controversial and in many ways unresolved. This makes it difficult to judge specific managerial alternatives against the stated objective of share price maximization. Although empirical research and financial theories can provide guidance, they have to be supplemented by managerial judgement in the many areas in which the evidence is less than perfect.

2. Limitations of the Free-Market Framework

More general and fundamental criticisms of the free-market framework can be grouped as follows:

1. Given that the assumptions of "perfect markets"—such as perfect competition and no externalities—are not met in practice, a narrow pursuit of wealth maximization by market participants need not lead to the desired result of economic efficiency.[10]

2. The objective of economic efficiency is too narrow to represent a justifiable overriding goal for society. It leaves unanswered many of society's important concerns such as protection of the environment, equity in distribution of wealth and income among economic agents, or measurable material wealth versus quality of life.

---

[9] The question as to what time span represents "the long run" is a thorny one that is normally side stepped. Clearly, the time horizon should be of sufficient duration to allow the investment community to absorb fully all relevant information. Even then, one can argue that investors on occasion have sustained speculative booms that had little economic justification and that they have done so for significant periods of time. In retrospect and with the hindsight knowledge that such booms subsequently collapsed, it is easy to say that firms should not have been misled by such temporary aberrations. Obviously, it is much more difficult for managers to ignore current signals from the market because they believe that the market is acting irrationally. Unless managers have inside information, such a disregard would imply a claim to superior judgement. Even if the future should prove these managers to be right, how long can they afford to be at odds with a market to which they are ultimately responsible?

[10] Externalities are costs or benefits that one party imposes on others without paying or receiving compensation. For example, through careless practices, a logging firm may jeopardize a salmon run in a particular river. If the company is not forced to bear all the resultant costs of such action, someone else will have to. Policies that may be optimal for the logging firm need not be optimal for the overall economy.

3. A single-minded focus on share price maximization does not correspond to observed managerial behaviour. Rather, management is viewed as an arbitrator and moderator between sometimes conflicting stakeholder groups including shareholders, debt holders, unions and employees, customers, governments, and management itself, all of which have a justifiable interest in the operations of the firm.

We elaborate on the final item in the next section.

ROLE OF MANAGEMENT AND AGENCY COSTS   1.7

Role of Management

Management serves an important role as an arbitrator and moderator between often-conflicting interest groups or stakeholders and objectives. Critics question whether the criterion of maximizing benefits solely from the standpoint of shareholders is appropriate in a setting that comprises many participating parties, each with a limited role. The parties consist of the following:

- creditors, who are interested in the security of their loans and collateral
- management, which is often interested in growth and continuity of operations
- customers, who are interested in quality of products and lower prices
- unions and employees, who are interested in higher compensation, job satisfaction, and security of employment
- host communities, which are interested in tax revenues and in social and environmental issues
- stockholders, who are interested in larger dividends and/or price appreciation

There is, however, a sense in which shareholders truly are different from other stakeholders. Creditors, managers, customers, employees, and the local community all hold **contractual claims** against the firm's revenues. That is, their stakes in the company give them legal rights to specific, well-defined amounts of money, goods, or services from the firm at specific times. Creditors, for example, have legal rights to timely payment of interest and principal. Managers and employees have legal rights that guarantee regular wage payments. Customers have a legal right to receive goods they have on order, and the community has a right (via its government) to taxes. If the business breaks the laws, it is subject to fines or other legal settlements.

Shareholders, in contrast, have **residual claims** against the company. They are paid only *after* all contractual claims are settled. Thus, if wages, taxes, interest, and fines reduce the firm's cash flow, shareholders must accept a lower dividend. Therefore, they bear the most immediate risk. For this reason, it is often argued that management should respond primarily to the concerns of shareholders.

EXAMPLE   **VALDEZ OIL SPILL**

After the Exxon tanker *Valdez* spilled large amounts of oil off the coast of Alaska in 1989, Exxon management was bitterly criticized at the subsequent annual shareholders' meeting. Some shareholders were upset that Exxon had damaged the environment. Others were upset that the company was forced to pay a record fine and would be vulnerable to future lawsuits, which would reduce the firm's future ability to pay dividends.

Agency Costs

A problem arises because managers may choose not to maximize share values. Managers have personalities and objectives of their own, and their goals need not always coincide with those of shareholders. For example, growth may be appealing to managers whose status and financial rewards are linked to the size of the organization that they manage even if it does not result in an increase in shareholder wealth. A number of takeovers—whereby one business bought out another often at a price that was a substantial premium over the prevailing market price—have been criticized on these grounds. It has also been argued that based on the perception of their own reward structure, management may tend to play it safe even when more aggressive or entrepreneurial attitudes might be supported by the market. For example, if a particular investment decision turns bad and results in substantial losses, a manager has more than a drop in earnings per share at risk. The manager's job and career may terminate, even if the original decision was the best that could have been reached under the circumstances. It is not surprising that a manager whose personal and professional future is tied to showing at least acceptable performance may be more risk averse than a shareholder who holds a diversified portfolio of securities and whose investment in the company may be purely temporary.

The possible discrepancies between management and shareholder objectives have given rise to increasing attention on **agency relationships** or **agency theory**.[11] This agency relationship arises due to the separation of management from ownership, which results in the employment of management by shareholders to act as agents on their behalf. Potential conflicts of interest arise when actions that are in the best interest of the shareholders do not coincide with those that are in management's best interests. Financial theory recognizes that this agency relationship does not work without friction and that shareholders may incur significant costs—referred to as **agency costs**—as a result of this relationship. These include the expenses of monitoring and controlling the actions of management and the costs of suboptimal actions by managers. These costs detract from shareholder value, and it is shareholders who ultimately bear the impact since the valuation of shares by investors should reflect such anticipated agency costs.

One of the most common and controversial types of agency costs is management compensation in the form of stock options, which give the executive the opportunity to

---

[11] Much of agency theory is based upon the classic article by M. Jensen and W. Meckling, "Theory of the Firm: Managerial Behavior, Agency Costs and Ownership Structure," *Journal of Financial Economics* (October 1976), pp. 305–60. They argue that to keep managers acting in the owners' best interests, shareholders must incur agency costs.

buy shares in the company at a given price. This is a common form of compensation for management often representing the largest percentage of overall compensation received by managers. For example, in 1997, over 85 percent of the chief executive officers (CEOs) for the 300 companies included in the Toronto Stock Exchange 300 Composite Index had a stock option plan, and stock option gains accounted for about 80 percent of total compensation for the 10 highest-paid CEOs.[12]

Stock options have grown in popularity because they alleviate the potential conflict of interest between shareholders and management since management's compensation is now based to some degree on the company's stock price. However, they do so at a cost: a number of new shares are provided to the managers at prices *below* the market price because managers will exercise their options when the stock price is higher than the exercise price—the price at which they can purchase the shares. As the preceding paragraph indicates, the costs associated with these options can be very substantial, which has led to debate as to whether they justify the benefit of aligning management's interests with those of shareholders. For example, in 1998, Peter Munk, the chairman of the board and former CEO for Barrick Gold Corp., was the highest-paid executive in Canada at $38.9 million, $33.6 million of this amount representing the exercise of 2 million stock options he had received in 1991.[13]

Another type of agency cost arises due to a potential conflict of interest between shareholders and debt holders whose best interests may conflict at times. For example, when a company is in severe distress with little hope for survival, it is unlikely that the shareholders will get anything for their shares since debt holders are paid first before any residual funds are distributed to shareholders. In this situation, it would be in the shareholders' best interests to have management gamble by investing in high-risk, high-potential-payoff investments since they have everything to gain and nothing to lose (because they are essentially gambling with the debt holders' wealth and not their own). Alternatively, it may be beneficial to shareholders to distribute large cash dividends to shareholders when the company recognizes it is in trouble, thus expropriating wealth from the debt holders. To eliminate the potential for such actions, debt holders impose debt covenants (such as restricting dividend payments or forcing management to comply with limits on future borrowing) that restrict the actions of management in order to protect their own best interests. Sometimes, these covenants restrict management's ability to make the best value maximization decisions, and that represents a cost to the shareholders.

Management plays a broad role in reconciling the legitimate and possibly conflicting interests of various groups. However, even within a broader range of objectives, it is clear that management's responsibilities to the owners of the business—its shareholders—continue to occupy an important position. Shareholders have a unique legal status that ensures that their interests are not disregarded: they can elect directors and challenge management's voting control through proxy fights, and they can tender their shares for sale when

---

[12] J. White, "How to Compensate Your CEO," *Benefits Canada* 23-1 (January 1999), pp. 51–52.

[13] M. MacKinnon, "Barrick's Munk Leads Pay Parade: $38.9m [*Globe and Mail's* Annual List of Canada's Best-Paid Chief Executives]." Canadian Press Newswire, April 26, 1999.

outsiders attempt to take over the firm in order to replace inefficient management. Furthermore, in an attempt to bridge the gap between managers' and shareholders' interests, executive compensation has been increasingly tied to some extent to the enterprise's financial performance. Again, agency theory has provided interesting insights into the structuring of employment contracts and compensation packages that maximize shareholder wealth in otherwise imperfect markets. It has also recognized that shareholders may face a trade-off between monitoring costs to ensure reasonable management behaviour and forms of compensation that will provide appropriate self-motivation in this regard.

1.8 IMPORTANCE OF MAXIMIZING FIRM VALUE

Maximizing firm value may seem like a very narrow objective, and most companies recognize that they cannot afford to turn a blind eye to major social concerns and problems on which its actions impinge. Indeed, most Canadian businesses are sensitive to these issues, and their statements of objectives incorporate social goals and responsibilities alongside economic considerations. At the same time, one of businesses' primary roles will continue to be striving for efficiency in providing the goods and services demanded by the market, and in this regard, one important dimension of company objectives will have to be financial performance. Without adequate financial performance, a firm may not survive in a competitive environment. This implies that managers of corporations cannot ignore the objective of shareholder wealth or long-run maximization of share prices. To quote Will Stinson, former chairman and chief executive officer of Canadian Pacific Ltd.:

> Obviously, a corporation exists only by public consent. So you have obligations there. You have obligations to your employees, to your customers, and to the communities they operate in. Unfortunately, if you don't satisfy your obligation to your shareholders, you're never in a position to do the rest.[14]

We conclude with some real-world evidence that attests to the importance many Canadian companies attach to the principle of maximizing firm value. The report below includes excerpts from a recent newspaper article dealing with BCE Inc.'s spinoff of its ownership stake in Nortel Networks Corp. This article makes direct reference to the importance of maximizing shareholder value and cites it as the motivating factor behind this key corporate decision. For example, BCE president and chief executive Jean Monty refers to shareholder maximization as the paramount reason for BCE's proposed spinoff of its ownership stake in Nortel. In particular, he states: "It would have been my personal view to stay closely associated with Nortel, but it's in the best interests of our shareholders, and they will be mighty proud of BCE in the months and years ahead."

---

[14] As quoted in the *Financial Post*, April 20, 1986, p.5.

■ *Finance in the News*

Nortel Deal a $73-Billion Windfall for Investors

BCE Inc., the telecommunication parent of Nortel Networks Corp., announced on January 26, 2000 that it will divest its 39.2 percent stake in its high-tech subsidiary, keeping just 2.2 percent worth $4.5 billion. BCE's half-million shareholders will be the beneficiaries of the largest transaction in Canadian corporate history, worth $73 billion at current share prices.

BCE CEO Jean Monty declared an end of the 105-year relationship because the soaring stock price of the former Northern Telecom was masking the value of the rest of BCE's holdings of other subsidiaries such as Bell Canada, Bell Mobility, Bell Emergis, Bell ExpressVu, and Telesat Canada. Robert Bertram of the Ontario Teachers Pension Plan, a major BCE shareholder, called the move "courageous" and added that it would "release a lot of value that has been held back."

BCE shareholders will get another gift in higher stock prices. Speculation about the spinoff saw BCE shares rise $6.55 to $142.45, and experts predict another $6 rise following the news. Monty saw the move as positive for both BCE and Nortel but stated that it was a "hard decision for all of us." He added, "It would have been my personal view to stay closely associated with Nortel, but it's in the best interests of our shareholders, and they will be mighty proud of BCE in the months and years ahead."

The Nortel divestiture was first mentioned by Monty in October 1999 and has been on the rumour mill particularly in the month preceding the announcement. BCE's market value was set at $91.7 billion of which $77.3 was its Nortel stake, leaving all its other assets worth just $14.4 billion. Monty values them at $30 billion and stated that BCE's shares were trading at a 30 percent discount. BCE hopes that with Nortel out of the way, shareholders will take another look and invest in the remaining BCE assets.

Source: Globe and Mail, "Nortel deal a $73-billion 'windfall' for investors," Mark Evans; Jacquie McNish; Lawrence Surtees, January 27, 2000, pp. A1, A6. Reprinted with permission.

The importance of maximizing firm value as a key corporate objective is echoed in Figure 1.3, which provides excerpts from a number of Canadian companies' 1999 annual reports. While the companies included in Figure 1.3 are from a variety of industries and refer to different items that are important to their own company's success, they all allude to the importance of maximizing shareholder value.

Company	Quotes
Royal Bank of Canada (1999 Annual Report, p. 3)	"Our vision is to be Canada's premier financial services provider, with committed people working as a team to create customer and **shareholder value**. Our focus is on improving performance in each of our businesses **to achieve consistent and superior returns for our shareholders**."
Barrick Gold Corporation (1999 Annual Report, p. 8)	"**Making more money for our shareholders** is our main objective. It is the key to creating the kind of corporate strength that is inevitably recognized by the stock market, especially when coupled with dynamic growth."
Empire Company Limited (1999 Annual Report, inside front cover page)	"Guided by conservative business principles, our goal is to **build long-term shareholder value** through income and cash flow growth, and equity appreciation. We accomplish this through direct ownership and equity participation in businesses that have the potential for long-term growth and profitability."
Nortel Networks (1999 Annual Report, p. 6)	"Through our commitment to building high-performance networks that support and accelerate the growth of eBusiness, we'll work to **deliver value to our customers and to our shareholders**."
Imperial Oil (1999 Annual Report, inside front page cover)	"The company's mission is to **create value for its shareholders** through the development and sale of hydrocarbon energy and related products."
Sears Canada (1999 Annual Report, p. 2)	"The Company's Vision is to be Canada's most successful retailer by providing our customers with total shopping satisfaction, our associates with opportunities to grow and contribute, and our **shareholders with superior returns on their investment**: a Great Place to Shop, Work and Invest."

Further evidence supporting the use of maximizing firm value as a key corporate objective can be found in a recent Canadian survey entitled "Shareholder Value Measurement in Canada—1997 Survey."[15] This study indicated that 88 percent of the

---

[15] N. Buhr and J. Desjardins, "Shareholder Value Measurement in Canada—1997 Survey," Toronto: The Canadian Institutes of Chartered Accountants and the Financial Executives Institute Canada, 1997.

111 companies with shares listed on a stock exchange that responded to the survey explicitly referred to "creating shareholder value" as a key corporate objective and linked it with strategic decision-making. The comparable figure for the 57 unlisted companies included in the sample was lower but still substantial at 67 percent.

SUMMARY   1.9

1. With the increasing complexity and uncertainty in the marketplace, finance is emerging as the business function that holds the corporation together at the top management level. Financial management is oriented toward the future, with a strong emphasis on forecasting and forward planning.

2. If markets are "perfect" (perfect competition, perfect information, rational market participants, no externalities), economic theory has demonstrated that an efficient allocation of resources will result.

3. Profits have to be viewed in relation to capital invested because the general theory of profit maximization ignores the amount of capital invested to generate a given profit, different patterns of profits across time, and the risks inherent in future profit projections.

4. Market preferences are expressed in prices—share prices in our case. The issue of valuation is concerned with establishing what determines the value of shares in capital markets.

5. Maximization of share prices can be criticized on the grounds that real markets are not perfect, that management also has responsibilities to other groups that have legitimate interests in the firm (employees, customers, and various sectors of government), and that the objective of economic efficiency is too narrow.

6. In a competitive market environment, profitability and good shareholder relations are a prerequisite to the pursuit of many additional concerns, and high share prices will assure the firm's continued access to financial markets for further expansion.

QUESTIONS AND PROBLEMS

Questions for Discussion

1. List and describe the three basic functional areas of finance.

2. Distinguish between proprietorships, partnerships, and corporations.

3. What benefits do corporations hold over proprietorships and partnerships? How have these benefits contributed to their growth and dominance of business activity?

4. "The sole corporate objective should be the maximization of share prices because this will lead to the most efficient allocation of resources in our economy." Discuss this statement.

5. What are the operational difficulties in using the maximization of shareholder wealth as a financial objective? Why is the issue of share valuation so complex and still unresolved?

6. In several countries, unions have gained official representation on boards of directors. What do you see as the potential advantages and/or disadvantages of such a development, and how might this affect the objectives of financial management?

7. Consider the objectives that shareholders, management, and employees may have in the operation of a firm. In what areas would you expect the objectives of each of these three groups to coincide, and where would you expect to find conflicts? Provide specific examples of managerial decisions in which conflicts may surface. How do you think such conflicts are resolved in practice? How should they be resolved?

8. In most industries that exploit natural resources, governments have interfered in various ways with free-market behaviour and have imposed a variety of constraints that regulate such exploitation. Take a specific natural resource-based industry with which you are familiar, and list various ways in which governments have interfered with free markets. In each case, discuss the arguments that can be made for and against such interference. Would a completely free market result in an optimal exploitation of the particular resource under consideration? Why or why not?

9. Prepare numerical examples to illustrate the potential weaknesses of the following criteria as objectives to be maximized by a company: (a) profits after taxes, (b) total sales revenue, (c) earnings per share.

10. (a) List and discuss some of the factors or variables that you think influence the prices at which the share of a firm will trade. To what extent are share prices a reflection of managerial decisions, and to what extent are they influenced by factors that are outside management's control?

(b) Assume that you want to formalize your answer under (a) above and support it through statistical testing. That is, you want to relate share prices (dependent variables) to various explanatory factors (independent variables). How would you proceed, and what, if any, difficulties might you encounter? Provide a detailed step-by-step outline for a statistical testing procedure.

11. Discuss the appropriateness of economic objectives such as profit maximization or share price maximization in the area of privately delivered medical care. To focus your discussion, you may take as specific examples (a) companies in the pharmaceutical industry, (b) nursing homes, (c) private hospitals. What, if any, other goals should be used to supplement economic objectives? Why? Prepare a complete statement of objectives that you would deem to be appropriate for such a business. Be as specific as you can, and outline how you would resolve potential conflicts and trade-offs between various subgoals.

12. What is meant by the term "perfect markets"? Do real-world markets fit this description? Why or why not?

13. Consider two firms. Last year, Firm A had total profits of $10,000, while Firm B had total profits of $10 million. Can you determine which is the better company based on this information? What other factors would you need information about in order to compare the profitability of these firms?

14. What is meant by agency problems? How can the issue of stock options help to alleviate them?

APPENDIX 1–A

CAREERS IN FINANCE

Below is a brief description of some careers within the field of finance that is found at the Careers in Business website at the following location: http://www.careers-in-business.com. While the list is not comprehensive, it includes a fairly good representation of potential finance careers and covers eight of the main areas of finance:

1. corporate finance
2. commercial banking
3. investment banking
4. money management
5. financial planning
6. insurance
7. real estate
8. venture capital

Salaries will vary depending upon years of experience and actual job titles; however, compensation for a large number of these careers is often in the six-figure range after five to 10 years of experience have been obtained.

The list below identifies a number of finance careers and a brief description of the duties associated with them. For more details, go to the Careers in Business website.

Corporate Finance

1. **Treasurer**: Responsible for financial planning, raising funds, cash management, and acquiring and disposing of assets.

2. **Financial Analyst**: Determine financial needs, analyse capital budgeting projects, conduct long-range financial planning, analyse possible acquisitions and asset sales, visit credit agencies to explain firm's position, work on budgets, analyse competi-

tors, implement financial plans, monitor the market price of your company's securities, analyse leasing agreements, and determine needs and methods of dealing with derivatives.

3. **Credit Manager**: Establish policies for granting credit to suppliers, establish guidelines for collecting on credit, and consider whether to securitize receivables.

4. **Cash Manager**: Establish relationships with banks, manage short-term credit needs, ensure that sufficient cash is on hand to meet daily needs, put excess cash into a concentration account bearing interest, and handle international transfers of funds.

5. **Benefits Officer**: Manage pension fund assets, set up employee retirement plans, determine health care benefits policies, and work with human resources to set up cost-effective employee benefits.

6. **Real Estate Officer**: Find real estate locations for a company and negotiate lease agreements. Also responsible for acquisition of real estate and valuation of properties.

7. **Investor Relation Officer**: Deal with the investing public by disseminating financial information, respond to queries from institutional investors, issue press releases to explain corporate events, and organize teleconferences with investors.

8. **Controller**: Responsible for financial planning, accounting, financial reporting, and cost analysis. Will get involved in property, revenue, benefits, derivatives, leases, and joint interest accounting. May need to develop forecasting models to project revenues and costs. May be called on to implement or work with a complex costing system, financial re-engineering, transfer pricing issues, or interface with auditors.

Commercial Banking

1. **Credit Analyst**: Evaluate business and consumer loan applications made to your bank. Your duties include projecting a company's future cash flow, evaluating its current financial soundness, visiting and interacting with financial people at businesses, and dealing with lenders. You will learn a lot about business in this job.

2. **Loan Officer**: Make loans to businesses and consumers.

3. **Branch Manager**: Responsible for overseeing all activities at your branch including opening new accounts, loan origination, solving customer problems, foreign exchange, and safety deposit boxes. Most importantly, you are responsible for establishing relations with customers.

4. **Trust Officer**: Responsible for delivering trust services, financial products, and advice to bank customers (often more upscale ones).

5. **Mortgage Banker**: Responsible for making mortgage loans to homebuyers and businesses. This involves heavy contact with real estate professionals, credit checks, and dealing with new buyers.

6. **Other Jobs**: Other jobs in banking involve accounting, marketing and advertising, commercial card operations securities transfer, wire operations, private banking, cash management services, instalment loans, loan servicing, correspondent banking, personnel, operations, and communication.

Investment Banking

1. **Corporate Finance**: Responsible for helping companies raise capital needed for new projects and ongoing operations. Work to determine the amount and structure of funding needed by a client through equity, debt, convertibles, preferred, asset-backs, or derivative securities.

2. **Mergers and Acquisitions**: Setting up deals in which one company buys another, an important source of fee income for many investment banks. Responsible for helping out and working with a team that acts as an advisor to a client, values transactions, creatively structures deals, and negotiates favourable terms.

3. **Project Finance**: Involves funding infrastructure and capital projects.

4. **Trading**: Involves undertaking transactions in equities, bonds, currencies, options, or futures with traders at commercial banks, investment dealers, and large institutional investors.

5. **Structured Finance**: Create financing vehicles to redirect cash flows to investors, known as asset-backed securities (ABS). Typical ABSs securitize credit card receivables, auto loan receivables, or mortgages.

6. **Derivatives**: Many jobs associated with the sale or management of derivatives, which require substantial knowledge of technical details regarding derivatives and their pricing.

7. **Advisory**: Provide advice to the public and to private clients involved in mergers or financing.

8. **Equity and Fixed-Income Research**: Analyse stocks and bonds and make buy or sell recommendations based on your analysis.

9. **International Sales/Emerging Markets**: Analyse foreign markets and securities within those markets and/or act as a salesperson for investors who wish to invest in these markets.

10. **Public Finance**: Assist various government agencies (at the federal, provincial, and municipal levels) in raising funding.

11. **Retail Brokerage (Stockbroker)**: Involved in selling stocks, bonds, mutual funds, and other products to individual investors.

12. **Institutional Sales**: Convey information about particular securities to institutional investors (such as pension funds and mutual funds).

13. **Computer Guru**: Maintain computer and information systems and assist with the development of software.

14. **Ratings Analyst**: Assign credit ratings to the debt instruments of businesses and governments.

Money Management

1. **Portfolio Manager**: Responsible for selecting and managing investments to meet the goals of a group of investors usually working for a money management firm or pension fund.

2. **Portfolio Management Sales**: Attempt to attract and maintain clients for a portfolio management company.
3. **Investment Advisory**: Provide investment advice, performance evaluation, and quantitative analysis to the money management sector.
4. **Mutual Fund Analyst**: Analyse mutual funds and/or the variety of potential investment instruments that might be included in a particular fund.

Financial Planning

Financial planners help individuals plan their financial futures, which requires an understanding of investments, taxes, estate planning issues, as well as excellent interpersonal skills.

Insurance

1. **Actuary**: Use analytical skills and techniques to predict the risks associated with writing insurance policies on property, businesses, and people's lives and health.
2. **Agent and Broker**: Advise people and organizations on their insurance needs and sell them the appropriate products.
3. **Claims Adjuster**: Negotiate claims for people who have experienced a loss that is covered by insurance.
4. **Service Representative**: Serve as the link between agents who sell insurance policies and insurance companies that write the policies.
5. **Loss-Control Specialist**: Assist in maintaining accidents and losses to a minimum by identifying and helping to eliminate potential hazards and promoting precautionary mechanisms.
6. **Risk Manager**: Help organizations to identify the risks they face and make recommendations for dealing with them.
7. **Underwriter**: Evaluate applicants' exposure to risk, decide whether they meet minimum acceptable standards, and assist in product pricing.

Real Estate

1. **Real Estate Agent/Broker**: Sales professionals who contract their services to real estate companies for a commission-sharing agreement.
2. **Real Estate Appraisers**: Provide unbiased estimates of a property's value and quality, often working for banks or real estate companies.
3. **Property Managers**: Manage real estate properties for the owners. Duties include negotiating leases, ensuring tenants are satisfied, and collecting rents.
4. **Real Estate Advisory**: Help investors select properties that are likely to increase in value and help them care for their properties.

5. **Development and Construction**: Identify the potential for new real estate developments and work through to the ultimate completion of such projects. A high-risk, high-potential reward career that requires an entrepreneurial flair.

6. **Real Estate Entrepreneur**: Buy properties based on the expectations that they will increase in value because of improved market conditions or as a result of planned renovations.

Venture Capital

Venture capital firms provide funding (usually in the form of equity and/or long-term convertible debt) to private companies that are unable to obtain adequate financing from traditional channels. The companies they finance are usually in the early stages of their development, and their future is considered risky. Therefore, venture capitalists demand high returns to compensate them for the risk. They also provide business planning and other services to these companies.

Launching an IPO with Style

In the 1990s, venture capitalists fell over one another to fund high-tech startups founded by young computer-savvy entrepreneurs. But back in 1984, University of Waterloo co-op engineering student Mike Lazaridis and his partner Douglas Fregin started Research in Motion the hard way, scraping up loans from family and friends.

Lazaridis believed passionately in the future of wireless technology. In the early years, RIM designed and built interactive pagers, wireless modems, and tiny radios, all of which were incorporated in other manufacturers' products. "I spent the first three years looking for market for a major product," he says. "Wireless data was something I believed in." By the late 1980s, RIM was focusing solely on wireless data networks. "We created LANs (local area networks) for industrial applications before the term was even coined," says Lazaridis. "To finance it, I took in various partners."

This partnering philosophy has helped RIM to grow quickly under the guidance of Lazaridis and co-CEO Jim Balsille, who joined RIM in 1992 (co-founder Douglas Fregin is now head of operations). For example, in 1993 RIM partnered with Swedish communications giant Ericsson—then in 1995 bought them out. Provincial loans and federal grants have also helped the company at key junctures.

By 1997, RIM was ready to go public. The IPO raised $115 million through 13.8 million common shares, issued at $7.25 on the TSE.

The financing went, in part, to expand research and development activities. That R&D focus paid off when, in 1999, RIM launched what has become its signature product, the wildly successful Blackberry pager. It's been called a "sublime," "a pager on steroids," and "the most addictive application since the video game." It sent RIM's 1999 revenues soaring to $70 million with an income of $9.5 million. (During the contentious U.S. presidential race of 2000, Democratic nominee Al Gore travelled with a Blackberry, on which he exchanged both crucial, up-to-the-minute information with his campaign staff and love messages with his wife.)

RIM's stock, meanwhile, went on a roller-coaster ride, trading as high as $260 and as low as $50 on the TSE within a single year.

In January 1999 RIM was listed on the NASDAQ, and later that year raised $258 million by offering 5 million common shares in the United States. The earlier Canadian IPO had been carefully thought out to with a view to the future, explains Balsillie. "The two firms that were in the underwriting syndicate were both NASDAQ members," he says. "That helped raise US investor awareness ahead of a listing there." (In 2000, RIM switched its accounting currency to U.S. dollars, since so many of its customers are American, but continues to follow Canadian GAAP in producing its reports.)

Sources: Michael Newman, "Blackberry Preserve," *eCompany Now*, September 2000; Gary Will, *Waterloo Business Digest*, November 1997; Yasmin Glanville, "The Challenges of Growth," *CAmagazine*, May 2000; *Report on Business* April 2000.

The Canadian Financial Environment

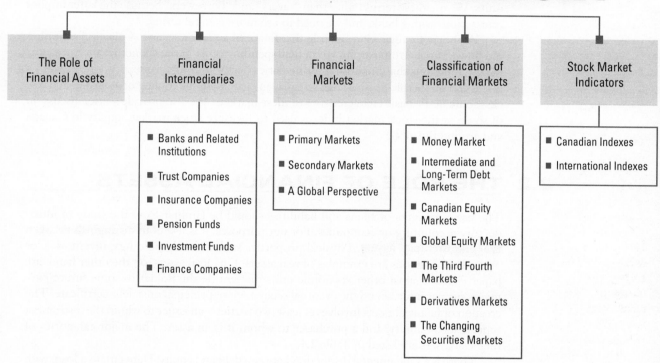

The Role of Financial Assets

Financial Intermediaries
- Banks and Related Institutions
- Trust Companies
- Insurance Companies
- Pension Funds
- Investment Funds
- Finance Companies

Financial Markets
- Primary Markets
- Secondary Markets
- A Global Perspective

Classification of Financial Markets
- Money Market
- Intermediate and Long-Term Debt Markets
- Canadian Equity Markets
- Global Equity Markets
- The Third Fourth Markets
- Derivatives Markets
- The Changing Securities Markets

Stock Market Indicators
- Canadian Indexes
- International Indexes

Learning Objectives

After studying this chapter, you should be able to:

1. *Describe the differences between surplus-spending units and deficit-spending units, and discuss how each contributes to the development of efficient financial markets.*
2. *Explain how financial intermediation operates in channelling funds between savers and users of funds.*
3. *Describe the different functions of primary and secondary markets.*
4. *Discuss the differences between traditional stock exchanges and over-the-counter (OTC) markets using examples from Canada and the United States.*
5. *Identify some major stock indexes, and discuss their strengths and weaknesses.*

2.1 INTRODUCTION

This chapter provides an overview of the financial environment within which Canadian companies and individuals operate. For brevity, we refer to the individuals, firms, and other institutions that participate in financial markets as **economic units**. Units that have more funds available than they wish to spend are called **surplus-spending units**, and those that have less funds available than they wish to spend are **deficit-spending units**. We use these terms rather than "savers" and "borrowers" because the latter implies transactions with a bank, and we need to use more general terms.

We begin by reviewing the role that financial assets or securities play in facilitating the flow of funds from surplus- to deficit-spending units in the economy, and we examine the functions that financial intermediaries perform in this context. We proceed to a discussion of the role financial markets play in facilitating the trading of securities and discuss some of the basic characteristics of these markets. We also provide a brief discussion of some of the stock market indexes used to measure stock market activity in Canada and around the globe.

2.2 THE ROLE OF FINANCIAL ASSETS

The basic concepts of assets and liabilities should be familiar from the study of introductory accounting or economics. For our purposes, it is useful to distinguish between real and financial assets. Physical properties such as land, buildings, inventories, or other durable goods are examples of real assets. Financial assets, on the other hand, are paper claims against other economic units that entitle the holder to some future payments such as interest and the eventual repayment of principal on a debt certificate. The creation of financial assets involves at least two parties—an issuer to whom the instrument represents a liability, and a purchaser to whom it is an asset. The major categories of financial assets are listed in Table 2.1.

There is a fundamental distinction between debt and equity. Debt entails a loan, with the purchaser becoming a creditor of the issuer. The future payments associated with debt, both interest and repayment of principal, represent contractual obligations. Financing through equity, on the other hand, means the sale of ownership certificates in a firm. Some of the legal implications of debt and equity will be reviewed in subsequent chapters.

There is also an important distinction between marketable and non-marketable assets. Marketable assets are those that can be easily sold to others through financial markets, whereas non-marketable ones are those that cannot be transferred to others and must be redeemed. Non-marketable financial assets have been included in Table 2.1 since they include some of the most commonly held financial assets by individuals: savings accounts, guaranteed investment certificates (GICs), Canada Savings Bonds (CSBs), and, more recently, provincial savings bonds.

TABLE 2.1

Major Categories of Financial Assets

Debt

Non-marketable assets

Savings deposits	—	demand deposits with financial institutions such as banks
Guaranteed investment certificates (GICs)	—	time deposits with financial institutions
Canada Savings Bonds (CSBs) and provincial savings bonds	—	issued by governments

Short-term: maturities of one year or less

Treasury bills	—	issued by governments
Commercial paper and Bankers Acceptances (BAs)	—	issued by corporations

Intermediate and long-term: maturities in excess of one year

Bonds	—	issued by governments or by corporations and secured by collateral
Debentures	—	unsecured corporate issues
Mortgages	—	issues secured by real estate
Asset-backed securities (ABSs)	—	created and sold by financial intermediaries

Equity

Preferred shares	—	typically provide fixed returns
Common shares	—	certificates of residual ownership

Other securities, including derivatives*

Options

Futures contracts

Forward contracts

Swaps

Options on futures

Swaptions

---

*Currency, which represents a claim against the issuing central bank, could also be included here.

In addition, a variety of new and more complex financial assets including derivatives have been introduced in recent years. Many of them are simply contracts between individuals that stipulate future payments as a function of conditions then prevailing in financial markets. Financial assets can be issued or held by governments, corporations, financial institutions, and individuals. Each type of financial instrument will be reviewed in detail in the appropriate chapters of the text that follow.

A barter economy is one that does not have money or other financial assets. Economic units within such an economy must supply their own current consumption and expenditures for real assets from the assets they produce or find willing trading partners who possess the goods they need to consume and who want the goods they produce. Each economic unit has to have a balanced budget in every time period because without financial assets, units can neither purchase more than they earn nor save more than is committed to real assets. To illustrate, consider a farmer who requires a plough to improve his output. He must either make the plough himself or trade part of his current crop to obtain one made by someone else. In all probability, however, he will not only be ill equipped and inefficient in plough construction but will also find it difficult to locate a person willing to make the trade. As a consequence, in a barter economy, we are unlikely to have resources allocated to their most productive use.

The introduction of money as a medium of exchange provides economic units with some flexibility. Money balances can be accumulated to save, and trading is facilitated. Nevertheless, the absence of other financial assets still constrains investment since savings cannot be transferred between economic units. Consequently, many worthwhile investments in real assets may be deferred or rejected, and resource allocation in the economy remains suboptimal.

The introduction of other financial assets improves the situation considerably. Economic units can now finance levels of investment in real assets in excess of current savings by, for example, incurring financial liabilities through borrowing. This entails the transfer of funds from a surplus-spending unit to a deficit-spending one (which issues new claims against itself). Such a transaction benefits both parties, because deficit-spending units no longer need to postpone promising investment opportunities for lack of accumulated savings, and surplus-spending units can hold their savings in the form of financial securities that yield a return.

Nevertheless, problems still remain. A deficit-spending unit must seek out a surplus-spending counterpart, and, if a sizeable project is to be financed, many surplus-spending units may have to be found. Such a search can involve significant transaction costs and, as a consequence, may produce relatively costly funds. Surplus units may face similar difficulties in placing their funds. Consequently, the allocation of resources in the economy remains suboptimal. For instance, a saver in one part of the country may be advancing funds to an entrepreneur at 12 percent, whereas a firm of comparable standing in another region, because of superior investment opportunities, may be eager to pay up to 18 percent.

The problem of suboptimal resource allocation may be even more severe across international borders particularly when capital controls restrict the international flow of funds. Other transaction costs that may be of special importance in the international context include: the cost of acquiring accurate and reliable information; costs attributable to differences in legal, taxation, or accounting environments; (currency) risk-management costs; and costs associated with political risk (e.g., expropriation).

To rectify these inefficiencies, a communication system emerges to provide more complete information to both surplus- and deficit-spending units in the form of financial markets. In time, **financial intermediaries** are formed to both simplify and reduce further the cost of contact between borrowers and lenders and to broaden the range of available financial assets to suit market participants better.

FINANCIAL INTERMEDIARIES   2.3

Financial intermediaries create a system of *indirect* financing. Rather than having surplus-spending units provide funds directly to deficit spenders, funds are channelled from units with surpluses to intermediaries who, in turn, make the monies available to deficit-spending units. Figures 2.la and 2.lb portray both direct and indirect financing. By issuing claims against themselves and thereby raising funds from ultimate lenders or investors, financial intermediaries introduce a new set of financial instruments—the so-called **indirect claims**. Indirect claims such as certificates of deposit with a bank are now held in the portfolios of surplus-spending units, while intermediaries commit their newly raised funds to the purchase of securities issued by deficit-spending units.

Surplus-spending economic units (savers)   Deficit-spending economic units

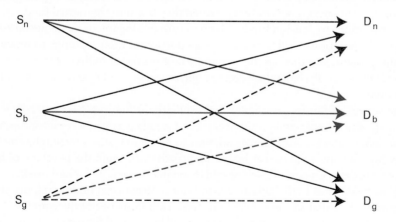

FIGURE 2.1a

Direct Financing

FIGURE 2.1b

Indirect financing

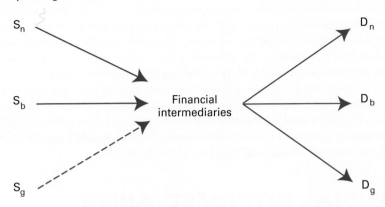

where S_n: households — savings
S_b: business — retained earnings, depreciation, depletion
S_g: government — budgetary surplus
D_n: households — new housing, durables, education
D_b: business — new plant and equipment, inventories, receivables
D_g: government — social capital, roads, schools, dams

Individuals represent the most significant source of indirect funding in Canada. In other words, they are the primary purchasers of the financial assets issued by deficit-spending units. They do so through a variety of mechanisms including bank deposits and direct purchases of financial assets issued by governments and businesses such as treasury bills, bonds, preferred stock, and common stock. They also purchase a wide variety of these financial assets indirectly when they buy units in mutual funds or through their contributions to pension funds, which in turn hold many of the financial assets listed above. Corporations tend to retain a large portion of their earnings to finance operations and growth, and they are not an important source of indirect funding. Canadian governments, generally, have also been net borrowers in recent years because of the need to fund their deficits.[1]

One source of funding not identified explicitly in Figures 2.1a and 2.1b is foreign investment, which has grown in importance in Canada partly as a result of funding government deficits and growth. Non-residents can invest in Canada by purchasing Canadian firms (which may be located at home or abroad) or through the purchase of bonds or stocks of Canadian companies that are sold through domestic or foreign markets. Foreign investment benefits us by helping to expand our international trading relationships, but the disadvantage is that this may take long-term cash flows out of the country. The optimal level of foreign investment is an issue that will be debated for some time to come, and it will no doubt continue to play an important role in our future as the world's economies become more integrated with each passing year.

---

[1] For example, the Canadian federal government balanced its budget in the 1997-98 fiscal year, which was the first time since 1969-70. While the budget has been in a surplus position since 1997-98, and is projected to be so for the near future, the government is still a net borrower.

Although financial intermediaries create new financial assets, the total amount of funding available remains unaltered. During any time period, the total amount of deficit spending has to equal net savings. Financial intermediaries will issue new indirect claims but only in the amount of direct obligations from deficit-spending units that they carry. In other words, the total amount of direct and indirect assets purchased over a given time period by surplus-spending units must equal the obligations issued by deficit-spenders.

A variety of financial intermediaries has evolved, reflecting the diverse financial needs of both savers and deficit spenders in an increasingly complex economy. Traditionally, in Canada, people have referred to chartered banks, trust companies, insurance companies, and investment dealers, as the "four pillars" of our financial system. The first three types of organizations represent financial intermediaries of the form reviewed earlier. Investment dealers have traditionally been somewhat different, and their particular intermediary services will be discussed separately in a subsequent section.

It is important to recognize that the distinctions between the different types of financial intermediaries have become blurred, and their functions increasingly overlapped in recent years as a result of numerous legislative changes. This is often referred to as the "erosion of the four pillars." Following international developments particularly in the United States, we continue to move toward integrated financial institutions or groups of interrelated firms that offer the broad range of financial services demanded in today's marketplace. The acquisition of securities firms (investment dealers) and trust companies by banks during the late 1980s and throughout the 1990s are two clear examples. There are numerous other examples of intermediaries offering services traditionally offered by others, and it is becoming increasingly difficult to distinguish between different types of intermediaries along a number of lines. Nonetheless, we have attempted to provide a brief description of the various types of financial intermediaries in the section below.

Banks and Related Institutions

These institutions accept deposits from individual savers under a variety of terms and conditions. The funds are pooled and lent out to borrowers for many purposes. Assets held by such institutions range from small consumer loans to significant debts of major corporations. The most important institutions under this heading are the chartered banks. Schedule I banks refer to those satisfying certain requirements. In particular, they must be widely held with no investor holding more than 10 percent, and foreign ownership is limited to 25 percent.[2] These include the so-called big six banks: Royal Bank, Canadian Imperial Bank of Commerce, Bank of Montreal, Bank of Nova Scotia, Toronto-Dominion

---

[2] These rules will be changed in the near future according to a new legislative policy framework introduced in June 2000. Under the new rules, there will be three classes of banks based on the size of their equity base: large (greater than $5 billion); medium ($1 to $5 billion); and small (less than $1 billion). Based on present figures, the $5-billion cut-off point would establish all of the present Schedule I banks as large banks except the National Bank (although it would be classified as such until deemed otherwise by the minister of finance). The large banks will have to remain widely held under new criteria, which eliminate the 25 percent foreign ownership rule and permit a single investor to own up to 20 percent of the voting shares of the bank and up to 30 percent of non-voting shares subject to a "fit-and-proper" test designed to evaluate their character and suitability. Medium banks would be allowed to have a single owner hold up to 65 percent of shareholdings and would be required to maintain a public float of at least 35 percent of voting shares. Small banks would face no ownership restrictions other than the fit-and-proper tests.

Bank, and National Bank. Schedule II banks, on the other hand, may be wholly owned by residents or non-residents. They are generally subsidiaries of foreign banks (41 out of a total of 45 by April 1997).[3] Until 1980, they were not allowed to accept deposits or call themselves banks, and most restricted their activities to making corporate loans. Non-U.S. banks are restricted to 12 percent of total assets of the banking system; however, as a result of the Free Trade Agreement of 1989, there is no such limit placed on U.S. banks.

Other institutions that have traditionally accepted deposits from individual savers include credit unions and caisses populaires. These are co-operative ventures originally formed to provide financial services to individuals with some common bond (for example, individuals residing in the same community or belonging to the same profession). As a result of years of financial deregulation, in today's environment, almost any financial institution readily accepts deposits including trust companies, insurance companies, investment dealers, and investment funds.

Trust Companies

The original mandate of trust companies was to operate in a fiduciary capacity (i.e., acting as a trustee in administering the assets of estates, pension plans, or other trust funds). This aspect of their operations is referred to as the estates, trusts, and agencies business. Over time, however, trust companies have also become deposit-taking institutions performing many banking functions such as accepting individual deposits and lending for a variety of purposes. Thus, trust companies today combine two different categories of services with particularly rapid growth of their banking-type business. Their deposits and loans tend toward somewhat longer maturities than those of banks, with a large proportion of their lending being in mortgages. That comprised over 40 percent of their total assets at the end of 1998. (See Table 2.2 toward the end of this section.) Unlike banks, which come under federal jurisdiction, trust companies can be chartered under either federal or provincial legislation.

Insurance Companies

Insurance companies accumulate large amounts of funds through regular premium collections from policyholders. The funds are invested in financial assets to provide a reserve for the payment of claims. In addition, many contracts available from life insurance firms involve a savings component. Under such arrangements, part of the premium is invested and the accumulated balance paid out upon retirement. Thus, life insurance companies also perform the functions of a savings institution and thereby play an important role as financial intermediaries.

Pension Funds

Regular contributions to such plans are invested for substantial time periods to provide benefits upon retirement. Pension fund portfolios have grown rapidly in recent years and are most often managed by trust companies or firms of professional money managers.

---

[3] Canadian Securities Institute, *Canadian Securities Course Textbook*, September 1998, p. 1-24.

In the past, pension fund assets were largely concentrated in high-quality debt and other "safe" investments. However, over the past few years, pension funds have become major players in equity and derivative markets, both domestic and foreign, as well as investing in real estate and even high-risk venture capital investments. For example, Canada's largest pension fund, la caisse de dépôt et placement du Québec, had close to 60 percent of its $105 billion in assets under management invested in equities and real estate as of December 31, 1999. The breakdown of their asset holdings was as follows:

- short-term investments and other net assets—2.8 percent
- mortgages—2.1 percent
- bonds—35.3 percent
- Canadian equities—27.5 percent
- foreign equities—27.2 percent
- real estate—5.1 percent.[4]

Investment Funds

Rather than investing in various types of securities directly, investors may pool their funds and employ professional money managers to administer their portfolios. The investor acquires shares in the fund, and the value of those shares reflects the value of the fund's investment portfolio. Open-end funds are referred to as mutual funds. Investors in these funds can redeem their shares in the fund at any time, perhaps subject to a redemption fee. The fund buys back these shares by liquidating part of its holdings. Closed-end funds do not redeem their own shares, which instead have to be sold in financial markets where they are traded in their own right, similar to common shares. Closed-end funds represent a very small proportion of available investment funds. For example, at the end of 1997, there were only 17 closed-end funds in Canada versus 1,023 open-end funds.

The benefits of investing in investment funds for the small investor include the ability to diversify by participating in a large and well-balanced portfolio and having the services of professional management. A variety of funds exist to satisfy different investor needs including:

- money market funds (invested primarily in money market instruments, which are discussed in Section 2.5)
- bond and mortgage funds
- equity funds that include income funds (invested mainly in stable, income-producing securities), growth funds (aimed toward riskier capital gains), and balanced funds (with an in-between strategy)
- real estate investment trusts (invested entirely in mortgages or other real estate securities)

There are also numerous international funds that focus on one or more countries and feature the same sort of investment strategy options available in purely domestic funds. As with pension funds, investment funds are often established and managed by other financial intermediaries.

---

[4] La caisse de dépôt et placement du Québec's website at http://www.lacaisse.com

Segregated funds are offered by insurance companies as an alternative to conventional mutual funds. These are legally considered to be insurance products, and they must be separated from the other assets of the insurance company. One distinguishing feature of these funds is that they guarantee investors a minimum percentage of their total contributions after a certain period of time. The minimum required by law is 75 percent after 10 years although most funds guarantee 100 percent. In recent years, there has been tremendous growth in the total assets of Canadian seg funds, which reached approximately $60 billion by the end of 1998, more than double the amount in 1994.

Finance Companies

These firms raise funds by issuing their own securities and by borrowing from other financial institutions. They provide short- and intermediate-term loans to both individuals and businesses for a variety of purposes. Some finance companies perform specialized functions. For instance, manufacturers of consumer durables sometimes form sales finance subsidiaries to assist customers with the financing of their purchases. An example of this type of finance company is General Motors Acceptance Corporation (GMAC).

Concluding Comments

Table 2.2 provides an overview of the relative importance of various types of financial institutions as measured by the size of their assets.

We see that the chartered banks continue to be the dominant force in financial intermediation at least in terms of total assets. Table 2.2 also shows that banks, trust companies, credit unions, and life insurance companies have a substantial portion of their assets in the form of loans although insurance companies have very little in the way of non-mortgage loans. Finance companies and other financial institutions, on the other hand, have a large proportion of their assets in cash and other short-term investments, with finance companies also maintaining a high proportion in the form of non-mortgage loans. The importance of intermediaries in financial markets is also highlighted by the fact that most of the trading that takes place on major stock exchanges such as New York or Toronto is accounted for by financial institutions. In fact, individual investors have been net sellers of stocks for the past 30 years, and in 1998, individual investors accounted for less than 20 percent of the dollar volume of the Toronto Stock Exchange (TSE).

In conclusion, the services provided by financial intermediaries and the range of indirect securities that they make available improve opportunities for both investors and businesses and contribute significantly to economic efficiency. While the development and growth of financial intermediation has associated costs such as driving a wedge between the ultimate providers of funds (savers) and the users of such funds (businesses), these costs are hard to measure. In any event, the benefits at this time appear to outweigh the costs, and a modern industrialized economy without extensive intermediation would be unthinkable.

Table 2.2

Asset Portfolios of Major Categories of Canadian Financial Institutions as of December 31, 1998, in Percentages of Total

Assets	Chartered banks and other deposit-accepting intermediaries	Trust companies	Credit unions	Life insurance companies	Property and casuality insurance companies	Consumer and business finance companies	*Other financial intermediaries
Cash, accounts receivable and investments with affiliates	5.9%	8.7%	15.7%	16.1%	17.4%	43.7%	45.2%
Portfolio investments	16.8%	20.3%	10.2%	53.1%	62.8%	4.1%	29.9%
Loans							
- mortgage	26.6%	40.0%	43.5%	23.9%	0.8%	2.2%	5.2%
- non-mortgage	36.0%	29.7%	28.5%	2.7%	0.0%	37.1%	3.7%
Customer liabilities under acceptances	5.1%	0.0%	0.0%	0.0%	0.0%	0.0%	0.0%
Allowances for losses, capital assets and other assets	9.6%	1.3%	2.1%	4.2%	19.0%	12.9%	16.0%
Total assets	100%	100%	100%	100%	100%	100%	100%
Total assets (millions)	$946,780	$54,178	$140,690	$177,913	$55,045	$110,186	$41,101

*Includes portfolio investment intermediaries, mortgage companies, trusteed pension funds, estate, trust and agency funds, security brokers and dealers, mortgage brokers, security and commodity exchanges, and other financial intermediaries not classified elsewhere.

Source: Statistics Canada website at http://www.statcan.ca, May 26, 2000.

2.4 FINANCIAL MARKETS

Financial markets encompass the institutions and procedures involved in the buying and selling of financial assets. Such markets facilitate the channelling of savings into the most attractive investment opportunities available, thereby fostering capital formation and economic growth. Their main purpose is to match buyers and sellers in an efficient way. The prices at which financial assets trade are determined by aggregate supply and demand and will reach a level at which the total offerings of all sellers will equal the total amount that buyers are prepared to purchase. This is referred to as the equilibrium price for a security.

Primary Markets

A **primary market** is one in which a borrower issues new securities in exchange for cash from an investor (buyer or lender). New sales of Government of Canada treasury bills, BCE Inc. common stock, or Ontario Power Generation (formerly Ontario Hydro) bonds all take place in the primary markets.[5] The issuers of these securities—the Canadian government, BCE Inc., and Ontario Power—receive cash from the buyers of these new securities who in turn receive financial claims that previously did not exist. Note that in all three of these examples, some amount of these securities is outstanding before the new sales occur. These primary distributions facilitate the efficient allocation of savings from surplus-spending units to deficit-spending units.

Table 2.3 indicates the total amount of net new securities issued by Canadian governments and businesses in both domestic and foreign markets for the years 1996-2000. Table 2.3 also shows that a substantial portion of this money is raised in foreign markets although we defer our discussion regarding the importance of global markets until later in this section.

---

[5] Sales of common stock of a company that is already publicly traded are called seasoned new issues. If the issuer is selling securities for the first time, these are referred to as initial public offerings (IPOs).

Table 2.3

Net New Security Issued by Canadian Governments and Businesses

	1996	1997	1998	1999	2000
			$ Millions		
Government of Canada bonds	33,364	18,439	9,895	2,214	−4,956
Provincial bonds	3,848	3,061	6,898	4,560	−5,578
Municipal bonds	235	32	−3,909	−84	−2,162
Corporations					
Bonds	20,278	38,623	36,252	39,179	9,182
Preferred and common stocks	21,489	21,721	15,615	18,507	21,511
Other institutions and foreign borrowers	−126	−90	173	−109	−54
Treasury bills and other short–term paper					
Government of Canada treasury bills and U.S.–pay Canada bills	−22,384	−25,492	−18,407	−41	−14,140
Provincial governments and their enterprises and municipal governments	−404	−847	231	967	−773
Sales finance companies and other commercial paper	4,882	6,828	21,814	24,405	23,023
Canadian dollar bankers' acceptances	4,095	3,264	6,208	5,749	1,140
Total net new issues	77,846	62,375	85,957	85,241	101,280
Of which placed in:					
Canada	52,766	36,836	64,856	47,945	97,210
Outside Canada	25,080	25,540	21,102	37,294	4,070
United States	18,803	23,981	13,927	28,142	5,080
Other	6,277	1,559	7,175	9,152	−1,010

Source: http://www.statcan.ca/english/Pgdb/Economy/Finance/fin34/htm

In the course of selling new securities, issuers often rely on an **investment dealer** (or an investment banker in the United States) for the necessary expertise as well as the ability to reach widely dispersed suppliers of capital. Along with performing activities such as helping corporations in mergers and acquisitions, investment dealers specialize in the design and sale of securities in the primary market while operating simultaneously in the secondary markets. For example, RBC Dominion Securities and the other major Canadian investment dealers offer investment services while operating large retail brokerage operations throughout the country.

Investment dealers act as intermediaries between issuers and investors. For firms seeking to raise long-term funds, investment dealers can provide important advice to their clients during the planning stage preceding the issuance of new securities. This advice includes providing information about the type of security to be sold, the features to be offered with the security, the price, and the timing of the sale.[6]

Secondary Markets

Once new securities have been sold in the primary market, an efficient mechanism must exist for their resale if investors are to view securities as attractive opportunities. Secondary markets give investors the means to trade existing securities. New securities may trade repeatedly in the secondary market, but original issuers will be unaffected in the sense that they receive no additional cash from these transactions. Secondary markets exist for the trading of commercial paper, treasury bills, Bankers Acceptances, bonds and debentures, common and preferred stock, and derivative securities.

Secondary trading is of importance because it provides liquidity to investors, and the existence of a reasonably efficient secondary market is a prerequisite for the issuance of securities especially those with longer maturities. For example, consider investors who purchased corporate bonds with a maturity of 20 years. Without a developed secondary market, the investors may have no choice but to hold such securities until maturity, and few investors would be willing to enter into such long-term commitments. However, given secondary markets, investors know that they can readily convert their holdings to cash by selling the bonds to other investors.

A Global Perspective

The global perspective of today's financial environment allows companies in various countries to raise new capital in amounts that would have been impossible only a few years earlier because these companies often were limited to selling new securities in their own domestic markets. The global equity offering has changed all that, and an important new development for investment dealers is the emphasis on managing the global offerings of securities. For example, Table 2.3 shows that over $30 billion of the total $78 billion (almost 40 percent) of net new financing for Canadian governments and businesses in 1998 was raised outside Canada.

---

[6] The details of how firms go about issuing new securities in the primary market are described in Chapter 14.

A lead investment banker can act as a "global coordinator," linking separate underwriting syndicates throughout the world in selling equity issues. In fact, a number of Canadian companies raise money from global markets, and there were more than 225 companies interlisted on both Canadian and foreign exchanges in 1998 (primarily on U.S. markets such as the Nasdaq Stock Market or the New York Stock Exchange—NYSE). This is an important trend with over one-third of all trading in Canadian stocks that do interlist occurring on U.S. markets. The importance of foreign trading varies from company to company. For example, during the first seven months of 1999, U.S. trading accounted for 95.9 percent of the total value of trading for Bowater Canada's stock and only 0.9 percent of Petro-Canada's.[7]

Global markets will represent attractive alternatives to companies when larger amounts of financing are required since they expand the potential demand for their securities. For example, when the Canadian National Railway Company (CN) completed its C$2.3-billion initial public offering in November 1995, the shares were handled by Canadian, U.S., and international underwriting syndicates. In addition, large investors may be drawn to international markets. This is one of the reasons given by Canadian financial institutions for their large investment in securities listed on the NYSE. They have argued that the size of this market makes it much easier to trade large blocks of securities thereby improving their flexibility and liquidity.

Some of the main reasons for raising funds in international markets include the following:

1. The limited size of the domestic Canadian market. The maximum size of a single issue that the Canadian market can absorb at any one time is about $1 billion. With many large projects requiring capital far in excess of such amounts, international markets have to be tapped.

2. Management of foreign exchange exposure for a firm with international operations. By matching the currencies for assets and liabilities and for cash inflows and outflows, the overall risk that arises from fluctuations in foreign exchange rates can be minimized.

3. Interest rate differentials. Interest rates vary from country to country, and a company may find it attractive to exploit such rate differentials in its financing. As will be discussed in Chapter 21, however, the benefit of lower interest rates has to be weighed against increased risks of foreign exchange exposure.

4. Availability of private placements. With U.S. financial institutions much larger than their Canadian counterparts, the U.S. market offers greater flexibility in placing large amounts with a single lender and tailoring the arrangements to the specific situation.

These points are explored in more detail in subsequent chapters. However, some illustrations are readily drawn from recent financing activities undertaken by Canadian firms and governments. We have already seen that CN's initial public offering was very large and that it was sold both domestically and abroad. Several other prominent Canadian companies that have announced financing involving international markets include (but are certainly not limited to) the following:

---

[7] Alexandra Eadie, "Where Canadian Interlisted Stocks Trade," *Globe and Mail Report on Business*, September 8, 1999, p. B12.

- TransCanada PipeLines Ltd., sold US$160 million in cumulative preferred securities in the United States, in part to finance pipeline construction
- Trizec-Hahn Corp. sold US$150 million in subordinated voting shares to U.S. investors
- Barrick Gold Corp. issued up to US$1 billion of non-convertible debt in the United States
- Inco Ltd., had a US$132-million initial public offering of American depositary shares in a business unit called Doncasters PLC with proceeds designed in part to retire debt taken on when Inco acquired Diamond Fields.

These examples provide some evidence of the variety of firms and securities involved in international corporate deals.

In addition to corporations, Canadian federal and provincial governments and provincial government enterprises like Hydro-Québec often borrow very large amounts in a single offering. They have become frequent participants in international markets. As an example, the Canadian federal government was awarded the title "Best Issuer of Globals" by *Euromoney* magazine for its issuance of two separate globals of US$1.5 billion each in 1995. A global bond issue is one that is simultaneously placed in Asia, Europe, and North America. Another frequent issuer of globals is Ontario, which alone raised over C$21 billion in 11 issues between 1992 and 1995, with most of this debt denominated in U.S. dollars. Québec has been particularly active in yen-denominated borrowing. Indeed, approximately 40 percent of outstanding provincial debt is now in currencies other than the Canadian dollar.

In addition to incentives relating to the size of an issue, some provinces appear to borrow in foreign markets in an attempt to take advantage of interest rate differentials that favour borrowing in the Euromarkets rather than domestically. In order to deal with the additional risk due to fluctuating exchange rates that such borrowing may generate, provinces frequently use swaps or other innovative financing techniques to reduce the risk. A swap is, roughly speaking, an agreement with another party to exchange debt-servicing obligations. Thus, for example, a Canadian province that has borrowed floating rate yen may agree to swap interest payment obligations with a Japanese company that has outstanding fixed-rate Canadian-dollar-denominated debt.

Apart from raising funds internationally, Canadian businesses may also choose to have their outstanding securities listed for secondary trading on various foreign stock exchanges. Although this provides broader market exposure, it forces firms to comply with foreign securities legislation and stock exchange regulations. Of particular importance in this context is U.S. legislation as administered by the federal Securities and Exchange Commission (SEC). Examples of Canadian companies listed on one or more foreign stock exchanges include each of the firms undertaking financing deals in international markets mentioned above as well as many others such as Canadian Pacific, Placer Dome, and Royal Bank.

Each country operates its own financial markets, and Canadian enterprises may tap such markets by, for example, selling debt instruments denominated in U.S. dollars to American investors. In addition, we have what has been termed **Euromarkets**, which function on a somewhat different basis. These markets involve securities and bank deposits denominated in currencies outside the country in which the currency is generally used. For example, bank deposits in U.S. dollars held in London or Kuwait are termed **Eurodollars**, whereas deposits in German marks held in Zurich or Tokyo are called Euromarks. Each major currency is available in a variety of international financial centres at an interest rate that reflects international supply and demand for that particular currency.

Funds in the Euromarkets are highly mobile and move freely from country to country on very short notice. Although it is claimed that this has contributed to instability in the international monetary environment, it has made such funds practically free from political interference. This is attractive to such important depositors as the oil exporting countries, and the Euromarkets have assumed a significant role in the "recycling" or lending of petrodollars.

An important reason for the existence of Eurocurrency markets is that such deposits are free from domestic banking regulations—reserve requirements, constraints on interest rates, and other impediments—that might otherwise apply.[8] For example, if a European-based bank does not have to maintain reserve requirements against a U.S. dollar deposit, it can simultaneously offer a higher interest rate to a depositor and a lower interest rate to a borrower than would be possible for a bank based in the United States or Canada that is subject to domestic regulations. Hence, terms offered to borrowers and/or lenders in the Eurocurrency markets can be more attractive than those available in various domestic markets, and this has contributed to the Eurocurrency markets' rapid growth. Eurobond markets are similarly free of government regulation.

All of these factors have helped to create an enormous pool of loanable funds available worldwide in a variety of currencies. Given the size of this pool and the magnitude of individual transactions, the global market has become very efficient, and banks operate on narrow margins. Borrowers are drawn to these markets because of economics, availability, and convenience. With the opportunity of borrowing more cheaply and the potential for sidestepping a variety of regulations, it is not unusual for a Canadian firm to float a Canadian-dollar Eurobond issue or to borrow Canadian dollars over the short term in the Eurocurrency market perhaps even through a Canadian bank. Japanese and U.S. corporations have been far more aggressive, issuing significant percentages of their debt in the Eurobond market. As far as convenience is concerned, a German importer requiring Canadian dollars may be better known to European bankers than to a Canadian lender. Therefore, the company may find it easier to borrow Canadian Eurodollars than to negotiate a loan in Toronto. Finally, when large amounts of capital have to be raised for single projects or over short time spans, the size of this market makes it an important source.

The rapidly increasing internationalization of financial markets with capital moving in a global context is also reflected in the dramatic growth in the volume of foreign exchange contracts in such leading markets as London, New York, and Tokyo. In value terms, daily trading in the international currency markets (spot, forward, futures, and options) dwarfs trading in equity markets like the NYSE. Estimates in 1998 place the value of trading in currency markets at approximately US$2 trillion *per day*. That year, Canada's average daily turnover in traditional foreign exchange transactions was estimated at US$37 billion. ⬆

---

[8] Limitations on borrowing domestically for the purpose of financing overseas firms or to otherwise expand abroad is one example.

2.5 CLASSIFICATION OF FINANCIAL MARKETS

It is usual to classify financial markets by the type of securities traded. Depending on the maturity of financial assets, we distinguish between **money markets** and **capital markets**. Money markets involve the trading of short-term debt typically with maturities of one year or less, whereas capital markets deal with more permanent sources of funds. Capital markets are further subdivided into markets for longer-term debt and equities. Each of these markets is characterized by a somewhat different institutional arrangement. Figure 2.2 provides an overview of the structure of the various secondary markets within which trading takes place. These markets will be discussed in the appropriate sections below.

FIGURE 2.2

The Structure of Secondary Markets

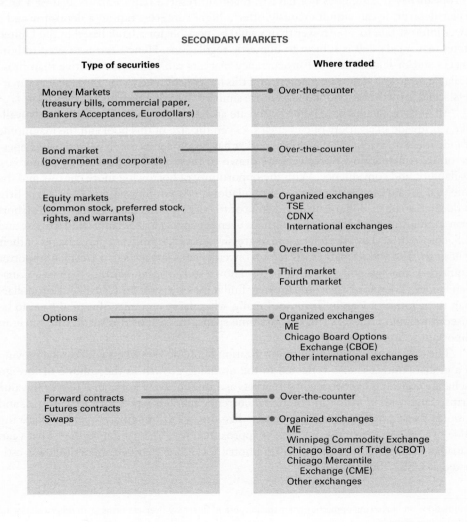

Money Market

Money market trading activity is dominated by financial institutions, particularly banks, and governments. The value of trading activity in the Canadian money market was approximately $5.9 trillion in 1997, which was slightly above the corresponding figure for the Canadian bond market of $5.5 trillion. Given all of the attention devoted to stock market activity in the media, it is surprising to note that this amount is over 10 times the 1997 volume of trading activity in Canadian stock markets, which was a mere $498 billion.

The Canadian money market basically consists of a number of major authorized dealers who are in constant contact with each other by telephone or computer, actively matching supply and demand. This type of market is referred to as a **dealer market** or **over-the-counter (OTC) market**. These dealers may either act as agents in bringing buyers and sellers of money market securities together, or they may act as principals trading on their own account. They enjoy special arrangements with the Bank of Canada, which acts as a "lender of last resort" in supplying such dealers with temporary credit when necessary, a facility that adds to the stability of this market. In addition, trading is restricted to securities of high quality, involving little risk of default. The total value of money market securities held outside the Bank of Canada as of December 1998 was $228 billion.

A wide range of different money market instruments exists, and the majority of them have maturities of less than one year. Most money market securities are sold in very large denominations (usually greater than $100,000), which has made them inaccessible to most individual investors (without the intervention of financial intermediaries). Recognizing this fact, several financial institutions now purchase large blocks of these instruments and break them up into smaller denominations (as low as $1,000) in order to make them available for their retail customers. The rates on these smaller denominations will be lower than those available on the larger blocks, which is how the intermediaries make a profit on these transactions. In addition, investment companies offer money market funds that allow the small investor to buy these securities indirectly.

In terms of volume outstanding, the most popular Canadian money market instruments in 1997 were Government of Canada treasury bills (T-bills), which accounted for about one-half of all outstanding securities. These are short-term promissory notes issued by the Government of Canada to finance ongoing expenditures in excess of current tax revenues. They are sold at a discount from face value in denominations of $5,000, $25,000, $100,000, and $1 million. The greater the discount at the time of purchase, the higher the return earned by investors. Typical maturities are 91, 182, and 364 days although shorter maturities are also offered. Because of their government backing, there is no risk of default.[9] In addition, their wide distribution and active trading guarantee a high degree of liquidity, making it easy to buy and sell on short notice at a predictable price. This has made T-bills a favoured vehicle for investing short-term surplus cash. New T-bills are auctioned every other week by the Bank of Canada, and the yield at which they sell is widely observed as an indicator of current interest rates since it represents what the government must pay to obtain short-term financing. Some T-bills are also issued by provincial governments.

---

[9] In fact, in subsequent chapters, we will use government T-bill rates as a measure of the "riskless rate" available to investors; this is commonly referred to as the risk-free rate.

Other common money market instruments include commercial paper, Bankers Acceptances (BAs), repurchase agreements, and Eurodollars. Commercial paper and BAs provide corporations with access to money market funding and are very similar to T-bills in that they are issued and traded at a discount from their face value. These securities and their use in business financing are reviewed in detail in Chapter 24, which deals with short-term sources of funds.

Commercial paper refers to short-term unsecured promissory notes issued by large, well-known, and financially strong corporations (including finance companies). Denominations start at $100,000 with maturities of 30 to 365 days, and they are sold either directly by the issuer or indirectly through a dealer with rates slightly above those for T-bills. The secondary market for commercial paper has grown in importance in recent years. BAs are time drafts drawn on a bank by a customer whereby the bank agrees to guarantee payment of a particular amount at a specified future date. They differ from commercial paper because the associated payments are guaranteed by a bank and thus possess the credit risk associated with that bank. BAs are issued in minimum denominations of $100,000 with maturities typically ranging from 30 to 180 days, 90 days being the most common.

Repurchase agreements (repos) are contracts between a borrower and lender (typically institutions) to sell and repurchase money market securities. The borrower initiates a repo by contracting to sell securities to a lender and agreeing to repurchase these securities at a prespecified (higher) price on a stated future date. The effective interest rate is given by the difference between the repurchase price and the sale price. The annual interest rate implied by these transactions is referred to as the repo rate. The maturity of repos is generally very short, from three to 14 days and sometimes overnight. The minimum denomination is usually $100,000.

Eurodollars are dollar-denominated deposits held in foreign banks or in offices of Canadian banks located abroad. Although this market originally developed in Europe, dollar-denominated deposits can now be made in many countries including Asia. Eurodollar deposits consist of both time deposits and certificates of deposit (CDs), with the latter constituting the largest component of the Eurodollar markets. Maturities are mostly short term, often less than six months. The Eurodollar market is primarily a wholesale market with large deposits and large loans. Major international banks transact among themselves with other participants including multinational corporations and governments. Although relatively safe, Eurodollar yields exceed those of other money market assets because of the lesser regulation for Eurodollar banks. In addition, unlike deposits with Canadian banks, Eurodollar CDs are not covered by the Canadian Deposit Insurance Corporation (CDIC). These are discussed in greater detail in the section on international markets. ▲

The money market plays a vital role in the management of liquidity not only for corporations but also for financial institutions including the banking system. For example, it enables banks to borrow money on a daily basis to maintain a positive level of reserves.[10] At the same time, these markets allow corporate treasurers to minimize idle cash balances, a fact that is significant in an environment of relatively high interest rates. Finally, because of its national character and its ability to respond on very short notice,

---

[10] Formerly, banks were required to maintain a mandated percentage of their deposits in the form of reserves.

the money market effectively ties the economy together, channelling funds from where they accumulate to where they are needed and guaranteeing a uniform structure of interest rates across the country.

Intermediate and Long-Term Debt Markets

Longer-term debt in the form of bonds and other types of securities is issued by various levels of government, by government agencies such as Crown corporations, and by businesses usually to finance more permanent needs that commonly arise in the funding of capital projects. A variety of specific debt instruments that vary according to maturity, collateral, and related provisions exist. Generally, only large and well-established firms have access to intermediate and long-term debt markets, with smaller companies having to rely primarily on financial intermediaries such as banks. We defer our discussion of many of the specific features of debt until Chapter 13.

Bond markets represent the most important markets for intermediate and long-term debt. Investors can purchase either new bonds being issued in the primary market or existing bonds outstanding in the secondary market. Yields for the two must be in equilibrium. If, for example, Nortel bonds are trading in the secondary market to yield 9 percent over a 20-year period, comparable new Nortel bonds will be sold with approximately the same yield.

Although some bonds trade on stock exchanges such as the Toronto Stock Exchange (convertible bonds only) and the Canadian Venture Exchange, the secondary bond market is primarily an over-the-counter (OTC) market with a large network of dealers making markets in the various bonds. Investors can buy and sell bonds through their brokers who in turn trade with bond dealers. The volume of bond trading in the OTC market in Canada dwarfs that of the exchanges. The situation is similar in the United States in which OTC trading of bonds dominates although a few thousand bonds are traded on exchanges such as the NYSE and a very few on the American Stock Exchange.

The Canadian bond market represents a relatively small percentage of the global bond market. For example, in 1997, it had approximately US$506 billion in outstanding debt—2 percent of the global market.[11] The size of the Canadian market pales in comparison to several international bond markets such as those in the United States and Japan, in which there was US$12.4 and $4.4 trillion in outstanding debt in 1997.

The government bond market comprises the majority of the Canadian market, and the major component is Government of Canada bonds. These are widely purchased, held, and traded resulting in a broad and deep market with a large volume of transactions.[12] The market is not as deep for provincial or municipal bonds or for corporate bonds. Corporate issues accounted for less than 20 percent of the total bonds outstanding in Canada in 1997 with a total of US$75 billion outstanding. That was a mere 0.8 percent of the world corporate market. At the same time, there was over US$5 trillion in outstanding corporate bonds in the United States.

---

[11] Bank for International Settlements (BIS) website at http://www.bis.org "International Banking and Financial Market Developments."

[12] A "deep" market is one that possesses a large number of active buyers and sellers, while a "thin" market is the opposite.

The money and capital markets are constantly adapting to meet new requirements and conditions that have given rise to new types of securities that were not previously available. An important debt market that has emerged in recent years is the market for **asset-backed securities (ABS)**, which are traded in OTC debt markets similar to traditional bond markets. These assets have been created through securitization, which refers to the transformation of illiquid, risky individual loans into more liquid, less-risky securities known as asset-backed securities. The best example of this process is mortgage-backed securities (MBS). These are created when a financial institution purchases (or originates) a number of mortgage loans, which are then repackaged and sold to investors as mortgage pools. Investors in MBSs are, in effect, purchasing a piece of a mortgage pool. MBS investors assume little default risk because most mortgages are guaranteed by a federal government agency as described below.

The Canada Mortgage and Housing Corporation (CMHC) introduced MBSs in Canada in 1987, and similar instruments are backed by a number of government agencies in the United States. The CMHC issues fully guaranteed securities in support of the mortgage market. ABSs are created when an underwriter such as a bank bundles some type of asset-linked debt (typically consumer oriented) and sells the right to receive payments made on that debt to investors. As a result of the trend to securitization, other asset-backed securities have proliferated as financial institutions have rushed to securitize various types of loans.

Marketable securities have been backed by car loans, credit card receivables, rail car leases, small business loans, photocopier leases, aircraft leases, and so forth. The assets that can be securitized seem to be limited only by the imagination of the packagers. For example, ABSs have been created on a wide variety of asset types including royalty streams from films or recording artists, student loans, mutual fund fees, tax liens, monthly electric utility bills, and delinquent child support payments.

Canadian Equity Markets

Common stocks, preferred stocks, and warrants are traded in the equity markets. Many equity securities are traded on stock exchanges, which are **auction markets**. On organized stock exchanges, brokers who act on behalf of their clients arrange to match buy-and-sell orders through an auction system. Trading takes place either on the floor of an exchange or by computer link between representatives of brokers who are members of the exchange. For their services, brokers charge a commission that is a percentage of the value of the transaction.

Canadian stock exchanges underwent significant changes in 1999 and 2000. At the start of 1999, there were five stock exchanges in Canada: the **Toronto Stock Exchange (TSE)**, the Montreal Exchange (ME), the Vancouver Stock Exchange (VSE), the Winnipeg Stock Exchange (WSE), and the Alberta Stock Exchange (ASE). In March 1999, a complete overhaul of that structure was proposed and is now in place. As a result of this restructuring, there are three remaining stock exchanges in Canada: the TSE, the ME, and the newly created Canadian Venture Exchange (CDNX).

The first objective of this restructuring was to make the TSE the official exchange for trading of Canadian senior stocks—big companies with solid histories of profits. This was finalized in December 1999 when over 400 senior stocks that traded on the ME began trading exclusively on the TSE. Even prior to this reorganization, the TSE was the largest stock exchange in Canada and dominated trading in large companies. For example, the TSE accounted for almost 90 percent of the dollar volume of stock market transactions in Canada in 1998.

Incorporated in 1878, the TSE is one of the 10 largest stock exchanges in the world and is the third largest in North America, behind the New York Stock Exchange (NYSE) and Nasdaq-Amex Stock Market. The total dollar value of trading reached a record level of $523 billion in 1999, averaging over $2 billion per day in trades.[13] There were more than 1,400 listed companies on the TSE in 1999, and the total market capitalization (which is defined as the total number of shares outstanding times the market price per share) was about $1.5 trillion. The requirements for companies wishing to list on the TSE are much more stringent than for the other Canadian exchanges and tend to preclude smaller companies.

The second objective of the restructuring was to create a single national exchange for trading of junior company stocks—the CDNX, which was originally to include junior stocks trading on the ASE, VSE, ME, and WSE. The CDNX came into existence on November 29, 1999 with the merger of the VSE and ASE, and the WSE joined in March 2000. While the ME continues to list approximately 120 junior stocks, they trade on the same electronic system as those on the CDNX, and it is anticipated that all remaining ME stocks will list on the CDNX in 2001.

The third major objective of the restructuring was to transform the ME into a national derivatives market that would combine all trading in futures and options that previously occurred on both the TSE and ME. This was officially accomplished in March 2000 with the final transfer of all equity options from the TSE to the ME.

An interesting new development, discussed in the report below, is the recent agreement between the Quebec provincial government and the U.S.-based Nasdaq-Amex Stock Market to create Nasdaq Canada, a Canadian market for Nasdaq-listed companies. Due to the popularity and rapid growth experienced by Nasdaq, this announcement has created serious questions about the future for the TSE and the CDNX and the achievement of some of the objectives proposed for the recent restructuring of Canadian stock exchanges. Some of these issues are discussed in the report below.

---

[13] TSE website at http://www.tse.com.

■ *Finance in the News*

Quebec Wins Nasdaq, Takes on Bay Street

On April 26, 2000 the Quebec government announced the creation of Nasdaq Canada, to be established in Montreal. The memorandum of agreement with the Montreal Exchange offered Nasdaq Canada "certain fiscal advantages" and seems to eliminate the Toronto Stock Exchange, which had also been in talks with the U.S. exchange. Speculation is that the TSE's high-tech sector may suffer. ScotiaMcLeod's Fred Ketchen saw it as "a challenging problem to overcome" and commented that it was "going to be interesting to see how this does work out."

The deal seems to reverse 1999's reorganization of Canadian stock exchanges, which saw Montreal become the centre for derivatives, with all senior shares moving to the TSE and junior shares being traded on the Canadian Venture Exchange. With this deal Montreal is back in the equities market as a branch of the U.S. giant Nasdaq.

TSE president Barbara Stymiest stated that the exchange intended to push "to gain equal opportunity within the U.S. market." John Wall, president of Nasdaq International, declared that his exchange "will embrace Toronto as well when they're ready to come in." William Hess of the Canadian Ventures Exchange saw the development in a positive light, saying, "It looks like the big leagues have just expanded." This means more opportunities for his junior players.

Source: Globe and Mail, April 27, 2000, p. A1. Reprinted with permission.

All of the exchanges rely heavily on computerized trading systems. The TSE closed its trading floor on April 23, 1997, and trading is now completely computerized. Stock exchange memberships (in the form of stock exchange seats) are sold to individuals, which permits them to trade on the exchange. These seats are valuable assets that may be sold, subject to certain exchange conditions. Exchange member firms must be publicly owned, they need to maintain capital reserves, and key personnel must complete required courses of study.

Exchanges have the power to suspend the trading or listing privileges of an individual security temporarily or permanently. Temporary withdrawals of trading and/or listing privileges include:

- delayed opening (which may arise if there exist a large number of buy and/or sell orders)
- halt in trading (to allow significant news to be reported such as merger activity)
- suspension of trading for more than one session until an identified problem is rectified by the company to the exchange's satisfaction (if the company fails to meet requirements for continued trading or does not comply with listing requirements)

Equities also trade on over-the-counter (OTC) markets, which do not have a physical location but consist of a network of dealers who trade with each other over phone or computer networks. These are negotiated markets, whereby only the dealers' bid and ask quotations are entered by those dealers acting as market makers in a particular security. Market makers execute trades from their inventories of securities in which they have agreed to "make a market." This market essentially handles unlisted securities—securities not listed on a stock exchange—although some listed securities are now traded in this market.

The volume of unlisted or OTC equity trading in Canada has traditionally been much smaller than the volume of exchange-traded equity transactions. While the exact size of Canadian OTC market activity has been difficult to measure due to lack of complete statistics, the reported trading volume grew from 281 million shares in 1991 to 3 billion shares in 1997. From 1991 to October 2, 2000, Canadian OTC trading for unlisted securities occurred through the Canadian Dealing Network Inc. (CDN), a subsidiary of the TSE. The CDN consisted of a large network linking dealers across Canada where trading went on longer than exchange hours.

On October 2, 2000, about 350 of the most actively traded stocks on the CDN were shifted to the CDNX for future trading. These stocks will initially be traded as tier-three stocks (existing CDNX stocks comprise tiers one and two based on size and other factors). The transition is intended to improve visibility and transparency of trade activity since the CDNX is generally perceived as having better market regulations than was the case for the CDN. In the following week, the remaining CDN stocks (as many as 800) began trading on the Canadian Unlisted Board (CUB), which is a new Internet-based reporting system owned by CDNX. Most of these stocks are very illiquid and experience very little trading activity (many are inactive). This system is not expected to differ much from the previous one at CDN.

Global Equity Markets

The U.S. auction markets include two national exchanges and several regional exchanges. The national exchanges include the **New York Stock Exchange (NYSE)** and the American Stock Exchange (Amex), which merged with the Nasdaq Stock Market in 1998 to form the Nasdaq-Amex Market Group. The NYSE is the oldest and most prominent secondary market in the United States and is the world's largest secondary market. Unlike many of the world's stock markets, the NYSE has resisted the change to complete computerized trading, and it continues to perform using its specialist system.[14] **Market specialists**, who own roughly one-third of all the seats on the NYSE, are assigned to trading posts on the floor of the exchange where they handle one or more of the stocks traded at that post. Specialists are exchange members that are responsible for maintaining an orderly market in one or more stocks by buying or selling shares for their own account. Some specialist firms are part of well-known brokerage operations, while many others are virtually unknown to the public.

---

[14] In actuality, the NYSE has become highly automated. An electronic system matches buy-and-sell orders entered before the market opens, setting the opening price of a stock. The NYSE has SuperDot, an electronic order routing system for NYSE-listed securities. Member firms send orders directly to the specialist post in which the securities are traded, and confirmation of trading is returned directly to the member firms over the same system.

As mentioned above, a number of Canadian companies are interlisted on the NYSE. The qualifying criteria for listing on the NYSE are far more stringent than they are for the TSE. For example, to list on the TSE, companies must have more than C$2 million in net tangible assets and have had pre-tax income of at least C$200,000 in the most recent year. To list on the NYSE, companies must have more than US$40 million in net tangible assets and have had pre-tax income at or above US$2.5 million in the most recent year and exceeding US$2 million in the preceding two years.[15] As a result of these criteria, only the largest Canadian companies are able to list their shares on this exchange. The NYSE is the dominant capital market in the world based on trading volume and on the market capitalization of its firms. During 1999, the NYSE had 3,025 listed companies, and trading volume reached US$8.9 trillion. By December 31, 1999, the market capitalization of the NYSE was US$12.3 trillion—by far the largest of any stock markets in the world.

The American Stock Exchange (Amex) is the only other national organized exchange in the United States, although it is very small relative to the NYSE both in terms of market capitalization and trading activity. The United States also has several regional exchanges patterned after the NYSE although their listing requirements are considerably more lenient.

Over 35,000 stocks trade in the OTC market in the United States. Many of these are small, thinly traded stocks that do not generate much interest. The most important part of the negotiated market is the **Nasdaq Stock Market (Nasdaq)**. It represents a national and international stock market consisting of communication networks for the trading of thousands of stocks. Technically, Nasdaq has insisted for several years that its market is not synonymous with the OTC market. It is a wholly owned subsidiary of the **National Association of Security Dealers (NASD)**, a self-regulating body of brokers and dealers that oversees OTC practices much as the TSE or NYSE do for their members. The Nasdaq Stock Market consists of a network of market makers or dealers, who compete freely with each other through an electronically linked network of terminals rather than on the floor of an exchange. Nasdaq features an electronic trading system as the centrepiece of its operations.

The common stock issues traded on Nasdaq vary widely in size, price, quality, and trading activity ranging from small start-up companies to giants such as Microsoft and Intel that have chosen to remain Nasdaq companies rather than move on to the NYSE. The Nasdaq Stock Market has become a major player in the securities markets and in all likelihood will continue to gain importance. In 1999, there were more issues listed on Nasdaq (5,210) than on the NYSE (3,025), and the dollar volume of trading ($11 trillion) exceeded that of the NYSE ($8.9 trillion). However, Nasdaz's year-end market capitalization was $5.2 trillion, well below the $12.3 trillion that the NYSE registered.

There are about 200 stock markets in over 60 nations in the world including 15 in North America. The New York, Nasdaq, Tokyo, and London stock markets are the largest, while the TSE is usually among one of the top ten in terms of market capitalization (it ranked seventh in 1999 and tenth in 1998). As noted, investors have become

---

[15] NYSE website at http://www.nyse.com.

increasingly interested in equity markets around the world, and important global equity markets exist in developed countries including the United Kingdom, France, Germany, Italy, Switzerland, Japan, Hong Kong, and Australia. Investors are also interested in emerging markets such as Mexico, Brazil, and Indonesia. Because of the large number and variety of foreign markets, we will consider only a few highlights here.

Western Europe has several mature markets including (in addition to those mentioned above) Belgium, Finland, Spain, and Sweden. The London Stock Exchange (LSE) is an important equity market that handles listed equities and bonds as well as unlisted securities. Germany has continental Europe's largest stock market, while Switzerland is home to some of the largest global companies in the world including Nestlé (food and beverage) and Hoffman La Roche (drug manufacturer).

Interestingly, analysts now refer to Europe's emerging markets including the Czech Republic, Hungary, and Poland where potential profits are great but risks are also significant. Illiquidity is a common problem, corporate information is difficult to obtain, and political risk can be an important factor. Turkey is another example of an emerging market.

The Far East is the fastest-growing region in the world with growth rates twice that of Canada and the United States. As a result, North American investors have been particularly active in the Far Eastern markets in recent years. These markets also have been very volatile, with large gains and losses because of illiquidity (a scarcity of buyers at times) as well as currency risks and political risks.

Japan, the dominant Asian economic power, has the third-largest stock market in the world, and although it has eight stock exchanges, the Tokyo Stock Exchange dominates that country's equity markets. Both domestic and foreign stocks are listed on the Tokyo Exchange, and among domestic issues, relatively few are traded on the floor of the exchange; most (as well as foreign stocks) are handled by computer.

Hong Kong is the second-largest Asian market in terms of market capitalization. Other Asian markets include India, Indonesia, Japan, South Korea, Malaysia, Pakistan, the Philippines, Singapore, Sri Lanka, Taiwan, and Thailand. Of course, some of these markets are quite small. The Four Dragons—Hong Kong, Singapore, South Korea, and Taiwan—dominate these markets when Japan is excluded.

The big unknown in Asian markets is China, an emerging economy of potentially great importance. The country is booming but with great risks, because politics strongly affects investments here. Its financial markets are still tiny by other countries' standards. Chinese companies do trade on the Hong Kong exchange as well as on exchanges in mainland China such as Shanghai and Shenzhen.

Latin America is the remaining emerging marketplace that has been of great interest to investors recently. The markets in Latin America include Argentina, Brazil, Chile, Colombia, Mexico, Peru, and Venezuela. Mexico's market is the largest, followed by Brazil, with the others small by comparison in terms of market capitalization. As we would expect in emerging markets, profit potentials are large, but so are risks—volatile prices, liquidity problems, and political risks.

Mexico's Bolsa has enjoyed popularity as a result of the North American Free Trade Agreement (NAFTA) and a general strengthening of the Mexican economy. Although

Mexico is the largest Latin American stock market, one well-known stock, Telefonos de Mexico, accounts for about 20 percent of the entire market's capitalization.

Figure 2.3 shows the market capitalization for the top 10 major world stock markets for 1998 and 1999. As we can see and as discussed earlier, New York was by far the largest market in 1999, followed by Nasdaq, Tokyo, London, and so on. The Toronto Stock Exchange ranked seventh in 1999 and tenth in 1998. Based on market capitalization (and on trading volumes), the TSE is the dominant Canadian stock market, while the NYSE remains the dominant market in the United States followed by Nasdaq. ⬆

FIGURE 2.3

The 10 Largest Stock Markets in the World by Market Capitalization (in Billions of U.S. Dollars) 1998–99

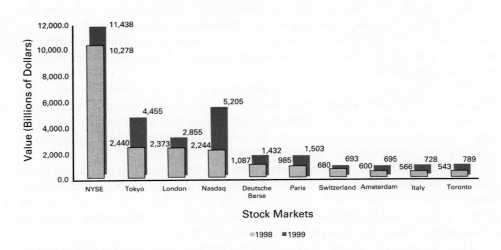

The 10 Largest Stock Markets in the World by Market Capitalization (in Billions of U.S. Dollars) 1998—99

Source: International Federation of Stock Exchanges website at www.fibv.com

The Third and Fourth Markets

The **third market** is an OTC market for the trading of securities that are listed on organized exchanges. This market has traditionally been important in the United States for block trades, which are extremely large transactions involving at least 10,000 shares or $100,000 in value. This is done in order to avoid minimum exchange-regulated commission fees. The use of third markets for block trading has not been essential in Canada because commission fees on large block trades are negotiable.

The **fourth market** refers to transactions made directly between large institutions (and wealthy individuals) bypassing brokers and dealers. Essentially, it is a communication network among investors interested in trading large blocks of stock. Several different privately owned automated systems exist to provide current information on specific securities that the participants are willing to buy or sell. **Instinet (Institutional Network)**, owned by Reuters, is an electronic trading network that has become the world's largest computerized brokerage. It is a system designed only for brokers and institutions, which pay commissions of about one cent per share and receive free proprietary terminals. Instinet Corporation is a New York-based registered broker that is a member of 20 exchanges around the world including the Toronto Stock Exchange. Instinet is always open for trading stocks on the exchanges to which it belongs.

Instinet offers anonymous trading, allowing large traders to bypass brokers and avoid information leaks regarding who is transacting. Trades are often less than 10,000 shares each, and an institution can do multiple trades to get into or out of a position in a stock without others knowing. Much of Instinet's volume is coming at the expense of Nasdaq. Some estimates are that Instinet's trades account for 20 percent of Nasdaq's volume on some days. Instinet volume amounted to roughly 100 million shares daily by mid-1996, and by 1998, over 90 percent of the U.S. institutional funds under management were Instinet clients.

Derivatives Markets

Derivative securities are so called because they derive their value from some underlying asset such as common shares or bonds. We discuss the details of derivatives markets in their respective chapters, but in this section, we provide a brief overview of their trading.

An **option** is a contract that grants the holder the right to purchase or sell a particular asset (typically a security) at a given price on or before a specified date. Options can be bought or sold through an exchange facility or privately arranged (OTC options). All exchange-traded options in Canada are presently traded on the ME as a result of the restructuring of Canadian exchanges discussed above.

The Chicago Board Options Exchange (CBOE) was formed in 1973 to begin trading in options, and it remains the best-known options market in the world. It operates using a system of market makers. Bid and ask prices are quoted by the market maker, and floor brokers can trade with the market maker or with other floor brokers. Liquidity problems, which had plagued the OTC options markets, were overcome by: (1) standardizing option contracts and (2) introducing a clearing corporation that would guarantee the performance of the seller of an options contract (i.e., effectively, it becomes the buyer and seller for each option contract).

In Canada, all equity, bond, and stock index positions are issued and guaranteed by a single clearing corporation, the Canadian Derivatives Clearing Corporation (CDCC), formerly Trans-Canada Options Inc. (TCO). The CDCC is wholly owned by the ME as of March 2000. In the United States, all listed options are cleared through the Options Clearing Corporation (OCC). Exercise of options is accomplished by submitting an exercise notice to the clearing corporation, which assigns the exercise notice to a member firm, which then assigns it to one of its accounts.

Futures contracts are agreements to trade a given asset at a specified price and time in the future. When the underlying asset is a real commodity, the term **commodity futures contract** is used, and when it is a financial obligation such as a currency, bond, or stock portfolio, the term **financial futures contract** is used. In contrast to options, futures contracts are traded on exchanges in designated pits using an open-outcry process as a trading mechanism. Under this system, the pit trader offers to buy or sell contracts at an offered price, and other pit traders are free to transact if they wish. This open-outcry system is unique in securities trading. There are few sights in the financial system that can rival the frenzied trading activity in a futures market pit. Another unique feature of these markets is that the delivery time period can vary from four to six weeks for commodities such as corn or wheat to one day for an index contract.

In Canada, the only commodity futures exchange is the Winnipeg Commodity Exchange (WCE) where canola futures are by far the most active commodity futures traded. For example, canola futures accounted for approximately 80 percent (1.42 million) of the total number of futures contracts (1.78 million) traded on the WCE from May 1999 to April 2000. The ME trades contracts on three-month Bankers Acceptances (which call for cash delivery) as well as on Government of Canada bonds. The 1999 volume for Canadian Bankers Acceptances was 6.055 million contracts (73 percent of all futures contracts cleared through the CDCC that year), while the volume for Government of Canada bonds was 1.607 million contracts. The Toronto Futures Exchange (TFE) ceased operations in December 1999, and the futures contracts that used to trade there now trade on the ME. These include futures contracts on the S&P/TSE 60 Index, which replaced index contracts that used to trade on the TSE 35 Index and the TSE 100 Index. Trading volume for the S&P/TSE 60 Index futures was approximately 262,000 contracts from September 7, 1999 (when trading began) to December 31, 1999 and approximately 743,000 for January 1, 2000 to August 31, 2000.

The centre of commodity futures trading in North America is the Chicago Board of Trade (CBOT) and the Chicago Mercantile Exchange (CME). However, there are several other important exchanges in New York including: the Commodity Exchange; the New York Mercantile Exchange; the New York Coffee, Sugar, and Cocoa Exchange; the New York Cotton Exchange; and the New York Futures Exchange.

The Changing Securities Markets

For the past 15 to 20 years the securities markets have been changing rapidly with many more alterations and transformations expected over the coming years. At least two factors explain why markets have undergone such rapid changes. First, institutional investors have different requirements and often different views from individual investors, and their emergence as the dominant force in the market has necessitated significant transformations in market structure and operation.

Institutional investors often trade in large **blocks** involving at least 10,000 shares or $100,000 in value. Large-block activity is an indicator of institutional participation, and the average size of trades on the TSE and NYSE has grown sharply over the years. In fact, block trading now accounts for more than 50 percent of all TSE and NYSE trading volume.

Another factor stimulating changes in our markets is the growth of computerized trading of securities, which has made possible the inter-market trading of securities. Inter-market trading permits brokerage houses to route orders electronically to whatever market is offering the best price to a buyer or seller. This system should enhance market efficiency by promoting competition and lowering bid-ask spreads because the dealers with the most attractive prices would automatically receive the orders.

Most of the world's major stock exchanges (including the TSE) have moved to computerized trading, the most notable exception being the NYSE. The NYSE continues to defend and justify its nearly 200-year-old specialist system despite criticisms that it is not attuned to the needs of the modern market. The NYSE vigorously defends its system citing such evidence as the 1987 market crash; the specialists stayed at their posts to handle orders while many over-the-counter dealers refused to answer the phone.

While after-hours trading is not presently permitted for Canadian securities, the move toward round-the-clock trading—which many expected to be the wave of the future—began in the early 1990s. The Nasdaq International Market started in 1991, trading OTC stocks early in the morning during regular trading hours in London. Evening sessions for futures trading were started on the Chicago Board of Trade. In mid-1991, the NYSE began two after-hour crossing sessions, which last from 4:15 p.m. to 5:30 p.m. One session is for individual stocks, and the other is for baskets of stocks. The Pacific Stock Exchange now has an expanded-hours session that lasts until 4:50 p.m. EST.

The following report describes a new development on the global stock exchange scene that should contribute to 24-hour trading of stocks. It refers to the TSE's announcement that it will join the NYSE and six other major equity markets throughout the world "to discuss the creation of a round-the-clock Global Equity Market or 'GEM'." The basic purpose of the GEM will be to "provide an orderly, continuous, low volatility and liquid trading environment for top-tier, high-market capitalization stocks."

■ *Finance in the News*

TSE to Join Global Equity Market Alliance

On June 7, 2000, the Toronto Stock Exchange (TSE) announced that it would join the New York Stock Exchange (NYSE) and half a dozen other exchanges around the world to "discuss the creation of a round-the-clock Global Equity Market" (GEM). The main purpose of the GEM will be to "provide an orderly, continuous, low volatility and liquid trading environment for top tier high-market capitalization stocks." Barbara Stymiest, president and CEO of the TSE, was upbeat about the possible benefits of GEM. She sees GEM as being "a global solution that is compatible with our market structure, technology, clearing and settlement protocol, and regulatory environment." The eight international exchanges will be linked electronically across time zones to allow around-the-clock trading.

Richard Grasso, chairman and CEO of the NYSE, predicted that the agreement will "strengthen and globalize our markets" and will "allow the GEM Exchanges to define the business and operating template." The alliance partners are pledged to work out the terms of the agreement with regulators and other interested parties over the coming months. ▲

Source: "TSE to Join Global Equity Market Alliance," *TSE News Release*, June 7, 2000, TSE website at: http://www.tse.com

None of the above marketplaces offering extended-hour trading has matched the success of Instinet. This electronic trading mechanism discussed previously allows large investors (primarily institutions) to trade with each other electronically at any hour. While Instinet trading of Canadian stocks outside of trading hours is not presently permitted, Canadian investors may trade foreign securities through Instinet. The Instinet system offers investors privacy and low trading costs because regular brokerage fees do not have to be paid. In addition, institutions are able to negotiate prices electronically with each other.

Through such sources as Instinet, stock prices can change quickly, although the exchanges themselves are closed. The after-hours trading is particularly important when significant news events occur or when an institutional investor is simply anxious to trade a position. Such activity could, in a few years (or months), lead to the 24-hour trading of stocks, such as what already exists for currencies.

What about bonds? In today's world, bonds are increasingly being traded at all hours around the globe, more so than stocks. The emergence of global offerings means that bonds are traded around the clock and around the world. The result of this global trading in bonds is that bond dealers and investors are having to adapt to the new demands of the marketplace. They need to be available to react and trade at all hours of the day and night, resulting in new employees in various locales, expanded hours, and computer terminals in the home.

PERSPECTIVES

Corporate Manager

The movement toward increased round-the-clock trading of securities implies that the timing of significant corporate announcements is not as important as it used to be. For example, many companies used to make major announcements after the markets closed for the day in order to allow time for investors to digest the news adequately before trading on such information.

Investor

This movement implies that investors must remain abreast of trading activity on all markets at all times. This accentuates the importance of having access to such information on a timely and continuous basis.

STOCK MARKET INDICATORS   2.6

Canadian Indexes

In order to assess the performance of stock markets, we need a composite report on market performance, which is what stock market averages and indices are designed to provide. Because of the large number of equity markets, both domestic and foreign, there are numerous stock market indicators.

An index is a time series of numbers that measures stock prices so that percentage changes in this series over time may be calculated. They are used primarily for performance comparisons and to gauge the overall directional move in the stock market. An average is used in the same manner as an index but differs from it because it is composed of equally weighted items.

The present TSE 300 Composite Index System was introduced in 1977 with historical series dating back to 1956. The **Toronto Stock Exchange (TSE) 300 Composite Index** measures changes in market values of a portfolio of 300 Canadian stocks due to changes in the total market capitalization (the number of common shares outstanding times the market price per share) of these stocks. Thus, a stock's weight changes in response to changes in share price and/or the number of shares outstanding. The actual stocks composing the TSE 300 are reviewed annually, and stocks that no longer satisfy the criteria are replaced by others that do. The 300 stocks included in the TSE300 are classified by industry to form 14 major group indices; 40 subgroups are also tracked.

The base value of 1,000 was set for the TSE 300 and related indices for the base year of 1975. The TSE has several other indices that determine values in the same manner as the TSE 300. Until recently, one of the most important of these was the TSE 35 Index. Introduced in 1987, it was used for stock index futures and options products. The TSE 100 and TSE 200 were introduced in 1993 and were designed primarily for institutional investors as an instrument for index or passive management. The TSE 100 includes the 100 largest and most liquid TSE stocks. The TSE 200 includes the remaining 200 stocks in the TSE 300 and is often used as a proxy for returns on small-cap stocks. Total Return Indices were introduced in 1980 and measure the return on the indices if all dividends had been reinvested. As such, they demonstrate the compound return available from investing in stocks on a continuing basis.

On December 31, 1998, the TSE introduced a new index, the **S&P/TSE 60 Index**, which has now officially replaced the TSE 35 Index and the TSE 100 Index as the basis for derivative products including index funds and index-linked GICs. The S&P/TSE 60 was developed in conjunction with Standard & Poor's (S&P) Corporation, which maintains several major market indices including the S&P 500 Composite Index (discussed below).

The S&P/TSE 60 Index is designed to mimic the performance of the TSE 300, which remains the broad stock market benchmark for Canada. In addition to designing the new index, S&P has assumed management responsibilities for all TSE indices and the marketing and management of related derivative products. The index base value was set equal to 100 as of January 29, 1982 (which differs from the base year of 1975 for the

TSE 300 Index). This base period was chosen due to concerns regarding data reliability prior to this date. The index closing value was reported as 375.98 on December 31, 1998—its inception date.

The CDNX maintains four indices: a main index (**CDNX**) and three sector indices (mining, oil and gas, and technology). The indices are equally weighted, and each is composed of the top 80 percent of index-eligible securities by market capitalization. Component securities are reviewed for continued eligibility at the end of each calendar quarter, at which time the component securities included in each index are reset. The indices were set to a value of 2000 at the start of CDNX trading on November 29, 1999.

International Indexes

The **Dow Jones Industrial Average (DJIA)** is the most widely quoted measure of NYSE stock performance despite the fact that it includes only 30 of the 3,000-plus stocks that trade on the NYSE. The DJIA is computed from 30 leading industrial stocks, which change slowly over time to reflect shifts in the economy. This average is said to be composed of blue chip stocks—large, well-established, and well-known companies.

The DJIA is price weighted and is therefore affected more by changes in higher price stocks. It is calculated by adding the prices of the 30 stocks together and dividing by a divisor, which has been revised downward through the years to reflect the impact of stock splits. The DJIA includes only blue chip stocks that have a low-risk profile, and it tends to underperform broader-based indices in the long term as a result of this lower risk. Other Dow Jones indices include the transportation average (20 companies), a utility average (15 companies), and a composite average (65 companies), all of which are price weighted.

There are several other U.S. indices, of which the **S&P 500 Index** is the most important. That index is a broader-based market-weighted index, which measures U.S. stock performance. The S&P 500 is obviously a much broader measure than the Dow, and it should be more representative of the general market. However, it consists primarily of NYSE stocks, and it is clearly dominated by the largest corporations. Nevertheless, the S&P 500 Index is typically the measure of the market preferred by institutional investors who most often compare their performance to this market index.

Other U.S. indices include NYSE-maintained market-valued indices that encompass all listed equities for a given group: composite, industrials, transportation, finance and real estate, and utilities. The Amex index includes all stocks (about 800) that trade on the American Stock Exchange, and it is value weighted. The Nasdaq Composite Index includes over 3,700 OTC stocks, and it is market valued. The Value Line Composite Index is an average percentage change in about 1,700 stocks that are mainly second-tier issues. Finally, the Wilshire 5000 Total Market Index is a market-valued index that attempts to measure all stocks for which quotations are available, and it is the broadest-based U.S. index.

Stock market indices are available for most foreign markets, but the composition, weighting, and computational procedures vary widely from index to index making comparisons difficult. To deal with these problems, some organizations have constructed their own set of indices to facilitate consistency in international market performance comparisons. The largest provider of international indices is Morgan Stanley Capital International (MSCI). It maintains several global indices including the MSCI World Index, which is a market-valued index that includes more than 2,200 stocks from 22 developed countries. MSCI also maintains 45 country and 18 regional indices including the **EAFE Index** (the Europe, Australia, and Far East Indices), the Emerging Markets Index, and several others.

Similar to the MSCI World Index, the Dow Jones World Stock Index covers the Pacific Region, Europe, Canada, Mexico, and the United States. It is designed to be a comprehensive measure and represents approximately 80 percent of the world's stock markets. Unlike the DJIA, the World Stock Index is a value-weighted index.

The best-known measure of the Japanese stock market is the Nikkei 225 Average, an arithmetic average of prices for 225 actively traded stocks on the Tokyo Stock Exchange. Similar to the Dow Jones Average, it traditionally has been a price-weighted series. In contrast, the Financial Times Actuaries Share Indexes are market-value indices covering stocks on the London Stock Exchange, the most widely followed being the FT London FT-SE 100 Index. These indices as well as those for other foreign markets can be found daily in Canadian financial newspapers. ▲

SUMMARY 2.7

1. Efficient financial markets are required to channel funds from surplus-spending units (savers) to deficit-spending units. Typically, such securities entitle the holder to a stream of periodic future cash payments.

2. Financial intermediaries allow economies of scale to be realized when matching surplus-spending units with deficit-spending units. Greater opportunities for portfolio diversification and money management can be gained.

3. Financial markets encompass the institutions and procedures involved in the trading of financial assets. They include the money market (trading of short-term debt instruments) and the capital market (trading of long-term securities). The capital market can be subdivided further into equity markets and bond markets.

4. Equities are traded either on organized security exchanges, or on the over-the-counter market.

5. The Toronto Stock Exchange (TSE) is the largest secondary market in Canada. The New York Stock Exchange (NYSE) is the world's premier secondary market.

6. Canadian OTC trading takes place through the Canadian Venture Exchange (CDNX). Most OTC trading in the United States takes place on the Nasdaq Stock Market.

7. The best-known market indicator in Canada is the TSE 300 Composite Index. The best-known stock market indicator in the United States is the Dow Jones Industrial Average (DJIA).

QUESTIONS AND PROBLEMS

Questions for Discussion

1. Briefly explain the term "financial assets" giving several examples. Why do savers purchase financial assets, and why are they issued? Could a modern industrialized economy function without financial assets?

2. What are some of the useful functions performed by financial intermediaries?

3. Why is it important to have financial markets that provide for efficient secondary trading of securities?

4. Why have so many Canadian companies turned to international debt and equity markets to raise new financing?

5. Distinguish between the third market and the fourth market.

6. What are two primary factors accounting for the rapid changes in securities markets?

7. What is the TSE 300 Composite Index?

8. What is the Dow Jones Industrial Average? How does it differ from the S&P 500 Composite Index?

9. What is meant by the statement, "The bond market is primarily an OTC market?"

10. Why do some large Canadian firms want to be interlisted on U.S. stock exchanges?

11. Discuss the importance of financial markets to the Canadian economy. Can primary markets exist without secondary markets?

12. List the major distinctions between debt and equity financing.

13. Why do you think that Schedule I banks have been subject to the "10/25 Rule" (no more than 10 percent held by any one investor and no more than 25 percent total foreign ownership)?

14. What are the main benefits to investors of investment funds?

15. Compare and contrast the role of banks and investment dealers in raising funds for companies.

The 1999 annual report for BCE Inc. is provided in Appendix II at the end of this text. Note that only an abridged version of the annual report is provided. A full version can be obtained from the website www.sedar.com or www.bce.ca.

The following questions should be answered by referring to the annual report.

1) Read the Report to Shareholders and the Chairman's Message at the beginning of BCE Inc.'s 1999 annual report. How important is growth of the firm in the current strategy of BCE? Give several examples of the company's growth strategy (both international and domestic). How could this growth strategy help BCE fulfill its goal of creating "long-term value for our shareholders"?

2) The Report to Shareholders discusses BCE's divestiture of Nortel Networks. For more details, see also the *Finance in the News* Box in Chapter 1 of this text, as well as the Management's Discussion and Analysis section of the annual report. Given that divesting Nortel Networks will shrink the size of BCE overall, how can you reconcile this decision with BCE's growth strategy and with the goal of shareholder wealth maximization?

3) The Report to Shareholders notes that divesting Nortel Networks will "enable markets to more accurately assess…the true value" of BCE. As well, the article in the *Finance in the News* Box of Chapter 1 states that the Nortel unit was "masking the value of the rest of BCE's holdings." Discuss these statements in terms of market prices acting as processors of information and the difficulties of using maximizing share price as a goal for a firm.

4) On what stock exchanges does BCE Inc. list its shares? Discuss why it might choose to list on multiple stock exchanges. How might this help fulfill the goal of shareholder wealth maximization?

5) Under "Forward Looking Statements" in the Management's Discussion and Analysis, general risk factors affecting BCE are discussed.

   a) Describe what is meant by "risk" in this context.

   b) BCE Inc. is engaged principally in the telecommunication industry. Would you think that this industry today is more or less risky than a more "traditional" industry such as consumer products? Why?

   c) Consider a small start-up company involved in e-commerce on the Internet. Would you consider BCE Inc. to be more or less risky than this type of firm? Explain fully why or why not.

2

Financial Analysis and Planning

In Part 2, we deal with financial analysis, planning, and control. Although some of this material may be familiar from accounting courses, it is reviewed here because an understanding of these topics is essential to financial management. In Chapter 3, we provide basic coverage of financial statement analysis including ratios and common-size analysis. In the two concluding sections of this chapter, we discuss the impact of inflation and operations that account in different currencies on financial statement analysis. In Chapter 4, we analyse the basic flow of funds through a business and review statements of sources and uses of funds. We also introduce financial planning through the preparation of *pro forma* financial statements.

Ratio Analysis in Annual Report Tells It Like It Is

Four years in a row, Calgary-based specialty menswear retailer Mark's Work Wearhouse has taken home the gold medal in its category from the Canadian Institute of Chartered Accountants' Awards of Excellence for annual reports. Exceptional clarity and readability are what make a Mark's annual report stand out. Eschewing euphemisms and jargon, it tells investors exactly where the company stands.

One feature that makes a Mark's annual report so readable is its inclusion of numerous ratios that help readers interpret the financial statements. Mark's also uses ratios extensively to set concrete corporate goals, which are reproduced—with their results—in the report.

One of four identified financial goals in Mark's 2000 Annual Report was "to maintain a current ratio of not less than 1.50 to 1 at the Company's fiscal year end." Presented with this goal is the information on current assets, current liabilities, and working capital needed to calculate this ratio, as well as the ratio itself, not just for fiscal 2000 but for two previous years, as well as both conservative and optimistic forecasts for 2001. (Mark's met this goal handily, achieving a current ratio of 1.77 to 1.)

Two of the other financial goals were also expressed as ratios and presented with the related information: to obtain a liabilities-to-equity ratio of no greater than 1.75 to 1 and a return on average equity (ROE) in excess of 15 percent. Mark's exceeded the first of these at 1.40 to 1, but missed the second; its ROE was just 11.3 percent. (The fourth goal was a simple profit target.)

The Mark's Work Wearhouse annual report also publishes the concrete business objectives of its senior managers. In the 2000 report, we learn that Rick Harrison, Senior Vice President, Merchandising, Mark's Division, came just shy of meeting his objective of an inventory turnover rate of 2.1 in the corporate store operation, while John Murphy, Senior Vice President, Treasurer and Secretary exceeded his objective of holding the 12-month rolling funded debt-to-equity ratio to no more than 1.13 to 1—it came in at .94 to 1.

The final years of the millennium have been challenging ones for Mark's Work Wearhouse. Its share price has suffered from slow growth in the specialty retailer sector generally and some warmer-than-usual winters that affected earnings (cold-weather gear accounts for a substantial portion of Mark's sales). But if its management is as focused and successful as its reporting, there are clearly brighter days ahead.

Financial Statement Analysis

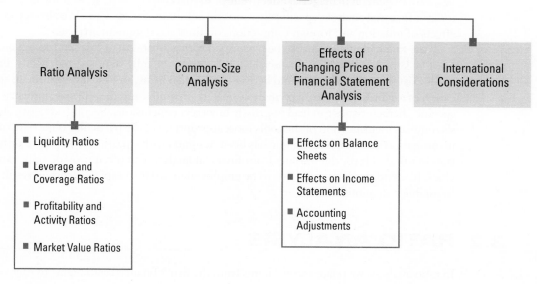

Learning Objectives

After studying this chapter, you should be able to:

1. *Compare and contrast the four categories of ratios used in financial analysis.*
2. *Discuss the three ratios used in the DuPont system of financial analysis of return on equity.*
3. *Understand what common-size analysis is, what it measures, and why it is used.*
4. *Name the four types of distortions in financial statements caused by changing prices and the impact they can have on income statements.*
5. *Discuss some of the implications of foreign exchange rates for Canadian companies with global operations.*

3.1 INTRODUCTION

At any given time, a variety of interest groups may wish to analyse the financial conditions of a firm. Trade creditors are interested in establishing a company's ability to meet its short-term obligations; bondholders will want to determine a business's cash-generating capacity over the long run; financial analysts and shareholders may focus on a company's present and expected cash flows, earnings, and dividends; and corporate executives must be aware of general managerial effectiveness. In this chapter, we discuss some of the basic tools of financial analysis, specifically ratio and common-size analysis. We also review the effects of inflation and foreign transactions on financial statement analysis.

Any financial analysis has to be performed with a great deal of care, and several points must be kept in mind. First, financial analysis cannot be fully standardized. Many differences exist between industries and between individual firms, and the indiscriminate application of a standardized form of analysis to all companies regardless of size, industry, and specific characteristics can lead to grossly incorrect conclusions. Second, effective analysis requires identification of the tools most appropriate to the particular objectives of the investigation since each technique has been designed with a particular objective or function in mind. Third, the outputs from financial analysis can often provide only general clues. In-depth analysis may have to be employed in order to explain a certain result and to establish its significance.

3.2 RATIO ANALYSIS

In ratio analysis, we relate various items from the firm's financial statements to each other with the aim of assessing and analysing the organization's financial position. Ratios are probably the most widely used technique of financial statement analysis. The following report contains excerpts from *Hardware Merchandising* magazine that highlight the benefits of using financial ratios to track business performance. The points made in the article apply to most businesses although the key ratios that the firm should focus on will vary from one business or industry to the next.

■ *Finance in the News*

Financial Ratios: How to Use Them to Track Your Business Performance

Financial ratios are accounting tools that can help you answer questions about your levels of debt, receivables, inventory, and operating expenses, and whether you are getting adequate return on your investment. Ratios simply divide one number by another to see how they relate regardless of the size of the numbers. Simple as that seems, ratios can be confusing, given the many types of ratios and how they are described and defined.

Seven of the main financial ratios are as follows:

1. Current Ratio—measures solvency by dividing current assets by liabilities. If your ratio is too high, you may have too much invested in current assets or too little in current debt.

2. Debt-to-Equity Ratio—measures financial risk by dividing all your liabilities by your equity. A high ratio here means you may be overextended, and interest on your debt may be eating into profits. On the other hand, too low a ratio indicates that you may be missing out on opportunities.

3. Inventory Turnover Ratio—measures turnovers (turns) per year, which is arrived at by dividing cost of goods sold by total inventory. Dividing the result by 360 gives you inventory days. High turns mean an inadequate supply of goods for sale, and low turns show too much inventory.

4. Return on Investment (ROI) Ratio—measures where you should be investing and is calculated by dividing net profit by your equity. A low ROI means that your money would do better elsewhere. This ratio can never be too high.

5. Accounts Payable Days Ratio—shows how quickly you are paying your creditors. If this ratio is high, you are probably paying penalties and interest, whereas if it is short, you may be able to use that money elsewhere.

6. Accounts Receivable Days Ratio—tells you how fast you are collecting your receivables. The longer this period is, the more you are financing your customers, which is not desirable.

7. Gross Margin Ratio—reveals good or bad buying practices. A low ratio implies bad buying and its associated problems of poor pricing, shrinkage, and lack of discounts.

Source: Hardware-Merchandising, 110 (May, 1998), pp. 30, 32. Reprinted with permission.

Ratios are particularly helpful for comparisons. Specifically, by comparing financial statements of the same company over time, we may discern important trends occurring for that firm. We can also compare a company's performance relative to similar firms at a given point in time or through time by comparing it to so-called industry standards. These are generally measured by average values of ratios broken down by industry classification. These averages are provided by organizations such as Dun & Bradstreet, the *Financial Post*, the chartered banks, various trade associations, and Robert Morris Associates (RMA). Statistics Canada also publishes detailed corporate financial statistics on balance sheet and income statement data that are broken down by industry classification and business size.

Table 3.1 provides a sample of key ratios for several Canadian industries in 1998 as provided by the *Financial Post*. The wide variation between ratio averages across industries emphasizes the importance of selecting the proper industry grouping when comparisons are made. However, even proper industry comparisons are not without their problems. For example, the increasing diversification (both across industries and geographical borders) of many firms may make it difficult to establish a proper industry classification. Also, wide differences may exist in accounting methods, size, age, and growth rates between companies in the same industry. In addition, within a given industry, some firms may have different fiscal year ends, which has the potential to affect the validity of comparisons for some ratios. All of these factors affect financial statements, making comparisons difficult.

Table 3.1

1998 Industry Ratios for TSE 300 Companies

Industry	Avg. price/ earning	Current ratio	Acid test	Total debt/ equity	Interest coverage	Net profit margin	Return on equity	Sales/ receivables	Sales/ inventory
Auto parts & transportation	15.70	2.09	1.11	0.66	121.24	4.42	13.57	8.12	8.54
Banks & trust	13.90	na	na	0.50	na	17.13	14.19	na	na
Biotech & pharmaceuticals	25.90	5.91	5.41	0.40	(52.93)	13.24	(4.13)	5.62	6.39
Building material	16.40	1.80	0.91	0.51	9.14	8.01	14.98	6.01	6.72
Chemical & fertilizer	13.50	3.44	2.66	0.65	4.11	4.62	7.69	7.10	7.67
Communication & media	21.10	1.51	1.06	0.87	14.40	6.63	(3.74)	7.51	29.71
Consumer products	15.30	2.05	1.36	0.84	5.36	5.86	14.92	8.57	10.89
Fabricating & engineering	17.70	2.66	1.74	0.66	16.50	3.05	13.35	5.48	7.37
Financial management	21.00	na	na	0.44	5.08	82.85	5.56	5.07	na
Food & beverage	20.00	1.92	0.72	1.30	27.13	1.27	4.20	9.67	8.12
Gold & precious minerals	25.30	6.45	5.93	0.38	(41.85)	(59.41)	(20.24)	14.99	24.54
Hospitality	21.30	1.39	1.10	1.11	3.88	1.12	0.20	6.61	54.23
Insurance	17.50	na	na	0.29	8.69	4.45	7.53	12.34	na
Metals & minerals	44.70	2.12	1.00	0.51	(1.42)	(5.35)	(3.78)	5.92	3.94
Oil & gas	36.40	1.52	1.18	0.54	0.92	(32.46)	(4.32)	4.66	25.59
Paper & forest products	22.90	2.11	1.16	0.66	3.15	(0.79)	(1.10)	8.60	6.45
Pipelines	25.50	0.81	0.60	2.48	1.58	5.14	9.19	7.18	23.30
Real estate	18.90	na	na	1.86	2.80	16.55	14.47	11.64	na
Steel	14.50	2.21	0.90	1.06	2.65	2.20	1.33	7.59	4.53
Technology	33.20	3.72	2.96	0.27	(22.44)	(16.49)	(5.37)	4.58	29.02
Telephone & utilities	15.90	0.78	0.60	0.12	2.24	(28.82)	3.41	8.44	66.46
Transport. & envir. services	22.10	1.13	0.87	1.39	15.96	4.99	10.72	9.69	70.72
Wholesale & retail	15.30	1.65	0.52	0.77	10.34	0.62	2.39	58.76	9.24

Source: Financial Post DataGroup, June 2000.

The availability of computerized data files, which provide extensive collections of corporate financial statements, has prompted statistical testing with the aim of providing a more solid foundation for ratio analysis. Modest success has been achieved particularly in testing the ability of ratios to predict bankruptcy and corporate bond ratings. As this progress has continued, ratio analysis has become more solid and comprehensive.

Ratios can be divided into four basic categories:

1. Liquidity Ratios
2. Leverage and Coverage Ratios
3. Profitability and Activity Ratios
4. Market Value Ratios

Although the relationships that one could compute are virtually without end, we will introduce a limited set of widely used ratios to illustrate each category. The numerical examples that follow are based on the financial statements of a retailing firm, Superior Enterprises, as reproduced in Tables 3.2 and 3.3. For ease of presentation, trailing zeros are omitted throughout the calculations with all figures given in millions of dollars.

TABLE 3.2

Superior Enterprises' Consolidated Balance Sheet (in 000s)

	End of fiscal 1999	End of fiscal 2000
ASSETS		
Current assets		
Cash	$ 2,000	$ 4,000
Marketable securities	1,000	1,000
Accounts receivable	189,000	203,000
Inventories*	120,000	114,000
Prepaid advertising	10,000	11,000
Total current assets	$322,000	$333,000
Investments and other assets		
Investments (at cost)	$ 13,000	$ 9,000
Notes receivable (from ABC Ltd.)	4,000	5,000
Total investments and other assets	$ 17,000	$ 14,000
Fixed assets		
Land	$ 14,000	$ 16,000
Buildings	64,000	99,000
Equipment	45,000	54,000
Total fixed assets	$123,000	$169,000
Less: Accumulated depreciation	(34,000)	(40,000)
Net fixed assets	$ 89,000	$129,000
Unamortized goodwill	$ 2,000	$ 3,000
TOTAL ASSETS	$430,000	$479,000

LIABILITIES
Current liabilities

Short-term notes payable	$ 72,000	$ 63,000
Accounts payable	31,000	40,000
Salaries payable	10,000	11,000
Interest payable	6,000	6,000
Income tax payable	5,000	8,000
Dividends payable	4,000	3,000
Total current liabilities	$128,000	$131,000
Long-term debt	$148,000	$183,000
TOTAL LIABILITIES	$276,000	$314,000

SHAREHOLDERS' EQUITY
Capital stock
  Common shares (no par value)

13,200,000 authorized, issued, and outstanding	$ 55,000	$ 55,000
Preferred shares (no par value)		
3,300,000 authorized 2,500,000 issued and outstanding	20,000	20,000
Total capital stock	$ 75,000	$ 75,000
Retained earnings	$ 79,000	$ 90,000
TOTAL SHAREHOLDERS' EQUITY	$154,000	$165,000
TOTAL LIABILITIES AND SHAREHOLDERS' EQUITY	$430,000	$479,000

*valued at the lower of cost or market

TABLE 3.3

Superior Enterprises' Consolidated Income Statement (in 000s)

	Fiscal 1999	Fiscal 2000
Net sales	$615,000	$647,000
Investment income	1,000	1,000
Gross income	$616,000	$648,000
Less:		
Cost of goods sold	$556,000	$589,000
Depreciation	6,000	6,000
Interest on long-term debt	9,000	12,000
Other interest	5,000	5,000
Other expenses	9,000	9,000
Total expenses	$585,000	$621,000
Earnings before tax	$ 31,000	$ 27,000
Less: Income tax	(12,000)	(11,000)
Net Income	$ 19,000	$ 16,000

Liquidity Ratios

Liquidity ratios reflect a company's short-term ability to pay its debts. Basically, they highlight the relationship between cash and "near-cash" on the one hand and short-term obligations on the other.

Current Ratio: The most widely used liquidity ratio is the **current ratio**, which is defined as:

$$\text{Current ratio} = \frac{\text{current assets}}{\text{current liabilities}}$$

From Table 3.2, the current ratios for Superior Enterprises for 1999 and 2000 are:

1999	2000
$\dfrac{322}{128} = 2.52$	$\dfrac{333}{131} = 2.54$

The major categories of current assets are cash and marketable securities, accounts receivable, and inventories. It is expected that during the normal course of business, accounts receivable and inventories revert to cash (as inventories get sold and accounts receivables are collected). Hence, they provide some indication of the firm's ability to generate cash in the short run. Prepaid expenses (normally a minor category of current assets) are sometimes excluded in calculating the current ratio because they do not revert to cash and cannot be used to cover current liabilities.

A crude rule of thumb cited from time to time suggests two as a suitable value for the current ratio.[1] This standard of two to one relays the expectation that at least one-half of current assets are to be financed by long-term or permanent sources of funds. Consequently, if the enterprise failed to realize full value on the liquidation of current assets (which is very likely in times of distress), current liabilities could still be met with a wide margin of safety. For example, in 2000, Superior Enterprises would only have needed to realize 39 cents (1/2.54) on every dollar of current assets to meet its current obligations. Clearly, however, no universal guideline can be given as to what represents a reasonable value for the current ratio since this depends on a variety of factors including the stability of the firm's cash flows and the liquidity of its current assets. Thus, a current ratio of 1.5 may be more than adequate for a company with large stable levels of cash flows and high quality receivables. For another company, a ratio of 2.5 may be inadequate if it has unstable cash flows and many of its receivables are due from customers of dubious credit quality.

Acid Test or Quick Ratio: In evaluating a business's ability to meet current obligations, inventories often create problems because it is difficult for an outsider to assess their sales potential and also because valuation methods may differ both over time and between firms. They are also usually less liquid than cash and accounts receivable. When

---

[1] See, for example, The Canadian Securities Institute. *The Canadian Securities Course Textbook.* (1998), Chapter 3.

there are concerns regarding the quality of inventories or if one wants to differentiate between inventory and other more liquid current assets, we can compute the **acid test ratio** or **quick ratio**, which is generally expressed as:[2]

$$\text{Acid test or quick ratio} = \frac{\text{current assets} - \text{inventories}}{\text{current liabilities}}$$

From Table 3.2, the values for Superior Enterprises are:

1999	2000
$\dfrac{202}{128} = 1.58$	$\dfrac{219}{131} = 1.67$

Inventory Turnover: The quality of inventories may be reflected in the **inventory turnover ratio**, which can also indicate the organization's efficiency in inventory management. Because inventories are valued at cost, they should in theory be related to the cost of goods sold.[3] We obtain:

$$\text{Inventory turnover ratio} = \frac{\text{cost of goods sold}}{\text{average inventory}}$$

Typically, the denominator is estimated by taking the average of beginning and ending inventories for the period.[4] The reason for using average inventories is that we are relating a balance sheet item that is estimated at one point in time (inventories) to an entry from the income statement covering a given period (cost of goods sold), and we want to make the balance sheet item as representative of the period as we can. This logic can be (and sometimes is) applied to other ratios that entail a combination of balance sheet and income statement entries (such as the receivables turnover ratio discussed below). For Superior Enterprises in 2000, we have:

Cost of goods sold $= \$589$

$$\text{Average inventory} = \frac{114 + 120}{2} = \$117$$

$$\text{Inventory turnover ratio} = \frac{589}{117} = 5.03$$

This annual turnover ratio of 5.03 is equivalent to inventory being replaced once every $365/5.03 = 73$ days, which is generally referred to as the days inventory ratio.

---

[2] Sometimes prepaid expenses will also be subtracted from the numerator of this equation.

[3] In practice, cost of goods sold is often replaced by net sales due to the difficulty in obtaining information for a large number of companies regarding their cost of goods sold. For example, the inventory turnover ratios for the various industries presented in Table 3.1 were determined using sales in the numerator.

[4] Again, for simplification purposes, it is not uncommon to see the ratio calculated using the ending inventory value rather than the average.

A high inventory turnover is often regarded as a signal of efficient management whereas a slipping ratio may flag both overstocking and obsolete inventories. Once again, however, caution is indicated since an unusually high inventory turnover could also be associated with too low a level of inventories and corresponding stockouts. In seasonal businesses, the inventory turnover ratio must be interpreted with particular care because its value can change dramatically depending on the date of the financial statements. For example, a department store with its fiscal year end in January will have a far higher inventory turnover than if its balance sheet had been drawn up in late November when inventory levels are built up in anticipation of the Christmas rush. Fortunately, companies in the same industry often use the same fiscal year-end dates, but this is not always the case. For example, Sears Canada has a December 31 year end, while Hudson's Bay Company uses January 31.

Average Collection Period, Receivables Turnover, and Ageing of Receivables:
We can examine the quality and liquidity of accounts receivable by using the **average collection period**. It is calculated as:

$$\text{Average collection period} = \frac{\text{receivables}}{\text{average daily credit sales}}$$

It indicates the average number of days that credit sales are outstanding and uncollected. When the credit sales figure is unavailable or difficult to ascertain, the total sales figure is often used as an approximation. This is reasonable as long as the majority of sales are on credit. Receivables could be either the average for the year or ending receivables. Ending receivables are more commonly used because they reflect the firm's current situation. Ideally, they should be related to current average daily sales, but this figure may not always be available. From Tables 3.2 and 3.3, the average collection periods for Superior Enterprises in 1999 and 2000 using ending receivables and average daily sales for the year are:

1999	2000
$\dfrac{189}{615/365} = 112 \text{ days}$	$\dfrac{203}{647/365} = 115 \text{ days}$

The **receivables turnover ratio** is defined as:

$$\text{Receivables turnover ratio} = \frac{\text{annual credit sales}}{\text{receivables}}$$

For Superior Enterprises, the receivables turnover ratios are:

1999	2000
$\dfrac{615}{189} = 3.25$	$\dfrac{647}{203} = 3.19$

The average collection period and the receivables turnover ratio indicate the speed of collections, which, in turn, is influenced by the efficiency of the firm's credit and collection policies. Again, too low a figure could stem from excessively restrictive credit policies that jeopardize sales and profitability. As with inventory turnover, seasonal or otherwise uneven sales can also distort the ratios.

A more thorough analysis of the liquidity of receivables is accomplished by an **ageing of accounts**. Although not a ratio technique, this useful auxiliary procedure categorizes receivables according to the length of time that they have been outstanding. An example might be as follows:

Age of accounts since billing (days)	Percentage of total value of receivables outstanding
0-15	40%
16-30	30
31-45	10
46-60	6
61-90	4
over 90	10
	Total: 100%

If credit terms are net 30 (meaning that payments are due in full after 30 days), this ageing schedule shows that 30 percent of the receivables' value is past due and that there may be some real questions about the likelihood of collecting on accounts in the over-90-days category.

In analysing the liquidity of a company, all of the above ratios should be computed since the information they provide is complementary. Whereas the current and quick ratios indicate the safety margin that a firm may have in meeting its current obligations, the inventory and receivables turnover ratios indicate the quality of the establishment's more important current assets. These measures of quality influence the safety margins with which creditors may feel comfortable. For example, the analyst may be more comfortable with a lower current ratio if it is attributable to a high inventory turnover ratio, which results in a lower inventory value and a lower current asset value.

Leverage and Coverage Ratios

There are basically two relevant aspects of debt or financial leverage (as it is often referred to): the relationship of borrowed funds to funds contributed by the owners, and the ability of the firm to service its borrowings. Consequently, we distinguish between leverage and coverage ratios. **Leverage ratios** measure the degree to which a company relies on debt and on other senior securities in its capital structure, whereas **coverage ratios** essentially relate the firm's cash flows to its ongoing financial obligations.

Debt-to-Equity: One of the most frequently used measures of financial leverage is the debt-to-equity ratio, which is commonly defined as:

$$\text{Debt-to-equity ratio} = \frac{\text{long-term debt}}{\text{shareholders' equity}}$$

Creditors may use this ratio as a rough indicator of the safety margin that shareholders are provided in the event of liquidation. Consequently, the treatment of preferred shares in calculating this ratio depends on the analyst's perspective. From the standpoint of common shareholders, one could argue that preferred shares should be included in the numerator under debt since they represent a senior or prior claim. However, when the analysis takes place from the bondholders' point of view, preferred shares are shifted to the denominator and are included under equity (or net worth) because of their subordinate position vis-à-vis creditors. This is the more common way of estimating this ratio. Some analysts may subtract intangible assets such as patents and goodwill from the value of shareholders' equity to obtain the tangible net worth, which is used in the denominator since it is difficult to determine their economic value.

Drawing on Table 3.2 with preferred shares included in shareholders' equity (in the denominator), we obtain the following ratios for the two years under consideration:

1999
$$\frac{148}{154} = 0.96$$

2000
$$\frac{183}{165} = 1.11$$

In other words, during 1999 and 2000, for every dollar contributed by the common and preferred shareholders, $0.96 and $1.11 had been contributed by long-term creditors.

When a company has relatively stable cash flows, the ability to service borrowings is enhanced, and a higher ratio is generally acceptable. For example, utilities often can carry a relatively high proportion of debt because cash flows are fairly stable and, consequently, creditors are less concerned about the size of the cushion provided by the owners.[5] Whether or not the analysis of a firm's financial leverage should recognize short-term debt (i.e., with maturities less than one year) could be problematic. Basically, in situations in which short-term debt is temporary and will be paid off after seasonal inventories and receivables revert to cash, it is reasonable to include only long-term borrowings. However, when businesses continually roll over short-term debt, which then becomes a semi-permanent form of financing, all outstanding debt may have to be considered.

[5] For example, the Canadian Securities Institute suggests that the debt-to-equity ratio should not exceed 0.5 for industrial companies as a general rule of thumb. However, the corresponding rule-of-thumb figure for industrials is much higher at 1.5. Refer to: The Canadian Securities Institute. *The Canadian Securities Course Textbook*. (1998), Chapter 3.

Total Debt-to-Assets: The more encompassing **total debt-to-assets ratio** looks at the proportion of the firm's total assets that is financed through debt and other liabilities and is defined as:[6]

$$\text{Total debt-to-assets ratio} = \frac{\text{total debt}}{\text{total assets}}$$

For Superior Enterprises, we obtain:

1999	2000
$\dfrac{276}{430} = 0.642$	$\dfrac{314}{479} = 0.656$

This indicates that the company finances 65.6 percent of its assets with debt in 2000, slightly above the 64.2 percent in 1999.

Leverage Ratio or Equity Multiplier: Another measure of the amount of assets a firm finances with debt (or equity) is the **leverage ratio** or **equity multiplier**. It is calculated as:

$$\text{Leverage ratio (or equity multiplier)} = \frac{\text{total assets}}{\text{equity}}$$

The higher this ratio is, the lower the proportion of the company's assets is financed through equity, and, therefore, the higher the proportion financed through debt.

For Superior Enterprises, we obtain the following estimates:

1999	2000
$\dfrac{430}{154} = 2.79$	$\dfrac{479}{165} = 2.90$

The increase in this ratio indicates that the proportion of assets financed by debt increased from 1999 to 2000.

Times-Interest-Earned: Although borrowing can enhance financial performance, the firm has to ensure that it is not jeopardized by excessive leverage. A widely used indicator of the safety of periodic interest payments is the **times-interest-earned ratio** or **interest coverage ratio**, given as:

$$\text{Times-interest-earned ratio} = \frac{\text{earnings before interest and taxes}}{\text{interest charges}}$$

---

[6] As with most ratios, there are several alternative formulations for determining this ratio. For example, some analysts use tangible total assets in place of total assets, while others may use long-term debt rather than total debt.

From Table 3.3, we obtain the following times-interest-earned ratios for Superior Enterprises:

1999	2000
$\dfrac{45}{14} = 3.21$	$\dfrac{44}{17} = 2.59$

Earnings are taken before taxes because interest payments, being a tax-deductible expense, are paid before taxes on income. For 2000, **earnings before interest and taxes** (EBIT) covered total interest charges 2.59 times suggesting that there is a substantial, although declining, margin of safety.

Fixed-Charges-Coverage: A serious shortcoming of the narrowly defined times-interest-earned ratio is that it may ignore both lease obligations and sinking fund requirements. Sinking fund requirements force the company to make periodic payments of funds to a trustee who uses the funds to retire the debt. These payments may involve equal instalments although less rigid repayment schedules designed to meet the borrowers' particular circumstances can be negotiated. Clearly, lease payments and sinking fund requirements are also fixed charges and can on occasion become more burdensome than interest payments. The broader **fixed-charges-coverage ratio** addresses this problem and is defined as:

$$\text{Fixed-charges-coverage ratio} = \frac{\text{earnings available to meet fixed charges}}{\text{fixed charges}}$$

It typically takes the form of:

$$\text{First-charges-coverage ratio} = \frac{\text{earnings before interest, lease charges, and taxes}}{\text{interest, lease charges, and before-tax sinking fund payments}}$$

We work from Table 3.3 and note from the annual report (not reproduced here) that sinking fund payments of \$4.2 million were required during 2000. Repayment of debt is not a deductible expense for tax purposes, and a firm has to have sufficient operating revenue to first pay taxes and then meet sinking fund charges. Sinking fund payments are made to retire the principal amount of outstanding debt, which is why the payments are not tax deductible. Therefore, in order to determine the earnings before taxes required to meet such obligations, sinking fund payments must be divided by $(1-T)$, where T is the applicable tax rate. Assuming a tax rate of 40 percent, the company will need earnings before interest and taxes of $4.2/(1-.4)=\$7$ million to cover its sinking fund payments; this is the figure used in the denominator of the ratio. The fixed-charges-coverage ratio for 2000 becomes:

$$\frac{44}{17+7} = \frac{44}{24} = 1.83$$

There are several variations in the fixed-charges-coverage ratio. One common formulation adds the preferred share dividend amount to the denominator because in many respects, it represents a fixed obligation of a set amount that must be paid. In such circumstances, dividend payments must be divided by $(1-T)$ since they are paid out of after-tax earnings. Depreciation may be included in the numerator as a further source of available cash since depreciation is a non cash expense. Although this may be appropriate in dealing with short-run emergencies, over the long term, we should not look to the cash flow counterpart of depreciation to service fixed charges because this would impair a firm's ability to maintain its asset base.

Profitability and Activity Ratios

We use profitability and activity ratios in an attempt to assess the overall managerial efficiency and profitability of an enterprise.

It is useful to relate profits to the volume of sales, to the value of assets employed, and to shareholder equity. Before defining specific ratios, we review briefly the various measures of profit that can be used depending on the particular purpose at hand.

We have:

Sales

Less: $\dfrac{\text{Cost of goods sold}}{\text{Gross operating profit}}$

Less: $\dfrac{\text{Operating expenses (including depreciation)}}{\text{Net operating profit (or earnings before interest and taxes)}}$

Less: $\dfrac{\text{Financing charges (interests on debt and lease charges)}}{\text{Profit before tax}}$

Less: $\dfrac{\text{Income tax expense}}{\text{Net profit}}$

Less: $\dfrac{\text{Dividends on preferred shares}}{\text{Profits available to common shareholders}}$

Gross operating profit measures the firm's performance in the areas of production and purchasing. Net operating profit, also termed earnings before interest and taxes (EBIT), measures the company's overall operating performance. Since it does not include financing charges, it is independent of how the firm elects to finance its operations. Before- and after-tax profits measure the combined effects of operating performance and financing decisions (or capital structure) with the net profit margin reflecting the effect of all costs faced by the company—operating, financing, and taxes.

Gross and Net Operating Margins: A firm's **gross operating margin** or **gross margin** is defined as:

√Gross operating margin $= \dfrac{\text{sales} - \text{cost of goods sold}}{\text{sales}}$

√= know these

For Superior Enterprises, we obtain:

1999	2000
$\dfrac{59}{615} = 9.59\%$	$\dfrac{58}{647} = 8.96\%$

The **net operating margin** is given as:

Net operating margin $= \dfrac{\text{earnings before interest and taxes } (EBIT)}{\text{sales}}$

The figures for Superior Enterprises are:

1999	2000
$\dfrac{45}{615} = 7.32\%$	$\dfrac{44}{647} = 6.80\%$

√**Net Profit Margin:** A company's **net profit margin** is defined as:

Net profit margin $= \dfrac{\text{net profit}}{\text{sales}}$

The figures for Superior Enterprises are:

1999	2000
$\dfrac{19}{615} = 3.09\%$	$\dfrac{16}{647} = 2.47\%$

√**Asset Turnover:** In conjunction with the net operating margin and the net profit margin, it is useful to consider the **asset turnover ratio**, which is defined as:

Asset turnover ratio $= \dfrac{\text{sales}}{\text{total sales}}$

It measures the sales generated by each dollar invested in assets and indicates the efficiency achieved in employing assets to produce a given level of output. For Superior

Enterprises we obtain:

$$\underline{1999} \qquad\qquad \underline{2000}$$

$$\frac{615}{430} = 1.43 \qquad\qquad \frac{647}{479} = 1.35$$

Once again, values computed for this ratio must be interpreted in their particular context. What may be an inadequate asset turnover for a food or department store might be unattainable by an electric utility. For example, the 1998 average asset turnover ratio was 2.45 for retail and wholesale firms versus 0.44 for telephone and utility companies. Furthermore, an older firm may show a better turnover than a newer one because its assets are depreciated and carried on the books at values that are low relative to current replacement costs. Similarly, a company that has expanded rapidly may show heavy investments in new assets and hence a lower turnover than a firm that has remained static. When one company leases a substantial portion of its properties and another owns its assets, comparisons are further complicated because some leased assets may be excluded from the balance sheet.

Return on Assets: The **return on assets (ROA)** measures the dollar return per dollar invested in assets and can be viewed as a broad measure of how well management is employing assets to earn profits. It is usually defined as:

$$\text{Return on assets (ROA)} = \frac{\text{net profit}}{\text{total assets}}$$

For Superior Enterprises, we obtain the following values for this ratio:

$$\underline{1999} \qquad\qquad \underline{2000}$$

$$\frac{19}{430} = 4.42\% \qquad\qquad \frac{16}{479} = 3.34\%$$

Return on Equity: A firm's **return on equity (ROE)** is a measure of how well management serves shareholder interest, which determines the profits generated per dollar of equity invested in the company. It is computed as:[7]

$$\text{Return on equity (ROE)} = \frac{\text{net profit}}{\text{shareholders' equity}}$$

Its value is the result of both the firm's operating performance (as measured by profitability and asset turnover) and the leverage afforded by the use of debt in the capital structure. For Superior Enterprises, we obtain the following values for this ratio:

---

[7] Some analysts prefer to use the return on common equity, which is the earnings available to common shareholders divided by the value of common equity.

$$\underline{1999} \qquad\qquad \underline{2000}$$

$$\frac{19}{154} = 12.34\% \qquad\qquad \frac{16}{165} = 9.70\%$$

The Dupont System: The ROE is the end result of several important variables, which are often broken down by what is referred to as the DuPont system of analysis because it originated at the DuPont Corporation. The idea is to decompose the ROE into its critical components in order to both identify adverse impacts on ROE and help analysts predict future trends in ROE.

Different combinations of financial ratios can be used to decompose ROE. We use three financial ratios multiplied together to produce ROE as shown below:[8]

$$ROE = \frac{net\ profit}{shareholders'\ equity}$$

$$= \frac{net\ profit}{sales} \times \frac{sales}{total\ assets} \times \frac{total\ assets}{shareholders'\ equity}$$

$$= net\ income\ margin \times asset\ turnover\ ratio \times leverage\ ratio\ (or\ equity\ multiplier)$$

The first two terms can be multiplied together to determine the ROA, which we have shown is an important measure of a company's profitability. In other words,

$$ROA = \frac{net\ profit}{total\ assets} = \frac{net\ profit}{sales} \times \frac{sales}{total\ assets} = net\ income\ margin \times asset\ turnover\ ratio$$

Therefore, we could also say that:

ROE = ROA × leverage ratio (or equity multiplier)

This expression shows that we can decompose ROE into three components, which give insight into three different areas of company performance. In particular, we have expressed ROE as a product of: a measure of profit margins (net income margin), a measure of debt (the leverage ratio or equity multiplier), and a measure of the sales generated per dollar invested in assets (asset turnover). This allows the analyst to see what is contributing to strong (or weak) company profitability as measured by ROE. In most cases, we would prefer to see high ROEs driven by strong profitability and/or high asset turnover rather than higher levels of debt. However, sometimes higher debt levels may be warranted as well. For example, two firms could have the same asset turnover ratios and the same net profit margin (and thus the same ROA), but one could display a higher ROE if it used more debt than the other. This could indicate that one firm is using too much debt or that the other is using too little.

---

[8] There are many other ways to decompose the variables, which may involve breaking down ROE into multiplicative components of several ratios. This is one of the most basic and most commonly used formulations.

P E R S P E C T I V E S

Corporate Manager

The DuPont system can assist managers in assessing the influence of some of the main factors (profitability, asset turnover, and leverage) that are causing changes in the firm's ROE. This may provide guidance for taking appropriate future actions such as increasing or reducing the level of debt and the like.

Investor

The DuPont system provides investors with preliminary information about the firm's profitability, asset management, and leverage position and how these factors affect the return on equity invested in the company (from an accounting point of view).

For Superior Enterprises, we observe the following:

1999

$$\text{ROE} = \frac{19}{615} \times \frac{615}{430} \times \frac{430}{154} = 0.0309 \times 1.43 \times 2.79 = 0.1233 \text{ or } 12.33\%$$

and the ROA = $0.0309 \times 1.43 = 0.0442$ or 4.42%

2000

$$\text{ROE} = \frac{16}{647} \times \frac{647}{479} \times \frac{479}{165} = 0.0247 \times 1.35 \times 2.90 = 0.0967 \text{ or } 9.67\%$$

and the ROA = $0.0247 \times 1.35 = 0.0333$ or 3.33%

The slight differences from the calculations above for ROE and ROA are due to rounding.

This process shows that the decline in ROE from 1999 to 2000 is attributable to a decline in profitability as measured by net income margin and a reduction in the asset turnover ratio, both unfavourable trends. It also shows that the ROE would have been even lower if firm leverage had not increased, which is indicated by the increase in the leverage ratio. This may also be an unfavourable trend.

Market Value Ratios

Market value ratios relate data from the company's financial statements to financial market data, thereby providing some insights into investors' perceptions of the firm and its securities.

Price-Earnings Ratio: The **price-earnings (P/E) ratio** (or **earnings multiplier**) is widely used and reflects what investors are prepared to pay for each dollar of reported annual earnings available on a common share. A higher number indicates that investors are willing to pay more for every dollar of the company's earnings. This may be due to expected growth in earnings or lower riskiness associated with the earnings. This ratio will be discussed in detail from the investor's point of view in Chapter 6. It is generally defined as:

$$\text{Price-earnings ratio} = \frac{\text{price per common share}}{\text{earnings per common share}}$$

The P/E ratio is typically reported using the earnings per share (EPS) figure over the past 12 months in the denominator and the current market price in the numerator. This is sometimes referred to as the "trailing" P/E ratio since it relates today's market price to the business's most recent earnings figures. As we shall see in Chapter 6, analysts often use the "forward" P/E ratio to try and establish a reasonable price for common shares. The forward ratio uses expected earnings in the coming period (usually a year) in the denominator. The problems associated with obtaining a consensus forecast of these future earnings figures explains why the trailing ratio is the one normally reported in newspapers and other financial publications.[9]

Given year 2000 dividends on preferred shares of $1 million, earnings available to common shareholders are $16−$1=$15 million. Dividing $15 million by the number of common shares outstanding, we obtain the earnings per common share figure:

$$\text{Earnings per common share} = \frac{\text{earnings available to common shareholders}}{\text{number of common shareholders}}$$

$$= \frac{\$15 \text{ million}}{13.2 \text{ million}} = \$1.14 \text{ per share}$$

If the company's common shares were trading at $10 in 2000, the earnings multiplier or

$$\text{price-earnings ratio} = \frac{\$10}{\$1.14} = 8.77$$

This means that the market was willing to pay $8.77 for each $1 of Superior's earnings based on its present market price per share of $10.

Dividend Payout Ratio and Dividend Yield: Two commonly used measures of a firm's dividend policy are the **dividend payout ratio** (payout) and the **dividend yield**. The dividend payout ratio indicates the percentage of earnings paid to shareholders in the form of dividends. It is generally calculated as follows:

$$\text{Dividend payout} = \frac{\text{common share dividends}}{\text{earnings available to common shareholders}}$$

$$\text{or} \quad = \frac{\text{dividends per common share}}{\text{earnings per common share}}$$

---

[9] In addition, some analysts use the average price for the stock over the past year in the numerator to determine the P/E ratio.

Common share dividends are not provided directly in the information above for Superior Enterprises, but we can easily determine the amount paid in 2000 using information provided. In particular, the net income for 2000 was $16 million, and $1 million of this was paid out in preferred share dividends resulting in earnings available to common shareholders of $15 million. Since the retained earnings item on the balance sheet increased only $11 million during 2000 (from $79 million in 1999 to $90 million in 2000), Superior must have paid out $4 million ($15 million $-$ $11 million) in common share dividends during fiscal 2000.

Using this information, we can estimate Superior's 2000 dividend payout ratio:

$$\text{Dividend payout} = \frac{4}{15} = 0.267$$

Alternatively, we could have arrived at the same result by first estimating the dividend per common share figure to be $4 million/13.2 million shares=$0.30 per share and dividing this by the earnings per common share figure:

$$\text{Dividend payout} = \frac{\$0.30}{\$1.14} = 0.263 \text{ (difference due to rounding)}$$

This ratio indicates that Superior Enterprises paid out approximately 26 cents of every dollar it earned to common shareholders. Alternatively, the company reinvested approximately 74 cents out of every dollar earned.

The dividend yield ratio is calculated as follows:

$$\text{Dividend yield} = \frac{\text{dividends per common share}}{\text{price per common share}}$$

For Superior Enterprises for fiscal 2000, we obtain the following estimate:

$$\text{Dividend yield} = \frac{\$0.30}{\$10} = 0.0300 \text{ or } 3.00\%$$

The dividend yield is a market value ratio commonly used by investors and analysts. It relates the dividend income received by shareholders to the price investors are willing to pay for the shares. This is similar to the P/E ratio in that it measures how much investors are willing to pay for the firm's dividends (instead of earnings). Unlike the P/E ratio, the price is in the denominator of this ratio. Therefore, a lower dividend yield implies investors are willing to pay more for each dollar of a company's dividends, and a higher value indicates they are willing to pay less.

Tobin's q Ratio and the Market-to-Book Ratio: A very useful measure of a firm's overall financial well-being is its q **ratio** defined as:[10]

$$q \text{ ratio} = \frac{\text{market value of both the firm's debt and equity securities}}{\text{replacement cost of the firm's assets}}$$

The numerator includes the market values of preferred shares as well as debt and common stock, while assets in the denominator are taken net of depreciation. Specifically, the denominator would be based on the replacement costs of such assets as plant, equipment, inventories, patents, and goodwill. Depreciation would be a realistic estimate and not just one based on accounting figures. It would reflect the impact of technological advances and current market prices of purchasing replacement assets. Clearly, computation of this ratio can be quite complex and requires more information than is provided here. Because of this, an approximation called the **market-to-book ratio** is more commonly used:

$$\text{Market-to-book ratio} = \frac{\text{market value of the firm's debt and equity securities}}{\text{book value of assets}}$$

Interpretation of the q ratio (or market-to-book ratio) is based on recognition that the numerator reflects the company's stream of revenues being capitalized in competitive security markets. It is generally viewed as a measure of future growth opportunities for the firm. This is because it relates market prices (which are determined based on future expectations) to the value of existing assets today. Higher values for these ratios are associated with higher future growth opportunities and vice versa. A ratio above one indicates that the company is worth more as an ongoing entity than the sum of the replacement value of its existing assets.[11] This may be traced to clever management, expected future gains, or a monopolistic position. It would tend to encourage more investment by the firm.

Conversely, a q ratio below one indicates that the market value of the enterprise is below the replacement cost of its assets. This could be due to perceived poor management, strong competition, a regulated industry, or even a declining industry. In such circumstances, the company may become a target for takeover since it could be broken up into individual pieces that could be resold for values exceeding the purchase price of the firm as a whole. In other words, it may be "worth more dead than alive." The implicit assumption is that on liquidation, assets would realize close to net replacement values. Alternatively, a takeover may be attempted, in the belief that better management could increase the flow of revenues to shareholders.

A summary of all of the ratios discussed above is provided in Table 3.6 at the end of this chapter.

---

[10] This ratio is named Tobin's q because it was made prominent by the work of James Tobin. See "A General Equilibrium Approach to Monetary Theory," *Journal of Money, Credit and Banking*. (1969), p. 15-29.

[11] We shall see in Part 4 of the text that this implies that the firm possesses one or more positive net present value (NPV) projects.

3.3 COMMON-SIZE ANALYSIS

In common-size analysis, we simply convert the dollar amounts given on the financial statements into percentages. Specifically, all balance sheet items are expressed as a proportion of total assets, and entries on the income statement are expressed as a proportion of net sales. Through common-size analysis, it becomes easier to compare financial statements and to pinpoint shifts that are not caused simply by a change in the overall size of the business. It also enables valid comparisons of companies of different sizes with regard to sales levels and/or asset values. Tables 3.4 and 3.5 set out the common-size financial statements of Superior Enterprises for 1999 and 2000. Increases in various cost categories and their impact on net earnings can readily be identified.

TABLE 3.4

Superior Enterprises' Common-Size Consolidated Balance Sheet[a]

	End of fiscal 1999 (%)	End of fiscal 2000 (%)
ASSETS		
Current assets		
Cash	.47	.84
Marketable securities	.23	.21
Accounts receivable	43.95	42.38
Inventories[b]	27.91	23.80
Prepaid advertising	2.33	2.30
Total current assets	74.88	69.52
Investments and other assets		
Investments (at cost)	3.02	1.88
Notes receivable (from ABC Ltd.)	.93	1.04
Total investments and other assets	3.95	2.92
Fixed assets		
Land	3.26	3.34
Buildings	14.88	20.67
Equipment	10.47	11.27
Total fixed assets	28.60	35.28
Less: Accumulated depreciation	(7.91)	(8.35)
Net fixed assets	20.70	26.93
Unamortized goodwill	.47	.63
TOTAL ASSETS	100.00	100.00

LIABILITIES

Current liabilities

Short-term notes payable	16.74	13.15
Accounts payable	7.21	8.35
Salaries payable	2.33	2.30
Interest payable	1.40	1.25
Income tax payable	1.16	1.67
Dividends payable	.93	.63
Total current liabilities	29.77	27.35
Long-term debt	34.42	38.20
TOTAL LIABILITIES	64.19	65.55

SHAREHOLDERS' EQUITY

Capital stock
Common shares (no par value)

13,200,000 authorized, issued, and outstanding	12.79	11.48
Preferred shares (no par value)		
3,300,000 authorized		
2,500,000 issued and outstanding	4.65	4.18
Total capital stock	17.44	15.66
Retained earnings	18.37	18.79
TOTAL SHAREHOLDERS' EQUITY	35.81	34.45
TOTAL LIABILITIES AND SHAREHOLDERS' EQUITY	100.00	100.00

---

[a] because of rounding, figures in the last decimal may not add up exactly.

[b] valued at the lower of cost or market.

TABLE 3.5 ▬▬▬▬▬▬▬▬

Superior Enterprises' Common-Size Consolidated Income Statement

	1999 (%)	2000 (%)
Net sales	100.00	100.00
Investment income	.16	.15
Gross income	100.16	100.15
Less:		
Cost of goods sold	90.41	91.04
Depreciation	.98	.93
Interest on long-term debt	1.46	1.85
Other interest	.81	.77
Other expenses	1.46	1.39

Total expenses	95.12	95.98
Earnings before tax	5.04	4.17
Less: Income tax	(1.95)	(1.70)
Net income	3.09	2.47

3.4 EFFECTS OF CHANGING PRICES ON FINANCIAL STATEMENT ANALYSIS

aka effect / inflation

Financial statements summarize transactions that have taken place over extended time periods. In preparing and interpreting financial statements, one has traditionally assumed that both relative prices and the unit of measurement—the dollar—remain constant through time, so that dollar transactions that occurred at different times are comparable. In today's rapidly changing environment, these assumptions are increasingly open to question. For example, inflation erodes the purchasing power of money, and equal dollar amounts at two different times are no longer equivalent. When financial statements are prepared in such an environment without adjusting for price-level changes, serious distortions can occur. The issue of accounting for price-level changes is complex, and a detailed discussion is beyond the scope of this text. However, if we want to be able to draw valid conclusions from financial statement analysis in today's environment, we need to be aware of some of the main distortions that inflation can cause. We note that although accounting for price-level changes received particular attention during the high-inflation years of the late 1970s and early 1980s, the issue continues to be relevant for several reasons. First, although inflation rates have decreased, they have not been eliminated, and the long-term effect of even relatively low annual rates can still be substantial. Second, some of the distortions caused during the high-inflation years of the past are still reflected in today's financial statements. And finally, distortions are also caused by shifts in relative prices across items (for example, the dramatic changes in the price of oil). We consider some of the main impacts below.

Effects on Balance Sheets

historical vs replacement

The main distortions to the balance sheet as a result of inflation occur because asset values are shown at historical costs. Consider fixed assets such as land and buildings that were acquired many years ago at costs well below current replacement or even liquidation values. By not adjusting the historical costs of such assets to reflect price changes, a serious understatement of asset values on the balance sheet will occur. This can be particularly severe for older firms owning valuable assets such as real estate or usable plant and equipment. As a consequence, ratios such as the asset turnover or ROA could be grossly overstated and appear to be improving over time.

A second distortion to the balance sheet occurs in periods of unanticipated changes in inflation because debt is shown on the books at its original face value. For example, escalating inflation normally brings with it increasing interest rates. As we shall see in

Chapter 6, increasing interest rates depress the market value of outstanding debt. The market value of outstanding debt issued some years ago at comparatively low (high) interest rates is often lower (higher) than the value that is shown on the books. Inasmuch as the firm has the opportunity to retire debt at current prices by, for example, repurchasing its own bonds or debentures in the market, its indebtedness as shown on its balance sheet may be overstated if interest rates have risen. Even when the company chooses not to retire its debt, gains accrue because the real value of outstanding debt decreases due to inflation.

The two distortions discussed above have the potential to cause a severe understatement of the firm's equity position and an overstatement of its leverage as measured by, for example, the debt-to-equity or total debt-to-assets ratios. Appropriate adjustments for inflation might change the values of these ratios and paint a different picture of indebtedness.

Effects on Income Statements

The effects of inflation on reported earnings can be just as misleading, with several factors causing distortions that may have an impact in opposite ways. Some of the more important aspects that should be recognized are described briefly below:

1. During periods of sustained inflation, replacement values generally exceed historical costs, and depreciation is therefore understated. This, in turn, leads to artificially inflated earnings.

2. During periods of inflation, profits often result from holding inventory that was purchased earlier and subsequently sold at higher prices. As long as the firm intends to stay in business, however, such profits are largely illusory since the items sold will have to be replaced at prevailing prices. Nevertheless, these holding profits are included in reported earnings and unless inventory-holding profits are identified separately, it becomes difficult to assess a company's normal operating performance from its earnings statement.

3. Sizeable holding gains can also result from fixed assets—notably land and buildings—but they are not included in reported earnings unless they are realized through disposition of such assets. Even then, they are usually identified as extraordinary items.

4. Interest payments associated with long-term debt instruments such as bonds are fixed in nominal dollar terms. However, when inflation is high, the real value of these future dollar payments declines although this is not reflected in the financial statements.[12]

5. In addition to inventories, other working capital items may be affected by inflation. Specifically, firms realize unreported inflationary gains on their accounts payable, the values of which erode over time. Conversely, they incur losses on holdings of idle cash and receivables.

The overall impact of these often-conflicting distortions on earnings is difficult to ascertain although we recognize that in aggregate, a significant overstatement of business earnings results. The amount of the overstatement increases with accelerating inflation. The consequences can be serious affecting not only financial reporting but also impor-

---

[12] This issue will be discussed in Chapter 6.

tant financial decisions. For example, when dividend payments are viewed in relation to properly adjusted earnings, payout ratios increase substantially, and some companies actually pay out dividends in excess of true earnings.

Accounting Adjustments

Given the magnitude of possible distortions, past practices are reviewed to adjust accounting procedures for inflation, but, as indicated above, the conceptual and technical issues that arise are exceedingly complex and cannot be dealt with here. In broad terms, however, some of the main issues are the actual method to be used in adjusting for price-level changes and in determining which of the distortions discussed above should be addressed.

In accounting for price-level changes, one has to distinguish between general inflation that affects the overall purchasing power of money and specific price-level changes that affect the relative value of individual goods and services. Put another way, given that accounting is concerned with measuring economic value, we have to decide on the scale of measurement and on the attributes of the objects to be measured. The scale of measurement is money—Canadian dollars, in our context. Because of general inflation, the purchasing power of money is eroded, and as a consequence, the scale of measurement changes. To correct for this distortion, dollar amounts that occur at different times can be made equivalent by applying a uniform inflation factor as measured by, for example, the Consumer Price Index (CPI). Such general adjustments that attempt to stabilize the scale of measurement fall under the heading of general price-level accounting.

In addition to remedying distortions that occur because the scale of measurement (money) does not remain constant, changes in price levels have increasingly forced a debate as to which attributes of an asset or a liability should be measured. Traditionally, accountants have measured historical costs that were incurred at the time of the original transaction, but such costs often bear little resemblance to current market value or replacement costs. Given that the latter are often more relevant for decision-making, accountants have attempted to supplement their traditional statements by providing current cost information about individual assets and liabilities. This approach, which adjusts individual balance sheet entries to reflect their worth today, is called current cost accounting.

3.5 INTERNATIONAL CONSIDERATIONS

The financial ratios of similar corporations in different countries can be quite different. Part of this may be attributed to accounting differences, while part may be explained by other country-specific features including institutional, cultural, political, and tax differences. These factors often have a major impact on the proportion of debt financing that is used by companies and hence, on the financial ratios of firms.

Many Canadian companies derive a substantial portion of their income from international transactions, but they also maintain active foreign operations and/or the finance part of their operations abroad. Thus, various assets and liabilities shown on their balance sheets are ultimately denominated in foreign currencies. For example, when a Canadian firm owns a U.S. subsidiary, the subsidiary maintains its own books in U.S. dollars. These have to be translated into Canadian dollars when its financial statements are consolidated with those of the parent. Similarly, a firm that issued bonds denominated in British pounds on European capital markets will translate this debt into an equivalent Canadian dollar amount at the time of issue. This equivalent dollar amount is then carried as a liability on its balance sheet. Subsequent changes in foreign exchange rates create problems in that the dollar amount that was originally entered on the company's books may no longer be consistent with current currency values. For example, if the pound appreciates vis-à-vis the Canadian dollar, the firm actually faces an increased Canadian dollar liability and, hence, has sustained a loss. The question arises as to whether (and how) such changes in the valuation of foreign assets and liabilities that come about by movements in foreign exchange rates should be reflected in the company's financial statements. On the one hand, we can argue that shareholders should know when the firm sustained a loss or gain as a consequence of its foreign investment or financing activities since currency gains or losses may be just as real as gains or losses from operations. On the other hand, a full integration of such effects into financial statements would make a company's performance strongly dependent on unpredictable foreign exchange markets. Given the significant realignments of currencies that take place, often over relatively short time periods, foreign exchange effects could well overshadow the operating performance of firms active in international markets.

Needless to say, the topic of how to account for foreign exchange movements is controversial, and early U.S. experience with accounting adjustments was fraught with difficulties. In Canada, the Accounting Standards Committee of the Canadian Institute of Chartered Accountants (CICA) has established recommendations for uniform foreign currency translations. Because of their complexity, a review of these guidelines is beyond our scope. The analyst, however, needs to be familiar with their effects when significant balance sheet items are ultimately denominated in foreign currencies. The introduction of a consistent accounting treatment by Canadian enterprises at least ensures comparability between firms. ⬆

SUMMARY   3.6

1. The four categories of ratios used in financial analysis are:
   - Liquidity ratios highlight the firm's short-term ability to meet financial obligations.
   - Leverage ratios reflect the company's long-term financing decisions, while coverage ratios indicate its long-term ability to service outstanding debt.
   - Profitability and activity ratios portray the earning power of an enterprise and the efficiency with which its resources are used.
   - Value ratios relate financial statement data to market data.
2. The three ratios used in the DuPont system of financial analysis of return on equity are Profitability, Leverage, and Asset Turnover.

3. Financial statement categories are expressed as percentages of total assets for the balance sheet and total sales for the income statement. These are useful when comparing financial statements particularly if there are variations in the size of operations.

4. The four types of distortions in financial statements caused by changing prices are depreciation based on historical costs, inventory and other holding gains, revaluation of debt, and inflated interest expenses.

5. Proper measurement and implementation of required adjustments are difficult and controversial, and the resulting errors can be substantial.

6. When firms hold assets and liabilities denominated in foreign currencies, the procedure for recognizing the gains or losses resulting from changes in foreign exchange rates becomes important.

TABLE 3.6 ▬▬▬▬▬▬▬▬▬▬▬▬▬▬▬▬▬▬▬▬▬▬▬▬▬▬

Summary of Commonly Used Financial Ratios

RATIO	DEFINITION
LIQUIDITY RATIOS	
Current	$\dfrac{\text{current assets}}{\text{current liabilities}}$
Quick (acid test)	$\dfrac{\text{current assets} - \text{inventories}}{\text{current liabilities}}$
Inventory turnover	$\dfrac{\text{cost of goods sold}}{\text{average inventory}}$
Average collection period	$\dfrac{\text{receivables}}{\text{average daily credit sales}}$
Receivables turnover	$\dfrac{\text{annual credit sales}}{\text{receivables}}$
LEVERAGE AND COVERAGE RATIOS	
Debt-to-equity	$\dfrac{\text{long-term debt}}{\text{shareholders' equity}}$
Total debt-to-assets	$\dfrac{\text{total debt}}{\text{total assets}}$
Leverage (or equity multiplier)	$\dfrac{\text{total assets}}{\text{shareholders' equity}}$
Times-interest-earned	$\dfrac{\text{earnings before interest and taxes}}{\text{interest charges}}$

✓ = Know

Fixed-charges-coverage

$$\frac{\text{earnings before interest, lease charges, and taxes}}{\text{interest} + \text{lease charges} + \text{before-tax sinking fund payments}}$$

PROFITABILITY AND ACTIVITY RATIOS

Gross operating margin

$$\frac{\text{sales}-\text{cost of goods sold}}{\text{sales}}$$

Net operating margin

$$\frac{\text{earnings before interest and taxes}}{\text{sales}}$$

Net income margin

$$\frac{\text{net profit}}{\text{sales}}$$

Asset turnover

$$\frac{\text{sales}}{\text{total assets}}$$

Return on assets (ROA)

$$\frac{\text{net profit}}{\text{total assets}}$$

Return on equity (ROE)

$$\frac{\text{net profit}}{\text{shareholders' equity}}$$

MARKET VALUE RATIOS

Price-earnings (P/E)

$$\frac{\text{price per common share}}{\text{earnings per common share}}$$

Dividend payout

$$\frac{\text{dividends per common share}}{\text{earnings per common share}}$$

Dividend yield

$$\frac{\text{dividends per common share}}{\text{price per common share}}$$

Tobin's q

$$\frac{\text{market value of both the firm's debt and equity securities}}{\text{replacement cost of the firm's assets}}$$

Market-to-book

$$\frac{\text{market value of both the firm's debt and equity securities}}{\text{book value of assets}}$$

QUESTIONS AND PROBLEMS

Questions for Discussion

1. "The indiscriminate application of a standardized routine of ratio analysis to all companies regardless of size, industry, and peculiar characteristics might well lead to grossly incorrect conclusions." Explain why, and provide specific examples.

2. Is it possible for a firm to have a high current ratio and still be unable to pay its current liabilities? Explain.

3. Why may reviewing a list of aged accounts receivable be useful even if the company's average collection period is felt to be acceptable?

4. Explain how some firms can influence many of their ratios through a judicious choice of their fiscal year end. In what industries do you think this might be a particular problem?

5. Assume that a company's sales have changed rapidly either because of seasonality or because of rapid growth. What, if any, problems might this cause in calculating and interpreting an average collection period?

6. One often finds that regulated utilities such as telephone companies or pipelines earn a much higher net operating margin than manufacturing or retail enterprises that are subject to free competition. Why would regulators allow this to happen, and how can it be justified?

7. Some industries such as the real estate industry in 1990 and the oil industry in 1985 have been subject to dramatic decreases in the value of their primary assets. Discuss how such a decrease in relative prices may affect a firm's financial statements and any possible distortions that an analyst should consider.

8. What would a q ratio of 1.4 imply about a company's business prospects? In particular, what would you infer about investor beliefs?

PROBLEMS WITH SOLUTIONS

Problem 1

Painter Wally owns a small wall washing and painting company. His accountant has just projected his financial statements for the current year as follows:

BALANCE SHEET

ASSETS

Current assets:
Cash	$10,000
Accounts receivable	25,000
	$35,000

Fixed assets:
Trucks, scaffolding, garage, etc.	25,000
Less: Accumulated depreciation	(10,000)
	$15,000
TOTAL ASSETS	$50,000

LIABILITIES AND SHAREHOLDERS' EQUITY

Current liabilities:
Taxes payable	$ 1,000
Finance company loan	10,000
Accounts payable	9,000
	$20,000

Long-term liabilities:
Mortgage on storage garage	7,000
	$27,000

Shareholders' equity:
Shares held by Wally	20,000
Retained earnings	3,000
	$23,000
TOTAL LIABILITIES AND SHAREHOLDERS' EQUITY	$50,000

INCOME STATEMENT

Revenues		$100,000
Less:		
Cost of goods sold	$50,000	
Salaries and wages (including Wally's salary)	40,000	
Provision for depreciation	4,000	
Interest on short-term debt	1,500	
Interest on mortgage	700	
		96,200
Net income before taxes		$ 3,800
Income taxes		$ 1,000
Net earnings		$ 2,800

There are currently several decisions that Wally must make about his operations and financing that could affect his ratios.

(a) He can use $8,000 of the company's cash to pay off some accounts payable. How would this alter his current and total debt-to-assets ratios?

(a) Wally normally carries no paint inventory, but a nearby paint store is going out of business and is selling a paint inventory valued at $40,000 for $25,000. Wally feels that he can use this paint for special contracts next year. Wally's wife has some cash with which she can buy the inventory and gain a share of the firm herself. How would this transaction alter the company's current ratio, quick ratio, total debt-to-assets ratio, and the times-interest-earned ratio? What would happen to these ratios if, instead, Wally borrowed the $25,000 at 15 percent interest for three years with the principal to be paid off only at the end of the term? What would happen if he borrowed $25,000 at 15 percent for one year? How would the purchase of the inventory (by any method) affect the return on assets ratio? In computing the above, we ignore the negligible effects of interest payments on after-tax income and retained earnings.

Solution 1

(a) *Current ratio*

Original: $\dfrac{35,000}{20,000} = 1.75$ Modified: $\dfrac{35,000-8,000}{20,000-8,000} = 2.25$

Total debt-to-assets ratio

Original: $\dfrac{27,000}{50,000} = 0.54$ Modified: $\dfrac{27,000-8,000}{50,000-8,000} = 0.45$

The firm's position seems safer and more conservative if Wally uses cash to reduce his current liabilities. We note, however, that Wally would be foolish to pay off any accounts payable before they were due unless he receives a discount for doing so; otherwise, he could at least earn bank interest on these funds in the interim.

(b) *Current ratio*

Original: 1.75

After inventory financed by equity: $\dfrac{35,000+25,000}{20,000} = 3$

After inventory financed by long-term debt: 3

After inventory financed by short-term debt: $\dfrac{35,000+25,000}{20,000+25,000} = 1.33$

Quick ratio

Original:
$$\frac{35,000}{20,000} = 1.75$$

After inventory financed by equity: 1.75
After inventory financed by long-term debt: 1.75

After inventory financed by short-term debt:
$$\frac{35,000}{20,000+25,000} = 0.78$$

Total debt-to-assets ratio

Original: 0.54

After inventory financed by equity:
$$\frac{27,000}{50,000+25,000} = 0.36$$

After inventory financed by
short- or long-term debt:
$$\frac{27,000+25,000}{50,000+25,000} = 0.69$$

Times-interest-earned ratio

Original or after inventory
financed by equity:
$$\frac{3,800+1,500+700}{1,500+700} = 2.73$$

After inventory financed by
short- or long-term debt:
$$\frac{3,800+1,500+700}{1,500+700+(.15\times25,000)} = 1.01$$

Return on assets

Original:
$$\frac{2,800}{50,000} = 5.60\%$$

After inventory purchase:
$$\frac{2,800}{50,000+25,000} = 3.73\%$$

This problem illustrates the need to use several ratios when analysing financial decisions. For example, equity or long-term debt financing of the inventory improves the current ratio seemingly implying an improvement in liquidity. The inventory, however, would not be needed for a year and may not have much of a resale value. Thus, the quick ratio, which did not rise, may reflect the liquidity position more fairly. Note how the current ratio falls if the inventory is financed by short-term debt (the opposite effect to using cash to pay off current liabilities).

The total debt-to-asset ratio was shifted in obvious ways depending on the method of financing the inventory. The times-interest-earned ratio shows that the safety of coverage of interest charges is not hampered by equity financing but by debt financing. However, if the inventory had contributed to the current year's income, this ratio might not have been impaired. Finally, the fall in the return-on-assets figure illustrates the immediate opportunity cost of purchasing inventory now for later use.

Problem 2

Below are some excerpts from the Falling Timber Company's annual reports. Falling Timber is a vertically integrated, forest resource conglomerate that concentrates on cutting timber and producing lumber. It also transports, wholesales, and retails some of its products. At 1997 year end, the estimated replacement cost of the firm's assets totalled $1.4 billion with a market value of $1.5 billion. Comparable 2000 values were $1.7 billion and $1.95 billion respectively. Calculate all the relevant ratios defined in this chapter, and also prepare common-size financial statements. Then, comment on any significant changes in the company's position from 1997 to 2000.

BALANCE SHEET (in 000s)

	2000	1997
ASSETS		
Current assets:		
Cash	$ 6,049	4,203
Short-term investments and deposits	15,383	14,927
Accounts receivable	149,206	111,984
Inventories	229,637	119,982
Prepaid expenses	5,406	3,033
	$ 405,681	$254,129
Investments:	$ 90,388	$ 33,019
Fixed assets, at cost:		
Buildings and equipment	$ 983,627	$788,623
Less: Accumulated depreciation	486,323	375,267
	$ 497,304	$413,356
Timber less accumulated depletion	75,798	73,997
Logging roads and land	45,654	27,498
	$ 618,756	$514,851
Intangible assets:		
Goodwill	$ 26,583	$ 28,503
	$1,141,408	$830,502

LIABILITIES

Current liabilities

Bank loans	$ 46,181	$ 43,867
Notes payable	40,962	—
Accounts payable and accrued liabilities	128,796	63,931
Income taxes payable	1,260	3,269
Current portion of long-term debt	11,537	7,929
	$ 228,736	$118,996
Bonds and debentures	$ 317,429	$270,410
Income tax allocations in respect of future years	92,454	63,352
	$ 409,883	$333,762

SHAREHOLDERS' EQUITY

Common shares	$ 169,343	$141,440
Retained earnings	$ 333,446	$236,304
	$ 502,789	$377,744
	$1,141,408	$830,502

EARNINGS STATEMENT (in 000's)

	2000	1997
Sales and other income:		
Sales of products and services	$1,401,657	$790,775
Income from investments	3,256	1,787
Profit (loss) on disposal of assets	$ (602)	$ 201
	$1,404,311	$792,763
Costs and expenses:		
Cost of sales and services	$1,053,134	$586,273
Depreciation	108,936	88,735
Depletion	12,610	10,695
Selling and administrative expense	93,275	46,835
Long-term debt interest	16,261	14,106
Bank and other interest	4,467	4,198
	$1,288,683	$750,842
Earnings before taxes	$ 115,628	$ 41,921
Income taxes:		
Current	$ 44,781	$ 21,672
Future years	16,674	(2,160)
	$ 61,674	$ 19,512
Net earnings (after-tax)	$ 53,954	$ 22,409

Relevant notes to financial statements (in 000's)

	2000	1999	1997	1996
1. Ending inventories	$229,637	$159,367	$119,982	$98,928

Financial commitments
  (at beginning of year):

	2000	1997
Payment for acquisition of cutting rights	$ 2,410	$ 2,273
Sinking fund requirements for debt	8,657	5,336

Solution 2

The data allow us to compute the following:

Current ratio

$$2000: \frac{405,681}{228,736} = 1.77 \qquad\qquad 1997: \frac{254,129}{118,996} = 2.14$$

Quick ratio

$$2000: \frac{459,681-229,637}{228,736} = 0.77 \qquad 1997: \frac{254,159-119,982}{118,996} = 1.13$$

Average inventory

$$2000: \frac{229,637+159,367}{2} = \$194,502 \qquad 1997: \frac{119,982+98,928}{2} = \$109,455$$

Inventory turnover ratio

$$2000: \frac{1,053,134}{194,502} = 5.41 \qquad\qquad 1997: \frac{586,273}{109,455} = 5.36$$

Average collection period
As most of Falling Timber's sales are to industrial consumers, we assume, in the absence of other information, that all sales are credit sales.

$$2000: \frac{149,206}{1,401,657/365 \text{ days}} = 38.9 \text{ days} \qquad 1997: \frac{111,984}{790,775/365 \text{ days}} = 51.7 \text{ days}$$

Receivables turnover ratio

$$2000: \frac{1,401,657}{149,206} = 9.39 \qquad\qquad 1997: \frac{790,775}{111.984} = 7.06$$

Debt-to-equity ratio

$$2000: \frac{317,429+92,454}{502,789} = 0.815 \qquad 1997: \frac{270,410+63,352}{377,744} = 0.884$$

Total debt-to-assets ratio

2000: $\dfrac{428,736+317,429+92,454}{1,141,408} = 0.560$ 1997: $\dfrac{118,996+270,410+63,352}{830,502} = 0.545$

Leverage ratio (or equity multiplier)

2000: $\dfrac{1,141,408}{502,789} = 2.270$ 1997: $\dfrac{830,502}{377,744} = 2.200$

Times-interest-earned ratio

2000: $\dfrac{115,628+16,261+4,4676}{16,261+4,467} = 6.58$ 1997: $\dfrac{41,921+14,106+4,198}{14,106+4,198} = 3.29$

Fixed-charges-coverage ratio

The fixed charges include payments for cutting rights and sinking fund requirements (neither of which affect income and thus are not added back to the numerator). In the denominator, sinking fund requirements and payments for cutting rights have to be given on a before-tax basis; they are divided by $(1-\text{tax rate})$. We use an average tax rate of 45 percent for the firm.

2000: $\dfrac{115,628+16,261+4,467}{16,261+4,467+(2,410+8,675)/.55} = 3.34$ 1997: $\dfrac{41,921+14,106+4,198}{14,106+4,198+(2,273+5,336)/.55} = 1.87$

Gross operating margin

2000: $\dfrac{348,523}{1,401,657} = 24.87\%$ 1997: $\dfrac{204,502}{790,775} = 25.86\%$

Net operating margin

2000: $\dfrac{115,628+16,261+4,467}{1,401,657} = 9.73\%$ 1997: $\dfrac{41,921+14,106+4,198}{790,775} = 7.62\%$

Net profit margin

2000: $\dfrac{53,954}{1,401,657} = 3.85\%$ 1997: $\dfrac{22,409}{790,775} = 2.83\%$

Asset turnover ratio

2000: $\dfrac{1,401,657}{1,141,408} = 1.23$ 1997: $\dfrac{790,755}{830,502} = 0.95$

Return on assets

2000: $\dfrac{53,954}{1,141,408} = 4.73\%$ 1997: $\dfrac{22,409}{830,502} = 2.70\%$

Return on equity (ROE)

2000: $\dfrac{53,954}{502,789} = 10.73\%$ 1997: $\dfrac{22,409}{377,744} = 5.93\%$

DuPont Analysis

	ROE	= net profit margin×asset turnover ratio×leverage ratio
2000:	ROE	= 0.0385×1.23×2.270=10.75% (difference due to rounding)
1997:	ROE	= 0.0283×0.95×2.200=5.91% (difference due to rounding)

We are not provided with the necessary share price information and earnings per share (EPS) information to calculate the P/E ratio, nor the necessary dividend information to determine the dividend payout ratio and dividend yield figures.

Tobin's q ratio

$$2000: \frac{1.95}{1.7} = 1.15 \qquad\qquad 1997: \frac{1.5}{1.4} = 1.07$$

Market-to-book ratio

$$2000: \frac{1.95}{1.141408} = 1.71 \qquad\qquad 1997: \frac{1.5}{0.830502} = 1.81$$

Comments

From the viewpoint of performance, the company's prospects seem to have brightened considerably from 1997 to 2000. First, the firm is using its assets more effectively to generate sales because both the asset turnover ratio and the inventory turnover ratio have improved with a substantial improvement in the former. Also, the net operating margin increased by over 2 percent from 1997 to 2000, and the net profit margin increased by more than 1 percent. As a result of the compounding effect of the improved net profit margin and asset turnover ratio, the company's return-on-assets figure almost doubled. This improvement in the return on assets was the primary factor causing an increase in return on equity of almost 5 percent since the leverage ratio increased only slightly from 1997. All of these points are evident from the DuPont analysis.

Because of temporary changes in business conditions, net income can change sharply from year to year. Therefore, in order to distinguish trends from temporary variations, any conclusive judgement of these performance indicators should include a comparison of several successive years.

To find the cause of the improved performance, we may examine the comparative common-size earnings statement. The cost of goods and services actually rose by 1 percent from 1997 to 2000, but depreciation and depletion charges as a proportion of sales volume showed a combined drop of 3.9 percent. This was the major cause of the fall of 3 percent in costs and expenses. After taxes, the difference in earnings is reduced to 1 percent.

Since the proportionately lower depreciation and depletion charges are an important factor in the improved performance (consistent with the higher asset turnover ratio), these improvements could have resulted from improved technology and management producing a higher volume with the same assets. Alternatively, they could also result from the cumulative effects of inflation, understating the value of assets and hence the required depreciation and depletion charges. The firm could also be failing to upgrade its capital assets (avoiding new depreciation charges) that would harm its long-run position. This is unlikely, however, because the balance sheet reports roughly the same proportion of accumulated depreciation of fixed assets for both years.

Finally, inflationary inventory profits could be a further factor in improved performance; but, again, that is unlikely, since the cost of sales as a proportion of sales actually increased from 1997 to 2000. We see the limitations of financial statement analysis in pinpointing the exact nature of any changes in the company's performance.

Considering the firm's ability to continue operating, we may examine, for example, the current and quick ratios. From the common-size balance sheet, we see that the corporation has increased the proportions of both its current assets and current liabilities, the net result being a decrease in the current ratio. As the increase in current assets was almost solely owing to the increase in inventories (as evident from the common-size analysis), the quick ratio fell even more sharply. Whether or not it is dangerously low requires comparison with other firms in the industry. However, given that the company has reduced its average collection period by about 13 days, we might contend that it has improved its liquidity insofar as it is able to turn receivables into cash more readily. This may tend to offset the trend toward poorer liquidity as evidenced by a falling quick ratio.

The firm's inventory figures deserve further analysis. Although the sharp increase on the common-size balance sheet suggests that inventory levels may be getting excessive (slow sales, obsolete inventory, etc.), the higher inventory turnover ratio actually points in the opposite direction. One possible reason could be that inflation increased the cost of inventory. Although this cost increase was immediately passed on to the consumer thereby preserving the inventory turnover ratio, inflation had little effect on the historic costs of fixed assets, so that inventory increased as a proportion of total assets.

From the point of view of debt, the company decreased its proportionate reliance on long-term debt, resulting in a decline of the debt-to-equity ratio. However, the substitution of current liabilities for long-term liabilities as evident from common-size analysis caused the total debt-to-assets ratio and the leverage ratio to increase. The development in Falling Timber's coverage ratios has been favourable. The times-interest-earned ratio increased mainly because of higher net earnings combined with the fixed interest charges on long-term debt that was issued several years earlier. Fixed charges are all covered by earnings and cash flows several times over and consequently provide some margin of safety both to creditors and to the liquidity of the firm.

A rise in the q ratio between 1997 and 2000 probably suggests ongoing investor optimism about the company's prospects although this is not reflected in the market-to-book ratio, which actually decreased.

COMMON-SIZE BALANCE SHEET*

	2000 (%)	1997 (%)
ASSETS		
Current assets:		
Cash	.53	.51
Short-term investments and deposits	1.35	1.80
Accounts receivable	13.07	13.48
Inventories	20.12	14.45
Prepaid expenses	.47	.36
	35.54	30.60
Investments:	7.92	3.98
Fixed assets:		
Buildings and equipment	86.18	94.96
Less: Accumulated depreciation	42.61	45.19
	43.57	49.77
Timber less accumulated depletion	6.64	8.91
Logging roads and land	4.00	3.31
	54.21	61.99
Intangible assets:		
Goodwill	2.33	3.43
	100.00	100.00
LIABILITIES		
Current liabilities:		
Bank loans	4.05	5.28
Notes payable	3.59	—
Accounts payable and accrued liabilities	11.28	7.70
Income taxes payable	.11	.39
Current portion of long-term debt	1.01	.95
	20.04	14.32
Bonds and debentures	27.81	32.56
Income tax allocation in respect of future years	8.10	7.63
	35.91	40.19
SHAREHOLDERS' EQUITY		
Common shares	14.84	17.03
Retained earnings	29.21	28.46
	44.05	45.49
	100.00	100.00

*Because of rounding, figures in the last decimal may not add up exactly.

COMMON-SIZE EARNINGS STATEMENT*

	2000 (%)	1997 (%)
Sales and other income:		
Sales of products and services	100.00	100.00
Income from investments	.23	.23
Profit (loss) on disposal of assets	(.04)	.03
	100.19	100.25
Costs and expenses:		
Cost of sales and services	75.13	74.14
Depreciation	7.77	11.22
Depletion	.90	1.35
Selling and administrative expense	6.65	5.92
Long-term debt interest	1.16	1.78
Bank and other interest	.32	.53
	91.94	94.95
Earnings before taxes	8.25	5.30
Income taxes:		
Current	3.19	2.74
Future years	1.21	(.27)
	4.40	2.47
Earnings after-tax	3.85	2.83

*Because of rounding, figures in the last decimal may not add up exactly.

ADDITIONAL PROBLEMS

1. The management of GHM Technology Company was particularly pleased with its financial performance over the past year. Sales had increased rapidly to $340 million, net operating profit had increased, and nearly all other ratios had improved. The firm's banker had noted, however, that the average collection period had steadily deteriorated to 83 days at present. All of the company's sales were made on credit, and its present policy was to offer terms of 2/30, net 60 (2 percent discount if bills are paid within 30 days, or the full amount is due on day 60).

   Calculate the dollar volume of receivables outstanding and the receivable turnover ratio for the company. Before being able to fully assess this aspect of the company's management, what additional information do you think the firm's banker should have?

2. Complete the following balance sheet based on the information provided below:

ASSETS		LIABILITIES AND EQUITY	
Cash	$	Accounts payable	$
Accounts receivable		Common stock	63,000
Inventory		Retained earnings	
Plant and equipment	$56,000	Total liabilities and	
Total assets	$	net worth	$135,000

The values of selected ratios are given as follows:

Quick ratio	1.4
Average collection period	38 days
Total debt-to-assets ratio	0.38
Asset turnover ratio	2.45

3. You are given the following information on the Prestige Department Store:

Annual sales	$50,000
Gross operating margin	35%
Beginning inventory	$8,000
Inventory turnover ratio	4.3
Average collection period	62 days
Asset turnover ratio	1.4
Times-interest-earned ratio	7.5
Tax rate	50%

Current assets consist of cash ($26,000), receivables, and inventory. Current liabilities are $18,000.

(a) Assume that all sales are credit sales. Calculate the current and quick ratios.

(b) Assume that 25 percent of sales are on a cash basis. Complete the following income statement:

Revenue
    Cash sales
    Credit sales
        Total revenue
Cost of goods sold
    Beginning inventory
    Add: Purchases
    Less: Ending inventory
        Cost of goods sold
Operating profit
    Less: Interest expense
Profit before tax
    Less: Income tax
Net income

(c) Calculate the net operating income margin.

4. Using the financial statements provided below for First Manufacturing Company, calculate all the ratios listed below for both 1999 and 2000. On the basis of compar-

isons with the industry averages given below, what do you see as possible areas of financial and operating weakness for the firm? Assume that all sales are credit sales.

Industry Averages

Current ratio	1.98
Quick ratio	0.83
Inventory turnover ratio	3.09
Average collection period	63 days
Debt-to-equity ratio	1.53
Total debt-to-assets ratio	0.59
Times-interest-earned ratio	3.90
Gross profit margin	14.22%
Net operating margin	3.93%
Asset turnover ratio	1.12
Return on equity	8.92%

First Manufacturing Company, Income Statement (in 000s)

	2000	1999
Sales	$241,319	$201,099
Cost of goods sold	193,055	171,074
Gross profit	$ 48,264	$ 30,025
Operating expenses:		
Selling and administrative	23,733	10,211
Depreciation	12,548	9,953
Net operating income	$ 11,983	$ 9,861
Interest expense	4,800	3,800
Income before taxes	$ 7,183	$ 6,061
Income tax	2,585	2,182
Net income	$ 4,598	$ 3,879

First Manufacturing Company, Balance Sheet (in 000s)

	2000	1999
ASSETS		
Cash	$ 5,500	$ 13,431
Accounts receivable	32,326	29,223
Inventory	43,762	41,622
Total current assets	$ 81,588	$ 84,276
Plant and equipment net of depreciation	106,270	80,988
Total assets	$187,858	$165,264

LIABILITIES AND SHAREHOLDERS' EQUITY

Accounts payable	$ 27,497	$ 26,883
Notes payable	28,011	24,610
Total current liabilities	$ 55,508	$ 51,493
Bonds and debentures	89,000	74,300
Total liabilities	$144,508	$125,793
Class A preferred shares 7%	7,500	7,500
Common shares	7,000	7,000
Retained earnings	28,850	24,971
Total liabilities and shareholders' equity	$187,858	$165,264

5. The following data were taken from the financial statements of a large integrated oil company (in 000s)

CONSOLIDATED BALANCE SHEET

	2000	1999
Current assets:		
Cash, including time deposits	$ 44,289	$ 46,808
Short-term commercial notes	100	3,095
Government securities	1,194	1,458
Accounts receivable	275,763	231,331
Prepaid taxes, insurance, and rentals	3,443	2,664
Inventories	170,625	163,579
	$ 495,414	$ 448,935
Fixed assets:		
Property, plant, equipment, less depreciation	811,365	713,034
Long-term accounts receivable	90,693	85,648
Total assets	$1,397,472	$1,247,617
Current liabilities:		
Bank loans	$ 36,600	—
Accounts payable and accrued liabilities	166,860	148,370
Income and other taxes payable	21,814	26,490
Long-term debt due within one year	20,000	—
	$ 245,274	$ 174,860
Long-term liabilities and deferred credit:		
Long-term debt	128,500	102,350
Employee annuity contributions	12,724	12,724
Deferred income tax	105,340	87,645
Total liabilities	$ 491,838	$ 377,579
Shareholders' equity:		
Capital stock	257,993	255,081
Retained earnings	647,641	614,957
Total shareholders' equity and liabilities	$1,397,472	$1,247,617

(a) Prepare a common-size balance sheet for both years, and note any variations that you consider significant.

(b) Calculate the current and acid test ratios for both years.

(c) Calculate the debt-to-equity and total debt-to-assets ratios.

6. Following are the financial statements of Western Forest Resources for 2000 and 1999 (in 000s)

CONSOLIDATED BALANCE SHEET

	2000	1999
ASSETS		
Current assets:		
Cash and short-term deposits	$ 100	10,577
Accounts receivable	38,540	33,968
Inventories	66,789	44,635
	$105,429	$ 89,180
Investments in partly owned companies		
(less than 50% owned) at cost	$ 9,695	$ 8,700
Fixed assets:		
Land, buildings, and equipment	$408,380	$357,236
Less: Accumulated depreciation	186,477	163,482
	$221,903	$193,754
Timber and cutting rights		
Less: Accumulated depletion	18,435	19,087
	$240,338	$212,841
Intangible assets:		
Unamortized goodwill of subsidiaries	1,032	1,073
Patent rights of plywood process	620	705
	$ 1,652	$ 1,778
Total assets	$357,114	$312,499
LIABILITIES		
Current liabilities:		
Bank loan	$ 6,200	$ 1,085
Short-term notes payable	12,635	—
Accounts payable and accrued liabilities	33,649	23,172
Income taxes payable	4,650	14,742
Current portion of long-term debt	1,259	787
	$ 58,393	$ 39,786
Long-term debt	$ 99,650	$ 94,839
Deferred income taxes	$ 62,563	$ 56,675
Total liabilities	$220,606	$191,300

SHAREHOLDERS' EQUITY

5.75% cumulative preferred shares	$ 9,775	$ 10,160
Common shares (no par value)	62,132	61,872
Retained earnings	64,601	49,167
	$136,508	$121,199
Total shareholders' equity and liabilities	$357,114	$312,499

CONSOLIDATED EARNINGS STATEMENT

	2000	1999
Net sales	$285,163	$257,670
Costs and expenses:		
Cost of products sold	203,841	174,192
Depreciation	22,995	20,890
Depletion	1,902	1,838
Selling and administration expense	9,652	10,031
Interest on long-term debt	7,998	6,673
Other interest expense	1067	1,320
	$247,455	$214,944
Net sales minus costs	$ 37,708	$ 42,726
Other income:		
Interest earned	1,838	1,271
Dividends from partly owned companies	50	100
Equity in retained earnings (loss) of partly owned companies	(408)	565
Earnings before income tax	$ 39,188	$ 44,662
Income taxes:		
Current	11,653	14,893
Deferred	6,271	5,051
	$ 17,924	$ 19,944
Net income	$ 21,264	$ 24,718

Other relevant data (in 000s)

	2000	1999	1998
1. Inventories	$66,789	$44,635	$38,290

	2000	1999
2. Sinking-fund requirements for bonds and debentures	3,010	$ 2,870
Lease payments (under prior commitments)	$ 2,850	$ 2,600

(a) Calculate all of the ratios defined in this chapter, for both 1999 and 2000. Set out the needed assumptions to come up with appropriate q ratios.

(b) Prepare common-size financial statements for 1999 and 2000.

(c) Comment on any significant changes in the firm's position and performance. How would such changes affect your view of Western as:

(i)   A common shareholder;

(ii) A preferred shareholder or bondholder;

(iii) Western's chief executive officer.

Assume that economic conditions for 2000 were: (1) Start of a recession (2) High rates of inflation and interest.

Other relevant data (in 000s)

1. Inventories	2000	1999	1998
	$66,789	$44,635	$38,290

2. Sinking fund requirements for bonds and debentures	2000	1999
	$ 3,010	$ 2,870
Lease payments (under prior commitments)	$ 2,850	$ 2,600

(a) Calculate all of the ratios defined in Table 3.6 for both 1999 and 2000. Set out the needed assumptions to come up with appropriate q ratios.

(b) Prepare common-size financial statements for 1999 and 2000.

(c) Comment on any significant changes in the firm's position and performance. How would such changes affect your view of Western as:

(i) a common shareholder

(ii) a preferred shareholder or bondholder

(iii) Western's chief executive officer

Assume that economic conditions for 2000 were (1) a normal period of growth, and (2) relatively low rates of inflation and interest.

7. A firm has a net income margin of 6.8 percent and an asset turnover ratio of 2.3. If the company's total debt-to-assets ratio is 0.2, what is the return on assets? Return on equity?

8. Given its current situation, a firm is projecting a return on assets of 12 percent and a return on equity of 18 percent. The company has total debt outstanding of $200 million. The corporation is considering issuing $75 million of common stock and using the proceeds to repay debt. If it does this, what will be the effect on return on equity if return on assets remains the same?

9. Consider the following two firms, both of which operate within the same industry:

	Firm A	Firm B
Revenue	$10,000	$5,000
Cost of goods sold	5,000	3,000
Other operating expenses	1,400	100
Depreciation	2,000	500
Interest expense	100	500
Tax rate	34%	34%
Number of shares outstanding	10,000	20,000
Price per share	$1.98	???

(a) You are an analyst attempting to put a value on the shares of Firm B. As a first attempt, calculate what the price per share of Firm B would be if it had the same price-earnings ratio as Firm A.

(b) If the trailing price-earnings ratio for Firm B was actually 15, what is the share price of Firm B? What factors might account for the difference in price-earnings between the two companies?

10. Income statements for the past four years for a company are shown below:

Year:	2000	1999	1998	1997
Sales	$75,000	$55,000	$35,000	$25,000
Cost of goods sold	37,500	27,500	17,500	12,500
Administration expenses	25,000	15,000	7,000	5,000
Depreciation	1,500	1,500	1,000	1,000
Net operating income	11,000	11,000	9,500	6,500
Interest expense	3,000	3,000	1,500	500
Income before taxes	8,000	8,000	8,000	6,000
Tax (@45%)	3,600	3,600	3,600	2,700
Net income	$ 4,400	$ 4,400	$ 4,400	$ 3,300

(a) Calculate the total percentage change in sales over the 1997-2000 period.

(b) Calculate the total percentage change in net income over the 1997-2000 period.

(c) For each of the four years presented, calculate the gross operating margin, net operating margin, and net income margin. Discuss any trends in these ratios and whether they are positive or negative for the firm.

(d) Based on the ratios and their trends observed in (c), discuss the causes of the difference between your answers to parts (a) and (b).

11. Look at the industry average ratios in Table 3.1 to answer the following questions:

(a) For the auto parts and transportation, and pipelines industries, use the DuPont formula to calculate the average asset turnover ratios for the industries.

(b) If the average net profit margin for the auto parts industry rose from 4.42 percent to 5.42 percent, what effect would this have on return on equity? If the pipelines industry average net profit margin rose from 5.14 percent to 6.14 percent, what would be the effect on return on equity? Discuss the reasons for the differential effect of a 1 percent rise in net profit margin with reference to both the DuPont formula and the nature of the industries.

Statements Tell Much, But Not All

In Chapter 3, you were introduced to Mark's Work Wearhouse's exceptionally clear and readable annual reports. The cash flow statement in Mark's 2000 annual report is presented with the same care found in the rest of the document; the figures showing the sources and uses of cash for the fiscal year are clearly laid out, along with the ranges forecast for 2000 in the previous year's report and the actual figures for the previous two years. As a record of the funds that flowed into and out of the firm over the year, the cash flow statement is a valuable companion to the balance sheet for Mark's Work Wearhouse shareholders interested in seeing how their investments are being managed.

Mark's cash flow statement is fairly typical of a merchandising operation. The major items in the operations category, which totals $16.9 million cash inflow for the year, are net earnings of $6.4 million and depreciation/amortization of $10 million. Changes in noncash working capital included entries for accounts receivable, inventory, accounts payable, and income taxes payable.

The investing category includes outflows toward the acquisition of a subsidiary (Mark's bought clothier John Paul in 1999, but the price was adjusted in 2000 resulting in further outflows), for the purchase of a franchise, and for other capital assets, which included some Y2K-related expenses.

The financing category shows that Mark's acquired $1 million of long-term debt in 2000 but was able to retire $3.4 million (compared with $10.2 million borrowed and only $1.4 million retired in 1999, when it made the bulk of the John Paul purchase). It also includes the repayment of some capital lease liabilities, and an inflow of $1 million in deferred landlord inducements.

But as is usually the case with financial statements, the numbers only tell part of the story. Only clear explanations and notes from management really make clear what is going on.

For example, the statement shows that Mark's inflow of cash for 2000 consisted of $16.9 million of cash and cash equivalents from operations, compared with $15.8 million in 1999—an increase of 6.7 percent. However, the management discussion points out that the 1999 figure includes a provision for the closure of its two stores in the United States—a pilot project that didn't work out. Excluding this provision, the funds flow from operations for 2000 is an impressive $4 million, or 31.3 percent, higher than that of 1999.

Or consider the entry of $808,000 under financing in 1999 for share capital. The notes explain that this figure represents the issuance of 579,900 common shares in response to employees cashing in their stock options.

Accurate, well-designed financial statements are crucial for communicating financial information to shareholders and other interested parties. But they are only the beginning, not the end.

Funds-Flow Analysis and Financial Forecasting

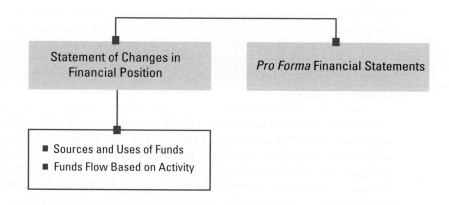

Learning Objectives

After studying this chapter, you should be able to:

1. *Recognize why statements of changes in financial position are important.*
2. *Describe the two ways of preparing statements of changes in financial position.*
3. *Explain what an increase or decrease in funds means in a statement of sources and uses of funds.*
4. *Discuss how an activity format evaluates a firm's cash flow.*
5. *Describe how* pro forma *statements are used as planning tools.*

4.1 INTRODUCTION

In addition to the techniques of financial statement analysis introduced in Chapter 3, other methods for assessing business performance are widely used. In this chapter, we discuss the analysis of changes in financial position based on the funds-flow statement (or statement of changes in financial position) and longer-term financial forecasting through preparation of *pro forma* financial statements. Short-term forecasting in the form of cash budgeting is discussed in Chapter 23.

The statement of changes in financial position (SCFP), which firms publish as part of their financial statements, answers two basic questions: over a given period, where have funds been used within the firm, and where have the funds come from? These questions bring us to the heart of financial management: the procurement and allocation of funds. Funds-flow analysis can most easily be carried out by comparing the firm's balance sheets at the beginning and at the end of the period under consideration and by noting any changes in the firm's financial position. Although funds-flow analysis is commonly applied to historical information, it can also be future oriented and based on projected financial statements.

Long-term financial planning through projected, or *pro forma*, financial statements assists management in forecasting a firm's future financial position. Such forecasting is important and serves a variety of functions. First, it promotes coordinated, future-oriented thinking. Once an overall financial plan has been established, every phase of management will be concerned with attaining the prescribed goals. Second, effective forecasting reduces surprises and curtails the need for hurried decisions. For example, if management can anticipate the timing and amount of needed external financing, it will be in a stronger negotiating position with prospective lenders than if it required funds on an emergency basis. Third, forecasting provides control through the analysis of budget variances because management can measure actual performance and compare it against projections. Finally, financial forecasts including detailed *pro forma* statements are often required by banks and other lenders that want to ensure that the borrowing firm has a coherent and viable plan that includes provisions for an orderly servicing and retirement of its debt.

PERSPECTIVES

Corporate Manager

Obviously, *pro forma* statements are essential for management to take the proper steps to prepare for the future.

Investor

Preparing *pro forma* statements can help prospective investors to forecast future earnings, cash flows, and dividends for a company. As we shall see in Chapter 6, these are key inputs into the process of estimating the value of common shares.

STATEMENT OF CHANGES IN FINANCIAL POSITION

Changes in a firm's financial position can be reported using both **sources and uses of funds** or in an **activity format**. While the second format is the one most often found in financial statements, both are used in practice, and we review each in turn noting that they contain equivalent information.

Sources and Uses of Funds

A statement of sources and uses of funds compares the balance sheets of a company at two different times. Changes in the various balance sheet entries indicate the net flows of funds resulting from both management decisions and external influences during the period under consideration. In the broadest type of analysis, which we use in this chapter, changes are recognized in all balance sheet accounts including the individual accounts that make up current assets and current liabilities.

Any increase in an asset account or decrease in a liability account represents a use of funds. Conversely, any decrease in an asset account or increase in a liability account becomes a source of funds. This is summarized in the chart below. For example, if assets such as plant and equipment or inventories are increased or if liabilities such as a bank loan or accounts payable are reduced, funds are used up. Similarly, funds can be provided either by liquidating assets such as inventories or by incurring additional liabilities. Clearly, over any given time period, total uses must equal total sources.

Sources and Uses of Funds

	Assets	Liabilities
Source of funds	Decrease	Increase
Use of funds	Increase	Decrease

Table 4.1 shows a statement of sources and uses of funds for fiscal 2000 for Superior Enterprises, financial statements of which were introduced in Chapter 3. The balance sheet changes indicate only the net shifts that occur in an account during the period under consideration. For example, a temporary building of inventories prior to the traditional Christmas rush would not be detected because by the end of December, most of those inventories would have been liquidated. To be more precise, the analyst would have to conduct funds-flow analysis based on shorter periods using, for example, quarterly or even monthly data.

For some individual entries, further detail may be useful. Thus, in analysing the fixed-asset account, we can break down the net change and record separately depreciation taken during the period as a source of funds and the gross change in buildings and equipment as a use of funds where:

Gross change in fixed assets	=	gross fixed assets at end of period
	−	gross fixed assets at beginning of period
	=	net fixed assets at end of period
	−	net fixed assets at beginning of period
	+	depreciation taken during period

TABLE 4.1

Superior Enterprises Statement of Sources and Uses of Funds, Fiscal 2000 (in 000s)

FUNDS DERIVED FROM

Decrease in inventories	6,000
Decrease in investments	4,000
Increase in accumulated depreciation*	6,000
Increase in accounts payable	9,000
Increase in salaries payable	1,000
Increase in income tax payable	3,000
Increase in long-term debt	35,000
Income earned	16,000
Total sources	$80,000

FUNDS USED FOR

Increase in cash	2,000
Increase in accounts receivable	14,000
Increase in prepaid advertising	1,000
Increase in notes receivable	1,000
Increase in land	2,000
Increase in buildings	35,000
Increase in equipment	9,000
Increase in goodwill	1,000
Decrease in short-term notes payable	9,000
Decrease in dividends payable	1,000
Dividends paid	5,000
Total Uses	$80,000

*Note that depreciation is shown as a source of funds from operations.

For Superior Enterprises, the change in net fixed assets for the period is $40 million. With an increase in accumulated depreciation of $6 million, however, the firm actually spent $46 million on land, buildings, and equipment during the year. A similar breakdown of the net change in retained earnings can also be incorporated. Rather than simply recording the net change in retained earnings as a source of funds, we can show total earnings as a source and dividends as a use. For example, the income statement for Superior Enterprises reports net earnings for 2000 at $16 million. With retained earnings increasing by $11 million over the year, dividends of $16 − 11 = $5 million must have been paid. The sources and uses of funds statement for Superior Enterprises, as shown in Table 4.1, include these extensions.

Funds Flow Based on Activity

It is useful to rearrange the statement of sources and uses of funds in Table 4.1 into the format shown in Table 4.2. This format is often called the **funds-flow statement**, the format found in the statement of changes in financial position in company financial statements. It categorizes the flow of funds according to major activities including cash flow from operations, financing, and investments, as well as any extraordinary items. These flows are then summarized in terms of their effect on the firm's cash position. Notice that the three major categories correspond to three main functional areas of financial management as described in Chapter 1: day-to-day management, long-term financing decisions, and long-term investment decisions.[1]

TABLE 4.2

Superior Enterprises Funds-Flow Statement, Fiscal 2000 (in 000s)

Opening balance of cash and marketable securities		$3,000
OPERATIONS		
Funds derived from		
Income earned		$ 16,000
Depreciation		6,000
Increase in accounts payable		9,000
Increase in salaries payable		1,000
Increase in income tax payable		3,000
Decrease in inventories		6,000
	Total	$ 41,000
Funds used for		
Increase in accounts receivable		$ 14,000
Increase in notes receivable		1,000
Increase in prepaid advertising		1,000
Increase in goodwill		1,000
Decrease in short-term notes payable		9,000
Decrease in dividends payable		1,000
	Total	$ 27,000
Net flow from operations		$ 14,000

---

[1] The funds-flow statement shown in Table 4.2 is computed using the "indirect" method, which is the method most commonly used in accounting statements. This approach estimates operating cash flow by starting with income, making adjustments to reflect non-cash items reflected in the income figure (such as depreciation), and making the necessary adjustments to reflect changes in the values of balance sheet items. These statements can also be prepared using the "direct" method. This method estimates operating cash flow starting with sales, which are adjusted to reflect "cash sales" and then moving on to attempt to estimate expenses on a cash basis. The financing and investing cash flows will be estimated in the same manner under either approach. We do not present an example of this approach here to avoid confusion for the reader.

LONG-TERM FINANCING

Funds derived from

  Increase in long-term debt $ 35,000

Funds used for

  Dividends paid   5,000

    Net flow from financing $ 30,000

INVESTMENTS

Funds derived from

  Decrease in investments $ 4,000

Funds used for

  Gross additions to fixed assets

    Land $ 2,000

    Buildings   35,000

    Equipment   9,000

        Total $ 46,000

    Net flow from investments $ (42,000)

    Total net flow $ 2,000

Closing balance of cash and marketable securities
(opening balance + net flow) $ 5,000

The emphasis on cash (including near-cash items such as marketable securities) and cash flows in the funds-flow statement was brought about in part by increased concerns about solvency and liquidity that were a consequence of the difficult economic conditions of the early 1980s. Although the income statement continues to be the main basis for evaluating normal operating performance, the funds-flow statement with its emphasis on cash flows has become a primary source of information for establishing liquidity. For example, bankers and debt-rating agencies use the funds statement extensively in assessing a firm's ability to meet obligations, relating items such as net funds provided by operations to debt-servicing commitments. The report below includes excerpts from the Online Women's Business Center website that indicate the importance of the cash flow (or funds-flow) statements to businesses. They state that, "without your cash flow statement, you will have an incomplete picture of your business."

■ *Finance in the News*

Preparing a Cash Flow Statement

The cash flow statement shows cash inflows (where the money came from) and outflows (where the money went) over a particular time period. It has three major components: **operations**, **investing**, and **financing**.

A cash flow statement is useful because it highlights some kinds of activities, such as substantial equipment purchases, increases in accounts receivable, and lump-sum debt payments, that an income statement does not. Your banker will want to see a cash flow statement before approving or extending a loan. In fact, without your cash flow statement, you will have an incomplete picture of your business.

One way to prepare a cash flow statement is to detail all the sources and uses of cash in your operations: cash revenues, purchases, salaries, rent, etc. But there is an easier method.

First, determine **operating** cash flow. Start with your net income and add back expenses, such as depreciation, that did not result in inflows or outflows of cash. Next, identify all the balance sheet accounts associated with your operations—trade receivables and payables, accrued expenses, prepaid expenses, and other current assets that are a part of day-to-day operations. For each one, determine the *change* in the account from the beginning to the end of the period.

Now divide the remaining balance sheet accounts into **investing** and **financing** activities. For each one, determine the change between the beginning and end of the period. Tally them up to create the other two sections of the cash flow statement.

Source: Online Women's Business Center website at http://www.onlinewbc.org/docs/finance/cashflow.wt (June 12, 2000). Reprinted with Permission.

Unlike the balance sheet, which represents the position of the firm at one point in time, the statements of changes in financial position provides insight into changes that have taken place over a given period. They thus provide a useful basis for evaluating past management decisions. For example, we may assess the firm's financing methods including the relative reliance on internal versus external sources, and for external sources, the proportions of equity and long- and short-term debt financing. We can then ask whether the financing methods employed were appropriate given the types of assets acquired. If, for example, new investments in plant and equipment were substantially financed through increases in accounts and notes payable and other short-term loans, we could become concerned about the future liquidity of the firm since short-term funds have been committed to finance long-term investments.

PRO FORMA FINANCIAL STATEMENTS　　4.3

In addition to reviewing a firm's past record, the financial officer or analyst will be interested in expected future performance. An important tool in this context is the projection of future balance sheets and income statements commonly called *pro forma* financial statements. Financial ratio and common-size analysis can be performed on these *pro forma* statements in the manner described in Chapter 3. Statements of projected sources and uses of funds or projected funds-flow statements can also be derived by comparing a *pro forma* balance sheet with the current one or with other *pro forma* statements.

In projecting financial statements, we begin by preparing an income statement for the period under consideration as anticipated retained earnings for the period are required to prepare a *pro forma* balance sheet. The balance sheet, in turn, is needed for undertaking a *pro forma* analysis of sources and uses of funds. Approaches employed in forecasting individual entries or accounts vary from simple historical projections to the use of sophisticated estimation techniques. Whatever approach is used, forecasting the future is one of the most difficult and challenging tasks facing the manager or the analyst particularly when longer time periods are involved, and any results derived have to be viewed as tentative and subject to revisions as new information becomes available.

The preparation of *pro forma* financial statements invariably starts with a forecast of sales or revenues as prepared by marketing personnel. This is perhaps the most crucial estimate, as most other variables depend on anticipated sales or revenues. The sales forecast can be derived by relying on an internal or an external approach or a combination of both. With internal forecasts, direct estimates concerning their particular product specialization are made by salespeople. Individual estimates are reviewed by the marketing manager, who then prepares a forecast of sales by product line and estimates overall sales for the period. In contrast, external forecasts start with an analysis of the general economic environment and of the particular industry under consideration. Once a forecast of industry sales has been made, the firm's market share is estimated by looking at competitive strategies. Finally, a forecast of the company's sales broken down by product lines is derived. Firms will often combine both internal and external forecasting, using managerial judgement in reconciling any differences that may arise.

Once a sales forecast has been completed, we relate other items in the financial statements—such as the cost of goods sold, inventories, and accounts receivable—to the projected sales figures and possibly to each other. Some entries may be estimated fairly accurately by simply taking an average historical proportion of sales. For example, if credit terms and hence payment patterns have remained unaltered, accounts receivable should be a reasonably constant proportion of sales. Relationships between sales and other items may be more complex. For instance, inventories may not be strictly proportional to sales since even with reduced sales, certain inventory levels are needed to operate efficiently. Nevertheless, the relationship may be assumed to be approximately linear. Regression analysis applied to historical data can sometimes be useful in establishing the nature of the underlying relationship.

Whereas long-term forecasts of current asset accounts typically are derived from aggregate projected sales as outlined, detailed schedules based on monthly sales forecasts are often prepared for short-term projections of one year or less. These projections are integral for the firm in determining short-term financing requirements and are usually required by prospective lenders. Such detailed breakdowns are particularly important when a firm's sales are seasonal because average annual figures may not be usable for the computation of current asset levels as of the particular date of the balance sheet.

Table 4.3 provides an example of a *pro forma* income statement. Sales for the year just ended were $8 million and are expected to increase to $10 million in the coming year. On the basis of this forecast, several major categories of costs are projected, specifically the cost of goods sold, selling and administrative expenses, and depreciation.

TABLE 4.3

Pro Forma *Income Statement for the Year Ended December 31, 2001 (in 000s)*

Sales		$10,000
Cost of goods sold	$6,900	
Selling and administrative expenses	800	
Depreciation	900	8,600
Earnings before interest and taxes		$ 1,400
Interest		600
Earnings before taxes		$ 800
Tax (@45%)		360
After-tax profit		$ 440
Dividends		140
Addition to retained earnings		$ 300

Often, a reasonable approximation for the cost of goods sold can be derived from gross operating margins in the past. Alternatively, for firms with more complex cost structures, detailed analysis of costs requires supporting cost accounting data and schedules concerning materials and direct labour costs, as well as anticipated inventory levels. Selling expenses are commonly based on a percentage of sales, and this may also be a reasonable approximation for general and administrative expenses, although fixed components in these costs often have to be recognized. Charges for depreciation are easily established from the book value of the firm's assets and the rates of depreciation to be applied. All of these costs are subtracted from projected revenues, which yields anticipated earnings before interest and taxes.

Earnings before interest and taxes reflect the profitability of the firm's operations before the deduction of financing charges. Traditionally, interest expenses could be predicted with a reasonable degree of accuracy, although the increasing incidence of variable interest rates on debt, coupled with volatile conditions in financial markets, now make such forecasts more challenging. Given taxable income and relatively stable tax rates, the derivation of after-tax earnings becomes relatively straightforward. For preparation of the *pro forma* balance sheet, we require the contribution to retained earnings forecasted for the period. Hence, the *pro forma* income statement also has to include projected dividend payments based on the firm's established dividend policies.

The current and *pro forma* balance sheets are reproduced in Table 4.4 below.

TABLE 4.4

Current and Pro Forma *Balance Sheets as of December 31, 2001 (in 000s)*

		End of current year		Dec. 31, 2001 (*pro forma*)
ASSETS				
Cash and marketable securities		$ 400		$ 200
Inventories		2,600		3,200
Accounts receivable		2,000		2,500
Total current assets		$ 5,000		$ 5,900
Plant and equipment	$7,000		$9,000	
Less: Accumulated depreciation	2,000		2,900	
Net plant and equipment		5,000		6,100
Total assets		$10,000		$12,000
LIABILITIES AND EQUITY				
Accounts payable		$ 1,500		$ 2,000
Bank loan		2,000		3,200
Total current liabilities		$ 3,500		$ 5,200
Long-term debt		2,000		2,000
Capital stock		1,000		1,000
Retained earnings		3,500		3,800
Total liabilities and equity		$10,000		$12,000

The anticipated 25 percent increase in sales from $8 million to $10 million may increase accounts receivable by the same percentage from $2 million to $2.5 million. Inventories may exhibit a linear relationship to sales, with the specific equation derived through regression analysis of past data.[2] Assume that for our example, we had found that inventories = $200,000 + (.3 × sales). With projected sales at $10 million inventory levels would be forecast at 200,000 + (.3 × 10,000,000) = $3,200,000. The value of plant and equipment is easily projected since plans for expansions are generally made well in advance and rates at which depreciation will be taken are known. Given the anticipated increase in sales, assume that the planned investment in new plant and equipment is $2 million. Assuming depreciation of $900,000 for the period, the ending balance becomes $6.1 million.

On the liability side, assume that the firm does not plan to raise new long-term funds externally so that the only change in this area of the balance sheet is given by the $300,000 in retained earnings as derived in the *pro forma* income statement. The firm anticipates that the most it can get in new bank loans is $1.2 million which would bring total outstanding bank loans to $3.2 million. To balance its projected accounts, the firm plans to draw more heavily on trade credit, perhaps foregoing some cash discounts. Accordingly, accounts payables are anticipated to increase by 33 percent to $2 million.

[2] Although a linear relationship between inventory levels and sales may provide a reasonable approximation for moderate fluctuations in sales, the general relationship could be more complex.

Given the completed *pro forma* balance sheet, a comparison with the current balance sheet enables us to prepare a *pro forma* statement of sources and uses of funds (shown in Table 4.5), and a funds-flow statement (shown in Table 4.6). Together with the other *pro forma* statements, these provide us with a basis for analysing the firm's projected operations. In our example, we could question the firm's plan to finance a significant portion of the investment in additional fixed assets from short-term sources. Should sales fall short of expectations, and with short-term borrowing pushed to the limit, the firm may have difficulty in meeting its obligations. Obviously, such planning statements are of vital importance because preventative or remedial action can be taken if undesirable developments are noted. Because *pro forma* presentations follow the same format as regular financial statements, ratio analysis and common-size comparisons are also possible, as mentioned above.

TABLE 4.5

Pro Forma *Statement of Sources and Uses of Funds for the Year Ended December 31, 2001 (in 000s)*

FUNDS DERIVED FROM

Decrease in cash and marketable securities	$ 200
Increase in accumulated depreciation	900
Increase in accounts payable	500
Increase in bank loans	1,200
Income earned	440
Total sources	$3,240

FUNDS USED FOR

Increase in inventories	$ 600
Increase in accounts receivable	500
Increase in plant and equipment	2,000
Dividends paid	140
Total uses	$3,240

TABLE 4.6

Pro Forma *Funds-Flow Statement for the Year Ended December 31, 2001 (in 000s)*

Opening balance of cash and marketable securities		$ 400

OPERATIONS

Funds derived from		
Income earned		$ 440
Depreciation		900
Increase in accounts payable		500
Increase in bank loans		1,200
	Total	$ 3,040

Funds used for			
Increase in inventories			$ 600
Increase in accounts receivable			500
		Total	$ 1,100
Net flow from operations			$ 1,940

LONG-TERM FINANCING

Funds used for	
Dividends paid	$ 140
Net flow from financing	$ (140)

INVESTMENTS

Funds used for	
Increase in gross plant and equipment	$ 2,000
Net flow from investments	$ (2,000)
Total net flow	$ (200)

Closing balance of cash and marketable securities	
(opening balance + total net flow)	$ 200

Our numerical example exhibits some patterns that are typical whenever there is a substantial growth in sales. Increasing sales are likely to force commensurate increases in various asset accounts such as inventories and receivables. If real growth is sustained, new investments in fixed assets may also be required. Therefore, a firm with increasing sales will have to find financing to fund such growth. Note that the projected increase need not be caused by increases in the physical volume of operations alone, but it may also reflect inflationary price-level changes that push up dollar sales. In fact, widespread inflation during the 1980s was a major factor that forced businesses into financial markets for additional funding. With erratic earnings, stock markets that often performed poorly, and long-term debt available only at record-high interest rates, we can understand why in the early 1980s firms drew heavily on short-term financing including trade credit with results quite similar to those portrayed in our example. The danger of this strategy became painfully evident during the subsequent recession.

The preparation of *pro forma* statements, which may extend over several years, can be tedious, but a variety of software packages is available to assist in this task. Such aids greatly reduce the time and costs of financial planning and make feasible much more thorough analyses than would otherwise be practical. For example, it becomes easy to perform sensitivity analysis by deriving various sets of *pro forma* statements for alternative forecasts of key variables. This enables management to explore the impact of alternative assumptions in projecting financial statements and to identify those factors that have the greatest impact on firm performance.

As a final word of caution, it should be noted that neither the computer nor quantitative models provide apparent solutions to the basic problem of forecasting in our volatile economic environment. Although we have tools that can assist in preparing forecasts and *pro formas*, there is no substitute for good judgement, and a significant amount of uncertainty invariably remains.

SUMMARY 4.4

1. Statements of changes in financial position can be prepared using either a source and uses format or an activity format, with both providing essentially equivalent information.

2. A statement of sources and uses of funds is derived by comparing the balance sheet of a firm at two different points in time. It provides information about a firm's investments over the period under consideration and how such investments were financed.

3. An activity format summarizes the various flows of funds in terms of their effect on the firm's cash position over a given time period. The resulting funds-flow statement, which is widely used by creditors, is particularly useful in highlighting the firm's liquidity position.

4. Any increase in an asset or decrease in a liability represents a use of funds. Similarly, any decrease in an asset or increase in a liability represents a source of funds.

5. Projected financial statements, also called *pro forma* statements, can be used as planning tools. In projecting financial statements, the forecast of sales or revenues is the basic forecast from which most other entries are derived.

QUESTIONS AND PROBLEMS

Questions for Discussion

1. In the context of funds-flow analysis, why does depreciation represent a source of funds?

2. Given inflationary growth in sales, what changes would you expect to note on a firm's balance sheet? How would such changes be reflected in a statement of sources and uses of funds?

3. Discuss the statement: "Carefully prepared *pro forma* statements reduce uncertainty."

4. Discuss the potential and limitations of regression analysis in relating projected balance sheet entries to the sales forecast.

5. How would you determine the overall planning horizon for a firm and the basic time unit (for example, yearly, quarterly, monthly) for which *pro forma* financial statements should be drawn up?

6. Funds-flow analysis may be defined in several ways, depending on the objective or approach of the analysis. In the narrowest sense, funds-flow statements simply reconcile cash balances from one period to another, and any transactions that do not

directly affect the cash account are excluded. In a somewhat broader context, funds-flow analysis concentrates on net working capital, or the excess of current assets over current liabilities. Changes in the non-current items of the balance sheet are analyzed only in terms of their combined effects on working capital.

7. Classify the following balance sheet changes as either sources or uses of funds:

   a) increase in equipment

   b) decrease in long-term debt

   c) increase in accumulated depreciation

   d) decrease in retained earnings

   e) decrease in accounts payable

   f) increase in accounts receivable

PROBLEM WITH SOLUTION

Problem

Prepare a sources and uses of funds statement and a funds-flow statement for the period of 1997–2000 for the Falling Timber Company, the financial statements of which were given in Problem 2 with Solution at the end of Chapter 3. Assume that cumulative net earnings for this period are $155.197 million.

Solution

Recalling that decreases in assets and increases in liabilities are sources of funds, and increases in assets and decreases in liabilities are uses of funds. By taking the difference of all accounts on the balance sheets, we draw up the following statement of balance sheet changes (in 000s).

FUNDS DERIVED FROM

Increase in bank loans	$ 2,314
Increase in notes payable	40,962
Increase in accounts payable and accrued liabilities	64,865
Increase in current portion of long-term debt	3,608
Increase in bonds and debentures	47,019
Increase in income tax allocations	29,102
Increase in common shares	27,903
Increase in accumulated depreciation	111,056
Income earned	155,197
Decrease in goodwill	1,920
Total sources	$483,946

FUNDS USED FOR

Increase in cash	$ 1,846
Increase in short-term investments and deposits	456
Increase in accounts receivable	37,222
Increase in inventory	109,655
Increase in prepaid expenses	2,373
Increase in investments	57,369
Increase in buildings and equipment	195,004
Increase in timber, less accumulated depletion	1,801
Increase in logging roads and land	18,156
Decrease in income tax payable	2,009
Dividends paid	58,055
Total uses	$483,946

Note that the increase in retained earnings of $97,142, which is derived by comparing the balance sheets, has been broken down into cumulative income earned of $155,197 with consequent dividend payments of $155,197 − 97,142 = $58,055$ during the years under consideration.

In summary, we see that the major uses of funds were increases in buildings and equipment, in inventories, investments in partly owned companies, and the payment of dividends. These uses of funds were primarily financed by earnings, depreciation, an increase in notes payable and accounts payable, and an increase in bonds and debentures.

Rearranging the above statements of sources and uses of funds, we obtain the funds-flow statement.

Opening balance of cash and marketable securities	$ 19,130

OPERATIONS

Funds derived from

Income earned	$155,197
Depreciation	111,056
Increase in accounts payable and accrued liabilities	64,865
Increase in bank loans	2,314
Increase in notes payable	40,962
Increase in current portion of long-term debt	3,608
	$378,002

Funds used for

Increase in accounts receivable	$37,222
Increase in inventories	109,655
Increase in prepaid expenses	2,373
Decrease in income tax payable	2,009
	$151,259
Net flow operations	$226,743

LONG-TERM FINANCING
   Funds derived from
      Increase in bonds and debentures $47,019
      Increase in income tax allocations   29,102
      Increase in common shares   27,903
                                             $104,024

   Funds used for
      Dividends paid   58,055
                                            $ 58,055
      Net flow from long-term financing $ 45,969

INVESTMENTS
   Funds derived from
      Decrease in goodwill   1,920
                                             $ 1,920
   Funds uses for
      Increase in investments $ 57,369
      Gross additions to fixed assets
         Buildings and equipment   195,004
         Logging roads and land   18,156
         Timber, less accumulated depletion   1,801
                                             $272,330
      Net outflow from investments $270,410
      Total net flow $ 2,302
Closing balance of cash and marketable securities
   (Opening balance + total net flow) $ 21,432

ADDITIONAL PROBLEMS

1. The current income statement and balance sheet for Antigua Ltd. are given as follows:

Income Statement

Sales		$9,000,000
Less: Cost of goods sold	$7,125,000	
Depreciation expense	375,000	
Selling and administration expenses	1,125,000	
Interest and debt expense	200,000	8,825,000
Income before taxes		$ 175,000
Less: Tax		70,000
Net income		$ 105,000

Balance Sheet

Cash	$ 112,500	Notes payable	$ 225,000
Marketable securities	50,000	Accounts payable	875,000
Accounts receivable	1,012,500	Other liabilities	450,000
Inventory	1,312,500	Long-term debt	2,625,000
Investments	231,250	Preferred shares	200,000
Other assets	1,425,000	Common shares	837,500
Plant and equipment $5,625,000		Retained earnings	2,306,250
Less: accum. depreciation 2,250,000			
Net pland and equipment	3,375,000		
	$7,518,750		$7,518,750

Prepare *pro forma* income statements and balance sheets for the next three years given the following predictions and information:

- Inflation is expected to increase dollar sales by 8 percent annually, while real sales growth will contribute 2 percent annually.

- Cost of goods sold, accounts receivable, inventories, and accounts payable are all expected to remain at a constant percentage of sales over the next three years.

- Selling and administrative expenses will grow at a rate that equals half the percentage increase in sales plus an expected fixed increase of $30,000 per year.

- Cash, investments, and preferred share accounts are expected to remain at current levels.

- $100,000 of 10 percent long-term debt will be issued in year 2, and the number of common shares outstanding will remain unchanged.

- Other assets will decrease by $200,000 in year 1.

- Plant and equipment purchases will be $200,000 in year 1, $100,000 in year 2, and $300,000 in year 3.

- $40,000 in dividends are to be distributed each year.

- Assets are depreciated at the current average rate over the next three years.

- Any excess funds are used first to reduce other liabilities, then notes payable. If any funds are left after these two liability accounts are reduced to zero, such surplus funds will be invested in additional marketable securities. Otherwise, no additions to the marketable securities account are contemplated.

2. You have been provided with the 2000 financial statements (reproduced below) and the following additional information (all figures are in 000s):

- The demand for XYZ's products is highly seasonal, but the firm employs level production because of its limited plant capacity and the need to reduce operating costs.

- Costs of goods sold are 70 percent of sales and are composed of materials purchased and wages. Estimated costs of goods sold for 2001 are $3,010. The value of goods produced each month is 3,010/12 = $250.83.

- Accounts payable are paid in the month following purchase and owing to level production, are constant at $125 per month.
- Wages are equal to the cost of goods sold less accounts payable, and for 2001, they are approximately $3,010 - (125 \times 12) = \$1,510$ or $126 per month.
- Operating expenses are $46 per month.
- Depreciation is taken on a straight-line basis at $525 per year.
- Accounts receivables are collected after 60 days, and bad debts are negligible.
- Monthly cash balances must not fall below $150. A short-term loan from the bank is expected to meet any cash needs.
- Taxes are levied at a rate of 50 percent and are paid or refunded each December.
- Long-term debt repayments of $100 and interest payments of $50 are made each June and December.
- Annual dividends of $15 are paid at the end of December.

Income Statement for the Year Ended December 31, 2000
(in 000s)

Sales	$4,149
Cost of goods sold	2,904
Gross profit	$1,245
Operating expenses	552
Depreciation	525
Income before interest and taxes	$ 168
Interest	100
Taxable income	$ 68
Income tax	34
Net income	$ 34

Balance Sheet as at December 31, 2000
(in 000s)

ASSETS		
Cash		$ 300
Accounts receivable		1,750
Inventory		310
Total current assets		$2,360
Plant and equipment	$10,500	
Less: Accumulated depreciation	3,900	
Net plant and equipment		6,600
Total assets		$8,960

LIABILITIES AND EQUITY

Accounts payable	$ 125
Notes payable	365
Accrued taxes	0
Current portion long-term debt	200
Total current liabilities	$ 690
Long-term debt	3,400
Common shares	1,800
Retained earnings	3,070
Total liabilities and equity	$8,960

Actual sales for 2000 (in 000s)

November	$820	December	$930

Projected sales for 2001 (in 000s)

January	$ 55	July	$ 80
February	55	August	550
March	55	September	690
April	55	October	830
May	60	November	850
June	60	December	960

(a) Prepare quarterly *pro forma* financial statements for 2001.

(b) Assume that sales during the second half of 2001 could drop 20 percent below fore-casts but that neither production nor purchases could be reduced. Prepare revised *pro forma* statements for the final two quarters of 2001. Why would such information be of interest to a bank manager reviewing XYZ Company's short-term loan request for 2001?

3. A firm had a book value of fixed assets of $25 million in 1999 and a book value of fixed assets in 2000 of $25 million. The 2000 income statement showed depreciation of $5 million. How much actual cash must the firm have spent on fixed assets during the year?

4. A company's income statement for last year is presented below:

Revenue	$10,000,000
Cost of goods sold	3,000,000
Administration expense	1,000,000
Depreciation	500,000
Earnings before Interest and Tax	5,500,000
Interest expense	1,500,000
Taxable income	4,000,000
Tax (@30%)	1,200,000
Net income	$ 2,800,000

Over the next five years, it is projected that the company's net operating margin will remain at 55 percent. Interest expense will remain unchanged, and the firm's tax rate will remain at 30 percent. Sales are forecast to grow at 10 percent per year.

    a) What is the total forecast percentage growth in sales over the five-year period?

    b) Forecast net income for each of the next five years.

    c) Calculate the total percentage growth in net income over the five-year period.

    d) Compare your answers to parts (a) and (c). What accounts for the difference?

6. Consider the following financial statements:

Balance Sheet

	1999	2000
	Assets	
	(in 000s)	
Current Assets:		
Cash	$1,500	$1,200
Accounts receivable	600	500
Inventory	1,000	1,300
Investments	2,000	1,800
Fixed Assets:		
Land	14,500	15,000
Buildings	30,000	32,000
Equipment	5,000	5,000
Accumulated depreciation	(3,000)	(3,500)
Total assets	$51,600	$53,300
	Liabilities	
	(in 000s)	
Current Liabilities:		
Accounts payable	$ 500	$ 300
Debt due within one year	200	0
Long-term debt	20,000	20,400
Deferred income tax	500	600
Shareholder's equity*	30,400	32,000
Total liabilities	$51,600	$53,300

*Note: The firm has issued no new equity.

Income Statement

	2000 (in 000s)
Net sales	$12,000.00
Cost of goods sold	5,500.00
Administration expense	1,120.00
Depreciation	500.00
Net operating profit	4,880.00
Income from investments	150.50
Interest expense	2,000.20
Earnings before tax	3,030.30
Tax	1,030.30
Net profit	$2,000.00

Prepare and comment on a sources and uses of funds statement for the firm for 2000.

6. Using the financial statements presented with Question (4), prepare a funds-flow statement for the firm.

7. You work for a venture capital firm that has been approached by a small technology company wanting to obtain financing. The firm is engaged principally in development of a new type of computer network card. The network card is in only the developmental stage right now, and further investment is needed to complete it and bring it to market. The firm has a few other products right now, but sales are small on these. The most recent income statement for the firm looks like this:

Sales	$2,000,000
Cost of goods sold	250,000
Salaries	1,500,000
Depreciation	100,000
Other developmental expenses	1,000,000
Earnings before interest and tax	(850,000)
Interest	0
Earnings before tax	(850,000)
Tax	0
Net income	(850,000)

The firm expects that sales on its existing product lines will increase at 5 percent per year (all sales are cash). Cost of goods sold will remain a constant percentage of sales. Salary and depreciation expenses are estimated to remain constant for the next five years. Developmental expenses (for the new network card) are expected to increase at a rate of 15 percent per year. The firm does not need to invest in any new fixed assets in the foreseeable future. The firm currently has no debt and no plans on obtaining debt financing in the future.

The current owners of the technology firm tell you that the company is losing money right now, but the new network card will be ready for market in five years. They need an investment of cash now in order to fund its development. Currently (at the end of the period described in the income statement above), they have $500,000, in their cash account (and no other current assets). For an investment of $2.5 million your venture capital company would receive a 50 percent stake in the tech firm. The current owners assure you that the new product will be ready in five years, and at that point, the profitability of the firm will increase dramatically.

Forecast the cash account for the tech firm over each of the next five years (you might find this easiest to do on a spreadsheet). How would you interpret this in terms of whether the venture capital firm should make the investment in this company?

1) During 1998, Nortel Networks, a major subsidiary of BCE, purchased the company Bay Networks. Nortel issued a large number of new shares in order to pay for this acquisition. As a result of this, BCE's ownership stake in Nortel was reduced to less than 50 percent. After the purchase, Nortel was no longer consolidated in the BCE financial statements. In effect, this means that in 1999 the revenues and expenses of Nortel are not included in the BCE statements, but rather BCE's share of Nortel's net profit is recorded under non-consolidated subsidiaries. For the 1998 numbers, Nortel's revenues and expenses are included in the BCE numbers. This makes the dollar figures presented for 1998 and 1999 hard to compare.

Prepare common-size income statements for BCE for 1998 and 1999. Comment on any major changes between those years and discuss whether this is a positive or negative trend for BCE. You may make the simplifying assumption that whether Nortel is consolidated or not would not affect the common-size statements.

2) Consider the following average ratios for firms in the Telephone and Utilities industry in 1999:

	Telephone and utilities average
Current ratio	0.97
Long term debt to equity	0.58
Times interest earned	2.20
Net operating margin	18.51%
Net profit margin	(20.19%)
Asset turnover	0.42
Return on assets	1.03%
Return on equity	(0.96%)

Source: *Financial Post Industry Reports*

Calculate these ratios for BCE for both 1998 and 1999. Based on these ratios, write a report commenting on BCE in terms of its liquidity, leverage, and profitability. Include a discussion of how BCE compares against its industry and any changes for BCE between 1998 and 1999.

Use the Du Pont system to break down BCE's return on equity into its three component parts. Use this to discuss the underlying reasons for any changes in the profitability of BCE.

For all of the above, whenever possible, link your comments to the discussion of the common-size income statements from part (1).

3) Construct a funds-flow statement for BCE for 1999.

4) Construct a pro forma income statement for BCE for 2000 under the following assumptions:

- BCE is pre-committed to buying $775 million worth of equipment next year. BCE will make no other purchases of fixed assets.
- Dividends will stay the same for both preferred and common shares.
- There will be no gains on sales of subsidiary companies.
- To estimate depreciation and amortization (D&A): Take 1999's D&A as a percentage of 1998's fixed assets plus goodwill. Use this percentage and the 1999 level of fixed assets plus goodwill to estimate depreciation in 2000
- There will be no restructuring charges.
- Operating revenues are projected to grow by 10 percent.
- Other operating expenses are projected to grow by 8 percent.
- All other income statement entries will stay at the same proportion of operating revenues as in 1999.

Based on 642.8 million common shares outstanding and the pro forma income statement, calculate the estimated earnings per share for BCE for 2000. (Your answer should be based on the earnings applicable to common shares, i.e., after preferred dividend payments.)

The closing price for 1999 for BCE was $131.15 per common share. Calculate the price-earnings ratio for the end of 1999 for BCE. Assuming the same price-earnings ratio will apply in 2000, what is your projected stock price for 2000?

If your forecast for revenue growth changes (all other assumptions remain the same) from 10 percent to 15 percent, what would be your projected stock price? What if revenues grow at 20 percent? What if revenues experience no growth? What if revenues decline by 10 percent? Re do the analysis, projecting a stock price under each case, and present a table of projected stock prices under the different forecasts. (Note: this part is easiest to perform by setting up the *pro forma* income statement on a spreadsheet.)

Valuation of Financial Securities

In this section of the book, we are concerned with the determination of economic value or valuation. First, we examine the concepts that underlie the valuation of financial assets by investors. We begin by reviewing compounding and discounting in Chapter 5. In Chapter 6, we apply these concepts to the valuation of debt and equity securities and discuss the determination of interest rates in financial markets. In Chapter 7, we develop the concept of risk and discuss how investors trade off risk against expected return and the importance of modern portfolio theory. In Chapter 8, we extend modern portfolio theory and discuss capital market theory, which provides investors with some approaches for estimating reasonable risk-adjusted rates of returns for common shares. This provides us with the basis for valuing risky securities such as common stocks. Chapter 9 concludes this section with a discussion of market efficiency and what this topic means to investors and corporate officers.

The Magic of Compound Interest

"According to legend, when Einstein was once asked, 'What is the most powerful force in the world?' he replied, 'Compound interest.'"

Dr. Allan Gould, author of several books on finance and investment, has a seemingly endless supply of anecdotes about compound growth, and he loves to tell them-in print, on speaking tours, and even in casual conversation.

"Then there's the one about the native Americans who sold the island of Manhattan to the British for $24. If they had invested that $24 in 1626, at 7.2% interest-about what you might get on a good bond, say-then by 1999 they would have had over $4 trillion. It's a theoretical example, of course, but it gets people's attention."

And that's important. Because compound growth affects so many areas of finance, both corporate and personal: equity returns, borrowing, lending, inflation, annuities-all are affected by the time value of money. And while the math involved in compounding is actually quite simple, it's hard for many people to really "wrap their minds around" the concept. "I tell them money doesn't grow linearly, but 'expotentially,'" says Dr. Gould."

Perhaps the most important lesson he tries to drive home is that small differences in the rate of return can have huge effects on profits over the long run. "If you invest a lump sum of $10,000 at 5% for 20 years,"

says Mr. Gould by way of illustration, "you'd end up with a little over $17,126. But if you invested it instead at 10%, at the end of the same 20 years you would find yourself with over $63,000! You've doubled your interest rate, but you've increased your return by 350%."

The concept of compounding is, of course, a two-edged sword; the same math that increases your investments astronomically if the rate of return rises slightly also increases the total amount you use to repay a long-term loan. But if you understand this, says Mr. Gould, you can use it to your advantage in your decisions.

For example, if your corporation, XYZ Widgets Inc., needs capital to expand the widget factory, you'll know to negotiate for the lowest possible interest rate; even a fraction of a percent can make a difference. You may also opt for flexible payments, so that if profits on widgets rise faster than expected, you can make additional payments early on, saving you a bundle over the long haul. It may even be worthwile to make more frequent, smaller payments.

"With careful planning, you can avoid the worst of the 'dark side' of compound interest, and make sure it works in your favour," whether you are a major corporation or a working person buying a home.

Economist John M. Keynes is credited with coining the phrase "the magic of compound interest." It isn't magic, of course, it's just math-but its effects are nonetheless amazing enough that they impressed even Einstein.

chapter 5

Time Value of Money

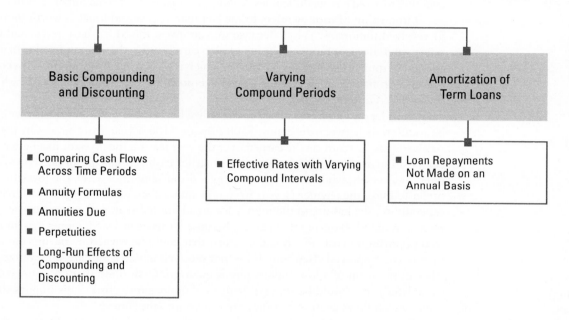

Learning Objectives

After studying this chapter, you should be able to:

1. *Describe how compound interest works.*
2. *Explain what is meant by the time value of money.*
3. *Define discounting and compare it to compounding.*
4. *Explain the difference between the nominal and the effective rate of interest.*
5. *Discuss how discounting and compounding affect effective yields and payment levels of term loans.*

5.1 INTRODUCTION

This chapter introduces the process of compounding and discounting, which forms the basis for valuation procedures in finance. It is one of the most important topics in the text since most of the subjects we address deal with economic valuation in one form or another. As a result, it is critical that students gain an understanding of compounding and discounting to avoid having difficulties dealing with many of the remaining topics in finance.

Time value of money refers to the fact that $1 received today is worth more than $1 received tomorrow. Why? Because we can invest the $1 we have today and earn a return on it. Because funds can be invested to earn returns, the economic value of a given amount of money depends on the time at which it is received or disbursed. This concept is crucial in finance since most financial decisions involve consideration of cash flows across different time periods.

Consider an investor wanting to maximize her wealth. Such an investor would not be indifferent between receiving $100 now or $100 a year from now. On the $100 received now, a return can be earned over the year leaving the investor in a better financial position at year end. In other words, earlier cash receipts are preferred over later ones. Conversely, when faced with making a disbursement of $100, the investor would prefer to make the payment a year from now rather than immediately. By deferring the expenditure, she has use of the money for an additional year, and, again, she can earn a return on the $100 during that period. Because it can be invested, money has an associated opportunity cost, which is the return that could be earned by having the money invested or employed elsewhere. If it is not received until a later date, an economic sacrifice in the form of a lost opportunity is incurred. Cash flows that do not occur until some later time should be charged with such opportunity costs. This implies that the value of cash flows decreases as they are moved into the future.

Because of the changing economic value of money as a function of time, cash flows that occur at different points in time cannot be compared through simple addition or subtraction; the time value of money has to be considered if we want economically meaningful results. The main purpose of compounding and discounting is to make money comparable across time periods by establishing a scale that translates future dollars into economically equivalent current dollars and vice versa.

This chapter deals with the mathematical foundations and the mechanics of compounding and discounting and the many applications of these processes.

5.2 BASIC COMPOUNDING AND DISCOUNTING

We begin this section by showing the ending wealth that an investor could have accumulated by the end of 1998 if he had invested $1,000 at the beginning of 1938. The figures assume all income from the investments was reinvested and that it earned the average annual compound return for the following asset categories:

1. T-bills
2. Bonds
3. Canadian stocks
4. U.S. stocks

The ending wealth figures depicted in Table 5.1 show that the investor would have accumulated the following amounts associated with the various investment categories:

1. T-bills—$23,253
2. Bonds—$37,720
3. Canadian stocks—$485,068
4. U.S. stocks—$2,260,413

   The results in Table 5.1 are somewhat shocking in several regards. First, it is hard to believe that $1,000 can grow to over $2 million even if left invested for 60 years (as is the case for U.S. stocks). Perhaps even more striking is the dramatic difference in ending wealth depending on where the $1,000 was invested. While the actual annual returns varied from year to year on all of these investments over this period, T-bills offered an average annual compound return of 5.2935 percent while the corresponding figures for bonds, Canadian stocks, and U.S. stocks were 6.1318 percent, 10.6699 percent, and 13.4976 percent respectively.[1] We observe that the average annual compound return for U.S. stocks was only about 3 percent higher than on Canadian stocks; however, the ending wealth for U.S. stocks is more than four times that for Canadian stocks. This dramatic difference demonstrates the nature of compounded returns, which is the essence of the time value of money. We now turn our attention to an examination of how compounding works.

TABLE 5.1

Cumulative Wealth ($000s)

	1938	1948	1958	1968	1978	1988	1998
Stocks	1,091	2,103	10,128	27,639	51.038	193,038	485,068
Bonds	1,056	1,434	1,623	2,084	3,691	10,480	37,720
T-bills	1,006	1,058	1,244	1,893	3,678	11,489	23,253
U.S. stocks	1,344	2,651	15,602	44,804	66,815	303,322	2,260,431

Source: Canadian Institute of Actuaries (CIA) website at www.actuaries.ca (June 14, 2000)

---

[1] Technically, these averages are geometric, which differ slightly from the more commonly referred to arithmetic averages. For more details regarding the distinction between the two, refer to W.S. Cleary and C. P. Jones, *Investments: Analysis and Management*, Canadian ed., (Toronto: John Wiley & Sons Canada Ltd., 1999), Chapter 6.

Given that we derive a number of formulas throughout this chapter, it is useful to define some standard notations. The following variables, most of which will be discussed in detail later on, will be used:

P	=	a current cash flow
F	=	a future cash flow
A	=	the amount of an annuity, where A is the amount paid at the end of each period for a given number of periods
i	=	the stated (or nominal) annual interest rate in percent
I	=	the dollar amount of interest per period
r	=	the effective period rate of return or yield in percent
n	=	the number of periods under consideration
m	=	the number of compounding periods per year
PV	=	the present value of a future cash flow(s)
FV	=	the future value of a cash flow(s)
$a_n r\%$	=	the discount factor for an annuity of n periods, discounted at r percent

Finally, before proceeding, we note that returns can be earned from sources other than interest—such as dividends and capital gains (or losses). We focus on interest returns in this chapter to simplify things. However, all of the results apply equally to the other forms of returns.

If an amount P is currently invested to earn interest at r percent, the interest payments are given as $I = rP$. Interest that is paid only on the amount originally invested but not on any interest that accrues subsequently is called **simple interest**. If simple interest is paid over n periods, total interest payments amount to nrP, and the sum originally invested will grow to:

$F = P + nrP$, or

(5.1) $F = P(1 + nr)$

EXAMPLE

SIMPLE INTEREST

A firm borrows $1,000 at 8 percent simple interest with all payments due at the end of four years. What amount must be repaid?

$F = P(1 + nr)$

$= 1,000[1 + (4)(.08)]$

$= 1,000(1.32)$

$= \$1,320$

Notice that this amount equals the original $1,000 plus four payments of $80.

Simple interest is not common in finance since interest earned in a given period is normally reinvested immediately to earn interest on itself. When interest is earned not just on the amount originally invested but also on any subsequently accrued interest, the process is called compound interest. Most applications in finance involve compound returns.

COMPOUND INTEREST

Assume that the prevailing interest rate at which borrowing and lending takes place is 8 percent compounded annually. A person invests $1,000. How would this investment grow over time?

The following table illustrates the basic process of compound growth and shows how the general formula for compound interest is derived.

Year	Amount at beginning of year	Interest earned	Amount at end of year
1	$1,000 = P$	80	$1,000(1+.08) = 1,080 = P(1+r)$
2	$1,080 = P(1+r)$	86.40	$1,080(1+.08) = 1,166.40 = P(1+r)^2$
3	$1,166.40 = P(1+r)^2$	93.31	$1,166.40(1+.08) = 1,259.71 = P(1+r)^3$
4	$1,259.71 = P(1+r)^3$	100.78	$1,259.71(1+.08) = 1,360.49 = P(1+r)^4$
n	$P(1+r)^{n-1}$	$P(1+r)^{n-1}(r)$	$P(1+r)^n$

The $1,000 invested at the beginning of year 1 earns interest of $.08 \times 1,000 = \$80$ during the first year so that the total wealth at the end of year 1 becomes $1,000+(.08 \times 1,000) = \$1,080$. Year 2 begins with an investment of $1,080 (original investment plus interest earned during the first year), and during the second year, interest of 8 percent will be paid on this amount. At the end of year 2, the total investment has grown to $1,080+(.08 \times 1,080) = \$1,166.40$. Year 3 begins with an investment of $1,166.40 to which interest again is applied and the process continues in the same manner.

Mathematically, the amount of interest earned during the first year is rP, and the value of principal plus interest at year end becomes:

$$F_1 = P + rP = P(1+r)$$

During the second year, interest is paid on this amount, and the ending value after two years is:

$$F_2 = F_1(1+r) = [P(1+r)](1+r) = P(1+r)^2$$

Similarly, we obtain:

$$F_3 = F_2(1+r) = P(1+r)^3$$

and generally, for the ending value after n years:

$$F_n = P(1+r)^n \tag{5.2}$$

Assume that a person is interested solely in maximizing his wealth. If the prevailing interest rate is 8 percent, such a person ought to be indifferent between receiving $1,000 today and receiving $1,360.49 four years hence since $1,000 received today could be invested immediately to grow to $1,360.49 by the end of year 4. Alternatively, an amount of $1,360.49 to be received in four years' time could be converted into $1,000 of immediately available cash by borrowing this amount today from a bank. At 8 percent annual interest, this debt would grow to $1,360.49 by the end of year 4, at which time one would use the receivable to pay off the bank. Similarly, the person ought to be indifferent between paying $1,000 now and $1,360.49 at the end of year 4. If the latter option is chosen, the $1,000 that does not have to be paid now can again be invested for the four years, and $1,360.49 will be available for payment at the end of year 4. We see that the process of compounding allows us to establish economic equivalence for different amounts of money across different time periods. In our example, $1,000 today is economically equivalent to $1,080 at the end of year 1, $1,259.71 at the end of year 3, or $1,360.49 at the end of year 4 based on an 8 percent discount rate.

Before leaving our example to explore more general economic implications, we introduce some basic definitions and terminology. In the context of the above example:

- $1,360.49 is called the **future value** at the end of year 4 of $1,000 received today if the annual interest rate is 8 percent.
- $1,000 is called the **present value** in today's dollars of $1,360.49 received at the end of year 4 if the annual interest rate is 8 percent.
- 8 percent is the **effective annual interest rate**, or **effective yield**, or **internal rate of return** if $1,000 invested today grows to $1,360 at the end of year 4.

Equation 5.2 represents the basic compounding relationship that is the basis for determining economically equivalent future and present values of cash flows. It depicts the relationship between present value, future value, and interest rates (or rates of return). If we know the present value of a cash flow and want to calculate its economically equivalent future value, we use the process of compounding where:

(5.3) $FV = PV(1+r)^n$

Similarly, if we know the future value or cash flow and want to calculate its economically equivalent present value, we rearrange Equation 5.3 to obtain:

(5.4) $PV = FV \times \dfrac{1}{(1+r)^n}$

This process of converting future values of cash flows into their present value equivalents is called **discounting**, and Equation 5.4 depicts the basic discounting relationship.

The factor $(1+r)^n$ in Equation 5.3 is called the **compound factor** and is calculated for several interest rates and time periods in Table 1 in Appendix III at the end of the textbook. Its reciprocal $1/(1+r)^n$, which is used in Equation 5.4, is called the **discount factor**, and some values assumed by this factor are provided in Table 3 in Appendix III at the end of the book. Pursuing our previous example, the compound factor for $n=4$, $r=8$ percent is found in Table 1 to be 1.360. The corresponding discount factor is given in Table 3 as 0.735 where $.735 = 1/1.360$. The tables for compounding and discounting are rounded to three decimal places, and because of this, results derived with a calculator may differ slightly from those in the tables.

Throughout this chapter, we derive our results using the equations above and a calculator as opposed to relying solely on the figures provided in the tables. We do so because we feel it is important for students to know how to perform the actual calculations using the equations and a calculator rather than using the tables alone. This is because the tables include the factors for only interest rates that correspond to round numbers such as 8 percent. In reality, one must deal with odd rates such as 8.12 percent. On the other hand, the tables do speed up our calculations in certain circumstances, and they also provide students with a means of checking their calculations for these compound and discount factors. For example, if you used your calculator to determine the four-year compound factor for 8.12 percent and obtained an answer of 1.23678, you could immediately recognize that you made a calculation error. This is obvious because the four-year compound factor for 8 percent is 1.360, and the factor for 8.12 must be greater.

In general, we see that the basic equations of compound interest contain four variables: PV, FV, r, and n. Clearly, if we know the values for any three of these variables, we can derive the fourth. Most business calculators have one key for each of these four basic variables, and if any three values are keyed in, the resulting value of the fourth will be computed.

DETERMINING THE RATE OF RETURN

EXAMPLE

An investment of $500 today will grow to $1,500 at the end of 10 years. What is the effective annual interest rate at which compounding takes place?

Given that $PV=\$500$, $FV=\$1,500$, and $n=10$ years, we can derive the value of the compound factor $(1+r)^n$. We have:

$$500(1+r)^{10}=1.500$$

$$(1+r)^{10}=\frac{1,500}{500}=3$$

Using a financial calculator, we can determine that:

$$r=11.612\%$$

We could have also solved for r in the following manner:
Since $(1+r)^{10}=3.0$, we can put both sides of the equation to the power of 1/10 without changing the equality:

$$(1+r)=(3.0)^{\frac{1}{10}}=(3.0)^{0.10}=1.11612,$$

so, $r=1.11612-1=0.11612$ or 11.612%

Alternatively, we could use an approximation technique referred to as linear interpolation. Searching Table 1 in Appendix III at the back of the book in the row for $n=10$, we find the entry with a value as close to 3 as possible. It is easy to see that compound factors increase continuously with increasing r. Given compound factors of 2.839 and 3.106 for $r=11$ and 12 percent, the effective interest rate must be between 11 and 12 percent. We can obtain a better approximation through linear interpolation as follows:

$$\begin{bmatrix} \text{at } 11\% & 2.839 \\ \text{at } r\% & 3 \\ \text{at } 12\% & 3.106 \end{bmatrix}$$

We find r by setting

$$\frac{r-11}{12-11} = \frac{3-2.839}{3.106-2.839}$$

$$\frac{r-11}{1} = \frac{0.161}{0.267} = 0.603$$

so, $r = 11.603\%$

This is close to the exact solution (11.612%) on a calculator obtained above.

Comparing Cash Flows Across Time Periods

The discussion above shows how compounding and discounting allows us to make valid economic comparisons of cash flows that occur at different points in time. Through compounding, we can shift any given cash flow forward in time, while discounting allows us to move any future cash flow back toward the present. However, the examples above deal with only one future cash flow and one present cash flow. What if we have several cash flows occurring through time that we wish to compare or determine present or future values for them? This is the case for the example included in the report below, which includes excerpts from an article in the *National Post*. One of the examples described in this article demonstrates the power of the time value of money. It shows that a 22-year-old would have accumulated the same amount upon retirement if he or she invested $2,000 per year for six years and then ceased all contributions as if he or she had waited six years then contributed $2,000 per year until age 65—assuming a 12 percent compound annual return. This is a very eye-opening example to many young investors!

In order to determine the present and future values associated with multiple cash flows that are received or paid through time, we follow the process described below:

1. Choose a particular point in time as the basis for economic comparison.
2. Shift all cash flows that occur at different times into economically equivalent amounts at the chosen point in time through compounding or discounting.
3. Add or subtract all of these equivalent cash flows to obtain a net total.

The time selected as the basis for economic comparison is essentially arbitrary. In most cases, one brings all future cash flows back to the present through discounting to derive an overall net present value. This figure is easy to interpret economically since it represents the current dollar amount that is equivalent to the set of cash flows under consideration.

■ *Finance in the News*

Early Investing Pays Off Big Time

Any financial adviser will tell you that it is best to start saving early to take advantage of the accumulative effects of compounding interest. The earlier you start to save, the larger the accumulation will be as years go by. As Canadian investment authority Gordon Pape advises, the sooner you start, the greater the accumulations because "the greatest growth takes place in the later years." He gives a startling example that someone who opens up an RRSP in his or her early twenties and then stops investing at age 35 will end up with more money in his or her RRSP at age 65 than another person who waited until 35 and contributed every year for the next 30 years.

Geoff Anselmo acknowledges the difficulty in getting the "invest early" message to young people and illustrates it with the story of twins, Bill and Linda. Bill starts investing $2,000 per year at age 22 and after six years, stops. Sister Linda waits until she is 28 and invests the same amount at the same return (12 percent). Despite the fact that Linda continues to invest for 38 years and Bill for only six, and that she invested $76,000 and he only $12,000, they both end up with $1.4 million at age 65. This story demonstrates the importance of early investing, says Anselmo.

Source: "Get Head Start on RRSP: It Pays to Begin Saving for Retirement in Your 20s," by David Howell, *Financial Post* (***National Post***), May 20, 1999, page D4. "Reprinted with Permission" (National Post)

We illustrate these concepts by calculating the economic value of annuities. An **annuity** is a series of payments over a specified period that are for the *same amount* and are paid at the *same interval* and where the *same discount rate* is applicable to all cash flows. For ordinary annuities, the payments are assumed to take place at the end of each period. Such sequential payments occur frequently in finance. Examples include periodic interest payments on debt and repayments on loans such as mortgages that are made in equal instalments at regular intervals.

FUTURE VALUE OF AN ANNUITY

EXAMPLE

Assume that an amount of $A=\$1,000$ will be received at the end of each year for $n=4$ years. The prevailing interest rate at which the proceeds can be invested is $r=10$ percent. We want to calculate the terminal wealth that would accumulate by the end of the fourth year.

In computing the terminal wealth, we have chosen the end of year 4 as the time for the comparison and aggregation of cash flows. Through compounding, we must first transform each individual $1,000 cash flow into an equivalent value at the end of year 4 and then total these amounts. The first payment of $1,000 will earn three years of compound interest by the end of the fourth year, yielding $A(1+r)^3=1,000(1+0.10)^3=\$1,331$. Similarly, the payment at year 2 will have grown to $A(1+r)^2=1,000(1+0.10)^2=\$1,210$, the payment in the third year to $1,000(1+0.10)^1=\$1,100$, with the fourth payment remaining at $1,000. It is often useful to visualize problems of this kind through a simple graph as follows:

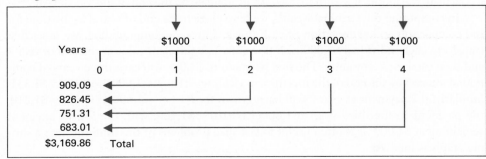

Numerically, the total future value of this four-year annuity is given as:

$$FV = A(1+r)^3 + A(1+r)^2 + A(1+r) + A$$
$$= \$1,000(1.331 + 1.210 + 1.100 + 1)$$
$$= \$1,000(4.641) = \$4,641$$

If each of the annual \$1,000 cash flows is invested upon receipt at the prevailing interest rate of 10 percent, a total wealth of \$4,641 will accumulate by the end of year 4. Hence, one should be indifferent between receiving a four-year annuity of \$1,000 or receiving \$4,641 at the end of year 4; in an economic sense, the two are equivalent.

EXAMPLE

PRESENT VALUE OF AN ANNUITY

Find the economically equivalent present value of the annuity in the example above.

We have now chosen the present as the point for comparison and aggregation of cash flows. By converting each individual flow to a current equivalent through discounting, the total present value becomes:

$$PV = A \times \frac{1}{(1+r)^4} + A \times \frac{1}{(1+r)^3} + A \times \frac{1}{(1+r)^2} + A \times \frac{1}{(1+r)}$$

$$= \$1,000(0.68301 + 0.75131 + 0.82645 + 0.90909)$$
$$= \$1,000(3.16986) = \$3,169.86$$

The graphical illustration is as follows:

If money can be invested at 10 percent, we should be indifferent between receiving $3,169.86 today and an annuity of $1,000 over four years. Note also the economic equivalence of the present value of $3,169.86 and the future value of $4,641. We have:

$4{,}641=3{,}169.86(1+0.10)^4=3{,}169.86(1.4641)=\$4{,}640.99$. The minor difference is due to rounding.

This means that $3,169.86 invested today at 10 percent would yield the terminal wealth of $4,641 after four years of annual compounding as computed above.

Annuity Formulas

Because of the frequency with which annuities occur in finance, special formulas have been developed to simplify the compounding and discounting of such flows.

Based on the above example, it is easy to see that the future value of an annuity over n years at the end of year n is given as:

$$FV=A(1+r)^{n-1}+A(1+r)^{n-2}+\ldots+A(1+r)+A \qquad (5.5)$$

When n is large, it would be tedious to work with the individual compound factors. Fortunately, it is easy to transform this formula into an equivalent but shorter and more convenient form, which is shown in Equation 5.6.[2]

$$FV=A\left[\frac{(1+r)^n-1}{r}\right] \qquad (5.6)$$

The factor $[(1+r)^n-1]/r$ is referred to as the future value annuity factor. It is shown in Table 2 in Appendix III at the end of the textbook, and it simply equals the sum of the individual compound factors from Table 1, which we would have to apply if we were using Equation 5.5. Pursuing the above numerical example, for $r=10\%$ and $n=4$ years, we find that the compound annuity factor equals 4.641 as shown below. This equals the sum of the compound factors from $n=0$ to $n=3$, which correspond to the ones used to determine the future value of this annuity in the calculations shown above.

$$FV=A\left[\frac{(1+r)^n-1}{r}\right]=1{,}000\left[\frac{(1+.10)^4-1}{0.10}\right]=1{,}000\left[\frac{1.4641-1}{0.10}\right]=1{,}000\,[4.641]=\$4{,}641$$

Similarly, we can express the present value of an annuity as:

$$PV=A\times\frac{1}{(1+r)^1}+A\times\frac{1}{(1+r)^2}+\ldots+A\times\frac{1}{(1+r)^n} \qquad (5.7)$$

---

[2] Multiplying both sides of Equation 5.5 by $(1+r)$ results in:
$(1+r)FV=A(1+r)^n+A(1+r)^{n-1}+\ldots+A(1+r)$
If we subtract Equation 5.5 from this equation, we obtain:
$rFV=A(1+r)^n-A$
which can be rearranged to produce Equation 5.6: $FV=A\left[\frac{(1+r)^n-1}{r}\right]$

It is straightforward to show that this expression is equivalent to the following equation:[3]

$$(5.8) \quad PV = A \left[\frac{1 - \frac{1}{(1+r)^n}}{r} \right]$$

The discount factor for an annuity (or the present value annuity factor) of n years at r percent is often designated by the symbol $(a_n r\%) = [1 - (1+r)^{-n}]/r$. Values for given interest rates and time periods are reported in Table 4 in the Appendix at the end of the book. This factor equals the sum of the appropriate individual discount factors. For the numerical example above, we find that $(a_4 10\%) = 3.16987$ as shown below. This corresponds to the sum of the discount factors from $n=1$ to $n=4$ that were used to solve the problem above (with a slight difference due to rounding).

$$PV = A \left[\frac{1 - \frac{1}{(1+r)^n}}{r} \right] = 1,000 \left[\frac{1 - \frac{1}{(1+0.10)^4}}{0.10} \right] = 1,000 \left[\frac{1 - 0.683013}{0.10} \right] = 1,000 [3.16987] = \$3,169.87$$

Business calculators normally have a separate annuity key, and, upon entering the appropriate values for r, n, and A, they will compute present and future values of annuities directly.

EXAMPLE

DETERMINING ANNUITY PAYMENTS

A person plans to retire in 10 years and, through annual savings, wants to build her wealth to $100,000 by that time. Money can be invested to yield interest of 14 percent per year. How much will she have to set aside at the end of each of the next 10 years in order to achieve her objective?

We use Equation 5.6, with $FV = \$100,000$, $n=10$ years, and $r=14\%$:

$$100,000 = A \left[\frac{(1+.14)^{10} - 1}{0.14} \right] = A \left[\frac{3.70722 - 1}{0.14} \right] = A[19.3373]$$

So, $100,000 = A \times 19.3373$

and, $A = \dfrac{100,000}{19.3373} = \$5,171.35$

Therefore, the person will have to save $5,171.35 each year.

The present value of that annuity can be calculated as:

$$PV = 5,171.35 \left[\frac{1 - \frac{1}{(1+.14)^{10}}}{0.14} \right] = 5,171.35 \left[\frac{1 - 0.26974}{0.14} \right] = 5,171.35 [5.21612] = \$26,974.38$$

---

[3] This can be derived by applying the technique shown in Footnote 2, namely multiplying both sides of Equation 5.7 by $(1+r)$ and then subtracting the second equation from Equation 5.7.

Note that we would have obtained the same value from:

$$PV = 100,000 \times \frac{1}{(1+.14)^{10}} = 100,000 \times .2697438 = \$26,974.38$$

If a person wants to accumulate \$100,000 by the end of year 10, she can either invest a lump sum of \$26,974.38 immediately or set aside \$5,171.35 at the end of each of the next 10 years. At an effective annual interest rate of 14 percent, all three quantities are of equal economic value: the annuity of \$5,171.35, the current amount of \$26,974.38, and the future wealth of \$100,000.

Annuities Due

Sometimes the payments of an annuity are made at the beginning of each year, for example, with leasing arrangements. Such annuities are often called **annuities due** (as opposed to the ordinary annuities discussed above). Calculators typically have a separate function key that allows direct computation of present and future values for an annuity due. Alternatively, the annuity formulas are easily modified, and the tables may still be used. In order to derive the future and present value factors for such annuities, we need only to multiply the future value and present value annuity factors by $(1+r)$ to shift them by one period.

FUTURE AND PRESENT VALUE OF AN ANNUITY DUE

EXAMPLE

Pursuing the previous example, assume that the person sets aside \$5,171.35 for investment at the *beginning* of each year instead of at year end. The ordinary annuity (payment at the end of each period) has been transformed into an annuity due (payment at the beginning of each period) with all cash flows shifted forward by one period. Hence, one additional compounding period has to be applied to derive its future value:

$$FV = A \left[\frac{(1+r)^{n-1}}{r} \right] (1tr)$$

$$FV = 5,171.35 \left[\frac{(1+.14)^{10}-1}{0.14} \right] (1.14) = [100,000](1.14) = \$114,000$$

Alternatively, one less discounting period has to be applied to compute the present value, which again is achieved by multiplying the normal present value annuity factor by $(1+r)$. We have:

$$PV = A \left[\frac{1 - \frac{1}{(1+r)^n}}{r} \right] (1+r) = 5,171.35 \left[\frac{1 - \frac{1}{(1+.14)^{10}}}{0.14} \right] (1+.14) = [26,974.38](1.14) = \$30,750.79$$

Because of the additional compounding period that is gained through the earlier payments, both the present and the future values increase by the factor $(1+r) = 1.14$. The fact that the future value is higher is intuitive if you make the same dollar contributions but make them earlier, there is more time for returns to accumulate. Similarly, it makes sense that the present value of annuities due will exceed those of corresponding ordinary annuities since they would be more attractive to investors who would prefer to receive their payments sooner and would therefore pay more for them.

Before proceeding to the next topic, we conclude with the comprehensive example below.

EXAMPLE

COMPREHENSIVE REVIEW

(a) Determine the present value of $1,000 invested at year end for the next four years and $2,000 (at year end) for years 5 to 7 assuming a 10 percent effective annual rate of return.

(b) How much will you have accumulated at the end of seven years based on these payments?

(c) Suppose you need $15,000 at the end of seven years and can invest only $1,000 per year for years 1 through 4 (as above). How much will the payments in years 5 through 7 have to be assuming they are all for equal amounts?

Solutions:

(a) We can view this problem in several ways. We could simply discount all seven cash flows back to the present using the 10 percent discount rate. Alternatively, we could view the cash flows as consisting of two separate annuities: a four-year annuity with payments of $1,000 (which we denote as $A1$), followed by a three-year annuity with payments of $2,000 ($A2$). The second annuity does not start until four years in the future, which means we must discount the present value of this annuity back four years. Following this approach, we obtain the following solution:

$$PV(A1) = 1,000 \left[\frac{1 - \frac{1}{(1.10)^4}}{.10} \right] = 1,000(3.16987) = \$3,169.87$$

$$PV(A2) = 2,000 \left[\frac{1 - \frac{1}{(1.10)^3}}{.10} \right] \left[\frac{1}{(1.10)^4} \right] = 2,000(2.48685)(0.68301) = \$3,397.09$$

So, $PV(total) = PV(A1) + PV(A2) = 3,169.87 + 3,397.09 = \$6,566.96$

(b) This is easily solved by recognizing that the present value determined in part (a) has converted all of the cash flows into one economic equivalent. This amount can be compounded to determine the future value at the end of seven years:

$FV_7 = 6,566.96(1.10)^7 = 6,566.96(1.94872) = \$12,797.17$

(c) The problem becomes more complicated here. If you need $15,000 by the end of year 7, the deposits outlined above would be insufficient since the future value of these payments is $12,797.17 according to the solution to (b). Since you can invest only $1,000 in years 1 through 4, the payments in years 5 through 7 must be increased. In fact, the amount of these payments is what we must determine. There are many ways to approach this problem. The method we demonstrate determines the future value of the first four payments (A1) and then subtracts this amount from $15,000 to determine the amount that must be accumulated through the last three payments (A2). Then we estimate the amount of these payments.

$$FV_7(A1)=3,169.87(1.10)^7=3,169.87(1.94872)=\$6,177.18,$$

so, $FV_7(A2)$ *must* $=15,000-6,177.18=8,822.82$

so, $A=\dfrac{8,822.82}{\left[\dfrac{(1.10)^3-1}{0.10}\right]}=\dfrac{8,822.82}{3.311}=\$2,664.70$

Therefore, the required year-end payments in years 4 through 7 are $2,664.70.

Perpetuities

Situations exist in which, at least theoretically, an annuity is to be paid in perpetuity. These cash flow streams are commonly referred to as perpetuities. Under such circumstances, it is not meaningful to talk about a terminal value. However, the present value can still be computed. As n becomes very large, $1/(1+r)^n$ approaches zero and the present value annuity factor in Equation 5.8 reduces to $1/r$. Thus, for perpetuities, Equation 5.8 becomes:

$$PV=A/r \qquad (5.9)$$

This simple expression also provides a convenient approximation for the present value of long-term annuities.

PRESENT VALUE OF A PERPETUITY

A contract promises annual payments of $1,000 in perpetuity. The time value of money is 12 percent. How much should we be willing to pay for this contract?
The present value of the contract is:

$$PV=\frac{A}{r}=\frac{1,000}{.12}=\$8,333.33$$

and this is the amount we should be willing to pay.

Using Equation 5.8, we find that the value of a 30-year contract would be:

$$PV=1,000\left[\frac{1-\dfrac{1}{(1.12)^{30}}}{0.12}\right]=1,000\,[8.05518]=\$8,055.12$$

This shows that the present value of all payments received after year 30 (from year 31 to infinity) is only ($8,333.33 − $8,055.12) − $278.21.

Similarly, the value of a 100-year contract would be:

$PV = \$8,333.23$

This demonstrates that the present value of all payments received after year 100 is a mere 10 cents, which implies that a 100-year annuity and a perpetual annuity are essentially equivalent. This is because discounting reduces the present value of payments more the further we move into the future so that very distant payments in the annuity have very little effect on its present value.

Long-Run Effects of Compounding and Discounting

An illustration of the long-run effects of compounding was provided in Table 5.1, which showed how much $1,000 would grow to after a certain number of years of compounding at the historical rates of return associated with several asset categories over the 1938–98 period. Table 5.1 illustrates that in spite of modest initial increases in cumulative value, compounding over long periods of time, even at low rates, leads to explosive growth. This is because the compound factor $(1+r)^n$ is a function that grows exponentially with increasing n. For example, after 31 years (by the end of 1968), $1,000 invested in T-bills would have grown to $1,893, but after 61 years, it would have grown to $23,253. At higher rates of return, this growth is accentuated as shown by the accumulated wealth associated with an investment in U.S. stocks. In particular, this amount

P E R S P E C T I V E S

Corporate Manager

The converse of the fact that very distant cash flows have little impact on the economic value of an investment in today's dollars is that the cash flows to be received in the near future have a large impact on the values of such investments. This implies that managers who use discounted cash flow approaches to evaluate long-term investments should take every effort to make short-term cash flow projections as accurate as possible. It also suggests that simplifying assumptions about very distant cash flows is reasonable since these assumptions should have little impact on the final results of the analysis.

Investor

Table 5.1 clearly demonstrates to the average investor that the benefits associated with earning compound returns are magnified as time passes. This shows the importance of starting to invest as early as possible, which was the focus of the discussion in the report earlier in this chapter.

would have grown to a "mere" $44,804 after 31 years and to an astounding $2.26 million after 61 years—quite a dramatic difference!

Given that discounting is just the reciprocal of compounding, it is easy to see why cash flows that occur in the distant future will have insignificant present values. Applying the reciprocals of the figures given in Figure 5.1, we can see that the present value of $2.26 million received at the end of 61 years equals $1,000 using a discount rate of 13.5 percent. It will be important to bear this in mind when we discuss the economic evaluation of long-term investments in Part Four of this text.

VARYING COMPOUND PERIODS   5.3

Clearly, there is no reason why compounding has to take place on an annual basis. Although yearly compounding is prevalent, any other time period can be chosen. The underlying process and its mechanics are not affected by the choice of the base period. However, we must ensure that the interest or discount rate applied is appropriate for the particular period chosen. If we define n as the number of compound periods and r as the interest rate per compound period, all of the formulas for compounding and discounting derived in the previous section remain unaltered.

QUARTERLY COMPOUNDING

EXAMPLE

Assume that compounding takes place quarterly, and the effective quarterly interest rate is 3 percent. If $100 is invested today, what will it grow to by the end of year 1 and by the end of year 3? We have:

$$FV = PV(1+r)^n$$

For one year, $n=4$, and

$$FV = 100(1+.03)^4$$

$$= 100 \times 1.1255 = \$112.55$$

Similarly, for three years, $n=12$, and

$$FV = 100(1+.03)^{12} = \$142.58$$

Given any compounding period, it is possible to compute an equivalent effective annual interest rate by calculating the value to which $1 will grow over a period of one year. Looking at the one-year figure of $112.55, we see that quarterly compounding at 3 percent is equivalent to annual compounding at approximately 12.55 percent. Note that this effective annual rate of 12.55 percent exceeds the rate that we would have obtained by simply multiplying the quarterly rate of 3 percent by 4. This is so because interest earned during the early quarters is immediately reinvested and will itself earn a return before year end.

Assume now that we want to calculate the present value of $500 received at the end of five years. With $n=20$, we have:

$$PV = FV \times \frac{1}{(1+r)^n} = 500 \times \frac{1}{(1+.03)^{20}} = 500 \times \frac{1}{1.8061} = 500 \times 0.55368 = \$276.84$$

We would have obtained the same result if we had discounted on a yearly basis at the effective annual rate of 12.55 percent. That is:

$$PV = 500 \times \frac{1}{(1+.03)^{20}} = 500 \times \frac{1}{(1+.1255)^5} = 500 \times \frac{1}{1.8060} = 500 \times 0.55371 = \$276.86$$

(The difference is due to rounding.)

This relationship between effective rates and compounding intervals is important because financial institutions often state neither the interest rate per compound period nor the equivalent effective annual interest rate when compounding takes place more than once a year. Rather, it is customary to state a nominal (or quoted) annual interest rate, which is simply given as the interest rate per compound period multiplied by the number of compound periods per year. In the above example, we would have stated that a savings account offers interest at 12 percent compounded quarterly. This means that an interest rate of 12/4=3 percent will be applied and compounded on a quarterly basis. As we saw, this translates into an effective annual interest rate of 12.55 percent.

As a result of this convention, it is useful to provide a general formula that determines the effective annual rate of return for any compounding interval. Defining i as the nominal interest rate (quoted as an annual rate) and m as the number of annual compound periods per year, we can determine the effective annual interest rate (r_{annual}) as follows:

(5.10) $$r_{annual} = (1+\frac{i}{m})^m - 1$$

Applying this equation gives us the result we obtained intuitively above as follows:

For i=12 percent with quarterly compounding (m=4), the effective annual rate (r_{annual}) is:

$$r_{annual} = (1+\frac{0.12}{4})^4 - 1 = (1.03)^4 - 1 = 1.1255 - 1 = 0.1255 \text{ or } 12.55\%$$

It is obvious in this example that the effective quarterly rate is 3 percent since each dollar grows to \$1.03 by the end of one quarter. However, what if we were interested in knowing the effective monthly rate associated with an annual effective rate of 12.55 percent—perhaps because we had to make monthly payments on a loan. We cannot simply divide 12.55 percent by 12 since it is an effective rate not a nominal or quoted one. What we are trying to determine is the effective monthly rate ($r_{monthly}$) that would make \$1 grow to \$1.1255 by the end of one year (or 12 months). In other words, we want to solve the following expression:

$1(1+r_{monthly})^{12} = \$1.1255$

or $(1+r_{monthly})^{12} = 1.1255$

Taking the 1/12th root of both sides and rearranging gives us:

$$r_{monthly} = (1.1255)^{\frac{1}{12}} - 1$$

$$r_{monthly} = 1.009901 - 1 = 0.009901 \text{ or } 0.9901\%$$

We now denote f as the number of times per year the period in question occurs (in other words, $f=12$ for monthly periods, $f=4$ for quarterly periods, etc.). This enables us to express the relationship above for determining the effective period rate (r) for any period as shown in Equation 5.11:

$$r = (1 + \frac{i}{m})^{\frac{m}{f}} - 1 \qquad (5.11)$$

This equation works for any situation. For example, with $i=12$ percent and quarterly compounding ($f=4$), Equation 5.11 shows that the effective quarterly rate is 3 percent (which we knew already):

$$r = (1 + \frac{0.12}{4})^{\frac{4}{4}} - 1 = (1.03)^{1} - 1 = 0.03 \text{ or } 3\%$$

It also works when we are looking for determining annual effective rates. In fact, Equation 5.10 is just a special case of Equation 5.11 with $f=1$.

EFFECTIVE RATES WITH VARYING COMPOUND INTERVALS

EXAMPLE

A bank offers an annual interest rate of 12 percent on its savings accounts. What is the effective annual rate if interest is compounded semi-annually? Monthly? Daily?

For this example, $i=12\%$, $f=1$, and m varies.

With semi-annual compounding, $m=2$, so:

$$r = (1 + \frac{0.12}{2})^{\frac{2}{1}} - 1 = (1.06)^{2} - 1 = 0.1236 \text{ or } 12.36\%$$

With monthly compounding, $m=12$, so:

$$r = (1 + \frac{0.12}{12})^{\frac{12}{1}} - 1 = (1.01)^{12} - 1 = 0.1268 \text{ or } 12.68\%$$

With daily compounding, $m=365$, so:

$$r = (1 + \frac{0.12}{365})^{\frac{365}{1}} - 1 = (1.000328767)^{365} - 1 = 0.1275 \text{ or } 12.75\%$$

The example above demonstrates that as a given rate of nominal interest is compounded more frequently, the effective rate of interest increases. To further illustrate this point, Figure 5.1 shows the effective annual interest rate as a function of the frequency of compounding for $i=10$ percent.

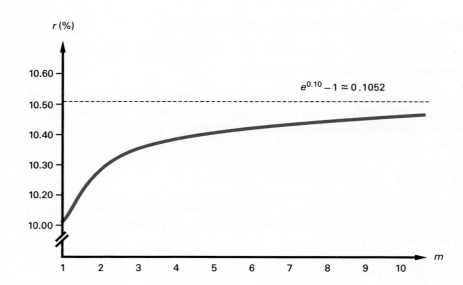

The curve in Figure 5.1 approaches the line at $r = 10.52$ percent as the frequency of compounding increases. The 10.52 percent is the effective annual rate that corresponds to continuous compounding based on a quoted rate of 10 percent. Continuous compounding assumes that the compounding frequency increases indefinitely so that interest is calculated and added to the principal amount invested at every instant in time. Although it may be difficult to visualize what that would imply on a loan transaction, there are many processes in nature that exhibit continuous growth, and interest on loans and deposits by some financial institutions is calculated on this basis.

Formulas for continuous compounding are easily derived. For example, when interest is compounded continuously, that is, when m increases indefinitely, the equation to determine the effective annual rate (Equation 5.10) becomes:

$$r_{annual} = \lim_{m \to \infty} \left(1 + \frac{i}{m}\right)^m - 1$$

Drawing on basic mathematics, one can show that:

$$\lim_{m \to \infty} \left(1 + \frac{i}{m}\right)^m = e^i$$

where $e \simeq 2.718$ is the base of the natural logarithms. Thus, we can express the equation above as:

(5.12) $r_{annual} = e^i - 1$

Equation 5.12 gives the annual effective rate associated with any given quoted rate when compounding is continuous.

CONTINUOUS COMPOUNDING

A firm borrows $1,000 at 8 percent interest compounded continuously with all payments due at the end of three years. What is the equivalent effective annual interest rate? What amount must be repaid?

Using Equation 5.12, we can determine the effective annual interest rate:

$$r = e^i - 1 = 2.718^{.08} - 1 = 1.0833 - 1 = 0.0833$$

Hence, $r = 8.33$ percent.

Thus, the amount due at the end of three years is:

$$FV = PV(1+r)^n = 1,000(1.0833)^3 = 1,000(1.27129) = \$1,271.29$$

Although continuous compounding is not common in financial transactions, continuous functions are of great importance in the development of financial theory. As can be seen from the previous example, results obtained through continuous compounding do not differ significantly from results obtained through monthly or even quarterly compounding. Use of continuous functions, however, allows for the application of calculus, and this often facilitates analysis. Therefore, continuous compounding and discounting are encountered frequently in academic literature, but for purposes of this book, they are of limited significance.

AMORTIZATION OF TERM LOANS 5.4

Important applications of compounding and discounting are found in debt financing. Under most term loans or mortgages, the borrower repays the original debt in equal periodic instalments. Each of these instalments encompasses two portions—interest and principal—and these vary over time. At the end of the loan period (that is, at the date of the last instalment), the principal and interest of the loan are fully amortized. Knowing the amount of principal on the loan, the typical computational problems that we encounter are:

1. Given the amount and duration of the repayments, what is the effective interest rate being charged?

2. Given an effective interest rate to be charged, what is the amount of the periodic repayments that have to be made over a given period of time, or what is the duration over which payments have to take place given their amount?

3. Given a particular set of repayments over time, what portion of each payment represents interest on principal outstanding, and what portion represents repayment of principal?

The calculations for loans with level repayments are relatively straightforward since the future cash flows represent an annuity. Drawing again on the notation defined in Section 5.2, the equation that forms the basis for all of our calculations is:

(5.13) $$P = A \left[\frac{1 - \frac{1}{(1+r)^n}}{r} \right]$$

where

P = the amount of principal originally outstanding (and is equivalent to the present value of the subsequent loan payments)

A = the amount of the loan payments

n = the number of periods for which repayments have to be made

r = the effective period interest rate on the loan

This equation states that the present value of the future repayments discounted at the effective rate of interest equals the amount of principal originally loaned. It contains four variables, and it is clear that if we know any three, we can compute the fourth. The equation can be solved directly for either P or A; solving for n or r entails the use of approximation techniques such as linear interpolation or a financial calculator, most of which provide functional keys for direct computations of loan amortization problems.

EXAMPLE

DETERMINING THE EFFECTIVE RATE OF A LOAN

A $10,000 loan calls for annual repayments of $3,500 per year for four years with payments due at the end of each year. What is the effective annual interest rate being charged?
Using Equation 5.13, we have:

$$10,000 = \left[\frac{1 - \frac{1}{(1+r)^4}}{r} \right] \times 3,500$$

$$\text{or} \quad \left[\frac{1 - \frac{1}{(1+r)^4}}{r} \right] = \frac{10,000}{3,500} = 2.85714$$

Searching Table 4 in Appendix III at the back of the book, in the row for $n=4$ years, we look for an entry that comes as close as possible to 2.857. We find that the effective interest rate is approximately 15 percent ($a_4 15\% = 2.855$).

Similarly, Equation 5.13 can be used to establish the amount of the regular payments (A) if the principal and duration of the loan and its effective interest rate are known.

EXAMPLE

DETERMINING LOAN PAYMENTS

A $10,000 loan carries an effective annual interest rate of 12 percent and calls for equal annual repayments over three years. What is the amount of each repayment? We have:

$$A = \frac{P}{\left[\dfrac{1 - \dfrac{1}{(1.12)^3}}{0.12}\right]} = \frac{10,000}{2.40183} = \$4,163.49$$

Finally, it is often necessary to divide the payments into the portion that constitutes interest and the one that constitutes repayment of principal since only the interest portion is deductible as an expense for tax purposes. The interest portion is calculated by applying the effective period interest rate to the principal outstanding at the beginning of each period. The remaining portion of the payment is then used to reduce the amount of principal outstanding.

LOAN AMORTIZATION SCHEDULE

Pursuing the previous example, we have:

Year	Principal outstanding at beginning of year	Annual repayment	Interest on principal outstanding	Repayment of principal	Principal outstanding at end of year
	(1)	(2)	$(3) = r \times (1)$	$(4) = (2) - (3)$	$(5) = (1) - (4)$
1	$10,000.00	$4,163.49	$1,200.00	$2,963.49	$7,036.51
2	7,036.51	4,163.49	844.38	3,319.11	3,717.40
3	3,717.40	4,163.49	446.09	3,717.40	0.00

We see that the annual repayments of $4163.49 indeed incorporate interest of 12 percent on the amount of principal outstanding each year and provide for a total repayment of the loan by the end of year 3.

The calculations in the example above that break down each payment into interest and principal can be tedious. Fortunately, it is easy to derive general formulas to simplify the computations. We note that the amount of principal outstanding on a loan at any time just equals the present value of the remaining annuity payments discounted at the original interest rate on the loan. Based on this, one can readily show that:[4]

$$P_t = A \times \frac{1}{(1+r)^{n-t+1}} \tag{5.14}$$

$$I_t = A - P_t = A\left(1 - \frac{1}{(1-r)^{n-t+1}}\right) \tag{5.15}$$

---

[4] The amounts of principal outstanding at times 0, 1, 2 ... t are $A(a_n r\%)$, $A(a_{n-1} r\%) A(a_{n-2} r\%)$ ... $A(a_{n-t} r\%)$ respectively. The amount of principal repaid in period t equals the amount of principal outstanding in period $(t-1)$ minus the amount of principal outstanding in period t or $P_t = A\ [(a_{n-t+1} r\%) - (a_{n-t} r\%)]$. Inserting the full expression for the annuity discount factors from Equation 5.8 and simplifying, we obtain $P_t = A/(1+r)^{n-t+1}$.

where

P_t=the amount of principal to be repaid in period t

I_t=the interest to be paid in period t

Note that the total annual repayment always equals the interest payment plus the repayment of principal so that $I_t+P_t=A$.

DETERMINING INTEREST AND PRINCIPAL REPAYMENTS

EXAMPLE

Applying these formulas to the previous example for year 2:

$$P_2 = 4{,}163.49\times \frac{1}{(1+.12)^2} = \$3{,}319.11$$

$$I_2 = 4{,}163.49-3.319.11=\$844.38$$

This corresponds with the results derived above.

Loan Repayments Not Made on an Annual Basis

In practice, many loan repayments are not made on an annual basis. For example, term loans and mortgages may call for monthly or even weekly repayments. As we saw above, the transition to other base periods for compounding and discounting is straightforward. Long-term loans such as mortgages offer to lock investors in at a fixed rate for a fixed period (called the term), which may be shorter than the period over which the loan is scheduled to be repaid (called the amortization period). The payments on such loans are determined using the interest rate as specified and assuming these payments are made to the end of the amortization period. For example, a loan with a 20-year amortization period (or a 20-year loan) may offer an interest rate of 11 percent for a term of five years. The payments for this loan would be determined using the 11 percent rate and assuming equal payments to the end of 20 years. Of course, after five years, the regular payments may increase (if interest rates rise) or decrease (if interest rates fall).

Mortgages pose a peculiar problem with regard to estimating the effective period interest rate. While payments must be made at least monthly, compounding on mortgages in Canada must be done on a semi-annual basis. Referring back to Equation 5.11 for estimating the effective period rate, this means that the compounding interval for mortgages will always be semi-annual ($m=2$); however, we will have to determine the effective interest rate for a period other than semi-annually ($f\neq2$). In fact, f must be greater than 12 since payments must be made at least monthly and are usually made on a monthly, biweekly, or weekly basis. Therefore, we need to know the effective rate corresponding to the time between payments since the principal amount will be reduced with each payment.

DETERMINING MORTGAGE PAYMENTS

Determine the monthly payments and amortization schedule for the first three months of a $100,000 mortgage loan with an amortization period of 25 years, a nominal rate of 12 percent, and a five-year term.

All mortgages are compounded semi-annually in Canada, so $m=2$. For this mortgage, we need to know the effective monthly rate since payments are made every month, so $f=12$.

We begin by determining the effective monthly rate using Equation 5.12:

$$r = (1+\frac{.12}{2})^{\frac{2}{12}} - 1 = 0.97588\%$$

Then, we can determine the required monthly payments (A). There are 300 payments in total since $n=25$ years $\times 12$ months $=300$.

$$A = \frac{P}{\left[\dfrac{1-\dfrac{1}{(1+r)^n}}{r}\right]} = \frac{100,000}{\left[\dfrac{1-\dfrac{1}{(1.0097588)^{300}}}{.0097588}\right]} = \frac{100,000}{96.908663} = \$1,031.90$$

Finally, we construct an amortization schedule similar to the example above:

Period	(1) Beginning principal outstanding	(2) Payment	(3) Interest $[r \times (1)]$	(4) Principal repayment $[(2)-(3)]$	Ending principal outstanding $[(1)-(4)]$
1	100,000.00	1,031.90	975.88	56.02	99,943.98
2	99,943.98	1,031.90	975.33	56.57	99,887.41
3	99,887.41	1,031.90	974.78	57.12	99,830.29

SUMMARY   5.5

1. Compounding specifies how a given amount of money grows over time at a particular rate of interest. By compounding at a rate that represents the time value of money, we can calculate future values of current cash flows.

2. Discounting is the inverse of compounding; it allows us to calculate present values of future cash flows.

3. Because of the time value of money, cash flows that occur at different points in time can be compared only by transforming them through compounding or discounting into equivalent flows with reference to a particular point in time.

4. The basic formulas for compounding and discounting are independent of the choice of the base period. However, because of institutional conventions, one must adjust the formulas to distinguish between the nominal or quoted rate of interest and the effective rate of interest.

5. Loans with level repayments, can be split into interest and principal.

QUESTIONS AND PROBLEMS

Questions for Discussion

1. (a) If a person can invest money at 10 percent, and we say that therefore he should be indifferent between receiving $100 today or $110 a year from now, what assumptions are we making?

    (b) How reasonable are these assumptions in the context of a business firm?

2. (a) What is the relationship between the entries (at the end of the textbook) in Table 1 (Compound-interest factors: Future value of $1) and Table 4 (Present value of an annuity of $1). For example, how could we derive the entry $(a_3 10\%) = 2.487$ as found in Table 4 if we had access only to Table 1?

    (b) The tables as reproduced at the end of the textbook go up only to $n = 50$ years. How could you find the present value of $1 to be received in 55 years if you had access only to Table 1?

3. (a) Explain the difference between a nominal and an effective interest rate. Give a practical example of where these two rates may differ. Which is more relevant for financial decision-making?

    (b) Why do some financial institutions that lend money quote a nominal rate rather than the effective rate of interest?

    (c) What impact do service charges and commissions have on the effective interest costs of a bank loan to a borrower?

4. Assume that the market-given rate of interest at which money can be borrowed or invested is 10 percent. Is it reasonable for an individual or for a business firm to have a time value of money that differs from this market rate? What would you expect an individual to do whose time preference for money exceeds or falls short of 10 percent? Discuss.

PROBLEMS WITH SOLUTIONS

Problem 1

(a) A firm borrows $10,000 from the bank at an effective annual interest rate of 10 percent. This loan is to be repaid through three equal annual repayments. What is the amount of each payment?

(b) Break down each payment into repayment of principal and interest.

Solution 1

(a) $$P = A \left[\frac{1 - \frac{1}{(1+r)^n}}{r} \right]$$

$$10,000 = A \left[\frac{1 - \frac{1}{(1.10)^3}}{0.1} \right]$$

$$A = \$4,021.15$$

(b)

Year	Unamortized principal (1)	Annual repayment (2)	Interest on unamortized principal (3)=(10%)×(1)	Amortization payment (4)=(2)−(3)	New unamortized principal amount (5)=(1)−(4)
1	$10,000	$4,021.15	$1,000	$3,021.15	$6,978.85
2	6,978.85	4,021.15	697.89	3,323.26	3,655.59
3	3,656.59	4,021.15	365.56	3,655.59	0

Using Equations 5.14 and 5.15 in the chapter:

$$P_1 = \frac{4,021.15}{(1+.1)^3} = \$3,021.15 \qquad\qquad I_1 = 4,021.15 - 3,021.15 = \$1,000$$

$$P_2 = \frac{4,021.15}{(1+.1)^2} = \$3,323.26 \qquad\qquad I_2 = 4,021.15 - 3,323.26 = \$697.89$$

$$P_3 = \frac{4,021.15}{(1+.1)} = \$3,655.59 \qquad\qquad I_3 = 4,021.15 - 3,655.59 = \$365.56$$

Problem 2

(a) Suppose that you secure a personal bank loan for $3,200 that you are to repay by making three annual payments of $1,200 due on the anniversary of the loan date. What is the effective annual interest rate on your loan?

(b) If instead of annual payments of $1,200, the loan in part (a) now calls for quarterly payments of $300, would you expect the effective interest cost to be higher or lower? Calculate the new effective annual interest rate.

(c) Assume the situation given in part (a). If at the time of the loan the bank charges you a service fee of $51, what is the effective interest cost of the loan?

Solution 2

(a) Loan amount=(annual repayment) $(a_n r\%)$

$$a_n r\% = \frac{P}{A}$$

$$a_3 r\% = \frac{3,200}{1,200} = 2.67$$

From Table 4, for $n=3$ years, we find $a_3 6\% = 2.673$. The effective interest rate is $r=6\%$.

(b) Because parts of the payments are now made earlier, we expect the effective interest cost to increase. We define r as the effective interest rate per quarter-year period:

$$3,200 = \frac{300}{(1+r')} + \frac{300}{(1+r')^2} + \ldots + \frac{300}{(1+r')^{12}}$$

$$3,200 = 300 \, (a_{12} r'\%)$$

$$(a_{12} r'\%) = \frac{3,200}{300} = 10.67$$

From Table 4 at the back of the book, for $n=12$, we have:

$$\begin{bmatrix} 2\% & 10.58 \\ \begin{bmatrix} r' \\ 1\% \end{bmatrix} & \begin{bmatrix} 10.67 \\ 11.26 \end{bmatrix} \end{bmatrix}$$

and we derive:

$$\frac{r'-1}{2-1} = \frac{10.67-11.26}{10.58-11.26} = .87$$

$$r' = (2-1)(.87)+1 = 1.87\%$$

Considering the effect of compounding, we have an effective annual rate of:

$(1+r)=(1+0.0187)^4=1.0769$

$r=7.69\%$

As an alternative to using Table 4, one could use Equation 5.13 directly. For instance, we know that:

$$a_{12}r'\% = 10.67 = \left[\frac{1-\dfrac{1}{(1+r)^n}}{r}\right]$$

We might have simply made an initial guess that the rate per quarter was 2 percent and then, using the formula, calculate $a_{12}r'=10.58$. Because this is too low, we would know that the actual interest rate per quarter was lower, so we might guess 1 percent and again use the formula to calculate $a_{12}r'=11.26$. Then the same process of linear interpolation would be followed to arrive at the final answer.

(d) The service fee decreases the amount of the loan actually received, whereas the amount of the repayments remains the same. Therefore, we expect the effective interest cost to increase:

$$a_n r\% = \frac{\text{net loan amount}}{\text{annual repayment}}$$

$$a_3 r\% = \frac{3,200-51}{1,200}$$

$$= \frac{3,149}{1,200} = 2.624$$

From Table 4, we now find that $r=7\%$.

Problem 3

(a) You plan to retire in 10 years, and at that time, you want to have $100,000. Interest rates will remain constant at 10 percent. How much would you have to save each year in order to accumulate $100,000 by the end of year 10? Assume that you save an equal amount each year, which you deposit at year end.

(b) Assume that after retirement your life expectancy is 10 years. How much can you withdraw each year if you just want to have your account down to zero by the end of your expected life? Again, assume that you withdraw an equal amount each year and that withdrawals are made at year end.

Solution 3

(a) The future value of an annuity is given as:

$$FV = A \times \left[\frac{(1+r)^n - 1}{r} \right]$$

$$100,000 = A \left[\frac{(1+0.1)^{10} - 1}{0.1} \right]$$

$$A = \$6,274.54$$

(b) In order to derive the annual withdrawals A_w that can be sustained, we equate their present value with the amount accumulated in the account. The point that serves as a basis for this comparison is the time of retirement.

$$PV = A_w \left[\frac{1 - \dfrac{1}{(1+r)^n}}{r} \right]$$

$$100,000 = A_w \left[\frac{1 - \dfrac{1}{(1+0.1)^{10}}}{0.1} \right]$$

$$A_w = 16,274.54$$

Given that the present value of the annual payments equals the current balance in the account, the bank would be indifferent between paying out $100,000 now or an annuity of $16,274.54 per year for 10 years. Note that 10 annual payments of $6,274.54 as computed under (a) now allow for 10 annual withdrawals of $16,274.54. The cause for this discrepancy is the interest that money has earned while it was invested in the account. The cash flows of (a) and (b) are illustrated in the diagram below.

Future value = 100,000 = present value

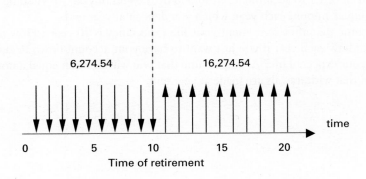

Problem 4

You are attempting to plan for your retirement. You plan on retiring 25 years from today. In order to fund your lifestyle after retirement, you have determined that you will require $27,000 per year. Your plan is to take $27,000 out of your retirement account in a lump sum at the beginning of each year (your first withdrawal will be the day you retire in 25 years). You expect to live long enough to need 21 withdrawals in total. In order to save for your retirement, you want to make annual deposits into your retirement account at the end of each year over the next 24 years. If the retirement account will earn 6 percent per year, what is the annual deposit needed in order to fully fund your retirement?

Solution 4

The first step is to determine how much you will need in the account the day you retire. The amount in the account should equal the present value of the $27,000 withdrawals you will be making. Because the withdrawals are made at the beginning of each year, they constitute an annuity due:

$$PV = A \left[\frac{1 - \frac{1}{(1+r)^n}}{r} \right] (1+r)$$

$$PV = 27,000 \left[\frac{1 - \frac{1}{(1+0.06)^{21}}}{0.06} \right] (1+0.06)$$

$$PV = \$336,687.87$$

If you have $336,687.87 in your retirement account the day you retire then it will be exactly enough to fund your retirement. That is, you will be able to rake 21 annual withdrawals out of the account at the start of each year and after the twenty-first withdrawal, there will be a zero balance in the account. Next, we have to determine how large each annual deposit must be over the next 25 years in order to accumulate $336,687.87 in the account. (Note: Because the withdrawals are at the beginning of the year and the deposits are at the end of each year, the last deposit and first withdrawal are actually at the same time. This is not a necessary assumption and the problem could be easily solved even if this were not the case.) We want the future value on 25 years of an annuity to equal $336,687.87.

$$FV = A \left(\frac{(1+r)^n - 1}{r} \right)$$

$$336,687.87 = A \left(\frac{(1+0.06)^{25} - 1}{0.06} \right)$$

$$A = \$6,136.71$$

Therefore, deposits of $6,136.71 at the end of each of the next 25 years would grow to $336,687.87, which in turn would be enough to fund your retirement.

Problem 5

Martha just purchased a new house for $120,000. She was able to make a down payment equal to 25 percent of the value of the house, and the balance was mortgaged. The rate quoted by the bank was 10 percent compounded semi-annually. The mortgage has a 20-year amortization period and a five-year term.

(a) If her payments are made monthly, what will be the payments?
(b) What will be the balance remaining at the end of the term?
(c) Assume that five years have passed, and the term of the mortgage is up. Martha must now negotiate a new mortgage for the remaining balance. Interest rates have now increased to 12 percent. She wants the new mortgage to have weekly payments and a 15-year amortization period. What will be her new payments?

Solution 5

(a) A mortgage of 0.75×$120,000=$90,000 will be needed initially. With a 20-year amortization and monthly payments, it will take a total of $n=20\times12=240$ payments to pay off the mortgage entirely.

Before determining the mortgage payments, we must first calculate the effective monthly interest rate being charged.

$$r=\left(1+\frac{i}{m}\right)^{\frac{m}{f}}-1$$

$$r=\left(1+\frac{0.10}{2}\right)^{\frac{2}{12}}-1$$

$r=0.00816$ per month

Next, we must calculate the monthly payment necessary to pay off a loan of $90,000 in 240 monthly payments when the interest rate is 0.00816 per month.

$$P=A\left[\frac{1-\dfrac{1}{(1+r)^n}}{r}\right]$$

$$90,000=A\left[\frac{1-\dfrac{1}{(1+0.00816)^{240}}}{0.00816}\right]$$

$A=\$856.15$

(b) After five years, the term of the mortgage will be up. The balance remaining will equal the present value of the payments that are left to be made. There are now 15 years' worth of payments that Martha has not made (on the original amortization period); this is equal to $15 \times 12 = 180$ monthly payments remaining. The present value of these remaining payments is:

$$P = A \left[\frac{1 - \frac{1}{(1+r)^n}}{r} \right]$$

$$P = 856.15 \left[\frac{1 - \frac{1}{(1+0.00816)^{180}}}{0.00816} \right]$$

$P = \$80,623.13$

So, after making five years' worth of mortgage payments, Martha still has a balance remaining on the mortgage of $80,623.13. Note that the principal has been reduced by a total of $(90,000 - 80,623.13) = \$9,376.87$ over the five years, but Martha has made 60 payments totalling $(60 \times 856.15) = \$51,369$. These numbers may help reinforce the idea that in the early stages of a mortgage, the majority of each payment goes to interest, and therefore, the balance of the mortgage does not decline very quickly. However, as more payments are made, the balance will start to decline more and more quickly.

(c) As in any situation in which we must figure out a loan payment, we need to know the number of payments, the principal amount of the loan, and the interest rate. With a 15-year amortization period and weekly payments (52 times per year), the new mortgage will be amortized over a total of $15 \times 52 = 780$ payments. The principal of the loan will simply be the balance remaining on the mortgage, which we know from part (b) to be $80,623.13. The only other piece of information we need is the effective weekly interest rate being charged:

$$r = \left(1 + \frac{i}{m}\right)^{\frac{m}{f}} - 1$$

$$r = \left(1 + \frac{0.10}{2}\right)^{\frac{2}{52}} - 1$$

$r = 0.00224$ per week

Given the information on the previous page, we can figure out the new mortgage payments (per week) as:

$$P = A \left[\frac{1 - \frac{1}{(1+r)^n}}{r} \right]$$

$$80{,}623.13 = A \left[\frac{1 - \frac{1}{(1+0.00224)^{780}}}{0.00224} \right]$$

$A = \$218.80$ per week

ADDITIONAL PROBLEMS

1. What is the present value of $1,000 received in two years if the relevant interest rate is:

    (a) 12 percent per year compounded annually?

    (b) 12 percent per year compounded semi-annually?

    (c) 12 percent per year compounded daily?

2. An annuity makes 10 annual payments of $1,000 each starting three years from now. What is the present value if the appropriate interest rate is 10 percent?

3. Bill wants to have $50,000 in 10 years to buy a boat. At the end of each of the 20 years after that, he will need $1,000 for upkeep on the boat. If he makes equal annual deposits into a bank account for the next nine years (first deposit one year from today) and the interest rate is 8 percent per year, what must the deposits be in order to fund Bill's boat?

4. (a) If $2,000 is placed in a savings account at the end of each year for five years, what is the value of this account at the end of the fifth year given that money paid into the account earns 10 percent simple interest?

    (b) What is the value of the account at the end of five years if all balances held in the account earn interest of 10 percent compounded annually?

    (c) Recompute your answer under (b) assuming that $2,000 is paid into the account at the beginning of each year. The first payment is made immediately.

5. Assume a nominal interest rate of 14 percent per year. Derive a diagram equivalent to Figure 5.2 that shows the effective interest rate as a function of the frequency of compounding per year. Show all of your calculations.

6. (a) Natasha plans to deposit $4,000 per year in her account for each of the next four years. Thereafter, she expects to deposit $1,500 per year for another four years. All deposits are made at year end. Interest rates are expected to be 8 percent for the next two years and 11 percent thereafter. Interest is compounded annually. What will Natasha's bank balance be at the end of year 8?

(b) How much would Natasha have to deposit as a lump sum today in order to accumulate the same bank balance at the end of year 8?

7. (a) What is the present value of $7,000 to be received at the end of each year for six years if the interest rate to be used for discounting is 10 percent compounded annually?

(b) What is the present value of $3,500 to be received at the beginning of every six-month period for six years if the nominal discount rate is 10 percent compounded semi-annually?

8. A property owner has to decide whether to repaint the wooden outside walls of her house or to install vinyl siding. Painting currently costs $3,500 and would have to be done every five years. Future painting costs would increase with the rate of inflation, which is expected to average 5 percent per year. In order to proceed with painting, some wooden boards with rot would have to be replaced at a one-time cost of $2,000; with these repairs, the wooden siding is expected to last for 25 years. Vinyl siding that can be installed over the old wooden boards without repairs costs $13,000 and is maintenance-free with an expected life of 25 years. Work on the house is to be financed by withdrawing funds from a bank account that earns 10 percent interest. From a financial point of view, which is the preferred alternative?

9. (a) If a bank pays 6 percent interest compounded annually on a $1,000 deposit, what will be the value of this deposit at the end of 10 years?

(b) If another bank pays 6 percent interest on the same $1,000 deposit but compounds interest quarterly, what will be the value of this deposit at the end of 10 years? What is the effective annual interest rate being paid?

(c) If interest were paid continuously at 6 percent on this $1,000 deposit, what would it be worth in 10 years?

10. Bank A offers an 8 percent nominal interest rate compounded monthly on its savings deposits. Bank B also offers an 8 percent nominal rate but compounds continuously. Compare the two alternatives on the basis of (a) the future value of $5,000 in five years and (b) the effective annual interest rate. Is continuous compounding a significant advantage over the more typical monthly compounding?

11. A mortgage of $250,000 has just been arranged for 25 years at an interest rate of 10.5 percent. It calls for equal payments made every two weeks.

(a) What is the size of each payment?

(b) After 26 payments have been made, what will be the outstanding principal?

(c) What will be the interest portion of the twenty-sixth payment?

12. (a) A five-year loan of $35,000 is to be repaid in five annual payments of $10,000. What is the effective interest rate on this loan?

(b) If this loan were to be repaid instead through payments of $2,500 every three months for five years, what would be the effective interest rate?

(c) Assume that the borrower had made a deal with an intermediary to pay him a 0.5 percent commission (of the loan amount) if he could locate a lender who would agree to certain terms. A lender was located, and the arrangement in part (a) was consummated. What was the effective interest rate to the borrower?

13. (a) Assume that a pension plan offers to pay a lump sum of $200,000 on a person's sixty-fifth birthday or an annuity of x for the remainder of the person's life. Interest rates are 10 percent, and a person's life expectancy has been determined statistically as being 80 years. What is the value of x (the amount of the annuity) that would make the two alternatives equivalent on an expected present-value basis?

(b) A person joins a pension plan at age 30. How much will she have to pay into the pension fund at the end of each year in order to accumulate a balance of $150,000 in the fund at age 65?

14. (a) Luke Smith wants to retire in 20 years and expects to live for another 15 years after that. During retirement, he wants to draw $12,000 at the beginning of each year from his savings account. How much will he have to deposit in his account at the end of each year for the next 20 years given that the interest rate is 10 percent compounded annually?

(b) How would the amount computed under (a) be altered if Mr. Smith expects his wife to live for five years after his death, and if, in addition to the amounts provided for under (a), he wants her to be able to draw $6,000 at the beginning of each year during this additional period?

15. Assume the inflation rate in Canada to be 5 percent per year for the indefinite future. How much would a Canadian dollar be worth at the end of 10 years in terms of today's dollar? How much at the end of 30 years?

16. Meena Lele is 60 years old and is attempting to plan for her retirement over the next 25 years. She owns a house worth $265,000 with no outstanding mortgage. She wants to utilize the equity her house to generate a supplemental income during this 25-year period. She has two alternatives:

Alternative A   The B.C. Trust Company offers her a special type of "reverse annuity mortgage." The trust company will pay Ms. Lele a 25-year annuity to supplement her annual income. In return, the company builds up a mortgage claim against Ms. Lele's house with the mortgage loan outstanding at any time amounting to the annual payments made to date plus interest of 10 percent compounded annually on payments that have been made. The annuity that the trust company is willing to pay is such that 25 years from now, the mortgage loan outstanding will amount to 80 percent of the currently assessed house value of $265,000.

Alternative B Lele can sell her house and rent equivalent housing accommodation at a fixed long-term rent of $19,000 per year. In selling her house, she would incur selling expenses of 5 percent of the sale price. Lele would invest the proceeds from the sale of her house to yield interest of 8 percent per year before tax. She would withdraw equal annual amounts from these savings so as to draw the balance down to zero at the end of 25 years.

(a) Assuming all other housing expenses are identical for the two alternatives and that Lele is concerned only with her before-tax annual income over the next 25 years, which alternative should she choose?

(b) What other considerations would be relevant in reaching a final decision between these two alternatives?

17. You have just bought a house. The house was priced at $175,000, and you had a down payment of $20,000 (the balance was mortgaged). The mortgage you took out was amortized over 25 years with monthly payments. You were able to get a special deal from the bank and get a 25-year term for the mortgage (this is unusual in Canada). The rate on the mortgage is 10.5 percent (compounded semi-annually). At the end of every year, you get a bonus from your employer. This bonus is typically $2,000 (and the amount of the bonus has not changed in many years, so you do not expect it to change in the future). Your plan is that every time you get your bonus, you will immediately use it to pay down the balance of your mortgage. Since the bank will keep your monthly payments the same, this means that your mortgage will probably be paid off in less than 25 years. Set up a spreadsheet that shows the balance remaining each month on the mortgage. Determine how long it will take to pay off the mortgage totally.

GTAA Bonds Deliver Value to Both Investors and Travellers

About 28 million passengers pass through Toronto's Lester B. Pearson International Airport each year—and sometimes, to a harassed traveller, it can seem like your feet have been trod on by every one of them by the time you get to the gate. Moreover, the air transport market is expected to double in size over the next 25 or so years.

This is why the Greater Toronto Airport Authority (GTAA), the not-for-profit corporation that operates Pearson, launched a major expansion project in 1997, including a massive new state-of-the-art terminal, additional runways, and an infield cargo area. The scale of the project is difficult to grasp; its total cost is estimated at over $4 billion, according to Todd Timmerman, Manager of Finance and Treasury at the GTAA.

How do you finance a huge project like this? "Well, I suppose we could've just hiked the landing fees sky-high," jokes Mr. Timmerman. Instead, the GTAA issued the largest bond offering in Canadian corporate history.

In December 1997, the GTAA completed an offering with record-breaking gross profits of $947 million. The bonds were in several series with different maturity dates—on demand, five, 10, and 30 year.

Several more substantial offerings followed in 1999 and 2000. Overall, the GTAA expects that its total gross cumulative debt from 1997 to 2007 may approach $7 billion. Its financial plan allows for a variety of debt instruments, and, beginning in 2001, travellers to and from Pearson will pay a small levy that will also go toward the development initiative. But bond issues are likely to be the major source of funds.

The Canadian Bond Rating Service (which merged with U.S. rating agency Standard and Poors in October 2000) rates the GTAA bond issues as A+, with a stable outlook. Investors clearly find the bonds attractive. Over 60 buyers participated in the 1997 offering, which was significantly oversubscribed.

How have the bonds fared in value? In December of 2000, the bonds in the five-year series from the 1997 issue, which have a coupon rate of 5.4 percent, were trading at 99.46, for a yield of 5.69. The thirty-year series (maturing in 2027), with a coupon rate of 6.45 percent, were trading at 93.68 for a yield of 6.87 percent.

Reasonable value for an investor. For a traveller, what the GTAA bonds will make possible—reducing congestion at Pearson airport, and therefore lowering the stress of flying—is priceless.

Bond and Common Share Valuation

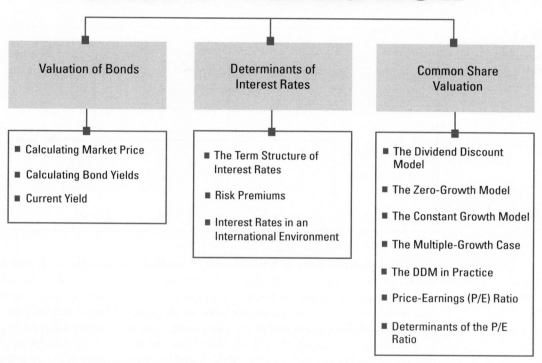

Valuation of Bonds	Determinants of Interest Rates	Common Share Valuation
■ Calculating Market Price ■ Calculating Bond Yields ■ Current Yield	■ The Term Structure of Interest Rates ■ Risk Premiums ■ Interest Rates in an International Environment	■ The Dividend Discount Model ■ The Zero-Growth Model ■ The Constant Growth Model ■ The Multiple-Growth Case ■ The DDM in Practice ■ Price-Earnings (P/E) Ratio ■ Determinants of the P/E Ratio

Learning Objectives

After studying this chapter, you should be able to:

1. *Name the five variables of a debt contract.*
2. *Describe how to estimate bond prices and bond yields.*
3. *Discuss the three leading theories on the term structure of interest rates, and explain how they differ.*
4. *Explain the dividend discount model (DDM) and how financial officers use it to value shares.*

6.1 INTRODUCTION

Most investments are characterized by a current commitment of cash that is made in anticipation of obtaining future cash inflows in return for this commitment. This is true whether it is an investment in financial assets such as common shares and bonds or in real assets such as plant and equipment. These inflows are expected to provide an adequate return on the initial investment, and this is portrayed graphically in Figure 6.1.

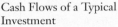

FIGURE 6.1

Cash Flows of a Typical Investment

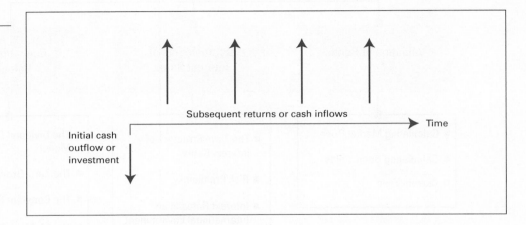

What investors want to know is how to establish an investment's economic value and its anticipated return. The question of investment worth is resolved by calculating present values: we discount expected future cash flows to the present to obtain their current economic value. This economic value of all expected future inflows may then be compared with the current cost of the investment to decide whether it should be pursued.

Similarly, we compute the effective return (or yield) of an investment by equating the present value of future cash flows with the initial investment and solving for the discount rate. To decide whether or not a particular investment is acceptable, we may compare this yield with what would be deemed an adequate return given current market conditions.

Although these basic concepts for the economic evaluation of investments are straightforward, their actual application often entails many complexities. For example, the expected cash flows that result from an investment may be difficult to estimate and generally are subject to uncertainty. Whereas a debt contract may specify all future payments to be made, this is not the case when one buys common shares or acquires new equipment. Even with debt payments, there is uncertainty because the borrower may be late with payments or default on them. In the previous chapter, we assumed a single discount rate that can be earned. Although this is a convenient simplification to introduce the mechanics of compounding and discounting, the actual determination of appropriate discount rates in financial markets is more complex, and significant variations can be found in both the costs of funds and in investment yields.

In this chapter, we explore the valuation of bonds and common shares. We also discuss how interest rates—the rates at which debt instruments are to be discounted—are determined in financial markets. We discuss the valuation of bonds and common shares without an explicit consideration of risk for the time being, aside from a brief discussion regarding the risk premiums associated with interest rates. We deal with the risk associated with common shares in detail in the following two chapters. Ignoring risk considerations is a convenient simplification that allows us to concentrate on the process of valuation itself.

PERSPECTIVES

Corporate Manager

It is an important prerequisite for financial managers to have a reasonable understanding of the valuation process that is applied to financial assets in the marketplace. If managers strive to maximize shareholder wealth as postulated in Chapter 1, valuation by financial markets becomes the foundation for the financial executive's own decision-making. Clearly, the shareholders' interests will be served only if the firm's evaluation and selection of real assets is consistent with expressed market preferences. Consequently, the financial executive has the responsibility of ensuring that the company uses criteria for the commitment of funds that are consistent with those prevailing in the financial markets in which those funds are raised.

Investor

The process of valuation is critical for investors. They need to know what determines the values of financial securities and where their returns will come from. This allows them to make adjustments to their investments based on their beliefs regarding the future. It also enables them to understand what caused their past investments to perform above or below expectations.

VALUATION OF BONDS   6.2

A **bond** is a debt instrument that entitles the owner to specified periodic interest payments and eventually to the repayment of principal (the face amount of the debt) at the stated date of maturity. From a lender's point of view, the relevant cash flows are illustrated in Figure 6.2. Unlike the term loans discussed in Chapter 5, this type of debt has a constant amount of principal outstanding. For example, consider a corporation that has issued bonds each with a face value of $1,000. The stated interest rate (or coupon rate) is 8 percent to be paid annually, and the bonds mature in 20 years. The pattern of payments that the holder of such a bond can expect to receive is: interest payments (or coupons) of $80 at the end of each year for 20 years and a lump-sum repayment of principal of $1,000 at the end of year 20.

FIGURE 6.2

Cash Flows of a Bond

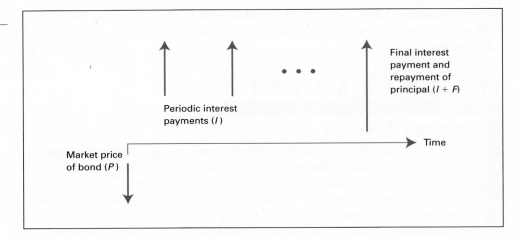

We saw in Chapter 2 that most financial assets are negotiable meaning that loan contracts bought by an investor can be resold before maturity. In selling the debt certificate, the original lender confers the right to future payments under the loan contract to the buyer. The price at which the debt contract is traded should equal the present value of its future payments. This present value will be a combination of the payments promised under the contract, the time value of money, and the prevailing interest rates at the time of the sale.

Pursuing the above example, consider the bond with a face value of $1,000 that pays 8 percent annual interest. The bond was originally issued several years ago and now has a remaining maturity of 20 years. Since the date of issue, prevailing interest rates have increased from the original 8 percent to the current 10 percent, so that the interest paid on the original bond is no longer competitive. In order to make the bond attractive to a prospective purchaser, the selling price has to be such that buyers will realize an effective yield of 10 percent on the investment if held to maturity. This is possible only if the bond sells at a discount below its face value. Thus, we have to distinguish between the face value (or the amount of principal outstanding under a loan contract) and the current market price at which the loan contract may trade. We also have to differentiate between the loan's stated interest rate and its effective market yield. The stated interest rate is the rate specified on the original debt contract in relation to the face value of the debt (8 percent in our example). In the case of bonds, it is also called the **coupon rate**. The **effective yield** or **yield to maturity** is the yield that investors realize by holding to maturity a debt contract that they have bought at a particular market price (10 percent in our example).

To summarize, a debt contract is characterized by the following variables:

- the face value, or amount of principal originally loaned
- the stated interest payments
- the particular time pattern of repayments to be made under the debt contract including its maturity or duration
- the current market price of the debt contract
- the effective yield of the debt contract, based on its current market price

The following report contains a list of bond quotations that is reported daily in the *Globe and Mail Report on Business* and includes the information above. In particular, the columns include information regarding: the issuer of the bond, the coupon rate, the maturity date, the closing bid price (as of 5 p.m. that day), the corresponding effective yield, and the price change from the previous day. The bond price is quoted assuming a $100 face value. Therefore, a bond price of $101.11 would translate into $1,011.10 for a bond with a face value of $1,000.

CANADIAN BONDS
Provided by RBC Dominion Securities
Selected quotations, with changes since the previous day, on actively traded bond issues yesterday.
Yields are calculated to full maturity. Price is the final bid-side price as of 5 pm yesterday

Issuer	Coupon	Maturity	Price	Yield	Price $Chg	Issuer	Coupon	Maturity	Price	Yield	Price $Chg
GOVERNMENT OF CANADA						Ontario Hyd	8.625	Feb 06/02	103.76	6.08	-0.04
Canada	7.000	Sep 01/01	101.11	5.98	-0.02	Ontario Hyd	9.000	Jun 24/02	105.31	6.08	-0.04
Canada	9.750	Dec 01/01	105.02	5.95	-0.03	Ontario Hyd	5.375	Jun 02/03	98.13	6.09	0.01
Canada	5.250	Dec 01/01	99.06	5.95	-0.01	Ontario Hyd	7.750	Nov 03/05	107.19	6.14	-0.01
Canada	8.500	Apr 01/02	104.14	5.95	-0.03	Ontario Hyd	5.600	Jun 02/08	96.20	6.21	0.02
Canada	10.000	May 01/02	106.84	5.97	-0.03	Ontario Hyd	8.250	Jun 22/26	124.41	6.32	0.32
Canada	5.750	Jun 01/02	99.74	5.89	-0.02	Quebec	10.250	Oct 15/01	104.95	6.11	-0.05
Canada	5.500	Sep 01/02	99.09	5.95	-0.02	Quebec	5.250	Apr 01/02	98.65	6.08	0.00
Canada	6.000	Dec 01/02	100.26	5.88	-0.03	Quebec	7.500	Dec 01/03	104.00	6.17	-0.02
Canada	11.750	Feb 01/02	113.51	5.99	-0.04	Quebec	6.500	Dec 01/05	101.20	6.23	0.00
Canada	7.250	Jun 01/03	103.40	5.95	-0.03	Quebec	6.500	Oct 01/07	101.10	6.31	0.00
Canada	5.250	Sep 01/03	97.98	5.96	-0.02	Quebec	11.000	Apr 01/09	130.50	6.38	0.00
Canada	7.500	Dec 01/03	104.65	5.96	-0.04	Quebec	5.500	Jun 01/09	94.15	6.37	0.00
Canada	10.250	Feb 01/04	113.40	6.01	-0.06	Quebec	8.500	Apr 01/26	124.45	6.52	0.15
Canada	6.500	Jun 01/04	101.88	5.95	-0.04	Quebec	6.000	Oct 01/29	94.04	6.45	0.13
Canada	5.000	Sep 01/04	96.67	5.92	-0.03	Sask	6.125	Oct 10/01	100.04	6.08	-0.01
Canada	9.000	Dec 01/04	111.62	5.95	-0.06	Sask	5.500	Jun 02/08	95.29	6.26	0.02
Canada	12.000	Mar 01/05	123.98	6.00	-0.08	Sask	8.750	May 30/25	130.07	6.33	0.33
Canada	6.000	Sep 01/05	100.62	5.86	-0.05	Tor -Met	6.100	Aug 15/07	99.12	6.25	0.00
Canada	8.750	Dec 01/05	112.82	5.94	-0.07	Tor -Met	6.100	Dec 12/17	96.38	6.45	0.27
Canada	14.000	Oct 01/06	141.12	5.99	-0.09						
Canada	7.000	Dec 01/06	105.63	5.93	-0.04	**CORPORATE**					
Canada	7.250	Jun 01/07	107.40	5.92	-0.07	AGT Limited	8.800	Sep 22/25	114.06	7.54	0.02
Canada	10.000	Jun 01/08	125.39	5.92	-0.11	Air Canada	6.750	Feb 02/04	95.00	8.40	0.00
Canada	6.000	Jun 01/08	100.71	5.88	-0.08	Associates	5.400	Sep 04/01	98.81	6.48	0.00
Canada	5.500	Jun 01/09	97.75	5.83	-0.08	Avco Fin	5.750	Jun 02/03	97.88	6.56	-0.13
Canada	9.500	Jun 01/10	127.12	5.85	-0.14	Bank of Mon	7.000	Jan 28/10	103.18	6.55	-0.09
Canada	5.500	Jun 01/10	97.72	5.81	-0.08	Bank of N S	5.400	Apr 01/03	97.76	6.30	0.08
						Bank of N S	6.250	Jul 16/07	98.25	6.56	-0.05
PROVINCIAL						Bell Canada	6.500	May 09/05	100.59	6.35	-0.04
Alberta	6.250	Mar 01/01	100.16	5.97	-0.02	Cdn Occ Pet	6.300	Jun 02/08	93.42	7.41	-0.06
B C	5.250	Dec 01/06	95.18	6.17	0.04	Clearnet	0.000	May 15/08	60.50	13.72	0.00
Hyd Quebec	10.875	Jul 25/01	104.78	6.06	-0.06	HydroOne	7.150	Jun 03/10	104.26	6.56	-0.09
Manitoba	7.875	Apr 07/03	104.43	6.09	-0.01	HydroOne	7.350	Jun 03/30	105.37	6.92	-0.02
Manitoba	5.750	Jun 02/08	96.88	6.25	0.02						

With bonds, the amount of principal and the coupon rate are generally specified in the debt contract, which is called the bond indenture. Usually, we are interested in calculating one of the following:

1. the market price that should prevail if the debt contract is to be sold given that one wants to obtain a particular market yield
2. the effective yield given the market price at which the bond currently trades

We adapt slightly the notation used in the previous chapter as follows:

B = the current market price of the bond

F = the face value or amount of principal of the bond

I = interest or coupon payments associated with a bond

r = the effective return (or yield to maturity) required by bond investors for a particular bond with all other variables remaining as defined at the beginning of Section 5.2.

Calculating Market Price

The price that a rational investor should be willing to pay for a bond is the present value of its future cash flows. The discount rate to be applied to obtain this market price is the effective yield that the investor wants to achieve. For regular coupon bonds, we can express this relationship as follows:

$$B = I \times \frac{1}{(1+r)} + I \times \frac{1}{(1+r)^2} + \ldots + I \times \frac{1}{(1+r)^n} + F \times \frac{1}{(1+r)^n}$$

It is obvious that the interest payments represent an annuity since they are for the same amount, paid at the same intervals, and we are using the same discount rate. Therefore, we can estimate the present value of the interest payments using the present value annuity formula presented in Chapter 5. This enables us to restate the relationship above as:

$$(6.1) \qquad B = I \times \left[\frac{1 - \dfrac{1}{(1+r)^n}}{r} \right] + F \times \frac{1}{(1+r)^n}$$

where, the term following I is the present value annuity factor.

If the market yield that an investor can obtain on similar investments is r percent, the investor should be indifferent to receiving the future payments under the debt contract (interest payments for n years plus repayment of principal at maturity) or receiving a current lump sum of B (the present value of those future payments). Hence, this is the value of the bond to the investor.

BOND VALUATION WITH ANNUAL COUPONS (semi-annual pay'ts)

EXAMPLE

We pursue the earlier illustration of a bond with a face value of $1,000, a remaining maturity of 20 years, and a coupon rate of 8 percent assuming annual payment of interest. If interest rates in the market have moved to 10 percent, at what market price should the bond currently trade?

We compute:

$$B = 80 \times \left[\frac{1 - \frac{1}{(1.10)^{20}}}{0.10} \right] + 1,000 \times \frac{1}{(1+.10)^{20}}$$

$$= 80 \times [8.5136] + 1,000 \times [0.14864] = 681.08 + 148.08$$

$$= \$829.16$$

This bond trades at a discount from face value since it provides interest payments that are below the current market rate.

Assume now that instead of rising, current interest rates have fallen to 6 percent. The market price of the bond becomes:

$$B = 80 \times \left[\frac{1 - \frac{1}{(1.06)^{20}}}{0.06} \right] + 1,000 \times \frac{1}{(1+.06)^{20}}$$

$$= 80 \times [11.46992] + 1,000 \times [0.31180] = 917.59 + 311.80$$

$$= \$1,229.39$$

The bond now trades at a premium over face value because it provides for interest payments that exceed current market rates.

The example above assumes that interest payments (or coupons) were made on an annual basis, but in reality, most bonds pay coupons semi-annually. The valuation process remains unchanged; however, we must make adjustments to reflect the fact we are dealing with semi-annual periods. We must:

- divide the annual coupon payments by two to determine the amount of semi-annual coupons
- divide the market yield by two to obtain the six-month market yield
- multiply the number of years to maturity by two to obtain the number of semi-annual periods to maturity.

This is demonstrated in the example below.

| EXAMPLE |

BOND VALUATION WITH SEMI-ANNUAL COUPONS

Using the example above, let's assume that the bond has a face value of $1,000, a remaining maturity of 20 years, and a coupon rate of 8 percent paid semi-annually. When interest rates in the market were 10 percent, we could compute:

Semi-annual market rate $r = 0.10/2 = 0.05$ or 5%

Term to maturity (in semi-annual periods) $n = 20$ years $\times 2 = 40$ periods

Semi-annual coupons I = coupon rate/2 $\times$ face value $= 0.08/2 \times \$1,000 = \$40$

$$B = 40 \times \left[\frac{1 - \dfrac{1}{(1.05)^{40}}}{0.05} \right] + 1,000 \times \frac{1}{(1+.05)^{40}}$$

$$= 40 \times [17.15909] + 1,000 \times [0.14205] = 686.36 + 142.05$$

$$= \$828.41$$

This amount is slightly below the value of the bond that was calculated above ($829.16) with annual coupons. If we repeated this exercise assuming that the market yield had fallen to 6 percent (3 percent semi-annually), we would arrive at a price of $1,231.15, which is slightly above the value of $1,229.39 that was determined in the example above assuming annual coupon payments.

The examples above illustrate the most important property of debt contracts such as bonds: their prices decline if interest rates rise and rise when rates fall. When the prevailing market rate is higher than the debt's nominal interest rate, the debt contract will have to trade at a discount to be attractive to investors (that is, the market price will be below the face value), and vice versa. Bonds are generally issued at or close to face value, which means the issuers must set the coupon rate at about the existing market yields at the time of issue. Since bonds are issued at various times, with different levels of prevailing interest rates, at any given point, some bonds will trade at discounts and others at premiums. This is reflected in the bond quotes included in the above report on Canadian bond quotations, in which most of the bonds are trading at premiums reflecting the fact that on average, bond yields in July of 2000 were below historical rates.

Another important property of bonds is that the longer the time to maturity, the more sensitive their market price is to changes in prevailing market rates.

BONDS WITH DIFFERING MATURITIES

We compute the current market prices for three different bonds, each paying annual interest of 5 percent on a face value of $1,000. The terms to maturity are (a) five years, (b) 10 years, and (c) 20 years. The present market rate of interest is 6 percent. We obtain:

$$\text{(a)} \quad B = 50 \times \left[\frac{1 - \frac{1}{(1.06)^5}}{0.06} \right] + 1{,}000 \times \frac{1}{(1+.06)^5} = 210.62 + 747.26 = \$957.88$$

$$\text{(b)} \quad B = 50 \times \left[\frac{1 - \frac{1}{(1.06)^{10}}}{0.06} \right] + 1{,}000 \times \frac{1}{(1+.06)^{10}} = 368.00 + 558.39 = \$926.39$$

$$\text{(c)} \quad B = 50 \times \left[\frac{1 - \frac{1}{(1.06)^{20}}}{0.06} \right] + 1{,}000 \times \frac{1}{(1+.06)^{20}} = 573.50 + 311.80 = \$885.30$$

The reason that the bond's market price in the above example declines with increasing maturity is easily explained. The bonds offer an interest rate that is below the prevailing market rate. The maturity of the bond specifies the time period over which an investor will be locked into this lower rate. The longer this period, the greater the economic sacrifice or opportunity cost, and, therefore, the lower the value of the bond. In this example, if interest rates had fallen below the coupon rate, say, to 4 percent, the premium would be greater for the bonds with longer terms to maturity. In particular, for the bonds in this example, we could determine the following prices if rates were 4 percent: five-year bond—$1,044.52; 10-year bond—$1,081.10; 20-year bond—$1,135.91.

P E R S P E C T I V E S

Corporate Manager

Since long-term bonds lock in the required amount of interest payments associated with debt for a long period of time, they represent an attractive source of funds since it lets the manager know what the levels of future outflows will be. It follows that long-term bond issues will be particularly attractive for companies when interest rates are low.

Investor

Bond investors will gain the most for a given bond when market interest rates fall below the rate prevailing at their time of purchase. All else being equal, the resulting gain in value will be greater the longer the term to maturity of the bond. Thus, if investors strongly believe that interest rates will fall in the future, they should purchase longer-term bonds. On the other hand, if they are concerned about interest rates rising, they would prefer to hold shorter-term bonds (if any at all) since the prices of such bonds will be less adversely affected.

Some bonds and other fixed-income securities have no maturities. They are called **perpetuals** or **consols** and generate interest payments indefinitely. Drawing on Equation 5.9 for perpetual annuities, the market price of such a perpetual is simply given as:

$$(6.2) \quad B = \frac{I}{r}$$

PERPETUAL BONDS

EXAMPLE

Pursuing the above example, consider a 5 percent $1,000 perpetual bond. With a prevailing market interest rate of 6 percent, the bond's price would be:

$$B = \frac{I}{r} = \frac{50}{.06} = \$833.33$$

An important innovation in the format of traditional bonds is the **zero coupon bond** (or **strip bond**), which does not pay any interest during its life. The purchaser pays less than face value for zeroes and receives face value at maturity; the difference in these two amounts is the rate of return. Similar to treasury bills, which are also issued at a discount from their face value, the lower the price paid for the coupon bond, the higher the effective return. Zeroes are created when financial intermediaries purchase traditional bonds, strip the cash flows from them, and sell the coupons and cash flows separately. These bonds first appeared in Canada in 1982.

Notice that for zero coupon bonds, the first term of the bond valuation equation (Equation 6.1) is zero since there are no coupons. Therefore, we are left with the following equation that can be used to determine the price of these bonds:

$$B = F \times \frac{1}{(1+r)^n} \qquad (6.3)$$

ZERO-COUPON BONDS

Calculate the price of a 20-year zero coupon bond with a face value of $1,000 when the prevailing market rate is 6 percent.

$$B = 1,000 \times \frac{1}{(1+.06)^{20}} = 1,000 \times 0.31180 = \$311.80$$

As with regular coupon bonds, if interest rates fell to 5 percent, the price of this bond would increase:

$$B = 1,000 \times \frac{1}{(1+.05)^{20}} = 1,000 \times 0.37689 = \$376.89$$

Alternatively, if rates rose to 7 percent, the price of the bond would decrease:

$$B = 1,000 \times \frac{1}{(1+.07)^{20}} = 1,000 \times 0.25842 = \$258.42$$

We conclude our discussion of bond pricing by applying the bond valuation process to a bond that is quoted in the *Globe and Mail Report on Business* on July 6, 2000 (from previous report).

VALUING BANK OF NOVA SCOTIA BONDS

The bonds issued by the Bank of Nova Scotia would mature on July 16, 2007, had a coupon rate of 6.25 percent, and a yield of 6.56 percent. The term to maturity of this bond is 7 years, coupons are paid semi-annually, and they have a $100 face value. We have:

$I = .0625/2 \times \$100 = \$3.125$

$n = 7 \text{ years} \times 2 = 14$

$r = 0.0656/2 = 0.0328 \text{ or } 3.28\%$

$$B = 3.125 \times \left[\frac{1 - \dfrac{1}{(1.0328)^{14}}}{0.0328} \right] + 100 \times \frac{1}{(1+0.328)^{14}}$$

$$= 3.125 \times [11.08346] + 100 \times [0.63646] = 34.64 + 63.65 = \$98.29$$

This figure is very close to the reported price of 98.25 with the difference due to rounding.

Calculating Bond Yields

The rate of return on bonds most often quoted for investors is the effective yield or **yield to maturity (YTM)**, which is defined as the promised compounded rate of return an investor will receive from a bond purchased at the current market price and held to maturity. This is the yield that was included for the bond quotes featured in the previous report on Canadian bond quotations. This yield captures the coupon income to be received on the bond as well as any capital gains and losses realized by purchasing the bond for a price different from face value and holding to maturity. It is the periodic interest rate that equates the present value of the expected future cash flows (both coupons and maturity value) to be received on the bond to the initial investment in the bond, which is its current price.

To calculate the YTM as quoted for a bond trading at a particular market price, we use Equation 6.1, but, we now want to solve for r as the unknown. Substituting YTM for r in Equation 6.1, we obtain the following:

$$(6.4) \qquad B = I \times \left[\frac{1 - \frac{1}{(1+YTM)^n}}{YTM} \right] + F \times \frac{1}{(1+YTM)^n}$$

Since price and the cash flows on the right side of Equation 6.4 are known, it can be solved for YTM. When the bond pays semi-annual coupons, all terms are expressed in semi-annual periods, and the resulting YTM will be a semi-annual rate that must be doubled to get the annual YTM.

Unfortunately, Equation 6.4 is complex because of the powers of YTM that appear in it. An algebraic solution that would allow us to find the value of YTM by simple computation is not available, and without access to a suitable calculator, we have to use trial and error or estimation techniques to derive an approximate value that satisfies the equation.[1] In particular, estimating the YTM requires a trial-and-error process to find the discount rate that equates the inflows from the bond (coupons plus maturity value) with its current price (cost). Different rates are tried until the left and right-hand sides are equal. It is relatively easy today to find financial calculators or computer software programs that are able to solve YTM problems; however, two approximation techniques are used in the example below.

DETERMINING THE YIELD TO MATURITY

EXAMPLE

We refer to the Bank of Nova Scotia bond that we valued in the example above. Suppose we had been given the price of that bond ($98.25) and were asked to determine the corresponding YTM. Denoting YTM_s as the semi-annual YTM and substituting the price of $98.25 plus the information from above ($I = \$3.125$ and $n = 14$) into Equation 6.4, we have:

---

[1] Extensive bond yield tables also exist to eliminate the need for tedious computations.

$$98.25 = 3.125 \times \left[\frac{1 - \dfrac{1}{(1+YTM_s)^{14}}}{YTM_s} \right] + 100 \times \frac{1}{(1+YTM_s)^{14}}$$

We will first solve this problem by trial and error and using linear interpolation (as described in Chapter 5). By substituting $YTM_s = 4$ percent, into the equation above, we get a price of \$90.76. Therefore YTM_s must be below this value since 90.76 is less than the price we want, \$98.25. Using 3 percent gives us a price of \$101.41, which is too low. Therefore, we know that the semi-annual rate we are looking for is between 3 and 4 percent.

We can obtain a close approximation using linear interpolation as follows:

$$\begin{bmatrix} \text{Rate} & \text{Price} \\ \text{at } 3\% & 101.41 \\ \text{at } YTM_s\ \% & 98.25 \\ \text{at } 4\% & 90.76 \end{bmatrix}$$

We find YTM_s by setting

$$\frac{YTM_s - 3}{4 - 3} = \frac{98.25 - 101.41}{90.76 - 101.41}$$

$$\frac{YTM_s - 3}{1} = \frac{-3.16}{-10.65} = 0.2967$$

so, $YTM_s = 3.30\%$ and the annual $YTM = 3.30 \times 2 = 6.60\%$

which is close to the exact solution of 6.57 percent obtained by financial calculator and the 6.56 percent provided in the bond listing.

An alternative technique involves the use of an approximation formula. This formula is generally less precise than using trial and error combined with linear interpolation; however, it is much easier to use. It relates the net annual effective cash flow associated with the bond to the average amount of money invested in the bond during the ownership period. Effectively, the investor is assumed to have an average investment of this amount in the bond since the price gradually converges to \$1,000 by the maturity date. This formula is given below:

Approximate YTM

$$= \frac{\text{Annual coupon interest} +/- \text{Average annual amortization of the discount (or premium)}}{(\text{Maturity value} + \text{Current market price})/2}$$

or

$$\text{(6.5)} \quad \text{Approximate } YTM = \frac{\text{Annual coupons} + \left[\dfrac{F-B}{n}\right]}{\dfrac{F+B}{2}}$$

where

n = number of years to maturity

For the bond in this example, we have annual coupons = 3.125 × 2 = $6.25, and we obtain:

$$\text{Approximate } YTM = \frac{\$6.25 + \dfrac{(100-98.25)}{7}}{\dfrac{(100-98.25)}{2}} = \frac{\$6.25+0.25}{99.125} = \frac{6.50}{99.125} = 0.0656 = 6.56\%$$

For this particular example, this formula worked perfectly producing the yield reported in the bond listing, but it is not always so precise especially for bonds with longer maturities.

Determining the YTM for a zero coupon bond is based on the same process, but because there are no coupons, the process reduces to Equation 6.6 with all terms as previously defined:

$$\text{(6.6)} \quad YTM = [F/B]^{1/n} - 1$$

EXAMPLE

DETERMINING THE YTM FOR A ZERO COUPON BOND

Determine the YTM for a zero coupon bond with 12 years to maturity that is sold for $300.

$YTM = [1000/300]^{1/12} - 1$

$YTM = [3.3333]^{1/12} - 1 = 1.1055 - 1 = 0.1055$ or 10.55%

We conclude our discussion of the yield to maturity by noting that it is a promised yield because investors earn the indicated yield only if the bond is held to maturity and the coupons are reinvested at the calculated YTM. Therefore, no trading can be done for a particular bond if the YTM is to be earned. The investor simply buys and holds.

Current Yield

The **current yield** is defined as the ratio of the annual coupon interest to the current market price. The current yield (CY) is clearly superior to simply citing the coupon rate on a bond because it uses the current market price as opposed to the face amount of a bond (almost always $1,000). However, current yield is not a true measure of the return to a bond purchaser since it disregards the bond's purchase price relative to its eventual redemption at par value. In effect, it is a one-period rate of return that measures the interest payment return relative to the initial investment. It is defined in Equation 6.7 below:

$$CY = \frac{\text{Annual interest}}{B} \qquad (6.7)$$

CURRENT YIELD

EXAMPLE

Determine the current yield for the Bank of Nova Scotia bond used in the examples above. Since this bond is trading at $98.25 and has associated annual interest payments of $6.25, we obtain:

$$CY = \frac{6.25}{98.25} = 0.636 \text{ or } 6.36\%$$

Notice from our example that the current yield does not equal the coupon rate of 6.25 percent or the YTM of 6.56 percent. This will be the case unless the bond is trading at its face value, in which case all three rates would be equal. It is obvious that whenever bonds trade at a discount, the CY will be greater than the coupon rate (as in this example), and whenever they trade at a premium, the CY will be less than the coupon rate.

DETERMINANTS OF INTEREST RATES   6.3

Thus far, we have said little about the determination of the proper discount rate or about what influences the effective interest yield that a particular debt contract commands in the marketplace. These issues are considered next.

The effective yield of a debt contract reflects the rates of interest that prevail in financial markets at the time, the characteristics of the borrower, and the particular terms of the instrument. In other words, it is established by general economic factors that affect the overall level of interest rates and by such features of the debt contract as its maturity, the currency in which it is denominated, and the perceived risk of default. We discuss each of these aspects in turn.

Interest is the price paid for borrowed money. It is commonly given in percent and expresses the annual rate of return provided. Changes in interest rates are often quoted in terms of **basis points**, where a basis point is 1/100th of one percent. For example, an increase of 25 basis points means that the interest rate has moved up by 0.25 percent.

Like other prices in a market economy, interest rates are determined by the laws of supply and demand. The general relationship between the supply and demand for funds is shown in Figure 6.3. The supply of capital through savings increases with rising interest rates, whereas the demand for funds decreases as their costs rise. At equilibrium, interest rates are such that demand equals supply. This framework for interest rate determination is called the **loanable funds theory**.

FIGURE 6.3

Interest Rates and the Supply and Demand for Capital

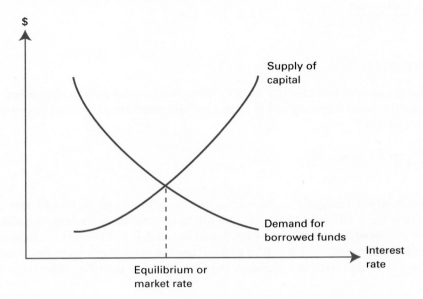

While interest rates measure the price paid by a borrower to a lender for the use of resources over some time period, the price differs from case to case based on the demand and supply for these funds, which results in a wide variety of interest rates. The spread between the lowest and highest rates at any point in time could be as much as 10 to 15 percentage points.

It is convenient to focus on the one interest rate that provides the foundation for others. This rate is referred to as the short-term riskless rate (designated RF in this text) and is typically equal to the rate offered by short-term government treasury bills. All other rates differ from RF because of two factors: (1) maturity differentials and (2) risk premiums.

The basic foundation of market interest rates is the opportunity cost of foregoing consumption representing the rate that must be offered to individuals to persuade them to save rather than consume. This rate is sometimes called the **real risk-free rate of interest** because it is not affected by price changes or risk factors. We will refer to it simply as the "real rate" and designate it RR in this discussion.

Nominal interest rates on T-bills consist of the RR plus an adjustment for inflation. A lender who advances $100 for a year at 10 percent will be repaid $110. But if inflation is 12 percent per year, the $110 that the lender receives upon repayment of the loan is worth only $(1/1.12) \times (\$110)$ or $98.21 in today's dollars. Therefore, lenders want to be compensated for the expected rate of price change in order to leave the real purchasing power of wealth unchanged or improved. As an approximation for discussion purposes, this inflation adjustment can be added to the real risk-free rate of interest. Unlike RR, which is often assumed by market participants to be reasonably stable over time, adjustments for expected inflation vary widely over time.

Thus, for short-term risk-free securities such as three-month T-bills, the nominal interest rate is a function of the real rate of interest and the expected inflationary premium. This is expressed in Equation 6.8, which is an approximation:[2]

$$RF \approx RR + EI \tag{6.8}$$

where

RF = short-term treasury bill rate

RR = the real risk-free rate of interest

EI = the expected rate of inflation over the term of the instrument

Equation 6.8 shows that the nominal rate on short-term risk-free securities rises point for point with anticipated inflation with the real rate of interest remaining unaffected. Turning Equation 6.8 around, the real risk-free rate of interest can be estimated by subtracting the expected inflation rate from the observed nominal interest rate. The expected rate of inflation can be determined by reference to various economic projections from the government information sources, banks, and securities firms.

ESTIMATING THE REAL RATE OF RETURN

EXAMPLE

If T-bill rates are presently 6.0 percent and the expected level of inflation is 2.0 percent, the real rate of return is expected to be (approximately):

$$RR \approx RF - EI$$

$$\approx 6.0 - 2.0 = 4.0 \text{ percent}[3]$$

Figure 6.4 plots historical annual inflation rates, T-bill yields, and long-term government bond yields in Canada over the 1965-97 period. While inflation during the past year does not necessarily measure expected inflation for the upcoming year, there is an obvious relationship. Figure 6.4 shows that T-bill yields have generally exceeded inflation levels, which was the case for 27 of 33 years (bond yields exceeded in 30 of 33 years). In fact, T-bill yields exceeded inflation levels by an annual average of 2.60 percent (bond yields by 3.64 percent) over this period, and they were never below the previous year's inflation rate after 1977. While this is only summary information, it is supportive of the existence of the Fisher relationship as described above.

---

[2] This is a simplification of the "Fisher Effect" [see Irving Fisher, "Appreciation and Interest," *Publications of the American Economic Association* (August 1896), pp. 1-100]. The precisely correct procedure is to multiply (1 + the real rate) by (1 + the expected rate of inflation) and subtract 1.0. For the purposes of our discussion, the additive relationship is satisfactory provided that levels of inflation are relatively low.

[3] More precisely, using the procedure described in Footnote 2, we could estimate the real rate as:
$$RR = (1.06)/(1.02) - 1 = 0.392 \text{ or } 3.92 \text{ percent.}$$

FIGURE 6.4

FIGURE 6.4

Canadian T-Bill, Bond
and Inflation Rates
(1965-97)

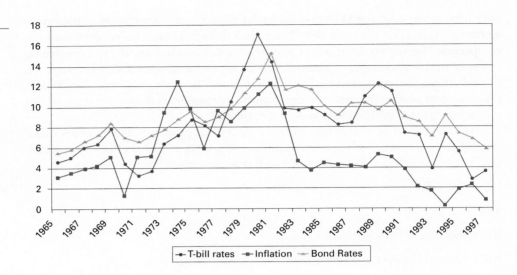

Sources: Canadian Institute of Actuaries (CIA) website at www.actuaries.ca (June 14, 2000) and Statistic Cana-da's CANSIM database.

The Term Structure of Interest Rates (Maturity Differentials)

All market interest rates are affected by a time factor which leads to maturity differentials. That is, although long-term Government of Canada bonds are virtually free from default risk in the same manner as government T-bills, long-term bonds usually yield more than medium-term ones, which typically yield more than T-bills. This pattern is evident in Figure 6.4 in which the reported long-term government bond yields exceeded government T-bill rates in 27 of the 33 years depicted in the graph. In fact, they exceeded T-bill yields by an average of 1.04 percent over the entire period. This typical relationship between bond maturity and yield applies to all types of bonds—federal, provincial, and municipal government debt securities, and corporate debt securities. While this relationship is characteristic, it is not always the case as shown in Figure 6.5 and Figure 6.6 below.

The **term structure of interest rates** refers to the relationship between time to maturity and yields for a particular category of bonds at a particular time. Ideally, other factors are held constant particularly the risk of default. Look at Government of Canada bonds. At any given time, there are bond issues of many different maturities. The term structure is usually plotted in the form of a **yield curve**, which is a graphical depiction of the relationship between yields and time to maturity for bonds that are identical except for maturity dates. The horizontal axis represents time to maturity, and the vertical axis represents yield to maturity. Figure 6.5 includes a graphical representation of the yield curve for government interest rates as of June 30, 2000. This graph depicts a yield curve with short-term rates increasing from approximately 5.5 percent for one-month T-bills to 6.0 percent for one-year securities before gradually declining to almost 5.5 percent for maturities greater than 10 years.

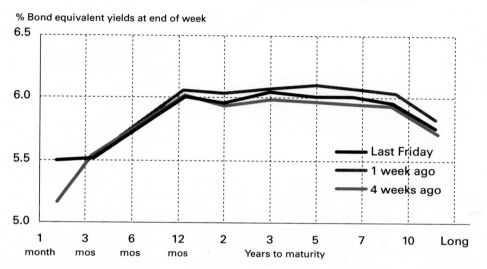

% Bond equivalent yields at end of week

FIGURE 6.5

CANADIAN BONDS
Government of Canada
Yield Curve

Source: Globe and Mail Report on Business, July 3, 2000, p. B9.

Figure 6.5 shows just one of the numerous possible shapes that the yield curve may assume and not the most common one. In fact, almost any shape is possible. Figure 6.6 shows three additional yield curves for government interest rates at the end of June in 1990, 1994, and 1998. The upward-sloping curve in 1994 is the most common since interest rates that rise with maturity are considered the "normal" pattern. The downward-sloping curve for 1990 is less common with short rates above long rates. These inverted yield curves are unusual, and some market participants believe they indicate that short-term rates will fall. In fact, short-term interest rates did decline in the subsequent 1991-1993 period. Another less-common shape is the relatively flat yield curve existing in 1998, which indicates that long- and short-term rates are very similar.

FIGURE 6.6

Yield Curves

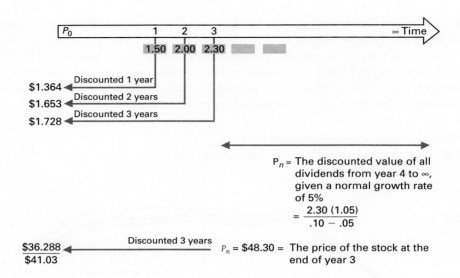

Several theories of the term structure of interest rates have attempted to explain the different shapes and slopes of the yield curve and why it shifts over time. The three most commonly referred to theories are: (1) the expectations theory, (2) the liquidity preference theory, and (3) the market segmentation theory.

The **expectations theory** of the term structure of interest rates asserts that financial market participants determine security yields such that the return from holding an n-period security equals the average return expected from holding a series of one-year securities over the same n periods. In other words, the long-term rate of interest is equal to an average of the present yield on short-term securities plus the expected future yields on short-term securities that are expected to prevail over the long-term period. For each period, the total rate of return is expected to be the same on all securities regardless of time to maturity. This hypothesis maintains that investors can expect the same return regardless of the choice of investment, and any combination of securities for a specified period will have the same expected return. For example, a five-year bond will have the same expected return as a two-year bond held to maturity plus a three-year bond bought at the beginning of the third year.

The second theory, the **liquidity preference theory**, states that as in the expectations theory, interest rates reflect the sum of current and expected short rates plus liquidity (risk) premiums. Because uncertainty increases with time, investors prefer to lend for the short run. Borrowers, however, would rather borrow for the long run in order to be assured of funds. Investors receive a liquidity premium to induce them to lend long term while paying a price premium (in the form of lower yields) for investing short term. The implication of this theory is that longer-term bonds should offer higher yields, which is consistent with the fact that yield curves are generally upward sloping. A key difference between the liquidity preference theory and the expectations theory is the former's recognition that interest rate expectations are uncertain. Risk-averse investors seek to be compensated for this uncertainty.

A third hypothesis for explaining the term structure of interest rates is the **market segmentation theory.** This theory states that the various institutional investors, who have different maturity needs dictated by the nature of their liabilities, confine themselves to specific maturity segments. Investors are not willing to shift from one maturity sector to another to take advantage of any opportunities that may arise. Under the market segmentation theory, the shape of the yield curve is determined by the supply and demand conditions for securities within each of the multiple maturity sectors.

Which of these theories is correct? The issue of the term structure has not been resolved; although many empirical studies have been done, the results are at least partially conflicting. Therefore, definitive statements cannot be made. In actual practice, market observers and participants do not tend to be strict adherents to any particular theory. Rather, they accept the reasonable implications of all of them and try to use any available information in assessing the shape of the yield curve. For example, many market participants will focus on expectations but allow for liquidity premiums.

Generally, upward-sloping yield curves have been the norm as would be predicted by the liquidity preference theory. This theory is more compatible than the others with the study of finance, which emphasizes the risk-return trade-off that exists. The liquidity preference theory stresses the idea that because of larger risks, longer maturity securities require larger returns or compensation. On the other hand, the most reasonable explanation for downward-sloping yield curves is that investors expect short-term rates to decline in the near future. Otherwise, investors could earn higher returns from short-term assets, which have less risk than long-term assets. One could not expect this relationship to persist for long periods of time since it runs counter to the risk-expected return trade-off we associate with financial assets.

Risk Premiums

Market interest rates other than those for riskless government securities are also affected by a **risk premium**—which lenders require as compensation for the risk involved. This risk premium is associated with the issuer's own particular situation or with a particular market factor. The risk premium is often referred to as the yield spread or yield differential.

The most prevalent risk premium is due to the risk of default by the bond issuer. In other words, creditors require higher yields to compensate them for the possibility that the borrower may default on the promised debt payments. The greater the risk, the higher the yield. We can approximate the amount of this risk premium by comparing the effective annual yields of otherwise similar debt issues with identical maturities and coupon rates.

We provide some evidence of these default risk premiums below in Table 6.1 using data from the previous report on Canadian Bond quotations. All of these bonds mature within one day of each other and have similar coupon rates except for the Clearnet bonds, which mature approximately two weeks earlier and pay no coupons (i.e., they are zeroes). Table 6.1 shows how the yields increase as we move from the

Government of Canada bonds, which have virtually no risk of default, to provincial bonds, to corporate bonds. In fact, the yield on Canadian Occidental Petroleum bonds was more than 1.5 percent higher than the Government of Canada bonds yield, while the Clearnet bonds had more than twice the yield on any one of the Government of Canada bonds, a substantial default risk premium.

Table 6.1

Comparison of Effective Yields on Debt as an Indication of the Risk of Default

Issuer	Coupon Rate (%)	Maturity Date	Effective Yield (%)*
Government of Canada	6.00	June 1, 2008	5.88
Ontario Hydro	5.60	June 2, 2008	6.21
Government of Manitoba	5.75	June 2, 2008	6.25
Government of Saskatchewan	5.50	June 2, 2008	6.25
Canadian Occidental Petroleum	6.30	June 2, 2008	7.41
Clearnet	0.00	May 15, 2008	13.72

*The effective yield assumes that all payments will be made, and the debt instruments are held to maturity. The figures are based on prices quoted on July 5, 2000 as reported in the *Globe and Mail* on July 6, 2000. Reprinted with permission.

Interest Rates in an International Environment

At any time, we can observe significant differences in interest rates from country to country. In today's world, money is one of the most mobile commodities flowing across most national borders via telecommunication links (telephone, fax, or computer) seeking the highest investment return. How, then, can such different interest rates persist without everyone seeking to borrow in the country with the lowest rate and investing in the country with the highest rate?

The answer is to be found mainly in anticipated foreign exchange movements. If we borrow or lend in a foreign country, we become exposed to foreign exchange risk, and this risk has to be balanced against any perceived advantages that may stem from interest rate differentials.

BORROWING IN FOREIGN CURRENCIES

Assume interest rates on one-year loans in the United States are 9 percent, while the equivalent Canadian rate is 11 percent. The current exchange rate is C$1 = US$0.72. We need to borrow C$1,000 and based on the lower rate, we decide to take the loan in the United States. We have:

C$ amount required	= C$1,000
US$ amount to be borrowed	= 1,000×0.72 = US$720
US$ amount to be repaid at year end	= 720(1 + 0.09) = US$784.80

The amount of Canadian dollars required to repay US$784.80 depends on the exchange rate that prevails at year end. Assume that, during the year, the value of the Canadian dollar falls slightly against the American and at year end, trades at C$1 = US$0.7070. The amount of Canadian dollars required to be repaid is:

$$= \frac{784.80}{.7070} = C\$1,110.04$$

We see that we are no better off than if we had taken out a loan in Canada at 11 percent. The interest rate differential of 2 percent (11 percent − 9 percent) that existed and that induced us to borrow in the United States has been offset by a slight decline in the value of the Canadian dollar during the year.

The well-known **interest rate parity theorem** states that in free markets, international differences in interest rates tend to be offset by expected changes in exchange rates. Otherwise, capital would flow from countries with low interest rates to those with high interest rates. Such flows would increase the supply of capital in the country with high rates thereby driving down the cost of borrowing. At the same time, funds would be withdrawn from countries with low rates causing interest rates to rise. More precisely, the exact link is again made through forward markets, and the fact that opportunities for arbitrage (or the making of a riskless profit through simultaneous borrowing and lending) should not persist.

Pursuing the previous example, assume that the exchange rate at year end of C$1 = US$0.7070 is in fact the forward rate at which U.S. dollars can be bought today for delivery one year from now. It is easy to show that any deviation from a forward rate that equates the effective riskless interest rates for loans of comparable maturities in both countries will result in covered interest arbitrage opportunities, with investors borrowing in the country with the lower rate to lend in the higher-rate country.

Specifically, assume interest rates as given above but with a forward exchange rate of C$1 = US$0.72. We could now take a one-year loan in the United States at 9 percent and fully protect against future exchange rate risk by buying U.S. dollars at this forward rate, which happens to equal the current spot rate. With foreign exchange risk thus eliminated, everyone would borrow in the United States and could then use the proceeds to lend in Canada at 11 percent for a riskless profit of 2 percent. Clearly, given free markets, it is economically inconsistent to have divergent interest rates across countries without expecting offsetting changes in foreign exchange rates.

According to the interest rate parity theorem, the relationship that links exchange rates and interest rates between two countries for any time period is given as:

$$(6.9) \quad \frac{f_{AB}}{s_{AB}} = \frac{1+r_A}{1+r_B}$$

where

$f_{AB} =$ current forward exchange rate expressed in number of units of currency A required to purchase one unit of currency B

$s_{AB} =$ current spot exchange rate again expressed in number of units of currency A required to purchase one unit of currency B

$r_A =$ interest rate in country A

$r_B =$ interest rate in country B

EXAMPLE

INTEREST RATE PARITY

Pursuing our earlier example in which we looked at one-year loans in the United States (country A) and Canada (country B), we have $r_A = 9\%$, $r_B = 11\%$, and $s_{AB} = .72$. Using the above equation, we can compute the equilibrium forward exchange rate as:

$$\frac{f_{AB}}{.72} = \frac{1+.09}{1+.11}$$

$$f_{AB} = .72 \times \frac{1.09}{1.11} = US\$0.70770$$

With foreign exchange controls or other market impediments, this balancing process may not work properly, which can lead to temporary distortions in market rates. The interest rate parity theorem is revisited in Chapter 20.

Earlier in this section, we saw that interest rates and inflation are closely linked, so that interest rates should be high in countries with high inflation and low in countries with low inflation. We would also expect exchange rates to be related to relative levels of prices and inflation. For example, if Canadian inflation significantly exceeded the rate in the United States, in time we would expect this to exert downward pressure on the Canadian dollar. With Canadian prices for goods and services increasing against those of the United States, we can remain competitive in international trade only if the value of our currency depreciates. Through inflation, we now have a link between interest rates and shifts in foreign exchange rates. Typically, we observe:

Countries with high inflation	Countries with low inflation
High interest rates	Low interest rates
Weak currency that is expected to depreciate against others	Strong currency that is expected to appreciate against others

so that

Interest rate + expected change in currency value = constant for all countries

Put another way, there are no bargains in international financial markets, and what you gain with one hand you are likely to lose with the other. This seems reasonable, for if we thought that we had discovered a bargain, we would immediately have to ask why this opportunity had not been recognized by others. There are many highly sophisticated players in international markets, and the international mobility of capital generally ensures that comparable yields will prevail even across national boundaries.

The above also explains why central banks of individual countries have limited discretion in influencing domestic interest rates through independent monetary policy. Assume, for example, that the Bank of Canada freely increased the domestic money supply in order to reduce interest rates, while rates in the United States remained high. Capital would immediately flow out of the country in search of higher yields. Such capital outflows would exert downward pressure on the Canadian dollar making imports more expensive. Because we import many goods and services, this would increase our inflation rate. We have seen that we cannot expect to maintain low interest rates given high inflation, since money would continue to leave the country. Thus, in the long run, such a one-sided policy could actually become counterproductive. Although this illustration is admittedly very cursory, it does underscore the fact that economic variables such as inflation, exchange rates, and interest rates are closely interrelated, and that domestic financial markets cannot be viewed in isolation. ▲

COMMON SHARE VALUATION   6.4

Two basic approaches to the valuation of common stocks using fundamental security analysis are the present value and the relative valuation methods.

The present value analysis is similar to the discounting process considered for bonds above. The future stream of cash flows to be received from a common stock is discounted back to the present at an appropriate discount rate (that is, the investor's required rate of return). We present the dividend discount model, which is the most common form of this approach.

The relative valuation approach values shares relative to some company characteristic based on a multiple that is deemed appropriate. We consider here only the price-earnings ratio, which is probably the most widely used by practising security analysts. A stock is said to be worth some multiple of its future earnings. In effect, investors determine a stock's value by deciding how many dollars (the multiple) they are willing to pay for every dollar of estimated earnings.

The Dividend Discount Model

Since dividends are closely related to earnings and represent the only cash payment a shareholder receives directly from a firm, they are often considered the foundation of valuation for common stocks. Following this rationale, the **dividend discount model (DDM)** uses these expected future cash flows as the basis for valuing common shares.

An investor or analyst using this approach carefully studies the future prospects for a company and estimates the likelihood of dividends being paid. In addition, the analyst estimates an appropriate required rate of return or discount rate based on the risk foreseen in the dividends and given the alternatives available. Finally, he would discount to the present the entire stream of estimated future dividends (properly identified as to amount and timing). This can be expressed in the form of the following equation:

(6.10)
$$P_0 = \frac{D_1}{(1+r_{cs})^1} + \frac{D_2}{(1+r_{cs})^2} + \dots + \frac{D_\infty}{(1+r_{cs})^\infty}$$

$$= \sum_{t=1}^{\infty} \frac{D_t}{(1+r_{cs})^t}$$

where

P_0 = the estimated value (or price) of a common stock today

$D_1, D_2, \dots$ = the dividends expected to be received in year 1, year 2, etc. for each future period

r_{cs} = the required rate of return for this stock, which is the discount rate applicable for an investment with this degree of riskiness

Many readers may be bothered by the fact that the DDM contains only dividends and an infinite stream of dividends at that. In addition to dividends, most investors are interested in capital gains, which by definition involve the difference between the price paid for a security and the price at which it is later sold. Therefore, a valuation model should seemingly contain a stock price somewhere. Thus, in computing present value for a stock, investors are interested in the present value of the expected price two years from now, six months from now, or whatever the expected holding period is. How can price be incorporated into the valuation, or should it be?

In truth, the only cash flows that an investor needs to be concerned with are dividends. Expected price in the future is built into the dividend discount model given by Equation 6.10; it is simply not visible. To see this, ask yourself at what price you can expect to sell a common stock that you have bought. Assume, for example, that you purchase today and plan to hold for three years. The price you receive three years from now will reflect the buyer's expectations of dividends from that point forward (at the end of years 4, 5, etc.). The estimated price today of the stock is equal to:

$$P_0 = \frac{D_1}{(1+r_{cs})^1} + \frac{D_2}{(1+r_{cs})^2} + \frac{D_3}{(1+r_{cs})^3} + \frac{P_3}{(1+r_{cs})^3}$$

But P_3 (the estimated price of the stock at the end of year 3) is, in turn, equal to the discounted value of all future dividends from year 4 to infinity. That is,

$$P_3 = \frac{D_4}{(1+r_{cs})^1} + \frac{D_5}{(1+r_{cs})^2} + \frac{D_6}{(1+r_{cs})^3} + \ldots + \frac{P_\infty}{(1+r_{cs})^{\infty-3}}$$

Substituting the second equation into the first one produces Equation 6.10, the basic DDM. Thus, the result is the same whether investors discount only a stream of dividends or a combination of dividends and price. Since price at any point in the future is a function of the dividends to be received after that time, the price today for a common stock is best thought of as the discounted value of all future dividends.

There are two problems associated with implementing Equation 6.10: we must estimate dividends to infinity, and the dividend stream is uncertain. The first problem is not as troublesome as it first appears from a practical standpoint. This is because as we showed in Chapter 5, at reasonably high discount rates such as 12, 14, or 16 percent, dividends received 30 or 40 years in the future are worth very little today. Therefore, it is reasonable to make simplifying assumptions with regard to dividends in the distant future. While we cannot alleviate the uncertainty associated with future dividend streams, we can deal with this problem in two ways:

1. by doing our best to estimate dividends as accurately as possible
2. by increasing the required rate of return on common shares in direct proportion to the level of uncertainty (or risk) associated with the expected dividends.

In order to operationalize the DDM, we make some assumptions about the expected growth rate of dividends. That is, the investor estimates or models the expected percentage rate of growth in the future stream of dividends. A timeline will be used to represent the three alternative growth-rate versions of the DDM. All stocks that pay a dividend or that are expected to sometime in the future can be modelled using this approach. It is critical to remember that in using the DDM, an investor must account for all dividends from now to infinity by modelling the growth rate(s). As shown below, the mechanics of this process are such that we do not actually see all these dividends because the formulas reduce to a simplified form. Nevertheless, we are accounting for all future dividends when we use the DDM.

In using the DDM, it is necessary to remember that the dividend currently being paid on a stock (or the most recent dividend paid) is designated as D_0 and is, of course, known. However, starting with D_1, investors must estimate the dividend expected to be paid in the next period future dividends.

The three growth-rate versions of the DDM are:

1. A dividend stream with a zero growth rate resulting from a fixed-dollar dividend equal to the current dividend D_0 being paid every year from now to infinity. This is referred to as the *no-growth-rate* or *zero-growth-rate* version of the DDM:

D_0	D_0	D_0	D_0	$+...+$	D_0	Dividends
0	1	2	3	$+...+$	∞	Time period

2. A dividend stream that is growing at a constant annual rate g starting with D_0. This is typically referred to as the *constant* or *normal-growth-rate* version of the DDM:

D_0	$D_0(1+g)^1$	$D_0(1+g)^2$	$+...+$	$D_0(1+g)^\infty$	Dividends
0	1	2	$+...+$	∞	Time period

3. A dividend stream that is growing at variable rates (e.g., g_1 for the first two years and g_2 thereafter). This is referred to as the *multiple-growth-rate* version of the dividend discount model:

$D_0 D_1=D_0(1+g_1)$	$D_2=D_1(1+g_1)$	$D_3=D_2(1+g_2)+...+$	$D_\infty=D_{\infty-1}(1+g_1)$Dividends
0	1	2	3 $+...+$ ∞ Time period

We examine each in turn.

No-Growth-Rate or Zero-Growth-Rate Version of the DDM

The fixed-dollar dividend model reduces to a perpetual annuity or perpetuity. Assuming a constant-dollar dividend, Equation 6.10 simplifies to Equation 6.11 below.

(6.11) $$P_0 = \frac{D_0}{r_{cs}}$$

where D_0 is the constant-dollar dividend expected for all future time periods.

The no-growth-rate version is equivalent to the valuation process for preferred shares (discussed in Chapter 13), which typically pay dividends of a fixed amount and have no maturity date. It is extremely important in understanding the valuation of common stocks using the DDM to recognize that in all cases, an investor is discounting the future stream of dividends from now to infinity. This fact tends to be overlooked when using the perpetuity formula involving the zero-growth-rate version because the discounting process is greatly simplified. Nevertheless, in this case, as in all others, we are accounting for all dividends from now to infinity. It is simply a mathematical fact that dividing a constant-dollar amount by the discount rate produces a result equivalent to discounting each dividend from now to infinity separately and summing all of the present values.

NO-GROWTH IN DIVIDENDS

Preferred shares with a par value of $100 specify a dividend rate of 8 percent implying annual dividend payments of $8, which we assume are paid at year end. If the market yield of 10 percent is currently applicable to these securities, the market price of these preferred shares is:

$$P_0 = \frac{8}{0.10} = \$80$$

Conversely, if the shares currently trade at $120, their effective rate of return becomes:

$$r = \frac{8}{120} = 6.67\%$$

The Constant- or Normal-Growth-Rate Version of the DDM

The other two versions of the DDM indicate that in order to establish the cash flow stream of expected dividends, which is to be subsequently discounted, it is first necessary to compound some beginning dividend into the future. Obviously, the higher the growth rate used, the greater the future amount, and the longer the time period, the greater the future amount.

A well-known scenario in valuation is the case in which dividends are expected to grow at a constant rate over time. This **constant-growth-rate version** is shown in Equation 6.12:

$$P_0 = \frac{D_0(1+g)}{(1+r_{cs})^1} + \frac{D_0(1+g)^2}{(1+r_{cs})^2} + \frac{D_0(1+g)^3}{(1+r_{cs})^3} + \ldots + \frac{D_0(1+g)^\infty}{(1+r_{cs})^\infty} \qquad (6.12)$$

where D_0 is the current dividend being paid and growing at the constant rate g.

Equation 6.12 can be simplified to the following equation:[4]

$$P_0 = \frac{D_1}{r_{cs} - g} \qquad (6.13)$$

where D_1 is the dividend expected to be received at the end of year 1. Notice that r must be greater than g or else the results are uninformative.

Equation 6.13 is used whenever the growth rate of future dividends is estimated to be constant to infinity. It is used quite often in actual practice because of its simplicity and because in many circumstances, it is a reasonable description of the actual behaviour of a large number of companies as well as the market as a whole.

---

[4] Equation 6.12 represents a geometric series that is being multiplied by $(1+g)/(1+k)$ every period. The sum of this series is represented by Equation 6.13 as the number of periods involved approaches infinity.

EXAMPLE

CONSTANT-GROWTH-RATE VERSION

A company is currently paying $1 per share in dividends on its common shares, and investors expect dividends to grow at the rate of 7 percent per year for the foreseeable future. For investments at this risk level, investors require a return of 15 percent a year. The estimated share price for this company is:

$$P_0 = \frac{D_1}{r_{cs} - g} = \frac{\$1.00(1.07)}{0.15 - 0.07} = \$13.38$$

We again stress the fact that the constant-growth-rate version of the DDM given in Equation 6.13 takes account of all future cash flows from now to infinity although this is not apparent from simply looking at the equation itself. In particular, the results produced by this equation are equivalent to the sum that would be obtained by adding together the discounted value of all future dividends. However, the mathematics of the process involving a constant growth rate to infinity reduces to a very simple expression masking the fact that all dividends from now to infinity are being accounted for.

Estimating the Growth Rate in Future Dividends

In order to implement the constant-growth-rate version of the DDM, we need three estimates:

1. the expected dividend at the end of the first year
2. the required rate of return by common shareholders
3. the expected growth rate in dividends.

Assuming constant growth in dividends from now to infinity, once we know the most recent dividend (D_0) and the expected growth rate (g), then the expected year-end dividend (D_1) can be estimated as: $D_1 = D_0(1+g)$. We defer our discussion of estimating the required rate of return until Chapters 7 and 8, and now turn our attention to determining a reasonable estimate of g, which will also enable us to estimate D_1.

The determination of a sustainable growth rate in earnings and dividends is one of the most important components of the stock valuation process. One of the most common growth estimates is referred to as the **internal** or **sustainable growth rate** of earnings or dividends. It is calculated as the product of the company's return on equity (ROE) and its retention ratio (which is calculated as 1.0 minus the dividend payout ratio) as shown below.

(6.14) $g = ROE \times (1 - \text{Payout ratio})$

This equation is often used by security analysts where g can be estimated using data for a particular year using long-term averages or "normalized" figures for ROE and payout ratio. The intuition behind this measure is that growth in earnings (and dividends) will be positively related to the amount of each dollar of earnings reinvested in the company (as measured by the retention ratio) times the return earned on reinvested funds (ROE). For example, a firm that retains all its earnings and earns 15 percent on its equity would see its equity base grow by 15 percent per year. If the same company paid out all its earnings, it would not grow. Similarly, a firm that retained a proportion (*b*) would earn 15 percent on that proportion resulting in $g = b \times ROE$. A weakness of this approach is its reliance on accounting figures that are based on book values and the accrual method of accounting. As a result, they may not always serve as reliable proxies for market values and cash flows.

ESTIMATING THE SUSTAINABLE GROWTH RATE

For 1998, Bombardier Inc.'s ROE was 0.145, and its dividend payout ratio was 0.2595. The internal growth rate estimate based on this data is 10.76 percent:

$$g = ROE \times (1 - \text{Payout ratio}) = (0.145) \times (1 - 0.2595) = 0.1076 = 10.76\%$$

The earnings growth rate or persistence in the earnings and dividend trends are seldom easy to predict. Investors cannot blindly use the current or past internal growth rate for earnings per share (EPS) or dividends to predict the future rate of growth. The internal growth rate estimate produced by Equation 6.14 is reliable only if a company's profitability as measured by ROE remains in balance and if the company maintains a stable payout ratio. If, for example, the ROE or payout ratio for a company increased or decreased significantly in the future, the actual growth rate will turn out to be quite different than the estimated one.

A problem associated with using a particular year to estimate the internal growth rate is that the year used may not be a normal year. Basing a projection on one year's results can lead to a faulty estimate; this is particularly true for companies in cyclical industries. While payout ratios for most companies vary over time, reasonable estimates can often be obtained for a particular company using an average of recent years. Estimating future ROE is more challenging.

It is critical to remember that what matters is the future "expected" growth rate not the actual historical growth rate. If investors expect the growth rate to be different in the future, they should use the expected growth rate and not simply the calculation based on current data. Despite this fact, one commonly used way of determining expected future growth rates is to examine historic rates of growth in dividends and earnings levels including long-term trends in these growth rates for the company, the industry, and the economy as a whole. Predictions regarding future growth rates can be determined based on these past trends using arithmetic or geometric averages or using more involved statistical techniques such as regression analysis.

Another important source of information regarding company growth, particularly for the near term, can be found in analyst estimates. Investors may be especially interested in consensus estimates because it is quite possible that market values are based to a large extent on these. Deviations from these estimates could signal that a security is mispriced in the market, which may represent an exploitable investment opportunity. This was evident when Nortel Networks saw the value of its stock plunge more than 25 percent on October 25, 2000 despite the company's announcement of strong third-quarter earnings.[5] The plunge was largely attributed to the fact that third-quarter revenue growth

---

[5] The value of the TSE 300 Composite Index declined by a record number of points (837.33) that day primarily due to Nortel's fall since it comprised about one-third of the TSE 300's value prior to October 25.

(of 42 percent) was weaker than expected, which caused concerns about the company's ability to sustain its rapid growth in the future.

Estimating Growth Opportunities

The constant-growth-rate version of the DDM can also provide a useful assessment of the market's perception of growth opportunities available to a company. For example, let's assume that a firm with no profitable growth opportunities would not reinvest residual profits in the company but rather pay out all its earnings in the form of dividends. This implies $g = 0$ and $D_1 = EPS_1$, where EPS_1 represents the expected earnings per common share in the upcoming year. Under these assumptions, the constant-growth-rate version of the DDM reduces to the following expression:

(6.15) $$P_0 = \frac{EPS_1}{r_{cs}}$$

Although we may not find many no-growth firms in practice, the result above can be applied to companies that do have growth opportunities. Thus, at any given time, we can view the share price of any common stock (that satisfies the assumptions of the DDM) as being comprised of two components: its no-growth component and the present value of growth opportunities (PVGO), which can be expressed as:

(6.16) $$P_0 = \frac{EPS_1}{r_{cs}} + PVGO$$

| EXAMPLE |

ESTIMATING THE PRESENT VALUE OF GROWTH OPPORTUNITIES

Assume that the expected year 1 earnings per share (EPS_1) for the company in the example above is $2.00. If their shares were trading at the intrinsic value of $13.38 estimated above, this implies that an estimate of only $0.05 for the present value of growth opportunities (PVGO) is factored by market participants into their share price:

$$PVGO = P_0 - \frac{EPS_1}{r_{cs}} = 13.38 - \frac{2.00}{0.15} = 13.38 - 13.33 = \$0.05$$

This implies that very little of the company's share price is attributable to future growth opportunities.

To fully understand the constant-growth-rate version of the DDM, it is also important to realize that the model implies that the stock price for any one period is estimated to grow at the same rate as the dividends, which is g. This means that the expected growth rate in price plus the expected percentage return received in the form of dividends will equal the required rate of return (r_{cs}). This is obvious if we rearrange the constant-growth-rate version of the DDM in the following manner using the present market price as a measure of the intrinsic value to obtain an estimate of the return required by investors on a particular share:

$$r_{cs} = \frac{D_1}{P_0} + g \qquad\qquad (6.17)$$

The first term in Equation 6.17 represents the expected dividend yield on the share; therefore, we may view the second term (g) as the expected capital gains yield since the total return must equal the dividend yield plus capital gains yield. This provides an appropriate approximation for required return only if the conditions of the constant-growth-rate version of the DDM are met (in particular, the assumption regarding constant growth in dividends to infinity must be satisfied). It also assumes that markets are reasonably efficient by assuming that the market price equals the intrinsic value.

ESTIMATING THE IMPLIED RATE OF RETURN ON A COMMON SHARE

EXAMPLE

For the company in the examples above, the estimated price today is $13.38, the estimated dividend at the end of this year (D_1) is $1.07, and the estimated long-term growth rate in dividends (g) is 7 percent. This implies an expected rate of return of 15 percent:

$$r_{cs} = \frac{D_1}{P_0} + g = \frac{1.07}{13.38} + 0.07 = 0.08 + 0.07 = 0.15$$

This suggests that the expected return is comprised of a dividend yield of 8 percent and a capital gains yield of 7 percent. In other words, we expect the company's share price to increase by 7 percent over this year. We can check this out by using Equation 6.13 to estimate the company's intrinsic value at the end of period 1:

$$P_1 = \frac{D_2}{r_{cs}-g} + g = \frac{\$1.07(1.07)}{0.15-0.07} = \$14.31$$

This estimated price at the end of period 1 is 7 percent higher than the estimated price today of $13.38 (rounding causes slight differences):

$$\text{Price change} = \frac{\text{ending price} - \text{beginning price}}{\text{beginning price}}$$

$$= (\$14.31 - \$13.38) / \$13.38 = 7\%$$

This result is intuitive since the equation used to determine P_1 is the same equation used to determine P_0 multiplied by $(1 + g)$.

IMPLIED RETURNS VERSUS PRICE

EXAMPLE

Notice that in the example above, our estimate of the expected return exactly equals the required return of 15 percent that we used to determine the intrinsic value in the previous example. This is because we assumed the share is trading at its intrinsic value. What if the firm was actually trading in the market at a price of $15? Under these circumstances, we estimate an expected return of 14.13 percent:

$$r_{cs} = \frac{1.07}{15.00} + 0.07 = 0.0713 + 0.07 = 0.1413$$

At a price of $15, the company's shares are not attractive investments since they offer a rate of return of 14.13 percent, which is below our required rate of return of 15 percent. In other words, based on our analysis, the shares are overpriced at $15.

Similarly, if the orgaization's shares were trading below $13.38, we would expect to earn above our required rate of return since they would be undervalued according to our analysis. For example, if they were trading at $12, the expected rate of return would be 15.92 percent, which is well above 15 percent:

$$r_{cs} = \frac{1.07}{12.00} + 0.07 = 0.0892 + 0.07 = 0.1592$$

An examination of Equation 6.13 readily demonstrates the factors affecting the price of a common stock, assuming that the constant-growth-rate version of the dividend discount model is the applicable valuation approach:

1. If the market lowers the required rate of return for a stock, its price will rise (other things being equal).

2. If investors decide that the expected growth in dividends will be higher as the result of some favourable development for the firm, its price will also rise (other things being equal).

Of course, the converse for these two situations also holds: a rise in the discount rate or a reduction in the expected growth rate of dividends will lower price.

The value calculated from Equation 6.13 is quite sensitive to the estimates used by the investor in the equation. Relatively small variations in the inputs can change the estimated price by a large percentage. For example, if we had used a discount rate of 16 percent instead of 15 percent with other variables held constant, our price estimate would have fallen from $13.38 to $11.89. Similarly, if we had used a 6 percent growth rate instead of 7 percent with other variables held constant, we would have obtained a price estimate of $11.78. If we had assumed that the discount rate rose to l6 percent while the growth rate declined to 4 percent, our estimate would have been $8.67, a change of 35.20 percent.

These differences suggest why stock prices constantly fluctuate as investors make their buy-and-sell decisions. Even if all investors use the constant-growth-rate version of the DDM to value a particular common stock (which in practice they do not), many different estimates of value will be obtained because they will use different estimates of variables as inputs into the model. Thus, at any time, some investors are willing to buy a particular stock whereas others wish to sell depending on their evaluation of the company's prospects. This helps to make markets active and liquid.

The Multiple-Growth-Rate Version of the DDM

Many firms grow at a rapid rate (or rates) for a number of years and then slow down to an "average" growth rate. Other companies pay no dividends for a period of years often during their early growth period. The constant-growth-rate version of the DDM discussed earlier is not formulated to deal with these situations; for that we have a variation of the DDM: the **multiple-growth-rate version**.

In addition, short-term earnings and dividend estimates should be much more reliable than those covering a longer period of time, which are often projected using some very general estimates of future economic, industry, and company conditions. In order to use the best information available, it often makes sense to estimate growth as precisely as possible in the short term before assuming some long-term rate of growth.

Multiple growth is defined as a situation in which the expected future growth in dividends must be described using two or more growth rates. Some companies (IBM, for example) have experienced rapid growth that could not be sustained forever. During part of their lives, their growth exceeded that of the average company in the economy, but later, the growth rate slowed. This seems reasonable since we would expect that competitive pressures and/or business cycle influences will prevent firms from maintaining extremely high growth in earnings for long periods of time.

To capture the expected growth in dividends under this scenario, it is necessary to model the dividend stream during each period of different growth. It is reasonable to assume that at some point, the company's growth will slow down to a steady rate similar to that of the economy as a whole. At this time, the company's growth in future dividends can be described by the constant-growth-rate version of the DDM (Equation 6.13). What remains, therefore, is to model the exact dividend stream up to the point at which dividends slow to a normal growth rate and to find the present value of all the components. This can be described in equation form as:

$$P_0 = \frac{D_1}{(1+r_{cs})^1} + \frac{D_2}{(1+r_{cs})^2} + \ldots + \frac{D_n}{(1+r_{cs})^n} + \frac{P_n}{(1+r_{cs})^n}$$

(6.18)

where $\quad P_n = \dfrac{D_{n+1}}{r_{cs}-g}$

n = the time at which constant growth in dividends to infinity is assumed to begin.

Essentially, we estimate dividends up to the beginning of the period at which it is reasonable to assume constant growth to infinity. Then we can use the constant-growth-rate version of the DDM to estimate the intrinsic value or market price of the stock at that time (P_n). Finally, we discount back to the beginning of the evaluation period (time 0):

1. all of the estimated dividends up to the beginning of constant-growth period

2. the estimated intrinsic value at that time, which provides us with today's estimate of the share's intrinsic value

How does this provide us with the present value of all expected future dividends from period 1 to infinity? Recall from the constant-growth-rate version of the DDM that the intrinsic value determined at time n (P_n) represents the present value of all expected dividends (at time $t = n$) from $n + 1$ to infinity. Because P_n is the expected price of the stock at the end of period n, it must be discounted back to the present. When we discount P_n back to time 0 and add it to the present value of all dividends from $t = 1$ to $t = n$, we end up with the present value (at time $t = 0$) of all expected future dividends from time $t = 1$ to infinity. According to the DDM, this is the estimated value of the stock today.

MULTIPLE-GROWTH-RATE VERSION

EXAMPLE

Figure 6.7 illustrates the concept of valuing a multiple-growth-rate company that is expected to pay a dividend of $1.50 at the end of this year, a $2.00 dividend at the end of year 2, and a $2.30 dividend at the end of year 3. It is estimated that dividends will grow at a constant rate of 5 percent per year thereafter. Determine the intrinsic value of this company's common shares if the required rate is 10 percent.

1. Estimate dividends up to the start of constant growth to infinity:

$D_1 = \$1.50$
$D_2 = \$2.00$
$D_3 = \$2.30$

2. Estimate price at the beginning of constant growth to infinity period:

$$P_3 = \frac{D_4}{r_{cs} - g} = \frac{(2.30)(1.05)}{0.10 - 0.05} = \$48.30$$

3. Discount back the relevant cash flows to time 0:

$$P_0 = \frac{1.50}{(1.10)^1} + \frac{2.00}{(1.10)^2} + \frac{2.30}{(1.10)^3} + \frac{48.30}{(1.10)^3} = 1.364 + 1.653 + 1.728 + 36.288 = \$41.03$$

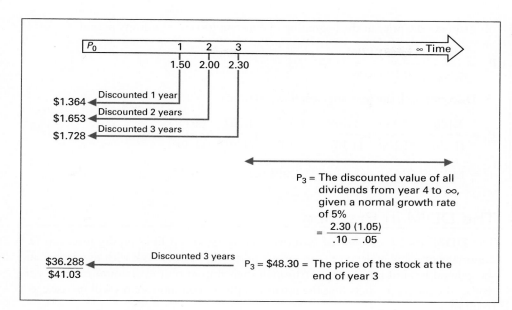

FIGURE 6.7

Valuing a Multiple-
Growth-Rate Company

Two-Stage Growth-Rate Version

A well-known multiple-growth-rate version of the DDM is the two-stage growth-rate version. This type assumes near-term growth at a rapid rate for some period (typically, two to 10 years) followed by a steady long-term growth rate that is sustainable (i.e., a constant-growth-rate version as discussed earlier).

TWO-STAGE GROWTH-RATE VERSION

EXAMPLE

Assume a company's current dividend is $1, which is expected to grow at the higher rate (g_1) of 12 percent per year for five years at the end of which time the new growth rate (g_c) is expected to be a constant 6 percent per year. The required rate of return is 10 percent.

1. Estimate dividends up to the start of constant growth to infinity. This can be done by compounding the beginning dividend $1 at 12 percent for each of five years producing the following:

$D_0 = \$1.00$

$D_1 = \$1.00(1.12) = \$1.120$

$D_2 = \$1.00(1.12)^2 = \$1.254$

$D_3 = \$1.00(1.12)^3 = \$1.405$

$D_4 = \$1.00(1.12)^4 = \$1.573$

$D_5 = \$1.00(1.12)^5 = \$1.762$

2. Estimate the price at the beginning of constant growth to infinity period:

$$P_5 = \frac{D_6}{r_{cs}-g} = \frac{(1.762)(1.06)}{0.10-0.06} = \$46.693$$

3. Discount back the relevant cash flows to time 0:

$$P_0 = \frac{1.120}{(1.10)^1} + \frac{1.254}{(1.10)^2} + \frac{1.405}{(1.10)^3} + \frac{1.573}{(1.10)^4} + \frac{1.762}{(1.10)^5} + \frac{46.693}{(1.10)^5}$$

$$= 1.018+1.036+1.056+1.074+1.094+28.993 = \$34.27$$

The DDM in Practice

The DDM has a great deal of intuitive appeal because it links equity prices to two important fundamentals: corporate profitability (through its link with dividends) and the general level of interest rates (through their impact on the discount rate). In particular, the model predicts that the intrinsic value of common shares will increase as a result of:

- increases in expected dividends (which are closely related to profitability)
- increases in the growth rate of these dividends
- decreases in the appropriate discount rate

From previous chapters, we know that the discount rate will be an increasing function of the general level of interest rates as well as the riskiness of the underlying security (which we discuss in the next two chapters).

Despite its intuitive appeal, it is often difficult to put the DDM into practice particularly for Canadian companies because the model is based on several assumptions that are not met by a large number of firms in Canada. It is best suited for companies with stable past and future dividend payouts and that are growing at a steady and sustainable rate. Hence, the DDM works reasonably well for large corporations in mature industries with stable profits and an established dividend policy. In Canada, the banks and utilities fit this profile, while in the United States, there are numerous NYSE-listed companies of this nature.

Not surprisingly, it does not work well for a lot of resource-based companies that are cyclical in nature and often display erratic growth in earnings and dividends. In addition, many of these companies (especially the smaller ones) do not distribute a great deal of profits to shareholders in the form of dividends. Thus, the DDM may not provide meaningful value estimates for a large number of Canadian corporations since resource-based and cyclical companies comprise a large proportion of the TSE and dominate the CDNX. Relative valuation approaches are generally used by analysts in most situations and are particularly important for situations under which the DDM is not applicable. The most commonly used approach is the price-earnings ratio discussed below.

Price-Earnings (P/E) Ratio

Relative valuation approaches determine the value of common shares by comparing the market prices of similar companies, relative to some common variable such as earnings, cash flow, book values, or sales. It is relatively simple to apply; however, using multiples based on comparable companies has the potential to build market errors into the value estimation process. This section discusses the application of the most common of these, the **price-earnings (P/E) ratio**, which is used by practising security analysts probably more often than dividend discount models.

The report below demonstrates the importance attached to the P/E ratio by analysts. It refers to Nortel's P/E ratio several times and discusses its valuation in the market as of September 15, 2000 (about six weeks prior to the collapse in Nortel's price referred to earlier in this section). The article suggests that Nortel was priced extremely high based on a P/E ratio that is "equivalent to more than 90 times the company's forecast profit for this year." This multiple is then compared to that of the U.S. giant microchip company Intel Corp. (35) and to the maximum multiple of 45 afforded Microsoft during the peak of its dominance in the late 1990s.

■ *Finance in the News*

Nortel Priced for Perfection

The fact that Nortel stocks are pricey merely reflects its great success, and that success is also reflected in the fact that Nortel represents 31 percent of the TSE300 Index. The performance of the high-tech giant has been instrumental in the stellar returns recorded by the TSE—32 percent gained this year, the best major stock exchange performance in the world, and 31.7 percent last year. Nortel's fourfold growth had a lot to do with those figures.

Some professional investors avoid Nortel despite the impressive gains, citing two major problems. 1) Nortel's valuation is seen as overinflated—"equivalent to more than 90 times the company's forecast profit for this year." Comparisons with microchip leader Intel Corp.'s price-earnings multiple of "only" 35 indicate that Nortel could cave in by more than 60 percent. 2) If the giant's earnings should fail to meet projections because of new competitors or a slowdown in fibre optic spending, Nortel could get hurt as well.

Richard Rooney of Burgundy Asset Management warned that "Nortel's current valuation surpasses one of the twentieth century's greatest business successes—Microsoft." It gives one pause to consider that the software doyen traded at less than 45 times earnings at the height of its power in 1998.

Source: Globe and Mail, September 16, 2000, p. N1, N4. Reprinted with permission

The P/E ratio is the number of times investors value earnings as expressed in the stock price. Although the P/E ratio model appears easier to use than the DDM, its very simplicity causes investors to forget that estimation of the uncertain future is also involved here. This is an important point to remember. Every valuation model and approach, properly done, requires estimates of the uncertain future.

The P/E ratio as reported daily in such sources as the *Globe and Mail* and the *National Post (Financial Post)* is simply an identity calculated by dividing the current market price of the stock by the latest 12-month earnings. As such, it tells investors the price being paid for each $1 of the company's most recent earnings. These P/E ratios provide no basis for valuation other than showing the underlying identity on which the P/E valuation model is based:

Current market price $= P_0 = EPS_0 \times P_0/EPS_0$

For valuation purposes, the typical P/E formulation uses estimated earnings for the next 12 months. The basic equation is given by:

Estimated value = estimated earnings × justified P/E ratio

or

(6.19) $P_0 = EPS_1 \times P_0/EPS_1$

To implement the earnings multiplier model and estimate the value of the stock today, we must estimate the values on the right-hand side of Equation 6.19.

EXAMPLE

USING P/E RATIOS

A stock with estimated earnings per share (EPS_1) of $3.00 for the next 12 months will sell for $45 ($P_0$) if investors are willing to pay 15 times expected earnings (P_0/EPS_1). In other words,

$P_0 = EPS_1 \times P_0/EPS_1 = (3.00) \times (15) = \$45$

This price will change as estimates of future earnings or the justified P/E changes.

Determinants of the P/E Ratio

The P/E ratio can be derived from the dividend discount model. We will illustrate this process only for the case of constant growth, which is the simplest case starting with Equation 6.13, the estimated price of a stock using the constant-growth-rate version of the model. We use P_0 to represent estimated price from the model.

$$P_0 = \frac{D_1}{r_{cs} - g}$$

Dividing both sides of this equation by expected earnings, EPS_1, we obtain:

(6.20) $$\frac{P_0}{EPS_1} = \frac{D_1/EPS_1}{r_{cs} - g}$$

Equation 6.20 indicates those factors that affect the estimated P/E ratio:

1. The expected dividend payout ratio (D_1/EPS_1)
2. The required rate of return (r_{cs})
3. The expected growth rate of dividends (g)

It is obvious from Equation 6.20 that the following relationships should hold other things being equal:

1. The higher the expected payout ratio, the higher the P/E.
2. The higher the expected growth rate g, the higher the P/E.
3. The higher the required rate of return r_{cs}, the lower the P/E.

It is important to remember the phrase "other things being equal" because usually other things are not equal and the preceding relationships do not hold by themselves. It is quite obvious, upon reflection, that if a firm could increase its estimated P/E ratio and therefore its market price by simply raising its payout ratio, it would be very tempted to do so. However, such an action would in all likelihood reduce future growth prospects, lowering g and thereby defeating the increase in the payout. Similarly, trying to increase g by taking on particularly risky investment projects would cause investors to demand a higher required rate of return thereby raising r_{cs}. Again, this would work to offset the positive effects of the increase in g.

Variables 2 and 3 are typically the most important factors in the preceding determination of the P/E ratio because a small change in either can have a large effect on its value.

ESTIMATING THE P/E RATIO

EXAMPLE

Assume that the expected payout ratio for the company used in the examples above is 53.5 percent (i.e., $D_1/EPS_1 = 1.07/2.00 = 0.535$). By varying r_{cs} and g and therefore changing the difference between the two (the denominator in Equation 6.20), investors can assess the effect on the P/E ratio as follows:

Assume $r_{cs} = 0.15$ and $g = 0.07$

$$\frac{P_0}{EPS_1} = \frac{D_1/EPS_1}{r_{cs}-g} = \frac{0.535}{0.15-.07} = 6.69$$

Now if r_{cs} increases to 0.16 while g falls to 0.06, the justified P/E ratio falls to 5.35.

$$\frac{P_0}{EPS_1} = \frac{D_1/EPS_1}{r_{cs}-g} = \frac{0.535}{0.16-.06} = 5.35$$

This is not surprising since both of these events produce a negative impact on the justified P/E ratio.

Finally, assume r_{cs} falls to 14 percent while g increases to 8 percent, which are both favourable events.

$$\frac{P_0}{EPS_1} = \frac{D_1/EPS_1}{r_{cs}-g} = \frac{0.535}{0.14-08} = 8.92$$

If we use each of these P/E ratios being used as a multiplier with an expected earnings for this company for next year of $2, the resulting prices would be $13.38, $10.70, and $17.84, respectively. This is quite a range given the small changes in r_{cs} and g that were made.

Estimates of the justified P/E ratio ultimately involve a great deal of subjectivity. While the valuation procedure itself is relatively easy, the estimation of an appropriate P/E ratio is difficult. Determining an appropriate P/E ratio requires much analysis and judgement regarding the firm's growth opportunities, position within the industry, and the riskiness associated with the firm, its industry, and the economy as a whole.

Despite the intuitive appeal of estimating the justified P/E ratio based on Equation 6.20, it is only appropriate under certain conditions since it is merely a reformulation of the constant-growth-rate version of the DDM. It will work well only for companies that exhibit stable and growing dividends at a rate below the required return on their common shares (i.e., r_{cs} must be $> g$). Another way is to find "comparable" companies, rate one relative to the others, and estimate a target P/E ratio for the company being analysed based on this comparison and on the P/E ratios of the comparable companies. Often, this approach involves scaling an industry average P/E ratio up or down based on the analyst's opinion regarding how well the company stacks up against its peers.

A comparison of one company with its peers also involves a great deal of subjectivity regarding several company-specific characteristics including risk, potential for growth, and overall financial health of the company. Some other approaches to estimating justified P/E multiples include using historical averages for the firm or its industry. An alternative is to determine the ratio based on its historic relationship to P/E multiples in the market as a whole. For example, a company or industry may historically have traded at P/E ratios that average 90 percent of the P/E ratio for the TSE 300, so you could estimate an appropriate P/E multiple based on 90 percent of the TSE 300's current P/E ratio. The problem with any of these approaches to estimating justified P/E ratios is that they may build market errors into the value estimation process. For example, we could overestimate the appropriate P/E multiple based on industry averages if the market has systematically overvalued the particular industry that the company is in. Similar results would occur if we scale the TSE 300 multiple by 90 percent but find that the entire market is overvalued.

Aside from the difficulties in estimating an appropriate P/E ratio, there are several other practical concerns regarding the informativeness of the P/E ratios themselves. One important matter is that P/E ratios are uninformative when companies have negative (or very small) earnings. Finally, the volatile nature of earnings implies a great deal of volatility in P/E multiples. For example, the earnings of cyclical companies fluctuate much more dramatically throughout the business cycle than their stock prices. As a result, their

P/E ratios tend to peak during recessionary periods and hit low points during the peak of business cycles. In response to some of these concerns, a number of other relative valuation approaches are often used in practice.[6]

SUMMARY 6.5

1. Market prices of debt such as bonds are calculated by discounting future cash flows specified under the loan contract (periodic interest payments and eventual repayment of principal) at the prevailing interest rate.

2. Interest is the price paid for borrowed money, and in free financial markets, it is determined by the laws of supply and demand. Interest rates tend to parallel inflation, and in an environment of general price-level changes, we have to distinguish between nominal and real interest rates.

3. The liquidity preference theory postulates that investors prefer short maturities, and borrowers desire long maturities. Therefore, the term structure should be upward sloping and exhibit a built-in liquidity premium. According to the expectations hypothesis, the yield curve reflects expectations about the future levels of interest rates. When investors expect short-term rates to fall, we may observe an inverted or downward-sloping yield curve.

4. According to the dividend discount model (DDM), the value of a stock today is the discounted value of all future dividends. To account for an infinite stream of dividends, stocks to be valued are classified by their expected growth rate in dividends.

QUESTIONS AND PROBLEMS

Questions for Discussion

1. (a) If the general level of interest rates rises, what do you think will be the effect on market prices of outstanding bonds? Give reasons

   (b) Further to your answer in (a) above, would you expect bonds with a longer or shorter term to maturity to be more significantly affected? Why?

2. How may investor uncertainty about future inflation rates affect the term structure of interest rates?

3. What effect would a sudden rise in the bond market (i.e., bond prices increasing) have on values in the stock market? Explain.

4. A firm currently pays no dividends and has never paid them in its history. If the dividend discount model (DDM) is true, why is the price of this stock not zero?

---

[6] For more details regarding these approaches, refer to Chapter 13 of *Investments: Analysis and Management*, Canadian Edition, 1999, W. S. Cleary and C. P. Jones, John Wiley & Sons Canada Ltd., Toronto.

5. When estimating a perpetual growth rate for a stock's dividends, most analysts assume that the dividend growth rate (in perpetuity) cannot be greater than the projected growth rate in the economy overall. Why is this so?

6. In the DDM with constant growth, the growth rate (g) cannot be larger than the required return on the stock (r). Explain intuitively why this situation would not be possible in the real world.

PROBLEMS WITH SOLUTIONS

Problem 1

A bond with four years to maturity, a face value of $1,000, and a coupon rate of 5 percent is selling in the market at $950. Calculate the effective yield if coupons are paid annually.

Solution 1

The market price of the bond is given as the present value of all expected inflows discounted at the effective yield r. We have:

$$\text{Market value} = \sum_{t=1}^{4} \frac{I}{(1+r)^t} + \frac{F}{(1+r)^4}$$

$$950 = \frac{50}{(1+r)} + \frac{50}{(1+r)^2} + \frac{50}{(1+r)^3} + \frac{50}{(1+r)^4} + \frac{1000}{(1+r)^4}$$

$$= 50 \left[\frac{1 - \frac{1}{(1+r)^4}}{r} \right] + \frac{1,000}{(1+r)^4}$$

We try to find the discount rate r that satisfies this equation. By trial and error, we find r between 6 percent and 7 percent.

For $r = 6\%$, the right side of the equation is $50 \times 3.465 + 1,000 \times .792 = 965.25$

For $r = 7\%$, the numbers become $50 \times 3.387 + 1,000 \times .763 = 932.35$

The true value of r must lie between these two figures because $932 < 950 < 965$.

Interpolating, we have:

$$\begin{bmatrix} 7\% & \$932 \\ \begin{bmatrix} r\% & \$950 \end{bmatrix} \\ 6\% & \$965 \end{bmatrix}$$

or graphically:

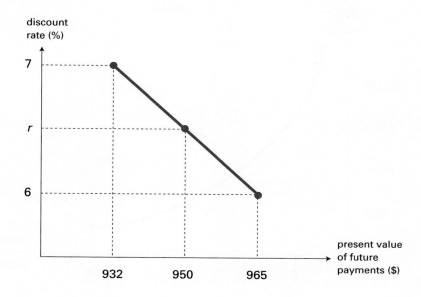

We derive:

$$\frac{r\%-6\%}{7\%-6\%}=\frac{950-965}{932-965}=\frac{-15}{-33}=.45$$

$$r=(7-6)(.45)+6=6.45\%$$

Problem 2

(a) Consider a bond that pays 12 percent interest on a face value of $1,000 with a maturity of 20 years. Plot the market price of the bond as a function of the prevailing market interest rate.

(b) A $1,000 bond pays 12 percent interest. Plot the market price of this bond as a function of its maturity if the current market yield is (i) 8 percent, and (ii) 16 percent.

Solution 2

(a) We calculate the market price using:

$$P=\frac{120}{(1+r)}=\frac{120}{(1+r)^2}+...+\frac{120}{(1+r)^{20}}+\frac{1,000}{(1+r)^{20}}$$

For various discount rates, we obtain:

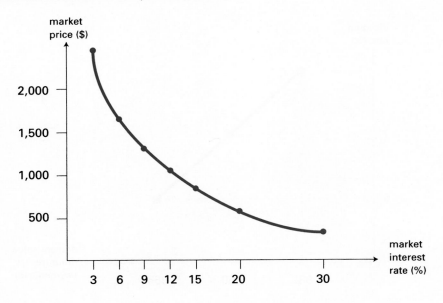

Market interest rate r	Market price of bond
3	$2,339.24
6	1,688.40
9	1,273.36
12	1,000.00
15	812.08
20	610.40
30	402.92

We see that the market price of the bond is a declining function of the market interest rate. As the market price of the bond decreases, its effective yield increases and vice versa. If the market yield equals the nominal yield of the bond, the bond just trades at face value.

(b) Again, we compute the market price using the formula:

$$120 \left[\frac{1 - \dfrac{1}{(1+r)^n}}{r} \right] + \frac{1,000}{(1+r)^n}$$

for $r = 8\%$ and 16%, and varying values of n.

For $r = 8\%$, we obtain:

Maturity n in years	Market price of bond
0	$1,000.00
1	1,037.12
5	1,160.16
10	1,268.20
20	1,393.16
30	1,449.96
perpetual	1,500.00

For $r = 16\%$, we obtain:

Maturity n in years	Market price of bond
0	$1,000.00
1	965.44
5	868.88
10	806.96
20	762.48
30	753.24
perpetual	750.00

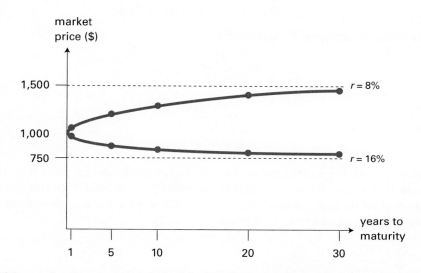

If the market interest rate is below the bond's nominal rate, the bond trades at a premium. Again, the premium increases with increasing maturity. Verify the results presented in this problem by looking up current market prices for various bonds in the financial pages of the newspaper.

Problem 3

A stock is expected to pay a dividend of $1 one year from today, a dividend of $1.50 two years from today, and a dividend of $2 three years from now. After that, dividends are expected to grow at a rate of 15 percent per year for the following four years. At that point, dividend growth is expected to slow down to a steady rate of 5 percent in perpetuity. If investors require a return of 12 percent on this stock, what is its fair value in the market?

Solution 3

As we need to calculate the present value of all future dividends, the first step is to map out what the dividends will be in the future up until the steady state growth rate of 5 percent is reached:

D_1	$1.00
D_2	1.50
D_3	2.00
D_4	$2(1.15) = 2.30$
D_5	$2(1.15)^2 = \$2.65$
D_6	$2(1.15)^3 = 3.04$
D_7	$2(1.15)^4 = 3.50$

Next, we must estimate what the price of the stock will be at the beginning of the steady-state growth period, seven years from now. The dividend in year 8 can be estimated by taking the estimated D_7 and considering the effect of the 5 percent growth rate:

$$D_8 = D_7(1.05) = 3.50(1.05) = \$3.68$$

Our estimated future price, P_7, is therefore:

$$P_7 = \frac{D_8}{r_{cs} - g}$$

$$= \frac{3.68}{0.12 - 0.05}$$

$$= \$52.57$$

This price at year 7 represents the present value of all dividends that come from year 8 and onward. If we take the present value of this future price and add on the present value of each dividend through the first seven years, we will arrive at today's value for the stock (the present value of all future dividends):

$$P_0 = \sum_{t=1}^{8} \frac{D_t}{(1+r)^t} + \frac{P_7}{(1+r)^7}$$

$$= \frac{1}{(1.12)} + \frac{1.50}{(1.12)^2} + \frac{2}{(1.12)^3} + \frac{2.30}{(1.12)^4} + \frac{2.65}{(1.12)^5} + \frac{3.04}{(1.12)^6} + \frac{3.50}{(1.12)^7} + \frac{52.57}{(1.12)^7}$$

$$= \$33.38$$

Problem 4

Two companies have the same required return (10 percent), and both have projected earnings per share of $1.25 for next year. Firm A has a price-earnings ratio of 20, while Firm B has a price-earnings ratio of 50. What is the price of each stock? Compare the present value of growth opportunities for each. Use this to explain why investors would pay a higher price-earnings multiple for Firm B.

Solution 4

To calculate the price for each stock, simply multiply the earnings-per-share (EPS) figures by the price-earnings ratios given:

Price of Firm A = $1.25 × 20 = $25

Price of Firm B = $1.25 × 50 = $62.50

The interesting question is why Firm B has the same level of earnings but investors are willing to pay a much higher price for its shares. To see why, we should first look at the relationship between price-earnings ratios and the present value of growth opportunities (PVGO). We know from Equation 6.16 that:

$$P_0 = \frac{EPS_1}{r_{cs}} + PVGO$$

Dividing both sides by EPS_1, we get an expression for the price-earning ratio in terms of future growth opportunities:

$$\frac{P_0}{EPS_1} = \frac{1}{r_{cs}} + PVGO$$

This shows that, all else equal, firms with higher growth opportunities will have higher price-earnings multiples. In this case, we know that $r_{cs} = 0.1$ for both firms so that for Firm A, we have:

$$20 = \frac{1}{0.1} + \frac{PVGO}{EPS_1}$$

$$\frac{PVGO}{EPS_1} = \$10$$

and PVGO = ($10)(1.25) = $12.50

and for Firm B:

$$50 = \frac{1}{0.1} + \frac{PVGO}{EPS_1}$$

$$\frac{PVGO}{EPS_1} = \$40$$

and PVGO = (40)(1.25) = $50

Investors value the growth opportunities in Firm A at $12.50 per share, while they value the growth opportunities in Firm B at four times that amount, $50. Obviously, investors see much more growth potential in Firm B than in Firm A. This means that they are willing to pay more for each dollar of current earnings for B (higher P/E ratio) because they believe that the "future" earnings potential is much greater for Firm B. It is important to remember that when investors buy a stock, they are buying not only a share of the current earnings of the company, but also of all future earnings.

Problem 5

Given current capital market conditions and the risk characteristics of XYZ Corporation, investors demand a return of $r = 15$ percent on the common shares that currently trade at $30 per share. Dividend payments for the current year are expected to be $1.50 per share.

(a) What is the implied long-term average growth rate in dividends that shareholders expect?

(b) If, because of changed business conditions, investors adjust their expectations down to a zero growth rate but still demand a 15 percent market return on the shares, what will happen to the market price of the shares?

(c) Conversely, if because of a buoyant economy, investors reassess their growth expectations to 15 percent per year but still demand a 15 percent market rate of return, at what price should the common shares trade?

Solution 5

(a) We have:

$$r = \frac{D_1}{P_0} + g$$

$$g = r - \frac{D_1}{P_0} = .15 - \frac{1.50}{30} = 0.10 \text{ or } 10\%$$

(b) Using the formula $P_0 = \frac{D}{r-g}$, and setting $g = 0$, with r staying constant at .15, the price of the shares (P_0) must fall. We obtain:

$$P_0 = \frac{1.50}{.15-0} = \$10$$

Note the fairly dramatic change in share price from $30 to $10 as investors adjust their growth expectations from $g = 10\%$ to $g = 0\%$.

(c) Again, we use:

$$P_0 = \frac{D_1}{r-g}$$

Here, it is obvious that the formula cannot be solved as the denominator $(r - g)$ becomes zero for $g = r$, implying $P_0 = \infty$ for $g = 15\%$. If the dividends that the firm pays are expected to grow at a rate of g, and the return that investors require is $r = g$, the growth in future dividends just cancels the effect of discounting. We have:

$$P_0 = \frac{D_1}{(1+r)} + \frac{D_1(1+g)}{(1+r)^2} + \ldots + \frac{D_1(1+g)^t}{(1+r)^{t+1}} + \ldots$$

which for $g = r$ reduces to:

$$P_0 = \frac{D_1}{(1+r)} + \frac{D_1}{(1+r)} + \ldots + \frac{D_1}{(1+r)} + \ldots$$

With this infinite stream of dividends, $P_0 = \infty$.

The economic implications of this mathematical derivation are that such a situation is unstable and cannot prevail. A company cannot grow at a rate that forever exceeds the growth of the general economy or of competing, similar firms because in time, it would take over the entire economy. Conversely, if general growth expectations for the economy were to increase, so would the yield, r, which investors would demand on their investments. Although a firm's projected growth rate may exceed r temporarily, such a situation cannot prevail indefinitely.

Problem 6

This problem, which is conceptually more difficult (and which the beginning student can omit without loss of continuity), illustrates an important application of the dividend growth model, which we will discuss further in subsequent chapters.

Assume that a company reinvests a certain proportion of its earnings at a return k_r to provide for constant growth of future dividends at a rate g. Show that the share price will remain unaltered only if $k_r = r$, that is, if the return on the reinvestments just equals the return required by shareholders.

Solution 6

Assume constant annual expected earnings per share of E, all of which are paid out in dividends, so that $E = D$. The share price becomes $P = D/r$.

The company now retains a constant portion of its earnings for reinvestment, and in the current period, pays out only $D'<D$, with retained earnings $= E-D'$. If it achieves a return k_r on its reinvestments, this implies an average growth rate on its total current earnings of:

$$g = k_r \frac{(E-D')}{E}$$

That is, the growth rate that can be sustained on 0 earnings (dividends and retentions) equals the reinvestment rate multiplied by the proportion of funds reinvested. The market price per share was derived in the chapter as:

$$P_0 = \frac{D'}{r-g}$$

For the price of the shares to remain unchanged as a consequence of the change in dividend policy, we need to have:

$$\frac{\text{share price with}}{\text{constant dividend}} = \frac{\text{share price with}}{\text{retention and growth}}$$

$$\frac{D}{r} = \frac{D'}{r-g}$$

from which we derive:

$$g = r \frac{(D-D')}{D}$$

Remembering that $D = E$, we see that this will be the case only if $k_r = r$. If at any time $k_r > r$, the growth rate will increase, and the share price will go up as a consequence of retention and vice versa.

As a numerical illustration, assume that earnings have been constant at $2 per share. Investors demand a return of $r = 20$ percent. With full payout, we have:

$$\text{share price} = \frac{2}{.2} = \$10$$

The firm now retains 25 percent of all earnings to reinvest at k_r. Retentions for the current year are $0.50 per share, leaving a dividend of $D' = \$1.50$. A growth rate of k_r on retained earnings that equal 25 percent of total earnings represents an average overall growth rate of $.25k_r$ that can be maintained on dividends. We obtain:

$$\text{share price} = \frac{D'}{r-g} = \frac{1.50}{.2-.25k_r}$$

Setting both share prices equal yields:

$$\frac{D'}{r-g} = \frac{D}{r}$$

$$\frac{1.50}{.2-.25k_r} = \frac{2}{.2}$$

from which we obtain $k_r = 0.2$.

This point will become more important in subsequent chapters. It indicates that share prices (and shareholder wealth) will increase if the company can find investment opportunities with yields that exceed the cost of financing (which equals the return that investors demand when buying the firm's securities). Conversely, if a business can only find investments with returns below its cost of financing, share prices will fall as a consequence of such investments, and it will be better off to pay its earnings out in dividends rather than to retain them for reinvestment.

ADDITIONAL PROBLEMS

1. (a) Calculate the market price of a bond having the following characteristics: face value of $1,000, matures in two years, coupon rate of 10 percent (with coupons paid semi-annually) and effective yield of 12 percent. – *have to figure out for 6 mos.*

   (b) Compute the market price of the bond in part (a) assuming that it matures in 20 years. *Same formula   use 40 instead of 4*

   (c) What would be the market value of the bond if it had no maturity (perpetual)? *—use perpetuity formula*
   50
   5.83%

2. (a) A $1,000, 20-year bond with an interest rate of 14 percent that pays coupons annually is selling at $1,300. Compute the effective yield.

   (b) What is the effective yield if interest of 7 percent ($70) is paid semi-annually (instead of the 14 percent annual payment)?

3. (a) Suppose a 12 percent, $1,000 bond with seven years left to maturity is selling for $1,208.25. What is the effective yield, assuming that interest is paid annually?

   (b) If, in part (a), interest were paid quarterly, what would the bond sell for, given that the effective yield remained unchanged?

4. A zero coupon bond has 15 years to maturity, a face value of $1,000, and currently sells for $750 in the market. What is the effective yield on the bond?

5. Consider two zero coupon bonds with par values of $1,000 and yields of 8 percent (expressed as annual effective rates). Bond A has a 10-year term to maturity, and Bond B has a five-year term to maturity. Assume that interest rates rise so that the yields on both bonds increase to 9 percent.

(a) By what percentage does the price of Bond A change? Bond B?

(b) Intuitively, why are the answers to (a) not the same? What does this say about the relationship between the term of a security and its sensitivity to interest rate changes?

6. A coupon bond has a $1,000 face value, a coupon rate of 10 percent (coupons paid semi-annually) and seven years to maturity. Similar bonds are priced to yield 14 percent (compounded semi-annually) in the market. What is the market price of this bond?

7. A bond has a $1,000 face value, a coupon rate of 10 percent, 15 years to maturity, and currently sells at par. What is the yield to maturity?

8. Assume that a stock is currently priced at $15 per share. It is due to pay a dividend of $1 per share tomorrow. Show what will happen to its stock price after it pays the dividend.

9. A firm is expected to pay dividends of $2 per year to each common share of stock. If investors require a return of 12 percent, what should be the price of each share?

10. A company is expected to pay a dividend of $1 per share in one year. Each year after that, the dividend will grow by 5 percent. If investors require a return of 10 percent, what is the value of one share?

11. (a) You are a stock analyst in charge of valuing high-technology firms, and you are expected to come out with buy-sell recommendations for your clients. You are currently analysing a firm called eGreg.com that specializes in Internet business communication. You are expecting explosive growth in this area. However, the company is not currently profitable even though you believe it will be in the future. Your projections are that the firm will pay no dividends for the next 10 years. Eleven years from now, you expect the stock to pay its first dividend of $2 per share. You expect dividends to increase at a rate of 25 percent per year for the nine years after that. At that point, the industry will start to mature and slow down; dividends will continue to grow but only at a rate of 9 percent per year.

The stock is priced in the market at $15 per share. If you believe that a fair rate of return on a stock of this type is 14 percent, what is your estimate of the value of the stock, and should you issue a recommendation to buy or to sell?

(b) The day after you make your estimate in part (a) news indicates that things are not going as smoothly as predicted for this business. Your estimates of the initial dividend and the growth rates remain the same, but the timing has changed. You now decide that the firm will pay its first dividend ($2) in 16 years. The high-growth period (25 percent per year) will last for only four years before slowing to growth of 9 percent per year.

Given a rate of return of 14 percent, what is your new estimate of the value of the stock, and should you change your recommendation?

12. An enterprise is expected to pay a dividend of $0.50 in one year. The dividend is

expected to grow at a rate of 15 percent per year for the next five years as the firm goes through a period of rapid growth. After that, it is expected to grow at an average rate of 5 percent per year forever. If the required return is 20 percent, what is the value of a share? $1038 $438

13. A company in Colombia is a subsidiary of a Canadian firm. The parent company has the choice of having its subsidiary borrow Colombian pesos, or borrowing itself in Canada. The interest rate in Canada is 9.5 percent and in Colombia, 105 percent. The current spot exchange rate is 1485 pesos per Canadian dollar. If the Canadian dollar is expected to appreciate 50 percent against the peso over the next year, where should the company borrow?

14. One-year interest rates in Canada are 6 percent and in the United States, 7 percent. If the spot exchange rate is currently 1.45 $Can/$U.S., what is the one-year forward rate between the currencies?

15. As a financial analyst, you are trying to place a value on a stock. The company has projected earnings per share of $1.50 for the next year. You have identified three other firms in the same industry, which are similar to this one. The others have the following price-earning multiples:

	P/E Ratio
Firm 1	25
Firm 2	19
Firm 3	21

What value would you assign to this stock based on the above information?

16. This question is best answered using a spreadsheet.

(a) Consider three bonds. The first has a 6.5 percent coupon, $1,000 face value, 20 years to maturity, and currently sells for $1,000. The second has a 6.5 percent coupon, 20 years to maturity, and currently sells for $900. The third has a 6.5 percent coupon, 20 years to maturity, and currently sells for $800. Use Equation 6.5 to approximate the yield on each bond. Use a spreadsheet or financial calculator to derive an exact solution for the yield on each bond. What can you say about the approximation formula?

(b) Consider two bonds. One has a 7 percent coupon, $1,000 face value, and five years to maturity. The other has a 7 percent coupon, $1,000 face value, and 30 years to maturity. Create a graph of bond price versus yield for both bonds by valuing each bond yields of 1, 2, 3, to 20 percent. Comment on the graph and the relative interest rate risk in each bond.

(c) Consider two bonds. Both have $1,000 face value and five years to maturity. One bond pays a 6 percent annual coupon, and the other is a zero coupon bond. Create a graph of bond price versus yield for both bonds by valuing each bond yields of 1, 2, 3, to 20 percent. Comment on the graph and the relative interest rate risk in each bond.

It's All about Balance

Susan Pozer's job is a balancing act. Ms. Pozer is an investment consultant with James P. Marshall (a Canadian firm with offices in Toronto, Regina, Vancouver, Calgary, and Montreal that recently became part of Hewitt Associates, a human resources consulting firm with offices around the world). In that role, she gives fund management advice to clients such as pension funds, endowments, and other organizations responsible for sizeable pools of assets. She and the 15 other consulting professionals in the firm are responsible for 64 retainer clients. The clients' asset pools range from about $20 million to $10 billion. But whatever the client's size, the challenge is the same: it's all about balancing risk and return.

"The first step we take with clients is to examine the combination of their liabilities—for example, the benefits promised to the members of a pension plan—and their assets, and work with them to come up with an appropriate long-term policy asset mix." This generally translates into finding the right mix of bonds and Canadian and foreign stocks.

To find this mix, say Ms. Pozer, the consultant "examines the risk profile of each client's fund. This involves considerations such as a fund's time horizon, the fund's financial position, and the client's attitude toward risk. We look at each asset class separately and in combination to assess what asset mix will best meet a client's objectives." She explains "that clients with longer time horizons can usually afford to take more risk as they are able to ride out market downturns."

Once the asset mix is established, Ms. Pozer says, "we help clients choose an appropriate managements structure and investment manager—or managers. James P. Marshall then monitors the client's fund's performance over time, with regular reviews to ensure that the portfolio is being managed according to the client's needs and within the client's investment policy."

Risk, Return, and Portfolio Theory

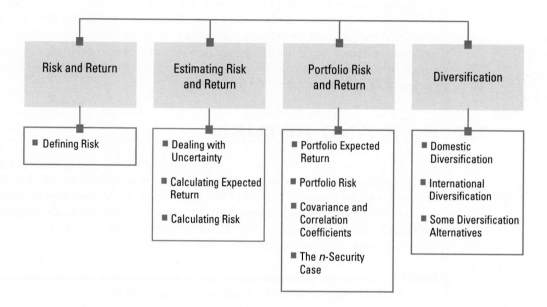

Risk and Return	Estimating Risk and Return	Portfolio Risk and Return	Diversification
■ Defining Risk	■ Dealing with Uncertainty ■ Calculating Expected Return ■ Calculating Risk	■ Portfolio Expected Return ■ Portfolio Risk ■ Covariance and Correlation Coefficients ■ The *n*-Security Case	■ Domestic Diversification ■ International Diversification ■ Some Diversification Alternatives

Learning Objectives

After studying this chapter, you should be able to:

1. *Define the term "risk," and explain how is it related to expected return.*
2. *Define and discuss expected return and risk with regard to individual securities and a portfolio as a whole.*
3. *Explain the meaning of correlation coefficient, and discuss how it compares to covariance.*
4. *Identify the main aims of diversification, and explain the principal benefits of international versus domestic diversification.*

7.1 INTRODUCTION

In Chapter 1, we identified the two key dimensions affecting most financial decisions as the time value of money and risk. In the preceding two chapters, we considered the time value of money and its application to the valuation of debt and equity securities. Risk was not explicitly recognized in our discussion of valuing of equity securities. The discussion of risk and return is central to all financial management decisions at the corporate and individual level since almost all of these decisions involve a trade-off between risk and expected return.

In this chapter, we concern ourselves with measuring the risk associated with financial securities—common stocks in particular. We begin by defining measures of total return and expected return. We then introduce the most commonly used measures of total risk—variance and standard deviation. Next, we look at combining risky securities into portfolios and the calculation of return and risk for portfolios. We conclude with a discussion of the importance of diversification.

7.2 RISK AND RETURN

Table 7.1 provides some historical evidence regarding the average returns on Canadian stocks, bonds, and T-bills as well as U.S. stocks over the 1938-98 period. The first row of numbers shows that both U.S. and Canadian stocks offered much higher returns than bonds or T-bills over the entire period. Based on total returns, stocks also outperformed both bonds and T-bills during all five 10-year subperiods with the exception of the 1989-98 period when bonds outperformed Canadian stocks.

Table 7.1

Average Annual Returns for Stocks, Bonds, and T-Bills (1938-98)

	Canadian Stocks	Bonds	T-bills	U.S. Stocks
1938-98	11.84	6.53	5.39	14.83
1939-48	7.71	3.16	0.50	8.30
1949-58	18.75	1.35	1.64	20.85
1959-68	11.32	2.62	4.29	11.86
1969-78	7.53	6.18	6.88	5.83
1979-88	15.43	11.78	12.11	17.16
1989-98	10.58	14.17	7.36	23.03

Source: The Canadian Institute of Actuaries (CIA) website: http://www.actuaries.ca.

Table 7.1 shows that stocks have historically offered much higher returns than T-bills and bonds, while Table 5.1 from Chapter 5 showed that a little bit of extra return can translate into tremendous differences in ending wealth when funds are invested for long periods of time. This explains why investors, both professional and individual, spend so much time trying to earn extra returns on their investments. Combining these observations leads to an obvious question: why would anyone bother to invest in T-bills or bonds given the low historical returns they have produced? The answer is that T-bills and bonds have lower risks associated with them than do common stocks. Before we formally define risk, we refer the reader to the report below, which illustrates the types of risks that investors attempt to avoid, or reduce their exposure to, by investing in T-bills and bonds rather than stocks.

■ *Finance in the News*

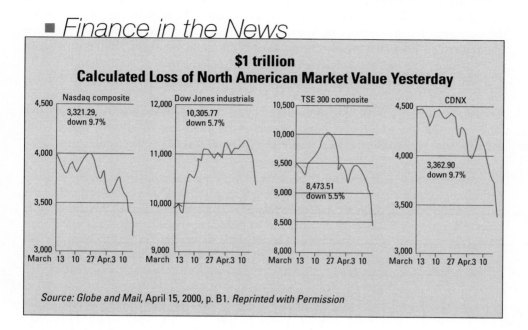

$1 trillion
Calculated Loss of North American Market Value Yesterday

Source: Globe and Mail, April 15, 2000, p. B1. Reprinted with Permission

The headline above shows the type of risk or volatility associated with stock returns. It refers to the great drop in value of North American stock markets on April 14, 2000. On that day, the value of both the Nasdaq Stock Market (Nasdaq) and Canadian Venture Exchange (CDNX) Indexes fell 9.7 percent in value, while the Dow Jones Industrial Average (DJIA), which measures activity on the New York Stock Exchange (NYSE), fell 5.7 percent, and the TSE 300 Composite Index fell 5.5 percent. In fact, during that particular week, common stocks had very high negative returns: the Nasdaq Composite Index fell 25.3 percent, the TSE 300 10.5 percent, and the DJIA 7.2 percent. During the same period, Canadian bonds (as measured by the DS Barra bond market index) provided a modest gain of 0.3 percent, while T-bills had a return of 0.0 percent. It is also noteworthy that the volatility displayed by Nasdaq and the resulting loss in value was much higher than that of the TSE or the NYSE. This is because of the large number of high-technology stocks that trade in this market, and these stocks are considered riskier than the average ones. The heavy concentration in high-tech stocks also means that Nasdaq is less diversified across industries than the TSE or NYSE, which also implies greater risk. We defer our discussion about diversification until later in this chapter.

Defining Risk

It is not sensible to talk about investment returns without talking about risk because investment decisions involve a trade-off between the two. Investors must constantly be aware of the risk they are assuming, know what it can do to their investment decisions, and be prepared for the consequences.

Risk may be defined as the chance that the actual outcome from an investment will differ from the expected outcome. Specifically, most investors are concerned that the actual outcome will be less than the expected outcome. The broader the range of possible outcomes, the greater the risk. We can see from the example on the previous page that the returns on stocks fell greatly during April 2000, while bond and T-bill returns were less variable. The fact that stock returns are more volatile than those of bonds and T-bills can be seen clearly in Figure 7.1 below, which provides a graph of the annual returns for Canadian T-bills, bonds, and stocks over the 1938-98 period. This graph shows the dramatic swings in annual returns displayed by stocks, both in the positive and negative direction. On the other hand, bond returns swing much less drastically, while T-bill returns were very stable and were never negative over this 61-year period.

FIGURE 7.1

Graph of Canadian Asset Returns (1938–98)

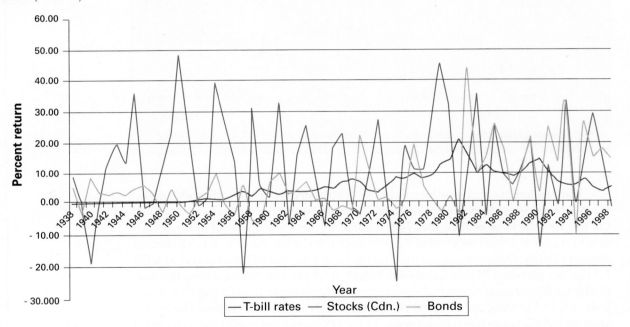

Investors should be willing to purchase a particular asset if the expected return is adequate to compensate for the risk, but they must understand that their expectation about the asset's return may not materialize and the realized return will differ from the expected return. In fact, realized returns on securities show considerable variability. Although investors may receive their expected returns on risky securities on an average long-run basis, they often fail to do so on a short-run basis.

It is important to remember how risk and return go together when investing. An investor cannot reasonably expect larger returns without being willing to assume larger risks. Consider the investor who wishes to avoid any risk (on a practical basis). Such an investor can deposit money in an insured savings account thereby earning a guaranteed return of a known amount. However, this return will be fixed, and the investor cannot earn more than this rate. Although risk is effectively eliminated, the chance of earning a larger return is also removed. To have the opportunity to earn a larger return, investors must be willing to assume larger risks. This is clear from the high long-term returns earned by common shares as well as the large volatility in these returns. We now turn our attention to the determination of the expected returns and risks associated with risky assets.

ESTIMATING RISK AND RETURN   **7.3**

In the section above, we discussed the returns that investors have experienced over the years from investing in the major financial assets available to them. Realized returns are important for several reasons. For example, investors need to know how well their investments have performed. Realized returns can also be particularly important in helping investors to form expectations about future returns because investors must concern themselves with their best estimate of return over some future time horizon.

How do we go about estimating future returns, which is what investors must actually do in managing their investments? We begin by noting that investors are concerned with total returns whether one is measuring realized returns or estimating future (expected) returns. The **total return** on a typical investment consists of two components: yield and capital gain or loss.

The basic component that usually comes to mind when discussing investing returns is **yield**, which is the periodic cash flows (or income) on an investment. It will consist of interest payments in the case of bonds, or dividends in the case of equities. The distinguishing feature of these payments is that the issuer makes the payments in cash to the holder of the asset. Yield measures such as the dividend yield or the current yield relate these cash flows to a price for the security such as the purchase price or the current market price.

The second component **capital gain (loss)**, is also important particularly for common stocks but also for long-term bonds and other fixed-income securities. This component is the appreciation (or depreciation) in the price of the asset commonly called the capital gain (or capital loss). We will refer to it simply as the price change. It is the difference between the purchase price and the selling price. If the latter exceeds the former, a gain occurs, while if the selling price is below the purchase price, a loss occurs.

Given the two components of a security's return, we need to add them together to form the total return, which for any security is defined as:

Total return = yield + price change

where:

the yield component can be 0 or +

the price change component can be 0, +, or −

The important point to note from the equation above is that any security's total return consists of the sum of two components—yield and price change. More formally, the total return (TR) for a given holding period is expressed as a decimal (or percentage) number relating all the cash flows received by an investor during any designated time period to the purchase price of the asset. Total return is defined as:

$$TR = \frac{\text{any cash payments received} + \text{price changes over the period}}{\text{price at which the asset is purchased}}$$

The general equation for calculating TR is:

(7.1) $$TR = \frac{CF_t + (P_E - P_B)}{P_B} = \frac{CF_t + PC}{P_B}$$

where
CF_t = cash flows during the measurement period t
P_E = price at the end of period t or sale price
P_B = purchase price of the asset or price at the beginning of the period
PC = change in price during the period, or P_E minus P_B

Although one year is often used for convenience, this calculation can be applied to periods of any length. In summary, the total return concept is valuable as a measure of return because it is all-inclusive, measuring the total return per dollar of original investment. It facilitates the comparison of asset returns over a specified period whether the comparison is of different assets, such as stocks versus bonds, or different securities within the same asset category such as several common stocks. Remember that using this concept does not mean that the securities have to be sold and the gains or losses actually realized.

EXAMPLE

CALCULATING TOTAL RETURN

The total return for the TSE 300 Composite Index for 1999 may be calculated given the following information: beginning value—6,485.94; ending value—8,413.75; dividends (adjusted to the index value)—110.46.[1]

$$TR = \frac{(8413.75 - 6485.94) + 110.46}{6485.94} \times 100 = 31.43\%^{[2]}$$

---

[1] *TSE 1999 Annual Review.*
[2] This TR is slightly different than that reported for the TSE Total Return Index for 1999, which was 31.43 percent since the Total Return Index assumes the dividends are reinvested as soon as they are received not at year end as the calculations above assume. For example, the TSE 300 Total Return Index for 1999 was 31.71 percent.

Dealing with Uncertainty

The return an investor will earn is not known and must be estimated. Future return is an expected return and may or may not actually be realized. Risk or the chance of an unexpected return is involved whenever investment decisions are made. To deal with the uncertainty of returns, investors need to think explicitly about a security's distribution of probable TRs. In other words, investors need to keep in mind that although they may expect a security to return 10 percent, this is only a one-point estimate of the entire range of possibilities. Given that investors must deal with the uncertain future, a number of possible returns can and will occur.

In the case of a Government of Canada bond paying a fixed rate of interest, payments will be made with virtual certainty barring a financial collapse of the entire economy. Thus, the probability of receiving the fixed payments is 1.0 (or very close to it). With the possibility of two or more outcomes, which is the norm for common stocks, each possible likely outcome must be considered and a likelihood of its occurrence assessed. Considering these outcomes and their probabilities together results in a probability distribution of the likely returns that may occur and their associated probabilities. Probabilities represent the likelihood of various outcomes and are typically expressed as decimals or fractions. The sum of the probabilities of all possible outcomes must be 1.0 because they must completely describe all the (perceived) likely occurrences.

How are these probabilities and associated outcomes determined? In the final analysis, investing for some future period involves uncertainty and therefore subjective estimates. While past occurrences and historical frequency distributions may be useful for estimating probabilities, there is no guarantee the past will repeat itself. It is important to monitor current economic and company variables that affect security returns and to forecast the future values of these variables.

Calculating Expected Return

To describe the single most likely outcome from a particular probability distribution, it is necessary to calculate its expected value. The expected value is the average of all possible return outcomes, where each outcome is weighted by the probability of its occurrence. Since investors are interested in returns, we will call this expected value the expected rate of return, or simply **expected return**. For any security, it is calculated as:

$$E(R) = \sum_{i=1}^{m} R_i pr_i \tag{7.2}$$

where

$E(R)$ = the expected return on a security

R_i = the ith possible return

pr_i = the probability of the ith return R_i

m = the number of possible returns

| EXAMPLE | **DETERMINING EXPECTED RETURN** |

An analyst anticipates three possible states of the economy next year: normal, recession, or boom. She estimates the following probabilities for each of these occurences as well as the following expected returns for securities A and B associated with these different states of the economy:

State (i)	Probability of Occurrence (Pr_i)	Stock A Return	Stock B Return
Recession	0.25	6%	0%
Normal	0.50	12%	12%
Boom	0.25	18%	24%

The expected return on stock A is:
$E(R_A) = (.25)(6\%) + (.50)(12\%) + (.25)(18\%) = 12\%$

The expected return on stock B is:
$E(R_B) = (.25)(0\%) + (.50)(12\%) + (.25)(24\%) = 12\%$

Calculating Risk

Investors must be able to quantify and measure risk. Variance or standard deviation is typically used to calculate the total risk associated with the expected return. These statistics measure the spread or dispersion in the probability distribution; that is, they measure the dispersion of a random variable around its mean and the larger this dispersion, the larger the variance or standard deviation. For example, we can relate the volatility of returns for the three major asset categories demonstrated in Figure 7.1 by referring to the standard deviations of the annual returns of T-bills, bonds, and stocks over the 1938-98 period. These values were 4.51, 9.56, and 16.15 percent respectively, confirming the greater variability in returns (or risk) of stocks evident in Figure 7.1.

To calculate the variance or standard deviation from the probability distribution, we must first calculate the expected return of the distribution using Equation 7.2. We can then measure the dispersion of possible outcomes from the expected return by using the possible returns as weighted by the probabilities associated with their occurence. The equations are given below:

(7.3)   Variance of returns $= \sigma^2 = \sum_{i=1}^{m} [R_i - E(R)]^2 \, pr_i$

and

(7.4)   Standard deviation of returns $= \sigma = \sqrt{\sigma^2}$

where all terms are as defined previously.

CALCULATING STANDARD DEVIATION

We use Equation 7.4 to estimate the standard deviation for securities A and B from the example above:

$$\sigma_A = \sqrt{.25(6-12)^2 + .50(12-12)^2 + .25(18-12)^2} = \sqrt{18} = 4.24\%$$

$$\sigma_B = \sqrt{.25(0-12)^2 + .50(12-12)^2 + .25(24-12)^2} = \sqrt{72} = 8.48\%$$

Notice that the variances are 18 for A and 72 for B.

Calculating a standard deviation using probability distributions involves making subjective estimates of the probabilities and the likely returns. This is unavoidable because future returns are uncertain since the prices of securities are based on investors' expectations about the future. The relevant standard deviation in this situation is the ex-ante standard deviation and not the ex-post one based on realized returns. In other words, we are interested in the variability associated with future expected returns.

Although standard deviations based on realized returns are often used as proxies for ex-ante standard deviations, investors should be careful to remember that the past cannot always be extrapolated into the future without modifications since standard deviations change through time. While historical (ex-post) standard deviations provide convenient proxies, they should not be relied upon exclusively to estimate future risk.

PORTFOLIO RISK AND RETURN   7.4

Given that the number one principle of portfolio management is to diversify and hold a portfolio of securities, we now focus our discussion on the expected return and risk for portfolios. When we analyse investment risks and returns, we must be concerned with the total portfolio held by an investor. Individual security risks and returns are important, but it is the risk and return to the investor's total portfolio that ultimately matters because investment opportunities can be enhanced by packaging them together to form portfolios.

As we will see, portfolio risk is a unique characteristic and not simply the sum of individual security risks. A security may have a large risk if it is held by itself but much less when held in a portfolio of securities. Since investors are concerned primarily with the risk of the total wealth position of their overall investment portfolio, individual stocks are risky only to the extent that they add risk to the total portfolio.

Portfolio Expected Return

The expected return on any portfolio is easily calculated as a weighted average of the individual securities' expected returns. The percentages of a portfolio's total value that are invested in each portfolio asset are referred to as portfolio weights, which we will denote by w. The combined portfolio weights are assumed to add up to 100 percent of total investable funds or 1.0, indicating that all portfolio funds are invested.[3]

The expected return on any portfolio, p, can be calculated as:

$$(7.5) \quad E(R_p) = \sum_{i=1}^{n} w_i E(R_i)$$

where

$E(R_p)$ = the expected return on the portfolio

w_i = the portfolio weight for the ith security;

$\sum w_i = 1.0$

$E(R_i)$ = the expected return on the ith security

n = the number of different securities in the portfolio

EXAMPLE

CALCULATING PORTFOLIO EXPECTED RETURN

Consider a two-stock portfolio consisting of stocks C and D, which have expected returns of 12 and 15 percent respectively. Assume that 20 percent is invested in security C and the remaining 80 percent in D. The expected return on this portfolio is:

$E(R_p) = 0.2(12\%) + 0.8(15\%) = 2.4\% + 12.0\% = 14.4\%$

Regardless of the number of assets held in a portfolio or the proportion of total investable funds placed in each asset, the expected return on the portfolio is *always* a weighted average of the expected returns for individual assets in the portfolio.

Portfolio Risk

The remaining computation in investment analysis is that of the risk of the portfolio. We measure risk as the variance (or standard deviation) of the portfolio's return, exactly as in the case of each individual security.

It is at this point that the basis of modern portfolio theory emerges, which can be stated as follows: although the expected return of a portfolio is a weighted average of its

[3] For now, we ignore the possibility of short-selling, which can create negative weights in securities. In other words, we assume that all the weights are positive, which implies that we are talking about long positions in the individual securities. This assumption can be relaxed without affecting our results.

expected returns, portfolio risk (as measured by the variance or standard deviation) is less than the weighted average of the risk of the individual securities in a portfolio of risky securities.[4] Symbolically,

$$E(R_p) = \sum_{i=1}^{n} w_i E(R)_i$$

but

$$\sigma_p < \sum_{i=1}^{n} w_i \, \sigma_i \qquad (7.6)$$

Precisely because Equation 7.6 is an inequality, investors can reduce the risk of a portfolio below the weighted average of the individual securities' risk. We will now analyse portfolio risk in detail in order to see how this risk reduction can be accomplished.

In order to develop an equation that will calculate the risk of a portfolio as measured by the variance or standard deviation, we must account for two factors:

1. weighted individual security risks (i.e., the variance of each individual security weighted by the percentage of investable funds placed in each individual security)

2. weighted co-movements between securities' returns as measured by the correlations between the securities' returns weighted again by the percentage of investable funds placed in each security

The co-movements between securities' returns is often measured using the **correlation coefficient** (pronounced "rho"). This is a statistical measure of the relative co-movements between the returns on securities A and B. It measures the extent to which the returns on any two securities are related; however, it denotes only association not causation. In other words, it measures how security returns move in relation to one another but does not provide information regarding the cause of this relationship. It is a relative measure of association that is bounded by

$+ 1.0$ and $- 1.0$, with

$\rho_{AB} = +1.0$

= perfect positive correlation

$\rho_{AB} = - 1.0$

= perfect negative (inverse) correlation

$\rho_{AB} = - 0.0$

= zero correlation (uncorrelated).

---

[4] This is always true except for one special case, which will be discussed later on in this chapter.

If two stocks A and B display perfect positive correlation, the returns have a perfect direct linear relationship. Knowing what the return on one security will do allows an investor to forecast perfectly what the other will do. When stock A's return goes up, stock B's does also, and when stock A's return goes down, so does stock B's. With perfect negative correlation, the securities' returns have a perfect inverse linear relationship to each other. Therefore, knowing the return on one security provides full knowledge about the return on the second. When one security's return is high, the other is low.

With zero correlation, there is no relationship between the returns on the two securities, and knowledge of the return on one is of no value in predicting the return of the other. In the real world, these extreme correlations are rare. Rather, securities have some positive correlation with each other since all security prices tend to move with changes in the overall market and/or economy. Figure 7.2 shows a graphical representation of returns that are positively correlated, negatively correlated, and uncorrelated (or independent).

FIGURE 7.2

Examples of Security Returns that Are Positively Correlated, Negatively Correlated, and Uncorrelated (Independent)

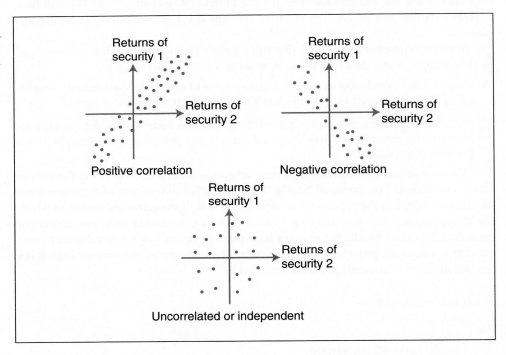

Using the correlation coefficient to measure co-movements of security returns, the risk of a portfolio as measured by the standard deviation of returns for the case of two securities A and B is given by the following equation:

(7.7) $$\sigma_p = \sqrt{w_A^2 \sigma_A^2 + w_B^2 \sigma_B^2 + 2 w_A w_B \rho_{AB} \sigma_A \sigma_B}$$

Equation 7.7 shows us that the risk for a portfolio encompasses not only the individual security risks but also the correlation between the returns on these two securities.

It also shows that three factors determine portfolio risk: the variance of each security, the correlation between the securities' returns, and the portfolio weights for each security.

Equation 7.7 shows that the standard deviation of the portfolio will be directly related to the correlation between the two stocks as discussed previously. The only case in which there are no risk-reduction benefits to be obtained from two-security diversification occurs when the correlation coefficient is $+1.0$. For this case only, the portfolio standard deviation will be a weighted average of the standard deviations of the individual securities.[5] Since $\sigma_p = w_A\sigma_A + w_B\sigma_B$ when $\rho_{AB} = +1$, and since $+1$ is the maximum value for the correlation coefficient, it must be the case that for all other possible correlation coefficients $\sigma_p < w_A\sigma_A + w_B\sigma_B$. That means that there will be benefits from diversification as long as $\rho_{AB} < +1$. The benefits will be greater as the correlation coefficient approaches -1.

ESTIMATING RISK FOR A TWO-SECURITY PORTFOLIO

Assume that the estimated standard deviations for two securities E and F are 37.3 and 23.3 percent respectively. To see the effects of changing the correlation coefficient, assume weights of 0.5 each (i.e., 50 percent of investable funds are to be placed in each security). With this data, the standard deviation or risk for this portfolio is:

$$\sigma_p = \sqrt{(0.5)^2(0.373)^2 + (0.5)^2(0.233)^2 + 2(0.5)(.05)(0.373)(0.233)\rho_{E,F}}$$

Carrying out the multiplication, this can be reduced to the following expression

$$\sigma_p = \sqrt{0.0348 + 0.0136 + 0.0435\rho_{E,F}} = [0.0348 + 0.0136 + 0.0435\rho_{E,F}]^{1/2}$$

The risk of this portfolio clearly depends heavily on the value of the third term, which in turn depends on the correlation coefficient between the returns for E and F. To assess the potential impact of the correlation, consider the following cases: $\rho_{E,F}$ of $+1$, $+0.5$, $+0.15$, 0, -0.5, and -1.0. Calculating portfolio risk under each of these scenarios produces the following portfolio risks:

$$\rho = +1.0: \sigma_p = [0.0348 + 0.0136 + 0.0435(1)]^{1/2} = 30.3\%$$

For this case only the portfolio standard deviation is a weighted average of the individual standard deviations (i.e., $0.303 = [0.50][0.373] + [0.50][0.233]$).

$$\rho = +0.5: \sigma_p = [0.0348 + 0.0136 + 0.0435(0.5)]^{1/2} = 26.5\%$$
$$\rho = +0.15: \sigma_p = [0.0348 + 0.0136 + 0.0435(0.15)]^{1/2} = 23.4\%$$
$$\rho = +0.0: \sigma_p = [0.0348 + 0.0136]^{1/2} = 22.0\%$$

---

[5] This fact is easy to show. Using Equation 7.7 and substituting $+1$ for ρ_{AB}, we obtain $\sigma_p = \sqrt{w_A^2\sigma_A^2 + w_B^2\sigma_B^2 w(1)\sigma_A\sigma_B} = \sqrt{(w_A\sigma_A + w_B\sigma_B)^2} = w_A\sigma_A + w_B\sigma_B$, which represents the weighted averge of the individual standard deviations.

$$\rho = -0.5: \sigma_p = [0.0348 + 0.0136 + 0.0435(-0.5)]^{\frac{1}{2}} = 16.3\%$$
$$\rho = -1.0: \sigma_p = [0.0348 + 0.0136 + 0.0435(-1.0)]^{\frac{1}{2}} = 7.0\%$$

Notice that for all of these values of $\rho < +1$, the standard deviation is less than the weighted average of the individual standard deviations. In fact, for this example, the portfolio standard deviation is less than either of the individual standard deviations for correlations of 0 or below.

The calculations above clearly show the impact that combining securities with less than perfect positive correlation will have on portfolio risk. In general, we can see there will always be risk reduction benefits available from diversification as long as the correlation coefficient between the returns is less than one, and the lower the correlation coefficient, the greater the benefits. The risk of the portfolio steadily decreases from 30.3 percent to 7 percent as the correlation coefficient declines from +1.0 to −1.0.

In general, we would expect correlations to be higher between stock returns for companies that are similar in nature and lower among stock returns for companies that have large dissimilarities. Over the period from July 1990 to June 2000, for example, the correlation coefficient between the monthly returns for Royal Bank of Canada common stock and Barrick Gold Corporation stock was 0.21, and the correlation between Royal Bank returns and Canadian Imperial Bank of Commerce common stock was 0.69.

The calculations in the example above consider the two-security portfolio, which is equally weighted with respect to securities E and F. What if we allowed the weights in each security to vary from 0.0 to 1.0? Using correlation coefficients of +1.0, +0.15, and −1.0, we obtain the following portfolio standard deviations for different weights in each security:

		Portfolio Standard Deviation (%)		
w_E	w_F	$\rho = +1.0$	$\rho = +0.15$	$\rho = -1.0$
1.0	0.0	37.3	37.3	37.3
0.8	0.2	34.5	30.9	25.2
0.6	0.4	31.7	25.5	13.1
0.4	0.6	28.9	21.9	0.9
0.2	0.8	26.1	21.1	11.2
0.0	1.0	23.3	23.3	23.3

Figure 7.3 plots the three curves that result if we join the standard deviations for the various portfolios that would arise assuming correlation coefficients of +1.0, −1.0, and +0.15 and including all possible variations in weighting schemes. While this particular graph relates to securities E and F, the shape of the three curves will be the same for any two securities given these three correlation coefficients.

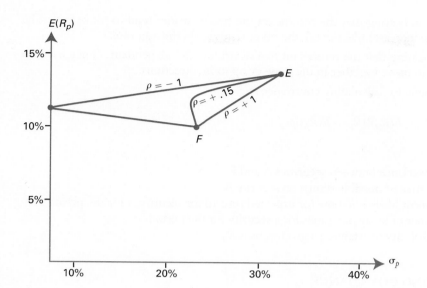

FIGURE 7.3

Two-Security Portfolio
Risk and Correlation
Coefficients

Notice the straight line connecting the individual risks that emerges in Figure 7.3 assuming a correlation coefficient of +1.0. This shows clearly that the standard deviation of the portfolio is a weighted average of the individual risks for this case only. For the case of $\rho = -1$, we have two straight lines from each individual risk to the vertical axis. This shows that for one particular weighting scheme ($w_E = 0.384$; $w_F = 0.616$), the portfolio will have zero risk.[6] One such point will always exist whenever we have two perfectly negatively correlated securities. However, it is highly unlikely that any two stocks would display such a relationship.[7] Finally, we observe the parabola-shaped curve that emerges when $\rho = +0.15$. This is of most interest to investors since most stocks display positive correlations between 0 and +1.

Covariance and Correlation Coefficients

Another commonly used measure of co-movements between security returns that is closely related to the correlation coefficient is **covariance**. This is an absolute measure of the degree of association between the returns for a pair of securities. Covariance is defined as the extent to which two random variables covary, or move together, over time. As is true throughout our discussion, the variables in question are the total returns (TRs) on two securities. Similar to the correlation coefficient, the covariance can be:

1. Positive, indicating that the returns on the two securities tend to move in the same direction at the same time. When one increases (decreases), the other tends to do the same.

---

[6] Technically, this point occurs for the following weight in security E whenever $\rho_{EF} = -1$: $w_E = \dfrac{w_F}{w_E + w_F}$.

[7] However, securities that approach this condition can be created synthetically, which is the principle underlying many portfolio hedging strategies, some of which are discussed in Part 7 of this text.

2. Negative, indicating that the returns on the two securities tend to move inversely. When one increases (decreases), the other tends to do the opposite.

3. Zero, indicating that the returns on two securities are independent. They have no tendency to move together in the same or opposite directions.

The formula for calculating covariance is:

$$(7.8) \qquad \sigma_{AB} = \sum_{i=1}^{m} [R_{A,i} - E(R_A)][R_{B,i} - E(R_B)]pr_i$$

where

σ_{AB} = the covariance between securities A and B
$R_{A,i}$ = one estimated possible return on security A
$E(R_A)$ = the most likely outcome (or expected return) for security A for the period
m = the number of likely outcomes for a security for the period
pr_i = the probability of attaining a given return $R_{A,i}$

EXAMPLE

CALCULATING COVARIANCE

Two securities G and H have the following expected returns associated with four possible states of the economy:

State (i)	Probability of Occurrence (Pr$_i$)	Stock G Return	Stocl H Return
1	0.20	6%	5%
2	0.40	10%	7%
3	0.30	11%	15%
4	0.10	14%	27%

The expected returns for each security are:

$E(R_G) = (0.20)(6) + (0.40)(10) + (0.30)(11) + (0.10)(14) = 1.2 + 4 + 3.3 + 1.4 = 9.9\%$

$E(R_H) = (0.20)(5) + (0.40)(7) + (0.30)(15) + (0.10)(27) = 1 + 2.8 + 4.5 + 2.7 = 11.0\%$

Using Equation 7.8, we can determine their covariance as follows:

$\sigma_{GH} = (0.20)(6 - 9.9)(5 - 11) + (0.40)(10 - 9.9)(7 - 11) + (0.30)(11 - 9.9)(15 - 11)$

$+ (0.10)(14 - 9.9)(27 - 11) = 4.68 + .016 + 1.32 + 6.56 = 12.58 \, (\%)^2$

The covariance and the correlation coefficient are related in the following manner:

$$(7.9) \qquad \rho_{AB} = \frac{\sigma_{AB}}{\sigma_A \sigma_B}$$

This equation shows that the correlation coefficient is simply the covariance standardized by dividing it by the product of the two standard deviations of returns.

CALCULATING THE CORRELATION COEFFICIENT

Continuing with the example above, we could determine the correlation coefficient for securities G and H. First, we need to estimate the indivdual standard deviations, which are:

$$\sigma_G = [(0.20)(6-10)^2 + (0.40)(10-10)^2 + (0.30)(11-10)^2 + (0.10)(14-10)^2]^{1/2}$$

$$= [3.2 + 0 + 0.3 + 1.6]^{1/2} = [5.1]^{1/2} = 2.26\%$$

$$\sigma_G = [(0.20)(5-11)^2 + (0.40)(7-11)^2 + (0.30)(15-11)^2 + (0.10)(27-11)^2]^{1/2}$$

$$= [7.2 + 6.4 + 4.8 + 25.6]^{1/2} = [44.0]1/2 = 6.63\%$$

Combining these results with the covariance we calculated above, we get:

$$\rho_{GH} = \frac{\sigma_{GH}}{\sigma_G\,\sigma_H} = \frac{12.58}{(2.26)(6.63)} = 0.84$$

Given this definition of the correlation coefficient, the covariance can be rewritten as:

$$\sigma_{AB} = \rho_{AB}\,\sigma_A\sigma_B \tag{7.10}$$

Therefore, knowing the correlation coefficient, we can calculate the covariance because the standard deviations of the assets' rates of return will already be available. Similarily, knowing the covariance, we can easily calculate the correlation coefficient.

Noting that $\sigma_{AB} = \sigma_A\sigma_B\rho_{AB}$, we can re-express Equation 7.7 as:

$$\sigma_P = \sqrt{w_A^2\sigma_A^2 + w_B^2\sigma_B^2 + 2w_Aw_B\sigma_{AB}} \tag{7.11}$$

ESTIMATING PORTFOLIO RISK

Using Equation 7.11 and the information for stocks G and H, and assuming that a portfolio is formed with 40 percent invested in G and the other 60 percent in H:

$$\sigma_P = \sqrt{w_A^2\sigma_A^2 + w_B^2\sigma_B^2 + 2w_Aw_B\sigma_{AB}}$$

$$= \sqrt{(.40)^2(2.26)^2 + (0.60)^2(6.63)^2 + 2(0.40)(0.60)(12.58)} = \sqrt{22.6801} = 4.76\%$$

The *n*-Security Case

We have so far considered risk for only a two-security portfolio. The same principles apply when this case is generalized to the *n*-security case. In particular, portfolio risk can be reduced by combining assets with less-than-perfect positive correlation. Furthermore, the smaller the positive correlation, the better.

Portfolio risk is a function of each individual security's risk and the covariances between the returns on the individual securities. Stated in terms of variance, portfolio risk for a portfolio comprised of n securities is:

$$(7.12) \quad \sigma_P^2 = \sum_{i=1}^{n} w_i^2 \sigma_i^2 + \sum_{i=1}^{n} \sum_{j=1}^{n} w_i w_j \sigma_{ij}, (i \neq j)$$

where

$\sigma_P^2 =$ the variance of the return on the portfolio

$\sigma_i^2 =$ the variance of return for security i

$\sigma_{ij} =$ the covariance between the returns for securities i and j

$w_i =$ the portfolio weights or percentage of investable funds invested in security i

$n \quad =$ the number of securities in the portfolio

$\sum_{i=1}^{n} \sum_{j=1}^{n} =$ a double summation sign indicating that n^2 numbers are to be added together

(i.e., all possible pairs of values for i and j).

The number of relevant covariances for an n-security portfolio equals $n(n-1)$. In the case of two securities, there are two covariances. Since the covariance of A with B is the same as the covariance of B with A, we simply multiply the weighted covariance term in Equation 7.8 by two. In the case of three securities, there are six covariances; with four securities, 12 covariances; and so forth. The number of covariances grows quickly based on the calculation of $n(n-1)$, where n is the number of securities involved. For example, the number of relevant covariances in a 100-security portfolio would equal $100(100 - 1) = 9,900$.

An important point emerges with respect to the relative importance of the variances and covariances in determining portfolio risk. As the number of securities held in a portfolio increases, the importance of each individual security's risk (variance) decreases, while the importance of the covariance relationships increases. In portfolios consisting of a large number of securities, the contribution of each to the total portfolio risk will be extremely small, and portfolio risk will consist almost entirely of the covariance risk between securities. For example, in a 100-security portfolio, there will be 9,900 weighted covariance terms and only 100 weighted variance terms. As n becomes larger, the influence of the individual variances becomes smaller and approaches zero for large values of n. Therefore, the risk of a well-diversified portfolio will be largely attributable to the impact of the second term in Equation 7.12 representing the covariance relationships. This fact has important implications regarding the benefits of diversification, which are discussed in the next section.

7.5 DIVERSIFICATION

The discussion above identifies the importance of risk and discusses the most common measures of total risk—standard deviation and variance. Much of this risk is difficult to avoid and is part of the risk of being an investor in today's financial environment. However, **diversification** helps investors reduce their exposure to risk to the greatest extent possible while still attempting to maximize their returns.

We begin by considering an example related to the report entitled, "$1 trillion Calculated Loss of North American Market Value Yesterday," in section 7.2, which shows how diversification helps to eliminate risk. We have seen previously that the value of the TSE 300 Composite Index fell 5.5 percent on April 14, 2000. At that time, what would have happened if you had invested all of your $100,000 in one common stock—that of Certicom (a Canadian high-technology stock trading on the TSE)? That particular stock dropped from $82.25 to $65 that day—a 21 percent decline. During that day, you would have lost $21,000 of your $100,000 available for investment purposes—a significant loss indeed. On the other hand, if you had only $5,000 (5 percent) invested in Certicom with the other 95 percent in a well-diversified Canadian stock portfolio that matched the TSE 300 decline of 5.5 percent, your losses would have been $1,050 (21 percent of $5,000) on Certicom, plus $5,225 (5.5 percent of $95,000) on your remaining stock portfolio. Your total loss would have amounted to $6,275 or 6.275 percent of the original investment—quite a dramatic difference. This example demonstrates the benefits of holding a well-diversified portfolio to eliminate risk. Obviously, if the investor held some bonds and/or T-bills in the portfolio, the risk could have been reduced even further. We now turn our attention to why diversification works in this manner.

We have seen that individual security returns and risks are important, but it is the return and risk to the investor's total portfolio that ultimately matters because investment opportunities can be enhanced by packaging them together to form portfolios. As a result, portfolio risk is a unique characteristic and not simply the sum of individual security risks. A security may have a large risk if it is held by itself but much less risk when held in a portfolio of securities. Since investors are concerned primarily with the risk of their total wealth position, as represented by their overall investment portfolio, individual stocks are risky only to the extent that they add risk to the total portfolio. In particular, while the return of a portfolio is always equal to the weighted average of the returns of its individual securities, the total risk of a portfolio is less than the weighted average of the risk of the individual securities in a portfolio (as long as the returns are not perfectly positively correlated).

The basic idea behind diversification is that as we add securities to any portfolio, the exposure to any particular source of risk becomes small, and the risk of the portfolio declines rapidly as more securities are added. This is especially true if the returns of the individual securities in the portfolio have low (or even negative) correlations with one another. However, as we have already seen, most stocks are positively correlated with each other since they display a significant level of co-movement with the overall stock market as measured by market indexes such as the TSE 300 Composite Index. Therefore, risk cannot be eliminated entirely because common sources of risk affect all firms.

Domestic Diversification

Diversification is the key to the management of portfolio risk because it allows investors to minimize risk without adversely affecting return, which is always a weighted average of the individual returns. Random or naive diversification refers to the act of randomly diversifying without regard to relevant investment characteristics such as expected return, company size, and industry classification. An investor simply selects a relatively large number of securities randomly (i.e., the proverbial "throwing a dart at the newspaper page containing the stock quotes"). We provide some actual Canadian evidence regarding naive diversification in Figure 7.4 and Table 7.2.

Table 7.2

Portfolio Risk January 1985 to December 1997

Number of stocks in portfolio	Average monthly portfolio returns (%)	Standard deviation of average monthly portfolio returns (%)	Ratio of portfolio standard deviation to standard deviation of a single stock	Percentage of total achievable risk reduction
1	1.51	13.47	1.00	0.00
2	1.51	10.99	0.82	27.50
3	1.52	9.91	0.74	39.56
4	1.53	9.30	0.69	46.37
5	1.52	8.67	0.64	53.31
6	1.52	8.30	0.62	57.50
7	1.51	7.95	0.59	61.35
8	1.52	7.71	0.57	64.02
9	1.52	7.52	0.56	66.17
10	1.51	7.33	0.54	68.30
11	1.52	7.17	0.53	70.02
12	1.51	7.03	0.52	71.58
13	1.51	6.91	0.51	72.90
14	1.51	6.80	0.50	74.19
15	1.52	6.72	0.50	75.07
16	1.52	6.63	0.49	76.04
17	1.52	6.56	0.49	76.82
18	1.52	6.51	0.48	77.41
19	1.52	6.45	0.48	78.00
20	1.52	6.39	0.47	78.65
21	1.52	6.32	0.47	79.48
22	1.52	6.25	0.46	80.30
23	1.52	6.20	0.46	80.79
24	1.52	6.15	0.46	81.32
25	1.52	6.11	0.45	81.80
26	1.52	6.07	0.45	82.25
27	1.52	6.03	0.45	82.66
28	1.52	5.99	0.44	83.18
29	1.52	5.94	0.44	83.66
30	1.52	5.91	0.44	84.06
35	1.52	5.76	0.43	85.68

40	1.52	5.62	0.42	87.24
45	1.52	5.50	0.41	88.56
50	1.52	5.41	0.40	89.64
60	1.52	5.25	0.39	91.40
70	1.51	5.12	0.38	92.86
80	1.51	5.02	0.37	94.00
90	1.51	4.93	0.37	94.94
100	1.51	4.86	0.36	95.70
150	1.51	4.64	0.34	98.18
200	1.51	4.51	0.34	99.58
222	1.51	4.48	0.33	100.00

Source: Table 1 in "Diversification with Canadian Stocks: How Much is Enough?" S. Cleary and D. Copp, *Canadian Investment Review*, Fall 1999.

FIGURE 7.4

Monthly data for 222 Canadian stocks between 1985 and 1997

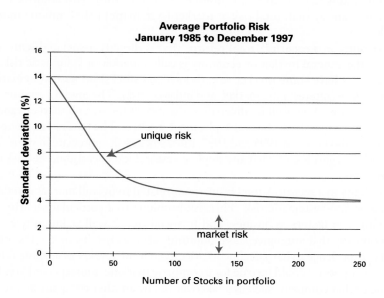

Average Portfolio Risk
January 1985 to December 1997

Source: Adapted from Figure 1 in "Diversification with Canadian Stocks: How Much is Enough?" S. Cleary and D. Copp, *Canadian Investment Review*, Fall 1999.

Figure 7.4 plots the actual monthly data for 222 Canadian stocks between 1985 and 1997 as reported in Table 7.2 to illustrate naive diversification. As we can see, portfolio risk for a randomly selected portfolio was reduced to approximately 4.48 percent per month over this period from an average of 13.47 percent for each individual stock. As more securities are added to the portfolio, the total risk associated with the portfolio of stocks declines rapidly. The first few stocks cause a large decrease in portfolio risk. Based on this data, 26 percent of portfolio standard deviation is eliminated as we go from one to three securities, 46 percent as we go from one to 10, and 60 percent as we go from one to 50. Unfortunately, the benefits of random diversification do not continue indefinitely. As more and more securities are added, the marginal risk reduction per security added becomes extremely small, eventually producing an almost negligible effect on total portfolio risk.

This evidence indicates that a large number of securities are not required to achieve substantial diversification benefits. On the other hand, the monthly portfolio risk reported above levels out at approximately 5 percent once there are 80 securities in the portfolio and beyond. Therefore, no matter how many additional securities are added to this portfolio, the risk does not decline by a significant amount.

The part of the total risk that is eliminated by diversification in Figure 7.4 is **unique (or non-systematic) risk**. The part that is not eliminated by diversification is the **market (or systematic) risk**. That is because all the securities in the portfolio will be directly related to overall movements in the general market or economy, so diversification cannot eliminate this risk. Total risk is often divided into these two additive components. Thus, we can say that: total risk = market (systematic) risk + unique (non-systematic) risk.

The variability in a security's total returns that is directly associated with overall movements in the general market or economy is called market or systematic risk.[8] Virtually all securities have some market risk, (bonds and stocks) because systematic risk directly encompasses interest rate, market, and inflation risks. The investor cannot escape this because no matter how well he diversifies, the risk of the overall market cannot be avoided. If the stock market declines sharply, most stocks will be adversely affected; if it rises strongly as it did between 1995 and 1997, most stocks will appreciate in value. These movements occur regardless of what any single investor does. Clearly, market risk is critical to all investors.

The variability in a security's total returns not related to overall market variability is called unique or non-systematic risk. This risk is unique to a particular security and is associated with such factors as business and financial risk as well as liquidity risk. For example, a company that announces disappointing earnings results, or the loss of a key executive may experience a sharp decline in price even if the market as a whole is having a good day. The opposite could be true for a company that offers unexpected good news that is unique to that company, such as a takeover bid by another company at a substantial premium over its present market price. Although all securities tend to have some non-systematic risk, it is generally connected with common stocks.

The declining relationship between portfolio risk and the number of securities in a portfolio illustrated above for Canadian stocks, is a well-known result that holds for diversification among domestic stocks in all developed stock markets around the world. It highlights the benefits of holding a well-diversified portfolio in terms of risk reduction when diversification is achieved by random security selection.

---

[8] The most commonly used measure of market risk is beta, which is discussed at some length in Chapter 8.

Not surprisingly, diversification can be achieved more efficiently when we take a more structured approach to forming portfolios. In particular, if we consciously diversify across stocks in different industries and/or with regards to other firm characteristics such as company size, we can obtain greater benefits of diversification. This structured approach works better because we are implicitly seeking out securities with returns that are not very highly correlated with one another. Finding securities with returns that have low correlations with each other provides the maximum diversification benefits. Consider, for example, a portfolio made up of only two securities. If the returns on these securities had very little relationship to one another, and the returns on one security were highly negative for a given time period, it is still quite possible that the other security may have provided a positive return. On the other hand, if the two securities were highly correlated, they would both likely provide negative returns at similar times. Although there would still be benefits associated with diversifying, they would be much smaller than if the returns were weakly correlated.

P E R S P E C T I V E S

Corporate Manager

Since rational investors will attempt to hold well-diversified portfolios consisting of the stocks of several companies in different industries, it is relatively unimportant for corporate managers to diversify their operations across different industries. Rather, they should focus on being the best within their industry.

Investor

Rational investors should avoid putting all their eggs in one basket by holding well-diversified portfolios. This enables them to eliminate unique, company-specific risk especially when they diversify across stocks with returns that display low correlations. This implies that they should hold stocks from several different industries and/or geographical areas. Investors are assuming unnecessary risks if they fail to diversify adequately.

International Diversification

The discussion above assumed diversification in domestic securities such as stocks traded on the TSE or NYSE. However, in today's world, increasing attention is devoted to the importance of taking a global approach to investing. What effect would this have on our diversification analysis?

FIGURE 7.5

International Diversification

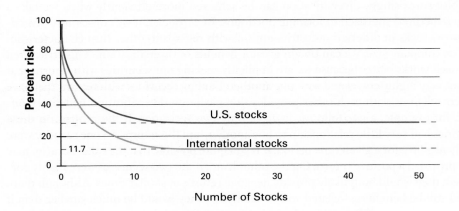

Source: "Why Not Diversify Internationally Rather than Domestically?" Bruno Solnik,
Financial Analysts Journal, July/August 1974. *Reprinted with permission.*

Considering only the potential for risk reduction and ignoring the additional problems in foreign investing such as currency risk, we could reasonably conclude that if
domestic diversification is good, international diversification must be better. This is consistent with the notion that the correlations between the returns on domestic and foreign
stocks will be lower than those across domestic stocks.

Figure 7.5 illustrates the benefits of international diversification in reducing portfolio risk. It is taken from a classic article by well-known researcher Bruno Solnik. He
shows that throughout the entire range of portfolio sizes, the risk is reduced when international investing is compared to investing in only domestic stocks (U.S. stocks, in this
example). The difference is dramatic—about one-third less risk. Several studies have
shown that similar risk-reduction benefits are available to Canadian investors who diversify internationally. For example, excerpts taken from a newspaper article that are included in the Finance in the News feature in Chapter 8, suggest that a portfolio containing
75 percent foreign content would have offered the maximum diversification benefits
available to Canadian investors over a recent 25-year period. ▲

Some Diversification Alternatives

This section has demonstrated that holding a well-diversified portfolio can help investors
eliminate risk without adversely affecting returns. Investors who do not diversify are
assuming risk unnecessarily, and the market may not provide compensation for this additional risk.

Given the importance of diversification, we close this section by answering the following question: how can investors in general, and small investors in particular, benefit
from diversification given their budgetary constraints? In other words, while it is relatively straightforward to diversify across several stocks if you are managing a portfolio
worth several hundred thousand or millions of dollars, it could prove very difficult to do
so if you have only three thousand dollars.

Investment funds provide one answer to this problem. Recall from Chapter 2 that **investment funds** sells shares or units in a trust fund to the public and uses the funds it raises to invest in a portfolio of securities such as money market instruments, stocks, and bonds. By pooling the funds of thousands of investors, a widely diversified portfolio of financial assets can be created. Investors can purchase units in these funds with required initial investment amounts as low as $200 and through a number of alternative purchase plans that may involve contributions at regular intervals, such as on a monthly basis. Since these funds are well diversified, they provide investors with the opportunity to achieve the benefits of diversification in a relatively straightforward manner.

Another convenient alternative for investors attempting to diversify is to purchase index participation units (IPUs), which are units of a trust that holds shares of companies in market indexes in proportion to their weights in the underlying index. In Canada, investors can purchase I-60 units, which are units in the S&P/TSE 60 Index. Similar to mutual funds, I-60s are eligible for deferred tax-savings plans such as Registered Retirement Savings Plans (RRSPs) and Registered Retirement Income Funds (RRIFs). However, the management expense ratio (approximately 0.1 percent) is very low in comparison to the average expense ratio (approximately 2.3 percent) for actively managed Canadian equity mutual funds. As a result, these instruments offer individual investors a cost-effective method of holding a well-diversified portfolio of equities. IPUs also make international diversification straightforward, since similar global products are available. Popular U.S.-based IPUs exist for the Dow Jones and S&P indexes, referred to as Diamonds and Spiders respectively. In addition, since 1996, Morgan Stanley Capital International (MSCI) has issued IPUs that replicate the total return performance of MSCI market indices. These IPUs are called iShares (formerly WEBS), and they are presently available for indices of 18 countries including: Australia, Austria, Belgium, Canada, France, Germany, Hong Kong, Italy, Japan, Malaysia, Mexico, Netherlands, Singapore, South Korea, Spain, Sweden, Switzerland, and the United Kingdom.

SUMMARY   7.6

1. Uncertainty can be quantified in terms of probabilities, and risk is commonly associated with the variance or standard deviation of probability distributions.

2. When securities are combined, the combined risk of the resulting portfolio depends not only on the individual risk of the underlying securities but also on the statistical correlation that exists between the individual returns.

3. Correlation coefficients of +1, 0, and -1 indicate perfect positive correlation, statistical independence, and perfect negative correlation respectively.

4. Portfolio diversification reduces risk, and most investors hold diversified portfolios.

5. Diversification enables the reduction of risk through the elimination of company-specific or unique risk. Because the returns of most securities are related to the general state of the economy, they are positively correlated with each other.

6. International diversification offers additional benefits in terms of risk reduction.

QUESTIONS AND PROBLEMS

Questions for Discussion

1. A common saying advises, "Don't put all your eggs in one basket." Explain the underlying reasons for this statement in statistical terms, and discuss the implications for investor behaviour.

2. Why are some risks diversifiable, whereas others are not? Provide specific illustrations of each.

3. Explain the role of total and of systematic risk in financial decision-making. As an investor, which of the two would you be concerned about? As a manager, which of the two appears more relevant? Can you see situations in which a manager may have difficulty with the notion that she should consider only systematic risk? Discuss.

4. An investor forms a portfolio consisting of the stocks in two different banks. Another develops a portfolio consisting of the stock of a bank and the stock of a biotechnology firm. Which investor is probably obtaining a greater benefit from diversification? Explain.

5. If investors construct a very well-diversified portfolio with many different securities, then it is very unlikely that they will suffer great losses on their investment over a short period of time. Do you think it is likely that they might have very large gains on that portfolio over a short period of time? Discuss your answer in terms of a "cost" to diversifying.

PROBLEM WITH SOLUTION

Problem

Consider two stocks, A and B. Stock A is currently priced at $10 per share, and Stock B, at $25 per share. For each, there are four possible prices that may occur one year from now, depending on how the economy performs over the next year.

Economy	Price of A	Price of B
Boom	$13.00	$27.50
Above average	11.50	27.50
Below average	10.50	27.00
Recession	9.00	25.00

There is a one-in-four chance of each type of economy occurring. Neither company will pay any dividends over the year.

a) What is the expected return of Stock A? Stock B?

b) What is the standard deviation of returns for Stock A? for Stock B?

c) What is the correlation coefficient between the stock returns of A and B?

d) If investors formed a portfolio with 60 percent of their money in Stock A and 40 percent in Stock B, what would be the expected return and standard deviation of the portfolio?

Solution

First, before solving the problem, notice that the future possibilities are presented in terms of stock prices rather than returns. We must convert these future possible prices into total returns before preceding. Since we assume that neither stock will pay dividends, the total returns simply correspond to the percentage change in the price in each case. For example, for a boom economy for Stock A, the total return will be (13-10)/10 = 30 percent. Similarly, you can convert the rest of the future prices into returns to get:

Economy	Total return on A	Total return on B
Boom	0.3	0.1
Above average	0.15	0.1
Below average	0.05	0.08
Recession	-0.1	0

(a) $E(R_A) = (0.25)(0.3)+(0.25)(0.15)+(0.25)(0.05)+(0.25)(-0.1) = 0.1 = 10\%$
$E(R_B) = (0.25)(0.1)+(0.25)(0.1)+(0.25)(0.08)+(0.25)(0) = 0.07 = 7\%$

Stock A has a higher expected return than does Stock B.

(b) Given the expected returns found in part (a), we can now calculate the standard deviations of each stock:

$$\sigma_A = \sqrt{0.25(0.3 - 0.1)^2+0.25(0.15 - 0.1)^2 +0.25(0.05 - 0.1)^2+0.25(-0.1 -0.1)^2}$$
$$= 0.1458$$

$$\sigma_B = \sqrt{0.25(0.1 - 0.07)^2+0.25(0.1 - 0.07)^2 +0.25(0.08 - 0.07)^2+0.25(0 - 0.07)^2}$$
$$= 0.0412$$

So, while Stock B has a lower expected return, it is also less risky than Stock A.

(c) First, calculate the covariance between the stocks. We can then use this to calculate the correlation. To compute the covariance, we take each stock's deviation from its average for each state. For each state, we multiply the stocks' deviations together and then multiply by the probability of that state occurring. After doing that for every state, we simply add up the results to get the covariance.

(1) probability	(2) Stock A's deviation	(3) Stock B's deviation	(1) times (2) times (3)
0.25	(0.3 - 0.1)	(0.1 - 0.07)	0.0015
0.25	(0.15 - 0.1)	(0.1 - 0.07)	0.000375
0.25	(0.05 - 0.1)	(0.08 - 0.07)	-0.000125
0.25	(-0.1 - 0.1)	(0 - 0.07)	0.0035
		Total:	0.00525

The total of the last column is the covariance, 0.00525. Unfortunately, covariance has limited intuitive appeal. Using correlation is much more intuitive because correlation is bounded by +1 and −1. Therefore, one can get an idea of how strong the relationship between two securities is after seeing the correlation. The correlation is calculated as:

$$\rho_{AB} = \frac{\sigma_{AB}}{\sigma_A \sigma_B} = \frac{0.00525}{(0.1458)(0.0412)} = 0.874$$

With a correlation of 0.874, there is a fairly strong relationship between the two stocks. However, the stocks are not perfectly positively related, so there will still be benefits to diversification in holding both of them together in a portfolio.

(d) $E[R_p] = (0.6)(0.1) + (0.4)(0.07) = 0.088 = 8.8\%$

$$\sigma_P = \sqrt{w_A^2 \sigma_B^2 + w_B^2 \sigma_B^2 + 2w_A w_B \rho_{AB} \sigma_A \sigma_A}$$
$$= \sqrt{(0.6)^2(0.1458)^2 + (0.4)^2(0.0412)^2 + 2(0.6)(0.4)(0.874)(0.1458)(9.0412)}$$
$$= 0.1022$$

Notice that compared to Stock A, the portfolio has lower expected return as well as lower risk. Proportionally, though, the risk has been reduced more than the return. This shows that even with the fairly high correlation between these stocks, there are still benefits to diversification. The benefit, of course, would be even greater for stocks that were not highly correlated as these two are.

ADDITIONAL PROBLEMS

1. Two stocks have the following possible total returns (each economy is equally likely):

Economy	Stock X	Stock Y
Boom	35%	20%
Average	5%	10%
Bust	-25%	0%

(a) Calculate the expected return and standard deviation for each stock.

(b) Calculate the correlation coefficient between the two stocks.

(c) For a portfolio consisting of 75 percent in Stock X and 25 percent in Stock Y, calculate the expected return and standard deviation.

2. Two investment funds pursue different investment strategies. One is a fund investing in equities, and the other invests in bonds. There are four possible returns for each of the funds over the next year. The possibilities are:

Probability	Equity fund	Bond fund
1/4	30%	-10%
1/4	25%	5%%
1/4	10%	10%
1/4	-30%	15%

An investor puts 50 percent of her money into each fund. Calculate the expected return and standard deviation of each fund, the correlation between the funds, as well as the expected return and standard deviation of the portfolio.

3. Stocks X and Y have expected returns of 12 percent and 20 percent, respectively. They have standard deviations of 0.15 for X and 0.3 for Y. The correlation between the stocks is 0.3. If you invest in a portfolio comprised of 35 percent in stock X and the remainder in Y, what is the expected return and standard deviation of the portfolio?

4. A portfolio consists of two stocks:

Stock	Expected return	Standard deviation	Weight
Stock 1	13%	19%	0.45
Stock 2	15%	25%	?

The correlation between the two stocks' returns is -0.20.

(a) Calculate the expected return and standard deviation of the portfolio.

(b) Briefly explain the benefits of diversification, and describe whether the above portfolio exhibits any of these benefits.

5. Suppose we had the following investments:

Stock	Amount invested	Expected return
A	$5,000	9%
B	5,000	10%
C	6,000	11%
D	4,000	12%

(a) What are the portfolio weights?

(b) What is the expected return on the portfolio?

6. Stock A has an expected return of 15 percent and standard deviation of 0.20. Stock B has an expected return of 10 percent and standard deviation of 0.15. The correlation between the two stocks returns is 0.6. If you wanted to form a portfolio of these two stocks and wanted that portfolio to have an expected return of 13 percent, what weights would you put on each stock? What would be the standard deviation of this portfolio?

7. Stock 1 has a standard deviation of 0.1 and an expected return of 7 percent. Stock 2 has a standard deviation of 0.3 and an expected return of 25 percent. The correlation between the stocks is 0.5. Calculate the expected return and standard deviation for various portfolios of the two stocks using weights on stock 1 of 0, 5, 10, 15, to 100 percent. Plot these portfolios on a graph of expected return versus standard deviation. Repeat this process assuming a correlation of −0.5. Comment on your findings. (Note: It is easiest to answer this problem using a spreadsheet.)

Global Diversification: A Whole New World

In Chapter 7, we met Susan Pozer, an investment consultant for James P. Marshall. Founded in 1973 by Jim Marshall, the company was taken over after his death by his wife, Ann, a former teacher.

In April 2000, James P. Marshall merged with Hewitt Associates, a much larger, global human resources consulting firm. Hewitt's services focus on the design, financing, communication and administration of human resources, benefit and compensation programs. James P. Marshall joined Hewitt's Financial Services practice.

The company's new position as part of a global firm seems appropriate, since one of the most important principles its consultants recommend to their clients is diversification. "We are big proponents of diversification," says Ms. Pozer. "It's one of the only free lunches that exists when investing."

Ms. Pozer advises her clients to diversify both by asset class and by manager, giving two or more managers using different management styles responsibility for a portion of a portfolio. But above all, she recommends geographic diversity. "By looking beyond Canada to the rest of the world," she points out, " clients can widen their investment opportunities. When you consider the small percentage that Canada represents in terms of the world's market capitalization this seems obvious."

Global diversification also helps reduce overall risk. "Canadian stocks may be earning low returns during a period when other equity markets are posting strong returns, and vice versa, for example," says Ms. Pozer. A client with holdings in many markets will have better protection against the downswings in the performance of any specific one.

Capital Market Theory

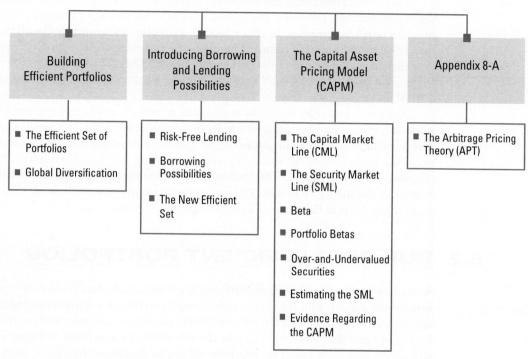

- **Building Efficient Portfolios**
  - The Efficient Set of Portfolios
  - Global Diversification

- **Introducing Borrowing and Lending Possibilities**
  - Risk-Free Lending
  - Borrowing Possibilities
  - The New Efficient Set

- **The Capital Asset Pricing Model (CAPM)**
  - The Capital Market Line (CML)
  - The Security Market Line (SML)
  - Beta
  - Portfolio Betas
  - Over-and-Undervalued Securities
  - Estimating the SML
  - Evidence Regarding the CAPM

- **Appendix 8-A**
  - The Arbitrage Pricing Theory (APT)

Learning Objectives

After studying this chapter, you should be able to:

1. *Explain the role of risk-free assets in an efficient portfolio.*
2. *Define the capital market line (CML), and explain what its slope indicates.*
3. *Compare and contrast systematic and non-systematic risk, and discuss the role of each in establishing the security market line (SML).*
4. *Define beta measure, and explain why is it more stable for large portfolios than for small ones than for individual stocks.*
5. *Identify some of the weaknesses in the capital asset pricing model (CAPM), and discuss alternative theories.*

8.1 INTRODUCTION

In Chapter 7, we discussed the evaluation of risky assets on the basis of their expected returns and risk as measured by the standard deviation. We also saw how portfolio expected return and risk can be calculated based on these inputs and the covariances involved. We analysed basic portfolio principles such as diversification and showed that investors should hold portfolios of financial assets in order to reduce their risk when investing.

This chapter completes our discussion of portfolio theory by analysing how investors select optimal risky portfolios and how the use of a risk-free asset changes the investor's ultimate portfolio position. In effect, we are analysing the optimal trade-off that exists between risk and expected return. This allows us to investigate asset pricing and market equilibrium using the capital asset pricing model (CAPM). This model sets out the basis for valuing risky securities such as stocks. Finally, we discuss some shortcomings of the CAPM and examine several alternative frameworks.

The pricing of risky securities in financial markets is an exceedingly complex phenomenon that cannot be captured wholly in a series of formulas. We provide only general rules for how rational investors should approach securities valuation. Our goal is to provide a basic framework that will serve as a starting point in dealing with the complexities of the real world. This chapter discusses some of the most important topics related to the theory of investments and portfolio management. Indeed, the development of the ideas in this chapter led to Nobel prizes in economics.[1]

8.2 BUILDING EFFICIENT PORTFOLIOS

As we saw in Chapter 7, even if portfolios are selected arbitrarily, some diversification benefits are gained. This results in a reduction of portfolio risk. However, random diversification does not use the entire information set available to investors and does not always lead to optimal diversification. To take the full information set into account, we use an alternative approach based on portfolio theory as developed by Harry Markowitz, a Nobel laureate, who is often referred to as the father of modern portfolio theory.

Portfolio theory is normative meaning that it tells investors how they should act to diversify optimally. It is based on a small set of assumptions, including:

1. a single investment period—for example, one year
2. liquidity of positions—for example, no transaction costs
3. investor preferences based only on a portfolio's expected return and risk, as measured by variance or standard deviation
4. homogenous expectations among investors regarding expected return and risk.

---

[1] James Tobin, Harry Markowitz, and William Sharpe all became Nobel laureates for work related to the material in this chapter.

The Efficient Set of Portfolios

Markowitz's approach to portfolio selection is that an investor should evaluate portfolios on the basis of their expected returns and risk as measured by the standard deviation. He was the first to derive the concept of an **efficient portfolio**, defined as one that has the smallest portfolio risk for a given level of expected return or the largest expected return for a given level of risk.

The construction of efficient portfolios of financial assets requires the identification of optimal risk-expected return combinations attainable from the set of risky assets available to the investor. This requires the expected returns, variances, and covariances for a set of securities as inputs. In economics in general and finance in particular, we assume investors are **risk averse**. This means that investors will require additional expected return for assuming additional risk. Based on this assumption, we can see that rational, risk-averse investors will prefer efficient portfolios because they offer the highest expected return for a given level of risk or the lowest risk for a given level of expected return.

Investors can identify efficient portfolios by specifying an expected portfolio return and minimizing the portfolio risk at this level of return. Alternatively, they can specify a portfolio risk level they are willing to assume and maximize the expected return on the portfolio for this level of risk. Rational risk-averse investors will seek efficient portfolios because these are optimized on the two dimensions of greatest importance to investors: expected return and risk.

To begin our analysis, we must first determine the risk-expected return opportunities available to an investor from a given set of securities as depicted in Figure 8.1. A large number of possible portfolios exist when we realize that varying percentages of an investor's wealth can be invested in each of the assets under consideration. This is referred to as the attainable set of portfolios or the opportunity set.

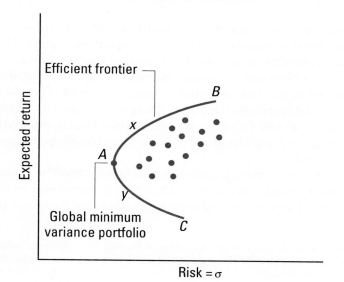

FIGURE 8.1

The Attainable Set and the Efficient Set of Portfolios

Fortunately, risk-averse investors should be interested in only those portfolios with the lowest possible risk for any given level of return. All other portfolios in the attainable set are dominated by these efficient portfolios. Therefore, it is not necessary to evaluate all the possible portfolios illustrated in Figure 8.1 because investors should be interested in only that subset of the available portfolios known as the efficient set.

Using the inputs described in Chapter 7—expected returns, variances, and covariances—we can calculate the portfolio with the smallest variance or risk for a given level of expected return based on these inputs. These are referred to as minimum variance portfolios, which fall along the minimum variance frontier, represented by the entire parabola-shaped curved line in Figure 8.1. Point *A* represents the global minimum variance portfolio because no other has a smaller risk. Portfolios on the bottom segment of the minimum variance frontier *(AC)* are dominated by portfolios on the upper segment *(AB)*. For example, since portfolio *X* has a larger return than portfolio *Y* for the same level of risk, investors would not want to own portfolio *Y*.

The segment of the minimum variance frontier above the global minimum variance portfolio, segment *AB*, offers the best risk-expected return combinations available to investors from this particular set of inputs. This segment is referred to as the **efficient set** or efficient frontier of portfolios. This efficient set is determined by the principle of dominance.

Technically, the basic Markowitz model is solved by a complex technique called quadratic programming.[2] Since the model is easily worked out by computer, we do not expand on the details. However, we note that the solution involves the determination of optimal portfolio weights or percentages of investable funds to be invested in each security. Because the expected returns, standard deviations, and correlation coefficients for the securities being considered are inputs in the Markowitz analysis, the portfolio weights are the only variable that can be manipulated to solve the portfolio problem of determining efficient portfolios.

Think of efficient portfolios as being derived in the following manner. The inputs are obtained, and a level of desired expected return for a portfolio is specified (e.g., 10 percent). Then, all combinations of securities that can be combined to form a portfolio with an expected return of 10 percent are determined, and the one with the smallest variance of return is selected as the efficient portfolio. Next, a new level of portfolio expected return is specified, and the process is repeated. This continues until the feasible range of expected returns is processed. Of course, the problem could also be resolved by specifying levels of portfolio risk and choosing that portfolio with the largest expected return for each specified level of risk.

The efficient frontier contains portfolios that are equally "good" in the sense that no portfolio on it dominates any other portfolio. Once the efficient set of portfolios is determined, investors must select the portfolio most appropriate for them since the efficient

---

2 In particular, the problem is to choose optimal weights in the available securities in order to minimize the risk of the portfolio for a given level of expected return. This optimization problem is subject to a wealth constraint (i.e., the sum of the weights in the individual securities must equal total wealth or 1.0) and is also constrained by the expected return-risk characteristics of the available set of securities.

set does not specify one optimum portfolio. The optimum portfolio for particular investors will depend upon their attitude toward risk. Stated on a practical basis, conservative investors would select portfolios on the left end of the efficient set *AB* in Figure 8.1 because these portfolios have less risk (and, of course, less expected return). Conversely, more aggressive investors would choose portfolios toward point *B* because these offer higher expected returns (along with higher levels of risk).

Global Diversification

Chapter 7 demonstrated that diversification worked the best when the returns for securities being combined in a portfolio displayed low correlations. Due to differences in overall market performance, economic activity, and industrial structure, the correlation between domestic stock returns and the returns on stocks trading in other countries will be low in comparison to those displayed among only domestic stock returns. Therefore, it is not surprising to observe the substantial benefits in terms of risk reduction obtained by diversifying internationally as depicted in Figure 7.5 of Chapter 7. Excerpts from a newspaper article in the report below demonstrate how Canadian investors could have expanded the efficient frontier significantly by diversifying internationally. The author goes on to suggest that Canadian investors could have minimized risk over the 1993-1998 period by holding 75 percent in foreign securities with the remaining 25 percent in domestic assets.

■ *Finance in the News*

About 75 Percent Foreign Content Seems Ideal for Equity Portfolios

In 1998, Canadians invested $22 billion in foreign stocks, which was more than twice the amount for 1997. About three-quarters of this was through Canadian mutual funds. But with the limits on foreign content in RRSPs and the lagging of Canadian stocks, experts are asking what is the optimal amount of foreign content. Using the TSE 300 and the Morgan Stanley Capital International World Index, the graph on the following page shows the efficient frontier, the line consisting of all the points representing the best risk-return blend for an infinite number of possible portfolios.

    The graph demonstrates that a portfolio consisting of only Canadian stocks has a relatively poor return for the level of risk, but as foreign stocks are added, the risk-return rate rises. Over the past quarter century, the optimal foreign content for Canadian portfolios has been 75 percent, but Canadians are nowhere near that level. Canadian investors have been leary of foreign markets perhaps in the belief that a stronger Canadian dollar will devalue foreign stocks. However, 75 percent foreign content appears to be a good target for investors to aim for.

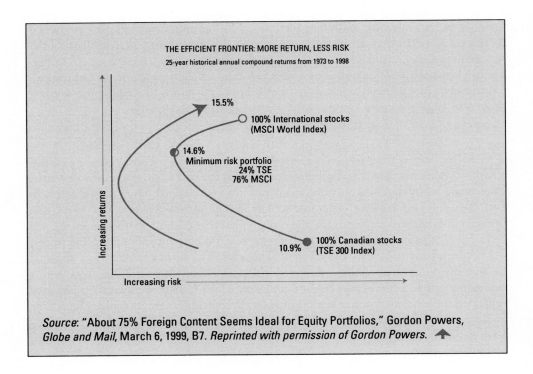

THE EFFICIENT FRONTIER: MORE RETURN, LESS RISK
25-year historical annual compound returns from 1973 to 1998

15.5%
○ 100% International stocks
(MSCI World Index)

14.6%
● Minimum risk portfolio
24% TSE
76% MSCI

100% Canadian stocks
10.9%   ● (TSE 300 Index)

Increasing returns

Increasing risk →

Source: "About 75% Foreign Content Seems Ideal for Equity Portfolios," Gordon Powers,
Globe and Mail, March 6, 1999, B7. *Reprinted with permission of Gordon Powers.* ▲

8.3 INTRODUCING BORROWING AND LENDING POSSIBILITIES

The section above shows how investors can determine the best available combinations of expected return and risk for a given set of inputs for risky assets. However, investors always have the option of buying a risk-free asset such as government T-bills. A risk-free asset can be defined as one with a certain return and a variance of return of zero.[3] Short-term T-bills are typically taken to be the risk-free asset, and the associated rate of return is referred to here as *RF*. Since the variance = 0, the nominal risk-free rate in each period will be equal to its expected value. Furthermore, the covariance between the risk-free asset and any risky asset *i* will be zero because:

$$\sigma_{RF,i} = \rho_{RF,i}\, \sigma_i\, \sigma_{RF}$$
$$= \rho_{RF,i}\, \sigma_i\, (0)$$
$$= 0$$

---

[3] Note, however, that this is a nominal return and not a real return, which is uncertain because inflation is uncertain.

where ρ denotes the correlation coefficient, and σ denotes the respective standard deviations of asset i and the risk-free asset. Therefore, the risk-free asset will have no correlation with risky assets.

Although the introduction of a risk-free asset appears to be a simple step to take in the evolution of portfolio and capital market theory, it is a very significant step. Investors can now invest part of their wealth in this asset and the remainder in any of the risky assets, resulting in a new efficient frontier. Assume that the efficient frontier as shown by the arc AB in Figure 8.2 has been derived by an investor. The arc AB delineates the efficient set of portfolios comprised entirely of risky assets. (For simplicity, we assume these are portfolios of common stocks.) We now introduce a risk-free asset with return RF and standard deviation of zero.

As shown in Figure 8.2, the return on the risk-free asset (RF) will plot on the vertical axis because the risk is zero. Investors can combine this riskless asset with the efficient set of portfolios on the efficient frontier. The discussion below demonstrates that we can draw a line between RF and any risky portfolio on the efficient frontier to represent obtainable combinations of risk-expected return possibilities that did not exist previously.

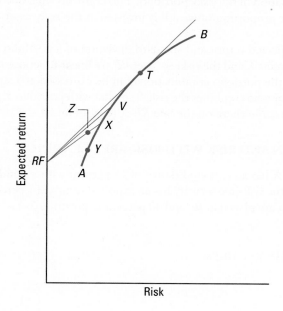

FIGURE 8.2

The Markowitz Efficient Frontier and the Possibilities Resulting from Introducing a Risk-Free Asset

Risk-Free Lending

Consider an arbitrary point on the efficient frontier depicted in Figure 8.2: risky portfolio X.[4] Assume this investor places w_{RF} of his investable funds in the risk-free asset and the remainder of his wealth $(1 - w_{RF})$ in portfolio X. As always, the expected return of a

---

[4] Recall from Chapter 7 that the portfolio weights must add up to 1.0 indicating that all wealth is invested.

portfolio is a weighted average of the expected returns of the individual assets, so the expected return on this combined portfolio p would be:

$$E(R_p) = w_{RF}RF + (1 - w_{RF})\, E(R_X)$$

Since portfolio X consists entirely of risky assets, it is assumed to have a larger expected return than that of the risk-free asset (RF). Therefore, the greater the percentage of an investor's funds committed to X, $(1 - w_{RF})$, the larger the expected return on the portfolio.

The standard deviation of this portfolio is:

$$\sigma_p = (1 - w_{RF})\, \sigma_x$$

because $\sigma_{RF} = 0$ and the correlation between RF and any risky portfolio is zero, which eliminates the second and third terms of Equation 7-11.[5] Thus, the standard deviation of a portfolio combining the risk-free asset with a risky asset (portfolio) is simply the weighted standard deviation of the risky portfolio. This confirms what one would expect: specifically, as a higher proportion of wealth is invested in the risky asset, the portfolio risk increases.

Since both the expected return and standard deviation of a portfolio comprised of any portfolio of risky assets X and the riskless asset RF are linear functions of the weights invested in RF and X, the portfolio combinations can be expressed as a straight line. In other words, an investor who combines the risk-free asset with portfolio X of risky assets would have a portfolio somewhere on the line RF-X (e.g., point Z).

EXPECTED RETURN AND RISK WITH RISK-FREE LENDING

EXAMPLE

Assume that portfolio X has an expected return of 15 percent with a standard deviation of 30 percent and that the risk-free security has an expected return of 7 percent. If 60 percent of investable funds are placed in RF and 40 percent in portfolio X (i.e., $w_{RF} = 0.6$ and $1 - w_{RF} = 0.4$), then

$$E(Rp) = 0.6(7\%) + 0.4(15\%) = 10.2\%$$

and

$$\sigma_\rho = (1.0 - 0.6)\, 30\%$$

$$= 12\%$$

---

[5] More formally, Equation 7-11 for this portfolio would reduce to

$$\sigma_p = \sqrt{(1 - w_{RF})^2 \sigma_x^2 + w_{RF}^2 \sigma_{RF}^2 + (1 - w_{RF}) w_{RF} p_{RF,X}\, \sigma_X\, \sigma_{RF}}$$

$$= \sqrt{(1 - w_{RF})^2 \sigma_x^2 + w_{RF}^2 (0) + (1 - w_{RF}) w_{RF} (0) \sigma_x (0)} = \sqrt{(1 - w_{RF})^2 \sigma_x^2 + 0 + 0^2} = (1 - w_{RF}) \sigma_x$$

An investor could change positions on the line RF-X by varying w_{RF} and hence $1 - w_{RF}$. As more of the investable funds are placed in the risk-free asset, both the expected return and risk of the portfolio decline.

It is apparent that the segment of the efficient frontier below X (i.e., A to X) in Figure 8.2 is now dominated by the line RF-X. For example, at point Z on the straight line, the investor has the same risk as portfolio Y on the Markowitz efficient frontier, but Z has a larger expected return. Thus, the ability to invest in RF provides investors with a more efficient set of portfolios from which to choose.

For example, in Figure 8.2 a new line could be drawn between RF and the Markowitz efficient frontier above point X, connecting RF to point V. Each successively higher line will dominate the preceding set of portfolios because it will offer higher expected returns for any given level of risk (i.e., they lie northwest of the other lines). This process ends when a line is drawn tangent to the efficient set of risky portfolios given a vertical intercept of RF. In Figure 8.2, we will call this tangency point T. The portfolio opportunities on this line (RF to T) dominate all portfolios below them.

Portfolio T is important in this analysis. The Markowitz efficient frontier set consists of portfolios of risky assets. In Figure 8.2, no other portfolio connected to the risk-free rate RF lies above the straight line connecting RF and portfolio T. This line has the greatest slope (and thereby provides the highest reward per unit of risk).

The straight line from RF to the efficient frontier at point T, segment RF-T, dominates all straight lines below it and contains the superior lending portfolios given the efficient set depicted in Figure 8.2. The term "lending portfolios" arises in reference to the fact that purchasing riskless assets such as T-bills to combine with some risky asset is a form of the investor lending money to the issuer of the securities—the federal government. We can think of this risk-free lending simply as risk-free investing.

Through a combination of risk-free investing (investing funds at a rate of RF) and investing in a risky portfolio of securities T, an investor can improve upon the opportunity set available from the Markowitz efficient frontier, which consists of only portfolios of risky assets. The set of efficient portfolios available to any investor with the introduction of the possibility of risk-free investing now lies along line RF-T.

Borrowing Possibilities

What if we extend this analysis to allow investors to borrow money? Investors are no longer restricted to their initial wealth when investing in risky assets. One way to accomplish this borrowing is to buy stocks on margin, which means investors can borrow part of the purchase price from their stockbroker. For example, some stocks have margin requirements as low as 30 percent suggesting that investors could purchase $1,000 worth of stocks by investing $300 of their own money, and borrowing the remaining $700 from their broker. Of course, investors must pay interest on borrowed money. We will assume that investors can also borrow at the risk-free rate RF.[6] Technically, borrowing at the riskless rate can be viewed as short-selling the riskless asset.

---

[6] While the assumption that borrowing rates equal lending rates is seldom met in practice since borrowing rates generally exceed lending rates, this assumption can be relaxed without greatly affecting our key results. Refer to W. S. Cleary and C. P. Jones, *Investments: Analysis and Management*, Canadian Edition, 1999, John Wiley & Sons Canada, Ltd., Toronto. P. 236.

Borrowing additional funds and investing them together with investors' own wealth allows them to seek higher expected returns while assuming greater risk. These borrowed funds can be used to lever the portfolio position beyond the tangency point T, which represents 100 percent of investors' wealth in the risky asset portfolio T. The straight line $RF\text{-}T$ is now extended upward as shown in Figure 8.3, and it can be designated $RF\text{-}T\text{-}L$.

FIGURE 8.3

The Efficient Frontier when Lending and Borrowing Possibilities are Allowed

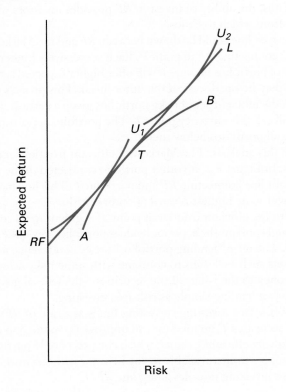

What effect does borrowing have on the expected return and risk for a portfolio? These parameters can be calculated in the usual manner. However, the proportions to be invested are now stated differently. Since the proportions to be invested in the alternatives are stated as percentages of an investor's total investable funds, various combinations must add up to 1.0 (i.e., 100 percent representing an investor's total wealth). Therefore, the proportion to be borrowed at RF is stated as a negative figure, so that:

$$w_{RF} + (1 - w_{RF}) = 1.0 = 100 \text{ percent of investor wealth}$$

Assume that an investor can borrow 100 percent of her investable wealth, which, together with the investable wealth itself, will be invested in risky-asset portfolio T (i.e., 200 percent of investable wealth is invested in portfolio T). The $1 - w_{RF}$ weight must now equal 2.0 to represent the sum of original wealth plus borrowed funds. To obtain this result, the proportion of investable funds associated with w_{RF} is negative; specifically, it is -1.0 representing borrowed funds at the rate RF. Therefore, the proportion to be invested in portfolio T is $[1 - (-1)] = 2$.

Overall, the combined weights are still equal to 1.0 since:

$$w_{RF} + (1 - w_{RF}) = 1.0$$

$$-1 + [1 - (-1)] = 1.0$$

$$-1 + 2 = 1.0$$

The expected return on the investor's portfolio P, consisting of investable wealth plus borrowed funds invested in portfolio T is now

$$E(Rp) = w_{RF}\, RF + (1 - w_{RF})\, E(R_T) = -1(RF) + 2\, E(R_T)$$

The expected return increases linearly as the borrowing increases. The standard deviation of this portfolio is:

$$\sigma_p = (1 - w_{RF})\, \sigma_T$$
$$= 2\sigma_T$$

Risk will increase as the amount of borrowing increases. Borrowing possibilities (i.e., leverage) are illustrated by the following example.

EXPECTED RETURN AND RISK WITH RISK-FREE BORROWING

EXAMPLE

Assume that the expected return on portfolio T is 20 percent with $\sigma_T = 40$ percent. The expected risk-free rate RF is still 7 percent as earlier. However, it now represents the borrowing rate or the rate at which the investor must pay interest on funds borrowed and invested in the risky asset T. The expected return on this portfolio would be:

$$E(Rp) = -1(7\%) + 2(20\%)$$
$$= -7\% + 40\%$$
$$= 33\%$$

The standard deviation of this leveraged portfolio would be:

$$\sigma_p = (1 - w_{RF})\sigma_T$$
$$= [1.0 - (-1.0)]\sigma_T$$
$$= 2\,(40\%)$$
$$= 80\%$$

The New Efficient Set

The end result of introducing risk-free investing and borrowing into the analysis is to create lending and borrowing possibilities and a set of expected return-risk possibilities that did not exist previously. As shown in Figure 8.3, the new risk-expected return trade-off can be represented by a straight line that is tangent to the efficient frontier at point T and that has a vertical intercept RF. The new efficient set is no longer a curve or arc but is now linear.

Investors simply borrow or lend desired amounts and invest the desired proportion of their wealth in one portfolio of risky assets T. This enables them to establish whatever risk-expected return combination they seek. In other words, investors can choose the point on the efficient set line that corresponds to their risk preferences. In practical terms, this means that more conservative investors would be closer to the risk-free asset designated by the vertical intercept RF in Figure 8.3. More aggressive investors would be closer to point T or on it representing full investment in a portfolio of risky assets. Even more aggressive investors could go beyond point T by using leverage to move up the line.

Unlike the case in which we considered the availability of risky assets, it is not necessary to match each client's risk preferences with a particular efficient portfolio of risky securities because only one efficient portfolio is held by all investors. Rather, each investor must determine how much of investable funds should be lent or borrowed at RF and how much should be invested in portfolio T. This result is referred to as the separation property.

The **separation theorem** states that the investment decision (which portfolio of risky assets to hold) is separate from the financing decision (how to allocate investable funds between the risk-free asset and the risky asset). The risky portfolio T is optimal for all investors regardless of their risk preferences. That is, T's optimality is determined separately from knowledge of any investor's risk-return preferences and is not affected by investor risk preferences. All investors, by investing in the same portfolio of risky assets (T) and either borrowing or lending at the rate RF, can achieve any point on the straight line RF-T-L in Figure 8.3. Each point on that line represents a different expected return-risk trade-off.

8.4 THE CAPITAL ASSET PRICING MODEL (CAPM)

Capital market theory is concerned with equilibrium security prices and returns and how they are related to the risk-expected return trade-off that investors face. One of the best known equilibrium models relating common stock returns to risk is known as the **capital asset pricing model (CAPM)**. It allows us to measure the relevant risk of an individual security as well as to assess the relationship between risk and the returns expected from investing. The traditional version of the CAPM was derived independently by Nobel laureate William Sharpe and by Lintner and Mossin in the mid-1960s. Although several extensions of this model have been proposed, the original CAPM remains a central tenet of modern financial economics.

The Capital Market Line (CML)

The market portfolio is defined as the portfolio that consists of all available assets. Its value equals the aggregate of the market values of all the individual assets comprising it. Since the market consists of all available assets and the CAPM assumes that all of these assets are priced correctly to reflect adequate compensation for the associated risk, the market portfolio will be the most efficient (or optimal) portfolio with respect to the weights attached to the individual securities comprising it. In other words, based on a number of simplifying assumptions, it can be shown that the tangent (or optimal portfolio) denoted as portfolio T in Figure 8.3 is the market portfolio.[7] An important implication of this is that all efficient portfolios will lie along the straight line drawn from the risk-free asset that passes through the point represented by the market portfolio since this line will represent the optimal trade-off between standard deviation and expected return available from the set of available assets.

This relationship is depicted graphically in Figure 8.4, which is the same as Figure 8.3 except that the point of tangency has been changed from T to M. Portfolio M in Fig-

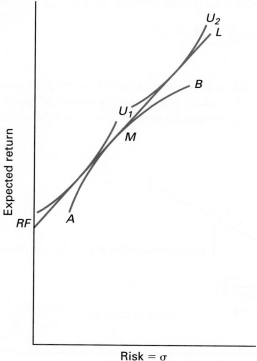

FIGURE 8.4

The Efficient Frontier with Borrowing and Lending

[7] The main assumptions are: all investors have homogeneous expectations with respect to expected returns, the variances, and correlation coefficients; all investors have the same one-period time horizon; all investors can borrow or lend money at the risk-free rate of return; there are no transaction costs; there are no personal income taxes; there is no inflation; there are many investors; investors are price-takers; and capital markets are in equilibrium. Most of these assumptions can be relaxed without significant effects on the CAPM or its implications.

ure 8.4 is called the **market portfolio** of risky securities. It is the highest point of tangency between *RF* and the efficient frontier and is the optimal risky portfolio. Because this line produces the highest attainable return for any given risk level, all rational investors will seek to be on this line.

The straight line depicted in Figure 8.4 is usually referred to as the **capital market line (CML)**. It depicts the equilibrium conditions that prevail in the market for efficient portfolios consisting of the optimal portfolio of risky assets and the risk-free asset. All combinations of risky and risk-free portfolios are bounded by the CML, and, in equilibrium, all investors will end up with efficient portfolios, which must lie somewhere on the CML.

The CML is shown as a straight line in Figure 8.5 without the now-dominated Markowitz efficient frontier. We know that this line has an intercept of *RF*. If investors are to invest in risky assets, they must be compensated for this with a risk premium. The vertical distance between the risk-free rate and the CML at point *M* in Figure 8.5 is the amount of return expected for bearing the risk of the market portfolio—that is, the excess return above the risk-free rate. At that point, the amount of risk for the market portfolio is given by the horizontal dotted line between *RF* and σ_M. Therefore:

$$\text{Slope of the CML} = \frac{E(R_M) - RF}{\sigma_M}$$

The slope of the CML is the *market price of risk* for efficient portfolios or the equilibrium price of risk in the market.[8] It indicates the additional expected return that the market demands for each percentage increase in a portfolio's risk as measured by its standard deviation of return.

FIGURE 8.5

The Capital Market Line (CML) and the Components of Its Slope

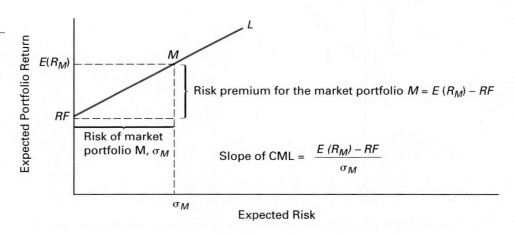

---

[8] The assumption throughout this dscussion is that $E(R_M)$ is greater than *RF*. This is the only reasonable assumption to make because the CAPM is concerned with expcted returns (i.e., ex-ante returns). After the fact, this assumption may not hold for particular periods; that is, over historical periods such as a year, *RF* has exceeded R_M, which is sometimes negative.

ESTIMATING THE SLOPE OF THE CML

EXAMPLE

Assume that the expected return on portfolio M is 12 percent with a standard deviation of 30 percent, and that RF is 6 percent. The slope of the CML would be:

$(0.12 - 0.06)/0.30 = 0.20$

In this example, a risk premium of 0.20 indicates that the market demands 0.20 percent of return for each one percentage increase in a portfolio's risk.

We now know the intercept and slope of the CML. Since the CML is the trade-off between expected return and risk for efficient portfolios, and risk is being measured by the standard deviation, the equation for the CML is:

$$E(Rp) = RF + \frac{E(R_M) - RF}{\sigma_M} \sigma_p \qquad (8.1)$$

where

$E(Rp)$ = the expected return on any efficient portfolio on the CML
RF = the rate of return on the risk-free asset
$E(R_M)$ = the expected return on the market portfolio M
σ_M = the standard deviation of returns on the market portfolio
σ_p = the standard deviation of returns on the efficient portfolio being considered
In other words, the expected return for any portfolio on the CML is equal to the price necessary to induce investors to forego consumption (RF) plus the product of the market price of risk and the amount of risk on the portfolio (σ_p) being considered where:

$$\frac{E(R_M) - RF}{\sigma_M} \quad \text{is the market price of risk}$$

It is important to recognize that the CML must always be upward sloping because the price of risk must always be positive. Remember that the CML is formulated in a world of expected return, and risk-averse investors will not invest unless they expect to be compensated for the risk. The greater the risk, the greater the expected return. On a historical basis for some particular period of time such as a year or two, the CML may appear to be downward sloping when the return on RF exceeds the return on the market portfolio. This does not negate the validity of the CML; it merely indicates that returns actually realized differed from those that were expected. Obviously, investor expectations are not always realized. (If they were, there would be no risk.). Historical evidence for the 1938–1998 period in Canada (provided in Table 7.1 of Chapter 7) suggests that the slope of the ex-post CML was $(11.84 - 5.39)/(16.15) = 0.40$ percent over this period.

The CML can be used to determine the optimal expected returns associated with different portfolio risk levels. Therefore, the CML indicates the required return for each portfolio risk level.

ESTIMATING THE EXPECTED RETURN ON AN EFFICIENT PORTFOLIO USING THE CML

Using the data for the example above, we can estimate the expected (or required) return on an efficient portfolio with a standard deviation of 35 percent as follows:

$$E(R_p) = RF + \frac{E(R_M) - RF}{\sigma_M}\sigma_p = 6 + \frac{(12 - 6)}{30}(35) = 6 + (0.20)(35) = 6 + 7 = 13\%$$

Notice that this exceeds the expected return on the market portfolio of 12 percent. This is the case because it has greater risk, as measured by standard deviation, than does the market portfolio (remember, higher risk always implies higher *expected* return).

The Security Market Line (SML)

The capital market line (CML) depicts the risk-expected return trade-off in financial markets in equilibrium. However, it applies only to efficient portfolios and cannot be used to assess the equilibrium-expected return on individual securities or inefficient portfolios. Since all investors will hold the risky portion of their portfolio in the market portfolio, the important issue with regard to individual securities is how they contribute to the risk of the market portfolio.

We know from Chapter 7 that the equation for portfolio standard deviation consists of many variance and covariance terms. With respect to the market portfolio, each security in the market portfolio (consisting of n securities) will have a variance term and $n - 1$ covariance terms multiplied by two (since we know that $Cov\,(1,2) = Cov\,(2,1)$ for securities 1 and 2). Chapter 7 also shows that for a well-diversified portfolio consisting of a large number of securities, the covariance terms will be the relevant risk factors with the individual variance terms having little impact on the overall portfolio risk. Based on this observation, the complex variance and covariance terms associated with estimating the risk of the market portfolio can be simplified to the following equation for the standard deviation of the market portfolio:

(8.2)
$$\begin{aligned}\sigma_M &= [w_1\,Cov\,(R_1, R_M) + w_2\,Cov\,(R_2, R_M) + \ldots +]^{1/2} \\ &= [\text{security 1's contribution to portfolio variance} + \\ &\quad\;\; \text{security 2's contribution to portfolio variance} + \ldots .]^{1/2}\end{aligned}$$

Equation 8.2 shows that the contribution of each security to the standard deviation of the market portfolio depends on the size of its covariance with the market portfolio. Therefore, investors should consider the relevant measure of risk for any security to be its covariance with the market portfolio. As a result, we can say that in order for market equilibrium to exist, investors will require that the excess reward per unit of covariance risk be equal for all securities. Thus, for any two assets i and j, we can say:

$$\frac{E(R_i) - RF}{\sigma_{i,M}} = \frac{E(R_j) - RF}{\sigma_{j,M}} \tag{8.3}$$

Since the covariance of the market portfolio with itself is its variance (i.e., $\sigma_{M,M} = \sigma_M^2$), we can express the market price of covariance risk as

$$\frac{E(R_M) - RF}{\sigma_{M,M}} \quad \text{or,} \quad \frac{E(R_M) - RF}{\sigma_M^2}$$

Recognizing that the market portfolio is efficient and is held by all investors, this market price of covariance risk must offer adequate compensation for risk, and it is the excess reward per unit risk required by investors for any asset. Formally, for any asset i, we can say

$$\frac{E(R_i) - RF}{\sigma_{i,M}} = \frac{E(R_M) - RF}{\sigma_M^2} \tag{8.4}$$

Equation 8.4 can easily be rearranged to solve for $E(Ri)$, which produces the following equation that shows the expected return on any risky asset is directly proportional to its covariance with the market portfolio:

$$E(R_i) = RF + [E(R_M) - RF] \frac{\sigma_{i,M}}{\sigma_M^2} \tag{8.5}$$

From Chapter 7, we know that $\sigma_{i,M} = \rho_{i,M}\sigma_i\sigma_M$, which implies we could alternatively express Equation 8.5 as

$$E(R_i) = RF + [E(R_M) - RF] \frac{\rho_{i,M}\sigma_i}{\sigma_M} \tag{8.6}$$

We now define a new term, the beta coefficient (β) or beta, as

$$\beta i = \frac{\sigma_{i,M}}{\sigma_M^2} = \frac{\rho_{i,M}\sigma_i}{\sigma_M} \tag{8.7}$$

Substituting beta into the last term of Equation 8.5 or Equation 8.6, we obtain the following expression for determining the expected return of a risky asset:

$$E(R_i) = RF + [E(R_M) - RF]\beta_i \tag{8.8}$$

Equation 8.8 is referred to as the **security market line (SML)**, which is the key contribution of the CAPM to asset pricing theory. It is depicted as the line *RF-Z* in Figure 8.6. In this diagram, beta is plotted on the horizontal axis and expected return on the vertical axis, with the intercept on the vertical axis occurring at the risk-free rate of return

RF. The SML represents the trade-off between systematic risk (as measured by beta) and expected return for all assets whether individual securities, inefficient portfolios, or efficient portfolios.

The SML implies that we measure systematic or market risk by a security's beta, which is simply a standardized measure of the security's covariance with the market portfolio. The reason that it is standardized in this manner reflects the fact that beta measures the sensitivity or responsiveness of the stock's returns to the returns on the chosen market portfolio. The reasons for measuring the relationship in this manner will be discussed later.

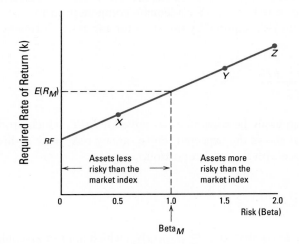

FIGURE 8.6

The Security Market Line (SML)

As we would expect, Figure 8.6 again demonstrates that if investors are to seek higher expected returns, they must assume a larger risk as measured by beta, the relative measure of systematic risk. The trade-off between expected return and risk must always be positive. In Figure 8.6, the vertical axis can be thought of as the expected return for an asset. In equilibrium, investors require a minimum expected return before they will invest in a particular security. That is, given its risk, a security must offer some minimum expected return before a given investor can be persuaded to purchase it. Thus, in discussing the SML concept, we are simultaneously talking about the required and expected rate of return.

In essence, the SML states that the expected rate of return on an asset is a linear function of the two components of the **required rate of return**—the risk-free rate and the risk premium. Thus:

$$(8.9) \quad k_i = \text{Risk–free rate} + \text{risk premium}$$
$$= RF + \beta_i[E(R_M) - RF]$$

where

k_i = the required rate of return on asset i
$E(R_M)$ = the expected rate of return on the market portfolio
β_i = the beta coefficient for asset i

This relationship provides an explicit measure of the risk premium. It is the product of the beta for a particular security i and the **market risk premium**, $E(R_M) - RF$. We note that the ex-post market risk premium in Canada over the 1938–1998 period was 6.45 percent $(11.84 - 5.39)$ according to Table 7.1. For any particular security, we can say:
Risk premium for security i

$$= \beta_i \text{ (market risk premium)}$$
$$= \beta_i \left[E(R_M) - RF \right]$$

Equation 8.9 indicates that securities with betas greater than the market beta of 1.0 should have larger risk premiums than that of the average stock and therefore, when added to *RF*, larger required rates of return. This is exactly what investors should expect since beta is a measure of risk, and greater risk should be accompanied by greater expected return. Conversely, securities with betas less than that of the market are less risky and should have required rates of return lower than that for the market as a whole. This will be the indicated result from the CAPM because the risk premium for the security will be less than the market risk premium and, when added to *RF*, will produce a lower required rate of return for the security.

Beta

Beta is a measure of the systematic risk of a security that cannot be avoided through diversification. It is a *relative* measure of risk—the risk of an individual stock relative to the market portfolio of all stocks. If the security's returns move more (less) than the market's returns as the latter changes, the security's returns have more (less) *volatility* (fluctuations in price) than those of the market. It is important to note that beta measures a security's volatility or fluctuations in price relative to a benchmark, the market portfolio of all stocks.

Securities with different betas have different sensitivities to the returns of the market index. If the beta is 1.0, it means that for every 1 percent change in the market's return this security's returns change 1 percent *on average*. The riskless asset has a beta of 0 since it is assumed to be known with certainty. The market portfolio has a beta of 1.0, which is intuitive since it moves exactly with itself. It is also obvious computationally since if we let $i = M$ in Equation 8.7, we obtain:

$$\beta_M = \frac{\sigma_{M,M}}{\sigma_M^2} = \frac{\sigma_M^2}{\sigma_M^2} = 1.0$$

A security with a beta of 1.5 indicates that on average, security returns are 1.5 times as volatile as market returns both up and down. A security with returns that rise or fall on average 15 percent when the market return rises or falls 10 percent is said to be an aggressive or volatile security. If the beta is less than 1.0, this indicates that on average, a stock's returns have less volatility than the market as a whole. For example, a security with a beta of 0.6 indicates that stock returns move up or down, on average only 60 percent as much as the market as a whole.

Stocks with high- (low) betas are said to be high- (low-) risk securities. Betas may vary widely across companies in different industries and within a given industry. They also change through time as the risk characteristics of the underlying security or portfolio change. Table 8.1 shows beta estimates for some Canadian common stocks as of Februaury 2000, which provide the reader with some insight into the nature of real-world betas. The companies included in Table 8.1 are chosen from many different industries, and as one would expect, the betas vary a great deal across the spectrum, ranging from a low of 0.35 for Loblaws to a high of 2.92 for Certicom Corp. (its volatility was referred to in Chapter 7).

Table 8.1

Canadian Betas

Company	Industry Classification	Beta*
Air Canada	Transportation	1.66
BCE Inc.	Utilities (Telephone Utilities)	1.22
Noronda Inc.	Mining (Integrated Mines)	1.57
Inco Limited	Mining (Integrated Mines)	1.04
Barrick Gold Corp.	Gold Producer (Precious Metals)	1.06
Nortel Networks	Comm. & Media (Telecommunications)	1.57
Research in Motion Ltd.	Comm. & Media (Telecommunications)	1.64
Clearnet Communications Inc.	Comm. & Media (Telecommunications)	1.77
Certicom Corp.	Industrial Products (Electrical & Electronic)	2.92
Bombardier Inc.	Industrial Products (Transportation Equip.)	0.68
Chapters Inc.	Merchandising and Lodging (Specialty Stores)	1.01
Loblaw Cos. Ltd.	Merchandising and Lodging (Food Stores)	0.35
Hudson's Bay Company	Merchandising and Lodging (Department Stores)	0.58
Petro Canada	Integrated Oil & Gas	0.91
Bank of Nova Scotia	Financial Services (Banks)	1.03
Fairfax Financial	Financial Services (Insurance)	0.92
Investors Group	Financial Services (Invest. Companies & Funds)	1.35

* Betas calculated over the previous 60 months.

Source: Compustat, February, 2000.

USING THE SML TO ESTIMATE REQUIRED RETURN

Table 8.1 provides a year 2000 beta estimate for BCE Inc.'s common stock of 1.22. If RF was 0.055 at that time while the expected return on the market was estimated to be 0.12, the required return for BCE would be estimated as:

$$k_{BCE} = 0.055 + 1.22(0.12 - 0.055)$$
$$= 0.1343 \text{ or } 13.43\%$$

The required (or expected) return for BCE is larger than that of the market because BCE's beta is larger. Once again, the greater the risk assumed, the larger the required return.

PERSPECTIVES

Corporate Manager

The SML provides corporate managers with one way for estimating the company's cost of common equity financing, which is important for determining the company's overall cost of capital (as discussed in Chapter 15). In fact, it is one of the most commonly used approaches to estimating this variable.

Investor

The SML provides investors with a method of estimating a reasonable risk-adjusted rate of return that they should require on an investment in an individual common stock or in a stock portfolio. This provides them with a key ingredient for estimating the intrinsic value of a common share using the methods described in Chapter 6 or using alternative estimation techniques.

Portfolio Betas

Unlike portfolio standard deviations, portfolio betas are weighted averages of the betas for the individual securities in the portfolio. For an n-security portfolio, this relationship is expressed in Equation 8.10:

$$\beta_p = w_1\beta_1 + w_2\beta_2 + \ldots w_n\beta_n \tag{8.10}$$

EXAMPLE

DETERMINING THE BETA FOR A PORTFOLIO

Consider a portfolio consisting of 20 percent invested in BCE, 40 percent in Certicom, and 40 percent in Loblaws. Using the betas for these securities provided in Table 8.1, the portfolio's beta would equal:

$$\beta_p = (0.20)(1.22) + (0.40)(2.92) + (0.40)(0.35) = 0.244 + 1.168 + 0.14 = 1.552$$

Over- and Undervalued Securities

The SML has important implications for security prices. In equilibrium, each security should lie on the SML because the expected return on the security should be what is needed to compensate investors for the systematic risk.

What happens if investors believe that a security does not lie on the SML? To decide this, they must employ a separate methodology to estimate the expected returns for securities. In other words, an existing SML can be applied to a sample of securities to determine the expected (required) return-risk trade-off that exists. Knowing the beta for any stock, we can establish the required return from the SML. Then, estimating the expected return from an alternative approach using, say, the constant-growth version of the dividend discount model from Chapter 6, an investor can assess a security in relation to the SML and determine whether it is under- or overvalued.

In Figure 8.7, two securities are plotted around the SML. Security X has a high expected return derived from fundamental analysis and plots above the SML; security Y has a low expected return and plots below the SML. Which is undervalued?

FIGURE 8.7

Overvalued and Under-valued Securities Using the SML

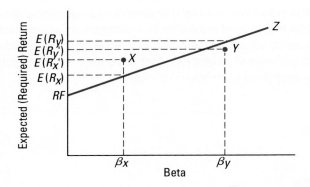

Security X, plotting above the SML, is undervalued because it offers more expected return than investors require given its level of systematic risk as measured by beta. Investors require a minimum expected return of $E(R_X)$, but security X, according to fundamental analysis, is offering $E(R_X')$. If investors recognize this, they will purchase security X because it offers more return than required, and as more of it is purchased this demand will drive up the price. The expected return will be driven down until it is at the level indicated by the SML.

Now consider security Y. According to fundamental analysis, it does not offer enough expected return given its level of systematic risk. Investors require $E(R_Y)$ for security Y, based on the SML, but Y offers only $E(R_Y')$. As investors recognize this, they will sell security Y (or perhaps sell it short) because it offers less than the required return. This increase in the supply of Y will drive down its price. The expected return will be driven up for new buyers because any dividends paid are now relative to a lower price as is any expected price appreciation. The price will fall until the expected return rises enough to reach the SML and the security is once again in equilibrium.

Estimating the SML

To use the SML to estimate the required return on an asset, an investor needs estimates of the return on the risk-free asset, the expected return on the market index, and the beta for an individual security. How difficult are these to obtain?

The return on a risk-free asset RF should be the easiest of the three variables to ascertain. In estimating RF, the investor can use the return on government T-bills for the coming period. Estimating the market return is more difficult because the expected return for the market index is not observable. Furthermore, several different market indexes could be used. Estimates of the market return could be derived from a study of previous market returns (such as the evidence on historical common stock returns provided in Chapter 7). Alternatively, expected future market returns could be determined by calculating probability estimates of market returns based on current market conditions and expectations of future market conditions. This would provide an estimate of both the expected return and the standard deviation for the market.

Finally, it is necessary to estimate the betas for individual securities. This is a crucial part of the CAPM estimation process. The estimates of RF and the expected return on the market are the same for each security being evaluated. Since beta is unique with respect to a chosen market proxy, it brings together the investor's expectations of returns for the stock with those for the market. Since beta is the only company-specific factor in the CAPM, risk is the only asset-specific forecast that must be made in the CAPM.

Betas are estimated by plotting the total returns for a security against the total returns for a chosen market index and fitting a line through the observations, as shown in the example in Figure 8.8. This line is referred to as the **characteristic line** and is determined using regression anlysis. The slope of the characteristic line is the security's beta. For the example in Figure 8.8, the slope coefficient is 1.30, which indicates the expected increase in a security's return for a 1 percent increase in market return is 1.3 percent.[9]

---

[9] The characteristic line is also often fitted using *excess returns*. The excess return is calculated by subtracting out the risk-free rate RF from both the return on the stock and the return on the market. In excess return form, the same analysis as before applies.

FIGURE 8.8

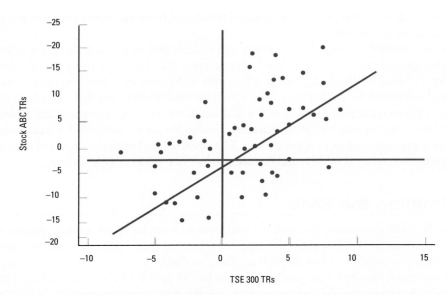

Many brokerage houses and investment advisory services report betas as part of the total information given for individual stocks. For example, the Nesbitt Burns Research Red Book reports betas for the companies included in its quarterly reports, while the globeinvestor website (located at www.globeinvestor.com) also includes betas for Canadian companies.

As noted, beta is usually estimated by fitting a characteristic line to the data, as called for in the CAPM. The market proxy used in the equations for estimating beta may not fully reflect the market portfolio specified in the CAPM. In addition, we must be aware that we are interested in estimating the future beta for a security, which may differ from the historical beta, since they change through time as the risk of the underlying common stock changes. This is particularly true for individual securities—their betas can change quite dramatically over relatively short periods of time.

On the other hand, betas estimated for large portfolios (e.g., 50 stocks) are much more stable because of the averaging effect. Although the betas of some stocks in the portfolio go up over time others go down, and these two movements tend to cancel each other. Furthermore, the errors involved in estimating betas tend to cancel out in a portfolio. Therefore, estimates of portfolio betas show less change from over time and are much more reliable than are the estimates for individual securities.

Evidence Regarding the CAPM

Extensive literature exists involving tests of capital market theory in general and the CAPM in particular. Although it is not possible to summarize the scope of this literature

---

[10] For a more detailed discussion of empirical tests of the CAPM, see Edwin Elton and Martin Gruber, *Modern Portfolio Theory*, 5th ed., (New York: Wiley, 1995).

entirely and reconcile findings from different studies that seem to be in disagreement, the following points represent a reasonable consensus of previous empirical results:[10]

1. The SML appears to be linear; that is, the trade-off between expected (required) return and risk is an upward-sloping straight line.

2. The intercept term is generally found to be higher than *RF*.

3. The slope of the SML is generally found to be less steep than posited by the theory. This means that CAPM systematically "underpredicts" realized returns for low-beta stocks and "overpredicts" realized returns for high-beta stocks.

4. Although the evidence is mixed, no persuasive case has been made that non-systematic risk commands a risk premium. In other words, investors are rewarded only for assuming systematic risk.

In addition to the evidence above, research by Fama and French contradicts the linear relationship between expected return and beta. They demonstrate that CAPM's sole risk factor—the market risk beta—possesses no explanatory power whatsoever in discriminating among the cross-sectional returns of U.S. stocks.[11]

Fama and French contend that two simple and observable variables—common market equity (ME) and the ratio of book equity to market equity (BE–ME)—combine to explain the cross-section of expected returns. Their analysis leads them to propose a three-factor pricing model, which has gathered much attention in recent years. Specifically, Fama and French suggest that an overall market factor and factors related to firm size and the book-equity to market-equity ratio explain cross-sectional differences in average returns of stocks.[12]

Fama and French's model to account for stock returns includes the following three factors:

1. the expected return to a portfolio of small market capitalization stocks less the return of a portfolio of large market capitalization stocks

2. the expected return to a portfolio of high book-to-market stocks less the return of a portfolio of low book-to-market stocks

3. the expected return on the market index

The Fama and French model has gained increasing acceptance in recent years. Its potential importance is evidenced by the fact that Ibbotson Associates (a major provider of financial information) now provides estimates of the required return on equity for companies based on this model in addition to estimates determined by the more widely recognized CAPM.

The major problem in testing capital market theory is that it is formulated on an ex-ante basis but can be tested only on an ex-post basis. We can never know investor

---

[11] See E. Fama and K. French, "The Cross Section of Expected Stock Returns." *Journal of Finance*, 47 (June 1992), pp.427-65.

[12] See E. Fama and K. French, "Size and Book-to-Market Factors in Earnings and Returns." *Journal of Finance*, 50 (March 1995), pp.131-55.

expectations with certainty. Therefore, it should come as no surprise that tests of the model have produced conflicting results in some cases and that the empirical results diverge from the predictions of the model.

Tests of return predictability over a long period of time using a model such as CAPM, inevitably must deal with the "joint hypothesis problem." This refers to the fact that we can test whether the asset pricing model (CAPM, in this case) fits the data well only if we also assume that assets are priced correctly in the market (i.e., if we assume that markets are efficient). Thus, we have two hypotheses that are being tested simultaneously. Evidence that rejects our overall hypothesis may imply a rejection of CAPM or of market efficiency or both.

Another important problem with attempting to test CAPM was identified by Richard Roll in his seminal article that advanced the argument that is commonly referred to as Roll's Critique.[13] He argued that CAPM has not been proven empirically, nor will it be. This is because CAPM is untestable since the market portfolio, which consists of all risky assets, is unobservable. This forces researchers or users of CAPM to choose a market proxy that may or may not be mean-variance efficient as defined in Section 8.3. In effect, Roll argues that tests of the CAPM are actually tests of the mean-variance efficiency of the chosen market portfolio. He shows that the basic CAPM results will hold whenever the chosen proxy is mean-variance efficient and will not hold if the converse is true.

Despite these and other criticisms, the CAPM remains a logical way to view the expected return-risk trade-off.

8.5 SUMMARY

1. An efficient portfolio has the highest expected return for a given level of risk or the lowest level of risk for a given level of expected return.

2. Capital market theory, based on the concept of efficient diversification, describes the pricing of capital assets in the marketplace. The new efficient frontier is called the capital market line (CML), and its slope indicates the equilibrium price of risk in the market.

3. Based on the separation of risk into its systematic and non-systematic components, the security market line (SML) can be constructed for individual securities (and portfolios).

4. Beta is a relative measure of risk, which indicates the volatility of a stock relative to a market index. While all betas change through time, betas for large portfolios are much more stable than those for individual stocks.

---

[13] Richard Roll, "A Critique of the Asset Pricing Theory's Tests; Part 1: On the Past and Potential Testability of the Theory." *Journal of Financial Economics*, 4 (March 1977), pp. 129-76.

5. Tests of the Captial Asset Pricing Model (CAPM) are inconclusive, which is not surprising since it is an *ex-ante* model that makes predictions about the uncertain future, and it is tested with *ex-post* data.

6. Alternative theories of asset pricing such as the arbitrage pricing theory (APT) also exist but also remain unproven. APT is not critically dependent on an underlying market portfolio as is the CAPM, which predicts that only market risk influences expected returns.

APPENDIX 8-A

The Arbitrage Pricing Theory (APT)

Another model of security pricing that has received a great deal of attention is based on the **arbitrage pricing theory (APT)**. APT represents an alternative theory of asset pricing, which is more general than the CAPM with less-restrictive assumptions. However, like the CAPM, it has limitations and is not the final word in asset pricing.

Similar to the CAPM or any other asset pricing model, APT posits a relationship between expected return and risk. It does so, however, using different assumptions and procedures. Very importantly, APT is not critically dependent on an underlying market portfolio as is the CAPM, which predicts that only market risk influences expected returns. Instead, APT recognizes that several types of risk may affect security returns.

APT is based on the **law of one price**, which states that two otherwise identical assets cannot sell at different prices. APT assumes that asset returns are linearly related to a set of indices, whereby each index represents a risk factor that influences the return on an asset. Market participants develop expectations about the sensitivities of assets to the factors. They buy and sell securities so that given the law of one price, securities affected equally by the same factors will have equal expected returns. This buying and selling is the arbitrage process, which determines the prices of securities.

The APT is based on the view that there are underlying risk factors that affect realized and expected security returns. These risk factors represent broad economic forces and not company-specific characteristics, and, by definition, they represent the element of surprise in the risk factor—the difference between the actual value for the factor and its expected value.

The APT model assumes that investors believe that asset returns are randomly generated according to an *n*-factor model. For security *i*, the actual return can be formally stated as:

$$R_{it} = E(R_{it}) + b_{i1}f_{1t} + b_{i2}f_{2t} + \ldots + b_{in}f_{nt} + e_{it} \qquad (8.A1)$$

where
R_{it} = the actual (random) rate of return on security *i* in any given period *t*
$E(R_{it})$ = the expected return on security *i* for a given period *t*
f_{nt} = the deviation of a systematic factor F_n from its expected value during period *t*

b_i = sensitivity of security i to a factor

e_{it} = random error term unique to security i during period t

The expected value of each factor F, is zero. Therefore, the f's in Equation 8.11 are measuring the deviation of each factor from its expected value. Notice in Equation 8.11 that the actual return for a security in a given period will be at the expected or required rate of return if the factors are at expected levels (e.g., $F_1 - E(F_1) = 0$, $F_2 - E(F_2) = 0$, and so forth) and if the chance element represented by the error term is at zero.

APT is an equilibrium theory of expected returns that requires a factor model such as Equation 8.11. The equation for expected return on a security is given by Equation 8.12.

(8.A2) $E(R_{it}) = a_0 + b_{i1}F_{1t} + b_{i2}F_{2t} + \ldots + b_{in}F_{nt}$

where

$E(R_i)$ = the expected return on security i during period t

a_0 = the expected return on a security with zero systematic risk

F = the risk premium for a factor

With APT, risk is defined in terms of a stock's sensitivity to basic economic factors, while expected return is directly related to sensitivity. As always, expected return increases with risk. The expected return-risk relationship for the APT can be described as: $E(R_{it}) = RF + b_{i1}$ (risk premium for factor 1) + b_{i2} (risk premium for factor 2)+ $\ldots$ + b_{in} (risk premium for factor n). Note that the sensitivity measures (β_i and b_i) have similar interpretations. They are measures of the relative sensitivity of a security's return to a particular risk premium. Also notice that we are dealing with risk premiums in both cases. Finally, notice that the CAPM relationship is the same as would be provided by APT if there were only one pervasive factor influencing returns (market risk). This is one reason that APT is more general than CAPM.

The problem with APT is that the factors are not well specified at least ex ante. To implement the APT model, we need to know the factors that account for the differences among security returns. The APT makes no statements about the number of risk factors or the size or sign of the F_i's. Both the factor model and these values must be identified empirically. In contrast, with the CAPM, the factor that matters is the market portfolio, a concept that is well understood conceptually. However, as noted earlier, Roll has argued that the market portfolio is unobservable.

Most empirical work suggests that three to five factors influence security returns and are priced in the market. For example, Roll and Ross identify five systematic factors:[14]

1. changes in expected inflation

2. unanticipated changes in inflation

3. unanticipated changes in industrial production

---

[14] Richard Roll and Stephen Ross, "An Empirical Investigation of the Pricing Theory" *Journal of Finace*, (December 1980), pp. 1073-1103.

4. unanticipated changes in the default-risk premium[15]

5. unanticipated changes in the term structure of interest rates

These factors are related to the components of a valuation model. The first three affect the cash flows of a company, while the last two affect the discount rate. According to this model, different securities have different sensitivities to these systematic factors, and investor risk preferences are characterized by these dimensions. Each investor has different risk attitudes. Investors could construct a portfolio depending upon desired risk exposure to each of these factors. Knowing the market prices of these risk factors and the sensitivities of securities to changes in the factors, the expected returns for various stocks could be estimated.

Roll and Ross have argued that APT offers an approach to strategic portfolio planning. The idea is to recognize that a few systematic factors affect long-term average returns. Investors should seek to identify the few factors affecting most assets in order to appreciate their influence on portfolio returns. Based on this knowledge, they should seek to structure the portfolio in such a way as to improve its design and performance.

A portfolio manager could design strategies that would expose them to one or more types of these risk factors or "sterilize" a portfolio so that its exposure to the unexpected change in the growth rate of profits matched that of the market as a whole. Taking an active approach, a portfolio manager who believes that she can forecast a factor realization can build a portfolio that enhances or reduces sensitivity to that factor. In doing so, the manager will select stocks that have exposures to the remaining risk factors that are exactly proportional to the market. If the manager is accurate with the forecast—and remember that such a manager must forecast the unexpected component of the risk factor—she can outperform the market for that period.

QUESTIONS AND PROBLEMS

Questions for Discussion

1. What does a security's beta measure, and how can it be estimated?

2. Why is it generally better to form a portfolio that combines a riskless asset with the market portfolio rather than to tailor-make portfolios of individual securities to match specific investor preferences?

3. Evidence indicates that a portfolio of stocks traded on the Hong Kong Stock Exchange has a standard deviation of returns more than twice the standard deviation of a representative portfolio of Canadian securities. Assume that the expected return (in Canadian dollars) on the Hong Kong Stock Exchange is less than the expected return on the Canadian portfolio. Would a rational investor ever combine the two portfolios? Why or why not?

---

[15] The default-risk premium is commonly defined as the yield on long-term corporate bonds minus the yield on long-term Government bonds.

4. "There may be some truth to the capital asset pricing model (CAPM), but over the past year, many stocks gave a substantially higher return than the CAPM predicted, and many others gave a substantially lower return; therefore, the model is badly flawed." Is the above statement a valid criticism of the CAPM? Give a brief explanation.

5. If the CAPM holds true, is it possible for a risky asset to have an expected return less than the risk-free rate of interest? Explain why or why not, and include an intuitive explanation.

PROBLEM WITH SOLUTION

Problem

The stock of Inert Technologies Ltd. paid a dividend last year of $1 per share. Dividends are expected to grow at a constant rate of 7 percent per year, forever. You have estimated (by using past data) that the correlation between the returns to Inert Technologies and the market overall is 0.3. The risk-free rate of interest is 8 percent, and the market overall typically returns 9 percent more than the risk-free rate. The standard deviation of returns to the market is 0.25 and to the returns to Inert 0.35. According to the capital asset pricing model, what should be today's price of this stock?

Solution

In order to value the stock, we can use the dividend growth model. The growth rate in dividends is given, and the next dividend can be easily calculated. However, we do not know the return required by investors. This is where the CAPM can be used.
The covariance between Inert and the market is:

$$\sigma_{IM} = \rho_{IM}\sigma_I\sigma_M$$
$$= 0.3(0.35)(0.25)$$
$$= 0.02625$$

This means that the beta of Inert must be:

$$\beta_{IM} = \frac{\sigma_{IM}}{\sigma_M^2}$$
$$= \frac{0.02625}{0.25^2}$$
$$= 0.42$$

Inert Technologies would therefore fall in the category of "defensive" stocks because it has a beta less than one. This means that it reacts less strongly than the market to market-wide changes. Given the beta, we can use CAPM to calculate the expected return for Inert. If CAPM is true, this is the same as the return that investors should require on the stock given its level of risk (its beta):

$$= E[R_{Inert}] = RF + \beta_{Inert}(E(R_M) - RF)$$
$$= 0.08 + 0.42(0.09)$$
$$= 0.1178$$

Notice that the risk *premium* on the market is given as 9 percent, which is equal to $(E(R_M) - RF)$. Given the above, we can then estimate the value of the stock using the constant-growth dividend model:

$$P_{Inert} = \frac{\$1(1.07)}{0.1178 - 0.07}$$

$$= \$22.38$$

ADDITIONAL PROBLEMS

1. An investor wants to form a portfolio from three securities and plans to invest $40,000, $60,000, and $25,000 respectively. The beta factors of these securities have been estimated at 0.25, 0.95, and 1.65. If the expected return on the overall market for the period under consideration is 14 percent, and the return on treasury bills is 8 percent, what is the expected return of this portfolio?

2. (a) An investor purchases $10,000 worth of shares in an index fund that closely parallels the overall market. She borrows $6,000 at the riskless rate to finance her purchase. What is the beta of her investments?

   (b) Does your answer under (a) depend on the assumption that the investor can borrow at the riskless RF? Explain.

3. Suppose we had the following investments:

Stock	Amount invested	Expected return	Beta
A	$5,000	9%	0.80
B	5,000	10%	1.00
C	6,000	11%	1.20
D	4,000	12%	1.40

   (a) What are the portfolio weights?
   (b) What is the expected return on the portfolio?
   (c) What is the beta of the portfolio?

4. A security is currently priced at $35. You expect its price in one year to be $40 and do not expect any dividends to be paid. The yield on T-bills is 7 percent, and the overall market is expected to return 15 percent. What will be the current price of the security if the expected future price remains the same but its covariance with the overall market suddenly doubles?

5. Suppose that you can borrow or lend at the risk-free rate of 9 percent. The overall market has an expected return of 15 percent and a standard deviation of 0.21. What are the expected returns and standard deviations of portfolios where:

   (a) you lend all of your wealth out at the risk-free rate

   (b) you lend out one-third of your wealth and invest two-thirds in the market portfolio

   (c) you invest all of your wealth in the market portfolio, and you borrow an amount equal to one-third of your wealth to invest in the market portfolio.

6. You are an investment advisor who believes that the capital asset pricing model (CAPM) will hold in the long run for all stocks. That is, the expected return on a stock does not always have to be the same as CAPM says, but eventually the price of a stock will adjust so that the CAPM does hold.

   You currently have holdings of two stocks, A and B, with the following characteristics:

	Expected return	Beta
A	14%	1.2
B	18%	2.9

   The current risk-free rate is 4 percent, and the expected return on the market is 10 percent.

   Both of these stocks are mispriced according to CAPM (i.e., they do not lie on the security market line—SML). If these stocks will eventually move back to the SML, how would you change your holdings of the two stocks (i.e., for each, would you sell or buy more)?

7. If the expected return of a firm's shares is 16 percent, the expected market return is 12 percent, and the risk-free rate of return is 6 percent, what should the beta of the stock be according to the CAPM?

8. The risk-free interest rate on one-year debt is 8 percent, and the expected return on the market is 14 percent. A stock that pays no dividends currently sells for $10. What is the expected price at which the stock should sell at year end if it has a beta of 1.4?

9. A stock that currently trades at $10 has a beta of 1.6. The risk-free interest rate for the coming year is 10 percent, and the market price of risk is $(R_M - R_F) = 5$ percent.

   (a) What is the expected return on the stock?

   (b) If the stock price is expected to remain unchanged, what would dividend payments have to be for the coming year?

   (c) What stock price (P_0) would you expect if dividends remain as calculated under (b), the stock price is not expected to change during year 1 $(P_0 = P_1)$, the risk-free rate is reduced to 6 percent, and the market price of risk remains unchanged?

   (d) Given the conditions under (c), what stock price (P_0) would you expect if the risk-free rate increases to 16 percent, with the market price of risk remaining unchanged?

(e) Generalize your findings under (c) and (d), and explain how you would expect stock prices to react to changing interest rates, other factors remaining constant.

10. The yield on treasury bills is 6 percent. The expected return on the market is 15 percent. It is possible to combine the market portfolio with treasury bills and end up with a portfolio that has an expected return of 12 percent and a standard deviation of 0.2. What must be the standard deviation of the market?

"I'm Not Out of a Job Yet" —One Investor's Views on Market Efficiency

In a perfectly efficient market, there should be no stock market crashes, theoretically. But major downturns do happen from time to time. So how does a consultant like Susan Pozer, whom we met in Chapter 6 and 7, advise her clients regarding this possibility?

"If the equities market in North America were perfectly efficient, I suppose I might be out of a job," muses Michael Decter, President and CEO of Lawrence Decter Investement Counsel, Inc., a Toronto company that manages portfolios, consisting largely of stocks, totalling about $150 million in about a hundred accounts. Mr. Decter is also the author of several books on investing.

"The purist view is that if you have perfect distribution of information, everyone will behave in the most rational manner because everyone will have the same knowledge. So it would be impossible to outperform the market; everyone would buy index funds."

While it's true, he admits, that index funds in fact outperform many discretionary managers, Mr. Decter isn't worried about losing his job at this point. "But the notion of a perfect market discounts a whole range of human emotion," is his opinion, "as well as disparities in education and other issues." He elaborates: "As I mentioned in my first book, *Michael Decter's Million-Dollar Strat-*egy, I believe that markets are heavily influenced by both fear and greed. People sell in a declining market out of fear; they buy in a rising market out of greed. These are sometimes rational reactions, but they are sometimes overreactions."

As a result, in Mr. Decter's view, the market will never be completely efficient. "It's certainly gotten much more efficient in recent years," he says. "The Internet has really levelled the playing field, giving small investors easy access to information that used to be much easier for bigger players to get." But even if everyone has the same information, he believes, the analysis they apply to it can be different.

There are structural issues too, he points out. Different kinds of players in the market behave differently. "Major players like large mutual funds need to have a float of a certain size, so they may overlook smaller companies."

In short, Mr. Decter believes that, "There will always be money to be made overall from picking good, solid companies likely to deliver growth over the long term. I'm not out of a job yet."

chapter 9

Market Efficiency

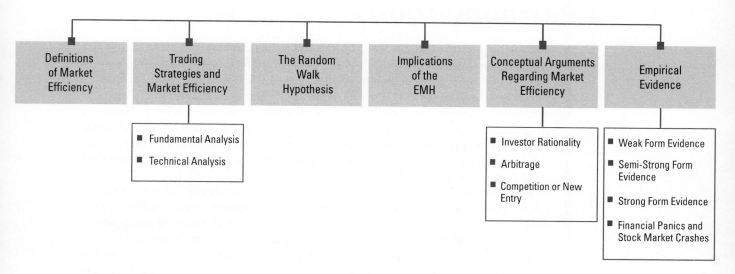

Definitions of Market Efficiency	Trading Strategies and Market Efficiency	The Random Walk Hypothesis	Implications of the EMH	Conceptual Arguments Regarding Market Efficiency	Empirical Evidence

Trading Strategies and Market Efficiency
- Fundamental Analysis
- Technical Analysis

Conceptual Arguments Regarding Market Efficiency
- Investor Rationality
- Arbitrage
- Competition or New Entry

Empirical Evidence
- Weak Form Evidence
- Semi-Strong Form Evidence
- Strong Form Evidence
- Financial Panics and Stock Market Crashes

Learning Objectives

After studying this chapter, you should be able to:

1. *Compare and contrast the three forms of market efficiency.*
2. *Define and compare fundamental analysis and technical analysis.*
3. *Discuss the random walk hypothesis and its implications for investors.*
4. *Explain the role of information in market efficiency and what this means to investors.*
5. *Discuss the empirical evidence about market efficiency and draw some conclusions.*

So far in this section, we have examined the time value of money, the valuation of debt and equity securities, and how to establish an appropriate level of return for risky assets. We conclude this section of the text with a discussion of market efficiency. In this chapter we examine how well capital markets establish security prices. This topic is central to much of the theory of finance that is developed throughout the text. In short, the relative efficiency (or inefficiency) of capital markets, as well as one's beliefs regarding this issue, has a large impact on the major investment and financing decisions made by individuals and corporations alike.

9.1 INTRODUCTION

Suppose the price of a share is $100. How is this price determined in the stock market? If you buy the stock, are you getting something worth $100? Is it possible to buy stocks that are worth more (or less) than their current prices? In short, how good are financial markets at getting the prices of stocks, bonds, and other securities "right"? And what does "right" mean? In one sense, the price in any free market is always right because it equates supply with demand. This means that buyers' demand matches sellers' supply and, thus, at the prevailing price, the asset cannot be an obvious bargain. This is particularly true when a large number of sophisticated market participants compete on either side in an increasingly global environment.

However, we need to probe the issues of market pricing in more depth in order to gain an appreciation of whether prices reflect "true economic value," and how prices adjust and move over time. As we shall see, these issues have far-reaching consequences not only for financial executives and investors, but also for the overall economy.

We saw in Chapter 2 that the main role of financial markets is to channel savings into the most productive investments, thereby contributing to economic growth. To achieve this, the market must function properly, without creating distortions or charging excessive transaction costs. In previous chapters, we also saw that securities should trade at prices that equal the present value of expected future cash inflows discounted at the appropriate market-given risk-adjusted rate. Therefore, the net present value (in our context, the present value of all future cash inflows minus the cash outflow associated with the current purchase price) of all securities should be zero[1] In other words, the expected future cash inflows from each security should just provide a return on the initial investment that is commensurate with its risk.

MARKET PRICES

Although actual results may vary from year to year depending on business conditions, assume that a firm's average earnings are $10 per share each year, and that all earnings

---

[1] Net present value will be discussed in greater detail in the next section of the text.

are paid out as dividends. Given the risk inherent in these projections, shareholders require an expected return of 10 percent. Thus, the shares should trade at:

$$\text{Market price} = \frac{10}{(1.10)^1} + \frac{10}{(1.10)^2} + \frac{10}{(1.10)^3} + \cdots$$

$$\text{Market price} = \frac{10}{.10} = \$100$$

Whether the price of $100 for the share is "right" depends on whether the market has chosen the proper discount rate, and on whether future cash flow expectations are correct. Expectations about the future are based on information, and the value of most assets depends on a wide variety of information. For example, expectations about a firm's future cash flows and, hence, the value of a firm's stock may depend on information about the overall economy, the industry, the firm's relative competitive position, and detailed information internal to the firm.

Generally, we call a market that gets future expectations and prices "right" an **efficient market**. Such efficiency implies that markets are good information-processing mechanisms, so that all relevant information is in fact embodied in security prices. As we shall see, various definitions of market efficiency are based on how quickly and how completely this information-processing task is performed.

We note that the term **information efficiency** used here is different from the ordinary meaning of economic efficiency. The latter implies that resources are used without waste, while information or market efficiency as discussed in this chapter implies proper forecasting and pricing. The two types of efficiencies need not go together.

The notion of market efficiency is controversial for two important reasons. First, if security markets are efficient, the investment advice professionals give may be of limited or no value. Advice such as "oil stocks are undervalued—buy them while they're a bargain!" is not helpful if prices are already at the "right" levels. Second, if markets are efficient and provide the proper signals to investors, the scope for government intervention in the economy is reduced.

It is important to emphasize in this context that financial market efficiency is not a law of economics but a *hypothesis*. As such, it represents one possible explanation of how markets work, and must be tested. At this time, there is no complete agreement among academics and finance professionals as to either the validity of the concept or the degrees of imperfection encountered in practice. Thus, we need to discuss both the idea of market efficiency and the evidence available to support or refute it.

Throughout this chapter, we concentrate on the efficiency of the stock market since most of the debate among financial researchers and practitioners has revolved around it. However, the concept of market efficiency can be applied to *any* market. Debt markets, commodities markets, foreign exchange markets, and even real estate markets can all be characterized, at least in principle, as processing information with varying degrees of efficiency.

9.2 DEFINITIONS OF MARKET EFFICIENCY

Figure 9.1 is a chart of a company's stock price, day-by-day, as new information relevant to the company is announced. The company's stock initially trades at about $45. To keep the illustration simple, suppose the company is paying a constant, expected (but not entirely certain) annual dividend of $4.50 and that the appropriate discount rate is 10 percent.

FIGURE 9.1

Stock Price as new Information is Released

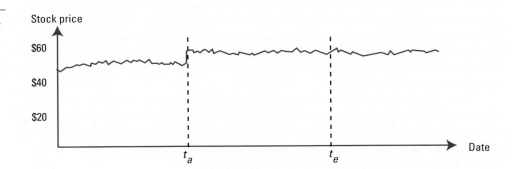

The business environment is constantly evolving and various events that might affect the firm's future profitability happen from time to time. For example, interest rates may move, a new competitor may appear, or a new product may be introduced. When information about events that may affect the firm becomes available, both potential buyers and sellers reconsider their calculations of what the share price should be. If something happens that is likely to increase the firm's future cash flows, shareholders may expect dividends to increase, and the share price should rise. The same would be true of an event that is likely to reduce the return required by the firm's common share investors, such as a decrease in interest rates. Conversely, an event that decreases anticipated cash flows and dividends or leads to an increase in the required return on the firm's common shares should lead to a drop in the share price.

For example, suppose that on day t_a, the repeal of a law that restricted the company's business is announced. This repeal greatly benefits the firm and is to take effect on date t_e. An analysis of the company suggests that, with the discount rate at 10 percent, profits should rise to a level that would sustain a constant $5.50 dividend, implying that the share price should rise to $55. If the market is efficient in processing new information, the stock price should immediately jump to $55. It should continue to trade in the $55 range, and the price should not change on date t_e, when the law actually changes. The increased dividends expected to result from this change would have been taken into account and **capitalized** (i.e., reflected in the price) when the announcement was made. Hence, there is no reason for the price to change further unless more new information becomes available.[2]

---

[2] Because of this reaction of stock prices to expectations about the future, economic forecasters often use stock market performance as a so-called *leading indicator*. However, efficiency does not mean that stock price movements always predict the future correctly. Prices may prove to be wrong *ex-post*.

Figure 9.1 and the example above illustrate what market efficiency means theoretically. Something happens that changes the value of the stock. In this case, there is a regulatory change that leads people to believe the company should be worth $55 per share.[3] Without waiting until the change actually occurs, the stock price adjusts instantly to reflect the new information. This example is analogous to the one discussed in Chapter 6, where the announcement of third-quarter results for year 2000 led to reduced expectations about Nortel's future sales growth, causing a dramatic and immediate decline in their share price

Market efficiency implies that new information disseminates quickly, with the market acting as a very fast information-processing system. Ideally, any new information is instantly reflected in share prices, making them "right" at any time, and no one can take advantage of temporary imperfections or time lags. The $10 gain per share simply becomes a windfall for those who happen to hold the stock at the time of the announcement.

If the market were less than perfectly efficient, however, the price in the previous example might move gradually, over some time, from $45 to $55. During this period of adjustment, which could last hours or weeks, the price would not fully reflect the new information. Hence, clever investors, with more information than others, could make money by buying the stock immediately and holding it until the price had fully adjusted upward to its new level. On the other hand, whoever sold at less than $55 after the announcement date would give potential value away; this is the price of ignorance.

For a market to be efficient, not every buyer and seller needs to have full access to all information. Different buyers and sellers may possess various bits and pieces of information relating to the value of a stock, and embody that in their buying and selling strategies which, in turn, may move security prices up or down. Such imperfect individual behaviour may, nevertheless, in aggregate result in security prices that are "right" and properly reflect all relevant information that is available in the marketplace.

The **efficient markets hypothesis (EMH)** states that securities markets are efficient, with market prices reflecting all available information at any given time. This is a very broad assertion. In order to structure the discussion on market efficiency, one useful and widely used approach is to classify information into major categories, and then explore how efficient the market is with regard to each class of information. Three definitions of market efficiency are commonly used in this context. Figure 9.2 depicts the relationship between these three levels of market efficiency.

1. The **weak form** of market efficiency states that stock prices fully reflect all information contained in past prices and volumes of trading. Expressed differently, future stock price movements are independent of what happened in the past, and investors cannot expect to achieve superior results by analysing past trading patterns.

2. In its **semi-strong form**, the EMH postulates that security prices adjust rapidly and fully reflect all *publicly* available information. This obviously includes historical price and trading information referred to above. Consequently, it is futile to

---

[3] The same reaction could have ocurred as a result of the release of information that leads market participants to believe interest rates would decline in the near future.

research a particular security through analysing past financial statements, industry records, trade statistics, and the like. Any such information is known widely enough to be embodied in current prices and does not confer an expected advantage on the prospective analyst.

3. The **strong form** of market efficiency implies that share prices reflect not only all public information, but also any relevant information, including insider information, that could potentially be gathered. Hence, no investor would ever be able to get an edge on the market by possessing superior knowledge.

FIGURE 9.2

Cumulative Levels of Market Efficiency and the Information Associated with Each.

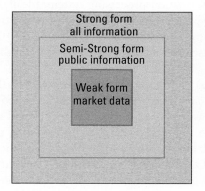

9.3 TRADING STRATEGIES AND MARKET EFFICIENCY

A practical starting point for understanding actual market behaviour is to examine the strategies commonly employed by financial analysts and managers to predict stock prices. Such strategies fall into two general categories. The first, called **fundamental analysis**, uses economic, industry, and company data (such as accounting information) to estimate a *fundamental value* for a stock. This is compared with the current market value and the stock is classified as either being over- or underpriced. The second, called **technical analysis**, tries to infer "market psychology" from recent patterns in stock price movements to discover what to buy and what to sell. In this section, we examine both types of approaches, and investigate how well they work.

Fundamental Analysis

Some of the most common methods used to determine the fundamental value of a firm's stock were discussed in Chapter 6. One widely used approach is the dividend discount model (DDM). A financial analyst might begin with general forecasts about the economy and about the future health of the industry in which the firm operates. The analyst might then examine the details of the firm's past and present financial reports and try to forecast what the firm's future financial statements might look like. Such forecasts are called *pro forma* financial statements, discussed in detail in Chapter 4. Using such information, and professional judgement, the analyst will try to forecast the firm's dividends and estimate an appropriate discount rate. This, in turn, provides an estimate of the stock price's fundamental value, denoted P_f, where:

$$P_f = \frac{D_1}{(1+r)} + \frac{D_2}{(1+r)^2} + \frac{D_2}{(1+r)^3} + \dots$$

with r representing the estimated discount rate and D_t, the estimated dividend at time t. Clearly, the DDM approach is as much an art as a science. Professional judgement is critical at each stage of analysis, and there is no single "right" estimate of future dividends or even of the discount rate.

Many financial analysts prefer a faster and more informal approach. One common way to estimate the underlying value of common stocks is based on price-earnings (P/E) ratios. The P/E ratio, its limitations, and its relation to other valuation techniques were discussed in Chapter 6. A further approach to valuing common stock that falls under the broad heading of fundamental analysis is based on estimating the breakup value of the firm. One tries to estimate how much the firm would be worth if it were closed down and it's component parts were auctioned off to the highest bidders. Both tangible and intangible assets must be included and valued at market prices rather than at how much they are carried on the books. The breakup value of the firm's shares then becomes the total value of all assets minus the total value of all liabilities. If the current stock price is lower than the breakup value per share, the stock may be undervalued. An alternative explanation is that the market price is low because current management is not using the firm's assets in the most advantageous way. Unless there is reason to believe that corporate policy is likely to change, the stock price could remain below the break-up value indefinitely.[4] Fundamental analysis based on break-up values is also difficult, since valuing individual corporate assets and liabilities, especially intangibles, is often quite subjective.

Technical Analysis

Technical analysis uses the historical trading record of securities in order to assess demand and supply for these securities. It is based on the notion that prices move in trends that repeat themselves through time. Practitioners of technical analysis are called **technicians**. Their analysis focuses on market data (historical price and trading volume information), rather than fundamental data.

The most prevalent group of technicians, called **chartists**, believe that stock prices follow patterns that can be exploited. They, therefore, use charts of stock prices against

---

[4] One way in which management policy can be changed quickly is if the firm is subject to a takeover bid. It explains why share prices in poorly performing firms may increase dramatically on any news that a takeover is imminent. This is discussed in Chapter 26.

FIGURE 9.3

Selected Charts (Stock Prices Against Time) Used in Technical Analysis

time to predict future stock price movements. Figure 9.3 shows a number of stock price patterns that are commonly thought by chartists to have significance in predicting the future. The arrows indicate the predicted future directions of prices based on the observed patterns up to the point where the broken line begins.

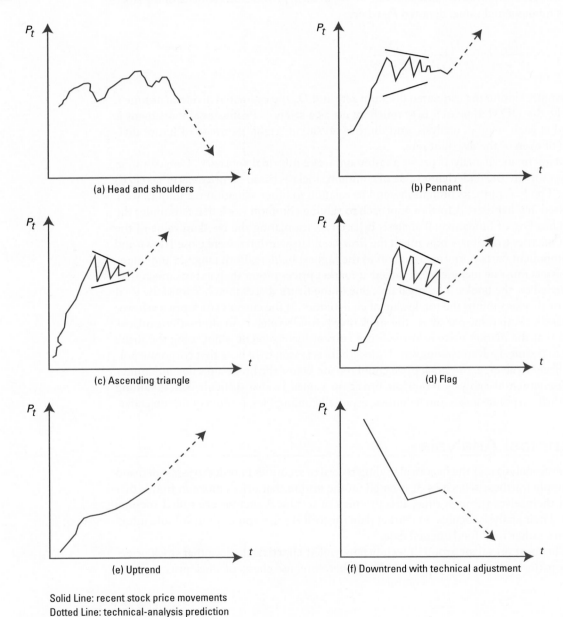

(a) Head and shoulders

(b) Pennant

(c) Ascending triangle

(d) Flag

(e) Uptrend

(f) Downtrend with technical adjustment

Solid Line: recent stock price movements
Dotted Line: technical-analysis prediction

Technicians also use terms such as *resistance level* and *support level*. In their view, the value of an individual stock, or of the market as a whole (as measured by an index such as the TSE 300) tends to stick at certain levels that have psychological significance. For example, if the TSE 300 is rising and suddenly pauses at, say, 10,000, technicians would say it has encountered *resistance*. If it were falling and suddenly paused, they would say it has found a *support level*.

A number of terms from technical analysis have been incorporated into everyday usage. For instance, a generally declining market is referred to as a **bear market**, and pessimistic forecasts are called *bearish*. A buoyantly rising market is called a **bull market**, and an optimistic prediction is called *bullish*. Bear and bull markets are thought to have momentum, in other words, a market in sustained decline is likely to continue down, and a market in a sustained rise is likely to hold its course as well. Temporary pauses or reversals in these trends are referred to as **technical adjustments**.

While the value of technical information is a hotly debated topic, its importance is highlighted by the fact that it is rare to see any type of analytical report that does not include some sort of historical price chart. Despite its prevalence, however, there are good reasons to believe that technical analysis should not work. One theory that leads to this conclusion is the **random walk hypothesis**, which has strong conceptual appeal. This hypothesis also casts doubt on the value of fundamental analysis as a predictive tool.

THE RANDOM WALK HYPOTHESIS   9.4

Assume that stock markets are efficient in the sense that investors are able to assimilate new information and recalculate stock prices quickly, as in the example at the beginning of this chapter. Assume also that stock prices move only because of new information. This is reasonable because only new information can change expectations about the future and, hence, about future dividends. By definition, new information has to be previously unknown and unanticipated. Therefore, it has to arise in an inherently unpredictable and random manner. If stock price movements are based on such inherently unpredictable new information, they themselves have to follow a random pattern. This is illustrated in Figure 9.4. When future changes in a quantity are unpredictable in this way, statisticians say that the quantity follows a random walk. Thus, the EMH is closely related to the idea that stock prices follow a random walk. This, in turn, casts serious doubt on the value of any of the security price analysis strategies outlined previously.

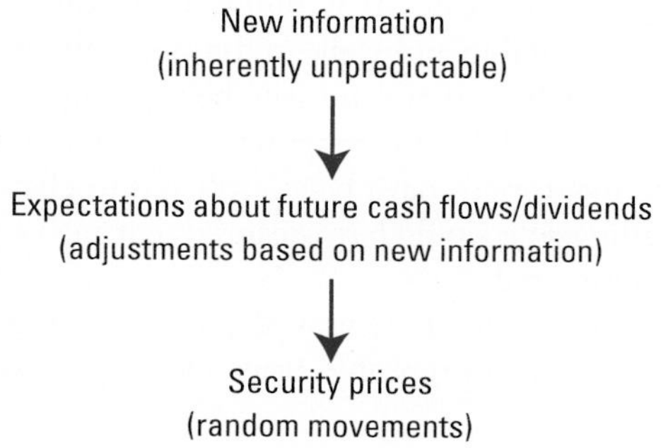

New information
(inherently unpredictable)

↓

Expectations about future cash flows/dividends
(adjustments based on new information)

↓

Security prices
(random movements)

FIGURE 9.4

Impact of Information on
Security Prices

The term random walk, which is taken from probability theory, can cause misunderstandings. The fact that stock prices follow a random walk does not imply that stock prices are random, like numbers generated by a roulette wheel, and thus do not follow economic logic. In fact, just the opposite is true. The random walk hypothesis assumes that investors gather and process all relevant information and perform accurate calculations for each stock to determine its correct economic price. If all existing information is embodied in the current stock price, any changes must be due to new information. Thus, the random walk hypothesis actually assumes that stock prices are calculated precisely and logically based on underlying economics and not arrived at randomly. Price changes appear random because they result from information that was previously unknown.

Another common misconception about the random walk hypothesis is that random movements imply an expected return of zero. Clearly, this cannot be the case because no one would have an incentive to invest. In fact, a random walk can well include a positive "drift": on average, one expects a positive return each period, thereby providing a fair reward for holding the security. However, actual returns can be distributed in a random and unpredictable manner around this expected value. For example, daily interest rates on treasury bills fluctuate in a random manner, but we know they will always be positive and provide a return to the savers who invest. Similarly, stock prices on average can be expected to provide a positive return, with actual prices following a random walk around this expected return.

Defenders of technical analysis argue that investors, like human beings in general, are not always rational, and they may be swayed by things that have little to do with economics. Also, the continual, precise recalculation of stock prices on the basis of new information may be more than can be expected from most, if not all, investors. It is argued, that investors are subject to psychological feelings of optimism or pessimism and to pressures to move with the crowd. Technicians claim their trading rules exploit these psychological effects.

The most famous advocate of psychological market effects, Lord Maynard Keynes, compared the stock market to a beauty contest in which the object is to guess which contestant everyone else will choose. There is no point, he argued, in paying $25 for a stock you feel is worth $30 if you are certain everyone else will value it at $20. Keynes was no armchair theorist. He made millions in the stock market and increased the value of the endowment of King's College in Cambridge by 1,000 percent.

While these arguments point to a possible momentum effect in stock prices and perhaps even to the existence of resistance and support levels, it is hard to see how they justify a mechanistic use of charts since it is highly questionable whether changes in psychological moods follow stable and well-established patterns. Also, the analysis of past trading patterns is something that can easily be replicated by many investors, particularly given the general availability of computers. If consistent gains were to be made, we would expect many investors to have been attracted to charting. This competitive search for the magic trading rule would have ensured that such a rule would have disappeared long ago, if it ever existed.

For example, let's consider one potential pattern in stock prices—runs. A run is a sequence of similar events such as repeated price increases during successive periods.

Assume that, at some time, runs that offered the potential for abnormal gains did exist. As more and more investors found out about them, this opportunity for profit would "self-destruct." Competitive investors, perceiving the beginning of an upward cycle, would rush to buy a particular share, bidding up its price immediately to the point where no further abnormal gains could be expected. If, in the process, the price had been bid up to an unjustified level, selling would set in, with investors searching for other potential runs. The price would drop back to the level where it provided its required rate of return - i.e., produced a net present value of zero. In a competitive environment, all of this would take place in a very short time span as each player tried to beat the other by being first. Thus, we would see the end of a run before it really ever got started.

Later in this chapter, we will examine the empirical evidence about stock price movements and whether or not technical analysis works. First, however, we will briefly analyse the more subtle implications of the random walk hypothesis for fundamental analysis.

The problem with fundamental analysis in an efficient market is not that it makes no sense, but that it makes sense to too many people too quickly for anyone to make a profit. For example, assume the price of Chapters Inc. common stock is currently $11.25. As an analyst following this industry, you have detailed information on all the projects in which Chapters is involved. You have analysed each part of the company and forecast future cash flows and have concluded that the stock is fairly priced at $11.25. Suddenly, a news flash appears on your computer screen, announcing that Chapters is spinning off its majority stake in a money-losing company. You feed the new data into your program for valuing companies and calculate that the stock price for Chapters should now be $12.55. You immediately place orders to buy as much Chapters stock as possible only to find that many others have done the same calculation you did—including the people who were previously offering to sell the stock at $11.25. Now, shares are not available anywhere for a price lower than $12.55.

The inability of fundamental analysis to generate profits can be linked to the semi-strong form of the efficient market hypothesis. The semi-strong form postulates that future stock price movements cannot be predicted using any current or past publicly available information. In the example above, such information formed the basis for a share price of $11.25, but the price movement from $11.25 to $12.55 was unpredictable from the information originally available. Once new information became available, the price moved so quickly that only the lucky few who placed their orders first made profits by trading on the information. Buyers and sellers immediately and simultaneously adjusted their prices. Thus, in a semi-strong form efficient market, fundamental analysis should not work.

Defenders of fundamental analysis (many of whom, by the way, are sharply critical of technical analysis) point out that such efficiency is an idealization not borne out in real markets. Even if new information were simultaneously available across the market, not all analysts in the previous example would conclude that the new price ought to be $12.55. Assessing the true impact on the firm's future cash flows can be highly subjective. Hence, some analysts' estimates will be higher and others lower. Indeed if this were not the case, few trades would ever occur. The analyst who has the best judgement should be able to outperform the others in forecasting the true new equilibrium price.

9.5 IMPLICATIONS OF THE EMH

Suppose that the market is perfectly efficient in the semi-strong sense and that prices do follow a random walk. What, then, is the smartest strategy for an investor, and what should a corporate financial executive do to best serve her company?

For an investor, the EMH implies that one cannot expect to beat the market and that any active trading strategy, on average over time, will not outperform a simple buy-and-hold approach. Specifically, it follows that:

1. There is no point in researching individual investments since all publicly available information is already reflected in current prices.

2. Investment counsellors and advisors do not provide a service that is of value when they recommend specific investments. Similarly, it is not worth hiring professional money managers in searching for consistently superior performance.

3. Timing with regard to buy-and-sell decisions is irrelevant. Since prices at any time reflect fair value, one should not be able to achieve consistently superior returns by playing the market and searching for optimal buy-and-sell strategies.

Consequently, the best strategy is not to even try for superior returns through active expert trading, thus avoiding unnecessary fees and commissions. If stocks are always priced at the "right" level, none are every under- or overvalued. There are no hot stocks, no ground floors to get in on, and no predictable peaks to sell at. Does this mean that an investor should just choose stocks at random and forget about any portfolio management strategy? The answer is no. All of the results we derived in Chapters 7 and 8, about diversification and the trade-off between risk and expected return, remain valid and are part of the description of an efficient market. This implies, first, that in order to minimize unnecessary risk, an investor ought to diversify as much as possible. Maximum diversification is, of course, obtained by "holding the market portfolio." This can be achieved through the use of index funds or index participation units, which were discussed at the end of Chapter 7.

Another implication of the material derived in Chapters 7 and 8 is that a higher expected return means higher risk. Because investors in aggregate are risk averse, they will only buy risky securities if the securities are priced to provide a superior expected return. In turn, in an efficient market, any investment that yields a higher-than-average return will expose its owner to higher-than-average risk, and no investment should ever consistently provide a higher return than other investments having the same level of risk. We note, in this context, that many investment funds advertise that they have dramatically out-performed the market (as measured by, say, the TSE 300). This is no great achievement if they have simultaneously exposed their investors to great risks. The right question to ask is: has the fund consistently outperformed other investments having the same level of risk?

Finally, the optimal investment strategy with regard to risk depends on each investor's specific needs and preferences. An investor willing to tolerate some risk may do best by putting all her money into an index fund or index participation unit. An investor more averse to risk should consider a combination of relatively risk-free assets such as Government of Canada bonds or T-bills and index investments. An investor who favours risk could invest in a diversified portfolio of higher-risk stocks. Alternatively, she might borrow money to buy more of a maximally diversified index product. These investment strategies were discussed in detail in Chapters 7 and 8, and are consistent with market efficiency.

The implications of the EMH for corporate financial officers are equally unsettling. Specifically:

1. The timing of security issues is unimportant since there is no good or bad time to sell. For example, if the firm's stock price has recently declined, it is because the future prospects for the firm, as viewed by investors in the marketplace, have deteriorated. The stock is still priced fairly, and management cannot justifiably claim that their stock is undervalued.

2. It does not make sense to "play" interest rates, for example, by rolling over short-term debt until long-term rates fall or by issuing long-term debt in order to lock in current "low" interest rates. The same holds for foreign exchange rates and commodity prices traded in efficient markets.

3. Since investors are always getting the prices of stocks and other assets "right," managers should pay close heed to changes in the prices of their firms' securities.

Managers should be concerned if, for example, as a consequence of a change in strategy, a firm's stock or bond prices suddenly drop.[5] According to the efficient market view, investors have busily recalculated the company's prospects in light of the new strategy and concluded that they are poor. For this to be reflected in security prices, it must be the shared and carefully considered opinion of many investors, and such "market judgements" should not be taken lightly. This is because shareholders in an efficient market use all available information to calculate the share price, and if shareholders value future cash flows less than managers do, then it is the managers who are mistakenly overvaluing the flows.

P E R S P E C T I V E S

If markets are semi-strong efficient and prices follow a random walk...

Corporate Manager

Corporate managers should react with concern to every change in their firms' security prices and try to respond to the markets' signals about investors' knowledgeable views.

Investor

Investors need worry only about picking a widely diversified portfolio with a risk that meets their tastes. They should be wary of investment managers (or advisors) who claim to be able to pick hot stocks or to know the best time to get into or out of the market.

---

[5] If other factors are not constant, then a price drop may not be caused by investor reassessment of future earnings and dividends. It could be, for example, that discount rates rose because of a change in general interest rates.

Needless to say, many investment counsellors, managers, and academics find this view somewhat unrealistic, and controversy remains about the extent of market efficiency. Before turning to a survey of the actual evidence on how efficient or inefficient markets appear to be, we will consider some conceptual arguments about what a realistic level of market efficiency might be.

9.6 CONCEPTUAL ARGUMENTS REGARDING MARKET EFFICIENCY

There are three major conceptual reasons for expecting financial markets to be reasonably efficient:

- investor rationality
- arbitrage
- competition or new entry.

We briefly discuss each of these in turn.

Investor Rationality

We have seen that markets are efficient if investors use available information promptly and reasonably to reassess future cash flows and then embody such projections in current prices. We should note that not all investors need to do this. It normally is sufficient if a significant number of large investors act rationally. Trading on all major markets is now dominated by institutional investors such as pension funds, insurance companies, and investment funds, all of which employ sophisticated professionals to manage their portfolios. In fact, well over 75 percent of the market value of all trading on major stock exchanges is attributable to such professionals. While small investors certainly participate, it is reasonable to argue that security prices are largely determined by rational professionals, who have access to the latest information and advanced computer programs.

Arbitrage

In a narrow sense, **arbitrage** is defined as making a profit through appropriate trading in mispriced securities, in a broader sense, it entails reaping any excessive gain or abnormal return that is not commensurate with prevailing market conditions. One principle that supports market efficiency is that in competitive markets, arbitrage opportunities should not exist since sophisticated investors would immediately buy any underpriced security (or sell overpriced ones) until prices are once more in equilibrium.

For example, consider an investor who believes that a stock is likely to pay $2 per year in dividends in perpetuity and feels that the risk inherent in those dividends warrants a discount rate of 20 percent. The stock should, therefore, be worth $10 according to the DDM. Whenever the stock is available for less than $10, the investor would buy it in the hope of making an arbitrage profit later, when its price rises, as other market participants discover their error.

Note that the investor above is exposed to the risk that new negative information about the stock might depress its value before the price correction to $10 takes place. Because of this possibility, the strategy in the previous example is called **risk arbitrage**. An investor should engage in such risk arbitrage if the returns from doing so can be expected to outweigh the risks involved. In a competitive environment, risk arbitrage is a powerful force that tends to keep prices in line.

Competition or New Entry

Finally, we know from basic economics that competitive imitation is a key ingredient to market efficiency. Ultimately, one can only make superior returns by exploiting advantages that others cannot readily replicate. In modern financial markets, it is exceedingly difficult to sustain such competitive advantage. Not only are there many local individuals and institutions seeking returns through investments, but also the international mobility of capital has created global competition. Few goods move so freely and quickly around the world in search of superior investment returns as money. Furthermore, there are no proprietary rights in finance, and clever investment schemes cannot be patented. In fact, they tend to be readily observable and open to almost immediate imitation; therefore, any inefficiencies should quickly disappear.

Assume, for example, that you develop a method of predicting the market. Perhaps you feed certain economic information and other data into a complex computer program and a buy recommendation for some stock emerges. Suppose, at first, your approach always works. You buy a large number of shares in the recommended stock and its price moves up substantially the next day. As you become rich, people will begin to wonder how you do it. They will watch your trades, and whenever you buy a stock, other people will begin to mimic your moves and also buy, ultimately driving the price up so quickly that you can only buy a few shares at a bargain price. Soon, someone will replicate your method of picking stocks. When you go to buy, you may find that the price has already been driven up by the purchases of other people taking advantage of your innovation. Eventually, your method might become so well known that it is discussed in finance textbooks like this one. Once everyone understands the method, it will stop working. People who would have happily sold you their stock at a low price in the past now know that its price will probably go up tomorrow. Consequently, they will demand a high price for it today, and the opportunity for arbitrage is lost.

Any systematic way of winning against the market should eventually defeat itself. Methods of beating the market must remain secret, or they stop working. Since market transactions transmit information, such methods cannot remain secret for long.

Do the above arguments imply that markets are perfectly efficient? Some hold that they do not and even maintain that perfectly efficient markets are impossible. One obvious objection is that trading costs such as commissions and bid-ask spreads limit arbitrage trading and thus the level of efficiency in the market. There is, however, a deeper concern, often referred to as the Grossman-Stiglitz paradox.[6] If markets were

---

[6] As developed in Sanford Grossman and Joseph Stiglitz, "On the Impossibility of Information Efficient Markets," *American Economic Review*, 1980, pp. 393-408.

perfectly efficient so that all information was properly evaluated and instantly factored into the price of every stock, no one could make money by buying underpriced stocks or selling overpriced ones. But in such a market, why would anyone bother to collect and evaluate information? There is no reward for doing so. Finding useful information and using it to estimate stock prices is costly, which is why there must be enough opportunities for profit to reward the people who gather and process information. Otherwise, no one would bother with any analysis. If no information is collected, stock prices cannot be set in an informationally-efficient way. In fact, perhaps, they could not be set at all, and the market could not operate, at least not in a rational way. Thus, the market cannot be perfectly efficient because it would not function at all.

At first glance, these arguments appear to imply a contradiction. On the one hand, market inefficiencies cause their own demise. On the other, without profit opportunities, there is no incentive to gather and process information. Therefore, a perfectly efficient market could not exist. This paradox is generally resolved by assuming that investors exert resources to collect information up to the point at which the marginal benefits of such information equal the marginal costs of obtaining it. This implies a revised form of the EMH, which suggests that no investor can earn risk-adjusted returns in excess of the return on the market *plus* the cost of information acquisition and analysis. That is, investors will earn back their information gathering expenses such that their *gross* returns exceed the market but their *net* returns exactly equal the market.

9.7 EMPIRICAL EVIDENCE

How efficient is the stock market? How quickly is new information reflected in stock prices? What sort of information is, or is not, so incorporated? To provide tentative answers to these questions, it is useful to provide an overview of the actual behaviour of financial markets.

Because of the significance of the EMH and the controversy surrounding it, a substantial body of evidence has been built up over the years regarding the efficiency of financial markets - most particularly the stock market. Much of the evidence has supported the notion of efficient markets; however, there has also been a number of questions raised about just how efficient the market really is.[7] In this section, we discuss some of the available evidence, which is separated into tests of the three forms of market efficiency previously discussed.

The key to testing the validity of any of the three forms of market efficiency is the consistency with which investors can earn returns in excess of those commensurate with the risk involved. Short-lived inefficiencies appearing on a random basis do not constitute evidence of market inefficiencies, at least in an economic (as opposed to a statistical) sense. Therefore, it makes sense to talk about an economically efficient market, in which assets are priced in such a manner that investors cannot exploit any discrepancies

---

[7] The U.S. evidence on this topic is quite extensive. Two of the most comprehensive sources can be found in: B. Malkiet, *A Random Walk Down Wall Street*, 5th ed. (New York: W.W. Norton, 1996); and, E. Fama, "Efficient Capital Markets: II," *Journal of Finance*, 46 (December 1991), pp. 1575-1617. Evidence for Canadian markets is summarized in J. Hatch and M . Robinson, *Investment Management in Canada, 2nd ed.*, (Scarborough: Prentice Hall, 1989).

and earn unusual returns after consideration of all transaction costs. In such a market, some securities could be priced slightly above their intrinsic values and others slightly below, and lags can exist in the processing of information but, again, not in such a way that the differences can be exploited.

What about the time period involved? In the short run, investors may earn unusual returns even if the market is efficient. After all, you could buy a stock today, and tomorrow a major discovery could be announced that would cause its stock price to increase significantly. Does this mean the market is inefficient? Obviously not; it means you are either very skillful or, more likely, very lucky. The question is can you and enough other investors do this a sufficient number of times in the long run to earn abnormal profits? Even in the long run, some people will be lucky, given the total number of investors.

Weak Form Evidence

As noted, weak form efficiency means that price data are incorporated into current stock prices. If price changes follow discernible patterns, they are dependent; otherwise, they are independent.[8] Therefore, weak form tests involve the question of whether all information contained in the sequence of past price changes is fully reflected in the current price.

One way to test for weak form efficiency is to statistically test the independence of stock price changes. If the statistical tests suggest that price changes are independent, the implication is that knowing and using the past sequence of price information is of no value to an investor. In other words, trends in price changes do not exist.

Two simple statistical tests of independence are the serial correlation test and the runs (or signs) test (which was discussed above). The serial correlation test involves measuring the correlation between price changes for various lags such as one day, two days, and so on. Most available evidence suggests that only a very small percentage of any successive price change could be explained by prior changes. The runs test evidence also supports independence. Although some runs do occur, they fall within the limits of randomness since a truly random series exhibits some runs (several + or - observations in succession).

A second way to test for weak form efficiency, after testing the pure statistical nature of price changes, is to test specific trading rules that attempt to use past price data. If such tests legitimately produce risk-adjusted returns beyond that available from simply buying a portfolio of stocks and holding it until a common liquidation date, after deducting all costs, it would suggest that the market is not weak form efficient.

Technical analysts believe trends in stock price changes do exist and can be used successfully. They argue that statistical tests do not detect more sophisticated or realistic strategies. Because an almost unlimited number of possible technical trading rules exist, not all of them can be examined. However, a substantial amount of evidence suggests that technical trading rules based solely on past price and volume data do not, after all proper adjustments have been made, outperform a simple buy-and-hold strategy.

---

[8] It should be apparent upon reflection that we are talking about price changes and not about the level of price itself. Obviously, a $50 stock has a price on any given day that will be related closely to its price tomorrow since it is unlikely on a typical day to go much above or below $50. The issue centres on whether percentage price changes over time are related or not.

Again, it is important to emphasize the difference between statistical dependence and economic dependence in stock price changes. Most of the statistical tests discussed detected some small amount of dependence in price changes. Not all of the series could be said to be completely independent statistically. However, they were economically independent in that one could not exploit the small statistical dependence that existed. After trading costs, excess returns disappear. After all, this is the bottom line for investors—can excess returns be earned with a technical trading rule after all costs are deducted? Therefore, the evidence is generally supportive of weak form market efficiency.

While markets are generally assumed to be efficient in the weak sense, there are two commonly cited contradictions of weak form market efficiency. The first refers to the existence of long-term reversals in stock returns. The existence of this pattern in U.S. stock returns was identified by DeBondt and Thaler, who tested an overreaction hypothesis, based on the notion that people tend to overreact to unexpected and dramatic news events.[9] As applied to stock prices, the hypothesis states that, as a result of overreactions, "loser" portfolios outperform the market after their formation. DeBondt and Thaler classify stocks as "winners" and "losers" based on their total returns over the previous three-to-five year period. They find that over a half century, the loser portfolios of 35 stocks outperformed the market by an average of almost 20 percent for a 36-month period after portfolio formation, while the winner portfolios earned about 5 percent less than the market. Their results are depicted below in Figure 9.5.

FIGURE 9.5

Average of 16 Three-Year Test Periods between January 1933 and December 1980 Length of Formation Period: Three Years

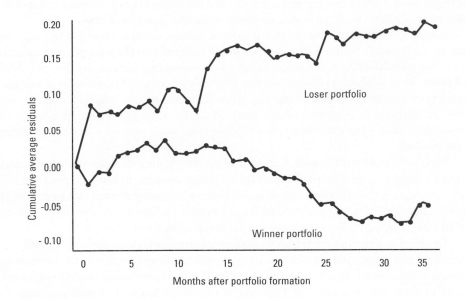

Source: W. DeBondt and R. Thaler, "Does the Stock Market Overreact?" *Journal of Finance*, (July 1985), p. 800

---

[9] W. DeBondt and R. Thaler, "Does the Stock Market Overreact?" *Journal of Finance*, (July 1985), pp. 793–805.

Trading strategies designed to exploit this pattern are commonly referred to as contrarian strategies, since the underlying rationale is to purchase or sell stocks in anticipation of achieving future results that are contrary to their past performance record. This tendency for long-term stock return reversals indicates the existence of a substantial weak form inefficiency. In other words, it suggests that knowing past stock returns helps significantly in predicting future stock returns. A more recent U.S. study of the overreaction hypothesis, which adjusts for several potential problems, also found an "economically important overreaction effect" even after adjusting for time variations in beta and for size effects.[10] Interestingly, Kryzanowski and Zhang find that no such pattern exists for Canadian stocks listed on the TSE over a similar period of time (1950-1988).[11]

Another apparent contradiction to weak form market efficiency is the existence of short-term persistence in stock returns in historical stock returns. In recent years, this pattern has received a great deal of attention in the finance academic and practitioner literature. Several recent studies have documented the success attainable by using momentum (or relative strength) indicators. The evidence suggests that stocks that have been top-performers over the past six- to twelve-month periods will continue to provide superior investment performance in the subsequent six- to twelve-month periods.

There is a substantial amount of supporting empirical evidence for the success of momentum trading strategies. One of the most influential studies was that of Jegadeesh and Titman (1993), who examined U.S. stock returns over three decades.[12] They formed portfolios by ranking stocks based on their past three- to twelve-month returns and showed that buying the top-performing decile of NYSE and AMEX stocks and selling the bottom-performing decile of stocks produced very significant positive abnormal returns. It is interesting to note that the persistence in short-term (six to twelve months) returns contrasts sharply with the longer-term (three to five years) reversals in return performance documented by DeBondt and Thaler.

Foerster, Prihar, and Schmitz, and Cleary and Inglis show that a similar pattern exists in Canadian stock returns.[13] The Cleary and Inglis results, which cover the 1978-90 period, are depicted graphically in Figure 9.6. In this diagram, the line for the Winner portfolio represents the wealth that would have been accumulated over their sample period by investing in a portfolio of stocks that displayed the best return performance over the previous 12-month period. The other line represents the cumulative wealth that would have been achieved by investing in the TSE 300 Index, which is well below that for the winner portfolio. Cleary and Inglis also demonstrate that the abnormal returns generated from "momentum trading" cannot be accounted for by transactions costs, size effects,

[10] See N. Chopra, J. Lakonishok, and J. R. Ritter, "Measuring Abnormal Performance: Do Stocks Overact?" *Journal of Financial Economics*, 1992, pp. 235-268.

[11] See L. Kryzanowski and H. Zhang, "The Contrarian Strategy Does Not Work in Canadian Markets," *Journal of Financial and Quantitative Analysis*, (September 1992), pp. 389-395.

[12] See N. Jegadeesh and S. Titman, "Returns to Buying Winners and Selling Losers: Implications for Stock Market Efficiency," *Journal of Finance*, (March 1993), pp. 65-91.

[13] See S. Foerster, A. Prihar and J. Schmitz, "Back to the Future: Price Momentum Models and How They Beat the Canadian Equity Markets," *Canadian Investment Review*, (Winter 1994/1995), pp. 9-13; and S. Cleary and M. Inglis, "Momentum in Canadian Stock Returns," *Canadian Journal of Administrative Sciences*, (September 1998), pp. 279-291.

or underlying risk characteristics. Finally, Rouwenhorst demonstrates that momentum performs well in 12 other international markets.[14]

FIGURE 9.6

Cleary and Inglis Results

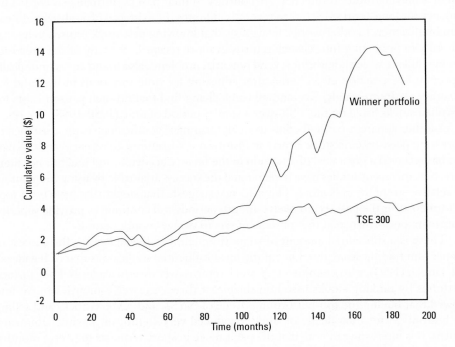

Source: Adapted from S. Cleary and M. Inglis, "Momentum in Canadian Stock Returns," *Canadian Journal of Administrative Sciences 1998, 15,* p.282

Another so-called market anomaly is the existence of seasonal patterns in stock returns. The most commonly referred to pattern is called the **January effect**. This refers to evidence produced by a number of studies that document unusually high stock returns during the first few days of each year. The January effect is often referred to as the "small firm in January effect" because it is most prevalent for the returns of small-cap stocks. For example, the average U.S. monthly return for January during the 1941–81 period was 1.34 percent for the S&P 500 Index versus an average monthly return of 0.92 percent for the remaining 11 months. During the same period, the average January return was 8.06 percent for the smallest quintile of NYSE stocks, versus 0.88 percent for the other 11 months. During the 1982–90 period, the average January return was 3.20 percent for the S&P 500 Index versus 1.23 percent for the other 11 months, while the January return for the smallest NYSE quintile was 5.32 percent versus 0.17 percent for the remaining 11 months. Canadian evidence also supports the existence of a January effect. For example, Vijay Jog shows that the average January return for the TSE 300 over the 1972–86

---

[14] See K.G. Rouwenhorst, "International Momentum Strategies," *Journal of Finance*, (February 1998), pp. 267-284.

period was 3.13 percent, versus an average monthly return of 0.82 percent for the other 11 months over the same time period. The difference in returns was even more pronounced for smaller stocks.[15]

A possible explanation for this pattern is that investors sell stocks at the end of each year to establish capital losses for tax reasons, and buy them back later in January. Since the January effect is most pronounced for small firms and such firms are least likely to be owned by tax-free investors like pension funds, this explanation may be correct, at least in part. However, most evidence suggests that tax-loss selling cannot account for the entire amount. In any event, the available evidence suggests that trading costs make exploiting the effect unprofitable for most investors. Therefore, this pattern does not represent a clear contradiction to weak form efficiency.

Other seasonal patterns include evidence of a **weekend effect**. Stock prices seem to decline from Friday close to Monday close slightly more often than a pure random walk would predict. This implies that one should buy on Monday afternoons but never on Friday afternoons or Monday mornings. Studies have also identified a day-of-the-month effect, where returns tend to be higher on the last trading day of each month.[16] This is similar to the January effect, but these effects are too small and uncertain to cover most investors' trading costs.

Semi-Strong Form Evidence

Weak form tests are numerous and are generally supportive of weak form efficient capital markets, with a few exceptions. Semi-strong tests are also numerous but more diverse in their findings. Although most of these studies support the proposition that the market adjusts to new public information rapidly, some do not.

One approach to testing semi-strong form efficiency involves conducting tests of the speed of price adjustments to publicly available information. The question is whether investors can use publicly available information to earn excess returns, after proper adjustments. This empirical research often involves an **event study**, which means that a company's stock returns are examined to determine the impact of a particular event on the stock price. The methodology generally uses an equilibrium model of stock returns, such as the CAPM, to predict what the expected return would have been had the significant event not occurred. The amount that the actual return deviates from this amount is denoted as is an **abnormal return** representing the impact of a particular event.

A large number of events have been studied using many different samples. The majority of evidence from event studies supports the notion that markets react quickly to reflect accurately the new information into security prices. For example, prices tend to adjust almost instantaneously to announcements such as dividend changes or takeovers.

---

[15] See V. Jog, "Stock Pricing Anomalies: Canadian Experience," *Canadian Investment Review*, (1988), pp. 55-62.

[16] This is an interesting observation in light of the recent dimissal of several members of RT Capital Management Inc. These individuals admitted to engaging in stock transactions designed to artificially inflate the prices of stocks held in various mutual funds or pension funds at the end of certain months. They did so to enhance the performance of the portfolio under their management during a given reporting period.

The second general approach to testing semi-strong market efficiency is to determine if investors can use publicly available information to generate consistently abnormal risk-adjusted returns over sustained periods of time.

Along these lines, perhaps the strongest evidence of semi-strong market efficiency is the fact that the average professional fund manager does not outperform the market benchmark on a risk-adjusted basis. The most abundant type of managed portfolios examined in the performance literature is U.S.-based equity mutual funds. The evidence does not support the hypothesis that the average manager outperforms the appropriate equity market indices.[17] There are also several U.S. studies regarding the performance of pension funds that indicate that these managers consistently underperform the appropriate benchmark.

The report below is exerpted from an article in the *Globe and Mail*, which suggests that very few Canadian Equity mutual funds have been able to perform above the average for their fund category on a consistent basis. Making matters worse, the average return for these funds is below the return for the TSE 300 Composite Index during the period examined. Unfortunately, there are very few rigorous empirical studies of the performance of Canadian mutual or pension funds. In addition, the existing studies deal with small numbers of funds over relatively short time periods. Overall, the available Canadian evidence is mixed; however, there is some indication of superior performance by professionally managed funds in Canada.[18]

■ *Finance in the News*

Few Funds Consistently Beat the Average

On a visit to Canada just last week, famed US investment superstar Peter Lynch made an interesting observation. "If you're right six or seven times out of 10," said the former portfolio manager of the worlds' largest mutual fund, "that's a terrific score."

Of course, Mr. Lynch, vice-chairman of Boston-based Fidelity Management & Research Co., was talking about picking stocks, a job he performed exceptionally well at the top-performing **Fidelity Magellan Fund** from 1977 to 1990.

But a detailed examination of the year-by-year returns of Canadian equity funds suggests that Mr. Lynch's words apply equally to picking mutual funds.

For a fund to perform merely better than the average in its category in a single year hardly seems worth of mention. But what's so surprising is how few funds manage to perform this feat more often.

---

[17] For example, see M. Grinblatt and S. Titman, "Mutual Fund Performance: An Analysis of Quarterly Portfolio Holdings," *Journal of Business*, (July 1989), pp. 393–416; and B. Malkiel, "Returns From Investing in Equity Mutual Funds 1971 to 1991," *Journal of Finance*, (June 1995), pp. 549–572.

[18] For example, see E. Coutere, "Investment's Smart Bomb: Passive Management With Style," *Canadian Investment Review*, (December 1992), pp. 43-48; and, R. Heinkel and R. Quick, "The Relative Performance of Canadian Institutional Portfolios and Canadian Indexes," *Canadian Investment Review*, (Fall 1993), pp. 33-39.

In fact, according to our examination of Canadian equity funds with ten years under their belt, fewer than half of funds can do it even half the time. So doing so six or seven times out of ten does indeed constitute a terrific score. Among the 76 Canadian equity funds in existence for the decade to September 30, 1997, not a single one managed to beat the category average in all ten years. And just one managed to beat the category average nine times. That fund — the $159-million **Bissett Canadian Equity Fund** — might well be called the consistency king of Canadian stock funds.

Possibly just as startling, only three funds managed to beat the average in eight years, and four more bested the average seven times. Just another seven managed to outperform in six out of 10 years — in other words, more than half the time. And another 14 outperformed five out of ten years, or exactly half the time.

The overall score: 34 of the 76 funds — fewer than half — beat the average at least five out of ten years. So beating the category average more than half the time really is a performance standard too few mutual funds ever meet.

What does this mean to you, the fund investor? Quite simply, these remarkable statistics reinforce the advice you've no doubt grown tired of hearing — invest for the long term. All funds and portfolio managers — the best and all the rest — go through periods when they simply fail to excel. So don't judge your funds harshly when they've suffered a single year of sub-average returns.

Year after year of consistently superior performance may be the most desirable trait any mutual fund can offer. That's because those few funds that manage to excel according to our criteria also exhibit relatively strong compound annual rates of return over time.

In fact, all four of the funds that beat the average at least eight times out of ten also turned in ten-year compound returns in the top ten per cent of their category.
These statistics may not seem to add much to the fund-selection process. After all, why not just pick the funds with the best long-term returns?

But they tell you a lot about why advisers constantly recommend staying with your existing investments. A year or two of below-average performance simply does not imply a poor fund. Even the best suffer periodic but temporary setbacks.

If you hold a fund that seems to be falling behind its peer group, by all means look for explanations. There may be something worng, such as a change of manager or a wandering of the manager's style. These reasons may suggest that a change in your portfolio is in order.

However, your fund may just be going through a temporary period when its style of stock-picking doesn't lead the charts. If you redeem and move on for that reason alone, you may find yourself selling low just before your fund begins to recover.

What's more, moving into another fund that's been hot recently may mean buying just before it suffers one of its inevitable setbacks.

When a fund's ten-year compound average annual growth rate places it firmly in the top 10 per cent of its category, it usually means the fund performed better than average more than half the time.

So the next time you're wondering how one of your funds could do so poorly, take a look at how many times it beat its category average. After all, even the best funds have a few off years.

Source: Excerpted from Peter Brewster, "Better than Average: Not Often Enough" *Globe and Mail*, A 15-Year Review, Mutual Funds, November 6, 1997 pp. C1-C2 Peter Brewster. *Reprinted with permission.*

On aggregate, the results indicate that the net performance of the average active portfolio manager (after management expenses) is substantially worse than the performance of the standard passive portfolio benchmarks. In fact, the average active portfolio manager may underperform the market index by 50 to 200 basis points. This infers that the gross performance (before management expenses) of the average active portfolio manager equals, at best, the performance of standard passive benchmarks, and it is likely marginally lower than these benchmarks.

Having considered the type of evidence supporting semi-strong market efficiency, we now consider some evidence to the contrary. We consider a few of these anomalies that have generated much attention and have yet to be satisfactorily explained. However, investors must be cautious in viewing any of these anomalies as a stock selection device guaranteed to outperform the market. There is no such guarantee because empirical tests of these anomalies may not approximate actual trading strategies that would be followed by investors.

The adjustment of stock prices to earnings announcements has been studied several times. The evidence shows that companies displaying the largest positive earnings surprises displayed superior subsequent performance, while companies with low or negative earnings surprises displayed poor subsequent performance. These studies also showed that, while a substantial adjustment occurs before the actual earnings announcement, a substantial adjustment also occurs after the day of the announcement. This is the unexplained part of the earnings surprise puzzle. In an efficient market, prices should adjust quickly to earnings rather than with a lag.[19]

In two recent studies, Sean Hennessey demonstrates that portfolios of Canadian stocks that have experienced positive earnings forecast revisions produce excess positive returns subsequent to the revision and the larger the revisions, the greater the excess returns.[20] This implies that investors can earn abnormal returns using publicly available information, which contradicts the semi-strong form of the EMH. Hennessey also shows that this effect is greater for small capitalization firms, which is consistent with less information being publicly available for these stocks.

One of the most prominent anomalies documented in the finance literature is the **size effect**. The firm size effect literature blossomed in the early 1980s with several U.S. studies that found that small market capitalization stocks tended to outperform large capitalization stocks, even after adjusting for CAPM market risk.[21] Keim found that 50 percent of the firm size effect occurs in January.[22] Several studies have confirmed the

[19] For example, see C. P. Jones, R. J. Rendleman, and H. A. Latane, "Stock Returns and SUEs during the 1970s," *Journal of Portfolio Management*, (Winter 1984), pp. 18-22.

[20] See S. Hennessey, "Can Active Managers Profit from Earnings Forecast Revisions?" *Canadian Investment Review*, (Spring 1993), pp. 39-45; and, S. Hennessey, "Get the Drift," *Canadian Investment Review*, (Winter 1995/96), pp. 23-28.

[21] A company's market capitalization is defined as the market price per common share times the number of shares outstanding.

[22] D. Keim, " Size-Related Anomalies and Stock Return Seasonality," *Journal of Financial Economics*, (June 1983), pp. 13-32.

persistence of this pattern for U.S. stocks in more recent periods, while Canadian studies have confirmed the existence of a size effect for Canadian stock returns.[23] Similar to U.S. studies, market betas cannot account for the returns, and a large portion of the return accrues during the month of January.

Stocks that carry above-average price-earnings (P/E) ratios, market-to-book (M/B) multiples, and below-average dividend yields are often referred to as "growth" stocks. This is based on the belief that investors are willing to pay a premium for these companies because they expect them to exhibit above-average future growth in earnings and share price. Stocks with below average P/E and M/B ratios and above-average dividend yields are referred to as "value" stocks. These stocks can be purchased at relatively inexpensive prices.

Several academic studies using U.S. evidence have shown that value stocks have outperformed growth stocks over long periods of time. For example, stocks with low P/E ratios have tended to outperform those with high P/E multiples, while those with low M/B values and/or high dividend yields have outperformed those with high M/B values and/or low dividend yields. Fama and French demonstrated that this relationship existed for stock portfolios of various sizes (i.e., small-, medium-, and large-cap stocks).[24] Bourgeois and Lussier provided Canadian evidence confirming the superior risk-adjusted performance of low P/E stocks relative to high P/E stocks and to the market as a whole.[25] There is also a substantial amount of evidence regarding the superior performance of value stocks in other financial markets around the world.[26]

This evidence seems to contradict semi-strong market efficiency unless the superior performance of the value portfolios is attributable to greater associated risk levels. However, Fama and French find that value portfolios appear to be less risky than the growth portfolios according to market betas. A 1997 study by Bauman and Miller also documents superior performance by value stock portfolios, with the standard deviation of the value portfolios being slightly lower than that of the growth portfolios.[27] All of this suggests that value investing is no riskier than growth investing, according to traditional risk measures. These results have lead many to adopt extreme views about market efficiency. For example, Haugen (1995) argues that the true risk-return relationship is negative—lower risk stocks provide higher returns, while riskier stocks provide lower returns.[28]

---

[23] For example, see S. Tinic, G. Barone-Adesi and R. West, "Seasonality in Canadian Stock Prices: A Test of the Tax-Loss-Selling Hypothesis," *Journal of Financial and Quantitative Analysis*, (March 1987), pp. 51-63; and, S. Foerster and D. Porter, "Calender and Size-Based Anomalies in Canadian Stock Returns," in Michael Robinson and Brian Smith, eds., Canadian Capital Markets, (1993).

[24] See E. Fama and K. French, "The Cross Section of Expected Stock Returns," *Journal of Finance*, (June 1992), pp. 427-465.

[25] See J. Bourgeois and J. Lussier, "P/Es and Performance in the Canadian Market," *Canadian Investment Review*, (Spring 1994), pp.33-39.

[26] See for example, C. Capaul, I. Rowley, and W. Sharpe, "International Value and Growth Stock Returns," *Financial Analysts Journal*, (January-February 1993), pp.27-36; and E. Fama and K. French, "Value Versus Growth: The International Evidence," *Journal of Finance*, (December 1998), pp. 1975-1999.

[27] S. Bauman and R. Miller, "Investor Expectations and the Performance of Value versus Growth Stocks," *The Journal of Portfolio Management*, (Sping 1997) pp. 57-68.

[28] R. Haugen, *The New Finance: The Case Against Market Efficiency*, (Toronto, Prentice Hall, 1995).

The reader should be wary of concluding that value stocks will always outperform growth stocks, and that small-cap stocks will outperform large-cap stocks. These results are based on historical data, and do not necessarily predict what will happen in the future especially in the short term. For example, while the 1982-98 average monthly return on the DS BARRA Large-Cap Growth Index of 0.77 percent was below the 1.13 percent monthly average for the corresponding Value index, in 1999 the Growth Index produced a return of 42.93 percent versus only 2.63 percent for the Value Index.

Strong Form Evidence

The strong form of the EMH states that stock prices immediately adjust to and reflect all information, including private information. Thus, no group of investors—even those with monopolistic access—has information that allows them to earn abnormal profits *consistently*. Note that investors are not prohibited from possessing monopolistic information—only from profiting from this information.

One way to test for strong form efficiency is to examine the performance of groups presumed to have access to "true" non-public information. If such groups can consistently earn above-average risk-adjusted returns, the strong form will not be supported. We will consider corporate insiders, a group that presumably falls into the category of having monopolistic access to information. A corporate insider is an officer, director, or major stockholder of a corporation who might be expected to have valuable inside information.

Insiders have access to privileged information and are able to act on it and profit before the information is made public. Therefore, it is not surprising that several studies of corporate insiders found that they consistently earned abnormal returns on their stock transactions, including two Canadian studies by Fowler and Rorke, and Lee and Bishara.[29] This evidence clearly contradicts strong form market efficiency, which suggests that no investor can earn abnormal profits on a consistent basis, whether they have access to private information or not, since prices should reflect *all* information.

Financial Panics and Stock Market Crashes

One of the more damaging pieces of evidence against market efficiency and rationality is the repeated occurrence of manias, panics, and crashes throughout the history of financial markets. Financial panics were a regular part of life for investors throughout the eighteenth and nineteenth centuries. Crashes or panics of various proportions occurred in 1763, 1772, 1792, 1810, 1816, 1819, 1825, 1836, 1847, 1873, 1890, and 1907. Many of these events have a disconcerting modern ring. For example, the panic of 1825 and the crisis of 1890 both involved defaulting Latin American securities. Often, a market crash was followed by a severe depression—as in 1873 and 1890. Other market slides were

---

[29] See D. J. Fowler and C.H. Rorke, "Insider Trading Profits on the Toronto Stock Exchange, 1967-1977," *Canadian Journal of Administrative Sciences*, (March 1988), pp. 13-24; and, M.H. Lee and H. Bishara, "Recent Canadian Experiences on the Profitability of Insider Trades," *Financial Review*, (May 1989), pp. 235-249.

stopped dead in their tracks. In 1907, for example, J.P. Morgan, upon hearing that the market was crashing, stormed onto the floor of the New York Stock Exchange and began buying vast amounts of stocks until prices returned to levels with which he was satisfied.

The best-known stock market crash occurred in October 1929, with Canadian stock markets tracking those of the U.S. The 1920s bull market in the United States reached a peak on September 7, 1929 when the Standard and Poor's Index hit 254. A modest decline in real industrial activity was already under way, with indices of industrial and factory output showing slight drops since June. The subsequent moderate market decline became a crash on Black Thursday, October 24, 1929, as panic selling consumed the markets. J.P. Morgan who had single-handedly stopped the panic of 1907 was dead, but his successors at the Morgan bank did undertake a massive buying effort to stabilize prices, and the steep slide was halted temporarily. On October 25, President Hoover announced "the fundamental business of the country is... on a sound and prosperous basis."[30] Panic selling resumed on October 28, and the decline accelerated on Black Tuesday, October 29, 1929. A short-lived recovery in late 1929 was followed by a sustained fall in prices. When the market hit bottom in July 1932, a typical stock was worth about one-tenth of its September 1929 value. Even more than the erased fortunes, the devastating depression of the 1930s made the crash of 1929 a momentous economic event.

Most popular accounts, such as John Kenneth Galbraith's *The Great Crash of 1929*, present a picture of lemming-like irrationality.[31] A buying mania pushed prices far above fundamentals in the late 1920s, and irrational panic caused the crash, implying a very inefficient stock market. A number of business historians have argued that things are more complicated than that. Some of the most prominent economists of the time felt that the price increases in the 1920s were entirely rational in an economy adapting to such new technologies as electricity, automobiles, and the radio. They held that the boom of the 1920s could have resumed quickly had wrong-headed government policies been avoided. The detailed arguments fill volumes, and certainly are beyond the scope of our discussion.

Advocates of market efficiency can (and do) argue that in 1929, investors simply foresaw the coming depression (including government reactions) and consequently adjusted their expectations of future dividends downward. This resulted in rapidly falling prices. Since people's expectations cannot be measured, this view can never be proved nor disproved. Supporters of an efficient market view of the crash must, however, explain why it was that everyone's expectations were revised on October 24, rather than, in say, August or November. Perhaps a combination of the various weakening of the fundamentals, together with an element of mania, is a reasonable explanatory compromise.

Stock markets throughout the world boomed in the mid-1980s. On Black Monday, October 19, 1987, stock markets around the world began to tumble. The first were in Asia, followed by those in Europe and finally the markets in the United States and Canada. Asian markets declined further on the twentieth, upon the news that U.S. markets had crashed. Politicians and journalists were quick to blame the crash on financial innovations

[30] Quoted in B. Malkiel, *A Random Walk Down Wall Street*, 5th ed. (New York: W.W. Norton, 1990), p. 49.
[31] See J. Galbraith, *The Great Crash of 1929* (Boston: Houghton Mifflin, 1955).

such as computer-directed program trading. It turned out, however, that stock markets in countries where program trading was widespread (Canada, France, Japan, the UK, and the U.S.) actually fell less than in countries where such trading was not prevalent. As in discussions of the 1929 crash, most commentators concluded that a speculative bubble had burst. Advocates of efficient markets again point to a sudden revision of expectations about future dividends. However, as with the 1929 crash, it is hard to see why the revision took place on October 19 rather than at some other date since no major news about changes in fundamentals was released on October 19.

9.8 CONCLUDING REMARKS

For a free-enterprise economy to function well, it is critical that markets be informationally efficient or at least not grossly inefficient since, as information processing mechanisms, they are fundamental coordinating devices for all economic activity. In this context, capital markets are especially important because the availability of capital determines which enterprises will grow and which will stagnate. In efficient markets, investors will correctly judge which new ventures should get funded, and will only make money available if adequate returns can be expected. Essentially, as in any other auction market, investment funds go to the highest bidder—in this case, to the venture promising the highest return for a given level of risk. Only if markets can correctly process information to select the most promising projects will economic welfare be served.

From the evidence above, some financial economists conclude that market efficiency is an unrealistic oversimplification. Others, viewing the same evidence, conclude that such efficiency is a self-evident truth. We take a compromise view. We regard market efficiency as a reasonable and useful concept. It is, however, a simplification that should not be carried to extremes. The stock market seems to be fairly efficient in general, but it may be influenced by investor psychology as well. As we discussed, however, if changes in mass psychology are difficult to predict, prices may still follow a random walk. Occasionally, when psychological factors come to dominate the market, manias and crashes can ensue.

It can be argued that the market is always efficient in the sense that stock prices always do reflect investors' expectations of future earnings and discount rates, however irrational those expectations may appear in hindsight. In our opinion, this trivializes the concept of market efficiency and deprives it of most of its importance. A major reason market efficiency is of interest to corporate finance is because it implies that managers ought to pay attention to the signals they receive from market prices. The importance of those signals stems from a belief that security prices reflect the calm and considered opinions of rational investors.

Finally, it is reasonable to expect that different markets might display different degrees of efficiency. Markets that are the centre of attention for a large number of sophisticated traders are likely to be more efficient than those attracting the interest of only a few local investors. Thus, the shares of large firms might be priced more efficiently than those of smaller companies. Furthermore, stocks might be priced more efficiently than real estate or art, while debt securities and currencies might be priced more efficiently than stock. Finally, U.S. stocks might be priced more efficiently than Canadian stocks, although we have no actual evidence of this.

   In summary, market efficiency is a good working hypothesis for describing financial markets and many others as well. However, it should not be viewed as an exact description of the real world, and the extent to which it fits actual markets is still a matter of intense debate and individual opinion.

SUMMARY   9.9

1. Various degrees of market efficiency, such as weak, strong, and semi-strong forms can be distinguished.

   - Weak form efficiency implies that market prices incorporate all the information that can be inferred from previous price movements.

   - Semi-strong form of market efficiency implies that market prices incorporate all publicly available information.

   - Strong form efficiency implies that all existing information is incorporated in current prices.

2. As in any other area of business, consistently superior returns can be achieved only through sustainable competitive advantage.

3. The random walk theory postulates that stock price movements are inherently unpredictable.

4. For investors, the existence of efficient markets implies that no benefits are to be derived from researching individual securities since all available information is already reflected in the price.

5. Both investors and corporate managers must pay careful attention to the concepts of market efficiency. "Playing the market" and reliance on expert advice may often not provide the consistent returns claimed or desired.

QUESTIONS AND PROBLEMS

Questions for Discussion

1. You judge the market to be semi-strong form efficient. Discuss whether your legal trading of stocks over the next few days, in search of abnormal returns, is likely to be influenced by:

   - the release of drilling results through an official announcement earlier in the day

   - a respected investment dealer's newsletter indicating a downward revision to the forecast of a particular company's earnings

- a casual comment by a corporate director over lunch about a major, impending environmental lawsuit against her company
- yesterday's announced cut in a particular company's cash dividends

Would any of your answers be different if, in your view, the market was only weak form efficient?

2. Discuss the real estate market in your area. How efficient does it appear to be? What sort of information is embodied in land prices? How do you explain land price changes in recent years?

3. In an inefficient stock market, one company may have its stock overvalued and another, its stock undervalued. The overvalued firm would be able to issue new stock at a price higher than its "true" worth and vice versa for the undervalued one. Given this, discuss how market inefficiency can result in a misallocation of society's resources.

4. As a chief executive officer, would you be content if your performance was judged solely on the price performance of your firm's stock? Discuss.

5. How efficient would you expect the market to be for the following commodities: (a) gold, (b) oil, (c) wheat? Discuss.

6. What statistical studies and techniques may one use to determine whether stock prices do indeed follow a random walk?

7. What are some of the difficulties in evaluating the performance of any investment manager? How would you evaluate an investment fund manager if you believed in market efficiency?

8. "In an efficient market, the price of a security is equal to the present value of its future expected cash flows. Because of this, there is no benefit to buying a security if the market is efficient." Discuss whether this statement is true or false.

9. Briefly describe and contrast fundamental and technical analysis. Under what conditions would each be of benefit to investors?

10. A friend of yours makes the following statement: "I have been watching a particular stock for a while, and now is the time to buy. It has gone up every day for the past seven days straight, so everybody knows it is going to go up again tomorrow." Comment on this statement with respect to market efficiency.

11. An actively managed mutual fund uses investment professionals to choose stocks, hoping to outperform the overall stock market. An index mutual fund simply buys the stock in a particular stock index and therefore attempts to perform at exactly the same level as the market. Because of the extra effort involved, actively managed funds charge higher fees to investors. If the stock market is efficient, which type of fund would be better for investors to choose? What if the stock market was not efficient?

12. Describe growth stock and value stocks. Which perform better on average according to past empirical evidence? Does this evidence mean that one type of stock will always be a better investment than the other?

1. You are a junior analyst with the research division of a brokerage firm. As one of your assignments, you have been asked to estimate a value for BCE stock. From the BCE Annual Report you have gathered the following information:

	1999	1998	1997	1996	1995
Earnings per common (after extraordinary items)	$8.35	7.07	(2.53)	1.70	1.12
Dividends per common share	$1.36	1.36	1.36	1.36	1.36

Source: BCE Annual Report, 1999

You have also gathered the total returns on BCE stock for each of the past 60 months, as well as the return on the TSE 300 stock index:

Month	BCE total return	TSE 300 return	Month	BCE total return	TSE 300 return	Month	BCE total return	TSE 300 return
Oct-95	0.0493	-0.0054	Jun-97	0.0822	0.0543	Feb-99	0.1321	0.0177
Nov-95	-0.0110	0.0118	Jul-97	0.1194	0.0258	Mar-99	-0.0849	-0.0577
Dec-95	0.0252	0.0406	Aug-97	-0.0048	0.0417	Apr-99	0.1401	0.0582
Jan-96	0.0563	0.0222	Sep-97	-0.0514	-0.0175	May-99	-0.0117	0.0663
Feb-96	0.0340	0.0487	Oct-97	0.0479	0.0563	Jun-99	0.0332	-0.0149
Mar-96	-0.0253	-0.0086	Nov-97	-0.0194	-0.0220	Jul-99	0.0528	0.0297
Apr-96	0.0537	0.0093	Dec-97	0.1263	-0.0369	Aug-99	-0.0225	-0.0232
May-96	0.0710	0.0233	Jan-98	0.0515	0.0087	Sep-99	-0.0342	0.0075
Jun-96	0.0177	0.0213	Feb-98	-0.0158	0.0091	Oct-99	0.0837	0.0064
Jul-96	0.0162	-0.0247	Mar-98	0.1123	0.0575	Nov-99	0.2358	0.0325
Aug-96	0.0138	-0.0122	Apr-98	0.1292	0.0671	Dec-99	0.1583	0.0747
Sep-96	-0.0208	0.0315	May-98	0.0771	0.0175	Jan-00	0.1649	0.0535
Oct-96	0.1207	0.0506	Jun-98	0.0406	-0.0314	Feb-00	0.3779	0.1240
Nov-96	0.0166	0.0374	Jul-98	-0.0425	-0.0124	Mar-00	-0.0211	0.0285
Dec-96	0.0908	0.0553	Aug-98	-0.0546	-0.0909	Apr-00	-0.0124	-0.0330
Jan-97	-0.0105	0.0031	Sep-98	-0.1316	-0.1421	May-00	0.0150	0.0308
Feb-97	0.0805	0.0397	Oct-98	-0.1677	-0.0378	Jun-00	-0.1539	0.0364
Mar-97	-0.0461	0.0029	Nov-98	0.2648	0.1556	Jul-00	0.0358	0.0578
Apr-97	-0.0568	-0.0534	Dec-98	-0.0028	-0.0028	Aug-00	-0.0739	0.0268
May-97	0.1138	0.0513	Jan-99	0.0997	0.0354	Sep-00	0.0075	0.0786

Source: Datastream

(a) Estimate the beta for BCE stock. Comment on your findings. Does this beta seem to make sense for a firm of this type? Compare your beta to the beta for BCE from Table 8.1 in the text. What might account for any differences?

(b) Calculate the required return for BCE stock based on the capital asset pricing model (CAPM)

(c) Estimate the growth rate of dividends three different ways:

1) based on past growth in dividends over the last five years;

2) past growth in earnings per share over the past five years;

3) and a sustainable growth rate based on the dividend payout ratio and return on equity. (You will have to look at the BCE financial statements in the appendix to calculate ROE.)

Using each of these growth rates, estimate the value of a share of BCE stock. Assume that the growth rate remains constant in the future. Comment on the suitability of each growth rate estimate and come up with a final estimate of value for BCE.

(d) Look up in the newspaper the current price per share of BCE stock. Based on this and your estimate in part (c), would you issue a buy, sell or neutral recommendation to your clients? What warnings might you give to your clients about your analysis (i.e., comment on the weaknesses in the analysis you have performed).

2. You are working in the finance department of BCE. The firm would like to get an idea of the average yield on its long-term debt. The table below contains details on the various bond issues that BCE and its subsidiaries have outstanding. However, since many of these issues are not widely traded, you cannot simply look up the current market prices for them. Based on current yields for government-issued bonds and estimated risk premiums, you have estimated what the yield to maturity should be for each issue (the yield is contained in the table).

(a) For each issue, calculate the current market price of the bonds.

(b) Calculate the total *market* value of all long-term debt. For each bond issue, calculate a weight equal to the market value of that issue divided by the total market value of all the issues. Based on these weights, calculate a weighted average yield for BCE's long-term debt.

For all the bonds, assume that coupons are paid semi-annually. Also assume that today is the beginning of 2000, and all bonds are due at the end of their maturity year (e.g., bonds due in 2002 have exactly two years to maturity; bonds due in 2003 have exactly three years to maturity etc.).

Issuer	Issue	Maturity	Face value (millions)	Estimated yield (%)
BCE Inc.	6.2% Notes	2007	300	6.32
Bell Canada	7.41% debentures	2001	171	6.38
	7.69% debentures	2002	323	6.40
	6.86% debentures	2003	497	6.45
	10.88% debentures	2004	207	6.41
	8.17% debentures	2010[a]	3,254	6.64
	9.21% debentures	2035[a]	1,425	6.70
	8.21% subordinated debentures	2028	275	6.80
	Other[b]	-	97	6.00
CGI and BCE Emergis	Other[b]	-	39	6.00
BCE Media	11.59% Notes	2001	50	8.38
	10.75% Notes	2002	75	8.40
	7.4% Notes	2006	150	8.50
	Other[b]	-	45	6.00
BCI	Floating rate note[c]	2002	346	8.30
	14% Senior notes	2004	226	8.40
	11% senior unsecured notes	2004	160	8.70
	9% debentures[d]	2004	212	8.80
	14.13% senior bonds	2005	367	8.44
	Other[b]	-	561	6.00
Total			8.780	

Source: *BCE Annual Report,* 1999

[a]These issues actually mature at various dates in the future; the maturity given is an average.

[b]"Other" refers mostly to lease obligations, other types of equipment financing, and bank debt. Assume that these things are valued at face value.

[c]Floating rate notes have coupon rates that change and are always equal to current market rates. Therefore, these notes always sell for face value.

[d]The coupon rate given is an average of a number of similar issues.

p a r t

Long-Term Investment Decisions

This section of the text considers the capital budgeting decisions made by firms, focusing on the valuation of non-financial assets such as investments in new plant and equipment. If companies want to maximize shareholder wealth, the criteria they apply to the evaluation of their investments must be consistent with the valuation preferences of investors in financial markets. Hence, the capital budgeting chapters are intimately related to, and build on, the concepts developed in Chapters 5 through 8. In Chapter 10, we introduce the basic framework for capital budgeting. In Chapter 11, we develop further procedures for evaluating risk within the firm, and in Chapter 12, additional topics in capital budgeting are reviewed.

Weighing Costs Against Returns Involves Both Calculation and Negotiation

Whether they know it or not, Kelowna, British Columbia is where millions of young people from across North America turn regularly for help in directing their futures.

Kelowna boasts the headquarters of pioneer e-learning company Bridges.com, the market leader in providing on-line career planning tools to North American middle and secondary schools. The company's market-leading resources, which include Career Explorer (CX Online) and the Choices line of product, provide service to over two million students in Canada and the United States.

The company is in the process of rapid expansion, both increasing the range of products it offers and broadening the market for its existing products. Rapid revenue growth over the past five years has earned Bridges.com recognition as one of Canada's fastest-growing technology companies; it placed 9th on the Canadian Technology Fast 50 list for 2000.

Rapid growth is great—but it comes with management challenges, such as careful allocation of capital. Michael Mooney, Executive VP for Information Technology, gives an example. Bridges.com currently realizes more than 80 million annualized Web page views on its self-directed career resources, and the number

increases daily. "As our server load increases as a result of increased traffic at our website," says Mr. Mooney, "we might decide to expand our server room capacity." This is an expensive proposition, and not one to be taken on lightly.

The decision, like so much in business, "involves weighing costs against returns," Mr. Mooney explains. "So our first step is to determine the costs. Some of these are known. We do a requirement analysis and determine the system architecture (which is like the blueprint for the new system). We then add the cost of the necessary new hardware and software, and any subcontracting fees. Then there are internal labour costs—we need to think about what parts of the job we can do in-house. Finally, there are more hidden costs, such as increased overhead and maintenance, that need to be factored in."

"Next we figure out the other half of the equation: the return on investment. There are several 'ROI drivers' for a project such as this." Mr. Mooney lists increased efficiency (how much will the new system make life easier for future programmers?), mitigation of technical risk (how much more reliable will it be?), and increasing the rate of growth (how much faster will it enable the company to get new products to market?).

All these factors and more "go into the mix" of internal rate of return calculations. Some can be calculated exactly; others have to be judged on more of a "gut feel." Ultimately, says Mr. Mooney, it "comes down to the negotiation around the boardroom table" as management balances the expected rate of return against the costs.

chapter 10

Capital Budgeting: Basic Framework

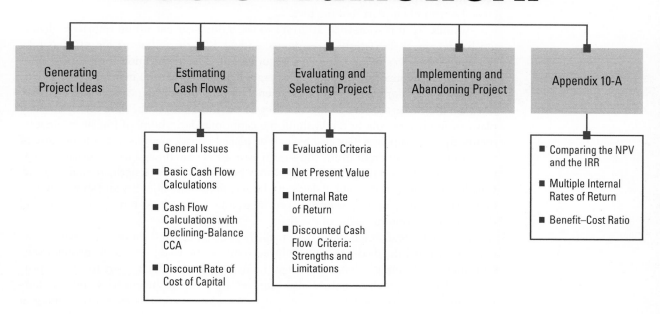

Learning Objectives

After studying this chapter, you should be able to:

1. *Explain net present value (NPV), how it is calculated, and why.*
2. *Discuss why generating project ideas and estimating cash flows are important?*
3. *Discuss the differences between operating profit, net profit, and cash flows in evaluating new investments.*
4. *Discuss the internal rate of return (IRR), how it is calculated, and why and how it differs from net present value.*
5. *Discuss some of the limitations of discounted cash flow criteria.*

10.1 INTRODUCTION

In this and the following two chapters, we examine the firm's capital expenditure decisions—that is, investment in projects expected to generate returns for more than one year. Examples include additions to plant or equipment, introduction of new products, or expenditures such as exploration and development by companies in natural resource industries. Short-term investments such as seasonal allocations to inventories and accounts receivable are considered as part of working capital management and are discussed separately in Part 8 of the text.

Admittedly, it is somewhat arbitrary to use a one-year cut-off on returns to distinguish long- from short-term investments, and we recognize that certain projects may not lend themselves readily to such categorization. The justification for treating long-term commitments of funds under a separate heading is that the managerial problems they raise differ significantly from those encountered in working capital management. For example, because cash flows accrue over an extended period, the time value of money plays an important role in establishing the economic desirability of long-term investments. Special emphasis may also have to be placed on risk analysis not only because of the uncertainties inherent in any long-term forecast of cash flows, but also because a significant percentage of the firm's resources may be committed for lengthy periods of time. Finally, whereas working capital decisions largely determine liquidity and short-run viability, capital budgeting decisions are crucial to establishing long-term profitability and therefore the economic value of the firm.

Note that the distinction we have made between long- and short-term investments does not parallel the distinction made by accountants between fixed and current assets. Consider, for example, a long-term investment in a new product. Apart from new production facilities, such a venture also requires additions to inventories and accounts receivable to support new sales. These investments in current assets form an integral part of the capital budgeting decision since the new product could not be launched without them, and they are expected to help produce returns over an extended period of time.

The relative magnitude of capital assets to total assets varies between industries. For example, this ratio is low in retailing, in which large sums are tied up in inventories and accounts receivable, and it is high in the telecommunication and energy sectors, which are characterized by massive investments in plant and equipment. Similarly, capital investments required to support a given level of sales vary widely. Data for selected Canadian industry categories is presented in Table 10.1.

Table 10.1

Median Ratios of Capital Assets to Total Assets and Capital Assets to Annual Sales for Selected Categories of Canadian Industries (1999)

Industry category	Capital assets as a proportion of total assets	Capital assets as a proportion of annual sales
Resource-based	0.73	1.84
Manufacturing	0.42	0.39
Retail & wholesale	0.27	0.09
Service	0.11	0.11

Source: Standard & Poor's Compustat Database, April 2000.

The discussion above emphasizes that the economic evaluation of capital expenditure decisions by firms should be consistent with the valuation processes that take place in financial markets. Only such consistency will ensure that the firm maximizes shareholder wealth. Essentially, we evaluate capital investments by discounting their cash flows to obtain a net present value, with the discount rate and risk adjustment determined by conditions that prevail in financial markets. There are, however, a number of institutional and conceptual complexities that need to be understood in order to apply this basic framework properly.

To structure our discussion, it is useful to recognize several distinct steps or phases in the capital budgeting process:

- Generating Project Ideas
- Estimating Cash Flows
- Evaluating and Selecting Projects
- Implementing and Abandoning Projects

We discuss each of these topics in turn.

GENERATING PROJECT IDEAS   10.2

Generating good project ideas is critical for success in capital budgeting, and in a competitive environment, it is not easy to find superior investments. Successful companies are often built around innovative concepts or ideas. For example, the rapid growth of Nortel Networks over the past few years can be attributed to the company's leadership position in providing optical infrastructure to the fast-growing segments of the Internet industry. In order to maintain this competitive strength, Nortel has continued to make substantial long-term investments in this area. The report below is excerpted from a newspaper article that suggests a significant portion of this investment has been accomplished through the acquisition of "early-stage companies with leading-edge technology."[1]

Ultimately, a firm should pursue only businesses in which it can create sustainable advantages. In a truly competitive environment in which everyone has the same capabilities, no company will be able to earn superior returns for its shareholders since in a world of perfect competition, investments tend to have a net present value of zero. Therefore, the achievement of superior returns hinges on the ability to have skills and/or resources that competitors cannot easily replicate and to use them to outperform competitors on at least some front.

There are two ways in which firms commonly build competitive advantages. Some gain an edge by differentiating themselves. They offer something that is not readily available elsewhere. Others become low-cost producers by operating more efficiently than their rivals. Through differentiation, firms may command a premium in price; through efficiency, they may reduce their costs. In either case, the firms achieve superior profits and as a result, can provide above-average returns to shareholders.

---

[1] We examine mergers and acquisitions in detail in Chapter 26. As we shall see, acquisitions represent a special type of capital budgeting decision; however, the basic framework developed in this section of the text is applicable.

■ *Finance in the News*

Nortel's Fibre-Optic Plan Becoming Clear

Nortel Networks Corp. purchased Xros Inc. for $3.4 billion in stock to bolster its presence in the fibre-optic market, which analysts are predicting will grow strongly over the next five years. This was just the latest move in the intense competition between Nortel and Lucent Technologies of New Jersey and Cisco Systems Inc. of San Jose, California for the lead in the transmission of voice, data, and video traffic over the Internet. Clarence Chandran, president of Nortel's service provider and carrier group, predicted that the fibre-optic market will explode to between $35 and $40 billion by 2004.

Xros is just one of the firms with "bleeding-edge technology"—that is, potentially lucrative technologies in development but no actual revenue—that are targets for Nortel, Cisco, and Lucent as they jockey for the lead in the fibre-optic race. Dan McLean of IDC Canada Ltd. noted "that in order to remain in a fast-growing market, Nortel, Lucent and Cisco must be willing to buy early-stage companies with leading-edge technology." All three are committed to fibre optics as the way of the future and will continue to acquire innovators.

Source: "Nortel's Fibre-Optic Plan Becoming Clear," by Mark Evans, *Globe and Mail*, March 15, 2000, page D5. *Reprinted with permission.*

10.3 ESTIMATING CASH FLOWS

General Issues

Next to generating good project ideas, estimating cash flows that result from new investments is probably the most critical prerequisite for successful capital budgeting. Invariably, such forecasting of cash flows over long periods of time is difficult. If, for example, a new product is to be launched, forecasts of the following variables must be made several years into the future:

- expenditures on new production facilities
- sales quantities and product prices
- possible effects of the new product on the sales of existing lines
- operating expenditures
- additional investments required in working capital

These forecasts must include estimates of future price-level changes and, when sales involve foreign markets, possible shifts in foreign exchange rates. With each forecast, uncertainties must be considered and quantified because risk affects economic value. Finally, all these individual projections have to be combined into overall cash flows that determine the attractiveness of the investment to the firm. The following are some general issues that commonly arise in the derivation of cash flows.

Relevance of Marginal or Incremental Cash Flows

In evaluating an investment, we compare the cash flows resulting from the new investment compared to what the firm would earn if the new investment were rejected. Hence, we are interested in the *marginal* or *incremental* effects that a new investment will have on the *total* operations of the firm. If, for example, the installation of a new machine allows you to sell the old model, your net investment will be the new purchase price less the receipts from the sale of the old machine. If a company introduces a new product, the sales of which will cut into the market of an existing product, the resultant decrease in existing revenues needs to be recognized. Further, when the new product can be produced in part on existing equipment that is idle because of excess capacity, the question arises whether the new investment should be charged for using this equipment. The answer hinges on what other opportunities the firm has for using the idle machines, and the concept of **opportunity cost** becomes relevant. If the firm expects a return to full production in the near future, the new product should be charged with such future expenditures as might be required to replace "borrowed" capacity. Even if the firm never expects to use the machines again, recognition should be given to any potential resale value. Finally, as indicated earlier, cash flows should encompass both the funds committed to the acquisition of fixed or long-term assets and any additions to current assets that may be required to support the proposed investment.

Time Horizon

Some investments such as equipment have limited and reasonably well-defined economic lives. Other projects such as a product line or an entire operating division of a firm may have an indefinite lifespan. Consider the case in which a firm invests in a new line of business by acquiring another company that becomes one of its divisions. The initial outlay will result in subsequent cash inflows that may continue indefinitely.

When an investment has a potentially long life, we have to determine the period of time over which forecasted cash flows are to be included in the analysis. We must also recognize that predictions are likely to become increasingly uncertain the further we move into the future. One approach is to specify a particular cut-off date and to ignore all cash flows beyond that time. Although arbitrary, this method is frequently used because of its simplicity. As we saw in Chapter 5, future cash flows that are discounted across reasonably long time spans have greatly reduced present values. Hence, if present values are relied on for investment evaluation, errors due to a neglect of cash flows that occur in the distant future may not be that significant.

Alternatively, and paralleling our discussion of future dividend streams in Chapter 6, we could assume constant annual cash flows beyond a certain time or perhaps cash flows that grow at some constant rate (e.g., at the rate of inflation) indefinitely. We could then determine the present value of such forecasts.[2]

---

[2] This assumptoin is often used in practice because it greatly simplifies the analysis, as we shall see later in this chapter.

Intangibles

Costs and benefits that are difficult to quantify in monetary terms are often referred to as intangibles. Rather than trying to provide for them quantitatively in cash flow forecasts, they are frequently noted in just a qualitative manner at the end of an investment proposal. Intangibles are often associated with benefits derived from research and development, marketing and public relations efforts, improved information systems, and enhanced organizational or management capabilities.

In many of these areas, hard numbers are difficult to find, and judgement often plays a dominant role. However, in deciding whether an investment should be accepted or rejected, such intangibles invariably have to be traded off against dollar amounts. The real issue is not whether intangibles are comparable to dollars since such comparisons are unavoidable, but, rather, who should make them. It could be the analyst drawing up the proposal or the final granting authority within the firm. No standard procedures can be offered because the optimal approach depends on the importance of the decision, on how knowledgeable various levels of management are, and on management's willingness to delegate.

External Effects

External effects are benefits or costs that accrue to units outside the firm as a consequence of the firm's investment decisions. Examples include recreational benefits of mining or logging roads that accrue to the general public or the costs of pollution that often are not fully borne by the polluters. With regard to external benefits, there is little debate as to their treatment in investment evaluations. They will generally be excluded from the firm's evaluation process since the investment has to be justified on the basis of benefits that accrue to the investor.

A more difficult issue is how, for example, the costs of pollution, which are largely shifted to the community, should be accounted for in evaluating the construction of a new smelter or pulp mill. It can be argued that in a free-market environment, a firm cannot afford to go beyond such basic requirements as are imposed on all competitors, for to do so could jeopardize its ability to compete. This suggests that it is the role of government to impose regulations that are binding on all concerned. Carrying the argument one step further, in markets that are competitive internationally, multinational co-operation may be called on to ensure both adequate and reasonably uniform regulation.

The situation may be different for corporations with significant market powers and, more particularly, for monopolies and Crown corporations. It can be argued that public utilities, for instance, should include consideration of external costs in their analysis of investment projects to ensure that such projects are in the best interests of society. The increased threat of legal and/or political action by parties that may suffer as a consequence of corporate activities or negligence is forcing firms to recognize potential externalities in their evaluations. Since shareholders are harmed if the firm is hit with major lawsuits or receives bad publicity, managers' traditional role of protecting shareholders' interests is pushing them to consider social costs and benefits more closely.

Effects of Price-Level Changes

In estimating cash flows, we have to decide how to provide for price-level changes that may occur over time. The relative prices for various goods and services may shift over time, and the general level of prices may increase as a result of inflation. Relative price changes always have to be included in cash flow forecasts. For example, if we expect labour costs to rise in relation to costs for equipment and machinery, that may provide an incentive to automate. We obtain valid investment evaluations only if such expectations are fully reflected in the projected cash flows of the various alternatives under consideration.

The issue of general inflation and how to account for it is somewhat more complex because it affects not only future cash flows, but also the time value of money at which discounting takes place. In order to simplify our presentation, we ignore general changes in the purchasing power of money for the time being and defer a discussion of inflation to Chapter 12.

Financial Charges and Taxes

Financial charges incurred in funding investments generally should not be included in cash flow forecasts. As will be explained shortly, the reason for that is that financing charges (such as interest on debt or returns expected by shareholders) are reflected in the *discount rate* that is applied when evaluating an investment. Hence, to avoid double counting, financial charges should not be considered in the project's cash flows. However, all cash flows should be on an *after-tax basis* since only after-tax dollars accrue to the investors.

Assumptions

Forecasts of future cash flows are based on a variety of assumptions both about the general environment and about the specific project. It is important that general assumptions that affect a variety of projects be made in a consistent manner; otherwise, projects cannot be compared in a meaningful way. For example, assumptions about future growth in the economy, price-level changes, or foreign exchange rates should be centrally specified and uniformly applied. Only project-specific assumptions such as future sales levels for a proposed new product should be made locally. In any event, all major assumptions on which cash flow projections are based ought to be clearly stated in any project proposal. As we will discuss in Chapter 11, sensitivity analysis regarding key assumptions is very useful for assessing the risks inherent in an investment.

Forecasting the cash flows to be generated by an investment can be a difficult task requiring sound judgement and may hinge on many assumptions. In reviewing various techniques for investment evaluation, we should bear in mind that even the most sophisticated approaches ultimately depend on the quality of subjective inputs, and regardless of the evaluation criteria used, poor forecasts are likely to result in poor investment decisions.

Basic Cash Flow Calculations

We now turn to the detailed calculations of the relevant cash flows. Specifically, we illustrate how the concept of incremental cash flows is applied and discuss the effects of **capital cost allowance (CCA)** and taxes in the derivation of net cash flows. In order to simplify our initial discussion, we assume that CCA expenses are charged on a *straight-line* basis, but this will seldom, if ever, be the case in practice. However, we defer our discussion of the *declining-balance* system of CCA as it generally applies in Canada until the following section.

Suppose a firm wants to purchase a new machine that costs $30,000. Its expected economic life is five years with an estimated salvage value of zero at the end of that time. The new machine is expected to generate before-tax net operating revenue of $9,000 annually, and the corporate tax rate is 40 percent. We assume that the machine can be depreciated on a straight-line basis over the five years. We want to isolate the net cash flows that would result from the new investment and ultimately decide whether the anticipated operating savings warrant the initial outlay.

The initial investment is $30,000, and deductions for CCA, based on straight-line deductions, are $30,000/5=$6,000 per year. To determine subsequent annual net cash flows, we need to take into account depreciation and its impact on tax payments. For many readers, this will be familiar from introductory accounting courses.

In arriving at taxable income, businesses may deduct CCA on depreciable assets. Through CCA deductions, provision is made for an investor to recover over some time frame the original amount invested without having to pay tax on that portion of proceeds. In other words, the investor can over the life of the project claim a series of tax deductions. The total amount claimed will eventually equal the original investment.

The term **depreciation** is sometimes used to denote the economic deterioration of an asset as a consequence of its productive use. CCA deductions are more narrowly defined as the depreciation claimed for tax purposes. As we will see, these two concepts can differ substantially, but in everyday usage, both terms are often used interchangeably. We follow this common practice through the book, drawing a careful distinction in those few places in which it is required.

With a given increase in net operating revenue (defined as all revenues from operations minus all operating expenses excluding taxes and CCA deductions), net after-tax cash flows for each year can be derived in two equivalent ways.

Alternative 1 for computing net cash flows:

Net operating revenue

Less: CCA

Taxable income

Less: Taxes payable

Net income or profit

Add: CCA

Net cash flow

Thus, net cash flows are determined by adding non-cash charges (CCA) back to net profits.

Alternative 2 for computing net cash flows:

Net operating revenue

Less: Tax on net operating revenue

After-tax net operating revenue

Add: Tax savings from CCA

Net cash flow

After computing tax on the full amount of net operating revenue, we add back the tax savings available from being able to claim CCA as a tax-deductible expense.

The preceding two methods for computing cash flows are equivalent, making the choice of which to use one of computational convenience.[3]

Computing the annual cash flows for our numerical example using Alternative 1 as follows:

Operating savings (or increase in net operating revenue)	$9,000	10,000
Less: CCA	6,000	4,000
Taxable income	3,000	6,000
Less: Tax payable (@40 %)	1,200	3,000 @40%
Net income	1,800	3,000
Add: CCA	6,000	4,000
Net incremental cash flow	$7,800	7,000

With Alternative 2, we obtain the same results as follows:

Operating savings (or increase in net operating revenue)	$9,000
Less: Tax on operating revenue (@40 %)	3,600
After-tax operating revenue	5,400
Add: Tax shield from CCA (40 % × CCA)	2,400
Net incremental cash flow	$7,800

The overall net after-tax cash flows for our example become:

	Years	
	0	1 to 5
Cash flows	−$30,000	+$7,800

Informally, we now define the net present value as the present value of all future incremental after-tax cash flows minus the initial incremental after-tax cash outlay or:

Net present value= − initial after-tax cash investment+present value of after-tax cash flows.

---

[3] Mathematically, this equivalence is easy to show. Letting T=tax rate, OR=operating revenue, NI=net income, and CF=net cash flows, we have $CF=(OR-CCA)(1-T)+CCA=OR(1-T)+(T\times CCA)$.

Assuming a time value of money of 10 percent and using the figures above, we obtain a total net present value for this example of:

$$\text{Net present value} = -\$30,000 + \$7,800 \times \left[\frac{1 - \dfrac{1}{(1.10)^5}}{0.10} \right]$$

$$= -30,000 + 7,800 \times [3.791] = -\$430$$

The negative net present value indicates that this investment falls short of providing the necessary 10 percent return.

Figure 10.1 clarifies the relationship between after-tax profits and net cash flows.[4] It is apparent from the diagram that CCA deductions are a part of the total cash flows available to the firm. In arriving at taxable income, CCA is a tax-deductible expense, and consequently, it reduces taxes payable. However, it is an expense that is simply an accounting entry with no corresponding cash outflows. Taxes are the only portion of cash flows that leave the firm.

FIGURE 10.1

Relationship Between
Cash Flows and Profits

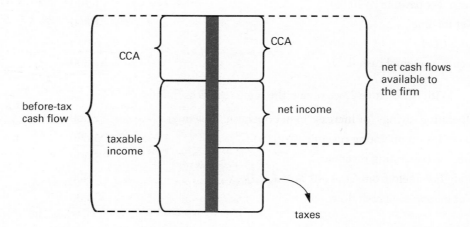

The cash flows that remain within the firm can be split into two components: CCA expense, which reflects the somewhat discretionary recovery over time of the original amount invested; and cash flows in excess of capital cost allowances, which are termed net income or profit after taxes. It is the sum of these two, or the total after-tax cash flows, that we use as the basis for investment evaluations.

Before we discuss the meaning and use of net present values in greater detail, we introduce the system of declining-balance CCA as it applies in Canada. The underlying concepts regarding CCA and the basic method of deriving after-tax cash flows remain

---

[4] We use the terms profit, income, and earnings interchangeably.

identical to those discussed in the simplified preceding example. The calculations, however, become more complex because the capital cost allowances and therefore the net operating cash flows are different in every year.

Cash Flow Calculations with Declining-Balance CCA

For the student who has not covered the topic in previous accounting courses, the general rules for the system of declining-balance capital cost allowance as it is used in Canada are set out in Appendix I of this text. In this section, we introduce only the key provisions and apply them to the derivation of cash flows that result from a capital investment. Major features include the following:

- Assets are grouped into classes, and CCA is charged against the aggregate book value of the class rather than on individual assets. In the year of acquisition, the claim is generally limited to one-half of the amount otherwise allowable. The rationale is that investments are undertaken throughout the year, and that it would be unnecessarily generous to allow a full claim for the first year for an asset that was acquired near year end. This provision complicates the otherwise straightforward formulas for declining-balance capital cost allowance. To simplify our exposition, we assume for all formulations and illustrations that follow that asset acquisitions are made at the beginning of the year and that CCA is claimed at year end. Different assumptions will alter the formula for finding the present value of the total tax shield, which is discussed momentarily.

- Different rates at which CCA is claimed apply to different asset classes.

- Typically, when an asset is purchased, its purchase price is added to the aggregate value of the asset class. Conversely, when an asset is sold, its selling price is subtracted from the asset pool.

- Each year, CCA is claimed at a constant percentage of the aggregate value in the asset class. The resulting pattern of book values over time is shown and contrasted with straight-line depreciation in Figure 10.2.

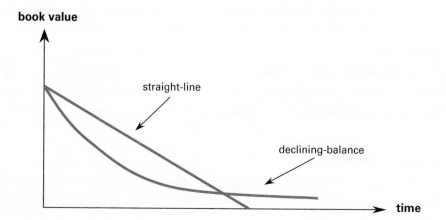

FIGURE 10.2

Book Value as a Function of Time

The system of declining-balance CCA and its effects on investment cash flows is illustrated in the following numerical example. A firm operates a machine purchased five years ago, which, if currently sold, would be worth $100,000. The machine is expected to last five more years, at which time it will have no residual value. A new and improved version of the equipment that could replace the old model is now on the market for $130,000. Its expected economic life is five years with an estimated salvage value of zero at the end of that time. Operating costs are $15,000 per year for the old machine, whereas the new machine would only require $9,000 annually. Both machines belong to the same asset class, and CCA can be charged at a rate of 30 percent on the declining balance. The corporate tax rate is 40 percent. Once again, we want to isolate the net cash flows that would result from the new investment over the next five years and to decide whether the anticipated operating savings warrant the initial outlay.

Initial Investment

If the new machine is acquired, the old one can be sold. Hence, the net or marginal investment in the new machine becomes $130,000 − 100,000 = $30,000 (cost of the new machine minus current market value of the old machine).

Operating Cash Flows

Continuing with the example, the incremental before-tax operating savings from investing in the new machine are $15,000 − 9,000 = $6,000 per year for years 1 to 5. To determine the investment's net cash flows, we need to derive the amounts of CCA to be claimed and the resulting tax savings (tax shields) in each year.

Effects of Capital Cost Allowance

If the new machine is acquired and the old one is sold, the resulting change in the undepreciated capital cost (UCC), or book value, of the asset class is as follows:

UCC of asset class	BV_{before}
Less: Proceeds from sale of old machine	$100,000
Add: Purchase price of new machine	$130,000
Equals: UCC of asset class after transactions	BV_{after}

That is:

$$BV_{after} = BV_{before} + \$30,000$$

As detailed above, when an asset is sold (purchased), its selling (purchase) price is generally subtracted from (added to) the UCC of the asset class, and future CCA claims are taken on the new asset value for the class.[5] In our example, we add a net $30,000 to

---

[5] We assume that there are always enough assets in the class so that a particular sale will not empty the asset class; otherwise, more complicated tax adjustments such as recapture of capital cost allowance or terminal losses may be necessary.

the asset class. Remembering that in year 1 only half the normal amount can be claimed, the incremental capital cost allowance that results from this addition is detailed below for the first five years:

Year	Incremental UCC at beginning of year (1)	CCA expense (2)=(1)×30%	Incremental UCC at year end (3)=(1)−(2)
1	$30,000	$4,500[6]	$25,500
2	25,500	7,650	17,850
3	17,850	5,355	12,495
4	12,495	3,749	8,746
5	8,746	2,624	6,122

We can now compute the annual net cash flows for the investment, using the two approaches outlined in the previous example. Using Alternative 1 we obtain:

	Year				
	1	2	3	4	5
Operating savings (or increase in net operating revenue)	$6,000	$6,000	$6,000	$6,000	$6,000
Less: CCA	4,500	7,650	5,355	3,749	2,624
Taxable income	1,500	(1,650)	645	2,251	3,376
Less: Tax payable (40%)[7]	600	(660)	258	900	1,350
Net income	900	(990)	387	1,351	2,026
Add: CCA	4,500	7,650	5,355	3,749	2,624
Net incremental cash flows	$5,400	$6,660	$5,742	$5,100	$4,650

With Alternative 2 we obtain the same results as follows:

	Year				
	1	2	3	4	5
Operating savings (or increase in net operating revenue)	$6,000	$6,000	$6,000	$6,000	$6,000
Less: Tax on operating revenue (40%)	2,400	2,400	2,400	2,400	2,400
After-tax operating revenue	3,600	3,600	3,600	3,600	3,600
Add: Tax shield from CCA (40%)	1,800	3,060	2,142	1,500	1,050
Net incremental cash flows	$5,400	$6,660	$5,742	$5,100	$4,650

---

[6] As set out in Appendix I, the maximum claim for CCA in year 1 is $Cd/2$ and in year n, $Cd(1-d/2)1-d)^{n-2}$, where $d=CCA$ rate, and $C=$original capital cost of the asset. The UCC at the end of year 1 is therefore $C(1-d/2)$, whereas at the end of year n, it is $C(1-d/2)(1-d)^{n-2}$. In this example, $C=\$30,000$, and $d=30\%$, so CCA for year 1 is $(\$30,000)(0.30/2)=\$4,500$. Therefore, UCC at the end of year 1 is $(\$30,000)(1-0.30/2)=\$25,500$.

[7] A negative taxable income results in tax savings when applied against income from other sources.

Considering only the first five years after investment, the net cash flows for an investment in the new machine are given as:

	Year				
	0	1	2	3	4	5

	0	1	2	3	4	5
Net incremental cash flows	−$30,000	$5,400	$6,660	$5,742	$5,100	$4,650

Present Value of Tax Shields from Declining-Balance CCA

Deriving CCA expense on a declining balance makes the computation of annual cash flows cumbersome since the process may go on indefinitely. In our example, at the end of year 5, we still have a UCC of $6,122, which will continue to be written off at 30 percent per year on a declining balance conceptually indefinitely.

The resulting tax savings in subsequent years cannot be ignored. Fortunately, it is easy to derive a formula for the total present value of the tax savings (or tax shields) due to CCA. This formula can then be used in the overall evaluation of investments. We use the notation and the concepts covered in Appendix I, in which we derive the following formulas for declining-balance capital cost allowance:

CCA claimed in year n: $Cd(1-d/2)(1-d)^{n-2}$

Tax shield from CCA in year n: $CdT(1-d/2)(1-d)^{n-2}$

where C is the starting value (or capital cost) of the asset, d is the rate at which capital cost allowance is taken, and T is the corporate tax rate. Given a discount rate k, the present value of all tax shields from CCA claimed on an asset is equal to the discounted sum of the individual tax shields for each year. Recalling that the tax shield from CCA in year 1 is $CdT/2$, it is easy to show that:[8]

(10.1) $$\text{Present value of CCA tax shield} = \frac{CdT}{(d+k)}\left[\frac{1+0.5\times k}{1+k}\right]$$

Applying this formula to our example and assuming a discount rate of 10 percent, the present value of the total tax shield from CCA, conceptually taken *ad infinitum*, becomes:

$$\text{Present value of CCA tax shield} = \frac{30,000\times.30\times.40}{(.30+.10)}\left[\frac{1+0.5\times.10}{1+.10}\right] = \$8,591$$

---

[8] The present value of the total tax shield from $CCA = \dfrac{CdT}{2(1+k)} + \dfrac{CdT(1-d/2)}{(1+k)^2} + \dfrac{CdT(1-d/2)(1-d)}{(1+k)^3} + \cdots$

$+ \dfrac{CdT(1-d/2)(1-d)^{n-2}}{(1+k)^n} + \cdots = \dfrac{CdT}{2(1+k)} + \dfrac{CdT(1-d/2)}{(1+k)^2}\left(1 + \dfrac{1-d}{1+k} + \dfrac{(1-d)^2}{(1+k)^2} \cdots + \dfrac{(1-d)^{n-2}}{(1+k)^{n-2}} + \cdots\right)$

Using the standard formula for deriving the sum of an infinite geometric series, the above expression simplifies to Equation 10-1.

This present value of the total tax shield associated with depreciating a capital investment can be used in the analysis of capital expenditure decisions. It eliminates the need for computing separate annual tax savings over the life of a project.

Total Cash Flows and Present Value of the Investment

We are now in a position to compute the total present value of all relevant cash flows associated with the investment. In order to be able to use Equation 10-1, we take the present value of after-tax operating revenues and add the present value of the CCA tax shield along the lines discussed above in Alternative 2 for computing cash flows. The total present value for all cash flows generated by the investment becomes:

Net present value = −initial investment+present value of after-tax operating savings
+present value of total tax shield from CCA

$$= -30,000 + (3,600 \times \left[\frac{1 - \frac{1}{(1.10)^5}}{0.10} \right]) + 8,591$$

$$= -30,000 + [3,600 \times 3.791] + 8,591$$
$$= -\$7,761.40$$

Effect of Salvage Value

To illustrate further the concepts introduced, we now assume a residual or salvage value $S_5 = \$20,000$ for the new machine at the end of year 5. If an asset is expected to be sold at the end of n years for S_n, this salvage value is deducted from the UCC of the asset class at the time of disposition, reducing the CCA deductions in subsequent years.[9] Ignoring the half-year-rule considerations at the time of disposition, a total tax shield is lost, with a present value at the end of year n of: $\dfrac{S_n dT}{(d+k)}$.

Discounted back to the present, this amounts to:

$$\text{Present value of lost } CCA \text{ tax shield due to salvage value} = \left[\frac{S_n dT}{(d+k)} \right] \left[\frac{1}{(1+k)^n} \right]$$

Combining this with Equation 10-1, we obtain a more generalized formula for the present value of the CCA tax shield associated with an asset acquisition:

$$\text{Present value of CCA tax shield} = \frac{CdT}{(d+k)} \left[\frac{1+0.5 \times k}{1+k} \right] - \left[\frac{S_n dT}{(d+k)} \right] \left[\frac{1}{(1+k)^n} \right] \qquad (10.2)$$

---

[9] As noted earlier, this assumes that other assets are in the asset class with an aggregate UCC exceeding S_n. If no other assets are in the class or if the salvage value exceeds the aggregate UCC of the asset class, the tax treatment is more complicated since recapture of capital cost allowance and capital gains or terminal losses may have to be recognized, as outlined in Appendix I.

This formula is commonly used to evaluate the present value of CCA tax shields for capital budgeting purposes.

Applying Equation 10-2 to find the new present value of the CCA tax shield for our example above, assuming a salvage value of $20,000, we obtain the following:

Present value of CCA tax shield=

$$\frac{30,000\times.30\times.40}{(.30+.10)}\left[\frac{1+0.5\times.10}{1+.10}\right]-\left[\frac{(20,000\times.30\times.40)}{(.30+.10)}\right]\left[\frac{1}{(1.10)^5}\right]$$

$$=8,591-3,725=\$4,866$$

Combining this result with the incorporation of the present value of the estimated cash flows to be received from the salvage value, we obtain the following net present value:

Net present value = −initial investment+present value of after-tax operating savings
+present value of total tax shield from CCA+present value of salvage value

$$= -30,000+[3,600\times3.791]+4,866+\frac{20,000}{(1.10)^5}$$

$$= -30,000+13,648+4,866+12,418$$

$$= +\$932$$

Notice how the present value is now positive due to the present value of the expected salvage value.

Denoting the annual incremental increase in net operating revenue as R_t, the formula used to derive the above result can be expressed as a comprehensive equation to determine the net present value of an investment, as expressed below:

Net present value $(NPV)=$ −initial investment+present value of after-tax operating savings
+present value of total tax shield from CCA+present value of salvage value

$$(10.3)\qquad NPV=-C+\sum_{t+1}^{n}\frac{R_t(1-T)}{(1+k)^t}+\left[\frac{CdT}{d+k}\right]\left[\frac{1+.5k}{1+k}\right]-\left[\frac{S_ndT}{d+k}\right]\left[\frac{1}{(1+k)^n}\right]+\left[\frac{S_n}{(1+k)^n}\right]$$

When the operating cash flows are assumed to be equal, therefore representing an annuity, Equation 10-3 reduces further to:

$$(10.4)\qquad NPV=-C+R_t(1-T)\left[\frac{1-\frac{1}{(1+k)^n}}{k}\right]+\left[\frac{CdT}{d+k}\right]\left[\frac{1+.5k}{1+k}\right]-\left[\frac{S_ndT}{d+k}\right]\left[\frac{1}{(1+k)^n}\right]+\left[\frac{S_n}{(1+k)^n}\right]$$

These two formulas are very commonly applied to solving capital budgeting problems.

The Discount Rate or Cost of Capital

We know from the discussion in previous chapters that the returns a firm's investments generate must be commensurate with the returns investors expect when they provide funds to finance these projects. We saw that investors are risk averse and trade off risk against expected returns. They are willing to make money available for risky investments but only if those investments promise higher expected returns.

Each project a firm undertakes contributes both risks and expected returns to the firm as a whole, which are ultimately borne by the firm's investors and creditors. Hence, when managers evaluate a new project, they should decide whether the expected returns it adds to the firm's cash flows are sufficient to compensate for the added risk investors must bear. In other words, one should ask how a new investment could be financed if it were a stand-alone proposition and what return would be required in today's financial markets to make money available given the project's risk. This required return is the firm's cost of capital to fund the project. It is the discount rate managers should use to derive the present value of the cash flows the investment is expected to generate. If a project produces more than the return investors require, it should be undertaken. If not, it should be passed by. In Chapter 8, we discussed in detail the extra return investors demand for bearing additional risk. We return to this topic and its application to the evaluation of risky capital investments in the following chapter.

A new project is often similar in risk to the firm's current business. In that case, the expected return the firm's investors are currently demanding can be used to evaluate the project, and the firm's current cost of funding its overall operations becomes the appropriate discount rate.

Most firms have reasonably well-defined policies regarding their capital structure, and they rely on various sources of funds (for example, debt and equity) in relatively constant proportions over time. If we know these proportions and the costs of each individual source of funds as currently reflected in financial markets, we can calculate a weighted average cost of capital for the firm. This average cost of capital represents the overall cost of financing the firm's new investments, and it is commonly used as the discount rate in capital budgeting evaluations. It is calculated on an after-tax basis and applied to the project's forecasted after-tax cash flows since both firms and investors are interested in after-tax wealth. If an investment is to provide an economic gain, it must at least cover these financing costs. A more detailed discussion of the firm's weighted average cost of capital and how it is derived is provided in Chapter 15.

As we already noted, since the costs of financing are reflected in the discount rate, they should not be included in the derivation of a project's cash flows. Thus, in evaluating a project's economic desirability, we first derive its cash flows without regard to any financing charges that may be incurred in funding the project. We then apply the costs of financing as a discount rate to see whether the project can support itself.

10.4 EVALUATING AND SELECTING PROJECTS

Evaluation Criteria

Once we have estimated cash flows, the next step in the capital budgeting process is to evaluate the project and decide whether it should be selected or rejected. There are several ways of doing this. The criteria commonly used, at least by larger and more sophisticated firms, recognize the time value of money and are based on the concept of discounting. For that reason, they are called discounted cash flow criteria. The most prevalent ones are the net present value, the internal rate of return, and the benefit–cost ratio (or profitability index). The net present value and the internal rate of return are discussed in this section. The benefit–cost ratio, which is primarily used in the public sector, is reviewed in the Appendix to this chapter.

Net Present Value (NPV)

The **net present value (NPV)** is defined as the sum of all cash flows generated by a project, with each cash flow discounted back to the present. The discount rate used is generally given by the firm's after-tax cost of capital. In equation form, the net present value is expressed as:

$$(10.5) \qquad NPV = \sum_{t=0}^{n} \frac{C_t}{(1+k)^t}$$

where:

C_t is the net after-tax cash flow (inflows minus outflows) in period t, and it is positive for net inflows and negative for net outflows

k is the discount rate used by the firm, typically represented by its weighted average cost of capital (or opportunity cost of investments foregone if capital rationing applies)

n is the number of periods comprising the expected life of the investment

For the typical investment and with capital cost allowances taken on a declining balance, this equation expands into Equation 10-3 as presented in the previous section. Applied to the numerical example of this section, we calculated a net present value of $932 for the investment (assuming a salvage value of $20,000 and a cost of capital of 10 percent).

The rationale for the NPV approach stems from the fact that an investment has to earn at least the costs incurred in funding it if it is to be considered attractive. A positive NPV indicates that a project contributes cash flows to the firm in excess of the costs required to finance it. These additional cash flows accrue to the benefit of the owners of the firm. It follows that projects with a positive NPV should be accepted because they enhance the value of the firm, and the amount of the NPV indicates conceptually the increase in shareholder wealth that accrues as a consequence of the investment.

Given its importance, it is useful to reinforce the economic meaning of the NPV through an additional simplified illustration.

CALCULATING NPV

Consider a project that requires an initial investment of $10,000 and which subsequently generates net cash inflows of $4,000, $5,000, and $6,000 assumed to occur at the end of years 1, 2, and 3.[10] Given a cost of capital of $k=10$ percent, we obtain:

Year	Cash flows (1)	Present value factors (2)	Present value of cash flows (3)=(1)×(2)
0	−$10,000	1	−$10,000
1	4,000	.909	3,636
2	5,000	.826	4,130
3	6,000	.751	4,506
		NPV=	$2,272

Alternatively,

$$NPV = -10,000 + \frac{4,000}{(1+.1)} + \frac{5,000}{(1+.1)^2} + \frac{6,000}{(1+.1)^3}$$
$$= \$2,272$$

The economic interpretation of this NPV is that the project is expected to generate a gain of $2,272 over and above the required return of 10 percent to cover financing charges that are levied each year on the unrecovered portion of the investment. Specifically, if the initial amount of $10,000 along with a return of 10 percent on any outstanding balance were to be repaid from cash flows subsequently generated, we would have:

Year	Investment outstanding at beginning of year (1)	Return on investment outstanding (2)=10%×(1)	Amount of inflow (3)	Repayment of investment (4)=(3)−(2)	Investment outstanding at year end (5)=(1)−(4)
1	$10,000	$1,000	$4,000	$3,000	$7,000
2	7,000	700	5,000	4,300	2,700
3	2,700	270	6,000	2,700*	0

*This leaves an additional amount of $3,030 in year 3. Thus, we can recover the initial investment, pay 10 percent each year on funds still tied up in the project, and in the third

---

[10] In Chapter 5, the possibility of discounting on a quarterly, monthly, or even continuous basis was noted. Annual discounting is, however, generally applied in capital budgeting and in most instances, yields sufficiently accurate results.

year given the $6,000 inflow, be left with a gain of $6,000-(2,700+270)=\$3,030$. The present value of this gain is $3,030/(1+.1)^3=3,030\times.751=\$2,276$, which equals the NPV of the project as computed above with the small difference between the two figures caused by rounding.

This example demonstrates that the NPV represents the amount by which the value of the firm increases as a consequence of undertaking the investment or the increase in shareholder wealth.

Internal Rate of Return (IRR)

Just as we did for financial assets in Chapter 6, we can also calculate the effective yield of capital investments. This effective yield is also called a project's **internal rate of return (IRR)**, and by definition, it is the rate of discount that when applied to the cash flows of an investment, will yield an NPV of zero. Arithmetically, it is the discount rate r that satisfies the equation:

$$(10.6) \qquad \sum_{t=0}^{n} \frac{C^t}{(1+r)^t} = 0$$

with the notation as defined earlier. Again, the IRR represents a project's yield before consideration of financing charges. If this yield exceeds the firm's after-tax cost of capital, the investment will generally make a positive economic contribution to the firm and to its shareholders. Therefore, it should be accepted.

To illustrate the derivation of the IRR, we first consider what is termed the **net present value profile** of an investment. This profile shows the NPV as a function of the discount rate applied.

EXAMPLE

NPV AT VARIOUS DISCOUNT RATES

Consider once again our previous example that called for an initial investment of $10,000, which was expected to generate net cash inflows of $4,000, $5,000, and $6,000 in years 1 through 3. We can compute the NPV for various discount rates as follows:

| Year | Cash flow | \multicolumn{4}{c}{Present value factors at discount rate} |
		0%	10%	20%	28%
0	-$10,000	1	1	1	1
1	4,000	1	.909	.833	.781
2	5,000	1	.826	.694	.610
3	6,000	1	.751	.579	.477
Net present values		$5,000	$2,272	$276	-$964

The resulting NPV profile is shown in Figure 10.3.

It is easy to see that the shape of the NPV profile will be similar for all investments that involve an initial outlay and subsequent inflows. The initial outlay is unaffected by discounting, whereas the present value of future cash inflows decreases as the discount rate rises. Hence, the NPV of a project typically decreases as the discount rate increases. Assume that the cash flows are such that a discount rate of zero yields a positive NPV (in other words, the total undiscounted cash inflows exceed the initial outflows). By increasing the discount rate, we decrease the NPV until at some stage, the NPV becomes negative. In the preceding example, the IRR is roughly 22 percent (the point at which the NPV profile crosses the horizontal axis in Figure 10.3).

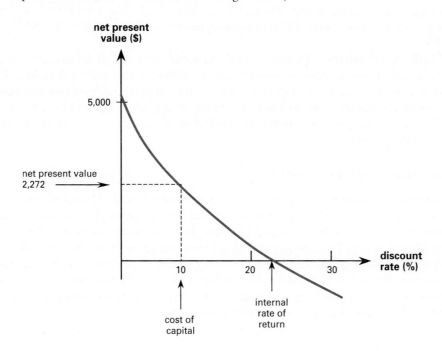

FIGURE 10.3

Net Present Value Profile Showing Net Present Value as a Function of the Discount Rate

As we saw in Chapter 5, an exact computation of r is generally not possible since it would require the solution of Equation 10-6, which is a polynomial of the nth degree. However, with the aid of calculators or computer programs (such as Excel) that have pre-programmed functions, one can readily derive IRRs. Because the NPV generally is a steadily decreasing function of the discount rate, one can also obtain approximate solutions manually by trial and error and interpolation. To do this, start by choosing any reasonable discount rate and compute the NPV. If the NPV is positive, increase the discount rate for the next calculation since the flows must be further reduced and vice versa. Repeat the process until a discount rate is found for which the NPV is close to zero. With some experience at straddling the actual IRR and then working toward it by interpolating, one can usually derive a reasonably close solution after a few trials.

Referring back to Figure 10.3, we see that the NPV and the IRR generally yield equivalent results. If for a desirable project the NPV is positive using as a discount rate the cost of capital, this normally implies that the IRR exceeds the cost of capital. Because returns in excess of the cost of financing accrue to the owners of the business, the IRR criterion also supports the objective of maximizing shareholder wealth. In fact, the two techniques can often be viewed as equivalent ways of looking at the same problem. In one case (NPV), we discount at the cost of capital and focus on the total benefit to be achieved after meeting the cost of funds invested. In the other case (IRR), we ensure that the effective yield of the project exceeds its costs of financing. Hence, the particular criterion chosen becomes almost a matter of taste. Given that each criterion portrays information about a project in a somewhat different manner, most firms compute both the NPV and the IRR.

Conflicts between the NPV and the IRR can occur under special circumstances (e.g., when one has to choose between two projects of a different scale and/or duration). We will deal with such situations in the Appendix to this chapter and limit our discussion here to a simple example that demonstrates the superiority of the NPV (which measures actual economic gain) over the IRR (which calculates the effective percentage yield on monies in the project).

EXAMPLE

COMPARISON OF NPV AND IRR

You can invest in one of two projects. One project provides a yield of 25 percent over one year, and the other provides a yield of 20 percent over 10 years. Assume that normal investment yields in your business are 15 percent. It is intuitively clear that you prefer to obtain 20 percent over 10 years over receiving 25 percent for one year since after the first year, you would have to reinvest at the prevailing rate of 15 percent. The 10-year project will have the higher NPV and leave you better off even if it provides the lower initial yield or IRR. A parallel argument applies if you have to choose between investing $100 in a 25 percent project or $1,000 in one that yields 20 percent.

Discounted Cash Flow Criteria: Strengths and Limitations

The strengths of discounted cash flow (DCF) criteria are that they:

- tie control over the disbursement of funds to the conditions under which funds have to be procured
- can be related directly to the goal of maximizing shareholder wealth

We saw that the discount rate to be used is the firm's cost of capital, which should embody all financing charges associated with an investment. Therefore, acceptance of projects according to DCF criteria will ensure that returns are commensurate with the costs of funding new investments and that all security holders receive the expected return they demand when making funds available to the company.

We also showed that the NPV measures the residual gain over and above normal financing charges. This gain accrues to the firm's owners. It represents the value that management has obtained for shareholders through its investment decision. With large investments such as the acquisition of another firm, one sometimes can observe share price changes that are linked directly to the market's estimate of the NPV that was created.

At the same time, DCF criteria are not without limitations including:

- ignoring the potentially negative impact that investments may have on financial statements
- ignoring non-economic aspects that, nevertheless, may be important

Major investments may affect a firm's financial statements in various ways. They may influence the total amount and composition of its assets and liabilities as well as reported profits or earnings per share. For example, a project with a positive NPV may well have negative effects on reported earnings in the initial periods either because of heavy start-up expenses or because of significant depreciation charges. In a world of perfect information and rational investors, this would not be disturbing because shareholders would accept the early decline in profits, recognizing that they would be adequately compensated through favourable cash flows and earnings in later periods. However, the real world is typically characterized by imperfect or asymmetric information, the latter of which suggests that management possesses information not available to investors. As a result, any decline in reported earnings may be interpreted as a sign of weakness, and management's concern about the immediate effect of its decisions on the firm's published financial statements becomes understandable. A practical compromise frequently implemented is to rely primarily on DCF criteria; at the same time, however, new investments are considered only if they do not bring about any serious deterioration of reported performance.

PERSPECTIVES

Corporate Manager

It is important for managers to communicate the expected future benefits associated with investment decisions especially if these decisions affect the firm's present financial statements in an adverse manner.

Investor

The observation above highlights the limitations of accounting data and reinforces the idea that investors should focus on the expected future earnings and cash flows of the companies they wish to invest in rather than examining their past and present profitability only.

DCF criteria measure economic value. However, we recall from Chapter 1, that the actual objectives that businesses pursue are often more complex and may have added dimensions. Inasmuch as other objectives exist, sole reliance on DCF criteria has obvious limitations. For example, it may be difficult to justify investments that support employee safety or environmental protection on the basis of an NPV.

10.5 IMPLEMENTING AND ABANDONING PROJECTS

The involvement of the financial officer does not end with evaluating and selecting a project and assigning it to operating divisions for implementation. Important control and follow-up activities remain to be performed. Continuous budgetary control and progress reports, including revisions of forecasts at periodically scheduled intervals, are required both in order to spot difficulties in implementation and to facilitate prompt remedial action. Proposals are approved on the basis of best estimates, and variations are common once a project is initiated.

Related to the above is the need for periodic reappraisals of the project to determine whether it should be continued or abandoned. If unforeseen difficulties are experienced or if at any point the present value of forecasted cash flows falls below a certain set threshold, the project should be abandoned no matter how much money has already been spent. The concept of sunk costs may be difficult to accept psychologically, and the temptation may be to keep a project alive based on efforts already expended. However, this is analogous to the gambler who having already lost a substantial amount and not wanting to face that fact, is determined to keep playing until she breaks even. Generally, it would be better for the gambler to accept the loss and withdraw rather than risk losing even more. In practice, it is often difficult to abandon an existing project that has gathered momentum and to which people are attached. Nevertheless, a realistic assessment of ongoing projects, including the willingness to abandon where necessary, can make an important contribution to the success of a firm.

EXAMPLE

ABANDONMENT DECISION

Consider an ongoing project that is expected to generate net cash flows of $10,000 for each of the next five years. The firm's cost of capital is 16 percent. The firm has just been offered $40,000 for various assets that are used in this project. Should the firm continue with the project or abandon it?

Clearly, continuing or terminating the project are mutually exclusive alternatives. Assuming that there are no other costs or benefits in terminating the project, the present value of abandonment is $40,000. The present value of continuing is:

$$PV = \left[\frac{1 - \dfrac{1}{(1.16)^5}}{0.16} \right] \times 10,000$$

$$= 3.274 \times 10,000$$

$$= \$32,740$$

Therefore, the project should be abandoned.

EXAMPLE

Alternatively, we could have charged the continuation of the project with an opportunity cost of $40,000 (the lost opportunity of selling the assets). The project's NPV then becomes:

$$NPV = -40,000 + 32,740 = -\$7,260$$

Its IRR is derived from:

$$0 = -40,000 + \left[\frac{1 - \dfrac{1}{(1+r)^5}}{r} \right] \times 10,000$$

$$\left[\frac{1 - \dfrac{1}{(1+r)^5}}{r} \right] = 4.0$$

We find that $r \approx 8$ percent, which confirms our decision to abandon since this is well below 16 percent.

Many financial managers find that a post-audit of investment projects can provide useful feedback for reappraising the soundness of established procedures, and that can contribute to improving the performance of participating management at all levels.

Finally, it is possible to evaluate the "options" of shutting down or abandoning a project or even the firm using criteria similar to those developed in Chapter 18 for the analysis of stock options. Such an approach, however, is beyond the scope of this text.

SUMMARY   10.6

1. The NPV of a project is defined as the present value of all cash flows discounted at the firm's cost of capital. It measures the economic gain to be derived over and above the costs of financing a project.

2. In evaluating new projects, we are concerned with identifying marginal, after-tax cash flows excluding any financial charges.

3. Proper identification of cash flows include the choice of an appropriate time horizon, and the incorporation of anticipated price-level changes. The effects on operating profits and net profits stem are viewed from this context.

4. The IRR measures the effective yield of a project, which is then compared to the cost of funding the investment. It relies on the concepts of discounting and explicitly recognizes the time value of money.

5. IRR differs from net present value in only the way a problem is analysed. Both criteria usually produce the same investment decisions.

6. The purpose of discounted cash flow criteria is to measure economic gain. They may ignore other non-economic objectives that a firm may have as well as short-run effects of new investments on reported financial statements, in particular on reported earnings

APPENDIX 10-A

ADDITIONAL SELECTED TOPICS

Comparing the NPV and the IRR

The NPV and the IRR are probably the most widely advocated criteria for sound capital budgeting, and as we have seen, they usually provide equivalent results. However, under special circumstances, the two methods may produce conflicting project rankings. We illustrate the nature and underlying reason for such conflicts through a simplified example.

EXAMPLE

RANKING MUTUALLY EXCLUSIVE PROJECTS

Consider two mutually exclusive projects. Each requires an initial investment of $1,000 and generates subsequent after-tax cash inflows as follows:

Year	Project A	Project B
1	$1,200	0
2	0	0
3	0	$1,643

The firm's cost of capital is 12 percent. The IRRs and NPVs are readily computed as:

	Project A	Project B
NPV	$72	$170
IRR	20%	18%

Project A is preferred according to the IRR, whereas project B has a higher NPV. The conflict arises because the cash flows generated by the two projects have different time patterns, and the two evaluation techniques imply different assumptions regarding the rates at which cash inflows can be reinvested.

The nature of the problem in the example above becomes clear if we calculate the terminal wealth at the end of year 3 for each of the two projects under consideration. If Project A is chosen, the terminal wealth clearly depends on the rate at which the early cash inflow of $1,200 in year 1 can be reinvested. Given that this cash inflow will be invested for two years, the terminal values of Project A for various reinvestment rates become:

Reinvestment rate	Terminal values for Project A
12%	$1,200 (1.12)^2 = \$1,505$
17	$1,200 (1.17)^2 = 1,643$
20	$1,200 (1.20)^2 = 1,728$

These terminal values have to be compared with the cash inflow of $1,643 at the end of year 3 for Project B. We see that Project B is superior if the reinvestment rate is below 17 percent and vice versa.

Reliance on the IRR approach implies that funds released from any project can be reinvested at that particular project's IRR. If reinvestment is possible at a rate of 20 percent in the example above (Project A's IRR), an investor's wealth will indeed be maximized by choosing Project A. The NPV method, on the other hand, implies that cash flows released from any project are reinvested at the discount rate that was used in calculating its NPV. Applied to our example, Project B becomes the preferred choice if the reinvestment rate equals the firm's cost of capital of 12 percent.

NPV profiles can be used to provide a more generalized view of this problem.

NPV PROFILES FOR MUTUALLY EXCLUSIVE PROJECTS

EXAMPLE

Consider two mutually exclusive projects, C and D. Each requires an initial investment of $10,000 and generates subsequent after-tax cash inflows as follows:

Year	Project C	Project D
1	$ 2,000	$10,000
2	4,000	3,000
3	12,000	3,000

The firm's cost of capital is 12 percent. The NPVs and the IRRs are computed as:

	Project C	Project D
NPV	$3,518	$3,457
IRR	27%	38%

Figure 10.4 shows the NPVs as a function of the discount rate applied for both projects. As discussed earlier, the IRRs are given by the intersections of the two curves with the horizontal axis.

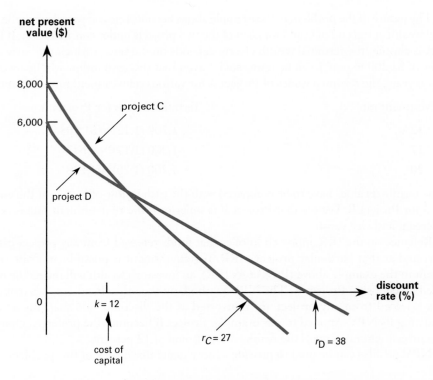

Contradictory rankings between the NPV and IRR criteria occur whenever the present value profiles of two projects cross over at some rate beyond or to the right of the cost of capital. In this instance, the crossovers are caused by differences in the time patterns of the projects' cash flows as illustrated in Figure 10.5. We note that conflicts may also occur because of a difference in scale between projects since the NPV as an absolute measure of investment worth varies with the size of the investment, whereas the IRR as a relative measure remains unaffected. This difference between absolute and relative measures of economic value is elaborated later in this Appendix.

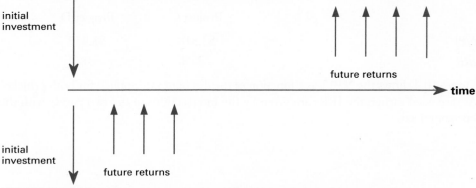

The NPV of Project C, with its more distant cash inflows, will be the more sensitive to changes in the discount rate. In applying a discount factor $1/(1+k)^t$, any increase in k is magnified by a large exponent t, and the resulting NPV profile is "steep." The relatively immediate cash returns of Project D, on the other hand, are much less sensitive to such change, which implies a "flatter" NPV profile with a more gradual slope. Given the different slopes of the two curves, it is easy to see why a crossover may occur.

Again, the desirability of Project D will depend on the rate at which its early cash returns can be reinvested. If this reinvestment rate is low, the larger but more distant cash returns of Project C will be preferred; as the reinvestment rate increases, Project D becomes progressively more attractive.

One possibility for resolving conflicts caused by contradictory rankings is to estimate the reinvestment rates that appear reasonable for the particular firm and to calculate terminal values for each investment project, as was done in one of our preceding examples. Although this approach is appealing conceptually, it is rarely implemented in practice. Estimating future reinvestment rates on a yearly basis for long time spans is a difficult task fraught with uncertainties that most managers shun. Instead, firms prefer to use currently observable discount rates and to apply them uniformly to all future cash flows under consideration.

If a choice between the two criteria is to be made, NPVs are generally superior to IRRs. An inconsistency of the IRR approach is the assumption that cash inflows from different projects can be reinvested at different rates depending on the particular project's effective yield. The NPV approach, on the other hand, assumes reinvestment of any cash inflows at one consistent rate for all projects. Moreover, there are good economic reasons for equating the assumed reinvestment rate with the discount rate used in NPV calculations. We saw earlier that the discount rate that a firm should apply is generally its cost of capital. We also saw that a firm should invest in all projects that provide a positive NPV or that yield returns in excess of the cost of capital. This implies that the returns on a firm's most marginal projects should be close to its cost of capital. Additional funds generated by the firm through its investments can be invested in such marginal projects or they can be used to pay back some of the capital that the firm has raised. In either case, the appropriate reinvestment rate in the absence of capital rationing is the firm's cost of capital.

Finally, it is reasonable to postulate that measures of economic value should be additive. That is, if we undertake two independent Projects A and B, the economic value of A and B together ought to equal the sum of the individual economic values:

Value (A+B)=Value (A)+Value (B)

The NPV, which as we saw measures the economic gain that an investment contributes to shareholders, possesses this property of additivity, whereas the IRR, which measures percentage returns, clearly does not. NPV additivity is particularly useful when having to select from among projects with different economic lives.

EXAMPLE

NPV ADDITIVITY AND PROJECTS WITH UNEQUAL ECONOMIC LIVES

Consider the production of red wines with the alternatives of ageing for either two, four, or six years. Assume that the NPVs of these three possibilities as stand-alone ventures are $15,000, $20,000, and $30,000 respectively. Producing the six-year wine offers the highest NPV. However, inside the six-year time span, it also would be possible to produce and sell outputs of both two- and four-year wines sequentially or just stay with two-year wines. Because of capacity constraints, these alternatives are mutually exclusive.

Evaluation of the above alternatives requires NPVs of various sequential alternatives to be discounted back to the present. For instance, the NPV of the four-year wine that would follow the production and sale of the two-year wine must also be discounted back to t_0. The following tabulation based on an assumed annual discount rate of 10 percent illustrates the point.

Alternative 1: six-year wine:

NPV_6 at t_0 = $30,000

Total NPV = $30,000

Alternative 2: sequential production of two- and four-year wines:

NPV_2 at t_0 = $15,000

NPV_4 at t_0 = $20,000/(1+0.1)^2$ = $16,529

Total NPV = 15,000 + 16,529 = $31,529

Alternative 3: sequential production of two-year wines only:

First NPV_2 at t_0 = $15,000
Second NPV_2 at t_0 = $15,000/(1+0.1)^2$ = $12,397
Third NPV_2 at t_0 = $15,000/(1+0.1)^4$ = $10,245
Total NPV = 15,000 + 12,397 + 10,245 = $37,642

Hence, sequential production of two-year wines with a total NPV of $37,635 is optimal. Only NPV analysis with its property of value additivity allows a meaningful comparison and appropriate recommendation for mutually exclusive projects with differing lives.

An advantage that is sometimes offered in defence of the IRR is that no discount rate need be specified in advance of any project evaluation. This point gains significance when we recognize that there can be substantial difficulties in estimating a firm's cost of capital, as will be detailed in Chapter 15. Such problems can be circumvented to some extent by ranking projects according to their IRRs. However, even then, it is necessary to establish a hurdle or cut-off rate that specifies the minimum return that a firm finds acceptable.

Multiple Internal Rates of Return

When an investment entails an initial cash outflow that is followed by cash inflows, the shape of its NPV profile will conform to the curve in Figure 10.3. Given that all future cash flows are inflows, the NPV decreases with increasing discount rates, and only one value for the IRR is possible. Such projects are characterized by one change in the direction or in the sign of cash flows over time. The initial investment (negative cash flow) is followed by subsequent returns (positive cash flows).

Some investments, however, can have more than one reversal of direction in the cash flows. Thus, we could start with an initial outlay followed by cash inflows, and at the end of the project's life, face cash outflows again. In strip mining, for example, costs may be associated with meeting legal requirements for restoring the environment after the ore body has been exhausted. Under such circumstances, a project can have two different IRRs, each of which satisfies the criterion of providing an NPV of zero.

MULTIPLE IRRs

EXAMPLE

We examine an often-cited example of an investment in a new pump that is larger than the one currently in use.[11] It would result in a larger immediate oil production but an earlier exhaustion of the supply. The net incremental cash flows from the investment are assumed to be as follows:

Year	Net cash flow
0	−$ 1,600
1	+10,000
2	−10,000

That is, the $1,600 investment in the pump shifts $10,000 of cash inflows from year 2 to year 1. It is easy to verify that this project yields IRRs of both 25 percent and 400 percent.

The reason for the multiple rates stems from the two reversals in the net cash flows that occur during the project's life. Using a zero discount rate, total outflows exceed total inflows, leaving a net balance of −$1,600. With positive discount rates, cash flows in the most distant period (year two) will be most heavily reduced. As these cash flows are negative, the NPV initially rises with increasing discount rates and at a discount rate of about 25 percent, discounted benefits start to exceed discounted costs. As the discount rate continues to increase, the cash inflow in year 1 is progressively more affected. The present value declines and again becomes negative. This is illustrated in Figure 10.6, which shows the project's NPV profile.

---

[11] See J. Lorie and L. Savage, "Three Problems in Capital Rationing," *Journal of Business* (October 1955), pp. 229-39 for the idea, and E. Solomon, *The Theory of Financial Management* (New York: Columbia University Press, 1963), pp. 129-30 for the numerical example.

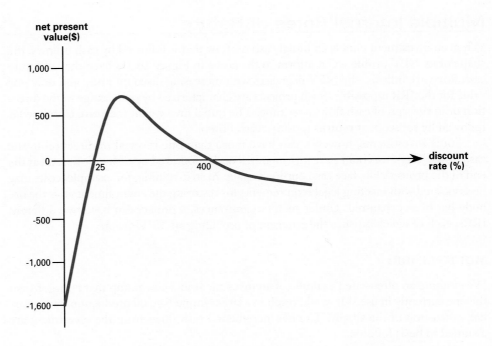

The interpretation of multiple rates is difficult, and mechanically derived results often are not meaningful economically. To illustrate, a full pattern of cash flows for our pump example might be given as shown in the following chart.

Year	With continued use of old pump	With new pump	Incremental cash flow on replacement
0	$ 0	−$ 1,600	−$ 1,600
1	$10,000	$20,000	10,000
2	10,000	0	−10,000

Given these figures, it is clear that the arithmetic solution does not provide a meaningful rate of return. By investing $1,600 in the new pump, the investor receives $10,000 one year earlier. The true economic desirability of the project again depends on the rate at which the $10,000 can be reinvested. Assume, for example, that the investor can earn 23 percent on the extra $10,000 received in year 1. This would provide an additional return of $2,300 in year 2. Under such circumstances, an economically meaningful IRR would be the discount rate that equates the initial investment of $1,600 with the extra return of $2,300 received in two years' time which is 20 percent.

We conclude that IRRs should not be relied on to evaluate investments that entail more than one change in the direction of their cash flows because this may give rise to multiple solutions.[12] As we saw in the previous section, the proper reinvestment rate for cash flow generated by a project is generally the firm's cost of capital. The NPV criterion is consistent with this reinvestment rate and hence, should be used. Unlike the IRR, it is unaffected by the particular pattern that cash flows may follow over time.

Benefit–Cost Ratio

A further criterion based on discounted cash flow analysis that is sometimes used is the **benefit–cost ratio** or **profitability index**. Particularly common in the public sector, it is defined as the ratio of a project's discounted net benefits over the initial investment. As with the NPV, the discount rate applied should reflect the cost of funds to the firm. Projects with ratios greater than 1 are acceptable, and larger ratios are favoured. In computing the benefit–cost ratio, the initial investment is placed in the denominator of the ratio, and subsequent discounted net inflows become the numerator. It is defined in Equation 10-7 below:

$$\text{Benefit–cost ratio} = \frac{\text{Present value (benefits)}}{\text{Initial outlay}} \qquad (10.\text{A}1)$$

BENEFIT–COST RATIO

EXAMPLE

Consider a project characterized by the following figures, where the cost of capital is 12 percent.

Year	Initial investment	Net cash inflows
0	-$12,000	
1		$6,000
2		6,000
3		6,000

We have:

$$\text{Benefit–cost ratio} = \frac{\left[\dfrac{1 - \dfrac{1}{(1.12)^3}}{0.12}\right] \times 6{,}000}{12{,}000}$$

$$= \frac{2.402 \times 6{,}000}{12{,}000} = 1.201$$

In comparing the benefit–cost ratio with the NPV, both methods generally yield equivalent results. The benefit–cost ratio is greater than 1 only if the present value of net benefits exceeds the initial investment, and this also ensures a positive NPV. Thus, both measures establish the same cut-off level. Conflicts can arise only when mutually exclusive projects are under consideration, in particular if the investments differ in terms of size.

---

[12] It can be shown that two or more reversals in an investment's cash flows are needed to produce multiple rates of return. However, not every project with more than one reversal in cash flows need result in multiple rates of return. In other words, more than one reversal of signs is a necessary but not sufficient condition for multiple rates. See G. D. Quirin and J. C. Wiginton, *Analyzing Capital Expenditures: Private and Public Perspectives* (Homewood, Ill.: Richard D. Irwin, 1981), pp. 97-98.

EXAMPLE

NPV VERSUS BENEFIT–COST RATIO

A firm that is considering purchasing a new machine receives two competing and mutually exclusive proposals. Cash flows have been estimated as follows:

	Project A	Project B
Initial investment	$50,000	$15,000
Present value of future net cash inflows	70,000	30,000

From these figures we obtain:

	Project A	Project B
NPV	$20,000	$15,000
Benefit–cost ratio	1.4	2

Project A is superior according to NPVs, whereas Project B has the higher benefit–cost ratio.

When conflicting rankings arise, the NPV is the better criterion because it measures the economic contribution of each project to the firm in absolute terms. The benefit–cost ratio like the IRR suffers from the usual limitations of percentages and index numbers in that it conceals absolute magnitudes. A project may have a high benefit–cost ratio but be small in terms of the absolute dollar amounts, in which case it could be less desirable than another opportunity characterized by a more modest ratio but a larger scale.

Pursuing the example above, we note that the initial investment in Project B is lower by $35,000 than the amount required to pursue Project A. The absolute economic contribution to the firm of choosing Project B depends on how these extra $35,000 can be invested. As was pointed out in previous sections, marginal investments should yield a return that is close to the firm's cost of capital, which implies NPVs that are close to zero. If, for example, the remaining $35,000 could be invested only to produce a net present value that is smaller than $5,000 (the difference in NPVs between Projects A and B), then the choice of Project B with its high benefit-cost ratio would have been wrong; the resulting economic contribution to the firm would be less than that available from Project A.

We conclude that in most practical situations, the benefit–cost ratio will produce the same results as the NPV. Both criteria can be computed and may supplement each other since they provide information regarding a project's relative and absolute profitability. However, NPV is superior in the evaluation of mutually exclusive investments that differ in size, and reliance on the benefit-cost ratio under such circumstances may lead to sub optimal decisions.

Note: All *asterisked* Questions and Problems relate to material contained in the appendix to the chapter.

QUESTIONS AND PROBLEMS

Questions for Discussion

1. Why are incremental cash flows rather than contributions to reported earnings the appropriate basis for evaluating investment projects? Should management or shareholders be concerned about earnings at all? Might a project with a positive net present value (NVP) make negative contributions to earnings? Explain.

2. (a) How can the government influence (stimulate or reduce) the attractiveness, and hence the level of business investments?

   (b) If the government provides for more generous capital cost allowances (CCA) what impact might this have on capital investments by industry? Explain.

3. We have seen that investment evaluations depend heavily on estimates of the future cash flows that a project may generate. Do you think that the people who are responsible for such estimates (managers or staff specialists) will always provide their best forecasts, or can you think of situations in which it would be in their best interest to introduce biases into their figures? Discuss.

4. Discuss some of the limitations of discounted cash flow criteria. What assumptions do we make when we advocate that investment decisions should be based solely on the NPV criterion? How realistic are these assumptions both for a firm and for an individual?

5. As the general manager of a firm, you are presented with an investment proposal from one of your divisions. Its NPV, if discounted at the cost of capital for your firm (which is 15 percent), is $100,000, and its internal rate of return (IRR) is 20 percent.

   (a) What are the economic interpretations of the NPV and IRR figures? In other words, what do they mean?

   (b) What, if any, additional information would you like to have before approving the project?

6. It has been said that many investment projects even in profit-motivated industries cannot be justified on a discounted cash flow basis. Examples cited include investments in antipollution devices, in improving employee safety and well-being, and in basic research and development. Do you agree? Discuss.

7. Some investments that a company undertakes will not produce a yield that exceeds the cost of capital. For example, some projects simply will not work out and will therefore produce losses. In time, these will have to be abandoned. Other projects such as investments for environmental protection are required by law and have to be undertaken even if they do not generate returns. Because of this, it has been argued

that the remaining projects will have to produce returns that are in excess of the firm's cost of capital if it is to be profitable. Thus, the yardstick by which the business judges the acceptability of new investments should not be the cost of capital but a figure that substantially exceeds the cost of capital. Do you agree? Carefully justify your position.

PROBLEMS WITH SOLUTIONS

Problem 1

A company contemplates the construction of a new production facility. Management wishes to determine the effective size of the initial investment (ignoring the tax shield of subsequent capital cost allowance). The building would be built on a piece of vacant land that the firm has owned for 10 years. When acquired, the land cost $200,000, but its current market value is estimated to be $1 million. The building itself can be erected for $350,000. Machinery worth $100,000 needs to be purchased. In addition, essential production equipment manufactured by one of the company's own divisions would be required. Production costs for this equipment are expected to total $50,000, and the equipment would have a ready market price of $60,000. Corporate taxes are 40 percent. Finally, additional investments of $30,000 in working capital (mainly inventories) are required.

Solution 1

In working toward a solution, we recognize that there are really two alternatives under consideration. Management may either build the facility or decide to pass up this particular investment. Therefore, we focus on the incremental cash flows attributable to building the facility as opposed to not doing so. If the new building were not erected, the land and the production equipment could be sold, and the following cash flows could be realized:

Receipts from sale of production equipment	$ 60,000
Less: Tax on profits from sale (60,000−50,000)×.4	4,000
Net cash inflow from sale of production equipment	56,000
Receipts from sale of land	$1,000,000
Less: Capital gains tax on profits from sale 1/2 (1,000,000−200,000)×.4	160,000
Net cash inflow from sale of land	840,000
Total potential cash inflows from sale of assets to be used in project (or total opportunity costs)	$896,000

It is immaterial whether or not the land is actually sold if the new facility is not constructed. The fact remains that the land could be sold, and if the project goes forward, the firm foregoes the opportunity of realizing cash inflows either from a sale or from an alternative use. Thus, the new project should be charged with such cash flows.

In building the new facility, we incur the following cash outflows:

Building	$350,000
Purchase of machinery	100,000
Investment in working capital	30,000
Total cash outflows relating to the new investment	$480,000

The effective size of the investment is given by the sum of the actual cash outflows of $480,000 and the cash inflows foregone by committing assets that could otherwise have been sold for $896,000 or a total of $1,376,000.

Problem 2

(a) A firm contemplates the purchase of a $10,000 machine that would save labour costs of $5,000 in each of years 1 and 2, and $6,000 in each of years 3 and 4. The machine is not expected to have a salvage value at the end of the fourth year, and capital cost allowance (CCA) on a declining balance may be claimed at a rate of 30 percent. If the company's tax rate is 40 percent and its cost of capital is 8 percent, calculate:

   (1) the net cash flows that the investment would generate during the first four years
   (2) the net present value (NPV) of this proposal
   (3) the internal rate of return

(b) Calculate the NPV of the proposal in part (a) if a salvage value of $1,000 is expected at the end of the four-year life of the machine.

(c) Assume that in order to stimulate investment, the government allows a fast write off on the machine with linear depreciation taken over two years. What is the NPV of the investment if the machine is expected to have no salvage value?

Solution 2

(a) (1) The cash flow in year zero is the initial outlay of $10,000. The inflows in years 1 through 4 are the after-tax labour savings plus the tax savings realized by claiming CCA. The schedule of CCA, the resulting tax savings, and the present value of the associated tax shields is provided in the table below.

Year	Undepreciated capital cost (1)	Capital cost allowance (2)	Tax savings (3)=40%×(2)	Discount factor at 8% (4)	PV of tax savings (5)=(3)×(4)
1	$10,000.00	$1,500.00	$ 600.00	.926	$ 555.60
2	8,500.00	2,550.00	1,020.00	.857	874.14
3	5,950.00	1,785.00	714.00	.794	566.92
4	4,165.00	1,249.50	500.00	.735	367.35
5	2,915.50	874.65	349.86	.681	238.25
6	2,040.85	612.26	244.90	.630	154.29
7	1,428.60	428.58	171.43	.583	99.94
8	1,000.02	300.01	120.00	.540	64.80
9	700.01	210.00	84.00	.500	42.00
10	490.01	147.00	58.80	.463	27.22
11 and subsequent					50.43
			Present value of tax shield =		$3,040.94

The cash flows for the first four years become:

	Year				
	0	1	2	3	4
Initial investment	−$10,000				
Before-tax labour savings		$5,000	$5,000	$6,000	$6,000
After-tax labour savings		3,000	3,000	3,600	3,600
Tax savings from CCA		600	1,020	714	499.80
Net cash flows	−$10,000	$3,600	$4,020	$4,314	$4,099.80

(2) The present value of all tax shields from CCA can be calculated by the formula:[13]

$$PV \text{ (CCA tax savings)} = \left[\frac{CdT}{d+k} \right]\left[\frac{1+.5 \times k}{1+k} \right]$$

$$= \left[\frac{10,000 \times .30 \times .40}{.30+.08} \right]\left[\frac{1+.5 \times .08}{1+.08} \right]$$

$$= \$3,041$$

The NPV for the project becomes:

$NPV=$ −initial investment+present value of after-tax inflows
+present value of tax shield CCA

$$= -\$10,000 + [\frac{3,000}{(1+.08)} + \frac{3,000}{(1+.08)^2} + \frac{3,600}{(1+.08)^3} + \frac{3,600}{(1+.08)^4}] + 3,041$$

$$= -10,000+[3,000(.926)+3,000(.857)+3,600(.794)+3,600(.735)]+3,041$$

$$= \$3,894$$

Instead of using the four separate present value factors to discount each annual inflow, we could view the operating cash flows as consisting of a two-year annuity of $3,000 (in years 1 and 2) and another two-year annuity of $3,600 (in years 3 and 4). In more complex problems with cash flows over many years, it may be advantageous to use this approach. We can rearrange the above equation as follows:

$$NPV= -10,000 + [3,000 \times \left[\frac{1-\frac{1}{(1.08)^2}}{.08}\right] + 3,600 \times \left[\frac{1-\frac{1}{(1.08)^2}}{.08}\right]\left[\frac{1}{(1.08)^2}\right]] + 3,041$$

$$= -10,000+[3,000(1.783)+3,600(1.529)]+3,041$$

$$= -10,000+[5,349+5,504]+3,041$$

$$= -10,000+[10,853]+3,041$$

$$= \$3,894$$

(3) The IRR is the discount rate r that provides an NPV of zero and satisfies the equation:

$$0= -10,000 + [3,000 \times \left[\frac{1-\frac{1}{(1+r)^2}}{r}\right] + 3,600 \times \left[\frac{1-\frac{1}{(1+r)^2}}{r}\right]\left[\frac{1}{(1+r)^2}\right]]$$

$$+ \left[\frac{10,000\times.30\times.40}{.30+r}\right]\left[\frac{1\times.5\times r}{1+r}\right]$$

The project's NPV for various discount rates is readily computed as follows:

Discount rate	0%	10%	20%	24%
NPV	$7,200	$3,234	$603	−$212

---

[13] Notice from the table above that the CCA tax savings accrue to the firm well beyond year 4. This fact is reflected in this present value tax-shield formula.

Interpolating, we find that the IRR is approximately 22.96 percent as shown below:

$$\frac{r-20}{24-20} = \frac{0-603}{-212-603} \text{ , so } \frac{r-20}{4} = 0.74, \text{ and } r = 22.96\%$$

(b) If the company receives $1,000 for the machine after four years, this inflow has to be discounted and added to the project's NPV. However, upon disposal of the machine, the undepreciated capital cost of the asset class will be reduced by $1,000. Consequently, at the end of year four, the present value of the tax shield lost owing to the disposal (assuming other assets remain in the asset class) becomes:

$$\left[\frac{(1,000)(0.30)(0.40)}{.30+.08}\right]\left[\frac{1}{(1.08)^4}\right] = \$232$$

Therefore, the project's net present value with salvage becomes:

$$NPV = NPV \text{ without salvage } + \frac{1,000}{(1+.08)^4} - 232$$

$$\uparrow \qquad\qquad \uparrow$$

PV of   PV of loss
salvage   of tax shield
inflow

$$= 3,894+735-232$$
$$= 3,894+503 = \$4,397$$

(c) Capital cost allowance of $5,000 will be claimed in both year 1 and year 2, resulting in tax savings of .4×5,000=$2,000 in each year. Net cash flows for the investment become:

	Year				
	0	1	2	3	4
Initial investment	−$10,000				
After-tax labour savings		$3,000	$3,000	$3,600	$3,600
Tax savings from CCA		2,000	2,000		
Net cash flows	−$10,000	$5,000	$5,000	$3,600	$3,600

The NPV becomes:

$NPV=$ −initial investment+present value of after-tax inflows+present value of tax shield CCA

$$NPV = -10{,}000 + 10{,}853 + \left[2{,}000 \times \left[\frac{1-\dfrac{1}{(1.08)^2}}{.08}\right]\right]$$

$= -10{,}000+10{,}853+[2{,}000\times1.783]$

$= -10{,}000+10{,}853+3{,}566$

$= \$4{,}419$

Problem 3

A firm operates a computer on which it has a five-year lease. The computer does not operate at capacity, and it is expected that this situation will prevail in the future. It is company policy not to rent spare computer capacity to outside clients. Management is currently investigating whether to develop a new computer program to automate certain aspects of production scheduling in the plant. Costs (before tax) of developing the program are estimated at $20,000. These costs would be capitalized, with CCA taken at a rate of 30 percent. In addition, a consultant would have to be hired at a fee of $3,000 with this amount being expensed in the current period. To recover its leasing costs, the company's computing centre normally charges departments for use of computer time at a rate of $200 per hour, and it would take 50 hours of computer time per year to run the above program. Savings (before tax) in production costs in the plant are expected to be $8,000 per year for five years if the new production-scheduling system is implemented. In addition, one of the machines that originally cost $20,000 and is currently required would no longer be needed and could be sold for $10,000. Assume that this machine belongs to the same asset class as the computer program under consideration and that there are other assets in this class. At the end of five years, it is expected that the entire production process will be obsolete. The firm's after-tax cost of capital is 15 percent, and the corporate tax rate is 40 percent. Should the program be developed if the evaluation is to be based on its net present value?

Solution 3

First, we isolate all relevant cash flows, specifying the time of their occurrence.

year 0	Initial cost of development	−$20,000
	After-tax cost of consultant ($3,000×0.60)	− 1,800
	Sale of old machine	+ 10,000
	Total initial outlay	−$11,800
years 1 to 5	Savings per year, after tax ($8,000×0.60)	+ $4,800

The present value of these savings is:

$$4,800 \times \frac{1 - \frac{1}{(1.15)^5}}{0.15} = 4,800 \times 3.352 = \$16,090$$

In addition, \$20,000 is added to the asset class with \$10,000 lost from the sale of the old machine for a net gain in depreciable assets of \$20,000 − \$10,000 = \$10,000. The present value of the tax shield from CCA will be:

$$\frac{10.000 \times .3 \times .4}{(.3 + .15)} \left(\frac{1 + 0.5 \times .15}{1 + .15} \right) = \$2,493$$

Note that leasing costs are not included in the analysis. Since it is company policy not to rent out spare capacity, the development of the new program has no effect on the leasing costs that the firm has to pay, which are essentially fixed. From the firm's point of view, there are no incremental cash flows with respect to leasing and hence, no opportunity cost.

We now compute the NPV of the program as:

$NPV = $ −total initial outlay + PV of production savings (after tax) + PV of the tax shield from additional CCA

$= -11,800 + 16,090 + 2,493$

$= \$6,783$

Problem 4

An investment criterion that was widely used in the past is the average or accounting rate of return (ARR). It is defined as:

$$\text{Average rate of return} = \frac{\text{average annual profits after tax}}{\text{average book value of investment}} \times 100\%$$

Profits are calculated ignoring financing charges, and normally straight-line depreciation is assumed in calculating the denominator. Use of the ARR is rapidly declining because it is easy to show that it generally produces misleading results.

Consider a new product line that requires an initial investment of \$100,000 and generates net operating revenue of \$40,000 per year for five years. The firm's tax rate is 40 percent. Assuming straight-line depreciation, calculate the ARR for the investment, and contrast it with the IRR.

Solution 4

Depreciation charges are $20,000 per year. We have:

Net operating revenue	$40,000
Less: Depreciation	20,000
Taxable income	$20,000
Less: Taxes payable	8,000
Net profit	$12,000

Net profit contributed by the investment is $12,000 per year, and the average book value over the life of the investment is:

100,000/2=$50,000

We obtain:

$$ARR = \frac{12,000}{50,000} \times 100\% = 24\%$$

In contrast, net annual cash flows from the investment would be $32,000 ($12,000 net profit+$20,000 depreciation). The IRR is calculated to solve the following expression:

$$0= -100,000 + \left[\frac{1-\frac{1}{(1+r)^5}}{r}\right] \times 32,000$$

which yields $r \approx 18\%$

It can be shown that the ARR generally overstates the true effective yield of any investment that has a limited economic life. Its weakness stems from the fact that it is based on average book values and accounting incomes rather than on cash flows.

ADDITIONAL PROBLEMS

1. The company is considering a project for which the total after-tax cash flows have already been calculated and the required return is 16 percent. The project will last 25 years, and the cash flows will be:

Year	Cash flows
0	−100,000
1	20,000
2	25,000
3	15,000
4	35,000

5	30,000
6 to 25	15,000

a) Calculate the NPV of this project.

*b) Calculate the profitability index of this project.

2. Last year, your firm paid $4,000 to a consulting outfit to recommend ways of increasing efficiency. The consultants have now given you their report, and they recommend the purchase of a particular piece of equipment for the factory. It would cost $1 million to purchase. It would also require $40,000 to be paid to the supplier in order to have the equipment installed, and $10,000 to a shipping firm to have the equipment delivered. The equipment would reduce labour costs by $210,000 per year for the five years that the equipment is operational. Costs of maintenance on the equipment are estimated to be $12,000 per year. The new equipment would require keeping an additional $12,000 in inventory on hand. In five years, the equipment would be sold for an expected $700,000 on the second-hand market.

   The equipment falls in an asset class with a CCA rate of 10 percent. The firm's tax rate is 35 percent. This equipment would take up a part of the factory that the has not been using. Prior to consideration of this equipment, the firm had considered renting out the space. It could get $6,000 per year in rent if it did not buy the equipment. If the firm could earn a return of 13 percent on other investments of equal risk, should it purchase this equipment?

3. You are an entrepreneur who delivers pizza for some of the large chains in the area and charge them on a per-pizza basis. To make your deliveries, you are using a 1989 Toyota Tercel, which costs $2,000 per year in gas and $2,000 per year in repairs. You expect that you could keep running the car for another five years, when you would have to sell it for scrap for $500.

   You are thinking about buying a new car to replace the Tercel and are considering a new 1997 Honda Civic. It would cost $19,000, plus a delivery charge of $500. The car will cost $1,500 per year in gas and only $100 in maintenance (it's under warranty). Also, because it is a faster car, you will be able to deliver more pizzas, and you expect your revenues to increase by $500 per year. If you buy the new car, you will sell the Tercel for $3,000. The Civic would be sold in five years and would bring $10,000 at that time. The new Civic would be financed through the dealership at an interest rate of 12 percent per year (compounded monthly).

   Your tax rate is 35 percent, and your cars are depreciable for tax purposes at a rate of 15 percent per year. The asset class for these cars will always remain open (as you have a few other cars which your part-time employees use) require a return of 15 percent on any money you invest in your business. Should you replace your car?

4. The company you work for requires a particular type of machine for its production process. The firm can choose between two competing models produced by different companies. Model A costs $10,000 to buy and would increase revenues by $7,000 per year. It would cost $1,000 per year to operate the machine which is expected to last five years before it must be replaced. After five years, the machine can be sold as scrap metal for $1,000. Model B costs $13,000 to buy and would increase revenues by $6,000 per year. This model costs $1,000 per year to operate

and it is expected to last for seven years after which time the machine can be sold as scrap metal for $1,000. Whichever machine is chosen, it will fall in an asset class with a CCA rate of 10 percent. The firm always has millions of dollars of other assets in this class. The company is subject to a tax rate of 40 percent, and its required rate of return is 10 percent. Which model of the machine should the firm choose?

5. The provincial government wants to clean up the Halifax harbour. It has invited businesses such as yours to bid on the contract. The government will pay you one lump payment today for the job (if your bid is the lowest and you win the contract). You figure that cleaning up the harbour would take your firm four years, and it would cost you $40 million per year to do the work. You require a return of 12 percent on projects of this type. You want to make your bid as low as possible in order to maximize your chances of winning the contract. Your firm generally loses money and therefore pays no taxes. What is the lowest bid you should submit?

6. (a) An organization considers purchasing a $20,000 machine and expects to realize annual operating savings of $4,000 per year for the first five years and $8,000 per year from the sixth to the tenth year inclusive. The company's tax rate is 50 percent, and its cost of capital is 12 percent. CCA on a declining balance is charged at a rate of 30 percent with no salvage value anticipated. For this investment, determine:

   (i) the net present value

   (ii) the internal rate of return

   (b) If the machine in part (a) can be salvaged at the end of its useful life for $3,000, recalculate the NPV of the investment.

7. Consider the following investment:

Initial investment	$10,000
Additional net operating revenues	
years 1 and 2	$3,500 each year
years 3 and 4	$4,000 each year

   Given a discount rate of 10 percent, a maximum rate for CCA deductions on a declining balance of 20 percent, and a corporate tax rate of 40 percent, calculate:

   (a) the net cash flows generated by the project during the first four years

   (b) the present value of the total tax shield from CCA

   (c) the NPV and IRR for this project

   (d) the NPV of the project assuming that a salvage value of $5,000 can be realized at the end of the fourth year

8. (a) A company considers a project that would entail new investments totalling $130,000. This amount is made up of $100,000 in new machinery and start-up costs of $30,000 that would be expensed. The firm's weighted average cost of capital (WACC) is 10 percent. Assume that the machinery is depreciated on a straight-line basis for tax purposes with no salvage value at the end of year 4. The investment is expected to result in the following incremental sales revenues, costs, CCA, and taxes:

	Year			
	1	2	3	4
Sales revenue	$80,000	$80,000	$80,000	$80,000
Operating costs	20,000	20,000	20,000	20,000
Operating income	$60,000	$60,000	$60,000	$60,000
Capital cost allowance	25,000	25,000	25,000	25,000
Taxable income	$35,000	$35,000	$35,000	$35,000
Taxes	17,500	17,500	17,500	17,500
Net income	$17,500	$17,500	$17,500	$17,500

Compute the NPV and the IRR for this investment.

(b) Assume the figures as given in (a), except that CCA is taken on a declining balance at a rate of 30 percent. Assume also that the machinery will have a salvage value of $20,000 at the end of year 4 and that the asset class will not be left empty by the sale of the machinery at that time. Recompute the NPV of the investment. Also, compute incremental net income and net cash flows that result from the investment for year 2.

9. (a) Consider a machine in use that can be sold for $4,000 or that could be used for another three years with no salvage value at the end. A new machine can be bought at a total cost of $18,000. It also has an estimated life of three years and no salvage value. If the new machine is purchased, operating savings are expected to be $12,000 in year 1 and $6,000 per year in years 2 and 3. The corporate tax rate is 40 percent, the maximum rate for CCA is 30 percent, and the discount rate is 11 percent. Calculate the IRR and NPV for the new machine.

(b) Recompute the IRR and NPV assuming that the salvage value of the new machine at the end of the third year is estimated at $2,000.

10. A restaurant chain considers opening a new restaurant. A suitable lot could be acquired for $450,000, and it would cost $300,000 to erect the building with CCA on the building taken at 10 percent. Kitchen facilities and furniture have already been bought for another restaurant, which at the last moment could not be put in operation. They were acquired a year ago at a cost of $70,000 and have a current market value of $50,000 with CCA taken at a rate of 20 percent. Landscaping can be done at a cost of $8,000 and would be expensed in the current accounting period. The firm's tax rate is 40 percent, and its cost of capital is 15 percent. Including the present value of tax shields from CCA in your calculations, what is the total net investment if the chain decides to go ahead with the new restaurant?

11. A firm currently operates a machine that was purchased at a cost of $200,000 two years ago. It has a current market value of $135,000. A new improved version of the equipment is now on the market at a cost of $175,000. The machines are part of an asset class with CCA taken at a rate of 30 percent. Special foundations for the new machine would need to be laid requiring 200 hours of labour. The work can be done by the company's own employees at the rate of $20 per hour. As there is currently

some slack and excess capacity owing to a sales slump, the 200 hours could be provided without disrupting other operations in any way. The firm does not contemplate laying off employees at this time since the current sales slump is expected to be short-lived. The costs for laying the foundations would be expensed in the current accounting period. The firm's tax rate is 40 percent, and its cost of capital is 12 percent. Including the present value of tax shields from CCA in your calculations, what is the total net investment if the firm disposes of the old machine and buys the new one?

12. A company considers building a new and improved production facility for one of its existing products. It would be built on a piece of vacant land that the firm owns. This land was acquired four years ago at a cost of $300,000; it has a current market value of $600,000. The building can be erected for $400,000. Machinery worth $160,000 needs to be bought. CCA on a declining balance will be taken on all depreciable assets at a rate of 20 percent. Operating savings from the new production facility are expected to be $220,000 per year for the next 10 years. The salvage value at the end of the 10 years is expected to be $800,000, which is solely the value of the land. The firm's tax rate is 40 percent, with capital gains taxed at two-thirds of their value. The firm's weighted average cost of capital (WACC) is estimated at 14 percent. Based on a discounted cash flow analysis, should the investment be undertaken?

13. A firm is re-evaluating one of its current product lines to determine whether it will continue to be profitable or whether it should be discontinued. Net operating revenues (sales minus all operating costs) are estimated to be $3,000 per year for each of the next six years, after which time they will drop to $2,000 per year. It is estimated that the product line has a useful life of 10 years; that is, after year 10, no further revenues are anticipated. If the product line were shut down, it would entail immediate expenses of $4,500. On the other hand, machinery used in the production could be sold for $12,000. This machinery is part of an asset class for which the applicable rate for CCA is 30 percent. The class is not left empty by the sale of the machinery. The floor space that is vacated by the shutdown could be leased out at $1,200 per year. The firm's tax rate is 40 percent, and the appropriate discount rate is 14 percent. Based on an NPV analysis, should the firm continue operations or close down the product line?

*14. You are presented with two proposals, A and B, with equal risks that require initial investments of $9,000 and $7,000. Subsequent net cash inflows are given as follows:

Year	Project A	Project B
1	$3,250	$2,500
2	3,500	2,500
3	3,500	3,000
4	3,500	3,000

(a) Assuming a weighted average cost of capital (WACC) of 14 percent, rank the two projects in terms of: (i) IRR and (ii) NPV.

(b) How do you account for the differences in ranking? Which project do you prefer? Why? How might capital rationing change your answer?

*15.Consider two projects, A and B, with the following data:

	Project A	Project B
Initial cash outlays	$25,000	$10,000
Present value of expected net cash inflows	50,000	30,000

(a) Compute the NPV and benefit–cost ratio for each project.

(b) Which project would you prefer if they were mutually exclusive? Why?

16. (a) Consider a project that requires an investment of $100,000 today and returns after-tax cash flows of $30,000 per year for five years. Using a spreadsheet, calculate the NPV of this project at all discount rates from 1 percent up to 25 percent in 1 percent increments. Use these numbers to plot the NPV profile of the project and then indicate what the internal rate of return for the project is.

(b) Consider a project for which no initial investment is required. It will generate after-tax cash flows of $15,000 per year for five years. In the sixth year, the firm will have to pay $100,000 in order to shut down the project. Using a spreadsheet, calculate the net present value of this project at all discount rates from 1 percent up to 25 percent in 1 percent increments. Use these numbers to plot the NPV profile of the project, and then indicate what the internal rate of return for the project is.

(c) Explain why the NPV profiles in (a) and (b) are different. Over what range of discount rates would the project in (a) be acceptable? Over what range of rates would the project in (b) be acceptable. Explain the difference.

Careful Planning Key to Keeping Risk at Bay

Any business activity has associated risks. When making capital budgeting decisions, the trick is to determine what those risks are, allow for them, and, above all, mitigate them as much as possible.

In Chapter 10, Michael Mooney, Executive Vice President for Information Technology at Bridges.com, outlined the process by which the company might decide whether or not to take on the capital expense of expanding server capacity. Risk assessment is a crucial aspect of that decision, though one, he says, that is often difficult to quantify.

"As a public company, we have a responsibility to our shareholders to show due diligence in making decisions," Mr. Mooney points out. Bridges.com, incorporated in 1994, went public in 1995 with an offering on the Alberta Stock Exchange. It has traded on the Toronto Stock Exchange since February 2000, under the symbol BIT.

"The fact is that one of the main reasons for undertaking an upgrade like this is to mitigate technical risks while at the same time taking advantage of emerging opportunities," he points out. "What if a database blows up on us? What if a fibre channel connection goes down?" These kinds of concerns have to be weighed against the business risks associated with undertaking a project like increasing server capacity.

To reduce those risks as much as possible, says Mr. Mooney, there are certain basic steps you can take, such as having parallel servers in case one goes awry during the upgrade. But the most important factor, he explains, is careful management. "Up-front thinking is the key to success. For example, a step in an upgrade like this might consist of one hour of work following four hours of planning.

"Minimizing risk," he believes firmly, "is largely a question of good project management."

So far, shareholders in Bridges.com have had little reason to question this wisdom. In five years, the company's revenue has increased more than 5,015 percent. At a time when many dot-com companies could be best classified by the rate at which they burn through investor cash, Bridges.com shows a positive operational cash flow. With a resubscription rate of 90 percent for four years running, it seems destined for long-term success. Mr. Mooney's challenge is ensuring its servers can keep up with the demand!

Capital Budgeting: Dealing with Risk

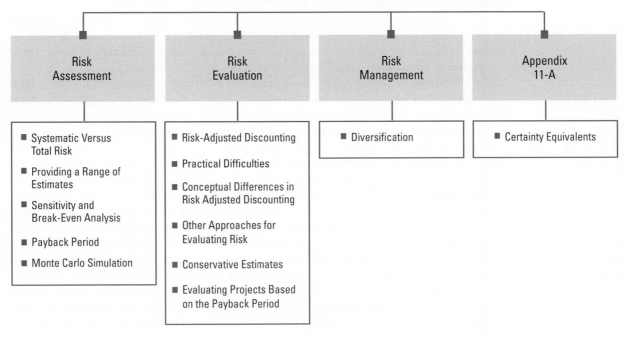

Risk Assessment

- Systematic Versus Total Risk
- Providing a Range of Estimates
- Sensitivity and Break-Even Analysis
- Payback Period
- Monte Carlo Simulation

Risk Evaluation

- Risk-Adjusted Discounting
- Practical Difficulties
- Conceptual Differences in Risk Adjusted Discounting
- Other Approaches for Evaluating Risk
- Conservative Estimates
- Evaluating Projects Based on the Payback Period

Risk Management

- Diversification

Appendix 11-A

- Certainty Equivalents

Learning Objectives

After studying this chapter, you should be able to:

1. *Describe four techniques used for risk assessment.*
2. *Define risk-adjusted discounting and discuss some of the challenges in using it in the real world.*
3. *Name two alternative methods of evaluating risk and explain how they differ from risk-adjusted discounting.*
4. *Name some techniques (three +) for managing risk within a firm.*
5. *Discuss the concept of diversification in terms of the individual investor and the corporation.*

11.1   INTRODUCTION

The previous chapter introduced discounted cash flow analysis as the basic framework for investment evaluations. In this chapter, we extend the previous analysis by explicitly recognizing uncertainty. First, we discuss how to measure or estimate risk. Second, we show how to incorporate risk into investment evaluations. Finally, we present various techniques that a firm can use to influence or manage its risk exposure. Additional considerations, including the handling of inflationary expectations and project interdependencies, are covered in Chapter 12.

Uncertainty plays an important role in any financial decision based on long-term business forecasts including capital budgeting. Given that investors and managers are generally risk averse, the risk associated with cash flow forecasts needs to be evaluated explicitly when assessing the economic desirability of investments.

Many firms report typical forecasting errors of over 10 percent when projecting future cash flows. Since in a competitive global environment many investment projects only promise modest returns to start with, it becomes understandable that both attention to formal risk analysis and the sophistication of methods employed have increased in recent years.

Based on the general concepts introduced in Chapters 7 and 8, in the following sections, we expand on how firms should incorporate risk into the evaluation of capital investments, and we review various techniques commonly used by business. In this context, it is useful to distinguish between risk assessment, risk evaluation, and the management of risk. **Risk assessment** is concerned with estimating the amount of risk inherent in an investment. After establishing this, the next step is **risk evaluation**. Here, one adjusts the economic value of the project to reflect its risk since investors view uncertainty as undesirable. This is what risk evaluation is about. Finally, there are various ways to limit or control risk. This is called **risk management**, and applicable techniques range from gathering additional information to buying insurance. All three aspects are important in dealing with the risk in a capital budgeting project, and we review each in a separate section.

11.2   RISK ASSESSMENT

The first step in dealing with risk is to estimate exposure. This is not easy because various definitions of risk are possible and because any estimate of future uncertainty is inherently subjective. We briefly review the various possible measures of risk that were discussed in detail in Chapters 7 and 8 and introduce some common techniques that enable us to quantify estimates of future uncertainty.

Systematic Versus Total Risk

Risk can be measured at various levels. It can be estimated for an individual project as reflected, for example, in the variability of its net present value. Risk can also be measured at the level of the firm by examining how much an individual project contributes to the overall variability in returns of the firm. At this level, the uncertainties inherent in all its projects interact to determine the overall risk of the firm, and the concepts of portfolio diversification from Chapter 7 apply. Finally, risk can be judged from the point of view of a well-diversified investor who, as we saw in Chapter 8, may be concerned solely with the systematic risk that an investment contributes to a broad-based market portfolio and that cannot be diversified away.

We reiterate that the measurement of risk depends on the context. In principle, since large investors are usually quite well diversified, only the systematic risk inherent in a project should affect shareholder wealth (as shown in Chapters 7 and 8). In practice, however, almost without exception, managers equate risk with the total variability inherent in a project. For example, engaging in exploration for minerals in a politically unstable country would be considered a high-risk investment. This is so despite the fact that their returns are probably not strongly correlated with the overall economy and hence could be eliminated through diversification.

One reason why managers behave in this way is that they themselves are usually not well diversified. Their jobs and salaries are not diversifiable, and their fortunes are generally tied closely to the success of the firms they lead. Executives whose firms face bankruptcy gain little solace from the fact that well-diversified investors face only a limited loss because many of the other firms in which they hold shares are doing well. It is therefore understandable that for managers, risk usually means total overall risk to their firms, to a particular division, or to a project with which she is involved.

There may also be instances in which managers pursue their own interests excessively and neglect those of the shareholders. When managers neglect their duties as agents for shareholders, we say that the firm faces an **agency problem**, a concept first introduced in Chapter 1. If such behaviour becomes prominent, it can lead to suboptimal economic performance. Some financial analysts have blamed such self-serving behaviour by management for the observable decline of some North American industries.

Assessing risk from the shareholders' point of view is simple in principle but often difficult in practice. As we saw in Chapters 7 and 8, diversified shareholders are concerned only with a project's undiversifiable (systematic) risk as measured by the project's beta. If a project has a high degree of undiversifiable risk (i.e., a high beta), it must generate a correspondingly high return. In practice, estimating the systematic risk or beta of a specific investment is often extremely difficult. While the beta of the firm's shares can be estimated by statistically relating the stock's return to those of a market index over many past periods, this approach is not feasible when dealing with a new product idea or a technological innovation. Without a statistical basis for estimating subjective risk, we may have only subjective judgement on which to fall back.

Assessing risk from the managers' or employees' point of view usually involves estimating a project's overall variability or how much variability the project adds to the company's overall cash flows. We next discuss the techniques most widely used in practice for measuring risk in this context.

Providing a Range of Estimates

While most enterprises use single-point estimates for cash flows and adjust for risk on a purely intuitive basis, many also estimate a range of possible figures that typically reflect a most-likely, an optimistic, and a pessimistic scenario. The optimistic and pessimistic forecasts are often defined as figures that have only a 10 percent probability of being exceeded on the positive or negative side. If more advanced, computer-based simulation techniques are used (which we will discuss shortly), standard probability distributions can be fitted to these ranges of estimates, thereby providing a reasonably good portrayal of the inherent uncertainties. To reduce the subjectivity associated with such forecasts, companies may require consensus estimates derived through discussions among several experts.

Sensitivity and Break-Even Analysis

A survey of large U.S. firms found sensitivity analysis to be the most widely used technique for assessing risk.[1] A more recent Canadian survey reached similar conclusions.[2] Sensitivity analysis determines how vulnerable a project's desirability is to changes in forecasted values.

BREAK-EVEN ANALYSIS

An investment in a machine costs $100,000, and net cash inflows of $30,000 per year are anticipated over the next five years. The applicable discount rate is 12 percent. Hence, the investment's net present value becomes:

$NPV = -100,000 + (30,000 \times 3.605) = \$8,150$

The NPV suggests that the project is acceptable. However, because cash flow forecasts are subject to uncertainty, a manager may be interested in knowing by how much the inflows of $30,000 per year could be reduced before the project's net present value becomes negative. Setting:

$NPV = -100,000 + 3.605 \times \text{annual cash flows} = 0$

we derive:

$$\text{annual cash flows} = \frac{100,000}{3.605} = \$27,739$$

With annual cash inflows of $27,739, the project just breaks even, implying that a drop of less than 10 percent from the original forecast will make the investment unattractive. Thus, the acceptability of the project is fairly sensitive to forecasting errors.

---

[1] T. Klammer and M. Walker, "The Continuing Increase in the Use of Sophisticated Capital Budgeting Techniques," *California Management Review* (Fall 1984), p. 142.

[2] V. Jog and A. Srivastava, "Capital Formation and Corporate Financial Decision Making in Canada," *Carleton University School of Business Working Paper* (Ottawa: 1992), p. 16.

Such sensitivity analysis and determination of break-even values can be carried out for a variety of factors influencing a project's cash flows. For instance, when launching a new product, we may determine how sensitive its NPV is with regard to future sales, selling price, useful life, production costs, and other forecasted variables. Not only does this information provide a manager with insights into the main determinants of risk in a particular situation, but it also allows him to concentrate on those variables that are most critical to the project's ultimate success.

Sensitivity analysis can also be used in the context of spreadsheet-type financial models that generate forecasted income statements and balance sheets. Thus, the impact of an investment proposal on the financial statements of the firm can be tested, including the sensitivity of the firm's projected financial performance to changes in forecasts.

Payback Period

The **payback period**, which is related to break-even analysis, is widely used in practice. As a quick way to assess exposure to risk, it can be quite useful. As a stand-alone evaluation criterion to determine investment decisions, however, it is simplistic and often misleading. In this section, we review its use as a simple technique for measuring risk exposure. In Section 11.4, we discuss why the payback period is inappropriate as a primary tool for measuring investment worth.

An investment's payback period is the time required for its expected after-tax cash inflows to equal (and thereby to recover) the original outlay. In other words, it is the time it takes for a project to break even. Since the uncertainty of cash flows typically increases the further one moves into the future, management may set a payback constraint. Also, if there is a chance an investment might have to be abandoned prematurely, knowing a project's payback period is useful in assessing exposure.

When a new product is launched, its useful life may be difficult to forecast because this will depend on such uncertain events as competitor reaction, technological obsolescence, and the like. If the project has an expected payback period of three years, management knows that at least the original investment should have been recovered by that time. The estimated useful life of the product can be viewed in relation to this figure; if the product's useful life is expected to exceed the payback period significantly, this may be perceived as providing adequate protection against risk.

The payback period can be made more useful by adding several refinements. For example, the "discounted payback period" accounts for the time value of money and is defined as the time required for the present value of cash inflows to equal the original investment. The firm has to be concerned not only with recovering the original investment but also with the cost of funding the investment over time.

DISCOUNTED PAYBACK PERIOD

EXAMPLE

An investment of $100,000 generates net cash inflows of $20,000 per year for seven years. The business's cost of capital is 15 percent. Without discounting, the payback period would be computed as five years because after that the undiscounted cash inflows have "repaid" the original investment. However, recognizing that returns have to be paid on the money that was used to fund the project, we should discount future cash flows and compare their present value with the current investment. In so doing, we find that this project will not pay back in the seven-year period. As Table 11.1 shows, the present value of $20,000 for seven years discounted at only 15 percent equals $83,220.

TABLE 11.1

	Year						
	1	2	3	4	5	6	7
Cash flows (undiscounted)	$20,000	$20,000	$20,000	$20,000	$ 20,000	$ 20,000	$ 20,000
Cumulative cash flows	20,000	40,000	60,000	80,000	100,000	120,000	140,000
Discount factor (at 15%)	870	.756	.658	.572	.497	.432	.376
Discounted cash flows	$17,400	$15,120	$13,160	$11,440	$9,940	$8,640	$7,520
Cumulative discounted cash flows	17,400	32,520	45,680	57,120	67,060	75,700	83,220

We see that the payback period as commonly computed without discounting understates the true time until break-even has been reached.

More generally, a firm may be interested not only in the break-even point as represented by the payback period but also in the magnitude of its exposure to loss if abandonment occurs prior to the payback period.

EXAMPLE

ABANDONMENT COSTS

Given a payback period of four years, it may also be relevant to know how much would be lost if unforeseen circumstances forced the project to be abandoned after only one or two years. As shown in Figure 11.1, we can plot the NPV of a project as a function of time assuming abandonment of the project at time t. Thus, the project shown in Figure 11.1 has an expected life of seven years with an ultimate NPV of $150,000. Its discounted payback period is four years, and if it is abandoned at that time, the total NPV of all cash flows is zero with the firm just breaking even. However, if unforeseen events force a liquidation after only one-and-a-half years, the firm would stand to lose $100,000 in present value terms since the initial investment and start-up expenses would have been incurred without the project having begun to generate cash inflows.

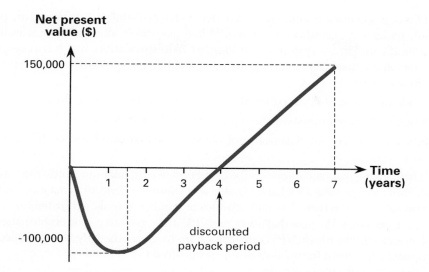

Net present value ($)

150,000

-100,000

1   2   3   4   5   6   7   **Time (years)**

discounted
payback period

FIGURE 11.1

Net Present Value
as a Function of Time,
Assuming Abandonment
at Time t

A curve as provided in Figure 11.1 shows the project's ultimate NPV, its payback period based on discounted cash flows, and the firm's exposure to potential loss throughout the project's life. It thus provides more complete information regarding risk than any single number.

Monte Carlo Simulation

Sensitivity analysis is most appropriate when the effects of deviations in various forecasts are to be assessed one at a time. In a typical investment, however, many variables interact in a complex way to determine the overall risk of the project. For example, a project's NPV is determined by net cash flows for several periods. The net cash flows themselves are made up of several costs and revenues, and each of these cost and revenue figures may, in turn, depend on several operating variables including production schedules and quantities, market variables, and so on. With uncertainties inherent in each of these interrelated variables, the overall impact on the economic desirability of the investment is in most instances far from obvious.

In mathematical terms, the problem can be expressed as follows. A measure such as the IRR is a function of a number of variables, which we may label $x_1, x_2 \dots, x_n$. In other words, IRR $= f(x_1, x_2, \dots, x_n)$. Each x is subject to uncertainty and has a probability distribution associated with it.[3] We may want to find the probability distribution for the IRR given that we know the function f and have received from operating personnel probability distributions for all of the individual variables and their statistical interrelationships.

---

[3] It should be noted that these variables need not be independent. For example, the sales forecast for a particular year may be influenced by the predicted selling price, which, in turn, may reflect expectations about labour costs.

Direct mathematical solutions that derive such a probability distribution are possible only under very special circumstances. When such direct solutions are not available, as is typically the case, we can resort to **Monte Carlo simulation**, which is a computer-based technique that offers solutions, based on sampling, to problems of this type. The technique calls for:

1. the identification of key variables that affect the investment's cash flows
2. the assignment of probability distributions to each variable
3. the specification of any statistical dependencies that may exist between different variables.

Then, giving due recognition to the likelihood of particular outcomes, the computer randomly selects values for each variable and combines them to generate cash flows and internal rates of return. Through a sufficient number of trials, a distribution of rates of return is provided. We note that use of the NPV in this context can be problematic since the discount rate on which NPV calculations are based presumably already reflects an appropriate adjustment for the overall risk of the project.

Figure 11.2 illustrates the use of Monte Carlo simulation to derive the probability distribution for a project's IRR (or some other evaluation criterion) given that the uncertainties associated with the project's forecasted variables and their statistical interdependencies have been qualified.

FIGURE 11.2

Monte Carlo Simulation Model

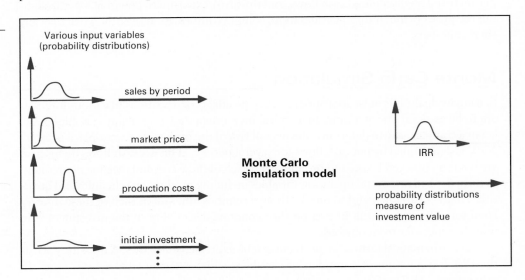

With Monte Carlo simulation capabilities being part of many financial software packages, this technique is becoming an increasingly useful and popular tool for companies analysing major investment decisions.

RISK EVALUATION   11.3

After obtaining a reasonable assessment of risk, the next move is to evaluate the risk or to estimate its likely cost. Since both investors and managers dislike uncertainty, risk detracts from a project's economic value. In this section, we discuss techniques that allow us to adjust net present values to reflect project risk.

Risk-Adjusted Discounting

In the previous chapter, we saw that expected future cash flows may be discounted at the firm's average after-tax cost of capital. This is true if the firm's investments are roughly of the same risk that investors perceive for the overall firm so that the new investments do not alter the terms under which the firm can obtain new financing. In practice, however, most firms are engaged in a variety of projects and possibly operate in several business areas, each subject to different risks. Within any one of these entities, investment projects may range from high-risk research and development investments to relatively low-risk automation expenditures.

Under such circumstances, it would be inappropriate to apply a single corporate-wide discount rate across projects and divisions. Such an averaging approach can cause serious economic distortions and imply a cross-subsidization by which low-risk projects are penalized (discounted at too high a rate), while high-risk ventures are subsidized (discounted at too low a rate). We discuss this issue further in Chapter 15, which deals with estimating a firm's cost of capital.

When projects differ substantially from the average risk of the company, individual risk adjustments should take place in investment evaluations. One of the most common approaches is to rely on risk-adjusted discount rates, which implies that we vary the discount rate applied to a project's expected cash flows on the basis of perceived risk. Typically, investments are grouped into several risk classes, and a separate discount rate is applied to each class of capital expenditures with higher rates used for more risky investments.

RISK-ADJUSTED DISCOUNTING

A company may use the following classifications:

Project class	Discount rate applied
Low-risk	12%
Normal business risk	15
Speculative	18

Consider a project that requires an initial investment of $100,000, with cash inflows of $30,000 per year expected for five years. Applying the various discount rates as set out above, the project's NPVs become:

Discount rate applied	Net present value of investment
12%	$8,150
15	560
18	−6,190

Although the project would be acceptable in the low-risk category and be marginally acceptable given normal business risk, it would be rejected if it entailed higher than usual risks.

Private investors provide the funds the firm invests in its various projects. They receive the returns those projects generate and bear the risks involved, which is why adjustments made to the discount rate have to reflect investors' preferences as revealed in financial markets.

We saw in Chapter 8 that the risk relevant for large and diversified investors is reflected in the beta for the project as if it were a stand-alone proposition. The capital asset pricing model (CAPM) tells us what return diversified investors should require of any asset with a given systematic risk, or beta. Specifically, the return a risky investment should yield r_i is given by:

$$r_i = r_f + \beta_i (r_m - r_f)$$

where r_f is the return on risk-free investments, r_m is the expected return on the market as a whole, and β_i is the beta of the risky investment, a measure of how much undiversifiable risk it exposes investors to. This formula can be used to produce a rough estimate of what return investors might expect from a given project.

RISK-ADJUSTED DISCOUNT RATE ESTIMATION

EXAMPLE

A natural gas transmission firm that is financed with 100 percent equity is thinking of setting up a new subsidiary that uses natural gas to produce polyethylene. The Value Line Investment Survey shows that small independent firms in the polyethylene business have betas of around 1.2. It seems reasonable to expect the new subsidiary to face business risks similar to those experienced by such firms. The risk-free rate is currently 6 percent, and the expected market return as measured by the TSE 300 Total Return Index is about 12 percent. Based on the CAPM, the project should produce a minimum expected return of:

$$r_i = r_f + \beta_i (r_m - r_f)$$

$$= 6\% + 1.2 \times (12\% - 6\%)$$

$$= 13.2\%$$

to compensate investors in the firm for the extra risk carried.

This return becomes the cost of capital against which the investment project should be judged. If it produces what investors require or more, it should be undertaken. If not, it should be rejected.

Practical Difficulties

A number of mostly large and diversified firms use market-based techniques as discussed in Chapter 8 to estimate risk-adjusted costs of capital for major areas of their business. However, in most cases, risk adjustments are made by management on a more or less intuitive basis, and there appear to be very few firms that apply the CAPM or other similar models to guide their capital budgeting decisions at the individual project level. Several reasons appear plausible in explaining this discrepancy between theory and practice.

First, as previously noted, there are the practical difficulties of estimating the systematic risk, or betas, for individual projects. Second, there is an agency problem. As was noted earlier, most managers are not diversified. They tend, therefore, to base investment evaluations on total rather than systematic risk, thus resulting in a potential agency problem. Finally, whereas financial markets are reasonably efficient, markets for real capital assets tend to be much less developed. For example, we can expect to sell shares of a large corporation on short notice and at a fair price. The sale of a specialized machine, however, may be considerably more difficult with a much less predictable end result. As a consequence, investors in securities can afford a reasonably short time horizon; after all, they can always adjust their plans as circumstances change. Companies, on the other hand, are tied to their investment projects on a much more permanent basis. Models such as the CAPM are developed on the assumption of efficient markets and are essentially based on a short-term (one period) time horizon. Their applicability is subject to serious questions when time and risk are interrelated in a more general way as typically would be the case in capital budgeting. We pursue this point in further detail below.

Clearly, intuitive adjustments by managers are subject to significant weaknesses of their own. Thus, managerial adjustments invariably give rise to questions such as:

- On what basis are risk adjustments made?

- How consistent are they between various divisions and managers?

- How can one prevent unwarranted distortions based on individual idiosyncrasies or personal objectives?

In this context, the corporate reward structure as perceived by managers can become important. For example, if a manager is penalized for failing to attain forecasts, and results that exceed projections are largely attributed to good fortune, conservatism becomes almost inevitable, and unrealistic adjustments for risk are likely to result. Hence, the control and reward system of an organization as sensed by management is an important instrument for promoting reasonable and consistent approaches toward the handling of risk. We note, however, that even when a manager's rewards are strongly tied to stock price performance (for instance, through stock options or performance-based bonuses as outlined in Chapter 1), this may not solve the problem of total versus systematic risk because the manager remains undiversified.

Conceptual Difficulties in Risk-Adjusted Discounting

Apart from the practical difficulties outlined above, **risk-adjusted discounting** in the context of capital budgeting is subject to some conceptual limitations. By adjusting discount rates to reflect risk, attitudes toward risk and the time value of money become linked together.

When we deal with short-term or single-period returns (as in the CAPM), we can ignore the problems that this linkage may cause. In the evaluation of longer-term projects, however, caution is in order. By linking together the time value of money and risk, we assume that the uncertainty of a project's cash flows increases over time in a narrowly specified manner. As we saw in Chapter 5, the process of discounting scales down cash flows more severely the further we move into the future. If we add a risk premium to the discount rate, this risk premium again becomes progressively more effective as it is applied to cash flows that are further away. Because of these characteristics inherent in the mathematics of discounting, the NPV of a short-term opportunity with a large element of risk is relatively unaffected by adjustments to the discount rate, whereas the adjustment effect on even a moderately risky project with longer-term benefits proves significant.

For example, consider the drilling of an oil well at the cost of $500,000 that may result in either a dry hole (probability of 85 percent) or a find (probability of 15 percent). In the latter case, a gain of $5 million is anticipated from a sale of the well. The results from the drilling will be known in one year. The expected cash inflow at the end of the year becomes $0.15 \times 5,000,000 = \$750,000$. Even if the discount rate is raised because of the high risk to 25 percent, the effect of such an increase is not very dramatic. As discounting is limited to one year, the expected benefits are reduced by a factor of only $1/(1+.25) = 0.8$. The project's NPV remains positive at:

$$NPV = -500,000 + \frac{750,000}{(1+.25)} = \$100,000$$

On the other hand, if another project's benefits accrued 10 years hence, a discount rate of 25 percent would reduce every dollar of future benefits by a factor of $[1/(1.25)^{10}] = 0.11$, or to just $0.11.

The use of risk-adjusted discount rates implies that the risk inherent in a project's cash flows increases as we move further into the future. Even if it is felt that risk increases over time (because the more distant future may be more difficult to forecast), it is unlikely that the increase in perceived risk would just parallel the decreases in present values brought about by a risk-adjusted discount rate. Furthermore, it is easy to find examples where risk and time may not be related in this manner. For instance, the initial construction costs of a new pipeline typically are subject to much greater uncertainty than the subsequent revenues once the pipeline is in place.

To overcome these deficiencies, we could vary the risk-adjusted discount rate over time, with the discount factor applied in each time period corresponding to the particular risks perceived. Such explicit specification of individual risk premiums for each period is not unlike the use of **certainty equivalents** (discussed in Appendix 11-A), whereby the cash flows for each period are individually adjusted for risk. However, although they are conceptually more appealing, such complex approaches become unwieldy and are rarely used.

In spite of these shortcomings, risk-adjusted discounting represents one of the most popular and useful practical approaches to handling the problem of risk, and it is often a good compromise between what is operationally workable and what may be conceptually desirable. Nevertheless, we should be aware of the limitations in order to make modifications when necessary—for example, when the perceived risk of a project's cash flows clearly does not match the adjustments effected through the use of a higher discount rate. We should also be aware that capital investment decisions, in which the dimensions of time and risk are interrelated in a general way, are complex enough to defy simple mechanistic solutions. Dealing with risk in this context remains a challenge both in terms of its assessment and evaluation.

Other Approaches for Evaluating Risk

Several other shortcuts to deal with risk are widely used often alongside risk-adjusted discounting. Not being tied to a systematic framework that links the firm's financing to its investments, they tend to be *ad hoc* and without prescriptive or normative substance. Nevertheless, firms and individuals obviously find them useful in providing at least some structure.

Conservative Estimates

The widely used approach of conservative estimates attempts to limit risk by scaling down original estimates. Thus, a manager presented with an uncertain forecast of $100,000 in inflows by a subordinate may use a scaled-down figure of $80,000 in her own evaluations. As we will see (when discussing certainty equivalents), this technique has some merit and can be useful if properly devised and implemented. In most practical settings, however, such subjective adjustments tend to be made in an *ad hoc* manner without much quantitative information about the underlying uncertainties. The decisions that result may be less than optimal.

To illustrate, the subordinate who provided the $100,000 figure may have already toned down his own forecast to protect herself should things not work out. If successive layers of management each make their own adjustments without knowledge of what others have done and without a full appreciation of the actual uncertainties underlying the original forecast, the figures on which the final evaluation is based may bear little relation to the actual project under consideration.

Evaluating Projects Based on the Payback Period

In situations with substantial uncertainty, managers sometimes measure a project's desirability by its payback period—the shorter the better. It is also common to impose payback constraints so that only investments with payback periods below the imposed limit are considered. Use of this simple technique predates the widespread availability of calculators and computers.

We saw earlier in this chapter that the payback period may be a quick intuitive way of assessing exposure to risk. However, as an evaluation criterion, it is often misleading and contradicts discounted cash flow analysis because it ignores both the timing of proceeds prior to the payback period and any cash flows that occur beyond the payback period. Furthermore, the choice of what constitutes an acceptable payback period is arbitrary.

EXAMPLE

PAYBACK PERIOD

Consider two mutually exclusive projects (A and B), a three-year payback requirement, and the following after-tax cash flows:

	Year				
	0	1	2	3	4
Project A					
Initial cash outlay	−$400				
Net cash inflows		$100	$100	$200	$200
Project B					
Initial cash outlay	−$400				
Net cash inflows		$200	$100	$100	$500

Both projects provide a three-year payback and hence appear equivalent. The extreme nature of the example makes it obvious, however, that B is superior to A not only because it generates larger inflows in the year following the payback limit ($500 versus $200 in year 4), but also because during the payback period, the larger $200 cash flow is generated earlier.

11.4 RISK MANAGEMENT

Risk is not entirely outside the firm's control. In addition to external factors, it is also determined by factors over which the firm has some influence. Examples of external factors include general economic conditions that affect product demand and prices that can be charged in a competitive market. Internal factors may include such things as the ability to control initial investment expenditures and ongoing operating costs.

Inasmuch as the firm has some control over sources of uncertainty, certain aspects of business risk can and should be managed. Even with regard to external factors, one may be able to shift risk through insurance-type arrangements. Since altering the risk of an investment may affect its economic viability, optimal risk management becomes important.

Reducing risk through internal actions typically entails improved forecasting, planning, and implementation. Numerous projects that at first look promising subsequently fail because of sloppy initial forecasting and/or poor controls during implementation.

Many factors influencing financial decisions are inherently risky including, for example, the price-level changes that may impact production inputs and/or outputs several years hence. Even if a firm cannot eliminate such risks, it can attempt to understand them more fully. Thus, collecting additional information may improve forecasting. Such added information could come from internal sources (better management information and control systems) or from external experts. Often, just waiting can provide useful information that helps to reduce risk. For example, it is generally more risky to pioneer new technology than to wait until it has proven itself in the marketplace. Finally, it can be useful to keep track of how accurate past predictions actually were through post-audits. By learning from past mistakes, one can often reduce future biases.

Smooth project implementation is also critical. Unforeseen increases in costs and/or slippages in schedules are a frequent source of risk. Thus, it is important that the firm's investment plans be thoroughly analysed by well-informed experts including engineers, economists, and accountants and then implemented without serious mistakes. A survey of senior executives found the following factors to be of primary importance in avoiding surprises during project implementation:

- committed senior management

- realistic plans and resource allocations

- good organization and monitoring systems

- proper motivation and reward structures

When such internal risks cannot be completely avoided, they must be managed. This may involve lowering break-even points through the reduction of fixed costs (becoming "lean"), designing flexibility into production processes, and reducing one's own exposure by subcontracting or leasing assets rather than owning them.

Risks that cannot be controlled internally may be shifted through some sort of insurance. The basic issue here as with the management of any insurance program is to determine the risks the firm should insure against and those it would assume itself through self-insurance.

Finally, a firm can enhance its ability to bear risk. This generally involves having some slack in its financial resources including cash, lines of credit, or assets that can be sold quickly without loss. A firm that is liquid and has unused borrowing capacity can withstand unexpected adversity far better than a firm that is financially stretched.

A variety of specific approaches is available for managing risk. Partly because of the increased volatility in financial markets, significant innovations have evolved. In fact, the use of new techniques and new financial instruments has led to the emergence of an entirely new area of financial management called **financial engineering**. Essentially, the aim is to design fairly priced insurance or **hedges** against a variety of adverse movements in interest rates, foreign exchange rates, or other prices. Such risk management is used not only by large multinational firms, but increasingly also by small- and mid-size companies. Since this type of risk management applies not only to capital budgeting but also to the entire financial management of the firm, we discuss it separately in Chapter 21 after we have covered both long-term investments and long-term financing.

Most techniques for managing risk entail costs, and their implementation lowers the returns the company can expect from its investments. Hence, managers once again are confronted with the difficult but pervasive trade-off between efficiency and flexibility or between expected returns and risk.

In summary, certain risks are difficult to avoid no matter how sophisticated the firm's risk-management techniques are. Others can be avoided, but doing so is simply too expensive. Finally, through effective management, some risks can be reduced or even eliminated, and this may make projects viable that would otherwise have been too risky to accept.

Diversification

We saw in Chapters 7 and 8 that diversification is one of the most effective ways to manage and reduce risk. Like individual investors, firms can reduce their overall risk through diversification, and many firms have pursued such strategies to stabilize their cash flows and returns. Often, firms have moved into related areas in which apart from diversification benefits, they have been able to create economic value through shared resources or skills. In the past, many firms moved into completely unrelated businesses for the sole purpose of diversification creating so-called conglomerates. Many of these conglomerates provided unsatisfactory results for shareholders, and they were subsequently split up into separate companies. An example of such a split-up is described in the report below, which includes excerpts from a newspaper article involving the recent split-up of RJR Nabisco into its respective food and tobacco businesses.

■ *Finance in the News*

RJR Nabisco to Split Food and Tobacco Business

RJR Nabisco Holdings Corp., makers of such international brands as Winston and Camel cigarettes and Oreo cookies, decided that it was time to reduce its staggering debt load resulting from one of the costliest hostile takeovers in history. Nabisco sold its international tobacco unit to Japan Tobacco Inc. for $8 billion (U.S.). RJR CEO Steven Goldstone confirmed that the dramatic move was necessary to reduce the staggering near-crippling debt resulting from the infamous hostile takeover. Goldstone stated, "We're going to let investors decide whether they want to invest in tobacco or Nabisco."

Things have changed since 1989 and the $25-billion leveraged buyout by Henry Kravis, which became the centrepiece of the best-selling *Barbarians at the Gate*, celebrating the era of greed. The controversial takeover led to a massive debt that stands at $10 billion a decade later even though large parts of the conglomerate had been sold off previously. The remaining parts will be split into three companies.

Source: "RJR Nabisco to split food and tobacco businesses," Brian Millner, *Globe and Mail*, March 10, 2000, page B1. *Reprinted with permission.*

Given that firms tend to operate most efficiently when they focus on their area of strength and that shareholders can readily diversify their own holdings, it is not surprising that internal diversification at the individual firm level has not been received with welcome arms by investors. In fact, the trend in today's business environment is for firms to focus on their core areas of strength, and it is common to see companies divesting unrelated businesses. In addition, most recent mergers have seen firms acquire others within the same industry or those in closely related or complementary industries.

P E R S P E C T I V E S

Corporate Manager

Given that investors can easily diversify their own portfolios as well as the difficulties associated with expanding into unrelated businesses, many companies have chosen to focus on their strengths and to leave the diversification to the investors.

Investor

Investors should try to find the "best" companies in many different industries and not concern themselves with how well "diversified" the companies that they purchase are.

SUMMARY 11.5

1. Widely used techniques for risk assessment include sensitivity and break-even analysis, payback period determination, and computer-based simulation.

2. Risk-adjusted discounting represents one of the most widely used techniques for evaluating risk. Here, the discount rate applied to individual projects is adjusted to reflect perceived risk. Conceptual difficulties of risk-adjusted discounting include the fact that time and risk become linked through the discounting process implying that risk increases with time in a specified manner.

3. Widely used alternative approaches to the evaluation of risk include conservative estimates and a shortening of the required payback period.

4. Risk can be managed, at least to some extent, within the firm. Different techniques for doing this include:

   • improving forecasting through the use of better information

   • implementing various operating measures that enhance flexibility (such as subcontracting and renting rather than owning)

   • shifting risk through insurance-type arrangements

- financial engineering
- diversification

5. Diversification depends largely on the correlation of cash flows between the various projects making up the firm's business portfolio. Because diversification to reduce such correlations can be pursued by both firms and investors, it is not clear whether diversification at the corporate level provides the economic gains often ascribed to it by management.

APPENDIX 11-A

CERTAINTY EQUIVALENTS

Certainty equivalents represent a relatively sophisticated approach to evaluating risk from an individual decision-maker's perspective. It overcomes some of the limitations of risk-adjusted discount rates previously noted.[4] As mentioned earlier, however, certainty equivalents are cumbersome to implement and consequently, are seldom used in practice. Furthermore, this method, which is based on an individual decision-maker's attitudes toward risk, cannot readily be linked to aggregate investor preferences as reflected in financial markets. Thus, it again lacks a normative economic foundation since it cannot be used directly, for example, to maximize shareholder wealth. Nevertheless, a brief discussion serves to clarify some interesting conceptual issues inherent in the evaluation of risk.

Assume that a financial officer is faced with the choice of (1) receiving at some point in time an uncertain cash flow characterized by a particular probability distribution, or (2) receiving x dollars with certainty. If the amount x is such that the financial officer is indifferent between the two alternatives, then x is termed the certainty equivalent of the uncertain cash flow.

ESTIMATING CERTAINTY EQUIVALENTS

Assume that net cash flows for the coming period are characterized by the following probability distribution:

---

[4] See, for example, G. Sick, "A Certainty-Equivalent Approach to Capital Budgeting," *Financial Management* (Winter 1986), pp. 23-32.

Cash flow	Probability
$17,000	.3
10,000	.4
3,000	.3

Expected value: $10,000

If a decision-maker is indifferent between either the prospect of such cash flows or a certain receipt of $8,000 in the same period, then $8,000 becomes the certainty equivalent of the uncertain cash flow. The discrepancy between the cash flow's expected value of $10,000 and the certainty equivalent of $8,000 reflects the person's risk aversion. The certainty equivalent can also be expressed as:

Certainty equivalent=Certainty equivalent coefficient×expected value of uncertain cash flows

This yields a certainty equivalent coefficient of 0.8 for this example.

We see that certainty equivalents are related to the approach of using conservative estimates to scale down uncertain forecasts. In using this method to evaluate investments, we first assign a certainty equivalent to the cash flow distribution specified for each period. These certainty equivalents are then discounted to derive the project's NPV. Because risk has been fully accounted for, the discount rate applied should reflect only the time value of money without in any way including a premium for risk (in other words, it should be the risk-free rate).

NPVS AND CERTAINTY EQUIVALENTS

EXAMPLE

Consider an investment of $900 that is to yield uncertain cash flows with expected values of $500 at the end of each of the next three years. We denote a_t as the certainty equivalent coefficient for period t, with $0 < a_t < 1$ for risk averse decision-makers and values of a_t decreasing with increasing risk. Assume that risk increases over time so that management views the certainty equivalent coefficients as $a_0=1.0$, $a_1=0.9$, $a_2=0.8$, and $a_3=0.7$. The time value of money for a riskless investment is given as $k=10\%$. We have:

Year	Uncertain cash flow (expected values)	Certainty equivalent coefficients	Certainty equivalents
0	−$900	1.0	−$900
1	500	0.9	450
2	500	0.8	400
3	500	0.7	350

The NPV for the investment becomes:

$$NPV = \sum_{t=0}^{n} \frac{a_t C_t}{(1+k)^t}$$

$$= -900 + \frac{.9(500)}{(1+.1)} + \frac{.8(500)}{(1+.1)^2} + \frac{.7(500)}{(1+.1)^3} = \$102.63$$

Because the project yields a positive NPV, after full consideration of the risks involved, it should be accepted.

Practical problems in implementation stem from the need to specify a certainty equivalent for every distribution of uncertain cash flows. This difficulty could be overcome to some extent if it were possible to measure comprehensively a decision-maker's attitudes toward risk, which could then form the basis for a repeated and more routine adjustment of cash flows for uncertainty. Utility theory provides for a more general measurement of attitudes toward risk; however, it is beyond the scope of this text.

Note: All *asterisked* Questions and Problems relate to material contained in the appendix to this chapter.

QUESTIONS AND PROBLEMS

Questions for Discussion

1. Why is an explicit evaluation of risk important in capital budgeting? How does risk affect a company and its financial management? How is the evaluation of risk related to the objective of maximizing shareholder wealth?

2. The most commonly used techniques for the evaluation of risk are conservative estimates, the payback period (including various refinements discussed in this chapter), sensitivity analysis, and risk-adjusted discount rates. Discuss the comparative advantages and weaknesses of each of these techniques. Which would you recommend using and why?

3. Discuss the relationship that may exist between the accuracy of forecasts obtained from an individual and the reward structure for performance as perceived by the individual.

4. Several researchers have found that many managers, especially in larger corporations, are very conservative in their forecasts and are overly risk averse in their evaluations of new projects. What are some possible reasons for this? If such behaviour is not in the best interests of the corporation's shareholders, how could it be overcome?

5. Discuss the concept of portfolio diversification. Why is this idea important in evaluating new investment projects? What are the difficulties in its implementation at the level of the firm?

6. It has been argued that companies should not be concerned about diversification because shareholders themselves can diversify their holdings by investing in shares of various corporations. Thus, diversification at the corporate level should be of no benefit to shareholders. Discuss your reactions to this argument. Why are many firms nevertheless concerned about diversifying their operations?

7. Discuss principal–agent problems in the context of major capital expenditure decisions, and suggest ways in which such difficulties may be reduced.

PROBLEMS WITH SOLUTIONS

Problem 1

Assume expected after-tax cash inflows of $100 a year for 20 years from two projects, whereby Project B is viewed to be somewhat riskier than Project A, and Project A corresponds to the company's usual investments. The risk-adjusted discount rate deemed appropriate for Project B is 15 percent, raised from the usual 10 percent applied to normal projects.

(a) Derive the ratio of present values for the annual net cash flows of Projects A and B for years 5, 10, 15, and 20; that is, derive PV (cash flows from A)/PV (cash flows from B).

(b) Based on your findings in (a), what is inferred about the riskiness of cash flows from Project B relative to those of Project A over time?

(c) Graph the present value of annual cash flows from each project as a function of their year of occurrence.

Solution 1

(a)

Year	Normal Project A Present value of annual cash flow discounted at 10%	Risky Project B Present value of annual cash flows discounted at 15%	Ratio A/B
5	$62	$50	1.24
10	39	25	1.56
15	24	12	2.00
20	15	6	2.50

All figures are rounded to the nearest dollar.

(b) The above figures illustrate the risk adjustment implied when using risk-adjusted discount rates. Through discounting, later cash flows are affected more severely by an increase in the discount rate. For example, the figures derived in part (a) imply that the riskiness of cash flows for Project B relative to the flows for Project A in period 20 is double that of period 5. Even if the relative risk of Project B increases over time, it would be unlikely that such increases in perceived risk would parallel the relationships implied by the ratios A/B in the above table.

(c) The present values of cash flows derived in part (a) result in the following graph:

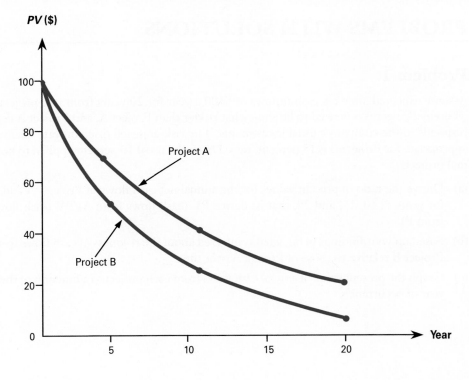

Problem 2

An organization with a cost of capital of 14 percent considers an investment project characterized by the following expected net cash flows over time.

Year	Net cash flows
0	−$100,000
1	− 20,000
2	+ 20,000
3	+ 40,000
4	+ 60,000
5	+ 60,000
6	+ 40,000
7	+ 20,000

(a) Compute the project's payback period, rounding up to the nearest year, without discounting cash flows.

(b) Compute the project's payback period, rounding up to the nearest year, using discounted cash flows.

(c) Draw the project's NPV as a function of time t assuming abandonment at time t.

(d) Given that the project might have to be abandoned early, what is the maximum amount that the firm stands to lose (in present value terms) if early abandonment comes at the worst possible time?

Solution 2

(a) Without discounting future cash flows, we compute the payback period as follows:

Year	Cumulative amount invested to date	Cumulative amount returned to date	Difference
0	$100,000	$0	$100,000
1	120,000	0	120,000
2	120,000	20,000	100,000
3	120,000	60,000	60,000
4	120,000	120,000	0

The payback period is four years.

(b) The payback period now involves discounted cash flows, which are computed as follows:

Year	Net cash flows	PV factor (14%)	Discounted cash flow
0	−$100,000	1.000	−$100,000
1	− 20,000	.877	− 17,540
2	+ 20,000	.769	+ 15,380
3	+ 40,000	.675	+ 27,000
4	+ 60,000	.592	+ 35,520
5	+ 60,000	.519	+ 31,140
6	+ 40,000	.456	+ 18,240
7	+ 20,000	.400	+ 8,000

The discounted payback period is derived from cumulative discounted cash flows in the same fashion as in part (a), so we obtain:

Year	Cumulative amount invested to date (discounted)	Cumulative amount returned to date (discounted)	Net present value to date (−investments +returns)
0	$100,000	$ 0	−$100,000
1	117,540	0	− 117,540
2	117,540	15,380	− 102,160
3	117,540	42,380	− 75,160
4	117,540	77,900	− 39,640
5	117,540	109,040	− 8,500
6	117,540	$127,280	+ 9,740
7	117,540	135,280	+ 17,740

The discounted payback period rounded up to the nearest year is six years.

(c) The following graph may be derived from the last column in the table above.

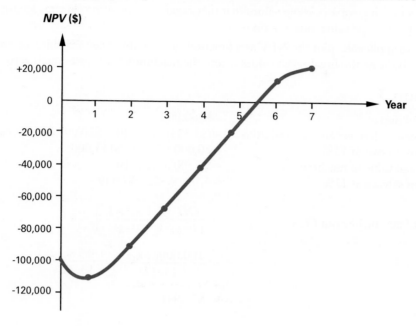

(d) From the graph, it is apparent that the worst time for abandonment occurs at the end of year 1, implying a loss of $117,540 (in present value terms).

Problem 3

Excellent Enterprises considers investing in a new machine that would cost $100,000 and is expected to produce before-tax savings of $33,333 per year for 10 years, at which point the machine could be sold for $4,500. CCA on a declining balance may be claimed at a rate of 30 percent. The company's cost of capital is 12 percent, and the tax rate is 40 percent.

(a) Based on the project's NPV, should the firm proceed?

(b) A more careful forecast is prepared by the divisional manager including possible variations in anticipated cash inflows. It is possible that sales could vary from expected values, which in turn would alter the before-tax savings achieved by the new machine by up to $15,000 per year. Once sales patterns are established in the first year, however, they are expected to remain at this level over the 10-year life of the machine. Also, it is possible that the new machine may last up to 12 years allowing savings to continue for another two years. Finally, the expected salvage value of the machine at the end of the 10th year, which is largely conjecture, may vary between zero and $6,000.

Perform a sensitivity analysis, and show the effects on the desirability of the project of the worst possible values that may occur for operating savings, length of life, and salvage value, one at a time.

(c) Where applicable, plot the NPV as a function of these three key variables, one at a time. Indicate the break-even values where the machine's NPV just equals zero.

Solution 3

(a) Initial outlay   =\$100,000

Expected after-tax annual cash inflows =(33,333)×(1−.40)=\$20,000 for 10 years

PV of inflows at 12%   =20,000×5.650=\$113,000

Salvage value of machine   =\$4,500 in year 10

PV of salvage at 12%   =4,500×.322=\$1,449

$$PV \text{ of tax shield from } CCA = \frac{CdT}{(d+k)}\left(\frac{1+.5\times k}{1+k}\right)$$

$$= \frac{100,000(.3)(.4)}{(.3+.12)}\left(\frac{1+.5\times.12}{1+.12}\right)$$

$$= \$27,041$$

$$PV \text{ of tax shield lost on sale} \atop \text{of machine in year 10} = \frac{4,500(.3)(.4)}{(.3+.12)} \times .322$$

$$= \$414$$

NPV= −initial outlay+PV of annual cash inflows+tax shield from CCA+salvage value of machine−tax shield lost on sale of machine

$$= -100,000+113,000+27,041+1,449-414$$

$$= \$41,076$$

Based on this figure, Excellent Enterprises should proceed with the project.

(b) After-tax savings of only .6(33,333−15,000)=\$11,000 per year (worst possible case) would reduce the NPV of annual cash inflows to \$11,000×5.650=\$62,150, yielding:

$$NPV= -100,000+62,150+27,041+1,449-414$$

$$= -\$9,774$$

Assuming the worst with respect to salvage value (\$0), the net present value of the project would change by only 1,449−414=\$1,035, and we obtain:

$$NPV=41,076-1,035=\$40,041$$

Since the useful life of the machine is not expected to be less than 10 years, we see that the only real concern regarding the project's economic desirability is the possible decrease in operating savings that may result from declining sales.

(c) To plot these functions, we compute three points for each variable.

(1) After-tax cash inflows:

We know if after-tax cash inflows are:

$20,000, NPV = $41,076

$11,000, NPV = -$9,774

$0, NPV = -100,000 + 27,041 + 1,449 - 414

$$= -100,000 + 27,041 + 1,286$$

$$= -$71,924$$

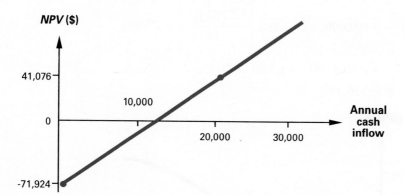

The general equation for the net present value as a function of annual cash inflows can be derived as NPV = -71,924 + 5.650×annual inflows. Hence, the break-even value for annual cash inflows becomes:

$$\frac{71,924}{5.650} = $12,730$$

(2) Length of life:

Varying the length of life of the project alters the discount factors. We already know that for a 10-year project, NPV=$41,076. Given eight years of operating life, we obtain:

$$NPV = -100,000 + 20,000 \times \left[\frac{1 - \dfrac{1}{(1.12)^8}}{.12}\right] + 27,041$$

$$+ 4,500(.404) - 1,286(.404)$$

$$= -100,000 + 99,360 + 27,041$$
$$+ 1,818 - 519$$

$$= \$27,700$$

A life of only two years would result in:

$$NPV = -100,000 + 20,000 \times \left[\frac{1 - \dfrac{1}{(1.12)^2}}{.12}\right] + 27,041$$

$$+ 4,500(.797) - 1,286(.797)$$

$$= -\$36,597$$

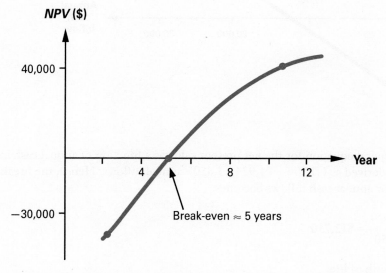

Break-even occurs for a project life of about five years.

(3) Salvage value:

This affects only the last two terms in the NPV equation. At a salvage value of $4,500, we had NPV=$41,076, and at a salvage value of $0 (worst possible case), NPV=$40,041. Given the insignificance of the change, it is not worthwhile to analyse the NPV function. There is no break-even value because the NPV remains positive regardless of the salvage value assumed.

Problem 4

The P. L. Company considers an investment with the following characteristics:

Initial outlay	$500,000
Net increases in net operating revenue	
year 1	400,000
year 2	300,000
year 3	180,000
Salvage value at the end of year 3	35,000

The corporate tax rate is 50 percent, capital cost allowance is taken at a rate of 20 percent on a declining balance, and the risk-free discount rate is 6 percent. Assume that risk increases over time so that management views the certainty equivalent coefficients for the cash flows anticipated in years 0 to 3 as $a_0=1.0$, $a_1=0.8$, $a_2=0.7$, and $a_3=0.6$.

(a) Using certainty equivalents, calculate the internal rate of return (IRR) of the investment. Would you accept the project?

(b) If instead risk-adjusted discount rates were used to evaluate this project, how high could the risk premium on the discount rate be (over and above the 6 percent risk-free rate) in order for the project to break even?

Solution 4

(a) Internal rate of return (IRR) calculation:

$$NPV = -500,000 + \frac{500,000(.2)(.5)}{(.2+r)}\left(\frac{1+.5\times r}{1+r}\right) + \frac{200,000(.8)}{(1+r)} + \frac{150,000(.7)}{(1+r)^2}$$
$$+ \frac{90,000(.6)}{(1+r)^3} + \frac{35,000(.6)}{(1+r)^3}\left[1-\frac{(.2)(.5)}{(.2+r)}\right] = 0$$

By trial and error, we find IRR $\approx$ 5%.

Because 5% < 6%, we would reject the project.

(b) Computing the IRR for the original cash flows as given above, we obtain:

$$NPV = -500,000 + \frac{500,000(.2)(.5)}{(.2+r)}\frac{1+.5\times r}{1+r} + \frac{200,000}{(1+r)} + \frac{150,000}{(1+r)^2}$$
$$+ \frac{90,000}{(1+r)^3} + \frac{35,000}{(1+r)^3}\left[1-\frac{(.2)(.5)}{(.2+r)}\right] = 0$$

Through trial and error, we derive:

for $r = 15\%$	$NPV = -\$3,511$
for $r = 14\%$	$NPV = \$6,311$

Interpolating, we obtain IRR $\approx$ 14.6%.

Only if the risk-adjusted discount rate is raised to above 14.6 percent would the project be rejected. Hence, any risk premium of less than 14.6%−6%=8.6% would imply that the project remains acceptable.

ADDITIONAL PROBLEMS

1. A firm is deciding about a potential project. It would involve an initial investment of $1 million. It would generate cash flows each year for the next 10 years. What must the after-tax cash flows be in order for this project to break even in a present value sense if the appropriate discount rate is 12%?

2. For the project in Problem 1, assume that cash flows over the 10-year life of the project will be as you calculated there. What is the payback period of the project in this case? What is the discounted payback period?

3. Consider the following after-tax cash flows on two projects:

	Year 0	Year 1	Year 2	Year 3
Project A	−100	50	50	25
Project B	−100	35	35	75

The company's cost of capital is 10 percent. Which of these projects would be preferred according to net present value? Which would be preferred according to payback period? Discuss which project the firm should choose.

4. A business has the opportunity to invest in a new factory. The total initial costs would be $2 million. The factory would operate for a maximum of 25 years and is expected to generate net after-tax cash flows of $150,000 each year it operates. The local government wants to encourage the firm to make this investment (in order to generate the extra employment in the region) and has agreed to pay $1 million toward the cost. If the firm closes the factory within the first five years, must repay the $ million, but if the factory stays open between five and 10 years, the company need only repay $500,000. If the factory stays open more than 10 years, it does not have to repay any of the money. Compute and graph the NPV of the factory up to year t assuming abandonment in year t for all t from 1 to 25.

5. A company has two projects to choose from with the following after-tax cash flows:

Project A

Year 0	−$500,000
Year 1	− 500,000
Years 2-8	300,000

Project B

Year 0	−$1,000,000
Years 1-8	250,000

The firm's cost of capital is 12 percent.

(a) Compute both projects' payback period on a non-discounted and a discounted basis.

(b) Compute and graph both projects' NPV as a function of time assuming abandonment at time t.

6. An investment would require an initial outlay of $600,000. Returns over the next eight years would be uncertain, but $140,000 per year is deemed to be a reasonable estimate. The cost of capital for the company is 13 percent.

(a) Derive the NPV of the investment.

(b) Do a sensitivity analysis, one variable at a time, that illustrates the effect on the NPV of changes in:

(i) the amount of anticipated annual cash inflows

(ii) the number of years that the inflows will last

(c) Plot the project's NPV as a function of these variables, and identify break-even points.

7. The R. M. Company requires risk-adjusted rates to be used when determining investment worth. Sample classifications and corresponding after-tax required rates of return include:

Investments in new lines of activity	16%
Substitution of capital for labour	10%
Expansion of existing product lines	12%
Replacement of existing equipment	8%

The firm is currently looking to invest internally generated funds totalling $400,000. No funds are to be raised externally. Project A requires $300,000 to replace existing equipment. Project B requires $400,000 to buy a more sophisticated piece of equipment as a replacement for existing machinery. This more sophisticated machine will enable R. M. Company to reduce the size of its workforce. A third project, C, would require an appropriation of $100,000, which would enable the firm to produce a brand new product line. There are no other projects available at this time.

Expected cash flows are as follows:

	Projects		
	A	B	C
		(in thousands of dollars)	
Investment ($t=0$)	−300	−400	−100
Net after-tax cash inflows			
($t=1$)	75	115	30
($t=2$)	85	145	45
($t=3$)	110	145	45
($t=4$)	20	130	40

Unused funds will be paid out to shareholders as an extra dividend. What would you recommend regarding the three projects under consideration?

*8. The LMS Company's usual after-tax required rate of return is 12 percent. Its after-tax risk-free rate is 6 percent.

The projected after-tax cash flows of two mutually exclusive projects and their certainty equivalent coefficients are:

Project A				Project B		
	Cash flow	CEC			Cash flow	CEC
$t=0$	−500	1.0		$t=0$	−500	1.0
$t=1$	305	0.9		$t=1$	190	0.9
$t=2$	370	0.7		$t=2$	210	0.9
$t=3$	300	0.6		$t=3$	305	0.8
$t=4$	240	0.5		$t=4$	385	0.7

Which project should be favoured?

9. (**Note**: This question is easiest to answer using a spreadsheet). A company is considering undergoing a major refitting of its production process, which would require an investment of $2.5 million in new equipment. The equipment would be depreciated for tax purposes at a CCA rate of 10 percent per year. The equipment would never be sold. The refitting would also require an immediate investment of $600,000 in training for the firm's workforce. If the refitting takes place, cost savings are expected to be (before tax) $300,000 per year. As well, the extra capacity in the factory will allow revenues to increase by $100,000 in the first year. The extra revenues are expected to grow by 5 percent each year after that. The firm's tax rate is 35 percent, the cost of capital is 10 percent, and the refitting project can be assumed to last forever.

(a) Given the projections, what is the net present value of the refitting project?

(b) Conduct a sensitivity analysis on the cost savings and the training costs. For cost savings, calculate the net present value if the savings were actually 50 percent lower than projected, then 45 percent lower, then 40 percent lower etc., continuing up to 50 percent higher than projected. Plot the resulting NPVs versus the error in the original projection. Do the same analysis for the training costs.

(c) Based on the plots in (b), which of the two projections (cost savings and training costs) is the source of the greatest amount of risk for the project? Discuss.

Taking the Long View with Student Residences

Simon Fraser University's townhouse-style residences, with their natural setting and names derived from regions of the province, are popular with students during the school year and conference-goers in the summer. Built in 1993, they are an example of a project where a public institution has to act more like a private corporation.

"Capital budgeting generally works very differently in a university than in a corporation," explains Denis Bérubé, Director of Accounting Services of the Burnaby, BC university, which has come in first in its category for three out of the last four years in the Maclean's magazine rankings. "Rather than looking for maximum return on an investment, we start with our program needs, demographic information, etc., and make requests to the government bodies that fund us. Student residences, however, are an exception."

Many universities in Canada operate student residences, but these are generally self-funding.

"Building residences is one area where Simon Fraser ends up involved in mortgages and long-term capital financing arrangements," explains Mr. Bérubé. "Typically, that means a 25- to 30-year mortgage."

"We calculate the finance costs over the long term and use that, together with the operating costs and market rates for comparable housing off campus as a basis for calculating the rent we charge students." The university also calculates a certain amount that goes into a reserve fund, to be used for major repairs and renovations as needed.

The townhouses were built with a shorter-term mortgage than most, to be paid off by 2002. The business plan called for dipping into the residence reserve fund each year to help finance this development. "In retrospect, this might not have been such a good idea," points out Jan Fialkowski, Simon Fraser's Director of Residences. "It is jeopardizing our ability to undertake renovations on the older structures, because the rents and residence fees have not increased as the business plan outlined."

"Raising the rent isn't necessarily an option, either," explains Mr. Bérubé. "Any increases need to be approved by a committee that is composed mostly of students. Naturally, they like to see rents kept low."

If rents can't keep up with inflation, and the reserve fund has been depleted to pay for ongoing costs, it may mean that there's no money available to replace a carpet or renovate a bathroom when it's necessary. "Students can be a little hard on buildings," points out Mr. Bérubé.

Capital Budgeting: Additional Topics

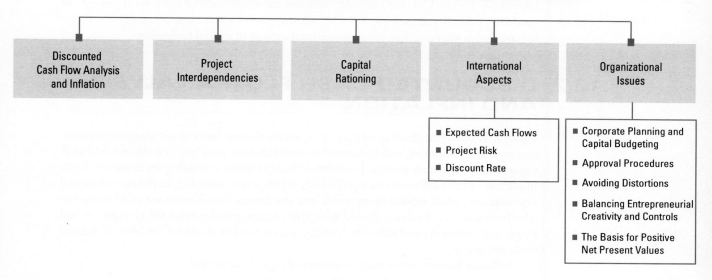

Discounted Cash Flow Analysis and Inflation	Project Interdependencies	Capital Rationing	International Aspects	Organizational Issues

International Aspects
- Expected Cash Flows
- Project Risk
- Discount Rate

Organizational Issues
- Corporate Planning and Capital Budgeting
- Approval Procedures
- Avoiding Distortions
- Balancing Entrepreneurial Creativity and Controls
- The Basis for Positive Net Present Values

Learning Objectives

After studying this chapter, you should be able to:

1. *Discuss why cash flows need to be projected in nominal terms when market discount rates are used.*
2. *Explain what discount rate is used and why, when a business faces capital rationing.*
3. *Explain why projects should be ranked according to their benefit-cost ratio.*
4. *Discuss the additional considerations of international capital budgeting.*
5. *Describe and define the relationship between capital budgeting, general corporate planning, strategic planning, and operating budgets.*

12.1 INTRODUCTION

In this chapter, we introduce a variety of additional issues that commonly arise in capital budgeting. They include dealing with inflation or general price-level changes in forecasting cash flows, the evaluation of interdependent projects, and making adjustments for capital rationing where because of resource constraints, not all positive NPV projects can be pursued. A section on international aspects introduces some of the additional complexities that are often encountered with foreign investments. All of these topics are important. Figure 12.1, for example, indicates the magnitude of price-level changes in particular periods and underscores why inflation must receive consideration. The chapter concludes with a review of the procedural aspects of capital budgeting.

12.2 DISCOUNTED CASH FLOW ANALYSIS AND INFLATION

Given that inflation, albeit at varying rates, seems to have become permanently embedded in most economies, it is important to establish how management should deal with expectations regarding general price-level changes when evaluating investments. Even moderate rates of inflation can significantly affect projections that, in the case of capital expenditures, often extend many years into the future. Specifically, we need to decide whether cash flow forecasts should fully reflect anticipated price-level changes caused by general inflation or whether such projections should be made on the basis of current costs and prices.

Inflation has an impact on two aspects of capital budgeting:

1. It influences the general level of future cash flows generated by a project.
2. It is incorporated in the cost of capital that is used as a discount rate.

In order to derive valid economic evaluations, it is essential that expectations about inflation be dealt with in a consistent manner both in the derivation of the firm's cost of capital and in the projection of future cash flows.

FIGURE 12.1

Inflation and T-Bill Yields (1938–98)

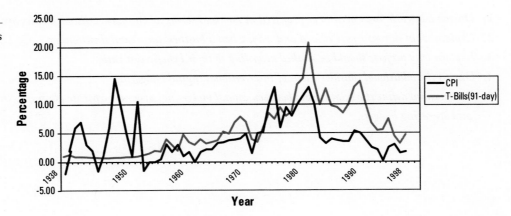

Source: Canadian Institute of Actuaries Website: www.actuaries.ca.

As we saw in our discussion of interest rates in Chapter 6, the cost of raising funds in financial markets reflects the expectations of investors about inflation. This is because investors normally demand a real return over and above the expected rate of general price-level changes, and, so, the inflation rate is embodied in the market's cost of raising funds. This is evident in Figure 12.1, in which we can see how T-bill yields in Canada have closely followed the level of inflation as measured by the Consumer Price Index (CPI). With the applicable discount rate fully reflecting inflationary expectations, consistency requires that projected cash flows also include anticipated price-level changes.

Consider what would happen if investors were inconsistent in their treatment of inflation. For example, assume that the inflation rate has risen to 50 percent per year. As a result, investors demand a return of 55 percent on any new capital that they advance (50 percent to protect them against inflation plus a real return of 5 percent). If a discount rate of 55 percent were applied to future cash flows that are based on current costs and prices, very few feasible investments would remain. In order to be accepted, an investment would have to provide a real return (in current dollars) of at least 55 percent per year, and it is unlikely that in a competitive environment, many such investments would exist.

Numerous enterprises still fail to incorporate forecasts of price-level changes into their cash flow projections, but they discount at rates that reflect the current market cost of funds. This may result in significant distortions. Consider, for example, an investment in reforestation with a harvest cycle of 80 years. If a 5 percent average inflation rate is applied over this time period, every $1,000 in current prices is equivalent to $1,000(1.05)^{80} = $49,561$ in prices 80 years from now—hardly a negligible effect to be ignored for reasons of convenience or ease of computation.

Forecasting the inflation rate over extended time periods is not easy and may appear to be a futile exercise. However, as we saw, current interest rates embody the market expectations regarding inflation and as such, can provide guidance to management.

An alternative that to some extent precludes the need to forecast the general level of inflation explicitly, is to take the inflation component out of the cost of capital and to forecast cash flows in terms of constant price levels. If applied consistently, this approach, which is common in public sector investment evaluations, will yield roughly equivalent results. This approach is called **constant dollar discounting** as opposed to the standard process of **current dollar discounting** as discussed above.

CURRENT DOLLAR VERSUS CONSTANT DOLLAR DISCOUNTING

EXAMPLE

A firm's weighted average cost of capital has been computed to be 14 percent. Based on current market interest rates, the annual average inflation rate over the next five years is estimated at 10 percent. A current investment of $1,000 is expected to produce cash inflows of $250 per year for five years measured at today's price levels.

The NPV of this investment can be calculated in two ways by:

1. including current expectations regarding inflation in both the discount rate and the cash flows

2. taking inflation out of the cost of capital and forecasting future cash flows at today's price levels

For Alternative 1, we apply the inflation rate of 10 percent to the annual cash inflows and then discount at the market-given cost of capital of 14 percent. We obtain:

$$NPV = -1,000 + \frac{250(1+.1)}{(1+.14)} + \frac{250(1+.1)^2}{(1+.14)^2} + \ldots + \frac{250(1+.1)^5}{(1+.14)^5}$$

$$= -1,000 + 250\,(.965 + .931 + .898 + .896 + .836)$$

$$= -1,000 + 1,124$$

$$= \$124$$

For Alternative 2, we reduce the market-given cost of capital of 14 percent by the inflation rate and discount at the real time value of money of 4 percent. Future cash flows are expressed in current dollars and remain at $250 per year. We have:

$$NPV = -1,000 + \left[\frac{1 - \dfrac{1}{(1.04)^5}}{.04} \right] \times 250$$

$$= -1,000 + (4.452) \times 250$$

$$= \$113$$

The two results are at least roughly equivalent, with the procedure under Alternative 1 yielding the more accurate figure.[1]

Contrast with the above an evaluation that discounts constant cash flows at an inflation-induced cost of capital. We have:

$$NPV = -1,000 + \left[\frac{1 - \dfrac{1}{(1.14)^5}}{.14} \right] \times 250$$

$$= -1,000 + (3.433) \times 250$$

$$= -\$141.75$$

By calculating this way, the project would be rejected, even though, in fact, it makes a positive economic contribution to the firm.

The reason the constant dollar discounting approach is used in the public sector but is not prevalent in private sector project evaluations is that there are interactions between the tax code and inflation. These are easy to deal with when inflation is included in both the cash flow and discount rate estimates. The constant dollar technique

---

[1] Defining k = nominal rate; i = inflation rate; r = real rate of return, in order to obtain an exact equivalence between these two results requires $(1+i)^n/(1+k)^n = 1/(1+r)^n$, or $(1+k) = (1+i)(1+r)$, from which we derive $k = i+r+ir$. The simple relationship $k = i+r$ as assumed in the example (14% = 10% + 4%) is an approximation that is valid only for small values of i and r, so that the term ir can be neglected.

used in the previous example makes it quite complex to deal with such interactions; hence, it is seldom used by taxable firms.[2]

As indicated earlier, changes in relative price levels of various cash flow components must always be recognized. That is, even if the average level of inflation as measured by the CPI is dealt with according to Alternative 2, individual components of cash flows may be expected to rise at rates that are higher or lower than the average level. For example, if average inflation is expected to run at 10 percent per year, but it is anticipated that the cost of labour will increase at a rate of 15 percent, the 5 percent increase in excess of the average inflation rate must be incorporated into cash flow forecasts.

DIFFERENCES IN RELATIVE PRICE LEVELS

EXAMPLE

Pursuing the previous example, it is estimated that labour costs will escalate at an annual rate of 15 percent, material costs for the firm's products will rise only 8 percent each year, while selling prices will keep pace with average inflation. Further assume that the $250 cash flow estimated for year 1 is derived as follows:

	Sales (constant quantity per year)	$1,000
Less	Cost of goods sold	
	Labour	250
	Materials	250
	Taxable income	$ 500
Less	Tax payable ($T=0.5$)	250
	After-tax income	$ 250

Assume there is no depreciation and there are no other costs or cash flows so that after-tax income equals the net cash flows.

In projecting net cash flows for the next five years, different rates of price-level changes have to be applied to various cash flow components as follows:

	Year				
	1	2	3	4	5
Sales (10%)	$1,000	$1,100	$1,210	$1,331	$1,464
Labour (15%)	250	288	331	380	437
Materials (8%)	250	270	292	315	340
Taxable income	$ 500	$ 542	$ 587	$ 636	$ 687
Tax payable	250	271	294	318	344
After-tax income or net cash flows	$ 250	$ 271	$ 293	$ 318	$ 343

---

[2] Depreciation deductions are based on historical costs. Inflation, therefore, erodes their real value. This is captured automatically if current dollars are used. If constant dollars are used, however, an adjustment to cash flows has to be estimated.

Even if forecasts are to be made in constant dollars net of general inflation, relative price changes or differences from the average inflation rate have to be recognized. Labour costs will escalate at a rate that exceeds general inflation by 5 percent, whereas material costs will lag inflation by 2 percent. We obtain:

	Year				
	1	2	3	4	5
Sales (constant $)	$1,000	$1,000	$1,000	$1,000	$1,000
Labour (15%−10%=5%)	250	265	276	289	304
Materials (8%−10%=−2%)	250	245	240	235	231
Taxable income	$500	$492	$484	$476	$465
Tax payable	250	246	242	238	233
After-tax income or net cash flows	$250	$246	$242	$238	$232

The previous point is important because the production factors that a given company employs will generally not coincide with the items that are included in the CPI. Cash flows will often be subject to price-level changes that differ from the average rate of inflation.

12.3 PROJECT INTERDEPENDENCIES

Our discussion thus far has assumed that investments are independent of each other and that each project can be evaluated in its own right. However, it may not always be appropriate to view each project in isolation since we often need to be concerned with interdependencies between them. Interdependencies exist when the cash flows generated by one project depend on other investments that the firm may consider. Extreme examples are projects that are **mutually exclusive** and projects that are **contingent** upon each other.

Location problems are a typical example of mutually exclusive projects. If a firm considers three different locations for a new warehouse, the alternatives are mutually exclusive since the choice of one site will preclude a warehouse in any other location even if a separate analysis of each alternative reveals that a positive net present value may have been attainable in more than one location. Another example would be the purchase of equipment whereby a choice of several different machines may be available for one particular task. To deal with such situations, all mutually exclusive alternatives are analysed as a group, and only the best one is chosen.

Contingent investments are those in which the viability of one project is conditional on the prior acceptance of another. Acquisition of a trailer may hinge, for instance, on the purchase of a truck and vice versa. Again, contingent projects have to be considered as a group and evaluated together. We note the possibility that a project upon which other projects are contingent may be accepted even if it, by itself, is not economically viable. This may be the case when an offsetting gain is provided by returns received from other projects in the contingent group.

More generally, the interdependence of projects may be either complementary or negative. For example, two new products may have some market overlap and therefore some negative interdependence, whereas two other products may complement each other, thus increasing total sales. Under conditions of dependence between projects, ideally, all possible subgroups of investments that make up a capital budget should be evaluated in order to find the best possible combination. Although this may be desirable, the operational consequences may prove prohibitive given the large number of combinations that might have to be considered. Thus, it may be possible to recognize only the most important interdependencies.

CAPITAL RATIONING 12.4

Under normal circumstances, a firm should accept all projects with cash flows that when discounted at the cost of capital, yield net benefits to shareholders as reflected in positive NPVs. At a given time, however, a firm may have limited resources at its disposal and be constrained in the activities it pursues. Although the following discussion focuses on financial constraints, we recognize that other constraints such as the scarcity of labour or managerial talent may also impose limitations.

When financial constraints prevent a firm from pursuing otherwise desirable investments, it is faced with **capital rationing**—money has to be rationed among projects that compete for scarce funds. We could argue that a firm that creates enough attractive investment opportunities to face financial constraints should simply raise additional capital to the point where marginal costs equal marginal benefits, thereby taking advantage of such opportunities. Efficient financial markets should make this possible, and as long as new investments yield more than the cost of raising the needed additional capital, they will make an economic contribution to the firm and increase the wealth of its owners.

PERSPECTIVES

Corporate Manager

Many managers attempt to have excess funds available for investment purposes in order to avoid creating capital rationing, which may force the firm to pass up profitable, positive NPV investments in the future.

Investor

Investors should evaluate the reasons for new security issues by corporations. If the proceeds are to be used to fund promising new ventures, this should be reflected in future security prices, if they are not already.

In practice, however, capital rationing is prevalent, particularly during business slow-downs. This is because firms typically feel that outstanding obligations have pushed them close to their debt capacity, and many firms are reluctant to sell new equity, particularly following declines in their share prices. This fact is evident in the results of a comprehensive survey of large Canadian corporations, which confirmed the presence of capital rationing. Over one-half of the respondents tied their firm's ability to undertake attractive investments to profit levels and the amount of internally generated funds available.[3] Figure 12.2 depicts this relationship between the availability of internally generated funds, via corporate profits, and corporate investment in Canada over the period 1980 to 2000. This figure shows that the pattern of corporate investment is highly correlated with corporate profits, with a lag.

FIGURE 12.2

Canada—Real Corporate Investments and Real Pre-Tax (Annual % Change)

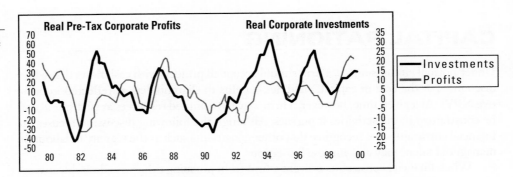

Source: "Economic and Financial Outlook", Montrusco Bolton and Andre Marsan, *Canadian Economy,* July 2000, Volume 16, No. 3, p. 5.

In efficient markets without impediments to the flow of information, such considerations may not be justified since current security prices should reflect fair-market expectations regarding the company's future performance. Given information asymmetries, however, whereby potential investors may know much less about a firm than its managers, the costs of raising outside equity can increase substantially and may become prohibitive. Also, managers may simply be more optimistic than investors about the firm's prospects. As a consequence, managers may find it psychologically difficult to accept the market's verdict regarding, for example, the price at which new shares could be sold especially when times are considered to be unfavourable.

Several other reasons may also contribute to the prevalence of capital rationing. For example, the raising of new capital often involves significant time lags so that in the short run at least, it may not be possible to lift the constraints. Also, the budgetary process, which is an important control tool particularly in large and decentralized firms, usually imposes limits on capital spending for each operating unit. Such constraints may be motivated in part by strategic policy considerations aimed at maintaining an overall

---

[3] V. Jog and A. Srivastava, "Capital Formation and Corporate Financial Decision Making in Canada," *Carleton University School of Business Working Paper*, (Ottawa: 1992), p. 27.

balance or direction in the firm's operations. Finally, in many closely held firms, in which both control and the use of debt could be of concern, external financing may be limited by policy.

A firm or division faced with capital rationing can no longer pursue all investment proposals that yield returns in excess of its cost of capital. Rather, it will accept the most desirable investment projects until its abilities to fund are exhausted, rejecting or postponing less attractive opportunities even if their returns exceed the cost of capital. As opportunity costs become the relevant yardstick against which new investments have to be measured, consequently, firms that operate under rationing will impose a discount rate that exceeds the cost of capital. Expressed another way, any accepted project should yield at least as much as the most desirable opportunity that had to be rejected or postponed. Hence, the discount rate to be applied is the effective yield of the most attractive investment foregone.

Consider, for example, a corporation with an overall cost of capital of 12 percent. If the firm has more investment opportunities than it can pursue with the limited capital currently available, then several investment projects promising returns of 16 percent must be foregone. It is clear that the opportunity cost of 16 percent becomes the standard against which new investment proposals must be measured, for this is the return that could be earned on any uncommitted funds.

However, even with the appropriate adjustment to the discount rate, a firm operating under capital constraints may no longer be able to simply rank projects on a net present value basis. Given limited funds, it becomes important that the feasible *combination of projects* yielding the highest net present value be accepted. From this perspective, capital rationing can be viewed as a special sort of project interdependency. Going ahead with one project may make another project infeasible.

CAPITAL RATIONING

EXAMPLE

Consider three investment Projects: A, B, and C, with the characteristics given below.

Project	Initial Investment	NPV
A	$10	$5
B	6	4
C	4	2

Assuming capital constraints of $10, the firm can either accept Project A, or Projects B and C. While Project A has the highest net present value, it should nevertheless be rejected in favour of accepting both Projects B and C since their combined net present value ($6) exceeds that of A ($5).

In situations of this type, firms can rank projects based on NPV per dollar of capital invested. These equal the benefit-cost ratio discussed in Appendix 10-A and reflect the "productivity of capital" per project. When capital is constrained, this becomes a reasonable criterion for the ranking of projects.[4]

---

[4] This approach works only if one constraint applies and if individual projects are independent of each other.

12.5 INTERNATIONAL ASPECTS OF CAPITAL BUDGETING

Firms invest abroad for a variety of strategic reasons. These include minimizing the cost of production factors (global sourcing), achieving economies of scale, circumventing trade barriers or regulations, and having a presence to be able to exploit future opportunities that may arise in various parts of the world. One such example is discussed in the report below, which considers Ipsco's plans to build a mill in Alabama. Most large multinational corporations view it as essential to be active in the three major industrialized trading areas of the world: North America, Europe, and the Asia-Pacific. Large firms that spend heavily on research and development are especially likely to have overseas subsidiaries because new products have to be marketed on a large scale to recover substantial development costs. Since firms often wish to keep research and development and technical know-how secret in order to retain competitive advantage, foreign subsidiaries are often preferred to licensing arrangements or joint ventures.

■ *Finance in the News*

Ipsco to Build $650-Million Alabama Mill

Regina-based steelmaker Ipsco Inc. announced plans to build a $650-million mini steel mill in Mobile County, Alabama, which will be a carbon copy of its plant in Montpelier, Iowa. The new mill is scheduled to go into production by mid-2001. Ipsco president Roger Phillips stated that they expected the new mill to supply the region that traditionally used imported steel. The mill will be financed by a $150-million stock issue, a private placement of another $150 million in junior subordinated notes, cash flow, and lines of credit.

President Phillips stated confidently that even if the worst happened in the economy or the steel sector, Ipsco could handle itself without any serious problems. The company recognized the U.S. Gulf of Mexico region as having the highest growth in steel consumption recently; it also has good transportation facilities and offers favourable electrical power rates. Alabama also made available training grants and income tax relief to help create jobs.

Industry analyst Jay Gordon of Maison Placements Inc. felt that the project was "very high risk" because "God knows where the steel cycle will be in two or three years." Ipsco president Roger Phillips disagreed, stating that he doesn't see another situation like the one in the early 1990s when the economy collapsed and steelmakers were forced to take whatever buyers offered or be stuck with millions of tons of steel inventory. He confidently stated that the company was better equipped than any other in the industry to carry out this project. Another analyst agreed that Ipsco's cash flow could easily finance the project over the next three years. The dramatic decline in steel prices this year makes this project look risky, but the analyst felt Ipsco had demonstrated its ability to grow. Some investors seem to agree since Ipsco shares rose 30 cents on the TSE to $26.50.

Source: "Ipsco to Build $650-Million Alabama Mill," by Greg Keenan, *Globe and Mail*, December 23, 1998, pages B1 and B4. *Reprinted with permission.*

The basic principles of investment evaluation, previously outlined, remain valid when moving abroad: we should derive net present values by discounting incremental net cash flows at the appropriate cost of capital. A number of additional difficulties arise, however, when one tries to operationalize this in an international context. These difficulties can be grouped into effects on expected cash flows, on project risk, and on the appropriate discount rate. We provide a brief overview of some common issues that one confronts in this context.

The analysis of a project may vary depending on whose point of view we take: that of the multinational parent company or that of a local subsidiary. It is clear that conceptually any analysis should be done from the point of view of the multinational parent company of which the shareholders ultimately own any new venture. In practice, managers may take a more local perspective, particularly if their own rewards are tied to success at the local level. This potential conflict between local and multinational interests may be accentuated when investments are arranged in the form of joint ventures with local participation.

Expected Cash Flows

Factors affecting expected cash flows may include special economic incentives provided at the local level, differences in tax rates and regulations, and restrictions on the free flow of funds. Many local governments provide special assistance to foreign investors, ranging from free advice to low-cost land or tax breaks. Such incentives can substantially reduce the initial capital outlay required.

Tax laws and rates vary from country to country. An example would be the rules that apply for computing capital cost allowances, which affect tax payments and, therefore, after-tax cash flows. Thus, if a foreign government offers generous, fast write offs on a new investment, this increases after-tax cash flows in the early periods thereby enhancing the NPV. If tax rates in the foreign country are below those at home, the home tax rate applies only when profits are repatriated. In addition, a firm may try to minimize taxes globally by shifting profits into low-tax countries—for example, through the setting of transfer prices or by charging management and licence fees to subsidiaries that operate in a high-tax environment.

Different norms of business conduct can also affect the expected cash flows of firms. For example, bribes or kickbacks to government officials are a part of everyday business in a number of Third World countries. From a financial point of view, these practices can be viewed as an additional tax the firm must pay. The problem is that the tax is unofficial and erratic. The unpredictability of such demands for payment by local government officials may discourage foreign investment and thus can be an important obstacle to the development of many countries.

Finally, some developing countries restrict the repatriation of profits. Cash flows that must remain in the host country may have a reduced economic value.

Project Risk

Important factors affecting the risk of international projects include political uncertainty and changes in foreign exchange rates. Political instability clearly can affect future cash flows and is a major consideration in international capital budgeting decisions. Locally earned cash flows ultimately have to be converted into the multinational home currency at exchange rates that, in recent years, have shown large variability.

If we add the fact that managers may be less well informed about distant markets and cultures, it comes as no surprise that foreign investments are often viewed as significantly more risky than domestic ones. If this is the case, adjustments for the added risk will have to be made at the evaluation stage.

Referring to our previous discussion of risk assessment, we note that risk need not be higher for foreign investments. In a global context, most political and foreign exchange risks are diversifiable since both shareholders and companies can spread their investments over many different countries. In fact, a business may find that international diversification reduces the risk of being dependent on a single market, even if the foreign investment, viewed in isolation, is risky.[5]

Finally, a variety of techniques are available to manage and insure against international risk. Such techniques include joint ventures, financing the investment in the local country, actual insurance against political risk (as provided, for example, by the Export Development Corporation), and a variety of tools for managing foreign exchange exposure that, because of their broader applications, will be discussed separately in Chapter 21.

Discount Rate

In efficient international financial markets in which capital is globally mobile, the costs of financing a project should be independent of its location. However, not all financial markets are fully integrated globally, and host governments sometimes offer favourable financing that is tied to specific investment decisions. Examples include loan guarantees or debt at subsidized interest rates. Such incentives can lower the effective cost of financing a project thereby once again affecting its NPV.

We conclude that while the basic principles of capital budgeting remain unaffected by location, many added factors have to be considered to derive the appropriate cash flows and discount rate in an international setting. We also note that most of the issues discussed in this section can also arise in a domestic setting; they just tend to be more prevalent and pronounced in an international context. For example, even foreign exchange risk is not restricted to international investments. If a new product launched domestically competes with an imported one, the future cash flows for the new product will be affected by foreign exchange rates, since they will influence the relative competitive position of the two products.   ▲

---

[5] Recall from Chapter 7 that it is also advantageous for investors to diversify internationally.

ORGANIZATIONAL ISSUES   12.6

Corporate Planning and Capital Budgeting

Investment planning is part of and takes place within general corporate planning. As we saw in Chapter 10, corporate planning normally begins at the strategic level at which market strategies (what business should the firm be in) and product strategies (how can the firm create sustainable competitive advantages) are formulated. Planning in the various functional areas of business, including finance, becomes subordinate to this overall corporate plan. As a consequence, from an organizational viewpoint, capital budgeting has both a "top down" and a "bottom up" component. The overall strategic framework within which capital budgeting takes place often is formulated at the top because it requires an overall vision of the firm and its environment. Detailed implementation of the strategy, however, requires input from the operating level in which people have the detailed "front-line" knowledge of what is needed to make things work. Achieving a good balance between top down and bottom up (i.e., between centralization and decentralization in decision-making) is one of the major organizational challenges in any planning including capital budgeting. Related to this issue is the balance between stimulating entrepreneurial initiative and maintaining reasonable control about which we will comment shortly.

Investment planning, which often covers a time span of at least three to five years, also has to fit with day-to-day planning and control, which is typically achieved through annual budgets. Once investment decisions are approved, they become part of the current operating budget.

Approval Procedures

Approval of investment proposals usually proceeds in several stages. Individual projects are aggregated at the divisional level and become part of a capital budgeting plan, which is reviewed and approved in principle by senior management. Prior to implementation, the appropriate operating department needs to submit an "authorization for expenditure," which contains the detailed economic justification of the project including a discounted cash flow analysis. Only after approval is obtained from the board of directors or the appropriate level of management (which depends on the size and importance of the project) are the funds released for investment.

Firms often group investment proposals into several distinct categories, and somewhat different procedures may apply in each case. A classification scheme may include:

1. projects required by law
2. safety and working condition improvements
3. essential replacements and additions
4. cost reduction and quality improvements
5. capacity expansion for existing products
6. new products or markets

For example, projects in Categories 1 to 3 may be subject to much less quantitative analysis than those in 4 to 6, and risk analysis may be particularly important for projects in Category 6. Also, there is much more discretion regarding investments in Categories 4 to 6. That is why total expenditures in these categories tend to expand and contract with the business cycle and the firm's ability to generate funding.

Table 12.1 provides a useful overview of Canadian corporate practices given different categories of projects. It is clear from the data that, in project evaluations, multiple techniques are commonly relied upon.

TABLE 12.1

Evaluation Techniques Used by Types of Projects

Type of Project	Evaluation Criteria		
	NPV	IRR	Payback
Replacement projects	34.6%	46.6%	48.9%
Expansion—existing operations	41.4	61.6	50.0
Expansion—new operations	45.1	61.6	47.4
Social expenditures	10.5	8.3	6.8

Source: V. Jog and A. Srivastava, "Capital Formation and Corporate Financial Decision Making in Canada," *Carleton University School of Business Working Paper,* (1992).

Avoiding Distortions

Quite often, divisions and departments are placed in a position in which they compete with each other for scarce corporate resources. Under such circumstances, it is understandable that investment proposals may become sales documents that attempt to portray the project in a positive light, and biases replace honest assessments in cash flow projections.

There are several ways in which management can deal with such distortions including the verification of projections through additional information (including reliance on outside experts) or by systematic post-audits of projects with feedback to the original proposers. Companies should also ensure that any calculations are based on consistent assumptions. That is a good reason to have forecasts of general economic variables that affect a variety of projects such as economic growth, raw material prices, escalations in labour costs, foreign exchange rates, and similar factors conducted centrally by corporate staff. Otherwise, varying NPVs among individual projects may have more to do with inconsistent assumptions than with differences in economic value.

A common approach for avoiding competitive bidding for every project at head office is to decentralize decision-making. For example, the firm allocates fixed amounts for investment to various divisions and departments, letting each organizational unit set its own priorities and then evaluates performance. The amounts allocated to departments may depend, in part, on past track records.

However, whenever distortions or other "game playing" become prevalent, management has to question the capital allocation procedures that are in place. Ideally, these procedures should be understood and supported throughout the organization. They should be viewed as helping the organization succeed rather than as hindrances that obstruct performance. If they are not supported by the people who work with them, it may be necessary to either educate the users or to improve the procedures.

Balancing Entrepreneurial Creativity and Controls

There are two basic types of errors that one can make in investment decisions:

1. accept a bad project (type 1 error)
2. forego a good project (type 2 error)

From the shareholders' point of view, both errors are equally serious. In one case, wealth is lost by assuming a negative NPV; in the other case, wealth or a positive NPV is given away, possibly to competitors.

In designing capital budgeting procedures, there clearly are trade-offs. If a control system is too "tight," it will avoid most type 1 errors, but strong conservatism normally also implies missed opportunities (type 2 errors). Conversely, in a "loose" environment, many initiatives may be encouraged. However, the looser the controls are, the more mistakes (type 1 errors) will be made. The "ideal" control system should balance these two types of errors.

In practice, many managers hold type 1 errors to be more serious than type 2 errors. The reason is that type 1 errors are measurable and are immediately reflected in financial performance. Missed opportunities are more elusive and may show up only indirectly and in the long run, for example, in the form of a deteriorating competitive position. That is why formal controls almost always tend to focus on avoiding the acceptance of bad projects. One should bear in mind, however, that a successful enterprise cannot be built through controls alone. The fostering of entrepreneurial initiatives and risk taking are essential to the success of business, and this implies a certain tolerance for type 1 errors.

The Basis for Positive Net Present Values

We saw earlier that in a truly competitive environment, net present values tend to be zero. In other words, a company may earn just a fair rate of return, but competition will erode any excess returns or economic rents. It follows that, if a manager is confronted with a proposal that shows a significant positive NPV, there are only three possible explanations:

1. The figures in the project are based on unreasonable assumptions. To check on this, it is important that all major assumptions are clearly spelled out. A sensitivity analysis regarding major assumptions may be useful.
2. The figures are biased, and the proposal is a sales document rather than an honest appraisal. We discussed this issue and how to deal with it previously.

3. The firm has identified some activity or output for which there is market demand and that it can perform better than the competition because of its superior skills and/or resources. Hence, there are market imperfections that give the enterprise, at least temporarily, some monopolistic powers.

Obviously, only item 3 above provides true economic value. When confronting positive NPV propositions, it is always useful to ask: "why cannot competitors replicate this endeavour easily, or what unique skills and/or resources do we possess that will make this asset more valuable in our hands than in the hands of the competition?" Only if these questions find satisfactory answers can one be confident that the forecasted positive NPV will, in fact, be forthcoming.

12.7 SUMMARY

1. Given inflation, it is important that in both the cash flow projections and choice of the discount rate, general price-level changes be reflected in a consistent manner.

2. Interrelations between projects can become important in affecting diversification and risk. Any direct interdependencies between investments need to be recognized. In extreme cases, projects may be either mutually exclusive or contingent.

3. When a firm faces capital rationing the discount rate to be used is the opportunity cost of funds, which equals the yield on the most attractive investment opportunity foregone.

4. Projects should be ranked on the basis of their benefit-cost ratio, which equals the net present value per unit of capital invested. The larger ratios are the more attractive.

5. International capital budgeting uses the same basic concepts and technologies, but added considerations affecting expected cash flows, risk, and the discount rate may exist.

6. Capital budgeting is linked to both strategic planning and to operating budgets. Ultimately, positive net present values are only created when a firm can do things better or cheaper than its competitors.

QUESTIONS AND PROBLEMS

Questions for Discussion

1. You have been asked to review a capital budgeting appropriation request finalized by a member of your staff. Cash flow forecasts have been prepared using constant price

levels. Payback is computed as well as NPV, with the flows discounted using the firm's weighted average cost of capital (WACC). Critique the approach taken.

2. Discuss why, given efficient financial markets, capital rationing is nevertheless prevalent in capital budgeting.

3. Using short examples, show why risk aside, the firm's weighted average cost of capital is an inappropriate discount rate to use, given capital rationing.

4. Illustrate why the benefit-cost ratio rather than the NPV should be used for ranking projects that are independent of each other in a situation of capital rationing.

5. In investment evaluations, why might there be conflicts between a multinational firm and its overseas joint venture? Assume the domestic partner in the joint venture has the controlling interest.

6. The production department of a bicycle manufacturer is proposing a significant investment for the retooling of part of its plant. The aim of the project is to produce a lighter and more luxurious mountain bike rather than just the fairly standard and slightly upscale models for which the company is known. The project's proponents have presented NPV data to show that the incremental investment will more than meet the firm's hurdle rate, given the risks involved. A recent graduate working in the finance department, suggests that the appropriation request from production, although backed by detailed NPV computations, is flawed in that it fails to take account of significant negative interdependencies. Describe what is probably at issue here and how it should be handled.

PROBLEM WITH SOLUTION

Problem

In Chapter 6 (see footnote 2 in that chapter), it was shown that the exact relationship between the nominal interest rate (R), the real interest rate (RR), and expected inflation (π) is given by:

$$1+R=(1+RR)(1+\pi)$$

This relationship can be approximated as $R \approx RR + \pi$.

Using the exact relationship, show that if a cash flow is going to be received t years from now, discounting the cash flow in constant dollar terms using the real discount rate gives exactly the same result as calculating the actual cash flow to be received in the future (i.e., including the affect of inflation) and discounting it at the nominal discount rate.

Solution

Let C be the cash flow in constant dollar terms. In other words, what would the cash flow be if we ignored inflation? The present value using the real interest rate would be:

$$PV = \frac{C}{(1+RR)^t}$$

If we incorporated the effect of inflation into our estimate of the cash flow, the actual cash flow to be received would be C^*, where:

$$C^* = C(1+\pi)^t$$

We can discount this cash flow at the nominal discount rate:

$$PV = \frac{C^*}{(1+R)^t}$$

$$PV = \frac{C(1+\pi)^t}{(1+R)^t}$$

If we now substitute in the relationship between the nominal rate, real rate, and inflation, we get:

$$PV = \frac{C(1+\pi)^t}{(1+RR)^t(1+\pi)^t}$$

which reduces to,

$$PV = \frac{C}{(1+RR)^t}$$

This is exactly the same as we would get if we had discounted the constant dollar cash flow at the real rate.

In the end, it should not matter if you use constant dollar cash flows or if your cash flow estimates incorporate inflation if you use the appropriate discount rate in your calculations.

This is the same as the PV using the nominal cash flow.

ADDITIONAL PROBLEMS

1. A company has total resources of $10 million available to invest in new projects. There are three possible projects that it is considering. The after-tax cash flows of the projects are as follows:

Project	Investment required	Year 1 cash flow	Year 2 cash flow
A	−10,000,000	30,000,000	5,000,000
B	−5,000,000	5,000,000	20,000,000
C	−5,000,000	5,000,000	15,000,000

In all three cases, the projects would be over after two years. Using a discount rate of 10 percent for all projects, calculate the net present value (NPV) for each. If the firm ranked the projects by NPV, which ones would they invest in and what would be the total NPV generated for the firm. Calculate the benefit-cost ratio for each project. If the organization ranked the projects based on this measure, which projects would it invest in, and what would be the total NPV generated for the firm?

2. There are three projects that the company could invest in, each lasting just one year:

Project	Investment	Cash flow in one year
A	−5	8
B	−5	7
C	−100	120

The firm has a limited investment budget of $100. Calculate the net present values and benefit-cost ratios of each project using a 10 percent discount rate. If the company ranked the projects based upon their benefit-cost ratios, which ones would it choose? Would this be the optimal solution? Explain why the benefit-cost ratio may not work correctly in this situation.

3. A sawmill produces studs that sell at about $200 per unit. Annual sales total 1,500 units. Chip sales average $100,000 per year. The value of the land, the salvage value of the mill including equipment, and the net working capital total $2.8 million, $50,000, and $150,000 respectively. If the mill were liquidated, working capital would just cover severance payments. The company has no debt, the mill is fully depreciated, and the firm's after-tax cost of capital is 12 percent. By investing $1 million in machinery, it would be possible for the mill to produce dimension lumber as well as the studs. This expansion would increase annual after-tax cash flows by the following projected amounts:

Year 1	$300,000	Year 6	$140,000
2	450,000	7	110,000
3	380,000	8	90,000
4	310,000	9	80,000
5	170,000	10	70,000

The equipment requires replacement after the tenth year, and it will have no salvage value. Because the price of dimension lumber fluctuates more than the price of studs, the company's new after-tax cost of capital is taken to be 14 percent rather than 12 percent. The after-tax cash flows from the stud mill are $280,000 annually and can be sustained for the next 10 years. In the tenth year, the total value of the land is expected to be $3 million, while working capital, as above, should just cover severance payments. Should the incremental investments be made? Show all of your computations and underlying assumptions.

4. The Triple-A Manufacturing Co. maintains that its after-tax cost of capital is 12 percent. A new machine to expand existing operations will cost a total of $50,000. The life of the machine is six years, and the current price levels are expected to rise by 6 percent annually. No additional working capital will be required because of expanded operations. The following projections are made:

- Incremental annual sales are expected to total 8,000 units.
- In the first year, each unit will sell for $5.00.
- Subsequent increases in selling price are expected to be 5 percent per year.
- Labour costs of $10,000 in the first year of operations are expected to rise by 10 percent each year.
- Materials will cost $12,000 in the first year and will rise by 6 percent annually.
- Other expenses total $1,500 in the first year and will rise by 2 percent a year.
- Corporate taxes are 50 percent.
- The appropriate CCA rate is 30 percent on the declining balance.

Should the purchase of the new machine be approved?

5. A firm is considering a project with the following forecasts:

- Initial investment will be $50,000.
- Revenues will be $500,000 at the end of the first year and will grow at 8 percent per year after that.
- Wage costs are paid monthly. The total wage costs will be $30,000 per month for the next two years. The union representing these employees has a history of signing two-year contracts (one of which was just signed) with fixed wages over the life of the contract. In the past, wage settlements for new contracts have risen at the rate of inflation (i.e., each new contract will reflect two years' worth of inflation).
- The project will last forever.
- The firm's required return is 18 percent in real terms.
- Assume that the firm pays no taxes.
- Inflation is expected to be 7 percent per year forever.

a) Calculate the NPV of this project.

b) Conduct a sensitivity analysis on this project. Change the growth rate in revenues to 8.5 percent and recalculate the NPV. Then change it to 9 percent and calculate the NPV, then change to 9.5 percent, then 10 percent and so on up to 15 percent. Also change it down to 7.5 percent, 7 percent, …, 0 percent. Create a graph of the growth rate in revenues versus the NPV of the project. Repeat this with the expected inflation rate. Calculate the NPV at different inflation rates from 0 percent up to 15 percent (in 0.5 percent increments). Create a graph of inflation rate versus NPV.

c) Comment on the graphs. What is the economic break-even point for the two variables? What can you say about the relative amount of risk in the project that comes from each variable?

*Bell Canada (an operating group of BCE Inc.) is considering building a small, new satellite reception and telecommunications switching centre in a remote region of Canada. If it does so, it will be able to provide additional value added services to telecommunications customers within the region as well as attract new customers because of increased capacity and services. Bell Canada must decide if the project will be worthwhile. Cash flow projections are presented below.

The centre itself will cost $45 million to build (you may assume that the entire cost of the centre will be paid immediately and that the centre will be built instantly if Bell Canada decides to go ahead with the project). The centre will fall in Asset Class 3 for Capital Cost Allowance purposes. The depreciation rate for this class is 3 percent per year. Bell Canada has many millions of dollars of other assets in this class.

Operation of the centre will require the laying of fibre optic cable in order to connect the centre to existing networks. This would require the purchase of some specialized cable equipment. The cost of buying this equipment (not included in the $45 million cost of the centre as given above) would be $1,500,000. The equipment would only be required for five years, at which time the fibre optic connections would be complete and Bell Canada could sell the equipment in the second-hand market. The current price of five year old machinery of this type is $700,000. The machinery would fall in an asset class with an allowable depreciation rate of 10 percent per year. The firm has no other assets in this class.

Also not included in the price of the centre ($45 million, as above) is the cost of acquiring state-of-the-art switching equipment for the centre. There are two different suppliers of this type of equipment who are each trying to get the firm to buy their particular equipment.

The first supplier's equipment (Brand A) costs $500,000 to buy. The costs of operating (mostly repairs and upkeep) this equipment would be $15,000 in the first year of operation and the annual operating costs are expected to rise at the rate of inflation after that (assume that all operating costs each year are paid at the end of the year). Brand A switching equipment lasts for ten years before it must be replaced. The cost of subsequent Brand A type equipment that Bell Canada buys will rise with the rate of inflation.

The second supplier's equipment (Brand B) costs $425,000 to buy. Its operating costs are expected to be $12,000 in the first year and rise annually at the rate of inflation (again, assume all operating costs are paid at the end of the year). Brand B machines last for

---

* Note that the project and all projections in this case are fictitious and do not represent actual projects that BCE may or may not have considered.

seven years before they must be replaced. The supplier of Brand B has stated that if Bell Canada signs a long-term contract, the price of future equipment that Bell Canada buys will only rise at a rate of 1 percent per year.

No matter which brand is chosen, the switching equipment will fall in an asset class with an allowable depreciation rate of 20 percent per year for tax purposes. The equipment will have no salvage value at the end of its life (as the technology required evolves rapidly), and the firm has many millions of dollars worth of other assets in this class.

The new centre would also require the hiring of new technicians to man the centre. Labour costs must be paid every two weeks (26 times per year) as that is how often the workers will receive their pay. The bi-weekly wage payments for the centre will be $200,000 during the first year of operation. Each year after that, the equal bi-weekly wage payments will jump up by one year's worth of inflation to reflect cost-of-living increases in the workers' wages.

As soon as the centre is built, an inventory of switching parts will be required to facilitate needed repairs as they arise. This will cost $2 million. Every year after that a new shipment of parts will be needed (as it is expected that the parts purchased at the beginning of each year will be entirely used up over the year) and the cost of future shipments is expected to increase at the rate of inflation.

Increased revenues due to the construction of the centre will be realized at the end of each year. The first year's revenues are expected to be $16 million. These revenues are expected to increase at a rate of 5 percent per year.

Assume that the effective tax rate for Bell Canada is 25 percent. Inflation is expected to average 4 percent per year for the foreseeable future. If Bell requires a return of 17 percent on investments of this type in order to consider them worthwhile, what is the net present value of the centre if Bell plans (if it decides to build it) on running it forever?

Long-Term Sources of Funds

This part of the text provides an overview of various long-term sources of funds available to a business. Long-term financing typically involves the sale of securities in financial markets, and in Part 5, we describe in some detail the main types of corporate securities: long-term debt, preferred shares, and common shares. Chapter 13 discusses the first two categories of financing: long-term debt and preferred shares. Both are generally referred to as senior securities since their claims on income and assets rank senior to those of common stock. Chapter 14 deals with common shares.

Brewing Up
Debentures At Molson

Molson used the proceeds to refinance its existing bank debt, as well as for "general corporate purposes." Longer-term issues (maturing in 2008, 20013, and 2018) were offered by Molson in 1998 and 1993.

Government issues have long dominated the bond market in Canada, but in recent years more and more corporations have been issuing debentures.

Molson, whose "back to beer" strategy and renewed corporate focus on shareholder value we looked at in the beginning of Chapter 1, has been using debentures as part of its financing strategy for years.

In April of 1999, for example, Molson—which was then called The Molson Companies Limited—announced an underwriting agreement for the issue of unsecured debentures in two series. Investors could choose between Series A 5.40 percent debentures, which mature May 3, 2002, and Series B 5.50 percent debentures, which mature May 3, 2004. Series A had an issue price of $99.84, for a yield of 5.56 percent, and Series B an issue price of $99.75 for a yield of 5.56 percent. Each series had an aggregate principle amount of $150 million.

The offer was underwritten by a syndicate that was led by RBC Dominion Securities Inc. and Nesbitt Burns Inc., and also included CIBC Wood Gundy Securities Inc. and Merrill Lynch Canada Inc. It was made in all provinces of Canada and closed on May 3, 1999. Both CBRS and DBRS rated this issue at A (low).

chapter 13

Debt and Preferred Equity

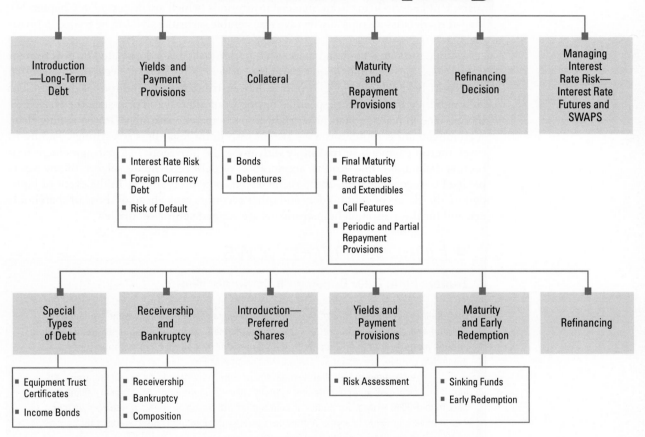

Learning Objectives

After studying this chapter, you should be able to:

1. *Identify the senior securities and explain why they are so designated.*
2. *Explain why the effective yield of a debt instrument seldom coincides with its coupon rate.*
3. *Name three types of options that allow for changes to the maturity dates of debt issues, and explain how they differ.*
4. *Describe the role of preferred shares from the point of view of the issuer and of the borrower.*

13.1   INTRODUCTION—LONG-TERM DEBT

Debt is a contractual liability. By issuing debt certificates, a company or government acquires funds under conditions that usually provide for both periodic interest payments and a definite repayment schedule. Although any definition is somewhat arbitrary, long-term debt commonly refers to issues with a final maturity of 10 or more years. In Canada, the average maturity of new long-term offerings is somewhere between 10 and 15 years. Unlike term loans from financial institutions (which are discussed in Chapter 24), long-term debt issues typically involve transferable securities that can be traded in financial markets.

While the Canadian bond market has traditionally been dominated by government bond issues, the corporate bond market has grown rapidly in recent years as discussed in the report below. Holders of corporate debt instruments are creditors of the firm, but although they are entitled to specified payments of interest and principal, they have neither a voice in management nor a right to participate in earnings. To the issuing firm, such indebtedness represents a consistent cash drain regardless of earnings. Failure to meet interest payments or to comply with any of the provisions of a loan agreement represents default and may lead to acceleration of debt repayment, seizure of any assets pledged to secure the loan, and possibly bankruptcy proceedings. In the event of liquidation, the claims of debt holders and other creditors rank ahead of those of shareholders, and for this reason, debt instruments are termed **senior securities**.

■ *Finance in the News*

Traders Form New Bonds with Corporate World

Best-sellers such as *Bonfire of the Vanities* and *Liar's Poker* portrayed bond traders as dashing and glamorous, but recent governmental fiscal responsibility has taken the glamour and big money out of fixed-income trading desks. Many traders have lost their jobs, and those that remain, are struggling with lower profit margins.

Fewer government bonds meant less supply, but the demand from money managers for lower-risk investments has actually risen. Canadian corporations are filling the gap. In mid-2000, corporate bonds accounted for $13 billion a month, which was as much as would have been sold in a year a decade ago. However, in the United States, that figure could be the result of a single deal by a single company.

But the new bond world is far more complicated than the old one. Corporations, unlike the federal or provincial government, can go bankrupt, so money managers are supplementing credit agency research with their own internal investigations.

More corporate paper is good news for investors because it gives them more choice for diversifying their portfolios and offers higher yields. It's also good news for Canadian companies, which can now more easily raise capital locally.

Source: "Traders Form New Bonds with Corporate World," Andrew Willis, *Globe and Mail*, August 30, 2000, p. B14. *Reprinted with permission.*

The actual debt contract, which is also called a **trust deed** or **indenture**, specifies all pertinent legal details. In a private placement, it is simply drawn up between the borrower and the financial institution with whom the debt is placed; in a public offering, a trust company normally acts as the trustee and contracting party for the creditors. Such a trust deed may cover various items including:

1. Size of the issue, maturity and repayment provisions, and redemption or call features, if any.

2. Amount and frequency of interest payments.

3. Collateral, including specification of assets against which creditors may have claims, the nature of such claims, and arrangements to be made for the protection of assets pledged.

4. Restrictions placed on the borrowing corporation with regard to further issues of debt, pledging of assets, maintenance of appropriate financial ratios, and dividend payments. These restrictions, also known as protective covenants, serve to protect creditors.

Should the issuer default on any of the provisions of the trust deed, the trustee on behalf of the debt holders will attempt to correct the situation. If that is unsuccessful, the trustee will inform the debt holders and with their consent, take action to force the borrower to comply. If this fails, the trustee will seek to satisfy the debt holders' demands by calling the entire issue for immediate repayment or by initiating bankruptcy proceedings.

A variety of debt instruments exists to suit the particular needs of borrowers and lenders. Although it is impossible to review all the detailed provisions that they offer, the key dimensions to consider when evaluating debt are yield, collateral, maturity, and retirement provisions. We discuss each of these in turn.

YIELDS AND PAYMENT PROVISIONS   13.2

Most long-term debt provides for a fixed interest rate that remains constant throughout the life of the debt. Payments are made at specified intervals, with semi-annual or annual interest payments being the most common. The actual method of payment varies depending on whether the debt certificates have been issued in bearer form or whether they are registered. When in bearer form, payments accrue to whoever possesses the certificate, whereas interest on registered debt is mailed to officially listed owners. Interest payments on bearer debt normally take the form of dated coupons that are attached to the certificate. On the appropriate dates, the holder simply clips the coupons and presents them to an intermediary such as a bank for payment. Bearer bonds are more convenient for trading, whereas registration affords greater protection against loss or theft. Ownership of registered debt may be transferred through written assignment, with the corporation's debt register being amended accordingly.

Interest payments are tax deductible for the issuer and are taxed as income in the hands of the recipient. This tax deductibility greatly reduces the effective cost of debt to the borrower and as we will see in Chapters 15 and 16, provides one of the main incentives for issuing debt. From the firm's point of view, debt is generally the cheapest source of financing; however, because of its contractual nature, it entails the greatest risk. Thus, we face the familiar risk-return trade-off that will be explored more fully in Chapter 16.

Note that yields are not always provided in the ways just described. For example, so-called pure discount or **zero coupon bonds** are issued at a significant discount from the face value payable at maturity. This approach to providing an investment return, although standard for short-term debt traded in money markets, is incorporated in longer-term debt issues to provide investors with tax and other advantages. As expected, the tax benefits (providing returns in the form of capital gains rather than interest income) were quickly blocked by governments, greatly reducing the advantages of this particular innovation.[1]

Interest Rate Risk

We saw in Chapter 6 that the effective yield of a debt instrument does not have to coincide with the interest rate quoted on the debt contract (also called the **coupon rate**) and that the market price of debt may differ from its face value. Specifically, movements in market interest rates will affect both the market price and the yield of outstanding debt.

EXAMPLE

BOND PRICES AND MARKET INTEREST RATES

On August 21, 2000, previously issued Government of Canada bonds that provide a coupon rate of 11.25 percent and mature in the year 2015 traded for $151.58 per $100 of par value, providing an effective yield (or yield to maturity) of 5.95 percent. Recall that the effective yield is the discount rate that equates the present value of expected future cash inflows with the current market price. Assuming a 15-year term to maturity and that coupons are paid annually, we have:

$$151.58 = 11.25 \times \left[\frac{1 - \dfrac{1}{(1.0595)^{15}}}{0.0595} \right] + 100 \times \left[\frac{1}{(1.0595)^{15}} \right]$$

As market interest rates decrease, the prices of previously issued bonds have to increase in order to provide competitive yields and vice versa. Over the past 10 years, we have seen falling interest rates that have generally paralleled decelerating inflation.

---

[1] Zero coupon bonds appeal to some investors for other than tax reasons. For example, it suits the needs of individuals and institutions wanting to achieve a predictable compounded yield to maturity without having to worry about the rate at which future interest receipts are reinvested. Investment dealers fill any void by taking bearer bonds and stripping off the coupons. The bonds and coupons are then sold separately to investors at appropriate discounts. Each, in fact, is the equivalent of a zero coupon bond, with varying maturities. The longer the maturity of the coupon or stripped bond, the deeper the discount. Such instruments, although available from investment dealers, have limited liquidity. Accrued interest on the "strips" has to be declared for tax purposes.

In the previous 20-year period during the 1970s and 1980s, interest rates were fairly high and increased quite dramatically in certain periods such as from 1977 to 1981. As a consequence, previously issued long-term debt generally fell in price with investors suffering significant losses. The experience, coupled with continued uncertainty about future levels of inflation and interest rates, made investors wary of accepting debt with long maturities at fixed interest rates. Thus, average maturities on new debt issues have been shortened in recent years, and financial futures markets have become more active. Finally, a variety of other provisions have been introduced to make investment in debt with longer maturities more attractive. Some examples of such innovations include:

1. Variable interest rates on long-term debt, where the interest rate is adjusted periodically to reflect changing market conditions. Such adjustments are commonplace in mortgages and have recently been offered on long-term corporate and government debt.

2. Inflation indexed or real return bonds, which offer a fixed real rate of interest. The principal to be repaid on which interest payments are based is adjusted in line with price level changes.

3. Interest payments that are tied to the price of some commodity such as gold or oil that is thought to provide protection against inflation.

Many companies have issued floating rate bonds or debentures in attempts to make long-term debt more appealing. In some cases, these floating rate provisions have enabled borrowers to extend maturities dramatically. As a vivid example, Hydro-Québec in 1986 was able to float a US$400-million variable-rate perpetual-debt issue, the principal of which never has to be repaid. At the same time, the proportion of corporate debt financing with fixed interest rates and maturities over 10 years declined steadily, and only recently, after several years of low inflation and relative interest rate stability, have we seen a hesitant and gradual return to the standard forms of long-term debt contracts that were previously common.

Investors can purchase bonds issued by the federal governments in Canada and the United States, the payments of which are linked to the rate of inflation. For example, in November 1991, the Government of Canada began issuing real return bonds that provide investors with a real return 4.25 percent above the level of inflation as measured by the CPI. This is achieved by applying the 4.25 percent coupon rate on the bond to the face value of the bonds, which change in value at the rate of inflation.

Many entities have also tied their required payments to levels of commodity prices that would influence their ability to make debt payments. For example, in 1979, an agency of the Mexican government offered its third issue of local currency debt backed by oil. Each Mex$1,000 (peso) bond was linked to 1.95354 barrels of oil. At maturity, the bonds would be redeemed at face value plus the amount by which the market value of the reference oil bundle exceeded the face value plus coupons received during the life of the instrument. Clearly, such provisions, which were originally introduced to make debt issues more attractive to investors, may also work to the issuing firm's advantage.

Foreign Currency Debt

We saw in Chapters 2 and 6 that firms may have reasons for issuing debt denominated in a foreign currency, but in such cases, they have to consider the additional risks owing to possible changes in foreign exchange rates. Unfavourable exchange rate movements have thwarted the attempts of many firms to save on their interest costs by issuing debt abroad. Increasing concern from both borrowers and lenders about the uncertainty of future movements in foreign exchange rates has led to innovations in the denomination of international debt issues. For example, in an attempt to spread the exchange risk, mixed currency instruments have been introduced providing for payments to be made in a weighted average of various currencies. One illustration of such a mixed currency unit is the Special Drawing Right (SDR) originally created by the International Monetary Fund (IMF). It is composed of a weighted average of several currencies, and its value in terms of any particular currency changes as the relevant exchange rates fluctuate. If debt is denominated in such a unit, the contracting parties are no longer tied to the fortunes of one particular currency but, rather, to a diversified portfolio of currencies that should be subject to reduced risk. Other common currency "baskets" include the European Currency Unit, which is based on a mix of European currencies. ⬆

Risk of Default

As discussed in Chapter 6, the yield that companies must offer on their debt is, among other things, a function of the perceived risk of default. To assist investors, several independent agencies provide rating information on a wide range of corporate and government debt to assess their ability to maintain uninterrupted payments of interest and repayment of principal. These ratings are important to both government and corporate borrowers because they affect the costs and conditions under which they can issue new debt. The specific procedures used to determine such ratings generally incorporate both objective information (based on the firm's financial statements, economic indicators, and the like) and subjective judgement. The following report includes a recent debt rating downgrading of a Canadian company—Fairfax Financial. The discussion touches upon a few of the areas that are monitored by debt rating agencies such as the company's balance sheet position, its earnings growth, and the rating agency's "near term expectations for the company."

■ *Finance in the News*

Fairfax Financial Holdings Ltd.—Downgrades to BBB (high)

Rating	Trend	Rating Action	Debt Rated
BBB (high)	Stable	Downgrade	Senior Unsecured Long Term Debt

Following the release of second quarter results, DBRS is downgrading the rating on the senior unsecured long-term debt of Fairfax Financial Holdings Limited ("Fairfax" or "the Company") to BBB (high) from A (low). With this action, the rating trend is changed to Stable from the previous Negative status. In our most recent comments on Fairfax, DBRS noted that the Company must achieve continuing steady progress in improving the combined ratio in 2000 while maintaining a satisfactory balance sheet position for the A (low) rating to be maintained. While Fairfax continues to maintain a satisfactory balance sheet and although it achieved a meaningful earnings increase in the second quarter, the latter improvement was due to higher capital gains and not reflective of an improvement in the combined ratio. The Company's progress in improving its combined ratio in 2000 has not met our expectation. Poor results at sizeable Crum & Forster in the U.S. have been a major limitation to progress. On the positive side there has been recent evidence of price firming in the troubled United States property casualty Industry, with Fairfax having achieved meaningful price increases in many lines, and ultimately, we expect that Fairfax will achieve better underwriting results. At this point, tangible improvement to date and near-term expectations are not strong enough to support the previous A (low) rating.

The BBB (high) rating and the Stable trend are based upon the size, diversity, management strength and focus on improving underwriting results at Fairfax. Within a competitive industry, the Company continues to be conservative in several areas, including financial flexibility. Specifically, cash at the holding company remains above $600 million, available bank lines remain at $1.3 billion and several steps have been taken to limit risk (including a sizeable re-insurance contract with Swiss Reinsurance). While past major acquisitions have very much contributed to the present challenges facing Fairfax, the Company has consistently maintained its balance sheet by including equity as part of the funding. Acquisition risk has also been reduced by the policy of either obtaining indemnification as to claims provision adequacy from the vendors or by purchasing below book.

Source: Dominion Bond Rating Service website at: www.dbrs.com, August 28, 2000. *Reprinted with permission.*

The Dominion Bond Rating Service (DBRS) and the Canadian Bond Rating Service (CBRS) are the two major Canadian bond rating services. Standard & Poor's (S&P) Corporation and Moody's Investors Service Inc. are two major U.S. rating agencies that rate bond issuers (both government and corporate) across the world. CBRS and S&P announced on October 31, 2000 that they will combine their Canadian operations. Table 13.1 includes the debt ratings categories for CBRS and DBRS.

TABLE 13.1

Debt Rating Categories

CBRS		DBRS	
A++	highest quality	AAA	highest credit quality
A+	very good quality	AA	superior credit quality
A	good quality	A	satisfactory credit quality
B++	medium quality	BBB	adequate credit quality
B+	lower-medium quality	BB	speculative credit quality
B	poor quality	B	highly speculative credit quality
C	speculative quality	CCC	very highly speculative credit quality
D	default	CC	extremely speculative
Suspended	rating suspended	C	extremely speculative
		D	in default of principal, interest, or both

Source: Dominion Bond Rating Service website at: www.dbrs.com, August 28, 2000.

Ratings of both services may also be modified by "high" or "low" to indicate the relative ranking within a category or the trend within the category. Other things being equal, bond ratings and bond coupon rates are inversely related. Investment grade bonds are defined as those with bond ratings of BBB (DBRS and S&P), B++ (CBRS), Baa (Moody's), or higher. Typically, institutional investors must confine themselves to investment grade bonds. Junk (high-yield or low-grade) bonds have bond ratings below these. These bonds are regarded as speculative securities in terms of the issuer's ability to meet its contractual obligations.

Despite their widespread acceptance and use, bond ratings have some limitations. The agencies may disagree on their evaluations. Furthermore, because most bonds are in the top four categories, it seems safe to argue that not all issues in a single category (such as A) can be equally risky. Finally, it is extremely important to remember that bond ratings are a reflection of the relative probability of default, which says little or nothing about the absolute probability of default. Table 13.2 includes a sample of debt ratings for some of the Canadian companies found in Table 8.1 (which listed their betas) according to DBRS as of August 2000.

TABLE 13.2 ▬▬▬▬▬▬▬▬▬▬▬▬▬▬▬▬▬▬▬▬▬▬▬▬▬▬

DBRS Long-Term Ratings

Company	Industry Classification	Rating
Air Canada	Transportation	BB
BCE Inc.	Utilities (Telephone Utilities)	A (high)
Noranda Inc.	Mining (Integrated Mines)	BBB (high)
Inco Limited	Mining (Integrated Mines)	BBB (low)
Nortel Networks	Comm. & Media (Telecommunication)	A (high)
Clearnet Communications Inc.	Comm. & Media (Telecommunication)	B (high)
Bombardier Inc.	Industrial Products (Transportation Equip.)	A
Petro-Canada	Integrated Oil & Gas	A
Bank of Nova Scotia	Financial Services (Banks)	AA (low)
Fairfax Financial	Financial Services (Insurance)	BBB (high)
Investors Group	Financial Services (Invest. Companies & Funds)	A (high)

Source: Dominion Bond Rating Service website: www.dbrs.com. The ratings were the most recent available as of August 28, 2000. They were determined at various times between August 30, 1999 and August 15, 2000.

COLLATERAL

13.3

Although the continued earning power of the issuing organization is of primary importance to investors in assessing the risk of a particular debt issue, the collateral offered is also important since these assets provide protection in case of default. A variety of collateral arrangements is possible, and debt instruments can be classified accordingly.

Corporate debt may:

1. be secured by the pledge of specific assets
2. be completely unsecured, backed only by the earning power of the borrower and a claim against residual assets
3. provide for a *floating charge* against assets ~can make a claim against any asset

Such a floating charge gives lenders an all-embracing claim against any corporate assets not otherwise pledged and effectively ranks them ahead of general, unsecured creditors in the event of liquidation. When specific assets are pledged, the debt instrument is commonly called a **bond**; the term **debenture** is used in the other two cases. However, this distinction is not always observed, and the term bond is sometimes used generically to refer to any debt security. For example, government bonds are not backed by any specific pledge of security and thus would technically be classified as debentures; however, they are almost always referred to as bonds.

Bonds

When specific assets are pledged, the market value of such collateral usually exceeds the amount of the bond issue by a reasonable margin. Assets commonly pledged include land, plant, and equipment. Debt instruments thus secured are labelled **mortgage bonds**.

It may become necessary for a firm to float additional debt using the same assets as collateral when an issue of mortgage bonds is already outstanding. Whether such a subsequent offering is possible depends on the provisions of the original trust deed, which may include constraints on the right to issue additional debt under the same mortgage. To protect the original bondholders against excessive new offerings that would erode the security provided originally, trust deeds that allow new offerings under the same mortgage normally limit bond issues to some fraction of the value of the pledged properties. When an existing trust deed prevents additional debt issues under the same mortgage, further offerings of bonds to be secured by the same property would have to be issued under a second mortgage with a separate contract. Such bonds are termed **second** or **general mortgage bonds**.

Trust deeds can provide for an open-end, closed-end, or limited open-end mortgage. With an open-end arrangement, subsequent debt can be issued freely under the same trust deed. To protect the original bondholders, however, an "after-acquired" property clause usually is included. It provides that all subsequently acquired properties will fall under the mortgage agreement and be pledged as further security. The limited open-end mortgage places a ceiling on the amount of bonds issuable under the trust deed, but at the time of issue, this maximum is not immediately binding. Closed-end mortgages prohibit the issue of debt under the same trust deed.

Clearly, the restrictions associated with closed-end and limited open-end mortgages are potentially attractive to investors or creditors. However, they may unnecessarily limit a company's future financing flexibility and lead to additional expenses on new issues. For example, consider a company that issued $10 million in bonds, initially pledging real property with a market value of $15 million in 1993. By 2000, about half of the debt had been repaid, and due to escalating land prices, the market value of the property had increased to $30 million. The now-generous safety margin of $25 million between the debt outstanding and the market value of the collateral would justify the issuance of additional debt. A closed-end mortgage precludes further debt from being issued under the existing trust deed. However, new bonds could be sold only under a new mortgage contract and would rank behind the original debt in terms of claims against the assets.

Provided that lenders are satisfied that the collateral will continue to have a realizable value, assets other than real property may be used to secure debt. For example, **collateral trust bonds** are secured by financial assets such as the common shares of other corporations. These shares are placed as collateral with a trustee.

Debentures

Debentures are not secured by claims against specific assets although floating charges are common. Typically, these instruments are used by firms that either have exhausted their ability to issue bonds or have a high enough credit standing to make the pledging of specific assets unnecessary. From the issuer's point of view, debentures afford increased flexibility not just in terms of future financing, but also for the management of corporate assets. A sale of assets, for example, would not be constrained by mortgage provisions.

When lenders perceive the earning power and general credit standing of a corporation to be high, debentures may find almost the same acceptance as secured debt. Generally, however, they must provide slightly higher yields than those available on comparable bonds. As with bonds, trust deeds covering debentures contain a variety of protective clauses or restrictive covenants that strengthen the creditor's position. A so-called negative pledge clause is common; it prevents the pledging of any of the firm's assets to others under subsequent borrowings. Although such a provision protects existing creditors, it does restrict management's ability to obtain additional financing.

Debt certificates with claims that rank behind those of ordinary debenture holders are termed **subordinated debentures**. A firm may have more than one subordinated debenture issue outstanding; in such cases, one offering may be subordinate to another and be labelled a junior subordinated issue. As the least secure form of debt, subordinated debentures must provide a higher interest yield in order to be marketable. Alternatively, borrowers may rely on either conversion features or warrants to "sweeten" the offering, thereby making it attractive to investors even at modest interest rates. Such option features are discussed in Chapter 19.

The use of relatively low-quality and, from an investor's point of view, high-risk subordinated debentures increased rapidly throughout the 1980s. Generally termed **junk bonds**, such debt pays interest at several percentage points above standard corporate rates. They have often been issued in substantial amounts to finance corporate takeovers, with the stock of the acquired firm sometimes providing limited collateral. Given deregulation, financial institutions have bought an increasing proportion of these issues, lured by their high yields that, in turn, allow the institutions to pay higher rates to depositors in an increasingly competitive environment. U.S. Savings and Loans companies, also known as thrifts, actually had their savings deposits guaranteed through U.S. federal deposit insurance. Having the risk insured by the government prompted thrifts to invest billions of dollars in junk bonds, keeping the interest rate spread over regular corporate issues very modest. When it was finally realized that these small spreads were inadequate compensation for the higher default risk on junk bonds and when the insurance coverage on such holdings was curtailed, the market for the bonds plunged. Hundreds of thrifts went bankrupt at an estimated total cost to the U.S. government of $500 billion over the next 30 years.[2]

---

[2] "When the Goalposts Move," *The Economist*, (April 27, 1991), pp. 20–23.

PERSPECTIVES

Corporate Manager

The company gains more flexibility in its future operations and financing activities by borrowing using instruments that are secured by less collateral or possess minimal restrictive provisions. However, creditors usually require additional compensation for the increased risk in the form of higher interest payments (or yields).

Investor

Investors can earn higher yields by purchasing debt instruments that are secured by less collateral or possess minimal restrictive provisions. However, they face additional risk with these instruments. Again, we have the familiar risk–return trade-off.

13.4 MATURITY AND REPAYMENT PROVISIONS

Final Maturity

A characteristic of debt is that it comes due and has to be repaid. Traditionally, most long-term debt issues provided for a specified maturity and outstanding certificates had to be redeemed at face value on that date. However, given the risks implied by fixed, long-term maturities in an environment characterized by uncertainty about future interest rates, such fixed maturities often have given way to more flexible arrangements that provide either the borrower or the lender the option of altering the maturity date. When the option rests with the investor, the bonds or debentures are termed *retractables* and *extendibles*, whereas *call features* provide the issuing firm with an opportunity for early redemption. In addition, many debt contracts contain *periodic and partial repayment provisions* of principal throughout the life of the debt. We review each of these features in turn.

Retractables and Extendibles

Many borrowers cater to investor concerns over future interest rate movements and consequent interest rate risk by issuing long-term **retractable debt**. These instruments give investors the right to move the maturity date forward and cash in the certificate at full face value on specified dates well before final maturity. Such redemptions are attractive if market interest rates rise above the coupon rate specified in the original offering.

For example, three years ago, a firm sold 20-year bonds at 5 percent with a retractable clause that allows investors to redeem after three years. Current interest rates have moved to 7 percent for this company. Without the retractable feature, the current market price on each $1,000 bond would have dropped to (assuming annual coupons):

$$\text{Market price} = 50 \times \left[\frac{1 - \frac{1}{(1.07)^{17}}}{.07} \right] + 1,000 \times \left[\frac{1}{(1.07)^{17}} \right] = \$804.73$$

Given the option to redeem at face value and to reinvest the proceeds at the current higher level of interest rates, investors would clearly cash in their securities.

Extendible debt is simply a variation of retractable debt. Here, the original debt contract specifies a relatively short maturity, but the investor has an option to extend the life of the debt. The feature is attractive if interest rates fall after the original offering because it allows the holder to lock in the higher original rate for a longer time. For example, a firm issued 7 percent debt to mature in five years, extendible to 20 years. If at the end of five years interest rates on comparable debt have fallen to below 7 percent, it will be advantageous to exercise the extendible option. The alternative would be to collect the face value with reinvestment yields limited to lower prevailing rates.

Because extendibles and retractables offer attractive options to lenders, they normally can be sold at lower yields than those required on comparable straight debt. However, what is attractive to creditors must be a burden for issuers since one group pays for what the other gains. If, for example, an extendible option is exercised because market rates have fallen, a borrower will face future interest payments higher than what would have been incurred under a straight debt issue with a limited maturity that could have been refunded at the prevailing lower rate. Alternatively, if rates had risen, the investors would not have extended the bond at the lower rate, and firms would have to issue new debt at the higher rates to refinance the old debt.

Consequently, what the firm gains with one hand it is likely to lose with the other. In addition, the borrower can no longer use the funds for a defined period. With a retractable, for example, the issuer may wind up with relatively short-term debt when long-term debt was needed. Despite such risks, extendible and retractable debt issues have become increasingly popular.

Another option sometimes available with debt securities is the convertible feature. This option allows the holder to convert the debt instrument into a predetermined number of common shares of the company. **Convertible debt securities** can be viewed as straight debt issues with a call option attached, which gives the holder the right to convert the debt to receive a specified number of common shares. This is discussed in greater detail in Chapter 17.

Call Features

When the option for early redemption rests with the borrower, the debt is said to have a **call feature**. This provision allows the issuing corporation to repurchase its debt before final maturity at a predetermined price. It is likely to be exercised if interest rates have declined significantly since the time of issue or if the borrower finds that the protective provisions in the trust deed are unduly restrictive and believes that a new issue can be floated under more favourable terms. If interest rates have declined and a security is called, investors will have to reinvest their funds at lower yields. Thus, call features are unattractive to lenders who normally demand a somewhat higher rate of interest on debt that includes such provisions due to the additional risks. In addition, when redemption is for other than sinking fund purposes (discussed in the next section), the call price generally exceeds the debt's face value.

Call provision details vary from issue to issue with some call options immediately operative, whereas others are deferred for a specified period. For example, a 20-year debt issue may specify that the firm has no right to call during the first 10 years. Thereafter, early redemption is possible with the call price set at $1,075 per $1,000 bond if the call is exercised between years 10 and 15, and at $1,025 if the debt is retired after year 15. This staggering of call premiums reflects the fact that investors stand to lose less from a call that comes during the later years of the issue's life.

Traditionally, most long-term debt has been issued with a call feature. Recently, however, many issuers have increased the attractiveness of their offerings by curtailing their right of early redemption. This guarantees investors potentially attractive returns over an extended period despite a possible subsequent decline in interest rates.

Periodic and Partial Repayment Provisions

To avoid possible problems at the time of maturity, trust deeds often call for a gradual repayment, or retirement, of principal over the life of the issue. Such a provision not only relieves the borrower of pressures that may be associated with a single large repayment, but it may also provide investors with increased liquidity by establishing a periodic demand for the outstanding securities. Gradual retirement may be achieved through a *sinking fund* or through *serial bonds*.

Under a **sinking fund**, the issuing firm makes periodic payments to the trustee, who uses the funds to retire the debt. These payments may involve equal instalments although less-rigid repayment schedules designed to meet the borrower's particular circumstances can be negotiated. For example, Maclean Hunter issued convertible debentures in 1984 with the conversion feature expiring in 1994 and the bonds maturing in 2004. For each of the years 1995 to 2003 inclusive, the trust deed called for minimum sinking fund payments of 5 percent of the aggregate principal amount outstanding on May 1, 1994. However, the company was entitled to retire up to an additional 2 percent each year.

Actual redemption of certificates may be accomplished either through purchases on the open market or by calling some portion of the issue for redemption. Such a call is normally effected through a random drawing based on serial numbers of the securities, and the redemption price may include a modest premium over face value. This provision avoids having to purchase the debt in the market at a significant premium if interest rates have declined.

Serial bonds also provide for a periodic retirement over the life of the issue; however, the procedure is somewhat different. When originally offered, such bonds provide for staggered maturities for different serial numbers in the issue. Although the effect for the borrower is very similar to that of a sinking fund, the specification of different maturities from the outset gives investors a choice and, consequently, broadens market appeal. The arrangements, however, are somewhat more complex since the coupon rate has to vary with maturities to reflect the term structure of interest rates. In Canada, municipalities have been the largest issuers of serial bonds. The poor resale market for municipal bonds has tarnished serial bonds to some extent and has restricted their use by corporate borrowers.

REFINANCING DECISION   13.5

A firm refinances or refunds debt when it replaces an outstanding issue at or before maturity with a new offering. Major reasons for refunding include:

1. The outstanding debt matures, but the firm wishes to extend the term of the borrowing. New debt is issued with the proceeds used to repay the old creditors.

2. A firm has debt outstanding at interest rates higher than current ones. The old debt may be called and new debt issued at a lower interest rate. Again, proceeds from the new issue are used to retire the old debt.

3. A company may have debt outstanding under terms that impose operating restrictions that management finds constraining. By issuing new debt to retire the outstanding issue, such restrictions may be removed.

Many firms have made long-term debt a permanent part of their capital structure. Hence, whenever an outstanding issue matures, refinancing takes place. When outstanding debt contains sinking fund provisions, earlier repayments may be financed through short-term borrowing. Eventually, however, accumulations of short-term debt along with any remaining payments at maturity will be refunded through new issues of long-term debt.

We saw that a call feature allows for refinancing when interest rates have declined. Without call premiums and transaction costs, a firm should call outstanding debt whenever interest rates fall below the level provided for in the original issue. However, should the old debt have to be retired at a premium and the new one involve issuing and underwriting expenses, any interest savings must be large enough to cover these additional expenses.

REFINANCING PERPETUAL DEBT

EXAMPLE

Consider an outstanding debt issue with a face value of $10 million and a coupon rate of 16 percent. Without a call premium and transaction costs, the firm should refund whenever it can float new debt at an interest rate below 16 percent.

Assume, however, that the old debt can be called only at a premium of 10 percent implying a redemption price of $11 million. In addition, issuing and underwriting expenses for a new issue would be $428,571 on an after-tax basis. Thus, new debt with a face value of $11,428,571 would have to be issued to finance the transaction. For simplicity, assume that both the old and new debt are perpetual and have no maturity. Refinancing would be indicated as long as interest payments on the increased amount of new debt are lower than the $1.6 million per year previously required. This implies that interest rates would have to drop below $1,600,000/11,428,571=.14 or 14 percent.

More generally, refunding can be viewed as a capital budgeting decision: the company incurs immediate costs (call premium plus transaction costs) in anticipation of future interest savings. Such an investment should proceed only if its net present value is positive implying that the present value of future interest savings has to exceed the initial incremental outflow. As in any capital budgeting evaluation, all cash flows and the discount rate have to be taken on an after-tax basis. For simplicity, we assume issuing and underwriting expenses to be deductible for tax purposes, whereas call premiums are not. [3] In addition, the discount rate applied should be commensurate with the risk of the corresponding cash flows. Future interest savings are highly predictable and accrue as long as the firm can meet interest payments. Hence, they entail essentially the same risk as the interest payments on the new debt. Furthermore, as we saw in the previous example, refunding expenses can be financed by issuing additional debt. It follows that the discount rate to be used is the after-tax interest cost on the new debt. The firm's average cost of capital, which may embody a substantial risk premium reflecting the overall risk of the firm, would be inappropriate.

In the previous example, let us assume that the firm faces a tax rate of 40 percent and that interest rates drop from 16 to 14 percent. Using the after-tax cost of new debt [14% $\times(1-.40)=8.4\%$] as the appropriate discount rate, with $10 million of perpetual debt outstanding, we have:

$$PV \text{ of after-tax interest savings } = \frac{(1,600,000-1,400,000)(1-.4)}{.14(1-.4)} = \$1,428,571$$

Confirming our earlier result, this is the maximum amount the firm can pay in call premiums and after-tax transaction costs.[4]

NPV OF A REFINANCING DECISION

Assume now that the old debt has a remaining life of only 10 years and is to be replaced with new 14 percent debt of identical maturity. We obtain:

---

[3] Actually, tax laws preclude such expensing of issuing and underwriting costs. They are to be capitalized and written off over varying time periods.

[4] To allow for unexpected delays in the placing of new debt, the date of the new issue usually preceeds the refunding date. Thus, a short overlap period exists during which both the old and new debt is outstanding and interest has to be paid on both. The additional interest costs on the old debt less any returns earned on the excess funds should be considered in the analysis of refunding. Usually, however, on an after-tax basis, the net cost is quite small.

$$\text{PV of after-tax interest savings} = (1,600,000-1,400,000)\,(1-.4)\left[\frac{1-\dfrac{1}{(1.084)^{10}}}{.084}\right] = \$790,882$$

Given the cost of "calling the issue" of \$1,428,571 that was estimated in the previous example, we obtain the following NPV:

$$NPV = -1,428,571 + 790,882 = -\$637,689$$

Therefore, refinancing becomes unattractive.

We see that the costs a firm can afford to bear for refunding (call premium plus after-tax transaction costs) depend on both the annual interest savings and the number of years those savings are available. Conversely, for a given decline in interest rates, the attractiveness of refinancing increases the longer the remaining maturity of outstanding debt.

Whether refunding to achieve such interest savings is actually undertaken may be influenced by additional considerations. For example, management may delay refunding in anticipation of even lower interest rates in the future. Also, if the call premium on outstanding debt declines in steps as it approaches maturity, refinancing may be postponed to take advantage of a reduced future call price.

We note that refunding to take advantage of lower interest rates, although potentially advantageous to the firm, does not create any economic value in an aggregate sense. What one group (the corporation and its underwriter, for example) gains, others (investors and perhaps the government in terms of lost tax revenues) must lose. In efficient markets, investors will protect themselves against expected losses by requiring higher yields, which is why debt that is likely to be called at some future time will have to bear higher interest payments.

Finally, refunding may be considered to remove restrictions imposed on a company by the terms of an old debt issue. Such provisions that may have been negotiated many years earlier could, for example, place limitations on additional borrowings, on the disposition of assets, or on dividend payments. Because of changed circumstances, the restrictions may now be inappropriate, and refunding may restore management's flexibility in pursuing actions that are in the firm's best interest. The assessment of such benefits weighed against the costs of refunding is largely a matter of subjective managerial judgement.

MANAGING INTEREST RATE RISK: INTEREST RATE FUTURES AND SWAPS 13.6

Rapid and large changes in interest rates and uncertainty about future interest rate movements have created a relatively high-risk environment for long-term debt from the position of both the borrower and the lender. Financial markets have responded to this situation by introducing various instruments that can at least partially provide protection against such interest rate risk. Financial futures contracts and interest rate swaps are two major ways of protecting your investment. With an interest rate futures contract, the seller agrees to deliver to the buyer a specified debt instrument at a fixed price on some future date. The value of these varies with changes in interest rates, but the aim is to enter into a forward commitment, the value of which is negatively correlated with the effects that interest rate changes would otherwise have on the firm. Under a swap, two parties exchange their respective debt-related commitments because each finds the other's obligation more attractive. Interest rate and currency swaps have become prevalent in the context of long-term debt. However, besides being vehicles that help manage interest rate risk, these contracts do contribute to financial management in other ways. Therefore, rather than focusing on them in this section with only a limited purpose in mind, discussion is deferred until Chapter 21. There, a wider and more complete perspective will be provided.

13.7 SPECIAL TYPES OF DEBT

Equipment Trust Certificates

Although **equipment trust certificates** are a form of long-term debt, they differ from the bonds or debentures previously discussed. They are mainly used by railways and other transportation companies to acquire long-lived equipment such as rolling stock. Under such financing, a firm orders equipment from a manufacturer and makes a modest down payment with the balance raised by selling equipment trust certificates usually to financial institutions. A trustee (typically a trust company) is then appointed to act on behalf of the certificate holders. The trustee takes title to the equipment when delivered and, in turn, leases it to the firm. The lease payments that the company makes to the trustee provide for both interest and the gradual retirement of the equipment trust certificates. The retirement schedule is designed so that at any time, the depreciated value of the equipment will exceed the certificates outstanding by a reasonable safety margin. Normally, this safety margin grows because the equipment pledged depreciates more slowly than the rate at which the certificates mature.

Although similar to debt, equipment trust certificates are a lease arrangement between the firm and the trustee, which provides creditors with additional security because the trustee retains title to the assets. Should the firm default, the lease can simply be transferred to another lessee without costly delays caused by bankruptcy proceedings. These and other features of leasing are discussed in Chapter 25.

Income Bonds

Interest payments on **income bonds** are not a fixed contractual obligation but become payable only when specified earnings are reported by the borrower. Such bonds, which can be viewed as a weak form of debt, typically are used in corporate reorganizations whereby the capital structure is readjusted because of actual or imminent default on payments to creditors. Given the choice of liquidating the business and recovering only a fraction of their debts or of accepting income bonds in exchange for their current claims, creditors may make the best of a bad situation and accept income bonds particularly if the company has reasonable long-term prospects for recovery. Alternatively, companies may issue income bonds as a substitute for preferred shares, which are discussed in the next chapter. Unlike the United States, Canadian tax legislation recognizes the similarity between income bonds and preferred shares and stipulates that interest on such bonds is to be treated as a preferred dividend by both the firm and investors. Such interest, therefore, is not a deductible expense to the issuer, but it qualifies for the dividend tax credit in the hands of the recipient.

RECEIVERSHIP AND BANKRUPTCY　13.8

A business that cannot meet its debts when they come due is said to be insolvent, and in such circumstances, remedies are needed for both the debtor and the creditors. The debtor will likely find it difficult to satisfy any obligations while under pressure from various sources and may need to be released at least partially from this predicament so as to attempt a fresh start. The creditors of an insolvent debtor will also require remedies. In most cases, they will be more interested in quickly salvaging what they can rather than waiting for the possibility of full payment in the distant future. Bankruptcy legislation exists for the benefit of both interests. Because few areas of corporation law are as complex as those touching upon corporate reorganization and the winding up of companies, we limit the discussion in this section to a brief overview.

To be specific, when default on required debt payments occurs, the mechanisms of receivership, bankruptcy, and composition are used to settle the claims between debtors and creditors.

Receivership

According to the Canadian Oxford Dictionary, receivership is "the state of being dealt with by a receiver." That is, an individual who has been appointed to protect the individual's or company's assets and for ultimate sale and distribution to creditors'. Corporations normally become insolvent when they are unable to meet their financial obligations as they become due. A receiver may be appointed to ensure that the assets remain intact. The receiver may be appointed directly by secured creditors or by creditors on application to the courts. The receiver may operate the business, seek a way to refinance the outstanding debt, or sell the operation or its assets and distribute the proceeds to the creditors. Debts and obligations of the insolvent debtor remain intact. The receiver is appointed to ensure that there is an orderly and equitable distribution of assets.

Bankruptcy

Bankruptcy is a legal state. It occurs because a person, partnership, or corporation commits an act of bankruptcy, the most common being failure to meet liabilities as they become due. Insolvent debtors may assign themselves into bankruptcy or may be petitioned by their creditors. Individual bankrupts are normally conditionally discharged meaning they have to pay only a portion of their obligations, and the remaining obligations are discharged. Discharge of a corporation occurs only if it pays 100 cents on the dollar of proved claims. The process of bankruptcy provides that a trustee gather in, realize, and distribute all non-exempt property of the bankrupt to the creditors.

Composition

A **composition** or **proposal** is an agreement between an insolvent debtor and her creditors whereby the creditors agree to accept less than their full claim in order to achieve some immediate payment. A proposal, whether informal or pursuant to the federal *Bankruptcy Act*, is an act of bankruptcy because it is an admission by the debtor of an inability to pay obligations. A formal proposal accepted by the creditors must be confirmed by the court. Any proposal that fails results in bankruptcy, but a proposal is not a bankruptcy; therefore, no discharge is required.

13.9 INTRODUCTION—PREFERRED SHARES

Technically, preferred shares are a form of equity financing since preferred shareholders have no contractual claim against the issuing firm and therefore, cannot be viewed as creditors. Preferred shares are often referred to as hybrid securities because their features stand somewhere between those of debt and those of common shares. Like debt, preferred shares generally provide for a fixed return, but unlike interest payments, dividends on preferred shares are not contractually guaranteed. Consequently, such payments involve lower risk to the issuing firm but provide investors with a less-certain return. Also, the tax treatment of the dividends is different from that of interest from the perspective of investors and the corporation.

In the event of liquidation, the claims of preferred shareholders rank behind those of creditors but ahead of those of common shareholders. Like common shares, preferred shares usually do not have a maturity date but become a permanent part of a firm's capital structure. Unlike common shareholders, however, preferred shareholders generally have no voice in management. Again, a variety of detailed provisions is possible. These are:

- Yields and Payment Provisions
- Maturity and Early Redemption
- Refinancing

We discuss each of these in turn.

YIELDS AND PAYMENT PROVISIONS 13.10

Preferred shares generally provide for constant dividend payments that are either specified as a dollar amount or as a dividend yield on the shares' par value (the equivalent of face value on debt).[5] Quarterly dividend payments are the norm, but such dividend payments do not represent a contractual obligation and can be suspended by the firm's board of directors without legal ramifications. Most firms issue preferred shares with every intention of maintaining dividends; however, when faced with severe adversity, payments may be curtailed in order to conserve cash. Although the consequences may be serious, in terms of investor reaction and future access to financial markets, they do not match the penalties imposed on a firm that defaults on its debt. Preferred share financing, therefore, provides a firm with more flexibility and reduces the risk of financial distress.

Because of this flexibility and because, in the event of liquidation, claims of preferred shareholders rank behind those of creditors, preferred shares are a riskier investment than debt. As a result, investors demand an expected higher return than prevailing yields on long-term debt. Although this is true on an after-tax basis, the different tax treatment that favours dividends over interest income often reverses this on a before-tax or gross basis. Appendix I shows that while interest is fully taxed, dividend income qualifies for a dividend tax credit, and if the dividend is received by another Canadian company, it could be exempt from taxes altogether. Therefore, even if the before-tax dividend yield on a preferred share is somewhat lower than the coupon rate on the same issuer's long-term bonds, the after-tax yield to an investor is likely to be higher. This explains why gross dividend yields on preferred shares in Canada have not generally exceeded long-term interest rates.

PREFERRED DIVIDEND YIELDS VERSUS BOND YIELDS

EXAMPLE

On August 28, 2000, Canadian Pacific (CP) had preferred shares trading on the TSE at a price of $24.70, which paid an annual dividend of $1.412. They provided an actual yield of $1.412/$24.70=5.72 percent. At the same time, the firm's 5.85 percent bonds maturing on March 30, 2009 were trading at $928.60, providing a somewhat higher effective yield of 6.97 percent. On an after-tax basis, however, the pattern is reversed. For instance, an investor subject to a 29 percent federal and a 50 percent provincial tax rate would realize 4.04 percent on the preferred shares and 3.94 percent on the bonds after tax. The effective rates were estimated in the following manner: [6]

---

[5] Under the *Canada Business Corporations Act*, shares of a corporation shall be without nominal or par value. However, this was not always the case.

[6] The yield to maturity is made up of both interest and changes in capital value. For investors, these two components are subject to different tax treatment, a subtlety not incorporated in our illustrations.

INTEREST:

Taxes paid on $100 in interest=federal taxes+provincial taxes

$= [(100)\times(0.29)]+[(100)\times(0.29)]\times0.50$

$= 29+14.50=\$43.50$ (for a 43.5% marginal tax rate)

Therefore, the after-tax return=6.97% $(1-.435)=3.94\%$

DIVIDENDS:[7]

Taxes paid on $100 in dividends=federal taxes+provincial taxes

In Canada, the dividend amount is grossed up by 25 percent (to $125 in this example), and then a 13.33 percent dividend tax credit it applied to reduce taxes payable.

$= [(125)\times(0.29)-(.1333)\times(125)]+[(125)\times(0.29)-(.1333)\times(125)]\times0.50$

$= 19.59+9.80=\$29.39$ (for a 29.39% marginal tax rate)

Therefore, the after-tax return=5.72% $(1-.2939)=4.04\%$

For the issuing firm, payment of preferred dividends cannot be claimed as a tax-deductible expense but has to come out of after-tax income. Therefore, for firms with taxable income, preferred share financing is significantly more expensive than long-term debt. Because of a distribution tax, preferred issues are also more expensive for businesses not subject to regular taxes. In choosing between the two alternatives, the firm faces the familiar trade-off between expected profitability for its common shareholders and risk. Debt is cheaper and should lead to higher expected profits for common shareholders, but its contractual obligations for payments entail increased risk; preferred shares are less risky but cost more.

EXAMPLE

CORPORATION COSTS OF DIVIDENDS VERSUS INTEREST

Staying with our previous example, let's assume that CP faced a corporate tax rate of 48 percent. Based on today's estimate of the cost of new funds based on prevailing market yields for both types of instruments, the after-tax cost of the preferred dividends would be 5.72 percent versus only 6.97 $(1-.48)=3.62$ percent on the debt. Expressed another way, CP would need to earn $6.97 before taxes to service $100 of debt. But in the case of $100 raised through preferred shares, before-tax earnings would have to equal $5.72/(1-.48)=\$11.00$ in order to be able to pay dividends of $5.72 after taxes.

---

[7] Dividends on most preferred shares issued after June 1987 are subject to a distribution tax. Specifically, the issuing corporation can either elect to pay a 25 percent or a 40 percent tax on the amount of the divident. If the lower rate is chosen, certain corporate recipients must then pay a further 10 percent tax. Regardless of the rate selected, the paying corporation may deduct 2.5 times the distribution tax in computing taxable income.

PERSPECTIVES

Corporate Manager

For the firm, it is more costly to pay $100 in dividends than $100 in interest since there is no tax deduction associated with dividend payments, which are paid from after-tax income.

Investor

All else being equal, the investor would prefer to receive $100 in dividends over $100 in interest because they can claim the dividend tax credit (if the dividends are from a Canadian corporation), thus reducing the effective tax rate applied to dividend income.

As with long-term debt, the yield originally specified on an offering of preferred shares need not coincide with subsequent market yields, and market prices of preferred shares will adjust to reflect current conditions in capital markets. Typically, returns demanded on preferred shares move in parallel with prevailing long-term interest rates. Because of their perpetual nature, however, swings in market prices of preferred shares can be more pronounced than those on long-term debt, and unless protected by other provisions, preferred shareholders bear significant interest rate risk.

Again, past experience with declining preferred share prices and uncertainty about future inflation and interest rates have made straight preferred share issues appear risky to both investors and issuers. In an effort to minimize such risks, options to shorten the maturity through early redemption have become common. Alternatively, some preferred share issues have offered variable dividend payments that are tied to current market yields. For example, the CP preferred shares referred to in the previous examples had no par value, and the associated dividend rate is based on the 90-day Bankers Acceptances rate, which is a short-term interest rate that fluctuates continuously.

Preferred shareholders recognize their weaker position relative to creditors. Though no dividends can be paid on common shares unless the current claims of preferred shareholders have been satisfied, this restriction provides only limited protection. Thus, a variety of additional provisions are commonly found in preferred share offerings to strengthen the investors' position. These include the following:

1. Preferred dividends are typically **cumulative**. This means that previous defaults on preferred dividends (also called arrears) must be paid up before any dividends can be paid on common shares. When preferred shares are non-cumulative, dividends not declared in any period do not accrue and are lost.

2. Preferred shareholders may obtain voting rights or automatic representation on the board of directors if the firm cannot meet preferred dividend payments for a specified period of time. The effectiveness of such voting rights depends on the number of votes that preferred shareholders receive in relation to the total votes that can be cast by common shareholders.

3. Protective covenants similar to those commonly found in trust deeds for debt may be provided. Examples include limitations on further issues of debt and preferred shares, and the maintenance of adequate working capital and liquidity.

On rare occasions, a **participating feature** may be included in an attempt to make preferred shares more attractive. Such a provision entitles preferred shareholders to participate in residual earnings over and above the regular preferred dividend. The basis and extent of such participation varies between issues. During the 1980s, several new and innovative features for preferred shares were developed in response to a changing economic environment. For example, in many natural resource industries, commodity prices were subject to increasing uncertainty. In an effort to share some of this risk with investors and to limit fixed commitments, several firms issued commodity-indexed preferred shares.

EXAMPLE

COMMODITY-INDEXED PREFERRED DIVIDENDS

For their 1999 fiscal year end, Cominco Ltd. had two series of cumulative redeemable preferred shares outstanding (1.44 million preferred shares in total). The cumulative cash dividends and redemption prices were based upon a rate of return index for world lead and silver prices.

Risk Assessment

A huge consideration for every preferred share investor is to determine the firm's ability to fulfill its obligations. This can be done through independent analysis; however, similar to debt instruments, the quality of preferred shares is rated by debt agencies. The following report provides a description of the DBRS preferred share rating scale, which ranges from a high of Pfd-1 (superior credit quality) to Pfd-5 (highly speculative) to D (in arrears).

■ *Finance in the News*

Preferred Share Rating Scale

The Dominion Bond Rating Service has devised a scale to help guide investors in their selection of preferred shares. Based on both quantitative and qualitative information, the rating does not consider such things as pricing or market risk. The six levels, which range from most secure to least, are:

Pfd-1	Superior Credit Quality
Pfd-2	Satisfactory Credit Quality
Pfd-3	Adequate Credit Quality
Pfd-4	Speculative
Pfd-5	Highly Speculative
D	In Arrears

■ *Finance in the News*

The rating Pfd-1, Superior Credit Quality, indicates companies with strong earnings and balance sheets, senior bonds rated AAA or AA, and where senior debt rating sets a ceiling for the preferred shares the company issues. The next best category, Pfd-2, includes firms with substantial dividend and principal protection, just not as outstanding as the first category; these companies generally have senior bonds rated A. Just below that is the adequate credit quality (Pfd-3), which encompasses companies with good dividend and principal protection but which are more susceptible to economic downturns or other financial adversities. The senior bonds of these organizations are rated at the higher end of the BBB category.

The speculative (Pfd-4) enterprises have uncertain protection of dividends and principal during economic slumps, and their senior bonds are from low BBB to BB. The second-lowest category, highly speculative (Pfd-5), are companies with problems that are serious enough that they could lead to default. It is "highly uncertain" whether these organizations can maintain timely dividend and principal payments in the future. Their senior bonds are rated B or lower. The bottom category, D, are companies that have not been able to meet their dividend or principal payments and are in arrears.

With each rating category, companies called high will be above average in their group, and low will be below average; no designation companies are in the middle of the rating. DBRS uses "n" as an alert for a non-cumulative security, which has a higher potential risk and the "y" designation for hybrid instruments with special characteristics of debt and equity.

Source: Dominion Bond Rating Service website: www.dbrs.com, August 28, 2000. *Reprinted with permission.*

The description in the above report relates the preferred share ratings to the debt ratings. For example, Pfd-1 corresponds to firms of which senior bonds are rated AAA or AA. For comparative purposes, we include Table 13.3, which includes preferred share ratings (where available) for those companies with debt ratings reported in Table 13.2. Notice that the only company to receive a rating in the Pfd-1 category was the Bank of Nova Scotia, and it was also the only firm with a debt rating of AA (or better). The three firms that were rated Pfd-2 had debt ratings of A, while Noranda had a preferred rating of Pfd-3 (high) and a debt rating of BBB (high), and Inco had a preferred rating of Pfd-4 (high) and a debt rating of BBB (low).

TABLE 13.3 ■■■■

DBRS Preferred Share Ratings

Company	Industry Classification	Rating
Air Canada	Transportation	N/A
BCE Inc.	Utilities (Telephone Utilities)	Pfd-2 (high)
Noranda Inc.	Mining (Integrated Mines)	Pfd-3 (high)
Inco Limited	Mining (Integrated Mines)	Pfd-4 (high)
Nortel Networks	Comm. & Media (Telecommunication)	Pfd-2 (high)

Company	Industry Classification	Rating
Clearnet Communications Inc.	Comm. & Media (Telecommunication)	N/A
Bombardier Inc.	Industrial Products (Transportation Equip.)	Pfd-2
Petro-Canada	Integrated Oil & Gas	N/A
Bank of Nova Scotia	Financial Services (Banks)	Pfd-1 (low)
Fairfax Financial	Financial Services (Insurance)	N/A
Investors Group	Financial Services (Invest. Companies & Funds)	N/A

Source: Dominion Bond Rating Service website at: www.dbrs.com. The ratings were the most recent available as of August 28, 2000, and they were determined at various times between July 14, 1999 and April 11, 2000.

13.11   MATURITY AND EARLY REDEMPTION

Although preferred shares typically have no maturity, early redemption may occur through the establishment of a sinking fund or a purchase fund for periodic retirement or by providing investors or the issuing firm with an option for early redemption.

Sinking Fund

Similar to debt issues, some preferred share issues have sinking fund provisions that allow for a gradual redemption of outstanding securities. Each year, a specified amount that may vary over time has to be committed either for the purchase of shares on the open market or for the redemption of shares on a random basis by serial number. Since no critical maturity dates need to be faced, sinking fund payments on preferred shares generally are more modest than would be the case with comparable issues of long-term debt. To protect preferred shareholders, dividend payments on common shares may be conditional upon sinking fund requirements being met.

Other things being equal, issues with a sinking fund are more attractive to investors since open-market purchases to meet sinking fund commitments increase demand for the shares. Also, the likelihood of being able to meet preferred dividends increases as the number of outstanding shares declines. For the firm, however, sinking fund payments represent an additional cash drain that over time, reduces the amount of capital available.

Early Redemption

To protect against interest rate risk (i.e., the risk of changing market yields and prices), an increasing number of preferred share issues provide options for early redemption to either investors or the issuing firm or both. Such an option allows the issuing firm to refinance at a lower rate if, for example, dividend yields on comparable preferred shares have fallen after the date of original issue. Conversely, if dividend yields have risen, investors would find an option for early redemption attractive because it protects them against capital losses and allows them to reinvest their funds at current yields. A retractable preferred share provides the option of early redemption to investors who can cash in their securities at face value on the dates specified in the retraction clause. When the option rests with the issuer, it is termed a call or redemption feature. Such features generally specify that the securities have to be redeemed at a premium over their original issue price. As with debt, the call premium may change through time. For example, both series of the preferred shares of Cominco Ltd. referred to in the example above were redeemable at a retraction price based on the rate of return index for world lead and silver prices.

RETRACTABLE AND REDEEMABLE PREFERRED SHARES

EXAMPLE

Consider retractable and redeemable preferred shares that provide both the firm and the investor with an option to terminate the securities at the original issue price 10 years after the original offering date. The shares provide an annual dividend of $12, and their issue price was $100 per share. If dividend yields on comparable securities have risen to 14 percent 10 years after the original issue, investors will find it attractive to turn in their shares. In the absence of a retractable option, the preferred shares would trade only at:

$$\text{Market price of preferred shares without retraction} = \frac{12}{.14} = \$85.71$$

Clearly, investors are better off if they cash in their shares for $100 and reinvest the proceeds to earn the higher current yield. The firm having to redeem the issue, however, will have to raise new funds at the prevailing rate of 14 percent.

Conversely, assume that dividend yields have decreased to 10 percent. Ignoring transaction costs for the moment, the firm should call the issue and refinance at the new lower rate. In this case, it is the investors who lose because they will have to reinvest the proceeds to yield only 10 percent. In the absence of the call feature, their preferred shares would have been worth:

$$\text{Market price of preferred shares without call feature} = \frac{12}{.10} = \$120 \text{ per share}$$

The above example shows that preferred shares that simultaneously offer the options of both redemption and retraction should be viewed essentially as preferred shares with a limited maturity. Unless market yields remain constant over many years (an improbable occurrence in today's economic environment), it is likely that one party or the other will find it advantageous to terminate the securities.

Whether we ascribe much importance to the choice of detailed provisions that can become part of a specific issue of preferred shares or debt depends on the extent to which we believe in market efficiency. Any feature that reduces risk to investors allows the firm to pay a lower return, and any feature that increases the risk they bear must be paid for with a higher return. If markets are reasonably efficient, investors price each feature at what it is worth, and any package of provisions must provide an expected yield that is commensurate with the risks to be borne. Whether, for example, a particular issue includes a sinking fund or a retraction feature is no longer terribly important because if such attractive features are provided to investors, they respond by accepting a somewhat lower dividend yield. Similarly, unattractive features such as early redemption rights by the company are compensated for with higher yields. Ultimately, the issuing firm should gain with one hand what it gives away with the other.

Convertibles illustrate another option sometimes provided to holders of preferred shares. This option allows the investor to convert the preferred shares into a predetermined number of common shares. As mentioned above, we defer an in-depth discussion of convertibles and other option-like securities until Chapter 19.

13.12   REFINANCING

The framework for analysing the possible refinancing of preferred shares in order to take advantage of lower dividend yields is identical to that developed in Section 13.5 for refinancing long-term debt. If anything, the calculations are simpler because dividends are viewed as perpetuities and are not subject to a tax shield. In the absence of a call premium and of issuing and underwriting expenses, a company would refund whenever dividend yields on comparable issues have declined below the yield originally offered. With a call premium and transaction costs, the present value of future dividend savings has to be sufficient to cover the initial after-tax outlays incurred in refunding. Once again, the discount rate applied to future dividend savings has to be commensurate with the risk of these anticipated cash flows. Following the reasoning outlined in Section 13.5, the savings in dividend payments accrue as long as the firm pays dividends and has the same predictability as the dividend payments themselves. The appropriate rate of discount is the dividend yield that the firm would have to pay on a new issue.

EXAMPLE

REFINANCING PREFERRED SHARE ISSUES

A company issued $10 million of preferred shares 10 years ago with a dividend yield of 12 percent and an initial value of $100 per share. Current dividend yields on comparable issues have fallen to 10 percent, and the firm has the right to call the issue at a premium of 10 percent. After-tax issuing and underwriting expenses on a new issue of similar magnitude would be $200,000. We have:

Initial after-tax outlay = call premium + expenses
$$= \$1,200,000$$

Present value of future dividend savings = $(1,200,000 - 1,000,000)/.10 = \$2,000,000$

Refinancing has a net present value = $-1,200,000 + 2,000,000 = \$800,000$ and so, should proceed.

Alternatively, we can view the problem as follows. The business currently faces annual dividend payments of \$1.2 million. If a new issue can be floated to replace the old one (including payment of all expenses associated with refunding) without increasing annual dividend payments, the firm should proceed. At current yields, dividend payments of \$1.2 million enable the firm to float $1,200,000/.10 = \$12,000,000$ in new preferred shares. This exceeds the amount required to replace the old issue by \$800,000 as computed above.

Note that in either case, we have assumed that future dividend savings accrue in perpetuity, which lets us use the simplified formulas for perpetual annuities from Chapter 5.

Although the value of options is discussed more fully in Chapter 18, we can illustrate the basic value of a call option by pursuing the above example. If the firm holds an option to redeem outstanding preferred shares at a given call price, then ignoring transaction costs and assuming that the decision to call has been made, the value of this option equals the difference between the preferred shares' market value and their call price. [8]

THE VALUE OF THE CALL FEATURE

EXAMPLE

In the absence of a call feature, the market price of the preferred shares from the previous example would be:

$$\text{Market price of preferred shares without call feature} = \frac{12}{.10} = \$120 \text{ per share}$$

or \$12 million in total. If the firm can repurchase these preferred shares for only \$11 million, it stands to make a gain of \$1 million. After transaction costs of \$200,000, the net gain on exercise of the redemption option is \$800,000.

SUMMARY   13.13

1. Long-term debt can be viewed as a promissory note with a life of ten or more years. Such promissory notes are transferable and traded in financial markets. They normally provide for periodic interest payments. The holders of debt instruments are creditors of the issuing firm, and are entitled to future payments as stipulated by the debt contract.

2. The effective yield of a debt instrument need not coincide with its coupon rate, as the market price of outstanding securities will adjust to reflect changing market rates of

---

[8] This same approach does not work with debt because of the limited maturity of such instruments and the tax deductibility of interest.

interest. In international markets, mixed currency instruments have been introduced to reduce foreign exchange risk.

3. Debt may be classified by collateral. Bonds are secured by the pledge of specific assets. Debentures are unsecured or backed only by a floating charge against remaining assets.

4. Most debt issues have provided for a specified maturity. Retractable and extendible bonds provide the right to alter the maturity date originally specified. Sinking fund payments or serial bonds with staggered maturities specify periodic retirement payments over the life of the issue.

5. A firm refinances or refunds debt when it replaces outstanding securities with a new issue at or before maturity. In the absence of call premiums or transaction costs, outstanding debt should be called whenever interest rates fall below the level provided for in the outstanding issue.

6. To deal with increased concern over interest rate risk, interest rate futures and swaps have become popular in financial markets. Other special types of debt include equipment trust certificates and income bonds.

7. The features of preferred shares place them somewhere between debt and common equity. They commonly contain a variety of clauses that strengthen the position of the investor because of the comparatively weak claim on income.

QUESTIONS AND PROBLEMS

Questions for Discussion

1. What do you see as the effects of inflation on the market for long-term debt? Does it make a difference whether such inflation was properly anticipated by financial markets? Are the major problems caused by inflation or by uncertainty regarding future inflation rates?

2. Assume that because of increased uncertainty regarding future inflation, debt instruments either provide for a relatively short maturity or for variable interest tied to prevailing market rates. In choosing between these two alternatives, what are the trade-offs for a borrower and for a lender? What, if any, are the potential costs to the overall economy if traditional markets for long-term debt cease to exist?

3. Why may debt denominated in a mix of currencies be advantageous for an investor or a borrower when compared with debt denominated in a single foreign currency?

4. As a lender, what type of protective covenants would you want to see in a trust deed to protect your position? What, if any, are the trade-offs that you would face when pressing for such protective provisions?

5. As a potential creditor, what trade-offs do you face when choosing between a straight bond and an extendible or retractable bond all issued by firms of comparable risk?

6. If you had to assess the risk of default on a particular issue of long-term debt, what information would you look for? What do you think are the most important items of information that debt rating agencies use?

7. As a financial officer, what trade-offs should you recognize in deciding whether your firm should issue new long-term debt with or without a call feature?

8. If current interest rates are high by historical standards, is it worthwhile to postpone long-term debt issues rolling over short-term debt in the interim? What are the trade-offs?

9. What, if any, implications does a belief in market efficiency have when choosing between alternative debt instruments as outlined in this chapter?

10. Compare financing through debt and through preferred shares. What are the similarities and differences?

11. Why do common shareholders view preferred shares as being similar to debt and often combine them with debt in their analysis of a firm?

12. With dividend payments on preferred shares being discretionary, what prevents unscrupulous common shareholders or management from simply stopping such payments even if the firm can afford to make them?

13. Why is the dividend yield on new preferred share issues the proper discount rate to use when we assess the present value of future dividend savings that accrue due to refinancing?

14. Consider two otherwise comparable issues of preferred shares. One contains a call feature that gives the firm the right to redeem at any time after 10 years, whereas the other does not contain such a provision. As an investor, how would you assess the difference in value between these two securities?

15. In financial reorganizations of companies in difficulty, creditors will sometimes exchange some of their claims for preferred shares. Why may that represent a compromise appealing to all parties concerned?

PROBLEMS WITH SOLUTIONS

Problem 1

A firm with a 40 percent tax rate has a $10 million, 25-year bond issue outstanding carrying an 18 percent interest rate. This issue was sold five years ago (it has 20 years left to maturity) and can be called by the company at a premium of 7 percent over face value. Currently, new 20-year bonds can be floated at an interest rate of 15 percent. After-tax issuing and underwriting expenses for the new debt would be $100,000. Based on discounted cash flow analysis, should refunding take place?

Solution 1

With a discount rate for future interest savings of $15\%(1-.4)=9\%$, we have:

Costs of refunding=call premium+issue expenses
Costs of refunding=700,000+100,000=$800,000
Present value of interest savings

$$= (1,800,000-1,500,000)(1-.4)\left[\frac{1-\dfrac{1}{(1.09)^{20}}}{.09}\right] \approx \$1,643,000$$

NPV of refunding=1,643,000−800,000=$843,000
Refunding should proceed.

Problem 2

A firm has $10 million in preferred shares outstanding at a dividend rate of 12 percent. The issue can be called at a premium of 10 percent, and after-tax issuing and underwriting expenses on a comparable new issue would amount to $200,000.

(a) By how much would market yields on similar preferred shares have to drop to make refinancing attractive?

(b) Assume that dividend yields on new issues have declined to 10 percent. How many years will it take before the present value of dividend savings exceeds the initial expenses of refinancing?

(c) If dividend yields have declined to 10 percent and dividend savings accrue in perpetuity, what is the maximum amount the firm can afford to pay in after-tax issuing and underwriting expenses if refunding is to proceed?

Solution 2

(a) Calling the dividend yield on new issues d, we have:

Initial costs of refinancing=present value of future dividend savings

$$1,000,000+200,000=\frac{10,000,000(.12-d)}{d}$$

$1,200,000\times d=1,200,000-10,000,000\times d$
$11,200,000\times d=1,200,000$
$d=1,200,000/11,200,000=10.71\%$

(b) We have:

$$\$1,200,000 = 10,000,000(.12 - .10) \left[\frac{1 - \dfrac{1}{(1.10)^n}}{.10} \right]$$

$$\left[\frac{1 - \dfrac{1}{(1.10)^n}}{.10} \right] = \frac{.12}{.02} = 6$$

from which we derive $n \approx 9.6$ years

(c) We obtain:

$$\text{Present value of future dividend savings} = \frac{10,000,000(.12 - .10)}{.10} = \$2,000,000$$

Given a call premium of $1 million, the maximum amount that can be paid in after-tax issuing and underwriting expenses is $1 million.

Alternatively, the maximum amount of new preferred shares that can be issued without increasing the current dividend payments of $1.2 million per year is 1,200,000/.1=$12,000,000. With $11 million required to retire the old issue, $1 million remains as a residual gain out of which issuing and underwriting expenses can be paid.

ADDITIONAL PROBLEMS

1. One year ago, you bought a newly issued 15-year bond with a face value of $1,000 and a coupon rate of 18 percent payable annually. Market interest rates have since fallen, and today the bond is priced to yield 13 percent.

   (a) Assuming that you sell the bond today, what price would you obtain?

   (b) What was your effective rate of return over the year?

2. (a) A previously issued bond carries a coupon rate of 16 percent, but current market rates on comparable debt have fallen to 10 percent. Assuming that interest is paid annually, plot the market price of this bond as a function of its remaining maturity.

   (b) A previously issued bond with a remaining maturity of 20 years carries an annual coupon rate of 16 percent. Plot the market price of this bond as a function of various possible market interest rates that may prevail.

   (c) Redo (b) assuming that the bond can be called at 5 percent over face value.

(d) Briefly interpret your findings under (a), (b), and (c) above.

3. The ABC Company currently has $50 million of 16 percent long-term debentures outstanding. These debentures are due in 10 years and can be called at a premium of 7 percent. At present, the company can float a new issue of similar debentures with a coupon rate of 14 percent. After-tax issuing and underwriting expenses will be $500,000, and the corporate tax rate is 40 percent. All interest is paid semi-annually, and you may assume that tax shields from interest payments are available at the time that each interest payment is made. Should refunding take place?

4. An outstanding bond issue of $25 million matures in 20 years and carries a 15 percent annual coupon rate. The existing indenture allows redemption at the following call premiums:

from   5-9 years: 10 percent

from   10-14 years: 6 percent

from   15 years: 2 percent

After-tax issuing and underwriting expenses would be $320,000 in all cases, and the firm's tax rate is 40 percent. To what level would interest rates have to decline in order to make refunding attractive in year 5? Year 10? Year 15?

5. A firm has to decide whether to replace an existing $35-million, 15-percent debenture that has 10 years to maturity and is callable at an 8 percent premium with a similar 10-year issue at a coupon rate of 12 percent. What is the maximum amount the firm could afford to pay in after-tax issuing and underwriting expenses for refunding to be feasible? The firm's tax rate is 40 percent and interest is paid annually.

6. A company issues 15-year, zero coupon bonds with a face value of $1,000 each. The current market yield for similar debt is 12 percent.

(a) At what price can the bonds be sold?

(b) Assuming that market interest rates do not change, plot the market price of the zero coupon bonds as a function of their remaining life. Compute their market price after two, five, and eight years.

(c) Assume that a few days after the bonds were originally issued, market interest rates for similar 15-year debt increased to 14 percent. At what price should the bonds now trade?

(d) Assume normal bonds specifying regular annual interest payments of 12 percent and sold at face value were issued at the same time as the zero coupon bonds. Given the conditions under (c) above, at what price should these bonds trade? Compare your answers under (c) and (d), and try to explain the difference.

7. A Canadian business has to raise $5 million and has decided to do so by selling zero coupon (or deep discount) bonds with a maturity of 15 years. Effective yields on such debt currently are 12 percent in Canada and 9 percent in the United States, and the current exchange rate is C$1.00=US$0.85. By how much would the exchange rate over the next 12 years have to shift to eliminate effectively any interest rate advantage that currently exists on borrowing in the United States?

8. An investor bought an apartment building some years ago and to finance it, she took

on a $350,000 mortgage at 14 percent interest, which is to be amortized through equal annual payments over 25 years. The mortgage has eight years left to run. She is offered an eight-year mortgage at 11 percent but must pay a penalty on the old mortgage of three-months' interest on the outstanding balance if she refinances. This penalty is tax deductible with the tax shield available at the time the penalty is paid. She plans to increase the new mortgage to cover the penalty. Her personal marginal tax rate is 40 percent. Should she undertake the change?

9. An investor faces a combined (federal and provincial) tax rate of 42 percent with provincial tax being 40 percent of federal tax. Current interest rates on long-term bonds are 11 percent. In order to invest in preferred shares, the investor demands an after-tax yield that is 2 percent higher than the after-tax yield on long-term debt. What before-tax dividend yield would preferred shares have to offer in order to become attractive? Assume that the investor has exhausted any tax-exempt amounts of investment income.

10. Consider preferred shares with a par value of $100 that entitle the holder to dividends of $9.00 per year. Compute the market price of these shares given the following conditions:

   (a) Current dividend yields are 12 percent on comparable issues.

   (b) Current dividend yields are 12 percent, but the issue is retractable and can be cashed in at par value in three years' time.

   (c) Current dividend yields are 7 percent.

   (d) Current dividend yields are 7 percent, but the issue can be called at any time at a price of $110.

   (e) The issue is retractable and redeemable, and both options can be exercised at par value at any time.

11. A firm has $10 million of preferred shares outstanding that provide a dividend yield on par value of 14 percent and are callable at a premium of 7 percent. After-tax issuing and underwriting expenses on a similar new issue would amount to $500,000.

   (a) To what level would market dividend yields (on comparable issues) have to drop to make refinancing attractive?

   (b) Assume dividend yields have dropped to 11 percent. How many years will it take before the present value of future dividend savings exceeds initial refinancing costs (that is, before the firm breaks even on the investment)?

   (c) With current dividend rates at 11 percent, what is the maximum number of new preferred shares the firm can issue without increasing aggregate annual dividend payments from their current level?

   (d) Assume current dividend rates have dropped to 12 percent. What would be the market price of the outstanding preferred shares if they were non-redeemable?

12. A company has issued a floating rate bond that pays coupons annually. Because it is a floating rate, the coupon rate on the bond is adjusted each year. The coupon rate on the bond is linked to the Bankers Acceptances (BA) interest rate (which changes continuously). The market demands a risk premium on the firm's debt so that the yield to maturity is always 2 percent higher than the BA rate. The coupon rate on the

bond is adjusted at the end of every year so that it is equal to BA rate+2% (i.e., if the BA rate is 5 percent, then coupon rate will be adjusted to 5+2=7% for the bonds).

(a) When the bonds were issued, they had 10 years to maturity. The BA rate at that time was 6 percent. What was the market price of the bonds at issue?

(b) One year after issue, the BA rate has risen to 8 percent. What should be the price of the bonds now?

(c) Two years after issue, the BA rate has fallen to 5 percent. What should be the price of the bonds now?

(d) Comment on the interest rate risk of floating rate bonds versus bonds that have fixed coupon rates. Explain why there is a difference.

13. An investor is trying to compare two bonds, both of which are zero coupon bonds. However, one is a real return bond while the other is a normal zero coupon bond. The current price of the real return bond is $600, and it has 10-years until maturity, when it will pay a sum equal to $1,000 adjusted for inflation over the 10-year life of the bond. The other bond currently sells for $450, has 10 years to maturity, and at maturity pays the holder $1,000. What must the investor expect the average inflation rate over the 10 years to be in order for the real return bond to be expected to provide a higher return?

14. A business has bonds outstanding that have a 6 percent coupon rate, 10 years to maturity, pay coupons annually, and are currently priced at par. The firm also has preferred shares outstanding that pay an annual dividend of $1.50 per share. To compensate for the higher risk, investors require an after-tax return on preferred shares 2 percent greater than the after-tax return on the firm's bonds. Assume that the effective tax rate on bond income is 45 percent and on dividend income is 30 percent. What should be the price of the preferred shares?

Meet the New Boss: Venerable Co-op Now a Public Company

If you buy shares under the symbol SWP.B on the Toronto Stock Exchange, you become a part owner of a the country's largest cooperative, the Saskatchewan Wheat Pool. Started in the 1920s to help ensure farmers got a fair price for their grain, over the years the Wheat Pool has diversified; it owns gas stations, newspapers, flour mills and even doughnut shops—it is the largest company in Saskatchewan.

And until recently it was 100% owned by 60,000 member farmers. But in April, 1996, the Wheat Pool issued public shares for trade on the TSE. It is now part of the TSE 300 Composite Index. As of fiscal 2000, over 37 million publicly traded Class B shares were currently outstanding.

Some members were appalled at the move, fearing that the interests of distant investors would prevail over those of farmers. A few pulled their money out rather than see it become part of a public company, and several dozen organized protest marches at the Pool offices when the public offering was announced. But the Pool's management felt outside investment was needed to keep enough capital in the pool; more and more farmers were retiring, withdrawing their stake in the pool, and few new ones were taking their place.

Control of the coop remains in the hands of members; the Class B shares do not come with a vote. Farmer members were issued Class A voting shares, which are not tradable and not eligible for dividends; there are currently about 73,000 Class A shares outstanding.

But the experience of other coops that have gone public suggests that, eventually, the situation may change. Investors, after all, tend to want a say in how their investment is managed.

Some observers claim the idea of a cooperative is outdated in today's marketplace, but others feel it simply needs to be reimagined. The Saskatchewan Wheat Pool is an example of a new breed of farmer coop emerging in both North America and Europe. As agricultural markets change, becoming more flexible and consisting of fewer, larger players, coops need both new skills within the organizations and new financial resources. At the same time, the market is increasingly populated with younger farmers with a different attitude towards what a coop should do for them.

Wheat Pool shares have fluctuated widely in price since they were issued at $12, from over $22 to under $3. They closed fiscal 2000 at $3.55. (The Class A voting shares have a par value of $25.) Only time will tell how successful the Wheat Pool's foray into the public market will ultimately be.

chapter 14

Common Equity

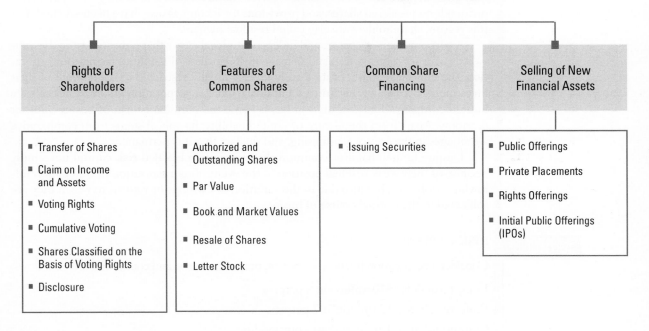

Rights of Shareholders	Features of Common Shares	Common Share Financing	Selling of New Financial Assets
■ Transfer of Shares ■ Claim on Income and Assets ■ Voting Rights ■ Cumulative Voting ■ Shares Classified on the Basis of Voting Rights ■ Disclosure	■ Authorized and Outstanding Shares ■ Par Value ■ Book and Market Values ■ Resale of Shares ■ Letter Stock	■ Issuing Securities	■ Public Offerings ■ Private Placements ■ Rights Offerings ■ Initial Public Offerings (IPOs)

Learning Objectives

After studying this chapter, you should be able to:

1. *Discuss the rights of shareholders.*
2. *Explain the difference between par value, book value, and market value.*
3. *Recognize two restrictions on the purchase or resale of securities.*
4. *Understand and explain the differences between the terms public offering, private placement, and rights offering.*
5. *Identify some of the challenges with initial public offerings (IPOs).*

14.1 INTRODUCTION

Common shares are certificates of corporate ownership that have no maturity date. Collectively, common shareholders own the company and assume the ultimate risk associated with ownership. However, shareholders are entitled to corporate earnings and assets only after all prior and senior claims—such as bond interest and sinking fund payments, dividends on preferred shares, and provisions for income taxes—have been satisfied. For this reason, shareholders are also called residual owners.

A corporation is a separate and independent legal entity that is distinct from the individuals who set it up, own it, and manage it. Regardless of liabilities facing the corporation, the financial liability of its shareholders is usually restricted to the amount of their investment. Because of this **limited liability** feature, a corporation is sometimes called a limited company. The corporation has become the dominant form of business in our economy. Apart from the feature of limited liability, its appeal stems from comparative advantages in the area of fundraising, and the fact that it is permanent.

Despite limited liability, common shares are often labelled **risk capital** not simply because of their weak residual position in the event of reorganization or liquidation following insolvency, but also due to the variation in earnings or returns to which they are subjected in the normal course of business.

EXAMPLE

RISK CAPITAL

Consider a corporation financed with debt, preferred shares, and common shares as follows:

Long-term debt: $10 million at 8 percent

Preferred shares: $5 million at 7 percent

Common shares: 1 million shares outstanding

The corporate tax rate is 50 percent, and annual net operating revenue before financing charges and taxes (also called **earnings before interest and taxes (EBIT)**) is normally $2.6 million. Case A below shows normal earnings per share. Cases B and C, on the other hand, illustrate the impact of a 50 percent shift in EBIT in either direction.

	Case A (Normal)	Case B (50% decline in *EBIT*)	Case C (50% increase in *EBIT*)
EBIT	$2,600,000	$1,300,000	$3,900,000
Less: Interest charges	800,000	800,000	800,000
Taxable income	$1,800,000	$ 500,000	$3,100,000
Income after tax	$ 900,000	$ 250,000	$1,550,000
Less: Dividends on preferred shares	350,000	350,000	350,000
Earnings available to common shareholders	$ 550,000	($100,000)	$1,200,000
Earnings per share	$0.55	($0.10)	$1.20

We see that the variations in EBIT primarily affect common shareholders since interest payments on debt and preferred share dividend payments are maintained at a constant level (barring a complete collapse in earnings). Furthermore, with senior securities (debt and/or preferred shares) outstanding, a given percentage change in EBIT will cause a magnified percentage change in earnings per share. Thus, the ± 50 percent change in EBIT assumed in the previous example caused earnings per share to fluctuate by ± 118 percent. The residual position of the common shareholder, who receives earnings only after all other financing changes have been met, gives rise to this more pronounced variability in returns and justifies the designation of risk capital.

RIGHTS OF SHAREHOLDERS 14.2

The principal parties that control corporate affairs, in descending order of authority, are the shareholders, directors, and officers of the company. Shareholders elect the board of directors, which acts on their behalf and sets general policies for the company. The board of directors also appoints and controls the firm's senior management and delegates to them the day-to-day running of the firm. Shareholders of broadly held corporations, as the ultimate owners of the business, have the following rights:

1. to do as they wish with their shareholdings
2. to share in the earnings of the company if and when dividends are declared by the board of directors
3. to benefit from retained earnings once all claims of senior securities such as bonds and preferred shares are satisfied
4. to elect directors
5. to vote on general questions that may be brought up at annual or special shareholder meetings, such as the selection of auditors and amendments to the corporate charter
6. to examine the company's books and records

At this point, we briefly elaborate.

Transfer of Shares

Incorporation allows for easy transfer of ownership since shareholders wishing to take their money out of a business may simply sell their shares. They are also free to bequeath shares in a will, and neither act will affect the life of the corporation.

A shareholder is not necessarily the agent of the company or of its other shareholders. This means that neither the corporation nor its other shareholders are liable for acts by individual owners, and, assuming shares are widely held, investors may feel safe buying shares in a company without knowing the other shareholders or knowing about their longer-term intentions and commitments.

Claim on Income and Assets

Common shareholders have no right to dividends or any other fixed return. They share in the earnings of the company only when dividends are declared. The amount, type, timing, and frequency of dividend payments are set by the board of directors. Shareholders have no legal recourse against a company for not distributing profits; their only recourse is to attempt to change the board of directors. At the same time, all earnings after taxes, interest charges, and preferred dividends accrue to the benefit of common shareholders. Even if such earnings are not paid out in dividends, they are significant because retained earnings may be used to finance new investments. This, in turn, should enhance the future earning power of the firm and should be reflected in an appreciating share price. Finally, shareholders also enjoy a residual claim against the corporation's assets in case of liquidation.

Voting Rights

Under the *Canada Business Corporations Act*, in the absence of other provisions, every shareholder is entitled to one vote for each share owned. This voting power may be exercised in person or by proxy. A **proxy** is a revocable power of attorney that authorizes an individual, other than the owner, to vote the shares at shareholders' meetings. It is usually given for one meeting only, though on occasion, the request is made for an assignment of the right to vote for one full year.

Because of the costs involved and because of general shareholder apathy, most small shareholders do not attend the company's meetings. If they vote at all, it is by proxy. Consequently, management will actively solicit proxies from shareholders. If shareholders are satisfied with company management, they will return the signed proxy and allow management to vote on their behalf. If dissatisfied but unwilling to sell their holdings, they may solicit proxies themselves, or they may assign their votes to some outside group desiring to replace the present directors. In general, management has a distinct advantage in any competitive solicitation of proxies because of its ability to solicit proxies and mail information to shareholders at the company's expense.

Alternatively, many common shareholders simply fail to vote, perhaps because they feel that their vote is unimportant. In this context, the Royal Commission on Corporate Concentration noted that: "In the large, widely held Canadian Corporation ... the voice of any single shareholder is normally so faint as to be inaudible."[1]

Given the weakness of the voting mechanism, it has been suggested that management can become self-perpetuating, especially as shares become widely distributed. This issue and the recent trend toward a concentration of shareholdings in the hands of financial institutions was discussed in Chapter 1.

In the Canadian context, however, it is also significant to note that a sizeable proportion of major corporations is effectively controlled by a single shareholder, frequently

---

[1] Canada, Report of the Royal Commission on Corporate Concentration (Ottawa: Ministry of Supply and Services, 1978), p. 283.

a family-owned holding company or a foreign multinational. For example, a recent study of 200 large publicly traded Canadian corporations showed that 42 percent of them had one shareholder controlling more than 50 percent of the outstanding shares. In fact, only 21 percent of the companies were truly widely held, with no shareholder owning more than 20 percent of the firm.[2] (In most situations, 20 percent ownership gives the holder effective working control.) This is consistent with evidence that, of the firms included in the TSE 300 Index, over one-third have a shareholder controlling more than 50 percent of the outstanding shares and less than 25 percent have no shareholder owning more than 20 percent of the firm.

By way of contrast, over 85 percent of the firms making up the Standard and Poor's 500 Index in the United States were widely held (with no shareholder controlling more than 20 percent of the shares). Clearly, this degree of concentration in shareholdings severely limits market depth and liquidity and poses special concerns in terms of protecting the rights of minority shareholders. In buying common shares, shareholders need to be concerned not only with the economics of the business, but also with the controlling shareholders' track record, including respect for minority owners.

Steps have been taken to protect minority shareholders. For example, majority shareholders must not vote so as to discriminate intentionally against a minority shareholder. Statutory court orders may afford some protection to minority owners in situations in which a controlling block of shares is voted in an oppressive way. The order could require an involuntary winding up of the company to allow the minority shareholders to get their money out or prescribe some other action that the court holds to be just and equitable. Unlike directors, however, shareholders may, in all other circumstances, vote any way they wish, even if they vote for their own best interests and against what may be best for the corporation.

The Ontario Securities Commission has enforced a set of rules to handle "squeeze-outs," which refer to the actions of a majority shareholder or group aimed at forcing minority shareholders to sell out at bargain prices. Squeeze-outs arise because majority shareholders are able to make important corporate decisions such as selling corporate assets, undertaking mergers, reducing dividends, and altering the capital structure without the consent of minority shareholders. At most, only a two-thirds vote in favour of such actions is required, and frequently a simple majority is sufficient. The rules provide for a "majority of the minority test," which requires that any actions that may be aimed at squeezing out minority shareholders should not be carried out unless approved by a majority of the minority shareholders affected.

Cumulative Voting

Under a normal voting system, each shareholder receives one vote for each share held. In elections of directors, votes can be cast for each vacant position. For instance, a shareholder with 10 shares can cast 10 votes for each contested position. To be elected, each

---

[2] S. Cleary, "The Sensitivity of Canadian Corporate Investment to Liquidity," the *Canadian Journal of Administrative Sciences*, September, 2000.

contestant requires a majority of the votes cast for that position. Thus, a minority group of shareholders may be precluded from winning any representation, and somebody controlling over 50 percent of the shares can elect the full board of directors.

In an attempt to strengthen the hand of minority shareholders, an increasing number of jurisdictions in the United States are requiring the use of cumulative voting. Unlike normal voting procedures whereby shareholders cast one vote per share for their choice on each vacant position, in cumulative voting the votes may be accumulated and cast for only one or a few contenders. No slates of candidates are involved, and the individuals garnering the largest number of votes are elected.

CUMULATIVE VOTING

EXAMPLE

A firm has 1,000 shares outstanding. Assume that all shares are to be voted at the annual meeting. Seven new directors are to be elected, and two opposing shareholder groups have a set of competing candidates. One group of shareholders holds 252 shares and the other group, 748 shares. Under normal voting, whereby each of the seven positions would be voted on separately, the minority group would be outvoted on the separate ballot for each position by 748 to 252, and the majority group would control the entire board of directors. Under cumulative voting, the minority group has a total of $252 \times 7 = 1,764$ votes versus $748 \times 7 = 5,236$ votes for the majority group. Only the seven candidates with the largest number of total votes win a position on the board. If the minority group concentrates its votes on just two candidates, each of these candidates will get $1,764/2 = 882$ votes. In order for candidates of the majority group to rank ahead in the election, each such candidate will have to exceed this figure of 882 votes. Given its 5,236 votes, the majority group can elect a maximum of five directors. (With 5,236 votes spread over five candidates, each candidate receives $5,236/5 = 1,047$ votes; with 5,236 votes spread evenly over six candidates, each candidate receives only $5,236/6 = 872$ votes, which falls short of the 882 votes that the candidates of the minority group have accumulated.) We see that cumulative voting ensures that the minority group, with 252 shares, obtains representation on the board with at least two directors even if all the other 748 shares are voted for competing candidates.

Clearly, cumulative voting gives minority interests a better opportunity to be represented on the board of directors. In Canada, this voting procedure is provided for federally as well as in a few provincial statutes, and it will likely gain greater future acceptance.

Shares Classified on the Basis of Voting Rights

For most companies, the common shares are **non-classified shares**, meaning that all common shares confer identical rights on their holders. A company may, however, have more than one class of common shares, classified on the basis of voting power.

MULTIPLE VOTING RIGHTS SHARES

Magna International provides a useful illustration. The company's capital stock consists of both Class A and B shares. The former carry one vote per share, whereas the B shares are equal in all respects except that the holders are entitled to 500 votes per share and Class B shares are convertible into an equivalent number of A shares at any time at the shareholders' discretion.

Classified shares are primarily used by the firm's original founders or promoters and corporate management to ensure that control of the company is retained within a select group in spite of subsequent sales of additional shares to the general public.

Institutional investors, however, have expressed increasing opposition to the use of classified shares, illustrating their desire to have an effective say in major decisions that affect their investments. Despite the protection generally provided to owners of shares with restricted (or no) voting rights, their market prices generally (but not always) fall below those with superior voting privileges. For example, Bombardier Inc. had two classes of common shares outstanding in 2000. The Class A shares entitled the holder to 10 votes per share, while the Class B shares received one vote per share, but also received $0.003 per share above the annual dividend for Class A shares. On August 21, 2000, the Class A shares closed at $23.95, while the Class B shares closed at $23.15. As illustrated in the example below, this price discrepancy becomes especially pronounced when votes are particularly important, such as when a takeover attempt is felt to loom on the horizon.

VOTING VERSUS NON-VOTING SHARES

In 1975, the non-voting Class A shares of Canadian Tire traded at a high of almost $53. The voting common shares, faced with a less-active market, only reached $49. By 1983, after a five-for-one stock split, the common shares traded as high as $17.75, whereas the Class A shares peaked at $13.75. In September 1986, spurred by takeover rumours, the voting shares traded at around $35, while the non-voting Class A securities lingered below $16. Finally, by the end of June 1998, the common shares traded at $46.05 and the Class A stock, at $43.50.

Disclosure

Shareholders are aided by statutory requirements regarding financial disclosure. Thus, all corporations must file annual income statements and balance sheets and make documents such as shareholder lists and the minutes of meetings available to their shareholders.[3] Widely held companies must release additional information including, for

---

[3] Annual reports, annual information forms, and much additional information for most publicly traded Canadian companies is available at the website for the System for Electronic Document Analysis and Retrieval (SEDAR) at: www.sedar.com. Similar information for U.S. companies can be found at: www.edgar-online.com.

example, reports on share transactions taking place on behalf of insiders. Insiders include directors, senior officers of the company, and individuals holding controlling blocks of shares. Furthermore, most provinces provide for an investigator to look into the affairs of a company if a sufficient number of shareholders approach the court to have one appointed.

Statutes also provide that shareholders are to be invited to attend shareholders' meetings at least once every year. Under certain circumstances, the shareholders may also require management to call special meetings. At any of the meetings, questions may be asked and criticisms voiced of the company's officers. Additionally, most common shares allow the holder to vote on issues raised at shareholders' meetings and to vote in the election of the directors. Through voting, a shareholder can express approval or disapproval with the way management is performing.

14.3 FEATURES OF COMMON SHARES

Share certificates are issued as engraved or printed forms, with space on the front for the owner's name and the number of shares owned. A street certificate is a document generally made out in the name of an investment dealer or a stockbroker. Like a bond in bearer form, the share certificate in street form is more conveniently traded because the name of the owner does not need to be altered every time the share changes hands. Dividend cheques, financial reports, and other communication reach the ultimate owner via the broker or dealer named on the certificate. Alternatively, share certificates can be registered in the name of the ultimate owner. Although less convenient from a trading point of view, such registration offers additional protection against theft or loss of dividend cheques.

Authorized and Outstanding Shares

A firm's corporate charter authorizes the maximum number of shares a corporation can issue. Although amending the charter is not difficult, it does require the approval of existing shareholders, and this will take time. Therefore, management typically prefers to have a significant number of shares authorized that are as yet unissued. These unissued shares introduce flexibility because it remains possible on short notice to grant stock options, to issue additional shares to pursue mergers, to obtain additional financing, and so on.

Outstanding shares represent the portion of authorized shares that have been sold or otherwise issued by the corporation and are presently held outside the company. If the firm has not repurchased any of its issued shares, then the amount issued equals the amount outstanding.

Subject to various constraints, several provincial statutes and the *Canada Business Corporations Act* allow companies to repurchase their own outstanding common shares. A purchase can be made by simply buying shares in the open market or through an invitation to all shareholders for tenders of shares. In the latter case, purchases must be made *pro rata* from the shares tendered. This means that if, for example, 10 investors tendered 100 shares each but the company only intended to repurchase 700 shares, they would be required to purchase 70 from each shareholder, as opposed to purchasing all 100 shares tendered by seven of the investors. The repurchase of shares and its motivations and effects will be discussed under dividends in Chapter 17.

Par Value

Shares can either have a **par value** or not. The par value of a share is its stated monetary face value. It is specified at the time of original issue and may be set at any amount. The more usual par value for mining stocks is $1, whereas par values of $5, $10, and $25 are common for shares of industrial corporations. At one time, all shares issued had a par value.

Today, however, shares are predominately without par value, and, since 1975, firms incorporated federally under the *Canada Business Corporations Act* may not issue shares with a par value. Even where it still exists, par value on common shares has limited significance. The only point worth noting is that shares with a par value (except for mining shares) cannot be issued as fully paid and non-assessable unless cash or a fair equivalent in property or past services at least equal to par value has been received by the company as consideration. Present shareholders are potentially liable for the difference between par and original issue price if the shares held were initially sold at a discount from par value and are still not fully paid. If the need arises, the company can call for payment of all or part of this difference.

The advantage of shares without par value is that such shares are always fully paid and non-assessable, regardless of the price at which they are sold to the public. That is, investors who purchase the shares and pay the full price for them cannot be required to make any additional payments.

Once shares are fully paid and non-assessable, a par value simply provides information identifying the lowest possible investment behind the company's historical offerings of shares. Also, the accounting treatment differs somewhat depending on whether or not the shares have a par value, as illustrated in the example below.

PAR VALUE SHARES

EXAMPLE

A newly formed, provincially incorporated company sold 100,000 common shares priced to net the company $20 a share, with a par value of $5 per share. The equity portion of the balance sheet appears as:

Common shares ($5 par value)	$ 500,000
Capital surplus	1,500,000
Total Common Equity (Net worth)	$2,000,000

The capital surplus indicates the amount by which proceeds from the issue exceeded the par value. If the same shares were without par value, the balance sheet would read:[4]

Common shares	$2,000,000
Net worth	$2,000,000

---

[4] Shares without par value may be carried on the books either at the market price at which they were issued or at some stated value. In the latter case, the difference between issuing price and stated value would be shown as paid-in capital.

Book and Market Values

The **book value** of a common share is the shareholders' equity (net worth) of a firm as shown on the balance sheet less the book value of preferred stock divided by the number of outstanding common shares. Book values are essentially determined by past investment and financing decisions as reflected on the balance sheet. They often bear little relationship to market values that, as we saw in Chapter 6, are primarily influenced by current investor expectations about the firm's future prospects.

EXAMPLE

BOOK VALUES VERSUS MARKET VALUES

The book value of the common shares of BCE Inc. as at December 31, 1999 may be determined from the equity section of the firm's balance sheet as set out below. It is found to be ($17,892 million − $1,700 million) / 643.804984 million shares = $16,192 million / 643.804984 million shares = $25.15 per share. At the same time, the market price at which the BCE's common shares traded during 1999 ranged from $56.75 to $136.00, closing out the year at $131.15 on December 31.

BCE Inc.
Shareholders' Equity as at December 31, 1999 (in $millions)

Preferred Shares		1,700
Common Shares		
Authorized:	unlimited	
Outstanding:	643,804,984 shares	6,789
Contributed Surplus		997
Retained Earnings		8,691
Currency Translation Adjustment		(285)
Total Shareholders' Equity		$17,892

In the case of common shares, it is sometimes useful to distinguish between two values: the **going-concern value** and the **liquidating value**. The going-concern value is reflected in the market price of shares during normal trading and represents the proportionate interest in the firm if it is sold as an operating entity. The liquidating value, on the other hand, is the proportionate interest in the residual amount to be realized when a firm's operations are wound up and its assets are sold off.

Conceptually, the liquidating value of the company could correspond to the aggregate book value of its common shares. In practice, however, the two values seldom coincide. Even if we disregard the costs of liquidating assets, we find the liquidation value to be lower for many firms because assets are often saleable only at distress prices, particularly if liquidation takes place on short notice. For example, a smelter somewhere in northern Canada may have a considerable book value based on its original costs, yet be almost worthless if it has to be liquidated. On the other hand, when a company's accounts show certain assets such as land and mineral rights at conservative values, the liquidating values can exceed book values. Inflation contributes to a relative increase in liquidation values over book values because market values are pushed up, whereas book values, based on historical acquisition costs, remain unaffected.

Because market prices of common shares depend on expected future returns and perceived risk—factors that bear only a very limited relationship to book and liquidating values—a firm's going-concern value will almost always differ considerably from its book and liquidating values. Clearly, book values are of very little economic significance, and liquidating values only become relevant if, because of poor performance or insolvency, it becomes advantageous to wind up the operations of the firm.

We note that, whereas the market prices for shares of listed companies and actively traded over-the-counter shares are easily obtainable, quotations for shares with thin or inactive markets or shares of closely held corporations may not be readily available. Although the concepts discussed in Chapter 6 still apply, the valuation of such shares or firms can present a serious challenge.

Resale of Shares

As we saw in Chapter 2, the trading of shares can take place either on organized stock exchanges or in the over-the-counter market. In either case, the purchase or sale of shares in widely held corporations is usually not constrained and involves no legal formalities.[5] We note, however, the following exceptions.

Letter Stock

Letter stock essentially involves a block of shares that is issued by a firm and sold to an individual or a corporate or institutional investor, but without the normal disclosures and other documentation that is required when shares are sold to the general public. In order to avoid the initial expenses and time delays that a public offering would entail, such sales are sometimes considered by smaller companies with an immediate need for capital. The resale of letter stock is generally restricted. They can be resold as a block only with the approval of the appropriate stock exchange and to the general public only when the term of the letter expires and the requisite documents have been prepared and filed. Given this lack of marketability, letter stock of six to 12 months' duration may initially sell at a discount of around 25 percent from the market price of the identical but publicly traded shares. This discount compensates investors for the additional risk they bear by being locked in.

Escrow Shares

Shares are said to be "escrowed" when they are turned over to a trustee, usually at the request of a securities commission or stock exchange. Once escrowed, such shares are not

---

[5] Widely held corporations should be distinguished from closely held ones, which are referred to as private companies in some jurisdictions and non-reporting corporations in others. The right to sell or transfer shares of closely held corporations is restricted.

transferable until the escrow agreement expires or consent is obtained from the appropriate securities commission or exchange following a formal request. Escrow agreements are used largely in connection with new offerings of common shares. Their purpose, in most cases, is to prevent the selling of shares by the original or founding shareholders who may have obtained significant blocks of shares in exchange for properties or services rendered because such selling could disrupt the public offering or depress the share price after the issuing has taken place.

14.4 COMMON SHARE FINANCING

By financing through common shares, the firm confronts the usual trade-off between risk and expected costs. Because of the lack of contractual obligations and the flexibility that they afford, common shares represent the least risky form of financing. In turn, shareholders bear more uncertainty than other security holders and, therefore, will expect compensation in the form of higher future returns, implying increased expected costs to the firm. In addition, dividends, unlike interest, have to be paid out of after-tax earnings.

An increasing number of common shares outstanding may result in a reduction in earnings per share. Whether the market price of the firm's common shares will drop as a consequence, to the detriment of existing shareholders, will depend on how effectively the firm uses the new funds that were raised. If these funds can be invested to yield a rate of return that exceeds the yield that shareholders view as commensurate with the risk that they bear (as discussed in Chapters 7 and 8), any drop in earnings per share should be temporary, and the market price of the company's shares should not depreciate.

For the issuing corporation, there may be other advantages and disadvantages to raising funds through common shares as opposed to other types of securities. On the positive side:

1. There is no critical maturity date, and funds received are made available permanently.

2. In case of financial difficulties, no fixed charges have to be met by the issuer, and any dividend payments are strictly at the discretion of the board of directors.

3. Because claims of creditors on the corporation's cash flows and assets rank ahead of those of common shareholders, the credit standing of the business is enhanced by any increase in shareholders' equity. This increased borrowing power provides flexibility in future financing.

Potential disadvantages include:

1. A controlling group of shareholders may suffer dilution of voting control if additional shares are issued.

2. Various costs and issuing expenses associated with the sale of common shares may be comparatively high.

It is generally argued that firms would want to issue securities when they have good uses for the funds and when market prices are high. The later observation is consistent with the observed record levels of initial public offerings (IPOs) on the TSE in 1997, in response to high stock market price levels.[6] That year, the TSE set a record

---

[6] IPOs are discussed in greater detail in the next section (14.5).

of $14 billion raised by 102 IPOs. On the other hand, IPO activity declined more than 70 percent to $4 billion in 1998 in response to falling equity prices and extreme market volatility.

In practice, the timing of share issues receives considerable attention. Clearly, in times of stock market buoyancy, the prices to be realized on the sale of new shares will exceed those that would prevail in a depressed market. The higher the market price per share, the lower the number of new shares that need to be issued to raise a given amount of new funds and, consequently, the lower the dilution suffered by current shareholders in terms of earnings per share or voting control.

TIMING OF STOCK ISSUES

EXAMPLE

A company needs to raise $30 million through an offering of new common shares. If they could net the company $15 per share, it would have to issue 30 million/15=2 million new shares. Assume that at present, the stock market is considered to be unduly depressed and that management expects a recovery of share prices, with the firm's share price climbing to at least $20 per share within the next 18 months. If shares could be sold to net $20 per share, only 30 million/20=1.5 million new shares would have to be issued. Alternatively, if 2 million shares were issued at $20 per share, the company would raise $40 million rather than $30 million.

The above example illustrates why new offerings of shares abound in times when share prices are high but dry up almost completely in times of depressed market conditions. Considerations regarding optimal timing confront the manager with the difficult task of forecasting future movements in the stock market. Whether it is fruitful to attempt such forecasting depends on our beliefs regarding market efficiency, an issue we discussed in Chapter 9.

Issuing Securities

For the protection of investors, there are restrictions on the way in which a corporation may seek financing from the general public. Securities legislation is a provincial responsibility and provides for the licensing of those in the securities business, establishes who may solicit public financing, and sets out the procedures to be followed. In part, protection of investors is achieved by requiring firms that seek public financing to issue a **prospectus**, a document containing extensive information about the securities being offered and about the corporation issuing the securities.[7] The prospectus is to contain full, true, and plain disclosure of all material facts relating to the proposed public offering. Several essential parts contained in a prospectus are:

- a set of financial statements, including the auditor's statements
- additional information likely to be of interest to investors, such as full details on securities to be issued, disclosures of interest in the corporation received or to be received

---

[7] Federally incorporated companies are also regulated by the prospectus provisions of the *Canada Busienss Corporations Act.*

by any experts or directors referred to in the prospectus, and the remuneration of directors and senior executives, including stock options
- the estimated amount to be raised and how the proceeds are to be used by the issuer
- a letter, signed by the company CEO, giving salient but broad facts about the company
- approval of the contents by the corporation's directors and appropriate certification by other experts whose statements or reports appear in the prospectus

It is worth noting that, within a limited time, a purchaser may have an agreement to buy securities rescinded if he or she did not receive a prospectus before placing the order. Rescission may also occur when false statements appear in the prospectus. Shareholders may, in addition, have a right of action against directors, investment dealers, and promoters for damages in case of deliberate misrepresentation. The next section deals in more detail with the process of issuing new securities.

14.5 SELLING OF NEW FINANCIAL ASSETS

A firm can sell new securities through a public offering, through private placements, or by offering them directly to its own shareholders. Each alternative entails different institutional arrangements.

Public Offerings

In a **public offering**, new securities are made available for sale to the general public. Sales of common shares of a company that already has publicly traded shares outstanding are called seasoned new issues. If the issuer is selling securities for the first time, these are referred to as **initial public offerings (IPOs)**. Once the original purchasers sell the securities, they trade in secondary markets. New securities may trade repeatedly in the secondary market, but the original issuers will be unaffected in the sense that they receive no additional cash from these transactions.

Although a few corporations may undertake to retail their own securities, they generally lack the expertise and required facilities for floating large public issues, so they usually engage an investment dealer to **underwrite** the issue. Underwriting, as applied to financing, is a term borrowed from the insurance field and refers to the purchase of a new offering of securities by the investment dealer. Most underwriting involves a **firm commitment** under which the investment dealer purchases the entire issue. The purchase takes place at a set price on a particular date, and once the underwriting is contracted, the success of the offering from the issuer's standpoint is assured. The dealer meanwhile arranges to retail the securities to investors at a somewhat higher price than was paid to the issuer, with the spread providing compensation for the dealer's services. Such services include not only marketing expertise and advice on timing, type, pricing, and other terms of the issue, but also the assumption of risks during the retailing process.

In order to reduce the risk associated with the selling price of the securities, underwriting arrangements may be made on a **best efforts** distribution basis. In such instances, the investment dealer undertakes to do little more than attempt to retail the securities for the issuer, receiving a commission on sales made. An example of a situation involving this distribution method is described in the report below, which refers to the 1999 initial public offering of Manulife Financial Corp.'s shares. The dealers received a commission of 3 percent per share sold. The shares were sold at $18 per share, with resulting commissions of $75 million. Best-efforts arrangements are used in several situations, particularly when there is price uncertainty. For example, with small and speculative issues involving relatively high risks, investment dealers may be willing to handle the offering but not to purchase the issue. On the other hand, since the fees are likely to be less, best-efforts distribution may also be favoured by a high-quality issuer wishing to reduce issuing expenses.

■ *Finance in the News*

Manulife Dealers Set to Cash in on a Big Payday

Manulife Financial Corp's newly public shares slipped another 1.4 percent. The two dozen investment dealers who sold the $2.49 billion IPO last week look forward to a windfall $74.7 million in underwriting fees. The underwriters sold 138.3 million Manulife shares at a commission of 54 cents each, or 3 percent of the $18 share price. The company had hoped for $23, but U.S. institutional investors refused to pay more than $18 per share. The dealers could have made an additional $20 million if the IPO had sold for $23 per share as Manulife had hoped—$95 million rather than $75 million in commissions.

Money-makers—top five dealers, number of shares, and commissions earned

ScotiaMcLeod: 33.1 million shares sold; $17.9 million in commissions

Merrill Lynch: 26.3 million shares; $14.2 in commissions

Credit Suisse First Boston: 23.7 million shares; $12.8 million in commissions

RBC Dominion Securities: 8.9 million shares; $4.8 million in commissions

Nesbitt Burns: 7.1 million shares; $3.8 million in commissions

Source: John Partridge, "Manulife Dealers Set to Cash in on a Big Payday." *Globe and Mail*, September 28, 1999, pp. B1, B10. *Reprinted with permission.*

Typically, underwriting commissions in the form of discounts have been 3 to 5 percent of the issue's dollar value for equity and 1.5 to 2.5 percent for debt offerings. Additional issuing expenses, usually several hundred thousand dollars, include audit and legal fees as well as other costs of preparing the prospectus.

TABLE 14.1

Top Underwriters of Canadian Issues (1999)

Underwriter	Number as Lead	Value as Lead ($million)	Number in Syndicate	Value in Syndicate ($million)	Total Number	Total Value ($million)
RBC Dominion Securities	123	9,533	199	5,462	322	14,995
CIBC World Markets	100	6,995	246	6,540	346	13,535
Merrill Lynch & Co.	40	5,446	163	5,112	203	10,558
TD Securities	60	4,944	202	5,597	262	10,541
Nesbitt Burns	58	5,129	208	5,345	266	10,474
Scotia McLeod	45	1,967	207	5,805	252	7,772
National Bank Financial	39	1,140	174	3,172	213	4,312
Goldman Sachs & Co.	20	3,479	15	536	35	4,015
Salomon Smith Barney	7	1,227	37	2,251	44	3,478
Deutsche Bank AG	10	3,088	9	389	19	3,478

Source: Barry Critchley, "RBC Dominion Securities Tops Underwriting Charts," *National Post*, January 29, 2000, p. C3.

Corporate underwriting in Canada has been dominated by a few large firms such as; RBC Dominion Securities, CIBC World Markets, Merrill Lynch & Co., TD Securities, Nesbitt Burns, and Scotia McLeod. Table 14.1 shows the top 10 underwriters of Canadian issues in 1999, which totaled over $65 billion.

In choosing an underwriter, a corporation may either stay with a dealer with whom it has an established relationship or select on a competitive basis. An informal agreement is drawn, usually in the form of a **letter of intent**, from the underwriter to the issuer. The letter broadly describes the securities involved, including the size of the offering, and it constitutes an offer by the dealer to purchase the issue under certain conditions. Should any pricing of the issue be discussed, it will be given in a range and not narrowed down until just before the securities are offered to the public. Upon acceptance of this letter, the underwriter assumes responsibility for coordination of the public offering, including preparation of the prospectus and other legal documentation in compliance with provincial securities laws.

Unlike the United States where securities legislation is a federal responsibility that is administered by the federal agency Securities and Exchange Commission (SEC), securities legislation in Canada comes under provincial jurisdiction, and each province has its own securities act. Among other things, these statutes set out the procedures to be complied with before a public offering of securities may be made in the jurisdiction. The requirements are similar but not identical from province to province, and for an issue to be sold nationally, separate registration must take place in each province.

In public offerings of securities, the issuing corporation has to publish a prospectus. Normally, before a final prospectus may be issued, it is necessary to prepare and distribute copies of a preliminary prospectus, or "red herring," to the securities commission and prospective investors. This contains most of the information to be included in the final prospectus except the price to the dealers and public and sometimes the auditor's report. A statement, in red—hence the nickname, red herring—must be displayed on the front page to the effect that it is not final and is subject to completion and/or amendment before shares can be issued. Clearance of the prospectus by all relevant securities commissions precedes the formal offering of the new issue. About four to five weeks elapse between submission of a preliminary prospectus and final clearance.

The actual marketing of a new issue begins as early as the initial filing of the preliminary prospectus and may overlap the waiting period for final clearances. During this period, initial discussions with potential buyers take place to ascertain market interest. The underwriter also takes steps toward forming a **banking group** or **underwriting syndicate**. The purpose of such syndication, which is common in the Canadian investment community, is to allow wider distribution of the issue and to spread risk. When securities are sold abroad, foreign banks are frequently part of the banking group, as was the case for the example presented in the earlier report, in which Credit-Suisse First Boston was one of the major dealers involved in the issue.

The banking group is often assembled on the basis of past relationships with the principal underwriter, who will be the banking group's manager. The managing firm's name will head the list of underwriters in a prospectus, a mark of prestige about which investment dealers are quite conscious. The agreement among syndicate members is fairly informal, consisting only of individual letters from the syndicate manager to prospective members. The letter provides tentative details on the securities involved and is an offer of specific participation. Acceptance of the offer constitutes a commitment to purchase an allocated participation from the managing firm. Expenses of the issue are borne by the members in proportion to participation.

Larger issues may also involve a selling group formed by the syndicate manager, who may invite orders from selected dealers to assist with the sale of securities. Unlike banking group members, however, members of the selling group do not take title to the securities but simply act as brokers who provide marketing services for a fee.

Due to constantly changing conditions in financial markets, the final terms of an issue and its price are not specified until the preliminary prospectus has been cleared. Should market conditions appear unfavourable at that time, the company and its underwriters have up to 75 days from the date of the first deficiency letter to bring the issue to market. Greater delays require the refiling of a revised preliminary prospectus.

The **underwriting agreement** is the contract between the company and its underwriters, and it sets out the various underwriting terms and conditions including the price at which the principal underwriter buys the issue. Provision is also made in this contract for a **market-out clause**, which gives the underwriter the option of terminating the agreement without penalty. Though use of this clause may be contingent on some extraordinary occurrence or governmental action, it often does provide that the agreement can be terminated on the basis of the underwriter's "assessment of the state of the financial markets," and thus it limits the risk that the underwriter assumes.

As soon as the issuer's board of directors approves the terms and price of the offering, **exempt institutions** are canvassed for orders.[8] A special percentage of each syndicate member's participation is reserved for sales to financial intermediaries such as insurance companies and pension funds, which make up the exempt list. The exempted institutions are approached only by the syndicate manager. In this way, large buyers are shielded from a flood of selling offers, and they are also prevented from attempting to break the minimum price.

The syndicate will work toward providing downside price support for an issue during and perhaps immediately after distribution. Thus, should the market price of the securities fall below the issuing price during this period, syndicate members will take an active role in the market, temporarily buying up excess supply in order to support the price. A significant break in the price during the offering period could obviously involve the underwriters in serious losses, whereas a weak aftermarket for the issue would likely produce disgruntled ex-clients.

Competitive pressures in the area of corporate underwriting, combined with growing annoyance about the market-out clause, have resulted in the introduction of the so-called **bought deal**, which is now the most commonly used distribution method for seasoned equity issues in Canada. Under such an arrangement, the investment dealer buys the entire issue outright and then decides when and how it should be marketed. To the issuer, the result is a faster, absolutely firm, and possibly less-costly sale of securities.

Bought deals are available only to large, well-known issuers, the same ones eligible to take advantage of a short-form or prompt offering prospectus (POP).[9] Under the POP system, much of the information contained in the normal prospectus is expected to have been filed annually, and only material changes and financial statements need be included and cleared by regulators. As a consequence, clearance can be achieved in a matter of days rather than weeks. The resultant speed and relative ease of clearance has facilitated the trend toward bought deals. It should be noted that a regular final prospectus must still be available before an issue is sold to the public.

In the United States, a number of regulatory bodies require competitive bidding for certain new issues as part of the underwriting process. This is not the case in Canada, but, nevertheless, some issuers have shown a preference for such auctions over the alternative of negotiated underwriting agreements with individual investment dealers. Evidence from the United States suggests that competitive bidding has made it possible for issuers to obtain higher prices for their securities. However, in evaluating the economic merits of competitive bidding, we should remember that the advisory facilities and financial counselling available to an issuer from its investment dealers of long standing may have to be arranged and paid for separately.

---

[8] Exempt institutions are large sophisticated investors who, in the view of securities commissions, do not need as much protection as small investors. Sales to them are *exempt* from rules requiring prior approval by the commission. If the entire issue is sold to exempt institutions, it is called a private placement. Such placements are considered in more detail in the next subsection.

[9] Technically, such companies qualify for the Prompt Offering Qualification System.

Partly because of the relatively high fixed costs of preparing a public offering and partly because of a reluctance of underwriters and investors to accept small issues of unseasoned firms, this avenue of financing is not available to most small businesses, and public issues usually exceed $1 million. As a consequence, small businesses enjoy much less flexibility in arranging their finances and are often restricted to internally generated funds and to loans through financial institutions. This leaves many small businesses in a difficult position. Several programs have been designed by various levels of government to remedy this situation and to supplement public financing available through financial markets. Some of these are reviewed in detail in Chapter 24.

Private Placements

As an alternative to a public offering, securities may be **privately placed** with one or more financial institutions such as trust or insurance companies. The financial institution purchases the entire issue of securities, with the terms and price of the offering determined through private negotiations. **Private placements** of both debt and equity issues have assumed significant importance.

One of the main attractions of private placements is the exemption from the registration and disclosure requirements of the various provincial securities statutes. Ontario, which is generally regarded as the model for provincial securities legislation, exempts certain securities transactions from prospectus filing requirements in instances in which buyers are adequately protected without such disclosure. Thus, the sophistication of institutional buyers allows for an **offering memorandum** to be used in place of the prospectus. Significant savings in both time and money are likely to result as the contents of an offering memorandum are less comprehensive and are not dictated by securities legislation but rather by generally accepted standards of the investment community. Other advantages of private placements are greater flexibility in negotiating individual terms (including possible later modifications) and costs and availability, particularly for smaller issues.

Even in private placements, the issuing corporation is likely to rely on the advice of one or more investment dealers on matters such as the nature and size of a proposed issue, its maturity, pricing, and other pertinent terms. The dealers will also act as coordinates between various parties to the transaction including company personnel, investment officers of the institutions, and legal counsel. Finally, they will assist the issuer in negotiating the best terms obtainable from the institutions. However, the investment dealers' fees for a private placement will be much lower than required in a public offering because the dealers act solely as agents, and none of the financial risk associated with a public underwriting is assumed. Issue expenses are also more modest, and the whole process may be completed in a few weeks rather than the several months required for a public offering.

Institutions generally expect private placements to be more attractive than comparably rated public offerings because such placements are not as readily marketable and are usually held until maturity. For example, privately placed debt normally provides for somewhat higher interest rates, shorter maturities, and possibly more restrictive covenants.

Rights Offerings

In a **rights offering** or privileged subscription, the firm's current shareholders are given the right to subscribe to a new issue of securities at a specified subscription price. Rights offerings are most common with issues of new common shares or securities convertible into common shares since this recognizes the shareholders' right to maintain their proportionate ownership in the firm. In fact, some firms have entrenched such pre-emptive rights of shareholders in their corporate bylaws, requiring rights offerings for all new equity issues.

Because the firm deals with its own shareholders, the marketing effort required is limited, and arrangements are relatively straightforward. The board of directors sets a **date of record**. Shareholders registered by that date receive one right for each share held. A certain number of rights will enable the holder to purchase one share of the new offering. Such rights are negotiable and are also termed a "subscription warrant." Fractional shares are not normally available, but a market for rights evolves almost immediately, thus permitting their purchase or sale as required. Shares will trade **ex rights** (meaning that ownership of a share no longer entitles the shareholder to the receipt of a right) two days prior to the date of record to allow for lags in registering changes on the company's list of shareholders, and because trades in common shares must be settled within three days. The time span within which rights can be exercised is relatively short (a few weeks), and, at the end of the period, the rights expire, thereby losing any value.

By offering new securities to existing shareholders who are presumably satisfied with the way that their firm is performing, the probability of a successful sale is enhanced, and issuing and underwriting expenses are reduced. Furthermore, rights offerings enable shareholders to maintain their proportional share of the business and to maintain their voting position. When this is of no concern, a shareholder may simply sell the rights.

Disadvantages associated with a rights offering include the time that it takes to complete the sale of the issue and the perpetuation of an existing base of ownership that may be narrower than desirable or perhaps fall too heavily outside of Canada. Also, the success of a rights offering depends on the relationship between the subscription price for new shares and their prevailing market price, because shareholders will only exercise their rights if the subscription price is below the current price at which shares can be bought in the market. If the share price should fall below the subscription price during the time when the rights are outstanding, the full subscription of new shares may not be taken up. To protect against such risks, the firm can enter into a **standby underwriting agreement** with an investment dealer. Under such an agreement, which entails additional costs, the underwriter stands ready to purchase any unsold securities. The effects of a rights offering on existing share prices, will be discussed in greater detail in Chapter 19.

Initial Public Offerings (IPOs)

We conclude this section with a brief discussion of initial public offerings (IPOs), which have received a great deal of attention from the financial press and many discussions surrounding investments. Pricing of IPOs is an extremely important and complex decision from the firm's perspective. Firms do not want to set their offering price too low since the higher the price obtained by the firm per share, the less shares have to be issued to raise the same amount of money. However, they do not want to overprice the issue and have it undersubscribed, thus not raising the required funds. The following report demonstrates the difficulties associated with determining a fair issue price for companies with no previous trading history, as shown by the wild swings in prices for some IPOs, with one stock increasing its value by 2,733 percent.

■ *Finance in the News*

IPO Market as Hot as it Gets: Appetite for E Commerce

The IPO of Neoforma.com, the Santa Clara, California-based business-to-business e-commerce enterprise that markets medical equipment, products, and supplies on the Internet, was a huge success. The January 24 launch was the first IPO issue over $10 million since December 16 and easily eclipsed Talisman Enterprises' $4.5 million the previous week. The stock, which was initially sold at $13 per share through the IPO, opened on Nasdaq at $39 7/8, hit a high of $60 15/16, and closed at $52 3/8—up an incredible $39 3/8.

This performance was reminiscent of that of 1999, when Internet IPOs soared an average of 90 percent their first day. The top 25 U.S. IPOs that year were all either technology or Internet companies. Leading the pack was Internet Capital Group, which gained 2,733 percent, followed closely by Commerce One Inc. (up 2,707 percent) and VerticalNet Inc. (+1,950 percent). These figures help explain how Nasdaq led all the major indexes with a gain of 85.5 percent.

Toronto software maker 724 Solutions Inc. hopes to catch the momentum with its IPO this week, when it plans a 6-million-share IPO. Priced between $11 and $13, many believe that the stock may trade as high as $18 and double its value on the first trading day. Mary Meeker, Internet stock analyst at Morgan Stanley Dean Witter, stated that she expected business-to-business e-commerce to be "significantly larger" than its business-to-consumer counterpart.

Source: Stephen Miles, "IPO Market as Hot as it Gets: Appetite for E Commerce." *National Post*, January 25, 2000, pp. D1, D2. *Reprinted with permission.*

Excerpts taken from the above report, refer to an upcoming IPO from 724 Solutions, which was expected to be priced at $11 to $13 U.S. and which some analysts thought could easily double in value. These estimates proved to be very conservative in hindsight, since the IPO was actually priced at $26 U.S. and was nine times oversubscribed. The shares closed their first day of trading on Nasdaq at $71.94 U.S., and during their first six months of trading, their price ranged from a high of $240 to a low of $28. Interestingly, the article also refers to the fact that the top 25 IPOs in 1999 were by technology or Internet companies; however, many of these types of companies either delayed or cancelled previously scheduled IPOs in 2000 after severe losses in value for these types of stocks in April 2000.

P E R S P E C T I V E S

Corporate Manager

The huge increases in value of many IPOs on their first day of trading do not result in any additional cash flows to the corporation since all it receives is the initial offer price per share. In this sense, there is a huge opportunity cost to the company associated with setting initial offer prices that are too low.

Investor

The investor who purchases shares in an IPO at the initial offering price can make enormous gains when the share begins trading well above this price. However, as we shall see below, this is not always the case, and such investments are not without risk.

The discussion above indicates the complexity and high degree of uncertainty involved in the pricing of some IPOs, particularly for companies with new products or those operating in rapidly changing industries. Other IPOs for well-known companies in well-defined industries are easier to price with relative accuracy.

There is substantial Canadian, U.S., and global evidence that, on average, IPOs are underpriced. Underpricing is generally measured as the difference between the closing price on the first trading day minus the issue price divided by the issue price. Loughran, Ritter, and Rydqvist provide summary evidence for international IPOs and find that average underpricing ranged from a low of 4.2 percent in France to highs of 78.5 percent in Brazil and 166.6 percent in Malaysia (during the 1970s and 1980s).[10] The authors also show that average underpricing in Germany (1978-92), the United Kingdom (1959-90), the United States (1960-92), and Japan (1970-91) was 11.1 percent, 12.0 percent, 15.3 percent, and 32.5 percent, respectively.

Jog and Riding provide Canadian evidence for 100 IPOs over the 1971-83 period and find average underpricing of 11.0 percent; however, the degree of underpricing varied significantly, and approximately 40 percent of the new issues were actually overpriced.[11] Jog and Srivastava extend Canadian evidence to the 1984-92 period and find that average underpricing falls to 5.67 percent during this period, with only 47.4 percent of the issues being underpriced.[12] It is important to note that not all IPOs are underpriced—some are overpriced. There is also substantial Canadian and U.S. evidence that the subsequent performance of IPOs is below average. In short, while IPOs may offer the opportunity for high returns, this is not always the case. Therefore, what you have is high return-high risk.

---

[10] T. Loughran, J. Ritter, and K. Rydqvist, "Initial Public Offerings: International Insights," *Pacific-Basin Finance Journal*, May 1994, pp. 165–200.

[11]. V. Jog and A. Riding, "Underpricing of Canadian IPOs," *Financial Analysts Journal*, Nov.–Dec. 1987, pp. 48–55.

[12]. V. Jog and A. Srivastava, "Underpricing of Canadian IPOs 1971–1992—An Update," Working Paper, Carleton University, 1994.

SUMMARY   14.6

1. Common shares are certificates of ownership in a company that bear substantial risks. They are the lowest obligation for a firm.

2. As owners of the company shareholders have many rights commiserate with their holdings. Minority positions can be strengthened by combined voting efforts.

3. We can distinguish among authorized, issued and outstanding shares. Shareholders have approved authorized shares for issue. Issued shares have been actually sold.

4. Shares may have par value or be without par value.

5. The book value of the common share is given as the net worth of a firm less the par value of preferred shares divided by the number of outstanding common shares. It may bear little relation to market value, which is based on the firm's current operations and future prospects.

6. Generally there are no restrictions on the purchase or resale of common shares. Exceptions are letter stock and escrow shares.

7. Issuing common shares is the least risky way to raise funds. But it can be the most expensive when the firm has to not only satisfy shareholder expectations by maintaining high returns, but dividends, which are paid out of after-tax earnings.

8. New securities can be sold through public offerings, private placements, or rights offerings.

9. Initial public offerings (IPOs) are securities issued for the first time.

QUESTIONS AND PROBLEMS

Questions for Discussion

1. You represent a minority group of shareholders with two representatives on the corporation's nine-member board of directors. Cumulative voting has enabled you to obtain such representation. Directors serve a three-year term, and it is being proposed that elections to the board be staggered, with three positions to be filled each year. What is your reaction and why?

2. Explain why the residual position of common shares makes such securities attractive to individuals electing to invest in more risky ventures. Why do some individuals favour risky investments?

3. The *Canada Business Corporations Act* specifically rules out the issuing of par-value shares by federally incorporated firms. What arguments can you advance to support the abolition of par-value common shares?

4. Some common shares have traded at prices that are considerably lower than their book values. How do you explain this? Do such shares necessarily represent bargains? Can shares trade at prices that are below their liquidating values? Explain.

5. Why is it often difficult to replace the existing board of directors of a corporation? What remedies do dissatisfied shareholders have, and how effective are they?

6. An increasing proportion of common shares is no longer held by individual investors but by financial institutions such as pension funds and insurance companies. What do you see as the potential advantages or disadvantages of this development? Discuss.

7. It is not uncommon for management to accept capital rationing rather than issuing new shares. In this context, it is often argued that the company's shares are under-valued and that management cannot justify the dilution, which existing shareholders would suffer as a consequence of a new issue. Discuss this position. Is it economical-ly justifiable?

8. The chief financial officer of a firm tells you that she likes to time new issues of com-mon shares. If the market is down and her shares are undervalued, she will not issue new shares. She only issues shares in up markets when the company can get a good price per share. Discuss this strategy from the viewpoint of someone who believes in market efficiency and from someone who does not.

9. Underpricing of shares in an initial public offering (IPO) represents an opportunity cost to a newly public firm. Provide some reasons why it might be optimal for a firm to choose to underprice its shares.

10. For a business engaging in an IPO, what inferences might you draw about the firm if you see that its investment dealer is selling the issue on a best-efforts basis?

11. The ability to issue new securities quickly and with minimal cost is extremely impor-tant to firms. Describe some of the innovations that have occurred in financial mar-kets that allow new securities to be issued quickly and cheaply.

ADDITIONAL PROBLEMS

1. Use the information provided in the preceding Problem with Solution. Assume that the existing board of directors is interested in keeping minority representation as small as possible and limiting the term of office to three years. The current board pro-poses that terms should be staggered, with five positions filled each year. What effect would this proposal have on minority representation, and how many representatives would the minority group have on the board of directors at any one time?

2. The Bjorn Gradin Blade Manufacturing Corporation has 800,000 common shares and 300,000 preferred shares outstanding. The preferred shares call for an annual dividend of $0.90 per share. The firm has just issued $5 million worth of 20-year debentures with an 8 percent coupon rate and sinking fund payments of $250,000 per year. Corporate income taxes are 40 percent. Compute (a) earnings per common share and (b) earnings per common share available after annual sinking fund pay-ments for different assumptions about future performance. Assume that earnings before interest and taxes could be $900,000, $1.7 million, or $2.5 million.

3. A company currently has earnings before interest and taxes (EBIT) of $150 million. It pays $20 million in interest on debt each year and has no preferred shares. Its tax rate is 35 percent, and it has a total of 50 million common shares outstanding.

a) Calculate the earnings per share of the firm.

b) The company is considering issuing 20 million new shares. If it does this and there is no change to its earnings, what will be the new earnings per share?

c) Assume the firm issues 20 million new shares and uses the proceeds of the issue to expand its capacity. This results in an increase in EBIT to $200 million. What will be the new earnings per share?

d) Assume the business issues 20 million new shares and uses the proceeds of the issue to expand its capacity. This time assume that this results in an increase in EBIT to $160 million. What will be the new earnings per share?

e) Given the scenario in part (d), comment on possible agency costs that might arise if managers desire to make the company larger by increasing EBIT.

4. Consider the following statements of shareholders' equity for two firms, A and B.

	Firm A	Firm B
Preferred shares	$ 50,000,000	$ 0
Common shares outstanding	$150,000,000	$200,000,000
Contributed surplus	45,000,000	44,000,000
Total shareholders' equity	245,000,000	244,000,000

Both firms' common shares have a par value of $10. The common shares of Firm A are currently priced at $39 per share in the market.

a) Calculate the ratio of market value to book value of common shares for Firm A.

b) Both companies are in the same industry. Because of this, you make the assumption that the ratio of market to book value should be the same for both. Under this assumption, what should be the market price of Firm B's common shares?

BCE Inc.
Case Part 5

1. Looking at the variety of bond issues outstanding for BCE (see the table in the Case at the end of Part 3), you can see that the maturity dates of the various issues are spread over many years in the future. Explain why BCE would choose to issue bonds with such a wide variety of maturities.

2. The BCE financial statements (in Appendix II located at www.wiley.com/canada /lusztig) contain details about the various issues of preferred shares which BCE has outstanding (see the note to the financial statements titled "Preferred Shares").

a) Given that dividends on most preferred shares are fixed, why would BCE choose to issue preferred shares rather than debt?

b) Note that all of BCE's outstanding preferred issues are redeemable. What does this feature of the preferred shares mean? What benefit might BCE see in issuing redeemable preferred?

c) The Series P preferred shares are convertible. What does this feature of these preferred shares mean? Why might BCE have chosen to issue convertible preferred?

3. BCE has an unlimited number of common shares authorized. Given that shareholders must approve the number of authorized shares, why would they choose to allow management to issue an unlimited amount?

4. The "Management's Discussion and Analysis" section of the BCE's financial statements contains a section discussing recent changes in BCE credit ratings. Discuss what these changes should mean for both current shareholders and current bondholders and whether these are positive or negative changes fore the two groups.

part 6

Long-Term Financing Decisions

In Part 6, we cover short-and intermediate-term financing. Institutionally, such financing differs from long-term funding in that it is typically negotiated and arranged with financial intermediaries. In Chapter 24, we review short-and intermediate-term financing, notably through banks. We also discuss the issuance of short-term promissory notes in money markets; trade credit, or funds advanced to the firm by its suppliers; and factoring. Finally, we cover financing available through various government programs, project financing, and venture capital. In Chapter 25, we review leasing which should be viewed as a form of intermediate-term debt.

Where the World Goes for Cost-of-Capital Information

Founded by Roger Ibbotson in 1977, Ibbotson Associates company markets a wide range of data and presentations products, consulting and training services, and software. Its customers range from financial planners and brokers to large investment managers and corporations. Ibbotson's Cost of Capital Center is often the first stop for finance professionals worldwide seeking information about the cost of capital, whether it's by country, by industry, or by company.

Based in Chicago, Illinois, Ibbotson has the United States as its major focus. But its information spans the globe; its customers include many Canadian professionals, since it has few competitors anywhere, including Canada, that provide similarly comprehensive data.

Michael Barad, a senior analyst at Ibbotson, puts this data to use every day. "If I had to create a cost of capital for a Canadian company," says Mr. Barad, "I would start by looking at the cost of a riskless asset - say, the yield on a 20- or 30-year government bond. You want something long term, since typically you are analysing a company as a going concern."

Under the CAPM method (see Chapter 8), the next step would be to "add the product of the company's beta with the appropriate equity risk premium," Mr. Barad continues.

"If it's a public company, of course, the beta can be derived by performing a regression on the stock's monthly returns. If it's a private com-

pany, I might instead have to take an industry average, or an average of some comparable companies."

The equity risk premium accounts for the higher risk of equity over bond investments. Mr. Barad can find the appropriate value in Ibbotson's publication, *Canadian Risk Premia Over Time*, which gives data

going back to 1936. "I would choose the longest period for which there is reliable data," he explains.

"Finally," says Mr. Barad, "unless it were a very large company, I'd apply a size premium based on the company's market capitalization." Few companies in Canada are so large as not to warrant some kind of size premium. "Ibbotson doesn't have specific data on Canadian company size, so I would try to match the company to the comparable category in our U.S. study data, which is found in Ibbotson Associates' Stocks, Bonds, Bills, and Inflation(s) Yearbook." The Yearbook, considered the industry standard, gives data going as far back as 1926.

Sometimes it's advisable to calculate the cost of capital using two methods to see how they compare. "It depends on how comfortable you are with your data," says Mr. Barad. "If you had to estimate some variables, you might be safer with two approaches."

chapter 15

Cost of Capital

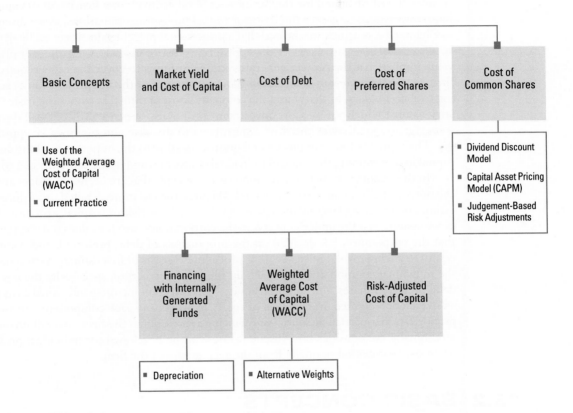

Learning Objectives

After studying this chapter, you should be able to:

1. *Show how to evaluate the cost of a given project within a company.*
2. *Demonstrate what weighted cost of capital (WACC) is and how it is used to calculate project costs.*
3. *Identify the components of a company's capital structure.*
4. *Name two reasons why the cost of a security to a company differs from its yield in capital markets.*
5. *Distinguish between market and book values in calculating WACCs of projects.*

15.1 INTRODUCTION

In previous chapters, we reviewed the various sources of funds that a company can draw on in financing its operations. In this chapter, we discuss how to estimate the costs of each of these sources of funds and how to combine the individual component costs into an overall cost of capital for the business. A good estimate of a firm's cost of capital is important because it forms the basis for capital budgeting evaluations, as we discussed in Chapter 10, in which we showed that a project's net present value is generally derived by discounting its cash flows at the appropriate cost of capital. A positive net present value implies that the project generates sufficient funds to cover the costs required to finance it and that it leaves a residual gain (the amount of the net present value) accruing to shareholders. In that sense, the company's cost of capital becomes the basic yardstick against which we measure investment proposals. When a project's risk deviates from the average risk for the firm, adjustments to this discount rate may be appropriate. The report below contains several quotes attesting to the importance of the cost of capital in determining the value of individual companies and to the economy as a whole.

In this chapter, we begin with some basic concepts that are useful in understanding the notion of a company's cost of capital. We then turn to more detailed procedures for estimating the cost of capital for a given level of business risk and capital structure. That is, we assume that the underlying risk in the corporation's cash flow does not change and that the corporation has decided on the proportions of debt, preferred, and common equity financing it will undertake. Our procedure consists of first estimating the costs of the individual components that make up the capital structure, specifically the costs of debt, preferred shares, and common equity. We then combine these individual costs into an overall or weighted average cost of equity by weighting each component cost by the proportion that particular source of financing represents in the firm's overall financing mix. Finally, we consider how discount rates can be developed for individual projects when risk deviates substantially from the average risk of the firm.

15.2 BASIC CONCEPTS

There are two fundamental ways of looking at a firm. The first is from the viewpoint of an investor, and it pictures a company as a collection of stocks, bonds, and other securities. Investing in these is a way of buying into the firm, and purchasing all outstanding securities results in clear ownership of the entire business. The second view, that of management, sees a firm as a collection of productive assets such as plant facilities and equipment. These can be grouped according to line of business, physical location, or other similar criteria. For the purpose of this chapter, however, it is most useful to think of the company's productive assets as a collection of individual projects, each of which was accepted following a net present value (NPV) analysis. We recall that a project's NPV is calculated by discounting its expected future cash flows at a rate equal to the project's cost

■ *Finance in the News*

Some Notable Quotes

"The cost of capital directly determines the hurdle rates Canadian firms use to evaluate investments of all kinds, including plants and equipment, acquisitions, research and development, brand building, and new market development. The higher the hurdle rates, the fewer the investments that clears them."

Source: David Pecaut, "Canada's high cost of capital: a barrier to investing for the future," *Canadian Investment Review*, Summer 1993, pp. 9-16.

"But for capital investments to be made, the prospective rate of return on their implementation must exceed the cost of capital. Gains in productivity and capacity per real dollar invested rose materially in the 1990s, while the increase in equity values, reflecting that higher earnings potential, reduced the cost of capital."

Source: Alan Greenspan, "Technology revolution: new efficiencies from the fast-evolving technology have been the driver for the powerful U.S. expansion," *Financial Post*, January 22, 2000, pp. D4 and D5.

Mr. Pardy of Goldman Sachs said, "there has been a capital strike as investors refuse to pump money into players that did not at least return their cost of capital. This is an industry that has typically generated less than a 10 percent after-tax rate of return," he said. Investors are standing back and saying: "Why am I going to supply capital to companies in this industry that are not generating real returns?"

Source: Ian McKinnon, "Sharply higher results should boost producer group: flight to liquidity," *Financial Post*, January 7, 2000, pp. D1 and D2.

"If an asset isn't delivering at least cost of capital returns, in the range of 10 percent, we'll either develop a plan to improve it or divest it and move on. You've seen us move forward on such asset divestitures in the first quarter," Mr. Brenneman told shareholders at the company's annual meeting here.

Source: Claudia Cattaneo, "PetroCan to sell assets that don't return 10 percent," *Financial Post*, May 2, 2000, p. C6.

of capital. When the NPV is positive, the project generates cash flows sufficient to cover the cost of the capital required to set it up and leaves a residual gain that adds to the overall value of the firm. If we view the business as a portfolio of projects with varying risk, the firm's investors can be viewed as having stakes in this portfolio. A theme of this chapter is that with efficient securities markets, these two views of the company must be consistent.

PERSPECTIVES

Corporate Manager

To satisfy its investors, the cost of capital used by management as a yardstick in capital budgeting must be consistent with the returns investors expect from holding the firm's securities. The risk-adjusted returns required by investors determine the company's cost of capital and hence the discount rate managers should use in NPV analysis of new projects.

Investor

Since investor's value securities on the basis of expected cash flows and risk, they demand a higher return on securities that carry higher risks. Thus, they will be dissatisfied when the firm does not earn an adequate appropriately risk-adjusted return on funds made available to them by investors. This is evident in one of the excerpts in the report above, which attributes the poor performance for certain shares to investor dissatisfaction with those firms' ability to earn an adequate return on invested funds.

The above points are best illustrated through an extended numerical example. We first look at the corporation from the perspective of investors, viewing it as a collection of financial securities. Firms can rely on various proportions of debt, preferred shares, and common equity for their financing. A decision on the particular financing mix determines a firm's **capital structure**, which simply is a summary of its outstanding obligations to investors.

EXAMPLE

FIRM MARKET VALUES

A firm has 1 million common shares and 500,000 preferred shares outstanding. The common shares trade at $20, and the preferred shares, at $12. The company also has 10,000 long-term bonds outstanding with each bond trading at $975.40. It has no short-term debt. The value of each type of investors' holdings defines the firm's capital structure. In this case, we have:

Value of common shares: 1 million shares at $20	$20,000,000
Value of preferred shares: 500,000 shares at $12	6,000,000
Value of long-term debt: 10,000 bonds at $975.40	9,754,000
Total market value of the firm	$35,754,000

Capital structure is usually expressed as a set of proportions giving the value of each type of investors' stakes as fractions of the value of the entire firm rather than as a list of dollar amounts. Thus, the more standard way of expressing this firm's capital structure is:

Value of common shares/value of firm   20,000,000/35,754,000=0.56, or 56%

Value of preferred shares/value of firm   6,000,000/35,754,000=0.17, or 17%

Value of long-term debt/value of firm   9,754,000/35,754,000=0.27, or 27%

The breakdown of the firm's value resembles the liability side of the balance sheet. Note, however, that in contrast to accounting statements, here we use the market values of the various components, not their book values. This is the case because when determining a company's cost of capital, we are interested in the return these various securities have to provide in the marketplace. The return investors demand depends on how much they have to pay for the stocks and bonds they buy (their market value) not the values at which the firm is carrying these obligations on its books. Despite this, for reasons of convenience, businesses may use book value weights to approximate their capital structures. We discuss this important issue more fully in a later section.

Once the firm's capital structure is known, we can derive its overall or **weighted average cost of capital (WACC)**. We first estimate the cost to the firm of providing an acceptable return to each category of investor. We then combine these individual costs into an overall cost by weighting each component cost by the proportion the particular source of financing represents in the firm's capital structure. If we denote B, P, and E as the existing market values of outstanding debt, preferred shares, and common equity respectively, and $V=B+P+E$ as the total market value of the firm, we have:

$$WACC = \text{cost of debt} \times \frac{B}{V}$$
$$+ \text{cost of preferred shares} \times \frac{P}{V}$$
$$+ \text{cost of common equity} \times \frac{E}{V}$$

(15.1)

TOTAL FINANCING REQUIREMENTS

EXAMPLE

Pursuing the previous example, under current market conditions, assume the after-tax returns investors expect on the various sources of financing are:

Common equity: 18%

Preferred shares: 12%

Long-term debt: 9%

Management has a strong incentive to meet such investor expectations. If the firm issues new bonds at 9 percent and then fails to provide the required return, it is in default, and bankruptcy proceedings may result. If it fails to provide the returns *its* preferred or common shareholders expect, the prices of those (and all other) securities will fall. If the shortfall in returns is substantial, the board of directors and senior management may be forced out by disgruntled shareholders.

In order to meet the above returns, the company must provide, annually, the following after-tax amounts to each class of investor:[1]

Funds for common shareholders:	18% of $20,000,000	=	$3,600,000
Funds for preferred shareholders:	12% of $ 6,000,000	=	720,000
Funds for long-term debt holders:	9% of $ 9,754,000	=	877,860
Total funds required for investors:			$5,197,860

Thus, the firm must generate at least $5,197,860 each year to provide the returns its various classes of investors require. Given that the firm's market value is $35,754,000, this amounts to a return of 5,197,860/35,754,000=14.5 percent. This percentage return is the firm's weighted average cost of capital. It could also have been derived directly using Equation 15.1 as:

$$WACC=9\%\times0.27+12\%\times0.\,17+18\%\times0.56=14.5\%$$

The above implies that if the firm's $35,754,000-worth of assets have an overall internal rate of return of at least 14.5 percent, the company can meet its cost of capital requirements. Equivalently, if the firm's overall expected cash flows, discounted at 14.5 percent, result in a non-negative net present value, the firm is again meeting its cost of capital, with each class of security holder receiving its required return.

We see that the return investors demand in order to buy and hold the firm's securities determine the return the firm must, in turn, obtain on its real assets. Indeed, if we now consider the business as a portfolio of productive assets, the expected returns on its various projects must combine to form a return consistent with that demanded by investors. The nature of this relationship is depicted in Figure 15.1 below.

FIGURE 15.1

The Firm as a Collection of Securities and Productive Assets

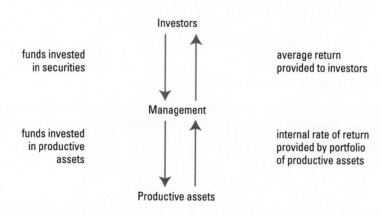

[1] Recall from previous chapters that firms can deduct interest expenses for tax purposes but not dividends. We deal with this issue in greater depth later in the chapter.

While the above example is simplistic, it captures the central issue behind cost of capital calculations: a firm's operating assets must produce sufficient cash flows to provide the expected returns its various investors require in funding them both collectively and individually. Collectively, all the company's projects must produce the overall or weighted average return demanded by all the firm's security holders. Individually, each project should produce a return that would allow it to be funded as an independent, stand-alone venture providing an adequate return to the investors who financed it. This implies that each project must produce a return that is commensurate with the risk it brings to the firm. In practice, taxes, transactions costs, and the fact that markets are less than perfectly efficient complicate the analysis. We explore the implications of these imperfections later in this chapter and again in Chapter 16.

Use of the Weighted Average Cost of Capital (WACC)

When an individual project's risk equals the overall risk of the firm, the cost of capital of the entire organization and of the individual project are the same. Hence, the company's overall cost of capital can be used to evaluate the cash flows of the project.

Assessing the individual risks and thus cost of capital for each individual project is operationally very difficult. Also, for companies that concentrate in one particular area of business, many projects have nearly the same risk. Therefore, a very commonly used approximation is to assume that a firm's individual projects have roughly the same risk as that for the overall company and to use the firm's WACC as a discount rate in capital budgeting. In fact, surveys indicate that this is the most common, formal approach managers use to estimate the discount rate in capital budgeting. Because of its prevalence, subsequent sections of this chapter focus on showing how to estimate this overall cost of capital. The broader framework for evaluating projects based on their individual risk will be pursued in Section 15.9. Before proceeding, we highlight some of the common misunderstandings that often surround applications of the cost of capital.

Common Complications and Pitfalls

We mentioned that when a project's risk deviates substantially from the company's overall risk, reliance on the firm's weighted average cost of capital is inappropriate. The example below provides one such case.

USING AN INAPPROPRIATE DISCOUNT RATE I

EXAMPLE

A stable firm that pumps and distributes natural gas has a WACC of 14 percent. Management evaluates a risky, new liquid natural gas (LNG) project using this 14 percent as the discount rate and obtains a positive NPV. The internal rate of return (IRR) of the new project is 16 percent. On this basis, the firm sells its gas transmission business and uses the proceeds to fund the new LNG venture. Although the company's capital structure has not changed, investors' perceptions about the risk of the firm's operations and thus its securities have changed. Shares are now seen to entail higher risk, and the refinancing of outstanding bonds may require a higher yield to compensate debt holders for a higher perceived probability of default. Given the increased returns demanded by its security holders, the firm's WACC now becomes 20 percent. This exceeds the LNG project's IRR of 16 percent, giving the project a negative NPV when its cash flows are discounted at 20 percent. In retrospect, the firm should not have proceeded with the project.

The problem is that undertaking the new project changed the business's risk and thus its cost of capital. Given the new strategy, the financial manager should have tried to estimate what returns the business's shareholders and bondholders would demand in the future not what they demanded in the past. As indicated, we pursue a more formal analysis of this in Section 15.9.

Another common error in capital budgeting is to relate a project's cost of capital only to the cost of the specific securities used to finance the undertaking. Clearly, it would lead to inconsistent decisions if, in one year, the firm accepted all investment projects yielding the cost of debt simply because debt financing was used. However, in succeeding years, investments of similar risk that promised similar yields were rejected based on the higher cost of using common equity.

In fact, issuing new securities to undertake a new project may alter the firm's capital structure. The financial manager must therefore consider the impact of the new financing on the existing security holders. Securities that seem safe given the old capital structure may seem risky given the new one.

EXAMPLE

USING AN INAPPROPRIATE DISCOUNT RATE II

A company has no debt outstanding. Its capital structure is 100 percent common shares, and shareholders expect a return of 14 percent. Management considers a new project that has the same level of risk as the company's existing projects. A capital budgeting evaluation shows that it has an IRR of only 12 percent and thus a negative NPV when discounted at 14 percent. The firm discovers, however, that the net cost of issuing new debt is only 8 percent. At 8 percent, the project's NPV is positive. Management decides to proceed, financing the project by issuing new debt. This, however, has shifted the firm's capital structure, which has now become 50 percent common shares and 50 percent long-term debt at 8 percent. Upon learning what it has done, shareholders become concerned that in any future recession, most of the firm's cash flows may be needed to service its debt. They reassess the company's dividends as now having significantly increased risk. To keep the share price stable, management discovers that it must increase its current dividends to provide shareholders with an expected 20 percent return. Given this additional cost, undertaking the new project was a mistake.

The error here was for management to assume that the cost of capital for a new project is only the cost of the securities issued specifically to finance it. When a firm changes its capital structure, the cost of capital for a new project is the return that must be paid on the securities issued to finance the project plus any additional returns that must be paid on previously outstanding securities to maintain their market value given the firm's new situation. As we saw, this latter effect can be large. Chapter 16 addresses the issue.

As a further complication, we note that actual financing may be "lumpy," with one type of security issued at any one time to reduce underwriting and issuing costs as well as management's time. Thus, a firm may float a significant issue of long-term debt in one year and then finance new investments out of internally generated funds over the next several years in order to rebuild its equity base and return its capital structure to the desired mixture of debt and equity. Clearly, if management knows in advance that the current capital structure is not permanent, it would make little sense to assume that it is for purposes of calculating a WACC. In this context, it would be preferable to base cost of capital decisions on a long-run average capital structure.

Finally, all of the analysis in this chapter is based on the premise that financial markets are reasonably efficient and that the returns demanded by investors and the prices they set on the company's securities are rational. If financial markets are seriously inefficient and market prices are not valid signals from investors to managers, the techniques discussed in this chapter become questionable. It is sometimes argued that temporary inefficiencies in financial markets may be justification for basing cost of capital estimates on book values rather than market values. There is little evidence to support this. Arbitrarily substituting one imperfect measure for another probably does not improve the final results. Book values based on historical costs and standard accounting rules can seriously distort a firm's value. For example, book values can be quite different when calculated using the accounting conventions of different countries.

Also, changes in accounting rules or their applications can sometimes substantially alter an organization's book value when no change has occurred in its actual cash flows. If financial markets really are badly inefficient (which in most cases is doubtful), an approach that balances market signals with managerial judgement, as illustrated in a crude way in Table 15.1, may actually be best.

Current Practice

Given these problems, in a rapidly changing business environment, it often is not easy to derive a reasonable estimate for the firm's cost of capital. In addition, in Chapters 7, 8, and 9, we saw the difficulties of accurately gauging how investors perceive risk and what premium they may require for bearing-added risk. Because of this, many managers do not attempt to estimate costs of capital with great accuracy and rely instead on approximations largely based on judgement. When evaluating investments, for example, they calculate the project's IRR and then intuitively ask whether the added return the project will contribute to the firm provides fair compensation for the risk it contributes. Typically, rough estimates are used for the returns investors may require given various levels of risk as illustrated in Table 15.1. Clearly, such approaches are rather *ad hoc*. Nevertheless, a major study of corporate decision-making in Canada found that a judgemental consensus among top managers is more important in capital budgeting decisions than the results of any quantitative analysis.[2]

---

[2] V. Jog and A. Srivastava, "Capital Formation and Corporate Financial Decision Making in Canada," *Carleton University School of Business Working Paper* #7 (1992).

TABLE 15.1

Discount Rates Used for Various Categories of Investment Project*

High-risk project (e.g., new product)	25%
Project with ordinary business risk (e.g., capacity expansion)	10%
Low-risk project (e.g., cost reduction)	5%

*Returns are usually based on the risk-free interest rate plus a judgemental premium for risk.

In many situations, we can hopefully do better than judgemental consensus. Thus, when the new project being evaluated does not significantly alter the firm's risk and when its financing does not change the firm's capital structure, a calculation of the WACC as in the examples above often provides a good approximation. Indeed, when formal techniques are used, the same survey confirms that the WACC is by far the preferred discount rate for evaluating investment decisions.[3]

To make this approach operational, we must consider certain aspects of the tax system and some of the costs involved in issuing securities. These topics are discussed in Sections 15.3 through 15.7.

15.3 MARKET YIELD AND COST OF CAPITAL

Given the general considerations outlined above, we now proceed with a more detailed discussion of required investor returns and the consequent costs of issuing various securities.

Any financial security issued by a corporation to raise funds results in an immediate cash inflow—arising from the sale of the securities to investors—followed by periodic cash outflows. The subsequent outflows take the form of interest and repayment of principal in the case of debt and of dividends in the case of shares. For investors who purchase such securities, the situation is reversed: they face an initial outflow when they purchase the securities, and they are compensated for this by expectations of future returns in the form of interest, repayment of principal, or dividends.

We saw in earlier chapters that the price investors are willing to pay for a security is given by the present value of the future cash inflows that the security is expected to generate. The discount rate used in this valuation process depends on the time value of money and the appropriate premium for risk both of which are determined in turn by current supply and demand conditions in capital markets. This yield that investors

---

[3] What is surprising, however, is that 25 percent of the firms surveyed identified their cost of capital with their cost of issuing debt. Unless the projects under consideration were very low-risk investments, this practice is difficult to justify. As noted earlier, even if projects are financed solely through debt issues, increasing a firm's debt increases the risk of its other securities most particularly its equity. The cost of the additional risk premium demanded increases the firm's cost of capital.

demand can also be viewed as the internal rate of return that equates anticipated future returns with the current price or outflow, and it is called the security's **market capitalization rate**. The term stems from the fact that the market converts future cash flows into an equivalent current capital amount by discounting at this rate. Similarly, the cost of funds to the firm is determined by the internal rate of return that equates the present value of future cash outflows with the funds originally received.

In the absence of taxes and issuing expenses, cash flows for the firm and those for the investor would be mirror images of each other with every outflow to the issuer representing an inflow of equal magnitude to the investor and vice versa. With all the cash flows the same and assuming everyone has the same expectations, for any security, the cost of capital to the firm would become identical to its market yield. However, taxes and the costs of issuing new securities drive a wedge between market capitalization rates and costs of funds. Issuing expenses on new securities have to be paid from the gross proceeds of an issue so that the firm's initial net cash inflow no longer matches the funds provided by investors. Furthermore, the tax deductibility of interest payments made by the firm further separates the cost of debt from the corresponding market yield.

For example, if a company sells bonds bearing an interest rate of 9 percent at their face value of $1,000, it may net only $980 for every bond sold because of issuing expenses. Furthermore, assuming a corporate tax rate of 40 percent, annual interest payments of $90 are tax deductible and thus result in tax savings of $36, reducing the after-tax outflow for the firm to $54 per year.

In addition, the yield to an investor is affected by individual taxes on investment income. However, because individual tax rates vary widely, it is customary to compute market capitalization rates before individual investor taxes. We follow this practice bearing in mind that individual tax adjustments have to be made by each investor to determine the effective after-tax yields.

To distinguish between a security's cost of capital to a firm and its market capitalization rate, we use the symbols k and r respectively. At this point, we introduce additional notation that will be used throughout this chapter:

r	= market yield or market capitalization rate
k	= cost of capital
b, p, e, re	= subscripts for debt, preferred shares, common shares, and internally generated funds
T	= corporate tax rate
I	= annual interest payment on debt
F	= face value of debt
n	= number of years to maturity
D	= annual dividend payment on shares
P	= market price of a security
NP	= net proceeds to firm when selling a security
t	= subscript for time (in years)

15.4 COST OF DEBT

Based on concepts developed in Chapter 6, we start by determining the cost of long-term debt. Consider a bond that is sold at face value *(F)* and pays annual interest *(I)* until maturity, at which time it is redeemed at face value. To determine the relevant cash flows to the firm, we must consider underwriting and issuing expenses as well as the possibility of selling the securities at a premium or discount from face value.[4] Underwriting costs, issuing expenses, and sales to the public at a discount reduce net proceeds to the issuer below the security's face value. With large debt issues, these reductions can amount to several hundred thousand dollars.

We simplify the subsequent discussion by assuming that costs and discounts on new issues of securities are fully expensed giving rise to a corresponding tax shield at the time of issue.[5] We note, however, that the actual tax treatment of issuing expenses, underwriting costs, and discounts can be complex with the *Income Tax Act* and its regulations providing for numerous special conditions and exceptions. Consequently, the basic framework as presented may have to be adapted to include any tax effects that may be applicable.

Net proceeds to an issuer are given by the face value minus underwriting and other discounts and issuing expenses taken on an after-tax basis. The market yield and the cost of debt are derived by finding the discount rates that equate the present values of future cash flows with the current market price or net proceeds as shown in Equations 15.2 and 15.3 below.

Market yield:

(15.2)
$$P_b = \frac{I}{(1+r_b)} + \frac{I}{(1+r_b)^2} + \cdots + \frac{I}{(1+r_b)^n} + \frac{F}{(1+r_b)^n}$$

$$P_b = I \times \left[\frac{1 - \frac{1}{(1+r_b)^n}}{r_b} \right] + F \times \left[\frac{1}{(1+r_b)^n} \right]$$

Cost of debt:

(15.3)
$$NP_b = \frac{(1-T)I}{(1+k_b)} + \frac{(1-T)I}{(1+k_b)^2} + \cdots + \frac{(1-T)I}{(1+k_b)^n} + \frac{F}{(1+k_b)^n}$$

$$NP_b = I(1-T) \times \left[\frac{1 - \frac{1}{(1+k_b)^n}}{k_b} \right] + F \times \left[\frac{1}{(1+k_b)^n} \right]$$

---

[4] Conditions in financial markets including interest rates may change during the final days of preparation preceding a new issue. If interest rates rise, for example, rather than increasing the coupon rate and revising documents including the prospectus, the bond may simply be offered at a discount to improve its yield.

[5] In practice, the expenses of issuing shares are to be amortized over five years. Similarly, expenses of debt financing are to be amortized over the greater of five years or the term of the obligation. Any unamortized costs are to be deductible in the year in which the debt is repaid.

From Chapter 6, we recall that we can solve for the appropriate discount rate in these equations: by financial calculator, by trial and error (using linear interpolation), or by using the following variations of the approximation formula that was presented in Chapter 6:

Market yield:

$$r_b = \frac{I + \left(\dfrac{F - P_b}{n}\right)}{\left(\dfrac{F + P_b}{2}\right)} \qquad (15.4)$$

Cost of debt:

$$k_b = \frac{I(1-T) + \left(\dfrac{F - NP_b}{n}\right)}{\left(\dfrac{F + NP_b}{2}\right)} \qquad (15.5)$$

COST OF DEBT

EXAMPLE

A 20-year $1,000 bond with an 8 percent coupon is sold to the public at a discount of 3 percent. The underwriting discount is a further 3 percent of the face value, additional issue expenses are $20 per bond, and the corporate tax rate is 40 percent. Assume that the discount as well as the underwriting and issuing expenses are fully deductible for tax purposes.

The net after-tax annual interest outflow per bond to the corporation equals $I \times (1-T) = 80 \times (1 - .40) = \$48$. Thus, the annual cash flows are:

Year	for investor	for corporation
0	$ 970 outflow	$ 952 inflow
1-19	80 inflow	48 outflow
20	1,080 inflow	1,048 outflow

The initial cash inflow for the corporation is the face value of $1,000 minus the discount to the public ($30), the underwriting discount ($30), and the issuing expenses ($20) plus the tax shields of these discounts and expenses, yielding:

$$NP_b = 1,000 - (30 + 30 + 20)(1 - .4) = \$952$$

Substituting the above cash flows into Equations 15.4 and 15.5, we obtain:

$$r_b = \frac{80 + \left(\dfrac{1{,}000-970}{20}\right)}{\left(\dfrac{1{,}000+970}{2}\right)} = \frac{81.5}{985} = 8.27\%$$

and

$$k_b = \frac{48 + \left(\dfrac{1{,}000-952}{20}\right)}{\left(\dfrac{1{,}000+952}{2}\right)} = \frac{50.4}{976} = 5.16\%$$

We recognize that a firm's debt may entail various maturities and forms other than bonds or debentures. For example, part of a firm's financial needs is usually met by short-term debt that may consist of trade credit granted by suppliers, loans from banks and other financial institutions, or short-term promissory notes issued by the company. As we will see in Chapter 25, leasing should be viewed also as a form of debt financing. These various short- and intermediate-term sources of borrowed funds and their costs are reviewed in detail in subsequent chapters. Basically, the techniques of discounted cash flow analysis presented above apply. For simplicity, examples in this chapter assume a single cost of debt (k_b) computed from bonds or debentures. It should be recognized, however, that in reality, a firm's cost of debt will often be an average of the individual costs of the various forms and maturities of debt that make up the its capital structure.

15.5 COST OF PREFERRED SHARES

Computation of the yield (r_p) and the cost of preferred shares (k_p) follows the same approach outlined above. As preferred shares generally have no set maturity only the stated dividends (D_p), the market price of the shares to investors at time of issue (P_p) and the net proceeds to the issuing firm (NP_p) need to be considered. Because dividends are not deductible by the corporation for tax purposes, future cash flows for investors and the firm are identical. Again, net proceeds are derived by subtracting from the market price any after-tax issuing and underwriting expenses.

To solve for the internal rate of return from an investor's point of view, we have:

$$P_p = \sum_{t=1}^{\infty} \frac{D_p}{(1+r_p)^t}$$

which, as we saw in our discussion of infinite annuities in Chapter 5, reduces to:

$$P_p = \frac{D_p}{r_p}$$

The market capitalization rate simply becomes dividends over market price:

$$r_p = \frac{D_p}{P_p} \tag{15.6}$$

Similarly, the cost of preferred shares to the firm is given as:

$$k_p = \frac{D_p}{NP_p} \tag{15.7}$$

COST OF PREFERRED SHARES

A corporation issues new $100 preferred shares that provide $8 annual dividends. The firm has identical preferred shares outstanding that also trade at $100 per share. Issuing and underwriting expenses are 5 percent of the issue price and are assumed to be tax deductible. The firm's tax rate is 40 percent. We have:

$$NP_p = 100 - (1 - .4)5 = \$97$$

$$r_p = \frac{8}{100} = 8\%$$

$$k_p = \frac{8}{97} = 8.25\%$$

In deriving the above formulas, we treated dividends as fixed. Although dividends on preferred shares do not represent legal obligations, few firms issue preferred shares without the intention of paying regular dividends because failure to do so has serious consequences for future financing flexibility, credit standing, management control, and dividends on common shares. Because dividends on preferred shares afford no tax shield to the issuing firm, the cost of preferred shares is generally higher than the cost of debt as discussed in Chapter 13.

COST OF COMMON SHARES 15.6

Common equity is available to a firm from internally generated funds (reinvested cash flows) and from the issuance of new common shares. The costs of these two sources may differ. We first analyse new share issues and then deal with internally generated funds.

Because future returns to common shareholders are subject to considerable uncertainty and dividend payments are discretionary, the cost of common shares is much more difficult to derive than the cost of debt or preferred shares. Ideally, we want to estimate the future returns that equity investors expect when they make funds available to the firm. If it then invests these funds to produce returns that exceed those expectations, share prices should increase and vice versa. Because there are no tax shields, future dividend payments that the firm makes are identical to the cash flows that investors receive, and the only difference between market yield and cost of capital stems from issuing and underwriting expenses that reduce the company's net proceeds.

We saw in Chapters 6, 7, and 8 that the most common ways of valuing common shares are the capitalization of expected future dividends and risk-expected return models. Given the difficulties of estimation in this area, analysts often use several approaches simultaneously and then attempt to reconcile the various results.

Dividend Discount Model

When a firm sells new common shares, investors provide funds in expectation of future cash returns, which according to the dividend discount model (DDM), take the form of dividends. We recognize that investors may purchase shares primarily in the hope of capital gains, which can become a significant part of the return they expect. We recall from Chapter 6, however, that capital gains should ultimately result from shareholders' expectations of higher future dividends since buyers should bid up the share price only if the expectation about the firm's future earnings and dividends support this. In fact, we shall see in Chapter 17 that paying out a current dividend or reinvesting funds to enhance the firm's ability to pay future dividends are alternative ways for management to provide a return to shareholders. Thus, the DDM considers the price of the shares at any time as the present value of future dividend payments.

Using the notation introduced earlier and D_t for the dividend paid at the end of period t, the market capitalization rate and the cost of equity for new common shares is found by solving for the internal rate of return in the following equations:

Market capitalization rate:

$$(15.8) \quad NP_e = \frac{D_1}{(1+k_e)} = \frac{D_2}{(1+k_e)^2} + \ldots + \frac{D_t}{(1+k_e)^t} + \ldots$$

$$= \sum_{t=1}^{\infty} \frac{D_t}{(1+k_e)^t}$$

Cost of new common shares:

$$(15.9) \quad P_e = \frac{D_1}{(1+r_e)} = \frac{D_2}{(1+r_e)^2} + \ldots + \frac{D_t}{(1+r_e)^t} + \ldots$$

$$= \sum_{t=1}^{\infty} \frac{D_t}{(1+r_e)^t}$$

We note that aggregate dividend expectations of investors in capital markets rather than management's own forecasts of future dividend payments are of relevance. Investor expectations determine share prices, and the objective of maximizing shareholder wealth requires that these expectations become the basis for financial decisions. Unfortunately, however, dividend expectations of investors are not readily observable, and actual dividend payments will depend on both the firm's uncertain future earnings and the discretionary decisions of the board of directors. Thus, as we saw in Chapter 6, simplifying assumptions regarding future dividends are normally made. The most commonly used version of the DDM assumes that dividends grow at some steady annual rate (g) to infinity. This constant growth rate of dividends version of the DDM can be expressed in equation form as:

$$P_e = \frac{D_1}{r_e - g} \tag{15.10}$$

This equation can be rearranged to derive the market capitalization rate as:

$$r_e = \frac{D_1}{P_e} + g \tag{15.11}$$

Similarly, the cost of capital becomes:

$$k_e = \frac{D_1}{NP_e} + g \tag{15.12}$$

COST OF COMMON SHARES USING THE DDM

EXAMPLE

Suppose a company has just paid an annual dividend of $2.00 per share. This amount is expected to grow at an annual rate of 5 percent indefinitely, and the firm's shares are presently trading at $21 per share. New shares could be issued to "net" the firm $20 after consideration of the after-tax cost of discounts and issuing costs.

Given this information, we can determine the market capitalization rate and the cost of new common shares using Equations 15.11 and 15.12 as follows:

$$r_e = \frac{2.00(1.05)}{21.00} + 0.05 = 0.1500 \text{ or } 15\%$$

$$k_e = \frac{2.00(1.05)}{20.00} + 0.05 = 0.1550 \text{ or } 15.50\%$$

Because of the underwriting and issuing expenses that the firm has to bear, NP_e is smaller than P_e implying that the cost of capital exceeds the shares' market yield.[6]

As noted earlier, the main difficulty in applying this DDM is the estimation of a growth rate that reasonably reflects investor expectations. We also saw that the assumption of indefinite compound growth at a constant rate may be unrealistic. In addition, many companies do not currently pay dividends, nor do they plan to do so in the immediate future. For these reasons, risk-expected return models are commonly used to estimate the cost of equity. We discuss the most commonly used of these models, the capital asset pricing model (CAPM), below.

Capital Asset Pricing Model (CAPM)

We have seen that investors in capital markets are risk averse and demand increased returns for bearing additional risk. As an alternative to forecasting future dividends, we can estimate a firm's required return on equity by assessing the risk of its common shares and relating this risk to the market-determined trade-off between risk and expected returns as set out in Figure 15.2. Once again, support for this approach can be derived from the objective of maximizing shareholder wealth. If a company's shares produce returns that are not deemed by the market to be commensurate with perceived risk, investors will sell their holdings thereby driving down share prices. The expected returns of shares in this context are made up of dividends and capital gains whereby, as we saw above, capital gains generally reflect improved earnings and dividend expectations.

FIGURE 15.2

Relationship in Capital Markets Between Risk and Expected Return

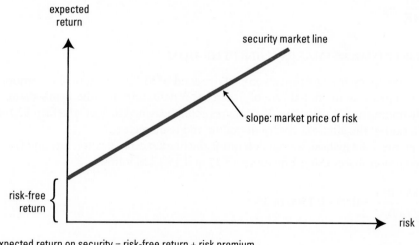

expected return on security = risk-free return + risk premium
$$r_e = r_f + \beta(r_m - r_f)$$

[6] Normally, new shares are offered at a discount from the prevailing market price to ensure the success of an offering. If management wants to ensure that the wealth position of existing shareholders is not impaired by such pricing to outsiders, it will have to maintain the yield on outstanding shares (r_e). Essentially, then, if dilution is to be avoided, the capital raised through the new common shares (those sold at a discount) will have to provide the higher yield to compensate for the discount.

We have seen that the CAPM is one of the most commonly used models that formalizes the general risk-expected return relationship described in Figure 15.2. Using the equations and notation introduced in Chapter 5, the expected return on common shares becomes:

$$r_e = r_f + \beta(r_m - r_f) \qquad (15.13)$$

where

r_e = rate of return expected on a share based on its perceived risk

β = measure of a share's systematic risk

r_f = risk-free rate of return

r_m = expected return on the market portfolio

Unfortunately, price does not appear anywhere in Equation 15.13, so we must approximate the impact of discounts and issuing and underwriting expenses on the cost of common share issues. We do so using the following adjustment:

$$k_e = \frac{P_e}{NP_e} \times r_e \qquad (15.14)$$

Because the firm's net proceeds from an issue are smaller than the current share price, in order to provide the desired return (r) to shareholders, the firm will have to earn a return (k) that exceeds the shares' current market yield.[7]

The CAPM was discussed in detail in Chapter 8 as were the many conceptual and practical difficulties that raise questions about this framework. However, an analysis based on the CAPM often provides a reasonable approximation, and many of the alternative risk-expected return models available are even more complex and difficult to apply. For these reasons CAPM is one of the most widely used approaches to estimating the cost of common equity.[8]

To use Equation 15.13, we need to estimate the risk-free rate, the return on the market portfolio expected by investors, and the shares' systematic risk as measured by its β as discussed in Chapter 8. The risk-free rate is commonly given by the current yield on federal government T-bills, which are virtually free of default risk, and any interest rate

---

[7] For example, assume $P_e = \$10$, $NP_e = \$8$, and $r_e = 10\%$. To provide shareholders with a return of $1 next year, the company has to earn $k = \$1/\$8 = 12.5\%$ on its net proceeds. We confirm that $ke = (10/8)10\% = 12.5\%$.

[8] For example, Ibbotson Associates, one of the world's largest suppliers of financial data, provides cost of capital estimates for a number of companies and industries based in the United States and in many other countries (including Canada). It has used CAPM to estimate the cost of equity for several years and continues to do so. Recently, it has also estimated this cost using the Fame and French three-factor model that was discussed in Chapter 8. For details regarding its cost of capital calculations, go to the following website: http://valuation.ibbotson.com.

risk is minimal because of their short maturity.[9] In estimating the return on the market, we first have to determine the relevant market portfolio. We typically use the return on the TSE 300 Composite Index to measure Canadian market returns, and the S&P 500 Composite Index for U.S. market returns.

Techniques for estimating a firm's beta were discussed in detail in Chapter 8. We saw that such estimates typically are based on regression analysis that relates historical returns on individual shares to the returns achieved by the market. A number of companies and websites also make beta estimates for many large Canadian companies available to the general public. For smaller or privately held corporations, one may have to look for a similar firm whose beta is published. Recall, however, that higher debt financing can increase equity risk. If the other firm has substantially different leverage, its beta must be adjusted. This is discussed further in Chapter 16. Given estimates of all the parameters, the calculation of the market yield for a company's common shares becomes straightforward.

COST OF COMMON EQUITY USING CAPM

EXAMPLE

The current interest rate on federal government T-bills is 6 percent, and a firm's beta has been estimated at 1.5. Using the historical market risk premium of approximately 6.5 percent over the 1938–98 period in Canada (excess return of the market portfolio over the risk-free rate), we obtain:

$$R_e = r_f + (r_m - r_f)$$
$$= .06 + (1.5 \times .065) = 15.75\%$$

If net proceeds on new shares issue are 5 percent below the shares' current market price of $21 so that net proceeds are $20 per share, the cost of equity to the firm becomes:

$$k_e = \frac{P_e}{NP_e} \times r_e = \frac{21}{20} \times .1575 = 0.1654 \text{ or } 16.54\%$$

Again, results derived through the CAPM can be viewed only as approximations. The model's limitations are both conceptual and practical. On the practical side, the model is limited by our inability to obtain accurate measures of various parameters. Once again, ideally, we would like to determine investors' expectations of risk (estimates of beta) and their attitudes about those risks (market price for risk). Because we cannot measure such expectations, we use past behaviour as a proxy and hope that the future will not be too different. In addition, we have to confront the usual statistical measurement problems.

---

9 Many argue that the use of short-term T-bill rates is inappropriate for estimating the cost of capital, which is to be used in evaluating capital budgeting decisions with cash flows that may extend over many years. They argue that the risk-free rate in this sense should have a time horizon that is at least roughly consistent with the period over which the cost of equity is to be applied and advocate the use of long-term federal government bond rates. The drawback of this approach is that long-term government bonds may experience substantial price changes as interest rates change due to inflation and other factors. Thus, they are not a truly risk-free investment, which is what is required for CAPM to hold. Thus, while we recognize the merits of this approach, in order to apply the CAPM consistently and in order to avoid confusion for the student, we will continue to use T-bill yields as the risk-free rate as we did in Chapter 8.

Overall, the model appears to perform better in describing and predicting risk–return relationships for portfolios of stocks than for individual securities in part because betas of individual securities are subject to greater instabilities over time. Such instabilities create difficulties because betas are computed from historical data. Also, the assumptions underlying the model imply that it is most useful in projecting short-term expectations since the model applies to a one-period investment horizon. These short-term expectations of performance may be applicable when managing security investments but are of more limited use in managing firms that invariably require a long-term approach to planning. As a consequence, though the model has gained relatively wide acceptance in the evaluation of portfolio management, at the corporate level, its use is more restricted.

Judgement-Based Risk Adjustments

In practice, probably the most common way of estimating a firm's cost of equity involves a judgement-based adjustment for risk as shown in Table 15.1. Management may start with the interest rate that the firm faces on new long-term debt since this provides a floor (or lower limit) and then add a premium for the risk that shareholders are expected to bear. Basically, one may ask: what expected return would the typical shareholder require in order to view investment in the firm's common shares as attractive? Again, in most cases, practitioners consider *total* risk in making this judgement rather than systematic or non-diversifiable risk as specified by the CAPM. Several reasons can be found for such behaviour. First, the validity of the CAPM in the Canadian context is subject to question, and many Canadian companys have major shareholders that choose not to be well diversified. Second, total risk is intuitively easier to understand and to estimate than systematic risk, a fact that has added significance in Canada because of the limited data (until recently) on betas. And finally, as we saw in Chapter 11, managers tend to associate much more with the stability and survival of their particular organization than with the interests of a well-diversified investment fund that may hold shares of the firm. After all, neither managers nor employees enjoy the benefits of such diversification because their jobs are linked directly to the fortunes of the firm.

Fortunately, this discrepancy is often not contentious because total risk and systematic risk tend to be correlated. Although exceptions exist, firms with high total risks commonly have high betas and vice versa.

In practice, analysts and managers are likely to use several approaches for estimating a firm's cost of equity simultaneously, and they will then attempt to reconcile the various results derived. When discrepancies arise, subjective judgement invariably tends to override any technical considerations.

FINANCING WITH INTERNALLY GENERATED FUNDS   15.7

In the previous sections, we examined the cost a firm incurs in issuing various types of securities. In fact, most firms finance a large portion of their new investments with internally generated funds (reinvested profits and other internal sources of cash flow such as depreciation).[10] Before we proceed to derive a firm's overall or weighted average cost of capital, we need to explore the implications of using such internally generated funds.

Unlike the use of new securities, reliance on internal funds does not commit the company to future cash outflows. Such internal funds, however, do entail opportunity costs. If earnings were not retained for reinvestment, they could be paid out to shareholders as dividends. Shareholders would willingly forego such current dividends only if the reinvested earnings generated adequate future returns. Such returns would then result in increased future dividends, which if anticipated by investors, should result in current stock price appreciation or capital gains. This trade-off between current dividend payments and capital gains resulting from reinvestment is discussed more fully in Chapter 17.

The important point is that reinvesting funds entails financing with shareholder money. Thus, we can view the costs of internal funds as being essentially identical to the costs of issuing new equity since both sources of funds must provide returns that shareholders deem adequate. The main difference is that reliance on internally generated funds avoids issuing and underwriting expenses that are associated with new stock issues. Hence, when a company relies on internal funds as the source of new equity capital, it can use the cost of common equity net of underwriting and issuing expenses in deriving the weighted average cost of capital. This is one reason why firms generally prefer to draw on internal funds first and issue additional shares only if retention proves inadequate. Figure 15.3 reflects this point.

FIGURE 15.3

Marginal Cost of Common Equity

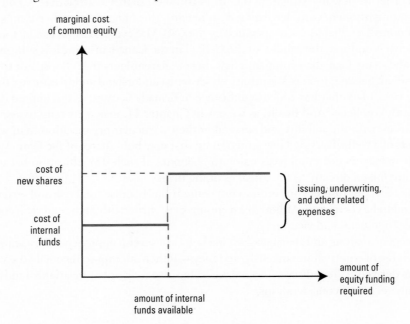

---

[10] For example, Colin Mayer showed that 76 percent of investments by Canadian companies were financed through internal funds over the 1970–85 period, with corresponding figures of 64, 61, 71, 52, 58, 102, and 86 percent for firms from Finland, France, Germany, Italy, Japan, the United Kingdom, and the United States respectively. C. Mayer, "Financial Systems, Corporate Finance, and Economic Development." In *Asymmetric Information, Corporate Finance and Investment*, ed. R. Glenn Hubbard, Chicago: University of Chicago Press, 1990.

The discussion above implies that the appropriate cost associated with the use of internally generated funds (denoted as k_{RE}) is the return required by the firm's common shareholders, who we have previously identified as r_e. Applying this to our approaches for estimating the cost of common equity using the DDM and the CAPM, we obtain the following equations that enable us to estimate the cost of using internal funds for a firm:

DDM:

$$k_{RE} = r_e = \frac{D}{P_e} + g \tag{15.15}$$

CAPM:

$$k_{RE} = r_e = r_f + \beta(r_m - r_f) \tag{15.16}$$

THE COST OF INTERNALLY GENERATED FUNDS

EXAMPLE

For the example above, using the constant-growth version of the DDM, we have the following estimate of the cost of internally generated funds:

$$k_{RE} = r_e = \frac{2.10}{21} + .05 = 0.1500 \text{ or } 15.00\%$$

Using CAPM as applied to the previous example, we obtain:

$$k_{RE} = r_e = .06 + 1.5(0.065) = 0.1575 \text{ or } 15.75\%$$

It is important to recognize that the discussion above does not mean that when a firm relies on internal funds, projects should have their cash flows discounted at the cost of equity. As discussed in Section 15.2, we should never match particular funding sources with individual projects, and reliance on internal financing is no exception for several reasons. First, financing through retained earnings is like financing through issuing new common shares. Relying on either source of funds increases the firm's equity base. Second, any new project must provide a return that is commensurate with the risk it brings to the company. If a project's risk is similar to the overall risk of the company as we assumed above, the required return on the project equals the firm's weighted average cost of capital regardless of what specific funds the corporation may appear to have used at the time.

Depreciation

We saw in Chapter 10 that part of an enterprises' internal cash flow is normally labelled as depreciation for tax purposes. Such depreciation (capital cost allowance) permits the firm to shield part of its cash flows from taxes. As a consequence, over the life of a project, it can recover the funds originally invested on a tax-free basis. While the distinction between depreciation and income as determined by the tax code is somewhat arbitrary, depreciation also represents an internal source of funds that should be included as part of the internally generated funds available to the business. Thus, the cost of these funds will also equal k_{RE} as defined above.

15.8 WEIGHTED AVERAGE COST OF CAPITAL (WACC)

Once the individual component costs have been determined, computation of a firm's weighted average cost of capital is relatively straightforward. We simply multiply each component cost by the proportion that that particular source of funds represents in the company's overall capital structure. Because the cost of capital will be used to evaluate new investments, we should use the current marginal cost of new funds from each source of financing. For example, in evaluating new capital expenditures, it is irrelevant that interest rates on some of the firm's debt issued in the past may have been higher or lower. The actual return any debt holder currently receives is the effective yield to maturity rather than its coupon rate. Since outstanding bonds rarely trade at face value, the two are not the same. New debt will have to provide the current market return demanded by investors not merely match the coupon rates of bonds that may have been issued in the past.

Similarly, dividend rates on shares expressed as a percentage of book value are irrelevant. Instead, the total returns current investors expect, consisting of dividends plus capital gains expressed as a percentage of the current market price, are needed. This is because the firm's discount rate for new projects depends on the current costs of raising funds. Those costs are in turn impacted by the risks investors see in the company now and in the future not what they may have seen in the past. The basic calculation of a firm's weighted average cost of capital is best illustrated through an example.

EXAMPLE

ESTIMATING THE WACC

A company with a tax rate of 45 percent has the following capital structure:

Debt: The firm has 35,000 bonds outstanding, which pay a coupon rate of 9 percent annually and mature in 20 years. They currently trade at a premium of $100 over their face value of $1,000. After-tax issuing and underwriting expenses for such bonds are typically about 2 percent of face value.

Preferred Shares: The company's 150,000 outstanding preferred shares currently trade at $100 and provide a dividend yield of 8 percent. After-tax issuing and underwriting expenses for preferred shares total 3 percent.

Common Shares: The business has 1 million common shares outstanding, which trade at $45 per share. The shares currently provide a $4 annual dividend, which is expected to grow at 4 percent per year. A new issue would net the company $40 per share.

The market yield on the firm's bonds can be determined using Equation 15.4:

$$r_b = \frac{90 + \dfrac{(1{,}000 - 1{,}100)}{20}}{\dfrac{(1{,}000 + 1{,}100)}{2}} = \frac{85}{1{,}050} = 0.0810 = 8.10\%$$

Thus, if the firm issued new bonds at a face value of $1,000 each, the coupon rate would be 8.10 percent, and the firm would "net" $980 per bond after issuing costs of 2 percent. Hence, the cost of debt to the firm can be estimated using Equation 15.5 as follows:

$$k_b = \frac{81(1 - .45) + \dfrac{(1{,}000 - 980)}{20}}{\dfrac{(1{,}000 + 980)}{2}} = \frac{44.55 + 1}{990} = 0.0460 = 4.60\%$$

The costs of preferred and common shares are:

$$k_p = \frac{D_p}{NP_p} = \frac{8}{97} = 0.0825 = 8.25\%$$

$$k_e = \frac{D_1}{NP_e} + g = \frac{4}{40} + .04 = 0.14 = 14.00\%$$

Given the costs of the various components of the firm's capital structure, we now calculate their weights based on the total market value of each type of security. With the total market value of the firm at $98.5 million, we find:

Capital structure component (1)	Number of securities outstanding (2)	Current market price (3)	Total market value (4)=(2)×(3)	Proportion of firm's total value (5)=(4/total)
Debt	35,000	$1,100	$38,500,000	38.5/98.5=0.391
Preferred shares	150,000	100	15,000,000	15/98.5=0.152
Common shares	1,000,000	45	45,000,000	45/98.5=0.457

Combining these estimates for the different component costs and the market value proportions of the firm's capital structure, the firm's weighted average cost of capital becomes:

$$WACC = 4.60\% \times \frac{35}{98.5} + 8.25\% \times \frac{45}{98.5} + 14.0\% \times \frac{45}{98.5} = 11.97\%$$

Therefore, the firm should use a discount rate of 11.97 percent in computing the NPV analysis of any new projects that have the company's typical risk level. This will ensure that each project provides a return that can fully cover the costs of its financing.

Alternative Weights

Ideally, the weights used in computing a company's average cost of capital should reflect the estimated proportions of the firm's future financing. It is often convenient, however, to estimate the weighted average cost of capital using existing financial data. The two main ways of approximating the weights of various sources of funds are to use book value proportions or proportions based on current market values of the various securities outstanding.

EXAMPLE

BOOK VERSUS MARKET VALUES

Consider the following balance sheet data:

Source	Book value	Proportion
Debt	$50,000,000	50%
Equity		
5,000,000 common shares at $5 each	25,000,000	
Retained earnings	25,000,000	50

The market price of the firm's debt equals 80 percent of its book value. However, reflecting growth potential perceived by investors, its shares currently trade at $16. This gives rise to the following market values:

Source	Market value	Proportion
Debt	$40,000,000	33.33%
Equity		
5,000,000 common shares at $16 each	80,000,000	66.67

Retained earnings do not appear explicitly in this tabulation, but they are reflected in the market price of the shares and do not have a separate market value. The same holds true for funds provided through depreciation. If we assume that $k_b = 8\%$ and

$k_e = 16\%$, we arrive at different results depending on how we weight these costs as shown below.

Using book value weights:

$k = (.5 \times 8\%) + (.5 \times 16\%) = 12\%$

Using market value weights:

$k = (.33 \times 8\%) + (.67 \times 16\%) = 13.36\%$

Whenever the market price of common shares is higher than the book value of equity, as is often the case, the use of market values implies that equity will weight more heavily in the calculations. Given that the cost of equity exceeds the cost of debt, the weighted average cost of capital will be pushed up.

Book value proportions reflect financial history and can be influenced strongly by the price at which shares were originally sold and by the earnings retained and reinvested in the past. Clearly, past market conditions that may have dictated such events have little relevance for current financing and investment decisions.

THE PROBLEM WITH BOOK VALUES

EXAMPLE

Consider an apartment building that was erected 10 years ago for $2 million. At the time, in light of projected net cash flows, a capital structure of 80 percent debt was deemed to be optimal, and $1.6 million of 30-year debt was raised at an interest rate of 8 percent. Because of inflation and a general escalation of land values, the building's market value is now estimated to be $5 million. Current interest rates for long-term debt have increased to 16 percent so that the market value of the building's debt (which has 20 years left to maturity) and its equity become:

$$\text{Market value of debt} = \sum_{t=1}^{20} \frac{128,000}{(1+.16)^t} + \frac{1,600,000}{(1+.16)^{20}} = \$841,108$$

Market value of equity $= 5,000,000 - 841,108 = \$4,158,892$

Given that depreciation was taken over the past 10 years, book values would indicate that over 80 percent of the project is debt financed. Clearly, neither an equity investor who bought the building today nor a creditor would view the situation that way. If rental revenues have kept pace with inflation, net cash flows plus the collateral value of the building would provide for substantial added-debt capacity, and current market values would provide a much more meaningful measure of capital structure and financial risk.

If, as discussed in Chapter 9, financial markets are efficient, there should be no controversy about which weights to use. In an efficient market, security prices are the result of thoughtful analysis by large numbers of sophisticated buyers and sellers and reflect the values they perceive a company to have. Hence, management should rely on the market values that investors ascribe to the firm's outstanding securities.

However, book values are readily obtainable while market values may not be. Many smaller enterprises have no publicly traded debt or equity, and even large firms may have entire classes of securities that are not regularly traded. Despite such operational difficulties, it may be better to estimate market values based on the techniques outlined in Chapter 6 rather than relying on arbitrary book values.

Despite these arguments, many firms continue to base WACC estimates on book values, and the main reasons are probably convenience, greater stability in the results, and accounting tradition. While this may yield reasonable approximations during stable times, when book and market values are likely to be similar, it will probably cause serious distortions during times of inflation, changing interest rates, or shifting economic conditions.

15.9 RISK-ADJUSTED COST OF CAPITAL

As indicated in Section 15.2, use of the WACC is justified only if the firm maintains a constant capital structure from which we can calculate the weights used to derive the WACC and if new investment projects do not alter the firm's risk. Essentially, while we have concentrated on the cost of financing, we have assumed that other major areas of financial policy—notably capital structure and capital budgeting—remain constant. As illustrated in Figure 15.4, all of these areas of financial decision-making are interrelated and interact. For example, capital budgeting decisions affect both the company's expected profitability and risk, which in turn affects its policies with regard to capital structure as will be discussed in Chapter 16. From our previous discussion, it is apparent that the firm's WACC depends on the particular financing mix being contemplated. Finally, the cost of capital affects capital budgeting as it becomes an important parameter in investment evaluations.

The simplification of holding everything else constant is reasonable only when we analyse normal decisions of ongoing enterprises operating in a reasonably stable environment. However, it is inappropriate when major departures from past policies are contemplated. For example, when a firm branches out into new and unrelated areas of business with significantly different risk characteristics or when it considers major

FIGURE 15.4

Interdependencies of Major Areas of Finance

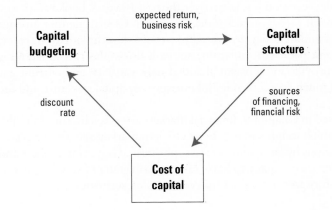

realignments of its capital structure, the interdependencies between various areas of financial decision-making need to be recognized, and consequently, the analysis becomes more complex.

Difficulties are also encountered when a firm operates in various areas of business that are subject to substantially different risk. Consider, for example, an integrated oil company that has divisions ranging from exploration to production including refining, transportation, and retailing. It is clear that exploration is subject to risk characteristics that are different from operating pipelines. Consequently, application of one average corporate-wide cost of capital may be inappropriate because it would result in too high a discount rate for low-risk operations and too low a discount rate for high-risk ventures. The consequences of such distortions can be serious.

To avoid such competitive distortions, firms with heterogeneous operating divisions will find it more appropriate to compute a separate cost of capital for each area of operation. When risk departs from the norm, it becomes necessary to use different discount rates for each operating area. This argument can be carried further to the level of individual projects. Conceptually, any project should provide a return that is commensurate with the risk it adds to the enterprise, and projects with differing risks should be discounted at different rates.

We discussed such risk-adjusted discounting in Chapter 10. The conceptual framework for estimating risk-adjusted required returns for individual projects using approaches such as the CAPM are just as applicable to the evaluation of productive assets as to financial securities. In fact, only if the firm's physical assets are evaluated on the same basis as its outstanding securities do we get the consistency between the two views of the firm that we addressed in Section 15.2.

As already noted, however, the practical implementation of models such as the CAPM in capital budgeting can be problematic. While we can often rely on past statistical information to estimate risk for financial assets, this method is usually not viable for new investments in plant and equipment. One approach that sometimes works for large new ventures in particular is to find a publicly traded company that operates in an equivalent business area and to use its beta as a surrogate.

FINDING COMPARABLE BETAS

EXAMPLE

An all-equity-financed firm wants to set up a new plant to manufacture ball bearings. This would involve risks that are different from those that affect the company's other operations. That is why using the same discount rate as used in other divisions seems inappropriate.

However, an independent, publicly traded firm that manufactures only ball bearings exists. It is all-equity financed, so the return on its shares is equal to its WACC and reflects the risk of operating in the ball bearing business. That company's beta is 1.3. We can use that figure to estimate an appropriate discount rate or cost of capital for the new plant. With a risk-free rate (r_f) of 8 percent and the market index return (r_m) expected to be 14 percent, using the CAPM, we derive the following discount rate:

$$r_e = r_f + \beta(r_m - r_f)$$

$$= 8\% + 1.3(14\% - 8\%) = 15.8\%$$

That is appropriate for the project. If the ball bearing project had to be financed in equity markets as a stand-alone venture, new shareholders would demand this expected return.[11]

The previous example not only assumes that a comparable stand-alone firm exists, but it also ignores issues of capital structure and tax. If the surrogate has debt or preferred shares outstanding, it is said to be **levered**, and the analysis to derive an equivalent beta is more complex. As a company becomes more levered, say through using debt, the risk in its common shares rises because bondholders have a legal right to be paid first if there is a shortfall in cash flows. Ups and downs in earnings are not shared equally by bondholders and shareholders. For example, in bankruptcy, bondholders are protected, and all risk in the firm's cash flows is borne by shareholders. Hence, the beta associated with a levered company's equity is not the same as the beta associated with its overall operating cash flows. The risk we are interested in is that associated with the overall cash flows the enterprise's assets generate regardless of who eventually receives them. This overall risk is measured by the company's "unlevered beta" or β. It equals the beta of a firm that has no senior securities outstanding. A general formula for calculating the unlevered beta is given in Chapter 16 in which the issue of how changing capital structures affect a business's beta are discussed in more detail.

In addition to having more risky equity, a levered company may also gain tax advantages from the deductibility of interest payments. A formula for taking this into account and calculating a tax-adjusted unlevered beta is also provided in Chapter 16. Finally, we note that if a Canadian project is to be evaluated, we should use a Canadian risk-free rate and expected market return even if the beta is estimated through a comparison with a U.S. firm.

Given these complexities, it is not surprising that individual cost of capital adjustments for risk, if made at all, are frequently based on just subjective judgements. Because it often represents a reasonable compromise between theoretical validity and operational simplicity, the WACC is widely used not only for internal evaluations but also by regulatory agencies in establishing fair rates of return for privately owned utilities and other regulated industries. However, as with any other approximations, its underlying assumptions and consequent limitations need to be recognized.

15.10 SUMMARY

1. In order to develop effective capital budgeting procedures, a firm needs to know the costs of funding new investments projects. One way to evaluate a new project is to view it as a freestanding venture and determine what return would be required by investors.

---

[11] The example assumes that the return the project produces is the return investors get. As we have already seen, the tax system and issuing costs can create a wedge separating investors' receipts from firms' payments. Introducing such factors into the analysis creates considerable complexity and given the overall uncertainty of the exercise, may add little precision.

2. The WACC is the discount rate that should be used for evaluating new investments under static conditions. A project producing a positive NPV guarantees that all financing charges incurred in funding the project can be met and a shareholder residual gain.

3. In order to calculate a WACC, we need to know a firm's capital structure and acquired returns to each security holder. The firm's overall cost of capital is the proportional weighting of these component costs in the firm's capital structure.

4. Estimating the cost of new common shares is more difficult as future returns are uncertain and decisions regarding dividends are discretionary. Two of the most commonly used approaches are the dividend discount model and reliance on risk-expected return models such as the CAPM.

5. Internally generated funds such as reinvested profits and depreciation are not free because the opportunity costs to investors need to be recognized.

QUESTIONS AND PROBLEMS

Questions for Discussion

1. What are some of the main practical difficulties in estimating a firm's weighted average cost of capital (WACC)? Discuss.

2. Why is it particularly difficult to estimate a firm's cost of common equity? In your view, what are the strengths and weaknesses of the various approaches described in the chapter? Specifically, discuss the comparative advantages and limitations of the dividend discount model (DDM) and the captial asset pricing model (CAPM).

3. Some successful firms in high-growth industries pay no dividends but reinvest all of their earnings to finance future expansion. Does this imply that their cost of new common equity is low? How would you apply a capitalization of future dividends in estimating their cost of equity?

4. A firm may previously have issued debt that is still outstanding at interest rates substantially below current market rates. Is this relevant when computing the firm's WACC? Why or why not?

5. A recent Canadian study found that about a quarter of the firms surveyed used the cost of debt as their cost of capital. Critique the following justification: new investments are never financed through share issues but rather through a mix of costless internally generated funds and new issues of debentures. As the capital structure remains unchanged, using the cost of debt is perhaps overly conservative. Only about half of project funding is actually provided through borrowing.

6. As an investor, would you base your assessment of a firm's capital structure and ensuing risks on the book values or market values of various securities outstanding? Discuss.

7. Why are regulators concerned about a firm's WACC when determining a fair rate of return for regulated monopolies? How should the WACC be used in this context?

8. Under what circumstances should a company with multinational operations and financing apply different discount rates to its investments in different countries? Under what circumstances should the company apply one rate worldwide?

9. If the cost of capital as derived in this chapter is used as the discount rate in investment evaluations, should it be applied to cash flows that embody inflation and are measured in nominal dollars or to cash flows net of inflation (real dollars)? Explain.

10. In using the CAPM to estimate r_e, is the stability of the firm's beta over time of concern? Why or why not?

11. A firm has the following proportions of different categories of funds in its capital structure:

	Book value proportions	Market value proportions
Debt	.50	.40
Equity	.50	.60

Can one tell from the above information with which weights (book or market value) the WACC will be higher? Justify your answer. Which should be used and why?

PROBLEMS WITH SOLUTIONS

Problem 1

(a) A company plans on financing major new expansion programs by drawing on funds in the following proportions that roughly correspond to its current capital structure:

Long-term debt	$30 million
Preferred shares	$10 million
New common shares	$40 million

Issuing and underwriting expenses can be ignored. Debt can be issued at a coupon rate of 12 percent, and the dividend yield on preferred shares would be 9 percent. Common shares currently trade at $45 per share. Next year's dividend is expected to be $2.25 per share. Management feels that, over the long run, growth in dividends should be about 10 percent per year. The corporate tax rate is 40 percent. What is the firm's WACC?

(b) The current interest rate on government debt is 10 percent, and the return on the market is expected to exceed this rate by 7 percent. What value of beta do we have to assume for the firm if the cost of equity as derived from the CAPM is to match the $k_e = 15\%$ calculated according to the dividend growth model under (a) above?

Solution 1

(a) The computations are greatly simplified by ignoring issuing and underwriting expenses:

$$k_b = (1-T)\, r_b = .6 \times 12\% = 7.2\%$$

$$k_p = r_p = 9\%$$

$$k_e \quad \frac{D_1}{P_e} + g = \frac{2.25}{45} + .1 = .15 \text{ or } 15\%$$

Source	Proportion (1)	Cost in % (2)	Weighted cost (3)=(1)×(2)
Debt	$\frac{30}{80} = .375$	7.2	2.7
Preferred	$\frac{10}{80} = .125$	9	1.13
Common equity	$\frac{40}{80} = .5$	15	7.5

weighted average cost of capital=11.33%

(b) We have:

$$r_e = k_e\, r_f + \beta(r_m - r_f)$$
$$.15 = .10 + \beta(.07)$$
$$\beta = .71$$

If the firm believes that its systematic risk is higher than indicated by a beta of 0.71, it should reassess the results derived from the dividend discount model (DDM). Perhaps investors expect a higher growth rate than indicated in management's initial projections.

Problem 2

Given current capital market conditions and the risk characteristics of XYZ Corporation, investors demand a market capitalization rate of $r_e=15\%$ on common shares that currently trade at $30 per share. Dividend payments for the current year are expected to be $1.50 per share.

(a) If a buoyant economy causes investors to assess their growth expectations at 15 percent per year, at what price should the common shares trade?

Solution 2

(a) We use:

$$P_e = \frac{D_1}{r_e - g}$$

Here, it is obvious that the formula cannot be solved because the denominator (re2g) becomes zero for g5re implying Pe5` for g515%. If the dividends that the firm pays are expected to grow at a rate of g and the equity capitalization rate that investors apply is re5g, the growth in future dividends just cancels the effect of discounting. We have:

$$?_e = \frac{D_1}{(1+r_e)} + \frac{D_1(1+g)}{(1+r_e)^2} + \ldots + \frac{D_1(1+g)^t}{(1+r_e)^{t+1}} + \ldots$$

which for $g=r_e$, reduces to

$$P_e = \frac{D_1}{(1+r_e)} + \frac{D_1}{(1+r_e)} + \ldots + \frac{D_1}{(1+r_e)} + \ldots$$

With this infinite stream of dividends, $P_e = \infty$.

The economic implication of this mathematical derivation is that such a situation is unstable and cannot prevail. A firm cannot grow at a rate that forever exceeds the growth of the general economy or of similar competing firms because before long, it would take over the entire economy. Conversely, if general growth expectations for the economy are to increase, so would the yield that investors would demand on their investments and hence, r_e. Although a firm's projected growth rate may exceed the required return by its shareholders temporarily, such a situation cannot prevail indefinitely.

ADDITIONAL PROBLEMS

1. A firm finances itself solely from internal sources. Shareholders expect a return of 18 percent on their equity holdings. What discount rate should the firm use in evaluating investments?

2. The XYZ Corporation intends to finance new investments in proportions of 50 percent debt, 10 percent preferred shares, and 40 percent equity that would come solely from retained earnings. The corporate tax rate is 40 percent. Debt with a maturity of 12 years can be sold at face value at an interest rate of 8 percent. Preferred shares would be sold at par with after-tax issue costs amounting to 1 percent of par value. The dividend yield to investors would be 7 percent. New common shares could be sold at 15 percent below the current market price of $20 per share. Additional after-tax issuing expenses amount to $0.50 per share. Growth in dividends has been steady at 5 percent per year, and it is assumed that this will continue. The dividend at the

end of the current year is expected to be $2.25 per share. What is the firm's WACC?

3. Equity Enterprises wants to estimate its cost of equity. The firm does not intend to issue new shares since internally generated funds have proven adequate for the funding of new investments. At a recent meeting of the board of directors, a fair return on equity was judged to be 14 percent subject to verification by the finance department. As a financial executive, you are reviewing this figure based on the following additional information.

Current interest rates on long-term government bonds are 9 percent. Historically, market returns have exceeded the risk-free rate by 5 to 7 percent. Although you do not have a beta for your firm, the beta for a similar firm in the United States is published by an investment house. Over the past few years, this beta has varied between 1.3 and 1.5. Earnings per share are currently $8, and dividends, $4.80. Over the past six months, the share price has fluctuated between $55 and $65. The average growth rate in dividends over the past 10 years has been 6 percent, which was about 3 percentage points higher than the average inflation rate. However, current interest rates seem to indicate long-term inflation expectations of 2 to 4 percent. For the next directors' meeting, prepare a brief memorandum outlining your thoughts regarding the firm's cost of equity. How reasonable does the judgmentally derived cost of equity of 14 percent appear to be?

4. ABC Corporation is deciding whether to undertake a new project that will not alter the firm's business risk. The following information on the project is available:

Initial outlay	$300,000
Net cash flows, years 1 to 10	$80,000
Salvage value at end of year 10	$ 5,000
Tax rate	50%
CCA rate	20%

Financing for the project would be provided in the proportions of the firm's current capital structure as follows:

Source	Proportion	Current market information
Debt	50.0%	$r_b=7\%$
Preferred shares	12.5%	$r_p=6\%$
Common equity	37.5%	$\beta=1.2, r_f=5\%, r_m=12\%$

Ignoring issuing and underwriting expenses, should the firm undertake the project?

5. A firm has the following balance sheet figures:

Debt: 11% coupon, 15 years to maturity	$ 35,000,000
Preferred shares: 10% dividend	15,000,000
Common stock: 4,000,000 shares at $5 each	20,000,000
Retained earnings	30,000,000

The firm's tax rate is 40 percent. Interest on a new 20-year debt would be 8 percent, and each $1,000 bond would net the firm $970. New preferred shares would be sold at par to provide a dividend yield of 8 percent with after-tax issuing and underwriting expenses amounting to 4 percent of par value. Common shares could be sold to an underwriting syndicate at $12.60 per share, which represents a 10 percent discount from the current market price. After-tax issuing and underwriting expenses would be 5 percent of the issue price. Current shareholders expect a yield of 15 percent on their investment. Internal funds are insufficient to fund anticipated new capital projects. Compute the firm's WACC based on current market value weights.

6. A firm can issue bonds with a coupon rate of 9 percent but only if they are sold at a discount of 2.5 percent, or at 97.5 percent of face value. Underwriting expenses amount to a further 2 percent of face value. Preferred shares with $25 par value, which can be issued to net 90 percent of par value after all expenses, carry a dividend of $2.00. The firm's common shares currently trade at $30, and a new issue would net the firm $27 per share. Growth in common dividends is anticipated to remain at 6 percent per year indefinitely, and the current dividend is $2.50. The firm's tax rate is 50 percent. Compute the cost of capital and market yield for each source of funds.

7. Gumball Corporation has the following capital structure based on market values that it wishes to maintain in the future:

Debt	25%
Preferred shares	20%
Common stock	55%

New debt financing is available in the form of 20-year, 7 percent bonds that can be sold at face value, and issuing and underwriting expenses can be ignored. New preferred shares would net the company $28 per share with a dividend of $2.10 per share. Common shares could be sold to the public at $8 per share with 4 percent issuing costs (after taxes). The firm has a beta of 0.6, the current yield on government T-bills is 6 percent, and the yield on the market portfolio is expected to be 11 percent. The firm's tax rate is 40 percent.

(a) Compute Gumball's WACC.

(b) If $10 million is provided through depreciation this year, what is the appropriate cost of such funds? Discuss briefly.

8. A firm has both debt and common shares outstanding. The firm has already estimated the cost of debt to be 6.5 percent and the cost of common equity to be 15 percent. Based on market values, the firm's debt-equity ratio is 0.5. What is the firm's weighted average cost of capital?

9. A firm wishes to determine the appropriate discount rate for a project it is considering undertaking. The project is very similar to the existing business of the firm. The project would require a total initial investment of $20 million. The firm has 1 million common shares outstanding which each sell for $65. You have determined

that the beta of the firm's common stock is 1.3, that the risk-free rate of interest is 6 percent and the expected return on the stock market as a whole is 13 percent. The firm also has 400,000 preferred shares outstanding each having a par value of $20 and a dividend set at 10 percent of par. The current market price of the preferred shares is $18. The firm's debt is in the form of bonds with an 8 percent coupon (paid annually) and 7 years left until maturity. The bonds currently sell at par. The firm's bonds have a total market value of $50 million. The firm is subject to a tax rate of 40 percent. Ignoring issuing costs for new securities, what is the appropriate required return for the project?

10. A firm has financed itself (based on market values) with 45 percent debt and 55 percent common equity. The firm's common stock has just paid a dividend of $2.50 per share. It is expected that the dividends of this firm will grow at a rate of 10 percent per year in the future. The current price of the common shares is $35. If new common shares are issued, it will be necessary to sell them at a 2 percent discount from the market price as well as pay $0.15 per share to the investment bank underwriting the issue. The underwriting fee is tax deductible. The firm's bonds have a par value of $1,000, a coupon rate of 8 percent, 10 years to maturity, and currently sell for $1,070 each. Flotation costs on new bonds would be 7 percent of the par value on an after-tax basis. The firm is considering a project with an initial required investment of $5 million. The firm has $10 million in cash that can be used for investment. What is the required return on this investment if the firm's tax rate is 35 percent and the project has the same level of risk as the firm as a whole?

No Shares, No Shareholders

Many issues can affect the mix of debt and equity that makes up a firm's capital, but some organizations have little manoeuvring room. In Chapter 6, we looked at some details of the largest corporate bond issue in Canadian history, from the Greater Toronto Airport Authority (GTAA). One reason the Authority's debt issues have been so massive is that it does not have the option of raising capital through selling shares. Its mandate when it was established in 1993 under an agreement with Transport Canada was to operate as a private, not-for-profit corporation without share capital.

No shares means no shareholders. "We're a community initiative," explains Manager of Finance and Treasury, Todd Timmerman. "Our directors are not elected by shareholders but are representatives from the municipalities we serve, and from the provincial and federal governments. Our mandate is not to generate profit but to manage and operate Lester B. Pearson International Airport within a regional system of airports to enhance regional economic growth and development."

Nevertheless, the Authority is a corporation that needs to finance its activities like any other. It is simply at one extreme of the capital structure spectrum—essentially 100% debt, to the tune of just over $3 billion, with the expectation of issuing another billion dollars in bonds in 2001 to finance the rest of its massive development initiative. "We should be finished borrowing by 2002," says Mr. Timmerman.

In many corporations, debt on this level would be worrisome. But the risk of over indebtedness is mitigated by the GTAA's special market situation. As the Canadian Bond Rating Service mentioned in its credit analysis, the Authority has the "durable advantage" of delivering necessary services in a monopoly-like context.

This finding was confirmed, says Mr. Timmerman, by a recent independent feasibility study of Pearson Airport. "All the projections seem to indicate that air traffic will continue to grow," and that Pearson will be the major player in the Toronto region. This means that the GTAA should continue to be a stable investment— "unless someone suddenly invents a new way to travel."

chapter 16

Capital Structure

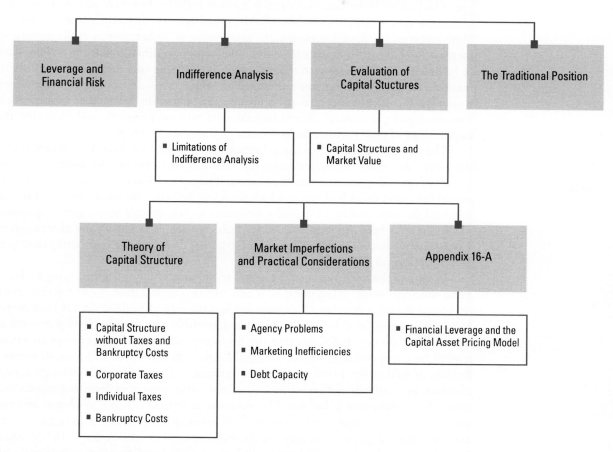

Learning Objectives

After studying this chapter, you should be able to:

1. *Describe leverage and how it affects companies.*
2. *Define indifference analysis, how it is used, and what it measures.*
3. *Explain how the value of a company is established.*
4. *Name two reasons why the cost of a security to a company differs from its yield in capital markets.*
5. *Describe how debt capacity affects a company.*

16.1   INTRODUCTION

In this chapter, we analyse the effects of alternative capital structures with respect to the consequences of varying the proportions of debt and equity within the overall financing mix of a firm. The use of debt in a company's capital structure creates leverage, which alters its balance sheet and influences earnings per share and, consequently, affects the claims that common shareholders have against corporate assets and income. With leverage, the basic trade-off is the expectation of higher returns at the expense of increased volatility. To maximize shareholder wealth, optimal financing policies have to be determined in relation to risk-expected return trade-offs that prevail in financial markets. After presenting some practical considerations that businesses face when formulating policies on capital structure, we introduce the theory that explores how various degrees of leverage should be valued by rational investors, and we review the implications of such theories for policies regarding capital structure.

The overall importance of capital structure is subject to debate. We can argue that the economic value of an organization is determined by its productive assets and by the stream of operating income that they create. The composition of those assets is determined through capital budgeting, which therefore becomes the most important area of financial decision-making. Financing decisions merely specify how a firm's operating income is split between various security holders such as creditors and shareholders. Consequently, decisions regarding capital structure do not create economic value; they merely apportion such value.

In spite of this view, financial executives spend much time and effort trying to determine the appropriate financing mix. There are two main explanations for this. First, payments to different types of security holders are subject to different tax treatments. Whereas interest on debt represents a tax-deductible expense, dividend payments to shareholders do not. It follows that the financing mix that a firm employs affects its overall tax payments and, hence, the total funds available for distribution to security holders as well as the firm's overall after-tax cost of funds. Second, although capital structure by itself may not create new economic value, improper financing can destroy value. A company that is burdened by excessive debt may become insolvent, and significant economic value can be lost through financial distress and bankruptcy. Thus, taxes and the threat of insolvency are the two key considerations that make decisions regarding capital structure important. In fact, one can argue that the critical trade-off in the management of capital structure is to obtain as large a tax benefit as possible through the issuance of debt without increasing the firm's risk to a point where potential bankruptcy costs become excessive.

16.2   LEVERAGE AND FINANCIAL RISK

Leverage is encountered whenever fixed costs are incurred to support operations that generate variable amounts of revenue. Thus, **operating leverage** is introduced when a portion of a company's operating costs are fixed, and **financial leverage** arises when a firm finances part of its business with securities that entail fixed financing charges such as bonds, debentures, or preferred shares.[1] Just as forces are magnified by physical levers, the financial results that accrue to equity investors are magnified through the use of operating and financial leverage, this is shown in Figure 16.1. Leverage at the operating level determines net operating profits or earnings before interest and taxes (EBIT) as a set function of sales, and the higher the proportion of fixed operating costs, the greater the percentage change in net operating profits for a given percentage change in sales. Financial leverage affects the transition from operating profits to earnings per share, and, again, relative changes in earnings per share are magnified as a consequence of fixed financing costs. The total leverage of a firm is given by the combination of operating and financial leverage, and measures the percentage variation in earnings per share for a given percentage change in sales.

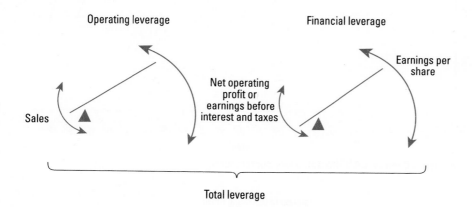

FIGURE 16.1

Operating and Financial Leverage

Most Canadian firms are levered to some degree. Complex, capital-intensive production processes lead to operating leverage, while many factors lead firms to use debt financing, which creates financial leverage. This levered position explains why relatively small changes in economic activity, as reflected in sales, can cause dramatic changes in profitability. For example, stock prices tend to be much more volatile than basic indicators of economic activity because investors value shares based on future dividends that typically depend on highly levered earnings per share. Figure 16.2 shows the book value of equity as a percentage of total assets for the average Canadian non-financial corporation between 1988 and 1999, which has generally been in the range of 39 to 41 percent. Figure 16.3 depicts the average ratio of interest costs to operating profits over

---

[1] Fixed financing charges are also incurred through financial leases. We note that the interest portion in such lease payments becomes part of the firm's total interest expense. This point is discussed more fully in Chapter 25.

the same period, which fluctuated much more widely through the period as a result of changes in the level of interest rates and corporate profits. For example, Figure 16.3 shows that on average, interest costs exceeded operating profits by the end of 1991, which was a recessionary year. In contrast, interest costs were less than 40 percent of operating profits during the pre-recessionary year of 1988 and during the subsequent growth period in 1997 and 1999, for example.

FIGURE 16.2

Capital Structure Trends for Canadian Non-Financial Corporations

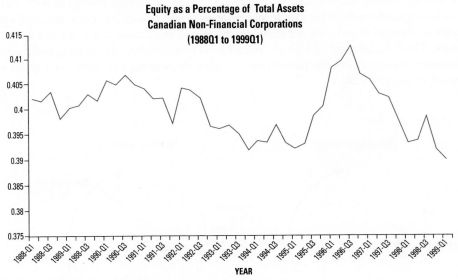

Source: Statistics Canada, CANSIM database, September 6, 2000.

FIGURE 16.3

Trends in Debt-Servicing Charges for Canadian Non-Financial Corporations

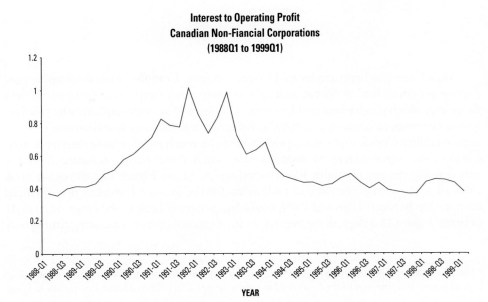

Source: Statistics Canada, CANSIM database, September 6, 2000.

Ultimately, total leverage is important in assessing and managing the firm's sensitivity to changing market conditions. Operating leverage, however, is largely determined by non-financial strategic considerations, and its effect should be familiar from basic accounting. Hence, our discussion will concentrate on the effects of financial leverage. Businesses use debt or preferred shares in their capital structure with the expectation that earnings per share will be magnified. However, increases in expected earnings per share through such leverage come at the expense of increased risk, for just as equity gains are magnified if operating results are favourable, potential losses to shareholders are enlarged if performance falls short of expectations.

FINANCIAL LEVERAGE

EXAMPLE

A new business venture requires an initial investment of $100,000. The company can either finance the investment entirely through common equity, or it can draw on a $50,000 loan at 10 percent interest that would reduce the equity investment to $50,000. The corporate tax rate is 50 percent.

In analysing the effects of alternative capital structures, we begin with net operating profits or earnings before interest and taxes (EBIT), as this measure of business performance is not affected by the capital structure employed. We look at before-tax operating profits because taxes are influenced by interest expenses and, therefore, are dependent on capital structure.

Assuming expected EBIT for the first year is $20,000, we obtain the following financial results for the two alternative capital structures:

	100% equity	50% debt
EBIT	$20,000	$20,000
Interest (at 10%)	—	5,000
Taxable earnings	$20,000	$15,000
Taxes payable	10,000	7,500
Earnings available to common shareholders	$10,000	$7,500
Return on equity investment	$\dfrac{10,000}{100,000}=10\%$	$\dfrac{7,500}{50,000}=15\%$

We see that debt financing has increased the expected return on equity from 10 to 15 percent. The reason is obvious: if the firm can raise funds through debt at an after-tax interest cost of 5 percent and is able to invest these funds to yield an after-tax return of 10 percent, the difference adds to the earnings available to common shareholders.

However, the increased expected gain comes at the expense of increased risk. Assume that the estimated EBIT of $20,000 is uncertain and could be as high as $35,000 or as low as $5,000. The following tabulation shows the consequences of such fluctuations.

	100% equity		50% debt	
EBIT	$35,000	$5,000	$35,000	$5,000
Interest	—	—	5,000	5,000
Taxable earnings	$35,000	$5,000	$30,000	0
Tax payable	17,500	2,500	15,000	0
Earnings to common shareholders	17,500	$2,500	$15,000	0
Return on equity	$\frac{17,500}{100,000}$=17.5%	$\frac{2,500}{100,000}$=2.5%	$\frac{15,000}{50,000}$=30%	=0%

Summarizing the percentage return on equity figures, we have:

EBIT	100% equity	50% debt
$35,000	17.5%	30.0%
20,000	10.0	15.0
5,000	2.5	0

Variations in EBIT are inherent in any business and result from general economic cycles, changing industry conditions, and the dynamics and operating cost structure of the individual firm. Such variations in operating results are termed the **business risk** of an enterprise. As we have seen, this risk is magnified through the use of financial leverage. The additional variability in equity returns caused by reliance on fixed-cost senior securities is labelled the financial risk of a company. In the above example, business risk caused EBIT to fluctuate by ± 75 percent, which resulted in an equivalent fluctuation in the return on equity for the all-equity-financed firm. Reliance on debt, however, introduced financial risk, with fluctuations in equity returns increasing to ± 100 percent. Management controls business risk through its capital budgeting decisions that determine the nature of the company's investments and its operating cost structure, and it exerts control over financial risk through its choice of capital structure when financing such investments.

The **degree of financial leverage** is sometimes defined as the percentage change on common equity or earnings per share divided by the percentage change in EBIT that caused the change in equity returns.

EXAMPLE

DEGREE OF FINANCIAL LEVERAGE

In the previous example, we saw that a 75 percent change in EBIT ($20,000 ± $15,000) resulted in a 75 percent change in the return on equity (10% ± 7.5%) for the equity-financed firm. Hence, the degree of financial leverage is 75/75=1. With 50 percent debt, the resulting change in the return on equity was magnified to 100 percent (15% ± 15%). Hence, the degree of financial leverage increased to 100/75=1.33.

If only common-equity financing is employed, changes in return on equity reflect only business risk, and the degree of financial leverage equals 1. A degree of financial leverage that exceeds 1 signals the use of senior securities in the capital structure, with magnified relative variations in returns on common equity.

We note that financial leverage, discussed above in terms of its effects on a company's income statement, also has an impact on shareholder wealth as reflected in the balance sheet. Debt represents an obligation of a fixed magnitude. The total value of a firm can be expressed as:

Value of firm = value of debt + value of equity

Therefore, a given percentage change in the value of a business's assets results in a magnified percentage change in the value of the firm's equity when debt is introduced into the capital structure.

EQUITY VALUE AND FINANCIAL LEVERAGE

EXAMPLE

A company has only one asset, which is land that was acquired a year ago for $10 million. Over the year, the value of the land has increased by 20 percent, so that it is now worth $12 million. If the firm is financed solely through equity, the value of the equity should increase by the same 20 percent.

Alternatively, the original land purchase could have been 50 percent financed through debt at an effective interest cost of $k_b = 10\%$. Market interest rates have not changed during the year; thus, the market value of the firm's original debt remains at $5 million. Interest payments for the year, representing an additional liability of $500,000, have not yet been made. The value of the equity at year end should be:

Value of equity = value of firm − value of liabilities

$$= \$12,000,000 - \$5,500,000$$
$$= \$6,500,000$$

The percentage increase on the $5 million of the equity originally invested is now magnified to 30 percent.

On the other hand, if the value of the land had fallen 20 percent to $8 million, the value of equity would have also declined 20 percent if the purchase had been all-equity financed. However, if the purchase had been financed with 50 percent debt, the value of the equity would now equal $8 − $5.5 = $2.5 million, representing a 50 percent decline in value. This represents the downside risk of using debt financing.

PERSPECTIVES

Corporate Manager

The use of debt can substantially magnify the variability in earnings, cash flows, and equity value of a company. This works to its advantage as long as things turn out favourably; however, it can create serious problems when results are worse than expected.

Investor

Companies with large amounts of debt tend to display more volatile earnings, cash flows, and equity values than those with less debt, all else being equal. The additional risk must be compensated for in the form of higher expected returns.

Because debt is a contractual obligation, default on debt provisions can lead to bankruptcy, and, if other things remain constant, the risk of bankruptcy increases with the amount of debt carried by a firm. We can again view the effects of such bankruptcy in terms of income statement or balance sheet quantities. Ignoring capital cost allowance, a firm is insolvent if EBIT is insufficient to meet financial obligations as they become due. Alternatively, a company can be viewed as bankrupt when the value of its assets has fallen below the value of its outstanding liabilities; in that case, equity holders have lost their investment, and, in fact, the debt holders have become the new owners. In the previous example, this situation would have arisen if the value of the land had dropped below $5.5 million.

16.3 INDIFFERENCE ANALYSIS

Indifference analysis is a common tool used to assess the impact of leverage. As we have seen, earnings per share (EPS) depend on both the level of earnings before interest and taxes (EBIT) that a company achieves from its operations and on the particular capital structure that the firm employs. The purpose of indifference analysis is to determine EPS as a function of EBIT for various capital structures and to identify the level of EBIT beyond which reliance on leverage produces higher earnings per share. For given expectations about future earnings before interest and taxes, such analysis may provide at least a rough indication of the relative desirability of alternative capital structures.

EXAMPLE

INDIFFERENCE ANALYSIS

A corporation has 10,000 common shares outstanding (n_1) and needs to raise $200,000 to finance expansion. It considers the alternatives of issuing 10,000 additional common shares (n_2) that can be sold to net $20 each or of issuing 8 percent debt with annual interest payments of I=$16,000. The firm's tax rate is T=40 percent. After the new financing has taken place, earnings per share under the two alternatives become:

Equity financing:

$$EPS = \frac{(1-T)(EBIT)}{n_1 + n_2} = \frac{.6\ EBIT}{20,000}$$

Debt financing:

$$EPS = \frac{(1-T)(EBIT - I)}{n_1} = \frac{.6\ (EBIT - 16,000)}{10,000}$$

$$= \frac{.6\ EBIT - 9,600}{10,000}$$

Computing earnings per share for various levels of EBIT, we obtain:

Equity financing:

EBIT	$16,000	$32,000	$48,000
Tax	6,400	12,800	19,200
After-tax earnings	$ 9,600	$19,200	$28,800
EPS (20,000 shares)	0.48	0.96	1.44

Debt financing:

EBIT	$16,000	$32,000	$48,000
Interest	16,000	16,000	$16,000
Taxable income	—	$16,000	$32,000
Tax	—	6,400	12,800
After-tax earnings	$ 0	$ 9,600	$19,200
EPS (10,000 shares)	0	0.96	1.92

Figure 16.4 shows the relationships between EPS and EBIT for the two alternatives. In both cases, EPS is a linear function of EBIT. The intercept on the horizontal axis represents before-tax interest cost, and with debt financing, EBIT must reach $16,000 before any earnings accrue to common shareholders. The slope of the line for the debt alternative is steeper because fewer common shares are outstanding. As a consequence, the change in earnings per share for a given change in EBIT is greater, confirming our previous conclusion that debt financing results in increased risk for equity investors.

We see that equity financing results in higher earnings per share for low operating incomes, whereas debt financing is superior for high levels of EBIT. The indifference point is the spot at which the company would be indifferent between either financing plan based solely on the resulting EPS figure. It is readily computed by setting EPS equal for both alternatives. Net operating income at the indifference point, $EBIT^*$, is derived as:

$$EPS_{equity} = \frac{EBIT^{*}(1-T)}{n_1 + n_2} = \frac{(EBIT^{*}-I)(1-T)}{n_1} = EPS_{debt}$$

Substituting our numbers from above, we obtain:

$$\frac{0.6EBIT^{*}}{20,000} = \frac{0.6EBIT^{*}-9,600}{10,000}$$

Multiplying both sides by 10,000, we obtain,

$$\frac{0.6EBIT^{*}}{2} = \frac{0.6EBIT^{*}-9,600}{1}$$

which yields,

$$0.6EBIT^{*} - 1.2EBIT^{*} = -19,200$$
$$EBIT^{*} = -19,200/-0.6 = \$32,000$$

This confirms the intersection of the two lines as depicted in Figure 16.4. Thus, for EBIT greater than $32,000, debt financing results in larger EPS, whereas for EBIT below $32,000, common share financing yields higher EPS. Notice that the EPS=$0.96 under either plan for an EBIT of $32,000, as shown in the table above. This could also be confirmed by substituting $32,000 into the EPS equations that were derived for each financing alternative:

Equity financing:

$$EPS = \frac{0.6EBIT^{*}}{20,000} = \frac{0.6(32,000)}{20,000} = \$0.96$$

Debt financing:

$$EPS = \frac{0.6EBIT-9,600}{10,000} = \frac{0.6(32,000)-9,600}{10,000} = \$0.96$$

These concepts can easily be extended to cover more complex situations that involve other financing alternatives. An illustration is provided in Problem with Solution 1 at the end of this chapter.

FIGURE 16.4

Indifference Chart

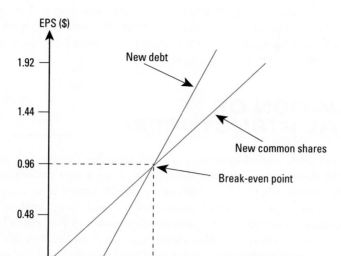

Limitations of Indifference Analysis

Indifference analysis demonstrates the sensitivity of earnings per share to changes in earnings before interest and taxes for different capital structures. Although this information is useful for analysis and planning, we must recognize its significant limitations. First, it ignores cash flow considerations such as sinking fund provisions for the periodic retirement of fixed income securities. These payments are made out of after-tax earnings available to common shareholders and therefore are not recognized in indifference analysis with its narrow focus on earnings per share. Sinking fund payments can, however, represent a sizeable cash drain. Pursuing our earlier example involving $3 million of 10 percent debt, assume that the issue is to be retired through annual sinking fund payments of $300,000 over 10 years. It is apparent that each year, sinking fund payments will exceed after-tax interest charges, and by an increasing proportion because the debt outstanding declines over the life of the issue. Therefore, although debt financing may result in higher earnings per share, unless new debt is issued to replace retired obligations, cash flows available to the corporation may actually be reduced.

Second, and most important, indifference analysis does not consider how equity investors may react to the increased risk imposed by leverage in the light of uncertain future operating performance. When projected EBIT levels are above the indifference point, leverage will result in higher expected earnings per share. However, future operating results are inherently uncertain, and, as we have seen, any deviations from expected EBIT values would result in magnified EPS fluctuations through leverage. Investors are risk averse and demand higher expected returns on their shares to compensate for this increased volatility or risk. Consequently, the use of cheaper debt financing will result in an increase in the firm's cost of equity and may even result in a drop in share prices despite higher expected EPS. This indirect or implicit cost of debt financing is ignored in simple indifference analysis. Clearly, however, such implicit costs must be recognized when considering the question of optimal capital structure.

16.4 EVALUATION OF CAPITAL STRUCTURES[2]

Before we can evaluate capital structures, we have to define the criterion against which we measure the desirability of various alternatives. If we accept the objective of maximizing shareholder wealth, the desirability of a capital structure is measured by its likely impact on the market price of a firm's common shares, and the optimal capital structure is one that maximizes share values. The report below shows an example of how a financing decision can affect company value directly. It refers to the decision by Cadillac Fairview Corp. to issue $100 million in convertible debentures and the subsequent 10 percent decline in the value of their shares upon making this announcement. While market reaction may not always be as immediate or dramatic as in this example, markets do pay attention to the capital structure decisions made by companies.

■ *Finance in the News*

Cadillac Shares Drop 10% After Financing Plan Unveiled: Developer's Bid to Raise $100 Million Triggers Heavy Trading

When developer Cadillac Fairview Corp announced plans to raise $100 million by selling convertible debentures, its stock price fell nearly 10 percent in heavy trading. An industry expert commented that investors were dismayed by the fact that the Toronto-based developer was raising the funds without any stated purpose beyond the company's Tuesday statement that it plans to use the money to pay down short-term debt and finance further growth. The unnamed expert stated that the market was skeptical of a business building up a "war chest" with money it doesn't really need.

Source: Karen Howlett, "Cadillac Shares Drop 10% after Financing Plan Unveiled: Developer's Bid to Raise $100 Million Triggers Heavy Trading," *Globe and Mail*, August 27, 1998, p. B13.

A capital structure that maximizes share prices generally will, at the same time, minimize the firm's weighted average cost of capital (WACC). Assume that a firm's investments produce given net after-tax cash flows. Any returns in excess of the firm's WACC are gains that accrue to common shareholders. Thus, if through judicious choice of its capital structure the company can reduce its WACC, shareholders will receive greater returns, and this

---

[2] For pioneering work on the theory of capital structure theory, see A. Durand, "Cost of Debt and Equity Funds for Business: Trends and Problems in Measurement," in *Conference on Research in Business Finance* (New York: National Bureau of Economic Research, 1952), pp. 215-47; and also F. Modigliani and M. Miller, "The Cost of Capital, Corporation Finance and the Theory of Investment," *American Economic Review* (June 1959), pp. 261-97.

should be reflected in increased share prices.[3] In the process, the total value of all of the firm's outstanding securities (equity plus debt) should also be maximized.

CAPITAL STRUCTURE AND MARKET VALUE I

A newly established corporation requires an initial investment of $1 million and considers two alternative capital structures. One involves no leverage, with 10,000 common shares to be issued at $100 each; the other consists of $500,000 of debt and only 5,000 common shares, also at $100 each. Debt can be issued at 10 percent interest, and the corporate tax rate is 50 percent. Throughout this section, we neglect underwriting and issuing expenses so that the cost of equity to the firm (k_e) equals the yield to investors (r_e). This simplifies the exposition, and it does not affect the derived results in any way.

EBIT is expected to be $300,000 per year and to remain at that level, with all earnings paid out in dividends. If no leverage is employed, shareholders require a return of $r_e = k_e = 15$ percent, which is commensurate with the anticipated business risk. With the added financial risk introduced through debt financing, the required return on equity has to increase. As we will see, the amount of this required increase in r_e is critical in determining which capital structure is superior. For the moment, assume that 50 percent debt financing causes r_e to increase to 20 percent. To establish which of the two alternatives represents the better capital structure, we perform the following computations:

	100% equity 10,000 shares	50% debt 5,000 shares
1. EBIT	$ 300,000	$ 300,000
2. Interest	—	50,000
3. Taxable earnings	300,000	$250,000
4. Tax	150,000	125,000
5. Net earnings to shareholders	$ 150,000	$ 125,000
6. Earnings per share	$ 15	$ 25
7. Required return on equity $r_e = k_e$	15%	20%
8. Market price per share: (6)/(7)	$ 100	$ 125
9. Market value of total equity	$1,000,000	$ 625,000
10. Total value of firm (debt and equity)	$1,000,000	$1,125,000
11. Total payment to all security holders (earnings plus interest): (2)+(5)	$ 150,000	$ 175,000
12. Average return on total market value (11)/(10)	15%	15.6%

---

[3] Only when operating income is independent of capital structure will minimizing the weighted average cost of capital (WACC) maximize the value of the firm. However, operating income need not always be independent of capital structure. See, for example, B. Schwab and M. Thompson, "Some Indirect Costs of Corporate Debt Financing," *Journal of General Management* (Winter 1980–81), pp. 53–7.

Clearly, the levered capital structure is superior. The firm raises debt at an interest cost (before tax) of 10 percent and invests the proceeds to earn an operating return (before interest and taxes) of 30 percent. The difference between the return from investments and the cost of debt financing accrues to shareholders and results in an increase in earnings per share from $15 to $25. Although shareholders require an increase in returns from 15 to 20 percent to compensate for the additional financial risk, the new level of earnings exceeds those requirements. Consequently, investors seeking to acquire such shares for their high yield will push up the market price until it reaches $125, at which point the shares just provide the required return of 20 percent.

The total market value of the firm is derived by adding the market values of all of the different types of securities outstanding. For the levered case, we have $500,000 in debt plus 5,000 shares with a market price of $125 each for a total of $1,125,000. We note that because of the tax deductibility of interest, the levered capital structure reduces tax payments by $25,000, thereby increasing the amount available to be paid out to security holders from $150,000 to $175,000. Because the total value of a firm (debt plus equity) is a function of the total cash flows (interest plus dividends) that it can distribute to its security holders, the tax savings that result from the use of debt contribute to making leverage attractive.

The WACC in the case of all-equity financing is simply $k=k_e=15$ percent. Given an after-tax cost of debt of $k_b=(1-T)10\%=5\%$, and using market value weights as computed above for the debt alternative, we obtain:

$$k = \frac{500}{1,125}\,(0.5) + \frac{625}{1,125}\,(.20) = 13.33\%$$

In summary, we have:

	100% equity 10,000 shares	50% debt 5,000 shares
Market price per share	$ 100	$ 125
Total value of the firm (V)	$1,000,000	$1,125,000
Weighted average cost of capital (k)	15%	13.33%

We see that the levered capital structure produces better results in terms of all three criteria; therefore, it should be selected. In fact, if a particular capital structure results in a higher market price per share, it will generally entail a lower WACC and a higher total value of the firm. Consequently, any one of these three criteria can be used to evaluate alternative capital structures, and the choice is one of convenience.

The numerical results in the above example depend critically on the assumed reaction of equity investors to the increase in financial leverage. If, for example, shareholders demand even higher returns as compensation for assuming additional financial risk, the preference ordering that we obtained could easily be reversed.

CAPITAL STRUCTURE AND MARKET VALUE II

Pursuing the previous example, assume that shareholders demand an expected return of 28 percent to compensate for financial risk under the levered capital structure. Replicating the calculations above, we obtain:

	100% equity	50% debt
Net earnings to shareholders	$ 150,000	$125,000
Earnings per share	$ 15	$ 25
Required return on equity	15%	28%
Market price per share	$ 100	$ 89
Market value of total equity	$1,000,000	$446,429
Total value of firm	$1,000,000	$946,429
Total payments to all security holders	$ 150,000	$175,000
WACC (market weights)	15%	15.8%

Although earnings per share and total payments to all security holders remain higher under the debt alternative, the high capitalization rate applied by equity investors more than counterbalances these increases and results in lower share prices, a lower firm value, and a higher WACC.

We see that the merit of alternative capital structures depends on how investors evaluate the increased financial risk introduced through leverage and how they trade off this risk against the added potential returns that result from the lower after-tax cost obtained through debt financing. In terms of this trade-off, conceptually, it is useful to distinguish three possibilities:

1. The cost of equity increases with leverage at a moderate rate so that when combined with the lower after-tax cost of debt, it causes the WACC to decrease with increasing leverage.

2. The cost of equity increases at a rate that just offsets any benefits gained through cheaper debt financing, with the WACC remaining constant regardless of leverage.

3. The cost of equity increases rapidly with leverage, and this increase more than offsets any gains from debt financing, resulting in a WACC that increases with leverage.

These three possibilities are illustrated in Figure 16.5.

FIGURE 16.5

Consequences of
Different Shareholder
Attitudes Toward Risk

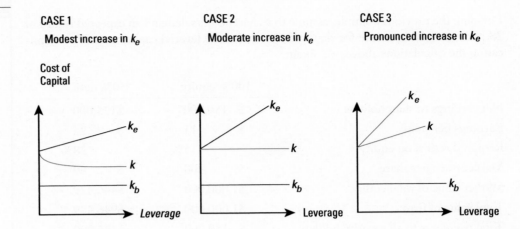

Initially, to simplify our discussion, we assume that the cost of debt remains constant regardless of the amount of financial leverage employed by the firm. This is a reasonable approximation for moderate degrees of leverage.

In the previous examples, we considered a \$1-million investment that could be financed with various proportions of debt and equity. The cost of debt was $k_b=5$ percent, and the cost of equity, assuming 100 percent equity financing (no financial risk), was $k_e=15$ percent. We measure leverage in terms of the proportion of debt in relation to equity in the capital structure (B/E). With $V=B+E$, the weighted average cost of capital is:

$$k = k_b \frac{B}{V} + k_e \frac{E}{V}$$

We considered 50 percent debt financing. Case 1 essentially implies:

$$k_b \frac{B}{V} + k_e \frac{E}{V} < .15$$

$$.05 \times .5 + k_e < .15$$

$$k_e < .25$$

That is, if the cost of equity remains below 25 percent in the levered case, the WACC is reduced through debt financing. Similarly, Case 3 implies $k_e >.25$ with indifference at $k_e=.25$ (Case 2).

The key question regarding capital structure centres around which of the above three cases we observe in practice and how investors at the margin actually do trade off the risks against expected returns arising from leverage. The answer to this question is not easy because it is generally not possible to poll shareholders directly, and such specific policy issues as a firm's capital structure are normally not brought before shareholders' general meetings. Alternatively, we could attempt to gather statistical data about otherwise similar companies to see, for example, how financial leverage is related to the earnings-price ratio at which a firm's shares typically trade. Such a ratio may be used as a rough but readily measurable substitute for the more elusive cost of equity. However, a variety of statistical and measurement problems that are discussed later in this chapter have prevented researchers from obtaining conclusive results.

Consequently, the problem has to be approached from a different angle, and we have to deduce through reasoning how we would expect investors to behave. This can be done at a more-or-less intuitive level. Alternatively, by making specific assumptions about investors and markets (e.g., assuming investor rationality and perfectly efficient markets), we can develop a formal theory as to how investors ought to react to various levels of financial leverage. Fortunately, we will see that the main results derived from these two approaches appear to coincide, at least in general terms. We first outline the less formal, traditional position that reflects reasoning commonly found in practice. Although it has intuitive appeal and avoids stringent assumptions about market behaviour, it lacks precision and depth and fails to properly explain the interrelationships between key variables. The theory of capital structure, which is presented in Section 16.6, overcomes these weaknesses and provides important conceptual insights, albeit at the expense of assumptions that sometimes may appear overly restrictive.

THE TRADITIONAL POSITION   16.5

In making their decisions on capital structure, most firms follow what has been termed as the **traditional position**. As shown in Figure 16.6, this position regarding financial leverage can be viewed as a mix of the three conceptual cases presented in Section 16.4.

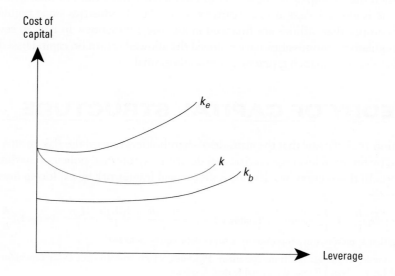

FIGURE 16.6

The Traditional Position on Capital Structure and the Cost of Capital

According to the traditional view, a corporation can issue a reasonable amount of debt with only modest effects on its cost of equity. With moderate leverage, the risk of insolvency or bankruptcy as a consequence of debt-servicing charges is low, and shareholders may not be unduly concerned about the greater variability in residual earnings. Because the after-tax cost of debt (k_b) is significantly lower than k_e, the addition of initial amounts of debt to the capital structure will reduce the average cost of capital and enhance the firm's value. As the amount of debt in the capital structure rises, however, so does the risk of financial distress. Clearly, any insolvency and possible bankruptcy may impose severe costs on the firm and its owners, which is why shareholders begin to require higher rates of return to compensate for the additional financial risk that they must bear.[4] If the proportion of debt financing increases even further, lenders will become reluctant to provide the corporation with additional funds. At a minimum, they will demand higher interest (k_b will increase), and in extreme cases, they may simply refuse to lend. Consequently, we see that the WACC initially falls, then flattens out, and finally increases again for high levels of debt, reflecting the basic trade-off between the benefit of low-cost debt financing, caused mainly by the tax deductibility of interest, and the risk of leverage as reflected in increasing probabilities of financial distress. This trade-off, which can be viewed as the key issue in selecting an appropriate capital structure, will be developed more formally in the theory section that follows.

Most corporations do use debt to take advantage of the positive aspects of leverage. At the same time, however, firms limit the amount of debt that they carry in most cases to amounts that fall well below any constraints imposed by lenders. Thus, their actions appear to be consistent with the traditional position and imply a belief that an optimal capital structure exists and is achieved by using moderate proportions of debt.

If Figure 16.6 represents capital market reactions to different amounts of leverage, it becomes important for companies to find the optimal point at which the WACC is minimized. By obtaining the lowest possible cost of financing, firms should be able to strengthen their competitive positions and to increase the wealth of their shareholders. The issue is also relevant at rate hearings of regulated industries since regulators will want to ensure that utilities are financed in an efficient manner. In fact, in several past cases, regulatory commissions have reduced the allowed return on capital based on their view that existing financing practices were suboptimal.[5]

16.6 THEORY OF CAPITAL STRUCTURE

In Section 16.4, we saw that the attitude of shareholders toward the risk-return trade-off implied by financial leverage is critical in determining optimal policies regarding capital structure. In this section, we develop a theoretical framework by exploring how rational

---

[4] When $k = k_b \dfrac{B}{V} + k_e \dfrac{E}{V} = $ constant, it follows that $k_e = \dfrac{kV - k_b B}{E} = \dfrac{k(B+E)}{E} - \dfrac{k_b B}{E} = k + (k - k_b)\dfrac{B}{E}$, implying that k_e increases in proportion to a firm's debt-equity ratio B/E.

[5] For example, in rulings on Trans Mountain Pipelines, which had no debt in its capital structure, the National Energy Board imputed reasonable debt financing.

and well-informed investors ought to react and by establishing the implications of such rational behaviour for the financing policies of the firm.

In presenting our arguments, it is easiest to start with a highly idealized framework and to introduce the various dimensions of real-life complexity one at a time. Not only does this simplify the exposition, but it also allows us to see more clearly how each factor influences the final conclusion. Consequently, we begin with an environment that assumes perfect financial markets, without taxes and bankruptcy costs. After developing some basic conclusions, we successively introduce each of these important dimensions and discuss how their inclusion modifies the results. Throughout, we ignore transaction costs such as the issuing and underwriting expenses, so that $k_e = r_e$ and $k_b = (1-T)r_b$. Although this simplifies the presentation, it does not affect our conclusions in any significant way.

Capital Structure Without Taxes and Bankruptcy Costs

In the introduction to this chapter, we postulated that decisions regarding a company's capital structure might not be as important as those that deal with capital budgeting. Investment decisions determine the composition of the firm's productive assets, which determine the overall value of the firm through the cash flows they generate. Decisions regarding capital structure merely apportion this stream of cash flows to various security holders. In the absence of taxes and bankruptcy costs, this splitting up of the pie neither creates nor destroys value. The total value of a firm ought to be independent of its capital structure, and as financing does not affect economic value, decisions regarding the particular financing mix that a company selects in funding its investments should become irrelevant.

An implication of this position is that the business's WACC has to remain constant regardless of the amount of financial leverage employed. As shown in Figure 16.7(a), it follows that the cost of equity increases in a linear fashion with leverage. Denoting k_e^u and k_e^L as the cost of equity for unlevered and levered firms, we have:

$$k_e^L \frac{E}{V} + k_b \frac{B}{V} = k_e^U = \text{constant}$$

from which we obtain:

$$k_e^L = \frac{V}{E} \left(k_e^U - k_b \frac{B}{V} \right) \tag{16.1}$$

$$= \frac{B+E}{E} \left(k_e^U - k_b \frac{B}{B+E} \right)$$

$$k_e^L = k_e^U + \left(k_e^U - k_b \right) \frac{B}{E}$$

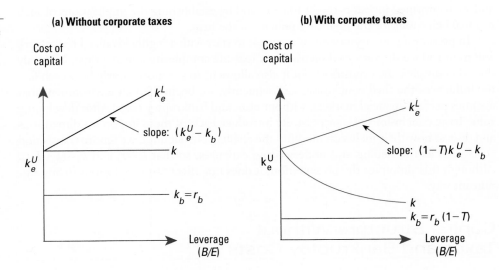

As the company introduces debt financing, it sets aside a clearly determined portion of its future cash flows to service commitments under the debt contracts. We saw in Section 16.2 that as a consequence, the residual cash flows to common shareholders are subject to greater relative risk. Rational shareholders should react by demanding a higher return on their equity, with the relation between this return and leverage determined by Equation 16.1.

In their pioneering work, Modigliani and Miller (M–M) have in fact proven that market forces will compel shareholders to react in exactly this way.[6] In setting out their arguments, M-M first provide the important insight that financial leverage through debt financing is not restricted to corporations but can also be achieved by the individual investor. That is, individual investors can create their own leverage by acquiring shares, which they purchase in part with borrowed funds; the effects will be the same as if the corporation had financed through debt. Thus, shareholders should be indifferent to corporate policies regarding capital structure and should not pay a premium for shares merely because a firm chooses to introduce financial leverage.

For example, assume that as an investor, I would like to see a high level of financial leverage in my investments. I can achieve this by purchasing shares of companies that are highly levered. I may discover a firm that is basically very attractive except that it is

---

[6] F. Modigliani and M. Miller, "The Cost of Capital, Corporation Finance and the Theory of Investment," *American Economic Review* (June 1958), pp. 261-97. Key assumptions made by Modigliani and Miller in developing their basic argument include: 1. Securities markets are perfectly efficient. There is equal access to information, there are no transactions costs, and interest rates at which borrowing and lending take place are the same for all corporations and investors; 2. Firms can be grouped according to business risk, with the EBIT stream for firms in the same risk class being subject to the same degree of uncertainty. Investors have common perceptions about firms and common expectations regarding the mean value and the risk of variability of future operating income.

financed solely through equity. According to M-M, this need not deter me since I can introduce the leverage myself by borrowing to purchase the shares. The effect will be identical to that created by corporate leverage, with expected returns increasing at the expense of higher risk.

Conversely, I may be a conservative investor who does not like financial leverage. If I find a firm that I consider to be too highly levered, I can still invest, but I now use part of my funds to acquire its shares and part to purchase its debt. The stream of cash flow from the debt will be highly predictable, reducing the expected return and the risk of my total holdings and, in effect, "undoing" the firm's leverage.

In the technical part of their argument, M–M demonstrate that the equilibrium price for shares can only prevail if Equation 16.1 is satisfied. Under any other situation, opportunities exist for immediate profit through arbitrage. Rather than attempting to reproduce their mathematical argument, a simple illustration will suffice to outline the basic reasoning.

Consider two firms that operate in the same industry, have identical assets, and produce the same stream of net cash flows from operations (X). However, they differ in their financing. Firm U is unlevered, financed solely through equity (E_U). Firm L is partially financed through equity (E_L), but it also has some debt outstanding (B) on which it pays interest (I). Using the notation introduced in Chapter 15, we have:

Firm	Cash flows	Capitalization rate	Market value
U from operations: X	shareholders: X	$r_e^U = k_e^U$	$E_U = V_U$
L from operations: X	$\left(\begin{array}{l}\text{to debt holders: } I \\ \text{to shareholders: } (X-I)\end{array}\right.$	$\begin{array}{l} r_b = k_b \\ r_e^L = k_e^L \end{array}$	$\left.\begin{array}{l} B \\ E_L \end{array}\right) V_L$

It is clear that the total value of the two firms should be identical ($V_u = V_L$), and we should be indifferent between owning the equity of U (cash flows = X) or both the debt and the equity of L (cash flows $I + [X-I] = X$). What matters when placing a total value on a company are the total cash flows generated, not the particular split of those cash flows between different security holders.

Assume for a moment that, contrary to this logic, the market responds favourably to financial leverage and is willing to pay a premium for the levered firm, so that $V_L > V_U$. M–M have shown that this condition cannot prevail, as it would allow shareholders of L to profit through arbitrage.

EXAMPLE

AN ARBITRAGE OPPORTUNITY

Assume V_L trades at a 20 percent premium over V_U, so that $V_L = 1.2 V_U$. You own 1 percent of the shares of L. It now pays you to go through the following sequence of transactions:

1. Sell your equity holdings in L, realizing $.01 E_L$.

2. Borrow an amount equivalent to 1 percent of L's debt $(.01B)$ on your own account. Assuming that you would pay the same interest rate as the firm, interest payments on this personal debt will amount to $.01I$.

3. Take the total proceeds from the previous two transactions $(.01E_L + .01B = .01V_L)$ to purchase shares in U. As $V_L = 1.2\ V_U$, you will be able to acquire 1.2 percent of U's outstanding stock.

Your cash flows before and after the transactions will be as follows:

	Stock ownership	Cash flows
Original position	$.01E_L$	$.01$(op. profit$-$corp. interest) $= .01(X-I) = .01X - .01I$
Position after above transactions	$.012E_u$	$.012$ op. profit$-$interest on personal debt$= .012X - .01I$

You have been able to increase your cash flows and your wealth without increasing your financial risk. The only difference is that leverage has now been shifted from the corporate to the personal level.

Clearly, this situation cannot prevail because arbitrage will continue and push down the price of L until once again, $V_U = V_L$. It is easy to show that $V_L = V_U$ implies that Equation 16.1 as derived above must hold.[7]

Critics have argued that the arbitrage process outlined above may not function perfectly because personal and corporate leverage may not be perfect substitutes. For example, the interest rate at which individuals can borrow may differ from the rate paid by the corporation, and investors may be reluctant to take on personal leverage because, unlike the corporation, they are not protected by limited liability.

Although M–M admit that corporate and personal leverage may not be perfect substitutes, these objections are hardly substantive enough to detract significantly from the basic argument. Many investors have margin accounts that allow them to borrow from their broker for the purchase of securities. Given that the securities purchased represent very liquid collateral, broker loan rates are generally not much different from interest rates paid by large corporate borrowers. Furthermore, borrowing could take place through incorporated investment funds, thereby preserving the advantage of limited liability for the ultimate investor. Hence, any distortions, if they exist at all, should be small.

---

[7] Assume that the firm's operating profit X remains constant and can be viewed as a perpetual annuity.

We have $E_U = X/k_e^U$, $B = I/k_b$, and $E_L = (X-I)/k_e^L$, obtaining: $k_e^L = \dfrac{X-I}{E_L} = \dfrac{(B+E_L)k_e - Bk_b}{E_L} = k_e^U + (k_e^U - k_b)\dfrac{B}{E_L}$, which is equivalent to Equation 16.1.

We conclude that in the absence of taxes and bankruptcy costs, the financing policies that a company pursues should not matter. The total value of a firm is independent of the way in which this value is apportioned to various security holders, and the ability to substitute personal for corporate leverage will ensure that investors do not pay a premium for any particular capital structure.

Corporate Taxes[8]

Corporate taxes exert an important influence on financing decisions because the amount of tax paid depends on its capital structure. Specifically, our tax system allows interest on debt to be claimed as a tax-deductible expense, and so, interest payments reduce a corporation's tax liabilities. If we allow for corporate taxes, then the operating cash flows that a business generates are now split into a portion that accrues to the firm's security holders and a portion that is paid to the government in taxes. As tax payments decrease, the total cash flows available for distribution to security holders have to increase.

Consider again the two firms U and L that are identical in every respect except for their capital structures. Assuming a corporate tax rate T, we now have:

Firm	Cash flows		Capitalization rate	Market value
U	from operations: X	to shareholder: $X(1-T)$ to government: XT	k_e^U	$E_U = V_U$
L	from operations: X	to debt holders: I to shareholders: $(X-I)(1-T)$ to government: $(X-I)T$	k_b k_e^L	B E_L $\Big\} V_L$

The total cash flows available for distribution to all security holders become:

For firm U:

Total cash flows to security holders $= X(1-T)$

For firm L:

Total cash flows to security holders $= (X-I)(1-T)+I = X(1-T)+IT$

In the levered case, the firm's taxes are reduced by the tax shield on interest (IT). This amount of taxes saved, which can be viewed as a subsidy from the government for debt financing, accrues as an additional gain to security holders. With cash flows to security holders no longer equal, the value of the two firms should not be the same, and $V_L > V_U$. Ignoring bankruptcy costs, we would now prefer to own the debt and equity

[8] In extending the analysis to account for corporate taxes, we are reflecting the subsequent work of M–M. See F. Modigliani and M. Miller, "Corporate Income Taxes and the Cost of Capital: A Correction," *American Economic Review* (June 1963), pp. 433-43.

of *L* over owning the equity of *U*. Although leverage has still not created any value, it has shifted value from the government (which now collects less in taxes) to shareholders. In fact, through its tax policies, the government subsidizes debt financing.

The magnitude of the value shifted depends on the rate at which we discount the stream of future tax savings. Typically, such tax savings are subject to a lower risk than the company's operating cash flows because they only depend on the tax rate and the enterprise's ability to earn taxable income. Corporate tax rates have not been subject to much variability, and the enterprise's ability to generate taxable earnings in the long run ought to be roughly equivalent to its ability to meet interest payments. Thus, the discount rate that we apply to future tax savings should be lower than that applied to residual cash flows available to shareholders, and a reasonable approximation would be to use the market yield on debt (r_b). This implies that the risk inherent in future tax shields is essentially the same as that inherent in the firm's interest payments on its borrowings. We ignore issuing costs, so that r_b equals the interest rate paid by the firm on its debt, and $I=Br_b$. Assuming that the debt outstanding (*B*) is perpetual, the tax shield generated by interest payments becomes a perpetual annuity of *IT*, with:

$$\text{Present value of tax savings} = \frac{IT}{r_b} = BT$$

so that

(16.2) $V_L = V_U + BT$

The value of a firm now increases with the amount of debt that it carries. Conversely, the WACC decreases with increasing financial leverage, implying that the cost of equity k_e^L has to increase at a slower rate than indicated in Equation 16.1. In fact, one can show that:[9]

(16.3) $k_e^L = k_e^U + \frac{B}{E_L}\left[(1-T)\,k_e^U - k_b\right]$

(16.4) $k = \frac{E_L}{V}k_e^L + \frac{B}{V}k_b = k_e^U\left(1 - \frac{BT}{B+E_L}\right)$

This is illustrated in Figure 16.7(b). The company's WACC continues to decrease with increasing leverage, indicating that firms ought to be levered to the fullest extent. Clearly, there are practical limitations to this recommendation, which we will recognize in a moment. The important conclusion at this point is that financial leverage owes any advantages that it may have solely to taxation and specifically to the tax deductibility of interest. Leverage introduced through preferred share financing, for example, should confer no benefits to common shareholders, as the framework outlined in the basic M–M position (presented in the previous section) remains valid.

---

[9] The reader is reminded that k_b is the after-tax cost of debt, as given by $k_b=r_b(1-T)$.

FIRM VALUE WITH TAX-DEDUCTIBLE CORPORATE DEBT PAYMENTS

A firm with a capital investment of $100,000 is financed solely through common shares and generates a steady stream of operating cash flows of $40,000 per year. The corporate tax rate is 50 percent, and the appropriate equity capitalization rate is $r_e^U = 20$ percent.

The company considers raising $50,000 through debt at an interest rate of 15 percent, using the proceeds to retire outstanding equity by repurchasing shares from its current shareholders. We should observe the following:

	Unlevered	Levered
Cash flows to debt holders	0	$I=7{,}500$
Cash flows to shareholders	$X(1-T)=20{,}000$	$(X-I)(1-T)=16{,}250$
Taxes paid to government	$XT=20{,}000$	$(X-I)(T)=16{,}250$
Total cash flows to all security holders	20,000	23,750
Total value of firm	$V_U=100{,}000$	$V_L=V_U+BT$ $=125{,}000$
Value of equity	$E_u=20{,}000/0.2$ $=100{,}000$	$E_L=V_L-B$ $=75{,}000$
Value of debt	0	$B=50{,}000$
Equity capitalization rate	$r_e^U=20\%$	$r_e^L=21.67\%$

The introduction of leverage has increased shareholder wealth by $25,000. Shareholders receive $50,000 in cash when the proceeds from the debt issue were paid out, and the equity that they retained should still have a market value of $75,000 after the transaction.

Individual Taxes

So far, we have considered taxes only at the corporate level. However, funds distributed by firms to security holders are again taxed in the hands of the individual investor, and investors presumably assign value to securities based on their own after-tax cash flows. Hence, individual taxes may affect the value of a company and, consequently, have a bearing on decisions regarding capital structure. With individual taxes, a firm can no longer concentrate on selecting a capital structure that minimizes its own taxes; rather, it should strive to minimize all taxes (both corporate and personal) paid on corporate income. By doing so, the firm maximizes total cash flows after corporate and personal taxes available to security holders. This should maximize the firm's market value and hence, shareholder wealth.

If, at the personal level, all investment income (i.e., interest, dividends, and capital gains) is taxed at the same rate, one can show that our previous conclusion remains unaltered and that leverage at the corporate level continues to provide the tax advantages we outlined. However, our tax system is not neutral with respect to investment income: although interest typically is taxed as normal income, the effective tax rate on dividends is reduced through the dividend tax credit, and capital gains are often not taxed at all. (When they are, a reduced rate applies, and tax can be postponed until the capital gain is realized.) With equity income taxed at a lower rate than interest, we are unable to ignore the effect of personal taxes on decisions regarding capital structure, since income from debt issues imposes an additional tax burden on the investor.

Figure 16.8 shows what happens to corporate cash flows when both corporate and personal taxes are considered. To illustrate the basic issue, we make the simplifying assumption that a firm pays out all of its net operating income to security holders, with its capital structure dictating the split between interest to debt holders and dividends to shareholders. As we will see, this assumption is easily relaxed without affecting our results. We define the following notation:

EBIT

I = total interest payments

E = taxable earnings

D = dividend payments

T_c = corporate tax rate

T_{pi} = personal tax rate on interest

T_{pd} = personal tax rate on dividends

We want to find the capital structure that minimizes total taxes or that maximizes total after-tax distributions, where:

(16.5) $$\text{Total after-tax distribution} = I(1 - T_{pi}) + E(1 - T_c)(1 - T_{pd})$$

If we can shift cash flows from E to I through taking on additional debt, it is clear from Equation 16.5 that we want to do so as long as the after-tax retention on interest is greater than the net retention on equity income, or as long as $(1 - T_{pi}) > (1 - T_c)(1 - T_{pd})$. In fact, it is easy to see that as long as the corporate tax savings on interest exceed the personal tax on interest (i.e., as long as $T_c > T_{pi}$ or $(1 - T_{pi}) > (1 - T_c)$), a company should always lever regardless of the personal tax rate on dividends.

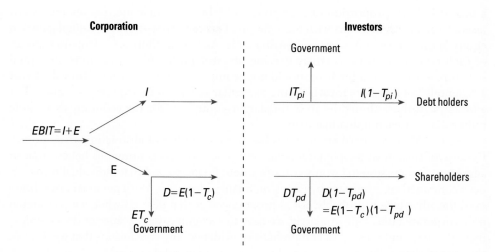

FIGURE 16.8

Cash Flow with
Corporate and Personal
Taxes

FINANCIAL LEVERAGE AND PERSONAL TAXES

EXAMPLE

A firm faces a corporate tax rate of 50 percent. The individual income tax rate that is applicable to interest income is 40 percent, but because of the dividend tax credit, dividends are taxed only at an effective rate of 25 percent. We have:

$$(1-T_{pi})=.6 > .375=(1-T_c)(1-T_{pd})$$

so that the firm should increase I by taking on financial leverage.

Our analysis can be extended to include capital gains as a form of equity income; in this case, T_{pd} simply becomes the effective tax rate that the investor pays on a given combination of equity income arising from dividends and capital gains.

Although, conceptually, we have had no difficulty in incorporating personal taxes into our discussion, at a practical level, this becomes almost impossible. The problem stems from the fact that firms have many security holders. Investors range from institutions that are exempt from taxes altogether to wealthy individuals subject to high marginal tax rates. Thus, there is no single T_{pi} or T_{pd} that could guide our decisions, and we have no hope of modelling the exceedingly complex world of individual taxes in a way that would allow us to determine analytically its effect on equilibrium prices of securities.

Several attempts have been made to come to at least some tentative general conclusions without such detailed modelling. One that has drawn much attention is that proposed by Merton Miller. He argues that individual investors will attempt to optimize their after-tax returns, and in doing so, will select a portfolio of securities that best suits their particular circumstances. For example, tax-exempt pension funds may invest a relatively large proportion of their funds in debt since their interest income is not taxed. Conversely, investors with high marginal tax rates may strive for capital gains on equity because taxes are lower and postponable. As long as there are adequate supplies of each type of security to satisfy varying investor preferences, decisions on capital structure at the level of the firm should not be important because each firm will attract a "clientele" of investors for whom the particular securities issued are best suited. Put another way, there should be an optimal debt-equity mix for the economy as a whole rather than for each individual firm.[10]

Again, Miller's formal argument is based on a number of abstracting assumptions. Because of this, most people (academics and practitioners) continue to believe that in aggregate, our tax system favours corporate debt financing and that individual firms can get a combined tax advantage by taking on financial leverage. With personal taxes, however, the advantage is probably not as pronounced as that derived when we considered only corporate taxes. Unfortunately, we have to recognize that because of the complexity of the issue and the lack of comprehensive evidence, any conclusions that we draw in this regard cannot be very precise and rest on less-than-solid ground.

Bankruptcy Costs

Because fluctuations in business results are magnified through leverage, a firm with debt in its capital structure enjoys greater upside potential but also faces greater downside risk than one financed entirely through equity. Therefore, as a firm increases its financial leverage, it increases the probability of insolvency with resulting financial distress and the potential for conflicts between owners and creditors. Financial distress is generally viewed with considerable apprehension by all parties concerned, and it is the threat of bankruptcy that limits the amount of debt that organizations will take on. We should analyse the costs imposed by bankruptcy more closely in order to gain a proper perspective on this important aspect of financing decisions.

Generally, one associates bankruptcy with significant losses of economic value. Visions of plant closures, scrapping and forced liquidation of valuable assets, and lost future potential invariably come to mind. However, it is important to distinguish between risk caused by a normal variability of returns from operations and losses of value attributed specifically to bankruptcy. Consider a firm that has incurred operating losses to a point where it defaults on its debt so that creditors lay claim to the assets. Assuming that the market value of those assets is less than the amount of debt outstanding, the equity investment of the original shareholders becomes worthless, and, in fact, the creditors become the new shareholders. They can either continue to operate the company, or they can liquidate by selling off assets to generate immediate cash.

Regardless of who ends up with ownership, any portions of the enterprise that generate cash flows sufficient to produce a positive net present value should survive and continue to be operated as usual, and only those assets with scrap or liquidation values exceeding the present value of future cash flows should be disposed of. In other words,

---

[10] See, for example, M. Miller, "Debt and Taxes," *Journal of Finance* (May 1977), pp. 261-75; and also, H. DeAngelo and R. Masulis, "Optimal Capital Structure Under Corporate and Personal Taxation," *Journal of Financial Economics* (March 1980), pp. 3-30.

although security holders may be disappointed in the economic returns of their assets, such results were part of the risk that they assumed when they made their original investment. If economic value is not destroyed, there is no reason to award bankruptcy any special treatment in investment and financing decisions.

Unfortunately, things are not quite so straightforward, and bankruptcies often entail costs that do reduce a firm's economic value. First, there are the direct costs such as fees for trustees, lawyers, and court proceedings. Most important, however, are indirect costs such as the lost profits caused by a loss of trust in the company and uncertainties surrounding its future.[11] Customers and suppliers may be reluctant to enter or maintain long-term arrangements with a firm that is perceived to be near bankruptcy. For example, many fliers avoided booking flights with Canadian Airlines during its period of financial difficulties prior to being taken over by Air Canada. In addition, it may be hard for such a firm to attract and retain good employees and managers. Indirect costs are also incurred because financial distress often leads management to operate in a suboptimal manner. Typically, such behaviour is caused by conflicts of interest between creditors and shareholders and possibly by market inefficiencies. A variety of specific circumstances can be found, but a few general illustrations will make the point:

1. Corporation shareholders are protected by limited liability so that if their firm is close to bankruptcy, they have little to lose, and this may provide an incentive to opt for high-risk strategies that under normal circumstances could not be justified and that would not be in the best interest of creditors. A relatively small probability of success may dominate considerations since downside risk is no longer of concern.[12]

2. Companies that have fallen behind the competition may require large new investments to turn the tide and catch up. Such investments may have long-term potential that is reflected in positive net present values. When a firm is in distress, however, it often becomes almost impossible to raise new funds in any form and on any terms. Shareholders may prefer to opt out and start afresh, leaving the excessive burden of debt behind them. This, in turn, may prevent creditors from realizing the full potential of the remaining assets. More generally, whenever liquidity and financing constraints dictate operations, enterprises will suffer not only from lost opportunities that cannot be funded, but also from suboptimal operating policies aimed solely at conserving cash.

3. Pursuing the previous point, shareholders who anticipate difficulties may go one step further and actually withdraw funds by continuing to pay dividends rather than retaining monies within the firm to enhance its competitive position and the creditors' collateral.[13]

---

[11] One study showed that, on average, indirect costs made up 63 percent of a firm's total bankruptcy costs. See E. Altman, "A Further Empirical Investigation of the Bankruptcy Cost Question," *Journal of Finance* (September 1984), pp. 1067-89.

[12] The common shares of companies with debt outstanding behave essentially like options. Because downside risk is limited, the value of options increases with the price variability of the underlying assets, which in the case of common shares are the assets of the firm. Consequently, shareholders may stand to gain from high-risk capital budgeting propositions. Options are discussed in Chapter 18.

[13] Restrictions set out in the several provincial companies acts and in the *Canada Business Corporations Act* are aimed at preventing company directors from abusing creditors. For example, dividends may not be declared when (a) a firm is insolvent; (b) its capital could be impaired as a consequence; and (c) such disbursements would render a company insolvent.

Significant agency costs can be involved when various parties try to ensure that management will not jeopardize their interests. These costs ultimately tend to be borne by shareholders. For example, creditors who recognize such risks will protect themselves through a combination of higher interest rates and protective covenants in debt contracts. Although such covenants may be aimed at safeguarding the legitimate interests of debt holders, in attempting to provide for all eventualities, they may become so confining that they interfere with management's ability to operate efficiently. The higher the perceived risk of distress, the more likely it is that creditors will insist on higher returns and stringent provisions.

Contrary to earlier assumptions, we see that the cost of debt no longer remains constant irrespective of leverage, but it increases with the probability of default as perceived by creditors. At some point, creditors may simply refuse to lend. Similarly, the cost of equity will reflect the potential loss of economic value owing to bankruptcy and rise more rapidly. As a consequence, the possibility of financial distress causes the WACC to increase and the organization's total value and the value of its equity to decrease.

The main challenge in devising an optimal capital structure now lies in trading off the tax savings from interest against the costs of potential bankruptcy. Unfortunately, the latter are difficult to quantify in advance, particularly if we also recognize the broader implications of insolvency. For example, financial distress may entail significant consequences such as loss of general confidence in the financial system caused by a major bank failure. Not only may insolvency impose costs on shareholders and creditors, but also on employees (including management), suppliers, host communities, and society at large. Major bailouts to avert bankruptcy (for example, the Canadian Commercial and Northland banks, Massey-Ferguson, and Dome Petroleum) attest to such broader concerns. From a narrow perspective, shareholders may not feel responsible for these broader implications; however, letting governments bear the burden is not without problems. Clearly, if firms come to rely on such assistance when in financial difficulty, it may become more difficult to resist government intervention on other, less-desirable occasions. For instance, significant deregulation in the financial services industry hardly seems feasible if, at the same time, the government is expected to assume the role of the insurer and backstop of last resort. We see, then, that in the longer run, it may well be in the shareholders' interest to take a broader perspective on bankruptcy and its associated costs.

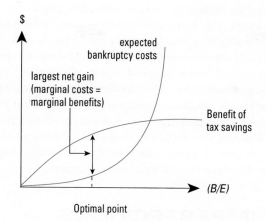

FIGURE 16.9

Benefit of Tax Savings,
Expected Bankruptcy
Costs, and Optimal
Capital Structure

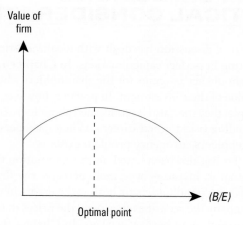

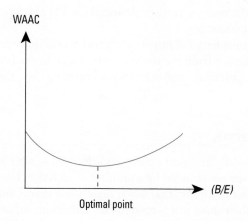

Regardless of what we include in the costs of bankruptcy, however, it is obvious that the probability of distress and, hence, the expected costs of bankruptcy increase with financial leverage, probably in a non-linear fashion. That is why, for low amounts of leverage, tax benefits will dominate and make debt financing attractive. At some point, though, the expected costs of bankruptcy will increase faster than the rate of tax savings, making further leverage undesirable. This confirms the existence of an optimal capital structure as postulated in the traditional position and illustrated in Figure 16.9. Because of our difficulty in quantifying bankruptcy costs, we are no closer in our attempts to find this optimal point. However, the discussion above should have provided us with a better understanding of the reasons that cause the WACC to be saucer-shaped and of the main factors that influence decisions regarding capital structure.

16.7 MARKET IMPERFECTIONS AND PRACTICAL CONSIDERATIONS

To this point, our theoretical discussion has dealt with idealized firms centred on value maximization and operating in perfect capital markets. In Chapter 1, we saw that managers, at least in theory, should act as agents for the shareholders who employ them and strive to maximize the value of their investment. In practice, however, managers may not always do this. For example, they may also be concerned about increasing their own prestige and rewards and avoiding risks to their careers. When managers fail to act solely in the best interests of shareholders, an agency problem exists.

Our discussion thus far has also been based on the assumption that capital markets are perfectly efficient—that is, investors accurately perceive the firm's cash flows and risks. If either shareholders or bondholders or both make errors in estimating the cash flows and risks that accompany the securities they own, the prices of those securities may deviate from what they would be in perfect markets. In Chapter 9, we saw that while investors are continually updating their estimates of share and bond prices to reflect newly available public information, realistic financial market efficiency does not mean a perfect understanding by investors.

In this section, we consider what impact such real-world imperfections might have on the conclusions we derived from the theories introduced in the previous section. We then consider some practical considerations relating to debt capacity and capital structure.

Agency Problems

How do shareholders typically interpret a company's decision to alter its capital structure? Empirical tests of this issue are clouded by a number of technical issues that are beyond the scope of this book, but it appears that when firms issue shares and use the proceeds to pay down their debt, their share prices tend to fall. Moreover, although there is greater disagreement on the reliability of this finding, there is some evidence suggesting that when organizations borrow money to buy back and retire shares, their share prices tend to rise.[14] It appears then that shareholders generally view equity issues to decrease leverage as bad news and, perhaps less clearly, view share buybacks connected with leverage increases as good news.

One interpretation of this might be that firms in general are not as levered as shareholders would like them to be. There are plausible reasons why this might be so. Managers might fear insolvency and possible bankruptcy more than shareholders do because managers lose their jobs and perhaps their reputations if their companies fail, whereas diversified shareholders lose only one asset among many in their portfolios.

Managers might also prefer to have discretion over whether or not to pay the firm's earnings out to investors. Interest payments on debts must be maintained, while there is some flexibility around the payment of dividends, and electing to reinvest earnings may contribute to higher profits in the future and to increased bonuses and salaries for management. Funds that can either be paid out to investors or reinvested in the company are called its free cash flow. Retained earnings and dividends are parts of this **free cash flow**, whereas interest payments are not. Clearly, managers can maintain control over a greater free cash flow by avoiding debt in their firms' capital structures.

In either case, such behaviour would be an example of the agency problems discussed in Chapter 1. Managers, acting in their own self-interests (and possibly in the interests of stakeholders such as other employees and creditors) rather than as sole agents of shareholders, may maintain a lower debt level than shareholders would want. If shareholders view new stock issues to decrease leverage as a sign of such agency problems, they may lower their expectations of managerial commitment to future returns, and the stock price would consequently fall.

Market Inefficiencies: A Financial Pecking Order

It appears that share prices have a tendency to fall whenever the corporation issues equity, not just when it plans on using the proceeds of the issue to reduce its debt. This may be a manifestation of other imperfections in financial markets.

Suppose that financial markets are not completely efficient so that investors do not have perfect information about the value of their investments. As a consequence, share prices sometimes may be higher (overpriced) and sometimes lower (underpriced) than they would be in an efficient market. Managers, quite sensibly, should want to issue new shares when the share price is highest. That way, the firm can minimize the number of shares it needs to issue in raising a given amount of capital. If, however, shareholders expect managers to behave in this way, they may view any new issue of securities as a clue that managers think those securities are currently overvalued. Given that managers have inside information about the company, news that more shares are to be issued would cause the share price to fall. In an imperfect market, in which shareholders, based on their more limited information, cannot tell which shares are overvalued and which are

---

[14] For a thorough overview of the evidence, see M. Harris and A. Raviv, "The Theory of Capital Structure," *Journal of Finance* (March 1991), pp. 297-355.

not, such price declines will occur even when the shares may have been valued correctly at the time of the announcement.[15] This phenomenon can give rise to yet another cost of issuing securities. In addition to underwriting and other fees, the firm may also have to contend with possible price-depression effects.

Since existing shareholders and bondholders are likely to be upset by any actions that reduce the values of their investments, management may want to avoid new issues when funds can be generated internally. Moreover, since common shares are harder to value than bonds, mispricing problems based on asymmetric information would be more acute for shares. Companies, therefore, should issue bonds when internal funds are unavailable and should only issue new common shares as a last resort. This gives rise to what has been called a **pecking order** of corporate financing, which holds that:

1. Retained earnings or depreciation should be used first to fund new projects in order to avoid price declines, which may result from issuing additional securities, as outlined above.

2. Once internal funds are exhausted, debt should be used. Because of its more predictable returns, debt is easier to value than equity and should suffer less from price declines caused by investor uncertainty.

3. New common shares should be issued only when further debt is likely to increase the chances of bankruptcy substantially.[16]

These prescriptions fit well with the actual practice of many corporations, as can be seen in the evidence provided in Table 16.1 by Colin Mayer, taken from a 1990 study of corporate financing behaviour in eight developed economies. The evidence shows that internally generated funds (or retentions) were the dominant source of financing for companies in all of the countries examined, while common share issues represented a relatively insignificant source of financing. In other words, firms issue stock when they first go public, but, under normal circumstances, seldom do so subsequently.[17] Healthy companies tend to issue little long-term debt, and finance much of their growth out of earnings, but weaker and rapidly growing ones must turn to debt markets to raise funds.

---

[15] This approach to capital structure issues is rather like the lemons problem associated with used cars. Any used car sold by its original owner, could have some unobservable defect known only to the owner. Because of such suspicions by potentional buyers, even an almost new, trouble-free used car has its resale price depressed relative to the price of an identical new car. The theory and empirical evidence relating to this view of capital structure are presented in S. Myers and N. Majluf, "Corporate Financing and Investment Decisions When Firms Have Information that Investors Do Not Have," *Journal of Financial Economics* (June 1984), pp. 187-221.

[16] Preferred shares lie somewhere between debt and equity on this scale.

[17] This is also consistent with a survey of chief financial officers and chief executive officers of large Canadian companies, which found that over 60 percent of such executives viewed the cost of new equity as high or very high. See V. Jog and A. Srivastava, "Capital Formation and Corporate Financial Decision Making in Canada," *Carleton University School of Business: Working Paper #7*, (1992).

TABLE 16.1

Unweighted Average Net Financing of Non-financial Enterprises, 1970-85

	Canada	Finland	France	Germany	Italy	Japan	United Kingdom	United States
Retentions	76.4	64.4	61.4	70.9	51.9	57.9	102.4	85.9
Capital transfers	.0	.2	2.0	8.6	7.7	.0	4.1	.0
Short-term securities	−.8	3.7	−.1	−.1	−1.3	N.A.	1.7	.4
Loans	15.2	28.1	37.3	12.1	27.7	50.4	7.6	24.4
Trade credit	−4.4	−1.4	−.6	−2.1	.0	−11.2	−1.1	−1.4
Bonds	8.5	2.8	1.6	−1.0	1.6	2.1	−1.1	11.6
Shares	2.5	−.1	6.3	.6	8.2	4.6	−3.3	1.1
Other	1.3	7.4	−1.4	10.9	1.0	−3.8	3.2	−16.9
Statistical adustment	1.2	−5.0	−6.4	.0	3.2	N.A.	−13.4	−5.1
Total	99.9	100.1	100.1	99.9	100.0	100.00	100.1	100.0

Source: C. Mayer. "Financial Systems, Corporate Finance, and Economic Development." In *Asymmetric Information, Corporate Finance and Investment*, ed. R. Glenn Hubbard, Table 12.1, p. 310. Chicago: University of Chicago Press, 1990.

It is interesting to note that pecking-order descriptions were popular before the theory in the previous section attained widespread acceptance. After years of being dismissed as "unsubstantial folklore" by academies, they are now seen as deriving from more realistic descriptions of capital markets and are undergoing a dramatic resurgence in popularity.

Debt Capacity

The tax and bankruptcy issues introduced in the theoretical discussions in the previous section may be more relevant for some companies than for others. So, too, might some of the issues relating to firm and market imperfections. For example, a business in a volatile industry or in an industry favoured by lower tax rates or substantial tax shelters (perhaps a small manufacturer) might have little to gain and much to fear from increased leverage, whereas a firm in an industry with low operating risk (perhaps a public utility) might envision few problems with fairly high levels of debt and welcome the opportunity to deduct interest costs. The ability of an enterprise to tolerate higher leverage indicates it has **debt capacity**. Several practical considerations, outside our theoretical treatment of capital structure, help determine the capacity of a firm to carry debt.

Debt capacity can be viewed as a function of both available collateral and stable cash flows. When a company faces financial distress, certain assets such as plant, land, and equipment are more readily valued and sold than patents, brand names, and other intangibles. It follows that a manufacturer with tangible assets available as collateral may be able to borrow more readily than a software company operating out of leased premises.[18]

However, not all tangible assets are equally attractive. Firms with assets that are easily marketable in recessions probably have higher debt capacities than those with assets that drop in value during economic downturns. For example, assets such as office buildings, aircraft, or resort hotels can suffer substantial price declines when the economy is weak. (In the terminology of Chapter 8, they have high betas.) During recessions, such assets cannot be sold to provide emergency liquidity without taking substantial write-downs. Thus, they afford poorer collateral than assets with values that remain steady during downturns and to which lenders react accordingly.

The variability of a company's net cash inflows and the level of such inflows during difficult times also have a bearing on debt capacity. In fact, knowing that the ability to service debt obligations will probably remain intact during a recession is far more comforting to both borrowers and lenders than having a safety margin around the liquidation value of the collateral. By focusing on expected net cash inflows over a business cycle, it is possible to estimate a corporation's reserve of unused borrowing capacity. A variety of financial statement ratios that were introduced in Chapters 3 and 4 can serve to assist in this task.

The stability of cash flows and corporate debt capacity are obviously influenced by both industry- and firm-specific factors. Sales by the heavy farm equipment industry, for example, are very volatile, dropping significantly when grain sales and prices fall. However, an equipment dealership that also has strong parts distribution and servicing capabilities or is otherwise diversified may enjoy much more stable cash flows than aggregate industry data would suggest.

Finally, it has been argued that firms with product lines that involve long-term commitments to customers probably have lower debt capacities than ones with products that do not. For example, users would hesitate to buy a computer system from a firm facing even the slightest chance of bankruptcy in the near future because long-term servicing and support are important aspects of the transaction. In contrast, commodity items such as steel ingots involve no such longer-term considerations. A steel company, therefore, may continue to get business even if its exposure to financial risk through leverage is abnormally high.

Numerous other factors influence the willingness and ability of firms to issue debt. Any complete analysis for a specific concern is beyond the scope of a general textbook and will require a detailed understanding of the business and the markets in which it operates.

---

[18] The shares of firms with significant intangible assets are more likely to be subject ot mispricing than those of firms with assets that are largely tangible.

Translating considerations such as those listed above into an optimal financing mix is not easy, and in setting appropriate targets for a firm's capital structure, senior management relies heavily on judgement. Although shareholders are rarely consulted directly, companies often seek the advice of investment dealers and consider the possible reactions by bond rating agencies. Many firms, particularly large ones, are concerned about maintaining a given rating on their debt, mainly to ensure future market access at reasonable costs, but also because they believe those shareholders could react negatively to any drop in ratings. In this context, future financing flexibility and the maintenance of an adequate flow of funds to finance operations, including any new investment opportunities, are issues of major concern to financial executives.

The process for translating such general judgements into specific decisions regarding capital structure vary, in part because there appears to be no consensus on what constitute the most appropriate measures for monitoring leverage. Whereas some firms rely primarily on measures taken from the balance sheet and others work with information derived from the income statement, most businesses recognize that leverage has to be evaluated in terms of its effects on both of these financial statements. In terms of the balance sheet, the most commonly monitored indicators are the proportions of long-term debt to total capital, long-term debt to shareholders' equity (or net worth), and total liabilities to total capital. Contrary to our discussion in Chapter 15, such measures are typically based on book values of outstanding capital rather than on market values. In terms of the income statement and cash flows, firms are concerned about their ability to service the contractual commitments incurred by financing through senior securities including interest, preferred dividends, and repayment of principal.[19] Rough measures of a firm's ability to meet such payments include various coverage ratios that were discussed in Chapter 3. Basically, by dividing the cash flows available to meet financing charges (such as earnings before interest and taxes—EBIT) by the anticipated required payments, we find some indication of the safety margin available to the company in meeting its financial obligations. More generally, however, in order to assess whether the organization enjoys sufficient leeway to be able to weather possible adversities, detailed projections of cash flows have to be prepared including forecasts under assumptions of unfavourable economic conditions.

NET CASH FLOWS WITH FIXED OBLIGATIONS

EXAMPLE

A firm operates with annual fixed cash obligations of $12 million. Of this amount, $7 million represent fixed costs incurred in operations; the remaining $5 million are required to service outstanding debt including $2 million for interest (tax deductible) and $3 million in sinking fund payments (to be met out of after-tax earnings). Annual sales are expected to total $44 million with variable costs at 50 percent of sales. Capital cost allowance (CCA) amounts to $5 million, and the corporate tax rate is 40 percent. We obtain:

---

[19] As discussed in Chapter 13, the charges referred to here are not always fixed. Corporate debt is sometimes issued with variable interest rates and/or flexible sinking fund provisions.

Sales		$44,000,000
Variable costs	$22,000,000	
Fixed costs	7,000,000	
Capital cost allowance	5,000,000	
Total expenses		34,000.000
Earnings before interest and taxes (EBIT)		$10,000,000
Interest		2,000,000
Taxable earnings		$ 8,000,000
Taxes		3,200,000
Net earnings		$ 4,800,000

We have:

Net cash flow = net earnings + CCA − sinking fund
$$= 4,800,000 + 5,000,000 - 3,000,000$$
$$= \$6,800,000$$

Based on these figures, the firm should experience no difficulty in meeting its obligations. If sales unexpectedly drop to half their forecasted level, we would have:

Sales	$22,000,000
Total expenses	
(11,000,000+7,000,000+5,000,000)	23,000,000
EBIT	($1,000,000)
Interest	2,000,000
Net earnings	($3,000,000)

Net cash flow = −3,000,000 + 5,000,000 − 3,000,000
$$= -\$1,000,000$$

Unless the previous year's tax payments are recaptured as a consequence of the loss, the firm may well face a liquidity problem.

When a company resorts to borrowing, it needs to assess the likelihood of adverse business conditions and to balance the risk of insolvency against any advantages that low-cost debt financing may provide. Most corporations keep such risk at low levels and incur fixed charges only as long as the probability of meeting obligations, given normal operating conditions, is very high. It follows that the anticipated stability of future revenues often becomes a key factor in determining a firm's debt capacity. Clearly, the stability of revenues and cash flows is strongly dependent on the particular type of business. Therefore, it is not surprising that, as shown in Table 16.2, financial leverage tends to vary by industry classification.[20] For example, regulated utilities, which enjoy stable revenues, resort to much higher financial leverage than firms in cyclical industries such as mining, which are significantly affected by changes in the economy and commodity prices. Such industry norms are watched by financial executives who may view them as indicators of the current consensus regarding optimal capital structure.

TABLE 16.2

Corporate Long-Term Financing by Industry in Proportions of Total Capital Employed (December 31, 1998)

Industry	Long-term debt	Preferred shares	Common equity
All non-financial industries	23.7	1.2	75.1
Financial services	27.8	4.5	67.7
Retail & wholesale	22.6	0.4	77.0
Resources	19.7	0.4	79.9
Manufacturing	23.8	2.2	74.0
Transportation & utility	43.0	1.7	55.3

Source: Standard & Poor's Compustat database, September 6, 2000.

Given that decisions about capital structure are strongly influenced by forecasts regarding the company's future ability to generate cash flows, it is worth noting that target leverage ratios may change over time, reflecting altered business conditions. In the 1980s, this was particularly evident in the oil industry. Based on forecasts of escalating oil prices, lenders willingly provided funds, and many firms (and even nations) went heavily into debt to finance major expansions. The unanticipated collapse of oil prices in the mid-1980s left these borrowers with a debt burden that they could no longer support. Companies that survived scrambled to bring their capital structures into line with new realities, often through painful programs of belt tightening and refinancing under adverse market conditions. At the same time, lenders faced massive write offs on bad loans.

A similar over-optimism in providing debt financing for takeovers in the late 1980s resulted in financial distress for many firms. A notable illustration is Campeau Corporation's takeover of the U.S. retailing giant, Federated Department Stores. Campeau went into bankruptcy shortly after completing the takeover.

Numerous real estate companies around the world faced similar problems in the early 1990s. When the upward escalation in land prices in major world financial centres that had prevailed through the late 1980s ended, firms such as Olympia and York were forced to reassess debt positions that suddenly were found to entail higher-than-anticipated risks. In a dynamic economic environment, the management of

---

[20] The amount of leverage appears much lower in this table than in Figure 16.2. This is because of the data sources. Figure 16.2 was compiled from data provided by Statistics Canada and included data on almost all Canadian companies regardless of size. On the other hand, Table 16.2 represents data for a total of 864 of the largest publicly traded Canadian companies that Compustat followed as of December 31, 2000.

capital structure has to be viewed as an ongoing process. In this context, we should also bear in mind that there are penalties for erring on either side: while a debt policy that is too aggressive can result in financial distress and bankruptcy, excessive conservatism may put a firm at a competitive disadvantage by giving rise to a comparatively high cost of capital. It may also make the company an attractive takeover target, enabling the acquirer to pay part of the takeover price with the target's own unused debt capacity. (We discuss takeovers in Chapter 26.)

16.8 SUMMARY

1. A firm that incurs fixed costs while generating variable revenues is subject to leverage. Leverage is used to increase the expected profitability of a firm. Financial risk is the added variability in returns to shareholders introduced by financing through fixed-cost senior securities.

2. Indifference analysis is used to evaluate the effect of leverage on profitability.

3. A firm's capital structure is optimal if it maximizes shareholder wealth. The desirability of financial leverage depends on equity investors' attitudes toward the implied trade-offs between risk and expected returns. The traditional position suggests, optional moderate leverage.

4. Given corporate taxes, interest on debt allows the firm to reduce its tax bill and to increase the amounts available for distribution to security holders.

5. Firms restrict debt financing in order to limit the probability of financial distress. Liquidation decisions entail capital budgeting analysis that is based on net present values. Total expected bankruptcy costs increase with financial leverage and reduce the value of the firm. The trade-off facing management is between the tax benefits that accrue through debt financing and the expected costs of financial distress that increase with leverage.

6. Since debt payments represent contractual obligations, high leverage reduces a firm's free cash flow. It thus limits management flexibility and discretion. A firm's debt capacity is mainly a function of the stability of its cash flows and its collateral's value and liquidity.

7. Financial leverage affects a firm's systematic risk. Beta, as specified by the Capital Asset Pricing Model, varies as a function of the debt proportion that the firm employs.

APPENDIX 16-A

FINANCIAL LEVERAGE AND THE CAPITAL ASSET PRICING MODEL

We saw in Chapter 15 that the capital asset pricing model (CAPM) is commonly used for estimating a company's cost of common shares. If financial leverage increases the return that shareholders demand and the CAPM is to remain valid, then such leverage must also increase a firm's beta.

It is easy to quantify the relationship between financial leverage and beta by developing formulas that parallel Equations 16.1 and 16.3.[21] Specifically, we obtain:

Assuming no taxes:

$$(16.6) \quad \beta^L = \beta^U \left(1 + \frac{B}{E}\right)$$

With corporate taxes:

$$(16.7) \quad \beta^L = \beta^U \left(1 + (1-T)\frac{B}{E}\right)$$

In either case, individual investor taxes and bankruptcy costs are ignored. The above equations enable us to estimate how a change in capital structure would alter a firm's systematic risk.

ESTIMATING UNLEVERED AND LEVERED BETAS

A company currently has 20 percent debt and 80 percent equity in its capital structure. Its beta has been estimated at 1.2, and its tax rate is 50 percent. It contemplates additional borrowing that would increase the proportion of debt to 40 percent of total capital, and we want to estimate what effect this would have on the firm's beta.

We first calculated the beta of the company's assets assuming 100 percent equity financing. That is, we "unlever" the current capital structure. Using Equation 16.7, we obtain:

$$\beta^U = \frac{\beta^L}{1 + (1-T)\,B/E}$$

$$= \frac{1.2}{1 + .5(.2/.8)} = 1.067$$

EXAMPLE

---

[21] With $r_e = k_e = r_f + \beta(r_m - r_f)$ we can rewrite Equation 16.1 ($k_e^L = k_e^U + (k_e^U - k_b)\frac{B}{E}$)as:

$r_f + \beta^L(r_m - r_f) = r_f + \beta^U(r_m - r_f) + [r_f + \beta^U(r_m - r_f) - k_b]\frac{B}{E}$. Assuming $k_b = r_f$ and solving for β^L, we obtain

$\beta^L = \beta^U(1 + B/E)$. Similarly, with taxes, we set $k_b = (1-T)r_f$ and we can derive Equation 16.7 from Equation 16.3.

We then "relever" this unlevered beta to reflect the new capital structure as follows:

$$\beta^L = \beta^U \left(1 + (1-T)\frac{B}{E}\right)$$

$$= 1.067\left(1 + .5 \times \frac{.4}{.6}\right) = 1.42$$

We have:

Capital structure (B/E)	Beta
0	1.067
$\frac{.2}{.8} = .25$	1.2
$\frac{.4}{.6} = .67$	1.42

Assume interest rates on government T-bills are at 6 percent, and the expected return on the market is 12 percent. If we ignore discounts and issuing and underwriting expenses so that $k_e = r_e$, the unlevered cost of equity becomes:

$$k_e^U = 6 + 1.067(12-6) = 12.40\%$$

Using β^L as derived, the cost of equity at 40 percent debt is given as:

$$k_e^L = 6 + 1.42(12-6) = 14.52\%$$

If we use Equation 16.3 and assume that the firm can also borrow at an interest rate of 6 percent, we obtain:[22]

$$k_e^L = k_e^U + \frac{B}{E}\left[(1-T)\,k_e^U - k_b\right]$$

$$= 12.40 + \frac{.4}{.6}\left[(.5)(12.40) - 3\right] = 14.35\% \text{ (difference due to rounding)}$$

In the last section of Chapter 15, we saw that a business's WACC is not an appropriate discount rate when the cash flows of new investment projects have risks different from those of the firm's portfolio of existing projects. In such circumstances, the new project's cash flows should be discounted at a rate appropriate to the risk it adds to existing systematic risk. We saw that one way of operationalizing this was to find another enterprise with a primary line of business that matches that of the new project. This benchmark firm's WACC is a more appropriate discount rate for the new project's risky

[22] The assumption of one interest rate at which all borrowing and lending takes place is commonly made in the development of financial theory, including the CAPM.

cash flows. However, the analysis in Chapter 15 did not take taxes and leverage differences into account. The example below shows how this may be done.

ESTIMATING RISK-ADJUSTED DISCOUNT RATES

Your firm is considering setting up a ball bearing plant, but ball bearing production is judged to be more risky than the firm's primary line of business. Consequently, your company's WACC of 11 percent is seen as too low a discount rate. After the new project is financed, your company's capital structure will remain at two-fifths debt and three-fifths equity. A benchmark firm that produces only ball bearings has a capital structure of two-thirds equity and one-third debt. The benchmark's equity has a published beta (i.e., levered beta) of 1.5, while its debt is seen as virtually risk-free. The risk-free rate, r_f, is 8 percent, the market return, r_m, is 14 percent, and the corporate tax rate is 40 percent. The relationship between the company's levered and unlevered betas is given by Equation 16.7 as:

$$\beta^L = 1.5 = \beta^U \left[1 + (1-T)\frac{B}{E} \right] = \beta^U \times \left[1 + (1-0.40)\frac{1}{2} \right]$$

Solving for β^U yields 1.15. This value can then be substituted into the CAPM to provide an estimate of the return a theoretical unlevered ball bearing firm would have to pay its investors:

$$k = r_f + 1.15 \times (r_m - r_f) = 8\% + 1.15 \times (14\% - 8\%) = 14.9\%$$

Thus, if your organization's capital structure were 100 percent equity, then 14.9 percent could be used as a discount rate for the proposed new ball bearing project. However, your firm does have debt outstanding. Therefore, the tax advantage of debt allows the project to compensate for the additional risk it brings to the company with a slightly lower return. If the ball bearing project were a stand-alone company with the same capital structure as your firm's two-fifths debt and three-fifths equity, its weighted average cost of capital (WACC) using Equation 16.4, would be:

$$k = k_e^U \left[1 - \frac{BT}{B+E_L} \right] = 14.9\% \times \left[1 - \frac{2(.4)}{5} \right] = 12.5\%$$

Thus, the ball bearing project requires an internal rate of return of only 12.5 percent, given the risk it adds to your firm's overall cash flows.

Although tax-adjusted unleveraged betas often are used, it should be recognized that they are rough approximations. Equations 16.4 and 16.7 clearly do not take into account the complexity of the tax situations of the two companies, nor do they consider personal taxes, potential bankruptcy costs, or capital market imperfections.

Note: All *asterisked* Questions and Problems relate to the material contained in the appendix to this chapter.

QUESTIONS AND PROBLEMS

Questions for Discussion

1. Explain the concept of leverage. What are the differences between operating and financial leverage; and between business and financial risk? As a manager shareholder, with which leverage and risk would you be mainly concerned?

2. The choice of an optimal capital structure is based on a trade-off between risk and expected return. Explain why this is so, and illustrate with a numerical example.

3. Why do we tend to observe different capital structures in different industries? Give examples of industries that you would expect to use large or small amounts of financial leverage. Discuss.

4. Discuss the usefulness and shortcomings of financial indifference analysis.

5. Why is it difficult to assess the optimal capital structure for a firm?

6. Why does a capital structure that minimizes the weighted average cost of capital (WACC) maximize shareholder wealth? How do we define shareholder wealth in this context?

7. Under what circumstances can personal leverage be viewed as a substitute for corporate leverage? What are the implications of such substitutability?

8. What are the theoretical justifications for a saucer-shaped WACC curve that has a minimum value for moderate amounts of leverage?

9. How does the choice of capital structure influence a firm's investment decisions? Do firms' investment decisions have any impact on the choice of capital structure?

10. Discuss the following statement: "As a company takes on more debt, it becomes riskier for both creditors and shareholders, and as a consequence, both bondholders and equity investors will demand rates of return that increase with financial leverage. Thus, a firm minimizes its cost of funding by taking on low amounts of debt."

11. "For small amounts of debt, the risk of bankruptcy as a consequence of financial leverage is minimal. Hence, moderate borrowing should not affect the expected rate of return that shareholders demand." Do you agree? Briefly discuss.

12. "Through the tax deductibility of interest, the government subsidizes corporate borrowing, and this subsidy increases during times of inflation. Conceptually, it would be more sensible if the tax treatment of all cash flows that accrue to various groups of security holders would be the same." Discuss.

13. Give three examples of direct and indirect bankruptcy costs.

PROBLEMS WITH SOLUTIONS

Problem 1

A firm has 500,000 common shares outstanding (n_1) and $10 million debt at 10 percent interest with annual interest payments of $I_1 = \$1$ million. The corporate tax rate is $T = 40$ percent. An additional $3 million has to be raised, and the following financing alternatives are under consideration:

Common shares:	The company can sell additional shares to net $30 per share. Therefore, 100,000 new shares (n_2) would have to be issued.
Debt:	Debt can be issued at 10 percent, requiring additional annual interest payment of $I_2 = \$300,000$.
Preferred shares:	An issue with a 7 percent dividend is possible, resulting in annual dividend payments of $D = \$210,000$.

Compute *EPS* as a function of *EBIT* for each of the above alternatives and derive the indifference points. Illustrate your results with a diagram.

Solution 1

Earnings per share for each alternative are computed as follows:

Common shares:

$$EPS = \frac{(1-T)(EBIT - I_1)}{n_1 + n_2} = \frac{.6(EBIT - 1,000,000)}{600,000}$$

Debt:

$$EPS = \frac{(1-T)(EBIT - I_1 - I_2)}{n_1} = \frac{.6(EBIT - 1,300,000)}{500,000}$$

Preferred shares:

$$EPS = \frac{(1-T)(EBIT - I_1) - D}{n_1} = \frac{.6(EBIT - 1,000,000) - 210,000}{500,000}$$

We note that the second term in the numerator always represents taxable income, which, when multiplied by $(1-T)$, yields after-tax earnings. Preferred dividends (D) are paid out of such after-tax earnings. The denominator simply gives the total number of common shares outstanding.

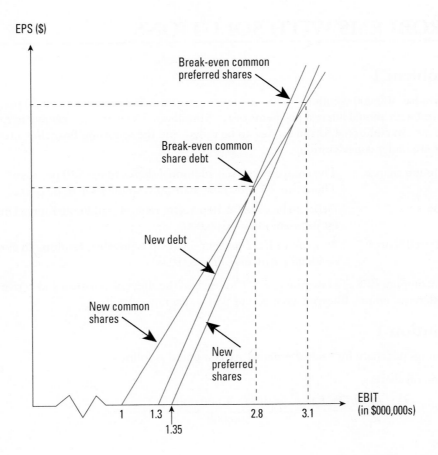

The previous equations are portrayed in the indifference chart. The intercepts of the various lines with the *EBIT* axis are found by setting *EPS*=0 in the above equations. For example, for the common share alternative we obtain:

$$EPS = \frac{.6(EBIT - 1,000,000)}{600,000} = 0$$

giving an intercept of *EBIT*=1,000,000. The slope of the line is determined by the coefficient of *EBIT*, which is .6/600,000=10^{-6}. This signifies that *EPS* increases by $1 for every $ 1,000,000 increase in *EBIT*. The indifference points are again derived by equating *EPS* for various alternatives. We have:

Between debt and common shares ($EBIT_1$):

$$\frac{.6(EBIT_1^* - 1,300,000)}{500,000} = \frac{.6(EBIT_1^* - 1,000,000)}{600,000}$$

$$EBIT_1^* = \$2,800,000$$

Between preferred and common shares ($EBIT_2$):

$$\frac{.6(EBIT_2^*-1,000,000)-210,000}{500,000} = \frac{.6(EBIT_2^*-1,000,000)}{600,000}$$

$$EBIT_2^* = \$3,100,000$$

The lines for the debt and preferred share financing in the graph have identical slopes, with debt providing higher EPS values at any level of *EBIT*. (In both instances, 500,000 common shares are outstanding and the slope is determined by this figure.)

Problem 2

Companies A and B are identical in all respects, except that A is financed entirely through common equity, and B has $20,000 debt at an interest rate of 15 percent in its capital structure. Assume perfect markets, with no taxes and no bankruptcy costs.

(a) Company A achieves annual net operating earnings of $10,000, which the market capitalizes at a rate $r=k=10\%$. What is the total value of A's stock?

(b) What should happen if the total market value of Company B is $120,000?

(c) Suppose you own 10 percent of Company B's stock. What net gain could you achieve through arbitrage?

Solution 2

(a) Market value of stock $= \dfrac{10,000}{.10}$

$= \$100,000$

Because Company A has no debt in its capital structure, the total market value of the firm is

$V_A=\$100,000.$

(b) If $V_B > V_A$, Company B is overvalued. Hence, shareholders of B can make a gain by selling their shares, borrowing on their personal accounts, and buying shares of A. In so doing, they will drive Company B's share price down, while A's shares could rise. These adjustments will stop when $V_A=V_B$. The working of this arbitrage process rests on the assumption that personal leverage is a substitute for corporate debt.

(c)

	Company A	Company B
Net operating income	$ 10,000	$ 10,000
Interest on debt	—	3,000
Earnings available to shareholders	$ 10,000	$ 7,000
Equity capitalization rate	0.10	0.07*
Market value of stock	100,000	100,000
Market value of debt	—	20,000
Total value of firm	$100,000	$120,000

*The equity capitalization rate of 7 percent for Company B is derived from the problem statement that specifies a total market value of V_B=$120,000, with $20,000 debt at 15 percent interest. Therefore, market value of stock=120,000−20,000=$100,000. Interest payments are 20,000×.15=$3,000, implying earnings to common shareholders of 10,000−3,000=$7,000. It follows that k_e=7,000/100,000=7%.

We have:

Expected annual returns from holding 10 percent of B's stock=.10×7,000=$700

Assume you sell your shares of B for $10,000 (0.01/10×$100,000) and borrow an amount equivalent to 10 percent of B's debt ($2,000) at an interest rate of 15 percent. You now have the following options:

(i) Invest $8,000 of the proceeds from the sale of B's stock plus the $2,000 borrowed on your personal account to purchase 10 percent of A's stock. You obtain:

Gross earnings	$1,000
Less: interest on personal account	300
Net income	$ 700

Results: net income unchanged,
same financial risk,
reduced investment (by $2,000)

(ii) Invest the entire $10,000 received from the sale of B's stock plus $2,000 borrowed on your personal account to purchase 12 percent of A's stock. You have:

Gross earnings	$1,200
Less: Interest on personal account	300
Net income	$ 900

Results: increased net income,
same financial risk,
same investment

ADDITIONAL PROBLEMS

1. A company manufactures an item that it sells for $24.50 per unit. Variable costs are $16.50 per unit, and total annual fixed costs are $700,000. In the fiscal year just completed, 880,000 units were sold. The company has $14 million of 13 percent long-term debt outstanding, no preferred shares, and 1.5 million common shares. The firm's tax rate is 50 percent.

(a) Compute earnings before interest and taxes for the past year.

(b) Calculate earnings per common share.

(c) What is the degree of operating leverage based on the volume for the year just completed?

(d) What is the degree of financial leverage?

(e) Calculate the combined or total leverage factor.

(f) How would an increase in the interest rate paid on outstanding debt affect the firm's leverage?

2. A firm that wants to raise $21 million has 500,000 common shares outstanding, with a current market value of $16 per share. The firm's tax rate is 45 percent.

(a) The alternatives are to issue an additional 1.4 million common shares that would net the company $15 per share or to place 20-year debentures at face value with annual interest payments of 12 percent. Issuing and underwriting expenses can be ignored. Carry out a financial indifference analysis illustrating the ranges of earnings before interest and taxes (EBIT) for which each of the above alternatives appears superior in terms of earnings per share alone. Provide a diagram and compute the indifference point.

(b) The $21 million could also be raised by issuing 525,000 preferred shares to net the company $40 per preferred share at an annual dividend rate of 10 percent. Include the proper line for the preferred share alternative in your diagram from part (a).

(c) EBIT is expected to be $5 million, but could be 20 percent higher or lower than this figure. What would be the resulting percentage change in earnings per share and the degree of financial leverage under each of the financing alternatives?

(d) What additional factors must be considered before a decision is taken? Discuss.

3. A firm that is financed solely through equity considers changing its capital structure to introduce financial leverage. To achieve this, the firm would issue debt and use the proceeds to repurchase some of its outstanding shares at their current market price of $50 per share. There are currently 20,000 shares outstanding. EBIT of $300,000 per year are expected to remain constant, and all net earnings are paid out in dividends. The firm can issue debt at an interest rate of 12 percent, and the corporate tax rate is 40 percent. Three alternative amounts of debt are under consideration, and the returns that shareholders demand in each case to compensate for the added financial risk are given as follows:

Amount of debt	0	$200,000	$400,000
Required return on equity	18%	20%	25%

(a) What is the optimal amount of debt to take on?

(b) Show that, at the optimal capital structure, the firm simultaneously minimizes the WACC and maximizes both the total value of the firm and the price of the outstanding shares.

(c) The required return for the unlevered firm drops to 16 percent. How would the required return on equity have to increase for the various amounts of debt under consideration if the WAAC is to remain constant regardless of leverage?

4. Wining Corporation feels that it must diversify its product lines in order to grow. The vice-president of finance has been looking for suitable investments and has come up with two projects of apparently equal potential. The first of these projects would require outside financing of approximately $500,000, whereas the second, would require $1.3 million. In either case, the new projects could be financed entirely

through debt, and because of the tax deductibility of interest this appeals to management. The first project could be financed by a 12 percent issue with sinking fund requirements of $80,000 per year. The second, which has different financial backing, could be financed with debt bearing only 10 percent interest; sinking fund requirements would be $160,000 per year.

In either case, it would take two years before the new projects would start to generate net inflows. Forecasts for the upcoming year suggest expected sales of $3 million that could fluctuate by ±5 percent. Variable costs have traditionally been 60 percent of sales, and fixed costs (excluding depreciation and interest on current debt) are $600,000 per year. Capital cost allowances on existing assets will be $200,000 for the coming year, while (CCA) on the new investments would be taken at a rate of 5 percent on a declining balance. Annual interest charges on debt currently outstanding are $150,000, with sinking fund requirements of $200,000. Wining's tax rate is 40 percent.

(a) Compute the expected net cash flow for the coming year, excluding any financing for the new projects.

(b) Suggest to the vice-president whether either of these projects appears acceptable from a cash flow point of view. Would 100 percent debt financing of either project be safe even if sales were at the low end of the anticipated range?

5. Firms U and L are identical in every respect except that the former is not levered, whereas the latter has $2 million in 14 percent debentures outstanding. Assume perfect markets and ignore taxes and bankruptcy costs. The current valuation of the two firms is as follows:

	Firm U	Firm L
Net operating income	$ 1,000,000	$1,000,000
Interest on debt	—	280,000
Earnings available to shareholders	$ 1,000,000	$ 720,000
Equity capitalization rate	.10	.12
Market value of stock	$10,000,000	$6,000,000
Market value of debt	—	2,000,000
Total market value of firm	$10,000,000	$8,000,000

An investor initially owns 10 percent of the unlevered firm.

(a) According to theory, can this valuation persist? Why or why not?

(b) Assuming that the investor wants to maintain the same proportionate ownership, outline the arbitrage process as put forth by Modigliani and Miller, and calculate the increase in return available to the investor.

6. A major bank has established a real estate investment trust (REIT) that issues trust units (which are essentially equivalent to ordinary shares) to investors, raises debt capital, and uses the proceeds to purchase mortgages. The REIT pays no corporate tax and distributes all of its net income in dividends to the investors.

Assume the REIT currently holds $20 million in mortgages yielding 13 percent. The company's capital structure consists of 500,000 trust units with a total book value of $5 million and $15 million of debt yielding 11 percent. The trust units have a market price of $12.50 per unit.

(a) What dividend yield do investors obtain on the trust units?

(b) Mrs. Sakamoto has $300,000 available to invest in mortgages, which currently yield 13 percent to maturity. She may also borrow at 11 percent, and her bank is prepared to lend her up to $900,000 if she invests the whole $1.2 million in mortgages. Mrs. Sakamoto is considering either purchasing units in the REIT or borrowing from the bank and purchasing mortgages herself. Based on the theory of capital structure, as developed by Modigliani and Miller, determine what Mrs. Sakamoto should do. Carefully explain your arguments and support them with numerical illustrations showing that your recommendations will maximize Mrs. Sakamoto's wealth.

(c) How would your answer to (b) change if Mrs. Sakamoto could only borrow from the bank at 13 percent?

(d) What other factors, if any, should Mrs. Sakamoto take into account in her decision?

7. Conglomerate Enterprises has grown rapidly by acquiring other firms. It is currently negotiating to take over Northern Manufacturing. Northern Manufacturing's capital structure consists of 20 percent debt and 80 percent equity, and the beta on its common stock has been estimated at 1.2. Northern's tax rate is 40 percent. The government T-bill rate is 14 percent, and Northern can borrow at this same rate. The expected return on the market is 20 percent. Conglomerate believes that Northern's financing mix is too conservative and plans to change its capital structure to 40 percent debt and 60 percent equity.

For simplicity, assume that any new shares can be sold at their prevailing market price, so that

$k_e = r_e.$

(a) What is Northern's beta and its cost of equity after the proposed change in capital structure?

(b) What is Northern's WACC both under the original and the proposed new capital structure?

(c) Plot Northern's beta, cost of equity, and WACC as a function of its debt-equity ratio, and briefly explain your findings. What assumptions are implied in your results?

Disappointing Results Mean No Wheat Pool Dividend for 2000

In Chapter 14, we saw how the Saskatchewan Wheat Pool co-operative began trading its shares on the TSE. Among the new responsibilities that accompanied this transition to a public company was the need for a dividend policy.

In 1997, 1998, and 1999, the Wheat Pool paid a dividend of 40 cents per share to holders of its Class B (publicly traded) shares. The dividends were declared each year at the end of the fiscal year in July and paid in September.

But in June 2000, the Pool declared its intention not to pay a dividend in light of disappointing financial results. It reported a loss of $44 million for the first three quarters of its fiscal year; during the same period the year before, it had a loss of $14.2 million. A 40-cent-per-share dividend in June 2000 would have represented a yield of over 9 percent on the stock's price, which closed June 21 at $4.35 a share. In 1997 and 1998, shares had closed on July 31 at $16.20 and $17.00 respectively.

The decision to go without a dividend in fiscal 2000 was taken in light of "significant challenges for agribusiness," the Pool's management stated, explaining that "intense competetion, consolidation, and deregulation in Western Canada have altered the dynamics of Prairie agriculture."

Said CEO Mayo Schmidt, "the Pool continues to have a solid balance sheet and the necessary resources to meet its debt obliga-

tions. However, we could not justify recommending a dividend until we see a return to consistent, improved earnings and a reduction in our debt levels."

Cash flow from operations during the third quarter was $800,000, comparied with $6.1 million a year earlier.

The Pool ended up posting a total loss for fiscal 1999-2000 of a whopping $90 million, including a fourth-quarter after-tax charge of $37.9 million stemming from the

Pool's decision to pull out of a port terminal development in Gdansk, Poland.

"Our strategic decisions have resulted in significant charges against this year's earnings," company CEO Mayo Schmidt said. "However, these issues are behind us now and we can turn our focus to managing our operations and improving profitability of our asset base." Schmidt pointed out that grain handling volumes had increased, from 7.95 million tonnes to 8.54 million tonnes, and that the Pool expects to reduce capital expenditures from $110 million last year to $60 million in the 2001 fiscal year. The Pool announced in March it was cutting 275 staff and accelerating the closure of several elevators made obsolete by new high-throughput grain handling facilities.

The Wheat Pool reviews its dividend policy annually, taking into account the company's cash flow, earnings, financial position, and other relevant factors.

chapter 17

Dividend Policy

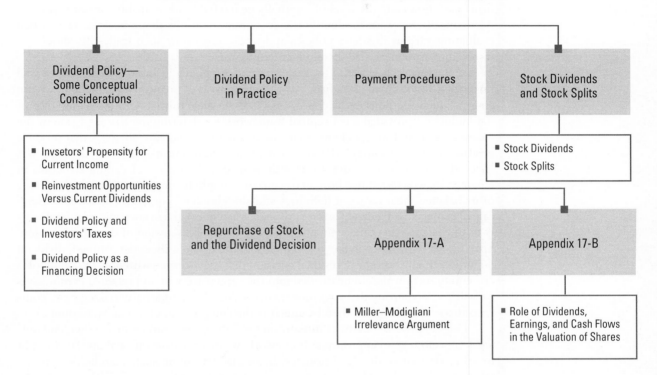

Learning Objectives

After studying this chapter, you should be able to:

1. *Discuss when a company should pay out dividends and why.*
2. *Explain how dividend policy may create value in its own right.*
3. *Define the terms ex-dividend date, date of record, and payment date, and demonstrate how they each play a role in share prices.*
4. *Describe stock splits, and compare them to stock dividends.*
5. *Understand how a company repurchases its own shares, and why and how this affects earnings per share (EPS) and the market price of shares.*

17.1 INTRODUCTION

Dividend policy is an important area of finance from both a practical and an academic perspective. Boards of directors pay considerable attention to dividend payouts since the decisions they make have an immediate affect on shareholders and also influence the firm's cash flows and the level of internally generated funds available for reinvestment. Academically, we want to identify the economic trade-offs that a business faces when evaluating various dividend policies and to establish how such trade-offs should be resolved so as to maximize shareholder wealth.

At the outset, it is useful to establish dividend policy in the context of the overall financial decisions made by a firm. As with other areas of financial management, we can consider such decisions in the context of a balance sheet format. Our discussion of capital budgeting provided a conceptual framework for determining the asset side of the balance sheet, and we concluded that a company should acquire all assets that produce positive net present values (NPVs). The management of a firm's long-term liabilities was covered in Chapters 13 and 14 as well as in our discussion of capital structure in Chapter 16, which outlined how an organization ought to apportion the right-hand side of its balance sheet between liabilities and shareholders' equity. Aside from working capital management (current assets and current liabilities), the major topic relating directly to the balance sheet that remains is a more detailed discussion of the equity section. Specifically, with other major components of the balance sheet determined, dividend policy essentially becomes a residual decision that is concerned with how the shareholders' equity section should be divided into the capital account and retained earnings. As we will see, a company that pays more generous dividends may have to issue more common shares and vice versa thereby affecting the composition of its equity accounts.

This chapter concentrates initially on the conceptual foundations of dividend policy. In developing an appropriate framework, we explore how rational investors ought to value alternative dividend policies. If we can determine such shareholder preferences, we should be able to establish, at least in a normative way, guidelines for optimal decisions in this area. Because investor preferences are reflected in share prices, the dividend policy that is most closely aligned with market preferences ought to maximize shareholder wealth.

After reviewing the conceptual foundations, we then consider various practical aspects that often influence the actual formulation of dividend policies by firms. We also review the relevant institutional setting and discuss alternative forms of dividend payments. Finally, we look to reconcile theory and practice.

In Appendix 17-A of this chapter, we present in simplified form an important model that has been proposed to deal with the issue of share valuation and dividend policy—namely, the theory developed by Miller and Modigliani.

Finally, Appendix 17-B confirms the relevance of dividends for share valuation. In contrasting dividends with earnings and cash flows, we demonstrate that investors should determine the value of a share by capitalizing its future stream of dividends.

DIVIDEND POLICY— SOME CONCEPTUAL CONSIDERATIONS

17.2

We noted in Chapter 6 that in valuing common shares, investors essentially should capitalize the stream of expected future dividends. Dividends are the only cash inflows that a shareholder is entitled to, and capital gains are the result of prospects for enhanced dividends sometime in the future. If, conceptually at least, the stream of future dividends is to be viewed as the prime determinant of share values, the question of how investors ought to value alternative dividend policies is of obvious importance. Specifically, we have to assess how a firm should decide on the proportion of earnings to be retained for reinvestment and, consequently, the proportion to be paid out in dividends.[1] The main purpose of this section is to clarify some basic issues at a conceptual level. How decisions on dividend policy are actually made in practice will be considered in the following section.

To clarify the issues that have a bearing on dividend policy, it may be useful if we place ourselves in the position of a shareholder with a controlling block of shares in a particular company. In that capacity, we would determine not only the dividend policy to be pursued, but we would also have complete information about the operations of the business, its investment opportunities, and prospective returns. This may help us to identify more closely with the well-informed and rational investor relevant to this discussion.

Assume that the firm's earnings for the current period are given and that a decision on the proportion to be paid out in dividends and the proportion to be retained for reinvestment has to be made. Several factors have a potential bearing on this issue. They include the following:

1. **The Shareholders' Current Consumption Needs:** To what extent do shareholders rely on dividend income to finance current consumption expenditures?
2. **The Shareholders' Own Reinvestment Opportunities:** If funds were to be paid out in dividends, what use could the shareholders make of such funds, and what rate of return could they obtain on outside investments?
3. **Tax Considerations:** How would shareholders be taxed on dividend payouts, and what are the taxes on capital gains that may occur if funds are retained for reinvestment in the business?
4. **The Firm's Investment Opportunities:** How would earnings retained in the business be invested, and what is the prospective return that can be earned on such new investments?

We briefly review each of these factors.

Investors' Propensity for Current Income

This point is not central to our discussion (any importance it may have basically stems from market imperfections), so we dispose of it first so as to concentrate on the main

---

[1] Throughout this chapter, we refer to the decision to reinvest or distribute "earnings" to shareholders. Technically, we should concern ourselves with all "internally generated funds" including capital cost allowance (CCA). We do this to simplify the discussion.

economic issues raised in points 2 to 4. Essentially, if shareholders are guided only by maximizing their wealth, dividend policy need not be influenced by their desire to use investment income in financing consumption expenditures because shareholders could always sell a fraction of their holdings to realize such income.

EXAMPLE

CREATING CURRENT INCOME

A shareholder holds 1,000 shares at a market price of $20 each. The company's earnings for the current year are $2 per share. These earnings could either be paid out in dividends or reinvested. If dividends are paid out, the share price will remain at $20. On the other hand, if these earnings were retained and reinvested, the market price of the shares would increase to $23 in anticipation of higher future earnings and dividends to be realized from the new investments. The shareholder requires investment income of $2,000 for the year to supplement other revenues. Rather than acquiring these funds through dividends ($2 dividends per share×1,000 shares=$2,000), the shareholder would be better off if earnings were reinvested and he sold 87 shares at the new price of $23 per share ($23×87 =$2,001). We have:

1. The firm pays a dividend of $2 per share, and the share price remains at $20.

   Shareholder's wealth position:

   Receipts from dividends:

$2 per share×1,000	$ 2,000
Value of shareholdings:	
1,000 shares at $20	20,000
Total wealth	$22,000

2. The firm pays no dividends, reinvests earnings, and the share price rises to $23.

   Shareholder's wealth position:

Value of shareholdings:	
$23 per share×913	$20,999
Cash from sale of shares:	
$23 per share×87	2,001
Total wealth	$23,000

As we saw in Chapter 1 and confirmed in the example above, the existence of efficient financial markets and the objective of maximizing share prices in such markets enables us to make financial decisions without regard to individual shareholder preferences. Thus, we conclude that a need for current income by shareholders probably should not be of major concern in formulating dividend policies, at least in widely held corporations. Rather, the company should concentrate on finding the dividend policy that maximizes shareholder wealth. Shareholders who desire current income can always sell some of their shares. Although brokerage costs and differential taxation of dividends and capital gains may have to be considered, the basic argument remains valid. For many investors, the limited exemption of capital gains from taxation may even favour this approach to supplementing income especially in light of the recent reduction in taxes on capital gains.[2] Because the issue of taxation is important and complex, it will be discussed separately.

We recognize that our argument may be of limited relevance for closely held or family enterprises in which transaction costs and non-economic objectives such as control or the desire for privacy may preclude a fractional sale of shares.

Reinvestment Opportunities Versus Current Dividends

An issue of greater importance is that of reinvestment opportunities both at the level of the firm and at the level of the individual investor. To simplify the exposition, we concentrate on one issue at a time and for the moment, ignore taxes that the investor may have to pay on dividends or capital gains. Under such circumstances, the firm should retain earnings for reinvestment whenever it can achieve yields exceeding those that a shareholder could get by reinvesting the same funds elsewhere at the same level of risk. Following such a policy will maximize shareholder wealth.

REINVESTMENT OPPORTUNITIES VERSUS CURRENT DIVIDENDS

EXAMPLE

For simplicity, we consider a company that is solely financed through common equity. It has 1,000 shares outstanding and has stable earnings of $1 per share. Historically, all earnings have been paid out in dividends and, given the firm's risk, shareholders demand an annual return of $r_e = 20\%$ on their investment. The enterprise now considers a new non-depreciable investment that would leave risk unchanged and require an initial cash outflow of $1,000. In order to fund this opportunity, the firm would have to withhold the current dividend. In return, earnings in subsequent years would increase by $300 per year indefinitely, which is an investment return of 30 percent. All subsequent earnings would again be paid out in dividends. The company faces the following two alternatives:

1. Continue dividend payments—no new investment:

   After payment of the current dividend of $1 per share, the firm's share should trade at $P_0 = D/r_e = 1/.2 = \$5$ per share. A shareholder's wealth is given by the current dividend plus the market price per share after the dividend has been paid so that:

   Shareholder's wealth $= D_o + P_o = 1 + 5 = \$6$ per share.

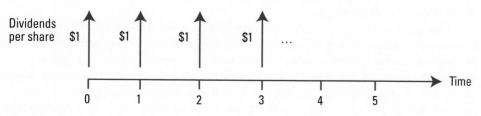

---

[2] In October 2000, revisions to the tax code provided for only one-half of capital gains to be taxable.

2. Withhold current dividend and undertake new investment:

That is, the current dividend is eliminated, but future dividends increase to $1.30 per share:

Shareholder's wealth $= P_0 = \dfrac{1.30}{.2} = \$6.50$ per share.

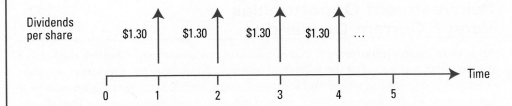

We see that the shareholder faces a trade-off between current dividends and capital gains. As a consequence of the increase in future dividend payments, the share price increases to $6.50. This more than compensates for the $1 loss in current dividends.

Note that the net present value (NPV) of the firm's investment is calculated as:

$$NPV = -1,000 + \frac{300}{.2} = \$500$$

or $0.50 per share. This is just the amount by which the wealth of a shareholder increases as a consequence of the new investment.

This example illustrates the important point that through appropriate reinvestment of current dividends, we can create capital gains that will occur in anticipation of enhanced future dividends. We saw in Chapter 10 that any investment with a positive NPV will enhance shareholder wealth. Our example confirms that any investment with a return that exceeds the market return required by shareholders should result in a share appreciation exceeding the value of current dividends foregone. Put another way, given equivalent risk, if a business can invest retained earnings to earn 30 percent and a shareholder can only reinvest the dividends that she receives at 20 percent, it is clear that it would be in the best interest of the shareholder not to draw dividends but rather to have the firm reinvest all earnings.

This leads to the following important conclusion for dividend policy: in deciding how to use earnings, a company should first look at its investment opportunities. As long as earnings can be reinvested at a rate of return that exceeds returns on opportunities with similar levels of risk available to shareholders, such investments should be undertaken. Any amount left after the firm runs out of promising investments should then be paid out in dividends. Conceptually, therefore, dividend policy becomes a residual decision that simply falls into place once a firm has determined its capital budget. Later in this chapter, the option of issuing additional securities to pay dividends is explored.

Dividend Policy and Investors' Taxes

Implied in our discussion so far has been the assumption that shareholders are indifferent between receiving dividends or realizing capital gains. However, investors strive to maximize *after-tax* returns. Insofar as differences in taxation may cause a systematic preference by shareholders for one form of investment income compared to another, our conclusion may need to be modified.[3] While we may be able to poll investor preferences for a closely held company in which the few shareholders and their tax brackets are known, this becomes impossible for widely held corporations with their constantly changing list of heterogeneous shareholders. Furthermore, given the complexities of tax legislation, it is difficult to ascertain whether a systematic general bias for dividends or capital gains exists in capital markets and, if it does, to determine its direction and magnitude. If, as seems likely, capital gains in aggregate receive a more favourable tax treatment than dividends, firms may reinvest earnings even if the yield is somewhat below r_e as postulated above. Companies may also repurchase their own shares. In both cases, this is so because investors are now willing to trade off a current dividend against a somewhat smaller capital gain. Problem 2 with Solution at the end of this chapter further illustrates the impact of tax differences between dividends and capital gains for an individual investor.

Paralleling Miller's point on the impact of individual taxes in the context of capital structure, it is worth noting that individual shareholders, in seeking to optimize their after-tax investment returns, are likely to buy shares in corporations with dividend policies that are compatible with their own tax-dictated preferences. For example, one may postulate that investors in low tax brackets as well as pension funds that are non-taxable will tend to hold shares in firms that pay out more generous dividends. On the other hand, investors subject to high marginal tax rates will seek out organizations pursuing strategies of high reinvestments for growth. Empirical studies have confirmed this process of self-selection whereby each firm tends to establish its own "clientele" of shareholders who are particularly attuned to its financial policies. If this is so, stability of dividend policy may become more important than fine-tuning the exact portion of earnings to be paid out. Any shift in policy would upset the existing shareholder base and, as long as all preferences are properly served by the market, there should be no abnormal gains from suddenly attempting to cater to a different shareholder group.

In summary, we see that because of the complexity of our tax system and the heterogeneity of individual investors, we face the same difficulties that precluded us from reaching precise and unequivocal conclusions on capital structure in Chapter 16.

Dividend Policy as a Financing Decision

A company can use its earnings to finance new investments or to pay dividends. If earnings are inadequate, additional funds can be raised through external financing. Capital cost allowance aside, the firm's total uses of funds for dividends and new investments

---

[3] For example, when the capital gains tax was introduced in Canada in 1972, Canadian corporations responded by significantly increasing their dividend payments. See N. Khoury and K. Smith, "Dividend Policy and the Capital Gains Tax in Canada," *Journal of Business Administration* (Spring 1977), pp. 19–37.

over any time period cannot exceed its sources of funds from earnings and external financing as depicted in the graph below:
Sources of funds

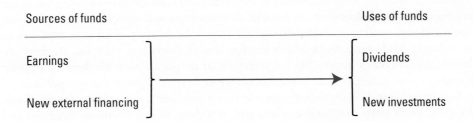

We argued that if a firm is to maximize shareholder wealth, it should accept all investments yielding positive net present values (NPVs) or returns in excess of its cost of capital. With the enterprise's investment budget thus determined, we see that dividend policy has immediate consequences for financing. If, for example, the firm wants to pay dividends in excess of earnings left over after all new investments have been funded, it will have to supplement its earnings through external financing.

DIVIDENDS AND EXTERNAL FINANCING

EXAMPLE

An all-equity company with 100,000 shares outstanding wants to maintain its historical dividend of $2 per share. Given current earnings of $300,000 and net new investment opportunities requiring cash outlays of $200,000, new external financing of $100,000 will have to be arranged. We have:

External financing = investments + dividends − earnings
$100,000 = $200,000   + $200,000 − $300,000

With net new investments and current earnings given, the amount of external financing becomes a direct function of dividend policy.

To illustrate the implications of such a view of dividend policy, let us assume that a firm finances itself solely through equity so that any external financing will be the result of issuing additional common shares. If we ignore taxes and expenses associated with the issuing of new shares, we can argue that the dividend policy pursued by the company does not matter. If dividends to be paid exceed earnings minus retentions for new investments, the firm can simply issue new shares to cover the deficit. Thus, dividend policy's only effect is to create a shift in the equity section of the business's balance sheet from retained earnings to the capital account. This conclusion was first proposed by Miller and Modigliani (their arguments are presented more formally in Appendix 17-A) and is intuitively reasonable: if nothing is lost through taxes and transaction costs, the firm can always pay dividends to shareholders and then ask them to reinvest these funds by buying new shares. Actually, many companies have introduced automatic reinvestment plans, which encourage shareholders to reinvest automatically all or at least a portion of any cash dividend they receive by buying additional shares.[4] The funds wind up where they started, namely in the hands of the firm, and all that has been accomplished is to circulate money from the company to shareholders and back again.

ISSUING SHARES TO FINANCE DIVIDEND PAYMENTS

EXAMPLE

Again, an all-equity firm has 100,000 shares outstanding. It has no productive assets and no earnings but just holds land with a market value of $10 million. Its shares are valued accordingly at 10,000,000/100,000=$100 per share. The firm decides to pay a dividend of $10 per share. In order to finance this dividend, 12,500 new shares are sold through a rights offering to existing shareholders, who can buy one new share at $80 each for every eight shares held. Consider a shareholder who holds eight shares and who exercises his rights: he will have received $80 in dividends ($10×8 shares) that he immediately reinvests to purchase one additional share.[5] He now owns nine shares, each of which should have a market value of 10,000,000/112,500=$88.89, and both his proportionate ownership of the firm and his total wealth remain unchanged. We have:

Shareholder's initial wealth	=8 shares×$100/share=$800
Shareholder's wealth after	=dividends−subscription price for new
dividend and rights offering	shares+value of shares
	=80−80+(9×88.89)
	=$800

In essence, the shareholder has financed his own dividend by providing the company with the cash that it required to make such a payment.

Needless to say, this appears to be an unproductive exercise. To pay dividends and to finance such payments by raising new funds externally becomes even less appealing if we consider taxes and transaction costs.

TAXES AND ISSUING COSTS

EXAMPLE

Pursuing the previous example, assume that the shareholder pays a net tax of 20 percent on dividends and that the corporation pays issuing expenses of $2 per share to implement the rights offering. We no longer have a senseless but harmless circulation of money from the company to its shareholders and back because the process now results in a draining of cash to pay taxes and expenses. The investor no longer has $80 in dividends to reinvest but only 80×(1−.2)=$64 net of taxes, and the corporation will have to sell each new share for $82. Hence, the investor has to pay 82−64=$18 out of his own pocket to close the circle, which is hardly an attractive proposition.

---

[4] There are presently more than 70 publicly traded Canadian companies that offer dividend reinvestment plans. A substantial portion of these offer shareholders a 5 percent discount on the purchase price of additional shares. Source: Stingy Investor website: http://www.stingyinvestor.com/SI/DRPs.html.

[5] In Chapter 19, in our discussion of rights offerings, we shall see that the wealth position of a shareholder is unaffected by his decision to exercise or to sell the rights, so that this assumption is not critical for our argument.

Clearly, it is not in the best interest of shareholders to maintain dividend payments when external financing is required to cover shortfalls in internally generated funds. Although the above argument was presented in the context of an all-equity-financed firm, it applies equally when new investments are funded through a mix of debt and equity. Assuming that the business has established the optimal capital structure it wants to maintain, any withdrawals of equity in the form of dividends have to be replaced with new equity financing.

In summary, the normative view on dividend policy, which is based on rational investors and efficient markets, stipulates that the primary determinant of share prices ought to be a firm's investment policy. Dividends become a residual to be paid out of whatever funds are left after all profitable investments have been financed.

17.3 DIVIDEND POLICY IN PRACTICE

Reviewing aggregate statistics on past dividend payments provides a reasonable indication of the overall dividend policies pursued by Canadian corporations. Approximately half of the firms that trade on the TSE pay dividends, while about three-quarters of those on NYSE do so. There is substantial evidence to show that the prevailing policy is one of stable or steadily increasing dividends per share. Wherever possible, unnecessary fluctuations and, in particular, any decreases in dividends, even temporary ones, are avoided. This is evident in the following report, which states that "Reducing or omitting dividends is not something companies, especially the blue chip corporations, do lightly." One analyst that is quoted in the following report goes on to say, "The big guys are so careful not to raise [their dividend] so they won't have to reduce it if they get into trouble. Their reputations are kind of on the line." The actual amounts paid out, however, are dependent not only on the level of dividends in proceeding periods but also on after-tax earnings.[6]

The **dividend payout ratio** is defined as the proportion of earnings that a firm pays out in dividends. Many firms appear to have a target payout ratio that they want to maintain over the long run. However, in order to achieve dividend stability in the face of fluctuating earnings, management usually hesitates to make changes in dividends. This produces drifts in the payout ratio.

---

[6] Early evidence regarding this issue, based on interviews with several large U.S. corporations, is found in the classic article by J. Lintner, "Distribution of Incomes of Corporations Among Dividends, Retained Earnings, and Taxes," *American Economic Review* (May 1956), pp. 97–113. Several subsequent studies have confirmed this matter. For example, see K. Dewenter and V. Warther, "Dividends, Asymmetric Information and Agency Conflicts: Evidence from a Comparison of Dividend Policies of Japanese and US Firms," *Journal of Finance* (June 1998), pp. 879–904.

■ *Finance in the News*

Firms Opt for Special Dividends

In 1997, 90 TSE-listed stocks paid extra dividends, up from 81 the year before and 33 in 1995. The reason, according to Royal Bank vice-president John Kellett, is conservative dividend policies. "They'd rather make special payments than lock into stone a higher quarterly payment. Reducing or omitting dividends is not something companies, especially the blue chip corporations, do lightly." As Tom Connolly, editor of a monthly newsletter, puts it, "The big guys are so careful not to raise [their dividend] so they won't have to reduce it if they get into trouble. Their reputations are kind of on the line." Steady dividends are attractive to many investors, especially retired ones.

In 1997, eight TSE stocks reduced their dividends, and another 11 failed to pay them at all. Most of them were small to mid-size firms. At the same time, half of the 1,700 TSE stocks paid dividends, and 121 of those increased their regular dividends. In January 1998, for example, 15 TSE listings raised their payouts.

Source: "Firms Opt for Special Dividends," by *Angela Barnes, Globe and Mail,* February 25, 1998, page B1. *Reprinted with permission.*

FLUCTUATING EARNINGS AND PAYOUT RATIOS

EXAMPLE

A company has a target payout ratio of 40 percent. In the face of fluctuating but generally increasing earnings, actual dividend payouts may appear as in the following table and graph.

Year	Earnings per share	Dividends per share	Actual payout ratio
1993	$5.00	$2.00	40%
1994	5.60	2.00	36
1995	6.00	2.50	42
1996	8.10	2.50	31
1997	6.50	2.50	38
1998	8.00	2.50	31
1999	8.25	3.30	40

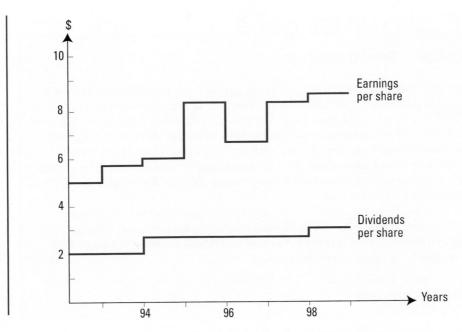

In this example, the lag is apparent in that after a sudden increase in earnings, it takes time for actual payout ratios to again reach the target. Such lags in payout ratios have been verified empirically. In addition, a survey of large U.S. firms listed on the NYSE found senior financial executives in strong agreement with the propositions that companies should:

(a) avoid making changes in their dividend rates that may soon have to be reversed

(b) strive to maintain an uninterrupted record of dividend payments

(c) have target payout ratios and periodically adjust the dividend payout toward the target

The first two statements echo the sentiments expressed in the above report regarding the dividend behaviour of TSE-listed companies. The survey also showed that there was strong agreement that dividend payout affects share prices.[7]

In this context, the separation of ownership and control and the principal–agent conflict view of the firm, as noted in Chapter 1, leads to an interesting theory.[8] Managers of firms with significant free cash flows may have a tendency to overinvest by accepting projects with negative net present values (NPVs).[9] Such projects may be appealing because, for example, they bring prestige, travel opportunities, or political connections. All else being equal, increasing dividends (thereby reducing free cash flows) will reduce the extent of such unattractive over investment and therefore, increase the market value of the firm. Any decrease in dividends has the opposite effect.

---

[7] H. Baker et al., "A Survey of Management Views on Dividend Policy," *Financial Management* (Autumn 1985), pp.78–83.

[8] The theory is strongly associated with the work of Michael Jensen. See M. Jensen, "Agency Costs of Free Cash Flow, Corporate Finance, and Takeover," *American Economic Review* (May 1986), pp. 323–9.

[9] The concept of free cash flows was discussed in Chapter 16.

Another frequently referenced ratio pertaining to a firm's dividend policy is the **dividend yield**, which was introduced in Chapter 3. It relates the dividend income received by shareholders to the price investors are willing to pay for the shares, and it represents the income component of a stock's return stated on a percentage basis. The dividend yield is typically calculated as the most recent 12-month dividend amount divided by the current market price. If the share price at the end of 1999 for the company in the example above had been $66.00, the corresponding dividend yield would have been $3.30/$66.00=5.0 percent.

Table 17.1 presents statistics on earnings, dividends, dividend yields, and dividend payout ratios for the TSE 300 Composite Index, with the earnings and dividends amounts adjusted to the value of the index. The figures illustrate the reluctance of firms to alter dividends, particularly if we look at the difficult years of 1991, 1992, and 1993. In each of these years, the dividend payout ratio exceeded 100 percent of earnings. This was because earnings declined dramatically in those years relative to previous years, dividend payments declined only modestly. Apparently, in the face of temporary adversity, most firms saw it as important not to jeopardize their dividends and instead allowed the aggregate dividend payout ratio to increase. The table also demonstrates that dividend payments over the past 14 years have been much more stable than after-tax earnings, ranging from a low of 91.67 to a high of 129.01 versus the range in earnings of 21.40 to 342.27.

TABLE 17.1

Prices, Earnings, Dividends, and Dividend Ratios (in Index Form) for the TSE 300 Composite Index, 1986–1999

Year	End-of-year index value (prices)	Earnings	Dividends	Dividend yield* (%)	Dividend payout
1986	3066.18	176.31	91.67	2.99	0.5199
1987	3160.05	220.67	97.32	3.08	0.4410
1988	3381.75	312.83	113.96	3.37	0.3643
1989	3969.79	268.41	129.01	3.25	0.4806
1990	3256.75	202.37	124.90	3.83	0.6172
1991	3512.36	76.63	111.93	3.19	1.4606
1992	3350.44	21.40	102.34	3.05	4.7822
1993	4321.43	34.68	97.81	2.26	2.8204
1994	4213.61	194.62	100.76	2.39	0.5177
1995	4713.54	342.27	107.44	2.28	0.3139
1996	5927.03	245.04	108.63	1.83	0.4433
1997	6699.44	293.05	110.27	1.65	0.3763
1998	6485.94	227.63	108.05	1.67	0.4747
1999	8413.75	210.18	110.46	1.31	0.5255

*Based on year-end prices.

Source: TSE Annual Review for the years 1986 to 1999.

We would expect there to be considerable variations in the dividend policies pursued by Canadian corporations. Table 17.2 confirms this variation as reflected in the average dividend payout ratios for several industries from 1980 to 1999. While the average payout ratio across all industry groups is 32.72 percent, the industry averages range from a low of 11.88 percent for resource companies to a high of 47.74 percent for the manufacturing segment.

TABLE 17.2

Average Canadian Dividend Payout Ratios (1980–1999)

Industry	Average payout ratio
All industries	0.3272
Financial services	0.3130
Retail & wholesale	0.4083
Resources	0.1188
Manufacturing	0.4774
Transportation & utility	0.4355

Source: Standard & Poor's Compustat database, September 11, 2000.

Even within the same industry, dividend policies differ, reflecting variations in operating performance, the need for funds, different ownership structures, or simply different management attitudes toward dividends. Table 17.3 reports the earnings, dividends, and payout ratios from 1990 to 1999 for two companies in the food distribution industry: Empire Company Limited and Loblaw Companies Limited. While the payout ratios for Empire swing widely from 0.08 to 16.00 due to fluctuating earnings levels, they remain in the range of 0.17 to 0.24 for Loblaws during the entire 10-year period. What is apparent from this table is the steady, slowly increasing trend in the actual level of dividends per share for both companies, which is maintained by Empire even in years of low (and negative) earnings.

TABLE 17.3

	Loblaw Companies Limited			Empire Company Limited*		
Year	Earnings per share	Dividends per share	Payout ratio	Earnings per share	Dividends per share	Payout ratio
1990	0.37	0.07	0.19	(0.17)	0.16	—
1991	0.39	0.08	0.21	0.01	0.16	16.00
1992	0.29	0.08	0.28	0.28	0.16	0.57
1993	0.36	0.08	0.22	0.52	0.18	0.35
1994	0.50	0.09	0.18	1.09	0.20	0.18
1995	0.60	0.12	0.20	0.93	0.20	0.22
1996	0.72	0.12	0.17	0.41	0.215	0.52

	Loblaw Companies Limited			Empire Company Limited*		
Year	Earnings per share	Dividends per share	Payout ratio	Earnings per share	Dividends per share	Payout ratio
1997	0.88	0.16	0.18	1.33	0.22	0.16
1998	1.06	0.20	0.19	2.33	0.2425	0.10
1999	1.37	0.24	0.18	3.55	0.2725	0.08

* Reported figures are for Empire's non-voting Class A shares.
Source: 1999 Annual Reports for Loblaw Companies Limited and Empire Company Limited.

Unexpected growth in earnings can also pose problems. Although management may wish to distribute some portion of such increased profits, the rise may be viewed as temporary, casting doubts on the firm's ability to sustain higher dividend payments. In such situations, a firm can declare **extra dividends**. By labelling a dividend "extra," management forestalls false expectations and loss of investor goodwill if in following periods such extras are not forthcoming. This practice is widespread in Canada, as discussed in the report earlier in the chapter.

As we have seen, management's behaviour in setting dividend policy can be described as cautious. It will increase dividends only when it is confident that the larger payments can be sustained, and it will decrease dividends only when absolutely necessary. Managerial reluctance is strongest when it comes to not paying dividends at all. Given the dividend clientele phenomenon noted earlier, such overall behaviour is understandable.

Interestingly, management's caution about dividends implies there is an information effect associated with changes in dividends. Management is generally perceived as having more complete knowledge than the market in general because of its access to inside information. With management's recognized preference for stable dividends, announcements of any changes in dividends are signals to the market, and share prices respond accordingly. For example, if earnings per share have fallen but dividends are maintained, the market may revise its expectations upward. The stable dividends indicate that insiders have more confidence in the firm's future prospects than current earnings levels might indicate, and, consequently, share prices will hold up better than if dividends were cut.

The extent to which such informational effects may be ascribed to dividend policy is subject to debate. On the one hand, one may downplay the issue, particularly in the well-developed capital markets of North America. Sophisticated investors, such as large financial institutions, certainly have access to a wealth of information that goes beyond the official announcements and financial statements issued by the corporations. Hence, there should be no need to look for "hidden information" in dividend announcements. On the other hand, it is difficult even for the most sophisticated outsider to assess the potential profitability of internal investments. Furthermore, again recalling our discussion in Chapter 1, management has considerable power to perpetuate its own decisions despite outside criticism. The need to provide a given dividend yield subjects management to the direct discipline of having to substantiate favourable returns on past investment decisions. Finally, if a sufficiently large number of investors and managers believe, rightly or wrongly, in the informational content of dividends, such a belief can become self-fulfilling and self-perpetuating. Managers will want and will be expected to avoid reductions in dividends if at all possible, and, consequently, any cut in dividends will be viewed as a sign of weakness. Despite the controversy over dividend signalling models, recent studies provide evidence that unexpected dividend changes signal information about firm performance to market participants.

Firms may have other reasons to keep their dividend policies consistent. Maintaining a stable dividend track record can enhance the attractiveness of common shares to potential investors. Institutional investors often require that a certain proportion of the equities they hold in their portfolio have a stable dividend history. For example, the Pension Benefits Standards Regulations used to require company dividend on earnings greater than 4 percent of its common share capital for four of the past five years, while the requirement was for all of the past five years for several provincial insurance acts. The purpose of these constraints is to maintain a relatively stable component in the equity portion of a portfolio as well as to provide dividend income. Foerster and Laroque provide Canadian evidence to support this assertion. They find that a stable dividend history is a valid predictor of the risk associated with an underlying stock, according to several traditional measures of risk.[10]

A number of other considerations may influence a company's dividend policy. These include:

1. Corporate Control
2. The Firm's Cash Position
3. Restrictions Imposed by Creditors
4. Restrictions on Foreign Transfers
5. Corporate Growth Potential

Corporate Control

When retained earnings prove inadequate for financing planned investments, management can either increase external financing or curtail dividend payments. If new common shares need to be issued, corporate control may become an important consideration, and controlling shareholders may opt to curtail dividends. The trade-offs, however, can be quite difficult. For instance, shareholders outside the controlling group may resent lower payouts and through their actions, encourage corporate raiders to challenge for control of the firm.

The Firm's Cash Position

Clearly, the availability of cash and the maintenance of corporate liquidity are important when deciding on dividend payouts. We reiterate in this context that although earnings

---

[10] Stephen Foerster and Stephanie Laroque, "History Lessons," *Canadian Investment Review* (Summer 1995), pp.21–25.

influence cash flows, the two are not the same. Furthermore, not all earnings may be available for distribution to common shareholders since sinking fund payments on debt and dividends on preferred shares have to be paid before any dividends can be declared on common shares. Cash budgeting and liquidity management will be discussed further in Chapter 22.

Restrictions to Protect Creditors

Trust deeds and other debt contracts often limit the size of dividends that can be paid by the debtor corporation. Restrictive covenants commonly aim at preserving the company's ability to service its debt and typically relate allowable dividend distributions to current earnings or cash flows or to the maintenance of appropriate levels of working capital.

There are also certain legal restrictions on dividend payments designed to protect creditors.[11] These restrictions seek to prevent unscrupulous management from distributing a firm's cash to shareholders prior to filing for bankruptcy, for example. Penalties for failure to comply can be levied against directors, and they may be held personally liable to creditors or shareholders.

Restrictions on Foreign Transfers

In an international environment, laws restricting the payment of dividends to foreigners may have to be recognized. Many countries with weak currencies exercise tight control over any outflow of funds that may influence their balance of payments unfavourably, and dividend payments abroad may be closely regulated. Such regulations, whether existing or anticipated, obviously become an important factor when evaluating foreign investments.

Corporate Growth Potential

In the previous section, we saw that a firm's dividend policy is interdependent with capital budgeting and financing decisions. Consequently, a firm may have to postpone profitable investments in order to maintain dividend stability. Faced with such a trade-off, it is clear that the firm's opportunities for growth will influence dividend policy even if not in such a complete way as our discussion in the previous section may have suggested. For example, we may expect dividend payout ratios to be lower for firms with unusual opportunities, while the reverse would be true in stagnant industries. Table 17.2 appears to be consistent with this conclusion.

---

[11] The question of legality is quite complex. In general, however, restrictions are aimed at preventing payments: 1. when the corporation is insolvent, 2. that will render the company insolvent, and 3. that will impair the firm's capital.

17.4 PAYMENT PROCEDURES

Dividends are payable if and when declared by the corporation's board of directors. A formal dividend declaration made at a directors' meeting specifies such particulars as: the type, amount, and form of the payment; the class of shares affected; and the dates of record and payment. Dividend distributions relate to a particular time period and are usually declared quarterly or semi-annually. The dividend may be labelled regular, extra, or liquidating, or it may be left unlabelled. Although dividends are usually paid in cash, alternatives include stock dividends (discussed in Section 17.5), property dividends, and scrip dividends. Property dividends involve distributions of assets other than cash, whereas scrip dividends entail a promissory note. Both forms of dividends are sufficiently rare as to not warrant further discussion. Once the declaration is made, shareholders are generally informed by publication of a notice in the financial pages of the press.

The corporation sets a date of record, and payment is made to shareholders appearing on the company's books as at the date of record. To allow for delays in cheque preparation and mailing, the date of record usually precedes the payment date by two or three weeks. Given the lag between a sale of shares and registration of new owners on the corporation's books, shares trade **ex dividends** two business days prior to the date of record, which is referred to as the **ex-dividend date**.[12] Shares are said to trade ex dividends when a purchaser is no longer entitled to the dividend just declared. Shareholder lists are often updated and maintained by separate institutions, notably trust companies. In performing this service, the trust company is said to act as the corporation's transfer agent. The treasurer or transfer agent will prepare and mail dividend cheques. A typical timeline including the declaration date, ex-dividend date, record date, and payment date is provided in Figure 17.1.

In the absence of taxes, we would expect the market price of a share to drop by the amount of the dividend when it goes ex dividends. While this is generally true, we have seen that investor taxes may affect the relative value that shareholders place on dividends as opposed to capital gains, and this can cause the drop in share price to differ from the dividend paid out. In addition, the drop in price that is caused by dividend payments is difficult to isolate because of many other factors simultaneously influencing share prices.

FIGURE 17.1

Dividend Payment Time Line

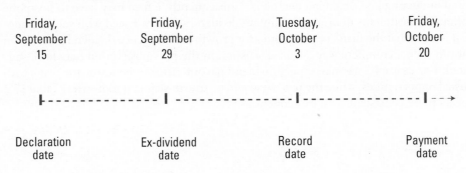

Friday, September 15	Friday, September 29	Tuesday, October 3	Friday, October 20
Declaration date	Ex-dividend date	Record date	Payment date

---

[12] Since the settlement date for common share trades is three business days after the purchase, this lag ensures that all owners of the shares on the record date would have settled their transactions.

STOCK DIVIDENDS AND STOCK SPLITS   17.5

Stock Dividends

Although most dividends are paid in cash, stock dividends are not uncommon. When such dividends are paid, the corporation distributes additional stock certificates to its shareholders on a *pro rata* basis. Therefore, there is no change in the proportionate ownership of any individual shareholder. The overall value of the firm should remain unchanged because the only effects that the payment of stock dividends have on a firm are the printing of new share certificates and an accounting transfer. From an accounting point of view, the disbursement simply involves transferring a portion of retained earnings to the capital account, leaving the aggregate net worth in the balance sheet unchanged. The amount transferred generally reflects the fair market value of the additional shares issued. It follows that, at least conceptually, shareholders receive nothing of value when stock dividends are declared and that each shareholder's wealth position should remain unaffected. More shares are outstanding, but each share should be worth less.

STOCK DIVIDENDS

EXAMPLE

Consider a firm that had the following shareholders' equity position before declaring a 5 percent stock dividend:

260,000 common shares without par value	$ 600,000
Retained earnings	5,000,000
	$5,600,000

With a 5 percent stock dividend, shareholders received one share for each 20 held so that a total of 260,000/20=13,000 new shares were issued. If the market value of each share was $12 at that time, 13,000×$12=$156,000 would be transferred from retained earnings to the capital account. This alters the shareholders' equity position to:

273,000 common shares without par value	$ 756,000
Retained earnings	4,844,000
	$5,600,000

As a consequence of the stock dividends, we would expect the market price of the shares to drop. If the price was $12 before the dividend, it should be 12/1.05=$11.43 after the dividend, leaving each shareholder's wealth position unaltered. For a shareholder who originally held 20 shares, we have:

Shareholder wealth before dividend=20×12=$240

Shareholder wealth after dividend=21×11.43=$240

Several side effects, however, may have to be recognized. When, following payment of a dividend, the corporation returns to its usual per share distribution, the stock dividend might have significance to those investors who value increased cash dividends. Since they now hold a greater number of shares, their total receipts from cash dividends increase. Investors may also ascribe an informational content to a stock dividend. For example, if a stock dividend is substituted for cash dividends, this may signal that the expected future productivity of earnings presently retained in the business will more than offset any dilution in earnings per share brought about by the increased number of shares outstanding. On the other hand, if shareholders are taxed on their stock dividend, they incur a real cost for such informational side effects, and it may become difficult to justify stock dividends economically. Since 1985, stock dividends in Canada have been taxed in the same way as cash dividends.

Stock Splits

Stock splits are similar to stock dividends in that, in both cases, additional share certificates are issued and distributed without cost to current shareholders. However, the motivation for issuing new shares is different. Stock dividends are issued as a so-called bonus to existing shareholders, and the number of new shares issued at one time is generally small compared to the total number of shares outstanding.[13] In contrast, the purpose of stock splits is to alter stock prices, moving them into a range that investors find more attractive.[14] This is illustrated in the report below, which refers to a recent announcement of a two-for-one stock split by Bombardier. The stated purpose of the split is "to make the company's stock more affordable to average investors." When a firm wants

■ *Finance in the News*

Bombardier Announces Stock Split, Dividend Increase

Transportation giant Bombardier Inc. says it will split its stock two-for-one and boost its quarterly dividends.

The aircraft and rail car maker said yesterday it will split its Class A and B shares after the company's annual meeting in June. The move, effective July 7, is meant to make the company's stock more affordable to average investors, Bombardier said.

The company also said it will boost its quarterly common share dividend to 6.75 cents a share from 5.5 cents.

Bombardier is enjoying one of the best periods in its history, with a fat order book and rapidly growing revenue from the sale of its business jets, regional aircraft, rail transportation equipment, and recreational products.

Source: "Bombardier Announces Stock Split, Dividend Increase," *Globe and Mail*, April 19, 2000, p.87. *Reprinted with permission.*

---

[13] The TSE views a distribution that exceeds 25 percent of outstanding shares as a stock split, whereas distributions falling below that figure are deemed to be stock dividends.

[14] Some empirical studies have shown that while stock splits are mainly aimed at restoring stock prices to a "normal range," there may also be a signalling motive—drawing attention to growing earnings and dividends. See J. Lakonishok and B. Lev, "Stock Splits and Stock Dividends: Why, Who, and When?" *Journal of Finance* (September 1987), pp. 913–32.

to reduce the price of its stock, it issues new share certificates in a number that is a multiple of the shares currently outstanding. With a two-for-one split, for example, each shareholder receives one additional share for every share currently held so that after the split, the number of shares outstanding has been doubled. As a consequence, the price of each outstanding share should roughly be cut in half. Conversely, a reverse split (or consolidation) reduces the number of shares outstanding, thereby increasing their market value.

Stock splits are common during periods of escalating share prices. Thus, after several years of rising share prices, 44 TSE-listed firms split their shares in 1985. This contrasts with only eight firms during the market slump of 1982.

Distinctions between stock dividends and stock splits also exist from an accounting point of view. For example, a two-for-one split doubles the number of shares outstanding, and when the shares have a par value, this figure is accordingly halved. With a stock dividend, the number of outstanding shares also increases, but the par value per share remains unaltered. In addition, unlike a stock dividend, the stock split requires no transfer between the balance sheet's retained earnings and capital accounts.

STOCK SPLITS

EXAMPLE

Consider a two-for-one split with the following entries for the equity section of the balance sheet before the split:

50,000 common shares, par value of $10 each	$ 500,000
Contributed surplus	300,000
Retained earnings	1,000,000
	$1,800,000

After the split, there would be:

100,000 common shares, par value of $5 each	$ 500,000
Contributed surplus	300,000
Retained earnings	1,000,000
	$1,800,000

In contrast, with a hypothetical 100 percent stock dividend if the shares were trading at $10 per share, there would be:

100,000 common shares, par value of $10 each	$1,000,000
Contributed surplus	300,000
Retained earnings	500,000
	$1,800,000

Conceptually, a stock split like a stock dividend is of no value to investors because both the value of the company and each shareholder's proportional ownership of it should be unaffected. Nevertheless, like stock dividends, splits may have informational content. They may suggest that the previous growth and prosperity that moved share prices above the preferred price range is expected to continue, thus prompting investors to bid the price higher. This view is supported by empirical research that found that when a split is anticipated or announced, the market price of the shares usually increases and sometimes remains higher than would otherwise be expected. This appears to be especially true when above-average dividend increases followed the split, as is the case for the Bombardier stock split described in the above report, which was accompanied by a dividend increase. Hence, reinforcement of growth expectations and prospects of a more attractive trading price may combine to increase value.

17.6 REPURCHASE OF STOCK AND THE DIVIDEND DECISION

An interesting alternative to the payment of cash dividends is a firm's repurchase of its own common shares. Repurchasing of shares is a well-established practice in the United States, but in some other countries, it is illegal because of fears about price manipulation. In Canada, it has been allowed since 1970.

A corporation with cash that it wants to distribute to shareholders can either pay dividends or buy back some of its own shares. Such share purchases can take place in the market or, after filing an appropriate notice, the company can offer to buy back a certain proportion of outstanding shares on a *pro rata* basis from existing shareholders. In any event, the company reduces the number of shares currently outstanding. As a consequence, earnings per share will increase, and the business's share price should appreciate. Potentially, under a repurchase program, shareholders trade off cash dividends against capital gains.

EXAMPLE

SHARE REPURCHASE

A firm with 1 million shares outstanding has total annual earnings of $1 million. The shares trade at a constant price–earnings ratio of 10. If the company distributes all of its earnings, it will mean a dividend of $1 per share. Alternatively, earnings can be used to repurchase and cancel shares. The consequences of such a repurchase program are tabulated below. With the number of outstanding shares reduced, earnings per share increase, and the market price of the remaining shares should appreciate. For those shareholders that retain their holdings, the choice is between receiving cash dividends or holding shares that increase in value.

Share Repurchase Program	Year 1	Year 2	Year 3
Earnings after taxes	$1,000,000	$1,000,000	$1,000,000
Shares outstanding	1,000,000	900,000	810,000
Earnings per share	$1.00	$1.11	$1.23

	Year 1	Year 2	Year 3
Price–earnings ratio (assumed constant)	10	10	10
Market price of shares	$10.00	$11.10	$12.35
Shares repurchased (total earnings/share price)	100,000	90,000	81,000

Clearly, the repurchase program does not alter the total value of the company nor total shareholder wealth before investor taxes.[15] That is, the number of shares outstanding times the share price should remain constant (with minor discrepancies in the example due to rounding).

Share repurchases may offer tax advantages to some shareholders because capital gains are substituted for dividends. However, such repurchases may pose other difficulties for management. Shares are purchased from current owners who are less well informed about the organization's current operations and future prospects than management engaged in buying on behalf of the remaining owners. For example, management may have good reasons to believe that in the light of future prospects, shares are currently undervalued, and it may use insider information to repurchase shares at bargain prices. Legislation governing the repurchase of shares seeks to limit such abuses and conflicts of interest. Protection is also afforded creditors who may not want to see cash, which could be used to service debt obligations, channelled into share repurchase programs. The effectiveness of the statutory provisions has, however, been questioned.

From a signalling perspective, the discussion above implies that management will be inclined to repurchase shares when it believes the shares are undervalued. This sends a positive signal to the market, and empirical evidence confirms that markets view such announcements positively, bidding up the price of the firm's shares (on average). This is consistent with the general proposition we established in Chapters 15 and 16, in which we saw that markets view new share issues as a signal that management believes the shares are overvalued and react accordingly.

It should also be noted that stock repurchases have also been undertaken for a variety of reasons that have little to do with dividend policy. Examples include changing the firm's capital structure (in which case, the dividend payment is financed with new debt) or attempts to block unfriendly takeovers by outsiders and to strengthen management's control. Recent studies indicate that like large special dividend payments, many share repurchases are actually part of a target company's defensive strategy in anticipation of a control contest.

While such repurchases have helped maintain the independence of a significant proportion of target firms, the resulting withdrawal of a potential hostile bidder generally results in a loss for target shareholders. Thus, it would appear that as a defensive strategy, decreasing cash balances through repurchases is for management's benefit and

[15] This simplified example assumes all else remains equal, as it seldom does.

[16] D. Denis, "Defensive Changes in Corporate Payout Policy: Share Repurchases and Special Dividends," *Journal of Finance* (December 1990), pp. 1433–56.

It has also been argued that management can use share repurchases to affect cosmetic improvements in financial data such as earnings per share. Because of the resulting reduction in the number of shares outstanding, a share repurchase program could be used to maintain reported earnings per share even if the company's operating performance is deteriorating. Unsophisticated shareholders may be lulled into a false impression of stability. Although the validity of these arguments depends on the efficiency of the markets in which the shares are traded, it is interesting to note that repurchased shares are frequently those selling at depressed prices because of inferior operating results and prospects.

17.7 SUMMARY

1. Dividends ought to be paid only if the firm has surplus cash that cannot be reinvested to yield a positive net present value or, equivalently, whenever the firm's returns on reinvestments fall below the returns that shareholders could achieve on their own in the marketplace. In practice, most firms have a strong commitment to maintain stable or steadily increasing dividends, and dividend payments often appear to take precedence over other uses of funds, including new investments.

2. Other practical considerations that influence dividend policy include the firm's cash and liquidity position, restrictions to protect creditors, and restrictions on foreign transfers.

3. Stock dividends are an alternative to cash dividends. Stock dividends involve issuance of additional share certificates to existing shareholders.

4. A stock split should not affect the wealth position of shareholders as it leaves the proportional ownership of each shareholder and the value of the firm unchanged.

5. The repurchase by a firm of its own shares may be an alternative to paying cash dividends. With the number of outstanding shares reduced, earnings per share will increase and the market price of the remaining shares should appreciate.

6. Miller and Modigliani developed the theoretical framework for analyzing dividend policy. The relevance of dividend policy for share prices stems from market imperfections such as transaction costs, taxes, and limited investor information.

APPENDIX 17-A

THE MILLER–MODIGLIANI IRRELEVANCE ARGUMENT

In this section, we formalize our view of dividends as a financing decision. One of the difficulties in any discussion of corporate finance is that the main areas of financial decision-making are interdependent. We saw that the payment of dividends represents a use of funds, and a change in the amount paid in dividends must be matched by a corresponding change in some other source or use of funds. Dividend policy may be regarded as more or less important for valuation depending on which other source or use is assumed to change. For example, an increase in dividend payments matched by a reduction in the size of the investment budget could have quite different implications than if it were matched by an increase in the amount of new external financing.

We made a strong argument for leaving the firm's investment decisions unchanged since any investment with a positive net present value should increase shareholder wealth. This is why dividend policy becomes a financing decision. With given earnings and investments, the external financing required becomes a direct function of dividend payments:

new external financing=dividends+new investments−earnings

In one of the most widely referred-to articles on this subject, Miller and Modigliani have shown that in the absence of transaction costs and taxes, this view of dividends leads to the conclusion that dividend policy is irrelevant and does not affect shareholder wealth.[17] Although we cannot develop all aspects of their complex arguments, it is easy to provide a simplified illustration of the basic reasoning. We use the following notation:

P =price per share just before dividend is paid

D =additional dividend per share

n_1 =number of shares outstanding before external financing takes place

V =total value of the firm, where $V=n_1$

n_2 =number of new shares that have to be issued to finance dividend payment

P_1 =price per share at which new financing takes place

At a particular time, a company decides to increase its dividend beyond residual earnings. Given that the investment budget remains unchanged, this requires subsequent outside financing. For simplicity we assume an all-equity-financed firm, so that only new common shares are issued. The additional dividend per share (D) requires total funding of n_1D, and we have:

External funding required=cash needed for dividend payment

$$n_2P_1 =n_1D \tag{17.A1}$$

The total value of the company is unaffected by this transaction because its operations and cash position remain unaltered. However, the price per share decreases because as a consequence of the financing, the company now has more shares outstanding. We have:

Original share price:
$$P=\frac{V}{n_1}$$

New share price:
$$P_1=\frac{V}{n_1+n_2}$$

---

[17] M. Miller and F. Modigliani, "Dividend Policy, Growth, and the Valuation of Shares," *Journal of Business* (October 1961), pp. 411–33.

Shareholder's wealth $=P$
position before dividend

Shareholder's wealth $=$ dividend $+$ new share price
position after dividend $=D+P_1$

Inserting $D=\dfrac{n_2}{n_1} P_1$ from Equation 17.1 and $P_1=V/(n_1+n_2)$, we obtain:

$$
\begin{aligned}
D+P_1 &= \frac{n_2}{n_1} P_1 + P_1 \\
&= P_1 \frac{(n_2+n_1)}{n_1} \\
&= \frac{V}{(n_1+n_2)} \times \frac{(n_2+n_1)}{n_1} \\
&= \frac{V}{n_1} \\
&= P
\end{aligned}
$$

We see that the shareholder's wealth position is unaffected by the dividend payment. As a consequence of the required share issue, the market price per share drops by just the amount of the dividend received, with $P-P_1=D$.

EXAMPLE

DIVIDEND IRRELEVANCE

A company has n_1 1,000 shares outstanding that trade at a price of $P=\$10$ per share. It contemplates paying a dividend of $D=\$1$ per share to be financed through a subsequent sale of new common shares. We have:

$n_2 P_1 = n_1 D = \$1,000$

and

$$
P_1 = \frac{V}{n_1+n_2} = \frac{1,000 \times 10}{1,000+n_2}
$$

Through simple substitution, we calculate a new share price of $P_1=\$9$/share and $n_2 \approx 111$ new shares. We confirm that each original shareholder who received a $1 dividend is faced with a corresponding drop in share price so that her wealth position remains unaffected.

In previous sections, we discussed how various market imperfections may dictate modifications to this conceptual framework. Specifically, factors that need to be considered include issuing and underwriting expenses on new security issues, taxes paid on dividends and capital gains, and possible informational effects of dividends. Although it is not possible to readily assess how these and other factors and their interactions affect share prices as a function of dividend policy, at least we have been able to show that the major reasons for concern over dividends as a practical policy issue are such market imperfections.

APPENDIX 17-B

THE ROLE OF DIVIDENDS, EARNINGS, AND CASH FLOWS IN THE VALUATION OF SHARES

The dividend discount model (DDM) argues that the price at which shares trade in financial markets should be the capitalized value of future dividend payments because dividends are the only cash flows that shareholders are entitled to. In practice, however, investment analysts often appear to ascribe primary importance to a firm's earnings per share (EPS) rather than to current dividend payouts. In the context of capital budgeting, we stressed that cash flows are the primary determinant of economic value. Figure 17-B.1 illustrates the relationship between these variables. To avoid possible confusion or misunderstanding, it may be useful to briefly review the relationship between a firm's

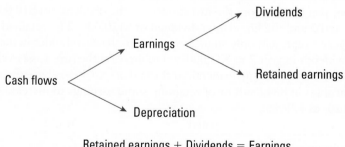

FIGURE 17-B.1

Relationships Between Cash Flows, Earnings, and Dividends

dividends, earnings, and cash flows and to explain why dividends may be viewed as the primary determinant of share prices.

Dividends Versus Earnings

We start with a numerical example that illustrates the significance of dividends versus earnings.

EXAMPLE

DIVIDENDS VERSUS RETAINED EARNINGS

At the beginning of year 1, we form a corporation by investing $100,000. Since the assets do not depreciate, no depreciation is charged. After-tax earnings per year are 20 percent of the amount invested, or $20,000 for the first year. At the end of the first year, $10,000 are paid out in dividends with $10,000 retained for reinvestment giving a net asset value of $110,000 for the second year. Earnings for the second year are 20%×110,000=$22,000, all of which are paid out in dividends. At the end of the second year, the firm is liquidated, and the assets are sold for $110,000, which are paid out as a liquidating dividend. Figure 17-B.2 summarizes the example as outlined.

FIGURE 17-B.2

Earnings Versus Dividends as a Basis for Valuing Common Shares

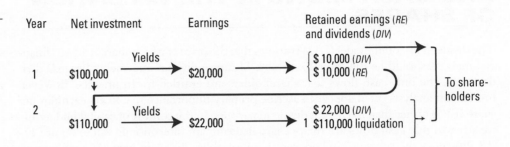

Assume that you are the sole shareholder evaluating this investment. It is clear that the only returns that you receive from the investment are the dividends of $10,000 and $22,000 in years 1 and 2 and the liquidating dividend of $110,000. The retained earnings of $10,000 in year 1 represent only an indirect value to the shareholder in that they serve to increase dividends in year 2 to $22,000 and to increase the firm's asset value by $10,000 as reflected in the liquidating dividend. At the end of year 1, you have the choice of paying out all earnings in dividends or of retaining some earnings to increase future dividends with returns as follows:

	Year 1	Year 2
No retentions, all earnings paid out in dividends	$20,000	$20,000+$100,000
Retention of $10,000 as outlined in example	$10,000	$22,000+$110,000

In order to increase future dividends, you, the shareholder, forego earlier dividends, which are reinvested instead. To consider these retained earnings, a return to shareholders in addition to dividends as outlined clearly would imply double counting.

Generalizing from this example, we see that the only value of retained earnings to shareholders lies in the fact that they are reinvested to increase future dividends. Ultimately, the only returns a shareholder receives are dividend payments. Retained earnings may provide an indication as to the likely growth rate of future dividends and therefore, may be of indirect relevance in valuing a firm's shares. If, however, an investor capitalizes a projected earnings stream, serious double counting may take place resulting in an overstatement of expected returns.

Dividends Versus Cash Flows

If cash flows were to form the basis for share valuation, we would need to include not only retained earnings alongside dividends but also depreciation. In this context, we view depreciation as an economic concept that measures the portion of an asset that wears out in a particular operating period. If funds set aside for depreciation are used to restore the asset to its original value, it is easy to demonstrate that depreciation cannot rightly be considered a return to shareholders.

DEPRECIATION AND DIVIDENDS

EXAMPLE

Consider again a company that was established with an original investment of $100,000. Ten percent of the asset base wears out each year. After-tax cash flows from operations are 20 percent of the amount invested, or $20,000 per year. Of these, $10,000 are set aside each year as depreciation to restore the asset base to the original $100,000. The remaining earnings of $10,000 are paid out in dividends. After 10 years, the firm is liquidated for $100,000, which corresponds to the book value of the assets. Thus, in return for the original investment of $100,000, shareholders receive $10,000 each year in the form of dividends and a return of their capital through a liquidating dividend at the end of year 10.

It should be obvious from the above example that the amounts set aside for depreciation to replace assets can hardly be viewed as direct returns to shareholders. Their only benefit lies in the fact that by replacing worn-out assets, the future earning power of the business is protected, which again is reflected in future dividends.

In Chapter 10, we advocated the use of cash flows as the basis for capital budgeting evaluations. Having just discarded use of the firm's cash flows as a basis for share valuations by investors may prompt the question as to how these two positions can be reconciled. In fact, there is no conflict, and basing the valuation of shares on the stream of future dividends is equivalent to advocating the evaluation of investments on the basis of net cash flows. Investors face a cash outflow when they purchase shares and in return receive future cash inflows in the form of dividends. What we have established above is that only those cash flows that accrue directly to the investors are relevant, whereas cash flows generated but also consumed by the company are not. To make the analogy with capital budgeting: when we derive the net cash flows on which a firm should base capital expenditure decisions, we do not include amounts that need to be plowed back to protect or generate a project's future cash flows as forecasted. If, as in the above example, funds from depreciation are required to maintain the asset base, such funds will not appear in the net cash flows for the project. The term net cash flows as used for capital budgeting includes only amounts available for use at the discretion of the owners after all the funding requirements of the projects have been met.

We conclude that any components of cash flows (depreciation or retained earnings) that remain within the company do so to protect and enhance future dividend payments to shareholders. Therefore, it is this stream of future dividends that we should look at when deriving the amount a shareholder ought to be willing to pay for a firm's shares.

Note: All *asterisked* Questions and Problems relate to material contained in the appendices to the chapter.

QUESTIONS AND PROBLEMS

Questions for Discussion

1. In practice, earnings per share (EPS) seem to be a more widely used indicator of share values than dividends per share. Discuss the reasons why this might be so. What are the limitations of EPS as an indicator in assessing the value of shares?

2. Some managers are unwilling to have dividends curtail free cash flows because such payouts to shareholders reduce the resources under their control. If a firm with corresponding management views and few investment opportunities available to them were to increase its dividend level, how might this affect its stock price and why? Are there ways to reduce the effects of such principal–agent conflicts?

3. Why may there be a direct trade-off between current dividend payments and capital gains? Illustrate your answer with a numerical example.

4. Many companies that pay regular dividends periodically raise new funds by issuing additional common shares. Is this reasonable, and why do they do this? What are the alternatives?

5. Is it sensible for a firm to have debt outstanding and at the same time, to pay dividends, or would it be better off using any available funds to reduce its indebtedness? Is it sensible for a firm to incur additional debt in order to finance dividend payments?

6. Why do companies issue stock dividends? As a shareholder, what would your reaction be if a firm substituted a stock dividend for cash dividends that were normally paid?

7. If you were on the board of directors of a firm and had to vote on dividend policy, what would be some of the main considerations that would have a bearing on your decision? What information would you try to gather before arriving at a decision?

8. Stock splits are used to alter the price range within which a company's shares trade. How would you determine what is a good trading range for a firm's shares? What factors would you consider to be relevant?

9. If you were the majority shareholder of a business and through electing directors could strongly influence its dividend policy, would stability of dividends be something you would value and try to implement? Discuss.

10. We have argued that in the absence of transaction costs and taxes, dividend policy is irrelevant and should not affect shareholder wealth. At the same time, we have shown that share prices should be determined by the present value of future dividend payments. Carefully explain how you can reconcile these positions which, at first glance, may appear to be contradictory.

11. Assets such as gold or objects of art are frequently held for investment purposes, but since they do not yield dividends, how do you explain their market value? How does your answer relate to the arguments presented in this chapter?

12. The following reasons have been given as to why a company may want to repurchase its own shares:

(a) Repurchase represents the best investment available.

(b) It repurchases shares to alter its capital structure.

(c) It repurchases shares in order to have stock available for general corporate purposes such as future acquisitions, stock options, and the like.

(d) Shares are repurchased to substitute capital gains for dividends since this may minimize taxes on investment income to be paid by shareholders.

(e) Share repurchases may improve the firm's financial performance indicators such as EPS. This may have a positive impact on share prices and increase shareholder wealth.

(f) Share repurchases by the company create demand for its shares and provides price support. At the same time, it "signals" to investors that management believes the shares are a good investment. Based on management's superior knowledge of the firm, this may result in an appreciation of share prices.

(g) Share repurchases represent a useful defensive strategy against potential hostile takeover attempts.

Briefly discuss the merits of each of these reasons. Which ones do you think are valid justifications for initiating a share repurchase program?

PROBLEMS WITH SOLUTIONS

Problem 1

A company has 100,000 shares outstanding. After-tax earnings have been constant at $3 per share with all earnings paid out in dividends at the end of each year. The yield that shareholders require is 12 percent.

(a) Compute the current market price of the shares.

(b) The firm considers retaining earnings for the current year to finance new investments. In subsequent periods, all earnings will again be paid out in dividends. Compute the new market price per share if the new investments promise an after-tax return of 10, 12, or 15 percent. For simplicity, assume that the investments generate a constant annuity for the indefinite future. Do the results derived depend on this assumption?

(c) Graphically portray the share price as a function of the yield provided by the investments.

(d) Is it reasonable for the firm to claim that it will always find enough good investment opportunities yielding at least 15 percent and thus, it will never pay dividends?

Solution 1

(a) The market price of the shares should be the present value of an infinite annuity of $3 discounted at the shareholders' required yield of 12 percent, or:

$$\text{Share price} = \frac{D}{r_e} = \frac{3}{.12} = \$25$$

(b) If the new investments are undertaken, no dividend would be received by investors until next year. However, future dividends would be larger. A return of 10, 12, or 15 percent on the current $3 foregone would result in future dividends of $3.30, $3.36, or $3.45, starting at the end of year 2. The new investments should be undertaken if the present value of the new annuity exceeds the $25 computed under (a).

Assuming a 10 percent return, the present value of a regular infinite annuity of $3.30 is 3.30/.12=$27.50. However, this amount must be discounted for one additional year since returns from the new investments do not start until year 2, so that:

$$\text{Share price} = \left[\left(\frac{3.30}{.12}\right)\left(\frac{1}{(1+.12)}\right)\right] = 27.50 \times .893 = \$24.56$$

Calculations for 12 and 15 percent returns yield:

$$\text{at 12\%: Share price} = \frac{3.36}{.12} \times .893 = \$25.00$$

$$\text{at 15\%: Share price} = \frac{3.45}{.12} \times .893 = \$25.67$$

Given a 12 percent return on the new investments, shareholders are indifferent between receiving a dividend this year or receiving increased dividends from next year onward. At 15 percent, they prefer the new investments, whereas at 10 percent, the new investments should not be undertaken.

These conclusions do not depend on the assumption that the return from the new investments accrues as a perpetual annuity. For example, for the 12-percent-return case, assume that the $3 foregone and invested at the end of year 1 results in a one-time extra return of 3(1+.12)=$3.36 at the end of the following year. Thus, we have:

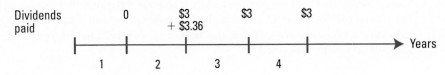

$$\text{Share price} = \frac{3.36}{(1+.12)^2} + \frac{25}{(1+.12)} = \$25$$

where the second term of the equation is the capitalized value of the regular $3 annual dividend paid from year 2 on.

We conclude that as long as investments yield a return that exceeds the firm's costs of capital, such investments should be undertaken because this should increase share values. We note that Problem 2 and Solution 2 in Chapter 6 deals essentially with the same issue and, in the context of the dividend growth model, derived the same conclusions in a more general way. It may be useful to review that problem at this time.

(c)

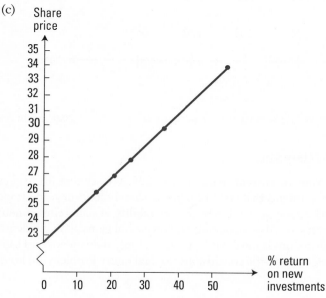

(d) If investments that are characteristic for the type of business the company is in typically provide a return of 12 percent as indicated by the rate of return that shareholders require, it is not reasonable to believe that the firm can grow forever at a substantially higher rate. Sooner or later, it would take over the entire industry. No part of a system can grow consistently at a rate that is higher than the aggregate growth rate of the system, and no part of the economy can grow forever at a rate that is higher than the overall economic growth rate. Abnormally high growth rates have to be viewed as temporary phenomena.

Problem 2

We pursue Problem 1 to analyse the effects of taxation. Assume that shareholders now pay a net tax of 25 percent on dividends received. The market continues to capitalize future dividends at 12 percent, which means that shareholders require an after-tax return of $(1-.25)12 = 9\%$. Compute the share price if the firm pays out all earnings in dividends. Also compute the share price if it retains the current dividend of $3 per share for reinvestment, with such investments yielding a return of 12 percent after corporate taxes.

Solution 2

If the company pays out all earnings in dividends, we have:

$$\text{Share price} = \frac{3}{.12} = \frac{3(1-.25)}{.09} = \$25$$

If the firm retains the current dividend for investments yielding 12 percent, dividends from year 2 on increase to $3.36, which after tax becomes $(1-.25)3.36=\$2.52$. We have:

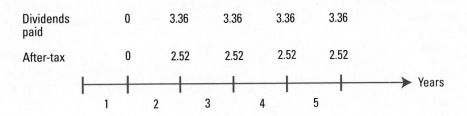

| Dividends paid | 0 | 3.36 | 3.36 | 3.36 | 3.36 |
| After-tax | 0 | 2.52 | 2.52 | 2.52 | 2.52 |

To provide an expected after-tax return of 9 percent at the end of year 1, shares would trade at:

Share price at year end $=2.52/.09=\$28$

providing a $3 capital gain over the current share price of $25. We see that if earnings are reinvested in marginal investments that yield 12 percent, shareholders in year 1 trade off a $3 dividend against a $3 capital gain. Clearly, the desirability of such reinvestment depends on the relative tax rates levied on dividends and on capital gains, with dividends preferred if the tax rate on dividends is lower and vice versa. Only if dividends and capital gains are taxed at the same rates do the conclusions reached under Problem l(b) hold.

Problem 3

National Profit Company had the following shareholders equity section before declaring a 5 percent stock dividend:

Shareholders' Equity

Authorized:	500,000 common shares without par value	
Outstanding:	200,000 common shares	$2,000,000
Retained earnings		600,000
		$2,600,000

(a) Show the change in the shareholders' equity section after the 5 percent stock dividend given that the firm's shares are currently trading at $15 per share.

(b) If an investor holds 100 shares of National Profit Company, what should the total value of those holdings be before and after the stock dividend?

(c) If the company continues to pay its earlier $2 per share cash dividend after the stock dividend, what is the incremental cash dividend received by the investor under (b)?

Solution 3

(a) *Shareholders' Equity*

Authorized:	500,000 common shares without par value	
Outstanding:	210,000 common shares	$2,150,000
Retained earnings		450,000
		$2,600,000

     The split does not affect the number of shares authorized. The number of shares outstanding increases by 5 percent. The value increases by the number of new shares issued times the current market value ($15×10,000=$150,000). The $150,000 increase in the value of shares issued is transferred out of retained earnings.

(b) After the stock dividend, the share price should drop in response to the increasing number of shares outstanding, where 105 shares after the stock dividend are worth as much as 100 shares before the stock dividend. We have:

$$\text{Share price after stock dividend} = 15 \times \frac{100}{105} = \$14.29$$

Value of holdings before stock dividend$=100\times15$ $=\$1,500$

Value of holdings after stock dividend $=105\times14.29=\$1,500$

(c) The shareholder's dividends increase by 5 percent. If the shareholder originally held 100 shares, his dividend income increases by $10, from 2×100=$200 to 2×105=$210.

ADDITIONAL PROBLEMS*

1. A firm's 500,000 common shares have a market value of $36 per share. All earnings have been paid out in dividends, which have been constant at $3.60 per year. The company considers retaining the next two years' dividends to finance an expansion that would yield a perpetual after-tax return of $450,000 per year, beginning in year three. How would this affect the share price, assuming all subsequent earnings are again paid out in dividends? What is the minimum yield the investment would have to provide in order to maintain the present share price of $36?

2. Atlantic Resources had the following shareholders' equity section in its balance sheet before a two-for-one stock split:

Shareholders' Equity

Authorized:	400,000 common shares with a par value of $12	
Outstanding:	250,000 common shares	$3,000,000
Contributed surplus		600,000
Retained earnings		200,000
		$3,800,000

(a) Show the change in the equity section after the two-for-one split.

(b) What should be the market value of Atlantic shares after the split if they were previously selling at $30 a share?

3. The share price of Morris Sports Ltd., a small but growing sporting goods company, has escalated rapidly. It has recently risen to $40, and management thinks this is too high for such a small company. Assume that Morris could meet this problem through either a two-for-one stock split or by declaring a 100 percent stock dividend.

The present equity section of Morris' balance sheet appears as follows:

Shareholders' Equity

10,000 common shares without par value	$100,000
Retained earnings	465,000
	$565,000

Show what the effects of the two-for-one stock split and of the stock dividend would be on the firm's balance sheet.

4. In 1997, Burns Ltd. adopted a policy of buying back its own outstanding common shares instead of paying cash dividends. Earnings after taxes for the four years 1997–2000 stayed at a constant $8 million and were used exclusively for the repurchase program.

(a) Assuming there were 32 million shares outstanding at the beginning of 1997 and that shares have traded at a stable price–earnings ratio of 16 since then, calculate earnings per share, the market price per share, and the number of shares repurchased for the four years 1997 through 2000.

(b) Determine the preference of a shareholder who owns 2,100 shares of Burns Ltd. from 1997 to the end of 2000 for either cash dividends or share repurchases. The shareholder's combined provincial and federal marginal tax rate is 38 percent with her federal tax being 29 percent. The shareholder has exhausted any tax-free amounts that may be available on dividend or capital gains income so that any investment income that she receives is taxable. Assume the shareholder is eligible to apply the Dividend Tax Credit (as discussed in Appendix I—The Tax Environment) to dividends received, and that 50 percent of capital gains are taxable. Ignore the time value of money and assume that earnings are either fully paid out in dividends or used for share repurchases.

5. A company currently has 1 million common shares outstanding and no debt. If it does not invest in any new projects, it expects to generate residual earnings of $10 million per year forever, which can be distributed as dividends. However, it has the opportunity to invest next year's profits in new machinery that will increase residual earnings by $1.5 million each year after that. Shareholders require a return of 10 percent on shares of this company given its risk.

(a) Without a new investment, what should be the share price of the firm?

(b) If the firm decides to make the investment, what will be its new stock price? Should it make the investment?

(c) What is the company's weighted average cost of capital? Use this to calculate the net present value of buying the new machinery? How does the net present value of the project relate to your answers to (a) and (b)?

6. A company has no productive assets and generates no earnings. Its sole asset consists of $1 million worth of real estate. The firm is 100 percent equity financed and currently has 100,000 shares outstanding. It does not currently pay dividends. However, management is considering paying a special one-time dividend of $1 per share. This would have to be financed via a new share issue (assume no issue costs).

(a) Calculate the new price per share if the business goes ahead with the dividend. What would be the new total wealth of a shareholder who held one share?

(b) What would be the new total wealth of a shareholder who held one share if dividends are taxed at a rate of 25 percent?

(c) Given (a) and (b), what can you say about the effect of dividend tax rates on the dividend policy of firms?

7. A business has earnings of $10 million per year. It has 1.5 million shares outstanding, which trade at a price-earnings multiple of 12. Up until now, the company has always paid out all of its earnings as dividends. It is now considering skipping the dividend due at the end of this year and instead using earnings to repurchase stock.

(a) What is the total market value of the company?

(b) If the same price-earnings multiple is applied to the firm, what will be the new price per share? What will be the total market value of the company?

(c) Assume that when the repurchase is announced, the market interprets this as a signal that the firm's shares are undervalued. Therefore, the firm's price–earnings multiple moves to 14. What will be the new price per share, and what will be the total market value of the company?

8. A business has 450,000 shares outstanding. The after-tax earnings of the firm have been constant at $1.50 per share, with all earnings paid out as dividends. Shareholders require a before-tax return of 15 percent. The personal tax rate on investment income (dividends and capital gains) is 20 percent. The corporate tax rate is 30 percent:

(a) What is the current share price of the company?

(b) If the firm announces that it will retain next year's dividend and invest it in projects returning 15 percent before corporate tax, what will be the price per share?

(c) If the company announces that it will retain next year's dividend and invest it in projects returning 20 percent before corporate tax, what will be the price per share?

(d) What return would the business expect to earn on its retained earnings in order for its share price to remain unchanged after announcing the new investments?

9. Jhana Corporation is a newly formed business financed solely through common shares with $3 million invested in assets. Assets depreciate at a rate of 15 percent per year, and the firm wants to maintain its asset base. After-tax cash flows amount to 20 percent of assets for each of the next four years. Plans call for $100,000 of earnings to be reinvested next year and $200,000 in each of the following three years, at which point Jhana will be liquidated and the proceeds distributed to

shareholders. At liquidation, the market value of the firm's assets will equal their book value. The company has 200,000 shares outstanding. Shareholders require an 8 percent annual rate of return.

(a) What is the current selling price for a share of Jhana?

(b) What would a share of Jhana sell for if all earnings were reinvested in the firm for the next four years?

BCE Inc.
Case Part 6

BCE has identified a number of potential investments that can be made in the near future*. The finance department has analysed the projected cash flows from each project and determined the internal rate of return for each. They are presented below:

Project	Investment Required	Internal Rate of Return
update some aging equipment	$100 million	9%
expand production in several factories	$250 million	5%
expand workforce in one division to meet increased demand	$50 million	25%
purchase computerized inventory tracking system	$25 million	4%
expand customer service department for corporate clients	$15 million	3%
build new call centre to provide retail customer service	$30 million	12%
buy a small firm with cutting edge technology	$400 million	7%

BCE must decide which of these projects to take on. In order to make this decision, it must determine an appropriate required return. It is estimated that the risk in each of the projects is the same as for BCE as a whole, therefore BCE's weighted average cost of capital is the appropriate required return. You have been assigned the task of determining the cost of capital.

Some information which may prove useful:

• BCE has a total of 68 million preferred shares outstanding (for simplicity, assume that there is only one issue of preferred shares, i.e., assume all BCE preferred shares are indentical for this case).

---

*The projects listed in this Case are fictitious, and do not represent actual projects that BCE may or may not have considered.

1. Look at the information on BCE's debt in question #2 of the BCE case at the end of Part 3. Based on that question calculate the total market value of BCE debt and the average cost of debt for BCE. Assume that BCE's tax rate is 35 percent.

2. Based on the information given above and in the financial statements in Appendix II, estimate the total market value of preferred shares and the cost of preferred shares for BCE.

3. In order to estimate the cost of capital for BCE, you need an estimate of the cost of common equity. To begin, you consider using the dividend growth model. In order to implement this you first need to estimate the future growth rate in dividends. You have the following information:

	1999	1998	1997	1996	1995
Earnings per common (after extra-ordinary items)	$8.35	7.07	(2.53)	1.70	1.12
Dividends per common share	$1.36	1.36	1.36	1.36	1.36

Source: BCE Annual Report, 1999

(a) What are the average annual growth rates in earnings per share and in dividends over this period? Why would BCE adopt this type of dividend policy?

(b) Do you think that either of the growth rates from (a) represent realistic estimates of the long term stable growth rate in dividends?

4. After some consideration, you decide to estimate the cost of common equity using the capital asset pricing model.

(a) Use the table of returns given in the case at the end of section 3 to estimate BCE's beta. Use a risk free rate of 5 percent and an expected return on the stock market of 12 percent to estimate the cost of internally generated funds for BCE. If issue costs would be $0.50 per share for new common shares, what would be the cost of new common equity?

(b) Note from the financial statements that BCE has a large amount of cash and cash equivalents on hand. At what total level of investment would the cost of new common equity be relevant? What benefits might there be to BCE in keeping this cash on hand rather than paying it out as a special dividend?

5. Based on your answers above (and using CAPM as your estimate of the cost of equity), calculate the weighted average cost of capital for BCE, both with and without issue costs for common shares. Which of the projects listed should BCE take on?

6. Assuming that the capital structure currently used by BCE is optimal, if they changed their capital structure (perhaps issuing more shares and then repaying debt) dramatically would they accept more or fewer of the projects listed above? Make some general comments on this in terms of the role which firms' optimal capital structures play in the overall economy.

Derivative Securities and Financial Risk

This part of the text begins with an introduction to options in Chapter 18, which describes the various forms that options take, and discusses their relationship to the underlying asset. An overview of the valuation of such derivative securities is also provided. In Chapter 19, we turn our attention to options that are written in conjunction with long-term financing. Specifically, we review rights, warrants, and convertible securities. Chapter 20 provides an introduction to futures markets and forward contracts and is written from the perspective of a corporate financial officer. Finally, in Chapter 21, the material is pulled together by illustrating the role that derivatives and, more generally, financial engineering can play in managing risk.

Options Allow Firms to "Manage the Managers"

A sked what one word or concept best represents Newcastle Capital Management, Robert Rafos, Executive Vice President for Client Services and Marketing, doesn't hesitate. "Innovation," he replies.

He would know; Mr. Rafos was one of three founders of Newcastle, a Canadian investment management and software development firm that now has 32 employees and manages about $8 billion of assets. Since 1989, the company, which is wholly owned by its employees, has provided portfolio management services based on innovative, often complex investment strategies, using its own sophisticated software, to a range of institutional clients that include universities, governments, and major corporations.

One of these innovative strategies is a "fund of hedge funds" that use a complex investment approach involving options, explains Mr. Rafos. Newcastle was the first retail financial services company to offer this unique instrument, in which a number of specialized portfolio managers are themselves managed "as if they were assets in a fund."

Mr. Rafos elaborates: "These underlying managers who are part of the fund of funds are all experts in some particular area. They tend to work in particularly inefficient areas of the market, and have specialized expertise and sophisticated models. This allows them to capture small returns on the difference in price between two options."

Thus, the Newcastle "fund of funds" managers act as arbitrageurs in the options market. "We choose market-neutral managers with an arbitrage strategy," confirms Mr. Rafos. "Most of them used to work at the trading desks of large U.S. banks, but eventually decided they would be better off using their expertise to help themselves."

Options

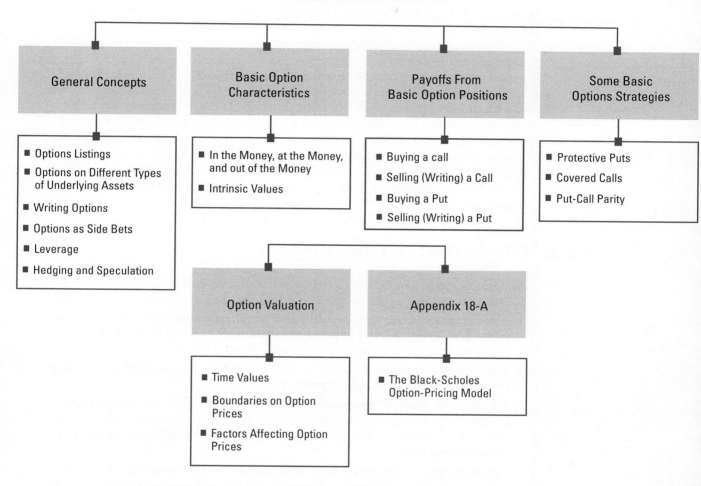

Learning Objectives

After studying this chapter, you should be able to:

1. *Explain the difference between a call option and a put option.*
2. *Identify four advantages of options.*
3. *Describe how options can be used to hedge a portfolio position.*
4. *Describe the factors that affect option prices.*
5. *Discuss the five aspects of the Black–Scholes option-pricing model.*

18.1 INTRODUCTION

Derivative securities are so called because they derive their value from the value of some underlying asset such as common shares or bonds. **Options** are contracts that grant the holder the right to purchase or sell a particular asset (typically a security) at a given price on or before a specified date. Holding the option entails no obligations. Since an option's value is contingent on, and derives from, the value of the asset this right applies to, options are also called **contingent claims** and are a type of derivative security. Options are bought and sold in financial markets.

Various types of options and related financial instruments have emerged as key tools that financial managers use to control their firm's risk exposure. At the same time, options have become very popular with investors, offering them the opportunity to engineer many more creative trade-offs between risk and return than is possible with stocks and bonds. In this chapter, we begin by examining standard options. In the next chapter, we consider options that firms sell along with their own securities in the context of long-term financing. In Chapter 21, we return to options in the more general context of how, through financial engineering, financial managers can control the risk inherent in a firm's various cash flows.

18.2 GENERAL CONCEPTS

We begin this section by defining some terminology and notation.

An option normally contains the following elements:

1. The right to either purchase or sell a given security. Options that provide the right to purchase are termed **call options**; **put options** grant the right to sell. The security that is the object of the option is called the underlying asset.

2. A specified price at which the option can be exercised. This is called the **striking price**, **exercise price**, or **subscription price**.

3. A limited time frame. The **expiration date** is the date at which an unexercised option becomes void. Options can be exercised either on the expiration date only or at any time before expiration. The former are called **European options**; the latter are **American options**.[1]

Although options may appear to be rather exotic tools for financial specialists, they are in fact a part of everyday life for most consumers. Simple financial arrangements such as rain checks at a store or insurance are actually options.

---

[1] This has nothing to do with geography. The nomenclature is purely historical. "American" options can be found in Europe and "European" options can be found in the United States. The equity options that trade on Canadian exchanges are generally American options, while index options are generally European.

RAIN CHECKS

A supermarket has a sale on frozen turkeys but is temporarily out of stock. You are given a rain check entitling you to return at any time during the next month to buy a turkey at the sale price. You have an option to buy an asset (the turkey) at a pre-arranged price any time between now and one month from now. This is an example of an American call option.

Although this may seem like a trivial matter, hardly worth the trouble of going through complex financial calculations, it does illustrate the basic concept of a call option. A corporate manager with a call option to buy a million barrels of oil at a specified price over the next month faces the same fundamental situation.

Next, we illustrate a put option.

CAR INSURANCE

You buy a new car for $50,000 and have it insured for $40,000. If you totally wreck the car, you have the right to sell the wreckage to your insurance company for $40,000. This is an example of a put option.

These two illustrations show that calls and puts can be thought of as general options to buy or sell almost any kind of asset. For simplicity, we shall focus our attention on options to buy or sell shares in companies—stock options.

ROYAL BANK CALL OPTIONS

An investor buys a call option that gives her the right to buy 100 shares of Royal Bank common stock for $90 per share any time before January 19 of next year. Suppose Royal Bank is trading at $95.25 in the stock market, and suppose the option costs $10.65 per share, or $1,065. This is a call option rather than a put because the investor is obtaining a right to buy rather than to sell. The underlying asset for this call option is 100 shares of Royal Bank common stock. The exercise price (striking price) of this option is $90 per share or $9,000. The expiration date or maturity of the option is January 19 of next year. The value of the underlying asset is $95.25 per share, or $9,525 for 100 shares. The price of the option is $10.65 per share, or $1,065. In this case, standard practice is to quote an option price of $10.65 since options are routinely for round lots of 100 shares.

Similar to common shares, options trade on organized exchanges or in the over-the-counter market. In Canada, exchange-traded options have been traded exclusively on the Montreal Exchange (which is the Canadian Derivatives Exchange™) since March 2000 as a result of the restructuring of Canadian financial markets, which was discussed in Chapter 2. As of that date, the Montreal Exchange is the whole owner of the Canadian Derivatives Clearing Corporation (CDCC), which acts as a clearing house for option trading and enforces standardized structures for Canadian options. For example, all stock options that expire in a given month do so on the third Friday of that month. For stocks priced above $35, options can have striking prices only at multiples of $5. For lower-priced stocks, option-striking prices can be multiples of $2.50 or even of $1.00. Option contracts are written for specific amounts of the underlying asset (e.g., 100 shares of common stock). Finally, the underlying asset may be shares of stock, foreign currencies, commodities, bonds, or portfolios of stocks. Table 18.1 shows the trading volume for exchange-traded options in Canada between 1996 and 1999. This table shows that equity option trading accounted for approximately 90 percent of total exchange-traded option volume during 1999.

TABLE 18.1

CDCC Optoin Volumes

Options Product Group	1996		1997		1998		1999	
	Millions	Percent	Millions	Percent	Millions	Percent	Millions	Percent
Equity	3.263	85.64	4.061	83.32	4.709	83.35	5.137	89.91
Index	0.305	8.01	0.495	10.16	0.541	9.62	0.290	5.08
Gov't bonds	0.030	0.79	0.023	0.48	0.019	0.33	0.009	0.16
Leaps	0.135	3.53	0.138	2.83	0.135	2.40	0.108	1.88
Metals	0.001	0.03	0.000	0.01	—	—	—	—
Options on futures	0.076	1.99	0.156	3.20	0.214	3.80	0.169	2.96
Totals	3.810	100.00	4.874	100.00	5.616	100.00	5.713	100.00

Source: Canadian Derivatives Clearing Corporation (CDCC) 1999 Annual Report.

A significant problem with the Canadian options markets is thin trading. As a result, many investors take their option trades to U.S. markets, which deal with much larger trading volumes. For example, the largest options exchange in the United States (and the world) is the Chicago Board Options Exchange (CBOE). The volume of trading in all options on this exchange for the 1999 fiscal year was 221.3 million contracts—almost 40 times the volume of all CDCC trades during that year.

The other major U.S. option exchanges include: the American, the Philadelphia, the Pacific, and the New York. Currently, the CBOE and the American Exchange are the most important U.S. markets and control roughly 75 percent of all trading in U.S. options. For the year ended June 30, 1999, the CBOE accounted for 50.1 percent of total U.S. option trading, 42.6 percent of U.S. equity option trading, and 90.7 percent of U.S. equity index option trading. Over the same period, the American Exchange accounted for 24.5 percent of all option trading, 28.4 percent of equity option trading, and only 4.7 percent of equity index option trading.[2] ▲

---

[2] Source: Chicago Board Options Exchange 1999 Annual Report at the following website location: http://www.cboe.com/exchange/annrpt2.htm.

Options Listings

Table 18.2 shows a typical options listing from a financial newspaper. In this case, data from the *Globe and Mail Report on Business* for options on the stock of the Royal Bank of Canada are shown. Note the name of the underlying stock in the upper-left-hand corner. Reading across, the value of Royal Bank stock when the market closed on September 19, 2000 was $95.25 and the total volume of trading of options of any sort on Royal Bank stock that day was 2,297 contracts. The total number of options of all kinds on Royal Bank that have been written and not yet exercised (the open interest) was 18,000 contracts.

This table lists prices for options expiring in October 2000 (Oct 00), November 2000 (Nov 00), January 2001 (Jan 01), April 2001 (Apr 01), January 2002 (Jan 02), and January 2003 (Jan 03).[3] Recall that stock options always expire on the third Friday of the month. For instance, the line beginning Jan 01 $90 contains information about options maturing on January 19, 2001 (the third Friday in January) and having a $90 striking price. Since there is no "p" after the striking price, these are call options; the options with a p after them are put options. The bid price being quoted as markets closed on September 19 for a call option to buy 100 shares of Royal Bank stock at $90 was $910 ($9.10 ×100). The ask price being quoted was $950 ($9.50×100). The last price at which a trade actually occurred (trades need not occur simply because bid and ask prices are quoted) was $1,065 ($10.65×100). The total volume of trade on September 19 in $90 January 2001 calls on Royal Bank stock was 34 contracts, while the open interest for these options was 577 contracts.

Options on Different Types of Underlying Assets

Note that options are available on a wide variety of different underlying assets. Equity options or stock options, the main focus of this chapter, have the common or preferred stock of traded companies as their underlying assets. "Commodity options" give their holders the right to buy or sell traded commodities such as oil, gold, soybean meal, and wheat at pre-arranged striking prices. If their business involves buying or selling such commodities, managers can use commodity options to reduce risk. "Foreign currency options" give their owners the right to buy or sell various international currencies at fixed striking prices. Again, these options are useful for reducing a company's risk exposure due to swings in exchange rates. "Interest rate options" let their owners buy or sell bonds at pre-arranged prices, and index options let their owners buy into the portfolios that make up various market indices such as the S&P/TSE 60 Index. The following report, features in *Finance in the News*, provides a list of the most actively traded options in Canada in August 2000, of which options on the shares of Nortel Networks were the most actively traded by a wide margin. While 23 of the top 25 are equity options, two of the top four include options on the S&P 60 Index (an index option) and on three-month Bankers Acceptances (an interest rate option).

Since commodity options, foreign currency options, interest rate options, and index options may often be **futures options** (giving their owners the right to buy or sell futures contracts—i.e., rights to buy or sell the underlying asset at some point in the future rather than immediately), we defer discussion of these until Chapter 20.

---

[3] The January 2001 and January 2002 options in the listing are referred to as long-term options or LEAPS, which is short for Long-Term Equity Anticipation Securities (LEAPS is a registered trademark of the Chicago Board Options Exchange). These are long-term options with maturities greater than one year and ranging to two years and beyond.

TABLE 18.2

Canadian Equity Options on Montreal Exchange

Stock Royal Bank		Close $95.25			Total Vol 2297	Tot Op Int 18000
	Series	Bid	Ask	Last	Vol	Op Int
Oct 00	$65.00	30.45	30.85	29.20	20	12
	$75.00	20.50	20.90	22.55	40	211
	$85.00	10.75	11.15	12.40	520	1755
	$85.00 p	0.30	0.55	0.55	5	132
	$90.00	6.50	6.90	7.35	27	1861
	$95.00	3.25	3.50	4.20	552	760
	$95.00 p	2.70	2.95	3.30	5	5
	$100.0	1.55	1.65	1.80	142	134
Nov 00	$100.0	2.50	2.75	2.85	755	760
Jan 01	$55.00	40.60	41.00	41.60	5	45
	$60.00	35.65	36.05	36.15	2	190
	$65.00	30.70	31.10	29.85	10	75
	$75.00	21.10	21.50	21.90	20	230
	$75.00 p	0.35	0.60	0.45	5	56
	$85.00	12.75	13.15	12.10	1	578
	$85.00 p	1.85	2.10	2.25	3	123
	$90.00	9.10	9.50	10.65	34	577
	$95.00	6.20	6.60	6.90	49	4973
	$95.00 p	5.35	5.75	5.10	7	35
	$100.0	4.05	4.30	5.00	24	1306
	$100.0 p	8.05	8.45	7.05	30	30
April 01	$80.00	17.55	17.95	18.30	3	108
	$85.00 p	2.70	2.95	2.50	1	10
	$100.0	5.50	5.90	6.00	7	50
Jan 02	$55.00	42.00	42.65	41.00	1	30
	$75.00	25.40	26.05	25.00	15	46
Jan 03	$75.00 p	4.00	4.65	3.90	3	4
	$80.00 p	5.50	6.16	5.85	4	14
	$100.00	16.55	17.20	16.25	7	7

Source: "Canadian Equity Options on Montreal Exchange," *Globe and Mail Report on Business*, September 20, 2000, p. B30. Reprinted with permission.

■ Finance in the News

On the Grid

Most-Traded Options in August 2000

An option on a financial instrument is the right to buy or sell the security at a specific price by a given date. Canadian options now trade on the Montreal Exchange. Not surprisingly, options on Nortel dominate the market. Here are the top 25 options by value traded in August 2000, which represent 86 percent of August's trading. A contract is an option on 100 shares. Open interest is the number of contracts available for trade.

	Open interest	No. of contracts	Trans-actions	($million) value
Nortel Networks*	91.0	93.7	11.6	$76.9
JDS Canada	6.5	13.9	3.2	18.5
S&P 60 index	19.3	4.1	0.3	15.2
3-month Bankers Acc.	50.5	17.8	0.4	8.6
Research in Motion	4.2	4.6	1.7	7.5
Celestica	8.7	8.8	0.9	7.2
BCE	19.8	15.3	2.9	7.1
CIBC	31.2	19.9	0.9	4.7
Alcan	23.8	19.5	0.9	4.6
Toronto-Dominion	24.8	17.7	1.7	4.4
Bombardier B	43.3	13.6	3.7	3.5
Bank of Montreal	12.2	6.1	1.1	3.2
Royal Bank	16.2	7.7	0.9	2.9
C-MAC	2.8	2.8	0.6	2.7
Ballard Power	2.6	3.6	0.7	2.5
Mitel	8.7	8.1	1.5	2.4
Seagram	6.2	5.1	0.5	2.3
Descartes Systems	2.2	4.2	1.7	2.3
Global Thermo.	5.7	5.4	1.1	2.0
Inco	12.2	11.5	1.3	1.8
S&P/TSE 60 units	6.4	6.9	0.4	1.7
Certicom	1.3	3.0	0.4	1.5
BCI	2.4	2.1	0.4	1.5
BCE Emergis	5.3	2.3	1.2	1.5
Bank of Nova Scotia	19.3	7.9	1.0	1.4

Source: Toronto Stock Exchange Review, August 2000. *Alexandra Eadie,* "Most Traded Options in August 2000," *Globe and Mail*, p. B21, September 20, 2000. *Reprinted with permission.*

Writing Options

In general, the options that investors can buy in options markets are written by other investors. In the case of the call option on Royal Bank in the example above, the investor who wrote the call undertakes to provide the investor who buys it with 100 shares of Royal Bank common stock for $90 per share any time until next January 19. If the owner of the option or any subsequent investor she sells it to exercises the option prior to its expiration, the writer must fulfill his obligation to sell the Royal Bank stock at the striking price. For example, if the option were exercised immediately, the writer would have to sell 100 shares of the Royal Bank (now worth $9,525) to the option holder for $9,000, thereby incurring a loss of $525. This means that his net profit from writing the option would be $540 (the $1,065 he got for originally writing the option minus his $525 loss when it was exercised).

The writer is, of course, hoping that the price of the Royal Bank will not remain above $90 so that the option will never be exercised, and he can simply keep the $1,065 he received for writing the option in the first place. In fact, he will make a net profit as long as the price of the stock does not rise above $100.65 per share (the striking price of $90 plus the option price $10.65).[4]

Most traded options are written by one investor and bought by another. However, some options, including rights and warrants as well as the options attached to convertible securities, are written by the company, the shares of which are the underlying asset. We shall deal with general options first. In the next chapter, we will turn to rights, warrants, and convertibles.

Options as Side Bets

Although options have value, the writing of an option does not create new economic wealth in the form of additional goods or services. Rather, it represents a potential transfer of value, and what the buyer gains, the seller loses, and vice versa. Thus, the writing of an option can be termed a "zero sum" game, and in that sense, options are similar to bets. The motivation for writing options stems essentially from different expectations by buyers and sellers about the future.

EXAMPLE

PAYOFFS TO OPTION BUYERS AND SELLERS

Suppose that I sell you an option to buy one share of Speculative Enterprises at any time during the next year at an exercise price of $E = \$25$, while the current market price of the shares is $S = \$20$. The option sells for $2. I do not own the shares but plan to purchase them in the market if you decide to exercise the option. Assume that at year end, the share price has increased to $35, and you exercise the option. Our wealth position as a consequence of writing the option has changed as follows:

Seller of option:

+initial option price+exercise price−market price of share

=2+25−35= −$8

---

[4] Actually, the price could rise slightly higher than this before the writer's gains are totally eliminated because the $1,065 earns interest while in the writer's possession.

Purchaser of option:

-initial option price-exercise price+market price of share

$= -2 - 25 + 35 = +\$8$

Notice that the loss to the seller equals the gain to the buyer.

Leverage

Part of the popularity of options among investors' stems from the very high returns they can provide as bets. In the example above, a \$2 investment provided an \$8 payoff—a 400 percent return even though the share price increased only from \$25 to \$35—40 percent. Thus, call options let investors magnify their returns on upward movements in stock prices much as buying on margin does. Put options, in contrast, let an investor magnify the returns a short sale would generate when a stock's price declines. Thus, it is common to say that options create "leverage" for investors. In addition, for the typical investor, it is easier to buy puts or calls than to set up margined or short positions.

It is important to note that with options, there may also be significant downside magnification to be considered. In the example above, you would lose your initial \$2 investment (a 100 percent loss) if the share price did not exceed \$25 (the striking price). Even if the share price rose from \$20 to \$25, exercising the option would provide you with no benefits. By contrast, if you had purchased a share for \$20, you would gain 25 percent (5/20) if the price increased to \$25.

Looking at options as if they were bets may give the impression that options markets are little more than financial casinos, but that may be misleading. Although no new goods come into existence when an option is written, options markets, as a whole, probably do add wealth to society in that they allow risk to be managed more effectively. In turn, this may facilitate investment and economic growth.

Hedging and Speculation

Call options provide a payment if the underlying asset rises in value, and puts pay if the underlying asset's value falls. Both types of options can thus be useful for managing corporate risk. For example, an oil refinery might find it advantageous to purchase oil call options during periods of high oil price volatility. These would let the company buy oil at a fixed price regardless of what happens to the market price of oil, thus protecting it against price hikes. Similarly, a money manager might fear a decline in the prices of some of the stocks in her portfolio. She can protect her clients by buying puts that let her sell the stocks at fixed prices even if their market prices drop sharply. The use of options to manage risk in this way is called **hedging**, and various hedging techniques are explored in Chapter 21.

Of course, options can also be used to gamble. An investor might be willing to bet that the price of a certain stock will soon fall and may try to make money by buying puts. If the price rises instead, the writer of the put benefits because he simply keeps what the buyer paid. Of course, another investor who expected the stock's price to move upward might then have made money by buying calls. This sort of trading on a perceived information edge is called speculation. Option markets are often criticized as being rife with speculators. Part of the reason is that they are attracted to the leverage provided by options, which magnifies their payoffs, as discussed above. This is probably true in the sense that the vast majority of option trades are by speculators. However, it is important to remember that this sort of trading is useful because it helps keep markets efficient and prices up to date. Speculators also add liquidity to markets. If there were no speculators, hedgers would often have no one to buy options from or to sell options to.

PERSPECTIVES

Corporate Manager

Options provide companies with mechanisms that can be used to protect profits from adverse changes in input prices (using call options) and in selling prices (using put options).

Investor

Options provide investors with a method to hedge the value of their investments. Alternatively, the leverage provided by options is attractive for speculation purposes.

18.3 BASIC OPTION CHARACTERISTICS

In the Money, at the Money, and out of the Money

Special terminology is used to describe the relationship between the exercise price of the option and the current stock price. If the price of the common stock S exceeds the exercise price of a call E, the call is said to be **in the money** and has an immediate exercisable value. On the other hand, if the price of the common stock is less than the exercise price of a call, it is said to be **out of the money**. Finally, calls that are near the money are those with exercise prices slightly greater than current market price, whereas calls that are **at the money** are those with exercise prices equal to the stock price.

These same definitions also apply to puts in reverse.

In summary,

If $S>E$, a call is *in* the money and a put is *out* of the money.

If $S<E$, a call is *out* of the money and a put is *in* the money.

If $S=E$, an option is *at* the money.

Intrinsic Values

The price of a call option can be dichotomized in the following manner. If a call is in the money (the market price of the stock exceeds the exercise price for the call option), it has an immediate value equal to the difference in the two prices. This value will be designated as the **intrinsic value** of the call; it could also be referred to as the option's minimum value, which in this case is positive. If the call is at or out of the money, the intrinsic value is zero, and the price of the option is based entirely on its speculative appeal. The intrinsic value can never fall below $0 since exercise is optional. Summarizing, where S_0=current stock price:

Intrinsic value of a call=Maximum $\{(S_0-E), 0\}$ (18.1)

INTRINSIC VALUE OF A CALL OPTION

EXAMPLE

We observed a closing price of $95.25 for the common shares of Royal Bank of Canada on September 19, 2000 in Table 18.2. The January 2001 call option on Royal Bank stock with a $90 strike price was available and last traded at a price of $10.65. This option would be considered in the money because the stock price was greater than the exercise price. The intrinsic value of the January 90 call is

Intrinsic value of Royal Bank January 90 call
=Maximum $\{(\$95.25-\$90.00), 0\}=\$5.25$.

Puts work in reverse. If the market price of the stock is less than the exercise price of the put, the put is in the money and has an intrinsic value. Otherwise, it is at or out of the money and has a zero intrinsic value. Thus:

Intrinsic value of a put=Maximum $\{(E-S_0), 0\}$ (18.2)

INTRINSIC VALUE OF A PUT OPTION

EXAMPLE

There was a January 2001 put option on Royal Bank stock available on September 19, 2000 with an exercise price of $95, which last traded at a price of $5.10. Given the market price for Royal Bank shares of $95.25 at that time, the intrinsic value for this put can be determined in the following manner:

Intrinsic value of Royal Bank January 95 put
=Maximum $\{(\$95-\$95.25), 0\}=\$0$

PAYOFFS FROM BASIC OPTION POSITIONS

18.4

We can better understand the characteristics of options by examining their potential payoffs and profits. The simplest way to do this is to examine their value at expiration. At the expiration date, an option has an investment value, or payoff, that equals the option's intrinsic value at that time. In addition, we can also examine the net profit, which takes into account the price of the stock, the exercise price of the option, and the cost of the option. We consider both variables because option traders are interested in their net profits, but option valuation is perhaps better understood by focusing on payoffs.

As part of this analysis, we use letters to designate the key variables:

S_T=the value of the stock at expiration date T

E=the exercise price of the option

Buying a Call

Consider first the buyer of a call option. At expiration, the investment value or payoff to the call holder is:

Payoff to call buyer at expiration:

$=S_T-E$ if $S_T>E$

$=0$ if $S_T\leq E$

Notice that this payoff is the intrinsic value for a call option at time T, as presented in Equation 18.1. This payoff to a call buyer is illustrated in Figure 18.1(a). The payoff is $0 until the exercise price is reached, at which point the payoff rises as the stock price rises.

FIGURE 18.1

Payoff Profiles for Call and Put Options at Expiration

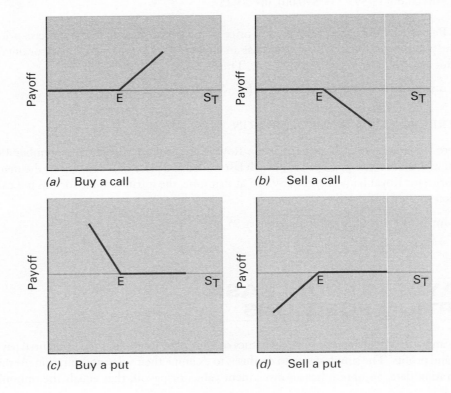

(a) Buy a call

(b) Sell a call

(c) Buy a put

(d) Sell a put

CALL BUYER PAYOFFS

Assume an investor buys a BCE November call option with an exercise price of $30. The payoff for the call at expiration is a function of the stock price at that time. For example, at expiration, the value of the call relative to various possible stock prices would be calculated as in the following partial set of prices:

EXAMPLE

BCE stock price at expiration	$20 25 30 35 40
BCE call value (payoff) at expiration	$ 0 0 0 5 10

Notice that the payoff is not the same as the net profit to the option holder or writer. For example, if BCE is trading $40 per share, the payoff to the option buyer is $10, but the net profit must reflect the cost of the call. In general, the profit to an option holder is the value of the option less the price paid for it. For the example above, if the cost of the BCE November 30 call option was originally $5.75, the net profit to the option holder (ignoring transactions costs) would be:

Net profit (option holder)=option payoff−option cost

Net profit (option holder)=$10−$5.75=$4.25

Figure 18.2 illustrates the *profit* situation for the call buyer in the example above. If the call expires worthless, the maximum loss is the $5.75 premium per option. Up to the exercise price of $30, the loss is $5.75 per option. The break-even point for the investor is the sum of the exercise price and the premium, or $30+$5.75=$35.75. Therefore, the profit-loss line for the call buyer crosses the break-even line at $35.75. If the price of the stock rises above $35.75, the value of the call will increase with it at least point for point, as shown by the two parallel lines above the $0 profit-loss line.

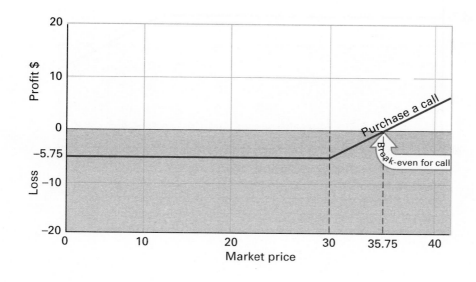

FIGURE 18.2

Profit and Losses to the Buyer of a Call Option

Selling (Writing) a Call

A naked or uncovered option writer is one who does not hold a position in the underlying stock. Naked call writers do not have their position covered in the underlying stock—in other words, they do not own shares in the underlying stock that can be made available if the call option is exercised. Naked call option writers (or sellers) incur losses if the stock's price increases, as shown by the payoff profile in part (b) of Figure 18.1. The payoff is flat until the exercise price is reached, at which point it declines as the stock price rises. The call writer loses if the stock price rises, whereas the call buyer gains if the stock price rises.

Payoff to naked call writer at expiration:

$$= -(S_T - E) \text{ if } S_T > E$$
$$= 0 \qquad\quad \text{ if } S_T \leq E$$

The net profit line depicted in Figure 18.3 is the mirror image of that for the call buyer, with a positive profit level (of $5.75) up to the exercise price because the call writer is receiving the premium. The horizontal axis intercept in Figure 18.3 occurs at the break-even point for the option writer. It is the sum of the exercise price and the option premium received. (Note that the break-even point is identical to that of the call buyer.) As the stock price exceeds the break-even point, the call writer loses. In fact, there is no conceptual limit to the call option writer's losses since there is no upward limit on the price of the underlying share.

FIGURE 18.3

Profit and Losses to the Writer of a Call Option

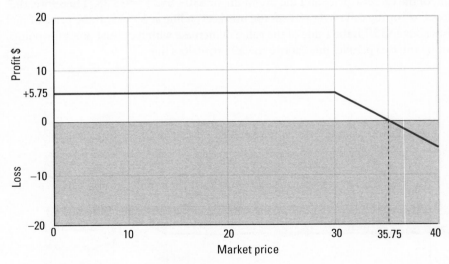

The mirror images of the payoff and net profit profiles for the call buyer (Figure 18.1(a) and Figure 18.2) and the call writer (Figure 18.1(b) and Figure 18.3) illustrate the point we made earlier about option trading being referred to as a zero sum game.

Buying a Put

A put buyer makes money if the price of the stock declines. Therefore, as part (c) of Figure 18.1 illustrates, the payoff pattern is flat at the $0 axis to the right of the exercise price; that is, stock prices greater than the exercise price result in a $0 payoff for the put buyer. As the stock declines below the exercise price, the payoff for the put option increases. The larger the decline in the stock price, the larger the payoff.

Payoff to put buyer at expiration:

$= 0$ if $S_T \geq E$

$= E - S_T$ if $S_T < E$

Notice that, as with call options, this payoff corresponds to the intrinsic value of the option at the expiration date.

PUT BUYER PAYOFFS

Suppose an investor believes the price of BCE will decline and purchases a November put option with an exercise price of $30. The payoff for the put option at expiration relative to various possible stock prices would be calculated as in the following partial set of prices:

BCE stock price at expiration	$20	25	30	35	40
BCE put value (payoff) at expiration	$10	5	0	0	0

Again, we note that the payoff does not equal the net profit to the option holder or writer. For example, if BCE is trading at $20 per share, the payoff to the option buyer is $10, but the net profit must reflect the cost of the put. For the above example, if the cost of the BCE November 30 put option was originally $0.30, the net profit to the option holder (ignoring transactions costs) would be:

Net profit (option holder)=option payoff−option cost

Net profit (option holder)=$10−$0.30=$9.70

Once again, the profit line parallels the payoff pattern for the put option at expiration. As Figure 18.4 illustrates, the investor breaks even (no net profit) at the point at which the stock price is equal to $29.70 (the exercise price minus the premium paid for the put). Beyond that point, the net profit line parallels the payoff line representing the investment value of the put.

FIGURE 18.4

Profit and Losses to the
Buyer of a Put Option

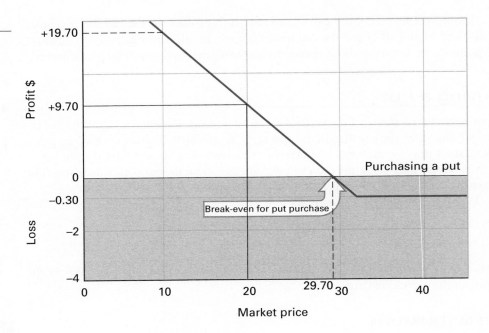

Selling (Writing) a Put

Selling (Writing) a Put

The payoff pattern for the naked put writer is the mirror image of that for the put buyer as shown in part (d) of Figure 18.1. The put writer retains the premium if the stock price rises and loses if the stock price declines. The put writer exchanges a fixed payoff for unknown losses.

Payoff to naked put writer at expiration:

$$= 0 \qquad \text{if } S_T \geq E$$
$$= -(E - S_T) \text{ if } S_T < E$$

Writers of puts are seeking the premium income exactly as are call writers. The writer is obligated to purchase a stock at the specified exercise price during the life of the put contract. If stock prices decline, the put buyer may purchase the stock and exercise the put by delivering the stock to the writer who must pay the specified price.

Note that the put writer may be obligated to purchase a stock for, say, $30 per share when it is selling in the market for $20 per share. This represents an immediate paper loss (less the premium received for selling the put). Also, note that the put writer can cancel the obligation by purchasing an identical contract in the market.[5]

---

[5] Of course, if the price of the stock has declined since the put was written, the price of the put will have increased and the writer will have to repurchase at a price higher than the premium received when the put was written.

PUT WRITER PROFITS

Figure 18.5 illustrates the profit-loss position for the seller of a put. Using the previous figures, we see that a November put is sold at an exercise price of $30 for a premium of $0.30. The seller of a naked put receives the premium and hopes that the stock price remains at or above the exercise price. As the price of the stock falls, the seller's position declines. The seller begins to lose money below the break-even point, which, in this case, is $30 - $0.30 = $29.70. Losses could be substantial if the price of the stock declined sharply. The price of the put will increase point for point as the stock price declines. The maximum loss for the put writer is limited, unlike that for the call writer, since the price for the underlying share cannot fall below zero. In this example, the most the put writer could lose is $0.30 - $30 = -$29.70 (where -$30 is the payoff if the shares became worthless).

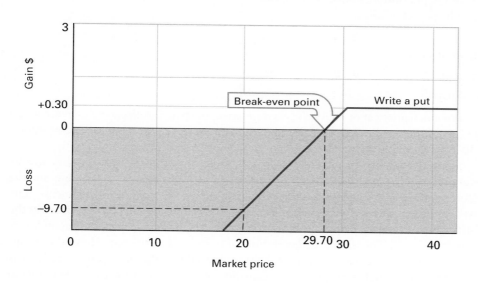

FIGURE 18.5

Profit and Losses to the Writer of a Put Option

SOME BASIC OPTIONS STRATEGIES   18.5

So far, we have examined the payoffs and profit/losses for the four basic uncovered (or naked) positions involving options:

1. buy a call
2. write a call
3. buy a put
4. write a put

In this section, we analyse "covered" positions involving hedges.[6] A **hedge** is a combination of an option and its underlying stock designed such that the option protects the

---

[6] For a discussion of spreads and combinations, which are also covered positions, refer to Chapter 21 of this text and also to Appendix 19-A of W.S. Cleary and C.P. Jones, *Investments: Analysis and Management*. (Toronto: John Wiley & Sons Canada Ltd., 1999).

stock against loss or the stock protects the option against loss. Before introducing the put-call parity option pricing relationship, we first consider two of the more popular hedges: protective puts and covered calls.

Protective Puts

A protective put involves buying a stock (or owning it already) and buying a put for the same stock; that is, it is a long position in both the stock and a put. The put acts as insurance against a decline in the underlying stock price, guaranteeing an investor a minimum price at which the stock can be sold. In effect, the insurance acts to limit losses or unfavourable outcomes. Possible profit is infinite although the profit is reduced by the cost of the put option, as discussed below.

The payoff profile is:

	$S_T < E$	$S_T \geq E$
Payoff of stock	S_T	S_T
+Payoff of put	$E - S_T$	0
Total payoff	E	S_T

For stock prices at or above the exercise price, the payoff reflects the increase in the stock price. Below the exercise price, the payoff is worth the exercise price at expiration ($30 in the example above).

Figure 18.6 shows the general case for payoffs from a protective put versus an investment in the underlying stock. As always, the payoff for the stock is a straight line, and the payoff for the option strategy is an asymmetrical line consisting of two segments. The payoff for the protective put clearly illustrates what is meant by the term truncating the distribution of returns. Below a certain stock price (the exercise price), the payoff line is flat or horizontal. Therefore, the loss is limited to the cost of the put. Above the break-even point, the protective put strategy shares in the gains as the stock price rises. This is one of the true benefits of derivative securities and the reason for their phenomenal growth since derivatives provide a quick and inexpensive way to alter the risk of a portfolio. Notice that this position is identical to purchasing a call except for a different intercept on the vertical axis.[7]

---

[7] The protective put illustrates a well-known concept called portfolio insurance.

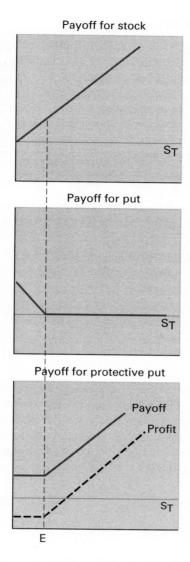

FIGURE 18.6

Payoff Profile and
Profit/Losses for a
Protective Put Position

Figure 18.6 illustrates how a protective put offers some insurance against a decline in the stock price. This insurance feature limits losses but at a cost if the insurance turns out not to be needed—the cost of the put. Above the exercise price, the profit is less than the payoff profile for the investment because of the cost of the put. Below the exercise price, losses in the stock price are partially offset by gains from the put, resulting in a constant loss equal to the cost of the put, as reflected in the profit line depicted in Figure 18.6.

EXAMPLE

PROTECTIVE PUT PAYOFFS

Using the November 30 BCE put referred to in the example above, assume that an investor had purchased BCE shares in a prior period for $30 and wished to ensure a minimum selling price of $30. We obtain the following payoffs to holding the share, buying the put, and the combined position for various share prices. The total profit for the combined position is shown in the bottom line.

Share Price	10	20	25	30	35	40	50
Payoff of stock	+10	+20	+25	+30	+35	+40	+50
+ Payoff of put	+20	+10	+5	0	0	0	0
Total Payoff of combined position	+30	+30	+30	+30	+35	+40	+50
Total Profit of combined position (assuming the put costs $0.30 and the shares cost $30 for a total cost of $30.30)	−0.30	−0.30	−0.30	−0.30	+4.70	+9.70	+19.70

Covered Calls

A **covered call** involves the purchase of stock and the simultaneous sale (or writing) of a call on that stock; that is, it is a long position in the stock and a short position in a call. The position is covered because the writer owns the stock and could deliver it if called on to do so as a result of the exercise of the call option by the holder. In effect, the investor is willing to sell the stock at a fixed price (the exercise price), limiting the gains if the stock price rises in exchange for cushioning the loss by the amount of the call premium if the stock price declines.

Using our previous notation, the payoff profile at expiration is:

	$S_T < E$	$S_T \geq E$
Payoff of stock	S_T	S_T
+Payoff of put	$E-0$	$-(S_T - E)$
Total payoff	S_T	E

Figure 18.7 illustrates the payoffs on the covered call hedge by showing all three situations: payoff for stock, payoff for writing a call, and payoff for covered call. Notice that the position is identical in shape to the payoff diagram from writing a put option as shown in Figure 18.1(d). The sale of the call truncates the combined position if the stock price rises above the exercise price. In effect, the writer has sold the claim to this gain for

FIGURE 18.7

Payoff Profiles for a
Covered Call Position

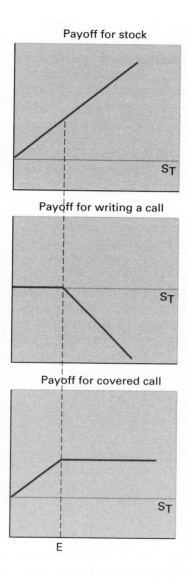

Payoff for stock

S_T

Payoff for writing a call

S_T

Payoff for covered call

S_T

E

the call premium. At expiration, the position is worth, at most, the exercise price and the profit is the call premium received by selling the call.

As Figure 18.7 shows, if the stock price declines, the position is protected by the amount of the call premium received. Therefore, the break-even point is lower compared to simply owning the stock, and the loss incurred as the stock price drops will be less with the covered call position by the amount of the call premium.

COVERED CALL PAYOFFS

Consider the position of the writer of a three-month BCE call option with a $30 exercise price, who also owns BCE and wants to sell his share in three months. Ignoring payment received for this option itself, the top row in the following table shows the losses the writer of a naked call suffers as a function of the price of BCE's stock at the time the option is exercised.

Share Price	0	10	20	25	30	35	40	50
Payoff of writing a call	0	0	0	0	0	−5	−10	−20
+Payoff of owning share	0	10	20	25	30	35	40	50
Total payoff of combined position	0	+10	+20	+25	+30	+30	+30	+30

When the price of the stock is below the exercise price of the option ($30), the option holder can buy stock more cheaply in the stock market. There is no reason for him to exercise the option, and, consequently, the option writer incurs no loss. She simply keeps the option price originally paid her. In contrast, when the value of the underlying stock is above $30, the call holder will exercise his option, and the writer must sell the stock at $30. If, for example, the stock is worth $40 at the time, the writer suffers a $10 loss when the option is exercised. If the call is covered, however, her risk exposure is different. Although she still loses $10 on having to sell stock worth $40 for $30, she also "makes" $10 since the stock she owns has risen from $30 to $40. The net result is that she is left in the position she would have been in had she not written the option and had the stock price remained at $30. This is illustrated in the last row of the table. Because writing a covered call is equivalent to writing a naked call and owning the underlying stock, the numbers in the last row are the sums of the numbers in the second and third rows.

Put-Call Parity

In this section, we develop a relationship between call and put prices for European options on the same underlying shares with identical exercise prices and expiration dates. We begin by noting that in addition to combining options with underlying positions in common shares, we can also combine options with risk-free T-bills (or bonds) and produce diagrams of the risk structures that result.

WRITING A PUT AND BUYING T-BILLS

Consider the position of the writer of a put option to sell one share of BCE at $30. The first row of the following table shows the loss the writer of the put suffers as a function of the price of BCE's stock when the option is exercised.

Share Price	0	10	20	25	30	35	40	50
Payoff of writing a put	−30	−20	−10	−5	0	0	0	0
+Payoff of T-bill	30	30	30	30	30	30	30	30
Total payoff of combined position	0	+10	+20	+25	+30	+30	+30	+30

When the price of the stock is below the exercise price of the option ($30), the put holder will exercise, and the writer of the put must purchase the stock at $30. For example, if the price has fallen to $10, the put writer must pay $30 for a stock worth $10. Her loss is $20.

Now consider a risk-free T-bill that promises to pay $30 (the exercise price of the put) three months from now at the time the option can be exercised. The third row in the table shows this value as a function of the price of BCE's stock. Recall that the definition of a risk-free asset is that its promised payment is unaffected by other events in the economy such as changes in BCE's stock price (i.e., it always pays $30).

The last row shows the position of the writer of a put who also owns a risk-free T-bill that pays $30. This row is the sum of the rows that describe the positions of a put writer and a risk-free T-bill owner. More importantly, the last row in this table is the same as the last column in the previous table (for the example dealing with covered call payoffs). This shows that writing a put and owning a risk-free T-bill places an investor in precisely the same position as does writing a covered call. Figure 18.8 illustrates this point.

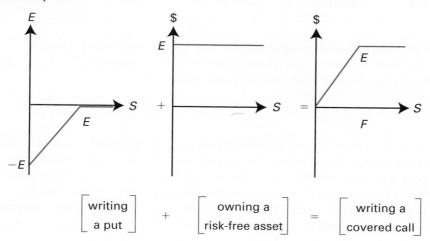

$$\begin{bmatrix} \text{writing} \\ \text{a put} \end{bmatrix} \quad + \quad \begin{bmatrix} \text{owning a} \\ \text{risk-free asset} \end{bmatrix} \quad = \quad \begin{bmatrix} \text{writing a} \\ \text{covered call} \end{bmatrix}$$

FIGURE 18.8

Payoffs Diagrams Showing the Positions of the Writer of a Put, the Owner of a Risk-Free Bond Paying the Striking Price of the Option at its Expiration Date, and the Writer of a Put who also Owns Such a Bond

The relationship between writing a put, owning a risk-free asset, writing a call, and owning the underlying stock is important in option pricing. It leads to the put–call parity relationship that we introduced at the start of this section and comes from combining the results shown in Figures 18.7 and 18.8. The put–call parity equation is a general result connecting the values of options immediately prior to exercise. We state the equation as:

(18.3) $\begin{bmatrix} \text{writing} \\ \text{a call} \end{bmatrix} + \begin{bmatrix} \text{owning under-} \\ \text{lying stock} \end{bmatrix} = \begin{bmatrix} \text{writing a} \\ \text{covered call} \end{bmatrix} = \begin{bmatrix} \text{writing} \\ \text{a put} \end{bmatrix} + \begin{bmatrix} \text{owning a risk-} \\ \text{free asset} \end{bmatrix}$

The put–call parity equation is illustrated in Figure 18.9. Each diagram shows the exercise value of a different position in options, risk-free assets, and the stock underlying the options. Writing a European put and owning a risk-free asset is shown to be equivalent to writing a European call (with the same expiry date and exercise price) and owning the underlying stock.

FIGURE 18.9

Payoff Diagrams
Illustrating the Put–Call
Parity Equation

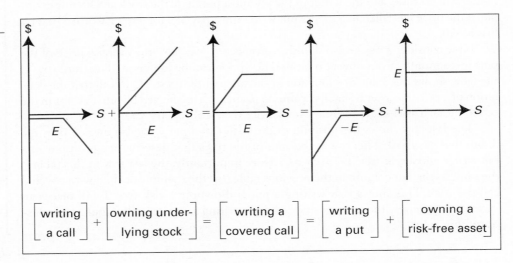

Since European options are not subject to early exercise, the put–call parity equation is the theoretical relationship between the price of a European call and a European put. We can therefore write the put-call parity equation as:

(18.4) $-V_c + S = -V_p + Ee^{-rt}$

where V_c is the price of a European call, S is the price of the underlying stock, V_p is the price of a European put, E is the striking price (which must be the same for the two options), r is the interest rate, and t is the time until the expiration of the two options. The present value, assuming continuous compounding, of a risk-free asset with face value E maturing as the options expire is thus Ee^{-rt}. This is important because it means that if we know the prices of any three of the four assets in the put–call parity equation, we can solve for the fourth. So, if we know the price of a European call, the underlying stock, and a risk-free bond, we can immediately calculate the price of a corresponding European put.

USING THE PUT–CALL PARITY RELATIONSHIP

EXAMPLE

A European call option on ABC Inc. stock costs $6.22. The call has a striking price of $30 and will expire in 18 months. The annual interest rate is 10 percent. ABC is currently trading at $28. We can calculate what a European put on ABC expiring in 18 months with a striking price of $30 should be. We begin by rearranging Equation 18.4 to solve for V_p.

$$V_p = V_c - S + Ee^{-rt}$$

We then insert the values into the equation:

$$V_p = \$6.22 - \$28 + \$30e^{-.10 \times 1.5}$$
$$= \$6.22 - \$28 + \$25.82$$
$$= \$4.04$$

Thus, we find that a European put maturing in 18 months (1.5 years) with a striking price of $30 is worth $4.04.

The valuation of American options, especially puts, is complicated by the possibility that the option holder might exercise his option before it expires. This means that we cannot be sure an American put and its corresponding call will be exercised simultaneously even if they have the same expiration date. Since it is based on an equivalence of exercise values, the put-call parity equation is, only a rough approximation for American options and can be misleading if early exercise is likely.

OPTION VALUATION

18.6

In this section, we examine the determinants of the value of a put or call. An option's premium almost never declines below its intrinsic value. The reason is that market arbitrageurs, who constantly monitor option prices for discrepancies, would purchase the options and exercise them, thus earning riskless returns. **Arbitrageurs** are speculators who seek to earn a return without assuming risk by constructing riskless hedges. Short-lived deviations are possible, but they will quickly be exploited.

ARBITRAGE PROFITS

EXAMPLE

Suppose a call option with an exercise price of $20 is selling for $2 when the price of the underlying share is $23. Notice that the intrinsic value of this option is $3 since the call enables you to purchase a share that is worth $23 for only $20. An arbitrageur (or anyone else recognizing that the option price is below its intrinsic value) could purchase an option contract (or contracts) at a cost of $200 (or $2×100). The investor could then immediately exercise the option, purchasing 100 shares at a cost of $2,000 ($20×100 shares). These shares could be sold in the market at a price of $23 per share for a total of $2,300. The net result (ignoring transactions costs) would be a profit of $100: ($2,300 −$2,000 (cost of exercising the options)−$200 (cost of the options)). This profit is earned without assuming any risks and is referred to as arbitrage profit; hence the name arbitrageurs. Clearly, these opportunities should not exist in efficient markets since rational investors will recognize these opportunities, exploit them, and therefore eliminate them.

Time Values

Option prices almost always exceed intrinsic values, with the difference reflecting the option's potential appreciation typically referred to as the **time value**. This is somewhat of a misnomer because the actual source of value is volatility in price. However, price volatility decreases with a shortening of the time to expiration; thus the term time value.

Because buyers are willing to pay a price for potential future stock price movements, time has a positive value—the longer the time to expiration for the option, the more chance it has to appreciate in value. However, when the stock price is held constant, options are seen as a wasting asset that reaches its intrinsic value as expiration approaches. In other words, as expiration approaches, the time value of the option declines to zero.

The time value can be calculated as the difference between the option price and the intrinsic value:

(18.5)   time value=option price−intrinsic value

EXAMPLE

TIME VALUE PREMIUMS

BCE stock was trading at $34.95 at the time we referred to the prices of the BCE options in the examples included in Section 18.4:

Time value of November 30 call=$5.75−$4.95=$0.80

Time value of November 30 put=$0.30−$0.00=$0.30

We can now understand the premium for an option as the sum of its intrinsic value and its time value:

(18.6)   premium or option price=intrinsic value+time value

EXAMPLE

OPTION PRICES

For the BCE options:

Option price for BCE November 30 call=$4.95+$0.80=$5.75

Option price for BCE November 30 put=$0.00+$0.30=$0.30

Notice an important point about options based on the preceding discussion. An investor who owns a call option and wishes to acquire the underlying common stock will always find it preferable to sell the option and purchase the stock in the open market rather than exercise the option (at least if the stock pays no dividends). Why? Because otherwise, the investor will lose the speculative premium on the option.

EXERCISING VERSUS SELLING AN OPTION

EXAMPLE

Consider the BCE November 30 call option with a market price of the common share of $34.95. An investor who owned the option and wanted to own the common share would be better off to sell the option at $5.75 and purchase the common share for $34.95 for a net investment of $29.20 per share. Exercising the call option, the investor would have to pay $30.00 per share. Thus, selling the shares reduces the required investment to own a share of BCE by $0.80 ($30−29.20). That is the amount of the time value (ignoring brokerage commissions).

On the other hand, under some circumstances it may be optimal to exercise an American put early (on a non-dividend paying stock). A put sufficiently deep in the money should be exercised early because the payment received at exercise can be invested to earn a return. Under certain circumstances, it may also be desirable to exercise an American call option on a dividend-paying stock before the expiration date. This is because dividends reduce the stock price on the ex-dividend date, which, in turn, reduces the value of the call option.

Boundaries on Option Prices

In the previous section, we learned what the premium or price of a put or call consists of, but we have not considered why options trade at the prices they do and the range of values they can assume. In this section, we learn about the boundaries for option prices, and in the next section, we discuss the exact determinants of options prices.

The value of an option must be related to the value of the underlying security. The basic relationship is most easy to understand by considering an option immediately prior to expiration when there is no time premium. At that point, if the option is not exercised, it will expire, leaving it with no value. Obviously, investors will exercise it only if it is worth exercising (if it is in the money).

We focus our attention on the pricing boundaries for call options. At expiration, a call must have a value equal to its intrinsic value. Therefore, the line representing the value of a call option must be horizontal at $0 up to the exercise price and then rise as the stock price exceeds the exercise price. For the BCE call option referred to in the previous section, on the expiration date, above $30 the call price must equal the difference between the stock price and the exercise price.

What is the maximum price an option can assume? To see this, think of a call. Since the call's value is derived from its ability to be converted into the underlying stock, it can never sell for more than the stock itself. It would not make sense to pay more for a call on one share of stock than the price of the stock itself. Therefore, the maximum price for a call is the price of the underlying stock.

Based on the preceding, we can establish the absolute upper and lower boundaries for the price of a call option, as shown in Figure 18.10. The upper boundary is a 45-degree line from the origin representing a call price equal to the stock price. The lower boundary is the price of the option at expiration, which must be either zero or its in-the-money value. This is represented by the 45-degree line starting at the exercise price. Once again, the lower boundary can be interpreted as the value of the call at the moment the call is exercised, or its intrinsic value.

FIGURE 18.10

Option Value as a Function of Share Price

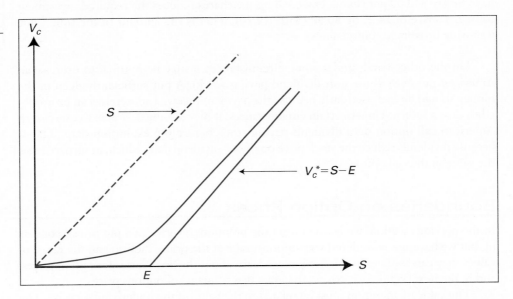

The range for call option prices established by these bounds is shown in Figure 18.10, which also portrays in a qualitative way the function that relates the actual option value V_c to share prices. When the share price is zero, the firm is bankrupt and the options are worthless. At positive share prices, options with some time left to expiry will have a positive value even if the lower boundary is zero ($S \leq E$) because, as we saw, there is always the possibility that during the remaining life of the option, share prices will appreciate sufficiently ($S > E$) to exercise the option at a profit. At share prices that are very high in relation to the striking price, eventual exercising of the call option is virtually guaranteed, and in owning the option, we ultimately acquire the underlying shares.

We showed earlier that a call option's price should exceed the gain from exercising it until just before the option expires. This being the case, an option owner who is thinking of exercising the option will find that he actually can make more money by selling it to another investor in the options market. There are, however, situations in which early exercise may be advisable. For example, if a large dividend is due, it is reasonable to expect the stock price to fall on the ex dividend date. This is because investors who buy the stock prior to the dividend are buying the dividend plus the same cash flows that investors who buy afterwards expect to receive. The value of the option holder's position from exercising the call while the stock price remains high prior to the dividend could exceed the value of the option after the stock has gone ex dividend.

In situations in which early exercise is never advisable, the early-exercise feature that distinguishes an American from a European call is of no value. In such a case, the price of an American call should equal the price of a similar European call. In contrast, if the underlying stock is due to pay a large dividend prior to the option's expiration, then an American option might be worth more.[8]

Early exercise is optimal for put options under a much broader set of conditions than is the case with call options. Indeed, if a put is sufficiently far in the money, it will almost always be exercised prior to its expiration. This means that American puts are, in general, worth more than corresponding European puts.

It is clear that it usually does not pay to exercise a call option before its expiration date, even if the price of the underlying shares exceeds the striking price (as long as no dividends are paid on the underlying stock). Determination of the exact function that relates option values to share prices is complex. Such a functional relationship is discussed in Appendix 18-A and is extensively relied on by professional traders and investors. The section below provides a brief discussion of the main qualitative factors that influence option prices.

Factors Affecting Option Prices

If we allow for stocks that pay dividends, we can summarize the main factors affecting option prices into a table with six elements, as shown in Table 18.3. The plus sign indicates a direct relation, and a negative sign, a negative relation. The assumption behind Table 18.3 is that all other variables remain fixed as we consider any of the six variables.

TABLE 18.3

Effects of Various Variables on Options Prices

Variable	Calls	Puts
Stock price	+	−
Exercise price	−	+
Time to expiration	+	+
Stock volatility	+	+
Interest rates	+	−
Cash dividends	−	+

[8] Unlike that of an American call option, where the underlying asset is a dividend-paying stock, the minimum price of a European call option may fall below $S - E$.

The following discussion provides a basis for the intuition regarding how these six factors affect option prices (holding all other factors unchanged). Recall that the option price=intrinsic value+time value (or speculative premium). Based on this framework, we note the following:

1. As share prices increase, the intrinsic value (IV) of calls increase and the IV of puts decrease.

2. As exercise prices increase, the IV of calls decrease and the IV of puts increase.

3. As share price volatility increases, there is a greater chance that shares will end up in the money, so the time value or speculative premium increases.

4. As the riskless rate increases, the advantage of delayed ownership increases for call options. Conversely, the delay of exercising put options, which involves selling assets for cash today, becomes more costly.

5. The greater the time to expiration, the greater the chance the option will be in the money, and hence, the greater the time value (or speculative premium).

6. Share prices fall by roughly the amount of dividend paid. Thus, dividend increases tend to reduce share prices, which reduces the IV of calls and increases the IV of puts.

18.7 SUMMARY

1. An option is a contract. It either grants the holder the right to purchase (call option) or to sell (put option) a given asset at a particular price for a specified time period.

2. Buyers of calls expect the underlying stock to perform in the opposite direction from the expectations of put buyers.

3. Although options have a value, it is a net zero transaction—what the holder gains, the other loses.

4. Options provide investors with opportunity to create leverage, to know their maximum loss in advance, and to expand their investment opportunity set.

5. Option prices are affected by:
   • underlying stock prices,
   • exercise price,
   • time expiration,
   • underlying stock volatility,
   • interest rates,
   • and cash dividends paid on the underlying assets.

APPENDIX 18-A

THE BLACK-SCHOLES OPTION-PRICING MODEL

Fischer Black and Myron Scholes have developed a model for the valuation of European call options that is widely accepted and used in the financial community.[9] While the equation estimates the price of European call options on non-dividend paying stocks, it is also used to evaluate American call options on non-dividend paying stocks. This is a reasonable application since we have seen that it is never optimal to exercise such American options before expiration date, so they should be worth approximately the same as the equivalent European option.

The formula itself is mathematical and appears to be very complex; however, it is widely available on calculators and computers. Numerous investors estimate the value of calls using the **Black-Scholes model**. The model is considered to be of such importance that Myron Scholes shared the 1997 Nobel Memorial Prize in economics largely for this work. Black would almost certainly have shared in the award had he not died in 1995.

The Black-Scholes model uses five of the six variables included in Table 18.3 to value the call option of a non-dividend-paying stock.[10] These five variables, all but the last of which are directly observable in the market, are as follows:

1. the price of the underlying stock
2. the exercise price of the option
3. the time remaining to the expiration of the option
4. the interest rate
5. the volatility of the continuously compounded rate of return on the underlying stock

We have already discussed the relationship between each of these factors and the price of a call option in Section 18.6.

The Black-Scholes option-pricing formula can be expressed as[11]

$$C = S[N(d_1)] - E\,[N(d_2)] \times \frac{1}{e^{rt}} \qquad (18.A1)$$

where

C = the price of the call option

S = current market price of the underlying common stock

---

[9] See F. Black and M. Scholes, "The Pricing of Options and Corporate Liabilities," *Journal of Political Economy*, Vol. 81 (May-June 1973), pp. 637-54.

[10] Since the model applies to non-dividend-paying stocks, the sixth factor included in Table 18.3—dividends—is not relevant.

[11] This version of the model applies to non-dividend-paying stocks. Adjustments can be made for stock that pay dividends.

$N(d_1)$ = the cumulative density function of d_1 (assuming this variable is normally distributed)

E = the exercise price of the option

e = the base of natural logarithms (or, approximately 2.71828)

r = the continuously compounded riskless rate of interest quoted on an annual basis

t = the time remaining before the expiration date of the option, expressed as a fraction of a year

$N(d_2)$ = the cumulative density function of d_2 (assuming this variable is normally distributed)[12]

To find d_1 and d_2, it is necessary to solve these equations:

(18.A2)
$$d_1 = \frac{ln\ (S/E) + (r + 0.5\sigma^2)t}{(\sigma[(t)^{1/2}])}$$

(18.A3)
$$d_2 = d_2 - (\sigma[(t)^{1/2}])$$

where

$ln\ (S/E)$ = the natural logarithm of (S/E)

σ = the standard deviation of the annual rate of return on the underlying common stock

The five variables previously listed are needed as inputs. Variables 1 to 4 are immediately available, but variable 5 is not because what is needed is the variability expected to occur in the stock's rate of return. Although historical data on stock returns are used typically to estimate this standard deviation, variability does change over time. A formula user should try to incorporate expected changes in the variability when using historical data. To do so, the user should examine any likely changes in either the market's or the individual stock's variability.

Variables 1 to 3 should be identical for a given stock for everyone using the Black-Scholes model. Variable 4 should be identical or very close among formula users, depending on the exact proxy used for the riskless rate of interest. Variable 5 will vary among users, providing different option values. Empirical studies have shown that estimates of the variance obtained from other than historical data are more valuable than the estimates based on historical data. Because the price of an option can be observed at any time, it is possible to solve the Black-Scholes formula for the implied standard deviation of the stock's return. This is an important application of the Black-Scholes equation that is frequently used by practitioners. In fact, some researchers have found that better forecasts of the actual standard deviation could be obtained by preparing forecasts from the model itself.

---

[12] This assumption does not imply that stock returns themselves are normally distributed, but that the variables d_1 and d_2 are normally distributed. In fact, one of the technical assumptions of the model is that stock prices are "log-normally" distributed.

USING THE BLACK-SCHOLES EQUATION

Assume

$S = \$40$

$E = \$45$

$r = 0.10$

$t = 0.5$ (6 months)

$\sigma = 0.45$

Step 1: Solve for d_1.

$$d_1 = \frac{ln(40/45) + [0.10 + 0.5(0.45)^2]\ 0.5}{0.45\ [(0.5)^{1/2}]}$$

$$= \frac{-0.1178 + 0.1006}{0.3182}$$

$$= -0.054$$

Step 2: Use a cumulative probability distribution table (such as the one provided in Appendix III located at www.wiley.com/canada/lusztig) to find the value of $N(d_1)$.

$N(d_1) = 0.4801$

where $d_1 = -0.054$

Step 3: Find d_2.

$d_2 = -0.054 - [0.45((0.5)^{1/2})]$

$\quad = -0.372$

Step 4: Find $N(d_2)$.

$N(d_2) = 0.3557$

Step 5: Solve for C.

$$C = S[0.4801] - E[0.3557] \times \frac{1}{e^{(.10)(0.5)}}$$

$$= 19.20 - (45)(0.3557)\ (0.9512)$$

$$= 19.20 - 15.23$$

$$= \$3.97$$

The theoretical (fair) value of the option, according to the Black-Scholes formula, is $3.97. If the current market price of the option is greater than the theoretical value, it is overpriced; if less, it is underpriced, according to the Black-Scholes model.

Put Option Valuation

To establish put prices, we can take advantage of the principle of put-call parity relationship established in Section 18.5. The put-call parity can be expressed as:

$$\text{Price of put} = Ee^{-rt} - S + \text{Call price}$$

where all terms are as defined before.

PUT OPTION PRICES

EXAMPLE

Use the information for the call given earlier. Since the Black-Scholes model uses continuous interest, the discount factor is expressed in continuous form. It is equal to e^{-rt} or $e^{-10(.5)}$. Using a calculator, this value is 0.951. Therefore:

$$\text{Price of put} = 45(0.951) - 40 + 3.96 = \$6.76$$

Options have an intrinsic value ranging from zero to the in-the-money value. Most sell for more that this, representing a speculative premium referred to as the time value. According to the Black-Scholes option valuation model, value is a function of the price of the stock, the exercise price of the option, time to maturity, the interest rate, and the volatility of the underlying stock.

Note: All *asterisked* Questions and Problems relate to material contained in the appendix to the chapter.

QUESTIONS AND PROBLEMS

Questions for Discussion

1. What is the difference between an American and a European option? Other factors remaining equal, which type of option is generally worth more? Is it true that it will never pay to exercise an American option before its expiration date? Discuss.

2. Consider an option that entitles the holder to purchase one share at any time during the next four years. The striking price, however, is a function of time and is set at $10 for the first two years, increasing to $12 thereafter. At the end of year 2, the underlying shares trade at $11. On what basis would you decide whether to exercise the option at that time? Discuss.

3. Given the claim that the writing of options does not create value, how do you explain their widespread use by both investors and firms?

4. What is a riskier investment: an option or the underlying stock? Explain. What are the main factors that influence the risk an investor bears when investing in an option?

5. How do each of the following events affect the value of a call option?

   (a) an increase in the risk or volatility of the underlying common stock

   (b) a decrease in the general level of interest rates

   (c) an increase in the dividend being paid on the underlying common stock

   (d) an increase in the exercise price

   (e) a decrease in the time to expiration of the option

6. (a) What is the value of an option to buy one common share if the exercise price is zero?

   (b) What is the value of an option to buy one common share if the life of the option is infinite? Assume that the underlying stock does not pay dividends.

7. How does the payoff from an option differ from that of a bond or share of stock? In what situations would the payoffs derived from options be especially desirable?

8. State the lower- and upper-bound values of an American call option. How could risk-free profit be made if either bound was violated?

PROBLEMS WITH SOLUTIONS

Problem 1

(a) Consider a call option for which $S=\$10$ and $E=\$6$. Assume that the price of the underlying shares increases by 20 percent. What is the corresponding percentage increase in the intrinsic value of V_C^* of the option?

(b) Recompute (a) assuming that the initial share price is (i) $7 and (ii) $20.

Solution 1

(a) We have:

$S=\$10$ $\qquad V_c^*=S-E=10-6=\$4$

$S_1=\$12$ $\qquad V_1^*=6$

percentage increase in $V_c^* = \dfrac{6-4}{4} \times 100\% = 50\%$

(b) (i) We obtain:

$S=\$7$ $\qquad V_c^*=\$1$

$S_1=\$8.40$ $\qquad V_c^*=\$2.40$

percentage increase in $V_c^* = \dfrac{2.40-1}{1} \times 100\% = 140\%$

(ii)

$S = \$20$ $V_c^* = \$14$

$S_1 = \$24$ $V_1 = \$18$

percentage increase in $V_c^* = \dfrac{18-14}{14} \times 100\% = 28.57\%$

We see that the leverage potential of options decreases as S increases in relation to E.

Problem 2

You own one share of Excellent Enterprises and one put option that entitles you to sell one share for $50. Plot your wealth position on the expiration date of the put option as a function of the share price at the time.

Solution 2

We obtain the following graphs:

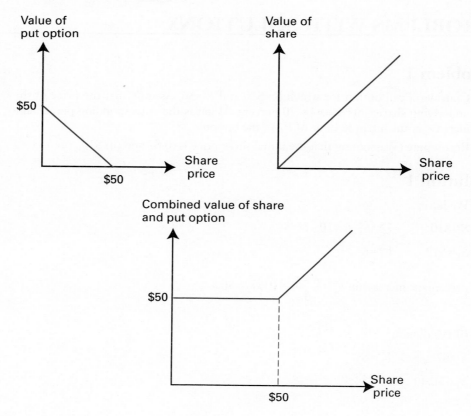

The put option entitles you to sell a share for $50. If on the expiration date the share is worth more than $50, you would rather sell in the open market; the put option expires and is worthless. On the other hand, if the shares trade at $20 on the expiration date, the put option is now worth $30 and will be exercised (you could buy a share for $20 in the market, exercise the option, and sell the same share for $50). We see that combining a put option with ownership of a share protects against losses caused by declining share prices. The price that we pay for this "insurance" is what it costs us to acquire the put option.

Problem 3

A call option to buy one share of ACME common stock has an exercise price of $100 and expires in 15 months. ACME stock is now at $85, and its return over the past year exhibited a standard deviation of 34 percent. The interest rate is now 10 percent. ACME is not currently paying dividends.

(a) What should be the price of this call option?

(b) Suppose the price of the call is $4.25. What does this say regarding traders' beliefs about the risk in ACME stock over the 15 months?

(c) Suppose the standard deviation of the return is actually expected to be 34 percent. What should the price be of a European put on ACME stock with a striking price of $100 and 15 months to expiration?

Solution 3*

(a) The Black-Scholes equation can be used to value this call since early exercise is not optimal (as there are no dividends).

First, calculate d_1:

$$d_1 = \frac{ln\left(\frac{S}{E}\right) + (r + 0.5\sigma^2)t}{\sigma(t)^{1/2}}$$

$$= \frac{ln\left(\frac{85}{100}\right) + (0.1 + 0.5(0.34)^2)1.25}{0.34(1.25)^{1/2}}$$

$$= 0.0914$$

Second, calculate the value of d_2:

$$d_2 = d_1 - \sigma(t)^{1/2}$$

$$= 0.0914 - 0.34(1.25)^{1/2}$$

$$= -0.2887$$

Next, using the values in Table 5 at the end of the text, find values for $N(d_1)$ and $N(d_2)$:

$N(d_1)=0.5364$ (note that you must interpolate between the

$N(d_2)=0.3864$ numbers in the table)

Now, solve for C using the Black-Scholes formula:

$$C = SN(d_1) - EN(d_2)\frac{1}{e^{rt}}$$

$$= 85(0.5364) - 100(0.3865)\frac{1}{e^{0.1(1.25)}}$$

$$= 11.49$$

The call option should be priced at $11.49.

(b) Recall that the only subjective estimate used in the Black-Scholes formula is the standard deviation σ. If the price of the call is actually $4.25, then we can work the calculation in (a) backwards to derive the standard deviation that must have been used in pricing the option. Mathematically, solving for the standard deviation implied by the option price can be tedious because of the complexity of the equation. Fortunately, many sources provide tables that you can use to determine call option prices. These same tables can be used to determine volatilities implied by option prices. For instance, the Black-Scholes equation can be rewritten as:

$$\frac{C}{Ee^{-rt}} = aN\left(\frac{ln\,(a)}{b} + \frac{b}{2}\right) - N\left(\frac{ln\,(a)}{b} - \frac{b}{2}\right)$$

where:

$$a = \frac{S}{Ee^{-rt}} \quad \text{and} \quad b = \sigma(t)^{\frac{1}{2}}$$

We could make up a table based on values of a and b to solve for option prices. For example, a small table would contain the values (tables covering broad ranges of a and b are available from many sources):

		$a=\sigma(t)^{1/2}$		
		0.160	0.170	0.180
	0.950	0.040	0.044	0.047
$b=S/Ee^{-rt}$	0.960	0.044	0.048	0.052
	0.970	0.048	0.052	0.056

The numbers in the table represent the value of the right-hand side of the equation above at different levels of a and b. To calculate a call option value, one could simply calculate a and b, look up the corresponding number in the table, and multiply that amount by Ee^{-rt} to get the call option value.

In this case, we have an option value and want the standard deviation implied by that value.

First, we determine what value from the table above, called X here, must have been used to get a price of $4.25.

$$C=\$4.25=X \times Ee^{-rt}=C \times \$88.25$$

Solving, we see that X must equal $4.25/$88.25 = 0.048. Reading across the row in the table that corresponds to 0.96 (this part of the calculation is the same because the parameters that go into it are known), we find that 0.96 is under $\sigma\sqrt{t}=0.170$. Since t is still equal to 1.25 years, we have:

$$\sigma\sqrt{t}=\sigma \times \sqrt{1.25}=0.170$$

Hence, σ is .152 or 15.2 percent. Options traders seem to expect that the standard deviation of the stock's return will be lower over the next year and three months (15.2 percent) than it was in the past (34 percent). The standard deviation derived in this way is known as the **implied standard deviation**.

(c) Given that the standard deviation is 34 percent, we calculated in (a) that the price of a call with the characteristics given is $11.49. We can use the put-call parity equation to calculate the price of a European put with the same underlying asset, striking price, and expiration date. We begin by rearranging Equation 18.4 to solve for V_p:

$$V_p=V_c-S+Ke^{-rt}$$

Substituting the values for the parameters of the equation,

$$V_p=\$11.49-\$85+\$100_e{}^{-.10 \times 1.25}$$

$$=\$11.49-\$85+\$88.25$$

$$=\$14.74$$

Thus, a European put maturing in 1.25 years with a striking price of $100 is worth $14.74.

ADDITIONAL PROBLEMS

1. A stock is currently priced at $10 per share. You purchase a call option contract on 100 shares with an exercise price of $10. You pay a premium of $1.50 per share.

   (a) If on the expiration date the share price has risen to $13, what is the percentage change in the stock price? What is the total dollar profit on the option? What is the percentage profit on the option?

   (b) If on the expiration date the share price has fallen to $9, what is the percentage change in the stock price? What is the total dollar profit on the option? What is the percentage profit on the option?

2. (a) What is the break-even point for a call option with an exercise price of $12.50 and a premium of $0.50?

(b) What is the break-even point for a put option with an exercise price of $70 and a premium of $2.25?

3. Consider the following options on Air Canada, with a current stock price of $12.70:

Call or put	Months to expiry	Exercise price	Premium
call	1	13	$0.25
call	2	12	1.40
call	2	13	0.90
call	2	14	0.55
put	4	12	1.15
put	4	14	2.25

For each option, calculate its intrinsic value and its time value.

4. A call option has an exercise price of $10.00 and an expiry date in six months. The underlying stock is currently trading for $12.00.

(a) What is the minimum price an investor would pay for this option? Could an investor profit if the call option was actually trading at $1.00?

(b) What is the maximum price an investor would pay for this option? If the option was trading for $13.00, how could an investor earn a risk-free profit?

5. You are given the following information:

Acme stock is trading at $21.00. A call option on Acme stock, expiring in nine months, with a striking price of $20, is trading at $3.35. The one-year risk-free rate is 8 percent.

(a) What would you be willing to pay for a nine-month put on Acme stock with a striking price of $20?

(b) If the above-mentioned puts were trading at $1.00, what trades could you make to exploit the price discrepancy?

(c) What assumptions are made when arriving at your answer in (b)?

*6. A call option has a striking price of $8.10 and an expiry date six months hence. The underlying stock is currently trading at $7.60 and has historically exhibited a standard deviation of 10.6 percent. The standard deviation is not expected to change. The interest rate is 5.4 percent. Using the Black-Scholes equation, estimate the value of the call option described above. What are some of the limitations of using the Black-Scholes equation?

7. You find the following quotes from a financial newspaper for Alpha Inc.'s options.

Striking price	Option price	Exercise date
7.50	2.25	6 months
7.50p	1.35	6 months

Alpha Inc. stock is currently trading at $8.25, and the one-year risk-free rate is 7 percent.

(a) Using the put-call parity equation, at what price should Alpha put options trade?

(b) Is it possible to make a risk-free arbitrage profit from the situation outlined above? What trades could you, as an investor, make to exploit the price discrepancy?

(c) What assumptions must be made to arrive at your answer in (b)? Under what circumstances might the situation described in (b) actually exist?

8. A put and a call option (both European) are written on the same stock and have the same maturity date and the same strike price. If the current price of a share of stock is equal to the strike price of these options, which option will have the higher premium?

9. You wish to write a put option on the stock of ABC Inc. However, the options exchange does not allow puts to be written on that stock (it does allow trading in calls, though). Devise a portfolio of securities that has the same payoff at maturity as a put option.

10. The current price of XYZ Inc. stock is $45. You observe the following premiums for options on that stock:

Put: expiry in three months	Strike=$35	Premium=$0.30
Put: expiry in one month	Strike=$35	Premium=$0.15
Call: expiry in three months	Strike=$35	Premium=$12.00
Call: expiry in one month	Strike=$35	Premium=$9.50

(a) One of the options is clearly mispriced. Which one and why?

(b) What should be the price of the mispriced option in (a) (assuming the other three options are priced correctly)?

11. (a) Consider an investor who buys a call option with an exercise price of $15 for a premium of $1.50. At the same time, the investor also buys a put option on the same stock with the same exercise price and expiration date as the call for a premium of $1.25. A portfolio of options such as this is a strategy known as a straddle. Using a spreadsheet, calculate the total profit at expiration to this strategy for the stock prices $0, $1.00, $2.00, …, $29.00, $30.00. Plot your results on a graph such as that in Figure 18.2 in the text. Under what circumstances would an investor want to follow such a strategy?

(b) Consider an investor who writes a call option with an exercise price of $20 for a premium of $2.50. At the same time, the investor also buys a put option on the same stock with the same exercise price and expiration date as the call for a premium of $1.95. A portfolio of options such as this is a strategy known as a straddle. Using a spreadsheet, calculate the total profit at expiration to this strategy for the stock prices $0, $1.00, $2.00, …, $29.00, $30.00. Plot your results on a graph such as that in Figure 18.2 in the text. Under what circumstances would an investor want to follow such a strategy?

Special Warrants Raise Both Funds and Investor Awareness

Back in Chapter 2, we followed the founding of Waterloo-based Research in Motion (RIM) and its two public offerings. The technical savvy and business perseverance founder Mike Lazaridis is certainly a large part of RIM's success.

But Lazaridis is only one of two co-CEOs at RIM. In many ways, the company really took off when Jim Balsillie joined. A chartered accountant with a passion for managing high-tech companies, in 1992 Balsillie left a vice-presidential post with Sutherland Schultz, a Kitchener, Ontario firm that was RIM's largest customer at the time, and bought his way in. He soon became RIM's chair and co-CEO; Lazaridis takes care of the technical side of things, and Balsillie handles the financial aspect.

When he arrived in 1992, RIM had sales of about $500,000 a year and a staff of ten. It was Balsillie who shepherded it through its fantastic expansion of the next few years, continuing and expanding on Lazaridis's strategy of acquiring strategic partners in the telecommunications business to leverage the business for fast growth.

In 1996 the company raised $35.7 million through special warrants. These securities, which could be converted to common shares when the company went public, were marketed to sophisticated investors. The tactic not only raised immediate funds, but also contributed to the success of its initial public offering the following year.

"What that did was give us a near-public valuation, and raise our profile in the investment community," Balsillie explains. "In effect, we were getting $35 million, which gave us the capital to grow." The week before the IPO, the warrants were listed on the TSE. They traded for as much as $10.20, finally settling at $7.80 on closing day (the IPO shares were offered at $7.25).

With a management degree from Harvard, Balsillie tends to handle more of the financial side of the CEO role. His theory is to "always have an eye on the next move and de-risk it through the moves you make today." Lazaridis, the wireless network guru, focuses on the technical side. Job sharing at the top of the pyramid is an unusual arrangement, but it suits both men. Lazaridis calls the job "way too complicated for one person." Balsillie points out that having two views of a problem helps guard against blind spots.

Options and Long-Term Financing

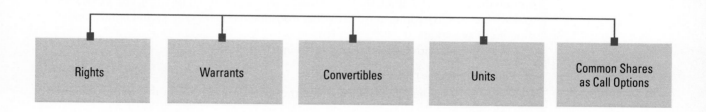

| Rights | Warrants | Convertibles | Units | Common Shares as Call Options |

Learning Objectives

After studying this chapter, you should be able to:

1. *Describe how rights work for existing shareholders.*
2. *Explain the gains and losses involved in the exercise of rights.*
3. *Identify what warrants are, and how they differ from options and rights.*
4. *Discuss convertible securities, conversion price, and conversion ratio.*
5. *Explain why a company issues convertible securities over common stock.*

19.1   INTRODUCTION

In the previous chapter, we introduced call and put options as independent investments. We now turn our attention to options that firms write on their own securities in the context of long-term financing. Corporations issue options either to provide current shareholders with an opportunity to subscribe to new share offerings on a preferential basis or as "sweeteners" that may make new issues of senior securities such as debt or preferred shares more marketable.[1]

In the following sections, we review each of these uses and the various forms of options that can arise. Specifically, we review rights, warrants, and convertible securities. Although each of these instruments is issued for different purposes, the underlying concepts are similar in all three cases. Indeed, all three are generalizations of the simple options discussed in Chapter 18. We conclude the chapter by considering circumstances under which ordinary long-term financing instruments such as stocks and bonds can be thought of as options.

We continue with the same notation as in Chapter 18:

S = market price per share

E = exercise price per share, often called the subscription price in the context of this chapter

t = time to expiry of an option

IV = intrinsic value of an option

To the above, we add the following additional notation:

N = number of options required to buy one share

19.2   RIGHTS

Rights are privileges granted to shareholders to acquire additional shares at a predetermined (subscription) price that is generally lower than the current market price. This creates value for shareholders and induces them to exercise this option. Rights generally have short maturities consisting of a few weeks to three months. Certificates are mailed to shareholders on the record date and are usually transferable. Shares trade ex rights two business days prior to a record date, which means they trade without the right privilege attached.[2] Prior to the ex-rights date, the stock is said to trade cum rights (or "rights on") since it trades with the right privilege attached. Typically, the share price will drop by the theoretical intrinsic value of the right on the ex-rights date.

---

[1] Stock option plans for executives, frequently used to encourage management to align their interests with those of the shareholders, are another example of options issued by corporations.

[2] Notice the similarity between the record dates and ex-rights dates, and the record and ex-dividend dates associated with dividend payments, which were discussed in Chapter 17.

Rights may be offered for the following reasons:

1. Current market conditions are not conducive to traditional common share issues.
2. Management wants to give existing shareholders the opportunity to acquire shares, possibly at a discount to present market price.
3. It enables new funds to be raised while providing existing shareholders the right to maintain their proportionate ownership of the company (i.e., the pre-emptive right).

The following report shows an example of a recent rights offering by Com Dev International Ltd. that was used to raise $37 million in financing in March 2000.

■ *Finance in the News*

Rights Offering

In February 2000, Com Dev International Ltd. announced a rights offering to expire on March 10. It was fully subscribed and raised $37 million, to be used to reduce its $12 million debt and provide working capital. A right allows existing shareholders to purchase additional shares at a discount or sell the right to others. Com Dev issued 8,055,726 shares, the maximum number available under the rights issue.

Source: Canadian Press Newswire, March 23, 2000.

No commission is levied on the exercise of rights, and a ready secondary market can develop, permitting the sale of rights by holders who do not wish to exercise. If the shares trade on an exchange, the rights are listed on the exchange automatically, and trading takes place until they expire.

A rights holder may take four courses of action:

1. exercise some or all of the rights
2. sell some or all of the rights
3. buy additional rights for trading or exercise purposes
4. do nothing and let the rights expire (which would represent suboptimal behaviour since the investor would gain nothing through this action)

Usually, each shareholder receives one right, and a certain number of rights (N) is required to purchase one share (purchase of fractional shares may or may not be permitted, depending on the details of the issue). The theoretical intrinsic value (IV) of a right, by necessity, is calculated using two methods described below.

During the cum-rights period:

$$IV = \frac{(S-E)}{N+1} \tag{19.1}$$

The addition of 1 to N reflects the fact that the market price of the share includes the value of one right.

EXAMPLE

THE CUM-RIGHTS INTRINSIC VALUE

A share is trading for $40 cum rights. Four rights are required to purchase a share at the subscription price of $35.

$$IV = (40 - 35)/(4 + 1) = \$1.00.$$

During the ex-rights period:

(19.2) $$IV = \frac{(S - E)}{N}$$

EXAMPLE

THE EX-RIGHTS INTRINSIC VALUE

Two days after the ex-rights date, the share price above has fallen to $39.20.

$$IV = (39.20 - 35)/4 = \$1.05.$$

Depending on the time to expiry and the other variables relevant to option pricing as discussed in Chapter 18, rights are likely to trade somewhat above the intrinsic value. As we can see, rights have an intrinsic value that is proportional to the difference between the market price and the subscription price. That is, the lower the subscription price is set in relation to the market price, the more shareholders receive when they sell a right. In the previous chapter, we pointed out that we cannot create value through options and that one party must lose what another gains. If rights have a value when distributed, where does this value come from, and who is paying for it? The answer is clear: if options have value in the hands of the recipient, the writer must lose an equivalent amount. In our case, the writer is the firm, and any value that the firm transfers has to come ultimately at the expense of its shareholders. On the one hand, shareholders may get "cheap" new shares that appear attractive because they are priced below market. On the other hand, the increased number of outstanding shares that were sold at a discount dilute the original shareholdings, depressing their value. In fact, shareholders gain with one hand what they lose with the other.

EXAMPLE

SHAREHOLDER WEALTH EFFECTS OF RIGHTS OFFERINGS

A firm with 1 million shares outstanding wants to issue 100,000 new shares, so that 10 rights are required to subscribe to one new share. The subscription price is set at $16. For simplicity, assume that the life of the right is very short, so that their market price equals their intrinsic value, and that the company is all-equity financed. Before rights were mailed, shares traded at $20.40, so that the total value of the firm before the offering was:
Value of firm before rights offering = 1,000,000 × 20.40 = $20,400,000

After the rights offering, the business, which is otherwise unchanged, has 100,000 new shares outstanding, and in return, it has collected 100,000 × 16 = $1,600,000. The total value of the company should now be:

Value of firm after rights offering=value before+cash collected from offering

$$=20,400,000+1,600,000$$

$$=\$22,000,000$$

and, consequently, the price per share after the offering should become:

$$\text{Share price after rights offering}=\frac{\text{total value of firm}}{\text{number of outstanding shares}}$$

$$=\frac{22,000,000}{1,100,000}=\$20$$

We see that as a consequence of the rights offering, the price per share has decreased by $0.40 (from $20.40 to $20), while shareholders have received one right worth $0.40 for each share held. Hence, shareholder wealth remains unaffected. Put another way, if a shareholder had owned 10 shares before the offering (total value=10×20.40=$204) and had exercised her rights, she would own 11 shares after the offering (total value=11 ×20=$220), having contributed the difference of $16 by paying the subscription price. Alternatively, the shareholder could have sold her 10 rights for $0.40 each and pocketed the $4.00. Adding this to the value of her stock position of $200 (10 shares worth $20 each) again leaves her wealth unchanged at $204. Only if she allowed the options to expire worthless would her wealth position be affected, since she would only have 10 shares worth $200 without the additional $4. Clearly, this would represent irrational behaviour.

The point just made is often not properly understood, and shareholders sometimes believe that they are getting a good deal when they can buy new shares at a discount. An extreme illustration should further clarify the issue. Assume that a firm sets the subscription price at zero, in effect giving away new shares. Clearly, the printing of new certificates does not affect the value of the firm in any way. With more shares outstanding, each share will be worth less. Although shareholders may hold more share certificates, their proportionate ownership in the firm remains unchanged and so does their wealth position.[3]

Denoting the share prices before and after the distribution of rights as S_o and S_x, we can generalize the results of the above example:

$$S_x=S_o-IV \tag{19.3}$$

That is, during a rights offering, we expect the share price to drop by the intrinsic value of the right on the ex-rights date.[4] While this is true conceptually, in practice, it is difficult to isolate this expected drop because a variety of other factors influence share prices

---

[3] Issuing new shares at a subscription price of zero is equivalent to declaring a stock dividend. Such dividends were discussed in Chapter 17.

[4] Though there may be a difference between the actual value at which rights trade and the intrinsic value IV, because of the short life of rights, this difference tends to be small and will be ignored to simplify the discussion.

at the same time. Among other things, the market price of the shares may be influenced by shareholder expectations as to how the new funds raised are to be invested. If, for example, the offering of new shares is seen as a positive action signalling the availability of good investment opportunities, the ex-rights price of shares may remain higher than we would otherwise expect.

Although the shareholders' wealth position should be unaffected by the subscription price, practical considerations often dictate its level. Clearly, should the market value of the shares have fallen below the subscription price by the time the rights expire, shareholders will not subscribe.[5] Rights owners would not buy new shares from the corporation and pay more than the price at which identical shares could be bought in the market. Thus, the offering would fail. To reduce this risk, an issuer will be tempted to offer a large discount because this will provide protection against fluctuations in share prices during the several weeks that may elapse between the announcement and the expiry of a typical rights offering. A significant spread between subscription price and current market price also enhances the value of a right, and this should encourage shareholders who elect not to exercise their rights to sell them rather than to just let them lapse.

On the other hand, the lower the subscription price, the more shares must be sold to raise a given amount of capital and the greater the drop in the price that can be expected on outstanding shares. Furthermore, adjustments to financial information to reflect the effects of a rights offering are not always made. Given the increased number of shares outstanding, the growth rate in reported earnings per share may decline in the short run, and the cash needed to maintain previous dividends per share will increase.

THE IMPACT OF SUBSCRIPTION PRICES

EXAMPLE

A firm currently has 1 million shares outstanding with a market price of $25 per share (cum rights). Earnings and dividends per share are $2.50 and $1 respectively, and $2.2 million in new equity capital needs to be raised. The tabulation below summarizes the immediate impact that we would expect on key financial variables as a function of the subscription price. These figures assume that the new funds raised would not increase current earnings for some time.

	Subscription price			
	$22.00	$19.80	$11.00	$4.40
Percentage discount of subscription price over previous market price: $(S_0-E)/S_0$	12%	20.8%	56.0%	82.4%
Number of additional shares to be issued: $2,200,00/E$	100,000	111,111	200,000	500,000
Number of rights required for one new share: N	10	9	5	2

[5] We recall that generally there is no incentive to exercise an option and, hence, a right until just before its expiry date.

Intrinsic value of a right: IV	$ 0.27	$ 0.52	$ 2.33	$ 6.87
Market value of share ex rights: S_x	$24.73	$24.48	$22.67	$18.13
Earnings per share	$ 2.27	$ 2.25	$ 2.08	$ 1.67
Annual cash required to sustain $1 dividend per share	$1,100,000	$1,111,111	$1,200,000	$1,500,000

EXAMPLE

It is apparent that if investors expect past dividend levels to be maintained, and if short-run earnings per share are viewed as important, firms may face real trade-offs when selecting the spread between market and subscription price. Although a low subscription price minimizes the risks of a failed offering, a large number of new shares will depress earnings per share and may cause a cash drain in terms of dividend payments. In trading off these conflicting considerations, firms in Canada typically set the subscription price at 15 to 20 percent below the market price of the shares prior to the offering.

WARRANTS   19.3

Warrants are long-term options that firms make available on their own shares. Although they may be issued for a variety of reasons—for example, to underwriters as partial compensation for their services—they are offered in conjunction with issues of senior securities such as debt or preferred shares. In this context, they are viewed as sweeteners that may make such issues more marketable and perhaps allow the firm to obtain somewhat improved terms in the form of lower interest or dividend payments or less restrictive covenants. The following report provides an example of a company that used warrants in such a capacity to raise equity financing during a period when similar firms were having difficulty doing so.

■ *Finance in the News*

Sweeteners

Leitch Technology Corp. was able to raise $52.8 million in the sale of two million shares at $26.40 each. The share offering, underwritten by BMO Nesbitt Burns Inc. and Yorkton Securities Inc., came at a time when many others in the sector were having a difficult time with new public offerings. Underwriters and investment bankers are often compelled to add sweeteners to attract investors. For example, Montreal biotech firm Haemacure Corp. raised $13 million from six million units, but only after underwriters Dloughy Investments Inc. and Loewen, Ondaatje, McCutcheon Ltd. created units of one-and-a-half share purchase warrants. Each of these allowed the investor to obtain an additional Haemacure share.

Source: Thomas Hirschmann,"Leitch Secures Fresh Financing: Bucks Sector Trend," *National Post,* June 20, 2000, pp. D1, D3. *Reprinted with permission.*

Once made available to purchasers of senior securities, warrants can normally be detached and traded in their own right. As a result, over 100 different warrants are listed on the TSE. Unlike rights, warrants generally have a life of several years, and one warrant may entitle the holder to subscribe to more than one share. The subscription price for warrants is commonly set at a level that is higher than the price of the underlying share at the time of issue. In other words, they are usually issued "out of the money" so that their intrinsic value is initially zero. On occasion, the subscription price may increase as a function of time.

BCE WARRANTS

EXAMPLE

In October 1999, BCE Inc. issued 4.7 million warrants that enabled the holders to purchase the company's non-voting common shares at a subscription price of $24.00 per share until October 2004. At the time, these shares were trading in the $8-$10 range.

The attraction of warrants lies in the fact that during the relatively long period until their expiry, the underlying share price may appreciate sufficiently to provide a gain when the option is exercised. When exercised, the firm makes new shares available and receives cash inflows from the subscription. This amount, however, is normally small in comparison to the funds that were raised through the original offering of senior securities. Moreover, whether or not such a capital inflow will occur is not under the firm's control but is determined by the movements of the overall stock market.

Clearly, the extent to which investors in senior securities are willing to accept reduced yields and less attractive provisions in exchange for warrants that are attached to debt or preferred shares depends on the attractiveness of the option offered. The duration of the warrants and the exercise price in relation to the current share price are of particular significance. Once again, what is of value to the investor has to be viewed as a cost to the firm. If, some time in the future, the warrant becomes valuable because the share price exceeds the exercise price, the firm will be forced to sell new shares at a discount. As these shares are sold to outsiders, existing shareholders will suffer a dilution in their holdings. This is the price they pay for the more attractive terms the company received on the original offering of senior securities.

Following a trend toward innovative financing through a variety of new instruments, some companies have issued warrants on assets other than common shares including preferred shares, corporate debt instruments, Government of Canada bonds, precious metals, and even various mixes of such assets. Also, in some cases, the exercise price of the warrants has been set at zero, and the warrants have been used as a primary financing vehicle that essentially has provided the firm with delayed equity or debt financing.

INNOVATIVE FINANCING ARRANGEMENTS

EXAMPLE

In January 2000, MGI Software issued 1 million special warrants at $25 apiece, each exchangeable for one common share at no additional cost. This translates into an exercise price of zero, which guarantees that the warrants will eventually be exercised. Hence, they have to be viewed as delayed equity financing.

In August 1987, Canadian Pioneer Energy Inc. issued $6 million of cumulative, redeemable, convertible, second preferred shares. As a sweetener, one gold purchase warrant was attached to each preferred share. Each warrant gave the holder an opportunity to purchase 0.02 troy ounce of gold at $11 until May 31, 1990. That amount of gold was then trading around $9. Thus, these preferred shares provided investors with an option to take advantage of any future rise in gold prices. It was believed that this gold option feature permitted a larger issue than would otherwise have been possible.

In 1987, BCE Development Corporation issued $88 million in retractable preferred shares that entailed a "currency warrant." Essentially, with each future receipt (dividends and eventual redemption), investors can decide whether they want payment in Canadian or U.S. dollars, where the respective amounts were equivalent given the exchange rate that prevailed at the time of issue. If, for instance, the Canadian dollar subsequently appreciates vis-à-vis the U.S. dollar, investors will be better off receiving future payments in Canadian dollar, and vice versa. Thus, these preferred shares provide investors with an option to take advantage of any future shift in currency values. It was claimed that this currency feature permitted a larger issue than would otherwise have been possible.

Clearly, there are few limits to human ingenuity when it comes to financial engineering and creating new types of financial instruments. The real question is whether such instruments truly broaden the spectrum of alternatives available to investors, or whether there are significant market imperfections that can be exploited. Otherwise, as we saw in our earlier discussion on market efficiency, the firm should just get with one hand what it gives away with the other when various features are incorporated into an offering.

Investors may be attracted to warrants because they provide "leverage," which is attractive to speculators. In other words, the market price of a warrant is generally much lower than the price of the underlying security, yet its price moves together with the underlying asset price. The result is greater percentage swings in warrant prices than for the underlying asset, which magnifies gains (or losses) in percentage terms. A ratio that may be used to measure this leverage potential is:

$$\text{Leverage potential} = \frac{\text{market price of the underlying share}}{\text{market price of the warrant}} \qquad (19.4)$$

Generally speaking, the larger this ratio, the greater the leverage effect. However, other factors such as the amount of overvaluation must also be considered. When selecting warrants, investors must also consider marketability and protection against stock splits and/or stock dividends (which is usually provided).

Like all options, warrants have an intrinsic value and a time value. The intrinsic value refers to the amount by which the market price of the underlying stock exceeds the exercise price of the warrant. It can never go below zero since exercise is at the option of the warrant holder. Time value refers to the amount by which the market price exceeds the intrinsic value.

There is also usually an overvaluation associated with warrants, which is calculated as follows:

(19.5)   Overvaluation=market price of warrant+exercise price of warrant
                          −market value of underlying asset

This will equal the time value whenever there is a positive intrinsic value, but it may exceed the time value when the intrinsic value is nil.

EXAMPLE

WARRANT CALCULATIONS

Determine the intrinsic value, time value, percentage overvaluation, and leverage potential of the following warrants:

Warrant (1): share price is $50, warrant price is $8, and exercise price of warrants is $52.

IV=Max (50−52, 0)=0; Time Value=8−0=$8;

Overvaluation=8+52−50= 10

Percentage overvaluation=10/50=0.20 or 20%

Leverage potential=50/8=6.25

Warrant (2): share price is $40, warrant price is $15, and exercise price of warrants is $30.

IV=Max(40−30, 0)=10; Time Value=15−10=$5;

Overvaluation=15+30−40=5

Percentage overvaluation=5/40=0.125 or 12.5%

Leverage potential=40/15=2.67

PERSPECTIVES

Corporate Manager

Warrants provide corporations with a mechanism to sweeten alternative security offerings and obtain improved initial financing terms.

Investor

Warrants can provide investors with leverage, which is ideal for speculation purposes.

CONVERTIBLES   19.4

Convertible instruments, whether preferred shares or debt, are securities that, at the option of the holder, may be converted into the common shares of the issuing firm. Such conversion features are another form of sweetener relied on by corporations to make their senior securities more attractive to investors. To facilitate exposition, we focus our discussion largely on **convertible debt**, noting that the concepts covered apply equally to issues of convertible preferred shares.

Convertible debt can be viewed as a combination of normal debt and an option to acquire common shares. In that sense, it is similar to a package of debt and warrants. When the call on common shares is exercised, however, the investor does not pay additional money in the form of a subscription price but rather surrenders the debt certificate. Thus, debt is transformed into common shares.

The basis for switching a convertible security into common shares is spelled out in terms of either a **conversion price** or a **conversion ratio**. The conversion price is defined as the portion of the senior security's face value to be surrendered for each common share when the option to convert is exercised. The conversion ratio specifies the number of shares received for each senior security.[6]

CONVERSION PRICE AND CONVERSION RATIO

EXAMPLE

Given a convertible debenture with a face value of $1,000, a conversion price of $25 indicates that the security is convertible into 1,000/25=40 common shares. Hence, the conversion ratio is 40.

We have the following relationship between conversion price, conversion ratio, and face value of a convertible security:

Face value=conversion price×conversion ratio   (19.6)

The conversion price is generally set above the prevailing market price of the common shares at the time of the offering and may increase over time.

In valuing convertible debt, it is easiest to consider the debt and the conversion feature separately. The **straight debt value** identifies the value of the debt alone, whereas the **conversion value** specifies how much the feature is worth if immediately converted. Clearly, the value of a convertible security is determined by the combination of these two components.

The straight debt value is determined by the standard debt valuation formulas outlined in Chapter 6 and is given as the present value of future cash flows (interest plus repayment of principal) discounted at the current interest rate on similar non-convertible debt. It is a function of both the interest rate paid on the convertible in relation to prevailing market rates and of the remaining maturity of the debt.

---

[6] Normally, appropriate provisions are made to protect the holders of both convertibles and warrants against stock dividends or stock splits, which dilute the value of their options. This is provided through adjustments to the conversion or subscription price.

EXAMPLE

STRAIGHT DEBT VALUE

Convertible debentures with a face value of $1,000 and a maturity of 20 years were issued three years ago with an interest rate of 8 percent. The current interest rate on similar debt is 10 percent. Assuming interest payments are made annually, we have:

$$\text{Straight debt value} = \$80 \times \left[\frac{1 - \dfrac{1}{(1.10)^{17}}}{0.10} \right] + \$1,000 \times \left[\frac{1}{(1.10)^{17}} \right]$$

$$= \$641.72 + \$197.84 = \$839.56$$

Given a conversion feature that is attractive to investors, convertible securities can often be issued with a yield that is somewhat below prevailing market rates. Therefore, at the time of issue, the straight debt value of convertibles is generally below their face value.

(19.7)   The conversion value of a convertible security is simply given as:

Conversion value=conversion ratio×current market price per share

If an investor chose to convert immediately and to liquidate his holdings, he would realize the conversion value.

EXAMPLE

CONVERSION VALUE

In the previous example, if the conversion price was set at $20 and the shares currently trade at $25, we would have:

Conversion ratio=1,000/20=50

Conversion value=50×25=$1,250

Convertible debt offers an investor the rights pertaining to both debt (payment of interest and principal) and to the conversion option (ability to convert at any time). Hence, a convertible security cannot trade at less than either its straight debt value or its conversion value. In fact, the conversion value and straight debt value combine to provide a price floor for the convertible. This is shown in Figure 19.1 together with the likely price of a convertible as a function of the underlying share price.

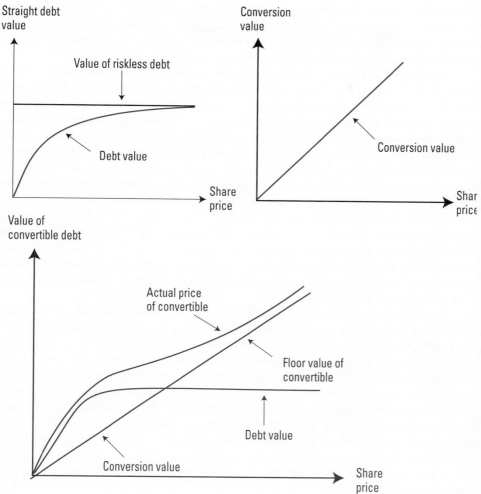

FIGURE 19.1

Value of Convertible
Debt as a Function of
Share Price

At low share prices, the option to convert has little attraction, and the holder of a convertible will prefer the more secure position of a creditor. Consequently, when share prices are depressed, the value of a convertible is determined mainly by the value of its debt. Apart from interest rates and maturity, the value of debt is a function of the risk of default. Decreasing share price is an indication of financial difficulty, and when a share price hits zero, a firm is bankrupt. Thus, the debt value becomes a function of share price and decreases rapidly for low share values, which indicates financial distress. As share prices increase, the debt value levels off, whereas the conversion value continues to increase. At some point, the conversion value will begin to dominate, and at high share prices, the value of a convertible security is determined mainly by its conversion feature.[7]

---

[7] When this situation prevails, it is common to say that the convertible is "selling off the stock."

We should recognize that the lines specifying the floor value of a convertible might shift over time. For example, the straight debt value will be influenced by any shift in prevailing interest rates and by the time left to maturity. Similarly, the conversion value may change if the conversion ratio does not remain constant.

As indicated in Figure 19.1, the actual price at which a convertible trades will normally be higher than the floor value for the reasons we explored in our discussion of options. As long as the option has time left to expiry, there is the potential for further capital gains through an appreciation in share prices. Moreover, investors, while waiting for such potential to be realized, are entitled to periodic interest payments on the debt, and the debt feature limits downside risk. Basically, convertible debt provides upside potential for price appreciation that is similar to owning stock and, simultaneously, the downside protection inherent in owning debt. Therefore, it is worth more than either pure security. Finally, certain institutional factors make convertibles attractive. Some financial intermediaries are legally constrained regarding their investments in common shares but not in convertibles, and they can enjoy the potential of capital gains from stock price appreciation by owning convertible securities. In addition, investors may face lower margin requirements that enable them to borrow more when investing in convertibles compared with a direct investment in common shares, and commission costs may be lower.

From a firm's point of view, convertible securities are often issued when new equity is required, but current market conditions and share prices are viewed as less than favourable. Ideally, the company would like to postpone the sale of new shares until share prices have recovered. However, if funds are required now, a convertible issue may appear attractive. As we saw, the conversion price is generally set above the prevailing market price of the common shares at the time of the issue. Thus, convertible securities are designed to net the corporation more for each issued share than could have been obtained under market conditions at the time of offering, thereby minimizing dilution. This is the rationale provided for a 1997 issue of convertible debentures by TVX Gold that is described in the report below. TVX vice-chairman John Hick said that the convertible debentures suited their needs since they were "not interested in selling equity at its current share price."

■ *Finance in the News*

Gold-Linked Convertible Debt

TVX Gold Inc. raised US$250 million through an offering of subordinated gold-linked convertible notes that mature in five years. At that time, note holders will receive their principal back as well as compensation based on the increase in the price of gold over that time. Vice-chairman John Hick said that the convertible debentures suited their needs since they were "not interested in selling equity at its current share price." He further explained that TVX used the financing as an alternative to traditional equity issues or debentures because they felt that the company's stock was underpriced. And, even though convertible debentures would allow TVX to issue stock later at a 20 to 25 percent premium, Hick felt the price would still be too low.

The financing was developed by TD Securities and was designed specifically for a gold company like TVX that did not want to sell shares at their low values. TD's Denys Calvin (equity capital markets) sees it as the "ultimate cross-markets instrument" because it has "option-like characteristics" that appeal to derivatives investors as well as "fixed-income attributes" such as the "return of principal at maturity." Equity investors are attracted by "uncertain payoff."

Other Canadian commodity-linked financings include Cominco Ltd.'s 1985 sale of three million units at $18 each to raise $54 million. These units consisted of a preferred share and warrants indexed to the price of zinc or copper. Investors earned returns on the warrants depending on which metal had appreciated the most.

Source: Barry Critchley, "Gold-Linked Issue Fits the Bill," *Financial Post*, March 8/10, 1997, p. 49. *Reprinted with permission.*

CONVERTIBLES AS DELAYED EQUITY FINANCING

EXAMPLE

A firm needs to raise $10 million. Its shares currently trade at $40 each, but management believes that they are undervalued and expects the price to increase to at least $50 over the next few years. The company intends to sell 20-year convertible debentures of $1,000 each with an interest rate of 8 percent. Each debenture can be converted at the option of the holder into 20 common shares. If the firm were to issue otherwise comparable straight debt, it would have to pay an interest rate of 10 percent.

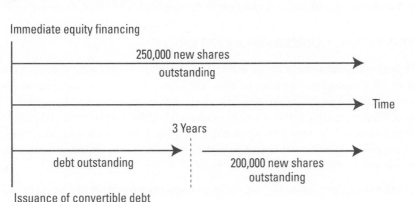

FIGURE 19.2

Consequences of Immediate Equity Finacing versus Issuance of Convertible Debt

Figure 19.2 contrasts the effects of immediate financing through new common shares at $40 per share with issuing convertible debentures. Under the latter alternative and given the conversion price of $50, upon conversion, only $10 million/50=200,000 new common shares would have to be issued. If, on the other hand, the $10 million had been raised through a straight issue of common shares at $40 per share, an additional $10 million/40=250,000 common shares would be outstanding.

Usually, convertible securities are viewed as deferred equity financing and are issued with the expectation that conversion will eventually become attractive and will take place. To enable the issuing corporation to force conversion once the price of its common shares has made conversion viable, convertible securities are generally issued with a call feature. This allows the firm to redeem the securities at a given call price. If, at the time, the conversion value exceeds the call price, investors have an incentive to convert.

FORCING CONVERSION

EXAMPLE

Pursuing the previous example, assume that three years after the original issue, the firm's common shares trade at $55 per share. If the convertible was subject to a call feature that allowed the corporation to redeem the debentures with a call premium of 5 percent, or at $1,050, investors would be forced to convert. Given a deadline of a few weeks and faced with the prospect of receiving the call price of $1,050 for each debenture, investors would choose to convert before the call date because the securities' conversion value of $20\times\$55=\$1,100$ exceeds the call price.

It is easy to see from the previous example why the market price of convertible securities that are subject to being called will not exceed substantially their conversion value. Because they limit potential price appreciation, call features are not attractive to investors. To protect investor interests, many convertibles can be called for redemption only after a specified period of time has elapsed since the date of issue.

Other features that a firm may include in order to provide an incentive to convert include a conversion ratio that declines over time, stipulation of a limited life for the option to convert, and coupon rates on the convertible debt that decrease with time.

TIME-VARYING CONVERTIBLE FEATURES

EXAMPLE

A 20-year convertible debenture with a face value of $1,000 may specify a conversion ratio of 20 if converted during the first five years and of 16 if conversion takes place between years 5 and 10. If the securities have not been converted by year 10, the conversion feature expires. Interest on the convertible debt may be set at 10 percent during the first five years, declining to 8 percent thereafter. It is easy to see that as time goes by, the convertible debenture becomes less attractive, providing investors with an incentive to switch into common shares.

In summary, the following are the main reasons why firms use convertibles:

1. It may permit cheaper initial financing or financing with fewer restrictive covenants. The conversion privilege is a sweetener with broad appeal to investors because it combines the safety of a senior security with the capital gains potential of common shares.

2. It provides a vehicle for possible common share financing at prices above those prevailing at the time. This could minimize dilution.

3. It enables the issuer to enlarge the market for its securities by attracting investors such as financial institutions that are faced with legal constraints restricting direct investment in common shares.

4. Underwriting costs are likely to be lower than for straight new equity financing.

Given these potential advantages, convertibles must also impose additional costs on the issuing firm. These costs include the value of the option that the company provides and the uncertainty as to whether and when conversion will take place. If share prices increase significantly above the conversion price so that the conversion option confers a capital gain to investors, the option forces the firm to sell shares at a discount. The enterprise may have been better off resorting to short- or intermediate-term straight debt financing initially and then selling stock when share prices rose because this would have minimized dilution. On the other hand, share prices may fail to appreciate sufficiently to force conversion, and this also entails costs, although of a different form. Convertible securities on which conversion cannot be forced are said to be "overhanging" and are normally an embarrassment since they remind investors that past management expectations have not been fulfilled. More importantly, the equity will not be forthcoming at a time when it may be needed most, and instead, the firm will be burdened with additional debt that is likely to restrict future financing flexibility.

Finally, investors recognize the dilution potential inherent whenever a corporation issues options on its own shares, and the earnings per share (EPS) figure reported in financial statements normally has to be supplemented by a disclosure of EPS on a fully diluted basis. Such diluted EPS are calculated on the assumption that all outstanding options—warrants, convertibles, and the like—have been converted, with an increasing number of common shares shown to be outstanding as a consequence.

DILUTED EARNINGS PER SHARE

EXAMPLE

We pursue an earlier example. A company that is solely financed through common equity has 750,000 shares outstanding, which currently trade at $40 per share. To finance new investments, the firm needs to raise $10 million and is considering 12 percent convertible debentures with a face value of $1,000 each and a conversion ratio of 20. Earnings before interest and taxes (EBIT) for the current year are $16 million. Because of start-up expenses on the new investments, it is expected that EBIT for the coming year will increase only to $18 million. The corporate tax rate is 40 percent. The impact of dilution in terms of EPS is illustrated in the calculations below:

	Presently	Coming year: convertibles outstanding	Coming year: debentures converted
EBIT	$16,000,000	$18,000,000	$18,000,000
Debenture interest at 12%	—	1,200,000	—
Taxable income	$16,000,000	$16,800,000	$18,000,000
Tax at 40%	6,400,000	6,720,000	7,200,000
Profit after taxes	$ 9,600,000	$10,080,000	$10,800,000
Number of shares outstanding	750,000	750,000	950,000
EPS	$12.80	$13.44	$11.37[8]

[8] This figure represents the fully diluted EPS figure.

Note, however, that dilution would have been even greater if the additional $10 million had been raised through an issue of straight common shares at $40 per share. With 250,000 new shares issued, EPS would drop to $10.8 million/(750,000+250,000)=$10.80.

It has been suggested that financing through convertibles is attractive when new investments require a substantial gestation period to become fully productive. As illustrated above, a resulting negative impact on EPS can be avoided while the debentures are outstanding. Once the new investments realize their potential, even conversion should not dilute prior returns to shareholders. The merits of this argument again depend on the extent to which markets are efficient since temporary fluctuations in reported EPS should be of limited concern to investors who are well informed about the firm's potential and are aware of earnings per share on a fully diluted basis.

P E R S P E C T I V E S

Corporate Manager

Convertible debt may be issued as sweeteners to provide delayed equity financing or to improve marketability or underwriting terms of alternative security issues.

Investor

Convertible debt provides investors with the upside potential associated with a company's underlying equity but with downside protection in the form of debt. However, they usually pay for this benefit in the form of reduced interest payments versus those that would be associated with similar non-convertible debt.

19.5 UNITS

On occasion, corporations package two or more different types of securities and options together in an attempt to increase the marketability of an offering or to appeal to a wider range of investors. Specific forms of packaging vary, and there is no standard unit or approach.

EXAMPLE

UNITS OFFERING

In January 2000, Digital Gem Corp. raised $7 million through a rights offering of 13.1 million units. Each unit consisted of one common share and one-half share purchase warrant. Each whole warrant entitles the holder to purchase one common share for $0.75 up to June 1, 2001.

The components of a unit may be tied together for some specified period after the issue in an attempt to curb, or at least defer, speculation that might otherwise develop around certain component securities of the unit, such as warrants. Practice in this regard varies and hinges on the particular circumstances and the judgement of the underwriters involved.

We can question whether such packaging serves a useful purpose. Clearly, the sale of units restricts investors' flexibility because investors would have a wider choice if the various securities were issued separately. Furthermore, in efficient markets, there is little reason to believe that the price of a unit would differ substantially from the sum of its parts. That is, a firm should not be able to reduce its cost of financing just because it packages securities in a specific fashion, particularly since investors who choose to do so can easily replicate any packaging on their own. However, the existence of units indicates that at least some underwriters and financial executives do not concur with this judgement. Indeed, in recent years a wide variety of complex securities have been issued by firms attempting to create innovative financing instruments that might appeal to investors.

COMMON SHARES AS CALL OPTIONS　19.6

We have reviewed the principal types of options that firms issue in connection with their long-term financing. Before ending this chapter, however, we briefly consider how more traditional long-term financing instruments such as common stock can be viewed as options.

A share of stock has a value that is contingent on the value of the real assets the company owns. Because of this, a share of common stock can be viewed as a call option on the firm's real assets. This is best illustrated through a simplified example.

Consider a business that is founded for the sole purpose of acquiring and developing a tract of real estate. Development will take place during the coming year, with the property to be sold at year end. The total capital required to cover all development costs is $1 million, of which $200,000 is equity in the form of common shares that you, as the only shareholder hold. The remaining $800,000 is raised through debt in the form of a mortgage, repayable at the end of the year.

Clearly, the value of your equity at year end is a function of the price at which the property can be sold. If the selling price is less than $800,000 (the amount of debt owing), you receive nothing. The firm would be bankrupt, and the debt holders would receive any proceeds from the sale to satisfy their claims. If the selling price exceeds $800,000, you receive the difference between the selling price and the value of the debt. This is illustrated in Figure 19.3. Note that this diagram is identical to Figure 18.1(a) of Chapter 18, which showed the value of an option at its expiration date as a function of the price of the underlying asset.

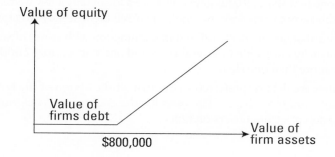

FIGURE 19.3

Equity as Call Option

Assume now that six months have gone by since the start of the project. Real estate prices are currently such that your property could be sold for only $800,000. If the project were terminated at that time, your equity would be worthless because you could only just repay the debt. But since you have another six months to go, you should be able to find buyers who would be willing to pay you something for your shares. If, for example, someone paid you $50,000 for your equity, his downside risk would be limited to a loss of $50,000, whereas on the upside, his gain would parallel any appreciation in real estate prices over the next half year. The actual value of your equity as a function of the asset value of your firm would be given by the curve showing option values V_c in Figure 18.10 of Chapter 18. We see that your equity behaves in a way that is identical to a call option on the property, with an exercise price of $800,000.

Generalizing from the above, a company's common shares can be viewed essentially as a call option on the assets of the firm, with an exercise price equal to the value of the enterprise's outstanding debt. Because of the feature of limited liability, common shareholders face the same limited downside risk as option holders. At the same time, if circumstances warrant, they can claim full ownership benefits by paying off the debt holders (this is equivalent to exercising the option). This view of common shares, apart from its conceptual interest, has two important implications:

1. The theory of option valuation provides important insights into the valuation of common shares. Given the mathematical sophistication of developments in this area, however, any further exposition is beyond our scope.

2. The view of common shares as options with limited downside risk and asymmetric payoffs as a function of asset values provides valuable insights into risk sharing between shareholders and debt holders, with implications for debt contracts and decisions regarding a firm's capital structure.

19.7 SUMMARY

1. Firms issue options either to provide current stockholders with an opportunity to subscribe to new share offerings on a preferential basis or as "sweeteners" to make new issues of senior securities more marketable.

2. Rights are issued when a firm offers new shares to current shareholders on a privileged subscription basis. Normally, one right is issued for each outstanding share and, depending on the number of new shares to be offered, several rights may be required to obtain one new share. Rights generally have a life of only a few weeks and shareholders who choose not to exercise their rights may sell them in the marketplace.

3. Warrants are options that are normally offered in conjunction with issues of senior securities. They normally have a life of several years and one warrant may entitle its holder to purchase more than one share.

4. Convertible securities are debt or preferred shares that, at the option of the holder, can be converted into common shares. The basis for the conversion is determined through the conversion price or conversion ratio.

5. On occasion, corporations package together two or more different types of securities and options and offer them as a unit in an effort to increase marketability.

6. Common shares generally can be viewed as options on the firm's assets with an exercise price equal to the value of the firm's outstanding debt.

QUESTIONS AND PROBLEMS

Questions for Discussion

1. (a) From an investor's point of view, what is the difference between purchasing rights and purchasing warrants?

   (b) Contrast rights and warrants from an issuer's point of view with particular reference to how they come into being, what the issuer expects to receive, and any balance sheet implications.

2. It has been said that convertible securities offer the best of two worlds to the issuing firm. While debt is outstanding, the company pays a lower interest rate than it would on straight debt, and after conversion, the number of shares outstanding will be smaller than if new shares had been sold initially. Do you agree?

3. Assume that for the same price you could purchase either a convertible debenture or a straight debenture with warrants that would entitle you to purchase the number of shares specified by the conversion ratio of the convertible. Assuming the same coupon and term to maturity, which would you prefer? Explain.

   (a) Compare and contrast convertible debentures and debentures with warrants from an issuer's point of view. What are the main differences, and how do they affect the issuing firm?

4. A company is contemplating a rights issue to raise new funds. Three investors each hold an equal number of shares in this company. The first investor subscribes to the rights issue, the second sells the rights on the open market, and the third investor does not act upon the rights issue at all. Contrast the wealth position, total number of shares, percentage ownership, and cash position of the three investors before and after the rights offering.

5. The common stock of a leveraged firm can be described as a call option on the underlying firm's assets. Following this analogy, identify the writer of the call option, and what is the exercise price of that option? What is the result if the company's value is less than the exercise price?

6. Why would a firm choose to issue its securities as units rather than separately? Would a separable unit be more or less valuable than a non-separable one? Why would a business issue non-separable units? Can you justify the use of units given efficient markets?

7. An investor holds a convertible debenture. Under what circumstances would that person choose to convert the convertible debenture? Discuss.

8. Consider a firm that decides to undergo a rights issue. Will its value change after the rights have been issued? Will the firm's value change if the rights issue is fully subscribed? What trade-offs must it make when deciding on a subscription price for a rights offering?

PROBLEMS WITH SOLUTIONS

Problem 1

A company currently has 5 million shares outstanding at a market price of $20 per share. New capital in the amount of $16 million is to be raised through common shares that are to be sold through a rights offering.

(a) If the subscription price is set at 20 percent below the current market price, how many new shares have to be issued? If one right is associated with each outstanding share, how many rights will be required to subscribe to one new share?

(b) Compute the total value that the firm's outstanding shares should have just before and just after the new offering as well as the market price per share.

(c) Compute the intrinsic value of a right during the cum-rights and ex-rights periods.

(d) Show that the total wealth of shareholders remains unchanged through the offering regardless of whether they exercise or sell their rights.

Solution 1

(a) Subscription price per share:

$E = .8 \times$ current market price $= \$16$

Number of new shares to be issued:

$n = 16,000,000/16 = 1,000,000$

Number of rights required to purchase one new share:

$N =$ current shares outstanding/new shares to be issued

$= 5,000,000/1,000,000 = 5$

(b) Before offering:

Price per share $= \$20$

Total value of firm's shares

$= 5,000,000 \times 20 = \$100,000,000$

After offering:

Total value of firm's shares

$$=\text{value before offering}+\text{amount raised through offering}$$
$$=100{,}000{,}000+16{,}000{,}000$$
$$=\$116{,}000{,}000$$

$$\text{Price per share}=\frac{\text{total value}}{\text{number of shares}}$$

$$=116{,}000{,}000/6{,}000{,}000$$
$$=\$19.33$$

(c) Formula based on rights-on market price:

$$IV=\frac{S_0-E}{N+1}=\frac{20-16}{5+1}=\$0.67$$

Formula based on ex-rights market price:

$$IV=\frac{S_X-E}{N}=\frac{19.33-16}{5}=\$0.67$$

(d) Assume that an investor held five shares before the offering and exercises his rights. We have:

Wealth before offering	$5\times20=$	$100
Shareholdings after offering	$5\times19.33=$	116
Minus: Subscription price paid for new share	$.8\times20=$	16
Total wealth after offering		$100

If the investor sells his rights, we obtain:

Shareholdings after offering	$5\times19.33=$	$96.65
Proceeds from sale of five rights	$5\times.67=$	3.35
Total wealth after offering		$100.00

Thus, a shareholder's wealth position should remain unaffected by a rights offering regardless of the subscription price.

Problem 2

A firm's common shares currently trade at $10 per share, and it has warrants outstanding that entitle the holder to purchase two shares at an exercise price of $9 per share. The expiry date is three years hence.

(a) Compute the intrinsic value for the warrants.

(b) Show that the warrants cannot trade at a price that is below this intrinsic value.

(c) Show the percentage change in the intrinsic value of the warrants given a 20 percent change in the market price of the shares.

(d) Assume that a year later the company's shares trade at $20 per share. Recompute the intrinsic value of the warrants and again derive the percentage change in this intrinsic value of the warrants for a 20 percent change in the market price of the shares.

Solution 2

(a) We have $S=\$10$, $E=\$9$, $N=2$; we obtain:

$$IV = \frac{S-E}{N} = \frac{10-9}{0.5} = \$2.00$$

(b) Suppose that the warrants traded below this intrinsic value at $1. An investor could then buy a warrant for $1, exercise and purchase two shares for a total of $18, and immediately sell these shares for $20 for a net riskless profit of $20-18-1=\$1$. Ignoring transaction costs, this arbitrage process would continue until the price of the warrants reached at least the intrinsic value of $2.

(c) We obtain:

S	IV
$ 8	$0
10	$2(10-9)=2$
12	$2(12-9)=6$

The percentage changes are:

$$+20\%: \frac{6-2}{2} = 200\%$$

-20%: IV becomes 0, so the change is -100%

(d) We have:

$$IV = \frac{20-9}{0.5} = \$22.00$$

Notice the leverage effect, a 100 percent increase in the share price (from $10 to $20), results in a 1,000 percent increase in the warrant's intrinsic value (from $2 to $22). For a share price change of 20 percent we obtain:

S	IV
$16	$14
20	22
24	30

Hence, a price change of 20 percent in S now results in a change of $8/22=36.36\%$ in IV

ADDITIONAL PROBLEMS

1. The shares of P.X. Company are trading at $48 ex rights. Shareholders were offered one new share for every five shares held at a subscription price of $42.

   (a) What is the intrinsic value of one right?

   (b) Show that the wealth position of a shareholder should be unaffected by the rights offering regardless of whether she chooses to exercise or to sell her rights.

   (c) A speculator, who has $6,480 to invest, believes that the price of P.X. shares should increase to $53 within a month. Should the speculator buy shares or rights assuming that rights trade at $2 and have one month left to expiry? What are the trade-offs?

2. Mechanical Industries Inc. wants to raise $100 million through a rights offering. It currently has 50 million shares outstanding with a market price of $12.40 each. It has decided to set the subscription price for the rights offering at $10 per share.

   (a) What will be the value of one right?

   (b) Assuming that no other news about this firm comes out, what will be the stock price:

          i) after announcement date but before ex-rights date?

          ii) after ex-rights date but before holder of record date?

          iii) after the holder of record date?

3. ABC Industries is planning a rights offering of 50,000 shares at a subscription price of $40 each. The following timetable is planned:

       March 27 – announcement date

       April 27 – ex-rights date

       April 29 – record date

       May 30 – rights expire

   The market price on March 27 is $50 per share, and four rights are required to purchase each additional share. Assume that there are no changes in the market price except as a result of the rights offering.

   (a) What is the value of one right?

   (b) How many shares of common stock will ABC have outstanding after the rights offering?

   (c) Suppose you own 200 shares of ABC stock. Discuss the effects on your wealth if on May 29, you decide to take the following actions:

          i) exercise the rights

          ii) sell the rights

4. A company is currently 100 percent equity financed. It has earnings per share of $1.50 and 5 million shares outstanding. It wants to raise funds through the issue of debt. If it issues straight debt, it will pay an interest rate of 6.7 percent resulting in total interest payments of $670,000 per year. However, it could issue bonds with warrants allowing purchase of a total of 100,000 new shares attached as a sweetener. If it

attaches warrants, then it will be able to sell bonds to yield only 5.8 percent resulting in a total interest payment of $580,000 per year. Whatever way the firm raises the capital, it will be able to invest the proceeds and raise earnings before interest and tax by 10 percent. Assume that the total earnings before interest and tax of the firm are not expected to change after that and that the firm's tax rate is 30 percent.

(a) If the enterprise issues straight debt to raise the funds, what will be its earnings per share?

(b) If it issues debt with warrants attached and the warrants are never exercised (as the stock price remains below exercise price), what will be the earnings per share?

(c) If the firm issues debt with warrants attached and the warrants are exercised, what will be the earnings per share (assume that the proceeds from exercise of warrants does not affect earnings)?

5. Successful Enterprises currently has 15 million common shares outstanding that trade at $12 per share, and $18 million of new equity capital is to be raised through a rights offering. Management has been debating whether to set the subscription price for the new shares at $11, $10, or $9 per share.

(a) For each alternative, compute the number of additional shares to be issued, the number of rights required for subscription to one new share, the intrinsic value of a right, and the market price per share ex rights.

(b) If after the offering, total after-tax earnings for the coming year are expected to be $20 million and dividends of $0.70 per share are to be maintained, compute the impact of various subscription prices on earnings per share and on total cash needed to pay dividends.

(c) What are the practical trade-offs in setting the subscription price?

6. Warrants for the purchase of shares of Child Corp. entitle the holder to purchase three shares per warrant at $12.50 per share. The warrants currently have an intrinsic value of $7.50.

(a) Compute the current market price per share.

(b) Calculate the percentage change in the warrants' intrinsic value for a 15 percent change in the market price of the shares.

(c) Assume that the share price moves to $11. Compute the new intrinsic value of the warrants and the effect of a 15 percent change in the new share price on the warrants' intrinsic value.

7. Several years ago, a firm issued convertible debentures with a coupon rate of 7.5 percent, callable at a 4 percent premium. The conversion price was set at $20. Today, its common shares trade at $23 and interest rates are 9 percent. The firm is considering whether or not to call the issue.

(a) What is the conversion ratio?

(b) If an investor were to convert his debentures into common shares today, how much would he receive in value? Can the firm force conversion?

(c) Why may the company want to call the debentures when the current interest rate is higher than the coupon rate?

8. Two years ago, Sixtue Corp. issued 20-year, 9 percent convertible debentures with a face value of $1,000 each and a conversion ratio of 40. Had Sixtue issued otherwise similar straight debt, it would have faced an interest rate of 12 percent. Interest rates have increased by about two percentage points during the past two years. Shares of Sixtue currently trade at $22.50.

(a) Compute the current straight debt value and the current conversion value of the convertibles. What is the present floor price for the convertibles?

(b) Two years later (four years after the date of the original issue), interest rates on comparable straight debt have decreased to 9 percent, and Sixtue's share price has increased to $32. Recompute the straight debt value and the conversion value.

(c) What would yearly dividends per share have to be for you to receive a higher annual cash return through converting rather than through holding the convertible debentures?

9. A company that is currently financed solely through common equity has 2 million shares outstanding that trade at $25 per share. To finance new investments, the firm wants to raise $5 million. The alternatives are to sell new common shares, to finance through convertible debentures, or to finance through ordinary debentures. Assume that new shares could be sold to net the firm $25 per share. The convertible debentures would carry interest of 10.5 percent and the straight debentures, a coupon of 12 percent. Earnings before interest and taxes were $14 million last year (year 0) and are expected to remain at that level for the coming year (year 1). After that time, the new investments are expected to be fully productive, resulting in EBIT for year 2 of $16 million. The corporate tax rate is 40 percent.

(a) Compute earnings per share (EPS) for year 0.

(b) Compute EPS for years 1 and 2 for new common share financing, for financing through convertible debentures assuming that conversion has not taken place, and for financing through straight debentures.

(c) With financing through convertible debentures, compute EPS on a fully diluted basis for years 1 and 2 assuming alternative conversion ratios of (i) 30 and (ii) 35 per $1,000 debenture.

(d) Briefly discuss the implications of your findings, and suggest what trade-offs the company faces in choosing between the various financing alternatives.

10. The following financial statements of Depliant Industries were released for the year just ended:

Balance Sheet

Current assets	$ 2,500,000	Current liabilities	$ 1,200,000
Investments	200,000	Long-term debt	
		(8% coupon)	5,000,000
Plant and equipment	6,000,000	Common shares	
Land	4,000,000	($2 par value)	
		authorized 2,000,000	
		issued 1,000,000	2,000,000
		Contributed surplus	3,500,000
		Retained earnings	1,000,000
	$12,700,000		$12,700,000

Income Statement

Sales	$4,000,000
Cost of goods sold	2,600,000
Earnings before interest and taxes	$1,400,000
Interest	400,000
Taxable income	$1,000,000
Tax (40%)	400,000
Net income	$600,000

Shares have generally traded at seven times earnings.

Depliant's vice-president Kay Smith would like to pursue new investment opportunities that would require additional capital of $4 million. She believes that if the new investments are undertaken, earnings before interest and taxes would grow at a rate of 8 percent per year for five years and that the price-earnings ratio for Depliant's shares would immediately adjust upward to 10.

Preliminary indications are that a straight debt issue could be floated at 14 percent interest, debt with warrants at 12 percent interest, and convertible debt at 11 percent interest. New common shares could be sold to net $4 per share. If the debt with warrants were issued, each $1,000 debenture would carry 100 warrants, and each warrant would entitle the holder to purchase one share at an exercise price of $4.75 during the next four years. Under convertible debt, the conversion price would also be set at $4.75.

(a) Compute the present market price of Depliant's shares.

(b) Given the above projections, show the effects on earnings per share and share price at the end of the coming year and also at the end of year 4 if the $4 million is raised by (i) straight debt, (ii) common shares, (iii) debt with warrants, and (iv) convertible debt. Assume that investors base their valuation of Depliant's shares on fully diluted earnings per share.

(c) Assume that all earnings for the four years will be paid out in dividends and that any increase in capital will go 60 percent to plant and equipment and 40 percent to land. Show the balance sheet as it would appear at the end of year 4 assuming issuance of (i) issuance of straight debt, (ii) issuance of common shares, (iii) issuance of debt with warrants with all warrants exercised prior to expiry, and (iv) convertible debt not yet converted.

11. The Manufacturing Company is planning an expansion program that requires new capital of $32 million. The firm currently has 12 million shares outstanding and $25 million in long-term debt at an interest rate of 10 percent. Earnings before interest and taxes for the year just ended were $14.5 million. With the new financing, they are expected to increase to $18 million for the current year and to grow at a rate of 8 percent annually thereafter for the indefinite future. The firm's shares have generally traded at a price-earnings ratio of 15, and it is expected that they will continue to do so. The corporate tax rate is 40 percent.

(a) Compute the current market price of the firm's shares.

(b) Assume that new shares could be issued to net the company 10 percent less than the current market price. If the new capital were raised through an issue of common shares, how many new shares would have to be issued? Compute earnings per share and the market price per share at the end of the current year (year 1) and at the end of year 3.

(c) Alternatively, the new capital could be raised by issuing 20-year convertible debentures with a face value of $1,000 each at an interest rate of 11 percent. The conversion price would be set at 20 percent above the current market price of the shares. A call feature would allow the corporation to redeem the issue at any time after year 3 at a premium of 3 percent over face value. Current interest rates on otherwise comparable straight debt are 12.5 percent.

(i) Assuming that the projections materialize and that interest rates remain unchanged, compute the straight debt value and the conversion value at the end of year 3. Can the corporation force conversion at that time?

(ii) Assuming that conversion has taken place, compute earnings per share and market price per share at the end of year 3.

(d) Based on the information given, what method for raising the funds appears preferable? What are the risks and trade-offs?

Synthetic Indexing:
When is a Foreign Investment
Not a Foreign Investment

In Chapter 18, we saw how Newcastle Capital Management exploits the possibilities of options in innovative ways. Options and hedge funds are relatively new ventures for Newcastle; however, it is perhaps best known as the first company to offer synthetic indexing, a sophisticated strategy that uses futures to replicate the behaviour of any index without actually holding the assets of that index.

Newcastle Vice President Robert Rafos, one of the company's founders, explains how this works. "Suppose you give us $1 million in Canadian money-market instruments. We take it, and put $1 million into futures contracts in such a way that their returns exactly match the return of the target index." This complicated operation requires sophisticated software, which Newcastle develops in-house.

"It's important that the amount we put into futures matches the amount of the orignal asset fund," says Mr. Rafos. "If we use any less, we don't exploit the market fully. If we use more, we expose the funds to higher risk."

The big advantage of a synthetic index for Canadian investors is that it allows them to gain exposure to return on U.S. and other foreign markets using Canadian investment instruments. "When we started the firm," points out Mr. Rafos, the limit on foreign investment for pensions and RRSPs was 10 percent," so investors were missing out on some pretty big opportunities in foreign markets. Today the limit is 30 percent, but the chance to increase foreign participation even further is still very attractive.

When Newcastle was first started on the strength of the synthetic indexing concept, which Mr. Rafos credits to co-founder David Paterson, now company chairman, there was some uncertainty as to whether or not Revenue Canada would allow assets invested this way to be treated as Canadian funds. "Once we got the okay from the government, however, things took off quickly," Mr. Rafos says. By now, "synthetic indexing has become very popular. Virtually every bank or investment firm offers it today."

But Newcastle was the first.

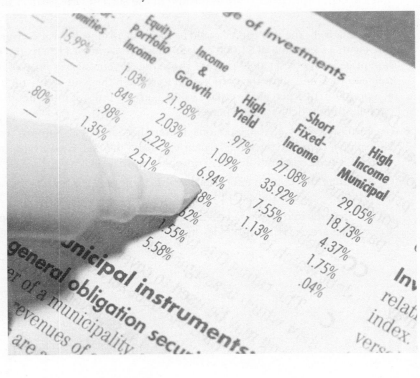

Futures

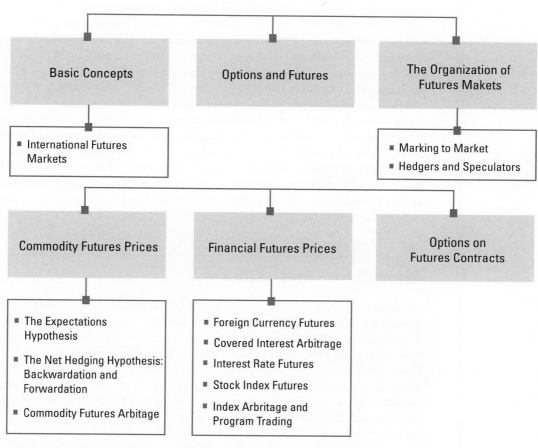

Learning Objectives

After studying this chapter, you should be able to:

1. *Explain how futures contracts differ from options.*
2. *Discuss the difference between futures contracts and forward contracts.*
3. *Define the terms backwardation and forwardation.*
4. *Explain arbitrage and demonstrate how it works in commodity and financial futures.*
5. *Describe how different types of futures (foreign currency, interest rate, stock index, etc.) contribute to risk management.*

20.1   INTRODUCTION[1]

Physical commodities and financial instruments are typically traded in cash markets. A cash contract calls for immediate delivery and is used by those who need a commodity now (e.g., food processors). Cash contracts cannot be cancelled unless both parties agree. The current cash prices of commodities and financial instruments can be found daily in such sources as the *Globe and Mail*, the *Financial Post* (*National Post*) and the *Wall Street Journal*.

There are two types of cash markets: spot markets and forward markets. Spot markets feature immediate delivery.[2] The spot price refers to the current market price of an item available for immediate delivery. Forward markets have deferred delivery. The forward price is the price of an item that is to be delivered at some specified time in the future.

Much of the uncertainty financial managers face concerns future prices since they are exposed to the risk of price declines in their products, and the risk of price increases in their inputs. One common way to mitigate such risks is to enter into **forward contracts**. A forward contract is a negotiated agreement between a buyer and a seller to lock in a price at which a future transaction will occur.[3] This price is called a **forward price**. Normally, under the contract, no money changes hands until the delivery time specified in the contract. Each contract is a unique legal liability and generally cannot be traded to another party.

■ *Finance in the News*

Barrick Defends Hedging Strategy

Peter Munk, chairman of Barrick Gold Corp., defended his company's use of gold hedging, a practice that it introduced into the gold mining industry 15 years before when Barrick was still a small petroleum concern. It is now the most profitable gold mining company in the world. A company spokesperson suggested that its hedging strategy had "brought in an additional $1.5 billion in revenue or $66 per ounce" over the previous 12 years. This has allowed the Toronto-based giant to overcome the problem of low gold prices. Barrick's chief financial officer, Jamie Sokalsky, noted that in 1999 alone, hedging produced $391 million additional profit, or $106 a\per ounce more than the market price.

Munk stated that hedging was "a distinguishing feature" of the company, one that allowed it to generate "massive additional income." Hedging also allowed Barrick to disregard specific delivery dates on gold being hedged. The chairman added that his company can offer the spot price or the hedge price, whichever is higher. For example, the spot price of gold is $276 per ounce, but Barrick is selling its gold for $360 per ounce and has sold forward 13.4 million ounces at that higher price. That represents all of its production for the next two years and one-quarter of its future production.

Source: Allan Robinson, "Barrick Defends Hedging Strategy," *Globe and Mail*, May 17, 2000, p.B4. *Reprinted with permission.*

---

[1] Parts of this chapter draw from Z. Bodie et. al. *Investments* (Homewood, Ill.: Richard D. Irwin, 1989).

[2] "Immediate" means in the normal course of business. For example, it may take two days for an item to be delivered after being ordered.

[3] Forward contracts are centuries old, traceable to at least the ancient Romans and Greeks.

The report above discusses the importance to Barrick Gold Corp. of hedging its selling price of gold by selling gold forward. The article states that Barrick had "sold forward 13.4 million ounces of gold" as of March 2000. A company spokesperson suggested that its hedging strategy had "brought in an additional $1.5 billion in revenue or $66 an ounce" over the previous 12 years.

The example below provides a simple illustration of how forward contracts can be used to hedge price risk.

USING FORWARD CONTRACTS TO SET A GIVEN SELLING PRICE

EXAMPLE

An oil producer, wishing to lock in a price for its output, enters a forward contract with a refinery that wants to lock in a price for its input. They agree to a forward contract whereby the refinery will purchase 50,000 barrels of oil in 18 months at a forward price of $30 per barrel. Payment of $1.5 million will be made in 18 months when the oil is received.

Forward contracts provide a useful and flexible approach to managing business, but they can have drawbacks. Negotiating an acceptable, legally binding forward contract may be time-consuming and expensive, and getting out of a forward contract when conditions change may create legal problems. Often, the possibility of default by the other contracting party must also be factored into any risk-management strategy.

In response to such difficulties with forward contracts, an alternative way of locking in futures prices, called **futures contracts**, has gained prominence. Futures contracts, like forward contracts, are agreements to trade a specified asset at a specified price and time in the future. They are, however, different from forward contracts in several important ways. First, futures contracts are standardized, and hence, no complex legal negotiations are involved. Second, they are traded on **futures markets** and consequently can be entered into and withdrawn from through straightforward market transactions. Thus, they offer liquidity. Finally, they are contracts with a financial intermediary called a **futures market clearing house**, so futures contract holders need not fear default by any other party. In Canada, the Canadian Derivatives Clearing Corporation (CDCC), introduced in Chapter 18, serves this function for all exchange-traded interest rate and equity futures contracts. The CDCC has also begun providing clearing, settlement, and administrative services to the Winnipeg Commodity Exchange (WCE) and the WCE clearing corporation.

These features have proven so attractive that futures have become an indispensable part of risk-management strategies for many industries. Because of this, we concentrate our attention on futures contracts rather than forward contracts. We note, however, that forward contracts are used when greater flexibility in contracting is required. For instance, forward contracts in foreign currencies, which are available from large banks, can be set up in a wider variety of currencies and further into the future than is possible with futures contracts. Since the overall structure of forward and futures contracts is broadly similar, most of the following discussion applies to forward contracts as well.

The value of a forward or futures contract depends on what happens to the price of the underlying asset. For example, if the price of oil rises to $40 per barrel, a contract to buy it at $30 is clearly worth more than it would be if the oil price fell to $20 per barrel. Thus, forward and futures contracts, like options, are a type of derivative security.

20.2   BASIC CONCEPTS

Futures trading has traditionally been associated by most people with trading in commodities such as gold, wheat, and oil. However, conceptually, forward or futures contracts can be written on anything as evidenced by the recent introduction of "weather derivatives," which arose in response to the fact that about $1 trillion of the $7-trillion U.S. economy is weather sensitive.[4] Many of these derivatives trade on over-the-counter markets, although some have recently begun trading on the Chicago Mercantile Exchange. There are a variety of weather derivatives available, and their values are based on numerous measures such as temperature, rainfall, snowfall, and humidity.[5]

In addition, money can be thought of simply as another commodity, and financial futures have become a particularly viable investment alternative for numerous investors. Therefore, futures contracts currently traded on futures exchanges can be divided into two broad categories:

1. commodities—agricultural, metal, and energy-related products
2. financials—foreign currencies as well as debt and equity instruments

Typical underlying assets for futures contracts include agricultural commodities, oil and gasoline, metals, foreign currencies, treasury bills, government bonds, and portfolios of stocks. In December of 2000, the U.S. Congress passed legislation that would permit futures on single stocks. This move is expected to cause a dramatic change in the U.S. derivatives markets. This will allow U.S. markets to compete with derivatives exchanges outside the U.S. (such as the London International Financial Futures and Options Exchange) that plan to launch such products in 2001. In fact the Montreal Exchange has recently begun trading futures on the common stock of Nortel Networks. When the underlying asset is a real commodity, the term **commodity futures contract** is used. Futures contracts for trade goods other than metals are referred to as soft-commodity futures. When the underlying asset is a financial obligation such as a currency, bond, or stock portfolio, the term **financial futures contract** is used. Forward contracts are widely used to lock in prices for foreign currencies and short-term debt. The price set out in a futures contract is called the **futures price**.

| EXAMPLE |

CANOLA FUTURES

The November 2000 futures price of canola was $252.20 per metric tonne for a standardized contract size of 20 tonnes. This means that a trader who entered a futures contract to buy or sell canola that month agreed that $252.20 per tonne would be paid when the 20 tonnes of canola was delivered in November.

---

[4] Simon Challis, "Bright Forecast for Profits," *Reactions*, June, 1999; and M. Hanley, "Hedging the Forces of Nature," *Risk Professional*, Issue 1, July/August 1999, 21-25.

[5] Weather derivatives will be discussed in greater detail in Chapter 21. For a complete survey, see Hanely (1999) from footnote 4.

An investor who took a **long position** in such a contract promised to buy the canola the following November and pay the futures price of $252.20 per tonne at that time. An investor who took the **short side** of the contract promised to sell the canola at that price in November. The futures price is usually compared to the spot price—the price at which the commodity itself is currently trading. Pursuing the previous example, if one were to buy canola for immediate delivery, one would have to pay the spot price of $238.80 per tonne. The difference between the November futures price and the spot price is called the basis of November futures. In this case, the basis is $13.40 per tonne ($252.20 minus $238.80).

Figure 20.1 shows how futures prices are listed in a financial newspaper. The listings shown are Canadian futures contracts traded on October 13, 2000 on the Winnipeg Commodity Exchange (WCE) and the Montreal Exchange (ME). We refer to the listing for canola futures traded on the WCE. The standard size of the canola futures contract is 20 metric tonnes per contract. The estimated volume of trade in canola futures contracts for the most recent trading day (Est sales—Estimated Sales) is 260 contracts,

Montreal Exchange

Futures

SeaHi	SeaLow	Mth.	Open	High	Low	Settle	Chg.	Opint
3-month bankers' acceptances, $1M, pts. of 100%								
94.24	94.15	Dec00	94.23	94.24	94.20	94.22		58776
94.32	94.19	Mar01	94.30	94.32	94.26	94.28	−0.01	57437
94.31	94.19	Jun01	94.29	94.31	94.25	94.28		21968
94.30	94.16	Sep01	94.30	94.30	94.23	94.23	−0.02	15465
94.28	94.14	Dec01	94.24	94.28	94.22	94.22	−0.01	6098
94.10	94.02	Sep02	94.10	94.10	94.10	94.10	−0.03	928

Est sales	Prv Sales	Prv Open Int	Chg.
14498	33600	160412	+12828

10-year Cda bonds, $100K, pts of 100%, 1 pt = $10

102.26	101.40	Dec00	101.98	102.04	101.70	102.01	+0.03	58700

Est sales	Prv Sales	Prv Open Int	Chg.
3228	4496	58553	+148

5-year Cda bonds, $100K, pts of 100%

Est sales	Prv Sales	Prv Open Int	Chg.
		0	+0

S&P Canada 60

631.00	605.50	Dec00	606.00	631.00	605.50	628.50	+17.20	58358

Est sales	Prv Sales	Prv Open Int	Chg.
2791	4023	56782	+1576

Options

Price	Calls	–	Last	Puts	–	Last
3-mo. bankers' acceptances futures,$1M,pts of 100%						
	Dec	Mar	Jun	Dec	Mar	Jun
9275.00	1.47	15.30	r	r	r	r
9300.00	1.22	12.80	1.28	r	r	0.02
9325.00	0.97	10.30	1.03	r	0.10	0.04
9350.00	0.72	7.80	0.82	r	0.20	0.07
9375.00	0.47	5.70	0.62	r	0.40	0.11
9400.00	0.23	3.80	0.46	0.02	1.00	0.18
9425.00	0.07	2.10	0.30	0.10	2.00	0.27
9450.00	0.01	1.20	0.19	0.28	3.30	0.49
9475.00	r	0.50	0.11	0.53	5.10	0.56
9500.00	r	0.20	0.05	0.78	7.20	0.75
9525.00	r	r	0.02	1.03	r	0.97
Prev day call vol		200 Open int.				21815
Prev day put vol		0 Open int.				20725
Canada bond futures, $100,000, pts. of 100%						
	Nov	Dec	Jan	Nov	Dec	Jan
100.00	2.01	2.07	218.00	r	0.07	19.00
101.00	1.03	1.25	143.00	0.02	0.25	43.00
102.00	r	r	84.00	0.28	0.62	83.00
Prev day call vol		0 Open int.				0
Prev day put vol		0 Open int.				0

Winnipeg Commodity Exchange

Futures

SeaHi	SeaLow	Mth.	Open	High	Low	Settle	Chg.	Opint
CANOLA 20 tonnes, $Cdn/tonne								
313.00	250.70	Nov00	256.40	256.60	252.00	252.20	−4.20	28368
303.20	256.50	Jan01	262.50	262.80	258.50	258.70	−3.80	28434
301.00	262.50	Mar01	268.00	268.00	264.80	265.00	−3.50	10892
280.50	267.70	May01	274.00	274.00	269.00	269.50	−4.00	1803
287.30	275.00	Jul01	277.50	277.80	275.00	275.00	−3.70	1872

Est sales	Prv Sales	Prv Open Int	Chg.
260	191	73522	−1754

FLAXSEED 20 tonnes, $Cdn/tonne

241.00	239.00	Nov00	241.00	241.00	239.00	240.40	−0.10	1838
243.20	240.50	Jan01	240.50	242.00	240.50	240.60	−2.00	1940
245.00	240.20	Mar01	245.00	245.00	244.70	244.90	−1.30	434

Est sales	Prv Sales	Prv Open int.	Chg.
33	24	4460	+157

OATS 20 tonnes, $US/tonne

Est sales	Prv Sales	Prv Open Int	Chg.
		0	+0

WESTERN BARLEY 20 tonnes, $Cdn/tonne

129.60	114.00	Dec00	118.50	118.50	117.70	117.90	−0.70	6801
132.50	117.80	Mar01	122.50	122.50	121.90	122.10	−0.50	6393
128.50	120.40	May01	125.00	125.00	124.70	124.70	−0.70	1322

Est sales	Prv Sales	Prv Open Int	Chg.
45	39	14779	−22

WHEAT 20 tonnes, $Cdn/tonne

153.50	129.80	Dec00	134.50	134.90	133.70	133.70	−1.30	3322
156.10	134.50	Mar01	141.00	141.20	139.90	139.90	−1.80	3830
158.00	137.50	May01	144.00	144.50	143.00	143.00	−2.00	865
148.50	146.00	Jul01	147.00	147.40	146.00	146.00	−2.00	485

Est sales	Prv Sales	Prv Open Int	Chg.
34	30	8922	−285

Source: "Cdn. Futures & Options," *Globe and Mail Report on Business*, October 14, 2000, p.B23.

FIGURE 20.1

Canadian Futures and Options Listings

while the volume of trade the previous day (Prv sales—Previous Sales) was 191 contracts. The previous open interest was 73,522 contracts. This means that as of the previous day, a total of 73,522 futures contracts for canola trades had been set up through the WCE and had not yet been fulfilled by the delivery or by other means (which we will discuss in Section 20.4). Reading across the first line of data, the highest and lowest prices recorded for November 2000 canola futures contracts, since they began trading, were $313.00 and $250.70 per metric tonne. The futures price of November canola futures, when the market opened on October 13, was $256.40, while the high and low prices during that day's trading were $256.60 and $252.00. The price at which the market's books were balanced at the end of the day's trading, the **settle price**, was $252.20. This was $4.20 lower than that for the previous day. The total number of WCE November 2000 canola futures contracts in existence was 28,368 contracts.

The existence of organized exchanges is crucial to the usefulness of futures contracts as risk-management tools. They allow futures contracts to be bought and sold quickly with low transaction costs. An investor who has signed a futures contract and then wants to get out of it can simply sell the contract on the futures exchange at the current market price. We shall return to this in more detail in Section 20.4.

Future contracts seldom have maturities longer than about two years. Only the maturity month of a futures contract is specified. In most cases, the underlying asset can be delivered any time during the expiration month to fulfill the contractual obligation. Stock index futures contracts, however, mature on the third Friday of the month. As well, with such contracts, payment in cash is substituted for actual delivery of the underlying asset.

Futures contracts are standardized. For example, one standard futures contract for canola on the WCE is for delivery of 20 metric tonnes. Delivery is accomplished by transferring a warehouse certificate for canola stored at Thunder Bay or Vancouver. The quality of the canola must meet standards set by the Winnipeg market. Standardization of futures contracts is important because it means that the precise legal obligations of the buyer and seller of the canola are well established. It also means that there is no call for lawyers to negotiate the contract. The signer of a futures contract need not fear being outmanoeuvred by the other party or that the fine print in the contract contains additional obligations.

Futures contracts are traded on organized exchanges. In Canada, commodity futures such as those for wheat, canola, flaxseed, oats, barley, and rye have traded on the WCE for several years, although lumber futures trade on the ME. Futures on canola are by far the most active commodity futures traded in Canada, as shown in Table 20.1.

TABLE 20.1

Listed Futures Products on the Winnipeg Commodity Exchange (September 30, 2000)

	CROP YEAR-TO-DATE VOLUME	OPEN INTEREST
	2000/01	SEP 30 2000
FUTURES		
Canola	238,652	64,684
Feed Wheat	33,319	9,815
Field Peas	0	0
Flaxseed	12,347	4,936
Oats	214	0
Western Barley	35,086	15,504
Futures Total	319,618	94,939
OPTIONS		
Canola	6,903	16,053
Feed Wheat	0	5
Flaxseed	890	1,241
Western Barley	1,570	1,423
Options Total	9,363	18,722
Grand Total	328,981	113,661

Source: Winnipeg Commodity Exchange website at http://www.wce.mb.ca (October 16, 2000).

Financial futures contracts presently trade in Canada on the ME. Currently, the ME trades contracts on three-month $1-million Canadian Bankers Acceptances (which call for cash delivery) as well as on five- and 10-year Government of Canada bonds with a notional 6 percent coupon rate. Table 20.2 shows that the 1999 volume for Canadian Bankers Acceptances was 6.048 million contracts, the volume for 10-year Government of Canada Bonds was 1.598 million contracts, while five-year bond contracts traded infrequently. Trading in the TSE 35 Index and the TSE 100 Index used to be carried out on the Toronto Futures Exchange (TFE); however, both of these products ceased trading in March 2000. They have been replaced by futures contracts on the S&P/TSE 60 Index, which commenced trading on the ME in September 1999. These contracts trade at 200 times the value of the S&P/TSE 60 Index and call for cash delivery.

TABLE 20.2

Financial Futures Volumes on the ME and TFE (1997-August 31, 2000)

Futures Product Group	1977		1998		1999		2000 (January 1– August 31)
	Millions	Percent	Millions	Percent	Millions	Percent	Millions
Three-Month Canadian Acceptances (ME)	4.140	71.37	6.803	74.41	6.048	72.74	3.152
10-Year Government of Canada Bonds (ME)	1.273	21.95	1.837	20.09	1.598	19.22	0.960
Five-Year Government of Canada Bonds (ME)	0.051	0.88	0.045	0.49	0.024	0.29	0.0002
S&P /TSE 60 Index Futures (ME)					0.262*	3.15	0.7443
TSE 100 Index Future (TFE)	0.019	0.33	0.017	0.19	0.008	0.09	N/A
TSE 35 Index Futures (TFE)	0.317	5.47	0.441	4.82	0.375	4.51	N/A
Totals	5.800	100.00	9.143	100.00	8.314	100.00	

*These contracts began trading on September 7, 1999.

Source: CDCC 1999 Annual Report and Montreal Exchange website at: http://www.me.org.

The centre of commodity futures trading in North America is the Chicago Board of Trade and the Chicago Mercantile Exchange (CME). However, there are several other important exchanges in New York including: the Commodity Exchange, the New York Mercantile Exchange; the New York Coffee, Sugar, and Cocoa Exchange; the New York Cotton Exchange; and the New York Futures Exchange. Futures markets in Canada are very small and much less developed than those in the United States, both in terms of the variety of available products and trading volume. For example, the CME alone traded over 200 million contracts in 1999, more than 600 times the number of contracts traded on the WSE for the year ended September 30, 2000 and about 24 times the volume of financial futures traded on the ME and TFE in 1999.

International Futures Markets

European futures exchanges are quite competitive, with the Germans and French now striving to compete with contracts offered by the London International Financial Futures Exchange.[6] Most of these systems are fully automated order-matching systems.

Japan, which banned financial futures until 1985, is now very active in developing futures exchanges. The 10- and 20-year yen bond futures contracts introduced on the Tokyo Stock Exchange in 1985 are one of the most heavily traded futures in the world. With regard to stock index futures, the Nikkei 225 contract, the most active Japanese index futures contract, trades on the Osaka Securities Exchange. ⬆

OPTIONS AND FUTURES   20.3

Futures or forward contracts can be used for risk management in many of the same situations in which options can be used. Recall from Chapter 18 that options give their owners the right (but not the obligation) to buy or sell the underlying asset at a locked-in price. Futures and forward contracts, in contrast, carry an obligation to trade the underlying asset at the locked-in price. Options thus provide greater flexibility. However, unlike futures and forward contracts, buying options requires an upfront payment. The following example illustrates these points.

OPTIONS VERSUS FUTURES

EXAMPLE

A company is concluding a sale to a British corporation and expects to receive 100,000 British pounds in six months. Management would like to use the funds to buy equipment from a U.S. supplier and would like to sign a contract now. Unfortunately, if the pound falls against the U.S. dollar, the firm might find it has insufficient dollars to pay the supplier.

One solution is to buy a put option to sell British pounds for U.S. dollars. Another is to enter a futures contract to sell pounds for dollars. The advantage of the option is that if the pound rises or if something goes wrong and the money does not arrive from Britain on time, the option need not be exercised. The option gives the company a right to trade pounds for dollars at the striking price, but the company can always back out. If it bought a put option, however, it would have to pay money to the option writer immediately. The advantage of a futures contract is that it involves no upfront payment.[7] Entering a futures contract is therefore cheaper if the amount and timing of the British pound payment are certain.

---

[6] This discussion is indebted to Peter A. Abken, "Globalization of Stock, Futures, and Options Markets," reprinted in *Financial Derivatives*, Federal Reserve bank of Atlanta, 1993, pp.3-24.

[7] As we shall see, an investor in futures need only establish a margin account.

The difference between futures (or forward contracts) and options can be further clarified by diagrams giving the gain or loss from holding a futures contract as a function of the price of the underlying asset. These are analogous to the payoff diagrams introduced in connection with options in Chapter 18.

EXAMPLE

VARYING FUTURES AND OPTION POSITIONS

The one-year futures price of pork bellies is currently 60¢ per pound. We consider the following investment strategies:[8]

1. a long position in pork belly futures at 60¢
2. a short position in pork belly futures at 60¢
3. a call option on pork bellies with a 60¢ striking price
4. a put option on pork bellies with a 60¢ striking price

Assume that the options and futures contracts listed above are all due to expire in one year. Table 20.3 lists the gain or loss from each strategy as a function of the spot price of pork bellies one year from now.

TABLE 20.3 ▬

The Gain or Loss from Positions in Futures and Options as a Function of the Price of the Underlying Asset*

Price of the underlying asset	Value of a long futures position	Value of a short futures position	Call option exercise value	Put option exercise value
0¢	−60¢	60¢	0¢	60¢
10	−50	50	0	50
20	−40	40	0	40
30	−30	30	0	30
40	−20	20	0	20
50	−10	10	0	10
60	0	0	0	0
70	10	−10	10	0
80	20	−20	20	0
90	30	−30	30	0
100	40	−40	40	0

*The futures contracts are entered at a futures price of 60¢, and the options have a 60¢ striking price. All figures are in cents per pound.

---

[8] Options on pork bellies are generally agreements to enter a futures contract at the striking price of the option. For our purposes, this is equivalent to being able to buy the commodity at that price. An option holder can wait until the option and futures contracts are due to expire and then exercise the option to enter the futures contract, which, in turn, calls for almost immediate delivery of the underlying asset. For simplicity, we ignore the effect of interest rates on option values as discussed in Chapter 18.

A buyer of pork bellies who is concerned about a possible price increase can protect herself either by buying a call option or by taking a long position in a futures contract. In either case, if the price of the underlying asset does increase, the buyer is protected. Pursuing the above example, the call option gives her a right to buy at 60¢, and the futures contract locks in a commitment to trade at 60¢. As Table 20.3 shows, the benefits from a call option are identical to those from a long position in a futures contract if the spot price of the underlying asset rises above 60¢. For instance, if the price of pork bellies rises to 70¢ per pound, the right to buy at 60¢ per pound through either the call option or a long position in futures results in a gain of 10¢. If the price rises to 80¢ per pound, the gain rises to 20¢ per pound.

The difference between a call option and a long position in a futures contract is what happens if, contrary to the buyer's fears, the price falls. If the price falls below 60¢, the holder of a call option will not exercise her option and will simply have to write off the price she paid for the call. In contrast, a long position in a futures contract at 60¢ commits the buyer to purchase pork bellies at that price. If the price falls to 50¢ per pound, she must still fulfill her obligation to buy at 60¢ per pound, and thus she loses 10¢ per pound. If the price falls to 40¢ per pound, she loses 20¢ per pound, and so on. Table 20.3 illustrates this increasing loss for the long position in futures as the price of the underlying asset falls.

A buyer who fears a price increase and is certain that the price will not fall is better off going long in futures since buying calls means paying an upfront price. A buyer who fears a price increase but feels there is some chance the price may fall instead might be better off with call options. She must balance the price of the options against the potential losses in futures if the price does fall.

A seller of pork bellies who is fearful of a price decrease could protect himself either by purchasing a put option or by taking a short position in a futures contract. As Table 20.3 shows, a fall in the price of the underlying asset gives rise to identical gains for the put owner and the short futures trader. If the price falls to 50¢ per pound, both have locked in a 60¢ per pound selling price, and both thus gain 10¢ per pound. If the price falls to 40¢, both gain 20¢ per pound. Again, the difference between the two is the consequence of a price movement that should be to the seller's advantage—a price rise. The put holder can simply refrain from exercising his put and can sell his pork bellies at the higher market price. A futures contract, however, locks the seller into a 60¢ price. If the price rises to 70¢ per pound, this means a 10¢ per pound loss, but if the price rises to 60¢ per pound, the loss is 20¢ per pound. Again, a seller who fears a price decline and who is confident that the price will not rise is better off in futures since the upfront price of entering a futures contract is zero. A seller who fears a price decline but who feels that the price might rise instead might be better off buying puts. He must balance the price of the puts against the potential losses stemming from a short position in futures if the price rises.

The information shown in Table 20.3 is represented graphically in Figure 20.2. These payoff diagrams, which parallel those introduced in Chapter 18 for options, show the gains at maturity from having entered a futures contract at an initial futures price of 60¢. We compare this with the gain from having bought an option with a 60¢ striking price. Note that the payoffs to futures contracts are linear, while those of options are asymmetric around the striking price.

FIGURE 20.2

Payoff Diagrams for
Positions in Futures
and Options*

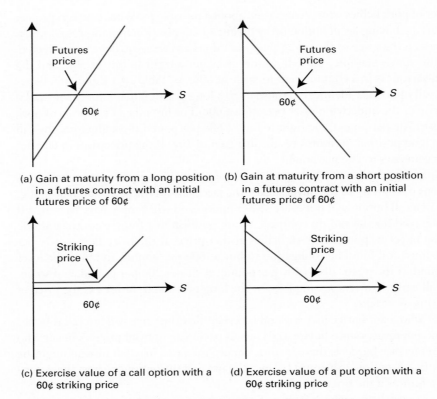

(a) Gain at maturity from a long position
in a futures contract with an initial
futures price of 60¢

(b) Gain at maturity from a short position
in a futures contract with an initial
futures price of 60¢

(c) Exercise value of a call option with a
60¢ striking price

(d) Exercise value of a put option with a
60¢ striking price

* The horizontal axis measures the price, S, of the underlying asset—at the maturity of the futures contract
for graphs (a) and (b) and when the option is exercised for graphs (c) and (d). The vertical axis is defined
below each graph.

Graphs (a) and (b) in Figure 20.2 show the gains from holding a long and short position respectively in a futures contract. Note that the gain from taking a long position
always precisely matches the loss from taking a short position. Thus, we see that futures,
like options, are a zero sum investment: one trader's gain is always another's loss.

Comparing graphs (a) and (c), we note that a long position in futures and a call
option provide the same gain when the price of the underlying asset rises above 60¢.
Thus, both offer the same protection against price increases. However, the call option
entails no loss when the price falls below 60¢, whereas the long futures position carries
a loss that increases cent for cent as the price falls. So, we see from their payoff diagrams
that a call option provides a better pattern of returns than does a long position in a
futures contract. At any price of the underlying asset, the gain from a call option match-

es or exceeds the gain from a long position in a futures contract. If the call option were free, it would dominate the futures position. Of course, call options are not free, whereas entering a futures contract involves no upfront payment. A financial manager must thus balance the better pattern of returns that a call provides against its higher cost relative to a long position in futures.[9]

Similarly, when we compare graphs (b) and (d) we see that a put option provides a better pattern of returns than does a short futures position. Both provide the same gain when the price of the underlying asset falls. They are both, therefore, equally effective hedges against price declines. However, when the price of the underlying asset rises, the put option entails no loss, whereas the short futures position does. Thus, at any price of the underlying asset, the put option's returns match or exceed those from a short position in a futures contract. Hence, if put options were free, they would always dominate short positions in futures. However, they are not free, so financial managers must again balance the better pattern of returns from options against their higher costs before forsaking futures contracts.

The decision to use options rather than futures to hedge against risks is difficult and often involves subjective judgements. We return to this issue in the next chapter.

THE ORGANIZATION OF FUTURES MARKETS

20.4

Each futures market has slightly different regulations. In Canada, provincial regulators are responsible for futures trading, so the rules across the provinces may vary somewhat. In the United States, futures markets are regulated by the Commodity Futures Trading Commission (CFTC), which also gives individual futures markets considerable leeway to set their own rules. In today's global economy, many Canadian businesses take positions in futures markets in London and Tokyo to hedge against foreign currency risk. We can, therefore, only give a broad overview of the general considerations involved in trading futures contracts.

In order to trade, investors in futures contracts must establish a commodity or margin account with a broker to establish evidence of solvency and to facilitate the process of marking to market, which is discussed in the next subsection. Margin requirements for futures trading are usually between 5 and 10 percent of the value of the position.

FUTURES MARGIN ACCOUNT

EXAMPLE

Standard futures contracts for cocoa are for delivery of 10 metric tonnes, so that if the price of December cocoa is $813 per tonne, the value of a contract is $8,130. If the margin requirement is 10 percent, a trader wishing to take either a long or short position in one cocoa futures contract must place $813 in her margin account.

---

[9] In a perfectly efficient market, pricing should be such that neither alternative is superior.

If the price of the futures contract changes so that more money is required, the investor will receive a margin call to deposit more funds.[10] If the futures price changes so that less money is required, the investor can withdraw funds. Margin accounts for futures trading normally earn interest; however, brokers may sometimes insist on zero interest margin accounts for smaller clients.

Futures markets usually are subject to **daily limits** on price fluctuations. If the price of a futures contract rises or falls by more than some preset limit, trading automatically stops and does not resume until the next business day. For example, the daily limit for futures price movements for Government of Canada bond futures are $3,000 per contract, while S&P/TSE 60 Index futures trading is halted when "circuit breakers" on the TSE are triggered. Daily limits have been introduced as a safety mechanism to help stabilize what was perceived as a highly volatile market. It is possible, however, that daily limits increase rather than decrease price swings. If prices are decreasing, the daily limit may encourage people who would otherwise sit tight to sell quickly before the limit is triggered. In practice, during very volatile periods, the limits may be expanded.

Investors in futures may also be subject to **position limits**. These limit the number of contracts a single investor can hold. For example, no single investor is allowed to hold more than 30,000 futures contracts to buy the stocks that make up the S&P/TSE 60 Index. The position limit for five-year Government of Canada bond futures is 4,000 contracts, while the limit is 10,000 contracts for 10-year bond futures and 36,000 for hedgers (5,000 for speculators) using Canadian Bankers Acceptances futures. Sometimes the position limits can be relaxed if the investor declares that he is in the market to hedge risks rather than to speculate.

Marking to Market

A critical problem that the organizers of a futures market face is being sure that people who have contracted to deliver a commodity or financial asset at a particular price and time fulfill their obligation. For example, a farmer who has entered into a futures contract to sell his wheat in September at $130 per metric tonne might regret entering the contract if the spot price of wheat in September turned out to be $150 per metric tonne. He might be motivated to sell his wheat on the spot market and renege on his futures contract commitment.

To prevent this, futures markets have an elaborate system of daily adjustments of contract prices and margin accounts called **marking to market**. Also, neither party deals directly with the other. Instead, their contracts are with the clearing house for the futures market. The following example illustrates how futures contracts are set up and how marking to market is done.[11]

---

[10] In many jurisdictions, a distinction is made between an initial margin and a maintenance margin. The initial margin is the margin requirement for new positions. The lower maintenance margin is used for existing positions as long as no change in the position is initiated by the investor.

[11] Forward contracts, in contrast, are generally not marked to market.

MARKING TO MARKET

EXAMPLE

A farmer, wanting to lock in a price for the wheat he expects to harvest, opens the short side of a futures contract by committing to sell wheat at $130 per metric tonne next September. A baker, wanting to guarantee herself a supply of wheat at a known price, opens the long side of a wheat futures contract by committing to buy wheat at $130 per metric tonne in September. Both parties simply check what price September wheat futures are trading at and then have their brokers arrange for the opening of their futures positions.

Both the farmer and the baker must set up margin accounts with the clearing house in order to trade. In this case, the contract is for 20 metric tonnes of wheat at $130 per metric tonne with a total value of $2,600. If the margin requirement is 10 percent, both the farmer and the baker must deposit $260 with the clearing house. The brokers would normally set this up as the contracts were opened. The initial positions of the farmer and baker are illustrated in Figure 20.3.

FIGURE 20.3

Long and Short Positions in a Futures Contract

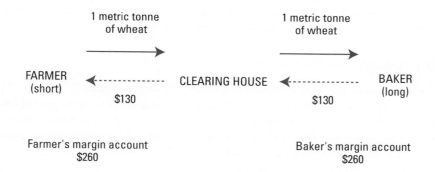

Now suppose that the next day, the price of September wheat rises to $135 per metric tonne and remains at this level on the news that China is buying large amounts of wheat. The market price is now higher than the price the farmer is committed to selling at in his contract. He, therefore, has an incentive to renege. To prevent this, immediately after the close of trading, all futures contracts are rewritten at the latest settle price. As a consequence, the farmer now has a contract to sell his wheat at $135 in September, and the baker is obliged to buy at that price. This gives the farmer $5 more per metric tonne than he originally contracted for and forces the baker to pay $5 more per metric tonne as well. Since the contract is for 20 metric tonnes, this gives the farmer $100 more ($5 per metric tonne times 20) and costs the baker the same amount. To redress this, the clearing house removes $100 from the farmer's margin account and deposits it in the baker's margin account. This is shown in Figure 20.4.

FIGURE 20.4

EXAMPLE

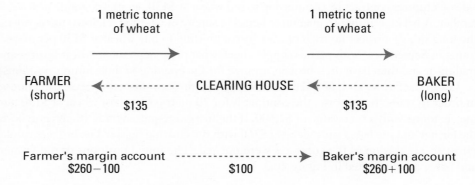

Contract size: 20 metric tonnes

1 metric tonne
of wheat

1 metric tonne
of wheat

FARMER   CLEARING HOUSE   BAKER
(short)   (long)
$135 $135

Farmer's margin account ----------------> Baker's margin account
$260 − 100 $100 $260 + 100

Financially, both are where they would have been had the terms of the futures contract not been changed. However, the new arrangement means that both parties have no incentive to renege on their obligations. Thus, the futures price always reflects market supply and demand. Also, marking futures contracts to market means that speculators need not wait for the contracts to mature to collect their gains.

EXAMPLE

OFFSETTING BY A SPECULATOR

Suppose a speculator thinks that the price of wheat will soon rise from $130 to $135 per metric tonne because of impending large Chinese purchases. If farmers are currently happy to sell wheat at $130, the speculator can take a long position in wheat futures to profit from his foresight. This is illustrated in Figure 20.5. Essentially, the speculator takes the same position as the baker did in Figure 20.3.

Now, as in the previous example, the price of September wheat rises to $135 per metric tonne. The speculator, who is due to receive wheat from the farmer in September at $130, can now resell the same wheat to the Chinese at $135 per metric tonne. The speculator does this by taking a short position in September wheat at $135. This offsetting transaction is called a "reversing trade" and is depicted in Figure 20.6.

FIGURE 20.5

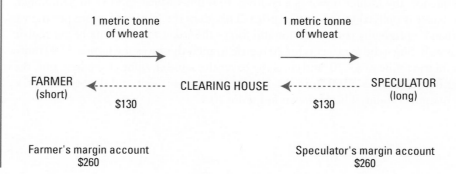

Contract size: 20 metric tonnes

1 metric tonne
of wheat

1 metric tonne
of wheat

FARMER   CLEARING HOUSE   SPECULATOR
(short)   (long)
$130 $130

Farmer's margin account   Speculator's margin account
$260 $260

Contract size: 20 metric tonnes

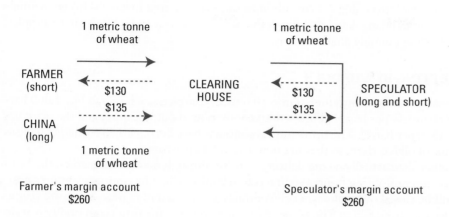

FIGURE 20.6

Speculative Long
Position and Reversing
Trade Following a
Futures Price Rise

When the clearing house marks the contracts to market at the end of the day, it transfers $100 from the farmer's margin account to the speculator's. It then checks through its records and finds that the speculator has a long position and a matching short position in September wheat. These two positions cancel each other out and are eliminated. This is termed closing the position. Thus, the speculator does not have to wait until September to buy wheat from the farmer and sell it to China. Instead, the speculator immediately gets the money that was added to his margin account, all of which can now be withdrawn. This final position is illustrated in Figure 20.7.

Contract size: 20 metric tonnes

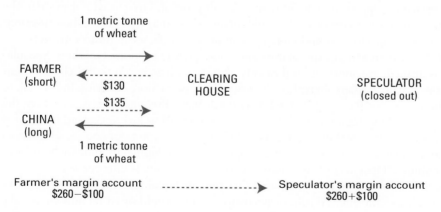

FIGURE 20.7

Closing Out a Speculative
Long Position in a
Futures Contract

Most futures positions are eventually closed out in this way. In fact, actual delivery generally takes place for less than one percent of futures contracts. However, the fact that a contract is closed out before it matures does not mean that it was entered into for speculation. Firms engaged in pure hedging commonly close out futures positions early and use the cash from doing so to subsidize trades in the spot market. This is essentially equivalent to taking delivery through the futures contract, and it often can be simpler. The following example illustrates this.

EXAMPLE

OFFSETTING BY A HEDGER

One year ago, a company entered into 10 futures contracts, each one to buy 1,000 barrels of oil at $23 per barrel. These contracts are now about to expire, and the price has risen to $30 per barrel. The firm's futures contracts have been marked to market daily as the price of oil has risen, so they are now also at $30 per barrel.

Rather than actually taking delivery of its oil through the futures market, the business can enter offsetting futures contracts to sell oil at $30. The company's futures position will be closed out that day when contracts are marked to market. Over the year as the price rose from $23 to $30, $7 per barrel was added to the firm's commodity margin account. On 10 1,000 barrel contracts, this amounts to $70,000.

The price of 10,000 barrels of oil in the spot market is now $300,000. The $70,000 from closing out its futures position means that the business need only spend $230,000 of additional funds to buy the oil it needs. It is essentially buying oil at $23—the futures price at the time the contract was entered into.

Hedgers and Speculators

Traders who open futures positions to help manage risk that arises from other business activities they engage in are called **hedgers**, and those who open futures positions expecting to close them again at more advantageous prices are called **speculators**. In a typical futures exchange, approximately 90 percent of all positions are closed out prior to the maturity of the futures contracts. Although hedgers also may often close their positions before maturity, speculation undoubtedly is an important factor in futures markets.

Much scorn attaches to speculators and consequently to futures markets. Speculators, it is argued, are short-sighted rascals who destabilize markets and cheat honest investors—usually farmers. In reality, the situation is much more complex. In general, to make money, a speculator must buy low and sell high. Buying low tends to drive the price up, and selling high tends to drive it down. Increasing low prices and decreasing high ones amounts to stabilizing, not destabilizing, the market. Of course, speculators might sometimes make money by buying high and selling higher, thereby fuelling speculative bubbles. The effect of speculators on market volatility is thus unclear.

Speculators also are important in that they provide liquidity to the market and probably increase its efficiency. Without speculators, there would often be nobody to take the opposite position from a hedger. Thus, speculators help the market to function for hedgers. Speculators presumably bring information to the market as well, thus causing prices to adjust more rapidly to new conditions and increasing the efficiency of the market as discussed in Chapter 9.

Speculators are in the market to make money. They are taking risks and gathering information, activities that are rewarded in financial markets with high returns. Hedgers, on the other hand, might expect to lose some money. They are in the futures market to buy insurance, and such protection, after all, is not free.[12]

Moreover, the distinction between speculators and hedgers is often quite blurred. Tax authorities make a clear distinction: the gains from trading in futures for speculative purposes generally are classified as capital gains, while those from hedging usually are deemed ordinary income. In reality, it is often difficult to classify a trader as either a speculator or a hedger. A large bank might consider itself a hedger in foreign currency futures markets yet take speculative positions from time to time when it believes it has an information advantage.

PERSPECTIVES

Corporate Manager
Futures enable companies to lock in input and selling prices in advance without having to pay an up-front fee.

Investor
Futures enable investors to speculate or hedge current investment positions without any immediate costs.

COMMODITY FUTURES PRICES   20.5

Commodity futures prices are, of course, set by supply and demand. If more people want to buy September wheat than want to sell it, its price will rise. If the reverse is true, its price will fall. There is, however, a great deal more we can say about futures prices. We begin by exploring the relation between the price of a commodity in a futures contract F and the spot price S expected to prevail at the time the contract matures—denoted $E(S)$.

The Expectations Hypothesis

The expectations hypothesis is probably of more interest to economists than to practical financial managers. We therefore discuss it only as a benchmark against which to compare more realistic descriptions of futures markets. The expectations hypothesis states that the futures price of a commodity should be what traders expect the spot price to be in the future:

---

[12] There is some controversy over who actually benefits when a company decides to hedge. Given efficient markets, an investor with a fully diversified portfolio may not value a firm that hedges more than one that does not. In fact, given the costs of hedging a firm's risk, a company that does not engage in hedging could actually be worth more to an investor than one that does. Some argue that the rationale for companies hedging their unsystematic risk is attribulatble to the principal-agent conflict between shareholders and management. Management, in effect, may be hedging for their own interests despite the cost to shareholders.

$F=E(S)$

This means that if September wheat futures are priced at $130 per metric tonne, we can conclude that traders expect that the spot price for wheat next September will be $130 per metric tonne.

However, many futures traders claim that they are actually setting futures prices higher or lower than the spot price they expect to see at maturity. We now explore why this might happen.

The Net Hedging Hypothesis: Backwardation and Forwardation

Suppose everyone agrees that the best estimate of the spot price of wheat next September is $130 per metric tonne. Assume further that a large number of farmers wish to hedge against price movements by locking in a price for their harvests using futures contracts, while there are only a few bakers who wish to buy September wheat. For supply to equal demand, speculators must be induced to take long positions in September wheat, and they will do so only if they expect to be able to sell the wheat at a small profit in September. If the futures price falls below the $130 estimate that everyone agreed upon, say to $120 per metric tonne, speculators can anticipate profits of $10 per metric tonne, and, consequently, they will enter the market.

A futures market with a shortage of hedgers in long positions means that the futures contract price will fall below the spot price expected in the future. In other words, where:

$F<E(S)$

the market is said to display **normal backwardation**. In this case, the September wheat futures market displays normal backwardation.

If, in contrast, bakers want more long positions in September futures contracts than farmers want short positions, there will be a market imbalance. This time, however, speculators will have to be induced to take short positions. Such positions will appear profitable to them if the futures price is slightly higher than the expected spot price. For example, if the futures price is $140 per metric tonne, a speculator could anticipate buying wheat in September at $130 and selling it with the futures contract at $140.

A futures market in which a shortage of hedgers on the short side of the contract has caused the futures price to exceed the expected spot price is said to display normal forwardation. More formally, **normal forwardation** means:

$F>E(S)$

The term **contango** is often used interchangeably with normal forwardation.[13]

In the cases of both backwardation and forwardation, an imbalance of hedgers on the long and short sides of the contract causes the futures price to deviate from what it would

[13] The terms backwardation and forwardation are also used informally to describe the relation between futures prices and contract maturity. If futures prices rise with the maturity date, the market is said to display forwardation or contango. If they fall with the maturity date, the market is said to display backwardation.

be if the expectations hypothesis were true. The futures market is acting as an insurance market. Hedgers are taking positions with an expected loss in order to get insurance. Speculators are taking positions whereby they can anticipate making money in return for providing insurance to hedgers. Thus, we see that the expectations hypothesis should hold only in a futures market in which the potential trading volume of hedgers seeking short positions matches exactly that of hedgers wanting long positions. In this case only, there is no need for speculators and, consequently, no expected gain or loss built into the futures price.

The same commodity may show a different pattern of futures prices for futures contracts with different maturities. For example, farmers may create a surplus of hedgers on the short side of September wheat contracts, while active trading by bakers may create an excess of long positions in March wheat futures. Thus, September wheat futures might display backwardation, while March wheat futures might display forwardation. Speculators are buying wheat from farmers in September and storing it until March when they sell it to bakers. They expect a small gain from each transaction, and as long as this covers their storage costs, they can make a profit. This view of futures prices as reflecting a balance between hedging and speculation is called the **net hedging hypothesis**.

Commodity Futures Arbitrage

We can take this analysis a step further by considering the concept of arbitrage. When the futures contract is about to mature, the futures price must equal the spot price. If it does not, a speculator could make large amounts of money with very little risk.

AN ARBITRAGE OPPORTUNITY

The spot price of wheat is $130 per metric tonne, and futures contracts that are about to mature price wheat at $125. A speculator could take a long position in wheat futures to buy wheat at $125 and then sell it at $130 in the spot market, earning a profit of $5 per metric tonne. A standard contract for 20 metric tonnes yields a profit of $100, and a long position in 1,000 contracts produces an arbitrage profit of $100,000. If the futures price were too high rather than too low, taking a short position in wheat futures would generate similar profits.

Making money by exploiting the mispricing of any good or security, as illustrated in the previous example, is called arbitrage. Traders who make money by performing arbitrage are called arbitrageurs. Arbitrageurs tend to drive prices toward levels that make arbitrage impossible.

For example, in the above case, if the spot price of wheat is $130 per metric tonne and the futures price in contracts is $125, arbitrageurs would be trying to set up large long positions in maturing wheat futures contracts. By doing this, they push up the futures price of the maturing contract until it equals the current spot price. An analogous argument works if the futures price in maturing contracts is higher than the spot price. In that case, arbitrageurs drive down the futures price by taking large short positions. Thus, an expiring futures contract should price its underlying asset at the current spot price.

A futures contract that is not due to expire for some time can price its underlying asset at a futures price quite different from the current spot price. However, even here, arbitrage sets limits on the difference between the futures price and the current spot price. We use the following notation:

F=futures price

S= spot price

r=annual risk-free interest rate

t=time until maturity of the futures contract measured in years

c=annual storage, insurance, transportation, and other costs for carrying an inventory of the underlying asset

If there are net benefits to having an inventory of the underlying asset, c can be negative and is then called a **convenience yield**. For example, if the market for copper were characterized by sudden temporary shortages and consequent price peaks, carrying an inventory of copper would let one take advantage of this and thereby earn a convenience yield.

Arbitrage sets an upper bound on futures prices of storable assets even for contracts that are not due to mature immediately. This bound is given by:

(20.1) $F \leq S(1+r)^t + ct$

If a futures price exceeds this upper limit, arbitrageurs can earn risk-free profits and, in doing so, drive the futures price back below the limit in Equation 20.1. They are able to do this by buying the commodity at today's spot price and storing it for future delivery against short positions they have simultaneously taken on futures contracts.

EXAMPLE

AN ARBITRAGE OPPORTUNITY

Suppose the spot price of wheat is $130 per metric tonne, and the six-month futures price is $145. The interest rate is 10 percent, and the storage cost of wheat is $10 per metric tonne per year. To make a risk-free arbitrage profit, do the following:

Step 1. Open a short position in a six-month wheat futures contract, agreeing to sell one metric tonne of wheat in six months for $145. Borrow $130 at 10 percent to buy wheat immediately and then store it for six months.

Step 2. Six months later, take the wheat out of storage and sell it for $145 to fulfill the futures contract obligation. Use this money to pay the storage cost, ct, of $5 ($10 per metric tonne per year for six months) and to repay the loan, which costs $S(1+r)^t$ or $130 \times (1+.10)^{.5} = \$136.35$. This leaves an arbitrage profit of $3.65 per metric tonne ($15-$5-$6.35). On a standard futures contract for 20 metric tonnes, this amounts to $73, and on a position of 1,000 contracts, the arbitrage profits are $73,000.

Note that these profits are risk-free. Once the terms of the loan are established, the futures contract is entered, the storage terms are arranged, and the profits are locked in.

Notice in the example above that the arbitrageur's strategy puts downward pressure on the futures price of wheat. The futures price should fall quickly to a level at which arbitrage ceases, defined by Equation 20.1:

$$F \leq S(1+r)^t + ct = 130 \times (1+.10)^{.5} + 10 \times .5 = \$141.35$$

When this happens, the arbitrageur can make a reversing trade. When marking to market is effected, her position is closed out, and she receives $3.65 per metric tonne immediately. On 1,000 contracts for 20 metric tonnes each, this adds up to $73,000.

In general, arbitrageurs can make profits by taking short positions and buying the commodity with borrowed money if the futures price is too high. This drives the futures price down until arbitrage is no longer possible. Arbitrage is impossible when the futures price is at the limit defined in Equation 20.1.

The underlying idea is that the futures price of any storable commodity cannot exceed the spot price plus financing and storage costs; otherwise, it would pay to hoard the commodity and sell it through futures contracts.[14] The balance between hedgers and speculators thus determines commodity futures prices but is subject to an upper bound set by arbitrageurs.

FINANCIAL FUTURES PRICES   20.6

As we shall see in this section, financial futures prices and corresponding forward prices are determined precisely by risk-free arbitrage possibilities. If a financial futures price moves above or below this level, arbitrage quickly forces it back. Thus, we can provide exact equations for what the price of each type of financial futures contract must be. We begin with foreign currency futures because they were the first type of financial futures contract to come into widespread use. We then turn to interest rate futures—contracts that let a trader buy a debt instrument, such as Bankers Acceptances or Government of Canada bonds, at a preset price in the future. Last, we examine stock index futures. These futures contracts let a trader buy a portfolio of stocks in the future at a preset price. Stock index futures contracts are especially controversial because they are the basic tool used in computerized program trading. We therefore consider this use of stock index futures contracts at the end of the section.

---

[14] Equation 20.1 is usually expressed as an inequality, although it is also theoretically possible to run arbitrage if the futures price is below an analogous lower bound. To do this, one would have to sell the underlying commodity short. Pursuing the example here, if the futures price were $135, one would borrow a tonne of wheat and sell it for $130 in the spot market, simultaneously entering a futures contract to buy a tonne of wheat at $135 in six months. The $130 would earn $6.35 in interest, so a $1.65 arbitrage profit would result. Such trading would drive up the futures price until it reached $136.35, in which case arbitrage would cease to be profitable. In practice, commodity short sales are not common, so the effectiveness of this lower bound is unclear. Companies that normally carry substantial inventories of the commodity may engage in some trading of this sort, effecting short sales by "borrowing" from their inventories; however, the extent of such trading is limited by the firms' minimum business inventory requirements. Financial assets, however, can readily be sold short, so equalities can be derived to define financial futures prices. This is discussed further in the next section.

Foreign Currency Futures

Foreign currency futures contracts allow one to lock in an exchange rate at a specified point in the future. They are available for most major currencies: U.S. dollars, Canadian dollars, Australian dollars, Japanese yen, UK pounds, and Euros. Currency futures are traded primarily on the International Money Market—a part of the Chicago Mercantile Exchange. Trading volumes and open interests are reasonably large for contracts with maturities of up to six months. Beyond that, the market can be much thinner and is non-existent for maturities in excess of two years. For hedging foreign currency risk over longer time periods, specially constructed forward contracts, as described earlier in the chapter, must be arranged through banks or other financial institutions.

Foreign currency forward and futures contracts are valuable risk-management tools for firms that engage in international business.

EXAMPLE

FOREIGN EXCHANGE HEDGING

A Canadian firm agrees to purchase software support from a U.S. company for one year. The U.S. firm charges US $1 million every three months for this service, with the first payment due in three months. When a business has net contractual obligations in a foreign currency, this is called its **foreign currency exposure**.[15] In this case, the Canadian firm is exposed to U.S. dollar exchange rate changes on $4 million throughout the year. Its managers are worried that if the U.S. dollar rises sharply against the Canadian dollar, these payments could become unmanageable. This risk can be controlled by taking short positions in a series of Canadian dollar futures contracts in U.S. markets. The futures prices of Canadian dollars quoted there are as follows:

	US$/C$
Spot rate	0.6608
3-month futures rate	0.6623
6-month futures rate	0.6637
9-month futures rate	0.6650
12-month futures rate	0.6662

Canadian dollars trade in contracts of C$100,000. The company should take short positions in 15 futures contracts in each of the maturities listed above. Its obligations under the futures contract are then to sell C$1.5 million three months, six months, nine months, and 12 months from now at the exchange rates listed above. This gives the Canadian firm approximately US$1 million at three-month intervals for the next year, which is what it needs to pay its U.S. partner. For instance, in three months, the business must sell C$1.5 million (15 contracts of C$100,000) for U.S. dollars at US$0.6623 per Canadian dollar. This means that the firm has locked in a cash flow of US$993,450 ($1.5 million×0.6623) in three months. Since this is not precisely equal

---

[15] Foreign currency exposure is a "net" concept. If the firm in this example had inflows of US $1 million every three months from some other part of its business, its U.S. dollar exposure would net out to zero.

to the $1 million to be paid to the U.S. partner, a small foreign currency exposure of $6,550 still exists. The enterprise's remaining exposure is shown below.

Time from now	Liability to U.S. partner	Receipt from futures contract	Remaining exposure
3 months	US$1,000,000	US$993,450	US$ 6,550
6 months	1,000,000	995,550	4,450
9 months	1,000,000	997,500	2,500
12 months	1,000,000	999,300	700

By using foreign currency futures contracts, the firm has reduced its exposure to exchange rate fluctuations from millions to a few thousand dollars.

Note that forward contracts for foreign currencies often provide more flexibility in the timing and amount of currency to be exchanged than do futures contracts. Canadian banks have considerable sophistication in setting up forward contracts to hedge foreign currency exposure. Remember that forward contracts cannot be traded in organized markets and are not marked to market, so that once the contract is set up, the company has little flexibility to alter the arrangement.

Covered Interest Arbitrage

Foreign currency forward and futures prices are determined precisely by arbitrage constraints. If the price of a foreign currency in a futures contract is even slightly too high or too low, arbitrage profits quickly become possible, and as these profits are taken, the futures price is driven back to its equilibrium value. In Chapter 6, we saw that foreign currency forward prices are forced toward levels at which arbitrage ceases. The same process determines foreign currency futures prices.[16] To illustrate, we consider an example analogous to one used in Chapter 6 for forward contracts.

COVERED INTEREST ARBITRAGE

EXAMPLE

The exchange rate between U.S. dollars and Canadian dollars is US$.72/C$. The annual risk-free interest rate is 9 percent in the U.S. and 11 percent in Canada. Given this, we can calculate precisely what the 12-month futures price of U.S. dollars in Canadian dollars must be.

Consider an investor who has US$720,000. She has two risk-free ways of investing her money for one year:

1. At the current U.S. interest rate of 9 percent, she can invest US$720,000 for one year and end up with US$784,800.

---

[16] The formulation presented here is valid for futures contracts if interest rates are fixed and is valid for forward contracts regardless. If interest rates fluctuate, traders' earnings on their margin accounts cannot be predicted precisely. This brings an additional complication to the problem but does not alter the basic framework.

2. Alternatively, she can convert her US$720,000 to C$1 million at the current spot rate, invest this in Canada at a risk-free rate of 11 percent to get C$1,110,000 in one year, and enter into a futures contract to convert this back to U.S. dollars at that time.

These two possibilities are shown in Figure 20.8.

FIGURE 20.8

The Framework for Covered Interest Arbitrage

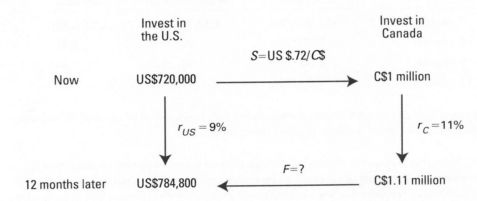

Since both of these investment plans are riskless, both must yield the same return. In particular, the C$1.11 million generated next year by the second alternative must be convertible by the futures contract into precisely US$784,800. This implies that the 12-month futures price of U.S. dollars in Canadian dollars must be US$.707/C$.

If the forword rate were not equal to US$.707/C$, large risk-free arbitrage profits could be made. Suppose, for instance, that the forword rate is US$.72/C$. To make risk-free arbitrage profits with no money down, take the following two steps:

Step 1.   Borrow US$720,000 at 9 percent and convert this to C$1 million in the spot market. Invest this at 11 percent in Canada and enter a futures contract to convert C$1.11 million into US$799,200 next year.

Step 2.   One year later, collect the US$799,200 from the futures contract, pay off the loan with US$784,800 (US$720,000 plus 9 percent interest) and retain US$14,400 in arbitrage profits.

Note that this is entirely risk-free and that the arbitrageur need invest none of her own money. As more and more arbitrageurs take larger and larger positions, the futures price of U.S. dollars should begin to fall. It will continue falling until it reaches US$.707/C$ and no further arbitrage profits are possible. Normally, this happens very quickly in futures markets with significant arbitrage possibilities seldom lasting more than minutes. Of course the arbitrageur need not wait for a year to collect her profits. She can close her position once the futures price has reached US$.707/C$, and when her position is marked to market and closed out, she will receive $14,400 immediately.

If the futures price had been below US$.707/C$, a similar strategy of borrowing money in Canada and investing it in the United States would have generated similar profits and put upward pressure on the futures price.

This type of arbitrage, called **covered interest arbitrage**, precisely defines foreign currency futures (and forward) contract prices. Formally,

$$F_{AB} = \left[\frac{1+r_A}{1+r_B}\right]^t S_{AB} \qquad\qquad (20.2)$$

where:

F_{AB}=current foreign exchange futures price, expressed in number of units of currency A required to purchase one unit of currency B

S_{AB}=current spot exchange rate, again expressed in number of units of currency A required to purchase one unit of currency B

r_A =risk-free interest rate in country A (annual)

r_B =risk-free interest rate in country B (annual)

t =time until maturity of the futures contract (measured in years)

Equation 20.2 is called the **interest rate parity equation** and can be used to price foreign currency futures contracts.[17]

INTEREST RATE PARITY

In the previous example, the spot rate S_{AB} is US\$.72/C\$; the U.S. interest rate r_A is 9 percent; the Canadian interest rate r_B is 11 percent; and the time until the futures contract matures is one year. Note that if annual interest rates are used, t must be measured in years. Inserting these values into Equation 20.2 gives us:

$$F_{AB} = \left[\frac{1+r_A}{1+r_B}\right]^t S_{AB} = \frac{1+.09}{1+.11} \times \text{US\$.72/C\$} = \text{US\$.707/C\$}$$

The 12-month futures rate that precludes arbitrage is US\$.707/C\$. ⬆

EXAMPLE

Interest Rate Futures

Interest rate forward and futures contracts allow one to lock in a price at which a debt instrument is to be bought or sold in the future. In Canada, interest rate futures on three-month Bankers Acceptances and on 10- and five-year 6 percent notional coupon Government of Canada bonds are traded on the Montreal Exchange. Minimum contracts are for $1 million and $100,000 respectively. A wider variety of U.S. interest rate futures are available, and Eurodollar futures contracts are traded on the London International Financial Futures Exchange (LIFFE). In addition, interest rate forward contracts are widely used by banks.

---

[17] The idea behind Equation 20.2 is the same as that behind Equation 20.1: a comparison is made between carrying an inventory and buying a futures contract. In this case, an inventory of a foreign currency brings the investor a different interest rate from that earned on local currecy. This difference, expressed as a ratio, relates the futures price to the spot price.

We saw in Chapter 6 that the market price of interest-bearing securities is determined by prevailing interest rates. If we purchase an interest rate futures contract, we stand to make a gain or suffer a loss if market interest rates decrease or increase during the contract period. We can use such gains or losses from futures contracts to offset, at least partially, losses and gains that we may suffer in the normal course of business as a consequence of interest rate movements. Hence, interest rate futures provide the possibility of hedging against interest rate risk.

HEDGING WITH INTEREST RATE FUTURES

EXAMPLE

A firm has started a major construction project, but because its completion is expected to take several years, some of the funds that will be issued in the form of long-term debt will not be required for another two years. To ensure the economic viability of the project, however, the company would like to protect itself against the risk of rising interest rates during the next two years. At least partial protection can be obtained by resorting to interest rate futures.

In using this market, the firm may commit to selling long-term Government of Canada bonds at a specified forward price two years hence. If during the next two years interest rates increase, the spot price of such long-term bonds will decline, and the business will make a profit through the futures contract. This profit will offset, at least in part, the increased interest cost to be borne when the new long-term debt is issued.

To illustrate, assume that the firm needs to raise $10 million in two years and that current interest rates on long-term debt are 10 percent. Consequently, 10-year Government of Canada bonds with a coupon rate of 6 percent as offered in Canadian futures markets will trade at:

Market price=

$$60 \times \left[\frac{1 - \frac{1}{(1.10)^{10}}}{0.10} \right] + 1,000 \times \left[\frac{1}{(1.10)^{10}} \right] = 60 \times [6.14457] + 1,000 \times [0.38559] = \$754.21$$

per $1,000 face value.

Assume further that the market does not expect interest rates to change much, so that the two-year forward price of these bonds equals their current market price of $754.21. The company sells a futures contract and commits itself to deliver 13,259 such bonds at a price of $754.21 each for a total of $13,259 \times 754.21 \approx \$10$ million in two years' time. Contrary to market expectations, interest rates increase to 12 percent. As a result, the market price of each 10-year, 6 percent Government of Canada bond decreases to:

Market price=

$$60 \times \left[\frac{1 - \frac{1}{(1.12)^{10}}}{0.12}\right] + 1{,}000 \times \left[\frac{1}{(1.12)^{10}}\right] = 60 \times [5.65022] + 1{,}000 \times [0.32197] = \$660.98$$

The firm can now close out its interest rate futures position. Marking to market will have generated a profit of $754.21 - 660.98 = \$93.23$ per bond, or $13{,}259 \times 93.23 = \$1{,}236{,}137$ in total. This gain can be used to offset the higher interest costs to be borne on the new debt offering.

The above example illustrates in a general way how interest rate futures may be used to protect against interest rate risk. Because gains or losses from standardized futures contracts typically will not be perfectly correlated with the company's exposure to interest rate fluctuations, such hedges are rarely perfect, and the actual design of a transaction package that minimizes exposure can be difficult. The complexities of this sophisticated tool of financial management are revisited in Chapter 21.

The use of interest rate futures should be considered in the following cases:

1. Borrowers want to protect against future interest rate increases either on variable interest rate loans or on delayed funding, as illustrated in the above example.

2. Investors want to protect against future interest rate decreases, locking in current rates that are perceived to be attractive.

3. Financial institutions are exposed to interest rate risk because of a mismatch in the maturities of their assets and liabilities. For instance, if a trust company finances long-term fixed-rate mortgages with short-term variable-rate deposits, interest rate futures can be used to reduce vulnerability to increases in the short-term rate that has to be paid on deposits.

4. Speculators simply want to bet on interest rates moving in a particular direction. Low margin requirements on futures contracts provide leverage that adds speculative appeal.

The pricing of interest rate futures contracts is complicated because one cannot assume fixed interest rates, as was done in pricing commodity and foreign currency futures. This is so because interest rate futures are used to manage risk related to interest rate fluctuations. An analysis of interest rate futures pricing is thus beyond the scope of this text.

With the growing maturity of these markets and an increasing awareness and understanding of the products available, financial institutions and other corporations have become more active participants. We note that because of the limited volume and liquidity of Canadian futures markets to date, much of the hedging activity of Canadian firms takes place on foreign exchanges, notably in the United States. The fact that large Canadian companies often raise debt denominated in foreign currencies in international markets provides further impetus for hedging abroad.

Stock Index Futures

Stock index futures contracts allow one to lock in a future price at which one can buy the portfolio of stocks that makes up a stock market index. Futures contracts based on the S&P/TSE 60 Index trade on the Montreal Exchange. In the U.S., stock index futures based on a wide variety of different indices are available. These include the Standard and Poor's 500 Index, the Value Line Index, the New York Stock Exchange Composite Index, and the Major Market Index. Stock index futures are also available on a number of important stock market indices in other countries such as France, Japan, and the United Kingdom.

Stock index futures, like commodity futures contracts, are for specified amounts of the underlying asset. For example, the S&P/TSE 60 Index futures contract is a commitment to buy or sell stocks worth 200 times the value of the index. Thus, if the futures price is at 628.50, an investor who takes a short position in one contract is committing to sell a bundle of stocks for 200 times 628.50 or $125,700. The actual value of the stocks will be 200 times whatever the index actually is when the contract matures. The quantity 200 is referred to as the stock index futures contract's multiplier. Multipliers for index futures typically range from 200 to 500.

Of necessity, stock index futures contracts are settled in cash because market indices often consist of non-integer numbers of shares of their component stocks. It is, of course, not possible to deliver a bundle of fractions of shares of stock to settle a futures contract obligation. Cash settlement circumvents this problem.

This means that an investor in a short position in a stock index futures contract need not physically deliver all of the shares that make up the index when the futures contract matures. Rather, he need only deliver enough cash to allow a person on the long side of the contract to buy the stocks.

EXAMPLE

USING STOCK INDEX FUTURES I

An investor enters a six-month futures contract to buy the S&P/TSE 60 Index. The futures price at the time the position is taken is 600. Six months later, when the contract matures, the S&P/TSE 60 is at 630. One futures contract is for 200 times the value of the index. This means that the futures contract was originally to buy a portfolio of these 60 stocks for 200×600, or $120,000. When the contract matures, the value of this portfolio has risen to 200×630, or $126,000. Over the intervening period, the investor's margin account is credited with the $6,000 difference. In effect, this lets the investor buy the portfolio for $120,000 if he desires to do so.

Unlike commodity futures contracts, stock index futures contracts mature on a specific date of the maturity month. For example, S&P/TSE 60 and S&P 500 futures contracts mature on the third Friday of March, June, September, and December. This gives rise to so-called **triple witching hours** when large orders to buy and sell shares hit stock markets, since stock options, stock index options, and stock index futures contracts expire simultaneously. Stock options and stock index options were discussed in Chapter 18.

Stock index futures contracts allow investors to move quickly in and out of diversified positions in stocks. Indeed, they can be used to replicate the gains (or losses) one would get by "buying the market." Moreover, the commissions and other transaction costs associated with taking a position in stock index futures are a small fraction of the fees one would have to pay to take an equivalent position in the actual stocks that make up the index.[18] Index futures have thus become increasingly popular with institutional investors and corporate financial managers.

USING STOCK INDEX FUTURES II

A firm has just sold off a division for $10 million in cash and expects to reinvest the money by entering a joint venture in six months. During the intervening six months, the financial manager must obtain a reasonable return on the funds. The S&P/TSE 60 Index is currently at 625 and, its six-month futures price 631.25. The return on six-month treasury bills is 2.5 percent (per six months). Over a six-month period, the stocks in the index can be expected to pay a 1.5 percent dividend yield. Suppose that the spot price of the index rises to 650 six months later—a 4 percent gain. Consider the following two investment strategies:

1. Investing the $10 million in the stocks that make up the S&P/TSE 60 Index would earn a 4 percent return, or $400,000, plus the $150,000 dividends the stocks paid during the six months. The total gain is thus $550,000, of 5.5 percent.

2. Putting the money in treasury bills and entering 80 futures contracts to buy the S&P/TSE 60 Index in six months at 631.25 earns precisely the same return. Since S&P/TSE 60 futures have a multiplier of 200, each contract is a commitment to sell a bundle of stocks for 200×631.25 or $126,250. When the contracts mature, the index is at 650, so the actual value of the portfolio of stocks is 200×650, or $130,000. The accumulated gain as the contract is marked to market is, therefore, $130,000 - $126,250 = $3,750$ per contract. The total gain on 80 contracts is $300,000 ($3,750 \times 80$). The interest from having $10 million invested in treasury bills for six months at 2.5 percent is $250,000. The total gain is therefore $550,000, again a 5.5 percent return.

The transaction costs of buying $10 million in stocks is likely to be large. Even a 0.5 percent transaction cost amounts to fees of $50,000. In contrast, the transaction costs for entering a futures contract is, at most, about $50 per contract. A position of 80 contracts thus involves transaction costs of $4,000.

Index Arbitrage and Program Trading

The previous example shows that positions in index futures can mimic the returns from stocks. For most investors, the transaction costs of quickly buying and selling large portfolios of stocks are so large that index futures positions are the preferred alternative. However, large investment houses with direct computer links to stock exchanges can

---

[18] Of course, index futures are not a perfect substitute for stock ownership. They do not entitle their owners to vote at shareholder meetings or to have board representation. Index futures are also available only on a few special portfolios. For a passive investor only interested in holding the market, however, they are a useful alternative.

EXAMPLE

assemble large portfolios of stocks quickly and with minimal transaction costs. Thus, they can take arbitrage positions that are based on the theoretical equivalence of positions in index futures and their underlying stocks. This is referred to as computer-directed **program trading**.

Again, we can use the theoretical relation between index futures and the underlying stock portfolio to solve for index futures prices. In this case, the spot price S is the current value of the stock index, or the current value in the stock market of the theoretical portfolio of stocks that the index represents. Let r be the risk-free interest rate, and let δ be the dividend rate of the index.[19] If, for example, δ is 3 percent, the value of the dividends paid by the stocks that make up the index is 3 percent of the value of the index. Both r and δ must be measured over the time period that corresponds to the maturity of the futures contract. Thus, if the futures contract in question runs for six months, both r and δ must be semi-annual rates. We want to solve for F the stock index futures price. To do this, we formalize the previous example. Again, we consider two possible investment strategies that result in owning the stocks in the index six months from now:

Strategy 1.   Buy the stocks now and hold them for six months.

Strategy 2.   Enter a futures contract to buy the stocks six months from now.

These two strategies are compared in Figure 20.9. Strategy 1 involves paying S dollars now (time zero) for the stocks and gives the investor six months' worth of dividends, or δS, while she holds the portfolio.[20] Thus, viewed from time zero, the cost of using Strategy 1 to acquire the portfolio of stocks six months from now, denoted by C_1, is:

$$C_1 = -S + \frac{\delta S}{1+r}$$

Strategy 2 involves no payment now and a payment of F dollars six months from now to buy the portfolio of stocks. The cost of this strategy, viewed from time zero, is the present value F, or:

$$C_2 = \frac{-F}{1+r}$$

FIGURE 20.9

The Framework for Program Trading on Stock Index Futures

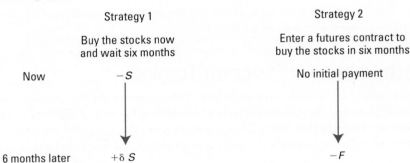

	Strategy 1 Buy the stocks now and wait six months	Strategy 2 Enter a futures contract to buy the stocks in six months
Now	$-S$	No initial payment
6 months later	$+\delta S$	$-F$

---

[19] For simplicity, we assume that the interest rate and the dividend yield are both known with certainty. When they are uncertain, as is the case in many practical situations, the solution is more complex. The basic framework as presented here, however, remains essentially correct.

[20] For simplicity, we assume that the dividends are paid at the end of the period.

Since these two strategies result in the same outcome, namely owning the underlying portfolio of stocks in six months, they should cost the same amount to set up. Thus,

$$-S + \frac{\delta S}{1+r} = \frac{-F}{1+r}$$

This simplifies to:

$$F = S(1 + r - \delta)$$

More generally, allowing for a multiperiod contract,

$$F = S(1 + r - \delta)^t$$

Equation 20.3 lets us solve for an index futures price F, given the spot price of the underlying index S, the risk-free interest rate r, and the dividend yield of the underlying portfolio δ.[21] Both r and δ must be measured over the time period that remains until the futures contract matures, t.

THE FUTURES PRICE FOR A STOCK INDEX

EXAMPLE

In the previous example, we had the spot price $S = 625$, the number of semi-annual time periods $t = 1$, the semi-annual interest rate $r = 2.5$ percent, and the semi-annual dividend rate $\delta = 1.5$ percent. Inserting these values into Equation 20.3, we can solve for the six-month futures price of the S&P/TSE 60 Index, F.

$$F = S(1 + r - \delta)^t = 625 \times (1 + .025 - .015)^1 = 631.25$$

To prevent arbitrage, the six-month index futures price must be 631.25. This is, in fact, the value in the previous example that results in the two investment strategies having the same return.

If the index futures price deviates from the value given in Equation 20.3, arbitrage profits are once again possible. To perform the required steps in this type of arbitrage, it is necessary to take positions in large numbers of stocks quickly.[22] To do this without facing prohibitive transaction costs requires a direct computer link to the stock exchange. The calculations that go into the arbitrage strategy require continual monitoring of the prices of all the stocks in the index that underlie the futures contract. Again, this requires a computer, and, as a consequence, arbitrage involving index futures is referred to as program trading.

ARBITRAGE WHEN S DECREASES

EXAMPLE

Let's pursue the previous example, with $S = 625$, $r = 2.5$ percent (six-month rate), $\delta = 1.5$ percent (six-month yield), and $F = 631.25$. Now suppose that bad news about

---

[21] Note again that the basic principle behind Equation 20.3 is the same as that used to value other financial futures and to provide a bound on commodity futures prices. The costs and benefits of holding an inventory of the underlying asset (in this case a portfolio of stocks) are compared with those of taking a futures position.

[22] Obviously, it is also necessary to take a sufficiently large position so that the index can be replicated with integer numbers of shares—preferably board lots.

a major stock in the index is released, causing its price to fall sharply. A computer that is continually recalculating the value of the S&P/TSE 60 Index based on the latest stock price data produces a new value of 612.50. If traders in the futures market do not react immediately by adjusting index futures prices to new levels, program trading arbitrage profits can be made as follows:

Step 1. The computer must issue an order to borrow $122,500 ($612.50×200) at the risk-free rate for six months. (Recall that the multiplier for the index futures is 200.) The computer must use its direct link to the stock exchange computer to spend this money immediately to buy the stocks that underlie one index futures contract. Simultaneously, it must enter one futures contract to sell those stocks for $126,250 ($631.25×200) in six months. Over the subsequent six months, the stocks being held will generate $1,838 in dividends (1.5 percent of $122,500).

Step 2. Six months later, the arbitrageur can collect the $126,250 from the futures contract and add this to the $1,838 in dividends to bring the total to $128,088. The arbitrageur can use this money to pay back the loan, which costs $125,563=$122,500×(1+ .025). The net arbitrage profit is, therefore, $2,525 per contract (128,088−125,563).

The position limit in S&P/TSE 60 index futures is 30,000 contracts. Therefore, a computerized arbitrageur with the maximum allowed position would earn arbitrage profits of 30,000×$2,525=$75.75 million.

The arbitrageur would not actually have to wait for six months to obtain her profits. The futures price would normally adjust within a few minutes to a new level consistent with a spot price of $612.50. This is given by Equation 20.3 as:

$$F=S(1+r-\delta)^t=\$612.50\times(1+.025-.015)^1=\$618.63$$

Once this adjustment takes place, the arbitrageur can make a reversing trade so that her position is closed out when it is marked to market. She originally had a contract to sell at $631.25. The selling price at which she closes out her position is $618.63. This means that the difference of $12.62 is deposited in her margin account. Since the multiplier is 200, the deposit is actually $2,524 per contract. For the maximum position of 30,000 contracts, this adds up to $75.72 million (difference from profit above is due to rounding).

Note that the profits in the example above are virtually risk-free and are obtained with no actual investment of the arbitrageur's own money. The dividend yield is slightly risky, so the strategy is not completely risk-free; however, the probability of any substantial change in the dividend yield of the portfolio before the contract is marked to market is small enough to ignore.

If the spot price of the S&P/TSE 60 Index had moved up instead of down and the futures price failed to adjust quickly enough, analogous arbitrage profit could again be made. This time, the strategy would be to engage in short sales of large quantities of the underlying stocks while entering a futures contract to purchase the shares that make up the index. Since the portfolio management divisions of large investment firms usually hold substantial amounts of stocks for various clients, the arbitrage division of such companies can affect short sales with minimal transaction fees by borrowing shares from the portfolio division and selling them.

ARBITRAGE WHEN *S* INCREASES

Suppose the situation begins as in the previous example, but that good news about a major stock in the index drives its value up to 637.50 and that the futures price remains temporarily at 631.25. Given a multiplier of 200, program trading arbitrage profits can be made as follows:

Step 1.   Sell $127,500 (637.50×200) of the underlying stocks short and invest the $127,500 at the risk-free rate of 2.5 percent. Over the subsequent six months, the stocks in the short sale would pay dividends equal to 1.5 percent of $127,500 or $1,913. Since the portfolio division of the firm must pay these dividends to its clients, the arbitrage division must transfer $1,913 to it.[23]

Step 2.   Six months later, collect the $130,688 from the risk-free investment ($127,500 plus 2.5 percent interest) and use $126,250 (631.25×200) to buy enough stock via the futures contract to close out the short sale. Given that $1,913 was transferred to pay dividend obligations, the net profit of the arbitrage division is again $2,525 per contract (130,688−126,250−1,913). With the maximum position of 30,000 contracts, after the futures price adjusts to the correct level and the contract is marked to market, the total arbitrage profit is $75.75 million.

We take the time to go through this side of the arbitrage argument because a few years ago, its mechanics became the subject of intense public concern. During the stock market crash of October 1987, stock exchange computers were often so overloaded with sell orders that they were quoting prices many minutes behind (and therefore higher than) the actual prices on the exchange trading floor. Arbitrageurs' computers linked to the exchanges' automated quotations systems were thus being fed "stale" prices and may have been using these prices to generate short sell orders as in the previous example. Because such sell orders were thought to have exacerbated the crash, this line of reasoning led to numerous calls to ban or restrict program trading.

These concerns do not appear to be justified. Periods of active program trading during the crash did not correspond to periods of steep price declines.[24] Moreover, exchanges that allowed program trading actually experienced smaller overall price declines than those that did not. Indeed, index futures may actually have stabilized the stock market by providing an alternative to massive sell orders. If the market is declining rapidly, a concerned investor can essentially get out of the market without selling his stocks. This is done by entering a futures contract to sell them in a few months at the futures price. Index futures may thus provide a form of emergency release valve for selling pressure in stock markets.

OPTIONS ON FUTURES CONTRACTS   20.7

It is possible to buy put and call options to enter futures contracts.

---

[23] Recall that a short seller is required to match the dividends paid on the securities he is shorting.
[24] See R. Barro, et al., *Black Monday and the Future of Financial Markets* (Homewood, Ill.: Dow Jones Irwin, 1989), for a good overview of these issues.

EXAMPLE

OPTIONS TO BUY CATTLE FUTURES

An American option to buy 12-month cattle futures at 70¢ per pound expires in one year. This means that at any time during the next year, the option owner can exercise her option and enter a futures contract to purchase cattle at 70¢ per pound regardless of the prevailing futures price. Once the option is exercised, the futures contract is marked to market, and the investor can either close out her futures position or keep her long position open for the remainder of the year.

Futures options are available for a number of heavily traded commodity futures contracts including wheat, corn, oats, pork bellies, and oil. Options are also available on a number of interest rate, foreign exchange, and stock index futures contracts. Although much of the trading activity in this area is in U.S. markets, futures options are widely used by Canadian enterprises especially to manage commodity price and interest rate risk.

EXAMPLE

OPTIONS ON GOLD FUTURES

A company wants to lock in a price at which it can buy gold for industrial use in one year. One way of doing this is through the purchase of an ordinary call option on gold at $300 per ounce, expiring in one year. Suppose that one year later, the price of gold is $325 per ounce. Exercising the option allows the firm to buy gold at the old price of $300, saving $25 per ounce on the current spot price.

Another way to achieve the same result is to buy a one-year call option to enter a long position in a futures contract to buy gold in one year at $300. For practical purposes, these two alternatives are equivalent. The call option lets its holder enter a futures contract any time during the next year and locks in a futures price of $300 per ounce for that contract. Again, suppose that one year later, the spot price of gold is $325 per ounce. The futures contract is about to expire, so the futures price must be very close to the spot price of $325. If the business exercises its futures option at $300, it enters a futures contract that is immediately marked to market at $325. The firm's margin account receives the $25 difference.[25] The firm can then accept delivery of the gold as the futures contract matures or close out its futures position and buy gold in the spot market. In either case, the gold costs $325 per ounce. However, proceeds from the marking to market of the futures contract subsidize the purchase by $25 per ounce, making the real cost to the company $300.

Options on futures are popular because, as the previous example shows, they are, effectively, commodity options with options for early cash settlement as an added feature. Some technical issues in valuing futures options arise from the possibility of early exercise and from differences in the expiration dates of the option and its underlying futures contract. However, these issues are beyond the scope of this text.[26]

---

[25] If the futures price had risen to $325 after just six months, the firm could have exercised its option early. It would then have a futures contract at the prevailing futures price as well as $25 (in its margin account). The company could use these monies as it saw fit.

[26] For a detailed treatment, see J. Hull, *Options, Futures, and Other Derivative Securities*, 3rd ed., (Toronto: Prentice-Hall Canada, 1997).

SUMMARY 20.8

1. Futures contracts and forward contracts are devices for locking in pricing for future transactions. They commit the investor to buying or selling in the future at that price. There is no choice on whether or not to exercise. Futures and forward contracts are less flexible than options. Their compensating benefit is that futures entail no up-front cost.

2. Futures contracts are standardized agreements with futures market clearing houses to buy or sell assets at specified times and prices. Commodity futures contracts are for important agricultural products, metals, oil, and other commodities. Financial futures contracts that allow one to buy or sell foreign currencies, debt instruments, and stock portfolios have become important risk-management devices.

3. If a commodity futures price is lower than the spot price traders expect to see at the time the futures contract matures, the market for that futures contract is said to display backwardation. If the futures price is higher than the expected spot price, the market is said to display forwardation.

4. Commodity futures prices are set by the interaction of the supply and demand for price hedging, but are limited by an arbitrage constraint. Futures contracts are important tools for risk management. Commodity futures contracts can be used to lock in prices for the firm's inputs and products and hedge against price changes.

5. Foreign currency futures can be used to lock in exchange rates and limit foreign currency risk. Interest rate futures lock in the prices and yields of debt instruments, allowing firms to hedge against the risk of interest rate fluctuations. Stock index futures contracts lock in the prices of stock portfolios based on widely used stock indices.

QUESTIONS AND PROBLEMS

Questions for Discussion

1. Why is the arbitrage constraint on commodity futures prices an inequality, while those on financial futures are equalities? What characteristics of commodities markets are involved? What would commodities markets have to look like for an equality to hold? Why are these conditions unlikely?

2. Are speculators likely to stabilize or destabilize futures markets? When might each possibility occur? Speculators are often seen as contributing nothing to society. Do speculators in futures markets fulfill any socially useful role?

3. Foreign currency futures contracts are seen by many as a way to circumvent overly conservative banking practices in setting up foreign currency forward contracts. What institutional features differentiate the two types of contracts? Why might these differences make banks act conservatively in arranging foreign currency forward contracts for customers?

4. Is it more likely that stock index futures contracts stabilize or destabilize the stock market during times of high volatility such as market crashes? What are the mechanisms by which stabilization or destabilization might happen? Which are likely to be more important as computer technology develops?

5. A "squeeze" play is an attempt to manipulate the price of the underlying asset so as to make money in the futures market. For example, one might enter a large long position in futures and then elevate the price of the underlying asset by spreading false rumours or cornering the market in that asset. This forces investors who took the short side of the contract to sell the underlying asset to the squeeze player at a large loss. This particular strategy is called "squeezing the shorts."

   Squeeze plays are not common, but they probably do happen occasionally. What effects does this have on the usefulness of futures as risk-management tools? What institutional reforms could be taken to eliminate squeeze plays?[27]

PROBLEMS WITH SOLUTIONS

Problem 1

A firm locks in a $1-per-pound price at which it can buy high-grade industrial copper in one year using futures contracts. The price is now 95¢, but the company's managers' fears subsequently prove correct, and the spot price rises to $1.10 one year later. Show how the firm need not hold its futures position to maturity in order to use futures contracts as an effective hedging tool. Why would this sometimes be a preferable strategy?

Solution 1

One year later, the business could, of course, accept delivery of its copper via the futures contract and pay $1 per pound for it (net of funds added to its margin account). Alternatively, the firm could close out its futures position with an offsetting short position. When marking to market takes place, the company would be left with only its margin account. Since the original futures price was $1 and the spot price at the time the contract matures is $1.10, total proceeds from marking to market over the year amount to $0.10 per pound. This $0.10 gain in the futures market lets the firm put up another $1 per pound and buy copper at the spot price. The real cost to the corporation is thus $1 per pound.

The advantage of not actually taking delivery from the futures contract is that it adds flexibility. Delivery via the futures contract involves the transfer of a warehouse receipt for copper stored in the location required by the rules of the futures exchange. If the firm would prefer delivery elsewhere, it can close out its futures position just prior to maturity and then arrange for delivery in the most convenient spot market.

---

[27] An attempt by American billionaires, the three Hunt brothers, to corner the silver market caused the silver futures market to crash. See S. Fay, *The Great Silver Bubble*, (London: Hodder and Stoughton, 1982).

Problem 2

The spot price of sugar is 9.62¢ per pound. The interest rate is 10 percent per year, and the cost of storing sugar is $5 per ton per month.

(a) What is the highest level the six-month futures price can attain?

(b) What happens if this level is exceeded?

Solution 2

(a) We know from Equation 20.1 that an upper bound on commodity futures prices is given by:

$$F \leq S(1+r)^t + ct$$

In this case, the spot price of sugar is $S = 9.62$¢ per pound, the interest rate is 10 percent per year, the time until maturity of the contract is $t = 0.5$ years, and the cost of carrying an inventory of sugar is $c = 3$¢/pound/year ($5/ton/month = $60/ton/year = $.03/pound/year). Note that all variables in the equation must have consistent units. Time must be measured in years to be consistent with the interest rate, and value must be measured in per pound to be consistent with the spot price.

Substituting into Equation 20.1 gives:

$$F \leq S(1+r)^t = ct = 9.62 \times (1+.10)^{.5} + 3 \times .5 = 10.09 + 1.50 = 11.59$$

The futures price cannot rise above 11.59¢ per pound.

(b) If it does, arbitrage is possible and will drive the price back down. Suppose the futures price rises past 11.59¢ to, say, 12¢ per pound. The following strategy lets one make large amounts of arbitrage profits with no risk and no money down:

Step 1. Open a short position in a six-month sugar futures contract agreeing to sell one pound of sugar in six months for 12¢. Borrow 9.62¢ at 10 percent to buy one pound of sugar, and store the sugar for six months.

Step 2. Six months later, take the sugar out of storage and sell it for 12¢ to fulfill the futures contract obligation. Use this money to pay the storage cost ct of 1.5¢ (3¢/pound/year for six months) and to repay the loan, which costs $S(1+r)^t$—or 9.62¢ $\times (1+.10)^{.5} = 10.09$¢, for a total cost of 11.59¢. This leaves an arbitrage profit of 0.41¢ per pound (12¢−11.59¢). On a standard futures contract for 112,000 pounds, this amounts to $45,920. On a position of 5,000 contracts, the arbitrage profit is $2.296 million.

Note that these profits are risk-free. Once the terms of the loan are set, the futures contract is entered, and the storage terms are arranged, the profits are locked in. Note also that this strategy by arbitrageurs puts downward pressure on the futures price since they all want to sell sugar in six months at 12¢. When the futures price falls to 11.59¢, arbitrage will stop. This will probably happen within minutes. When contracts are marked to market at the end of the day, the difference between 12¢ and 11.59¢, namely 0.41¢ per pound is deposited in the arbitrageur's margin account. On 5,000 112,000-pound. standard contracts, this equals $2.296 million. Thus, the arbitrage profit is also immediate.

Problem 3

In foreign currency spot markets, the Canadian dollar is trading at US$0.85. The risk-free interest rate is 6 percent in the United States and 9 percent in Canada.

(a) What should the one-year futures price of the Canadian dollar be?

(b) What arbitrage strategy is profitable if the futures price is too high?

(c) What arbitrage strategy is profitable if the futures price is too low?

Solution 3

(a) We can use Equation 20.2 to solve for a foreign currency futures price. We have a spot rate S_{AB} of US$0.85/C$; a U.S. interest rate r_A of 6 percent; a Canadian interest rate r_B of 9 percent; and the time until the futures contract matures of one year. Note that since annual interest rates are used, t must be measured in years. Inserting these values into Equation 20.2, we get:

$$F_{AB} = \left[\frac{1+r_A}{1+r_B}\right]^t S_{AB} = \frac{1+.06}{1+.09} \times US\$0.85/C\$ = US\$0.8266/C\$$$

The one-year futures price of the Canadian dollar must be US$0.8266.

(b) If the futures price exceeds US$0.8266/C$, arbitrage is possible. Suppose the one-year futures price is US$0.84/C$. The following strategy earns large amounts of risk-free arbitrage profits with no money down:

Step 1. Borrow US$779,817 in the United States at 6 percent, and convert this to C$917,432 in the spot market. Invest this at 9 percent in Canada for one year, and enter futures contracts to convert the future value of this C$1million into US$840,000 next year. Note that the original loan amount of US$779,817 was chosen to end up giving a round number of C$1 million to be exchanged via futures contracts.

Step 2. One year later, collect the US$840,000 from the futures contract, pay off the loan with US$826,606, and keep US$13,394 as arbitrage profits. This is entirely risk-free, and the arbitrageur need invest none of her own money. Moreover, arbitrageurs taking large short futures positions to sell Canadian dollars will drive down the futures price to US$0.8266/C$ at which level arbitrage is no longer possible. A reversing trade at this price means marking to market puts US$0.0134/C$ in the arbitrageur's margin account. On a futures position of C$1 million, this amounts to $13,400. Except for a rounding-off error, this is the same amount as before. Thus, the profits arrive immediately as well.

(c) If the futures price is below US$0.8266/C$, say, at US$0.81/C$, the arbitrage operation in (b) can be run backwards. Again, two steps are required.

Step 1. Borrow C$899,001 in Canada at 9 percent and convert this to US$764,151 in the spot market. Invest this at 6 percent in the United States for one year, and enter futures contracts to convert the future value of this US$810,000 into C$1 million next year. Again, the initial amount is chosen to produce a round number for trading in the futures market.

Step 2. One year later, collect the C$1 million from the futures contract, pay off the loan with C$979,911, and keep C$20,089 as arbitrage profits.

Again, this arbitrage strategy drives the futures price up until it reaches US$0.8266. A reversing trade once this futures price is reached delivers the arbitrage profits immediately.

Problem 4

The S&P/TSE 60 Index is now at 650. The one-year interest rate is 6 percent, and the dividend yield of the portfolio of stocks in the S&P/TSE 60 is 2.8 percent.

(a) What is the one-year futures price of the index?

(b) Describe how a program trading strategy could make money if the price of a major stock in the index suddenly fell pulling the index down to 648, and the futures price failed to adjust immediately?

Solution 4

(a) We use Equation 20.3. The spot price of the index is $S=650$, the one-year interest rate is $r=0.06$, and the expected dividend yield over the next year is $\delta=.028$. The one-year futures price F is:

$$F=S(1+r-\delta)=650(1+0.06-0.028)=670.8$$

(b) The following two-step strategy results in arbitrage profits:

Step 1. Borrow $648, and buy the shares that make up the index. Enter a futures contract to sell these shares in one year for $670.80.

Step 2. One year later, collect the $670.80 from the futures contract and $18.14 in dividends paid over the year (2.8 percent of $648). This totals $688.94. Pay off the loan, which, at 6 percent, costs $686.88. The remaining $2.06 is an arbitrage profit.

　　　The multiplier for S&P/TSE 60 futures is 200, so a position in one contract yields 200×$2.06 in profits or $412. The position limit is 30,000 contracts, which implies a maximum arbitrage profit of $12.36 million. Note that the futures price of the index should quickly adjust to its new value of:

$$F=S(1+r-\delta)=648(1+0.06-0.028)=668.74$$

Of course, it is not really necessary to wait for one year to get the arbitrage profits. A reversing trade and marking to market at the end of the day puts $670.80−$668.74 or $2.06 into the arbitrageur's margin account. On a position of one contract, this amounts to 200×$2.06 or $412. On a 30,000 contract maximum position, the total is $12.36 million. If something else affects the market before the close of trading, the profits are locked in and can be collected one year later anyway.

ADDITIONAL PROBLEMS

1. The spot price of corn is $2.85 per bushel. The storage cost is 5¢ per bushel per month. The term structure of risk-free interest rates is as follows:

   3-month rate: 2.1% over 3 months

   6-month rate: 4.0% over 6 months

   9-month rate: 5.9% over 9 months

   12-month rate: 7.9% over 12 months

   What are the upper limits for the 3-, 6-, 9-, and 12- month futures prices of corn?

2. The spot exchange rate between Euros and U.S. dollars is US$0.86/Euro. The one-year risk-free rate is 4 percent in Europe and 7 percent in the United States. What is the one-year futures price of Euros in U.S. dollars?

3. The spot exchange rate between Euros and U.S. dollars is US$0.86/Euro, while that between Australian dollars and U.S. dollars is US$0.53/A$. The European one-year risk-free rate is 4 percent, while that in Australia is 10 percent. What is the one-year futures price of Australian dollars in U.S. dollars if the one-year futures price of Euros is US$0.85/Euro?

4. The New York Stock Exchange Composite Index is at 638. The risk-free rate for one-year investments in U.S. dollars is 6 percent, and the dividend yield on the portfolio of stocks that makes up the index is 3.5 percent. The multiplier is 500, and a position limit of 5,000 contracts is in place.

   (a) What should be the one-year futures price of the NYSE Composite Index?

   (b) Suppose the price of an important stock falls dragging down the index to 630. What arbitrage profit can be earned by program trading if the futures price remains at the value calculated in (a)?

   (c) Suppose the price of an important stock rises pulling the value of the index up to 646. What arbitrage profits can be earned if the futures price remains at the value in (a)?

5. A speculator goes long three futures contracts on sugar for May delivery at a price of $0.2145 per pound (each contract is for 112,000 pounds). The speculator posts a margin of 10 percent. Two days later, the futures price has risen to $0.2200. Calculate the speculators percentage return on the investment.

6. The futures price for crude oil for delivery in three months is $31.30 per barrel. The risk-free rate of interest is 6 percent and the spot price of crude is $31.01 per barrel. Assuming that the futures trade at their upper-price bound, what is the annual convenience yield on oil? Why might there be a convenience yield for a commodity like this?

7. The spot price of coffee is $0.7454 per pound. The risk-free interest rate is 5.5 percent. The storage costs for coffee amount to $0.01 per pound per year. What is the upper bound on the futures price of coffee for delivery in one year? If the futures price for delivery in one year was $0.8500, how could an arbitrageur take advantage of this?

8. A firm is going to raise $60 million in six months and plans on borrowing. Currently, interest rates on the company's debt are 8 percent, and 6 percent on Government of Canada bonds. The firm is worried that interest rates will rise before it borrows the money. Consequently, it takes a short position on interest rate futures. It sells interest rate futures on 20,000 Government of Canada 6 percent coupon bonds (with $1,000 face value) for delivery in six months. This should provide a partial hedge against rate changes. Assume that the futures price equals the spot price. Any gains on the futures will be used to reduce the amount borrowed, while any losses will have to be covered through increased borrowing.

(a) If interest rates in six months are 9 percent on the firm's debt and 7 percent on Government of Canada bonds, what will be the annual interest payments on the company's debt?

(b) If interest rates in six months are 7 percent on the firm's debt and 5 percent on Government of Canada bonds, what will be the annual interest payments on the company's debt?

(c) If the firm had chosen not to hedge with futures, what would be its annual interest payments if rates on its debt had risen to 9 percent? What if rates on its debt had fallen to 7 percent? Based on this and the answers to (a) and (b), discuss the benefits and possible drawbacks of hedging risk.

9. A Canadian company is due to make a payment of £130,000 to a supplier in England in August. In order to hedge the foreign exchange rate risk that it is exposed to, the firm uses futures contracts from the International Money Market (IMM) in Chicago. It takes a position in pound futures contracts (each contract is on £62,500) for August delivery at a price of US$1.60/£. However, because futures on the IMM are for trade in U.S. dollars for a foreign currency, this will only hedge the value of the payment in terms of American dollars. In order to hedge the payment in terms of Canadian dollars, the corporation will also have to take a position in Canadian-dollar futures on the IMM. Each Canadian-dollar futures contract is on C$100,000. The August futures price for Canadian dollars is US$0.67/C$. In order to provide the best hedge:

(a) Should the firm be long or short in pound futures, and how many pound contracts should it enter?

(b) Should the company be long or short in Canadian-dollar futures, and how many Canadian-dollar contracts should it enter?

10. The interest rate for one-month deposits or loans in Canadian dollars is 7 percent (this is an annualized rate that is compounded monthly). The interest rate for one-month deposits or loans in U.S. dollars is 6 percent (again, compounded monthly). The spot exchange rate is C$1.35/US$, and the futures price for delivery in one month is C$1.37/US$.

(a) Show that there is an arbitrage opportunity available.

(b) Your bank tells you that you can borrow a maximum of C$10 million in Canada or US$7.40740741 million in the United States. How much profit (in Canadian dollars) can you make on the arbitrage opportunity?

Let's Swap

In Chapters 6 and 16, we looked at the Greater Toronto Airport Authority's (GTAA) large bond issues. The size of the GTAA's debt poses certain challenges from a treasury risk management perspective.

"Our only major concern is interest rate risk," explains Todd Timmerman, whose responsibility includes both Finance and Treasury at the GTAA. "Because of all the debt issues we have outstanding, all of which is at fixed rates, a drop in interest rates could be very costly for us." The GTAA's annual report for 2000 stated that just a 1 percent change in interest rates could amount to a $1 million additional expense for the Authority.

"The problem is that we would have to keep paying the set coupon rates on our bonds, while our reserve funds would be at the mercy of the market," explains Mr. Timmerman. Per the Authority's Capital Markets Platform, a reserve fund is established in trust with a full year's interest on each bond series issued to help reduce the risk to the bond's purchasers.

The solution? A kind of derivative instrument known as a "swap deal." "We basically swap our fixed-rate investments with a bank for flexible investments that we can manage month to month," explains Mr. Timmerman. "We set up the swap as soon as we take on a new major debt."

"The swap is like a hedge for us," he says. It allows the Authority to mitigate the risk of interest variations—and allows Mr. Timmerman to sleep a little better at night.

Treasury Risk Management

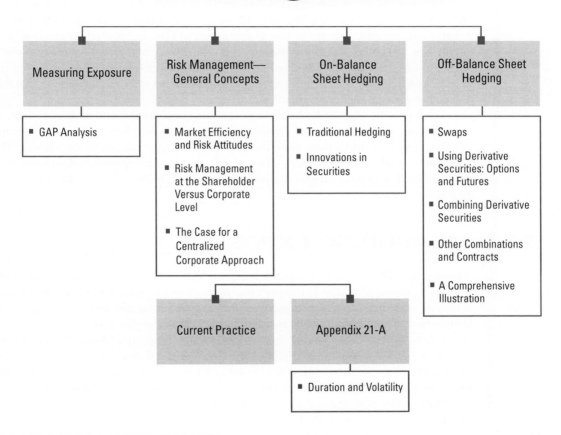

Learning Objectives

After studying this chapter, you should be able to:

1. *Define the term exposure, and describe how it affects effective risk management.*
2. *Explain why most firms use aggregate measures, and understand why they are preferable in defining exposure.*
3. *Identify some techniques used to quantify exposure.*
4. *Describe the role market efficiency plays in risk-management choices.*
5. *Compare and contrast on-balance-sheet hedging and off-balance-sheet hedging.*

21.1 INTRODUCTION

Treasury risk management is concerned primarily with managing the firm's exposure to unanticipated changes in interest and foreign exchange rates as well as exposure to changes in the prices of commodities that the company may buy or sell. The reallocation of risk that we will be reviewing is an important aspect of the activity and the financial innovating, or financial engineering, it may entail.

Treasury risk management has gained increasing attention for several reasons. First, prices in many financial markets have become more volatile, thus exposing firms to greater risk; second, because of the globalization of business (including international financing), foreign exchange exposure has become more pronounced for many companies; and third, deregulation and increased competition in the financial services industry have resulted in significant innovations in financial instruments and techniques that can be used to manage such risks effectively.

We begin the chapter by briefly laying some conceptual foundations. We look at exposure and how it may be measured and discuss how beliefs regarding market efficiency and risk attitudes determine the approach one may take in managing risk. We then survey various methods for reducing risk including traditional hedging and new approaches that rely on various derivative securities. Finally, we review briefly current trends in practice.

21.2 MEASURING EXPOSURE

Exposure to fluctuations in foreign exchange or interest rates is pervasive. It is not limited to companies that deal in international markets or that have large amounts of debt outstanding. When interest rates increase, for example, this could depress housing starts that, in turn, would reduce the demand for lumber. Thus, lumber producers are likely to suffer from decreased demand and prices quite apart from any additional interest they may have to pay on their outstanding loans. Similarly, a Canadian manufacturer who deals solely in the domestic market may suffer from a rise in the Canadian dollar that makes competing offshore imports cheaper. Exposure to changes in financial prices can take many forms and, in some way, affects most companies.

Exposure can be measured in different ways. The two most common concerns are how financial variables (such as interest or foreign exchange rates) affect operating performance as reflected in profits and how they influence the firm's value as reflected in share prices.

While profits and share prices obviously are related, their basic focus is clearly different. Profit reflects performance over a given time period—it is a **flow variable** measuring how much income flows into the business during a particular time span. Profit is also influenced by accounting conventions. Share price, on the other hand, measures economic value at a particular point in time. It, therefore, is a **stock variable**. As we saw in previous chapters, share prices are primarily determined by investors' expectations about the company's ability to generate cash flows in the future.

We have stressed previously that management, at least normatively, should focus on creating value for shareholders. Therefore, the primary concern of risk management should be to protect value as reflected in share prices. In practice, however, most treasury risk management programs focus on profits or earnings per share. This is the case because many managers are evaluated on that basis, with bonuses often tied to operating performance. Tradition and the fact that managers, at least over the short term, have more control over earnings than over share prices, reinforce this behaviour. Finally, erratic earnings per share may be difficult to explain to outside investors. If they are viewed with concern by shareholders, stock prices will suffer as a consequence.

Technically, exposure is commonly measured as the relative change in profits or share prices caused by a given percentage change in the particular financial variables of concern. Measuring how a firm's share price reacts to changes in interest or foreign exchange rates is not easy. Given the variety of other factors that influence share prices, managers may rely upon regression analysis. In a simplified form, this can be expressed as:

$$\frac{\Delta V}{V} = a + b_1 \frac{\Delta P_1}{P_1} + b_2 \frac{\Delta P_2}{P_1} + \ldots + b_n \frac{\Delta P_n}{P_n} \qquad (21.1)$$

where:

$\dfrac{\Delta V}{V}$ is the percentage change in the value of the firm's shares

$\dfrac{\Delta P}{P}$ are the percentage changes in various financial prices such as interest rates, foreign exchange rates, or commodity prices

b_i are the regression coefficients that measure the sensitivity of the corporation's stock prices to changes in the price of the ith factor price

By observing the firm's performance over many time periods, it is possible to establish a regression equation and obtain estimates for the various parameters.

WESTINGHOUSE RISK EXPOSURES[1]

EXAMPLE

Westinghouse is a multinational company that provides a diverse range of electrical, electronic, and mechanical products and services. To determine Westinghouse's sensitivity to interest rates, exchange rates, and the price of oil, the following regression equation was formulated:

$$R = a + b_1(\Delta 3ML/3ML) + b_2(\Delta 10YT/10YT) + b_3(\Delta P_{\pounds}/P_{\pounds}) + b_4(\Delta P_{\yen}/P_{\yen}) + b_5(\Delta P_{OIL}/P_{OIL})$$

where:

R = rate of return for holding Weestinghouse stock

$\Delta 3ML/3ML$ = percentage change in three-month LIBOR[2]

$\Delta 10YT/10YT$ = percentage change in the 10-year Government of Canada bond rate

$\Delta P_{\pounds}/P_{\pounds}, \Delta P_{\yen}/P_{\yen}$ = percentage changes in dollar prices of pounds sterling and yen

$\Delta P_{OIL}/P_{OIL}$ = percentage change in the price of crude oil

---

[1] This example is taken from W. Rawls and C. Smithson, "Strategic Risk Management." *Journal of Applied Corporate Finance* (Winter 1990), pp. 6-18.

[2] LIBOR is an acronym for the London Interbank Offer Rate, the rate at which banks borrow eurocurrencies from each other.

The coefficients b_1 and b_2 provide measures of the sensitivity of the value of the firm to changes in short- and long-term interest rates, while b_3 and b_4 estimate the sensitivity to exchange rates, and b_5 estimates the sensitivity to oil prices.

The time period from October 1987 to October 1989 was chosen for the analysis. The rate of return on holding Westinghouse stock was determined by calculating the rate of return on Westinghouse's equity using the daily data on share prices and dividends. Similarly, it was necessary to calculate the daily percentage changes in three-month LIBOR, the 10-year treasury rate, the dollar prices of sterling and yen, and the price of West Texas Intermediate crude oil.

The following results were obtained:

Sensitivity to	Coefficient	Parameter Estimate
3-month LIBOR	b_1	−0.263*
10-year bond yield	b_2	−0.681*
Price of sterling	b_3	−0.517
Price of yen	b_4	0.098*
Price of oil	b_5	0.023

* Statistically significant at the 95 percent confidence level.

The results indicated a statistically significant negative relationship between the three-month LIBOR, the 10-year treasury rate, and the value of Westinghouse equity. This meant that increases in interest rates were associated with decreases in the value of Westinghouse shares, and decreases in interest rates were associated with increases in the value of Westinghouse shares. In addition, the results showed a significant positive relationship between the price of yen and the value of Westinghouse shares but not a statistically significant relationship between the price of sterling or the price of oil over the two-year period.

Another way of estimating market value exposure is to assess how the values of the firm's major assets and liabilities are likely to change with fluctuating financial prices. Many companies ignore such fluctuations simply because they do not affect financial statements that are based on historical costs. Such price signals are relevant, however, when we are concerned with current shareholder wealth. For example, the market value of an oil well is clearly influenced by current oil prices even if the firm's investment in the well is shown on the balance sheet at constant historical costs. Similarly, the market value of a business's fixed interest rate debt will increase if market interest rates fall. A firm may argue that this is of no concern since at maturity, it needs to repay only face value. However, an increase in the market value of the debt signals that current and future interest payments exceed current market rates. They reflect an added burden on the company that its competitors may not have to bear.

Since share values are ultimately determined by the market value of the firm's assets and liabilities, enterprises should monitor how the prices of their major assets and liabilities may be affected by changes in financial or commodity prices and assess the resulting exposure.

While estimating market value exposure typically is more complex, even determining how a firm's profits are affected by simultaneous and interrelated changes in various interest and exchange rates may not be simple. However, various financial computer models (including the Monte Carlo simulation process discussed in Chapter 11) can provide reasonably good estimates.

There are other more limited measures of exposure that were developed primarily for use in the investment and banking industries but which also have more general applicability. One such measure that focuses mainly on interest rate risk—gap analysis—is discussed in the next subsection.

Gap Analysis

One way to measure exposure to interest rate risk is to classify assets and liabilities as having present values that are either sensitive or insensitive to changes in interest rates. The "gap" is defined as the difference between the values of interest-rate-sensitive assets and interest-rate-sensitive liabilities. As we know, the interest rate sensitivity of fixed income securities depends greatly on their maturity; thus, gap analysis may be accomplished by classifying such securities according to their maturities. Since the values of both interest-rate-sensitive liabilities and assets typically move inversely with the level of interest rates, by minimizing the gap, management is able to limit the firm's exposure to interest rate changes. Table 21.1 below is taken from a table in Scotiabank's 1998 Annual Report, which shows the company's "total interest rate sensitivity gap" and "cumulative gap" as of October 31, 1998.

Table 21.1

	1998						
As at October 31 ($ millions)	Immediately rate sensitive	Within 3 months	Three to 12 months	One to 5 years	Over 5 years	Non-rate sensitive	Total
Cash resources	$ 1,213	$ 11,828	$ 6,590	$ 312 $	—	$ 2,957	$ 22,900
Trading securities	600	2,470	472	2,300	2,997	3,269	12,108
Investment and loan substitute securities	691	2,192	2,717	3,979	4,175	3,638	17,392
Assets purchased under resale agreements	—	10,929	260	—	—	—	11,189
Loans	22,573	52,645	18,866	42,758	2,069	382	139,293
Other assets	—	—	—	—	—	$30,706	$ 30,706
Total assets	$ 25,077	$ 80,064	$ 28,905	$ 49,349	9,241	40,952	233,588
Deposits	10,502	91,798	35,468	18,678	50	9,864	166,360
Obligations related to assets sold under repurchase agreements	—	13,891	712	—	—	—	14,603
Obligations related to securities sold short	—	24	89	1,029	1,883	96	3,121

Subordinated debentures	—	171	463	583	4,265	—	5,482
Other liabilities	—	—	—	—	—	33,208	33,208
Shareholders' equity	—	—	—	—	—	10,814	10,814
Total liabilities and shareholders' equity	10,502	105,884	$ 36,732	20,290	6,198	53,982	$ 233,588
On-balance sheet gap	14,575	(25,820)	(7,827)	29,059	3,043	(13,030)	—
Off-balance sheet gap	—	(3,159)	8,235	(4,518)	(558)	—	—
Interest rate sensitivity gap based on contractual repricing	14,575	(28,979)	408	24,541	2,485	(13,030)	—
Adjustment to expected repricing	(39)	1,721	1,877	(4,051)	1,062	(570)	—
Total interest rate sensitivity gap	**$ 14,536**	**$ (27,258)**	**$ 2,285**	**$ 20,490**	**$ 3,547**	**$ (13,600)**	**$ —**
Cumulative gap	**14,536**	**(12,722)**	**(10,437)**	**10,053**	**$ 13,600**	**—**	**—**

Source: Scotiabank 1998 Annual Report, Notes to Financial Statements, (Note 17 B) Interest Rate Risk.

EXAMPLE

GAP ANALYSIS

A financial institution has the following assets and liabilities measured in millions of dollars:

Assets		Liabilities	
Fixed rate mortgages	$75	Long-term deposits	$30
Variable rate mortgages	50	Demand deposits	95

The present value of fixed-rate mortgages and long-term deposits are sensitive to changes in interest rates, while variable-rate mortgages and demand deposits are not (since their interest payments are adjusted to match any changes in general interest rates). The institution's gap is therefore $45 million. It has more interest-rate-sensitive assets ($75 million) than liabilities ($30 million) and, therefore, is faced with some exposure. If interest rates fall, both the value of its fixed-rate mortgages and the value of its term deposits will rise. Since the financial institution has a positive gap (more mortgages than long-term deposits), this will result in a net gain. Conversely, if interest rates rise, the institution will incur losses since the value of its assets will fall by more than the drop in value of its liabilities.

By managing the gap, one can control the extent and direction of exposure to interest rate risk. The limitation of gap analysis is the rough, binary classification on which it is based: assets and liabilities are assumed to be either sensitive or insensitive to interest rate changes. In most realistic settings, various assets and liabilities have differing degrees of interest rate sensitivity, and hence, a more differentiated approach is required.

One commonly used approach that deals with the sensitivity of the values of a specific asset, liability, or portfolio to changes in interest rates involves the use of the concept of **duration**. The basic idea is that portfolio managers can undertake appropriate measures ahead of time to guard against interest rate risk. Known as *portfolio immunization*, this is done by matching the duration of a portfolio of assets to the relevant liabilities that are outstanding. This analysis is somewhat technical in nature, and we defer our discussion of this matter until Appendix 21-A.

RISK MANAGEMENT— GENERAL CONCEPTS

21.3

Market Efficiency and Risk Attitudes

Faced with volatile financial prices (interest rates, foreign exchange rates, or other commodity prices), a company has three fundamentally different approaches, which may be termed as opportunistic, passive, or defensive. An opportunistic approach tries to take advantage of market swings through judicious timing of transactions. Essentially, one attempts to buy low and sell high. Illustrations include locking in long-term debt when believing that interest rates have bottomed and maintaining active cash balances in currencies that are perceived to be strong. With a passive approach, business is conducted without regard to potential changes in prices, and one simply rides out any fluctuations as they occur. Defensive risk management seeks to limit exposure through judicious hedging.

In the past, many firms behaved in an opportunistic manner, spending considerable effort in trying to forecast financial prices either in-house or with the help of outside consultants. The objective was to reap benefits through the judicious timing of transactions.

TIMING STOCK ISSUES

EXAMPLE

In an attempt to profit through the judicious timing of equity issues, companies undertake their issues when stock prices are at historical highs. Conversely, fewer offerings are made when stock prices are low. The months surrounding the October 1987 stock market crash illustrate the point. The following table compares the monthly close of the TSE 300 Index with the gross new equity financing raised through the Toronto Stock Exchange during the one-year period surrounding the stock market crash.

		Monthly close of TSE 300 Index	Gross new equity financing raised through TSE $(000s)
1987	April	3,717	1,578
	May	3,685	1,342
	June	3,710	1,305
	July	4,030	1,281
	August	3,994	1,161
	September	3,902	1,805
	October	3,019	579
	November	2,978	287
	December	3,160	164
1988	January	3,057	50
	February	3,205	277
	March	3,313	318

Clearly, many firms thought they could reap benefits through timing. Equity issues rose when the prices of equity were high. Conversely, when stock prices dropped, the number of equity issues declined.

An example of timing security issues is described in the report below. It discusses the decision made by two Canadian technology companies to cancel previously scheduled equity issues in response to "horrible" market conditions for technology stocks at that time.

▪ *Finance in the News*

Two Tech Firms Kill Share Issues: Anticipated IPO in Doubt

Two Canadian high-tech firms, Certicom Corp. and Look Communications Inc., have cancelled plans for scheduled public offerings, and 360networks Inc. may delay going public. Certicom spokesperson Lorraine Kauffman said that "the company decided not to proceed with the stock issue because of "horrible" market conditions". When the security software developer decided to go public in March, its stock was trading at around $225, but by mid-April, it was down to $65 on the TSE.

Look Communications Inc, an Internet and broadband wireless company, also decided to delay its offering. 360networks Inc., which had hoped to raise US$1 billion to expand its fibre optic networks in North America and Europe, is now expected to delay as well.

Source: Keith McArthur, "Two Tech Firms Kill Share Issues: Anticipated IPO in Doubt," *Globe and Mail*, April 15, 2000, B1.

Such an active response to market volatility is hardly surprising. Management culture, generally, is oriented toward exploiting opportunities created by change, and financial advisors benefit from selling their advice. Whether such an approach is justified, however, depends on our beliefs about market efficiency (see Chapter 9). In any market, one can expect to earn superior returns only through superior capabilities—in our case, if one enjoys sustainable competitive advantage in economic and financial forecasting. In such globally competitive arenas as money, bond, or foreign exchange markets, this seems unlikely. In fact, an increasing number of firms, after systematically reviewing their past record and finding that any gains did not exceed costs and periodic losses, have abandoned opportunistic strategies. Evidence indicates that even professional consulting firms offering forecasting services—sometimes based on elaborate econometric models—have not, on average, outperformed predictions that are embodied in the market through prevailing forward rates. Only for thinly traded currencies and other commodities that may also be subject to significant market interference (as is likely in some developing countries) could a more proactive approach prove appropriate.

PERSPECTIVES

Corporate Manager

Successful timing of new stock issues can result in increased cash inflows from such issues and/or less dilution of earnings among existing shares.

Investor

If investors believe that managers spend a great deal of time trying to "time" new share issues, then they should be wary of buying into such new issues at prices that may be inflated.

If we believe in market efficiency and, hence, our inability to benefit from judicious forecasting, we are left with either a passive or a defensive approach. Using the passive method, one simply rides out the fluctuations, believing that in the long run, any gains and losses will balance out. When in need of long-term debt financing, for example, such securities are issued regardless of what current interest rates may be, and foreign currency transactions are converted into the domestic currency at whatever exchange rates happen to prevail. This minimizes both transaction costs and the drain on management time, and it makes sense as long as the impact of possible fluctuations on the firm is modest so that the risk does not become a concern.

A defensive or insurance-type strategy is appropriate even when we recognize market efficiency but are exposed to significant risks that we wish to avoid. Such an approach has become increasingly attractive because of innovations in financial products that have made hedging easier and more convenient to arrange. Also, because of the depth and liquidity of financial markets and the fact that moral hazard problems do not exist, such insurance can often be arranged at low cost.[3]

---

[3] Moral hazard is the risk that, given insurance coverage, the insured's behaviour will change and increase the probability of loss. It is a key problem in insurance and can significantly increase the cost of coverage.

A compromise between a completely defensive and an opportunistic approach is represented by what has been called benchmarking. A firm first develops a complete hedging strategy that minimizes its financial exposure. This strategy becomes the benchmark. If management has good reason to believe that it can benefit by taking active positions in various financial markets, it may deviate from its fully hedged position. The risks and expected returns are then measured and evaluated against the benchmark position. This is how many companies manage their portfolio of liabilities.

If, on the other hand, we believe in market efficiency, a combination of a passive and defensive approach may be most appropriate; small fluctuations are absorbed as a normal risk of doing business, while large risks are hedged. Central to such a policy is the decision regarding what loss a company is willing to bear, for example, as a result of changes in current values. This, in turn, presupposes knowledge of how sensitive a firm's profits are to changes in factors such as the value of the Canadian dollar.

Risk Management at the Shareholder Versus Corporate Level

Exposure to financial risks can be managed not only at the level of the business, but also by shareholders themselves. If, for example, a firm's performance and, therefore, its share price is sensitive to changes in the value of the Canadian dollar, the company can enter into offsetting hedging transactions. However, the instruments and transactions that are open to the firm—such as options, futures contracts, or swaps (discussed in Section 21.5)—are also available to investors. Thus, if management can protect aggregate profits or share values, individual investors can do the same on a per-share basis.

In perfect markets with full information and no transaction costs, a strong case can be made for letting each individual shareholder manage his or her own risk particularly since personal preferences are likely to differ among various shareholder groups. The shares of many large businesses, for example, are held internationally. Why should a Japanese institutional shareholder of a Canadian firm who is concerned about its income and wealth in Japanese yen pay Canadian management to hedge the company's performance as measured in Canadian dollars? This is a particular problem for the many Canadian firms that are partially owned subsidiaries of foreign multinationals. Also, the relevant measure of risk for a well-diversified investment fund is likely to differ substantially from that of a majority shareholder who has concentrated a large investment in a particular enterprise.

At a practical level, it is often argued that information asymmetries and transaction costs make it advantageous for the firm's executives to engage in treasury risk management. As we saw, risk exposure may be difficult to measure and requires detailed inside information about the company and its operations that investors generally do not possess. Also, there may be some economies in transaction costs if this function is handled centrally. Finally, a more stable firm may enjoy other advantages such as better relations with creditors and customers. It may even be able to attract and retain better and more loyal employees and managers who value the stability of the business for which they work. These factors may be important to increasing share values.

It is interesting to note that empirical studies have found very little share price sensitivity to changes in foreign exchange rates even for strongly export-oriented firms.[4] Share prices are much more sensitive to a variety of other factors including the general state of the economy. A possible explanation may be that the large export-oriented firms examined had implemented effective hedging strategies, or, at least, shareholders believed that they had. In this context, it is important that companies communicate explicitly to investors what treasury risk management strategies they pursue; otherwise, it becomes difficult for shareholders to value and manage their own investments properly.

The Case for a Centralized Corporate Approach

Treasury risk can be managed at the level of the overall firm, at divisional levels, or even around individual transactions. Conceptually, at least, a centralized approach appears optimal. For example, a business with multinational operations should first try to match future receipts against obligations with a similar maturity in each currency. Only balances that remain after various inflows and outflows are netted out would have to be covered. Considerable savings can result as the need for contractual hedging in forward markets is minimized. At the same time, this requires a centralized approach to the management of foreign exchange risk.

USING FORWARD CONTRACTS TO ELIMINATE RISK

EXAMPLE

A major Canadian corporation may find that after matching and netting all of its projected flows in pounds sterling, it expects to have £100,000 of surplus on hand as of the first week in April. To protect itself against currency fluctuations, the firm could sell £100,000 forward to the first week in April and eliminate the exposure. The expense is clearly less than what would be incurred if a variety of individual transactions were entered into, with forward purchases and forward sales of pounds sterling arranged simultaneously, perhaps by different divisions of the same firm.

In practice, treasury risk management, generally, has not been dealt with in a comprehensive manner but rather left to individual managers and divisions, and, too often, it has been performed in a more-or-less *ad hoc* fashion around individual transactions. For example, as part of a loan arrangement, some lenders, to protect their positions, insist that exposure to interest or currency fluctuations be hedged. The firm then arranges protection for this particular debt issue. Arranging for such a hedge, in turn, may provide additional service-fee income for the financial institution that advanced the loan.

Reasons for not centralizing this vital function in the past included a failure to recognize its importance and the general trade-offs between centralized control and local autonomy that are found in many areas of management. A lack of comprehensive policies, however, has resulted in some spectacular fiascos.

---

4 See, for example, "Stocks and Currencies." *The Economist* (June 6, 1992), p. 87.

EXAMPLE | **SOME HISTORICAL CASES**

There have been some winners in speculation. In 1991, for example, the finance department of Intel reportedly earned $140 million in foreign exchange transactions. However, a number of companies lost significant amounts of money because individual managers took active positions in interest rates, foreign currencies, or commodities to take advantage of anticipated market swings. Quite typically, initial transactions were for legitimate purposes. After early successes, however, it appeared that quick-and-easy gains could be made through speculation. When the desired results failed to materialize, managers continued to play the market, hoping to recover their losses. Prominent examples include:

- Gibraltar Savings bought $6 billion in fixed-rate, long-term securities in a bet that interest rates would fall. They did not, and losses from this transaction significantly contributed to the company's collapse. With assets of US$13.4 billion, it became the second largest savings and loan failure ever.
- Local managers for Kloeckner, one of Germany's largest trading companies, lost over $400 million in speculative oil futures trading. It required a bailout by Deutsche Bank to prevent insolvency.
- Various British municipalities arranged over $10 billion in interest rate swaps (exchanging fixed-rate for variable-rate debt) and suffered massive losses when interest rates subsequently rose. The end result was a major political scandal and increased central control.

Based on such highly publicized disasters and given increased management attention and sophistication, the current trend is toward a more centrally controlled approach.

21.4 ON-BALANCE SHEET HEDGING

In this section, we deal with managing treasury risk through a judicious balancing of assets and liabilities and revenues and costs. Contrary to techniques discussed in section 21.5, "on-balance-sheet" transactions are directly reflected in the firm's financial statements.

Traditional Hedging

The basic concept of hedging to manage financial risk entails matching assets and liabilities and revenues and costs. Such matching can occur on a variety of dimensions. For example, one can match assets and liabilities according to the following:

- their maturity (funding short-term assets with short-term liabilities and long-term assets with long-term funds)
- the currencies in which the assets and liabilities are denominated
- the sensitivity of asset and liability values to changes in interest rates

Similarly, one can match revenues and costs. Invariably, the objective is to reduce the volatility of the firm's net worth, profits, or net cash flows caused by fluctuations in various financial variables.

HYDRO-QUÉBEC LONG-TERM DEBT DENOMINATION

EXAMPLE

Hydro-Québec is one of the world's largest corporate users of U.S-dollar-denominated long-term debt, with $16.1 billion (or 42.7 percent) of its total long-term borrowing denominated in that currency as at December 31, 1999. Less than half of its total long-term debt was in Canadian dollars ($16.5 million or 43.8 percent), with the remaining $5.0 billion (13.3 percent) denominated in other currencies. Hydro-Québec exports a great deal of the electricity it produces to the United States, thereby expecting to generate sufficient U.S.-dollar income to pay the total interest and principal on existing U.S.-dollar debt that is not otherwise hedged.

Since building activity is quite sensitive to mortgage rates, the revenues and, the values of construction companies usually are inversely related to the level of current interest rates. To offset such risk, a construction company may consider financing through fixed interest rate debt. As the value of fixed-rate debt is also inversely related to the level of interest rates, the market value of the firm's liabilities will, at least partially, offset any changes in income and value brought about by the volatility of interest rates.

The matching of assets and liabilities is particularly important for financial institutions such as banks. In fact, the widely publicized savings and loan (S&L) crisis in the United States in the 1980s can be attributed largely to failures in this regard.

To stabilize the banking industry after the Crash of 1929, U.S. Congress passed legislation fixing the interest rates banks could pay depositors at artificially low levels. This legal price fixing limited competition for depositors and let bankers provide mortgages at fairly low interest rates while still earning healthy profits. In the late 1970s, limited financial deregulation disrupted this arrangement by allowing money market funds and other high-yield investments to attract customers away. Congress responded with further financial deregulation that removed the interest rate caps on deposits to allow banks to compete more fully. This development exposed the fundamental interest rate risk of the S&Ls. While their investments were long term, their financing depended on short-term sources. They were the traditional providers of long-term, fixed-rate mortgages to local businesses and families, and they soon discovered that their assets (mortgages) were providing insufficient income to cover the returns they had to pay on their short-term liabilities (deposit accounts) to keep depositors from leaving.

Several techniques have been developed to help financial institutions match portfolios of assets and liabilities including the use of gap analysis and duration matching, which were referred to in section 21.2.

Innovations in Securities

Recent years have seen a flurry of innovations in the types and features of financial instruments that firms can issue to raise funds. Major factors that have spurred this development include deregulation, increased competition in financial markets, and a more complex global environment with significant economic uncertainties.

The range of new instruments and features has grown to a point where any comprehensive listing is almost impossible to prepare and, in any event, would be obsolete within a few months. What follows are some prominent illustrations taken from the debt markets.

Floating-Rate Debt: Debt with interest rates that rise and fall (float) in response to market shifts in interest rates. Generally, a benchmark rate is defined, and interest on the floating-rate instrument is set at a number of basis points above or below the benchmark. In Canada, most floating-rate issues have been private placements (i.e., they do not trade publicly). Floating rate debt shifts the risk of changes in nominal rates from the investors to the issuers. In return, the initial coupon rate is lower. Such issues are particularly useful for companies with revenues linked to inflation. Hydro-Québec, for example, had 25 percent of its debt at floating rates at the end of 1999.

Real Interest Rate Debt: Debt that protects investors from inflation. A fixed real interest rate is paid over and above the current inflation rate. In 1991, the Government of Canada began issuing inflation-indexed bonds, which have a 30-year term and are offered at a 4.25 percent fixed rate over changes in the consumer price index. In addition, inflationary adjustments of the principal will be paid at maturity. The U.S. federal government recently began offering similar bonds.

Commodity-Linked Debt: Debt with interest payments linked to the price of a commodity such as gold or oil. Such contracts are attractive to resource-based companies because they tie future interest payments to the firm's ability to pay as reflected in commodity prices. They also can become attractive when borrowers and lenders differ in their expectations about future commodity prices. For example, the 1997 issue of 5-percent gold-linked convertible notes by TVX Gold Inc. (referred to in the report entitled "Gold-Linked Convertible Debt," of Chapter 19) promised debt-holders the return of principal plus an extra payment based on the increase in the price of gold over the period.

 Debt Denominated in Currency Mixes and Cocktails: Rather than being denominated in a single currency, such debt provides for payments based on a weighted average of various currencies. The most important mixed-currency unit available today is the Euro, which was adopted by 11 European countries (Germany, France, Italy, Spain, the Netherlands, Belgium, Austria, Portugal, Finland, Ireland, and Luxembourg) on January 1, 1999 to replace their existing currency. Greece is scheduled to become the twelfth participating country on January 1, 2001. All interbank commerce and stock exchange trade is now denominated in this official currency; however, bills and coins of the local currencies will remain in circulation until January 1, 2002, at which time they will be exchanged for new Euro currency.

Another important illustration of mixed-currency units are the Special Drawing Rights (SDR), originally created by the International Monetary Fund. The SDR comprises a weighted average of five currencies—Euro (Germany), Euro (France), Japanese yen, British pound, and U.S. dollar—and its value in terms of any particular currency changes as the relevant exchange rates fluctuate. Table 21.2 below shows that the exchange rate of 1SDR was US $1.29164 on December 4, 2000. ▲

Table 21.2

SDR Valuation

Monday, December 4, 2000

Currency	Currency amount under Rule 0-1	Exchange rate*	U.S. dollar equivalent
Euro (Germany)	0.2280	0.88720	0.202282
Euro (France)	0.1239	0.88720	0.109924
Japanese yen	27.2000	110.92000	0.245222
Pounds sterling	0.1050	1.44870	0.152114
U. S. dollars	0.5821	1.00000	0.582100
			1.291642
		US $1.00=SDR	0.774208
		SDR1=US$	1.29164

*The exchange rate for the Japanese yen is expressed in terms of currency units per U.S. dollar; other rates are expressed as U.S. dollars per currency unit.

Source: International Monetary Fund website at: http://www.imf.org

Debt with Interest Rate Caps, Floors, and Collars: Caps and floors place upper and lower limits on the interest rate to be paid on floating-rate debt. When an issue has both a cap and a floor, we term it a collar, with interest rate movements restricted to a specified range. Such debt allows for any apportioning of interest rate risks between borrower and lender, with the borrower bearing the risk of fluctuations within the collar and the lender exposed if rates move outside this range. From the investor's point of view, caps imitate put options on debt, while floors mimic call options. For example, as of October 31, 1999, the Toronto Dominion Bank had US$150 million of debt maturing in October 2002 that required floating interest payments at a rate of LIBOR minus 0.13 percent. However, the debt had a collar that provided for a ceiling of 10 percent and a floor of 5 percent. Caps, floors, and collars will be discussed further in Section 21.5.

Zero Coupon Bonds: These bonds do not offer periodic interest payments. Instead, as in the case of treasury bills, the investor purchases the bond below its maturity value, with the difference between the maturity value and the purchase price representing the interest. This type of security eliminates the purchaser's reinvestment risk around the periodic interest payments. Pepsi Cola was the first firm to issue such bonds, and the market was so receptive that the implied interest rate dropped below that of U.S. government debt. This form of debt issue has become more popular in recent years. For example, Hydro-Quebec had over $300 million in zero coupon bonds outstanding as of December 31, 2000.

Index-Linked-Debt: Securities that attempt to offer the security of bonds with the potential return of stocks are called indexed-linked-debt. Holders are provided with some minimal fixed return as well as a certain percentage of the return reflected in a stock market index. For example, in 1992, the Export Development Corp. raised $75 million through an issue of such debt. Investors bought a five-and-a-half-year instrument and stood to receive 95 percent of the gain of the S&P 500 Index over that period.

In evaluating such new instruments, one has to determine whether and how they actually create economic value. Essentially, a new instrument creates economic value only if it makes financial markets more efficient or more complete. By more complete, we mean that the instrument provides issuers and/or investors with substantive alternatives that were previously unavailable and that could not be replicated by using existing instruments. More specifically, new securities could provide new ways of allocating risk, reducing overall taxes and/or issuing costs, responding to regulatory change, or mitigating agency problems. For example, commodity-linked bonds, when interest and/or principal repayments are linked to the future price of a commodity, enable a commodity producer to shift some of the risk of changing commodity prices to lenders. Lenders can readily diversify their investments and, hence, may have a comparative advantage in bearing such largely diversifiable risks.

Extendible interest rate reset notes, which allow for interest rates to be adjusted periodically and original maturities to be extended, entail lower issuing costs than debt that has to be retired and then replaced. At the same time, the periodic resetting of interest rates protects investors against the risk of management actions that may lower the firm's credit rating. This may also minimize agency problems and, in turn, may allow the issuing firm to reduce interest payments.

As with any burst of innovation, there appear to be decreasing marginal returns over time. Markets become more complete and efficient, making further innovations marginal. As in any other market, however, financial service companies have a vested interest in increasing their fees through new and differentiated products, which sometimes turn out to be nothing more than marketing gimmicks.

21.5 OFF-BALANCE SHEET HEDGING

In the previous section, we saw how financial risk can be managed by carefully structuring the future obligations that the corporation assumes. In this section, we explore how similar results can be achieved through side contracts that are not an inherent part of the firm's primary outside financing and, hence, are not reflected in the liability side of the balance sheet. A wide variety of such side contracts are available to companies. The most common ones are **swaps**, contracts based on the derivative securities (options and futures) discussed in Chapters 18 and 20, as well as various special contracts that can be viewed essentially as a combination of derivative securities.

The importance of these instruments is shown in Table 21.3, which shows that the notional value of global derivatives was over $98 trillion by the end of June 1999 ($81.46 trillion in over-the-counter (OTC) contracts and $17.26 trillion in exchange-traded contracts). The growth of usage of these instruments is dramatic if we consider that their total global value was slightly below $6 trillion in 1990, and only slightly above $1 trillion in 1986. We discuss each of these in turn and conclude with a comprehensive example.

Table 21.3

The Global Over-the-Counter (OTC) Derivatives Markets[1]
Amounts outstanding in billions of US dollars

	Notional amounts	
	End June 1998	End June 1999
A. **Foreign exchange contracts**	**18,719**	**14,899**
Outright forwards and forex swaps	12,149	9,541
Currency swaps	1,947	2,350
Options	4,623	3,009
B. **Interest rate contracts[2]**	**42,368**	**54,072**
FRAs	5,147	7,137
Swaps	29,363	38,372
Options	7,858	8,562
C. **Equity-linked contracts**	**1,274**	**1,511**
Forwards and swaps	154	198
Options	1,120	1,313
D. **Commodity contracts[3]**	**451**	**441**
Gold	193	189
Other	258	252
Forwards and swaps	153	127
Options	106	125
E. **Other[4]**	**9,331**	**10,536**
GRAND TOTAL	**72,143**	**81,458**
Memorandum item:		
Exchange-traded contracts[5]	*14,256*	*17,262*

Source: "The Global OTC Derivatives Market at end-June 1999," Bank for International Settlements (BIS). Obtained from BIS website at: www.bis.org.

[1] All figures are adjusted for double-counting. Notional amounts outstanding have been adjusted by halving positions vis-à-vis other reporting dealers. Gross market values have been calculated as the sum of the total gross positive market value of contracts and the absolute value of the gross negative market value of contracts with non-reporting counterparties. [2] Single-currency contracts only. [3] Adjustments for double-counting estimated. [4] For end-June 1998: positions reported by non-regular reporting institutions in the context of the triennial Central Bank Survey of Foreign Exchange and Derivatives Market Activity at end-June 1998; for subsequent periods: estimated positions of non-regular reporting institutions. [5] Sources: FOW TRADEdata; Futures Industry Association; various futures and options exchanges.

Swaps

In general terms, with a swap, two parties exchange their respective future cash flow commitments on loans with identical principal outstanding. They do so because each finds the form of the other party's obligations more attractive. A financial intermediary normally arranges the swap and, for a fee, may guarantee future performance under the deal. In the context of long-term debt, various types of swap arrangements are possible, with the most common one being the interest rate swap, as shown in Figure 21.3. It effectively involves the trading of fixed interest obligations on a loan for variable interest payments, and vice versa.

For example, a smaller firm lacking market appeal or influence may find it difficult to secure long-term debt at a reasonable fixed rate of interest; however, it wants to avoid the interest rate risk inherent in a floating-rate loan. A large financial institution, on the other hand, can readily issue a fixed interest rate bond. However, most of its assets are consumer loans made at variable interest rates, and to avoid exposure, the institution prefers to incur liabilities that also stipulate a floating rate. Under an interest rate swap, the financial institution borrows at a fixed rate, whereas the smaller company borrows at a floating rate. The interest obligations are then exchanged. Technically, however, each party retains a liability to its original creditor.

EXAMPLE

INTEREST RATE SWAP

A financial institution (F) can borrow at a 9-percent fixed rate or at a prime plus 0.5 percent floating rate, whereas a smaller firm (S) faces rates of 13 percent and prime plus 2 percent respectively. Through the swap, S agrees to satisfy the 9-percent fixed-rate debt-service obligations of F. In return for F providing the fixed-rate opportunity, it will usually not pay the prime plus 2 percent floating rate but rather something less than the prime plus 0.5 percent that F itself could have borrowed at, leaving the remaining payments to S. For this gain, F has, however, assumed the risk of S failing to live up to the terms of the swap. For a fee, such risk can then be transferred to financial intermediaries.

FIGURE 21.1

Schematic Diagram of Interest Rate Swap

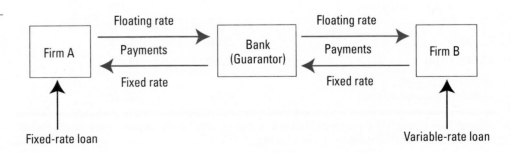

Another common swap arrangement entails the exchange of obligations on loans denominated in different currencies.

CROSS-CURRENCY INTEREST RATE SWAP

A Canadian company considers purchasing machinery in France to be financed in part by an agency of the French government through a subsidized long-term export loan denominated in Euros. The Canadian importer finds the terms of the financing attractive but is hesitant to take on the foreign exchange risk that the loan in Euros would entail. A swap may be the solution. If an intermediary can locate a European firm wanting to borrow Euros but able to raise an equivalent Canadian-dollar loan, it could then arrange to exchange this Canadian-dollar liability against the low-cost Euro loan. In fact, because of the subsidized interest rate on the Euro loan, the European business would probably be willing to pay the Canadian importer for the right to enter this transaction. Thus, through the swap (for which the intermediary would command a fee), both firms could share in the subsidized government loan without either having to assume foreign exchange risks.

The volume of swaps has grown rapidly, with most such transactions arranged in the Euromarkets through offices of international banks and other intermediaries. Recent estimates, as shown in Table 21.3, place the value of outstanding swaps at over US$50 trillion (versus approximately US$3.5 trillion in 1992).

Using Derivative Securities: Options and Futures

In Chapters 18 and 20, we reviewed the basic features of options and futures contracts. Both of these derivative securities can be used to hedge financial risk, although the ultimate risk profile that a firm is exposed to differs somewhat depending on the instrument used.

FOREIGN EXCHANGE RISK HEDGING

A Canadian company has decided to issue US$1 million of 90-day commercial paper in the Eurodollar market. The spot exchange rate is US$1.00=C$1.43, and the 90-day forward exchange rate is US$1.00=C$1.44. In dealing with its foreign exchange exposure, the firm has three alternatives:

1. It can leave the funds unhedged and simply bear the exchange risk.
2. It can hedge through a forward contract.
3. It can hedge through a currency option.

If the firm does not hedge, it assumes foreign exchange risk over the 90 days. This may result in unanticipated gains or losses. For example, if the U.S. dollar strengthens to US$1.00=C$1.50 at the end of 90 days, the business will incur an unanticipated loss of C$70,000. (The firm had expected to repay US$1 million×1.43=C$1.43 million; it now has to repay US$1 million×1.50=C$1.5 million.) On the other hand, if the U.S. dollar weakens to US$1.00=C$1.36, the company will capture an unanticipated gain of C$70,000.

If the firm hedges through a forward contract, it can purchase US$1 million today for delivery in 90 days at a price of C$1.44 million. The repayment is now locked in, and any change in the exchange rate will not affect the company. This means that if the U.S. dollar strengthens to US$1.00=C$1.50, the loss of C$70,000 is avoided. If the U.S. dollar weakens to C$1.36, however, the firm will be unable to capture the windfall gain of C$70,000.

For a price, hedging with a currency option provides the company with a similar downside protection as the forward contract, but it retains the possibility of capturing upside gains. To illustrate, consider an option with three months to expiry, allowing the holder to buy US$25,000 at an exercise price of C$35,000 (implying an exchange rate of 35,000/25,000=C$1.40/US$1.00). The option currently sells for C$1,300. Its minimum value is calculated as C$750=25,000×(1.43−1.40). The firm can buy 40 such options now for C$52,000. The following scenarios are then possible:

 (i) The U.S. dollar strengthens, for instance to US$1.00=C$1.50. The company would exercise its options and purchase 40×25,000=US$1 million for 40×35,000=C$1.4 million at an effective exchange rate of US$1.00=C$1.40.

(ii) The U.S. dollar weakens, for instance, to US$1.00=C$1.36. The firm has no incentive to exercise its options since the market price of U.S. dollars has fallen below the exercise price on the options (1.36<1.40). The options become worthless, and the business simply leaves them unexercised, buying the required U.S. dollars on the spot market instead. It pays C$1.36 million and realizes an unanticipated gain.

(iii) The exchange rate remains constant at US$1.00=C$1.43. As under 1. above, it pays to exercise the option, buying at the rate US$1.00=C$1.40.

The calculations for these three alternatives are summarized below.

Net Amount Repaid on US$1,000,000 Commercial Paper
Three months from now, in Canadian dollars

| | Spot foreign-exchange rate (C$/US$) in 90 days | | |
	C$1.43 (unchanged)	C$1.50 (US$rises)	C$1.36 (US$falls)
Alternative			
Unhedged	$1,430,000[a]	$1,500,000	$ 1,360,000
Forward contract	1,440,000[b]	1,440,000	1,440,000
Currency option	1,452,000[c]	1,452,000	1,412,000[d]

a. Amount paid $= \dfrac{\text{face value of}}{\text{commercial paper}} \times \dfrac{\text{spot rate}}{\text{in 90 days}}$

$=$US$1,000,000×C$1.43/US$1.00
$=$C$1,430,000

b. Amount paid $=$face value×current 90-day forward rate
$=$US$1,000,000×C$1.44/US$1.00
$=$C$1,440,000

c. Amount paid $=$(face value×strike price)+price of options
$=$(US$1,000,000×C$1.40/US$1.00)+(C$1,300×40)
$=$C$1,400,000+C$52,000
$=$C$1,452,000

d. Because it does not pay to exercise the options, we now have:

Amount paid   5(face value×spot rate in 90 days)+price of options
5(US$1,000,000×C$1.36/US$1.00)+C$52,000
5C$1,412,000

We see that hedging through forward contracts and through options provide essentially the same downside protection. The option provides greater flexibility than a forward contract, because forward contracts are binding while options can be either exercised or left to expire. Thus, with options, the potential for gains remains. This has to be traded off against the cost of buying the options.

In a simplified way, this is illustrated schematically in Figure 21.2. We note that the price we have to pay for buying an option shifts the net payoff downward, as indicated in graphs (c) and (e). For simplicity, we ignore the time value of money, which, as was detailed in Chapter 18, influences the value of an option before its expiration date.

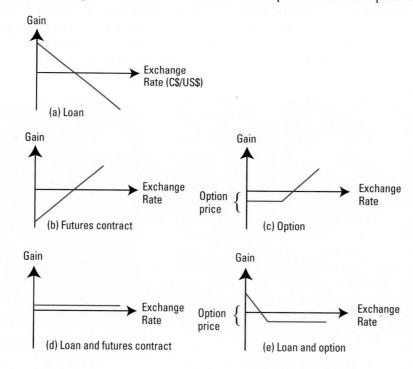

FIGURE 21.2

Gains and Losses from a Foreign Currency Loan, Futures Contract, and Option

Ideally, the underlying asset of any derivative security should be the same as that of the original transaction being hedged (i.e., U.S. dollars in the above example). This is called a **direct hedge**. Often, however, derivative securities are not available in that particular asset or are available only at a high cost; thinly traded currencies of small countries and more specialized commodities are examples. In such cases, one may use derivative securities denominated in an asset with a value that is highly correlated with the asset of the original transaction—a move called a **cross hedge**.

EXAMPLE

CROSS-HEDGING

Assume that the loan in the above context was in Swedish kronas, but futures contracts or options on that currency may be unavailable in Canada. However, since the krona is strongly correlated with the Euro, an effective cross-hedge is obtainable by using derivatives having the Euro as the underlying asset. ⬆

While we have focused most of our attention on managing currency and interest rate risk, in today's environment of continual financial innovations, companies have several alternatives available to them to manage many other types of risks faced by their business. One interesting example was first mentioned in Chapter 20, in which we mentioned the recent development of weather derivatives. The report below discusses the motivation for the creation of the exchange-traded version of these options and futures contracts on the Chicago Mercantile Exchange (CME). The example below was adapted from the CME brochure, "Weather Futures & Options." The example demonstrates how a utility company can use weather futures to hedge its potential losses from a really mild winter, although it would forego the potential additional profits it would normally realize if a very severe winter occurs.

▪ *Finance in the News*

Weather Futures & Options

Something like 20 percent of the U.S. economy is directly affected by the weather, which is why abnormally hot summers or cold winters can affect business earnings. On the other hand, mild weather can hurt the incomes of utilities such as power producers with the decline in air conditioning and heating. To allay some of the risk, a weather derivative market was established to allow companies that could be hurt by unseasonable weather shifts. This market gives weather-sensitive businesses the opportunity to hedge their risk on weather much as others do with interest rates and foreign exchange.

The Chicago Mercantile Exchange (CME) Heating Degree Day (HDD) and Cooling Degree Day (CDD) futures and options are pioneering weather derivatives that allow businesses to protect themselves against unforeseen weather developments. These futures and options are available for specific population and energy centres throughout the United States that have weather-related risks.

Source: "Weather Futures & Options," brochure obtained on the Chicago Mercantile Exchange website at: www.cme.com/weather/weather.html.

EXAMPLE

USING WEATHER FUTURES CONTRACTS

ABC Utility Co. sells electricity in Chicago, and its projected revenue for a normal winter is $80 million. The company's research department has concluded that its revenue is highly correlated with the CME Chicago Heating Degree Day (HDD) Index, so ABC decides to enter into a cross-hedge on their revenues using futures contracts on this index. On October 1, they short 576 of the January HDD futures at a price of 1,250.

Suppose the winter is very mild, and the contract settles at 1,150. The mild winter reduces ABC's sales to $74.24 million ($5.76 million below the projected normal level of $80 million). However, the company's loss in revenues is offset by a $5.76-million gain on its futures position ($100 per tick×[1,250−1,150]×576 contracts).

On the other hand, suppose the winter is very severe, and the contract settles at 1,400. The severe winter increases ABC's sales to $88.64 million ($8.64 million above the projected level). However, their increase in revenues is offset by a $8.64-million loss on its futures position ($100 per tick×[1,250−1,400]×576 contracts). This is the cost of the hedge.

Combining Derivative Securities

By combining different types of derivative securities, it is possible to set up positions that provide almost any payoff pattern. Option traders have developed a wide variety of such combinations, but detailed treatment of the topic is beyond the scope of this book. To illustrate, however, we discuss two payoff patterns that can be achieved by combining simple options: namely the **straddle** and the **butterfly spread**. We then examine some other financial products made available through banks.

The Straddle

A straddle combines a put and a call on the same underlying asset with the same strike price, and with the same expiration date. If the price of the asset rises, the call option provides a return. If the price falls, the put option becomes valuable. Only if the price of the underlying asset remains approximately unchanged does the holder of a straddle lose. The following example and Figure 21.3 illustrate the payoffs for a straddle. Again, we ignore the time value of money and its impact on option values. This is reasonable when the option life is relatively short.

A STRADDLE

EXAMPLE

Consider a put and a call option on the same security with the same strike price of $45. Ignoring the costs of buying the options, the payoffs at expiration for a put, call, and straddle are as follows:

(a) ignoring option prices, the payoffs are:

Stock price at expiration	Put payoff	Call payoff	Straddle payoff
$ 0	$45	$ 0	$45
20	25	0	25
30	15	0	15
40	5	0	5
45	0	0	0
50	0	5	5
60	0	15	15
70	0	25	25

(b) assuming the call option costs $6, and the put option is bought for $5, the net profits become:

Stock price at expiration	Put payoff	Call payoff	Straddle payoff
$ 0	$40	−$6	$34
20	20	−6	14
30	10	−6	4
40	0	−6	−6
45	−5	−6	−11
50	−5	−1	−6
60	−5	9	4
70	−5	19	14

These results are represented graphically in Figure 21.3.

FIGURE 21.3

Payoff Diagram for a Put, Call, and Straddle at Expiration

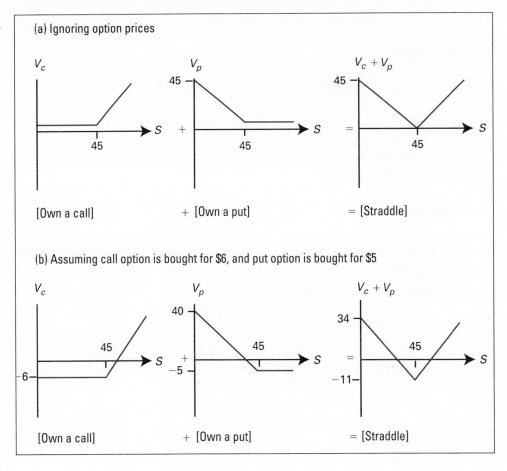

Straddles are often used by speculators to bet on either an upward or a downward movement in the price of the underlying asset. For example, a speculator who feels a stock's price is sure to change when new information is released but is unsure whether the information will bode well or ill for the firm, might buy a straddle.

Straddles also can be useful as hedging devices—for example, for companies that act as intermediaries, transferring commodities from producers to ultimate purchasers.

STRADDLES FOR HEDGING PURPOSES

EXAMPLE

A pipeline company that transmits oil from Alberta to markets in the United States has committed itself to offer oil to a buyer at $25 per barrel. A different branch of the company has extended an offer to an Alberta producer to buy oil at $25 per barrel. Both offers are to remain valid for a limited time.

Management saw no problem in extending such offers at the time but now is concerned because an unexpected political crisis has increased the volatility of oil prices. If the price rises, the firm is committed to sell at $25, but its offer to buy at $25 will certainly be declined. Similarly, if the price falls, its offer to sell oil at $25 will be turned down, but its offer to buy oil at $25 will be accepted. In either case, the business will lose. To hedge its position as a purchaser, the firm buys a put option to sell oil at $25. That way, if the price falls, it can sell the oil it has committed itself to buying with no loss (except the price of the option).

To hedge its position as a seller, the company also buys a call option to purchase oil at $25. If the price rises, it can then buy the oil it must sell at $25.

It is interesting to note that in the above example, the contract offers the enterprise makes in the everyday course of its business can be viewed as writing options. This is because the first stage in any of its contract negotiations involves making a firm offer that the other party is free to accept or reject during a limited time—precisely what writing an option is all about. Extending a firm offer to buy is equivalent to writing a put option, while extending a firm offer to sell is equivalent to writing a call. Sometimes such options are extended with no immediate payment, but often the party extending the offer requires a deposit from the potential acceptor. This is essentially payment for the option.

PERSPECTIVES

Corporate Manager
Straddles provide management with a method of hedging existing risk exposure.

Investor
Straddles provide investors with a method of speculating on substantial movements in a stock's market price when the investor is uncertain of the direction of the price movement.

It follows, therefore, that the firm in the example above is doing nothing more than explicitly recognizing the options it has written by buying offsetting option positions to eliminate its risk.

The Butterfly Spread

The butterfly spread combines several call options to obtain payoffs only if the price of the underlying asset remains within a given range. Specifically, it involves the following :

- buying an option with a very low striking price E_L
- writing (i.e., selling) two options with a mid-range striking price E_M
- buying an option with a high striking price E_H.

The price range against which the firm wants to hedge is between E_L and E_H.

EXAMPLE

HEDGING WITH BUTTERFLY SPREADS

An agribusiness produces oats and is concerned that future declines in oat prices may reduce its profits at harvest time. The company could buy put options on oat futures contracts to protect itself. However, if the price of oats falls to very low levels, government assistance would probably be made available, and owning puts would have been unnecessary. Thus, the firm really wishes to hedge against the possibility that the price of oats will be low but not very low. One way to do this is to assemble call options to create a butterfly spread. In this case, E_L is the very low oat price below which government assistance makes hedging unnecessary, and E_H is the oat price above which the business's profits are satisfactory without hedging. The half-way point between E_L and E_H is E_M. The payoff diagrams in Figure 21.4 illustrate the combination of call options that produces a butterfly spread and the payoff diagram of the butterfly spread itself.

In general, the cost of buying the low- and high-striking-price options, net of the proceeds from writing the two mid-range striking-price options, will be less than the price of a put with striking price E_H. The firm thus gets the hedging it needs but does not pay for unnecessary protection.

We see that the butterfly spread provides a payoff if the price is between E_L and E_H but not otherwise, and that the payoff is greatest at the midpoint E_M. By appropriately designing such positions, it is possible to hedge against the occurrence of any range of values for the underlying asset.

Other Combinations and Contracts

A wide array of derivative combinations have been introduced by banks and other financial institutions. Again, a complete survey of these products is beyond the scope of this text, but a partial listing is provided below.

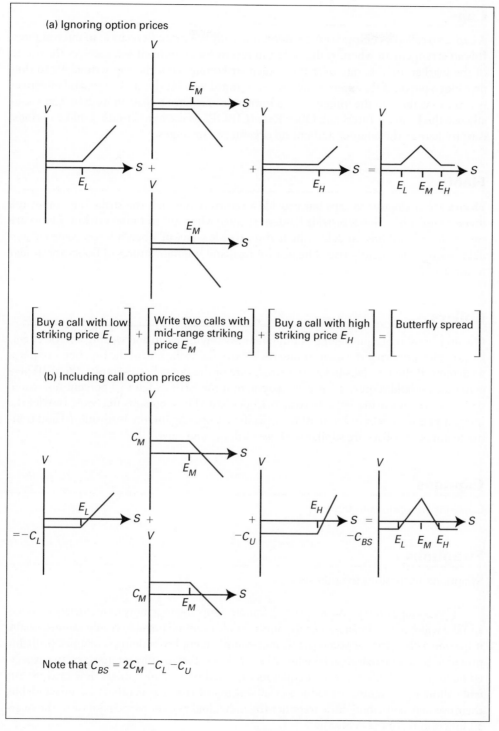

FIGURE 21.4

Payoff Diagram for a
Butterfly Spread at
Expiration

Caps

A **cap**, also called a **ceiling arrangement**, normally is written in relation to interest rates. It is an arrangement whereby the buyer, in return for an upfront fee, receives the excess of the market interest rate over the agreed strike rate from the cap writer. A cap thus provides a payoff if the interest rate moves upward beyond the strike rate and effectively places a ceiling on the interest rate a borrower may have to pay on its debt. Caps usually use the London Interbank Offer Rate (LIBOR) as the market rate. Unlike options, caps trade over the counter and not on organized exchanges.

Floors

Floors are analogous to caps but provide a return that equals the strike rate minus the market rate. Thus, floors provide lenders a return when interest rates are low. Floors are similar to call options on debt, which also provide a payoff when interest rates fall and debt prices consequently rise. The institutional and trading features of floors are similar to those of caps.

Collars

Owning a **collar** is equivalent to simultaneously buying a cap and writing a floor. A collar provides a return if the interest rate rises above the strike rate of the cap, but it requires a payment if the rate falls below the strike rate of the floor. For example, a 6 to 10 percent collar would require a 2 percent payment if the LIBOR fell to 4 percent but would pay 3 percent if the market rate rose to 13 percent. Thus, collars effectively restrict the interest rate on a debt instrument to a specified range. Again, the institutional and trading features of collars are similar to those of floors and caps.

Captions

Captions are options to buy caps.

Swaptions

Swaptions are options to enter swaps.

This listing could go on almost indefinitely. Only the ingenuity of financial engineers and the willingness of market participants to trade limit the possible combinations. Again, it becomes clear that at some point, increasingly complex hedging strategies probably provide decreasing marginal benefits. Also, we know that in efficient markets, the expected benefit from hedging should equal its expected cost. Thus, unless new instruments truly allow for a significant reduction or shifting of risk that is otherwise unavoidable, their use may contribute little to either the individual market participant or to the overall functioning of the economy.

A Comprehensive Illustration

The variety of potential applications of financial risk management through off-balance-sheet contracts and the integrative nature of any hedging strategy, is best illustrated through a comprehensive example. We note that the risk a company faces ultimately derives from its operations, both present and future. The risk of future operations is reflected in the economic value of its assets and of any capital investment projects under consideration. Since these are carried at historical costs on the firm's accounts, they appear stable in the context of the balance sheet. Their economic values, however, may fluctuate substantially as prices, currency values, interest rates, and other economic factors change. We saw that, at least normatively, financial risk management should be concerned with protecting economic value. Thus, one of its most important applications arises in the context of evaluating and managing major capital investments.

D'Anconia Copper, a multinational copper producer, has decided to invest heavily in new electrolytic extraction equipment for its Chilean operations. The schedule of upgrading costs involving the purchase and installation of equipment from a Japanese supplier is as follows:

Immediate costs	1.955 billion yen
Costs in 6 months	2.552
Costs in 12 months	1.180
Costs in 18 months	1.320

These payments are part of a binding contract with a clause exposing D'Anconia to heavy penalties should the schedule not be met. Moreover, once the upgrading begins, it must be completed to be of any benefit to the firm.

For the new equipment to operate, an upgraded electricity supply must be provided to the region in which the mine is located. The Chilean government has agreed to provide such an upgrade if D'Anconia enters a joint venture with it to do so. The terms of the joint venture are that D'Anconia is to provide US$30 million, or 50 percent of the capital cost of the new grid, and is to receive 50 percent of the revenue the grid generates from all its users over the first 10 years. This revenue stream will be in Chilean pesos, and it is projected as follows:

Year	
1	200 million pesos
2	250
3	313
4	391
5	488
6	610
7	763
8	954
9	1,192
10	1,490

Revenue is expected to increase because of an expected inflation rate of 20 percent per year and because several smaller copper producers in the area are expected to piggyback on the system to upgrade their own facilities, thereby adding to revenues. After 10 years, the ownership of the power grid will revert fully to Chilean ownership. Management expects to lose money on the power grid, but it is willing to undertake it anyway because the increased profits from its copper mines will more than offset the loss.

Copper trading in international markets is conducted in U.S. dollars. If copper prices remain at current levels, the new equipment can be financed entirely out of retained earnings. The worldwide economy has grown steadily for the past several years, and copper demand has been strong. However, a few leading economic indicators are beginning to show signs of softening, and some forecasters are predicting a downturn in the near future. Should copper prices fall significantly, it would be necessary to raise funds from external sources.

Management nevertheless views the Chilean investment as sound in the long run. Its net present value (NPV) has been calculated assuming a 20-year life, and it is positive under most reasonable assumptions. The board has made it clear, however, that the investment should be undertaken in a way that avoids any possibility of additional external financing. Following a debt issue required to finance the firm's participation in the new power grid, the board feels that the company will have borrowed as much as is prudent. On the other hand, D'Anconia's major shareholder is opposed to equity issues because she wishes to retain a controlling stake.

The president has requested the chief financial officer to develop as wide a set of hedging strategies as possible to limit exposure to changes in financial and commodity prices.

There are at least six dimensions in which the firm can control the risk in its cash flows over the coming period, and we briefly review each in turn.

1. Because world copper trading is usually in U.S. dollars, most of the company's revenues are in that currency. While the initial equipment payment of ¥1,955 million can be met out of current cash flows from copper sales, the subsequent three payments must be hedged against changes in the yen–dollar exchange rate. To avoid foreign currency exposure in Japanese yen, management decides to buy options to purchase futures contracts to convert U.S. dollars to yen in six, 12, and 18 months. Futures options rather than futures contracts are chosen because management thinks there is a reasonable chance that the Japanese yen will soon fall against the U.S. dollar. A futures contract would lock in the exchange rate, depriving the firm of the benefits of a depressed yen. Although the company must pay the option price upfront, this is regarded as a worthwhile expenditure to retain future flexibility.

   The relevant striking prices for the exchange rate between U.S. dollars and Japanese yen are as follows:

   - Spot price   115 ¥/US$
   - Six-month options   116 ¥/US$
   - 12-month options   118 ¥/US$
   - 18-month options   120 ¥/US$

The striking prices with the highest open interest are chosen so that the firm is in the deepest (i.e., most liquid) part of the options market. Standard futures options are for 12.5 million yen.

The following option contracts are purchased:

- 204 options at 116 ¥/US$ that let the firm convert US$21,983,000 to ¥2,550 million in six months

- 94 options at 118 ¥/US$ that let the company convert US$9,958,000 to ¥1,175 million in 12 months

- 106 options at 120 ¥/US$ that let the firm convert US$11,037,000 to ¥1,325 million in 18 months

By entering futures options contracts to convert U.S. dollars to yen, the company buys the right to translate its obligation into a series of U.S. dollar payments:

- Due in six months: US$21,983,000

- Due in 12 months: US$ 9,958,000

- Due in 18 months: US$11,037,000

With the firm's revenues from copper sales primarily in U.S. dollars and its capital costs now in the same currency, the foreign exchange exposure has been largely eliminated.

2. Although it is now covered against adverse changes in the U.S. dollar–yen exchange rate, the firm may still experience problems if copper prices fall sharply. To protect itself from such an occurrence, it could hedge with copper commodity futures. The futures prices of copper contracts with various maturities are:

- Spot price   100¢US/lb.

- Six-month contracts   98¢US/lb.

- 12-month contracts   96¢US/lb.

- 18-month contracts   94¢US/lb.

Standard copper futures contracts are for 25,000 pounds. To offset the risk of a copper price collapse should a recession occur, the business enters a series of short futures positions (i.e., it commits itself to sell copper in the future at specified prices) as follows:

- 897 contracts at 98¢ provide US$21,977,000 in six months

- 415 contracts at 96¢ provide US$9,960,000 in 12 months

- 470 contracts at 94¢ provide US$11,045,000 in 18 months

By locking in selling prices for these amounts of copper, D'Anconia guarantees itself sufficient cash flows to meet the U.S. dollar contractual obligations to purchase Japanese yen through the futures market, which, in turn, will allow it to meet its Japanese yen obligations to the equipment supplier.

The corporation uses futures short positions rather than put options for this part of its hedging strategy because:

- D'Anconia's worldwide copper reserves are large. There is no danger of having insufficient copper to fulfill the futures contract.

- Although management fears a price downturn, it has little expectation of a copper price rise. There is, therefore, no real concern about committing the company to sell at the locked-in price.

3. To finance its US$30-million participation in the Chilean power grid, D'Anconia decides to issue bonds. Since D'Anconia's Swedish subsidiary is facing higher taxes than its other subsidiaries, management decides that the Swedish unit will represent the firm in the joint venture. The Swedish subsidiary will be able to deduct the interest costs of the US$30-million loan from its taxable income. Also, since management expects to lose money on the power grids, it makes sense to let a high-tax subsidiary claim the losses. This practice of shifting interest payments and losses to the highest-taxed subsidiaries is called tax arbitrage or income shifting. Although illegal in many jurisdictions including Canada, income shifting remains widespread among multinationals.

4. D'Anconia must decide in what currency to have its Swedish subsidiary issue the bonds. Because another branch of the company has recently concluded a 10-year agreement to sell copper to a German manufacturer for German marks (DM), D'Anconia presently has a foreign currency exposure there. If the DM falls, D'Anconia's revenues from its German deal, when measured in U.S. dollars, would also fall. To hedge against this, the Swedish subsidiary issues debt denominated in marks to provide funds for its Chilean joint venture. The spot exchange rate is DM1.60/US$, so the firm issues DM48 million in 10-year, fixed-rate mark-denominated bonds and converts the proceeds into US$30 million.

5. D'Anconia's revenues from its power grid joint venture are to be in pesos. If the value of the peso falls, D'Anconia's revenues will fall. Futures contracts in Chilean pesos are not available and, in any case, would not be available for more than two years. To hedge the exchange rate risk in these cash flows, the firm must therefore resort to forward contracts. D'Anconia, through its bank, arranges a 10-part forward contract to convert pesos into U.S. dollars, each part defining a forward rate for one particular year's expected cash flow.

6. Finally, management may be concerned in general about a possible recession that might leave it short of cash. There are several ways in which one can hedge, at least partially, against a general economic downturn. The most obvious alternative is through stock market index puts or futures. These would provide the company with a cash infusion in the event of a general market downturn, as typically experienced in a recession. Another approach is to use interest rate futures. During recessions, short-term rates tend to fall relative to long-term rates. The firm could therefore take positions in interest rate futures or time the maturity of debt issues or refinancings to take advantage of this. After some debate, management decides not to pursue these alternatives. ▲

Taking such market positions would create some risk. Not only are future economic developments inherently uncertain, but the relationship between share prices, interest rates, and levels of general economic activity is complex and not entirely predictable.

Hence, what was intended as hedging could also be viewed as speculation. In fact, the dividing line between hedging and speculation is not clear-cut. Also, one must question whether operating management has any comparative advantage in anticipating and/or hedging against general economic conditions, or whether this, legitimately, should be left to shareholders who clearly have the same techniques at their disposal.

The example above provides some illustration of the variety of possible exposures to risk that are commonly encountered by firms operating in an increasingly global business environment and reinforces the importance of measuring and managing such risks in a systematic manner. The range of instruments now available greatly increases management's ability to engineer its own solutions to these problems.

CURRENT PRACTICE   21.6

In light of the complexities discussed above and the rapid rate of change and innovation in this area, it is not surprising that the policies of companies with respect to treasury risk management vary considerably. Some companies such as Barrick Gold hedge extensively, while others within the same industry such as Placer Dome remain relatively unhedged.

As noted earlier, the overall trend has been toward a more deliberate approach to treasury risk management. An increasing number of businesses are formulating comprehensive policies involving senior management, often doing so with the aid of specialized consultants. Settling on the approach to be taken involves developing consensus on such basic issues as market efficiency and attitudes toward risk. In fact, a straightforward attempt to discuss and confront these issues explicitly is, on its own, often of major benefit. Based on their own experiences, many firms have also moved away from an "opportunistic" approach to financial markets after having recognized that many such markets are probably efficient enough so as to preclude consistent speculative gains. Instead, financial managers now concentrate on ensuring adequate funding at reasonably predictable costs. This makes it easier to manage capital budgeting and operations in which most of the enterprise's economic value is after all created.

The move toward comprehensive treasury risk management is often triggered by past losses and failures, by major new individual transactions that entail significant exposure (e.g., a major new export contract or a large debt issue), and by contacts with financial advisors including the firm's bank. Financial institutions and consultants that are active in this area obviously have an incentive to promote their products and services by increasing managerial awareness.

Nevertheless, many corporations still neglect treasury risk management and continue operating in an *ad hoc* and uncoordinated manner. Impediments to a more systematic approach include complacency ("we have done fine in the past, so why change?"); an ongoing belief that it is possible to selectively "beat" the market through judicious forecasting and timing; a lack of sophistication and familiarity with the many new instruments and elaborate techniques that are available; and management incentives that may favour a local and divisional perspective rather than a global corporate-wide orientation.

21.7 SUMMARY

1. Treasury risk management activity has become increasingly important as volatility in financial markets increases. Financial markets and institutions have responded with new vehicles for apportioning risk, reducing taxes and issuance costs, or otherwise enhancing efficiency and value.

2. Effective risk management requires systematic and reasonably accurate measurement of exposure. Exposure is defined as the variability in a firm's value or cash flows that results from changes in financial variables such as interest rates, exchange rates, and commodity prices.

3. Regression analysis and computer simulation can be used to quantify aggregate exposure. Other techniques commonly used by financial institutions include gap and duration analysis.

4. Optimal risk management is closely related to beliefs about market efficiency.

5. On-balance sheet hedging entails the matching of assets and liabilities, and revenues and costs, on the basis of maturities, currencies, and value sensitivity to changes in interest rates or commodity prices.

6. Off-balance sheet hedging relies on derivative securities whose usage does not directly affect the firm's financial statements. Swaps, options, and futures, alone or in various combinations, allow for the design of a variety of creative solutions to risk management.

APPENDIX 21-A

DURATION AND VOLATILITY

Assets or liabilities with fixed cash flows that extend over longer periods of time typically have higher volatilities. This can be formalized mathematically by developing the concept of duration, which has become important in managing interest rate risk. Duration essentially enables us to measure the sensitivity of a portfolio of assets or liabilities, with varying cash flows distributed over many time periods to changes in interest rates. For simplicity, we illustrate its use in the context of a single bond with periodic interest payments and a final repayment of principal.

EXAMPLE

ESTIMATING A BOND'S DURATION

Consider a five-year 8 percent coupon bond with a face value of $1,000. The current interest rate and, therefore, the discount rate appropriate for valuing this bond is 10 percent. The bond's current price is equal to the present value of the cash flows it pays, or $924.18. We perform the following calculations:

Time period	Bond cash flows	Present value of cash flow paid	Present value of period cash flows as a percentage of total present value ($924.18)
Year 1	$ 80	$ 72.72	7.87
2	80	66.12	7.15
3	80	60.11	6.50
4	80	54.64	5.91
5	$1,080	$670.59	72.56

Thus, the bondholder waits one year to get the first payment, which amounts to 7.87 percent of the bond's total present value. She waits two years to get the second payment, which amounts to 7.15 percent of the total present value; three years for the third payment of 6.50 percent of the present value; and so on.

The bond's duration (D) measures the weighted average time the investor must wait for the present value of cash flows to be received. Specifically,

$$D = 0.787 \times 1 \text{ year} + .715 \times 2 \text{ years} + .0650 \times 3 \text{ years} + .0591 \times 4 \text{ years} + .7256 \times 5 \text{ years} = 4.28 \text{ years}$$

In other words, the investor waits an average of 4.28 years to receive the present value of cash flows from her bond.

It can be shown that the volatility v of any asset or liability is equal to a simple function of its duration D:[5]

$$v = \frac{-D}{(1+r)} \tag{21.2}$$

Alternatively, duration can be interpreted directly as the price elasticity of a bond with regard to changes in interest rates, or as the percentage change in the bond value for a given percentage change in $(1+r)$.

[5] This equation comes from applying basic calculus to the problem. The price of a bond with face value F, coupon payment I, maturity n, and yielding r, is: $P = \frac{I}{(1+r)} + \frac{I}{(1+r)^2} + ... + \frac{I+F}{(1+r)^n}$. The change in the bond's price when the discount rate changes are:

$$dP/dr = \frac{-I}{(1+r)^2} + \frac{-2I}{(1+r)^3} + ... + \frac{-n(I+F)}{(1+r)^{n+1}} = \frac{-1}{(1+r)}\left[\frac{I}{(1+r)} + \frac{2I}{(1+r)^2} + ... + \frac{n(I+F)}{(1+r)^n}\right]$$

Volatility, v, is the change in the price of the bond as a percentage of its current value since the term in square brackets in the equation below is precisely the bond's duration,

$$v = \frac{dP/dr}{P} = \frac{-1}{(1+r)}\left[\frac{I}{P(1+r)} + \frac{2I}{P(1+r)^2} + ... + \frac{n(I+F)}{P(1+r)^n}\right] = \frac{-D}{(1+r)}$$

EXAMPLE

DURATION AND BOND VOLATILITY

Pursuing the previous example, the bond's volatility becomes:

$$v = \frac{-4.28}{(1+.10)} = -3.9\%$$

If the interest rates rise one percentage point to 11 percent, the value of this bond should fall by 3.9 percent to $914.18 \times 0.961 = \$878.53$. Alternatively, if $(1+r) = (1+.1) = 1.1$ changes by 1 percent (to either 1.089 or 1.111), the average change in the value of the bond will be 4.28 percent.

Duration can be expressed more formally as the sum of the products of the bond's cash flows in present value terms multiplied by the time period in which they are received, all divided by the total present value of the bond. Mathematically, we have:

(21.3)
$$D = \frac{\displaystyle\sum_{t=1}^{n} \frac{tC_t}{(1+r)^t}}{\displaystyle\sum_{t=1}^{n} \frac{C_t}{(1+r)^t}}$$

C = the future cash payments from the bond

t = time period of the payments

n = the number of years to maturity

r = the discount rate or current yield[6]

Since the concept of duration is applicable to any portfolio of assets and liabilities with any pattern of future cash flows, it has become a tool widely used by portfolio and pension fund managers who need to assess the volatilities of the assets and liabilities for which they are responsible. Even in the corporate context, it enables us to readily determine, for example, the interest rate sensitivity of a firm's varied liabilities.

Essentially, if a company's assets and liabilities have the same duration, the firm is hedged in that any changes in their values, as a consequence of varying interest rates, move in parallel. In practice, several complications may arise. As time and interest rates change, the duration of assets and liabilities need not remain the same, thus necessitating periodic "rebalancing." Also, short- and long-term interest rates may change in different ways over time, resulting in shifts in the term structure of interest rates. Finally, debt instruments such as bonds may not have fixed predetermined maturities (investors, for example, have the option to alter maturities when bonds are convertible, extendible, or retractable). Thus, actual applications of duration analysis can become rather technical and complex, with the details clearly beyond the scope of this introductory discussion. **Note**: All *asterisked* Questions and Problems relate to material contained in the appendix to the chapter.

---

[6] We assume the interest rate is not expected to change over time—that we have a flat term structure of interest rates. More generally, duration analysis can be extended to include discount rates that vary over time.

QUESTIONS AND PROBLEMS

Questions for Discussion

1. What is the difference between hedging, speculation, and investing? Discuss.

2. It has been argued that not limiting exposure is speculation. Discuss.

3. What, if any, are the similarities and differences between buying standard property insurance and protecting one's financial position through a futures contract or option? Do the writers of the above contracts have equal concerns about the "moral hazard" involved?

4. Contrast the hedging of foreign exchange exposure using forward markets, futures markets, and options on futures.

5. Discuss and illustrate the relevance of the following concepts to the management of interest rate risk: (a) bond volatility, (b) off-balance-sheet hedging, (c) immunization, (d) duration.

PROBLEMS WITH SOLUTIONS

Problem 1

A regression analysis relating the percentage change in a real estate firm's share value to various types of risk gives the following results:

Sensitivity to	Parameter estimate
3-month LIBOR	−.315
10-year Government-of-Canada-bond yield	−.199
3-month lumber futures price	.766
S&P/TSE 60 Index	.348

(a) Suppose the LIBOR rate rises 1 percent while 10-year rates remain constant. Lumber futures prices simultaneously fall 3 percent, and the S&P/TSE 60 Index drops 2 percent. What should happen to the value of the firm's stock?

(b) Consider the economics that give rise to the parameter estimates above.

Solution 1

(a) $\Delta V/V = -.315 \times 1\% - .199 \times 0\% + .766 \times -3\% + .348 \times -2\% = -3.3\%$

The stock price should fall by 3.3 percent.

(b) The negative relation between short-term interest rates and the value of the real estate company probably arises from the procyclical nature of both short-term interest rates and real-estate values. Both rise and fall with the general level of economic activity. The negative relation between long term rates and the firm's value is simply picking up the sensitivity of the company's value to its long-term cost of capital as discussed in Chapter 15. The lumber futures price may be driven by changes in demand due to the health of the real estate industry. Recall from basic statistics that regressions only measure correlation not causation. That is, the regression says that a 1 percent change in the lumber futures price is on average accompanied by a 0.766 percent change in the firm's value. The regression does not say which is cause and which is effect. The positive parameter estimate relating the firm's value to the market is simply reflecting the capital asset pricing model (CAPM).

Problem 2

A pulp and paper company sells most of its output to Japanese newspapers in yen-denominated contracts. The contracts are long-term agreements with reliable and stable buyers, and the firm has reliable agreements with lumber companies. It wishes to expand its Canadian facilities by purchasing new equipment from a Swedish manufacturer. The Swedish firm is to be paid in Swedish krona in four semi-annual installments. The equipment is to be financed through a debt issue. The pulp and paper company is concerned about a downward trend in the yen and an upward trend in lumber prices. Futures contracts in Swedish currency are not readily available. Devise a hedging strategy for the pulp and paper firm.

Solution 2

The enterprise should arrange to sell yen and buy lumber through the futures market. It should use futures contracts rather than options to hedge its yen and lumber price risk because the amounts it must sell are already set, and since management is not fearful of missing the benefits of high yen or of low lumber costs, there is little advantage in paying for the flexibility options provide. As Swedish krona futures are not available, the firm must design a forward contract with its bank to hedge against possible fluctuations in that currency by the four points in time when payments are required. Alternatively, the firm could issue debt in Swedish krona. The disadvantage of this is that the market for krona-denominated debt may be quite thin.

Problem 3

A fund manager is considering a transaction using Arctic Fuel Corp. options. She rules out the use of a straddle. The manager is aware of the fact that Arctic Fuel Corp. is engaged in a major court case and that the outcome will impact the firm. If the decision is in its favour, she believes the stock price will appreciate by 30 percent. However, if the judgement is against the firm, she estimates the stock price will depreciate by 40 percent. The manager is confident that the court case will be decided in the next three months. However, if the case has not been decided, the stock price is expected to remain unchanged. The company's common shares currently trade at $100. Three different three-month call options can be purchased or written. An option with a $75 striking price costs $35; an option with a $100 striking price costs $15; and an option with a $125 striking price costs $5.

(a) What combination of call options will provide a (i) positive payoff if the price of the underlying security varies a great deal and a (ii) negative payoff if the security remains relatively unchanged?

(b) What is the portfolio's payoff (ignoring option costs) if the verdict is (i) positive, (ii) negative, or (iii) not decided yet?

(c) What is the manager's payoff (net of option costs) if the verdict is (i) positive, (ii) negative, or (iii) not decided yet?

(d) Plot the manager's return for various stock prices using a payoff diagram. Graphs should show: (i) option prices ignored and (ii) option prices taken into account. Mark all intersections with the x and y axes.

Solution 3

(a) To produce the desired payoffs, the investor could create a reverse butterfly spread. This involves shorting one low- and one high-striking-price option and purchasing two mid-striking-price options. This is the exact opposite of a butterfly spread.

(b) Ignoring the costs of the option, the portfolio payoff is as follows:

	(i) Positive verdict $S_1=\$130$	(ii) Negative verdict $S_1=\$60$	(iii) No verdict $S_1=\$100$
Short position of $75 strike call	−55	0	−25
Long position of two $100 strike calls	+60	0	0
Short position of $125 strike call	−5	0	0
Total payoff	0	0	−25

(c) Taking into account the costs of the option, the portfolio has the following returns:

	(i) Positive verdict $S_1=\$130$	(ii) Negative verdict $S_1=\$60$	(iii) No verdict $S_1=\$100$
Short position of $75 strike call	−20	+35	+10
Long position of two $100 strike calls	+30	−30	−30

	(i) Positive verdict $S_1=\$130$	(ii) Negative verdict $S_1=\$60$	(iii) No verdict $S_1=\$100$
Short position of $125 strike call	0	+5	+5
Total payoff	+10	+10	−15

(d) The following payoff diagrams result:
(i) Ignoring options prices

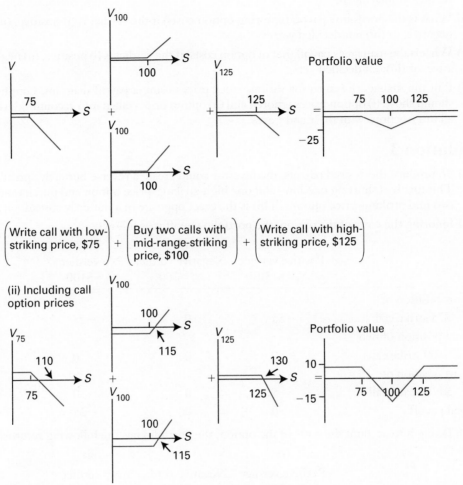

$$\begin{pmatrix} \text{Write call with low-} \\ \text{striking price, \$75} \end{pmatrix} + \begin{pmatrix} \text{Buy two calls with} \\ \text{mid-range-striking} \\ \text{price, \$100} \end{pmatrix} + \begin{pmatrix} \text{Write call with high-} \\ \text{striking price, \$125} \end{pmatrix}$$

(ii) Including call option prices

Problem 4

Calculate the duration and volatility of a five-year $1,000 face value 8 percent coupon bond yielding 9 percent.

Solution 4

First calculate the market value of the bond:

$$P = \frac{\$80}{1+.09} + \frac{\$80}{(1+.09)^2} + \frac{\$80}{(1+.09)^3} + \frac{\$80}{(1+.09)^4} + \frac{\$1,080}{(1+.09)^5}$$

$$= \$73.39 + \$67.33 + \$61.77 + \$56.67 + \$701.94$$

$$= \$961.10$$

Now the bond's duration can be calculated as:

$$D = 1 \times \frac{\$73.39}{\$961.10} + 2 \times \frac{\$67.33}{\$961.10} + 3 \times \frac{\$61.77}{\$961.10} + 4 \times \frac{\$56.67}{\$961.10} + 5 \times \frac{\$701.94}{\$961.10}$$

$$= 4.3 \text{ years}$$

The volatility of the bond is then:

$$v = \frac{-4.3}{1 + .09} = -3.9$$

A 1 percentage-point increase in the interest rate will trigger a 3.9 percent fall in the bond's value.

ADDITIONAL PROBLEMS

1. You are the treasurer of a German corporation looking to purchase a significant volume of light, sweet crude oil. All of your sales are in Euros, but the price of crude is generally quoted in U.S. dollars. Discuss your risk exposure, and illustrate how you might handle the situation. Use the financial pages to obtain realistic numbers.

2. You are the senior manager of a chartered bank and have been approached by one of the bank's important clients who is seeking advice on how to handle an unwanted interest rate exposure attributable to a major capital expenditure commitment that is about to be finalized. Specifically, major equipment is to be installed with payment of $15 million due in three months. All $15 million is to be raised at that time through 10-year debt. The current interest rate on such debt is 12 percent, but the client believes that interest rates could increase by at least one percentage point within the next three months. The client has already asked you to illustrate *numerically* how interest rate futures might be used to limit exposure. It was agreed that the explanatory numerical illustration could ignore taxes and transaction costs.

3. Following board approval, the chief financial officer of the Ruper Pulp Co. is looking to issue US$50 million 20-year debentures with an 8 percent coupon. Regulatory clearance of the prospectus and other necessary steps associated with the issue are expected to delay the actual pricing of the issue for three months. This lag is troublesome to the CFO because, despite current expectations, long-term rates could rise. He is not worried about foreign currency risk because pulp prices are quoted in U.S. dollars. He has asked you to look in the financial pages and suggest a way in which Rupert Pulp's interest rate risk could be hedged using futures options and to assume that comparable yields will not rise beyond 10 percent. (Hint: If yields rise to 10 percent, what would that do to the pricing of the issue?)

4. The North Island Credit Union has a loan portfolio of $5 million. The portfolio's duration is six years, and its yield is 12 percent. Funding is largely from deposits, and the duration of all liabilities is one year. The appropriate discount rate for calculating portfolio volatility is 12 percent. What problems will the credit union face if interest rates rise by 1 percent? What steps would you encourage the credit union to consider?

5. (a) Calculate the duration of a six-year 8 percent coupon bond with a face value of $1,000. The prevailing yield to maturity of this bond is 11 percent.

   (b) What is the bond's volatility?

   (c) Of what significance are these calculations to the asset/liability management of a financial institution?

6. You work for a Canadian-based firm that has just opened a sales division in India. It is planned that all revenues will be kept in the Indian division and then transferred to the Canadian parent company in two years. Revenues to be transferred to the parent are expected to total 30 million rupees two years from today.

   In order to finance the new division, your company took out a loan denominated in Japanese yen (which it then converted to Indian rupees to open the division). The loan has unusual characteristics in that it is to be paid off in one lump sum of ¥45 million due two years from today.

   Yields on two-year treasury securities are 6 percent in Canada, 2 percent in Japan, and 15 percent in India (these are annual effective interest rates).

   Current exchange rates are:

   2.4510 yen/rupee

   29.4154 rupee/$Can

   You know that these exchange rates will most likely change over the next two years and estimate that the rupee will depreciate against the Canadian dollar. Your forecast is that the rupee will depreciate somewhere between 5 percent and 20 percent in value against the dollar. For the yen, you forecast that over the next two years, it will be somewhere between a 1 percent depreciation and a 9 percent appreciation against the dollar.

   (a) Based on the forecasted ranges of possible future exchange rates, what is the maximum possible total profit in Canadian-dollar terms of the division (in two years), and what is the minimum possible total profit (in Canadian dollars) of the division?

   (b) Assume that when the division was set up, the loan was taken out in rupees. The total lump sum due in two years would be 25 million rupees. What is the maximum possible total profit in Canadian-dollar terms? What is the minimum possible profit in Canadian dollars?

   (c) Comment briefly on your answers to (a) and (b) in terms of the potential benefits and risks of exchange rate changes to a firm and ways to manage that risk.

7. A floating rate bond has a coupon of LIBOR+1 percent. The coupon on the bond is adjusted each year (it makes annual coupon payments) to equal the current level of LIBOR plus an extra 1 percent. The bond has 10 years to maturity and a $1,000 par value.

(a) If, on the interest adjustment date, LIBOR equals 5 percent, what is the market value of the bond?

(b) If, on the interest adjustment date, LIBOR equals 7 percent, what is the market value of the bond?

(c) What is the duration of a floating-rate bond?

8. A farmer expects to manufacture 80,000 pounds of cheese this season. The current cash price for block cheddar cheese is US$1.58 per pound. The farmer is concerned about possible fluctuations in the price of cheese before he is ready to sell in December. He does not want to lock in a price with futures because that means he cannot benefit if the price of cheese rises; therefore he is interested in options. Options on cheddar cheese are available on the Chicago Mercantile Exchange (each contract is on 40,000 pounds). A put option on cheese is available with an exercise price of $168 per 100 pounds for a premium of $2 per 100 pounds (note that the prices are quoted per 100 pounds even though the contracts are on 40,000 pounds each). Plot the farmer's total revenue versus the price of cheese in December if he uses options to hedge his risk. What would be the upfront cost of instituting this strategy?

9. The U.S. firm for which you work has won a contract with the Japanese government. The contract involves paying workers in yen. (All revenues for the project come in U.S. dollars.) The total liability is ¥12.5 million and will have to be paid in six months. Today's spot exchange rate is 100¥/US$. The firm wishes to hedge its exposure to foreign exchange risk with options. Call and put options that mature in six months are available. All options on yen are written on ¥12.5 million per contract. A call option with a striking price of 0.01 US$/¥ has a premium of US$4,000 per contract. A put option with striking price of 0.01 US$/¥ has a premium of US$3,500 per contract.

(a) How much, in U.S. dollars will the business gain or lose (relative to the value at today's spot exchange rate) if it does not hedge and the spot rate in six months is 110 ¥/US$?

(b) How much, in U.S. dollars will the firm gain or lose (relative to the value at today's spot exchange rate) if it hedges with options and the spot rate in six months is 110 ¥/$US? (Remember to include the cost of hedging.)

(c) How much, in U.S. dollars will the company gain or lose (relative to the value at today's spot exchange rate) if it does not hedge, and the spot rate in six months is 90 ¥/US$?

(d) How much, in U.S. dollars will the firm gain or lose (relative to the value at today's spot exchange rate) if it hedges with options and the spot rate in six months is 90 ¥/US$? (Remember to include the cost of hedging.)

10. Options on the Euro are available on the Chicago Mercantile Exchange with the following characteristics:

call option—exercise=$0.84 per Euro, premium=$0.012 per Euro

call option—exercise=$0.85 per Euro, premium=$0.005 per Euro

call option—exercise=$0.86 per Euro, premium=$0.002 per Euro

Consider a strategy whereby you buy one of the first option contract, write two of the second option contract, and buy one of the third option contract. Each contract is on 125,000 Euros. Create a diagram showing the total dollar profit on this strategy as a function of the value of the Euro at maturity of the options. Make sure to include the prices paid for the options as in Figure 21.4(b) in the text. When might a speculator use such a strategy?

11. A bank has the following balance sheet, where all values are market values (in billions of dollars):

Assets		Liabilities	
Floating-rate loans	15	Notice deposits	30
Fixed-rate loans	29	Zero coupon bonds	10
		Equity	5
	45		45

Notes:

- Floating-rate loans make annual interest payments and have their coupon rates reset to market rates each year.
- Fixed-rate loans are in the form of bonds. They have annual coupons and three years to maturity. (The next coupon is one year from now.) The coupon rate is 10 percent and yield to maturity is 12 percent.
- The zero coupon bonds have four years to maturity.
- Notice deposits are deposits held by the bank. The interest rate paid on these can be adjusted by the bank at any time.
- Assume that 12 percent is the market rate of interest for all assets and liabilities.

(a) Calculate the volatility of each type of asset and liability. (You may want to do Question #7 before attempting this question.)

(b) Based on your answer to (a), if interest rates rise by 0.5 percent, what will be the market value of equity of the bank?

(c) Based on part (b), what is the volatility of the bank's equity with respect to changes in interest rates?

(d) The bank is considering changing its marketing strategy and heavily promoting fixed-rate rather than floating-rate loans. Its plan is to gradually change the assets that are currently floating rate into fixed rate. Using a spreadsheet, plot the volatility of equity versus the percentage of assets held as fixed-rate loans. Comment on the bank's proposed strategy with respect to the risk they are exposed to.

This case examines the use of derivative securities from the perspective of both the investor and the corporation.

1) *Investor's Perspective:*

The following are listings for options on the stock of BCE Inc. All options listed mature in four months. The current price of BCE stock is $41:

Exercise	Put/call	Premium	Volume	Open interest
$30.00	c	$11.10	68	495
35.00	c	6.75	12	990
37.50	c	5.20	50	1276
40.00	c	3.40	76	1480
40.00	p	2.15	5	103
42.50	c	2.30	19	72
45.00	c	1.35	41	36

You work with a financial advisory firm specializing in individual investors. A client of yours is interested in beginning to use options in his investments.

(a) The client understands some of the basic concepts about put and call options but needs some things explained about how they are priced. Briefly explain what is meant by the terms intrinsic value and time value for options. For each option listed, calculate the intrinsic value and the time value.

(b) The client has been reading the financial press about BCE for some time and believes that there will be major changes in the telecommunication industry over the next four months. However, the client is unsure whether this will be good or bad news for BCE. Devise a strategy for the client that will profit regardless of whether the stock price of BCE changes up or down. Draw a diagram showing the net profit of the strategy over a range of stock prices (at maturity of the options) from $0 to $65. Assume that the client has a maximum of $5,000 available to invest in your strategy. If the client follows your strategy, what will be his dollar profit and percentage return if the stock price of BCE in four months is $50? What if the stock price in four months is $30? What if the stock price is unchanged at $41? What if the stock price changes to $43? (Remember that each option contract is on 100 shares.)

(c) A second client comes to you for advice. She currently holds shares in BCE that she purchased six months ago. In that time, the share price has risen. She has decided that if the share price rises from its current level to $45, then she will immediately sell her shares to lock in the profit. Given this, what advice could you give this client in terms of an option strategy that would be in line with her objectives but increase her profits? Explain exactly what the client could do and how this would increase her profits while still being in line with her objectives.

2) *Corporation's Perspective:*

(a) BCI, a subsidiary of BCE, has an issue of floating-rate bonds outstanding (see the table at the end of the Case in Part 3 for details). The bonds have their coupon rate adjusted each year to market levels (assume that they pay annual coupons and have exactly two years to maturity). BCI is worried about interest rates rising in the future, which would lead to higher interest payments. There is a plan under consideration to use interest rate futures to hedge against the risk of a rise in rates. Any profits from the futures would be used to retire a portion of the debt. Any losses would be covered through additional borrowing.

The firm would use futures on 10-year Government of Canada bonds with a 6 percent coupon rate (assume that they make annual coupon payments). Each futures contract is on a bond with a $100,000 face value. The firm would take a position in 5,000 contracts. Assume that the futures price is equal to the spot price and that the yield on 10-year Government of Canada bonds is currently 7 percent.

  (i)   If BCI does not hedge and the yield on its bonds rises to 9.3 percent, what will be its annual interest payments on the bond issue? If rates fall to 7.3 percent what will be its annual interest payments?

  (ii) IF BCI adopts the interest rate futures hedge, what will be its total annual interest payments (after retiring debt or borrowing more to cover futures losses) if the yield on its bonds rises to 9.3 percent and the yield on 10-year Government of Canada bonds rises to 8 percent? What if the yield on its bonds falls to 7.3 percent and the yield on 10-year Government of Canada bonds fall to 6 percent?

  (iii) What happens to BCI's total interest payments if there is a shift in the yield curve (short-term rates increase but long-term rates decrease) and yields on its two-year bonds rise to 9.3 percent while yields on 10-year Government of Canada bonds falls to 7.75 percent?

  (iv) Comment on your answers to parts (i) to (iii), concentrating on the benefits, drawbacks, and difficulties in hedging.

(b) In BCE's annual report, Management's Discussion and Analysis (see Appendix II at: www.wiley.com/canada/lusztig) contains a section entitled "Risk Factors" in which it outlines some of the major sources of risk for each of the company's divisions. For each source of risk, discuss whether or not it would be possible for BCE to hedge this risk, and if so what business procedures or securities BCE could use to manage that risk. If there is more than one method in which the risk could be managed, discuss the relative benefits and drawbacks of each method.

part 8

Working Capital Management

In Part 8, we cover working capital management, reviewing the major categories of current assets, current liabilities, and their management. In Chapter 22 we deal with the basic concepts of working capital management and also discuss the management of cash and marketable securities including cash budgeting. Chapter 23 discusses the management of accounts receivable and inventories, while Chapter 24 considers short-term and intermediate-term financing.

UPS Delivers on Managing Capital

Where do you live? No matter what your answer, United Parcel Services delivers there. Its delivery service covers every address in Canada and the United States—not to mention 200 other countries and territories.

The largest package delivery company in the world, UPS delivers about 13.6 million packages a day—that's over 3.5 billion a year. It employs over 359,000 people worldwide, including about 6,000 at UPS Canada. Some 152,500 UPS ground vehicles are at work around the world, as well as a fleet of 238 jets and another 384 chartered aircraft.

Teamwork and co-ordination, needless to say, is key for a global courier company. This holds true not only for operations but for finance. Which is why representatives from all UPS regional companies get together every year at the company's world headquarters in Atlanta prior to finalizing their regional budgets.

"There were people from Europe, from Asia Pacific, from Latin America and the Caribbean," explains Shivani Thakur, who represented UPS Canada at the Atlanta meeting in 2000. "Because we are a global company, with packages, information and funds flowing across borders, it's important for us to share information. It can get pretty complicated for a company this size."

Back at UPS Canada headquarters in Mississauga, Ms. Thakur co-ordinates the business plan for the next twelve months, then works with the rest of the finance team to manage the working capital throughout the year.

The most important elements for working capital management, she finds, are good cash flow projections and accurate management reporting systems. "So many important decisions are based on the numbers," she explains.

These decisions include, for example, whether to invest in new vehicles if volume increases, or to lease them, or simply charter space temporarily on other carriers. Or how to handle payments from small-business customers; "The standard in the courier industry is 7-day billing," explains Ms. Thakur, "but for many small businesses, cash flow considerations mean they prefer to pay monthly. So we now offer the opportunity for them to pay with a corporate credit card."

Carrying out these decisions means careful management of cash. "We have to balance what we need against when we have the cash available," says Ms. Thakur. "For example, should we make this expenditure this month or next month?" Luckily, says Ms. Thakur, having the needed cash on hand is never a problem at UPS, which manages its cash flow "carefully and conservatively."

Like many businesses, UPS experiences seasonal fluctuations, which are an added challenge. Managing staffing levels can be a challenge—one that UPS approaches with team spirit.

After all, "through stock benefit plans, management personnel are all partners in the business," explains Ms. Thakur. "At peak times, we all help out where we can."

chapter 22

Cash and Working Capital Management

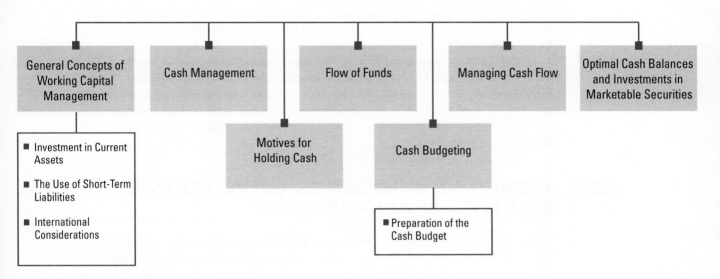

Learning Objectives

After studying this chapter, you should be able to:

1. *Explain why the efficient utilization of working capital is so important for companies.*
2. *Define the difference between short-term and long-term financing.*
3. *Identify the four motives that influence the proportion of a company's assets to be held in cash.*
4. *Discuss the circular flow of funds in a business and the role of the various types of expenses and incomes.*
5. *Describe the types of inflows and outflows in a cash budget and how they interact.*

22.1 INTRODUCTION

Working capital can be defined in various ways. A narrow definition might only encompass a firm's current assets (notably cash, marketable securities, accounts receivable, and inventories), while a more useful definition includes both current assets and current liabilities (such as various payables and short-term borrowings). **Net working capital** is defined as the difference between current assets and current liabilities, and it is a single figure derived from the company's balance sheet. For the purposes of this chapter, we use a broad definition of working capital such that working capital management is concerned with managing both current assets and current liabilities, as well as the interrelationships between them.

We begin this chapter by introducing some general concepts that should guide a firm's investment in current assets and its financing through current liabilities. We then discuss the management of cash and marketable securities. In the next chapter, we review investments in accounts receivable and inventories before reviewing short-term financing sources, which are generally reflected in the current liabilities' section of the company balance sheet.

22.2 GENERAL CONCEPTS OF WORKING CAPITAL MANAGEMENT

Table 22.1 provides aggregate statistics on working capital for all Canadian corporations. We see that both the absolute levels and relative proportions of current assets and current liabilities are sizeable. Consequently, the efficient management of working capital is vital to the overall success of most firms. For example, overinvestment in

Table 22.1

Aggregate Figures of Current Assets and Current Liabilities for all Canadian Companies (in $000,000s)

	First Quarter 1989	First Quarter 1994	First Quarter 1999
Cash and deposits	84,543	94,111	121,996
Accounts receivable and accrued revenues	134,862	174,210	217,398
Inventories	122,673	127,687	163,297
Investments and accounts with affiliates	311,491	476,082	674,657
Total current assets	**653,569**	**872,080**	**1,177,348**
Accounts payable	168,792	242,297	282,418
Loans and accounts with affiliates	107,847	191,086	274,696
Bank loans and other short-term loans	273,877	278,374	312,627
Bankers acceptances and paper	39,812	37,155	72,987
Total current liabilities	**590,328**	**748,912**	**942,728**

Source: Statistics Canada's CANSIM database.

unproductive current assets will reduce the profitability of a business, whereas mismanagement of current liabilities will have a negative impact on both the firm's cost of capital and its risk. Also, in the short run, current assets and liabilities may be the only items that a firm can adjust to meet changed circumstances. Given a volatile economic environment, it is not surprising that working capital management demands a large proportion of management's time.

Table 22.2 shows wide differences in the relative importance of working capital across various industries. The current and quick ratio industry averages range from a low of 0.94 and 0.70 for pipelines to a high of 8.08 and 7.54 for gold and precious metals. The ratio of working capital to total assets shows similar variability, ranging from -3.05 percent for pipelines to 39.20 percent for biotechnology and pharmaceuticals. It is evident from these statistics that one cannot derive general guidelines regarding either absolute or relative amounts that firms should carry in various working capital accounts.

Table 22.2

Working Capital and Liquidity Ratios for Selected Canadian Industries

	Current ratio (current assets/ current liabilities)	Quick ratio ([current assets– inventory]/current liabilities)	Working capital to total assets (%) ([current assets– current liabilities] /total assets)
Auto, parts and transportation equipment	1.75	0.89	0.98
Biotechnology and pharmaceuticals	6.93	6.33	39.20
Building material	2.16	1.18	21.01
Chemical and fertilizers	4.35	3.46	21.73
Communication & media	1.44	0.97	7.29
Consumer products	1.68	1.00	17.18
Fabrication & engineering	2.23	1.32	28.15
Food & veverage	2.24	1.14	17.93
Gold & precious minerials	8.08	7.54	20.57
Hospitality	1.63	1.33	9.03
Metal & minerals*	2.26	1.08	15.69
Oil & gas	2.04	1.80	6.66
Paper & forest products*	2.00	1.01	15.98
Pipelines*	0.94	0.70	(3.05)
Steel	2.27	1.04	23.60
Technology	3.34	2.60	27.83
Telephone & utilities*	1.38	1.16	0.50
Transportation & environmental services*	1.26	0.99	4.12
Wholesale & retail	1.70	0.61	22.52

Source: Financial Post Industry Reports, May 6, 2000.

* The ratios are the seven year averages for the 1992 to 1998 period except for metal & minerals, paper & forest products, pipelines, telephone & utilities, and transportation & environmental services which are the averages for the period 1993–99.

A survey of large corporations asked what factors treasurers considered to be most important in the management of corporate liquidity.[1] The factors that obtained the highest rankings were:

1. good cash flow projections
2. maintaining adequate earnings
3. good relations with bankers
4. proper management of receivables, inventories, and capital expenditures
5. a timely and accurate management reporting system

It is also interesting to note that almost one-third of the largest U.S. corporations reported that they had been subject to some liquidity problems during the previous five years, with the incidence among smaller firms probably being much higher. The most important warning signs indicating potential liquidity problems were reported as:[2]

1. a buildup of inventories and declining inventory turnover
2. increases in debt and debt ratios
3. increases in costs that cannot be passed on
4. increases in accounts receivable and longer collection periods
5. a decline in net working capital and daily cash flows

Consequently, trimming of inventories, tighter collection policies, and greater cost control of overhead were seen as key actions that should be pursued to resolve liquidity problems.

Investment in Current Assets

An important characteristic of current assets is that they tend to grow automatically with increasing sales. Thus, assuming a constant credit policy, investments in accounts receivable will rise proportionally with the dollar volume of sales. Similarly, increased inventories and larger cash balances are typically required to support expanded sales. Although, over the longer term, the physical volume of sales will also affect a firm's investments in fixed assets, the effects on working capital management are more direct and immediate. Furthermore, whereas new investments in plant and equipment may be required only if the physical volume of sales expands, an increased dollar volume of sales caused by price-level increases will affect the dollar investment in current assets and create a need for additional funds.

Conceptually, a company should increase current assets until the marginal benefits to be derived from additional investments equal the marginal costs of carrying additional current assets. At that point, net benefits will be maximized.[3] This is illustrated in Figure 22.1, using inventories as an example. The graph assumes that the cost

---

[1] See J. Johnson, et al., "Problems in Corporate Liquidity." *Financial Executive* (March 1980), pp. 44-53.

[2] See J. Johnson, et al., "Identifying and Resolving Problems in Corporate Liquidity." *Financial Executive* (May 1982), pp. 41-46.

[3] The marginal cost or benefit curve is the first derivative of the total cost or benefit curve. At the point at which marginal benefits equal marginal costs, the slope of the total cost and total benefit curves are identical; this is a necessary condition for the distance between the two curves to be at a maximum.

of carrying inventories increases proportionately with the level of inventories, which is often a reasonable approximation. Consequently, the marginal costs of carrying additional inventories are constant. On the other hand, marginal benefits typically decrease as more current assets are carried. For instance, initial investments in inventories are likely to have a major impact on the efficiency of production and the quality of customer service. As additional inventories accumulate, however, improvements in these areas become less pronounced, with benefits increasing at a decreasing rate. The optimal level of inventory is at the point at which marginal benefits equal marginal costs because here, the difference between total benefits and total costs is largest. Similar arguments can be made for investments in accounts receivable or for the holding of cash or marketable securities.

Just as with any other investment, we see that funds should be provided to expand current assets so long as such commitments yield positive net returns. The main difference between investments in current assets and fixed assets is the time frame of the analysis. Because current assets are expected to revert to cash in the near future, benefits are not normally discounted to derive net present values (NPVs), but rather are compared with costs on a period-by-period basis. As current assets tend to be relatively low-risk investments, a large proportion can normally be financed through short-term debt, and their financing cost is commonly taken as the after-tax interest cost on short-term bank borrowings.[4]

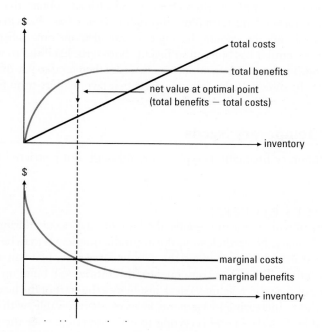

FIGURE 22.1

Optimal Investment in Inventory: Marginal Benefits Equal Marginal Costs

---

[4] Although useful as an approximation, we should recognize that this approach need not be entirely correct. First, inventories can often be financed in part through trade credit that may not entail direct costs. Second, some portion of current assets normally has to be financed with more permanent sources since most firms will maintain current ratios (current assets/current liabilities) that exceed one. The firm's weighted average cost of capital may be more appropriate for this portion of permanent funding.

The practical difficulties of translating this general framework into specific decisions stem from our inability to measure the relevant cash flows as accurately as we would like. For example, the benefits from increasing inventories depend not only on the change in probabilities of stockouts but also on the costs associated with such stockouts. Loss of customer goodwill because of delivery delays, which is often of major concern in this context, is very elusive and typically classified as an "intangible." Also, costs and benefits from investments in current assets may be subject to significant fluctuations over relatively short time periods. Consequently, decisions need to be constantly adapted. For example, in an expanding and prospering industry, liberal credit policies may entail little risk; but if the same policies are maintained through a recession, losses from bad debts could become significant. The exercise of informed judgement in estimating various costs and benefits in a timely manner is a key ingredient of good working capital management.

The Use of Short-Term Liabilities

Firms may draw on short-term liabilities to finance their operations for three main reasons. First, the need for funds may be only temporary. For example, it would be wasteful to finance seasonal peaks on a permanent basis because the company would then have excess cash balances in off-seasons, incurring higher financing costs than necessary. Second, debt with shorter maturities is often cheaper and easier to obtain than long-term debt. Finally, because raising long-term funds through an issue of securities in capital markets is "lumpy" with significant amounts having to be raised at one time, a firm may draw on temporary sources until it has built up sufficient short-term liabilities to warrant new long-term financing. The proceeds from such an issue are then used to pay off short-term obligations. We briefly discuss each of these aspects that favour short-term financing.

Financing of Temporary Needs

The need for temporary financing is typical for, although not restricted to, seasonal businesses.

SEASONAL SALES PATTERNS

For manufacturers of winter sporting goods, the bulk of sales occurs during the period from October to January. Nevertheless, uniform production levels may be maintained throughout the year in order to retain a stable labour force and obtain an efficient utilization of production facilities. As a consequence, inventories will build up throughout the first two-thirds of the year, reaching a peak just before the start of the heavy sales season. Large sales lead to increasing investments in accounts receivable, with both inventories and receivables liquidated and reverting to cash sometime after the peak selling period or early in the new year. Actual sales, production, and investments in current assets may follow the patterns shown in Figure 22.2.

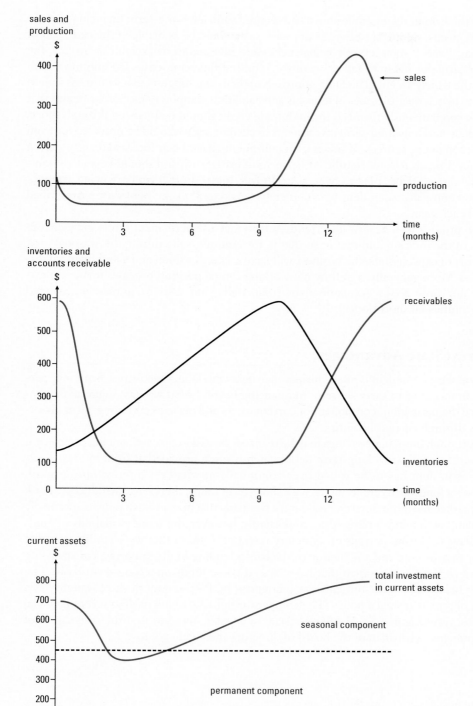

FIGURE 22.2

Seasonal Sales: Production, Inventories, and Accounts Receivable as a Function of Time

If the firm in the example above had secured sufficient long-term financing to meet its peak needs, significant balances of excess cash would be available in the early half of the year. Even if such temporary balances were invested in marketable securities, the return earned is likely to fall short of the required financing costs. To minimize such costs, the widely accepted hedging approach to financing suggests that a business should strive to match the maturities of its assets and liabilities. Temporary increases of assets that are not spontaneously financed through trade credit should be financed through short-term debt, and only long-term investments in current assets should be provided for from more permanent sources. If financial requirements have been forecasted accurately, a firm never needs to have significant balances of excess cash and should be able to liquidate all current debt at least once a year. In fact, many short-term borrowing arrangements require that such debt be completely repaid and off the books for a prescribed period each year.

To protect itself against uncertainty, a firm may use permanent funds somewhat in excess of the indicated minimum so that if, for example, sales during the seasonal peak fall short of expectations, the business will have a safety cushion and avoid financial difficulties. More generally, a healthy net working capital position provides financial flexibility not only to meet unanticipated shortfalls, but also to pursue unexpected opportunities on short notice.

Interest Rate Advantages

Because short-term debt is often cheaper than debt with longer maturities, firms may perceive an incentive to carry short-term financing beyond what was just suggested and to finance the permanent component of current assets and perhaps even long-term investments through current liabilities.[5]

Although immediate savings may be realized, the risks of such financing policies are obvious. In contrast to long-term debt, which is often provided at fixed interest rates, short-term debt has to be rolled over continually at whatever interest rates prevail. Financing long-term requirements with short-term funds, therefore, introduces the risk of unpredictable future interest costs, and a company that pursues such policies essentially speculates with interest rates. More importantly, however, the actual availability of funds can change. During periods of monetary restraint, sources that were readily available earlier may dry up, and a reduction in the bank's lending limits can prove embarrassing or lead to trouble for a firm that has invested those funds on a long-term basis. The report below shows the difficulties experienced by Patriot American Hospitality as a result of pursuing such a policy. The company eventually found itself in severe financial distress, resulting in a $3.45-billion rescue by outside investors and the resignation of the company's chairman of the board of directors and chief executive.

---

[5] Recall from Chapter 6, that the yield curve of interest rates is upward-sloping a large percentage of the time, which implies that short-term rates are quite often below long-term interest rates.

■ *Finance in the News*

Patriot Chief Resigns Amid Restructuring: Rescue for Hotel Chain

Investors Leon Black and Thomas Lee announced a US$3.45-billion rescue of U.S. hotel chain Patriot American Hospitality Inc. The financial rescue is in the form of $1 billion in direct investment and $2.45 billion in loans to cover Patriot's $3-billion debts, which will come due at the end of 2000. The company will be renamed Wyndham International Inc. after its upscale hotel division. James Carreker, who had managed this division, will replace Paul Nussbaum as the new CEO of the renamed company. The Dallas-based hotel company ran into trouble when it used short-term financing to acquire properties that would only be profitable in the long term.

Source: "Patriot Chief Resigns Amid Restructuring: Rescue for Hotel Chain," by Adam Steinhauer, *Financial Post* (*National Post,*) March 2, 1999, p. C12. *Reprinted with permission.*

Stop-gap Financing

The use of short-term debt as a stop-gap measure while preparing for a new long-term issue is common. For example, although long-term debt may be viewed as a permanent part of a firm's capital structure, sinking fund features that require a gradual retirement of an outstanding issue are often prescribed. Such payments could be financed through short-term borrowings, with another long-term issue placed once short-term liabilities reach a level that warrants the new offering. New long-term financing could also be delayed temporarily in anticipation of falling interest rates by relying on short-term borrowings. We have already noted the risks associated with such a strategy.

Overall, selection of the appropriate level of current liabilities is once again subject to the familiar trade-off between risk and expected returns or between efficiency and flexibility. An overly liquid company, with current assets that exceed current liabilities by a wide margin incurs little risk but sacrifices profit potential. On the other hand, a firm that attempts to minimize costs by maintaining high current liabilities relative to current assets may maximize expected profits but at the expense of increased risk of illiquidity. The optimal balance depends on not only the risk attitudes of managers and shareholders but also on the characteristics of the particular business. When cash flows are highly predictable, safety margins in net working capital can be more modest than would be appropriate for businesses that operate in less-stable environments.

International Considerations

For firms operating internationally, foreign exchange exposure can be an important consideration in managing current assets and liabilities. Foreign exchange risk and its management affects both short-term and long-term assets and liabilities. A review of this topic was provided in earlier chapters, most notably in Chapter 21.

22.3 CASH MANAGEMENT

Cash management is concerned with determining the cash balances that will adequately sustain the operations of the company, managing the firm's payments and collections to ensure efficiency, and investing any temporary surplus funds in liquid assets such as marketable securities in order to earn a return.

When dealing with cash management, we should appreciate the difference between profitability and liquidity. A firm is liquid if it can meet its obligations as they come due, whereas profitability implies that a company's revenues exceed the costs incurred in producing these revenues. For example, a profitable firm can go bankrupt by becoming illiquid through an overcommitment of funds to new long-term investments. On the other hand, a business that has been unprofitable for some time may remain solvent by drawing on cash balances built up in the past or by liquidating assets. Just as capital budgeting decisions are crucial in determining long-term profitability, the liquidity of a firm hinges on its cash management. In any volatile environment, cash management has to be an ongoing process. Financial officers must devote a relatively high proportion of their time to this responsibility.

P E R S P E C T I V E S

Corporate Manager

A company that has too much money tied up in cash may be missing out on opportunities to earn additional returns for its shareholders. However, a company that does not maintain sufficient cash reserves runs the risk of having the company become illiquid, which often entails even more severe consequences for shareholder wealth.

Investor

Investors should monitor company measures of liquidity such as cash levels as well as the current and quick ratios (discussed in Chapter 3). These measures should be compared to identical measures for similar companies in order to obtain an indication of whether the company appears to be too aggressive or too conservative in its cash management policies since the investors ultimately bear the costs of either of these decisions.

Proper cash management is essential to the financial well-being of any corporation (or any individual, for that matter). This is evident in the report below, which discusses the crashes of the share prices of many "e-tailors." This market reaction was largely attributed to the concerns of investors that many of these companies would not survive because "they are spending cash reserves at a faster rate than they can be replenished."

■ *Finance in the News*

More Online Retailers Feeling the Heat: But Amazon.com Gets Some Relief from Upbeat Report

Shares of dozens of small Internet retailers (e-tailers) have crashed amid fears that "they are spending cash reserves at a faster rate than they can be replenished." The shares of online health information provider Drkoop.com fell 26 percent in a single day due to investor profit taking. Just a few days before, the company had announced that it had arranged US$1.5 million

in short-term financing. Drkoop has been short of cash for months. In fact, in mid-June, *Barron's* magazine stated that the company had only 45 days of cash remaining.

Experts are predicting the demise of many e-tailers, which will simply run out of cash reserves before they can generate sufficient revenue. Other Internet retailers will probably be the victims of competition. For example, e-tailer HomeGrocer.com has been taken over by rival Webvan Group Inc. for US$1.2 billion. HomeGrocer was spending its cash reserves at the rate of more than US$25 million per month and was expected to be out of money within a year.

Source: "More Online Retailers Feeling the Heat: But Amazon.com gets Some Relief from Upbeat Report," by Stephen Miles, Financial Post (*National Post*), January 27, 2000, pp. D1, D4. *Reprinted with permission.*

We note that in the context of our discussion, cash has to be broadly defined. It includes all demand deposits at banks and other financial institutions as well as term deposits and investments in marketable securities that can be converted into cash on short notice. (Such assets are often called "near-cash.") Furthermore, firms may also make payments by overdrawing their accounts and relying on lines of credit or other short-term borrowing arrangements. A company's short-term borrowing capacity is directly related to its cash management.

We start by briefly reviewing the motives for holding cash. We then discuss the typical flow of funds through a business and the forecasting of cash requirements through cash budgeting. Next, we explore how a firm can manage its payments and collections efficiently. Finally, we look at the risk-expected return trade-off in determining actual cash balances and consider how surplus funds may be invested temporarily in marketable securities.

MOTIVES FOR HOLDING CASH   22.4

Economists have analysed and categorized the various reasons for maintaining cash balances. We can identify the transactions motive, the precautionary motive, the speculative motive, and the finance motive for holding cash. A brief review of these motives provides a useful framework for the analysis of cash management.

The **transactions motive** looks at the holding of cash to meet current transactions. The need for spare cash to transact business arises because cash inflows do not always equal outflows, and there are definite and often fixed costs involved in converting even highly liquid assets such as marketable securities into cash. Consequently, it is both impractical and expensive to make such conversions too frequently and for small amounts each time. Even as individuals, we do not withdraw cash from our savings accounts several times a week in $10 amounts simply because to do so would prove inconvenient and time-consuming. Reasonable cash balances are, therefore, maintained to meet daily transactions and to minimize the nuisance and costs of having to replenish holdings too frequently. The amount of cash held depends on the typical volume of business and possibly on the interest that can be earned if excess cash is invested.

The **precautionary motive** focuses on cash balances that are held to provide a cushion for unexpected events such as business declines. During economic downturns, sales may fall below expectations, resulting in reduced cash inflows. At the same time, outflows could prove higher than was budgeted, for example, due to unanticipated price level changes. Because of such uncertainties, some cash in excess of anticipated requirements may be maintained. In this context, the term "cash" is used broadly to include near-cash and even unused short-term borrowing capacity.

The **speculative motive** arises when cash is held to take advantage of special situations such as sudden price declines or increases in interest rates. For instance, an investment manager may temporarily hold large balances of cash in anticipation of a further rise in interest yields or declines in security prices. Similarly, manufacturing or trading enterprises purchasing raw materials that are subject to cyclical price fluctuations may build up cash in order to acquire inventories when prices are relatively low.

Finally, the **finance motive** for holding cash deals with the buildup of funds required to finance capital budget appropriations, dividend payments, and other large outlays. Cash (again defined in a broad sense) may have to be accumulated over an extended period of time to finance such "lumpy" expenditures.

We see from the above that the determinants of cash management are reasonably complex since the various motives are normally superimposed on one another. Furthermore, circumstances vary depending on the particular business situation, making it impossible to derive rules that are universally applicable for the determination of optimal cash balances. Instead, we have to consider general principles and techniques that can then be applied to specific situations in order to arrive at actual decisions.

22.5 FLOW OF FUNDS

Before dealing with the details of cash budgeting, it is useful to examine the typical flow of funds through a business. As shown in Figure 22.3, such flows can be depicted as a circular movement originating from a pool or source that is the outgrowth of capital originally contributed by the owners. In most instances, this pool is augmented by credit received from lenders including suppliers. Available funds are then committed to expenses of operations, the purchase of fixed assets, and to governments in the form of taxes or royalties. As sales are generated and accounts receivable collected, funds flow back to replenish the pool. Miscellaneous inflows, through the sale of fixed assets, for example, also add to the cash reservoir, whereas additional outflows include interest on and repayment of debt as well as dividends paid to shareholders.

Of considerable importance to cash management and cash budgeting are the time lags that are typically encountered in this circular flow of funds. Thus, operating costs are incurred to produce in-process and finished goods inventories. Normally, items remain in inventory for some time before sales are made. Further delays are incurred until accounts receivable are collected and cash flows back into the business. Funds will be required to bridge these time lags and to finance investments in inventories and accounts receivable.

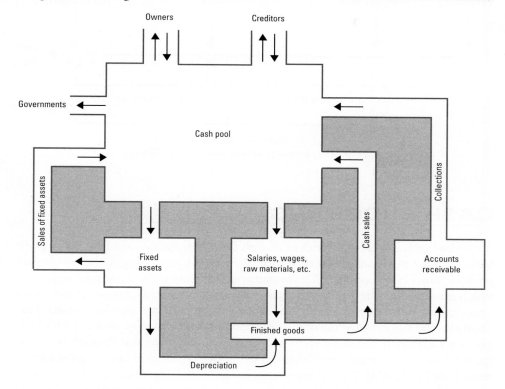

FIGURE 22.3

Typical Flow of Funds through a Business

TIME LAGS IN CASH FLOWS

EXAMPLE

Consider a wholesaler who purchases goods on terms of net 10 and sells on terms of net 60. With an inventory holding period (or days inventory) of 90 days (which translates into an an inventory turnover ratio of 4.56 times), the time lag between cash outflows required to procure goods and the time until collections are made on sales is 140 days, as shown in Figure 22.4.[6] Hence, 140 days of average daily purchases will have to be financed. If, for example, annual purchases increase by $1 million so that daily purchases rise by 1,000,000/365 = $2,740, this implies increased investments in current assets (inventories and accounts receivable) of $2,740 × 140 = $383,600 for which funds will have to be found.

The example above illustrates why time lags in the flow of funds are important in preparing cash budgets. It also shows that a combination of such time lags with growth in sales (real or inflationary) can pose problems in the procurement of funds. Finally, we note that seasonal peaks in sales can have a major impact on a firm's cash flows and may necessitate temporary borrowing to finance buildups in inventories and receivables. We expand on this below.

---

[6] This time lag is often referred to as the firm's cash conversion cycle.

FIGURE 22.4

Time Lags in the Flow of
Funds and their Impact
on Financing

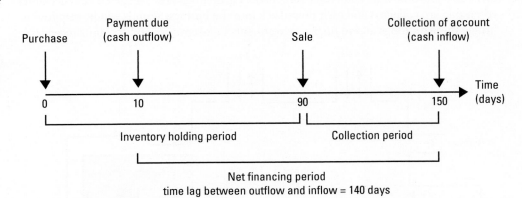

Time pattern of typical purchase and sale:

FIGURE 22.4

Time Lags in the Flow of
Funds and their Impact
on Financing

22.6 CASH BUDGETING

A cash budget is a detailed forecast of all cash flows into and out of a firm over a given period. Rather than being concerned with profits or account changes, the cash budget projects actual cash receipts and disbursements including their cumulative impact on cash balances. The budget period may cover a year or more, and it may be broken down on a monthly, weekly, or even daily basis depending upon the company's operating characteristics and the intended use of the projections. Because they are detailed, cash budgets are particularly useful for short-term forecasting; projections through *pro forma* financial statements (which were reviewed in Chapter 4) are more common for longer-term financial planning. If *pro forma* statements and cash budgets are based on a consistent set of assumptions and projections, they obviously have to lead to identical forecasts of the firm's future cash position, albeit using different formats. In showing the magnitude, timing, and duration of any expected cash shortage or surplus well in advance, the cash budget is essential in planning for adequate external financing or the temporary investment of excess funds. Also, cash budgets are often required by banks as part of loan applications, and, in this context, they usually prove to be useful control tools.

Preparation of the Cash Budget

The preparation of a cash budget may require inputs from many departments within the firm, and the accuracy of the budget depends directly on the reliability of these inputs. After deciding on the time period to be covered and the breakdown of this period into smaller segments, the financial manager must first obtain a forecast of sales or revenues for the budget period. This is the most crucial estimate for financial planning, because most other variables depend on the sales forecast.

Based on the sales forecast, schedules of purchases, production, and inventories are drawn up so as to meet anticipated demand. Projected payments and collections are derived from these schedules in accordance with current experience, leading to detailed schedules of inflows and disbursements from operations. Finally, we add non-operating cash flows such as capital expenditures and flows associated with financing to obtain a complete cash budget.

PREPARING A CASH BUDGET

EXAMPLE

Consider the preparation of a cash budget for a merchandising company covering the six-month period from July to December broken down into monthly segments. The firm retails a single product that it sells at $10 per unit. Forecasted sales are as follows:

Month	Sales forecast (in units)
July	1,000
August	1,000
September	1,000
October	1,200
November	1,500
December	1,200
January	1,200

All sales are credit sales on terms of net 30, and experience indicates that 75 percent of accounts receivable are collected one month following the date of the sale, with the balance collected after two months. No bad debts are expected. Table 22.3 indicates the firm's expected cash receipts from sales during the budget period. We note how seasonality in sales affects the magnitude and timing of cash inflows.

The forecast of cash outflows is also based on the sales forecast. Assume that the business purchases enough units each month to cover sales expected during the following month. Purchase terms are net 30, and the company avoids any stretching of its accounts payable. Costs of purchase are $7 per unit, wages paid are $1,000 per month, and miscellaneous operating expenses (excluding depreciation) are $1,500 per month.

Table 22.3

Schedule of Cash Receipts

	May	June	July	August	September	October	November	December
Sales	$8,000	$9,000	$10,000	$10,000	$10,000	$12,000	$15,000	$12,000
Collections: on previous month's sales		6,000	6,750	7,500	7,500	7,500	9,000	11,250
on sales 2 months previous			2,000	2,250	2,500	2,500	2,500	3,000
Total collections			$8,750	$9,750	$10,000	$10,000	$11,500	$14,250

Know this for exam

Table 22.4

Schedule of Cash Disbursements

	June	July	August	September	October	November	December
Purchases	$7,000	$7,000	$7,000	$8,400	$10,500	$8,400	$8,400*
Cash outflows:							
Accounts payable		7,000	7,000	7,000	8,400	10,500	8,400
Wages		1,000	1,000	1,000	1,000	1,000	1,000
Miscellaneous		1,500	1,500	1,500	1,500	1,500	1,500
Total operating outflows		$9,500	$9,500	$9,500	$10,900	$13,000	$10,900

*Based on expected January sales of 1,200 units.

By combining Tables 22.3 and 22.4 and adding non-operating cash receipts and disbursements, we obtain a typical, though simplified, cash budget as shown in Table 22.5. Incorporated are an assumed receipt of $750 from the planned sale of a fixed asset in September, dividend payments of $100 in August and November, income tax payments of $1,000 in September and December, and loan payments (including interest) of $100 per month. As the budget demonstrates, a policy requiring minimum cash balances of $1,000 for precautionary reasons would entail borrowing beginning in July and building up to $3,350 by November. The large negative cash flows in October and November are caused by payments on larger purchases made in anticipation of the seasonal peak. By December, increasing collections result in a large net inflow that can be used to reduce borrowings. We note that if the cash budget had been prepared on a quarterly basis, the large outflows in October and November would have been averaged with the inflows for December, and this would have concealed the true peak in cash requirements. When sales are seasonal, care has to be taken to choose a basic time period that is small enough so that temporary peaks in the requirement for funds are fully disclosed.

Table 22.5

Cash Budget

	July	August	September	October	November	December
Receipts:						
Total sales receipts	$8,750	$9,750	$10,000	$10,000	$11,500	$14,250
Sales of fixed assets			750			
Total receipts	$8,750	$9,750	$10,750	$10,000	$11,500	$14,250
Disbursements:						
Operating expenses	$9,500	$9,500	$9,500	$10,900	$13,000	$10,900
Dividend payments		100			100	
Income taxes			1,000			1,000
Loan payments	100	100	100	100	100	100
Total disbursements	$9,600	$9,700	$10,600	$11,000	$13,200	$12,000
Net cash flow	($850)	$50	$150	($1,000)	($1,700)	$2,250

Beginning cash balance	$1,000	$1,000	$1,000	$1,000	$1,000	$1,000
Ending cash balance	150	1,050	1,150	0	(700)	3,250
Minimum cash balance	1,000	1,000	1,000	1,000	1,000	1,000
Net borrowing (repayment)	$850	($50)	($150)	$1,000	$1,700	($2,250)
Cumulative borrowings	$850	$800	$650	$1,650	$3,350	$1,100

The cash budget, like any other forecast, is invariably subject to uncertainty. Deviations from the budget are likely, and the numbers should be revised as new information becomes available. As a consequence, cash budgeting becomes a continuous process. For instance, if sales for a given month were below expectations, we need to consider whether sales forecasts for subsequent months should be adjusted accordingly. Computerization has made continuous updating and extended analyses feasible at minimal cost and inconvenience. Given the uncertainty inherent in operating environments, it is also helpful to prepare separate cash budgets for alternative forecasts of key variables since this highlights the risk that the firm may face. For example, if sales during the seasonal peak fell 10 percent short of the values forecasted, what would the impact be on the firm's cash position and its ability to meet payments on its short-term debt? Based on such analysis, we can determine the safety margin to be maintained on cash balances.

We illustrate the trade-off between risk and expected profitability by pursuing the example above. According to Table 22.5, cumulative borrowings of $3,350 are anticipated by November with a substantial repayment of $2,250 projected for December. Assume that a short-term loan with the bank has been arranged based on these figures and that actual sales in September exceed forecasts. The firm may take this as an indication of a good season and commit itself to increased purchases in October, thus requiring additional funds. Should sales for November then prove disappointing, the company may sit on unsold inventory and find itself unable to meet previously contracted loan repayments. To protect against such a contingency, the borrower could have arranged for a larger loan. However, although risk would have been reduced, this is achieved at a price. If subsequent results actually deviate in the opposite direction with cash requirements below those projected, the firm would incur unnecessary financing costs and reduce its profitability.

We will continue our analysis of optimal cash balances below. First, we briefly look at various techniques that enable a firm to manage its collections and payments efficiently.

MANAGING CASH FLOW 22.7

In managing cash flows, the basic approach is to ensure that inflows are received as soon as possible and that payments are not made any sooner than necessary. Such a policy maximizes the firm's available cash.

The first step in attempting to speed up collections involves prompt invoicing including interim billing on lengthy contracts and negotiating possible advances on large specialized orders. Credit and collection policies are discussed further in the next chapter.

Next, it is necessary to ensure the efficient handling of receipts. The majority of business payments are made by cheque. When a customer mails a cheque, several days generally elapse before the payment can be credited to the recipient. Time is lost while the cheque is in the mail, and until it is cleared.[7] The time that elapses from the initial mailing until the funds are available to the recipient is called the **float**. Since cheque clearing in Canada is highly automated and efficient, the main source of float is the time that cheques spend in the mail and possibly with the recipient before being deposited.

Clearly, float works to the disadvantage of the company that is collecting and to the advantage of the business making payment. For firms with large collections, reducing the float even by one day can be significant. For instance, a firm with annual sales of $100 million will have average daily collections of $274,000; thus, speeding up collections by one day will free up this amount of cash for the company's use.

Two commonly used techniques employed to reduce mail float include **concentration banking** and **lock boxes**. Under concentration banking, customers are instructed to make payments to the firm's closest office, which deposits collections daily into a local branch bank account. The bank, in turn, concentrates the individual branch balances into a central account. As internal bank transfers are effected within the same day and branch banks are closer to the customers, mailing time can be reduced.

This system can be streamlined further through lock boxes. Here, the firm establishes local, locked post office boxes that customers use as mailing addresses for their payments. The local bank branch is authorized to empty these boxes and deposit the receipts, cancelling the need for the company to handle cheques and make deposits. Some Canadian banks even offer selected lock box services in the United States, and banks will assist customers in devising an optimal system of concentration banking with or without lock boxes using sophisticated computer-based modelling techniques.

Finally, when appropriate, pre-authorized payment services can be used to eliminate any float, since customer accounts are automatically debited by the bank on the payment date. In addition, this system simplifies invoicing and eliminates late payments. More advanced electronic collection systems such as electronic funds transfer (EFT) and electronic data interchange (EDI) systems eliminate mail and processing float entirely.

On the disbursement side, the main concern is to ensure that payments are not made before they are due except when cash discounts make an early payment advantageous. A firm may even stretch its payables. Although minor delays in payments are common, a systematic abuse of credit privileges is likely to entail indirect costs in terms of lost goodwill and a deteriorating credit rating. As mentioned, any float provides the advantage of delaying the date on which funds are actually withdrawn from the account.

Many firms use a centralized body to control and time disbursements as efficiently as possible. In addition, rather than keeping cash balances in several accounts to pay cheques, companies often have their funds concentrated in a central account. Funds are then transferred from this account to individual accounts referred to as zero balance accounts (ZBA) as cheques are presented against these accounts. This reduces the need for excess cash in aggregate since the balance in the concentration account is generally lower than the total that would be required to maintain balances in several accounts. Firms also typically tie their operating loans to this central account, which reduces the total amount of borrowing.

---

[7] The cheque is deposited by the recipient at the bank, but the bank may not credit the account until it has received payment from the issuer's bank.

OPTIMAL CASH BALANCES AND INVESTMENTS IN MARKETABLE SECURITIES

22.8

A business must decide on the total amount of liquid reserves it wishes to hold (including cash, marketable securities, and access to short-term borrowing). Normal and unanticipated payments can be made from such reserves, and they determine the firm's liquidity or its ability to meet obligations in the short term. The company also has to apportion this liquid reserve between cash and demand deposits, investments in marketable securities, and possibly open lines of credit. The objective is to minimize the overall costs (including opportunity costs) of holding reserves.

Optimizing Cash Balances

In holding cash balances, the firm invariably faces an opportunity cost, since such funds are withdrawn from productive investments that otherwise should yield at least the company's cost of capital. At the same time, we saw that cash balances are held for good reasons and provide benefits to the firm. Conceptually, the optimal cash balance is one in which the marginal benefits from holding additional cash just equal the marginal opportunity costs. Given the complexity caused by various motives for holding cash including the need to act as a buffer in a volatile and uncertain environment, formal derivations of such an optimum are difficult.

Empirical evidence suggests that the transactions and precautionary motives are of particular importance in determining cash balances in business. In terms of the transactions motive, cash can be essentially viewed as a commodity that, like raw materials, is required to sustain the operations of the firm. Therefore, one may attempt to apply inventory control methods to the management of cash, although this has met with only limited success.

The precautionary motive, which is often critical, relates to ensuring that the firm has sufficient liquidity to avoid financial embarrassment in what is generally an unpredictable environment. Clearly, the trade-off here is between risk and expected returns. Tight cash management increases the risk of insolvency, whereas excessive holdings of unproductive cash balances detract from the firm's profitability. The balance between these conflicting objectives will be influenced by the volatility of the company's operations and by the opportunity costs of holding excess cash. For example, a firm in a stable operating environment can afford lower liquidity; similarly, a business that suffers severe capital rationing and, as a result, has a high opportunity cost for funds will be tempted to reduce its liquidity. In spite of attempts to formalize these trade-offs, optimal cash balances are mostly determined through judgement essentially because information that would allow a statistical quantification of risk is seldom available.

Obviously, cash management is particularly important for large businesses with substantial absolute amounts. Difficulties arise because most large firms have decentralized operations, and decentralization is only meaningful if it includes at least some local control over cash flows. On the other hand, cash management can be much more effective if it is optimized from the point of view of the overall firm. Cash management often entails a delicate balance between the interests of decentralized operations and centralized financial control. As discussed previously, the use of centralized accounts may improve overall cash management. Alternatively, banks may give customers access to their bank accounts through computer terminals installed on the customer's premises, with the ability to obtain instant information about cash balances broken down or aggregated in a variety of ways (such as by branch, by organizational unit, or by region). Customers can also initiate transfers of funds between various accounts and obtain other information such as foreign exchange and money market rates. Finally, various cash budgeting and cash flow planning models can be accessed through such terminals.

We see that in recent years, some of the greatest improvements in cash management have come through the introduction of electronic communication and transfer systems. This area, which may ultimately result in full-fledged electronic funds transfer systems, is subject to continued rapid developments that, no doubt, will have an impact on future cash management.

Investments in Marketable Securities

A firm can live with minimal cash balances if it has unused short-term borrowing capacity such as unused lines of credit that it can draw on to pay its obligations. Short-term borrowing is discussed in Chapter 24, and the extent to which a firm relies on short-term debt becomes part of its overall strategy regarding capital structure. At the same time, temporary surplus cash balances may accrue for a variety of reasons. Such balances may arise in the ordinary course of business or they may be built to meet larger outlays due on specific dates such as tax or dividend payments. Excess funds are typically invested in short-term securities that provide a return but involve limited risk and are quite liquid, allowing for rapid conversion into cash at a fair price should the need arise. Various types of short-term securities that are available for investment purposes were reviewed in Chapter 2 and will be discussed again in Chapter 24.

When investing temporary cash balances, the following factors must be considered:

1. The amounts to be invested and/or the period over which the funds are available for investment should be sufficiently large to cover transaction costs and to justify the managerial time required to arrange and oversee such investments.

2. In the choice of securities, we must deal with the typical risk versus expected return trade-off.

3. The balance between holdings of cash and marketable securities needs to be determined based on anticipated returns and transaction costs.

We briefly discuss each of these considerations.

Investment of temporary surplus cash is of limited interest to small businesses simply because typical balances are of an insufficient size, and the costs of buying and selling securities, including the management attention required, would likely exceed the returns. Consequently, although a small company may obtain some return on excess balances through a savings account, it is unlikely to be involved in managing a portfolio of money market instruments. In large firms, on the other hand, periodic cash buildups may warrant attention even if they are available only for a few days. For example, assuming an effective annual return of 6 percent on short-term paper, the availability of $1 million for just 10 days would result in a gross return of approximately $1,644. Such investments may be important to many larger businesses, which often have specialists in their finance departments to manage the productive investment of excess balances.

Individuals charged with investing the firm's surplus cash face the typical risk and expected return trade-off. When investing in debt instruments, the risks include default, interest rate risk, and the risk of not being able to convert the security into cash at a fair market price on short notice. Some of the more commonly used investment vehicles include repurchase agreements (also called repos), negotiable certificates of deposit, commercial paper, Bankers' Acceptances, and Eurodollar securities.

Repurchase agreements entail an arrangement whereby a bank or security dealer sells specific marketable securities to the firm and agrees to repurchase them at a specified later date (often the next day) and for a specified price. Thus, the company faces minimal risk and can obtain investments with tailored maturity dates. In return, the expected yield may be somewhat lower than if the same securities were bought without a repurchase agreement. In terms of usage, Eurodollar securities experienced the largest rate of increase in recent years, indicating greater international sophistication by financial managers. Clearly, if investments are denominated in foreign currencies, foreign exchange risk has to be considered. At the same time, treasury bills seem to have lost some of their earlier appeal, mainly because of their comparatively low yield.

The importance of liquidity for short-term investments will in part depend on the predictability of the firm's anticipated cash flows. Ideally, the maturity of any investment should be matched with the anticipated duration of a cash surplus. Concerns about liquidity become relevant only when projections do not materialize and when the invested cash is required sooner than anticipated. If under such circumstances securities have to be liquidated at depressed prices, this can more than offset any interest that was earned over the investment period. On the other hand, a large portfolio committed entirely to treasury bills or commercial paper is likely to be more liquid than necessary with income being sacrificed as a consequence. Referring back to the various purposes for which cash or near-cash may be held, it is useful to divide portfolio holdings into:

1. instruments convertible into cash on demand that are used to provide for general liquidity
2. securities maturing on or near specific payment dates, relating, for example, to taxes, dividend payments, or capital expenditures
3. longer-term notes for general contingency purposes

In the absence of transaction costs, the financial manager's strategy should be one of keeping the firm's cash balances close to zero by investing any net inflows and selling off security holdings to cover net outflows. The split between cash and marketable securities is basically determined by transaction costs that make it impractical to carry out small adjustments to investment holdings on a continuous basis. Consequently, investments must be limited to situations in which returns are expected to exceed transaction and management costs.

22.9 SUMMARY

1. Efficient utilization of working capital is important due to the effects on profitability and liquidity of a firm. Conceptually, the optimal levels of investment in current assets occur when marginal costs equal marginal benefits.

2. The use of short-term liabilities is primarily used to satisfy temporary, seasonal needs. Short-term funding may act as a stop-gap measure while temporarily postponing long-term financing, or while waiting for requirements to have grown sufficiently to warrant a public issue of long-term securities.

3. Cash management is concerned with determining the optimal cash balances that a business should carry. The proportion of assets that a firm should maintain in cash derives from the imposition of the transaction motive, the precautionary motive, the speculative motive, and the finance motive on each other.

4. The flow of funds in a business can be depicted as a circular movement. Funds are committed to expenses of operations, purchases of fixed assets, servicing of outstanding capital, and payment of taxes. As sales are generated and accounts receivable collected, funds flow back to replenish the pool. Investment in inventories and accounts receivable result in time lags in the flow of funds.

5. A cash budget is a detailed plan that lays out projected cash inflows and outflows over a given period. The cumulative net flow determines the cash balance that will be available, or the amount of borrowing that will have to take place.

6. Excess balances of cash may be invested temporarily in marketable securities. Anticipated returns should exceed transaction and management costs.

QUESTIONS AND PROBLEMS

Questions for Discussion

1. What are the marginal benefits and the marginal costs of holding additional cash or near-cash? How would you attempt to estimate these marginal benefits and costs in a specific situation? Why do they change over time?

2. Discuss the trade-off between risk and expected return that a company faces in the context of:

    (a) allowing net working capital to decline

    (b) increasing the yield on the firm's holdings of marketable securities

    (c) minimizing holdings of cash and near-cash

    (d) hedging foreign exchange exposure

3. Why and how do changing interest rates affect an enterprise's policies in the area of working capital?

4. Is the cash budget affected by the amount of capital cost allowance (CCA) taken? Discuss.

5. How can a firm shorten the time lags involved in the flow of funds as illustrated, for example, in Figure 22.4? What are the trade-offs in contemplating such actions?

6. What are the main determinants that influence how far into the future a cash budget should be projected and the basic periods into which the cash budget is to be broken down?

7. Define the term liquidity from the point of view of a business that invests in marketable securities. What are some of the factors that influence the liquidity of a particular type of security?

8. What are some of the risks that investors face when they invest in debt instruments? From the point of view of a firm investing temporary short-term cash, which of these risks are typically of greatest concern?

PROBLEM WITH SOLUTION

Problem

Christmas Cracker Corp., a subsidiary of Party Stuff Inc., manufactures novelties for the Christmas trade for nine months of each year. The corporation owns no assets except for $75,000 in earnings retained from previous years which are lent without interest to the parent corporation for the idle three months of the year, but that are available as cash at the beginning of the season in July. Christmas Cracker has access to funds from Party Stuff and for purposes of budget forecasting, interest is charged at an annual rate of 7 percent on the average amount of the loan outstanding for whatever time a loan is needed. Interest is paid at the end of the season.

Sales forecasts for the coming season are as follows:

July	$ 6,000
August	50,000
September	400,000
October	600,000
November	500,000
December	200,000
January	6,000

Ten percent of sales are in cash, 40 percent of sales are collected after 30 days, and the remaining 50 percent, after 60 days. Costs of goods sold—80 percent of sales—are incurred in the month in which the sale is made. These goods are paid for 30 percent in cash and 70 percent within 30 days. Selling and administrative expenses are $10,000 per month plus 1 percent of monthly sales during the selling season, and are zero in months when there are no sales. Start-up costs in July are $30,000, and taxes for the entire operating period paid in April are 40 percent of net income. Christmas Cracker feels that it is necessary to maintain a minimum cash balance of $25,000 during the selling season.

(a) Prepare a cash budget for Christmas Cracker for the coming fiscal year, which starts July 1, broken down by months.

(b) Calculate net income for the coming fiscal year.
(c) Prepare the cash budget on a quarterly basis. Comment on any inadequacies of such a quarterly budget compared to the monthly budget prepared under (a).

Solution

(a) The first step in the preparation of the cash budget is to calculate the amount and timing of all receipts and expenditures. These are found in Table 22.6.

Table 22.6

Christmas Cracker Corporation

Schedule of Inflows and Outflows

	July	August	September	October	November	December	January	February	March
Sales	$6,000	$50,000	$400,000	$600,000	$500,000	$200,000	$6,000	—	—
Receipts from sales:									
cash (10%)	600	5,000	40,000	60,000	50,000	20,000	600	—	—
net 30 (40%)	—	2,400	20,000	160,000	240,000	200,000	80,000	2,400	—
net 60 (50%)	—	—	3,000	25,000	200,000	300,000	250,000	100,000	3,000
Total collections	$ 600	$ 7,400	$ 63,000	$245,000	$490,000	$520,000	$330,600	$102,400	$ 3,000
Total cost of goods sold	$4,800	$40,000	$320,000	$480,000	$400,000	$160,000	$4,800	—	—
Cash disbursements:									
cash (30%)	1,440	12,000	96,000	144,000	120,000	48,000	1,440	—	—
30 days (70%)		3,360	28,000	224,000	336,000	280,000	112,000	3,360	—
Total payments on cost of goods sold	$1,440	$15,360	$124,000	$368,000	$456,000	$328,000	$113,440	$3,360	—

Next, we calculate sales and administrative expenses as $10,000 plus 1 percent of sales for the period July-January:

July	$10,060
August	10,500
September	14,000
October	16,000
November	15,000
December	12,000
January	10,060

Based on this and the information supplied above, we can prepare the monthly cash budget as shown in Table 22.7

Table 22.7

Christmas Cracker Corporation

Monthly Cash Budget

	July	August	September	October	November	December	January	February	March
Opening cash balance	$75,000	$34,100	$25,000	$25,000	$25,000	$25,000	$25,000	$207,740	$306,780
Cash collections	600	7,400	63,000	245,000	490,000	520,000	330,600	102,400	3,000
Cash balance before disbursements	$75,000	$41,500	$88,000	$270,000	$515,000	$545,000	$355,600	$310,140	$309,780
Payments on cost of goods sold	$1,440	$15,360	$124,000	$368,000	$456,000	$328,000	$113,440	$3,360	
Sales and administrative expenses	10,060	10,500	14,000	16,000	15,000	12,000	10,060	—	
Start-up costs	30,000	—	—	—	—	—	—	—	—
Total disbursements	$41,500	$25,860	$138,000	$384,000	$471,000	$340,000	$123,500	$3,360	
Net balance at end of month	$34,100	$15,640	($50,000)	($114,000)	$44,000	$205,000	$232,100	$306,780	
Less: desired level of cash	25,000	25,000	25,000	25,000	25,000	25,000	25,000	25,000	
Net borrowing (repayment)	—	9,360	75,000	139,000	(19,000)	(180,000)	(24,360)	—	
Total loan outstanding	—	$9,360	$84,360	$223,360	$204,360	$24,360	—	—	

(b) Remembering that Christmas Cracker has no assets to depreciate, earnings before interest and taxes are simply given as the difference between the ending cash balance from operations in March and the beginning cash balance in July. Interest is taken on the average amount over the total time a loan was outstanding. Thus:

$$\text{Interest} = \frac{(9,360 + 84,360 + 223,360 + 204,360 + 24,360)}{12} \times .07$$

$$= \$3,184$$

Cash on hand at the end of March	$309,780
Cash on hand at the beginning of July	75,000
Earnings before interest and taxes	$234,780
Interest	3,184
Earnings before taxes	$231,596
Taxes (40%)	92,638
Net income for period	$138,958

Note that there is a further cash outflow in April consisting of taxes ($92,638) and interest ($3,184).

(c) The quarterly budget is prepared by combining the figures from the monthly budget as derived under (a).

	July–Sept.	Oct.–Dec.	Jan.–March
Opening cash balance	$ 75,000	$ 25,000	$ 25,000
Cash collections	71,000	1,255,000	436,000
Cash balance before disbursements	$146,000	$1,280,000	$461,000
Payments on cost of goods sold	$140,800	$1,152,000	$116,800
Sales and administrative expenses	34,560	43,000	10,060
Start-up cost	30,000	—	—
Total disbursements	$205,360	$1,195,000	$126,860
Net balance at end of quarter	($ 59,360)	$ 85,000	$334,140
Less: desired level of cash	25,000	25,000	—
Loan outstanding	$ 84,360	24,360	—

Note that according to this quarterly budget, the maximum loan outstanding is shown as $84,360. From the monthly budget under (a), we found that the loan outstanding at the end of October amounts to $223,360. We see that temporary peaks may be concealed when budget information is aggregated into longer time periods.

ADDITIONAL PROBLEMS

1. A firm purchases raw material inventory on terms of net 30. It sells its products on terms of net 60. It has an inventory turnover ratio of 9.125.

    (a) If sales are normally $15 million per year and annual purchases are two-thirds of sales, how much cash (or line of credit) will be required to fund the purchases?

    (b) If the company projects that next year's sales will increase by 10 percent, how will its requirements for funds to finance inventory change?

2. A firm currently has sales of $40 million per year. Cost of goods sold run at 60 percent of sales. It sells its products on terms of net 45, and purchases are on terms of net 90. The company's inventory holding period ("days inventory") is 60 days. The firm is considering the adoption of a just-in-time inventory system, and if it does so, purchases will only be made just before they are required. The result would be that the inventory holding period would fall to just 10 days. If it adopts this system, what will be the change in the funds required for funding purchases?

3. A firm has a days inventory ratio of 10. It is able to purchase goods on terms of net 30, but it makes sales on terms of net 10. What can you say about the company's needs for funds to finance inventory purchases?

4. Student Services Incorporated acts as a wholesaler to the various student retail shops that operate on campuses throughout Canada. It supplies clothing, records, and confectionary items. The company has a $75,000 line of credit with a local bank, and it draws on its account in amounts of $5,000 at a time. As at December 31, the firm had a cash balance of $7,000, which is the minimum balance that it wants to maintain. The following additional information is available.

Actual sales		Forecasted sales	
October	$100,000	January	$100,000
November	75,000	February	50,000
December	50,000	March	30,000
		April	100,000
		May	70,000
		June	70,000

Accounts Receivable: Terms are net 30 days. From past experience 50 percent of the accounts are collected within a month, 40 percent within 60 days, and 10 percent within 90 days. Bad debts are negligible.

Accounts Payable: Accounts are paid promptly at the time of purchase.

Cost of Goods Sold: The goods are ordered, received, and paid for in the month prior to sale. This makes up 90 percent of sales.

Administrative Expense: The administrative expense is $3,000 per month plus a bonus of 4 percent of gross sales realized during the last quarter of the calendar year. This bonus is paid in February of each year.

Dividends: In March, $6,000 in dividends will be paid.

Taxes: The tax rate is 40 percent. For the past year, $2,000 in taxes must be paid by January 15, and no other taxes are payable in the period January to April.

Salaries: Wages and salaries amount to 15 percent of the monthly dollar sales or $12,000, whichever is greater.

Capital Expenditures: No capital expenditures are planned.

Prepare a cash budget for the period January to April inclusive. In your budget, show the amount and timing of any bank borrowings. Is there a problem?

5. Prepare a cash budget for Carly Corp. for August, September, and October given the following information: as of July 31, the firm had a balance of $30,000 in cash, which Carly considers the minimum amount to have on hand. Forty percent of sales are for cash with the remaining sales collected equally in each of the following two months. Bad debts are negligible. Actual and projected sales are given as follows:

Actual sales		Forecasted sales	
April	$100,000	August	$140,000
May	100,000	September	160,000
June	120,000	October	200,000
July	120,000	November	200,000

Manufacturing costs are 70 percent of sales with 90 percent of these costs paid during the first month after they are incurred and the remaining 10 percent paid in the second month. Capital cost allowance amounts to $30,000, $32,000, and $36,000 for August, September, and October. Sales and administration expenses are $20,000 per month plus 10 percent of monthly sales. All of these expenses are paid in the month incurred. A semi-annual interest payment of $18,000 on outstanding bonds (6 percent coupon) is paid during October. A $100,000 sinking fund payment must also be made in October along with payments of $20,000 in dividends and $2,000 in taxes. Finally, the company plans to invest $80,000 in plant and equipment in September.

(a) Based on the above information, what is the cumulative borrowing of the firm in August, September, and October?

(b) Suppose that August receipts from sales come in uniformly during the month (assume a 30-day month), but payments for cost of goods manufactured, and sales and administrative expenses are made on the twelfth day of the month. How would this affect the cash budget for August prepared under (a)?

6. As a company's newly appointed treasurer, you notice that its cash balances regularly exceed $1 million. You appreciate that an opportunity to invest in money market instruments is being missed. Current annual yields are 6 percent in the one-to-six-months range, but they could rise slightly.

   Total transaction costs associated with each investment are estimated at $20,000. If $1 million in surplus cash is available for six months and three-to-six-month rates are expected to rise and settle at 9 percent in two months, would you elect to invest for two or for three months initially?

   Show all computations and state all assumptions. Taxes may be ignored.

7. The company for which you work makes purchases on terms of net 30. Its sales are now on terms of net 60. Currently, sales are $25 million per year, and cost of goods sold is 75 percent of sales. The average inventory level is 20 percent of cost of goods sold. The firm operates in a competitive industry in which customers are very sensitive to the payment terms offered. Your company is considering revising the terms offered to customers. However, if the business shortens the period until payment is required from customers, it knows that it will lose some sales. Specifically, the firm has forecast that for every day it shortens the financing period offered to customers, sales will decrease by 1 percent (e.g., if it offers terms of net 50, sales will decrease by 10 percent). Use a spreadsheet to calculate the company's funding requirements for purchases at different financing terms offered to customers. Create a plot of funding requirements versus sales terms.

"How Much for That Chisel in the Window?"

"... handle with hardwood scales complete with spots of wood filler. A tough, ugly tool that is perfect for the person whose usual solution is to use a larger hammer," reads one item of copy from the 1999 Lee Valley Tools catalogue. It's this straightforward approach to its products, together with a reputation for quality products and exceptional customer service, that has earned this family-run business based in Ottawa, Ontario, a following more devoted than most congregations. Lee Valley Tools has plenty of loyal-and some downright fanatical—customers in Canada. But many a woodworker and gardener from the United States, Asia, or Europe also pores lovingly over-and orders frequently from-the handsomely designed, unusually literate pages of its catalogues.

Lee Valley has nine storefronts across Canada, but their sales are also catalogue based; instead of open shelves of stock, the stores feature cases displaying the products, which customers ask for at the counter by catalogue number. This set-up is a significant advantage to a retailer in terms of managing inventory, since orders can be filled efficiently from a single central warehouse.

Business at Lee Valley is not as cyclical as at many retailers. "We sell a lot of gift items before Christmas, certainly—but we also sell a lot of gardening things in spring," points out Brenda Lamothe, responsible for accounts receivable. "And a lot of our gift sales are as gift certificates," so from an inventory point of view, the sales occur year round.

Otherwise, Lee Valley's receivables management is fairly typical of a mid-sized retail company. "For catalogue sales to individuals, we accept Visa or MasterCard, or they can pre- pay with a cheque. Or we can send items COD in Canada," says Ms. Lamothe. International customers can send a bank transfer, "but for the most part people send a cheque or money order in U.S. dollars."

The company has such large U.S. sales, in fact, it produces a separate American edition of its catalogue, with U.S. shipping information and prices in U.S. dollars.

Everyone pays the same price, though there are volume discounts available on some items. "Our terms are also the same for everyone on account—net 30 days," explains Ms. Lamothe. "We get a rating from Dun & Bradstreet when a new customer applies for credit." Some elements of the family-run business remain in this company of 500 employees, however; "a school would get an account automatically," Ms. Lamothe allows.

Not all Lee Valley policies follow traditional business rules. The company will sometimes stock-or even manufacture-an item that is not actually likely to be profitable, but is useful to some customers and is impossible to find elsewhere (such as a folding Japanese dozouki saw). But business is booming after 22 years, so founder Leonard Lee must be doing something right.

chapter 23

Receivables and Inventory Management

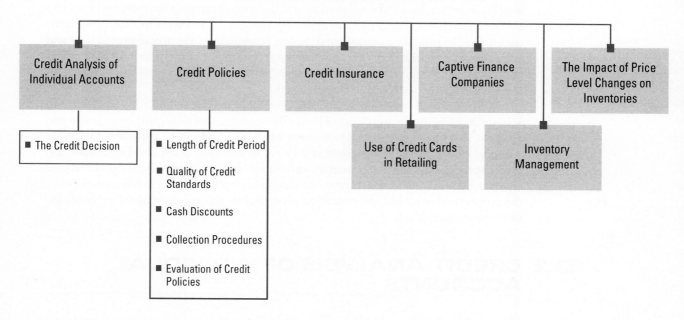

Learning Objectives

After studying this chapter, you should be able to:

1. *Discuss accounts receivable and inventories.*
2. *Name four major policy variables in the area of credit management.*
3. *Discuss the trade-offs between benefits from anticipated sales and the costs of carrying an account.*
4. *Compare the different types of insurance available against bad debts.*
5. *Explain the different benefits and costs involved in inventory control.*

23.1 INTRODUCTION

For most firms, accounts receivable and inventories are the largest categories of current assets, and they almost invariably arise in the process of doing business. Inventories are required at various stages of the production and distribution process and range from raw material inventories, through work in process, to finished goods. Accounts receivable are amounts that customers owe and result from trade credit granted for the purchase of goods or services.

The carrying of inventories and the granting of trade credit produce benefits for the company. Larger inventories, for example, may result in more efficient production and improved customer service, while more generous trade credit may stimulate sales. These benefits, however, have to be weighed against the costs of carrying the increased asset levels. Such costs include storage and financing charges. Investments in these assets ultimately have to produce a net gain and, hence, contribute to the overall profitability and economic value of the firm. This implies the commitment of funds as long as marginal benefits exceed marginal costs. In this chapter, we discuss how to apply this guideline to determine the optimal levels of current assets.

We begin by noting that an account receivable for the selling firm represents an account payable for the purchaser. Hence, the management of accounts receivable and accounts payable are concerned with many of the same variables, albeit from opposite points of view. Whereas trade credit as a source of financing is discussed in Chapter 24, this chapter reviews the investment in account receivable. Specifically, we deal with the credit analysis of individual accounts, the setting of overall credit and collection policies, the use of credit insurance, the evaluation of receivables management, and the role of captive finance companies.

23.2 CREDIT ANALYSIS OF INDIVIDUAL ACCOUNTS

The purpose of credit analysis is to assess the credit worthiness of potential customers and the corresponding risk of late payments or default. Such credit analysis consists of:

1. the gathering of information about the potential customer
2. the analysis of this information to derive a credit decision that establishes the terms of payment and the maximum amount of trade credit to be granted

Various sources of information are available to assist in credit investigations of prospective customers. As the gathering of comprehensive credit information can be time-consuming and expensive, the costs of such investigations have to be weighed against their potential benefits, which include a reduced risk of bad debts. Obviously, a large order from a new customer with potential for further development will warrant more comprehensive credit checks than a small routine order.

Important sources of credit information are commercial rating agencies such as Dun & Bradstreet (D&B), which monitors over 60 million companies around the globe. Credit agencies prepare both general credit ratings and comprehensive credit reports on individual firms. They gather financial data and analyse the firm's operations, managerial efficiency, competitive position, and past dealings with creditors including suppliers. On the basis of these inputs, companies are rated, and conclusions are condensed into symbols as shown in Table 23.1. The comprehensive individual reports include a summary of the rating, simplified financial statements, details of maximum credit obtained from key suppliers, promptness of payments made, banking background, history of the company, and some insight into operations. Excerpts from such a credit report are reproduced in Figure 23.1.

Table 23.1

Dun & Bradstreet Credit Ratings

Estimated Financial Strength*				Composite Credit Appraisal*			
				HIGH	GOOD	FAIR	LIMITED
5A		Over	$50,000,000	1	2	3	4
4A	$10,000,000	to	50,000,000	1	2	3	4
3A	1,000,000	to	10,000,000	1	2	3	4
2A	750,000	to	1,000,000	1	2	3	4
1A	500,000	to	750,000	1	2	3	4
BA	300,000	to	500,000	1	2	3	4
BB	200,000	to	300,000	1	2	3	4
CB	125,000	to	200,000	1	2	3	4
CC	75,000	to	125,000	1	2	3	4
DC	50,000	to	75,000	1	2	3	4
DD	35,000	to	50,000	1	2	3	4
EE	20,000	to	35,000	1	2	3	4
FF	10,000	to	20,000	1	2	3	4
GG	5,000	to	10,000	1	2	3	4
HH		up to	5,000	1	2	3	4

* In these ratings, estimated financial strength refers to tangible net worth (tangible assets minus all liabilities), while composite credit appraisal encompasses the more subjective evaluation of managerial ability, business prospects, and past treatment of creditors. Thus, a rating of 1A-2 refers to a firm with an estimated financial strength of between $500,000 and $750,000 and a good composite credit appraisal.

Although abbreviated financial statements are supplied with most credit reports from commercial agencies, a complete set of the firm's current financial statements may also be requested directly from the customer. In addition, banks often assist their clients in gathering credit information. Additional credit material may be obtained from such miscellaneous sources as better business bureaus, trade associations, and credit bureaus. Finally, if a company has had prior dealings with a prospective customer, past experience with the account obviously is a prime source of information, which the firm can also exchange with other companies with whom the client has done business.

FIGURE 23.1

Business Information Report

Dun & Bradstreet

Please note whether name, business and street address correspond with your inquiry.

BUSINESS INFORMATION REPORT

BASE REPORT

SIC	D-U-N-S	© DUN & BRADSTREET	STARTED	RATING
34 62	04-426-3226	CD 34 APR 7 19--	1957	DD1
	ARNOLD METAL PRODUCTS CO	METAL STAMPINGS		

53 S MAIN ST
TORONTO ON M4E 2V6
    TEL 416 925-6218

SAMUEL B. ARNOLD)
GEORGE T. ARNOLD) PARTNERS

SUMMARY

PAYMENTS	DISC PPT
SALES	$177,250
WORTH	$42,961
EMPLOYS	10
RECORD	CLEAR
CONDITION	STRONG
TREND	UP

PAYMENTS*

HC	OWE	P DUE	TERMS	APR 1 19--	SOLD
3000	1500		1-10-30	Disc	Over 3 yrs
2500	1000		1-10-30	Disc	Over 3 yrs
2000	500		2-20-30	Disc	Over 3 yrs
1000			30	Ppt	Over 3 yrs
500			30	Ppt	Over 3 yrs

FINANCE

On Apr 7 19-- S.B. Arnold, partner, submitted statement Dec 31 19--:

Cash	$ 4,870	Accts Pay	$	6,121
Accts Rec	15,472	Notes Pay (Curr)		2,400
Mdse	14,619	Accruals		3,583
	------------			------------
Current	34,961	Current		12,104
Fixed Assets	22,840	Notes Pay (Def)		5,000
Other Assets	2,264	NET WORTH		42,961
	------------			------------
Total Assets	60,065	Total		60,065

19-- sales $177,250. Gross profit $47,821. Net profit $4,204. Fire insurance on merchandise $15,000, on fixed assets $20,000. Annual rent $3,000; lease expires 19--.
    Signed Apr 7 19-- ARNOLD METAL PRODUCTS CO, by Samuel B. Arnold, partner. Johnson & Singer, C.A., Toronto.
    -----O-----
    Sales and profits increased last year due to increased sub-contract work, and this trend is reported continuing. New equipment was purchased last Sep for $8,000, financed by a bank loan, secured by a lien on the equipment, payable $200 per month. With increased capacity, the business has been able to handle a larger volume. Arnold stated that for the first two months of this year, volume was $32,075 and operations continue profitable.

BANKING

Medium to high four-figure balances are maintained locally. An equipment loan is outstanding, and being retired as agreed.

HISTORY

Style registered Feb 1 1965 by partners. SAMUEL, born 1918, married. 1939 graduated Queens University with B.S. degree in Mechanical Engineering. 1939-50 employed by Industrial Machine Limited, Toronto. 1950-56 production manager with Aerial Motors Ltd., Toronto. Started this business in 1957. GEORGE, born 1940, single, son of Samuel. Graduated in 1963 from Ryerson Polytechnical Institute. Served RCAF 1963-64. Admitted to partnership interest Feb 1965.

OPERATION

Manufactures light metal stampings for industrial concerns, and also does some work on a sub-contract basis for aircraft manufacturers. Terms net 30. 12 accounts. Employs 10, 5 production, 2 office employees, one salesman, and 2 partners. LOCATION: Rents one-storey cinder block building with 5,000 square feet, located in industrial section, in normal condition. Housekeeping is good.
4-8 (802 92)

* This section summarizes the firm's payments history with other suppliers. "HC" refers to the highest credit granted by that particular suppliers during the past year, "Disc" indicates that discounts were taken, "Ppt" indicates that payments have been prompt. Also included are amounts still owed, past due, and the creidt terms offered.

Source: Dun & Bradstreet Limited. *Reprinted with permission.*

The Credit Decision

Once credit information has been gathered, it must be analysed so that a credit decision can be reached. In general, the evaluation is aimed at establishing the applicant's liquidity, which, in turn, determines the applicant's ability to meet short-term obligations. In this context, financial analysis and projections, as discussed in Chapters 3 and 4, are often useful. However, financial ability and responsible behaviour toward creditors do not always coincide, and in addition to financial capacity and collateral, credit managers are concerned with assessing the applicant's attitude or character.

When a large number of new accounts have to be processed on a regular basis, point systems have been devised whereby numerical values are assigned to specific characteristics, and the applicant's total score serves at least as a preliminary screen in determining credit decisions. However, ultimate decisions are usually based on judgement. The final decision regarding the acceptance or rejection of a particular applicant and the maximum amount of trade credit to be granted entails an economic trade-off. Rejection may involve not only the loss of the current order but also the loss of any future orders that might have been placed. Assessing the magnitude of this loss is difficult since assumptions about the size and timing of future orders and about the customer's future paying habits have to be made. On the other hand, if the decision to accept an applicant proves incorrect, the net loss will be the amount of bad debts less the value of past profits that the firm realized on that customer's account. Since a customer's financial position can change rapidly particularly in a volatile economic environment, a periodic reappraisal of past credit decisions and a constant surveillance of critical accounts are essential.

On occasion, the credit decision may be partially a function of factors that do not relate to the applicant. For instance, a marginal customer's request for credit may be accepted when the supplier is operating below capacity, though an identical order would be turned away during normal or peak times. This is particularly significant in industries in which suppliers face high fixed and relatively low variable costs of production.

CREDIT POLICIES 23.3

A firm's credit and collections policy is mainly determined by the trade-off between higher profits from increased sales on the one hand and the costs of having to finance investments in accounts receivable and of additional bad-debt losses on the other. In light of this trade-off, we consider the evaluation of alternative credit policies based on the following policy variables:

- length of the credit period
- quality of credit standards
- cash discounts
- collection procedures

Length of Credit Period

Selling terms often entail a credit period, a cash discount, and a discount period. Thus, terms of 2/10 net 30 indicate that a customer is given a 2 percent discount if the bill is paid within 10 days of the invoice date. Failure to pay by the tenth day requires payment of the full amount within 30 days of the date of invoice. Hence, the discount period is 10 days, and the total credit period 30 days. Although industry practice often influences credit terms, there is little reason not to consider such terms as a competitive tool that can be altered.

To evaluate the suitability of lengthening the credit period, we must weigh the profits from added sales against the costs of increased receivables and bad-debt losses. We will also have to assess likely reactions by competitors and the effects of a longer credit period on the firm's cash budget.

EXAMPLE

CHANGING THE CREDIT PERIOD

A product is characterized as follows:

Current selling price	$5 per unit
Average cost	$4.50 per unit
Current annual sales	360,000 units
Current terms of sale	net 30

The firm contemplates an extension of its credit period to terms of net 60. Allowing for the reaction of competitors, it is anticipated that such a move will produce the following results:

1. Sales are expected to increase to 420,000 units.

2. Because of the additional 30 days it now takes to learn if a customer is delinquent, bad-debt losses are expected to increase by $6,000 per year.

The marginal cost per unit for the increased number of units to be produced is $3. The firm's tax rate is 40 percent, and its required minimum rate of return on such investments is 10 percent after tax.

In deciding whether or not the credit period should be extended, we first compute the increase in after-tax profits that results from the expected increase in sales. We obtain:

Increase in sales	60,000 units × $5	$300,000
Marginal cost of increased sales	60,000 units × $3	180,000
Increase in bad debts		6,000
Increase in costs before financing charges		186,000
Before-tax operating profit from additional sales		$114,000
After-tax operating profit	114,000(1 - .4)	$68,400

This incremental operating profit must be weighed against the cost of higher investments in accounts receivable. Assuming that all customers pay at the end of the credit period, the amount of receivables outstanding will increase from 30 days' sales to 60 days' sales. We have:

Sales per month at old level	$= 360,000 \times 5 \times \frac{1}{12}$
	$= \$150,000$
Sales for 2 months at new level	$= 420,000 \times 5 \times \frac{2}{12}$
	$= \$350,000$

This requires an investment of $200,000 in added receivables.[1]

To achieve an annual after-tax return of 10 percent on this investment, annual after-tax profits from operations would have to increase by $0.10 \times 200,000 = \$20,000$. Since the expected increase was calculated to be $68,400, the firm should proceed with the proposed change. Even if sales do not increase to 420,000 units per year as anticipated, the firm has a wide margin of safety because the expected increase in operating profits ($68,400) far exceeds the required financing charges on the additional receivables ($20,000).

However, we note two simplifying assumptions that underlie our analysis. First, we assume that the increase in sales does not require additional investments in fixed assets. This is valid only when a firm does not operate at full capacity. Second, we assume that incremental changes in sales that result from a change in credit policy do not require adjustments in other current assets. If, for example, an increase in sales requires additional investments in inventories, the costs of such added investments must also be recognized.

The hurdle rate or financing cost commonly used in evaluating alternative credit policies is the interest rate on short-term bank loans. This is reasonable, because receivables are generally a low-risk investment that can be financed largely through such debt. Hence, it would be inappropriate to apply a cost of financing that embodies a substantial risk premium such as the weighted average cost of capital (WACC).

Speeding up collections through curtailment of the credit period can be evaluated in the same manner. The greatest practical difficulties in such evaluations do not lie in the basic approach but in estimating the various consequences of altering the credit terms, including competitive reactions and the effects on sales, bad debts, and production costs. This makes it important to carry out sensitivity analysis in order to assess how vulnerable the ultimate conclusion is with regard to changes in the various forecasts. Furthermore, decisions regarding credit policy need to be re-evaluated continually since many of the underlying variables (such as interest rates or capacity constraints) can be subject to rapid change.

---

[1] Although the firm's actual investment is only the cost of these receivables and excludes the profit component, we base our analysis on the full amount (i.e., $200,000) since it captures the opportunity cost of not receiving cash from a sale at an earlier date.

Quality of Credit Standards

Alternative credit standards can be evaluated in a similar manner. A change in credit standards influences sales because a lowering of minimum requirements results in the acceptance of additional accounts of an inferior quality. Again, the increased sales potential has to be viewed against increasing losses from bad debts and additional carrying costs. Furthermore, acceptance of lower-quality accounts may imply slower payments and increasing costs of surveillance and collections.

Cash Discounts

Discounts on the selling price are commonly offered if payment is made at an early date. The purpose of cash discounts is to provide an incentive for early payments, in order to reduce the firm's investment in accounts receivable. On the other hand, such discounts reduce the profit margin on sales. Again, policies regarding cash discounts should be evaluated by weighing reductions in profits that result from discounts against the benefits of lower investments in receivables.

EXAMPLE

CASH DISCOUNT CHANGES

A firm offers terms of 2/10, net 30. Current sales are 600,000 units per year at a selling price of $5 per unit and an average cost of $4.50 per unit. Cash discounts are currently taken on 70 percent of the sales with payments received on the tenth day after the sale. For the remaining 30 percent of sales, payment is received in 30 days. The company's tax rate is 40 percent, and its required rate of return on investments in receivables is 10 percent after tax. The firm is considering elimination of the cash discount.

Assume that the total volume of sales would not be affected by such a move. Annual after-tax operating profits with the current policy are:
Annual after-tax operating profit

= [annual sales × (unit selling price − unit costs) − discounts given](1 − tax rate)
= [600,000(5 − 4.50) − (.7 × .02 × 600,000 × 5)] (1 −.4)
= (300,000 − 42,000) × .6
= $154,800

Under the new policy, discounts amounting to $42,000 (2 percent of 70 percent of annual sales) would be eliminated, increasing after-tax profits by 42,000 × .6 = $25,200 to a total of 300,000 × .6 = $180,000. We assume that under the new policy, all payments are made in 30 days. Thus, the 70 percent of sales on which discounts were previously taken will be outstanding for an additional (30 − 10) = 20 days. We have:

Daily sales = (600,000 × $5)/365 = $8,219
Daily sales on which discounts are currently taken = 0.70 × 8,219 = $5,753
Increase in receivables if discounts are eliminated   = 20 days of sales
                                                      = 20 × 5,753   = $115,060

Viewed against the annual increase in after-tax operating profits of $25,200, this incremental investment in receivables of $115,060 provides an annual after-tax return of 25,200/115,060 = 21.9 percent (well above the 10 percent cost of funds). Hence, discontinuation of the cash discount seems attractive.

Customers who in the past have taken advantage of such discounts may view their elimination as an indirect price increase and may react by investigating alternative sources of supply. Therefore, the assumption that sales would remain unaffected by an elimination of discounts would have to be validated before any final decision is taken.

Collection Procedures

Procedures for dealing with overdue accounts are a sensitive area of supplier-customer relations. The objective in establishing collection procedures is to maintain a balance between being overly aggressive and too relaxed. Should customers become irritated with collection efforts, they may well take their business elsewhere. This should be tolerated only if the lost customers are, in fact, unprofitable accounts.

In addition to interest being charged on overdue accounts, collection procedures typically consist of a series of steps that gradually increase the pressure on a customer. First, the customer may be sent a standard reminder that the account is past due, followed by a telephone call from the credit department. Continued failure to pay will prompt more formal correspondence, and a representative of the firm may call on the client. The final step involves either legal action or turning the account over to a collection agency. Both of these alternatives are costly, and fees paid to collection agencies can range up to 50 percent of any amounts eventually collected.

Clearly, the time and money spent on collection efforts should take into account the size of the outstanding balance and the likelihood of collecting. Exceptions are organizations such as banks and sales finance companies that are sometimes willing to spend more on their collection efforts than the actual sum to be collected. These institutions cannot afford to seem even remotely willing to write off bad accounts because such a policy may result in increased abuses by other customers who may withhold payments in the hope of being written off.

Evaluation of Credit Policies

The importance of implementing effective credit policies is discussed in the report below, which includes excerpts taken from an automotive wholesaler trade journal. The article suggests that "poor management of accounts receivable is one of many reasons that stores have been forced to close their doors." It goes on to suggest that "effectively managing your receivables not only keeps profits, it can also keep customers."

Unfortunately, the evaluation of how well a firm manages its accounts receivable is difficult particularly for an outsider. Commonly used indicators for assessing the quality of credit and collection policies include the turnover ratio of receivables and the average collection period supplemented perhaps by a more detailed ageing of accounts

■ *Finance in the News*

Managing Your Accounts Receivable Effectively: Helps Cashflow and Profits

An automotive wholesaler was profitable in a very competitive market, with strong sales and profit margins that were higher than the previous year. Nevertheless, the business was having trouble meeting payroll and paying suppliers because management had neglected to manage its accounts receivable. The main difference between an invoice and a payment is that the former is only in the mail, while the latter is actually in the bank. If revenue is not collected in a timely manner, trouble can ensue. Neglect of accounts receivable is a major reason for financial failure. "Poor management of accounts receivable is one of many reasons that stores have been forced to close their doors."

Accounts receivable management is a twofold process: credit management and revenue collection. Good credit management starts with understanding your clients and discovering the ones that are good credit risks. Collecting the money due to you is a matter of firm persistence—you must keep on top of things. "Effectively managing your receivables not only keeps profits, it can also keep customers."

Source: Jobber News, v.68(5), May 2000, pp. 14-15.

and an analysis of bad debts (as discussed in Chapter 3). Although widely used, these techniques are cursory and subject to biases if a company's sales pattern changes over time. Furthermore, such performance measures generally ignore the fact that decisions regarding credit policy involve both financial and marketing considerations. Hence, unless we have a detailed appreciation of various costs and also know how the firm's customers may react to any changes in credit policies, we cannot properly evaluate how well a company manages its accounts receivable.

PERSPECTIVES

Corporate Manager

Management must balance the increased costs of extending lenient credit terms to customers against the potential increase in sales and profits of doing so.

Investor

When evaluating a company's credit policy according to standard ratios such as the average collection period, investors should be sure to examine simultaneously ratios related to profit margins and growth in sales. This is because of the trade-off that exists between sales and profitability on the one hand and credit terms on the other. Because of this trade-off, above-average collection periods that are accompanied by above-average margins and/or growth in sales levels do not represent as big a concern as those that are not accompanied by such apparent benefits.

CREDIT INSURANCE   23.4

When receivables include a limited number of large accounts, credit insurance can be useful since default by a major customer could have serious financial consequences for a supplier. Credit insurance is designed to indemnify a firm for unexpected losses caused by the insolvency of its customers. However, such insurance coverage is often subject to various limitations and exclusions. For instance, under most insurance contracts, the amount recoverable for losses from any single account is limited, and the limit may depend on ratings by agencies such as Dun & Bradstreet. Furthermore, the normal loss experience that a particular company has come to anticipate may be excluded. Finally, so-called **co-insurance clauses**, or participating stipulations, may require the insured to bear a percentage of any loss incurred. These provisions aim at curtailing careless credit extensions by the insured.

In managing accounts receivable in an international context, additional problems arise. These were well described by the former chairman and president of the Export Development Corporation. He stated that:[2]

> ... financial aspects of export marketing pose different business problems than those encountered domestically. The commercial credit risks vary with and are complicated by the remoteness of geography and the differences of culture, language, legal systems, and business practice; all too often [they are] compounded by a scarcity of reliable information. These differences are further overlaid with the imponderables of political risks which bear heavily on foreign exchange availability. Finally, the competitive environment is very different, and all too often more ruthless, thereby frequently establishing a buyer's market for the foreign customer to choose amongst competing offers.

The Export Development Corporation (EDC) is a Crown corporation that operates as a commercial financial institution. It has done much to develop export trade and to facilitate the management of accounts receivable from foreign customers with particular emphasis on providing assistance to small- and medium-sized Canadian companies. For example, in 1999, the EDC supported over $40 billion in export and international investments through its 5,182 customers, of which 88 percent were small- and medium-size companies. As part of its wide-ranging activities, the EDC will insure Canadian firms against non-payment when Canadian goods and services are sold abroad. Risks covered include failure to pay because of insolvency, war or revolution in the buyer's country, and blockage of funds.

In the case of capital goods, in which sellers may have to offer intermediate-term credit in order to compete for the business, the EDC grants term loans to foreign

---

[2] J. MacDonald, "Financial Aspects of Selling to Export Markets," an address before the marketing conference of the Conference Board of Canada, Toronto, April 22, 1976.

buyers of Canadian capital equipment and technical services. It may also guarantee losses incurred by financial institutions making direct loans to such buyers.▲

The decision on whether to purchase credit insurance depends upon several factors including the financial strength of the credit-granting firm and, hence, its ability to absorb bad-debt losses. Insurance coverage can be costly and, like most other insurance, should only be purchased when unexpected losses may be of a magnitude that would severely affect the financial well-being of the firm.

23.5 USE OF CREDIT CARDS IN RETAILING

A retailer's management of accounts receivable can be influenced significantly by the decision to accept a general credit card such as Visa or MasterCard. These cards are sponsored and administered by the major Canadian banks and trust companies. By honouring such credit cards and limiting all other sales to cash, a retailer can dispense with credit decisions since the risk of losses from bad debts is shifted to the sponsoring bank. Invoicing and collection procedures are also unnecessary, and the retailer eliminates receivables because it receives cash immediately on depositing its sales slips with the bank. In return for these services, the retailer has to pay the bank a percentage on its credit sales. This percentage, which usually ranges between 2 and 6 percent, is determined primarily by the total volume of credit sales and by the average amount of each individual sale. In many ways, the acceptance of bank-sponsored credit cards by a retailer is similar to factoring. Factoring, which involves the sale of receivables to other companies, (factors) in return for financing, will be discussed in greater detail in Chapter 24. Factoring is mainly used by wholesalers and manufacturers, which do not sell to end-users.

In deciding whether or not to honour a particular credit card, we again have to weigh costs against the benefits in particular circumstances. For example, a business that operates on a small margin and competes mainly on price may find the costs of an extra few percent of sales prohibitive and may be forced to sell mainly on a cash basis. On the other hand, in cases in which some proportion of sales is attributable to impulse buying and markups are sizeable such as in the merchandising of fashion goods, the benefits provided by the acceptance of a widely held credit card often exceed the costs.

Some large retailers such as The Bay, Sears, and Zellers find it advantageous to retain the credit function and to administer credit through their own credit cards. This gives them more complete marketing information about their credit sales and credit customers. In addition, the term financing of receivables, which can be quite profitable, is retained.

23.6 CAPTIVE FINANCE COMPANIES

Firms that sell or manufacture high-cost equipment such as consumer durables and machinery occasionally establish wholly owned financing subsidiaries known as captive finance companies. Their purpose is to provide customers with term financing in the purchase of the company's products. Examples of firms that have established captive finance subsidiaries include Canadian General Electric and General Motors. The parent company sells financing contracts that arise from the sale of its products to its subsidiary, which in turn collects the customers' periodic payments.

Some businesses use captive finance companies because they believe that receivables can be financed at a lower cost. The assets of the finance subsidiary basically consist of financing contracts that provide predictable cash flows through the periodic payments made by customers. The subsidiary can borrow against these receivables, and, generally, such finance subsidiaries rely on a much greater proportion of debt financing than the parent company. As a consequence, it is argued that the cost of capital to the organization may be reduced. However, the validity of this position is questionable. In selling its receivables to a subsidiary, the parent company loses some of its better current assets. Consequently, the parent corporation's own debt capacity is reduced, and it appears likely that a simple transfer of debt capacity from parent to subsidiary has taken place.

An additional argument for captive finance companies, which essentially become financial institutions, is that their management is quite different from that of a manufacturing or trading enterprise. Consequently, the autonomy that results from a separate organizational entity can be beneficial.

INVENTORY MANAGEMENT 23.7

Although the control and management of inventories are not usually the direct responsibility of the financial manager, she may be expected to set broad guidelines on the matter since it is her responsibility to ensure that the firm's scarce funds are allocated efficiently.

As with other current assets, the concern is to balance the benefits and costs of carrying inventories. The actual benefits to be derived are varied. Increasing raw materials or purchased goods inventories may allow bulk purchases at lower prices. Higher in-process inventories may permit more efficient production, while added finished goods inventories could result in lower stockouts, hence improving customer service and sales. Finally, firms that face seasonal demands often carry seasonal inventories in order to level out production, thereby achieving a better utilization of equipment and a more stable labour force throughout the year. On the other hand, various costs such as the expense of warehousing, handling, insurance, obsolescence, spoilage, and financing are incurred in carrying added inventories.

An extensive body of technical literature attempts to quantify the trade-offs between these benefits and costs, and various models have been developed that have become a standard part of automated inventory control systems. Computers play a vital role in this context since firms often store thousands of different items. Through standard programs for inventory control, businesses can forecast demand routinely for each item based on previous sales, compute and adjust economic order quantities and order points, and keep up-to-date records on actual stock levels. Finally, through the use of computers, it becomes feasible to integrate inventory control with production planning, scheduling, and even some marketing and financial decisions. Such coordination obviously should lead to better overall decisions. The report below describes how the introduction of a new inventory management system at the Mississauga Hydro warehouse led to substantial costs savings and improved operating efficiency.

■ *Finance in the News*

**Tuning into New Automated Warehouse Technology:
Radio Frequency has Improved Inventory Management and Slashed
Costs at Mississauga Hydro Facility**

Mississauga Hydro's warehouse has undergone a transformation through its unique inventory system that uses scanners, PCs, barcodes, and radio frequency to efficiently control data collection of inventories. When the Intermec System Co. technology was installed in April 1995, the warehouse was inefficiently run by manual paperwork. Two-hour waits for materials were not uncommon, and there were no emergency weekend supplies. The $5 million in inventory in the warehouse—it processed $1 million in orders each month—was operating at only 60 percent accuracy.

　　Too many people see computers as the magical answer to just about everything, but it is all a matter of how they are used. For example, Mississauga Hydro had computers, but because data was still being collected manually, it had a very low accuracy rate. In less than a year, all that changed, and inventory accuracy soared to 98.6 percent. Systems consultant Geoffrey Dewhurst is confident that the company can reduce inaccuracy to "less than one percent." Other benefits of the new technology include savings of about $10,000 per year in overtime and for the salary of a data entry clerk, who is no longer needed. Also, because of shorter waiting times, line crews are on the road two hours earlier each day, and the lengths of cable and wire are more accurately measured out.

Source: Plant, v.55(6) April 22, 1996, pp. 10-11.

　　The main operational difficulties of inventory control involve accurate estimation of the relevant costs and benefits. For example, it is difficult to quantify the costs of being unable to fill a customer's order because of a stockout (including any loss of goodwill that may be reflected in lost future sales) or the marginal benefits to be derived from increasing inventory levels. In practice, therefore, we often have to work with rough estimates, and this limits the usefulness of sophisticated inventory control models. While a review of the extensive literature on inventory control is beyond the scope of this book, the decision as to what constitutes an optimal inventory level involves a basic trade off. The firm must trade off the carrying costs of holding inventory (as identified above) versus shortage costs (which were also discussed above).

We briefly describe four approaches to inventory management:

1. The ABC approach involves dividing inventory into three (or more) categories in relationship to their contribution to inventory value per unit. More attention is devoted to the management of higher-valued inventory items.

2. The economic order quantity (EOQ) model determines the optimal inventory level, which minimizes the total shortage and carrying costs. It relies on several technical assumptions to reach the conclusion that the minimum total cost occurs at the point at which carrying costs equal restocking costs. The EOQ model is useful for items that are sold evenly throughout the year; however, it is less valuable when inventory sales do not follow this pattern.

3. Materials requirement planning (MRP) refers to a computer-based system for ordering and/or scheduling production of demand-dependent inventory items. The basic idea is to determine the exact level of raw materials and work in process that must be on hand to meet finished-goods demand. With this capability and good sales forecasts, a company can run on extremely low levels of inventory.

4. Just-in-Time (JIT) inventory systems attempt to schedule delivery of raw materials and the completion of necessary work-in-process components exactly when they are required in order to reduce inventory to its lowest possible level. These systems were created and perfected by Japanese car companies that have close relationships with their suppliers.

A practical problem associated with the implementation of any inventory policy arises from the conflicting interests that different operating departments have regarding inventories. For instance, production and marketing departments normally are interested in high inventory levels: production, because its prime concern is with production schedules and costs that usually can be improved by allowing inventories to expand; and marketing, because it has to meet competitive pressures in customer service, which implies minimizing stockouts. The financial officer, on the other hand, is concerned with the best use of scarce funds and is likely to encourage the reduction of inventories in order to free resources for potentially more profitable employment elsewhere. These conflicting interests often result in friction and politicking. It is clear, however, that good overall decisions can be reached only if each party involved has a basic understanding of the more general overall implications that inventory decisions will have for the firm.

THE IMPACT OF PRICE-LEVEL CHANGES ON INVENTORIES

23.8

As we saw in Chapter 3, price-level changes can cause serious problems in financing and financial reporting. Inventories play a prominent role in this context because of their magnitude and their immediate susceptibility to price-level changes. For example, with the costs of most inventory items increasing during periods of inflation, firms have to commit larger amounts of cash even though the physical quantity of inventory on hand may remain unchanged. This can represent a serious drain of funds for the company, and it can also result in artificial changes in a company's financial statements. Thus, when other items on a company's balance sheet (such as fixed assets that are carried at historical costs) are not influenced by inflation, distortions in the relative magnitudes of various asset accounts can occur, with inventories representing an increasing portion of the total balance sheet amount.

As a further consequence of price-level increases, inventory profits accrue, and reported earnings may no longer accurately reflect the profitability of a firm's regular operations because they may be influenced by profits made from the holding of inventories. When a sudden major price change occurs in an industry's key commodity, the effects could be dramatic. Compounding the cash problem alluded to earlier is the fact that such inventory profits are subject to regular tax.

| EXAMPLE |

INFLATION AND INVENTORY PROFITS

Consider an inventory item that was bought some time ago for $1,000 per unit. The current cost to the firm of the inventory item has jumped to $2,000 per unit, and the corporate tax rate is 40 percent. If the firm sells one unit for $2,200 today, it realizes a net cash inflow of $1,720 per unit ($2,200 from the sale, minus $480 in taxes [(0.40 × $1,200)] on the inventory profit). If the company wants to stay in business, however, it faces an outflow of $2,000 per unit in replacing its inventory.

The problem of inventory profits is aggravated in Canada by the fact that the last-in, first-out (LIFO) method of inventory valuation is not acceptable for tax purposes. If, for example, the first-in, first-out (FIFO) method is used, the item that has been in inventory longest is deemed to be the one on which a current sale is based. Although this will result in a more accurate valuation of inventories for balance sheet purposes (inventory values will be closer to current costs), inflationary inventory profits become accentuated.[3]

We see that a sudden increase in price levels can simultaneously result in inflated earnings and cash shortages with the consequent temptation to increase prices in order to bolster cash inflows from sales. Needless to say, price increases at a time of high earnings elicit neither general understanding nor sympathy. Conversely, major decreases in the price of significant inventory items would have the opposite effect, depressing profits but enhancing cash flows. The impact of both inventory profits and losses could readily be observed in the oil industry following major price changes in that commodity in the 1970s and 1980s.

23.9 SUMMARY

1. For most firms, accounts receivable and inventories are the most important categories of current assets. Management is concerned with reaching optimal levels where the marginal benefits of added investment just equal incremental costs.

2. Returns from investments in accounts receivable are realized through increased profitable sales. Costs include the expense of financing and losses from bad debts.

3. Credit information on individual accounts is available from credit rating agencies, banks, other suppliers, and from customers themselves.

4. The cost of short-term bank borrowing is usually the cost of financing receivables. The most difficult aspect of credit analysis is the assessment of the effects of altered credit policies on sales and the estimation of bad debts.

5. Credit insurance is for accounts large enough that a default can cause serious financial difficulties for the supplying firm. For international sales, the Export Development Corporation provides export insurance and other assistance. In retailing,

---

[3] Revenue Canada recognizes both FIFO and the average-cost method for inventory valuation. However, because it is operationally easier to implement, the FIFO method is widely used. In order to minimize distortions in reported earnings, firms may use the LIFO method for internal reporting purposes.

acceptance of general credit cards sponsored by banks provides insurance against losses from bad debts and a reduced investment in accounts receivable. Captive finance companies are wholly owned subsidiaries set up by firms producing high-cost equipment in industries where extended credit is customary.

6. The main costs of inventories include warehousing, handling, insurance, obsolescence, spoilage, and financing. Price level changes can have a serious impact on inventories.

QUESTIONS AND PROBLEMS

Questions for Discussion

1. What are the major factors that a firm should consider before making a decision to lengthen or shorten the credit period?

2. In what ways might a change in credit standards affect a company's profit level? How would you assess the contribution to profits of accepting a new marginal account?

3. Discuss and critically evaluate the possible reasons for setting up a captive finance company.

4. What cost of financing should a firm use when evaluating alternative credit policies? Discuss.

5. What are some of the conflicts that could arise between the financial manager, the marketing manager, and the production manager regarding the desired inventory level?

6. Why are inventory levels in many companies subject to strong seasonal fluctuations? Give an example of an industry in which you would expect this to be the case. How could a firm in such an industry avoid seasonal inventories? What are the trade-offs?

7. What will be the effect on a corporation's inventories if the following actions are taken:
   (a) greater use of air freight for both purchases and shipments?
   (b) greater standardization of parts?
   (c) increases in the number of products produced?
   (d) the offering of discounts, if sales are seasonal, for orders placed in the slack season?

8. If interest rates go up and other things remain equal, how would you expect general inventory levels to be affected? Discuss.

9. During a period of continued inflation and other things remaining equal, would it be advantageous for firms to increase or decrease their physical level of inventories? Discuss.

PROBLEM WITH SOLUTION

Problem

business that currently sells on a cash basis only contemplates offering credit terms of net 30 in order to stimulate sales. Current sales are $6 million per year. If the proposal to offer credit terms is implemented, a credit department would have to be established at a monthly operating cost of $2,000. It is expected that all customers will take full advantage of the offered credit period. Losses owing to bad debts are estimated at 1.5 percent of credit sales. Additional investments in accounts receivable would be financed by drawing more heavily on a line of credit with the bank. The bank currently charges 12 percent interest on outstanding balances. The firm's tax rate is 40 percent. The cost of goods sold amounts to 60 percent of the selling price with variable marketing expenses at 25 percent of sales. By how much would sales have to increase to make the proposed change in credit policy worthwhile?

Solution

Current sales of $6 million yield a profit margin of 15 percent or $900,000 when the cost of goods sold (60 percent of sales) and variable marketing expenses (25 percent of sales) are deducted. Therefore, if the new credit policy is to be worthwhile, sales must increase to cover all credit expenses and still leave at least $900,000 in before-tax profits.

The annual costs of implementing the new credit policy are:

Cost of credit department $= 12 \times 2,000 = \$24,000$

Losses from bad debts $= 0.015 \times$ sales

If all collections occur at the end of the credit period, 30 days of sales (or 30/365 of annual sales) will be outstanding. We have:

Costs of financing receivables $= 12\% \times (30/365) \times$ sales

$\qquad\qquad\qquad\qquad\qquad\quad = .00986 \times$ sales

The 15 percent profit margin on the new sales level less all costs of implementing the new credit policy must yield at least $900,000. Solving the following equation, where x sales, we obtain:

$$.15_x - .015_x - .00986_x - 24,000 \;=\; 900,000$$

$$.12514_x \;=\; 924,000$$

$$x \;=\; \$7,383,730$$

Thus, sales must increase to $7.38373 million for the proposed change in credit policy to be worthwhile.

ADDITIONAL PROBLEMS

1. A small computer store is about to introduce credit terms of net 30 for its customers (before it required immediate cash payment). Previously, sales have been $750,000 per year, with cost of goods sold running 95 percent of sales. With the new credit policy, approximately 2 percent of accounts receivable will have to be written off as bad debts. Receivables are financed through the store's line of credit at an interest rate of 9 percent. To keep track of customer accounts receivable would require hiring a new employee at a cost of $25,000 per year. Assuming that all customers take the credit terms, to what level will annual sales have to increase for the introduction of the credit terms to be beneficial for the business?

2. Taran Ltd. is reviewing its credit policy. Currently, Taran offers terms of 1/10 net 45, and the selling price of its product is $25 per unit. Production costs (including variable overhead) for a range of 500,000 to 800,000 units per year are $21 per unit with current annual sales at 700,000 units. Accounts receivable are financed through a bank loan at 9 percent interest. Forty percent of the units sold are paid for within 10 days, and the remainder is paid for after 45 days. Two percent of sales on which the cash discount is not taken have to be written off as bad debts. Taran considers tightening its credit policy by offering terms of net 30. If this policy is put into effect, sales are expected to drop to 650,000 units, and bad-debt expenses would amount to a flat $45,000 per year. Taran's tax rate is 45 percent. Should the proposed change in credit policy be implemented?

3. The Imperial Socket Company has a subsidiary in Mexico. At present, the subsidiary offers its customers terms of 2/10 net 60. The Mexican operation has been under pressure to extend the terms granted to its customers in order to meet the competition. After an appraisal of the situation, the company believes that the demand for its product is not very sensitive to price. A proposal by the Mexican executive states that prices could be increased by 12 percent if terms of 1/30 net 90 were offered with overall sales unaffected by these changes. At present, 80 percent of the customers take advantage of the full credit period offered. On the remaining 20 percent of sales, any cash discounts offered are taken. These proportions are expected to remain the same if the new credit terms are implemented. Sales average $300,000 per month. All receivables are financed through the local bank, at which financing is available at 18 percent annual interest. Past experience has shown that 2 percent of sales that do not avail themselves of the cash discount are written off as bad debts. The corporate tax rate is 40 percent.

   (a) Should the company introduce the proposal suggested by the Mexican executive?

   (b) Are there other factors to be considered before implementing such a change?

4. At present, the Chocolate Cookie Company's products sell at $4.50 per unit with monthly sales of 150,000 units. Twenty percent of all sales are for cash, and the remainder are sold on terms of net 30. The present average cost per unit is $2.50, and the marginal cost for the next 15,000 units per month would be $2.00 per unit. If the credit terms are altered to 2/10, 1/30, net 60, sales are expected to increase by 12,000 units per month. Cash sales will remain at 20 percent of total sales. It is assumed that 35 percent of future credit sales will be paid after 10 days, 10 percent after 30 days,

and the balance after 60 days. Based on past experience, bad debts amount to 1 percent of credit sales, and it is assumed that they will remain at 1 percent of any sales not paid after 60 days. The company's tax rate is 50 percent, and its required rate of return on investments in receivables is 7 percent after tax. Should the firm alter its credit terms as indicated?

5. Prior to a change in credit policy, Slow Soils had lagged behind its competitors. It now has annual sales of $8.8 million. Previous credit terms were net 30; currently, terms of 2/10 net 30 are in use. Forty percent of customers take the discount, and all others pay at the end of the credit period except for bad debts, which increased by 50 percent to 3 percent of total sales. Accounts receivable are financed through a bank loan at 12 percent annual interest. As a result of the change in policy, total costs (financing charges, bad debt write offs, and amounts foregone through cash discounts) increased by $159,146. What was the percentage increase in annual sales following the change in policy?

6. Homeoil Limited distributes home heating oil to residential areas. It makes deliveries every month. Thirty percent of its customers pay cash on delivery, and the rest pay at the end of the month after delivery. Sales over the past year have been:

	Sales		Sales
January	$50,000	July	$4,000
February	$40,000	August	$4,000
March	$25,000	September	$6,000
April	$15,000	October	$15,000
May	$5,000	November	$35,000
June	$4,000	December	$40,000

Calculate the receivables outstanding, average collection period, and receivables turnover for each month based on average daily sales for the month. (Assume that the previous December had the same sales as this December.) Is there a problem with the figures?

7. A small retailer currently does not accept credit cards. It has a credit system whereby customers can delay paying for their purchases for 30 days. Forty percent of customers currently elect to delay payment, and the rest pay cash. The retailer is considering beginning to accept credit cards. If it does, it will get rid of its own credit system and require immediate payment on all purchases. It estimates that overall sales would remain unchanged, and about 50 percent of sales would be on credit cards. The credit card company charges the store 5 percent of sales as a service charge. Annual sales are projected to be $600,000, and the business currently finances accounts receivables through a bank line of credit at an interest rate of 10 percent. Should the retailer begin accepting credit cards?

8. A small firm builds and sells very large pieces of industrial equipment. Typically, it buys all the parts it will require at the beginning of the year and keeps them in inventory, selling the finished equipment at the end of the year. It has just purchased the parts for a new machine, for $2 million. The last sale was for a price of $3 million.

The company's tax rate is 40 percent. Assuming no other costs for the firm, calculate its net profit, the cashflow required to replace inventory, and the amount of financing that would be required for the new inventory if inflation (for both sale price and inventory costs) is 10 percent. Recalculate the numbers assuming that inflation is 15 percent and then 20 percent.

9. A company currently demands cash payments from all customers. Total sales are $5 million per year. The cost of goods sold equals 75 percent of sales. The firm is considering introducing credit terms of 1/10 net 30. Accounts receivable will be financed through a line of credit with the bank at an interest rate of 8 percent. It is estimated that 30 percent of customers will take the cash discount, and 70 percent will take 30 days to pay. Bad debts will amount to 1 percent of the sales that take 30 days to collect. With the new credit policy, sales will increase by 25 percent.

(a) What is the net benefit to the company of introducing the new credit policy?

(b) Using a spreadsheet, estimate the net benefits of the new credit policy under a range of assumptions about the sales increase. Use changes in sales ranging from 0 percent up to a 50 percent increase (looking at 5% increments in the sales growth assumption). Comment on the findings.

(c) Assuming that sales increase 25 percent, use a spreadsheet to estimate the net benefits of the new credit policy under a range of assumptions about the bad-debt exposure. Use bad-debt estimates ranging from 0 percent up to 5 percent (in 0.5 percent increments). Comment on the findings.

(d) Under the original sales and bad-debt assumptions, use a spreadsheet to estimate the net benefits to the firm of the new credit policy under a range of assumptions about the proportion of customers that take the cash discount. Use estimates ranging from 0 percent of customers up to 60 percent (in 5 percent increments). Comment on the findings.

Export-Import Bank Financing Helps WestJet Soar

WestJet Airlines of Calgary, Alberta, started small, but grew fast. The company commenced operations on February 29, 1996, with two Boeing 737s offering budget flights among five cities in British Columbia and Alberta. It grew steadily over the next few years; by 1999 it had fourteen aircraft serving twelve cities, going as far east as Thunder Bay, Ontario. In July it went public with an initial offering of 2.5 million shares.

Nineteen ninety-nine was a tumultuous year for the Canadian airline industry; after a prolonged "battle of the skies," Air Canada merged with Canadian Airlines, leaving a single major national carrier in the market. WestJet seized the opportunity to expand, and was soon flying 18 planes on routes that spanned the entire country, from Victoria to Moncton. By August 2000 it had announced plans to purchase 26 new aircraft between 2003 and 2005, as well as option and lease agreements by which it could acquire up to 68 more over the next eight years.

Financing this rapid growth involved two parts. One was home-grown: an issue of 2.2 million new common shares in December 2000, for total gross proceeds of $49.5 million. The other involved looking farther afield: to obtain medium-term financing for the 26-plane purchase from Boeing, WestJet turned to the Export-Import Bank of the United States.

This entity, analagous to the Export Development Corporation in Canada, is an independent U.S. Government agency that helps finance the overseas sales of U.S. goods and services. Ex-Im Bank's mission is to create jobs in the United States by encouraging exports. To this end, it guarantees working capital loans for U.S. exporters, and guarantees or makes loans to foreign purchasers of U.S. goods and services. The bank does not compete with commercial lenders, but assumes risks they cannot accept-only for transactions that are determined not to affect the U.S. economy adversely, and for which there is "reasonable assurance" of repayment.

In recent years, Ex-Im Bank's primary focus has been on developing nations, but it accepts applications from firms in any nation importing U.S. goods, including Canada.

Under its agreement with WestJet, Ex-Im bank guarantees up to $744 million (US), representing up to 85% of the purchase price of the 26 aircraft plus Ex-Im Bank's exposure fees. As required, about six months before the desired aircraft delivery year, WestJet can call for portions of this preliminary commitment to be converted into final commitments with lenders (as yet undetermined). The loans will be amortized over 12 years at interest rates reflecting the U.S. government guarantee.

Sandy Campbell, WestJet Senior Vice President and CFO, said of this financing arrangement, "Our philosophy is to maintain a strong balance sheet, and therefore it is not our intention to borrow to this extent. However, this commitment does provide a back-up source fo financing, if required in the future, on an aircraft by aircraft basis."

chapter 24

Short-Term Financing Options

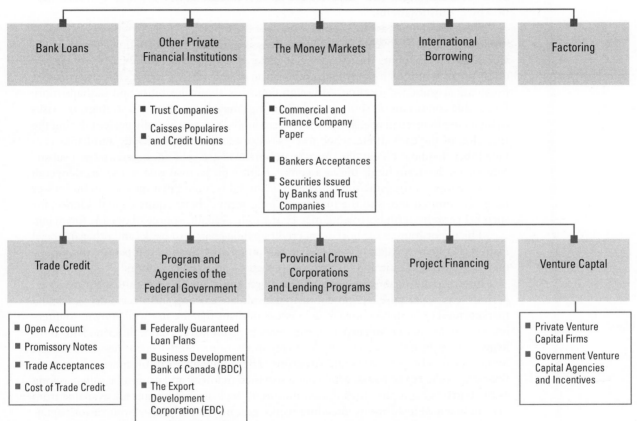

Learning Objectives

After studying this chapter, you should be able to:

1. *Discuss the different sources of short-term and intermediate-term loans.*
2. *Identify five common features of term loans.*
3. *Discuss the reason for hedging through forward or futures contracts or options.*
4. *Compare the informal and formal types of trade credit.*
5. *Explain the role of the venture capital firm.*

24.1 **INTRODUCTION**

We have seen that it is convenient to classify external sources of funds according to the time period that elapses between the raising and final repayment of such funds. Short-term financing generally encompasses loans with maturities of one year or less; inter-mediate-term financing implies maturities of from one to 10 years; and long-term financing extends beyond 10 years. Though such breakdowns are somewhat arbitrary, the institutional arrangements vary with the term of financing, thus making such classification by maturities useful.

Short-term funds are most appropriate for the financing of temporary needs such as seasonal buildups in inventories and accounts receivable. Short-term financing also provides flexibility in timing the issuance of long-term securities. For instance, firms may rely on short-term funds temporarily in anticipation of replacing them with more permanent financing at some future time. Although concerns about flexibility and perhaps more favourable conditions on short-term borrowings may motivate such a strategy, the risks of financing long-term needs with short-term funds became painfully evident during the recession of the early 1980s when interest rates escalated dramatically and banks curtailed their lending. Generally, short-term borrowing should not be viewed as a substitute for longer-term funds but as a complement with its own role in the firm's overall financing mix. At the same time, however, it should be noted that most small businesses have very limited access to the market for long-term debt or equity capital. Hence, for such firms, short-term borrowing may be the only available source of outside financing.

The major sources of short-term credit include chartered banks and other financial institutions such as credit unions and caisses populaires, finance companies, the money markets (both domestic and international), factors, and trade creditors.

Intermediate-term financing is useful when funds must be committed for extended periods (e.g., to acquire equipment or to consolidate existing short-term debt). Capital markets tend to be unreceptive to debt issues of firms that are not well known, so interest costs and underwriting expenses can become prohibitive. Hence, intermediate-term loans may be the only practical way for many small- or medium-size businesses to include longer-term debt in their capital structure. The dominant form of intermediate-term financing is the **term loan**, which has a specified maturity and cannot be called as long as the borrower complies with the conditions of the loan. Term loans are available from private financial institutions including banks and, increasingly, also from various agencies are set up and sponsored by different levels of government. Leasing also represents an important source of intermediate-term financing. However, we do not deal with this here but do so in Chapter 25, which is devoted entirely to the topic of leasing.

We may ask why governments have become active in this area rather than letting the free market determine the allocation of funds to various borrowers. Several reasons can be given. First, governments may view such agencies as vehicles for achieving social objectives, and loans may be used to subsidize endeavours that are deemed to be socially desirable even if they do not result in the greatest economic efficiency. Incentives to locate industries in depressed areas with high unemployment and subsidies to small businesses are examples of such reasoning. Often such government programs are viewed as complementing private institutions, and many government agencies stipulate that borrowers will qualify only if comparable loans under reasonable terms could not be obtained elsewhere. Second, government agencies may be set up to compete directly with private institutions. These actions usually stem from charges of monopoly power and/or excessive profits by private institutions, with the government claiming that it can provide better service at more reasonable rates. Needless to say, such arguments are controversial. Finally, various provincial and local governments have set up a variety of incentives including financial assistance to attract industries to their jurisdictions.

Without going into detail, we should also note that at the international level, many countries—developing countries in particular—have set up incentive programs and/or special agencies for the purpose of attracting businesses. A wide variety of services are offered, ranging from financial assistance to special tax concessions. Often, host country governments will also offer to become partners in new industrial ventures.

In this chapter, we discuss short- and intermediate-term financing. Institutionally, such financing differs from long-term funding in that it is typically negotiated and arranged with financial intermediaries. We review short- and intermediate-term financing available through financial institutions, notably through banks. We also discuss the issuance of short-term promissory notes in money markets, trade credit or funds advanced to firms by suppliers, and factoring. Finally, we cover financing available through various government programs, project financing, and venture capital.

BANK LOANS 24.2

The Canadian banking system has been termed a system of branch banking. It is characterized by banks that operate on a national scale with business conducted through branches spread across the country. In contrast, until recently, banks in the United States were restricted in the geographical range of their activities and commonly still confine themselves to a particular state. Such a system of geographically restricted activity is called unit banking.

Operating on a national scale, Canadian banks usually maintain a broad, balanced portfolio of loans. Hence, they are less susceptible to changes in economic conditions in any one geographic area, and individual credit offices need not be overly concerned about concentrating their lending in one particular industry. The advantages of such diversification became particularly evident during the recession of the early 1980s when several regional banks, which operated on a more limited scale, ran into serious difficulties because their loans were concentrated in problem industries such as energy and real estate in Western Canada.

The traditional view of banks has been that they should provide short-term credit. Since a large proportion of their own liabilities are deposits with short maturities, short-term loans provide banks with the necessary flexibility and liquidity and, therefore, continue to dominate their lending.[1] However, loans with longer maturities have become more common, and the 1980 revision of the *Bank Act* provided the chartered banks with

---

[1] For example, as of December 31, 1998, chartered banks and other deposit-accepting intermediaries had a total of $888 billion in total liabilities consisting of $604 billion (or 68 percent) of demand and short-term deposits.

additional sources of long-term financing including the right to issue convertible securities and preferred shares. Table 24.1 provides details regarding the amount of loans
outstanding to Canadian banks for selected years.

Table 24.1

Outstanding Bank Loans to Business Classified by Size of Authorization (in $000,000s)

Authorized Limit	1965	1975	1985	1990	1995	2000*
More than $5.0 million	994	10,906	35,238	41,857	93,487	135,853
$1.0 million to $5.0 million	1,418	5,084	13,023	19,998	29,190	36,505
Less than $1.0 million	3,361	9,048	26,983	33,483	43,233	47,887
Totals	$5,773	$24,038	$75,244	$95,338	$165,910	$220,243

* As of March 31, 2000.
Source: *Bank of Canada Review*, various issues.

Most short-term operating loans granted to businesses are part of a **line of credit**.
A line of credit is an open lending arrangement with a stated maximum that a bank may
be willing to lend to a customer for a set period of time. Once a line is approved, the borrower may draw on the funds as needed up to the specified limit. This loan is usually
linked to the firm's current (chequing) account, and it enables the business to borrow up
to a predetermined amount to finance temporary cash deficits. The amount of borrowing may be reduced at the borrowing firm's discretion, and for a fee they may have the
bank automatically "revolve" the loan for it. This involves having the bank pay down the
amount of the loan when there is sufficient cash in the company's current account or
increasing the borrowing when there is insufficient cash. These loans are typically secured
by accounts receivable and inventory since these are the assets they are intended to
finance. The bank normally charges a commitment fee to secure a line of credit.
The advantages of lines of credit include the following:

- The firm knows how much bank credit can be expected.
- Borrowings may be limited to amounts actually needed.
- The bank's credit manager can make instant advances up to the maximum amount
  prescribed without having to process additional loan applications.

Such lending arrangements also provide customers with an opportunity to develop
a solid banking relationship, which is important. Thus, lines of credit offer flexibility and
convenience in meeting fluctuating day-to-day requirements and are commonly used to
finance working capital including accounts receivable and inventories. Most lines of credit are subject to annual review, and to continue using the line, the business must maintain its credit standing and have fulfilled conditions that were agreed to when the loan
was negotiated. In addition, the bank often reserves the right to reduce the negotiated
maximum depending on general economic and market conditions or even to call any
outstanding amounts on demand.

The rate of interest on bank loans is usually expressed as some percentage over the
prime loan rate, which is the interest rate banks charge their most credit-worthy bor-

rowers. The prime rate is published by the banks and is adjusted frequently to reflect changes in market conditions. If loans are financed with short-term deposits on which current rates have to be paid, loans at fixed interest rates entail additional risks for the lender. To protect themselves against such risks on loans with longer maturities, banks normally charge variable interest rates that are adjusted periodically to reflect prevailing market conditions as evidenced by changes in the prime rate. Borrowers can use financial futures contracts to hedge against possible interest rate movements on variable interest rate loans. These and other risk-management techniques were discussed in Chapter 21.

Apart from interest, payments on a loan may include other service charges. As mentioned above, banks often charge standby fees for lines of credit in the form of a levy against the difference between the line granted and the maximum actually borrowed. These are used to discourage borrowers from requesting lines of credit that they do not really need. In addition, arrangement fees are sometimes charged for establishing lending facilities especially for real estate loans. Other loans entail compensating balance arrangements, which require the borrower to maintain a fixed percentage of a loan as an interest-free deposit. These also entail costs. However, their use has become rare in Canada. Clearly, the imposition of standby fees, service charges, and/or compensating balances increases the effective cost of borrowing.

A significant proportion of business loans are secured loans, with the borrower having to pledge assets as collateral. As mentioned previously, most lines of credit are secured by inventories and receivables. However, a variety of other assets may be acceptable as collateral against bank loans ranging from equipment to oil and gas reserves under the ground. The *Bank Act* regulates not only the types of assets against which banks may lend but also sets out the procedures to be followed when assets are pledged as security. Because interest costs increase with risk, a borrower who can pledge assets with stable values that can readily be converted into cash should be able to negotiate reduced interest charges.

PERSPECTIVES

Corporate Manager

Pledging security for loans may reduce the interest cost associated with the loan. However, this action may also restrict future borrowing capability and reduce flexibility with regards to asset management.

Investor

While the cash flows available to common shareholders increase when the firm reduces its interest costs by pledging security, this action also reduces the chances of obtaining any residual amount if a company should be dissolved since it implies that a certain amount of assets is already tied up.

With the rapid growth of their assets, banks have been able to diversify their loan portfolios more fully, and they now place more emphasis on intermediate-term loans for such varied purposes as plant expansion, export financing, and takeovers. As a result, the proportion of intermediate-term commercial bank loans and personal loans have increased in recent years.

The particular forms that term loans may take are too numerous to review and are often tailored to meet specific circumstances. Almost all the provisions that may be encountered are negotiable and depend on the comparative strength of both the borrower and the lender. However, most contracts contain at least some fairly standard clauses.

Generally, term loans are secured by some type of collateral. Although the most common forms of collateral are land, buildings, and equipment, a variety of other items can be used. For example, term loans for mine development have been granted on the strength of long-term ore-delivery contracts. Typically, the market value of the collateral exceeds the amount of the loan by some margin, with the margin demanded depending on the saleability of the asset. When the borrowing firm is a small- or medium-size incorporated business, lenders often require additional collateral in the form of personal guarantees from management or the principal owners. In addition, life insurance may have to be taken out on key personnel. Borrowers are frequently required to supply the lender with periodic information about their operations in the form of up-to-date financial statements. The debt contract may also impose restrictions on the borrowing firm's operations to protect the creditor. The provisions commonly found in trust indentures on long-term debt are typical in this context.

In contrast to long-term debt raised through a public offering, interest rates on term loans are often variable and tied to fluctuations in the prime rate. Given the uncertainty about future interest rate movements and the fact that institutions such as banks have to pay competitive current rates on the money they raise through deposits, this provision is understandable. It allows banks and other financial institutions to match variations in revenues (income from loans) with variations in costs (interest payments on deposits), thereby eliminating risks associated with changing interest rate levels. For the borrower, however, a variable interest rate loan may entail unwanted uncertainty in financing costs. In earlier chapters, we reviewed various techniques for managing such risk including hedging through futures markets and interest rate swaps, which clearly also apply in this context. Obviously, banks can also avail themselves of these hedging techniques and because of their size, diversity, and sophistication, may actually be in a better position to do so than individual firms.

In addition to granting more term loans, banks have also begun to take equity positions in some of their clients' firms. Although shareholdings by banks are restricted through the *Bank Act*, a number of bank financing arrangements entail stock options and other equity participation that is offered to the bank as part of an overall financing package particularly in the context of project financing, which is discussed in Section 24.10. We also note that in recent years, banks have sometimes acquired significant shareholdings as a consequence of loan defaults and the subsequent reorganization and financial restructuring of client firms.

OTHER PRIVATE FINANCIAL INSTITUTIONS

24.3

The chartered banks are the dominant source of short- and intermediate-term funds both to businesses and individuals. Trust companies grew in importance in the late 1980s and early 1990s; however, most of them have been acquired by major banks in recent years. Credit unions and caisses populaires continue to play an important role in particular for small- and medium-size businesses at the local level. In addition, a growing number of investment and financing companies that are often either wholly or partly owned subsidiaries of major financial institutions such as banks view term lending as one of their activities.

Trust Companies

As described in Chapter 2, one of the main original purposes of trust companies was to act as fiduciaries in administering estates, pension plans, and other trust funds. Over time, however, trust companies became deposit-taking institutions, performing many banking functions. As the nature of their liabilities shifted to short-term deposits, intermediate-term investment certificates, and term deposits, trust companies expanded their lending in the intermediate-term market. They eventually became a relatively important source of term loans to businesses, and their near-bank activities grew in importance. Today, most of the major trust companies operate as subsidiaries of the chartered banks, and the number of independent trust companies had decreased to 15 as of March 2000, down from 50 in 1990. This matter is elaborated upon in Box 24-1 below. Table 24.2 shows the impact of this phenomenon on the total assets of independent trust companies in Canada, which fell from $135.5 billion in 1990 to $10.6 billion by March 31, 2000.

■ *Finance in the News*

New Trust Companies Formed to Focus on Retail Clients

Consumers are concerned that the big banks are swallowing up Canada's trust companies. Over the past decade, they have declined from 50 to just 15. Two of the latest and largest takeovers were the 1997 Scotiabank buyout of National Trust for $1.25 billion and the TD Bank takeover of Canada Trust in early 2000 for nearly $8 billion. The establishment of Home Trust in March 2000 will be "welcome news to the retail market, where the loss of independent trust companies has been most sorely felt," said Gerald Soloway, CEO of Home Capital Group Inc., the trust's parent.

As a federally licensed trust, Home will be able to provide financial services such as self-directed RRSPs for mortgages and RRSP conversions to RRIFs in addition to the residential mortgages the company now offers. Soloway pledges that Home "will continue to be Canada's leading alternative lender" with even more products to offer.

Source: Canadian Press Newswire, March 28, 2000. Reprinted with permission.

TABLE 24.2

Selected Assets of Independent Trust and Mortgage Loan Companies (excluding Bank Trust and Mortgage Subsidiaries) (in $000,000s)

Year	Total assets	Mortgages	Loans Personal	Other
1986	84,217	50,072	3,276	6,288
1990	135,502	87,694	8,194	6,306
1995	72,441	44,034	9,106	2,279
Mar. 31, 2000	10,558	5,504	602	194

Source: Bank of Canada Review, September 2000.

Caisses Populaires and Credit Unions

Caisses populaires and credit unions are essentially savings and credit co-operatives. The first caisse populaire, modelled largely on the nineteenth-century European movement that established Peoples' Banks, was founded in Quebec in 1900. The caisses encouraged savings and provided loans to members for emergencies or to finance investments. Canadian credit unions first evolved in Nova Scotia in the early 1930s and trace their origins to Europe's eighteenth-century mutual savings banks. As reflected in Table 24.3, the growth and success of both movements has been substantial.

TABLE 24.3

Selected Assets of Caisses Populaires and Credit Unions (in $000,000s)

Year	Total assets	Mortgages	Loans Personal	Other
1975	12,791	5,072	3,243	407
1980	30,546	15,328	6,391	1,173
1985	44,045	21,769	7,736	3,948
1990	72,377	34,857	10,956	9,541
1995	100,356	54,322	13,409	10,563
Mar. 2000	116,066	62,744	14,970	14,503

Source: Bank of Canada Review, various issues

Although similar in many ways, the caisses populaires and credit unions have followed somewhat different policies regarding asset investment. Credit unions are heavily committed to lending to their members although some of them have started seeking unrelated business accounts. Caisses populaires, on the other hand, have held consumer and business loans to a more modest total while taking a more active role in the financing of local municipalities and school boards. Although there are significant variations in their size (ranging from small single-branch operations to credit unions with assets exceeding $1 billion), credit unions and caisses populaires are restricted in their activities to narrow geographical areas. This curtails their ability to service larger corporations with widely dispersed operations. Nevertheless, the contributions of these institutions to the total financial system has become significant, with local governments or their agencies and smaller businesses as the principal beneficiaries.

THE MONEY MARKETS   24.4

The money markets consist of the places and institutions in which debt instruments with relatively short maturities (sometimes referred to as "near-money") are traded. Though the definition sometimes relates to securities with maturities under three years, the bulk of activity centres around debt instruments coming due within one year. Table 24.4 shows the breakdown in money market trading in Canada by Government of Canada primary distributors during the month of March 2000, which totalled $142 billion. Corporate paper trading was the most actively traded category, accounting for approximately 58 percent of the total amount, while federal government T-bills (20 percent) and Bankers Acceptances (17 percent) were also important categories.

Table 24.4

Domestic Money Market Trading by Type of Security (as reported by government securities distributors) March, 2000 ($ millions)

Total	Gov. of Canada T-bills	Federal Crown Corp. Securities	Provincial Securities	Bankers Acceptances	Corporate and Finance Paper	Bank, Trust, and Mortgage Company Paper	Other Domestic Money Market Trading
142,237	29,127	2,139	3,354	24,658	62,294	19,779	885

Since its inception in 1954, governments and large corporations have used the Canadian money market to obtain short-term financing. Table 24.5 shows how rapidly this market has expanded in recent years. Notice the dramatic increase during the period from 1995 to 2000, when the dollar amount of outstanding securities more than doubled. This is primarily due to the huge increase in commercial paper and finance company paper, which more than tripled over this period.

TABLE 24.5

Estimates of Money Market Instruments Outstanding (in $000,000s)

Year	Total Commercial Paper and Finance Company Paper	Canadian Dollar Bankers Acceptances	T-bills	Total
1980	14,752	5,365	1,182	20,117
1985	13,187	17,007	7,462	30,194
1990	29,317	44,109	14,185	73,426
1995	40,482	30,701	17,132	71,183
June 2000	126,483	50,886	19,665	177,369

Source: Bank of Canada Review, September 2000.

In this section, we review some of the money market instruments that are most important for business financing. Rather than providing periodic interest payments, money market instruments normally sell at a discount from face value. The investor realizes a return when, at maturity, the borrower redeems the paper at face value. Given the relatively short maturities, it is more convenient to provide for returns in this way than by mailing out interest cheques or resorting to coupons. When such instruments are traded, the discount at which they sell gradually decreases as the maturity date approaches. The effective yield is the rate that equates the discounted future face value with the current market price.

EXAMPLE

YIELDS ON MONEY MARKET SECURITIES

A security with a face value of $100 currently trades at $98 and has 91 days to maturity. By purchasing this paper and holding it to maturity, an investor receives $2 on an investment of $98 for three months. Based on simple interest only, the approximate annual yield would be given as:[2]

$$\text{Approximate annual yield} = \frac{\text{discount}}{\text{market price}} \times \frac{365}{\text{days to maturity}}$$

$$= \frac{2}{98} \times \frac{365}{91} = 0.0819 \text{ or } 8.19\%$$

To be more exact, however, we should consider the effects of compounding. The interest rate for 91 days is computed as $2/98 = 2.04\%$. Referring to our discussion in Chapter 5 and compounding over 4 quarters, we find the effective annual interest rate r from the equation:

$$(1 + r) = (1 + .0204)^4 = 1.0841$$

Hence:

effective annual yield = $1.0841 - 1 = 0.0841$ or 8.41%

Commercial and Finance Company Paper

Tables 24.4 and 24.5 show that commercial paper and finance company paper comprise over half of the entire Canadian money market, which attests to the importance of these instruments. **Commercial** or **corporate paper** consists of short-term promissory notes issued by major corporations that are well known to investors and enjoy excellent credit reputations. Issued in large denominations often of not less than $100,000, the maturities vary from demand notes, which can be cashed on 24-hour notice to 365-day paper. However, by far the most common are 30-, 60-, and 90-day notes. Although most commercial paper is unsecured, the market generally expects issuers to have bank lines of

---

[2] This approximate rate is the one that is commonly referred to by market participants, when quoting money market yields.

credit available to cover the dollar value of outstanding issues. Banks may also provide revolving underwriting facilities particularly in conjunction with short-term international security issues. Under such arrangements, the bank will either purchase such securities or provide equivalent lending if the firm finds it difficult to resell (or roll over) the outstanding issue at maturity.

Paper issued by finance companies is similar except that it is usually secured by a pledge of receivables, with the value of the receivables amounting to anywhere from 112.5 to 125 percent of the value of paper outstanding. Unsecured finance company paper would almost certainly have to be guaranteed by a parent corporation.

To an issuer, the advantage of raising funds in the money market is that costs are generally lower than those faced when borrowing from a financial institution. At the same time, the borrower's relations with its creditors (investors who purchase such paper) are much less personal than when dealing with a bank. Good and continuous relations with a bank can be quite valuable, (e.g., when a firm faces a temporary credit squeeze). Unfortunately, the value of such bank support in periods of temporary difficulties is hard to assess beforehand, making comparisons between the alternatives of issuing commercial paper or drawing on bank loans difficult. Even if commercial paper is not used as a major source of short-term funds, the mere fact that a firm can issue such paper may prove useful in ensuring competitive terms when negotiating for a bank loan.

Actual access to the money markets is provided through investment dealers. If a dealer is unable to locate an investor willing to purchase the paper, he may buy such paper himself and temporarily hold it in his own inventory. When the dealer does not take title to the paper, commissions equivalent to 1/8 to 1/4 of 1 percent of the face value per year is charged to the issuer.

Once a firm decides to go to the market, an offering memorandum is prepared with the help of legal counsel and an investment dealer. This memorandum typically includes:

- details on the authority to borrow as set out in the corporation's bylaws
- an indication of the maximum amount of notes that the firm is authorized to issue
- a certificate of incumbency supplying signatures of the signing officers
- legal opinion on a variety of points that relate to the issue, including its suitability for insurance and trust company investment.

Commercial paper offerings are not subject to the scrutiny of provincial securities commissions the way long-term debt and equity issues are. This means fewer delays and lower underwriting costs for the issuing firm. It may also mean hidden risks for the investor.

Although such offering memoranda may help to build market acceptance, investors can also refer to various published ratings on the quality of commercial paper. Such ratings reflect the ability of a borrower to meet cash obligations on time. The Canadian Bond Rating Service (CBRS) commercial paper and short-term debt ratings range from A−1 to A−3 and are modified by plus or minus signs within these categories. A rating of A−1+ indicates the highest quality and implies the company's long-term senior debt generally enjoys an A++ rating. Such companies have ready access to alternative sources of borrowing, a long and proven record of earnings and cash flows, and a sound position in a strong industry. A rating of A−3, on the other hand, suggests an issuer of poor quality. Dominion Bond Rating Service (DBRS) commercial paper and short-term debt ratings range from a high of R−1 (high) to a low of R−3 (low). Table 24.6 displays these ratings for the companies with long-term debt and preferred share ratings that were displayed in Chapter 13.

Table 24.6

DBRS Commercial Paper Debt Ratings

Company	Industry Classification	Rating
Air Canada	Transportation	N/A
BCE Inc.	Utilities (Telephone Utilities)	R-1 (middle)
Noranda Inc.	Mining (Integrated Mines)	R-1 (low)
Inco Limited	Mining (Integrated Mines)	N/A
Nortel Networks	Comm. & Media (Telecommunication)	R-1 (low)
Clearnet Communications Inc.	Comm. & Media (Telecommunication)	N/A
Bombardier Inc.	Industrial Products (Transportation Equip.)	R-1 (low)
Petro Canada	Integrated Oil & Gas	R-1 (low)
Bank of Nova Scotia	Financial Services (Banks)	R-1 (middle)
Fairfax Financial	Financial Services (Insurance)	N/A
Investors Group	Financial Services (Invest. Companies & Funds)	N/A

Source: Dominion Bond Rating Service website at: www.dbrs.com, October 25, 2000. The ratings were the most recent available as at October 25, 2000. The ratings were determined at various times between August 30, 1999 and August 15, 2000.

Increased availability of assistance and advice to investors and the greater understanding and sophistication of corporate financial officers has encouraged growth in the use of commercial and finance company paper.

Bankers Acceptances

Bankers Acceptances, first introduced in Canada in 1962, are drafts or orders to pay, drawn on a chartered bank by the firm seeking funds. Once accepted and countersigned by a bank, these short-term debt instruments are essentially equivalent to commercial paper guaranteed by that bank. Because of this guarantee, Bankers Acceptances are virtually default-free. Their eligibility for purchase by the Bank of Canada makes them particularly attractive for money market dealers, who can either use such instruments as security for day-to-day loans from the chartered banks or rediscount them at the central bank.[3] Tables 24.4 and 24.5 provided an indication of their importance and their increased use.

---

[3] To the chartered banks, day loans are useful vehicles for investing temporary balances of surplus cash. They are granted to investment dealers in multiples of $100,000 and can be called by either party before noon for settlement that same day. Day loans form part of a bank's secondary reserves.

Bankers Acceptances are normally issued for periods of between 30 and 90 days and in multiples of $500,000. Although they generally are issued only to borrowers with a first-class credit standing, Bankers Acceptances may be relied on by firms that for various reasons find it difficult to sell commercial paper of their own. They are also common in financing export and import transactions. The combination of being extremely secure and liquid makes them saleable at relatively modest yields. An issuer must, however, add to such interest costs the charge levied by the chartered bank for the guarantee provided. This acceptance fee ranges between the annual equivalent of 1/2 to 1 percent of face value. The amount of any guarantees provided is viewed by banks as part of the overall credit extended to a particular firm and commonly becomes part of a line of credit arrangement. That is, when the bank has specified a limit on a firm's current loans, any guarantees obtained will count toward this ceiling.

Securities Issued by Banks and Trust Companies

Instruments used by the chartered banks to obtain short-term funds from savers include **certificates of deposit, deposit receipts**, and **bearer deposit** term notes. Certificates of deposit (CDs) are non-redeemable, registered, transferable, interest-bearing notes with maturities of between one and six years. Denominations vary but range upward from $5,000. Deposit receipts are transferable term deposits with maturities of between 30 and 364 days that can be cashed in at any time subject to an interest penalty. Bearer deposit term notes are issued in amounts exceeding $100,000 for fixed maturities of up to seven years. These securities are also transferable and sell at discounts from face value to provide the necessary yields.

Competing securities, such as deposit receipts, guaranteed investment certificates (GICs), and the like, have been issued by trust companies, credit unions, and other financial institutions. The instruments of trust companies may have terms as short as 24-hour demand.

Bank **swapped deposits** are somewhat more complex. These are foreign currency short-term deposits purchased by investors with Canadian dollars to take advantage of international interest rate differentials. To eliminate foreign exchange risks, a swap or hedge is arranged whereby the purchase of foreign currency necessary for the deposit is combined with a forward sale of a like amount of the currency to coincide with the term of the deposit.[4] The use of forward contracts is revisited in the following section. Yields quoted by banks on such swaps include both the deposit rate and effects of the spot purchase and forward sale of foreign exchange. The propensity of investors to purchase swapped deposits hinges on both international short-term interest rate differentials and forward exchange premiums or discounts. Swapped deposits most frequently involve U.S. dollars and terms of from one to six months.

---

[4] For example, purchasing U.S. dollar deposits for a 1/2 percentage point above what is available in Canada would make little sense if during the term of the deposit, the U.S. dollar depreciated by 1 percent against the Canadian dollar. Such exchange rate risk can be eliminated, however, through a forward exchange contract to sell the foreign currency at some future agreed-to date and at a pre-arranged price.

The report below provides an example of the relative yields of various money market instruments as published regularly in the financial press.

■ *Finance in the News*

MONEY RATES

Money Market Rates (for transactions of $1-million or more)		Administered Rates	
3-month treasury bills	5.63%	Bank of Canada	6.00%
6-month treasury bills	5.73%	Central bank call range	5.50-6.00%
1-year treasury bills	5.81%	Canadian prime	7.50%
10-year Canada bonds	5.67%		
30-year Canada bonds	5.57%		
1-month Bankers Accep.	5.84%		
2-month Bankers Accep.	5.84%		
3-month Bankers Accep.	5.84%		
Commercial Paper (R-1 Low)			
1-month	5.84%		
2-month	5.86%		
3-month	5.88%		
Call money	5.75%		

Source: "*Money Rates*," *Globe and Mail, Report on Business*, October 25, 2000, page B20. *Reprinted with permission.*

24.5 INTERNATIONAL BORROWING

The international money markets located in major financial centres such as New York, London, Zurich, Frankfurt, and Singapore are frequented by larger corporate borrowers. Apart from providing loans in their respective domestic currencies, banks located overseas also offer **Eurocurrency** transactions. A Eurocurrency generally refers to deposits at a commercial bank denominated in a currency other than that of the country in which the bank is located. A general introduction to such markets is provided in Chapter 2. Short-term interest rates in the Eurodollar market are often quoted in relation to the London Interbank Offered Rate (LIBOR), which is the below-prime rate at which major banks lend to each other.

Loans may be sought in international markets for a variety of reasons. For instance, borrowings may be part of a covering or hedging operation to reduce foreign exchange exposure.[5]

---

[5] We use the terms covering and hedging interchangeably for financial transactions undertaken for the purpose of reducing risk exposure.

INTERNATIONAL BORROWING FOR HEDGING PURPOSES

Consider a Canadian firm that exports to the United Kingdom. Receivables are denominated in pounds sterling and are payable in 60 days. In the absence of hedging, the sterling receivables represent a foreign exchange risk because their value in terms of Canadian dollars will be affected by the exchange rate that prevails in two months' time. However, the Canadian company could borrow an equivalent amount in pounds sterling with a maturity of 60 days, and immediately convert the proceeds of the loan into dollars at the current rate of exchange. The subsequent sterling receipts from the collection of the receivables are used to repay the sterling loan. By matching future receivables and liabilities in the foreign currency, foreign exchange risk has been eliminated. These and other procedures that relate to the management of working capital in an international environment were reviewed in Chapter 21.

Short-term borrowing may also be undertaken abroad to take advantage of interest rate differentials. If, for example, U.S. funds were available at a lower interest rate than that charged on comparable loans in Canada, foreign borrowing may seem attractive. When borrowers arrange for loans in a foreign currency they incur the added risk of fluctuations in the exchange rate over the term of the loan. Thus, if during a loan period the Canadian dollar depreciates relative to the U.S. dollar, a Canadian borrower who has to repay a loan denominated in U.S. funds would incur added costs in terms of Canadian currency.

SHORT-TERM INTERNATIONAL BORROWING

Consider a Canadian borrower requiring C\$1 million for one year who makes arrangements for a loan in New York. Assume that U.S. interest rates for such a loan are 9 percent against 11 percent in Canada, and that the current exchange rate is US\$1.00 = C\$1.3958. We obtain:

$$\text{US\$ amount borrowed} = \frac{\text{C\$ amount desired}}{\text{current exchange rate}}$$

$$\text{To obtain C\$1 million} = \frac{1,000,0000}{1.3958}$$

Interest on U.S. loan payable at year end = $716,435 \times .09 = \text{US\$64,479}$

Total amount to be repaid at year end   = principal + interest
$$= 716,435 + 64,479 = \text{US\$780,914}$$

The amount of Canadian dollars to be repaid at year end depends on the exchange rate at that time. Assume that the Canadian dollar has dropped in value, with the year end exchange rate given at US\$1.00 = C\$1.4343. We obtain:

Total C\$ amount to be repaid at year end   = US\$ amount exchange rate
$$= 780,914 \times 1.4343$$
$$= \text{C\$1,120,065}$$

Effective cost of loan $= \dfrac{\text{amount repaid}}{\text{amount borrowed}} - 1$

$$= \dfrac{1,120,065}{1,000,000}\ 1 \approx 0.12 \text{ or } 12\%$$

We see that the unfavourable shift in the foreign exchange rate has more than off-set the original interest rate differential, making the U.S. loan ultimately more expensive than domestic borrowing.

As noted in earlier chapters, the existence of foreign currency forward contracts, futures, and options permit borrowers to eliminate the foreign exchange risks associated with such transactions. Forward exchange rates vary depending on the future time period involved, and examples of rates quoted on various forward contracts are shown in the report below.

■ *Finance in the News*

Mid-Market Rates in Toronto at Noon, Oct 24, 2000. Prepared by BMO Nesbitt Burns, Capital Markets.

		$1 U.S. in Cdn.$ =	$1 Cdn. in U.S.$ =
U.S./Canada spot		1.5115	0.6616
1 month forward		1.5104	0.6621
2 months forward		1.5094	0.6625
3 months forward		1.5081	0.6631
6 months forward		1.5050	0.6645
12 months forward		1.4999	0.6667
3 years forward		1.4855	0.6732
5 years forward		1.4707	0.6799
1 years forward		1.4515	0.6889
10 years forward		1.4165	0.7060
Canadian dollar	High	1.4318	0.6984
in 2000:	Low	1.5239	0.6562
	Average	1.4750	0.6780
		Cdn. $ per unit	U.S. $ per unit
Country	Currency		
Britain	Pound	2.1912	1.4497
1 month forward		2.1908	1.4505
2 months forward		2.1906	1.4513
3 months forward		2.1900	1.4522
6 months forward		2.1881	1.4539
12 months forward		2.1844	1.4564

Europe	Euro	1.2643	0.8365
1 month forward		1.2652	0.8377
3 months forward		1.2664	0.8398
6 months forward		1.2682	0.8427
12 months forward		1.2715	0.9478
Japan	Yen	0.013990	0.009256
1 month forward		0.014058	0.009307
3 months forward		0.014180	0.009403
6 months forward		0.014366	0.009545
12 months forward		0.014744	0.009830

Source: Globe and Mail Report on Business, October 25, 2000, B25. *Reprinted with permission.*

USING FORWARD CONTRACTS

EXAMPLE

Pursuing the previous example, assume that a forward contract calling for the purchase of U.S. dollars with Canadian funds for delivery in one year is quoted at an exchange rate of US$1.00 = C$1.4227. By entering into such a contract, the borrower obtains the right to buy U.S. dollars one year hence at a forward exchange rate that is specified at the time the loan is arranged. Thus, the borrower can compute the effective cost of the foreign loan with all foreign exchange risk eliminated before entering into the arrangement. Applying the forward exchange rate to the year end repayment, we have:

Amount repaid at year end in C$ = US$ amount forward exchange rate

$$= 780,914 \times 1.4227$$
$$= C\$1,111,006$$

Effective cost of loan with forward exchange coverage $= \dfrac{\text{amount repaid}}{\text{amount borrowed}} - 1$

$$= \frac{1,111,006}{1,000,000} - 1 \approx 0.11 \text{ or } 11\%$$

As we saw in Chapters 6 and 21, the above result is typical. With full coverage against foreign exchange risk, the costs of foreign and domestic loans should be similar.[6] If, for example, the forward exchange rate had been such that fully covered borrowing in the United States was significantly more attractive, many Canadian borrowers would elect to finance there. At the same time, it would become profitable for U.S. lenders to deposit their money in Canada, for example, through fully hedged swapped deposits. These flows of funds would continue until the opportunity for profit had been eliminated implying roughly equivalent net yields on fully covered transactions in both countries (interest rate parity).

---

[6] This is the basis of the interest rate parity theorem.

Forward market activity is usually confined to the more important currencies, and forward contracts are sometimes available for periods of up to 10 years. For the financial manager who is concerned about foreign exchange risk, it is useful to watch forward rates because they reflect general market beliefs about the future movement of currencies. In the previous example, we quoted a one-year forward rate on the U.S. dollar that was above the spot rate, implying a belief by the market that the Canadian dollar would weaken.

Rate quotations as shown in the report above are available from banks. When the forward rate on a currency is given at a premium, this means that it is higher or more expensive than the spot rate, whereas a discount implies that it is cheaper. As we noted earlier, the currency of a country in which lower interest rates prevail will normally sell at a forward premium relative to a currency with a higher interest rate, so that hedging through a forward contract will eliminate at least part of the interest rate differential.▲

24.6 FACTORING

Factors are firms that provide financing to businesses by purchasing their accounts receivable. Traditionally, enterprises engaged in factoring have been finance companies and their subsidiaries. After years of severe competition and mounting losses, however, most finance companies have left the factoring business, which is now dominated by a few specialized U.S.-controlled companies.

When entering into a factoring arrangement, the seller's customers are normally instructed to remit directly to the factor, and all problems associated with the receivables such as collections pass on to this factor. The factor derives compensation by paying less than book value for the receivables outstanding, with the size of the discount reflecting the quality of the receivables. When funds are advanced before the maturity date of the receivables, an interest charge is also levied.

Because the factor assumes the risk of losses from bad debts, it generally takes on the tasks of credit checks as well as collections. The resultant savings to a business through curtailment of its own credit and collection functions may be significant. In particular, small or highly seasonal businesses may find it relatively uneconomical to maintain their own credit departments and may be attracted by the prospect of dispensing with these functions. The size of a factor's operations, its financial resources, and its expertise may also enable it to assume marginal credit risks more readily than its clients could.

We see that a factor can provide three services:

1. taking over credit screening and collections

2. assuming the risks of bad debt

3. financing by advancing funds that would otherwise be collected later

Factoring arrangements that include various combinations of the above three services are possible, and charges vary accordingly. The pure financing costs of factoring are generally competitive with those of other short-term sources although they can be substantially higher.

TRADE CREDIT

Trade credit is the financing suppliers extend by allowing customers to pay for goods or services sometime after delivery. Of course, sellers recognize this and incorporate interest charges on these loans in the price of the goods sold. Such credit is debt on the buyers' books, appearing as accounts payable. In terms of volume, trade credit is one of the more significant sources of short-term financing used by Canadian businesses. One of its key characteristics from the buyer's point of view is that when required, it arises spontaneously. For example, if standard payment procedures in an industry call for payment of the invoiced amount 30 days after receipt of the goods, a purchaser automatically receives a 30-day credit from the supplier equal to the amount purchased. When repeated purchases are made, such credit can be rolled over and becomes a semi-permanent source of financing. As the volume of business and therefore the purchase of supplies increases or decreases, so does the amount of trade credit generated.

TRADE CREDIT AND PURCHASES

EXAMPLE

If a firm buys $15,000 in materials every 15 days with payment due 30 days after receipt of the goods, it will at any time have $30,000 in accounts payable. Should the business expand and require a 20 percent increase in purchases, trade credit will increase spontaneously and add another $6,000 to accounts payable as illustrated in Table 24.7 below.

Table 24.7

Trade Credit and Purchases

Receipt of goods: Shipments numbered Sequentially	(1)	(2)	(3)	(4)	
	0	15	30	45	Time (in days)
Shipments of $15,000: accounts payable outstanding	$15,000	$30,000	$30,000	$30,000	
20% increase in purchases: accounts payable outstanding	$18,000	$36,000	$36,000	$36,000	

This automatic increase in trade credit can become particularly important in an inflationary environment. In the presence of price-level increases, even constant physical operations will require increasing dollar values of inventories and purchases. Such increases can be financed, at least in part, through corresponding increases in trade credit and accounts payable.

As shown in Table 24.8, trade credit (as measured by the level of accounts payable) has been an important source of funds over the years and represents a significant proportion of all short-term financing undertaken by Canadian businesses. Its relative importance in short-term financing, however, has varied from year to year, reflecting both new alternatives and changing economic circumstances.

TABLE 24.8

Accounts Payable for All Canadian Corporations, Selected Years

Year	Accounts Payable (in $000,000s)	Accounts Payable as a percentage of all current liabilities (%)
Q1, 1989	168,792	28.6
Q1, 1994	242,297	32.4
Q1, 1999	282,418	30.0

Source: Statistics Canada's CANSIM database.

One of the main reasons for the wide use of trade credit is its convenience to both suppliers and purchasers. Once the account has been accepted by the seller, trade credit becomes a continuing source of financing as long as the buyer maintains his credit standing. There are no negotiations to be entered into or detailed forms to be filled out as subsequent orders are placed. Furthermore, in contrast to many alternative sources, trade credit is generally unsecured. Consequently, assets that are suitable as collateral remain unattached, affording additional flexibility to the debtor. We review some major types of trade credit below.

Open Account

The most common and most informal form of trade credit is the **open account**. Once the seller accepts the account, she merely fills the buyer's order and sends out a dated invoice indicating the items forwarded, their price, and the credit terms. The supplier's only evidence of the credit extended consists of her book entries and the purchase and shipping documents. Of course, sellers include a markup in the prices they charge to cover occasional defaults. This, on top of interest charges already embedded in prices, may result in a substantial discount for immediate or early payment.

Open account trade credit is extended under a variety of selling terms that can be classified by the timing of called-for payments and by the discounts provided. Terms of **cash before delivery**, or (CBD) involve no credit and hence relieve the seller of any risk. Although such terms may reflect uncertainty about the buyer's credit standing, they also arise when a sale may not warrant the expense of credit analysis or when time constraints are pressing. Under terms of **cash on delivery**, or COD, the seller requires payment at the time that the buyer takes possession of the goods. Because shipment precedes payment, the supplier faces some risk of delayed payment.

The extension of credit for a particular period with no cash discount can be set out in several ways, as discussed in Chapter 23. Terms of net 45, for example, indicate a credit period of 45 days from the date of invoice, whereas terms of net/10 EOM call for payment within 10 days following the end of the month.

Cash discounts are often offered by suppliers to induce customers to make prompt payments. When offered, terms of trade credit comprise a percentage cash discount, a discount period, and a credit period. Thus, terms of 2/10 net 30 provide for a 2 percent discount on the invoiced amount if payment is made within 10 days, with the full payment otherwise due within 30 days. Terms of 2/10 EOM, net 30 may exist when a buyer places frequent orders. The discount period extends to 10 days following the end of the month in which the purchase is made, with full payment of the invoiced amount due 30 days after the end of the month. Such terms allow the buyer to make one payment for all orders placed within a single month without foregoing any discounts.

Manufacturers of products that have a strongly seasonal demand often encounter problems in forecasting sales and, therefore, in establishing production schedules. To minimize such difficulties, firms may attempt to stimulate orders during the off-season by means of seasonal datings. Thus, during the summer months, a ski manufacturer may offer terms of net/30 November 1, indicating that payment on the goods will not be required until 30 days after November 1. Although the supplier has to finance the cost of the skis during this period, sales may become more predictable with production problems and storage costs minimized. Customers, on the other hand, are ensured of early delivery of goods that may be in short supply during the seasonal rush, and if payment dates agreed to under such an arrangement are sufficiently liberal, they may obtain generous trade credit on early sales.

Promissory Notes

In certain lines of business, especially those involving high-cost items (such as jewellery wholesaling), suppliers may request formal evidence of indebtedness from the buyer. Formal evidence may also be asked for when a customer's credit worthiness no longer warrants selling on an open-account basis. One vehicle for formalizing the credit arrangement is the promissory note, which provides a written commitment to pay a stated obligation by a specified date.

Trade Acceptances

Formal acknowledgement of indebtedness to a supplier can also take the form of a trade acceptance. Under this arrangement, the supplier prepares a draft drawn on the buyer requiring payment of the invoiced amount by a particular date. The draft is signed as accepted by the buyer and only then are the goods turned over. The signed draft, now a trade acceptance, may be held by the seller until the due date, appearing on his balance sheet as a note receivable. It could also be sold at a discount to a finance company, for example. The marketability of a trade acceptance is determined largely by the signer's credit standing.

Because the acceptance is presented at maturity for payment at the debtor's bank, inability to meet the obligation quickly and significantly impairs the debtor's credit standing. Therefore, this form of trade credit is attractive to suppliers facing difficulties with particular customers.

Cost of Trade Credit

Trade credit is often thought of as a costless source of funds. This view is, at best, an oversimplification. Even excluding the effects of cash discounts, there are indirect costs to be considered. Financing credit terms has a cost to the supplier. When competitive forces permit, the supplier passes on the cost of extending credit to the purchaser in the form of higher prices.

When a purchaser foregoes cash discounts, additional explicit costs, which may be substantial, are incurred. These costs can be expressed as an equivalent annual interest rate.

EXAMPLE

ESTIMATING THE COST OF FOREGOING A DISCOUNT

Assume that selling terms specify 2/10 net 30, thus offering a cash discount if payment is made within 10 days of the date of invoice. If the invoice amount is $100, the purchaser has the choice of either paying $98 by the tenth day or paying the full $100 by the end of 30 days. The cost of not taking the discount is payment of an additional $2, and the benefit is to have the use of $98 for up to an additional 20 days as illustrated in Figure 24.1.

In order to compare the cost of not taking the discount with the costs of alternative sources of funds such as a bank loan, consider the effective annual interest rate implied in foregoing the cash discount. If we pay $2 to obtain the use of $98 for 20 days, the interest paid during this 20-day period is $2/98 = 2.04\%$. On an annual basis, such costs would be incurred $365/20 = 18.25$ times a year. A commonly used approximation gives the equivalent annual interest rate as:

$$\text{Approximate annual interest rate} = \frac{2}{98} \times \frac{365}{20} = 37.2\%$$

More exactly, the effects of compounding have to be recognized. Thus, $1 invested to earn 2.04 percent per period over 18.25 periods will grow to $(1.0204)^{18.25} = 1.446$, implying:

Effective annual interest rate = $(1.0204)^{18.25} - 1 = 0.446$ or 44.6%

Note that this interest rate is a before-tax figure. By foregoing the discount, the firm increases its expenses and hence reduces its taxable income and its tax liability. If the firm's tax rate is 40 percent, the after-tax annual interest cost of foregoing the cash discount can be approximated as:

After-tax effective annual interest rate $\approx (1 - .4)44.6\% = 26.8\%$

As demonstrated, the costs of foregoing cash discounts can be significant, and the effective interest rates implied are generally so high that borrowing from other sources is indicated. Nevertheless, when a business experiences an acute cash shortage, has exhausted other sources of financing, or is judged to be a poor risk, increasing accounts payable by not taking discounts may be the only way to generate additional funds.

Besides recognizing the convenience of drawing on trade credit, the financial officer should give consideration to the efficient management of accounts payable. For
instance, the time value of money suggests payment at the latest time specified. Once a
discount has been missed, payment should then be made at the end of the credit period.

FIGURE 24.1

Effects of a Cash Discount

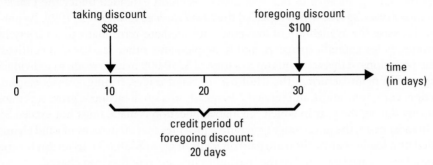

Assumed terms: 2/10 net 30

ESTIMATING THE COSTS OF DIFFERENT PAYMENT DATES

EXAMPLE

Consider once again the terms of 2/10 net 30. Foregoing the discount and then making
payment on the fifteenth rather than on the thirtieth day gives the firm the use of $98
for only an additional five days. This implies a significant increase in the annual percentage cost to approximately:

$$\frac{2}{98} \times \frac{365}{5} = 149.0\%$$

The cost of not taking cash discounts decreases the longer payments are delayed. For
example, if payment were made after 60 days, the implied annual cost of foregoing the
discount would be reduced to approximately (2/98)(365/50) = 14.9%.

To reduce credit costs, stretching payables beyond the credit period may appear
attractive. However, there also may be costs to such stretching. Given the high costs of
financing in recent years, many suppliers charge interest on overdue accounts. Also, credit analysts view a history of late payments negatively, and the buyer's credit standing may
suffer.

PROGRAMS AND AGENCIES OF THE FEDERAL GOVERNMENT

24.8

Federally Guaranteed Loan Plans

The first guaranteed loan plan, which was jointly sponsored by the federal and provincial governments to assist farmers, was introduced in the 1930s during the Depression.
Since then, varied federal legislation has extended such guarantees, thereby enabling

households, small businesses, fishermen, and students to have easier access to the credit facilities of chartered banks and certain other institutions. Under most plans, the federal government guarantees reimbursement on defaults up to an annual maximum. This limit is generally set as a percentage of total advances made under a particular lending program. No government funds are involved unless default occurs.

Of particular significance to business finance is credit extended under the *Canada Small Business Financing Act*, which replaced the *Small Business Loans Act* in 1999. Its purpose is to increase the availability of low-cost, intermediate-term loans to a variety of small businesses for capital expansion, and it supplements other tax-based incentives. Under the provisions of this act, loans up to a total of $250,000 may be made to individual firms engaged in manufacturing, the wholesale or retail trades, fishing, transportation, construction, communication, and services. To qualify as a small business, gross revenues of a company during the year in which the loan application is made must not exceed $5 million. In most cases, the government guarantee provides that 90 percent of valid claims of loss filed by a lending institution are paid on loans of up to $250,000. In return for the guarantees, lenders are restricted in the maximum interest rate they can charge.

Loans provided under this program represent a significant share of total term lending to small businesses. A study conducted for the Canadian Bankers Association concluded that the program not only increased the amount of financing available to small businesses but also reduced their costs of borrowing and lengthened loan maturities.[7]

Business Development Bank of Canada (BDC)

Prior to 1944, no financial institution in Canada provided regular sources of medium- or long-term financing for small businesses that were unable to raise funds in the capital markets. Short-term credit was available from the banks but, in general, medium- and long-term funds were difficult to obtain. Recognition of this situation led to the establishment of the Industrial Development Bank as a wholly owned subsidiary of the Bank of Canada. In 1975, the Industrial Development Bank was succeeded by the Federal Business Development Bank, which in 1995, was succeeded by the Business Development Bank of Canada (BDC).

Legislation empowers the bank to extend credit to any industrial enterprise in Canada provided that such credit would not otherwise be available on reasonable terms and conditions and provided also that the character of the investment and the amount invested by others afford the bank reasonable protection. Given these broad terms of reference, the BDC provides financing through loans, loan guarantees, leasing, or equity participation to a wide range of enterprises, primarily those in the small business sector.

Term lending represents the BDC's major activity although it is also heavily involved in providing venture capital (which is discussed in greater detail in Section 24.11). Both variable- and fixed-rate loans are available, and the borrower generally has the option to

---

[7] J. Hatch, et al., *Government Loan Guarantee Programs for Small Business*. London: School of Business Administration, University of Western Ontario, 1985, especially Chapters 2-6.

convert a variable-rate loan to one with a fixed rate. The interest rates on such loans are comparable to those levied by the chartered banks. The BDC traditionally secures its loans with a first charge against the borrowing firm's assets. By the end of fiscal 2000 (March 31), it had 18,708 customers, and total financing reached an all-time high of $5.446 billion.[8] During fiscal 2000, $1.4 billion in new lending was authorized, albeit 41 percent of this amount was repeat business. Its commitment to small business is evidenced by the fact that 56 percent of the volume of lending in 2000 was for amounts of $100,000 or less, as shown in Figure 24.2.

Lending Authorized Size for The Year Ended March 31, 2000

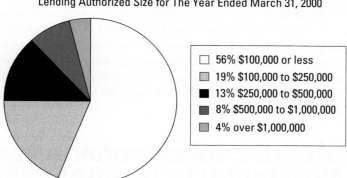

- ☐ 56% $100,000 or less
- ☐ 19% $100,000 to $250,000
- ■ 13% $250,000 to $500,000
- ■ 8% $500,000 to $1,000,000
- ☐ 4% over $1,000,000

Source: BDC *Annual Report* 2000.

For a fee, the BDC will act as a guarantor for a client dealing with private financial institutions. It also provides management services such as general counselling, training, and information through the BDC Consulting Group, which consists of a national network of private sector consultants. Revenues from the BDC Consulting Group reached $19.4 million in fiscal 2000.

The Export Development Corporation (EDC)

The Export Development Corporation (EDC) was established in 1944 and became a Crown corporation in 1969. The main functions of the EDC are to provide financial services to Canadian exporters and foreign buyers in order to facilitate and develop Canada's export trade. With these objectives in mind, the corporation provides a range of loan, insurance, and guarantee services not normally available through the private sector. Particular attention is paid to the needs of the smaller exporters. For example, 88 percent of its customers in 1999 were small- and medium-size businesses.

Federal government sponsorship of the EDC is in part a direct recognition that export trade involves particular risks and problems. For example, it insures against both commercial and political risks. Coverage is available against insolvency, cancellation or

---

[8] Source: BDC Annual Report, 2000.

default by the buyer, blockage of funds, war or rebellion in the buyer's country, and unexpected trade restrictions. Such insurance coverage may be assigned to a bank or other lender. Because appropriate insurance protection obviously enhances the collateral value of foreign receivables, this service provides valuable assistance to those who seek financing. During 1999, the EDC provided $27.6 billion in short-term insurance and $6.4 billion in medium-term insurance.[9] An exporter, through co-insurance, is expected to assume 10 percent of any loss.

The EDC also offers financing services to assist exporters and to stimulate foreign interest in Canadian technology and products in the form of direct loans, lines of credit, and equity investments. It provides export financing for up to 85 percent of the contract value (at both fixed and variable rates) to buyers of Canadian capital goods, equipment, and services. The corporation provided $6.1 billion in such financing during 1999. The EDC also provides guarantees to banks making export loans or issuing performance and bid securities.[10] In offering such guarantees, however, the EDC normally maintains at least partial recourse against the exporter. Loan guarantees are also given to financial institutions willing to advance funds to a foreign buyer of Canadian capital goods and services. ▲

24.9 PROVINCIAL CROWN CORPORATIONS AND PROVINCIALLY GUARANTEED LENDING PROGRAMS

Most provinces have public agencies to further economic development within the province by lending funds, guaranteeing private sector loans, and providing other services to particular types of businesses. Financing assistance is generally designed to complement the lending of private financial institutions and federal assistance programs with the intention that support be given only to firms that otherwise would be unable to obtain funding on reasonable terms. In some provinces, however, such agencies take more aggressive positions and compete directly with private institutions. The government of Quebec, for example, offers a significant array of assistance programs for businesses that are located or are considering the establishment of manufacturing plants in the province. Information offices have been set up in Europe, Asia, South America, and the United States to promote and provide details about the almost 30 support programs available across the province. The aim is to attract new capital investment to Quebec. There is little doubt that the decision of Hyundai in 1986 to locate its automobile plant in the province was prompted by grants and other assistance made available to it by a variety of provincial agencies working to convince manufacturers to locate in that part of Canada. Other provinces follow similar strategies and have set up competitive organizations. Examples of provincial development corporations include Ontario development corporations, the Alberta Opportunity Company, and Atlantic Canada Opportunities Agency

---

[9] Export Development Corporation. Annual Report, 1999.

[10] Such securities provide indemnification if a contractor fails to carry through on the specific duties agreed to.

(ACOA). The details of the range of services offered by these and similar organizations may be obtained from promotional materials, annual reports, and from the Industry Canada website at: http://strategis.ic.gc.ca.

PROJECT FINANCING   24.10

Project financing may be obtained from private financial institutions and/or government agencies to fund separately identifiable undertakings that usually involve large capital expenditures. Loans of this type are different from traditional debt financing because they are supported by the assets and the future income stream of the project rather than by the assets and earnings of the sponsoring corporation. Thus, the project is viewed as an independent economic entity separated from the sponsoring company that provides limited equity financing. Most of the project is normally financed through debt, which may provide up to 85 percent of the total funding. Chartered banks acting independently, in syndication with other private lenders, or in conjunction with government programs or agencies are the major source of project loans for both domestic and international undertakings. Customers interested in future output from the project or project suppliers may also participate in the funding. Because lenders have little or no recourse against the sponsoring firm in the event of default, project financing typically entails higher risk for the lenders than conventional loans.

To make project financing feasible, the risks of the venture have to be carefully assessed and apportioned between the equity sponsors and the lenders. As a first step, a sponsoring firm is expected to provide a detailed analysis of the project including forecasts of costs and potential returns as well as a sensitivity analysis to show the impact of any changes in key variables. An important aspect of this analysis is a detailed discussion of the various risks to which the project may be exposed. As set out in Table 24.9, such risks may include cost overruns, completion delays, cash flow deficiencies, and risks of political interference especially with foreign ventures. Lenders then perform a sophisticated risk analysis of their own, which often includes extensive computer modelling to identify critical assumptions, evaluate alternative scenarios and financing plans, and estimate the likelihood of violations of loan covenants or default.

TABLE 24.9

Typical Allocation of Risks in Project Financing

Risk	Sponsor	Lender
Overruns and completion delays	Completion guarantees	May assist if appropriate
Production, marketing, political	Demonstrates adequacy prior to completion	Bears risk after project completion
Cash flow deficiencies	Sometimes guarantees deficiencies	Normally borne by lender

The sponsor tries to reduce his risk exposure by obtaining financing or guarantees for the project that carry limited recourse from other parties. For example, customers may contract to purchase future output at specified prices, or suppliers may guarantee raw materials at a fixed cost. To fix the financing costs for the project, hedging techniques or swaps may be pursued. Typically, the sponsoring company assumes the risks until completion of the project; but once it is operational, lenders accept the remaining risks with security for repayment limited to the project's assets and earnings stream. In agreements with chartered banks, the sponsoring firm is generally expected to provide completion guarantees covering the major risks of completion delays and cost overruns, and it is only released from responsibility once predetermined criteria have been satisfied. For instance, the sponsor may be freed from such guarantees once the facility is physically completed and operating in a stable fashion for a specified period of time and with an acceptable level of quality output.

Besides apportioning risks, project financing may provide other advantages to the sponsoring corporation. A well-planned approach to project financing enables a venture to get under way with limited sponsor support, thereby preserving the sponsor's flexibility. Because the project is a separate borrowing entity carrying the burden of repayment, the company is free to commit to other projects requiring financing once its limited guarantees expire. Thus, it can move its debt capacity from project to project within a relatively short time, enhancing the company's potential for growth. This is particularly important in the natural resource and energy areas in which companies increasingly face projects that by historical standards involve massive capital requirements that can strain the financial resources of even large corporations. To share such financial burdens, joint ventures by several sponsoring firms have become common, making it convenient to set up the project as a separate legal and economic entity.

On the other hand, the costs associated with project financing need to be recognized. They may include additional management time and transaction costs, delays in meeting the requirements of various participants, possible price reductions granted to obtain customer guarantees, and the potential of higher interest charges to compensate lenders for additional risks.

It has been argued that project financing may enhance a firm's borrowing capacity. Because the project is set up as a separate entity, the debt associated with it is not a liability on the sponsor's balance sheet. Consequently, it becomes easier for the sponsoring firm to maintain reasonable debt-equity and interest coverage ratios and to meet restrictive covenants in trust deeds on its own debt. The validity of this assertion is subject to question. By setting up a good project as a separate venture, the firm loses valuable assets and future income that could otherwise enhance its debt capacity. In fact, if capital markets are efficient, it is difficult to see why a lender would provide funding for a separate project and would not do so if the same project had remained an integral part of the sponsoring organization. Perhaps the popularity of project financing owes more to institutional and legal factors than to basic financial advantages.

PROJECT FINANCING ARRANGEMENT

An American-based producer of specialty papers, controlled and managed by Canadians, planned to undertake a major capacity expansion that entailed the purchase of new machinery from an Ontario manufacturer at a cost of $50 million. Although the firm faced strong markets and operated profitably and with good management, its financial flexibility was very limited. The firm already had a total debt-equity ratio of over 0.85, and the local bank, which had a floating charge against all assets, was unwilling to advance additional funds.

Given the firm's demonstrated strength and the economic attractiveness of the expansion, the new investment was financed on a project basis. A Canadian bank in conjunction with the Export Development Corporation (EDC) was willing to lend $27 million secured by the value of the new equipment. Several large customers agreed to lend an additional $8 million of subordinated debt on the machine in return for assured future supplies at reduced prices. The manufacturer of the machine, obviously interested in selling his equipment, advanced a further $3 million. Finally, the firm's major pulp supplier had for some time been interested in a possible equity participation in this promising company, which, among other things, would guarantee an expanding market for its output. It agreed to purchase $10 million of convertible preferred shares. Thus, the firm had to contribute only $2 million in equity capital (which was just about the limit of what it had available) to make the expansion feasible.[11]

Given the existing operating arrangements with its bank, it appears that it would not have been possible to proceed without a project set-up because only this enabled the Canadian bank and the EDC to clearly separate their activities and interests from those of the firm's other lenders.

VENTURE CAPITAL   24.11

Venture capital may be defined as unsecured term funds provided to a non-public firm by an outsider. It can provide a financing alternative to promising smaller businesses that have found more traditional sources of funds inadequate. Private venture capital firms and government agencies such as the BDC provide such risk capital by buying common or preferred shares, convertible debt, or warrants of firms seeking financing for start-up, development, or expansion. In buying an illiquid and generally highly risky equity or potential equity position, venture capitalists look for rewards in the form of significant capital gains that may arise when a successful investment is sold, usually five to 10 years later. Firms suitable for venture capital financing must have the potential for substantial growth that may ultimately result in their becoming sizeable public companies.

A venture normally terminates in one of three ways:

1. a successful public offering of shares

2. the private sale of the investment to another party

3. bankruptcy

---

[11] See Toronto Dominion Bank, Innovations in Corporate Finance, (1980) which also includes other interesting case studies.

Typically, professional managers are hired to run both public and private venture capital firms. They invest considerable effort not only at the time of original negotiations but also after the arrangement is in place by taking an active role in monitoring, consulting with, and, in some instances, even replacing the entrepreneurial management in order to increase the likelihood of the venture's success. Thus, as a financing option, venture capital is not only costly, but it also can involve a considerable loss of managerial control and flexibility on the part of the entrepreneur. On the other hand, the entrepreneur may receive useful management advice as well as assistance in the public offering of shares once the venture has become successful.

Private Venture Capital Firms

Venture capital firms are formed specifically to seek, acquire, manage, and divest potentially successful business ventures. Although there have been wealthy individuals or families who were willing to advance risk capital, the development of venture capital firms as intermediaries for risk capital is a relatively recent phenomenon. In Canada, in 1952, foreign-backed Charterhouse Canada was the first to be established with an investment company orientation. Domestically funded firms took hold in the 1970s, and in 1974, the Association of Canadian Venture Capital Companies was created. Now called the Canadian Venture Capital Association (CVCA), it has over 100 full-time members. Table 24.10 shows the total number of financings and investments as well as the total dollar amount of venture capital provided by CVCA members during 1999, which reached an all-time high of $2.72 billion that year. This brought the total amount of venture capital under management to $12.1 billion at that time.

Table 24.10

Disbursements Surge to New Record High New vs. Follow-on Investments

	1999			1998		
	Financings	Investments	$ Invested (MM)	Financings	Investments	$ Invested (MM)
New	405	565	1,085	478	607	756
Follow-on	584	1,047	1,635	596	922	899
Total	989	1,612	2,720	1,074	1,529	1,656

Source: Table 1 of CVCA Statistical Review at: http://www.cvca.ca .

In the United States, pension funds were the dominant suppliers of capital to the venture industry. In contrast, Canadian venture capital firms started operations with private funds supplemented with financing from banks and insurance companies. In addition, some of the major chartered banks have become directly involved by establishing their own venture capital subsidiaries.

Significant growth in Canadian venture capital investments has taken place since the industry also sought capital from pension funds particularly through the use of limited partnerships. The limited partnership is an alternative to incorporation. It permits unrelated investors to contribute financially without assuming unlimited liability. One or more general partners manage the business and have unlimited liability. In contrast, limited partners remain uninvolved in the partnership's affairs except for providing capital and sharing in profits.

The advantage of a limited partnership over a corporation relates to taxation. Because income is taxed in the hands of the partners and not in the partnership itself, the partnership is more suitable for attracting a group of investors with different tax positions. Thus, pension funds, which are not taxable, are able to avoid tax entirely, through participation in limited partnerships thereby attaining a higher return without assuming additional risk.

There is considerable debate as to whether sufficient private venture capital is available in Canada to exploit opportunities for economic growth. The perception that entrepreneurial opportunities are being squelched by a scarcity of risk capital has been the justification for various government initiatives. Critics of market efficiency, with regard to risk capital, point to the low acceptance rates for venture capital proposals, which has historically averaged well below 5 percent. However, figures in the United States, in which venture capital financing is more developed, are not much different. Low acceptance rates may simply be characteristic of this high-risk industry. Certainly, total venture capital investment has grown in recent years indicating that the private market for venture capital in Canada is becoming more developed.

Government Venture Capital Agencies and Incentives

Government initiatives to provide venture capital are also relatively recent. As mentioned previously, the Business Development Bank of Canada provides venture capital for Canadian companies. By March 31, 2000, the BDC had authorized capital for 63 investments with $195 million committed. The Investment Banking Division provides services such as syndication of proposals to private venture capitalists, underwriting of private placements, purchase of minority interests, engagement in joint ventures, and assistance with mergers and acquisitions.

Several provinces have set up special venture capital funds commonly referred to as Labour Sponsored Venture Capital Corporations (LSVCCs). These funds have attracted a substantial amount of capital in recent years due to the provision of attractive tax incentives provided to investors.[12] Most of these funds have a particular orientation such as the promotion of investments in the area of high technology. Other provincial programs use incentives such as tax credits and loans to induce the private sector to undertake venture capital investments.

---

[12] For more details, see W. S. Cleary and C. P. *Jones, Investments: Analysis and Management,* Canadian edition, John Wiley & Sons Canada, Toronto: 1999. pp. 77-79.

24.12 SUMMARY

1. Short-term credit covers loans with maturities of one year or less. Primary sources of funds are banks and other financial institutions, money markets (both domestic and international), factoring, and trade credit.

2. Intermediate-term loans mature within one to 10 years. Sources of intermediate-term debt may be divided into two broad categories: private financial institutions including banks, and government agencies.

3. Most short-term bank loans are granted under lines of credit. They may be secured or unsecured, and the interest rate is normally quoted as a given percentage above the prime loan rate. Although provisions in term loans vary and are negotiable, the following features are common:

   - Most term loans are secured
   - Lenders often require personal guarantees from smaller companies
   - Borrowers have to provide the lender with periodic information about the operations of the firm
   - Various restrictions may be imposed on the operations of the borrowing firm in order to strengthen the position of the lender
   - Interest rates charged are typically variable and tied to fluctuations in the prime rate.

4. Money market instruments such as treasury bills, commercial and finance company paper, and banker acceptances, are short-term promissory notes issued by major corporations and governments. Most money market securities provide returns by selling at a discount from face value.

5. A country with lower interest rates will sell at a forward premium relative to the currency of a country with higher interest rates.

6. Factoring entails the sale of accounts receivable.

7. Trade credit is an important source of short-term funds for Canadian business. It arises spontaneously with the purchase of goods if payment is called for sometime after delivery.

8. Credit terms vary, and can be classified by the timing of called-for payments and the cash discounts provided. Datings, commonly used in seasonal industries, allow delayed payments to stimulate sales during the off-season.

9. Federal programs and agencies that provide term financing include the Business Development Bank of Canada, the Export Development Corporation, and federally guaranteed loan plans such as those extended under the *Canada Small Business Financing Act*.

10. Venture capital firms provide money for riskier equity investments that typically entail promising start-up or development situations.

QUESTIONS AND PROBLEMS

Questions for Discussion

1. Why do lines of credit represent the most popular form of short-term bank financing? Discuss.

2. Why are interest rates on commercial paper usually lower than those on bank loans? Why might firms use bank credit even though interest rates are lower on commercial paper?

3. From the financial press, obtain the current yields for finance company paper, commercial paper, bankers acceptances, and Canada treasury bills. Explain any differences in their yields.

4. Why and in what ways does a well-developed and efficient money market contribute to greater efficiency in the economy?

5. Why is the interest rate on most term loans granted by private financial institutions variable and tied to movements in the prime rate? As a business, would you prefer to receive a loan with a variable or with a fixed interest rate, and what are the trade-offs?

6. What are the advantages for a bank of matching the maturities of its loan portfolio with the maturities of its liabilities or deposits? Why have banks sometimes chosen not to match these maturities?

7. Are a bank's activities in connection with credit cards such as Visa or MasterCard a form of factoring? Discuss.

8. A supplier contemplates changing the credit terms offered to his customers. At present, the terms are net 30 days. The new proposal offers a 2 percent discount for payment within 10 days, or the balance due within 60 days. What effects might such a proposal have on both the supplier's and a purchaser's cash flows?

9. We saw that cash discounts are often set so that the effective cost to the purchaser of foregoing the discount is comparatively high. If a customer consistently fails to take advantage of cash discounts, what conclusions might you draw?

10. Why are suppliers often willing to grant trade credit to customers who would not be able to secure additional lending from their bank?

11. Do you see any dangers in the fact that, in their efforts to attract industry, various Canadian provinces may be in direct competition with each other? What possible remedies can you suggest?

12. What do you see as the main advantages/disadvantages of project financing from both borrowers' and lenders' points of view? Why do you think project financing has become popular?

PROBLEMS WITH SOLUTIONS

Problem 1

On a one-year loan of $1,000, a bank charges interest at 16.5 percent. In addition, the bank charges an application fee of $30 to cover processing expenses. What is the effective interest cost (computed at an annual rate) being paid by the borrower? Ignore taxes.

Solution 1

The borrower only receives a net amount of $970, but a year later must repay $1,000 plus interest of $165. We have:

$$\text{effective interest cost} = \frac{1,165 - 970}{970} = 0.20 \text{ or } 20\%$$

We see that service fees and other costs increase the effective interest rate implied in a loan.

Problem 2

A Canadian borrower in need of short-term funds wants to determine the maximum interest rate that he could pay on a loan of 10 million euros available for one year. He wishes to avoid foreign exchange exposure. The following data are relevant:

1-year forward rate on the euro	C$1.3145
Spot rate on the euro	C$1.3255
1-year borrowing rate in Canada	12%

Solution 2

10 million euros is the equivalent of C$13,255,000, which could be borrowed in Canada at interest of $13,255,000 × .12 = C$1,590,600. On 10 million euros, he could pay interest i, buy the necessary euros forward at $1.3145, while holding total outflows to $1,590,600 plus the principal repayment of $13,255,000. We have:

$$(10,000,000 + 10,000,000 \times i)(1.3145) = 1,590,600 + 13,255,000$$

$$(1 + i) = \frac{14,845,600}{13,145,000}$$

$$= 1.129$$

$$i = 12.9\%$$

Transaction costs aside, if borrowing in euros is available at an interest rate of less than 12.9 percent, this alternative is preferred to borrowing in Canada, and vice versa.

Problem 3

Compute the effective annual cost of not taking the discount if the terms of payment are 1/15 EOM, net 60.

Solution 3

A discount of 1 percent is available if payment is made within 15 days after the end of the month. Otherwise, full payment is due 60 days after the end of the month. Thus, if the discount is not taken, funds are available for an additional $(60 - 15) = 45$ days. The interest cost for 45 days is $1/99 = 1.01$ percent. On an annual basis, we have to apply $365/45 = 8.11$ compounding periods. Thus:

Effective annual interest rate $= (1 + 1/99)^{365/45} - 1 = 0.0849$ or 8.49%

Problem 4

Terms of trade credit are 2/10, net 90. You have an open and partially used line of credit with the bank at an interest rate of 12 percent (before tax). Rank the following three alternatives regarding payment in order of their desirability:

Payment in 10 days
Payment after 60 days
Payment after 90 days

Also show the implied annual interest rates for funds used in each of the three cases.

Solution 4

Not taking discount and paying after 60 days:

$(1 + 2/98)^{365/50} = 1.1589$, implying a cost of 15.89 percent

Not taking discount and paying after 90 days:
$(1 + 2/98)^{365/80} = 1.0966$, implying a cost of 9.66 percent

Where the cash discount is taken and payment is made on the tenth day, financing for such payment would come from the line of credit at 12 percent. As payment after 90 days implies an interest rate lower than the rate currently being paid for funds drawn from the line of credit, we should not take the discount. Funds obtained through drawing on trade credit (at 9.66 percent) can be used to reduce the balance owing to the bank (which costs 12 percent), resulting in a net saving of interest. On the other hand, payment after 60 days is clearly not attractive, and the ranking becomes:

Most desirable: payment after 90 days
Second choice: payment on 10th day
Least desirable: payment after 60 days

Note that all of the above calculations were made on a before-tax basis. The effect of taxes would be to reduce the costs under each alternative by a factor of $(1 - T)$, where T is the corporate tax rate. Clearly, the relative ranking of the three alternatives is left unaltered if each is multiplied by the same factor $(1 - T)$.

ADDITIONAL PROBLEMS

1. Assume that a Canadian firm needs to borrow $15,000 for 1 year. Interest rates for a 1-year loan are 8 percent in Canada and 9 percent in Europe. Assume that the current exchange rate is 0.7583 euro = C$1, and that the 1-year forward-exchange rate is 0.7603 euro = C$1. Would it be cheaper to borrow in Canada, or to arrange a fully hedged loan in Europe?

2. The financial vice-president of Mountain Watch Co., a Swiss corporation, is exploring the possibility of borrowing British pounds to finance short-term needs for the next six months. A lender has been found who would lend £3,000,000. If the 6-month forward rate for British pounds is Swiss Fr.2.5643 = £1 and the current spot rate is Swiss Fr.2.5159 = £1, what is the maximum interest rate that Mountain Watch would be willing to pay? The effective annual interest rate on a six-month loan in Switzerland is 6 percent.

3. (a) The Canadian spot rate for U.S. funds is C$1.1415/US$ and the 90-day forward rate is 1.1488. The current yield on 90-day Canadian treasury bills is 8.66 percent, and 90-day U.S. treasury bills yield 5.61 percent. Should a Canadian invest in Canadian or in U.S. bills?

   (b) Assuming that the effective yield after hedging for foreign exchange risk should be the same for investments in both countries, what should be the 90-day forward rate for U.S. funds?

4. You can borrow Canadian dollars at a rate of 7 percent. Alternatively, you can borrow U.S. dollars at a rate of 9 percent. Either loan would be paid off in one lump sum after one year. The current spot exchange rate is C$1.53 $US. What must you expect the spot rate to be one year from now in order for the U.S. dollar loan to be expected to be cheaper?

5. You are trying to decide between long term and short-term financing. You have narrowed the choices down to a 10-year loan versus a five-year loan. If you take the five-year loan, you will still require financing at maturity and therefore will have to negotiate a new five-year loan. The fixed interest rate on the 10-year loan would be 8.75 percent. For a five-year loan the rate is 7.75 percent.

   (a) What must the rates on five-year loans be five years from now in order for the 10-year option to be cheaper?

   (b) Discuss your answer to (a) in terms of risk.

6. The Nufit Shoe Company is experiencing a temporary shortage of funds. The treasurer has suggested two ways in which funds could be raised. First, the company could forego the cash discounts it has been taking and pay its invoices at the end of the credit period. The firm's suppliers offer terms of 2/15, net 60. Second, the company could borrow funds from the local bank at an interest rate of 12 percent (before tax). Which alternative should be chosen?

7. Exceptional Enterprises offers terms of net 45. Management considers introducing a cash discount in order to encourage earlier payments. The discount period would be 10 days.

(a) Find the discount that would have to be offered if management wants the cost of foregoing the discount to equal the current 11-percent interest rate on bank loans.

(b) Is it reasonable for management to determine the size of the cash discount offered by reference to the current bank borrowing rate?

(c) What interest rate would management have to charge on overdue accounts in order to discourage customers from stretching their payables?

8. Two suppliers offer the same goods at the same prices, but under different credit terms. Supplier A offers terms of 2/15 net 45, whereas supplier B offers terms of 3/10 net 90. The firm can borrow from a bank at an annual interest rate of 10 percent. Which of the following would be best for the firm to do?

(a) Purchase from A and pay after 45 days.

(b) Purchase from B and pay after 90 days.

(c) Purchase from A, pay after 15 days, and borrow any money needed from the bank.

(d) Purchase from B, pay after 10 days, and borrow any money needed from the bank.

9. A firm has found itself having cashflow problems. It pays its suppliers on terms of 3/10 net 30. In the past, it has always taken the cash discount. However, it finds itself in a situation where it cannot come up with the cash needed to pay within 10 days for purchases. In 30 days, it will have the necessary cash. If it chooses to borrow money to pay for purchases it would be forced to go to a finance company specializing in high risk loans. It would be forced to pay a rate of 4 percent per month on the loan. What should the firm do?

10. A large company wants to raise short-term funds in the money market. It prepares a $500,000 60-day draft which it takes to its bank to be accepted. It then sells the draft in the Bankers Acceptance market at 99 percent of face value. In order to get the draft accepted, the company had to pay a bank fee of 1/2 percent of face value. What is the effective annual rate the company is paying on its financing?

11. A Canadian firm will have to make a payment of 1 million euros to a supplier in France in six months. The Canadian firm will not have the necessary funds available until that time. The current spot exchange rate is C$1.3187 per euro. Because the payable is denominated in euros, the Canadian firm is exposed to exchange rate risk as the exchange rate may change by the time the payable comes due. While the risk could be hedged using a forward contract, the firm wants to explore other possibilities. The firm could borrow Canadian dollars at a rate of 11 percent, and could deposit Canadian dollars to earn a rate of 8 percent. It could borrow euros at a rate of 12 percent, and could deposit euros to earn a rate of 9 percent. How could the firm use loans and deposits in the two currencies to effectively lock in a exchange rate in six months? What would be the exchange rate locked in by this procedure?

12. Credit terms of 2/10 net 30 are offered on purchases. A penalty charge of 1/2 percent per day is charged on all accounts paid later than 30 days. Use a spreadsheet to plot a graph of the cost of not taking the cash discount as a function of the time of payment (use an exact approach which includes the effects of compounding).

1. Based on BCE's financial statements in Appendix II (see www.wiley.com/canada/lusztig) estimate the cash conversion cycle for BCE, i.e., the average time lag between cash outflows required to procure goods and the time until collections are made on sales. Assume that the asset category "other current assets" consists of inventory; that BCE pays for all purchased goods immediately and that the majority of its sales are on credit. You may find it useful to review some of the financial ratios presented in Chapter 3 in order to estimate the necessary numbers. (Note: Treat "operating revenue" as sales and "other operating expenses" as cost of goods sold.)

2. Suppose that BCE is considering revising the payment terms that it offers to customers across its entire organization. The end result would be an increase of one day in the average collection period for receivables. It is estimated that the more generous payment terms would result in a 0.25 percent increase in operating revenues. Assume that operating expenses will remain at a constant percentage of operating revenue and that the days inventory ratio would remain unchanged.

   (a) If BCE moves ahead with its plan to change the terms of payments to customers, what investment would be required to finance the necessary higher level of inventory? What investment would be required to finance the higher level of accounts receivable? [Note: When goods are sitting in inventory the relevant cost to the firm is the original cost. After a sale is made, and the firm is waiting to collect on the account, the relevant cost of that account receivable is the entire sale price (representing the fact that the firm must wait until the account is paid to recoup its initial cost and to collect its profit).]

   (b) If BCE moves ahead with the plan to revise payment terms, then it will finance any additional investments in working capital out of its cash on hand. The cash portion of its balance sheet is currently invested in liquid money market securities yielding an average rate of 5 percent. BCE estimates that any investments in working capital should yield that rate plus a 2 percent risk premium. Based on this (and a tax rate estimated from BCE's financial statements), should BCE begin revising its customer payment schedule?

part 9

Special Topics

In Part 9, we deal with two additional topics: leasing, and mergers and acquisitions. Leasing may generally be viewed as a form of intermediate-term debt. The decision of whether or not to enter into a leasing arrangement is a financing one which draws upon the concepts developed in Parts 5, 6, and 8 of the text. In addition, the leasing decision is often evaluated based on a discounted cash flow analysis using the procedures outlined in Part 4 and comparing its present value to that of available debt financing alternatives. Mergers and acquisitions are essentially business investments. Hence, the valuation principles outlined in Part 4 are also applicable to these decisions. However, mergers may also entail other aspects of financial management dealt with in other parts of the book such as financial analysis and planning, external financing, and considerations of capital structure.

Due to these complexities and the fact that their analysis may draw on various aspects of corporate finance, leasing and merger and acquisitions decisions are best discussed separately in this last part of the book. This also allows for omission without loss of continuity if time constraints or interest do not allow for complete treatment of this topic.

GECAS's Leasing Solutions Takes WestJet Into New Skies

In Chapter 24, we looked at how WestJet Airlines was able to secure some of the medium-term financing for a rapid expansion of its fleet by securing a loan guarantee for the purchase of up to 26 Boeing 737s from the Export-Import Bank of the United States.

Under another part of its expansion plan, WestJet entered into an agreement to lease 10 aircraft from GE Capital Aviation Services, with an option to lease another 10.

GECAS, one of several financing arms of General Electric, has been a leader in aviation financing since it closed its first aircraft lease in 1965. With a portfolio of over 1100 planes, it serves 170 customers in 60 countries around the world. Financing services offered include sales, finance leasing, trades, secured loans, and consulting.

The advantages of an operating lease with GECAS include individually tailored terms, 100 percent financing with no need for predelivery payments, and a wide range of aircraft to choose from. GECAS is also the only lessor in the industry with AAA-rated funding costs. The company has over 200 agents worldwide to work with customers on finding finance solutions; it is now even possible to make a preliminary application for an aircraft lease on the company's Web page, www.gecas.com. (Another financing arm of the electronics giant, GE Capital Canada Equipment Financing, which also provides some financing to the aviation industry, offers a "leasing calculator" on its Web page, which will calculate interest rates, residual values, amortizations schedules, and more.)

The first four of WestJet's ten leased Boeing 737-700s, expected in 2001, will be used to expand the company's fleet. The next six, expected in 2002, will replace some of the company's original 737-200s; WestJet's intention, President and CEO Stephen Smith told Airwise News in February 2000, "though a period of transition will exist for approximately five years… is to operate a single type [of aircraft], and we are focused on the 737-700."

WestJet's lease agreements run for 14 years, at a cost of approximately $45 million Canadian per plane.

chapter 25

Leasing

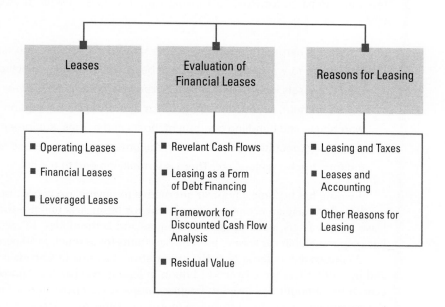

Learning Objectives

After studying this chapter, you should be able to:

1. *Discuss the advantages for the lessor and the lessee under a lease agreement.*
2. *Compare the differences between operating and financial (or capital) leases.*
3. *Discuss the three most important cash flows under a lease.*
4. *Compare the internal rate of return (IRR) and net present value (NPV) methods of evaluating leasing costs. State why one is preferable to the other.*
5. *Identify three major reasons for the popularity of leasing.*

25.1 INTRODUCTION

We have defined intermediate-term financing as debt contracts with final maturities of between one and 10 years; most forms of leases fall into this category. Under a leasing arrangement, the **lessor** who owns the asset makes it available to the **lessee** who has full use of it in return for periodic lease payments. In this way, a lease is similar to a rental agreement, although it normally covers a longer term. The following, taken from a brochure prepared for RoyNat Leasing Ltd., provides a useful foreword to this chapter.[1]

> Profits are earned through the use of equipment, not through its ownership. The extent to which this concept has been recognized is reflected in the wide range of assets leased for business purposes. To name only a few: manufacturing equipment, production lines, office and professional equipment, aircraft, warehouse and handling equipment, boats and barges, equipment for oilfields and mining operations, radio and TV equipment, printing presses, store fixtures, tractors, trucks, trailers, etc. There is virtually no end to the list.

Leasing has become a popular alternative to buying assets because it fills a definite need in the Canadian economy. This is true for businesses but also for individuals who lease several assets, most notably computers and automobiles. In fact, some estimates have suggested that car leasing presently accounts for as much as 50 percent of car sales.[2]

As illustrated in Table 25.1, the importance of leasing in Canada continues to grow, and by 1999, there were over $17 billion in leasing receivables. Approximately 78 percent of this amount was owed to finance companies, 20 percent to chartered banks and the remaining 2 percent to trust and mortgage companies. Table 25.1 does not include leases from manufacturers, which are major leasers of equipment to customers.

TABLE 25.1

Leasing Receivables Outstanding ($millions)

Leasing receivables	1995	1996	1997	1998	1999
Chartered banks	1,777	1,850	2,155	2,706	3,447
Trust and mortgage loan companies	859	750	486	373	332
Finance companies	3,545	5,424	8,572	12,127	13,297
TOTAL	6,181	8,024	11,213	15,206	17,076

Source: Business Credit, Statistics Canada website at: www.statcan.ca.

---

[1] RoyNat Ltd., "Equipment Leasing for Canadian Business", p. 5.

[2] For example, see Alan Toulin, "Fight Banks on Leasing, Martin Urges Car Dealers: Close Session." *National Post*, July 15, 2000, pp. D1, D8.

Before evaluating the benefits of leasing versus owning an asset, we need to distinguish several types of leasing arrangements.

Operating Leases

Operating leases are similar to straight rentals in that the contractual commitment covers a period that is short relative to the life of the asset. Compared with straight rentals, however, the commitment on operating leases is somewhat longer, sometimes running beyond one year.

Given terms that are fairly short relative to the asset's life, a leasing firm is likely to recoup the asset's cost through lease payments only if the original lease is repeatedly renewed or if the firm can enter into a second or third leasing arrangement with other lessees. Because the lessee can usually cancel an operating lease on relatively short notice, the lessor assumes any risk of obsolescence. This risk is likely to be reflected in comparatively high lease charges particularly for equipment that is subject to rapid technological change such as computers.

Operating leases may be advantageous in a variety of circumstances. First, financial managers may turn to operating leases when their assessment of the risk of obsolescence for a particular asset is higher than that of the lessor. Second, operating leases provide the lessee with flexibility for altering his operations since the leased assets can be exchanged on short notice and without penalties. Such flexibility may be of particular value to firms with operations that are subject to unpredictable changes. Finally, under an operating lease, maintenance for the asset is generally provided by the lessor so that the lessee avoids any risk of equipment deterioration or unexpected maintenance and repair costs.

Financial Leases

Financial leases, or **capital leases**, are also called "full-payout" leases. They provide for a contractual arrangement of sufficient length to allow the lessor to recover the full cost of the asset plus a return during the period of the lease. For practical purposes, the contractual commitment cannot be cancelled prior to its expiration. Costs of insurance, repairs, and maintenance normally rest with the lessee. Consequently, the lessor provides only a financing service. The lessor initially purchases the asset and then recovers this outlay plus an implied return through lease payments received over the life of the contract.

Financial leases can take two forms. In a **direct lease**, the lessee gets the use of an asset not previously owned. In a **sale and leaseback** arrangement, the lessee sells an asset to a financial institution, which then leases the asset back to the lessee. For the sale, the lessee receives immediate cash that like a loan, has to be repaid through periodic lease payments. The news report below discusses the recent growth in popularity of these type of arrangements, which have been around for a number of years.

■ *Finance in the News*

Leasing Trend on Upward Spiral: Firms Sell Property, Rent it Back

Many Canadian companies are selling their real estate assets then leasing them back. For example, Canadian Imperial Bank of Commerce and the Royal Bank of Canada both announced in late 1999 that they would be selling off their real estate assets and leasing them back. Gary Whitelaw, CEO of Penreal Capital Management, points to the advantages to the Royal Bank of being the major tenant in his company's $200-million Meadowvale North Business Park in Mississauga. With leasing, the bank has a long-term lease in a tailored facility "without the extra aggravation that being a landlord entails." He sees the shift to leasing as "one of the most significant trends" in the Canadian financial industry. The reason for it is the internal hurdle rate (IHR), whereby companies assess the return on investment with respect to their real estate holdings. When the return does not match up to the IHR, the investment is not considered profitable.

Source: Daily Commercial News, v. 72 (174) September 10, 1999, p. B6.

Leveraged Leases

A financial lease, whether it is a direct lease or a sale and leaseback arrangement, may be either a **two-party lease** or a **third-party, tax-leveraged lease**. In the conventional two-party lease, the leasing firm purchases the assets with its own capital and leases them to the lessee.

Tax-leveraged, third-party leases were developed to meet the need for lease financing of multimillion-dollar capital equipment projects with long economic lives in the 10- to 25-year range. The tax-leveraged lease differs from the two-party lease in size, complexity, the number of parties involved, and the thorough legal documentation required. Its principal distinguishing economic feature is that the owner/lessor provides only a portion of the capital needed to purchase the equipment, usually from 20 to 40 percent. The remaining capital is borrowed from institutional investors. The owner/lessor normally does not guarantee the loan, which is secured by a first lien on the equipment and by an assignment of the lease payments to the lenders. In part, therefore, lenders must look to the credit rating of the lessee to assess the security of their loans.

The lessor, as owner, is permitted to deduct capital cost allowance (CCA) on the leased assets for income tax purposes. In tax-leveraged leasing, the owner/lessor obtains the tax benefits with only a partial investment in the cost of the asset. The debt used to supply the remainder of the capital is not the lessor's obligation because creditors have no claim against the lessor. Nevertheless, as owners of the equipment, lessors may deduct interest payments on the debt for tax purposes.[3]

---

[3] Limitations are imposed on the amount of tax deductions that the lessor can claim. However, detailed review of the often-complex tax provisions that apply, is beyond the scope of this introductory treatment.

As noted, tax-leveraged leases are written for large-dollar projects involving a financially strong lessee. Often, a limited partnership composed of several equity investors is established to act as owner/lessor, and several lenders may jointly supply the borrowed funds.

EVALUATION OF FINANCIAL LEASES   25.2

We are interested primarily in the financing arrangements implied by leasing, so in the remainder of this chapter, we focus on financial rather than operating leases. We note that from the lessee's point of view, an operating lease can be analysed essentially as a financial lease with an added insurance coverage against risks of premature deterioration in the usefulness of the equipment.

We assume that the investment decision to acquire a particular asset has been made. That is, based on a capital budgeting analysis as outlined in Chapter 10, the firm has determined that an acquisition of the asset is desirable and will yield a positive net present value. All that remains to be established is whether leasing is an attractive form of financing.[4]

Relevant Cash Flows

In order to evaluate the economic desirability of leasing versus purchasing an asset, we first have to determine the relevant cash flows incurred under a lease. In leasing, the lessee avoids the initial outlay of capital required in a purchase. In return for this benefit, subsequent costs are incurred, which can be divided into two categories:

1. Direct cash outflows associated with the lease contract. These are the periodic lease payments minus the tax savings that result from being able to claim the payments as a tax-deductible expense.

2. Indirect or opportunity costs that result from the fact that ownership of the asset is not retained. Such costs include the tax shields from capital cost allowance (CCA) that the lessee loses as well as any net benefits derived from the asset's residual value at the end of the lease period.

If we purchase and own an asset, we are entitled to claim CCA that reduces our tax liability, but when we lease, these tax savings are lost to the lessor, who now owns the asset. Similarly, benefits derived from the residual value that an asset may have at the end of the lease contract accrue to the lessor as the legal owner of the asset. Consequently, such benefits of legal ownership, which are relinquished by resorting to a lease arrangement, have to be recognized as a cost in lease evaluations.

---

[4] This separation of the investment and financing decisions is reasonable in most situations. If, however, acquisition of a particular asset provides uniquely attractive financing opportunities such as a favourable lease available from a manufacturer, this financing advantage may have to be reflected in the investment evaluation.

EXAMPLE

NET CASH FLOWS FROM LEASING

A firm considers the acquisition of an asset with a purchase price of $10,000. CCA could be taken at a rate of 20 percent on the declining balance with only one-half the normal amount available in the first year. The company's tax rate is 40 percent. The asset has a useful life of four years, and no salvage value is anticipated at the end of that period. A finance company offers to lease the asset. The four-year lease contract calls for annual lease payments of $3,000 to be made at the end of each year. In notation, we have:

Capital value of asset	$C = \$10,000$
CCA rate	$d = 20\%$
Tax rate	$T = 40\%$
Annual lease payments	$L = \$3,000$

In evaluating the lease against a purchase, we recognize the following cash flows during the first four years:

	Year				
	0	1	2	3	4
Capital outlay avoided	+$10,000				
Lease payments		−$3,000	−$3,000	−$3,000	−$3,000
Tax shield from lease payments		+1,200	+1,200	+1,200	+1,200
Tax shield lost from CCA		−400	−720	−576	−461
Total cash flows	+$10,000	−$2,200	−$2,520	−$2,376	−$2,261

We see that the lease means an immediate benefit of $10,000 (avoidance of the outlay for purchase). In return, we commit ourselves to cash outflows in years 1 to 4 as indicated in the table above, and we continue to lose the benefits of the tax shield from capital cost allowance beyond year 4. The tax shields from declining balance CCA continue beyond year 4, conceptually forever (see Appendix I at the end of the book). The tax shield in year 1 is given as $CdT/2$, and in year n, it is given as $CdT(1 - d/2)(1 - d)^{n-2}$.

We note that many leases require monthly payments. Also, lease payments usually have to be made at the beginning of each payment period with tax shields available at year end. After one has determined the relevant cash flows under a lease, an economic evaluation of leasing simply entails the application of discounted cash flow analysis. Before calculating the net present value (NPV), however, we have to ascertain the appropriate discount rate for such an analysis.

The alternative to leasing is to purchase an asset, and the proper yardstick in any investment evaluation is the cost of capital. In this case, we have to resolve how buying the asset would be financed. This financing cost then becomes the standard against which we measure the cost of leasing, or the discount rate that we apply to lease evaluations.

Leasing as a Form of Debt Financing

The effects of a lease on the financial position of a firm are very similar to debt financing. In each case, the enterprise is committed to fixed payments that have to be met before any earnings or cash flows accrue to common shareholders. Thus, both arrangements affect the firm's financial risk and its discretionary cash flows in about the same way. The accounting profession has recognized this fact and now requires that financial leases be capitalized. Consequently, the capital value of the leased asset is included on the asset side of the balance sheet, and the present value of all lease payments is shown as a corresponding liability. We pursue the accounting treatment of leases in Section 25.3, but at this point, we merely note that the effects of debt and lease financing result in a roughly equivalent capital structure as reflected, for example, in the company's balance sheet. It follows that leasing should be viewed as a substitute for debt: it affects the firm's financial risk as measured both by its cash flows and its capital structure in almost identical ways. In fact, lease commitments reduce a business's ability to borrow and vice versa. Hence, the relevant comparison is between leasing and borrowing to purchase.

If borrowing is the standard of comparison for leasing, then the cost of borrowing has to become the standard against which we measure the cash flows under leasing. Because, in any economic analysis, a firm is ultimately interested in net after-tax cash flows and costs, we use the after-tax cost of the company's debt to discount the after-tax cash flows in lease evaluations. We saw in Chapter 6 that the interest cost a firm pays on its debt may be a function of the maturity of the loan. In order to ensure comparability, we base our analysis on the interest that would be paid on a term loan with a maturity that equals the length of the contract period under the financial lease.

Framework for Discounted Cash Flow Analysis

We saw in Chapter 10 that the two main criteria for investment evaluations are the net present value (NPV) and the internal rate of return (IRR). Although the NPV is conceptually superior, both criteria will often yield equivalent results, and both can be applied in the context of lease evaluations.

The IRR for a lease is the discounted rate that equates the future net cash flows under the lease plan with the initial capital value of the asset. It represents the effective financing cost incurred under the lease and is compared with the after-tax cost of borrowing. If the IRR exceeds the after-tax borrowing cost, borrowing is preferred and vice versa.

In applying the NPV criterion, we discount future net cash flows under the lease at the after-tax cost of debt. We compare this present value with the original purchase price of the asset. If the present value of the leasing costs exceeds the asset value, borrowing is preferred and vice versa.

ESTIMATING THE NPV AND IRR OF A LEASE DECISION

We pursue the numerical example introduced earlier. Assume that the firm can obtain a four-year debt at an interest rate of 10 percent. The relevant discount rate is the after-tax cost of debt, which becomes $(1 - .40) \times 10 = 6\%$.

In calculating the effective financing cost implied in the lease, we have to find the internal rate of return (r), or the discount rate that satisfies the equation:

$0 = +$ purchase price of asset
   $-$ discounted future after-tax lease payments
   $-$ present value of tax shield from CCA lost due to leasing
   $-$ present value of net benefit from residual value lost due to leasing

The residual value was assumed to be zero. Using the formula for the present value of the tax shield from CCA as derived in Chapter 10, we obtain:

$$0 = C - L(1 - T) \left[\frac{1 - \frac{1}{(1+r)^n}}{r} \right] - \frac{CdT}{d+r} \left[\frac{1 + .50 \times r}{1+r} \right]$$

or:

$$0 = 10,000 - 3,000(1-.40) \left[\frac{1 - \frac{1}{(1+r)^4}}{r} \right] - \frac{10,000 \times .20 \times .40}{.20+r} \left[\frac{1 + .50 \times r}{1+r} \right]$$

Solving for r through trial and error yields $r \approx 3.4\%$. Given that our equation contained only after-tax cash flows, this is an after-tax financing cost. The equivalent before-tax figure that could be compared with the 10 percent interest charged on the loan is $3.4/(1-.40) = 5.7\%$. Since the financing cost implied by the lease is lower than the cost of comparable debt, the lease should be accepted.

The present value of the cash outflows under leasing when discounted at the 6 percent after-tax cost of debt, is computed as:

$$PV = -3,000(1-.40) \left[\frac{1 - \frac{1}{(1+.06)^4}}{.06} \right] - \frac{10,000 \times .20 \times .40}{.20+.06} \left[\frac{1 + .50 \times .06}{1+.06} \right]$$

$PV = -\$9,227$

The benefit derived from the lease is an immediate saving of the asset's purchase price of \$10,000. This benefit exceeds the present value of future outflows, and the lease's net present value is positive. Specifically:

$NPV = 10,000 - 9,227 = \$773$

Since the lease provides the firm with an economic gain of \$773 over the purchase and borrow alternative, we confirm our decision that the company should lease.

Another way of interpreting the NPV of leasing is as follows. In the above example, the present value of the cash outflows under leasing discounted at 6 percent was $9,227. Assume that we wanted to take out a loan at an after-tax interest rate of 6 percent in such a way that the after-tax cash repayments on the loan equal the after-tax cash outflows under the lease. In this case, future cash obligations for both the lease and the loan alternative become identical. The maximum loan that such cash flows could support would be $9,227 because at this point, the future cash flows provide an effective yield of just 6 percent. Hence, we could sign the lease, or take out a loan of $9,227 and purchase the asset and in either case, face identical future payments. Again, it is clear that the lease alternative is superior since it provides financing for the entire $10,000 required to obtain the asset. The loan alternative with equivalent cash flows falls short by $10,000 - 9,227 = 773. This figure represents the economic disadvantage of borrowing versus leasing, or the net present value (NPV) of leasing.

The notion of a loan with equivalent cash flows is conceptually useful to an understanding of the present value framework for lease evaluations. Therefore, we provide an additional illustration.

LOAN-EQUIVALENT CASH FLOWS

EXAMPLE

A firm has decided to acquire an asset with a purchase price of $20,000. It has a useful life of five years and no residual value. To simplify our exposition, we assume straight-line depreciation over five years. The company can obtain a five-year term loan at an interest rate of 15 percent. The firm's tax rate is 40 percent so that the after-tax interest cost on the loan becomes $(1 - .40) \times 15 = 9\%$. The asset could be acquired under a five-year financial lease that calls for annual lease payments of $5,500 to be made at the end of each year.

Given straight-line depreciation, annual after-tax cash outflows under the lease alternative become constant. For years 1 to 5, we have:

Annual after-tax cash outflows
$= -$ after-tax lease payments $-$ annual tax shield lost from depreciation
$= -(1 - .40)5,500 - (4,000 \times .40)$
$= -\$4,900$

The lease entails paying a five-year annuity of $A = -\$4,900$. We now ask what size loan could be supported at an after-tax interest cost of 9 percent if we are willing to repay $4,900 per year after tax for five years. Recalling our discussion of term loans in Chapter 5, the loan amount that a given annuity of future repayments will sustain is given by:

$$\text{Amount of loan} = A \times \left[\frac{1 - \frac{1}{(1+r)^n}}{r} \right] = 4,900 \times \left[\frac{1 - \frac{1}{(1+.09)^5}}{.09} \right]$$

$$= 4,900 \times 3.890$$

$$= \$19,061$$

To the corporation, the consequences of the lease or of taking out a loan of $19,061 at 9 percent after tax are identical. In either case, the firm commits itself to paying $4,900 per year for five years. However, while the lease will secure use of the asset valued at $20,000, the equivalent loan falls short by 20,000 − 19,061 = $939. Thus, the lease is superior to the purchase-and-borrow alternative by the amount of its NPV, which is $939.

Residual Value

In the previous examples, we assumed that the asset under consideration had no residual value at the end of the leasing period. Clearly, this is not always the case, and for certain types of assets, such as real estate, the residual value could be substantial. As mentioned earlier, the residual value accrues to the lessor as the legal owner of the asset. Therefore, when evaluating the acquisition of an asset through a lease against the purchase alternative, we have to charge the lease with the loss of any residual value.[5] When incorporating a residual value into our analysis, we again have to isolate the relevant cash flows and then decide on the appropriate discount rate to apply.

We recall from Chapter 10 that in the case of a depreciable asset and without specifically adjusting for uncertainty, the net benefit from a salvage value of S_n to be realized at the end of year n is generally given as the present value of the salvage value less the loss of the tax-shield benefits associated with owning the asset beyond the salvage date. In other words, if we dispose of the asset, we realize the selling price S_n. However, we also lose subsequent capital cost allowance on this amount. Because the transaction occurs at the end of year n, we obtain the present value by discounting at the appropriate discount rate over n periods. This can be expressed as follows:[6]

$$\text{Present value of net benefit from salvage} = \left[\frac{S_n}{(1+k)}\right]+\left[\frac{S_ndT}{(d+r)}\right]\left[\frac{1}{(1+k)^n}\right]$$

The question of the proper discount rate (k) to be applied to the cash flows from a residual value requires additional discussion. We argued earlier that the cash flows from a lease are very similar to the cash flows from borrowing. In both cases, the company faces contractual obligations that are highly predictable. The fact that we used the after-tax cost of debt as a discount rate in lease evaluations reflects this predictability, and any discount rate embodying a substantial risk premium (such as the firm's weighted average cost of capital) would be inappropriate. However, when we incorporate a residual value into our analysis, we introduce a cash flow that is often subject to much greater uncertainty. Con-

[5] If the asset had originally been purchased and retained an economic value beyond the lease period, the company may continue using it rather than selling it. In such an event, in order to make the two alternatives comparable, we assume that under the lease alternative, the firm could purchase the asset at its fair market value at the end of the lease period. Leasing would then entail an additional outflow at the end of the lease equivalent to the asset's residual value minus tax shields from future capital cost allowance, and the relative desirability of leasing versus purchasing would remain as outlined above.

[6] This assumes that there are no capital gains, that the asset class is not rendered empty by the sale of the asset (as discussed in Appendix I), and that disposition of the asset occurs at the end of fiscal year n (see Chapter 10).

sider, for example, a financial lease on a computer. The computer industry is characterized by rapid technological change, which makes it difficult to forecast the future market value of equipment. Unless we explicitly adjust such uncertain future estimates for risk (for example, by deriving certainty equivalents as discussed in Chapter 11), it would be inappropriate to apply a low discount rate such as the after-tax cost of debt. Thus, the discount rate that we apply to the residual value has to be higher than the discount rate applied to the other cash flows in a lease evaluation since it should embody a risk premium that is commensurate with the uncertainty inherent in the particular forecast.[7]

ESTIMATING THE NPV WITH A RESIDUAL VALUE

Once again, we pursue the example introduced at the beginning of this section. Assume that the asset is expected to have a salvage value of $2,500 at the end of year 4. Given the uncertainty inherent in this estimate, a discount rate of 15 percent is deemed appropriate. Our NPV analysis is modified as follows:

NPV of lease = + original purchase price of asset
 − present value of after-tax lease payments
 − present value of CCA lost
 − present value of net benefit from residual value lost owing to leasing

Since leasing now has a negative NPV, the salvage value has made purchasing attractive.

$$= +10,000 - 3,000(1-.40)\left[\frac{1-\frac{1}{(1+.06)^4}}{.06}\right]$$

$$- \frac{10,000 \times .20 \times .40}{.20+.06}\left[\frac{1+0.5\times.06}{1+.06}\right]$$

$$- \left[\frac{2,500}{(1+.15)^4}\right] + \left[\frac{(2,500)(0.20)(0.40)}{.20+.06}\right]\left[\frac{1}{(1+.15)^4}\right]$$

$$= +10,000 - 6,237 - 2,990 + 440$$

$$= +773 - 989$$

$$= -\$216$$

Note that in the expression $\left[\frac{2,500}{(1+.15)^4}\right] + \left[\frac{(2,500)(0.20)(0.40)}{.20+.06}\right]\left[\frac{1}{(1+.15)^4}\right]$

the risk-adjusted discount rate of 15 percent is used to discount from year 4 to the present. However, the lower discount rate of 6 percent (after-tax cost of debt) is retained to

[7] Conceptually, the use of risk-adjusted discount rates in this context is not without problems. See B. Schwab, "Conceptual Problems in the Use of Risk-Adjusted Discount Rates with Disaggregated Cash Flows." *Journal of Business Finance and Accounting* (Winter 1978), pp. 281-93. Whereas other adjustments for risk may be preferable, however, risk-adjusted discount rates are commonly used as an operational compromise. Note that the application of risk-adjusted discount rate is sometimes extended to other components of cash flows. For example, if there is substantial uncertainty regarding the tax environment, future tax shields could also be discounted at increased rates.

discount tax shields lost beyond year 4 to the time at which the residual value is realized (end of year 4).

The reasoning for this subtle distinction is as follows. When signing the lease, the residual value is uncertain, which is the reason for the higher discount rate for the years until the residual value is realized. Once we reach the end of year 4, however, we will know what residual value we can realize, and the uncertainty is resolved. At that point, subsequent cash flows once again become predictable, justifying the low discount rate beyond year 4 for tax shields lost.[8]

Including a residual value in IRR calculations is even more problematic. Leasing now involves cash flows with different degrees of uncertainty since the lost residual value normally is less predictable than lease payments and tax shields. Unless risk is adjusted for in some other way (for example, by deriving the certainty equivalent of the residual value), it is inappropriate to apply one uniform discount rate, as implied in the IRR analysis, to such diverse cash flows. Furthermore, the uncertain cash flows implied in a residual value can make leasing a riskier form of financing than borrowing. Because of this risk differential, the costs of these two financing alternatives as given by their IRRs are no longer completely comparable.[9]

EXAMPLE

CALCULATING THE IRR WITH A RESIDUAL VALUE

The internal rate of return for the previous example is the discount rate that satisfies the equation

0 = + original asset value
  − discounted future after-tax lease payments
  − present value of tax shields from CCA lost due to leasing
  − present value of net benefit from residual value lost due to leasing

Solving for the IRR, we obtain:

$$0 = + 10,000 - 3,000(1-.40)\left[\frac{1-\frac{1}{(1+r)^4}}{r}\right] - \frac{10,000 \times .20 \times .40}{.20+r}\left[\frac{1+0.5\times.06}{1+r}\right]$$

$$- \left[\frac{2,500}{(1+r)^4}\right] + \left[\frac{(2,500)(0.20)(0.40)}{.20+r}\right]\left[\frac{1}{(1+r)^4}\right]$$

Through trial and error, we derive $r \approx 8.2\%$. This implies that we should reject the leasing alternative since this figure exceeds 6 percent, which is consistent with the conclusion of our NPV analysis above. However, this solution implies, that we are willing to

[8] Although this appears to be the prevalent and conceptually correct approach, some controversy exists on the issue. For practical purposes, however, differences obtained by applying various discount rates are rarely large enough to influence the decision.

[9] As an alternative for dealing with this issue, when calculating the internal rate of return, we could have discounted the residual value in the above example at $(r + x)$, where x is the risk premium that is deemed to be appropriate. Given a value for x, we can then proceed to solve the equation for r, which would become a more representative figure for the cost of leasing.

discount the residual value at the IRR of 8.2 percent. If the residual value is subject to significant uncertainty and if we rely on discounting to adjust for the risk, this would not be reasonable.

We conclude that simple IRR analysis is fraught with difficulties in situations in which the residual value is substantial and uncertain and that decisions based on NPVs will prove to be easier computationally and more valid. An additional illustration of the problems that may be encountered is provided in Problem 3 with Solution at the end of the chapter.

Given the difficulty of estimating residual values, sensitivity analysis with regard to the residual value is often useful. It helps to establish whether the issue of a residual value is critical in a particular situation. We may start by analysing a lease on the assumption that the asset's residual value is zero. If this leads to a preference for borrowing, then borrowing to purchase will always be superior, because a positive residual value imposes an additional cost on leasing that can only make leasing less desirable. If, on the other hand, leasing is preferred with a residual value of zero, we can determine what level the residual value would have to achieve to make leasing and borrowing equal. We can then consider the likelihood of the salvage value exceeding this level.

ESTIMATING THE BREAK-EVEN RESIDUAL VALUE

In the above example, leasing was preferred when the residual value was zero (NPV Leasing = \$773). We now determine what level the salvage value would have to reach in order to make the NPV for leasing equal to zero:

EXAMPLE

$$NPV_{leasing} = +733 - \left[\frac{S_n}{(1+.15)^4}\right] + \left[\frac{S_n(.20)(.40)}{(.20+.06)}\right]\left[\frac{1}{(1+.15)^4}\right]$$

$$= +733 - [.5717\, S_n] + [.1759\, S_n]$$

$$= +733 - .3958\, S_n$$

Setting the NPV eqaual to zero and solving for S_n, we obtain:

$$S_n = \frac{733}{0.3958} = \$1,953$$

If we are confident that the asset's salvage value will exceed \$1,953, borrowing will be preferred over leasing and vice versa. Careful estimation and evaluation of the residual value will become an issue only if its likely range moves the analysis close to the break-even point.

We have emphasized the residual value and its proper incorporation into lease evaluations because in an inflationary environment, residual asset values often become significant. Real assets, particularly land and buildings, normally increase in value with inflation, and in transactions involving real estate, residual values may well dominate the analysis. To estimate residual values under such circumstances requires not only an assessment of the asset's economic usefulness many years hence but also a prediction of likely inflation rates. It is easy to see that both the absolute magnitude of the residual value and the uncertainty inherent in any estimate can be substantial.

In summarizing the various techniques for lease evaluations, we conclude that NPV analysis is the most widely applicable and computationally the easiest approach. The appropriate discount rate is the after-tax cost of borrowing except for the residual value when a risk adjustment should be applied. The assessment of and adjustment for risk in this context is largely judgemental. Sensitivity analysis is useful in determining whether the issue of a residual value is critical to the decision at hand. Although the computations are slightly more cumbersome and dealing with the uncertainty of residual values becomes problematic, an assessment of implied financing costs through IRR calculations will often provide equivalent results.

25.3 REASONS FOR LEASING

In the previous section, we analysed leases from the lessee's viewpoint. The cash flows that a lease produces for a lessor are a mirror image of those incurred by the lessee. In fact, if tax rates and regulations are the same for the lessor and the lessee, we face exact symmetry: whatever the lessee loses, the lessor gains, and vice versa. For example, any tax savings from CCA or any net benefits of a residual value lost by the lessee accrue to the lessor. It follows that the effective cost of a lease to a lessee, as measured by its IRR, just equals the effective yield of the lease for the lessor.

Many financial institutions such as finance companies offer both leases and loans as part of their financing services. Given that the risks under both arrangements are similar, one would expect both leases and loans to be priced in such a way as to provide equivalent returns to the financial institution. Consequently, in competitive markets and with uniform tax treatments, the effective costs of leasing and borrowing should be the same. This fails to explain the popularity of leasing as reflected in Table 25.1, and the question arises as to why many firms find it more advantageous to lease rather than to borrow. A large part of the answer is found in differential tax treatments between lessors and lessees and in various other market imperfections. It is the purpose of this section to explore these tax implications and other factors that may influence the attractiveness of leasing.

EXAMPLE

Leasing and Taxes

We have noted that when the tax rates and regulations are identical for both lessor and lessee, there should be no advantage to leasing over borrowing. In fact, the NPV of any lease should be zero, which implies indifference between lease and debt financing.

EQUAL TAX RATES FOR LESSOR AND LESSEE

A firm plans to acquire new machinery worth $10,000. The machinery qualifies for accelerated CCA expenses on a straight-line basis over two years. At the end of its useful life of five years, the machine is expected to have no residual value. The company approaches a finance company for funding. The alternatives offered are either a five-year lease or a five-year term loan. The income tax rate facing both the firm and the finance company is 40 percent, and the appropriate market interest rate on a five-year term loan is 15 percent.

In setting the lease payments, the finance company will want to get an after-tax return of $15(1 - .40) = 9\%$ from the lease, which is commensurate with the return that it can obtain through lending. The necessary lease payments (L) are derived by solving:

$$10,000 = L(1-.40) \times \left[\frac{1 - \frac{1}{(1+.09)^5}}{.09} \right] + 5,000 \times .40 \times \left[\frac{1 - \frac{1}{(1+.09)^2}}{.09} \right]$$

That is, in order to achieve the desired return on the lease, future after-tax inflows from the lease (after-tax lease payments plus tax savings from accelerated CCA) discounted at the desired rate of return of 9 percent must equal the initial outlay of $10,000 required to purchase the machinery.

$$10,000 = L(.06) \times [3.8896] + 2,000 \times [1.7591]$$

$$L = \frac{[10,000 - 2,000 \times 1.7591]}{.60 \times 3.8896} = \frac{6,481}{2.33376} \approx 2,777$$

We obtain:

With lease payments set at $2,777, the finance company will earn an after-tax return of 9 percent on the lease, which is equivalent to the before-tax interest income of 15 percent on a loan. Given that the lessee's cash flows are a mirror image of those of the lessor, lease payments of $2,777, payable at the end of each year for five years, imply an after-tax cost of 9 percent, which once again is equivalent to the after-tax cost of debt. The NPV of the lease becomes:

$$NPV_{leasing} = +10,000 - 2,777(1-.40) \times \left[\frac{1 - \frac{1}{(1+.09)^5}}{.09} \right]$$

$$- 5,000 \times .40 \times \left[\frac{1 - \frac{1}{(1+.09)^2}}{.09} \right] = 0$$

If the lease payments in the example above had not been set so as to make both financing arrangements equivalent, shifts would occur in the finance company's business. If, for example, lease payments had been lower, customers would prefer to lease, and the finance company's leasing business would grow at the expense of its lending activities. Given that leases would then produce lower returns than loans, the finance company's overall profitability would decline.

Basic alterations in the above analysis arise when tax rates differ between the lessor and the lessee. Consider, for example, a firm that does not pay taxes either because it is a Crown corporation or because it has been subject to losses and has no taxable income. When such an organization purchases a depreciable asset, it cannot take advantage of tax benefits that arise from claiming CCA. If the company leased the asset, however, such tax benefits would shift to the lessor, which will be able to take advantage of them. Since the lost tax shield no longer implies an opportunity cost for the lessee, leasing may become comparatively more attractive. In fact, one of the major incentives for leasing is that it permits the shift of benefits from tax write offs such as CCA to firms that can best use them.

EXAMPLE

UNEQUAL TAX RATES

Continuing with our previous example, assume that the business seeking to acquire the asset pays no taxes. The analysis from the finance company's perspective remains unchanged: it either offers the loan at an interest rate of 15 percent or offers a five-year lease calling for annual lease payments of $2,777. For the lessee, however, these two alternatives are no longer equivalent. Because we can ignore any tax shields from CCA, the NPV of the lease becomes:

$$NPV_{leasing} = +10,000 - 2,777 \times \left[\frac{1 - \frac{1}{(1+.15)^5}}{.15} \right] = +10,000 - 9,309 = +\$691$$

Note that we have discounted at 15 percent since the tax rate is zero and there is no tax shield on interest. Thus, the relevant discount rate becomes the full interest cost on a comparable loan.

The finance company is no worse off than before, though the lessee can achieve an economic gain of $691 through leasing. This economic gain comes at the government's expense. By allowing the transfer of CCA from the lessee, which cannot benefit from them, to the lessor, which can use them to reduce taxes, the value of overall tax collections to the government is reduced. In fact, the government is subsidizing the lease. Therefore, this becomes the preferred form of financing.

Not surprisingly, beginning in 1976, the federal government introduced measures restricting the amount of CCA that may be claimed by lessors on leased equipment. Specifically, CCA on the leasing of movable property was limited to the lessor's net rental income, which is defined as leasing income less overhead and interest charges. Basically, this provision precludes the lessor from applying CCA on a leased asset against any other income not directly associated with the lease. Additional and much more restrictive changes were imposed on lessors in 1989. Lease payments were taken to comprise interest (as prescribed in regulations) and principal. The lessor was then permitted to claim as CCA only the lesser of the principal component of the lease payments or the traditionally allowable CCA (but with the half-in-first-year rule waived). These drastic limitations apply only to lessors for which leasing is their principal business. Also, certain properties were exempt from the ruling. High-cost heavy equipment was generally the target with assets under $25,000 exempt from the 1989 rulings. It also should be noted that lessees might continue to deduct the full amount of the lease payments.[10] These restrictions dealt certain segments of Canada's leasing industry a severe blow.

An additional concern to taxation authorities has been the fact that some leases have been used essentially to effect a sale, but the formality of drawing up a lease provided tax advantages to the transacting parties. Consider, for example, a lease that provides for high lease payments over a time period that is short relative to the useful life of the asset. At the end of the lease period, the lessee has an option to purchase the asset from the lessor for a nominal price far below the asset's market value at the time. Through the purchase option, all the benefits of ownership including any benefits from a residual value revert to the lessee. However, the high initial lease payments, which are tax deductible, may provide the lessee with greater tax savings than would be available through CCA under immediate ownership.

The tax department has not accepted such arrangements as *bona fide* financial leases and has classified them as conditional sales.[11] In essence, a lease is deemed to be a sale if it either provides for automatic transfer of ownership to the lessee at the end of the lease period or if the lessee is given an option to acquire the asset at less than fair market value. The tax implications of such reclassifications are complex and beyond the scope of our discussion, but they are essentially another attempt to prevent purchases from being arranged through the vehicle of a lease in order to avoid taxes.

Before leaving the area of taxation, a few comments on leasing in an international context are in order. Increasingly, various Canadian firms have found it advantageous to lease assets that are financed abroad. As usual, tax considerations play a major role in such transactions. Provisions for CCA expenses and other tax incentives vary from country to country, and leasing may provide an opportunity to shift ownership of the asset to the country in which the largest tax benefits can be realized. By taking full advantage of various tax incentives and deductions available in an international environment, a lessee may achieve lower effective financing costs. Although it is impossible to consider the complex and constantly changing details of international taxation in this chapter, the potential savings available through international leases should be borne in mind particularly when expensive machinery or equipment has to be imported from abroad. ⬆

Leases and Accounting

Traditionally, the accounting treatment of lease and debt financing has differed substantially. When a company purchases an asset and borrows to finance the acquisition, the transaction is fully reflected on the company's balance sheet with both assets and liabilities increasing by the purchase price. Leases, on the other hand, were generally not

---

[10] In certain instances and subject to lessor approval, provision is now made for a lessee to claim both capital cost allowance and the interest imputed in the lease payments.

[11] Under a conditional sale, transfer of the ownership of the asset sold is postponed until the purchaser has met certain obligations such as full payments on any financing provided

reflected on the firm's balance sheet but only disclosed through footnotes to the financial statements. As a consequence, various performance measures such as debt-equity ratios or return on assets could be influenced by the method of acquisition. Not only might a casual observer be deceived by financial statements that fail to fully disclose lease commitments, but corporations could also use this opportunity to circumvent various debt restrictions imposed by creditors. For example, a bond indenture may specify constraints on the maximum proportion of debt to total capital or on interest coverage as derived from the firm's audited financial statements. Although such restrictions may preclude the business from financing additional capital acquisitions through debt, lease financing would remain feasible as it was off-balance-sheet financing with no direct effect on the firm's financial statements.

To overcome these shortcomings, the Canadian Institute of Chartered Accountants (CICA) added guidelines to its handbook that provide for a more explicit treatment of financial leases. As these guidelines are complex and detailed, we can present only a brief overview of some key features. Their basic purpose is to ensure that true financial leases are fully disclosed and recognized as a liability on a firm's balance sheet.

The guidelines distinguish between capital (or financial) leases and operating leases. A capital lease is defined as one that transfers substantially all of the benefits and risks incident to ownership of property to the lessee. Specific tests may be applied to determine whether a particular lease meets the definition of a capital lease including the following:

1. The lease term is equal to a major portion (usually 75 percent or more) of the economic life of the leased property.

2. The present value of the minimum lease payments, excluding executory costs, is equal to substantially all (usually 90 percent or more) of the fair value of the leased property at the inception of the lease.

3. Ownership of the leased property is transferred to the lessee at the end of the lease term either automatically or by providing for a bargain purchase option at less than fair value of the asset at that time.

If any of the above conditions apply, the lease will normally be treated as a capital lease, and the lessee should account for such leases by recognizing both an asset and an obligation. The asset amount and the amount of the obligation, which are recorded on the balance sheet at the beginning of the lease term, would be the present value of the minimum lease payments (excluding any executory costs built into the lease). The discount rate to be used in determining this present value would be the lower of the lessee's rate for incremental borrowing and the interest rate implicit in the lease. However, the maximum value recorded for the asset and obligation should not exceed the leased asset's fair value. The capitalized value of a depreciable asset under a capital lease is then amortized over the period of expected use on a basis that is consistent with the lessee's depreciation policy for other similar fixed assets. Similarly, lease payments, like repayments on debt, are broken down and allocated to a reduction of the obligation, interest expense, and any related executory costs. The interest portion then becomes part of the overall interest expense shown in the firm's income statement.

The net effect of these regulations is to make the accounting treatment for financial leases similar to the accounting treatment for purchasing and borrowing, recognizing that in either case, the company has incurred long-term contractual obligations in return for the use of an asset.

Operating leases, like rental agreements, continue to receive a separate treatment and are not reflected in balance sheets. Some enterprises that are concerned about either the complexities of the guidelines or the effects of disclosing leases on their balance sheets have attempted to avoid such disclosure by rewriting their leases in ways that would allow them to be classified as operating leases. For example, many automobile leases have been changed as a consequence of the guidelines so that the present value of lease payments is just under 90 percent of the value of the leased assets. This has allowed the lease to be treated as an operating lease, thus escaping the capitalization requirement.

In summary, we doubt whether accounting considerations should play a major role in evaluating leasing against borrowing. The recent move by the accounting profession has made the accounting treatments of financial leases and borrowing quite similar. In any event, it is questionable whether cosmetic changes to financial statements through varying disclosure requirements would have a major impact on the firm. Most investors, analysts, and creditors are sophisticated enough to include lease commitments in their evaluations if they are substantial enough to make a difference.

P E R S P E C T I V E S

Corporate Manager

It is advantageous for companies to have leases recorded as operating leases rather than capital leases since operating leases will not have a detrimental effect on the company's debt ratios and may enhance profitability measures such as the return on assets ratio.

Investor

Investors should carefully read footnotes to company financial statements and consider operating leases as debt for the purposes of ratio analysis, cash flow projections, and for other matters relating to the evaluation of a company.

Other Reasons for Leasing

Leasing can be used to offset the risks of asset ownership, which is true to a certain extent. In the following report the author states that "leasing can provide a means to acquire equipment for a specified period of time without assuming the long-term liability of ownership and disposal." There are several other reasons often advanced for the use of lease financing as opposed to traditional asset purchases. Some of these are discussed in the report below.

■ *Finance in the News*

Balance Risk Through Leasing

Leasing is not a new business concept, but it is one that is not well understood. "Leasing can provide a means to acquire equipment for a specified period of time without assuming the long-term liability of ownership and disposal." The leasing company assumes those, but, of course, the lessee must pay for those risks. With any product, you pay for additional features, and in equipment leasing, risk is one of the primary features. One of the main attractions of leasing is that you are not responsible for the leased items beyond the term of the lease. Depreciation, disposal, and other liabilities of ownership are not your concern. Of course, there are a wide variety of leases, and costs will reflect the risks of the owners.

Source: "Balance Risk through Leasing," by Mike Fox, Canadian *Machinery and Metalworking*, Vol. 95(4) May 2000, p. 19. *Reprinted with permission.*

Ready Availability

Companies with a weak credit rating sometimes find that they can obtain 100 percent financing through a lease even though loans would be available for only a portion of any proposed asset acquisition. For example, banks generally stipulate that for the purchase of new machinery, only 75 percent of the funding may be provided through a loan. The balance would have to be financed internally by the firm. Because the asset would serve as collateral against the loan, the bank is essentially providing for a margin of safety in case of default. This raises the question of why, given the circumstances, a lessor would provide 100 percent financing despite the lessee's weak credit rating. The answer lies in the fact that on default, a lessor typically enjoys a more secure position than a creditor. Because the lessor retains title to the asset, it can simply repossess it, whereas a creditor may have to go through lengthy bankruptcy proceedings.[12]

Furthermore, a leasing company often has specialized marketing expertise that allows it to place the repossessed asset on a new lease with a different client without much loss of revenue. This is particularly true for standard equipment with relatively wide usage. In contrast, a bank may have to opt for a liquidation sale perhaps at depressed prices, making provision for a safety margin on its loan more important. As well, because of this risk, lenders may impose restrictions in the form of various debt covenants to protect their interests, whereas arranging a lease may be simpler, faster, less costly in terms of transaction costs, and less restrictive. These considerations are particularly important for smaller businesses that often have weaker credit ratings and less flexibility in arranging for debt financing.[13]

---

[12] Although the lessor can repossess the asset, its claim to subsequent lease payments is limited to one year's obligations at most.

[13] Where leasing increases the debt capacity of the firm, the analysis of leasing becomes quite complex. Leasing and purchasing now imply different amounts of debt financing, leading to different capital structures and to different financial risk. As such, they are no longer strictly comparable.

Payment Provisions

Because of uncertainty about future interest rate movements, most loans provide for variable interest rates that are tied in some way to the prime rate. Given that lessors often finance a large proportion of their investments through their own debt, some lease agreements also provide for variable lease payments that are tied to the general level of interest rates. Clearly, the evaluation of leases when payments and/or interest rates are variable is more complex and beyond the scope of our discussion although formal procedures have been developed. Essentially, they entail hedging programs that enable the lessee to transfer a variable-rate lease into an equivalent fixed-rate lease that can then be evaluated using standard procedures. When only one of the two alternatives (leasing or borrowing) provides for variable payments, this may affect its relative desirability. If payments on a loan are variable while lease payments are fixed, the borrowing alternative contains an additional element of uncertainty, and this may provide an incentive to lease.

Organizational Considerations

Most organizations have separate budgets for operating expenses and for capital projects. New proposals for capital outlays are subject to extensive evaluations, and capital appropriations may be subject to rigid ceilings. Under such circumstances, a manager may find that she can lease an asset with leases charged against the operating budget, whereas organizational approval for a purchase could not be secured. Clearly, sophisticated budget controls would assure that such loopholes could not be exploited. The fact remains, however, that some leases are written simply to circumvent organizational restrictions on capital expenditures.

Lease Financing through Manufacturers

It is common for manufacturers to offer leasing plans on their equipment. For example, terms on leases of computers and office equipment may not only be dictated by financing considerations but may also be used by the manufacturer to attain marketing or other objectives. As a consequence, the terms offered under a lease may be more attractive than those that a customer could get under a comparable loan.

To illustrate, consider the extreme case in which a manufacturer only leases its equipment. As a consequence, no used equipment market that could detract from new sales will develop, and the vendor can retain full control over maintenance and operating performance. Furthermore, when the manufacturer has significant market powers, leasing can offer the opportunity to increase profits through differential pricing particularly when lease charges are tied to equipment usage.

Flexibility and Obsolescence

As discussed, operating leases provide more than just financing. They provide the lessee with flexibility and insurance against obsolescence. The dividing line between an operating lease and a financial lease is not always clear-cut. For example, computer leases can be anywhere from 90 days to over five years. Even long-term financial leases, particularly if they are written with the manufacturer, may provide for flexibility that would be unavailable if the equipment were purchased. Thus, some computer leases provide for an option to upgrade equipment throughout the lease period without penalty. When such flexibility is important, it may well dispose any analysis toward leasing.

25.4 SUMMARY

1. The lessor retains title to the asset and makes it available to a lessee in return for periodic lease payments. The lessor takes capital cost allowance (CCA) and any residual value on the asset at the end of the lease agreement.

2. Operating leases provide for a contractual commitment that is short relative to the life of the asset. The risk of obsolescence rests with the lessor.

3. Financial (or capital leases) call for a contractual arrangement of sufficient length to allow the lessor to recover the full costs of the asset plus a return. From the viewpoint of the lessee, reliance on a financial lease is very similar to raising funds through debt. Financial leases may take the form of direct leases or sale-and-leaseback arrangements, and they may be two-party leases or third-party, tax-leveraged leases.

4. The quantitative analysis of leasing versus borrowing is carried out within the framework of discounted cash flow analysis. The relevant cash flows under a lease consist of:

   • the initial financing obtained in the amount of the purchase price of the asset (an inflow or saving)
   • subsequent direct cash outflows in the amount of the after-tax lease payments
   • subsequent indirect costs that consist of the tax savings lost by being unable to claim CCA on the asset, and net benefits lost through foregoing any residual value that the asset may have at the end of the lease period

5. The effective cost of a lease is given by its internal rate of return (IRR). This IRR is compared to the after-tax interest cost of a term loan, and the alternative with the lower cost is preferred.

6. The lease's net present value (NPV) is given as:

   NPV leasing = + purchase price of asset
   − present value of after-tax lease payments
   − present value of tax savings from lost capital cost allowance
   − present value of lost net benefits from residual value

7. The discount rate employed in calculating the NPV is the after-tax interest cost on a comparable term loan. A higher, risk-adjusted discount rate, however, may be appropriate for the residual value.

8. Major reasons that have contributed to the popularity of leasing include:

   • differences in tax rates and regulations applicable to lessor and lessee
   • different accounting treatments of lease and debt financing
   • different provisions governing lessors and creditors in case of default

9. Other considerations that may play a role in evaluations of leasing and borrowing include

differences in payment provisions (fixed versus variable payments), organizational restrictions regarding capital acquisitions, and differences in the flexibility afforded.

QUESTIONS AND PROBLEMS

Questions for Discussion

1. Is it correct to say that leasing is the best way to hedge against obsolescence without incurring any cost? Why?

2. "The effective cost of a lease can be computed if one knows the amount and duration of the lease payments." Is this statement true? Discuss.

3. A car rental firm can acquire its fleet of vehicles through either a financial or an operating lease. How would you evaluate and compare these two alternatives? Be as specific as possible in developing a detailed outline of the analysis that one would have to go though. What would be the main judgement inputs required for a final decision to be reached?

4. Is leasing a perfect substitute for debt, and vice versa? Why or why not?

5. "In competitive and efficient capital markets, and in a world without taxes, leasing would not exist." Discuss this statement.

6. If a financial lease can be written with substantially more favourable results for the lessee than would be possible under a loan, indications are that, under the lease, the government will lose potential tax revenue. Discuss.

7. Why might the taxation authorities be concerned about international or foreign source leases? Who do you think would be more concerned: the taxation authority in the country of the lessee, or the authority in the country of the lessor? Why?

8. Lessors lost part of their competitive advantage when restrictions were placed on the amount of capital cost allowances that such firms could claim on leased equipment. Explain why this is so.

9. "If, given relatively high rates of inflation, taxation authorities do not permit capital costs to be revised upward through some form of indexing, assets will be leased rather than purchased." Discuss this statement.

10. A Crown corporation that does not pay any taxes is evaluating whether to lease or purchase an asset; in the latter case financing could be obtained through a bank loan. Lease payments would be $4,000 per year, and loan repayments would amount to $5,000 per year, both to be incurred for the next seven years. Can you conclude from these figures alone that leasing is to be preferred? Give reasons.

PROBLEMS WITH SOLUTIONS

Problem 1

A firm wants to acquire a computer network system that costs $30,000. The system is expected to have a useful life of six years, and no residual value. Capital cost allowances could be taken at a rate of 30 percent on the declining balance, and there are other assets in the asset class. The firm, which faces a tax rate of 40 percent, could borrow under a six-year term loan at an interest rate of 15 percent. The manufacturer makes its computer network systems available either through a straight sale or through various leasing arrangements. The firm is negotiating with the manufacturer for a six-year lease. Lease payments would be made at the end of each year.

(a) What are the maximum lease payments that the manufacturer could demand in order for the firm to prefer leasing over purchase?

(b) Assume that lease payments sought by the manufacturer under the financial lease discussed in (a) are $7,500 per year. The manufacturer also offers an operating lease that can be cancelled on a year's notice. Annual lease payments would be $10,000. The useful life of the equipment is subject to uncertainty owing to rapid technological change. What is the minimum useful life that the equipment would need to have in order for the six-year lease to prove more attractive?

Solution 1

(a) We set the net present value of leasing equal to zero and solve for the lease payments, remembering to use the after-tax interest rate for discounting.

$$NPV_{leasing} = C - L(1 - T)\left[\frac{1 - \frac{1}{(1+r)^n}}{r}\right] - \frac{C \times d \times .T}{d+r}\left[\frac{1 + 0.5 \times r}{1+r}\right]$$

$$= 30,000 - (L \times .60 \times 4.486) - \frac{30,000 \times .30 \times .40}{.30+.09}\ \frac{1 + 0.5 \times .09}{1+.09}$$

$$= 30,000 - 2.692L - 8,850$$

We obtain:

$$L = \frac{21,150}{2.692} = \$7,857$$

(b) The net present value of the financial lease is:

$$NPV_{financial\ leasing} = 30,000 - (7,500 \times .60 \times 4.486)$$

$$- \frac{30,000 \times .30 \times .40}{.30+.09}\left(\frac{1 + 0.5 \times .09}{1+.09}\right)$$

$$= 964$$

We can express the NPV of the operating lease as a function of its duration. We then set the net present value of operating lease equal to the net present value of the financial lease and solve for the useful life. We have:

$$NPV_{\text{Operating Leasing}} = 30,000 - 10,000 \times .60 \times \left[\frac{1 - \frac{1}{(1.09)^n}}{.09}\right]$$

$$- \frac{30,000 \times .30 \times .40}{.30 + .09}\left(\frac{1 + 0.5 \times .09}{1 + .09}\right)$$

$$= \$964$$

or

$$\left[\frac{1 - \frac{1}{(1.09)^n}}{.09}\right] = (30,000 - 8,850 - 964) / 6,000 = 3.365$$

Problem 2

A steel distributor must acquire a piece of land for open-air storage. The distributor is weighing the alternatives of leasing the land for a 10-year period or of borrowing to purchase. The current market value of the land is $1 million. Annual lease payments would be $130,000 payable at the beginning of each year. The tax shields from lease payments are available at year-end. The value of the land at the end of year 10 (when it would be sold) is estimated to be $1,300,000. Assume that the firm's tax rate is 40 percent, with capital gains included for taxation at just half the amount realized. The firm can borrow at a before-tax interest cost of 10 percent. Given the uncertainty inherent in the estimate of the land's residual value, a risk-adjusted discount rate of 16 percent is deemed to be appropriate in computing its present value.

(a) Which alternative is more attractive?

(b) At what compounded annual rate would the value of the land have to appreciate for leasing to become unattractive?

(c) What difficulties would one encounter when trying to compare the cost of the lease as given by its internal rate of return with the after-tax cost of borrowing?

Solution 2

(a) As land is not depreciable, no CCA arises. The expected after-tax proceeds from the sale of the land at the end of year 10 are:

After-tax proceeds = selling price − capital gains tax
= selling price − .40(½) (selling price − purchase price)
= 1,300,000 − .40 × 150,000
= $1,240,000

Lease contracts often call for lease payments to be made at the beginning of each period.

As discussed in Chapter 5, annuity factors are easily modified to account for this. Multiplying by $(1 + r)$ shifts an annuity forward by one period. We obtain:

$$NPV_{\text{leasing}} = + \text{ purchase price of land}$$
$$- \text{ present value of lease payments}$$
$$+ \text{ present value of tax shields from lease payments}$$
$$- \text{ present value of after-tax residual value}$$

$$= +1{,}000{,}000 - 130{,}000(1 + .06) \times \left[\frac{1 - \dfrac{1}{(1+.06)^{10}}}{.06} \right]$$

$$+130{,}000 \times .40 \times \left[\frac{1 - \dfrac{1}{(1+.06)^{10}}}{.06} \right] - 1{,}240{,}000 \times \frac{1}{(1.16)^{10}}$$

$$= +1{,}000{,}000 - 1{,}014{,}220 + 382{,}725 - 281{,}088$$

$$= \$87{,}417$$

Because the NPV is positive, leasing is preferred.

(b) The NPV of leasing would have to decrease by $87,417. For this to occur, the after-tax proceeds from the sale of the land would have to increase by

$$87{,}417 \times (1 + .16)^{10} = 87{,}417 \times 4.411 = 385{,}596 \text{ to } 1{,}240{,}000 + 395{,}596$$
$$= \$1{,}625{,}596.$$

The required before-tax selling price of land (S_n) is computed from:
After-tax proceeds = selling price $- .4(\frac{1}{2})$ (selling price $-$ purchase price)
or

$$1{,}625{,}596 = S_n - .40(\tfrac{1}{2})(S_n - 1{,}000{,}000)$$

which yields:

$$S_n = \frac{1{,}625{,}596 - .20 \times 1{,}000{,}000}{1 - .20}$$

The compound annual rate of increase in land value is determined by setting:

$$1{,}000{,}000(1 + k)^{10} = 1{,}791{,}995$$

or

$$(1 + k)^{10} = 1.792$$

which, from Table 1 at the end of the text, yields $k \approx 5.9\%$. If the value of the land is expected to increase at an annual rate that exceeds 5.9 percent, borrowing to purchase would prove superior. It is easy to see that, in an inflationary environment, residual values may well dominate the analysis, in particular for transactions involving real estate.

(c) In this problem, as in many transactions involving real estate, the residual value, which is highly uncertain, is of significant importance. In calculating an IRR, we apply the same discount rate to all cash flows and do not differentiate between the low risk associated with lease payments and the high risk surrounding estimates of the residual value. Unless residual values are adjusted for risk in some other way (for example, by using certainty equivalents, as discussed in Chapter 11), results from

IRR calculations may contain significant biases.

To illustrate, solving the equation:

$$NPV_{leasing} = 1,000,000 - 130,000(1+r) \times \left[\frac{1 - \frac{1}{(1+r)^{10}}}{r} \right]$$

$$+ 1,300,000 \times .40 \times \left[\frac{1 - \frac{1}{(1+r)^{10}}}{r} \right] - 1,240,000 \times \frac{1}{(1+r)^{10}}$$

$$= 0$$

would have yielded an IRR of $r \approx 11\%$. Contrary to our result obtained in part (a), this would indicate that purchase is superior. The contradiction stems from the fact that under (a) the residual value was discounted at a risk-adjusted rate of 16 percent, whereas no such risk premium was applied when calculating the IRR.

Note that if we apply the technique discussed in footnote 9 of this chapter, we would obtain a more realistic IRR. Adding a risk premium of 10 percent to the discount rate applied to the salvage value, the IRR becomes $r \approx 11\%$, once again confirming the superiority of leasing.

ADDITIONAL PROBLEMS

1. Halifax Company has decided to acquire equipment costing $200,000. CCA can be charged at a rate of 20 percent. The estimated life of the equipment is 10 years and the scrap value at the end of the 10th year is estimated to be $8,000. The asset can be purchased using a 9 percent bank loan, which would be repaid in equal amounts for 10 years, or leased at $35,000 a year. Payments under both the loan and the lease are made at the end of each year. The firm's tax rate is 40 percent, and the discount rate appropriate for the residual value would be 14 percent. Should the firm lease or purchase?

2. You have decided to acquire a truck costing $18,000. You are offered a four-year lease of $4,500 per year payable at the beginning of each year, or a term loan of $18,000 with equal payments at the end of each year. The benefits of any tax shields are realized at the end of each year. The interest rate on the loan is 12 percent. The CCA rate is 30 percent. At the end of four years the truck has no salvage value, and the tax rate is 40 percent. Which way would you finance the truck?

3. A manufacturer of farm equipment offers to lease or sell a piece of machinery that has a useful life of eight years with no salvage value. The asset sells for $45,000 and CCA on a declining balance can be taken at a rate of 25 percent. At the option of the purchaser, the manufacturer will guarantee an eight-year, 12 percent bank loan to cover the purchase price. Alternatively, an eight-year lease would call for monthly payments of $750 due at the beginning of every month, with the corresponding tax shields available at year end. Having decided to acquire this piece of equipment, should a farmer with a 30 percent marginal tax rate purchase or lease the asset?

4. A firm has decided to acquire a particular asset. Annual lease payments, to be made

at the end of each year, amount to 20 percent of the asset's original value. The firm could borrow at an interest rate of 10 percent. CCA on the asset would be taken at a rate of 20 percent, and the firm's tax rate is 45 percent. The asset has no salvage value at the end of its economic life.

(a) Assume an economic life of 6 years. What is the after-tax cost implicit in leasing? Round to the nearest percentage point.

(b) Assume that the firm is uncertain about the economic life of the asset, and that a lease has been offered that can be cancelled on an annual basis. How long would the economic life of the asset have to be (round up to the nearest year) for owning and borrowing just to become attractive?

5. A government agency that pays no taxes is evaluating whether to lease or to purchase an asset. In the latter case, financing could be obtained through a bank loan at an interest rate of 8 percent. Lease payments would be $15,000 per year payable at the beginning of each year, and loan repayments would amount to $18,000 per year payable at the end of each year, both to be incurred over the next 5 years. The anticipated salvage value of the asset is $4,000. Given the uncertainty inherent in this estimate, the discount rate applicable to the residual value is 15 percent.

(a) Which alternative would you recommend?

(b) What would the expected salvage value have to be before you would reverse your decision under 5(a) above?

6. An asset worth $180,000 is leased by the XYZ Corporation for 5 years at $50,000 per year. Lease payments are due at the end of the year. Assume that if purchased, CCA expenses on the asset would amount to $72,000, $43,200, $25,920, $15,552, and $9,331 over 5 years. The XYZ Corporation faces a tax rate of 40 percent. What is XYZ's weighted average cost of capital if its capital structure is 60 percent common equity at an after-tax cost of 14 percent, and the remainder is lease financing?

7. In order to alleviate its somewhat strained cash position, Storerite Corporation considers signing a sale-and-leaseback arrangement with a finance company on one of its warehouses. Under the arrangement, Storerite would sell the warehouse for $1,500,000 and then lease it back over a 10-year term for annual lease payments of $200,000. Lease payments are due at the beginning of each year, with tax shields available at year end. $600,000 of the $1,500,000 selling price is deemed to be the value of the building, and the remaining $900,000 is the value of the land. CCA on the building are taken on a declining balance at a rate of 10 percent. At the end of 10 years, the building is likely to be worthless, but the land is expected to appreciate at the average inflation rate, which is anticipated to be 5 percent per year. An appropriate risk-adjusted discount rate for the residual land value would be 14 percent. Storerite can float 10-year debt at an interest rate of 12 percent, and its tax rate is 50 percent.

(a) Is the lease financing attractive?

(b) How high would the average annual inflation rate have to be so that Storerite becomes indifferent between leasing and borrowing?

8. A business friend has offered to sell you her truck for $17,000; she will then lease the truck back from you. The lease calls for annual lease payments over four years, payable at the beginning of each year, with tax savings available at year end. It is expected that the truck will have no residual value at the end of the 4 years, and CCA can be claimed at a rate of 25 percent on a declining balance. Assume that you have other assets in the class. Your tax rate is 30 percent, and you want to achieve

an effective after-tax return on your capital of 14 percent per year.

(a) How high would the lease payments have to be?

(b) Assume that you would finance $10,000 of the acquisition price of the truck by borrowing from the bank at an interest rate of 11 percent. Given the lease payments calculated under (a), what return would you then achieve on your remaining equity investment of $7,000?

(c) How would your answer under (a) change if the lease payments were monthly, payable at the beginning of each month, with tax shields still available at year-end?

9. The Lavish Carpet Manufacturing Co. has decided to acquire a new machine that has an economic life of 10 years, with no residual value. The machine can be purchased for $75,000, and the supplier is willing to advance $45,000 of the purchase price at 12 percent. The loan is to be repaid in equal instalments over 10 years. Lavish Carpet pays 40 percent corporate income tax and can claim 20 percent capital cost allowances on the purchased asset. It expects to negotiate a further $30,000, 10-year loan with a financial institution at 14 percent interest, thereby financing any purchase entirely through debt. Meanwhile, Midland Leasing Ltd. has also offered to make the equipment available under a 10-year financial lease. Lease payments of $11,200 are to be paid at the end of each year. How should the asset be acquired?

10. The firm for which you work requires the use of a particular type of machine. To purchase the machine would cost $12,000. The machine falls in an asset class in which the firm has many other assets (hundreds of thousands of dollars worth) and for which the allowable depreciation rate for tax purposes is 15 percent per year. The machine would be sold in six years and the firm estimates that it would be able to get $4,000 for it at that time. Instead of buying the machine, the firm also has the opportunity to lease it (the lessor would provide the machine and also cover the installation cost). The firm could sign a six year lease in which the first lease payment would be $2,000 and would be due immediately. A clause in the lease contract states that future payments will increase at the rate of inflation. If the firm's tax rate is 25 percent, its cost of borrowing (before tax) is 15 percent, its required return on investments of this type is 18 percent, and inflation is expected to be 7 percent, should the firm lease or buy the machine?

11. A firm requires a piece of machinery for its business. If the firm buys the machine it will cost $15,000. It would be sold in four years and the firm estimates that it would get $5,000 for it at that time. This machine would be the only asset in its asset class and that class has an allowable depreciation rate of 7 percent for tax purposes. The firm also has the opportunity to lease the machine for a yearly payment of $4,000 (each payment would be due at the beginning of the year). The tax rate for this firm is 40 percent and the cost of borrowing for the firm is 8 percent. The residual salvage value should be discounted at a rate of 10 percent. Should the firm lease or buy the machine?

12. In order to buy an automated packing machine for your factory, the cost would be $150,000. You have inquired at the bank about borrowing that amount and the bank would charge you a rate of 9.5 percent on the loan. The packing machine would be used for 10 years, at the end of which it would have no salvage value. It falls in an asset class with an allowable CCA rate of 10 percent per year. Use of the machine would reduce before-tax costs by $30,000 per year over its life. You also have the ability to lease the packing machine from the manufacturer for lease payments of $25,000 per year (due at the beginning of each year). Your firm's tax rate is 35 percent. Assuming that you will obtain the new packing machine in some way, should you lease or buy it?

Canadian Book Business Wakes with a Roar

Time was, the phrase "bookselling" conjured up images of sleepy little shops run by timid, bespectacled scholars. Hah! At the turn of the millennium, the fierce takeover battle between Canada's two biggest book retailers, Chapters and Indigo, made a better story than many of the bestsellers stacked in the windows of both chains.

The story begins back in 1996, when CEO Larry Stevenson launched Chapters, two years after a controversial purchase of both Coles and Smithbooks. The same year, Industry Canada nixed efforts by Heather Reisman, a noted Canadian businesswoman, and several partners to start a Canadian superstore book chain called Borders Canada—partly, it was reported, in response to lobbying by Stevenson. Undaunted, Ms. Reismann started up her own chain, Indigo, within the year, hiring away seven high-level Chapters executives in the process.

By 2000, Chapters was unquestionably the giant of the industry with 77 superstores and 230 smaller stores across the country. Indigo's 15 superstores, meanwhile - several of them no more than a block or two from a competing Chapters—occupied a slightly more "upmarket" niche.

Neither, however, appeared to be in perfect financial health.

Then, in November 2000, Ms. Reisman dropped a bombshell. Trilogy Retail Enterprises, a private company controlled by Ms. Reisman and her husband, Gerry Schwartz, a veteran of many major corporate takeovers, made a hostile takeover bid for Chapters, offering $63.5 million for 50.1% of shares—$13 a share in cash one day after it had been trading for $9.10.

The Chapters board promptly rejected the bid as "totally inadequate." Mr. Stevenson began an aggressive defense strategy, including a plan to buy back Chapters.ca online. Meanwhile, Trilogy was buying up Chapters shares, eventually increasing its holding to 14%. Eager to retain shareholders' confidence, Chapters issued a forecast on 28 December predicting an operating profit of over $60 million by March. Ten days into the new year, Trilogy raised its bid to $15 a share.

A week later, a new twist: Future Shop launched a counterbid of $200 million for all of Chapters—a bid supported by the Chapters board and executives. The giant electronic retailer offered $16 or two Future Shop shares for each Chapters share, with a maximum of $100 million cash. Some observers were puzzled by the combination, but executives predicted substantial "synergies."

Trilogy sweetened its bid to $17. Still Mr. Stevenson and his board resisted, planning a "poison pill" defense (issuing new stock so that the company would become too expensive to buy at a fixed per-share price). But the Ontario Securities Commission nixed the plan, ruling it not to be in the public interest. On January 28, the Chapters board finally capitulated, tendering their own shares to Trilogy and recommending that other shareholders do the same.

It's not yet clear what the outcome of this pitched battle means for such players as book buyers (how many stores will close? will discounts on bestsellers remain?), independent bookstores (is one giant competitor better than two?) or Canadian publishers (will the new, merged company refrain from using its huge size to "bully" its way to better prices and to get away with long-unpaid bills, as Chapters has been accused of doing?). But one thing is certain— few people will think of Canadian bookselling as a sleepy little industry from now on.

chapter 26

Mergers and Acquisitions

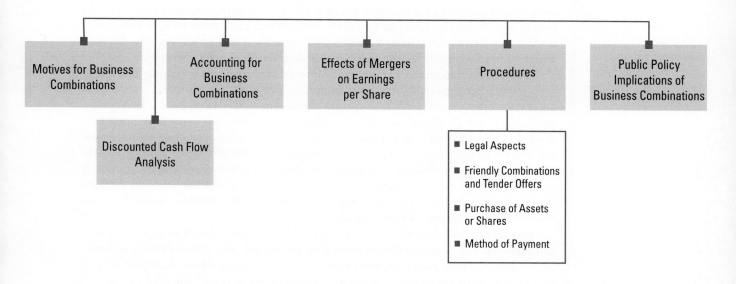

Learning Objectives

After studying this chapter, you should be able to:

1. *Identify the four types of external expansion that a company may pursue.*
2. *Define synergy, and explain what effect it can have on a merged company.*
3. *Describe some of the consequences for the acquiring company when it is paying more than the current market price for the shares of the firm it is taking over.*
4. *Identify the accounting concerns in an acquisition, and discuss some of their implications.*
5. *Discuss the major concerns involving corporate concentration, declining competition, increased debt loads, insider trading, and other such topics.*

26.1 INTRODUCTION

A firm can grow either by generating new internal investments or by acquiring other businesses through external expansion. External expansion possibilities should be evaluated in essentially the same way as internal investments, and if an acquisition is to contribute to shareholder wealth, its cash flows must produce a positive net present value. Thus, the basic framework for analysing business combinations is very similar to that outlined in the chapters on capital budgeting. The procedures for effecting external growth can be quite different, and they therefore warrant separate discussion. In addition, mergers and acquisitions may entail special legal, tax, and accounting considerations. We note in this context that divestitures—when, for example, a firm sells one of its subsidiaries or divisions—represent a mirror image of an acquisition and entail basically the same analysis and procedures. So, the concepts discussed in this chapter also apply.

Business combinations can take several forms including **holding companies**, **mergers**, and **amalgamations**. Holding companies are firms whose main assets are shares of other companies. These include corporate giants such as Canadian Pacific Enterprises, BCE, and Roger Communications. The parent corporation buys a sufficient number of shares in a subsidiary to establish effective control, but each firm retains its separate identity. With a merger of two firms, one loses its corporate identity and is absorbed by the other. In an amalgamation, both corporations disappear and are replaced by an entirely new entity. Mergers are the norm when companies of different sizes combine, with the smaller one usually being absorbed, whereas amalgamations, which are also called consolidations, are common between equals.

It is rare in today's world to read a financial newspaper or listen to or watch a program dealing with financial matters that does not include the announcement of a corporate merger, amalgamation, joint venture, or divestiture. Many examples of such activity in Canada have been referred to in previous chapters including the merging of the stock exchanges, the acquisition of Canadian Airlines by Air Canada, the acquisition of CTV Inc. by BCE Inc., and the sell-off of Nortel shares by BCE Inc.

Very significant corporate growth has taken place through external expansion, and the pace has accelerated in recent years. Total merger activity in the world exceeded US $3.3 trillion in 1999. More than one-third of the value of these transactions represented cross-border merger activity, which reflects the trend toward globalization. There were 1,057 mergers, worth more than $218 billion in Canada throughout the first half of 2000, which is a record-setting pace.[1] The technology sector accounted for the largest proportion of first-quarter activity with 139 deals worth a total of $32 billion, while the industrial products sector was the most active in the second quarter with 118 deals worth $7.5 billion. More than one-quarter of the total number of deals involved a Canadian and a foreign company with 177 Canadian ones acquiring foreign companies, and 110 foreign companies acquiring Canadians.

---

[1] Bessie Ng., "Mergers and Acquisitions Activity Hits $149 b in Second Quarter: On Record Pace." *National Post*, July 8, 2000, page D8; and, "Tech Deals Drive Mergers and Acquisitions Higher [First Quarter Data]." Canadian Press Newswire, April 7, 2000.

The reasons for this merger wave are varied and will be explored below. A quote included in the report below attributes the record pace of merger activity in the second quarter of 2000 to a variety of "fundamental" factors including "a strong Canadian economy, still relatively low interest rates, and the trend toward globalization of companies and the consolidation of industries." The trend toward globalization is indeed an important factor driving worldwide merger activity. The following report illustrates the dramatic increase in the value of worldwide cross-border mergers.

■ *Finance in the News*

Mergers and Acquisitions Activity Hits $149 Billion in Second Quarter: On Record Pace

Toronto investment banking house Crosbie and Co. Inc. stated that mergers and acquisitions were up 11 percent to 691 deals in the second quarter of 2000 compared to 621 the previous year. In dollar terms, the amount is more than double--$149 billion compared to $69 billion. Of this activity, 13 of the second-quarter megadeals were for more than $1 billion, led by the Segram-Vivendi $49-billion transaction. Even without that giant agreement, mergers and acquisitions were up 66 percent to $100 billion for the quarter.

Crosbie partner Ian Macdonell saw several factors at work including "a strong Canadian economy, still relatively low interest rates, and the trend toward globalization of companies and the consolidation of industries." Noting the slowing during the economic downturn, he has seen things "really come back since the markets have recovered."

The industrial sector had the most activity in the quarter, with 118, up 23 percent from 96 the previous year. This represented a total of $7.5 billion compared to $2.9 billion. Technology posted 31 deals worth $2 billion.

Canadian companies acquired 80 foreign ones to the tune of $7 billion, up from $4.1 billion in 68 transactions the previous year. However, Canadian firms were taken over 52 times, totalling $58.5 billion compared to just $6.2 billion in 41 deals.

Source: "Mergers and Acquisitions Activity Hits $149 Billion in Second Quarter: On Record Pace," by Bessie Ng, *Financial Post (National Post)* July 8, 2000, D8. *Reprinted with permission.*

Value of Cross-Border Mergers & Acquisitions Rising Fast

The United Nations, in its just-released World Investment Report, has detailed how cross-border mergers and acquisitions are in the process of integrating the world's economy. Here are total value & numbers of cross-border deals, 1987 to 1999.

Largest cross-border deals 1987 – 1999, with Canadian ones in top 50

Rank	Year	Value $billion	Acquiring co.	Acquired
1.	1999	$60.3	Vodafone Group PLC Britain, telecommunications	AirTouch Comm. United States, telecom
2.	1998	48.2	British Petroleum Britain, oil & gas; refining	Amoco United States, oil & gas
3.	1998	40.5	Daimler-Benz Germany, transportation equip.	Chrysler United States, trans. equ.
4.	1999	34.6	Zeneca Group Britain, drugs	Astra Sweden, drugs
5.	1999	32.6	Mannesmann Germany, metal & metal products	Orange Britain, telecom
18.	1998	9.3	Nortel Networks Canada, communications equip.	Bay Networks United States, comp. equ.
33.	1988	6.5	Campeau Corp. Canada, real estate	Federated United States, retail
35.	1998	6.4	Teleglobe Canada, telecom	Excel Comm. United States, telecom
42.	1995	5.7	Seagram Co. Canada, food & liquor	MCA Inc. United States, film

Sources: UNCTAD, cross-border M&A database, based on Thomson Financial Securities Data statistics;"Value of Cross-Border Mergers & Acquisitions Rising Fast," On the Grid, by Alexandra Eadie, *Globe and Mail Report on Business*, October 4, 2000, p. B17. *Reprinted with permission.*

Invariably, much of the analysis that precedes such combinations is the responsibility of financial officers. Therefore, a brief introduction to the analysis and procedures that apply to business acquisitions is essential.

26.2 MOTIVES FOR BUSINESS COMBINATIONS

Although the principal motivation for any business combination should be a creation of value that enhances shareholder wealth, the specific factors that may contribute to that are varied. This is reflected in the several directions that external growth can take. Though not all acquisitions fit categories neatly, we distinguish between horizontal, vertical, circular, and conglomerate expansion.

With **horizontal expansion**, a firm acquires competitors that produce or distribute similar products. The main motivations are usually to derive economies of scale and increased market share. Horizontal mergers have dominated merger activity in recent years. This is evident in the report below, which shows the 10 largest deals worldwide as of June 9, 2000, most of which involve mergers of companies in the same industry or industries that are closely related. The concern with these types of mergers is that they may result in a substantial decrease in competition. As a result this concern, these types of mergers are closely scrutinized by government regulatory agencies, and some are not permitted. A recent example of such a decision was the government's decision not to allow the proposed 1998 mergers of the Royal Bank of Canada with the Bank of Montreal, and the Canadian Imperial Bank of Commerce with the Toronto-Dominion Bank.

Vertical expansion occurs when successive stages of operation are integrated. In manufacturing, for example, integration may be backward toward the source of raw materials or forward into retailing. Maple Leaf Mills Limited provides a good illustration. The focus of its business was the milling of flour, but over the years, it moved to grain elevators, bakeries, poultry farming, animal foods, and seeds. Usually, motivations for vertical expansion include economies of scale and risk reductions that can be obtained from integrated business operations.

■ *Finance in the News*

Mergers and Acquisitions, the Biggest Deals to Date

A forced split up of Microsoft will be one of the biggest deals ever. Yesterday, the total market capitalization of the company was (US)$362-billion, and it hit its peak Dec. 27, 1999 at $615-billion. If the operating system, which is about 41% of the company, is spun off, the value of that divestiture would be $150-billion. Here we show the 10 largest deals so far, globally. At current market values, a forced Microsoft operating system spinoff would rank third.

	Target	Acquirer	Total value (000,000s)	Announced	Pend/ Completion date
1.	Time Warner	America Online	$187,215	Jan. 10, '00	Dec. 31, '00 P
2.	Mannesmann AG	Vodafone AirTouch	185,066	Nov. 14, '99	na P
3.	Sprint	Worldcom	110,065	Oct. 5, '99	June 30, '00 P
4.	Warner-Lambert	Pfizer	88,633	Nov. 4, '99	June 16, '00 P
5.	Mobil	Exxon	79,043	Dec. 1, '98	Dec. 1, '99 C
6.	SmithKline Beechham	Glaxo Wellcome Plc	71,187	Jan. 1 7, '00	June 30, '00 P
7.	GTE	Bell Atlantic	71,190	Jul. 28, '98	June 30, '00 P
8.	Ameritech	SBC Communications	68,680	May. 11, '98	Oct. 11, '99 C
9.	AirTouch Communications	Vodafone	57,471	Jan. 5, '99	June 30, '00 C
10.	Amoco	British Petroleum	56,347	Sep. 11, '98	Jan, 4, '99 C

Source: "Mergers and Acquisitions, the Biggest Deals to Date," On the Grid, Alexandra Eadie, Globe and Mail Report on Business, June 9, 2000, p. B14. *Reprinted with permission.*

Circular or **concentric expansion** brings together different products that can be handled by similar technologies or methods or distributed through the same channels. For example, the purchase of Canadian-based Seagram Co. Ltd. by Vivendi SA of France was motivated by the desire to combine Seagram's extensive entertainment content with Vivendi's pay-TV wireless telephone and Internet operations.

Conglomerate expansion involves companies with products or lines of business that bear no relation to one another. The main motivation behind conglomerate expansion is diversification and a corresponding reduction of risk. The recent attempt by Onex Corp. to acquire Canadian Airlines would have represented a conglomerate expansion. Onex Corp. is a large Canadian conglomerate that is involved in several businesses. These types of expansions were very common in the 1960s. However, many of them met with limited success with many of them undergoing subsequent divestitures in the 1970s. A relatively famous recent example is the 1988 merger of tobacco company R.J. Reynolds Tobacco Co. with food merchandiser Nabisco to form RJR Nabisco Holdings Corp. This takeover was heavily financed with debt, and the resulting conglomerate was subsequently split up into two separate companies in 1999 after several years of disappointing results.

When a business becomes an acquisition target, its share price generally rises sharply. This is because the acquirer frequently ends up offering to buy the target company's shares at a substantial premium over the market price. These premiums are generally in the 20-25 percent range for mergers (friendly takeovers) and in the 30-35 percent range for tender offers (which are normally associated with hostile takeovers). Generally, acquiring companies are willing to pay more than the going price for the target firm, sometimes bidding considerably more. This suggests that the acquiring establishment's managers anticipate substantial benefits from the acquisition. However, historical evidence suggests that on average, the bidding firm's common shares gain little in value and often decline.

PERSPECTIVES

Corporate Manager

The empirical evidence suggests that acquiring firms gain little on average as a result of acquiring other companies, which suggests they should be very thorough in their analysis before embarking on such endeavours.

Investor

Empirical evidence suggests that investors holding shares of so-called target businesses may receive substantial premiums for these shares if the firm is acquired by another. This means that investors can benefit from successfully identifying companies that have a high likelihood of becoming targets.

There are several possible sources of increased value when a merger or acquisition takes place. Some of the most likely are:[2]

Synergy

Synergy is said to exist when the value of the combined company exceeds the sum of the values of the two firms being merged. Because of this, synergy is sometimes referred to as the one-plus-one-equals-three effect. Synergies can arise from economies of scale because operating on a larger scale can improve efficiency. The greatest synergies often involve intangible assets such as research programs, marketing strategies, or organizational innovations. When the intangibles of one firm can be applied to improve the productivity of the other, synergy results.

Improved Management

We saw in Chapter 1 that although top managers are legally required to act in the shareholders' interests, often they do not, and agency problems arise. This is especially likely if the managers' own interests diverge from those of shareholders. For example, if a new investment project would provide glamour and status to the firm's top executives, it might be accepted even if it appears to have a negative net present value. Once investors become aware of what management has done, the company's stock price will fall. If managers pursue their self-interest to excess, the share price can become substantially depressed, which may make the firm an attractive takeover target. Following the takeover, management can be replaced and the enterprise restructured to improve operating performance.

When acquisitions are used as tools for ousting underperforming managers, they are referred to as the **market for corporate control**. Different groups of managers are seen as competing to gain control of the business. The group that can maximize the value of the firm's assets wins the takeover contest and assumes control. The market for corporate control is seen as a powerful check on agency problems in publicly traded corporations.

Many hostile takeovers are acquisitions of this kind. Since the managers of the target company are likely to be replaced following such a disciplinary takeover, it is hardly surprising that they resist. In contrast, synergy-motivated takeovers or mergers are more likely to be friendly since the target firm's managers have less reason to fear losing their positions.

---

[2] For a more detailed analysis of this material, see, J.F. Weston, K.S. Chung, and J.A. Siu, *Takeovers, Restructuring, and Corporate Governance* (Upper Saddle River, N.J.: Prentice-Hall, 1997).

Bargain Prices

We saw in Chapter 9 that stock markets can be considered reasonably efficient. However, if shareholders do place too low a value on a corporation's shares, a takeover might be profitable. The problem with this theory is that takeovers are most common during bull markets, when stock prices are usually high.

Market Power

When a small number of firms dominate the market, they can sometimes push prices up to the detriment of consumers. If new companies cannot enter the market, to inject competition, high prices may prevail for long periods. In such a case, the dominant firms are said to possess market power. Many economists are concerned that mergers lead to large enterprises exercising market power and a large branch of theoretical economics studies such situations. While imperfect competition may characterize many Canadian industries, there is no evidence that heightened market power follows periods of merger activity. Despite this, market power may be an important motivation for some mergers in some industries.

Improved Financing

Young, promising firms may experience difficulty in financing rapid growth without suffering significant dilution from new share issues. A merger with an established company that has sizeable cash balances or unused borrowing capacity may be the answer.

Tax Considerations

A profitable company may seek to take over one with losses that are not yet written off or with large unused deductions in order to reduce its own taxes.

Search for Liquidity and Management Skills

The owner/manager of a privately held firm may not have a successor and may be forced to sell out in order to obtain liquidity for eventual retirement while ensuring survival of the operation.

Not all of the motives identified above can necessarily be justified on economic grounds. For example, the corporate diversification benefits achieved through conglomerate mergers can normally be replicated by shareholders at lower costs and, therefore, may not convey benefits to them. If, for example, a shareholder of Onex Corp. had wanted to diversify into the Canadian airline business, she could have bought Air Canada shares on her own; management did not have to act on her behalf in attempting to take over Canadian Airlines. One can also question whether shares trading at prices that are below the replacement value of the underlying assets necessarily represent bargains. In valuing these shares, investors presumably capitalize the future cash flows that these assets are expected to generate. If this capitalized value is below replacement costs because of poor expected returns, perhaps capacity should not be expanded in the first place. Only if management possesses superior information or is consistently better at interpreting information than the market, can the argument of "bargain prices" be justified. Finally, we should recognize that management might have objectives of its own in pursuing external growth, and that those objectives not coincide with those of shareholders. For example, business combinations may provide an attractive and effective way of building an empire, or fostering power and growth. When this is the case, merger activity is a manifestation of the very sort of managerial self-interest that the market for corporate control is supposed to reign in.

Table 26.1 is excerpted from a recent study of acquisition activity in the United States from 1980 to 1996. The strategic motives provided for the 278 acquisitions are classified into six different categories.

1. geographic expansion (27 or 9.7 percent)
2. broaden product line (50 or 18.0 percent)
3. increase market share (37 or 13.3 percent)
4. vertical integration (47 or 16.9 percent)
5. diversification with overlap (53 or 19.1 percent)
6. diversification with no overlap (64 or 23.0 percent)

It is interesting to note from Table 26.1 that the motive of diversification is the stated objective of over 40 percent of the entire sample. However, they account for only 20 of 71 (or 28 percent) of the acquisitions in the 1990s versus 87 of 207 (or 42 percent) of the acquisitions in the 1980s. The decline in the importance of diversification is even more pronounced where it has no overlap. In this category, where we observe only 6 of 71 (or 8.5 percent) in the 1990s versus 58 of 207 (or 28.0 percent) during the 1980s. This is consistent with the limited success many such acquisitions had in the past and with the move to concentration on core strengths that many companies have undergone since the late 1980s. This trend is reflected in the heightened importance of increasing market share in the 1990s, which motivated 17 of 71 (23.9 percent) in the 1990s versus 20 of 207 (or 9.7 percent) during the 1980s.

Table 26.1

Strategic Objectives of Acquiring Firms

Year	N	Geographic expansion	Broaden product line	Increase market share	Vertical overlap	Diversification With overlap	With no overlap
1980	16	1	1	0	3	3	8
1981	17	0	4	0	2	1	10
1982	15	2	1	1	4	4	3
1983	18	1	4	0	3	2	8
1984	19	2	3	2	5	3	4
1985	28	5	3	2	7	7	4
1986	27	4	4	4	6	3	6
1987	26	2	2	4	2	7	9
1988	20	2	3	4	4	5	2
1989	21	3	6	3	1	4	4
1990	7	0	1	1	1	2	2
1991	13	1	3	4	2	2	1
1992	10	0	3	3	2	2	0
1993	4	0	2	0	1	1	0
1994	2	0		2	0	0	0
1995	15	3	3	2	2	4	1
1996	18	1	5	5	2	3	2
Total	278	27	50	37	47	53	64

Source: Table 1 on page 57 of "Corporate Takeovers, Strategic Objectives, and Shareholder Wealth," M.M. Walker, *Financial Management*, Spring 2000, pp. 53-66.

26.3 DISCOUNTED CASH FLOW ANALYSIS

In Chapter 10, we mentioned that an acquisition is merely a special type of long-term investment decision and should be valued according to the same general process used to evaluate any capital budgeting decisions. The value that an acquisition contributes to the acquiring firm is given by its net present value (NPV), which is calculated by subtracting the acquisition price from the present value of all incremental net future cash flows that accrue because of the acquisition. To compute the NPV, we have to establish the proper discount rate and estimate the future cash flows.

The discount rate used to evaluate an acquisition has to reflect the risk inherent in that firm's cash flows. Consider a pipeline company that acquires an oil exploration firm. Obviously, the risk characteristics of the two firms are quite different, and this may be reflected in different capital costs. It is clear that any valuation of the exploration company has to be based on its cost of capital, and that the pipelines cost of capital is irrelevant. Approaches to estimating a firm's cost of capital were discussed in Chapter 15.

Although it may be difficult to forecast future cash flows over many years, the problems are no different from those discussed in Chapter 10. Because most business entities have an indefinite economic life, the selection of a proper time horizon for the evaluation becomes critical.

Alternative approaches to this time horizon problem include the following:

1. Choice of an arbitrary cut-off date, after which subsequent cash flows are ignored. Ten years is a time horizon commonly used in this context.

2. Detailed estimation of cash flows for a number of years with some simplifying assumptions regarding cash flows beyond that date. Typical assumptions include either cash flows that remain constant or that increase at a constant rate (for example at the anticipated rate of inflation).

3. Projections of detailed cash flows to a specified cut-off date followed by an assumed liquidation of the investment at that time at an estimated fair market value. Because of the uncertainty inherent in any estimate of liquidating values, sensitivity analysis is normally performed regarding this variable.

ESTIMATING A FAIR PURCHASE PRICE WITH NO COMPLICATIONS

EXAMPLE

Starting with a simple illustration, consider a business planning to acquire a firm that has the following characteristics:

- It has 1,000 common shares and no senior securities outstanding.
- All its assets are useful to the acquiring firm and will be retained.
- Physical assets match the firm's readily identifiable lifespan of 10 years with no need for prior replacement and no residual value.
- No prospects for synergy exist.

After-tax net cash inflows anticipated from the acquisition are $10,000 per year for the first five years, increasing to $12,000 per year for the remaining five years. Given the risk inherent in these cash flow estimates, the appropriate discount rate is 18 percent. The present value of expected cash inflows becomes:

$$PV = 3.127 \times 10,000 + (4.494 - 3.127) \times 12,000 = \$47,674^3$$

It follows that the maximum price that should be paid for this acquisition is $47,674 or $47.67 per share.

---

[3] In this equation, 3.127 is the five-year present value annuity factor for 18 percent, while 4.494 is the 10-year present value annuity factor for 18 percent. These reflect that the cash flows can be viewed as a five-year annuity of $10,000 per year for the next five years and a five-year annuity of $12,000 per year for years 6 to 10.

In a more realistic setting, several adjustments may be required. For example, some assets of the acquired firm may not be needed after the fusion and can therefore be disposed of. On the other hand, periodic reinvestments may be required to sustain the cash flows as projected. Finally, adjustments to improve the target company's capital structure may be contemplated.

EXAMPLE

ESTIMATING A FAIR PURCHASE PRICE WITH ADJUSTMENTS

Expanding the previous example, the basic net cash flows anticipated remain at $10,000 per year for the first five years, and $12,000 per year for the following five years. However, the following additional factors need to be considered:

- The acquiring firm's management estimates that inventories can be reduced immediately by $5,000 without affecting its operations.
- To support the projected cash flows, a net investment of $10,000 (this includes the present value of tax savings from CCA) is required in year 5 to replace equipment.
- In addition to the above cash flows, synergy arising out of the merger is expected to amount to an additional $2,000 per year after taxes.
- It is felt that the target firm should carry some debt. Consequently, $10,000 of debt at an after-tax interest cost of 10 percent is to be issued immediately after the acquisition. The funds thus raised will be paid as a special dividend to the new parent to reduce its equity investment
- The company is estimated to have an after-tax terminal value of $60,000 at the end of year 10 after retiring its debt.

The net cash flows become:

Year			Cash flow
0	Special dividend from debt	$10,000	
	Selling off inventory	5,000	
			$15,000
1-4	Normal cash flows	$10,000	
	After-tax interest on new debt	−1,000	
	Synergy	2,000	
			11,000
5	Normal cash flows	$10,000	
	After-tax interest on new debt	−1,000	
	Synergy	2,000	
	Additional investment	−10,000	
			1,000
6-9	Normal cash flows	$12,000	
	After-tax interest on new debt	−1,000	
	Synergy	2,000	
			13,000
10	Normal cash flows	$12,000	
	After-tax interest on new debt	−1,000	
	Synergy	2,000	
	Net proceeds from liquidation	60,000	
			73,000

The contemplated change in capital structure will alter the appropriate discount rate. We assumed above that the proper discount rate under all-equity financing was 18 percent. Part of the financing will now come from debt that has an after-tax cost of only 10 percent. However, leverage increases the financial risk of the firm and, as a consequence, the cost of equity should increase. Nevertheless, assume that the resulting weighted average cost of capital (WACC) is lower than 18 percent, which justifies the change in capital structure. Assuming that the new WACC for the target company is now estimated at 15 percent, the present value of future cash flows becomes $83,400. Therefore, the acquiring firm can offer a maximum price of $83,400 or $83.40 per share.

Given its uncertainty, we may be concerned about the effect of changes in our estimate of the corporation's residual value at the end of year 10. It is easy to verify that every $10,000 change in the net terminal value will alter the present value of cash flows by $10,000/(1 + .15)^{10} = $2,472$, or $2.47 per share. As an alternative to estimating a terminal value directly, we could have assumed that the cash flows of $13,000 per year in years 6 to 10 would continue indefinitely. This would have implied a terminal value at the end of year 10 equal to the present value of subsequent cash flows, yielding $13,000/.15 = $86,667$. Finally, if we had assumed that after year 10, cash flows would increase at an average anticipated inflation rate of 8 percent per year, we would have obtained:

Implied   =   present value of

terminal value =   subsequent cash flows

$$\sum_{t=1}^{\infty} \frac{13,000(1+.08)^t}{(1+.15)^t}$$

$$= 15.43 \times 13,000$$

$$= \$200,590$$

This would have increased the present value of future cash flows from $83,400, as calculated above, to $118,146. We see how critical assumptions regarding time horizon and terminal value can be.

Typically, firms that are highly liquid or that have an overly conservative capital structure with unused debt capacity are attractive takeover targets because the acquisition can be financed in part by drawing on the target company's own financing abilities after the takeover. Liquidation of non-essential assets such as idle land holdings or excessive working capital also represents a potential source of cash in these situations. Under so-called **leveraged buyouts**, the acquiring firm puts up a minimal amount of equity using the expected cash flows and assets of the target company to obtain debt financing. Often, this includes significant amounts of high-risk-subordinated debt called **junk bonds** or **high-yield bonds**. Clearly, riskier debt has to provide higher expected yields, and the high degree of leverage enhances the residual risk to equity holders. This is illustrated in the

Quebec entrepreneur Robert Campeau's ill-fated 1989 acquisition of the U.S. retailing giant Federated Department Stores, a takeover accomplished through a record-breaking leveraged buyout. Following the buyout, Federated's cash flows proved insufficient to cover Campeau's interest costs, and his firm was quickly forced into bankruptcy.

Notwithstanding the associated risks, favourable economic circumstances and the potential for significant gains lured large numbers of acquisition-minded corporations and lenders into such transactions. In the late 1980s, the junk bond market was almost entirely the domain of investment banking firm Drexel Burnham Lambert, where the idea of junk bond financing had been developed by star financial expert Michael Milken. In 1990, Drexel Burnham Lambert collapsed, and Milken was later convicted of securities law violations. Although junk bonds are slowly regaining popularity, their market in the 1990s was far more staid than in the 1980s.

The above example helps to explain why firms are often prepared to pay a significant premium over the current market price when taking over another company's shares. Essentially, such premiums have to be justified on the basis of synergies by arguing that the target company was not managed optimally or one of the reasons listed above. Once the NPV of the acquisition is calculated, management must decide what proportion of that gain should be paid out to the target firm's shareholders to induce enough of them to sell their shares.

At the same time, it is questionable whether the above factors fully account for the very significant premiums that have been paid in some recent mergers, and on occasion, one can question the judgement and motivations of management. Mergers that do not enhance the enterprise's business prospects do not always meet with the approval of capital markets, and a number of merger announcements have triggered an immediate decline in the acquiring firm's share prices. Numerous examples of acquisitions that have failed to produce the expected improvements and resulted in the loss of shareholder wealth can be cited such as the RJR–Nabisco merger discussed in Section 26.2. Other examples include the 1994 takeover of Snapple by Quaker Oats for US $1.7 billion and its subsequent sale in 1997 for US$300 million; and AT&T's 1991 acquisition of NCR for US $7 billion before eventually spinning off the company for US$3 billion in 1995. In fact, empirical studies have found that nearly half of the mergers between 1990 and 1996 actually destroyed shareholder value, while a 1998 study concluded that "only 20 percent of major North American mergers made a significant contribution to shareholder value, with 58 percent of all mergers associated with shareholder erosion."[4]

Ex post, a fairly significant proportion of the sometimes-spectacular acquisitions that took place in the boom period of the 1980s, proved to be economic failures. However, the evidence is mixed. For example, a study by P. Healey et al found that post-merger performance improved, while another study by D. Ravenscraft and E. Scherer found the opposite result.[5]

[4] Ian Madell and Ralph Piller, "Merger Mania: The Financial Risks of Mergers and Acquisitions," *CMA Management*, volume 74 (3), April 2000, 25–29.

[5] P. Healey, et al."Does Corporate Performance Improve After Mergers?" *Journal of Financial Economics* (April 1992), pp. 135–75; D. Ravenscraft and E. Scherer, *Mergers, Sell-Offs and Economic Efficiency* (Washington: Brookings Institution, 1987).

Over a longer period of time, empirical research based on more than 1,900 business combinations that took place between 1964 and 1983 showed that in a majority of cases, shareholders of both firms gained from the fusion at least in the short term.[6] That is, share prices of both the bidder and target company tended to realize abnormal gains around the announcement date of a merger indicating that at the time, investors viewed such mergers as positive for both firms. Based on this evidence, abnormal gains tend to be much larger for shares of target companies than for those of bidders, with the magnitude in either case depending on the form of the takeover. In addition, the gains did not appear to be caused by increases in market power but rather by synergies and enhanced efficiency.

Abnormally high returns are also often observed in the period preceding the merger announcement, which suggests that inside information regarding merger negotiations filters out into capital markets well before it receives official sanction. This is confirmed by the major insider trading scandals that rocked Wall Street in the late 1980s.[7] Finally, it has been shown in this context that shareholders of acquired firms frequently experience a period of unusually low returns before the takeover, suggesting that performance could in fact be improved by strengthening managerial efficiency.[8]

ACCOUNTING FOR BUSINESS COMBINATIONS

26.4

In the overwhelming majority of cases in Canada, the surviving company will account for an acquisition through the so-called **purchase method**. Basically, the assets of the firm being acquired are revalued to reflect the purchase price and are integrated into the acquiring company's balance sheet at that revised value. Incomes of the two business entities are pooled as of the date of acquisition.

ACCOUNTING FOR A MERGER

EXAMPLE

In a merger, Firm A acquired Firm B and issued 100,000 new shares to pay for the acquisition. With a market value of $10 per share, the total acquisition price is $1 million. Firm B's assets have a current book value of $800,000, and corporate liabilities total $100,000. Assume the following pre-merger balance sheets (in $ millions):

---

[6] E. Eckbo, "Mergers and the Market for Corporate Control: The Canadian Evidence," *Canadian Journal of Economics* (May 1986), pp. 236-60. See also M. Jensen and R. Ruback, "The Market for Corporate Control: The Scientific Evidence," *Journal of Financial Economics* (April 1983), pp. 5-50.

[7] Investment banks are required to separate their mergers and acquisitions departments from their other operations to prevent leakage of inside information. In practice this so-called Chinese wall is often very difficult to maintain. Several spectacular insider trading scandals in the late 1980s such as that involving the financier Ivan Boesky were due to breaches in some investment banks' Chinese walls. See J. Stewart, *Den of Thieves* (New York: Touchstone, 1992).

[8] Morck, R. et al., "Alternative Mechanisms for Corporate Control" *American Economic Review* (September 1989), pp. 842-52.

Firm A				Firm B			
Assets	7.0	Liabilities	1.2	Assets	0.8	Liabilities	0.1
		Common stock	1.1			Common stock	0.2
		Retained earnings	4.7			Retained earnings	0.5
	7.0		7.0		0.8		0.8

Following the combination, the balance sheet of Firm A becomes:

Assets	8.1	Liabilities	1.3
		Common stock	2.1
		Retained earnings	4.7
	8.1		8.1

Because of the share issue, A's common stock increases by $1 million (from $1.1 to $2.1 million). The purchase price of $1 million exceeds the book value of Firm B's common equity by $300,000. As a consequence, B's assets are revalued (often accomplished by "writing up" the value of B's fixed assets) to a new book value of $1.1 million, which equals the book value of B's assets of $0.8 million plus the $0.3 million paid above B's book value of equity. In some circumstances, it may not be reasonable to revalue B's assets to $1.1 million, which gives rise to a contribution to the goodwill accounting entry for the new consolidated firm. For example, if B's assets had been revalued at $1 million, then the remaining $0.1 million would have been reflected in goodwill.

The revaluation of assets under the purchase method influences the amounts of future capital cost allowance that can be claimed, and, the after-tax cash flows that accrue after the merger. Similarly, the amount of goodwill reported on the balance sheet must be amortized through time, which affects the company's reported earnings adversely. In addition, when shares are issued to pay for the merger, the acquired assets are valued on the basis of share prices at the transaction date. Valuations of individual categories of assets and liabilities are the responsibility of the acquiring corporation's board of directors, but because of their potential significance, such valuations may come under the scrutiny of taxation authorities.

Both the accounting treatment of amalgamations, and the consolidation of financial statements for subsidiaries that are not wholly owned, are sufficiently complex to defy simple description in this context.

26.5 EFFECTS OF MERGERS ON EARNINGS PER SHARE

We saw in Chapter 10 that discounted cash flow analysis should not pay attention to the temporary effects that an investment may have on reported earnings. Given well-informed and rational investors, this omission is defensible since only the net present value (NPV) of a project should influence shareholder wealth. However, in practice, managers attach considerable importance to reported earnings not only because of possible links to their own remuneration but also because they believe that investors react to these earnings. The issue is important in business combinations, because most mergers will have an immediate and major impact on reported earnings. In fact, an improvement in earnings per share has provided a strong, albeit misguided, motivation for some mergers.

ACQUISITIONS AND EARNINGS PER SHARE

EXAMPLE

Examine the following information for two firms, only one of which will be acquired by Company A. The basis for the merger will be a share-for-share exchange based on market prices, with Company A issuing new shares in return for the shares received from shareholders of Company 1 or Company 2.

	Company A	Company 1	Company 2
Total earnings	$16,000	$15,000	$12,000
Common shares outstanding	4,000	5,000	2,000
Earnings per share	$4	$3	$6
Price–earnings ratio	15	20	10
Market price per share	$60	$60	$60

The different price–earnings (P/E) ratios in the above table reflect different future prospects for the three firms. Company 1 has exhibited a pattern of rapid growth, justifying its high P/E ratio relative to Company 2, with Company A being somewhere in between.

For simplicity, assume that there will be no synergy so that the expanded business entity will show earnings that are simply the sum of the earnings of the two firms being merged. Effects of the merger on earnings per share (EPS) are as follows:

	Total earnings after merger	Shares of Co. A outstanding	Earnings per share
Company A fused with	16,000	4,000	31,000/9,000
Company 1	+15,000	+ 5,000	= $3.44
	= $31,000	= 9,000	
Company A fused with	16,000	4,000	28,000/6,000
Company 2	+12,000	+ 2,000	= $4.67
	= $28,000	= 6,000	

The importance of the P/E ratio is apparent. If Company A uses market prices as the standard for the exchange of shares and merges with another firm that has a lower P/E ratio (Company 2), the expected EPS for Company A will increase. New EPS are a weighted average of the earnings of the two merging firms, so that:

$$\$4.67 = 4 \times \frac{4,000}{6,000} + 6 \times \frac{2,000}{6,000}$$

Conversely, a merger of Company A with Company 1, which has a higher P/E ratio, will lead to a decline in EPS to $3.44.

We note that owners of Company 2 need not object to receiving shares with projected EPS of $4.67 in exchange for previous EPS of $6 provided that the lower earnings stream of the newly formed company is more highly valued by the market. If, for example, the P/E ratio of Company A settled at 14 after the merger, a share in Company A would be worth 14 4.67 = $65.38, above the $60 per share price at which the merger took place.

Growth in EPS that is achieved through mergers with firms having low P/E ratios has been termed **phantasmic growth**. The label reflects the fact that such contrived growth is not the result of more profitable operations but is the side effect of financial transactions that basically leave the earning power of the underlying business entities unchanged. Clearly, in the absence of synergistic or other effects, the total market value of the new firm after a merger should just equal the sum of the market values of the two individual companies, and, accordingly, investors should revise the P/E ratio of the acquiring firm downward after the merger.

IMPLIED P/E RATIOS AFTER MERGERS

EXAMPLE

Pursuing the merger of Company A with Company 2 in the previous example, rational investors should react by revising Company A's P/E ratio down to 12.85 after the merger. We should observe:

$$\text{Market value of Co. A merged with Co. 2} = \text{market value of Co. A} + \text{market value of Co. 2}$$
$$= 60 \times 4{,}000 + 60 \times 2{,}000$$
$$= \$360{,}000$$
$$\text{Shares outstanding after merger} = 4{,}000 + 2{,}000 = 6{,}000$$
$$\text{Share price after merger} = 360{,}000/6{,}000 = \$60 \text{ per share}$$

Given earnings per share of $4.67 for the combined firm as computed above, this implies a new P/E ratio of 60/4.67 = 12.85.

If, however, investors and analysts are gullible enough to perceive this growth in EPS as real increased profit potential, they may fail to scale down the P/E ratio and, in extreme cases, may even revise it upward to reflect their growing optimism. In fact, during the late 1960s when the conglomerate merger movement was at its peak, several firms brought about dramatic increases in their EPS by acquiring corporations that investors deemed relatively unattractive and therefore had low P/E ratios. Increases in EPS were even more dramatic if acquisitions were financed through debt rather than through new common shares. Investors reacted by increasing P/E ratios, mistaking phantasmic growth for real potential. The higher ratio tended to facilitate, if not accelerate, the acquisition program, because it became even easier to find target firms meeting the lower P/E requisite. This game was made possible largely because an indiscriminate faith in reported EPS seemed to dominate investor thinking and stock prices. Like most speculative bubbles, it came to an abrupt halt when investors redis-covered fundamental economic values in the wake of a general recession. As discussed in Section 26.3, discounted cash flow analysis should be the primary evaluation crite-rion for acquisitions. However, it is reasonable to believe that considerations regard-ing EPS are likely still considered by many companies and analysts alike.

PROCEDURES   26.6

Legal Aspects

The *Canada Business Corporations Act*—the securities legislation and corporation statutes of the provinces—and stock exchange regulations all prescribe rules under which busi-ness combinations may take place. The main objectives of such legislation are to provide shareholders with both the necessary information and the opportunity to participate in any final decision. The legislation extends beyond mergers and amalgamations and also regulates major purchases of assets from other firms, private agreements to purchase a controlling block of shares, and moves to acquire a controlling interest in the open mar-ket. Because of substantial provincial jurisdiction in this area, there is no uniform regu-latory framework that applies across the country, and the legal complexities are such that we cannot attempt to review the several statutes and their detailed provisions.

At the federal level, competition policy as reflected in the *Competition Act* of 1986 also needs to be complied with. This legislation created a competition tribunal to adjudicate mergers. However, it does not apply to mergers or proposed mergers under the *Bank Act*, the *Trust and Loan Companies Act*, or the *Insurance Companies Act*. The minister of finance must deal with prospective mergers in these industries, and the recent rejection of the bank mergers was based on the recommendation of the minister of finance. Finally, it is worthy of note that in general, Canadian anticombines law is considered to be weaker than U.S. antitrust law.

A key criterion used by the tribunal in evaluating business combinations is whether any "merger or proposed merger prevents or lessens, or is likely to prevent or lessen, competition substantially." The dimensions of efficiency and international competition are recognized explicitly. Thus, the tribunal considers the existence of competition by foreign firms and products, and it can approve mergers if "gains in efficiency will be greater than, and will offset, the effects of any prevention or lessening of competition." The tribunal also assesses whether, as a consequence of efficiency gains, a merger may result in a significant increase in exports or a significant substitution of domestic for imported products. If mergers are not consistent with the provisions of the Act, the tri-bunal can prohibit the merger or negate certain provisions of it. The *Competition Act* specifies pre-merger notification requirements, and under certain circumstances, advance rulings may be obtained. With its focus on competition, the *Act* does not apply to mergers in unrelated industries (conglomerate mergers) and, does not address the issue of concentration of corporate power in general. We will discuss this broader pol-icy issue in the next section.

Friendly Combinations and Tender Offers

Business combinations may be initiated through friendly negotiations between the managements of the corporations involved or may be the outcome of a takeover bid. When negotiations are entered into, the boards of directors of the respective companies are fully apprised, and when a tentative understanding is reached, ratification by the boards is sought. Upon ratification and depending on the terms arranged, shareholder approval will have to be sought, supplementary letters patent or an alteration of the memorandum of association arranged, prospectus requirements (if any) accommodated, and various statutes complied with.

Clearly, a major issue in the bargaining process is the price that is to be paid for an acquisition or the value that shareholders of the respective firms will realize as a consequence of an amalgamation. Not only are estimates of value likely to differ between buyer and seller but the benefits of any synergies will have to be apportioned between the two shareholder groups. Although current market prices of the respective shares form a natural starting point in negotiations, we have seen in previous sections that the amounts ultimately paid will often involve a significant premium. In addition to offering a good price, the acquiring firm will also have to convince the target management that a fusion is in its best interest. This can prove to be a major stumbling block particularly if the company has become an acquisition target because of suboptimal management.

The alternative to negotiations, or the fallback once negotiations break down is the **tender offer**. In this case, the acquiring firm bypasses management and makes a direct appeal to shareholders of the target company, asking them to tender their shares for sale. When the bid comes as a surprise or in opposition to the target company's management, it is referred to as a hostile takeover or raid.

Management may fight such unfriendly takeovers and often does. Various defence strategies that have proven successful include the following:

1. Legal barriers and delays may argue that the substance or procedures set out in one of the many applicable statutes has been violated.

2. The target company may be changed to make it less attractive as a takeover candidate. Tactics might include depositing of attractive assets, issuing of additional voting shares to dilute voting power, or assuming a heavy debt burden (for example, buying back some of its own shares at prices higher than those offered by an unwanted suitor).

3. One specific variant of the previous defence is called the poison pill. It entails issuing special securities that entitle the holders to unusual rights and privileges if the issuing firms become the subject of a takeover bid. Such securities are issued to existing shareholders, and the special privileges (such as unusual voting rights, lucrative redemption features, or generous conversion options) apply only to shareholders who have not accumulated a substantial block of common stock, thereby shutting out a potential bidder.

4. Soliciting competing takeover bids from firms that are viewed with more favour may be attempted. Such more attractive suitors are labelled white knights.

5. A successful bidder, through contracts and company bylaws, may be prevented from quickly replacing the existing board of directors and/or management.

6. A counterattack may be launched by attempting to buy up the shares of the pursuing firm. On occasion, even smaller concerns have been able to gain control of larger suitors.

7. In the event of a takeover from outside Canada, it may be argued that the particular combination offers no benefits to the country and, hence, should come under particularly close government scrutiny.

One can question whether such defence tactics are in the shareholders' best interests, for example, by increasing the price that shareholders ultimately receive for their shares.[9] In this context, it is useful to distinguish between defences that require prior shareholder approval (such as antitake-over amendments to the corporate charter or bylaws) and those that can be pursued by management on its own authority (most of the above fall in this category). There is some evidence that when management acts on its own authority, it does so mainly to further its own self-interest to the detriment of shareholders. The fact that such defences are often preceded by periods of substandard corporate performance indicates that incumbent management has reasons to feel insecure should a takeover succeed.

It is not uncommon for a tender offer to elicit responses from other firms seeking external expansion, and this may result in various offers and counter-offers conducted in an auction-like atmosphere. The beneficiaries are normally the shareholders of the target firm who see the price of their shares increased through successive rounds of bidding. In the end, even a reluctant management may have little choice but to recommend acceptance. Obviously, any vigorous defence by the target firm's management virtually guarantees its ouster if the defence tactics fail. Even then, however, the management of the target company may take steps to protect itself while the board is still friendly by, for instance, arranging generous employment contracts for extended periods of time or setting up generous retirement packages. The latter are sometimes referred to as golden parachutes. Although these are often portrayed as scandalous rewards for poorly performing managers, they may serve a useful purpose. Managers protected by golden parachutes may be less likely to let their own self-interest sway them into opposing economically sensible mergers.

Purchase of Assets or Shares

External growth can be achieved either by purchasing another firm's assets or by gaining control over those assets through purchasing the company's shares. When only a firm's assets are acquired, the liabilities remain with the vendor, which will use the proceeds from the sale to meet these obligations. This method of expansion is attractive when the target has contingent liabilities such as unsettled lawsuits or warranty claims or when only a portion of the assets are sought. If all operating assets are disposed of, a liquidating dividend may be paid to shareholders followed by surrender of the corporate charter.

---

[9] An example of how resistance to takeover bids might ultimately increase the takeover premium that target shareholders receive is presented in R. Giammarino and R. Heinkel, "A Model of Dynamic Takeover Behavior," *Journal of Finance* (June 1986), pp. 465-80. The basic idea is that resistance to an initial bid encourages competition between potential acquirers and drives up the acquisition price.

With a purchase of shares and subsequent merger, both assets and liabilities are taken over by the new parent. Alternatively, the acquiring firm may purchase only a controlling block of shares and function essentially as a holding company. Because shareholders of most widely held corporations are relatively passive and often fail to exercise their votes, ownership of as little as 15 percent of the issued common stock may ensure effective working control, greatly reducing the investment required. In addition, the purchase of shares may take place gradually and informally (to legally prescribed limits), thereby minimizing the premium over current market price that has to be paid. On the other hand, partial ownership results in only partial benefits. Also, as the target firm's separate identity is preserved, such issues as separate financial disclosure, tax considerations, dividend policy, and the general treatment of minority shareholders need to be dealt with.

Method of Payment

Payment for a company's assets or shares may be by cash or through newly issued securities of the acquiring firm. Tax considerations for the recipient owners may play a major role in establishing the preferred method of payment. When payment is through shares of the new parent, an additional concern that arises is the valuation of these shares. This is true because the share prices of an acquiring company tend to be unusually unstable at the time of a contemplated acquisition. Nevertheless, an exchange of shares or the use of convertible securities appear to be the most common methods of financing business combinations. For example, mergers tend to increase during periods of soaring stock prices. This occurs as acquiring firms experience large increases in the price of their shares, which enhances their ability to offer larger offer prices for potential targets.

26.7 PUBLIC POLICY IMPLICATIONS OF BUSINESS COMBINATIONS

Because of its prominence and magnitude, the move toward business combinations has attracted significant public attention. The issue is well summarized in the following statement by Stanley Beck, then chairman of the Ontario Securities Commission:[10]
While Canada is a country which requires large economic units in some areas, the question is in what sectors does this make sense? There is concern in any society when too much power is concentrated in too few hands, and the problem is as much political and social as economic. How decisions are made, whose voices are heard, and, ultimately, how democratic our society is—these are the kinds of questions we must come to terms with, and the issue is far deeper than what is happening on Bay Street.

While this statement was made in 1986, many of the concerns expressed within are commonly seen in today's media. One of the most widely followed examples of such concerns in a global context involves the recommended split-up of Microsoft, which was

[10] Stanley Beck, "Concentration Concerns: How Much Is Too Much?" *The Financial Post*, March 29, 1986, p. 4.

alluded to earlier in this chapter. In Canada, public debate continues over whether or not the banks should be allowed to revisit the idea of mergers and whether the banks should be allowed to enter into the insurance business. Other discussions focus on how well served the average Canadian consumer is by having only one national airline company as a result of the acquisition of Canadian Airlines by Air Canada.

Specific concerns in this context include corporate concentration and power, declining competition, and foreign control and ownership. Although a detailed discussion of such complex topics is beyond our scope, an awareness of these issues is essential for financial executives, since governments may well take an active role in responding to related public concerns.

Canada's economy, more than that of most other major industrialized nations, is characterized by a high degree of concentration of corporate control, which was alluded to in Chapter 14. For example, over one-third of the companies on in the TSE 300 Composite Index have one shareholder controlling more than 50 percent of the firm's outstanding shares In contrast, less than 25 percent of TSE 300 companies are considered to be widely held, with no shareholder owning more than 20 percent of their shares. Compare that to over 85 percent of the firms included in the S&P 500 Composite Index in the United States.

A detailed look at any one of Canada's major corporate empires will reveal an astonishing degree of interlocking corporate ownership, with control of massive accumulations of assets exerted through complex structures involving several layers of subsidiaries. Often, synergies are not apparent. Coupled with a general distrust of big business, this leads to obvious questions regarding the economic, social, or other benefits and costs of corporate concentration. We note that the aggregate level of business concentration in Canada far exceeds that of Germany, the United States, or Japan, with our 100 largest non-financial corporations accounting for a large percentage of the total assets of all non-financial enterprises.

It can perhaps be argued that free-market forces are at work allowing efficient management to extend its control, and that large-scale operations are required to compete effectively in world markets for capital and goods and services. Indeed, this was the gist of the argument by the banks defending their desire to merge in order to be competitive globally. Furthermore, the potential threat of hostile takeovers is viewed as providing an effective control mechanism against inefficient management, ensuring that management self-interest cannot result in significant deviations from the goal of maximizing shareholder wealth. It is interesting in this context that corporate raiders, in bidding up share prices, often portray themselves as champions of the common shareholder's interests. In fact, a number of companies that have become takeover targets would probably be worth significantly more if they were broken up and their assets sold separately. Needless to say, this is rarely viewed as attractive by existing management.

One consequence of mergers is the huge rewards to financial advisers who help to arrange such deals. Some have pocketed amounts exceeding $100 million as a consequence of a single transaction. The opportunity for such inflated compensation has led to questions about the integrity, independence, and economic soundness of their advice.

Another aspect that has been viewed with concern is the large debt some firms burden themselves with as a consequence of extensive merger activity (or of defences against hostile bids). An excessive debt burden clearly can make a company more vulnerable and restrict its future flexibility in pursuing productive investments. At the same time, it introduces added risks of future loan defaults into the financial system. On the other hand, as we saw in Chapter 16, it has been argued that increased leverage reduces managers' scope for committing corporate funds to grandiose negative net present value projects since a highly levered firm can tolerate less misallocation of resources. Finally, the merger wave of the 1980s was also accompanied by a series of insider trading scandals. Although such scandals may have hurt the share prices of individual companies, there is no evidence that overall confidence in the integrity of stock markets has decreased.

Perhaps the most important issue related to corporate concentration is the concern about competition particularly when mergers expand market power. Although most developed countries have legislation to ensure reasonable competition, the effectiveness of such legislation in placing restrictions on business combinations and its interpretation in the courts, has varied. Proponents for an enforcement of tight legislation argue that only effective domestic competition will ensure economic efficiency. On the other hand, business people and many economists argue that the key to competition is not the number of domestic firms operating in a given market but rather competitive conditions in world markets. For example, it has been suggested that even if North America had only two major automakers, competition would be assured because of Japanese manufacturers, and, furthermore, in order to compete effectively with Japanese companies in world markets, the domestic car industry could not afford greater fragmentation. Canada's *Competition Act*, although recognizing that size may be important to compete internationally, has specific provisions dealing with anticompetitive mergers, which attempt to ensure that major business combinations, in particular in industries with a high degree of concentration (such as oil, retail chains, telecommunication, and newspaper publishing) receive adequate scrutiny. The perennial problem is that the anticompetitive effects of a merger cannot be directly observed but rather must be estimated through judgement or economic models. Consequently, the potential for error is large.

Foreign ownership remains a particular concern, partly because a significant proportion of our productive capacities in key industries is owned and controlled from abroad. In response to this concern, the federal government pays particular attention to the acquisition of Canadian corporations by foreign companies, although this type of activity continues to flourish, as mentioned earlier in this chapter in the report entitled "Mergers and Acquisitions Activity Hits $149 Billion in Second Quarter: On Record Pace."

Compromise is probably the key to resolving the above issues. Where the line is drawn undoubtedly will change from time to time and will depend not only on underlying economic conditions at the time but also on political considerations. It is clear, however, that the issues will remain with us, that they will influence the ground rules under which business combinations can take place, and that responsiveness by business to the concerns noted may well pre-empt additional legislative initiatives.

SUMMARY   26.8

1. The combination of separate business entities in the form of mergers, amalgamations, and the use of holding companies can achieve business expansion externally for a firm. Ultimately, the driving force behind any expansion should be a creation of value that increases shareholder wealth.

2. An acquisition should only be pursued if it generates a positive net present value. Estimated future cash flows that accrue as a consequence of an acquisition should reflect any actions that the new management may implement, and the discount rate applied should be commensurate with the target firm's perceived risk.

3. Business combinations affect reported earnings per share (EPS), the shares' price-earnings (P/E) ratio and market price of the surviving entity. EPS, however, may grow if one firm acquires another whose share trade at a lower P/E ratio.

4. Net assets of the acquiring firms are revalued to reflect the purchase price actually paid, and incomes of the two businesses are pooled as of the date of acquisition.

5. A combination may be arranged through negotiations between management followed by shareholder ratification or through a tender offer. Reluctant management can pursue a variety of strategies to fend off an unfriendly takeover and to protect their own interests.

6. A variety of statutes dictate the rules under which a business combination may occur because of economic concerns and past abuses.

QUESTIONS AND PROBLEMS

Questions for Discussion

1. Why might a preoccupation with increasing earnings per share (EPS) and a discounted cash flow evaluation of prospective acquisitions yield different results? Conceptually, why should management ignore short-term effects on EPS? In practice, is management justified in attaching importance to EPS? Explain.

2. Why does the acquiring firm in a merger usually offer a premium for the sought-after shares? In the absence of synergy, can such a premium be justified economically?

3. What relevance does a target firm's book value or replacement value have in determining an acquisition price?

4. Diversification is given as a major reason for many business combinations. From a shareholder's point of view, how justifiable is this reason? Why do managers consider it important?

5. Discuss some reasons why the interest of shareholders and management may not coincide in a business combination. What power does each group have to protect its own interests?

6. In evaluating an acquisition, would it be reasonable to take the net cash flows *after* interest payments, preferred dividends, and taxes and to discount these at the appropriate cost of common equity?

7. Why may a shareholder not tender his shares even if a substantial premium is offered? Is such behaviour irrational?

PROBLEM WITH SOLUTION

Problem

The A-2 Manufacturing Company is a machine shop that undertakes a mix of custom and production line work. The quality of their product is well regarded, partly because of the skills of the firm's owner, Bob Jones.

Because of a depressed economy, business has been slow lately. Meanwhile Bob Jones, having recovered from a recent heart attack, is looking forward to early retirement supported by proceeds from the sale of A-2. In his efforts to locate a buyer, he first found a holding company, Liqui-Date Ltd. that negotiated as though it simply planned to liquidate A-2 by selling its valuable site and other assets. A-2 had net income of $130,000 last year, down from $160,000 the year before, on roughly the same capital base. Liqui-Date offered $400,000 in cash for A-2 and the offer was rejected. Jones felt that his company had established substantial goodwill with its customers and that this should enable it to continue profitable operations and to command a higher price. He also had close personal relationships with his employees and realized that, under the Liqui-Date offer, their jobs might be lost.

On extending his search, Jones entered negotiations with a conglomerate, the Octa Company, as a possible buyer. Octa's management subsequently offered 10,000 shares of its own common stock that currently trade at $70 per share in exchange for ownership of A-2 Manufacturing.

The following data are available on the A-2 Manufacturing Company, the Octa Company, and financial conditions at the time:

A-2 Manufacturing is financed solely through common equity. Other manufacturing firms similar to A-2 also have such capital structures and betas of around 1.5; Octa has a beta of 1.1.

The interest rate on long-term Canada bonds is 14 percent, and the average annual return on common stocks was 18 percent over the past 15 years. This figure is deemed to be indicative of expected future returns from the market portfolio. All depreciable assets required by A-2 fall into a class allowing for maximum annual capital cost allowances at 20 percent on a declining balance. Both firms face a corporate tax rate of 50 percent.

A-2 anticipates net cash flows from operations of $120,000 this year, to be followed by flows of $140,000 in each of the next 4 years, and of $160,000 per year for years 5 to 10. These flows reflect the loss of Bob Jones' talents. Projections beyond the 10th year are difficult to make.

Octa expects to be able to reduce A-2's working capital by $50,000 following the merger without affecting business operations. Octa must also recognize unfunded pension liabilities with a present value of $20,000.

To sustain operations, A-2 would have to acquire new equipment valued at $400,000 at the end of the eighth year. The outlays associated with this investment have not been recognized in the above projections of operating cash flows.

Octa has 400,000 shares outstanding, and current earnings per share are $10. Octa has some unused borrowing capacity.

(a) Knowing that Octa's management uses a discounted cash flow approach to valuing target firms, would Bob Jones be wise to turn down the opening offer of 10,000 Octa shares? Base your analysis on after-tax cash flows up to year 10 only.

(b) Based on discounted cash flow analysis, what resale price or liquidating value for A-2, on an after-tax basis, to be received at the end of year 10, would be necessary for the Octa offer to be just adequate?

(c) Alternatively, what constant annual cash flow do we have to assume for A-2 beyond year 10 to make Octa's offer just adequate?

Solution

(a) The appropriate discount rate to be used is A-2 Manufacturing's cost of capital. Octa' cost of capital would be inappropriate for valuing A-2, as the risks of the two firms differ.

To derive the appropriate discount rate, we must estimate A-2's cost of common equity. Based on our discussions in Chapter 8 of the Capital Asset Pricing Model and assuming $r_e = k_e$ we have:

$$k = k_e = 14 + 1.5 (18 - 14) = 20\%$$

The cash flows to be considered in the analysis are as follows:

Year	Cash flows		
0	30,000	consisting of:	
		disposition of redundant working capital	50,000
		pension liability	−20,000
			30,000
1	120,000		
2-5	140,000		
6-7	160,000		
8	−220,000	consisting of:	
		operating inflows	160,000
		purchase new equipment	−400,000
		tax shield new CCA	
		(400,000 × .2 × .5 × 1/2)	20,000
			−220,000

9	196,000	consisting of:	
		operating inflows	160,000
		tax shield new CCA (360,000 × .2 × .5)	36,000
			196,000
10	188,800	consisting of:	
		operating inflows	160,000
		tax shield new CCA (288,000 × .2 × .5)	28,800
			188,800

Based on the above cash flows only, the present value at a discount rate of 20 percent becomes $548,000.

Given a market price of $70 per share, 10,000 shares should be worth $700,000, and Octa's offer appears attractive. However, the present value derived above ignores any residual value that A-2 may have at the end of year 10.

(b) A terminal value producing a present value of $700,000 - 548,000 = \$152,000$ after tax must be available at the end of year 10. We have:

Terminal value $= 152,000 (1+.2)^{10} \approx \$941,000$

(c) Again, the present value of these cash flows has to equal $152,000. The present value of a perpetual annuity (A) at the end of year 10, discounted at 20 percent, is A/.20. We obtain:

$$152,000 = \frac{1}{(1 + .20)^{10}} \times \frac{A}{.20}$$

which yields

$A \approx \$188,000$

ADDITIONAL PROBLEMS

1. Consider two firms with the following information:

	Firm A	Firm B
Net Income	$75,000,000	$50,000,000
Number of Shares	7,500,000	25,000,000
Stock Price	$100	$12

Firm A is going to takeover Firm B through an all share offer. Firm B shareholders will receive shares in A with the number of shares received based upon current market values.

(a) Assume that there are no synergies to the combination. If the takeover goes through and the market applies Firm A's price-earnings multiple to the combined firm, what will be the stock price of the new, larger Firm A?

(b) Assume that there are no synergies to the combination. If the market rationally analyses the combination of firms, what price-earnings multiple should it apply to the combined firm? What should be the new stock price of Firm A?

(c) Assume that there are synergies to the combination. In particular, by combining the two firms, the management team of firm A will be able to increase the growth potential of Firm B's earnings, making it more Firm A. The price-earnings multiple of the combined firm is expected to be the same as Firm A's original multiple. What is the total dollar value of the synergies created by the combination?

2. The balance sheets of two firms, Bidder Inc. and Target Inc., are as follows (all numbers in millions):

Bidder Inc.					Target Inc.			
assets	24	liabilities	20		assets	9	liabilities	5
		equity	4				equity	4
	24		24			9		9

Bidder Inc. takes over Target by paying a total price of $8 million. The entire purchase price is funded through an issue of Bidder Inc. shares at $20 each. If the takeover is accounted for using purchase accounting and any excess of the purchase price over the book value of Target is considered goodwill, what will the balance sheet of the combined firm look like?

3. The balance sheets of two firms, ABC Ltd. and XYZ Ltd., are as follows (all numbers in millions):

ABC Ltd.					XYZ Ltd.			
cash	5	liabilities	10		assets	5	liabilities	3
other assets	25	equity	20				equity	2
	30		30			5		5

ABC is about to purchase XYZ. It will pay $4 million for XYZ and the payment will come from ABC's cash reserves. Purchase accounting will be used to account for the combination and XYZ will be revalued to the purchase price upon completion of the deal. What will the balance sheet of ABC look like after the takeover?

4. You own a business with the following characteristics:

• the firm has no debt

• after-tax net cashflows are expected to be $450,000 next year, growing at 25 percent per year for the 4 years after that. After that, growth is projected to be 5 percent per year into the foreseeable future.

• similar firms which are publicly traded have beta's of around 1.6. The current risk free rate of interest is 5 percent and the risk premium on the stock market is estimated to be 7 percent. A competitor has offered to buy out your firm. Your competitor is a large, publicly traded firm with a stock beta of 1.2 and debt-equity ratio of 1.5. If you are taken over, it is estimated that synergies between the firms would result in after-tax cashflows being 10 percent higher than the estimates given above in all years.

(a) What is the minimum price which you would accept for your firm?

(b) What is the maximum price which your competitor would pay for your firm?

Is it possible to set a price at which both you and your competitor benefit from the takeover?

5. The Alpha Company plans to take over the Omega Company. Relevant data before the merger are as follows:

	Alpha	Omega
Earnings per share	$2.50	$3.50
Market price per share	$35.00	$35.00
Number of shares outstanding	2,000	2,000
Price-earnings ratio	14	10

Synergetic effects in a combination of Alpha and Omega are expected to produce after-tax cash flows of $2,000 annually.

(a) If Alpha offered a one-for-one share exchange with Omega (based on their identical market prices) and the share value of the combined firm remained unchanged at what would be the new price-earnings ratio and earnings per share for Alpha immediately after the acquisition?

(b) The management of Alpha, noting that its earnings per share would rise with the offer in (a), decides to entice shareholders of Omega with a more attractive offer. Specifically, for each 2 shares of Omega, the shareholder could receive 1 share of Alpha and a $50, 3-year note paying 12 percent interest annually. What would be Alpha's earnings per share immediately after the takeover?

(c) If this were a horizontal merger, discuss the likely impact of the fusion under alternative (b) above on the acquiring firm's cost of common equity.

6. The Huge Co., a conglomerate, is negotiating a takeover of the Tiny Co. and is using discounted cash-flow analysis to establish an appropriate value. Tiny would be the tenth small firm taken over in the past 15 months. Huge currently has a cost of capital of 20 percent, a tax rate of 40 percent, and, because it is so much larger than Tiny, expects that there is no need to re-evaluate its cost of capital after the takeover. Estimates of annual after-tax cash flows from operations for Tiny are:

Years 1 to 5: $20,000 in year 1, increasing by $5,000 annually
Years 6 to 10: $40,000 each year.

In addition, new equipment will have to be bought in year 5 at a cost of $50,000. Capital cost allowances on this equipment will amount to $5,000 in the first year and 20 percent on the declining balance thereafter. Furthermore, in year 6, a $6,000 investment in working capital will be called for. These cash flows are not included in the operating projections given above.

The estimated market value of Tiny at the end of year 10, net of taxes on recaptured depreciation and capital gains is $100,000. Tiny has no senior securities in its capital structure, and its cost of capital is estimated to be 21 percent.

(a) What is the maximum cash offer that Huge should make for the firm?

(b) If Tiny's assets include excess cash of $15,000 that is temporarily invested in Government of Canada paper, how would this alter your response under part (a) above?

(c) If Tiny had unused borrowing capacity, how might this alter your analysis? Briefly discuss and illustrate.

7. The Acquisitor Corporation, which is a tax-exempt financial institution (say a pension fund) is evaluating the purchase of the Bergon Co. The latter's only asset consists of an office building, the Bergon Tower, which is financed solely through common equity. Using discounted cash flow analysis, the maximum price that could be paid for the target company's shares is found to be $25 million. If the merger with Bergon proceeds, Acquisitor expects to take advantage of Bergon's unused debt capacity. Specifically, it would arrange a $14 million, 30-year loan and make use of the proceeds to offset the purchase price. Current interest rates on such debt are 16 percent. This move toward an optimal capital structure is reflected in the $25 million maximum price computed for the acquisition.

   Another corporation, Argon, owning as its single asset an identical office tower, has emerged as an alternative acquisition target. The Argon merger would differ in that the target company carries a 10 percent, 30-year loan of $14 million on the building that can be assumed in the takeover. Neither loan involves a sinking fund.

   (a) What maximum price would you recommend that the Acquisitor Corporation be willing to pay for Argon?

   (b) If the price you are willing to pay for Argon differs from the $25 million you are willing to offer for Bergon, explain the reasons for the difference. Assume your audience to be Acquisitor's board of directors, a group not necessarily well versed in the technicalities of finance.

   (c) In Chapter 15, we argued that historical costs on previously issued securities are irrelevant for investment evaluations. How do you reconcile that position with your answers derived above?

   (d) If the Acquisitor Corporation were not a tax-exempt financial institution, how would your answer to (a) differ? Assume a tax rate of 40 percent.

8. A company is expected to have after-tax cashflows of $150,000; $200,000; $300,000; $400,000; and $450,000 in each of the next five years, respectively. The firm for which you work is considering making an offer to take over this company. If your firm buys this company, it expects to reduce overall operating costs by $35,000 per year, after-tax, for the first five years. However, inventories will have to be immediately increased by $60,000. You estimate that the target company's cost of capital is 12 percent. If you purchase the company it is assumed that after five years, after-tax cashflows of the target company will grow at a constant rate forever. The company is in a maturing industry in which long-run growth is projected to be at roughly the same rate as growth in the general economy.

   (a) Using a spreadsheet, create a plot of the maximum price you would pay for the company versus the assumed long term growth rate in after-tax cashflows.

   (b) The owner of the target company is insisting on a price of $10 million for his company. Would you consider this a reasonable price? Why or why not? Give a range of prices which you might consider reasonable for this company based upon the projections above and possible growth rates in the general economy.

On February 25, 2000, BCE announced a takeover offer for the CTV Inc., the television broadcaster. BCE made a cash offer of $38 per share (eventually this was increased to $38.50 per share and accepted by CTV's Board of Directors and shareholders). Exhibits 1 and 2 below contain media reports on the offer. Exhibit 3 presents the closing share prices of BCE and CTV each day for the week of the initial announcement of the offer.

1. Section 26.2 of the text contains a variety of different motivations for mergers. Based on these classifications, write a short report on what you think the motivation is for the BCE takeover of CTV. Comment on how CTV fits in with the overall strategic plan of BCE (you might also want to review the management discussion in the BCE annual report in Appendix II).

2. Exhibit 1 contains a quote from Ted Rogers, CEO of Rogers Communications. Comment on what Mr. Rogers is saying in terms of the growth prospects of CTV's two major business areas and in terms of the price being offered by BCE. What response might BCE make to Mr. Roger's statement?

3. Look at the stock prices in Exhibit 3. How do you explain the closing price for CTV on February 25, given that the initial offer was for $38 per share. Based on the market reactions to the announcement, what would you say the market's opinion of the $38 price was?

EXHIBIT 1

The full name of Bell Canada Enterprises makes one think first of telephones—telephones, and monstrous, glacial, monopolistic utility companies. But the new swashbuckling image of BCE and its CEO, Jean Monty, shows what a little deregulation can do. In recent years, the face-lifted Bell has dabbled in every business from gas pipelines to trust companies. In January, BCE hived off its 39 percent stake in Canadian telecom heavyweight Nortel, rounding out an $8-billion media-convergence war chest. On February 25 a first shot was fired as BCE declared its intention to buy CTV Inc. for $2.3 billion.

That price would fetch BCE not only the CTV network but its subsidiary cable channels, which include Talk-TV, The Comedy Network, CTV SportsNet, and the Outdoor Life Network. Still, even in a souped-up market, the $2.3 billion figure is staggering. It's 70% more than the market thought CTV was worth as recently as January 1. The bid hiked the price of CTV nearly 19 times the company's annual earnings, a ratio that would have seemed gargantuan in the old days—say, 1993. It is not such a remarkable figure in today's market, but for a rather stodgy broadcaster in a small country, it is noteworthy. Now everyone is asking the question: is CTV really worth $2.3 billion?

Ted Rogers, chief executive of the cable and Internet concern Rogers Communications, thinks not. Or so he says. After the BCE bid, some expected Mr. Rogers to quarterback a consortium counterbid (his company is too small to contemplate launching one alone). But on March 1, Mr. Rogers declared BCE's bid to be unrealistic. "About half [CTV's earnings are] from the over-the-air television, which is declining, and half are from cable specialty channels, and are increasing," he noted. "If the average [price-earnings ratio] is 18 to 20, over-the-air is likely valued at nine to 10. That would mean that the cable specialty channels would be valued at, perhaps, 30…which is extraordinarily high. We must be careful because of the Internet. People will be able, in Canada, to have access through the Internet or other means without the regulator being able to block programming."

At his press conference, Mr. Monty justified the bid by pointing out the importance of content to new-media companies. "Our customers do not want to connect just to a network," he said, referring to BCE's underperforming on-line portal Sympatico. "They are looking for connections to destinations and experiences… That's why BCE must have greater access to distinctive and original content." The web of BCE media holdings, Mr. Monty conjectured, would become a rock-solid Canadian presence in a world where all forms of bandwidth—TV, e-mail, the Web, the telephone—are slowly melding. "It's the increasing capability to have a Canadian perspective on the TV and the Net, both at the same time, while having access to global perspectives," he said.

Source: "Betting on Canada: is BCE's $2.3b bid for CTV a brilliant media play or just hype in hyperspace," by Colby Cosh, Report News Magazine, March 27, 2000, vol. 26 (50) p. 30. *Reprinted with permission.*

EXHIBIT 2

BCE chief executive Jean Monty said yesterday he has already spoken to Ivan Fecan, CTV's chief executive, and has laid out a "welcome mat" to him and other executives to grow the broadcaster under his wing.

"CTV management isn't going to be very motivated to go and find other bidders who might end up slashing their jobs," said one analyst who did not want to be named. "Besides, a lot of people were interested when it was closer to $30, not $38…There is really nobody in Canada who can win a bidding war against BCE."

Other industry insiders say although CTV has missed some of its financial targets in the past, BCE needs the expertise the broadcaster used to bring to air such successful television shows as *Open Mike With Mike Bullard* and *The West Wing*.

In a conference call with analysts yesterday, Mr. Monty acknowledged BCE, while a powerhouse in the field of communications and the Internet, does not have the management team in place to build up the content division CTV could provide.

BCE has long been expected to follow a two-pronged approach for international and domestic growth and diversification, which includes the Internet, as well as news and entertainment content. For that reason its interest in buying CTV comes as no surprise.

CTV has been seen as a takeover target since early 1998 when its major shareholder, the Eaton family, sold its 40.2 percent stake. Speculation intensified late last year when it was revealed that Corus owns just under 10 percent of the broadcaster. CanWest Global Communications Corp. is believed to also own a similar stake.

Since the Stentor group was disbanded and provincial boundaries vanished, Mr. Monty, who cut his teeth in corporate finance at Merrill Lynch and Co., has moved like lightning to transform BCE and position it in the race for global survival. Some key dates:

Jan. 26   BCE spins off most of its 39.2 percent stake in Nortel to its 500,000 shareholders in a $73-billion stock freebie. Each company can now pursue its own growth strategy. BCE aims at being a full communication service provider.

Feb. 2   Bell Canada and Lycos Inc. create Internet company Sympatico-Lycos, intended to be the biggest business to consumer portal in Canada. Further portal deals rumoured.

Feb. 15   BCE is buying Teleglobe Inc.'s shares it doesn't own for $9.65-billion in stock—including entrepreneur Charles Sirois' 9 percent stake. BCE wants to become a global data-Internet company and can use Teleglobe's massive fibre-optic infrastructure. Mr. Sirois will focus on building his international wireless empire.

Source: "Welcome mat laid out for Fecan: nobody in Canada can win a bidding war against BCE," by Brenda Bouw, Financial Post (National Post) Feb. 26, 2000, p.D2. *Reprinted with permission.*

EXHIBIT 3

Closing share prices.

	CTV	BCE
Monday, Feb. 21	$27.50	$166.95
Tuesday, Feb. 22	29.80	165.10
Wednesday Feb. 23	31.50	171.50
Thursday, Feb. 24	31.25	167.00
Friday, Feb. 25	38.45	161.25

Source: Datastream

Index